THE WORLD FERTILITY SURVEY

An Assessment

The World Fertility Survey

An Assessment

EDITED BY

JOHN CLELAND *and* **CHRIS SCOTT**

in collaboration with
DAVID WHITELEGGE

PUBLISHED FOR
THE INTERNATIONAL STATISTICAL INSTITUTE BY
OXFORD UNIVERSITY PRESS
1987

Oxford University Press, Walton Street, Oxford OX2 6DP
London New York Toronto
Delhi Bombay Calcutta Madras Karachi
Kuala Lumpur Singapore Hong Kong Tokyo
Nairobi Dar es Salam Cape Town
Melbourne Auckland
and associated companies in
Beirut Berlin Ibadan Mexico City Nicosia

Oxford is a trade mark of Oxford University Press

Published in the United States
by Oxford University Press, New York

British Library Cataloguing in Publication Data

The World Fertility Survey : an assessment.
1. Fertility, Human — Statistical methods
I. Cleland, John II. Scott, Chris
III. International Statistical Institute
304.6'32'0724 HB901
ISBN 0-19-828525-6

Library of Congress Cataloging-in-Publication Data

World Fertility Survey.
Bibliography: p.
Includes index.
1. World Fertility Survey. 2. Fertility, Human.
3. Demographic surveys. I. Cleland, J. G. (John G.)
II. Scott, Christopher, 1927-
HB901.W664 1986   304.6'32'0732   87-23483
ISBN 0-19-828525-6

Set by Grestun Graphics, Abingdon, Oxfordshire
Printed and bound in Great Britain by
Biddles Ltd, Guildford and Kings Lynn

This book is dedicated to
the memory of V. C. Chidambaram,
Deputy Director of the
World Fertility Survey, 1978–84

The views expressed in the various chapters of this publication are those of the authors personally and should not be attributed to any particular institution.

PREFACE

This comprehensive contribution of social scientists to an assessment and over-all review of the findings and accomplishments of the World Fertility Survey is a clear demonstration of the significance of this unique research undertaking. The international collaborative twelve-year effort involved sixty-two developing and developed countries and several hundred scholars and experts from all over the world. The programme was designed to provide vitally important scientific information on one of the most crucial issues of our times – human fertility. The survey findings constitute a gold mine of information far surpassing in depth and quality that obtained from other sources such as population censuses or registration of vital events. The findings have already been widely discussed, evaluated, interpreted and utilized by research workers, policy-makers and administrators of population, health and social development programmes and they will continue to be of great value in this regard for many years to come. In the present volume only some of the highlights of survey findings are published due to limitation of space. For more detailed information on specific topics and countries it is necessary to examine the comprehensive range of publications of the International Statistical Institute on the World Fertility Survey programme.

Besides the substantive findings the programme, in at least two other respects, will continue to have a great impact for a long time to come. First, the fact that a large number of persons received practical training on various aspects of plan-ning, organization and execution of sample surveys has contributed considerably to strengthening the data collection and analytical capability in most of the par-ticipating countries. This important human resource development will stimulate and facilitate future social survey undertakings. The contacts and friendships which have been established within and between countries will contribute to promoting collaboration and exchange of experience in future survey research.

Furthermore, the most lasting effect may be the tremendous contribution the programme has made to the development of survey methodology and data analysis through its successes, as well as its shortcomings and failures, in applying and testing various techniques – many of them new and innovative. This book brings together the most important implications which the World Fertility Survey has for future survey work. It draws to a considerable extent on docu-ments, reports and articles already published but in many respects it also takes a new and fresh look at what has been learned and what will be the impact upon future research in this field.

Although the World Fertility Survey has been completed, it is not the end of international co-operative effort on fertility research and surveys on related topics. The International Statistical Institute, through its International Statistical Institute Research Centre, continues to make available to research workers the vast amount of materials obtained from the WFS surveys and still provides technical and other support for surveys, as for example those currently occurring through collaboration with the Government of the People's Republic of China.

The United Nations has established a programme of national multi-round household surveys which provides a framework for collection of data on fertility and related topics. Furthermore, the United States Agency for International Development has recently established a project of demographic and health surveys in some developing countries to be executed by the Westinghouse Public Applied Systems of Columbia, Maryland, and the Population Council, New York. It is clear that these schemes and other social surveys to be carried out in the future will benefit immensely from the World Fertility Survey experience.

It seems to me appropriate as the last Project Director of the WFS to take this opportunity to extend to the International Statistical Institute a sincere tribute for its vision and courage in establishing and taking responsibility for this daring international venture. Perhaps the most remarkable accomplishment of the programme is that it could be done at all. Great appreciation should also be extended to the international agencies and organizations as well as Governments and institutions which provided financial and other support for the programme.

Full recognition should also be given to the competent and energetic staff at the WFS headquarters and their collaborators in the participating countries for their devoted efforts and high scientific standards and integrity. One of the most outstanding contributions was made by V.C. Chidambaram, the Deputy Director for many years, who suddenly passed away during the closing days of the programme. This volume illustrates some of his many significant contributions to the success of the WFS. It is indeed appropriate that this publication is dedicated to his memory.

Halvor Gille

CONTENTS

LIST OF CONTRIBUTORS

Affiliations shown are those at the time of authorship

Michael D. Bracher	*Australian National University*
William Brass	*London School of Hygiene and Tropical Medicine*
John C. Caldwell	*Australian National University*
John B. Casterline	*World Fertility Survey*
Ramesh Chander	*World Bank*
V. C. Chidambaram	*World Fertility Survey*
John Cleland	*World Fertility Survey*
Sidiki Coulibaly	*International Development Research Centre (Canada)*
Trevor Croft	*World Fertility Survey*
Paolo De Sandre	*University of Padua*
Ronald Freedman	*University of Michigan*
Halvor Gille	*World Fertility Survey*
Christiaan Grootaert	*World Bank*
Trudy Harpham	*World Fertility Survey*
John Hobcraft	*London School of Economics and Political Science*
Hédi Jemai	*World Fertility Survey*
Gwendolen Johnson-Ascádi	*United Nations Population Division*
Robert E. Lightbourne	*World Fertility Survey*
Cynthia B. Lloyd	*United Nations Population Division*
Albert M. Marckwardt	*World Fertility Survey*
John W. McDonald	*World Fertility Survey*
Manuel Ortega	*Centro Dominicano de Organzaciones de Interes Social*
James Otto	*World Fertility Survey*
V. T. Palan	*International Planned Parenthood Federation*
Thomas W. Pullum	*University of Washington, Seattle*
Judith Rattenbury	*World Fertility Survey*
J. R. Rele	*United Nations Economic and Social Commission for Asia and the Pacific*
Beverley Rowe	*World Fertility Survey*
Lado T. Ruzicka	*Australian National University*
Chris Scott	*World Fertility Survey*
Susheela Singh	*World Fertility Survey*
Bob Thompson	*World Fertility Survey*
Ian Timæus	*London School of Hygiene and Tropical Medicine*
James Trussell	*Princeton University*
Martin Vaessen	*World Fertility Survey*
Vijay Verma	*United Nations Statistical Office*
Jane Verrall	*World Fertility Survey*
Mary-Beth Weinberger	*United Nations Population Division*
Andrew Westlake	*World Fertility Survey*

ABBREVIATIONS

Titles of Organizations and Programmes

CELADE	Centro Latinoamericano de Demografía
CES	Conference of European Statisticians
CICRED	Committee for International Co-ordination of National Research in Demography
DNISR	Danish National Institute of Social Research
ECIEL	Joint Studies on Latin American Integration (Spanish acronym)
FPA	Family Planning Association
FSO	Federal Statistical Office (Czechoslovakia)
ICP	International Comparison Project
ICSOPRU	International Comparative Study on Organization and Performance of Research Units
IDRC	International Development Research Centre (Canada)
IIPS	International Institute for Population Studies (Bombay)
ILO	International Labour Organization/Office
INE	Instituto Nacional de Estadística (Spain)
INED	Institut National d'Etudes Démographiques (France)
IPPF	International Planned Parenthood Federation
ISI	International Statistical Institute
ISPC	International Statistical Programs Center (US Bureau of the Census)
IUSSP	International Union for the Scientific Study of Population
LSHTM	London School of Hygiene and Tropical Medicine
LSMS	Living Standards Measurement Study (World Bank)
NAS	National Academy of Sciences (USA)
NCHS	National Center for Health Statistics (USA)
(N)CSO	(National) Central Statistical Office
NFS	National Fertility Survey
NHSCP	National Household Survey Capability Programme (United Nations)
NIDI	Netherlands Interuniversity Demographic Institute
OECD	Organization for Economic Co-operation and Development
PAA	Population Association of America
POPLABS	Laboratories for Population Studies
PRB	Population Reference Bureau
PSC	(WFS) Programme Steering Committee
RIPS	(United Nations) Regional Institute for Population Studies
SCBS	Swedish Central Bureau of Statistics
SS	Statistik Sentralbyra (Norway)

TAC	(WFS) Technical Advisory Committee
UKODA	United Kingdom Overseas Development Administration
UNDP	United Nations Development Programme
(UN)ECA	(United Nations) Economic Commission for Africa
(UN)ECE	(United Nations) Economic Commission for Europe
(UN)ECLA	(United Nations) Economic Commission for Latin America
(UN)ESCAP	(United Nations) Economic and Social Commission for Asia and the Pacific
UNESCO	United Nations Educational, Scientific and Cultural Organization
UNFPA	United Nations Fund for Population Activities
UNPD	United Nations Population Division
UNSO	United Nations Statistical Office
USAID	United States Agency for International Development
WFS	World Fertility Survey
WGSD	(UN) Working Group on Social Demography
WHO	World Health Organization
WPPA	World Population Plan of Action

Technical terms

AGFM	Age at First Marriage
AU	Area Unit
BAU	Basic Area Unit
CEB	Children Ever Born
COTA	Latin American occupational classification
CV	Coefficient of Variation
DEIR	Date Edit, Imputation and Recode (WFS computer software package)
DP	Data Processing
EA	Enumeration Area
ED	Enumeration District
FEA	Fertility Exposure Analysis
FOTCAF	Factors Other Than Contraception Affecting Fertility (WFS module)
FP	Fixed Probability
FRM	(WFS) Fertility Regulation Module
FT	Fixed Take
FW	Fixed Weights
GNP	Gross National Product
HFC	High Fertility Country
IQ	Individual Questionnaire
ISCO	International Standard Classification of Occupations
ISIC	International Standard Industrial Classification
IUD	Intra-Uterine Device

KAP	Knowledge, Attitudes and Practice (regarding contraception)
LFC	Low Fertility Country
MCA	Multiple Classification Analysis
PERT	Project Evaluation and Review Techniques
PES	Post-Enumeration Survey
PPS	Probability Proportional to Size
PPS-SW	PPS-Self-Weighting
PSU	Primary Sampling Unit
RE	Non-standard recoded (file)
SES	Socio-Economic Status
SHS	Shorter Household Schedule
SNA	System of National Accounts
SPSS	Statistical Package for the Social Sciences
SR	Standard Recode *or* Scientific Report (according to context)
SS	Supplementary Standard (data file)
TFR	Total Fertility Rate
TMDR	Total Marital Duration Rate
UAU	Ultimate Area Unit
XHS	Extended Household Schedule

Introduction

John Cleland and Chris Scott

The World Fertility Survey was a unique programme: for the first time in history an attempt was made to organize a sample survey comparable across a very large number of countries. Between 1973 and 1984 a total of 61 countries completed a survey of human fertility under the co-ordination of an office in London run by the International Statistical Institute. Fifty million dollars were spent and a huge volume of experience was amassed. This book attempts to record that experience while the memory of it is still alive. It represents the joint effort of many of those who were involved in the programme and, in particular, of the WFS staff.

In order to understand the context of the work some knowledge of the WFS programme is needed. The surveys were carried out by national staff in each country. Between 2 500 and 10 000 women in the age range 15–49 were interviewed in nationally representative samples. Questionnaires were largely, but not fully, standardized: there were many national adaptations and the questions were translated into local languages. The data were processed into a standardized data tape which is available for international research, subject to each country's agreement. The role of the internationally staffed headquarters was, first, to draw up the general survey specifications, embodied in a series of manuals, then to provide technical assistance to the survey execution, processing and analysis in each country, and finally to participate in the inter-country analysis and the numerous activities involved in international dissemination of the findings. The programme was funded by the United Nations Fund for Population Activities and the United States Agency for International Development, with a contribution from the United Kingdom Overseas Development Administration, but participating countries contributed resources in kind. Developed countries also took part in the WFS but their surveys were nationally funded, less standardized and largely independent of the WFS headquarters. Their surveys are considered in chapter 34 but elsewhere in this volume they are excluded.

An internationally standardized programme of surveys offers an unusual opportunity for the accumulation of technical knowledge, but this can only be achieved if a conscious effort is made to record the experience as it is acquired. This was recognized from the beginning of WFS. The project's 'Manual of Sample Design' contains the sentence: 'Efficient sampling, like civilization, depends on the recording of experience for the benefit of posterity'. What is true of sampling is true of all aspects of survey design. Thus WFS made special efforts to document procedures and evaluate their success, regarding this as an essential obligation owed by the survey organizer to his successors. The funding agencies, for their part, recognized the need to reap the maximum harvest from their investment by supporting a thorough-going technical assessment of the pro- gramme. Thus, 18 months before the project came to an end a special section was set up within the London headquarters with the specific objective of documenting and evaluating the WFS achievement. WFS set itself the objective of reporting its main conclusions to an international symposium, held in London in April 1984. The present volume is based largely on the papers prepared for this symposium; of the 39 chapters that follow, 27 were either presented and discussed at the symposium or were available as background documents. Many have been revised in the light of comments made by participants. The additional 12 chapters represent work done in the closing months of the programme.

Authors were asked not to confine themselves to factual descriptions but to attempt, as far as possible, an *evaluation* of WFS methods and achievements. Since many of the authors were themselves instrumental in devising or applying such methods, the writing of these papers has demanded a serious effort of self-criticism. It could be argued that a more objective assessment would have emerged had authors been recruited who had no personal involvement in the work under review. This issue was discussed intensively by the WFS's Programme Steering Committee and by the management of the WFS itself when the assess- ment project was first planned. In the end the decision was clear: only an assessment by those directly concerned could hope to take account of the volume and complexity of the material and the sheer range of experience that had to be evaluated. In certain areas, however, where the ratio of value judge- ment to fact would need to be particularly high or where considerations external to the WFS would dominate the issues, outside authors were sought.

Whether the authors' personal involvement has stood in the way of an objec- tive assessment, readers must judge for themselves. Certainly there is no lack of self-criticism in the contributions which follow.

No single publication, however large, can attempt to provide a complete account of WFS's achievements and failings. This is particularly true of the substantive findings of the programme; hundreds of reports and articles on survey results have already been published and the flow will continue for a number of years. This element of incompleteness also applies to a lesser extent to the assessment of WFS methodology, and we note below the more sub- stantive pieces that are not contained in this volume. WFS was discouraged from carrying out experiments, or research into methodology. This was unfortunate, since investment in such activities is the surest way of achieving advances. How- ever, there are a number of important exceptions. The Canadian International Development Research Centre supported a special four-survey study into response errors, which has so far generated three reports (O'Muircheartaigh 1982; 1984a; 1984b). The United Kingdom Overseas Development Administration financed a two-country study of effects on questionnaire translation. A preliminary account of the findings may be found in chapter 6 but more detailed results will be published elsewhere. WFS also sponsored a linguistic study in Cameroon (Ware 1977). A special field comparison of different data collection techniques in Bangladesh was funded from central resources (Becker and Mahmud 1984) and in the same country an evaluation of the interviewing process was made possible by a detailed analysis of tape-recorded interviews (Thompson, Ali and Casterline 1982). In a number of countries, repeat surveys on small subsamples of respondents were conducted and results have yielded valuable information on response consistency (MacDonald, Simpson and Whitfield 1978; Srikantan 1979; Paita 1984).

Apart from this limited number of field experiments, several important methodological papers have been based on secondary analysis. Examples include a study of sample design effects on the precision of results (Verma, Scott and O'Muircheartaigh 1980), an analysis of response rates and the efficacy of call-back procedures (Marckwardt 1984) and an investigation of the effect of data editing on results (Pullum, Özsever and Harpham 1984). Perhaps the most substantial contribution to self-assessment was the policy to subject each survey data set to thorough checks of the quality of information collected, undertaken usually in a workshop with full participation from the countries concerned. Each such evaluation resulted in a report, 25 of which have so far been published in the WFS *Scientific Reports* series. A summary of this extensive work is provided in chapter 24.

This volume is structured so that the sequence of chapters follows a logical path from the design and execution of surveys to analysis and dissemination of results and finally to their implications for future surveys and government policies. This spectrum underlines one of the great strengths of the WFS programme. Far from being simply a massive data collection exercise; it developed an equal strength in data analysis and was actively involved in the dissemination of findings and concerned with their practical utility.

PART 1

Origin and Nature

1

Origin and Nature of the World
Fertility Survey

Halvor Gille

1.1 Origin

In the late 1960s and early 1970s several factors led to the creation of the World Fertility Survey.

First there was the growing concern among governments and demographers about accelerating rates of world population growth, particularly in the developing countries, and sustained high levels of fertility. A crucial time had been reached in the history of mankind. The prospects for a decline in fertility in the developing countries were uncertain and there was little hard evidence that such a change was actually on the way.

At the same time, reliable information on birth rates was lacking in major parts of the world. Some statistics on current number of births were available in South America for 51 per cent of the population, in Africa for 73 per cent and in Asia for 89 per cent. Birth statistics by age of mother were available for 49, 19 and 17 per cent of the population in the three developing regions respectively and by birth order for only 32, 3 and 10 per cent respectively. For the world as a whole, only 34 per cent of the population were living in an area where birth registration was considered reliable, varying from 1 per cent in Africa to 8 per cent in Asia and 19 per cent in South America, as compared with almost 100 per cent in developed regions (United Nations 1971). Where the birth statistics available were unreliable, considerable efforts had to be made to correct and adjust for deficient data and provide reasonable estimations.

Some fertility data were becoming increasingly available from special surveys on knowledge, attitudes and practice of family planning – the so-called KAP surveys. By the end of the 1960s it was estimated that about 150 major studies of this kind had been carried out, of which one-third had taken place in the last five years. However, these studies had various deficiencies. Many of them did not follow the basic principles of sound survey design and management; objectives were often vague and the content and design correspondingly diffuse and imprecise; frequently little or no provision was made for evaluation of errors. The data collected were often insufficiently tabulated and analysed and sometimes never published. In addition, many of the surveys were of limited geographical scope and did not attempt to be representative of the entire country. Furthermore, they were in many cases carried out by independent research institutions having no direct links with the country's policy-making bodies and unconcerned with making the data comparable with those obtained in surveys elsewhere.

More adequate and reliable information on levels, trends and patterns of human fertility was stressed by many experts, governments and international conferences as a prerequisite for realistic development planning in many areas and the formulation and implementation of family planning programmes. The United Nations Population Commission, for example, urged in November 1971 that steps be taken to improve knowledge of fertility on an internationally comparable basis, in particular with regard to fertility differentials.

Second, in the late 1960s a dramatic increase took place in the funds made available by some industrialized countries to assist developing countries in population matters. International population assistance increased from around $30 million in 1967 to $125 million in 1970, $186 million in 1972 and $254 million in 1974. This rapid growth, which to a large extent was the result of growing concern about the impact of current and prospective population trends upon development, exceeded the number of sound projects available for implementation. Many developing countries were not immediately interested in initiating major population programmes, due to a large extent to lack of information on fertility trends and patterns and other demographic factors. In many countries a pre-condition for the initiation and exchange of demographic research and a better understanding of interrelationships between demographic trends and development was an improved data base. Human fertility was obviously a research area where useful investments could be made from the growing resources of international population assistance.

Third, in the late 1960s the International Statistical Institute (ISI) was undergoing an appraisal of its role and future responsibilities. This organization, which at that time was over 80 years old, had begun life as an association of national official statisticians having the primary aim of developing international statistical standards and promoting the progress of national statistics. Later, when the United Nations established the Statistical Commission, this body took over many of the functions of the ISI, which became mainly a professional society of government and academic statisticians holding biennial worldwide conferences for its members and other interested statisticians to discuss scientific papers submitted to them. In the mid-1960s a Reappraisal Committee of the ISI had been set up, chaired by the man who later became the first Project Director of WFS, Maurice Kendall. This Committee recommended that the Institute should make a strong effort to restore its previous position as the natural focus of international statistical work and 'reshape its work in a fundamental way by attempting to meet the challenge of the present and future needs of the profession'. A number of steps were proposed to accomplish this goal, including promotion of research on a wide range of topics, among them 'birth control and abortion'. The Committee also proposed that the Institute could fulfil a useful function by providing services to governments and other bodies on specific statistical problems.

As a first step towards the implementation of the Reappraisal Committee's recommendations, the Bureau of ISI established an Advisory Committee chaired by Alan Stuart to look into the feasibility of research in the various subject areas proposed. The Advisory Committee considered a number of proposals, including the study of demographic problems and adaptation of sample survey techniques to the conditions prevailing in developing countries. Members of the Committee and William Cochran, President of ISI, solicited ideas about research activities which ISI might pursue. During informal discussions at the time of the ISI Session in Washington DC, in August 1971, several leading American demographers and Dr R. T. Ravenholt, Director of the Population Office, United States Agency for International Development (USAID), indicated the need for a worldwide study on fertility somewhat analogous to the Growth of the American Family studies. Late in 1971 the Bureau of the ISI decided to develop such a major international research programme with the aim of 'obtaining systematic scientific knowledge on a worldwide scale concerning differential fertility, reproductive norms and family planning practices'. In January 1972 the Institute called upon the co-operation of its members in realizing this scheme. Some 50-60 persons were consulted directly or through correspondence and members of ISI generally expressed their interest and support. In March 1972 a meeting of consultants was convened which made recommendations about a number of steps to be taken by ISI including the establishment of several committees to prepare detailed proposals for a 'World Fertility Survey'.

In 1971 the United Nations General Assembly launched the World Population Year, 1974, and invited governments and non-governmental organizations to participate in this programme. ISI, together with some 15 other international scientific associations, was called upon to contribute to this major global effort. In response, ISI submitted early in 1972 tentative plans for a major international research programme called the World Fertility Survey (WFS) for statistical and research activities which it was prepared to promote as a part of this global effort. This research programme became the largest activity of the World Population Year. The World Population Plan of Action, adopted by consensus at the World Population Conference held in Bucharest in 1974, 'invited all countries to co-operate with the World Fertility Survey' (United Nations 1975).

1.2   Aims

In the official proposal prepared by ISI in early 1972, the aims of the programme were stated as follows:

(i) the *general purpose* (is) to assess the current state of world knowledge concerning fertility and family planning and to promote new, nationally representative, internationally comparable sample surveys in as many countries of the world as possible;

(ii) the *specific purpose* (is) to promote through technical assistance, selective subsidization and voluntary country co-operation, individual country surveys on the part of national statistical agencies or other competent research institutions in some thirty to forty key developing countries.

It was emphasized that the programme should aim to assist governments to institutionalize fertility research as a major and regular component of the work of their statistical offices.

These aims were discussed and revised in consultation with various experts within and outside ISI. An *ad hoc* advisory group of experts (see section 1.4) recommended that the primary objectives should be 'to improve the world's knowledge of fertility, fertility regulation and related topics by developing useful standard definitions and survey methods and by helping to strengthen national institutions'.

In the project proposals submitted to development assistance agencies, the final objectives were stated as follows:

The first and most basic aim of the WFS programme is to assist countries to acquire the scientific information that will permit them to describe and interpret their populations' level of fertility. Individual country surveys undertaken as part of the WFS will strive to identify meaningful differentials in patterns of fertility regulation, and to clarify factors affecting fertility. Improved data on these topics will facilitate national efforts in economic, social and health planning.

A second important purpose of the WFS is to increase national capacities for fertility and other demographic survey research, particularly in developing countries. It is hoped that by participating in the WFS a country will acquire an increased cadre of trained personnel who will be able to undertake further research programmes.

A third purpose of the WFS programme is to collect and analyze data on fertility which are internationally standardized and therefore permit comparisons from one country to another. The interpretation of national data on fertility is greatly enhanced when put into a comparative framework. There is also considerable scientific interest in having available comparable data on fertility for populations whose socio-economic characteristics differ widely.

These three main objectives have largely remained unchanged, despite much subsequent discussion.

The first technical advisory group established for the programme (see section 1.4) recommended, in 1972, that the objectives of WFS be formulated in broad and comprehensive terms. It recognized that the essential elements included sound data collection and analysis in participating countries and on an internationally comparable basis but little attention was given to developing survey capability and institution building as an objective. Some members suggested that WFS should aim at providing basic demographic data required for the preparation of improved population projections, but it was agreed that such a goal was unrealistic for the surveys envisaged and that the programme should primarily be a scientific study of the factors affecting fertility and fertility regulation.

An evaluation task force established by the two main funding agencies raised in 1976 the issue of priority ranking between the three initially established goals. The group felt that WFS in its work so far had given too much attention to international comparability of data and largely neglected the promotion of institution building in the participating countries. After considerable discussion among the policy-making bodies of the programme it was decided to maintain the three initial objectives without stipulating priorities between them. It was at the same time emphasized that all three objectives should be pursued as far as possible, recognizing that there were limitations on accomplishing all of them fully but also that they were not necessarily in conflict with each other.

The primary objective of WFS was to meet the need for reliable and up-to-date information on human fertility. The need for data on fertility and the factors affecting fertility behaviour came not only from demographers, sociologists and other scientists but also from government planners and policy-makers. The latter required information on fertility as a major component of population growth, on the effects of fertility on economic and social development, and on policies and programmes in population, health, social and economic fields which might have an impact upon fertility. It was therefore understood that the findings from the survey would be useful for policy-makers in various fields, although this was not explicitly stated among the major aims of the programme. It is in fact interesting to note that the two funding agencies – United Nations Fund for Population Activities (UNFPA) and USAID – did not initially insist upon emphasizing the potential role of the scheme for policy-making in economic and social development in general and population policies in particular, an area which both agencies were committed to support. It should be remembered, however, that in many countries rapid population growth was not at that time generally recognized as a topic of governmental concern, or was subject to considerable controversy. A strong emphasis on the role of WFS in providing much needed data for policy-making in the population field could have limited countries' responses and the full collaboration of the necessary local institutions and personnel. Further, at the international level the importance of the role of population policies for development and the influence of economic and social factors upon fertility and other population trends were subjects of considerable discussion and debate.

During the implementation phase, the usefulness of WFS data in relation to policy formulation and implementation became increasingly apparent. The programme's main objectives, as initially formulated and agreed, were never in fact amended or modified to reflect this. However, USAID in particular was anxious that WFS data and their analysis should contribute substantially to the measurement and evaluation of the impact of family planning programmes, and the 1977 additions to the core questionnaire relating to knowledge, availability and accessibility of family planning services exemplified the growing recognition of the contribution that the findings from the WFS programme could provide for policy-making.

The WFS management and staff themselves were initially concerned to limit the scope of the programme to fact-finding and to maintain neutrality with regard to population policies. However, this stance was modified as time went on, though without any change being made in the programme's objectives. The policy relevance of findings was given considerably more attention in later country reports as compared with the earlier ones. Further, the convening (from 1978 onwards) of high-level national meetings to publicize and discuss survey results helped to focus attention on the policy implications.

In the initial official announcement about the establishment of WFS, ISI stressed that the goal of the programme was 'to carry out a *World* Fertility Survey: that is, to solicit participation from all nations'. It was soon recognized, however, that not every country in the world could be expected to participate; nevertheless, universal participation was considered the ideal. In a press release (August 1972) ISI expressed the hope that at the beginning of the World Population Year, 1974 'a large number of countries, perhaps 50, will be interviewed'.

This ambitious goal created no problem as regards the developed countries, since here the role of WFS was limited to the provision of survey instruments, general promotion, and co-operation with the countries. There was to be no provision of technical or financial assistance. Ultimately, most of the developed countries (with a few notable exceptions) participated in the programme.

As regards the developing countries, the consultative groups of experts mentioned above recommended that WFS should, in principle, explore the interest of all countries in participating in the programme. It soon became clear, however, that most developing countries would not be able to participate unless considerable financial and technical assistance were made available. Moreover, many countries might not be prepared to participate even if the necessary external assistance was provided due to lack of manpower resources, conflicting national priorities or insufficient interest in or sensitivity about the substance of the surveys. It was expected that participation would gradually increase with increasing recognition of the importance of the subject matter. Several times the desired target was stated by ISI and the management of the programme as around 45 developing countries, with the aim of concentrating efforts on around 40 needing assistance. When recruitment was discontinued at the beginning of 1981, the final figure was 42.

With limited resources available for technical and financial assistance and for backstopping support from WFS headquarters, the selection of participating countries from the developing world became an important issue. Various approaches were proposed but no firm overall policy was ever established for the programme except for the following.

First, to avoid competing for scarce financial and manpower resources at the national level, it was decided that initially no efforts should be made to include those African countries which were currently engaged in carrying out a census within the scope of the African Population Census programme. Some 30 African countries participated in this major United Nations effort; about half of them (17) had never had any population census experience before. The result was that no African country was recruited in the early years and the sub-Saharan region of Africa never quite caught up with other developing regions before recruitment of new countries was discontinued.

Second, it was felt most desirable to include some of the largest countries, more specifically the most populous country in each major region. Special efforts were therefore made to include Brazil, the People's Republic of China, India and Nigeria. At one time Brazil decided in principle to participate but eventually abandoned the idea, mainly due to doubts in the Federal Office with which WFS was dealing about the timeliness of a national survey of the kind envisaged. China agreed, but only after the programme had passed the stage when it could accept new participants.[1] India felt it had adequate survey capability, and had in fact carried out some fertility surveys, but agreed to make use of the WFS survey instruments whenever desirable.[2] Nigeria joined as the last country included in the programme before recruitment was discontinued.

Aside from these two considerations a fairly representative selection of national surveys was clearly a desirable goal, but it was soon realized that such a policy was difficult to implement for political or other reasons. In actual fact, countries were included in the programme to a large extent on a first come first served basis. Over time it was possible to accept almost all developing countries which clearly indicated their interest and were ready to accept the conditions and guidelines for participation. However, several times participation of new re-cruits had to be delayed or postponed due to the limited technical and financial resources at the disposal of the programme. In 1981, when the funding agencies and the Bureau of the ISI decided that the programme should aim at completion and no more new surveys could be included, several developing countries were considering whether to join the scheme but were prevented from doing so by the decision.

The initial uncertainty about the geographical coverage of the programme created some difficulties in determining its proper title. The name 'World Fertility Survey' was decided upon to make the programme as spectacular and attractive as possible. It was also very much in line with terms used in several other major international undertakings under way in the field of population, such as 'World Population Year', 'World Population Conference', 'World Population Plan of Action' and a proposed 'World Population Institute'. A title closer to reality would have been 'International Fertility Survey Programme', but the more ambitious term was adopted with the unavoidable consequence that later mis-understandings sometimes arose about the actual scope of the programme. Except during the initial months of the planning phase, it was never expected that the programme could realistically become a world programme or that it would be able to establish world indicators on fertility and related topics.

1.3   Creation of WFS

The question of the executing agency for the programme was initially subject to considerable discussion between the two main funding agencies. In accordance with its policies, UNFPA favoured the United Nations, more specifically the Statistical Office and/or the Population Division, as the responsible organization for this emerging large-scale international research programme. The Fund recognized, however, the difficulties and shortcomings of the United Nations in carrying out an operational scheme of this kind due to its bureaucratic and other rules and regulations, in spite of the wealth of experience and local contacts with governments it could contribute. USAID was quite insistent that it would not be prepared to support the programme if it was to become a United Nations-executed activity. The outcome of these discussions was that ISI was accepted as the executing agency but that special arrangements were to be made to benefit from and collaborate with the United Nations. For this purpose, UNFPA allocated funds for the establishment of four posts of liaison officers in the United Nations Population Division and three Regional Commissions to monitor and assist the development of the programme.

ISI accepted the WFS programme as a major challenge tó strengthen its role in the international community and to contribute to knowledge and understanding in an area of major international concern. As the organization had very limited resources, it had to rely entirely on external funding. USAID indicated clearly an interest in, and willingness to support, the programme but could not do so until a certain amount of detailed planning had been done. In this situation UNFPA made a grant early in 1972 of $54 000 to enable ISI to prepare plans and to convene two consultative groups of experts for this purpose. The US Bureau of the Census as well as the Population Council offered to second a staff member to assist in the preparation of the project plans. Several international bodies voiced their support, for example the Conference of European Statisticians.

In May 1972, USAID approved a grant of $1 million for a two-year development phase of the programme beginning July 1972; later, UNFPA approved a grant of $1.5 million for activities in the calendar year 1973.

ISI sought wider support by approaching nearly 30 ex-officio members of the organization, all directors-general of statistics in Eastern and Western Europe, Canada, Australia, New Zealand and Japan. Governments were urged to make grants in the range $25 000–100 000. In the appeal it was estimated that around $10 million was required, excluding the cost of national surveys themselves, for a period of at least five years. This effort did not yield many results, which is not surprising since in all cases the approach was made to the above-mentioned ISI contacts and not to the authorities responsible for, and interested in, assistance to developing countries. The fact that ISI went on record as expressing the hope that USAID might contribute some 90 per cent of the budget for the five-year period may also have discouraged other governments for political or other reasons from participating. Only the Dutch Government pledged to contribute by making available office space and some services for the programme, and the Japanese Government by making a small initial grant.[3]

UNFPA and USAID agreed to divide the core cost about equally between them for the first five-year period. This did not include the cost of the countries' participation and of the surveys themselves. It was envisaged that the in-country cost would amount to around 40 per cent of the total.

The sponsorship of the programme was much discussed. Several international organizations had competence and experience in the field concerned. The International Union for the Scientific Study of Population (IUSSP), which is the international non-governmental organization of demographers and population scientists, played an important role in the development of the plans, including the survey instruments. Initially, the main preoccupation of the ISI and the funding agencies was the problem of gathering good quality data. But soon the importance of analysis and interpretation of the data became recognized, an aspect the Union was particularly interested in and in a good position to promote. The Union was designated as a co-sponsoring organization and not only contributed in the formative stages of the programme but also played an important part later in advising on the analysis of data.

The United Nations was another body which could provide considerable technical advice and guidance. The Statistical Office had long experience in data collection in the population field including population censuses, vital statistics and household surveys, which was most useful and important for the development of the WFS programme. The Population Division had a strong analytical capability and considerable experience in promoting demographic training and research in developing countries. In addition, the United Nations regional commissions had both statistical and demographic personnel and experience as well as contacts in the developing countries which could benefit the programme. The role of the various participating organizations and even the order in which they should be mentioned were agreed upon only after considerable discussion.

Another issue which was not easily settled was the location of the programme. Various possibilities were explored, including that of locating it in a developing country. This issue, together with the problem of designating a project director, was resolved in late 1972 when Maurice Kendall accepted the assignment on condition that the programme would be located in London. This location offered many advantages with regard to recruitment of competent professional and support staff, good telecommunications facilities and a centre for air connections to most parts of the world. Since ISI, the executing agency, had its headquarters in The Hague, it was decided that administrative and financial matters would be dealt with by the ISI's Permanent Office but that all the technical survey work would be located in London.

1.4   Development of WFS

The development phase of WFS began in July 1972 and extended until June 1974. The first step ISI took was to convene in mid-1972 two *ad hoc* groups of experts to advise on the feasibility, scope, nature and technical requirements of the programme. One group, attended by some 21 experts in addition to agency representatives, endorsed both the feasibility and desirability of launching a

WFS programme. It offered technical guidance on the requirements for carrying out the WFS and considered particularly the need for WFS, its objectives and general nature, subject matter, functioning and relationship to other activities. Another group, attended by nearly as many but different experts, was convened immediately after with the aim of discussing in detail the technical requirements for carrying out the recommendations made by the first group. A number of recommendations were made for conducting national surveys and the group considered detailed questions of survey methodology, from initial planning to analysis and publication of results. ISI adopted the recommendations of these two advisory meetings as the basis for the development of the WFS programme.

Several committees were established to assist ISI and WFS in the development and implementation of the programme.

First, a Programme Steering Committee (PSC) was set up to provide over-all substantive and managerial guidance to the programme. The Committee consisted of a chairman (President of the ISI at the time), four renowned statistical and demographic experts from developing countries serving in their individual capacities, and representatives from the main funding agencies and the two co-sponsoring organizations, IUSSP and the United Nations. The Committee, which met periodically for two or more days at a time, determined the policies of the programme, reviewed the progress of work and considered the budget. From the beginning this Committee was the key body in the organization of WFS.

A Technical Advisory Committee (TAC) was established to advise the PSC through the Project Director on all technical and substantive aspects of the programme. It consisted of 12 experts from various parts of the world acting in their personal capacities, half of them designated by IUSSP and the rest by ISI. The Committee held meetings during the first three years of the programme and prepared, with backstopping from the staff, proposals on the household schedule, the individual core questionnaire and the various questionnaire modules. It also reviewed and made comments on the draft survey organization manual, sample design manual, instructions for field supervision and tabulation manual. With the adoption of the survey instruments, the data processing guidelines and the basic tabulation plans, the task of this Committee was considered complete.

Further, a regional co-ordinating committee was created to advise on the co-ordination and exchange of information with non-governmental organizations and regional inter-governmental bodies, especially the United Nations regional commissions. The committee, which included representatives from the organizations most directly concerned, met only once, as its role to a large extent was obviated by the series of regional conferences sponsored by WFS and the establishment of three United Nations regional liaison posts to WFS at the respective headquarters of the regional commissions.

Finally, the Bureau of ISI established a small Executive Committee composed of three members of the Bureau chaired by the ISI President. It met once or twice a year to review and advise on managerial and administrative aspects of the programme but played only a minor role in the development of the programme and was disbanded in 1982.

In developing the plans for the programme, a primary goal was to strive for results of high scientific quality. This was to be achieved by recruitment of the most competent professional headquarters staff to prepare and test instruments and procedures, to train national staff and to assist the countries at all stages of survey work. In short, the ambition was to develop a programme which would become a model of excellence and serve as a standard against which subsequent surveys could be compared.

The major task in the project development phase was to develop the various survey instruments. Two core data collection instruments and accompanying optional modules were prepared for developing countries with high fertility. For developed countries a separate individual core questionnaire was prepared similar to that for developing countries but adjusted to the low fertility conditions.[4]

A detailed survey organization manual was prepared to advise the local staff on the planning and organization of surveys, sampling requirements, training, quality control, evaluation and standards for data processing and analysis.

Other manuals were prepared on sample design and training of personnel, instructions to supervisors and interviewers, editing and coding guidelines and guidelines for data processing and preparation of the main country report.[5] As a part of the preparatory work, a review of relevant methodological research that had been conducted in the past was carried out. In drafting the core questionnaires and making other plans, such as for coding and tabulation of data, considerable guidance was obtained from the work done by the IUSSP and published in a report entitled 'Variables and Questionnaires for Comparative Fertility Surveys'. Later, as a guide for analysis of survey results, a series of illustrative studies was carried out demonstrating the application of various analytical tools to WFS data.

An important initial task was to establish confidence in and secure support for the survey programme. While many had expressed enthusiasm and confidence in the undertaking, there was also considerable scepticism among others. Doubts were expressed about the concept of a worldwide survey, largely inspired by social scientists' research in some developed countries, in particular the United States, as well as about the feasibility of organizing a research project of such magnitude and complexity. Thus in the early stages of the development of the scheme considerable efforts had to be made to establish credibility, acceptability and support. The Project Director, a distinguished and well-known statistician, was successful in enlisting the co-operation of many statisticians and demographers, in recruiting some of the best and most experienced experts to join the staff and in persuading a number of governments and scientific communities in many countries to participate.

Various measures were taken to explain and promote the programme. An information brochure was prepared and distributed widely, a press release was sent out to all major mass-communication media, a six-page annnouncement was sent to some 65 professional journals and a newsletter was established. Recruitment of participating countries was stimulated by presentations at important international meetings convened at inter-governmental or non-governmental levels and by staff visits to countries. Further, regional meetings were organized by WFS for government officials and scholars in Africa, the Middle East, the Caribbean, Europe, Asia and Latin America to explain the programme, discuss its various aspects and learn about the interests and intentions of the countries as to possible participation.

An important activity during the development phase of WFS was the preparation and execution of a pilot survey which would guide future programme implementation. At a meeting of the Conference of Asian Statisticians, held in 1972, the Government of Fiji in response to a presentation concerning WFS offered Fiji as the location for a pilot survey. This offer was accepted, but the exercise was designed in such a way that it served the dual purpose of pilot project for the programme and national survey for Fiji. A complete survey apparatus was established, household and individual questionnaires prepared, pre-testing carried out, supervisors and interviewers trained and a probability sample drawn. Interviews with nearly 5000 women were carried out in early 1974 and a post-enumeration check implemented immediately afterwards. A critical review and assessment of the administration, survey design and implementation of the Fiji project were undertaken and the findings applied in the planning and execution of subsequent WFS surveys.

Several other pilot tests were carried out in mid-1974. In order to test the draft core individual questionnaire in a Spanish-speaking setting, a pilot survey of 300 interviews was carried out in Colombia. A pilot survey of 700 interviews was undertaken in Zaire to test the suitability and application of the WFS instruments in a relatively difficult setting, using a local language. In order to gain experience with the core questionnaire drafted for low fertility countries, a pilot test was carried out through interviews with some 200 women in the United Kingdom. All these tests provided useful guidance for the preparation of survey instruments to be applied under various local conditions.

1.5   Implementation

Around mid-1974 the implementation phase of the programme began. In the initial plans it had been envisaged that this phase would last for five years, but it was soon recognized that an extension would be necessary to accomplish the programme objectives. By mid-1979 the financial commitments of the two main funding agencies were extended first by three years and later by another two years, making the implementation phase ten years in all and establishing mid-1984 as the termination date for the programme.

The first regular surveys were carried out in Asia and the Pacific. In 1974 and 1975 interviewing was undertaken in six countries in that region in addition to Fiji. 1975 was the peak year, with fieldwork in eight countries, four in Asia and

and four in Central America and the Caribbean. In 1976 fieldwork was undertaken in six countries, two in Asia and the rest in Latin America. In 1977 the
first two African countries were included, in addition to one from Asia, two
from the Caribbean and one from the Latin American region. Seven more
countries were added in 1978, four of them from Africa, two from the Middle
East and one from Asia. In 1979 the number of new recruits decreased to five,
including the only one from Europe and the rest from Africa, Latin America
and the Middle East. In each of the following three years only two new countries
were added, all from Africa except one Middle Eastern country. As regards the
developed countries, the first WFS-type survey was initiated in 1973; participation gradually increased to the peak year of 1977, when fieldwork took place
in seven countries, thereafter only one new recruit being added in each of the
following years to 1981.

A complete list of participating countries with their population totals, sample
size and year of fieldwork is presented in table 1.1.

The survey instruments prepared and tested during the development phase
proved in general to stand up well to the requirements and needs of the various
countries implementing the programme. It was to be expected, of course, that
certain modifications and adjustments would be made in the course of time, but
major changes were avoided.

In the early days of WFS the inclusion of abortion as a major topic of investigation was the subject of considerable discussion between the three main partners
in the planning of the programme, the PSC, the TAC and the Project Director,
Initially the Project Director and his staff, supported by the TAC, took the
position that it was neither appropriate nor feasible to inquire specifically about
the incidence of induced abortion but only about various types of foetal wastage,
with the aim of improving completeness of live birth reporting (TAC 1973: First
Meeting). Some members of the PSC challenged this recommendation and urged
that such an important and widespread means of family planning could not be
ignored. Other members disagreed and warned that, apart from the difficulties
involved in defining abortion and obtaining accurate information about its
occurrence, the inclusion of this topic as a part of the basic survey instrument
would be politically sensitive and could result in refusal to participate by a
number of countries, particularly in Africa (PSC 1974a: Third Meeting). The TAC
reviewed the matter again, at the request of the PSC, and recommended that,
among the four modules which should be given priority in preparation, a module
on abortion be included for countries wanting to use it as a part of their survey.
However, some members of the Committee continued to have reservations about
the validity of the data which would be obtained (TAC 1974a: Fourth Meeting).
Several PSC members insisted that countries prepared to include the Abortion
Module should be given priority status with regard to technical and other assistance. In the end it was agreed that the Project Director and his staff would
recommend to all countries the application of the Abortion Module, as well as
other modules, but that no country would be rejected or given inferior treatment

TABLE 1.1

Countries participating in World Fertility Survey

Region and country	Year of fieldwork	Region and country	Year of fieldwork
A *Developing countries*			
Africa		**Europe**	
Benin	1981–2	Portugal	1979–80
Cameroon	1978		
Ghana	1979–80	**Latin America and Caribbean**	
Ivory Coast	1980–1		
Kenya	1977–8	Colombia	1976
Lesotho	1977	Costa Rica	1976
Mauritania	1981–2	Dominican Rep.	1975
Morocco	1980	Ecuador	1979–80
Nigeria	1981–2	Guyana	1975
Senegal	1978	Haiti	1977
Sudan (North)	1978–9	Jamaica	1975–6
Tunisia	1978	Mexico	1976–7
		Panama	1975–6
		Paraguay	1979
Asia and Pacific		Peru	1977–8
Bangladesh	1975–6	Trinidad & Tobago	1977
Fiji	1974	Venezuela	1977
Indonesia[a]	1976		
Iran	1977	**Middle East**	
Korea, Rep. of	1974		
Malaysia[b]	1974	Egypt	1980
Nepal	1976	Jordan[c]	1976
Pakistan	1975	Syria	1978
Philippines	1978	Turkey	1978
Sri Lanka	1975	Yemen AR	1979
Thailand	1975		
B *Developed countries*			
Belgium[d]	1975–6	Japan	1974
Bulgaria	1976	Netherlands	1975
Czechoslovakia	1977	Norway	1977–8
Denmark	1975	Poland	1977
Finland	1977	Romania	1978
France	1977–8	Spain	1977
Great Britain	1976	Sweden	1981
Hungary	1977	Switzerland	1980
Israel	1973–5	United States	1976
Italy	1979	Yugoslavia	1976

[a] Java and Bali only.   [b] Peninsular Malaysia only.   [c] East Bank only.
[d] Flemish part only.

if it declined to follow that advice (PSC 1975: Fifth Meeting). Further, it was decided to include in the core questionnaire a question on whether the respondent had ever had a miscarriage or abortion or still birth and if so how many, with the understanding that it be applied by the staff with some flexibility and only where its inclusion would not be considered offensive (PSC 1976: Seventh Meeting).

Several other modifications to the core questionnaire were considered from time to time. Thus, USAID urged that the topic of availability of, and accessibility to, various methods of contraception be included to contribute to the monitoring and management of family planning programmes (PSC 1974b: Fourth Meeting; PSC 1975: Fifth Meeting). After a specially designed test conducted in three countries at the request of the PSC, it was decided in 1976 to incorporate in the core questionnaire, as mandatory, three questions on community availability of major known methods of contraception, the time required to get there and the perceived costs of purchase. However, an item on presence of contraceptives in the respondent's home was not included in the core questionnaire but only in the optional Family Planning Module, together with a number of other facets of availability (PSC 1976: Seventh Meeting).

In general, the PSC and the Project Director were reluctant to expand or modify the core questionnaire as it would complicate the execution of the programme and possibly reduce comparability of the data from various national surveys. Therefore, proposals made in the TAC for additional topics to be included, such as factors affecting fecundity, perception of infant mortality and information on income (TAC 1973: First Meeting), as well as variation in questionnaire content between rural and urban respondents, were not adopted although attempts were made by the staff to formulate satisfactory questions. Furthermore, proposed questions on whether the most recent pregnancy was planned and the birth was wanted were not included in the core questionnaire but only in the fertility and family planning modules (TAC 1974b: Fifth Meeting; PSC 1975: Fifth Meeting). A proposal made by the International Labour Office to modify or add to the core questionnaire to cover certain aspects of migration and economic activities was not accepted, and rather than preparing a new module on these topics it was decided to respond on an *ad hoc* basis to requests, if any, from countries wishing to obtain data on these topics (TAC 1977: Eighth Meeting).

Throughout the implementation phase the policy was maintained that all countries wishing to participate had to accept and apply the general guidelines and principles of WFS. In several cases a potentially interested country expressed reluctance to include certain questions but usually gave in or withdrew its request. Only in one instance was a case brought before the PSC for decision, when a Latin American country which declined to include certain questions on availability of family planning was, after considerable discussion, maintained in the programme on the grounds that the questions concerned had only recently been included as mandatory and the survey as planned was technically sound.

Countries which were meeting many but not all the requirements could be granted 'associate status', which meant they would be granted full recognition by WFS on technical grounds but not be entitled to technical or financial assistance. This was a decision left for the Project Director to make. The main consideration was that the high quality of data collection and the overall purpose of WFS be maintained, while geographical and topical coverage was less important. Surveys in two non-self-governing territories (Hong Kong and Guadeloupe/Martinique) were granted associate status.

An important feature of WFS as originally conceived was that the surveys included should be based on nationally representative samples. This policy came up for review several times in view of the practical, often political, problems involved in specific situations. In four cases it was agreed to limit the surveys to a part of the country concerned but usually including the major part of it.[6] With growing interest in including some of the most populous countries in the developing world in the programme, it became increasingly clear that the policy of striving towards nationwide coverage might have to be modified if necessary. Such a modified approach was adopted in the case of the People's Republic of China, but only after the cut-off date for recruitment to the WFS programme as such had been passed.[7]

The WFS programme was in several respects unique in the field of international assistance on population and statistics. It promoted development, co-ordination and standardization of data collection and went much further than the United Nations Population Census Programme, which concentrated on standardization of concepts and development of plans. The WFS programme provided a comprehensive package of technical assistance to ensure that all the essential parts of a successful survey programme were available and that competent technical guidance and support would be available upon short notice and with little formality. Adequate financial resources were available to respond to countries' needs and if necessary to make personnel available for limited periods to meet deficiencies in local expertise.

1.6 Programme management

Because each WFS-assisted survey was conducted by the country itself, the key body in the organization was the national executing agency. In a large majority of countries (29) the national statistical office was designated as the responsible body, but in four countries the Ministry of Health and/or the national family planning agency played that role, in five the central population agency and in four the statistical office jointly with the relevant health or population agency. Within each country two administrators, usually senior staff from the national executing agency, were appointed to oversee the survey. One of them, the National Director, often the director of the national executing agency, provided the overall co-ordination of the survey while the other, the Survey Director, was responsible for the day-to-day management working full-time on the execution of the survey. The entire survey staff, including interviewers, editors, coders and computer personnel, were generally nationals of the country concerned.

For each survey a Co-ordinator was designated among the WFS headquarters staff to maintain liaison with the national staff and arrange advisory missions as required, as well as having overall responsibility for ensuring full support for the survey. Technical advisory services to the countries were provided in most cases through short-term *ad hoc* visits by the Co-ordinator and headquarters specialists. Only in a few cases were resident advisers provided.[8]

The WFS headquarters in London was built up from a tiny cadre of specialists during the development phase. In the early days the expectations about the size of the staff were quite modest and in 1973 the Project Director stated: 'We may eventually even have as many as five professional staff members'. However, during the implementation phase of the programme the professional staff increased rapidly to meet commitments, reaching 46 at its peak in mid-1980 and thereafter gradually declining to 23 by the end of 1983. Considerable efforts were made to recruit the most competent staff, with survey experience and from the various disciplines required. Special attention was paid to obtaining as wide a geographical distribution of the professional staff as possible, but shortage of candidates with the specific training and experience required, as well as reluctance to contribute to the brain drain from some developing countries, clearly created difficulties in reaching the desired goal. Around 40 per cent of the professionals recruited for the programme were from developing countries, nearly 25 per cent from the host country, the United Kingdom, and the remainder from various other developed countries.

In addition to the professional staff, support staff were employed at a strength usually below that of the number of professionals, reaching a maximum of around 40 at the peak of the programme in 1980. At the administrative and financial centre in The Hague, a small staff of up to six professionals and five support staff were employed. (The staffing of the programme is presented in table 1.2.)

It was the policy and management style of Maurice Kendall, and followed by his successors as Project Director, to delegate considerable authority to each staff member in dealing with the countries and in promoting the programme. The delegation of authority did not mean that the staff acted independently. Constant interaction, exchange of views and often lively discussions took place between the professional staff directly or in meetings and seminars. At the same time the decentralized management approach at headquarters made it possible for the staff concerned with field operations to establish and maintain close and direct relations with collaborators in the participating countries. Initially, and for a number of years, there was no organizational structure and none of the staff at headquarters had titles. A structure was established only when activities became diversified and the staff strength increased to such an extent that it became necessary.

While the internal management at the professional headquarters was decentralized, the overall management of the programme was very centralized. Close and direct contacts with the countries were maintained by not having a

TABLE 1.2
WFS staffing 1972-1984

End of	Headquarters London		Administrative office The Hague	
	Professional	Support	Professional	Support
1972	2	3	–	1
1973	9	7	4	1
1974	21	14	4	2
1975	29	17	6	2
1976	30	17	5	2
1977	34	21	5	3
1978	35	29	5	5
1979	46	40	6	3
1980	42	36	6	4
1981	37	31	5	5
1982	31	32	4	5
1983	23	34	4	5
1984 (June)	21	18	2	3

Note: Part-time staff and short-term consultants are excluded.

regional set-up, except in the case of Caribbean countries. WFS achieved a considerable degree of freedom to act independently of the funding agencies, and in most instances it was not required to use their headquarters, regional or country representatives as intermediaries or to seek prior approval of projects, appointment of staff or travel. The adequate financial resources made available throughout the programme also facilitated the work and made it possible to respond quickly to needs, particularly in the event of some urgent problems or shortcomings in the countries concerned.

The staff on its part had, and was prepared, to respond to the changing needs in a flexible manner. They were sometimes obliged to set aside other official responsibilities and personal plans to assist in dealing with cases of emergency, including making country visits at very short notice. Frequent and sometimes lengthy field trips were taxing for the management of the programme and often made it necessary for headquarters staff to accept responsibility for the duties of absent colleagues.

Contributing to the good management/staff relations was the policy adopted at an early stage of giving the professional staff members credit for their contributions by naming them as authors of papers and reports except in the case of the Basic Documentation and overall reports. In many international organizations research contributions of individual staff members remain anonymous but it was recognized that such a restrictive policy would not be appropriate for WFS. The programme was dependent upon the work not only of the professional staff but also of consultants and other outside experts, who usually expect acknowledgement of authorship. It was felt impractical and undesirable to treat the staff differently and discriminate against them. This liberal policy facilitated recruitment of high-level staff required for analysis of data and other report writing and contributed substantially to their career development.

Initially, the main emphasis was on the preparation of survey instruments, data collection and data processing. As an increasing number of surveys were carried out and the main tables became available, the priorities gradually changed towards analysis of the data and utilization of the results for research purposes and policy-making and implementation. This change in emphasis was reflected in the work priorities and the composition of the headquarters staff.

A first step to facilitate utilization of data was made by preparing a brief non-technical summary presenting the salient findings and highlights of each survey and publishing it in English, French and Spanish. A specialist group was convened in 1977 to outline policies on the analysis of survey data and the staff prepared a selected list of topics for research. A series of 12 illustrative analyses was initiated in 1978 on various topics to demonstrate the application of various statistical and demographic techniques to the data from a country in order to guide and stimulate other research workers and countries to undertake similar work on data becoming available elsewhere. Another change in emphasis was to give increasing attention to evaluation of the data from each survey, in particular by organizing three-month workshops with the participation of national staff, giving them an opportunity to work full-time on the data from their own country and prepare a comprehensive evaluative report. Also, the convening of national meetings was encouraged to promote dissemination of information and discussion of the policy implications of survey findings, and to stimulate further analysis among local research workers and policy-makers.

As the WFS programme approached completion, increasing emphasis was given to the archiving of the data tapes and documentation and the assessment of experience gained in various phases of survey development and implementation.

A high point in the programme was reached in 1980, when a major international conference with some 600 participants was convened in London to review the survey findings so far available, encourage use of the data and consider the future of WFS. Later in the same year, the significance of the programme was highlighted by the award of the United Nations Peace Medal to Sir Maurice Kendall. In the citation, the UN Secretary General expressed his 'sincere appreciation for the valuable support . . . extended to the United Nations particularly in the field of international population activities'. The citation concluded: 'The World Fertility Survey, which you directed with such distinction, has achieved results which will have a lasting impact on development and population planning'.

1.7   Completion of WFS and future surveys

In 1980 a comprehensive appraisal of the programme was carried out by six independent consultants with experience in the fields of statistics, demography, health and family planning. After a detailed review of WFS activities at headquarters, as well as a few selected participating countries, the group came to the following conclusion concerning the future of the programme:

The Mission considers it highly desirable that WFS continue to be funded to 1986 or 1987 to enable it to complete the current round of fertility surveys, facilitate second-stage analysis, give proper consideration to the long-term future of WFS archives, redesign the core questionnaire and modules in the light of experience and the constructive criticisms made at the World Fertility Survey Conference, review and revise the survey manuals, and assist and advise in a small number of selected countries that have completed first-round surveys and that wish to undertake further fertility surveys, using improved survey instruments and ensuring that WFS standards are maintained. (Smith *et al.* 1980, p. xxiii)

The Mission supported its recommendation by making the following observations:

In the long term, fertility survey results can only be put to maximum use if the surveys themselves are repeated at intervals of five or, at most, ten years. Many of the less developed countries that have participated in WFS will need some guidance and technical assistance, although not on the scale of the first round of fertility surveys, if the surveys are to be repeated regularly. Within WFS itself a vast fund of experience and expertise has been built up, and this must not be wasted. It is imperative that this expertise be put to good use to provide the required assistance in the future. The Mission does not express a view on the long-term future of WFS in its report; it does, however, take the view that the efforts made by the WFS will have been partially wasted if no organization is available in the future to take over the operation of such technical assistance, at as competent a level and with the same degree of flexibility that the WFS now has. (Smith *et al.* 1980, p. xxiii)

The funding agencies decided to extend financial support to the middle of 1984, at a somewhat reduced level but sufficient to ensure the completion of all on-going surveys and related work, including evaluation of the data, and furtherance of the programme of assessment of WFS experience and of the series of cross-national summaries including results from all surveys. The decision to terminate the project was made in spite of a general acceptance of the considerations which the Evaluation Mission had presented in favour of an extension over a longer period. Although the two main funding agencies agreed in this decision, their reasons were different.

In the case of UNFPA, fears that WFS would gradually become a permanent institution — almost another international organization — if it was again extended for a period of five years played a part, but of particular relevance also was the fact that the Fund had considerable difficulties in keeping its support to inter-country activities, of which WFS was a major one, within the limit repeatedly stipulated by its governing body. Furthermore, the newly established United Nations National Household Survey Capability Programme was to some extent seen as a scheme which could meet some of the needs of developing countries for assistance with data collection and analysis in the fields of fertility and family planning, although its primary objective was to assist developing countries to build up national skills and instruments for survey-taking required in the broad field of economic and social development. The problem of competition for scarce resources in support of two major international statistical programmes may also have played a role.

With regard to USAID, the decision was no doubt influenced by a desire to see the WFS programme changed more towards meeting the needs of national family planning service programmes for basic data, to be made available fairly quickly from simplified periodic surveys on knowledge, use and availability of family planning methods, as demonstrated in the Contraceptive Prevalence Surveys promoted by Westinghouse Health Systems with USAID support.[9] It was also possible that the execution of a major AID-supported programme by a non-US institution created increasing difficulties in view of procurement and other regulations.

In 1982 and 1983 ISI and the two main funding agencies took steps which clearly indicated that although WFS was to be brought to an end in its present form, the activities it had carried out in the past would, to a large extent, continue in the future but through other machinery. After preparatory exploration and consultation, the Bureau of ISI made a decision in late 1982, later endorsed by the organization's full assembly, to establish an International Statistical Institute Research Centre (ISIRC) to respond to requests for research, training and advisory services in the field of statistics. Most of the requests received by ISIRC so far and for which it has been possible to obtain funds are in the fields of fertility, family formation and family planning surveys of the WFS type. Thus, under the auspices of ISIRC such surveys are being supported in the People's Republic of China and Rwanda and under consideration in several other countries. UNFPA has fully recognized the importance of periodic fertility and family planning surveys and expressed its readiness to support such activities in developing countries but not on a global or inter-country basis. USAID decided to establish a new survey programme on fertility and family planning practice and availability of services, to become operational at the time when WFS and the Contraceptive Prevalence Survey programme both came to an end in the middle of 1984. Furthermore, USAID country programmes will continue to be available for support of individual surveys of this kind in selected countries.

In spite of maximum efforts to complete the WFS programme as scheduled by the middle of 1984, several activities by their nature inevitably continued beyond that date.

First, a number of manuscripts emerging from the work being undertaken in the concluding months became available for editing, preparation for publication and printing. Some of these were documents which could only be finalized at the very end, such as assessment essays, follow-up of the Symposium held in May 1984, and a Final Report on WFS. Others included the final round of cross-national. summaries, containing data from a number of surveys completed in early 1984, and reports of the last multi-national workshop on evaluation as well as a number of analytical studies.

Second, the very extensive amount of material accumulated by WFS in the form of tapes, documents and records on approaches applied and experience gained needed to be maintained and its accessibility to future research workers secured. Many institutions and scientists expressed great interest in and concern about the future availability of WFS data and urged that steps be taken to ensure their future dissemination and utilization. The process of completing the preparation of edited and standardized data tapes for the most recent surveys also had to be undertaken. ISI, acting together with IUSSP, prepared a proposal for the establishment of a so-called dynamic data base on survey research in fertility which would ensure the maintenance and availability of data from developing countries which participated in WFS and also data from surveys on fertility and related subjects to be carried out in the future in countries which had or had not participated in WFS. USAID agreed to support the operation of such a data base for the three-year period 1984-7, with the objective of maintaining the existing WFS datasets and stimulating efforts to further analyse and utilize WFS data, allowing also for the addition of new datasets to the existing collection.

Notes

1. With the assistance of the International Statistical Institute Research Centre of the ISI, the State Statistical Bureau of China carried out in 1985 representative sample surveys of the WFS type in three areas to obtain detailed information on family health, fertility and family planning.
2. WFS-type surveys have been carried out in several Indian states with the assistance of the World Bank, UNFPA and the United Kingdom. The International Institute for Population Studies in Bombay has collaborated with WFS in several areas of development of survey methodology.
3. Subsequently, the UK Government provided funding for three country surveys and, from 1982, a regular contribution towards headquarters expenses; support was also provided by the Government of France (secondment of personnel and certain analysis work) and the International Development Research Centre (IDRC) of Canada (response errors project).
4. Further discussion of these instruments may be found in chapters 2 and 3.
5. All of these manuals, constituting the WFS Basic Documentation, were published in English French and Spanish and, in the majority of cases, Arabic. An exception was the Data Processing Guidelines, of which only an English version and a French version of volume 1 were produced.
6. Malaysia (Peninsular Malaysia), Indonesia (Java and Bali), Sudan (North) and Jordan (East Bank).
7. Surveys in three areas with an aggregate population of nearly 100 million people, amounting to nearly 10 per cent of the total for the country as a whole (see note 1).
8. Further details may be found in chapter 8.
9. The programme of Contraceptive Prevalence Surveys was launched by USAID largely due to the reluctance of WFS to develop and implement quickly surveys which included questions on availability of contraceptives (Ravenholt 1984).

PART II

Data Collection Instruments

2

The Core Questionnaires

John Cleland
Gwendolen Johnson-Acsádi
Albert Marckwardt

2.1 Origins and nature of WFS core questionnaires

The main purpose of this chapter is to appraise the contents and design of WFS core data collection instruments and to make recommendations for future fertility surveys. Nevertheless it is necessary to start by describing the origins of WFS's approach.

The WFS core questionnaires drew on the experience of numerous fertility and family planning surveys[1] conducted mainly in the 1960s and, particularly, on earlier international efforts to establish comparability in this field. The issue of comparability of fertility and family planning studies was first raised in the 1961 New York Conference of the International Union for the Scientific Study of Population (IUSSP), which established a Committee on Comparative Studies of Fertility and Family Planning. The IUSSP Committee produced a report entitled 'Variables for Comparative Fertility Studies'.[2] In collaboration with the IUSSP Committee, the United Nations developed a core questionnaire for measuring the variables,[3] which, along with extensive explanatory notes, comments and definitions, was published as 'Variables and Questionnaires for Comparative Analysis' (United Nations 1969).[4]

The model questionnaires mentioned above were designed to be applicable anywhere regardless of the level of fertility or economic development. However, as their primary focus was on high fertility countries, they were less useful as models for developed countries with low fertility. For the latter, parallel efforts were made to design a standard questionnaire. WFS also followed this dual approach and issued separate core questionnaires for high and for low fertility countries. In this and following sections, we discuss the questionnaire for high fertility countries. The WFS low fertility questionnaire is described in appendix A.

The original drafts of the WFS core questionnaire and household schedule were prepared by Ryder and Westoff of Princeton University, drawing not only on the existing IUSSP/UN model questionnaires but also on their experience of fertility surveys in the USA. These were circulated to some 200 professionals with relevant experience and knowledge, whose views were collated by Harewood of the University of the West Indies and taken into account in the revision of the pro formae. These were presented to the Technical Advisory Committee (TAC) of the WFS at its first meeting in May 1973, revised in light of comments received and discussed at the four subsequent gatherings of the TAC. The materials were finalized in November 1974 and published in March 1975, after 18 months of work and a total of eight drafts.

The final household schedule contains eight main questions on name, relationship, residence, sex and age to be asked of all household members, two questions on marital status for all adults, and an additional eleven items on fertility, applicable only to adult females. The individual questionnaire, designed for administration to ever-married women in the reproductive age range, is composed of a total of 112 basic questions, with an additional four items for each pregnancy outcome and each former marriage. They are allocated over seven major sections as follows:

	Fixed number of questions	Variable number of questions
1 Respondent's background	12	Country-specific items on religion, ethnicity, language
2 Maternity history	22	4 items for each live and non-live birth
3 Contraceptive knowledge and use	23	—
4 Marriage history	8	4 items for each former marriage
5 Fertility regulation	23	—
6 Work history	14	—
7 Current (last) husband's background	10	—
Total	112	

This total of 112 basic questions with a variable supplement depending upon the number of demographic events in the respondent's life is a somewhat misleading measure of size because it makes no allowance for the inherent redundancy of the questionnaire, caused by alternative versions of the same question, and routing patterns. A fairer indication of its overall length is the estimate that an average respondent, with a total of four pregnancies, one marriage, reasonable contraceptive knowledge and employment experience would be required to answer about 80 questions, taking about 30 minutes to administer.

As the core questionnaire and household schedule were nearing their final form, a number of pre-tests were launched. A full-scale pilot survey was started in Fiji with fieldwork in February to April 1974. A more modest appraisal of the suitability of the questionnaire for Latin America was conducted in Colombia in the summer of 1974, with a sample of 300 women.[5]

It cannot be claimed that either of these pre-tests influenced the content or design of the core questionnaire. The version used in Fiji was already superseded by the time of fieldwork and, in any case, full appraisal of the results came too late to influence the core questionnaire. The Colombian experience could perhaps have affected the nature of the core but no major defects were revealed in this pre-test.

A comparison of the earliest drafts and the version published in 1975 reveals surprisingly few major changes of substance. The main casualties of content over the 18-month period of questionnaire development clearly reflect considerations of moral and political sensitivity. Items on coital frequency, post-partum sexual abstinence and attitudes towards induced abortion were dropped. In addition, attempts to measure media exposure of husband and wife, and kinship, were abandoned. Few appreciable additions were made. The employment history of women generated a great deal of discussion and the final version contains more detail than originally envisaged (but less than some of the intermediate versions). Questions on breastfeeding, initially confined to the last born child, were extended to the penultimate child and method-specific questions about use of contraception were asked of all methods known, rather than restricted to the current or open-interval experience.

The final published document displays one curious feature: alongside the core household schedule and individual questionnaire is an additional detailed set of questions called the fertility regulation module. This arrangement was the outcome of a prolonged and divisive debate about the usefulness of collecting data on the subject of reproductive motivations in large-scale, Third World surveys. Most experts conceded the need to include questions on desire for more children and on the total desired number of children. But opinion was deeply divided over such topics as the desired timing of the next birth, wives' reports on their husbands' attitudes and, above all, on the status of the last pregnancy (i.e. whether it had been planned or was the result of contraceptive failure and whether it had been wanted at all). By the time of the seventh draft, produced in August 1974, the solution was in sight. Questions on the status of the last pregnancy were relegated to a separate supplementary module. The core questionnaire, however, still contained items on contraceptive use prior to the last pregnancy and enquired about reasons for stopping contraception in the open interval. The relevant section 5 of this seventh and penultimate draft comprised a total of eight pages in different colours, designed for administration to different categories of respondent. This compromise was unacceptable to certain members of the TAC and, as a result of their protestations, the core section 5 was further simplified by the omission of the disputed items and compressed into four pages without colour coding. At the same time, a multi-coloured, 13-page fertility regulation module was finalized and published alongside the core questionnaire with a recommendation for use in *most* developing countries in preference to the core section 5.

How much does the final core questionnaire and its semi-voluntary accompanying module differ from the original starting point, the UN document 'Variables and Questionnaires for Comparative Analysis'? The differences between the

WFS core and the UN Short List, regarded then as 'indispensable for any fertility investigation', are revealing. Omitted by WFS were items on approval of, and interest in, contraception, knowledge of family planning services and how to use specific methods, and decomposition of additional and total children desired into desired number of sons and daughters. Conversely, the WFS document contains full marriage and pregnancy histories, which are missing from the UN Short List. Clearly, the WFS core reflects a shift away from attitudinal and family planning variables towards more traditional concerns of demography: fertility, nuptiality and infant and child mortality. A further comparison with the UN Short List, defined as 'desirable for all studies that have sufficient staff', confirms this diagnosis. Nearly all the items omitted by WFS in its core or fertility regulation module concern reproductive motivations or family planning matters.

It is ironical that the core data collection instruments of the WFS, a project funded by USAID and UNFPA, the two leading proponents of birth control, should differ in these respects from the model questionnaires advocated by the IUSSP and the UN Department of International Economic and Social Affairs, whose stance towards population matters has always been less closely tied to particular policy objectives. There are perhaps two main reasons. First, the period of the late 1960s and early 1970s saw a growing disillusionment with the attitudinal components of KAP-type enquiries. The contrast between their anodyne results (e.g. small family size ideals, approval of and interest in family planning) and the apparent failure, at that time, of family planning programmes tended to discredit the KAP approach. Secondly, the global nature of the WFS and the concomitant need to develop widely acceptable and uncontroversial core instruments clearly played a role in restricting the subject matter of the Survey.

At this juncture it is appropriate to consider the merits and demerits of the concept of a core questionnaire, which was mandatory for those participating countries dependent upon external financing. Clearly a model questionnaire, as carefully designed and widely discussed as the WFS core, guarantees some degree of substantive success for a survey. The questionnaire consists mainly of items which had proved feasible in previous surveys and which represented a consensus among demographers concerning substantive priorities. In our judgement, the 'guarantee' was honoured. None of the WFS surveys proved to be a total failure; despite wide variations in the reliability of data collected and in the elucidation of fertility, all have yielded data which are valuable at the national level and amenable to cross-national comparisons. This result could not have been achieved without carefully considered and strongly endorsed core instruments.

Furthermore, a degree of standardization in questionnaire content and design offered both financial and administrative advantages. The costs of developing a totally new questionnaire for each of the 42 participants would have been considerable and, of course, more vulnerable to errors and oversights of design or substance. Use of a common questionnaire made possible the preparation and application of other standard materials, ranging from interviewers' manuals to data processing guidelines and finally to the contents of the report.

There is also a price to be paid for standardization and comparability. Inevitably flexibility and innovation tend to be stifled. The WFS strove to introduce flexibility in substantive content by the design and promulgation of a set of modules on particular topics. These could be added in their totality or in part to the core questionnaire. Participating countries were also encouraged to modify the wording of the core questionnaire and the order of items to meet their particular needs and to add country-specific items of interest. However the constraints on the length of interview precluded major additions. The core questionnaire itself took about 30 minutes to administer and another 10-15 minutes were required for most of the modules. If 45-50 minutes is the practical upper limit of interview length, there was little scope for a country, which wished to use one module, to add further to questionnaire content. A discussion of the use of modules and country-specific additions are described by Singh in chapter 3.

It can also be argued convincingly that a single model questionnaire is insensitive to the varying priorities and situations within the developing world. Countries where family planning programmes or the habit of contraception are well established differ considerably in their data needs from settings where natural fertility persists and where there is little official interest in anti-natal policies. Though the modules gave some flexibility, the core itself was more suitable to the former than the latter situation.

Ultimately, however, it must be recognized that WFS had no choice in the decision to opt for standardization in questionnaire content. Cross-national comparability of results was part of the original WFS mandate and this goal could only be achieved by insisting upon a high degree of uniformity.

2.2 Changes to the core questionnaire and country-specific deviations

The need for cross-national comparability of results largely explains one of the more remarkable features of WFS core instruments: their durability. Although, after two years of experience, a number of suggested modifications was published in the WFS *Basic Documentation* series, most concerned minor matters of measurement. Apart from the addition of current or last husband's age, the single major substantive change concerned contraception. USAID had begun to urge the importance of gathering information on the availability of contraceptives, both in the household and in the community. Accordingly, at its sixth meeting in 1976, the Programme Steering Committee requested the WFS to conduct field trials to determine whether such questions could be asked, and, if so, the reliability of answers. Contingent upon a positive result of the trials, the questions would be added to the core.

Samples of approximately 300 women were selected and interviewed in India, Panama and Turkey. In light of the results obtained (Rodríguez 1977), the following questions, asked separately for the pill, IUD, condom and female sterilization, were added to section 3 of the core: 'Where would you go to get . . .?', 'How long would it take to get there?', and 'How much do you think . . .

may cost there?'. These were asked only if the respondent had earlier indicated knowledge of the respective method. Questions on the availability in the household of pills, condoms and other female scientific methods were not put into the core but they were added to the family planning module.

Other important modifications were made in the later surveys though they were never formalized in the WFS *Basic Documentation* series. In response to the growing realization that birth spacing generated an appreciable potential demand for contraception, the following question to be asked of women who wanted more children was added: 'Do you want to have the child soon or would you prefer to wait a few years?'. A less frequently adopted addition to section 5 was to ask women who indicated that they wanted no (more) children, 'Do you mean not for the time being, or not at all?'. The intention was to obtain better measurement of the limitation motive.

It has been noted that countries participating in the WFS were not expected to follow the wording and structure of the core questionnaire exactly, and were given scope for adding extra questions or topics, some of which were covered by the modules. But they were expected to collect the information sought in the core in a form that would guarantee a high degree of comparability across countries. For purposes of cross-national research it is essential to be aware of variations in question wording or in the ordering of questions which might affect comparability. A compendium of such variations and exceptions, titled 'Comparability of Questionnaires', may be found in Singh (1984a) and major departures are summarized in appendix B.

The general verdict is that the contents of the core questionnaire were faithfully reproduced in the majority of countries, a remarkable result in view of the great diversity of cultures and political attitudes towards population and family planning represented by the 42 participating countries, and a testimony to the prudence exercised at the design stage.[6] The main source of non-comparability concerns the female work history (section 6) where a number of countries chose to use a more restrictive definition of work. There is also clear evidence that respondent interpretation of the core questions on work varied widely between surveys (United Nations 1980b; 1982b, ch. 16). Important country-specific deviations occurred in the administration of certain fertility preference questions in Bangladesh, Cameroon and Senegal and the topic of nuptiality was handled quite differently from the core in the Caribbean and in Nepal.

2.3 Appraisal of substantive content: an overview

In attempting to appraise the substantive content of the WFS core questionnaire, fertility regulation module and household schedule, we are confronted by a number of problems. The aims of the programme are so broad that there cannot be precise criteria for evaluation. At various times, detailed demographic *description*, elucidation of the underlying *causes* of fertility behaviour and *policy* relevance have been considered as the prime substantive objectives of WFS. Clearly, these three requirements carry different, though overlapping, implications for questionnaire content and cannot all be fulfilled in a single instrument. There is the additional complexity, to which we have already referred, of the varying circumstances and priorities of participating countries. A topic which is relevant in one setting may be of little interest in another. Our reaction to these problems is to evaluate the questionnaire content by each major criterion in turn, bearing in mind that the conclusions may vary according to country situations.

Demographic description

Let us consider first the criterion of demographic description, which is generally admitted to be the main strength of WFS. In this regard, the decision to include complete maternity histories in the questionnaire has been fully vindicated. The collection of retrospective histories on such a vast scale has stimulated advances in analytic techniques, which are described in chapter 25. Together they have made possible detailed examination of the process of family formation and fertility trends, far beyond the limited scope afforded by more traditional, restricted household survey approaches, based on parity and date of last birth, or based on the last two births as in the recent surveys in the Indian states of Bihar and Rajasthan. Even in surveys where inaccurate dating of live births precludes straightforward reconstruction of the past, the existence of birth histories, with their opportunities for checks of internal consistency and external validation against previous estimates, have permitted analysts to identify the likely nature and direction of errors and reach more confident conclusions about the recent course of fertility than is possible with more restricted data sets. Thus, in terms of estimating current fertility, the crucial difference between the birth history and 'last birth' approaches lies not in the fact that the former necessarily gives superior estimates, but that histories can be subjected to more checks and are more amenable to adjustment. Aggregation over several years to reduce sampling error is a second important advantage of the history approach. Only in countries where the level and trend of fertility are well established from other sources might it be reasonable to omit a full maternity history from a fertility survey. However, such countries are usually characterized by low fertility and thus the cost of collecting a full history is slight.

The great unexpected bonus of WFS birth histories has been the quality of information on infant and child mortality. Perhaps the most substantial contribution to demographic description lies here. Even in surveys where analysis of fertility is problematic because of data defects, plausible levels and trends in childhood mortality over the previous 10-15 years have been derived and relationships between birth spacing and survivorship elucidated. In short, the experience of WFS has proved that birth histories bring substantial gains, even in innumerate and illiterate societies where this approach was hitherto considered too ambitious.

Similarly the incorporation of complete marriage histories in the core questionnaire has permitted detailed studies of nuptiality. The main analytic emphasis has been on timing of the first union. However, one important limitation in the study of age at first marriage from WFS surveys of ever-married women is the dearth of information on single women. The omission of educational items from the household surveys of many Asian surveys has proved a costly mistake, a point that will be discussed later in more detail. The data on dissolution and remarriage have received far less attention, perhaps in reaction to the realization that non-exposure due to dissolution acts as a less important restraint on fertility than hitherto assumed.

The proximate determinants of fertility may be subsumed under the label of demographic description. Following Bongaarts (1978), four major determinants may be identified: sexual exposure, post-partum infecundability, contraception and induced abortion. The WFS core and fertility regulation module contain relevant data on three of these. The missing item is induced abortion. Though a considerable number of countries in the WFS programme chose to add questions on induced abortion, the results, with the exception of those from the Republic of Korea survey, appear to suffer from underreporting (Casterline and Ashurst 1984). Thus the well-known deficiency of straightforward question and answer techniques in this regard is confirmed and we may conclude that little of substantive interest was lost by the absence of questions on induced abortion in the WFS core.

The marriage data have been extensively used as a surrogate for sexual exposure in descriptions of the proximate determinants of fertility. Supplementation of marriage histories with more direct information on sexual exposure would have been a major advance but was considered culturally unacceptable. This point will be discussed more fully in the next section.

Post-partum infecundability is now recognized as a major proximate determinant of fertility. The inclusion in the core questionnaire of breastfeeding data, from which mean durations of post-partum amenorrhoea may be estimated indirectly, is perhaps the single most important advance over the earlier IUSSP/ UN models. However, just as marriage is not an entirely satisfactory substitute for sexual exposure, so direct measurement of amenorrhoea would have been a valuable addition to breastfeeding.

The WFS core questionnaire has elicited occasional criticism for excessive orientation towards contraception. Ironically, measurement of this proximate determinant in the core and fertility regulation module is in some respects weaker than for the other two major direct determinants of fertility. There is little information on the timing of use and none on duration of use. This poses no problems for estimating the effect of contraception on fertility through Bongaarts's model, which requires current use data only. However, the deficiency has caused difficulties for more ambitious models which attempt to decompose reproductive time more directly (Gaslonde 1972; Hobcraft and Little 1984) and has greatly restricted analysis of contraceptive use effectiveness and fecundability.

While fertility and its proximate determinants, childhood mortality and nuptiality constitute the main contributions of WFS to demographic description, the role of the household schedule in providing age, and sex and marital status distributions of the whole population should not be forgotten. Admittedly this contribution has been a minor one, partly because these data are already widely available from other sources but also because the survey design of WFS encouraged distortions in the recorded age and sex structure (UN 1983a; Marckwardt 1984). In many WFS household enumerations, there is evidence of severe shifting of women beyond the boundaries which defined eligibility for the individual survey and evidence of a deficit of males. Perhaps the most interesting addition to demographic knowledge contributed by WFS household surveys is the nationally representative data provided on family structure. So far these data have not been fully exploited (though see Kabir 1980; Zoughlami and Allsopp 1985), but we foresee major use of them in the future.

Causal analysis

While a degree of favourable consensus can probably be reached concerning the suitability of WFS core instruments for demographic description, the same cannot be claimed for WFS's contribution to a deeper understanding of fertility behaviour and change. Comment upon this aspect of WFS has been almost universally unfavourable.

In the development of the core questionnaire, the view was expressed that the substantive content of the programme should be derived from a theoretical framework. These arguments were successfully countered by those who pointed to the absence of an agreed framework and who maintained that a pragmatic approach was more appropriate for an international project.

As a result, the WFS core questionnaires are essentially atheoretical. With the single exception of female employment, where selection of questions was influenced by the prolonged theoretical debate concerning the links between work and reproductive behaviour, questionnaire content reflects the traditional descriptive nature of demographic enquiries rather than theoretically derived hypotheses. Variables such as occupation, education, urban/rural residence are all too broad for illuminating analysis of causes, yet they are such powerful correlates of fertility that their presence is required.

Accepting that these criticisms are valid, can we identify, in retrospect, how the defect can be remedied? The search is for causal factors that meet the following five conditions:

1 They are widely thought to be important underlying determinants of fertility.

2 They are amenable to succinct and reliable measurement in large-scale national surveys, which are primarily directed towards women.

3 They are invulnerable to severe problems of circular or reverse causality when measured cross-sectionally.

4 They avoid intractable problems of cross-cultural comparability.

5   They vary sufficiently between individuals or families to permit statistical analysis.

We suspect that if twelve eminent population scientists were given this mandate, they would not only find difficulty in providing suggestions that met all five criteria but their recommendations would vary widely. This likely outcome reflects the total lack of consensus about the causes of fertility change and the severe limitations inherent in large single-round sample surveys designed to be widely applicable. No doubt household economists would urge measurement of the actual and perceived costs and benefits of children but to cover this topic in any but the most superficial way would surely be too costly in data collection terms and imbalance any model questionnaire. Many sociologists would place kinship structure and obligations as a top priority but this topic defies straightforward conceptualization and measurement. Changes in attitudes and aspirations of parents towards their offspring lies at the heart of much theoretical speculation, but cross-cultural comparability in such attitudinal data is very difficult to achieve and there is the additional problem of establishing the direction of causality. Similar objections apply to other hypotheses concerning moral and social acceptability of the idea of birth control and of particular methods. Correlations between such perceptions and attitudes and behaviour itself would be difficult to interpret because of the problem of *post facto* rationalization. In summary, the theory of the subject and the links between theoretical propositions and their empirical investigation are not sufficiently advanced to offer solutions that would command widespread endorsement.

These difficulties are not paraded to deflect the criticism that the WFS core questionnaires obtained relatively little data of direct relevance to the underlying causes of fertility change. The criticism is patently true. However, we stress the point that no obvious remedies exist, despite the intensive work on fertility determinants that has occurred since the inception of WFS.

The solution lies at least partly in serious questionnaire development. It is regrettable that, despite the huge sums spent on the execution of family planning and fertility surveys, so little attention has been paid to methodological work involving a reiterative process of defining clear hypotheses and concepts, intensive interviewing and the formulation, testing and refinement of questions. Attempts to produce more causally relevant approaches than that of WFS (e.g. Bilsborrow, Adlakha, Cross, Chao and Nizamuddin 1982) will remain unconvincing unless linked to coherent theories and tried and tested in the field.

In conclusion, we are inclined to the view that the atheoretical posture of the WFS core was not only justified but inevitable. Perhaps the failure of the programme lies in the dearth of theoretically relevant modules, where more speculative attempts to test particular hypotheses could have been made, without insistence that they be incorporated into all surveys. The WFS only produced two such modules, the economic module(s) and the community module. The limitations of the latter are discussed in chapter 33, while the economic module, or parts thereof, was only used in a handful of surveys. It is perhaps regrettable that greater use of the economic module was not made and that WFS did not develop additional modules on such factors as the education of children, and on modernism (following the ideas in Goldberg 1974).

Policy relevance

For reasons that we have outlined earlier, the original WFS core data collection instruments contain few items whose presence is justified largely or solely on grounds of their relevance to government policies or programmes. The exceptions to this generalization are the series of questions concerning reproductive preferences and the 1977 additions on contraceptive availability, though their inclusion can also be strongly defended on explanatory grounds. We are not asserting that WFS core data are irrelevant to policy issues. The descriptive data on fertility, childhood mortality, contraception, breastfeeding and other topics are of obvious interest to governments. Without such essential facts, population projections are largely guesswork and population policies have to be formed in a vacuum of knowledge. Nevertheless, this value of WFS data is a by-product of scientific objectives.

As described in section 2.2, the main changes made to the core questionnaire in 1977 were motivated largely by a desire to shift the WFS programme towards the collection of data that might be more operationally useful, particularly to the managers of family planning programmes. Yet the fact remains that, if family planning programme relevance had been the original, primary goal of WFS, the core questionnaire would have had a different balance of topics, more similar to the KAP surveys of the 1960s and the various 1970 model questionnaires. In addition to the measurement of knowledge and perceived accessibility of supply sources for important contraceptive methods, the criterion of policy-relevance might have led to more detailed questioning on knowledge of methods themselves, including how to use them, sources of supply, use-effectiveness, reasons for discontinuation and on attitudes towards birth control in general and towards particular methods. Many of these items may be found in the family planning module.

2.4   Detailed assessment of substantive content

In this section we consider the contents of the core questionnaires in detail. Issues of design will be discussed in the next section. This substantive review is important because WFS core instruments are already widely used by survey researchers independently of the WFS programme itself. Thus any improvements that we can suggest on the basis of the last decade of experience may make an appreciable contribution to future surveys. Our approach is that every single item in a model questionnaire must justify its presence in terms of analytic utility. We shall also invoke the principle that questions should yield reasonably reliable data. As issues of demographic measurement and fertility preferences are discussed separately in chapters 5 and 31, we give special emphasis to the background and socio-economic sections of the individual questionnaire. We start, however, with the household schedule.

Household schedule

Most items in the household schedule are simple and straightforward and require no further comment. The few points of interest stem from the relationship between the schedule and the detailed questionnaire and, in particular, from the fact that interviewing of eligible women usually followed immediately after completion of the schedule. We have already noted the regrettable omission in some surveys of the items on educational status. For survey designs in which all women aged 15–49 were interviewed in detail, this omission was not crucial, but for individual samples confined to ever-married women, it was a serious defect. As education is a powerful determinant of age at marriage, the failure to obtain the educational status of single women greatly restricted analysis of recent trends and differentials in nuptiality. Moreover, it precluded the computation of total fertility rates for educational subgroups of the population. The lesson is clear: in future surveys where the household schedule is the only source of data on single women, particular care must be devoted to the contents of the schedule. In some instances, it may be desirable to gather information on the religion and other characteristics of single women in addition to education, to allow computation of differentials in relation to these variables.

In a considerable number of WFS surveys, provision was made in the schedule to collect date of birth of each household member in addition to age. The rationale is discussed in chapter 5 and we accept the validity of the arguments deployed there in favour of allowing dates of birth to be collected in the schedule.

The core household schedule contains eleven columns in which lifetime fertility and date and survivorship of most recent birth are recorded. These items were generally retained for the large minority of surveys which employed an expanded household sample, but were typically omitted in other surveys on the grounds of duplication with the individual questionnaire. Obviously, in surveys where all women in the reproductive age range were eligible for the individual interview, the only possible advantage of retaining fertility items on the schedule is the extra information on older women, aged 50 or more. In our view, this gain does not usually justify the associated costs, because recall lapse erodes confidence in the data; furthermore, even where the prospects of obtaining reliable data are good, this information is of historical interest only. In the instance of ever-married individual samples, an additional possible advantage of household schedule fertility questions is the information concerning never-married women. The WFS provides a sufficient range of experience to provide a detailed assessment of the importance of gathering fertility data for never-married women and this topic, together with the wider issue of the costs and benefits of all-women samples, is discussed in chapter 11. Based on the experience of all-women samples and on the few instances such as Fiji, Peru and Lesotho which used ever-married samples but obtained household data on fertility for all adult women, the general conclusion is that the estimates of total fertility were affected little by the additional births relating to single women. Only in four surveys (Costa Rica, Mexico, Kenya and Cameroon) did the proportion of single women reporting any live births rise above 10 per cent. Note, however, that this conclusion would not necessarily apply in surveys which employ a less liberal definition of marriage.

The WFS recommended that all household surveys collect information on the physical characteristics of the dwelling, such as lighting, construction materials, toilet facilities, nature of water supply and the ownership of modern objects. The implementation of this guideline was patchy. While some countries collected extensive data (e.g. Morocco, Sri Lanka), others (e.g. Nepal, Colombia) collected none. For this reason and for the more prosaic reason that these household variables were not transferred routinely and quickly to individual survey data files, little analytic use has been made of this type of information until recently. But their potential value in permitting the construction of indices of economic living standards which can then be used in Country Reports (see Morocco) or in multivariate analyses of reproductive behaviour has already been demonstrated (e.g. Little and Perera 1981; Freedman, Khoo and Supraptilah 1981; Cleland, Little and Pitaktepsombati 1979). The use of particular items such as toilet facilities for analysis of infant and child mortality is perhaps greater (see Meegama 1980; Hobcraft 1984; Guerra 1981; Casterline (ed.) 1985). Their relative neglect in the WFS programme is unfortunate and symptomatic of a general tendency to overlook household data.

Respondent's and husband's backgrounds (sections 1 and 7)

We consider the first and last sections of the individual questionnaire together, because of their overlapping nature. Along with section 6, on the respondent's employment history, and the household schedule, they provide the sole data on social and economic characteristics of individuals and households.

Section 1 of the questionnaire starts with the following sequence of questions:

101   'Do you live in this house?'
102   IF NO TO 101 'Do you live in (name of sample locality)?'
103   IF NO TO 102 'Where do you live?'

The logic of these questions is clear. Because most WFS samples were *de facto* (i.e. they included temporary visitors to selected households), the urban-rural character and region of the respondent's normal locality of residence could not be assigned automatically for all individuals from the known character of the sampled cluster.

Despite their obvious justification, were these questions useful? Examination of data for five surveys indicates that only a small number of visitors from areas other than the sampled locality were interviewed, representing between one and five per cent of the total sample of women. The proportion who would have been misclassified in terms of urban-rural residence and region is of course even smaller. We believe that this level of measurement imprecision is acceptable and that questions 101–103 can be deleted from future questionnaires, unless population mobility is thought to be atypically high.[7]

Having established the usual place of residence, the core questionnaire proceeds to ascertain the urban–rural nature of residence in childhood, as follows:

104   'Have you always lived in (usual locality)?'
105   IF YES TO 104 'What kind of area would you say this was when you were growing up, say to age 12? Was it countryside, a town or city?'
106   IF NO TO 104 'In what kind of area did you live mostly when you were growing up, say to age 12? Was it in the countryside, in a town or in a city?'

There are two issues here: the substantive merit of the topic and the reliability of the childhood variable. These data permit crude classifications of respondents and their husbands (see the parallel question 708) into four basic categories according to the urban–rural character of current and childhood residence. In the few analyses in which this variable has been used, the reproductive behaviour of rural to urban migrant has been found to be intermediate between the 'pure' rural and 'pure' urban groups.

This finding is unsurprising, even banal. Furthermore the potentially more interesting category, rural residents with an urban childhood, have usually formed too small a group to sustain serious investigation. It seems to us therefore that the inclusion of questions 104–106 in future model questionnaires is unjustified. While the relationship between migration and fertility is undoubtedly interesting, it cannot be elucidated by such a grossly over-simplified approach.[8]

Even if these arguments are found unconvincing, the evidence from reliability studies points to the same conclusion. Table 2.1 shows the level of consistency in response between first and second interviews for two WFS surveys. Nearly one-third of respondents (31 per cent) gave inconsistent replies in Indonesia and 18 per cent did so in the Dominican Republic. These figures indicate that the childhood variable tends to be measured with the poor reliability which is usually found for attitudinal variables. Special cross-tabulations (confined to women who had always lived in the same locality) of current and childhood type of place of residence further underline the subjective nature of the childhood variable. In some surveys, appreciable proportions of these women who currently reside in areas classified as rural nevertheless claim an urban childhood.

The core questionnaire devotes three questions to the measurement of the respondent's schooling and an identical set for the husband. There can be no quarrel with this emphasis, as length of schooling is such a powerful predictor of reproductive behaviour. The addition of a question, for women and partners with less than six years of schooling, on literacy ('Can you read – say a newspaper or magazine?') requires some discussion, because few country reports or subsequent analyses have utilized this datum and the validity of self-reported literacy (or in the case of the husband, proxy-reported) is dubious.

Cross-classification of literacy by years of schooling shows very wide country

TABLE 2.1

Cross-classification of respondents according to answers given in first and second interviews, concerning childhood type of place of residence

	First interview		
	Village	Town	City
Second interview			
A Dominican Republic			
Village	506	49	10
Town	48	123	19
City	8	14	34
B Indonesia			
Village	235	44	13
Town	44	76	23
City	13	19	29

variations. For instance, among women who had no formal schooling (or less than a year), the proportions literate range from one-fifth or more in Indonesia, Republic of Korea, Malaysia, Thailand, Portugal, Colombia, Costa Rica and Mexico, to less than five per cent in 16 other countries. Similarly, among those with four complete years of schooling, the proportions literate range from about one-third in Egypt and Ghana to over 90 per cent in the majority of surveys. Does this reflect definitional or measurement error, genuine differences of curriculum content or of the popularity of adult literacy classes? Most likely, these cross-national variations reflect a mixture of all three factors,[9] but the lesson appears to be that literacy questions should not be dropped. Arguably, one of the main reasons for the powerful relationship between length of formal schooling and fertility behaviour is the exposure to new ideas and enhanced opportunities for participation in a modern way of life. Literacy is a component of this wider change and indeed may exert a more important influence on reproductive attitudes than length of school attendance, *per se*. There is scope for interesting analyses here which, to our knowledge, have not yet been attempted. Until this work is completed, we suggest that self-reported literacy be retained in future model questionnaires.

The core questionnaire devotes a whole section to the collection of employment data concerning female respondents. This will be discussed below. In contrast, only three items are collected on the husband's work: his current or most recent occupation; his employment status (self-employed, family employee, non-family employee); mode of payment (cash, kind, unpaid) if an employee, or number of employees if self-employed. Despite their sparseness, these data have been little utilized. The reasons for this neglect lie partly in the lack of conceptual clarity underlying the precise choice and administration of questions and partly in the highly uneven distributions across categories. Let us consider the conceptual issues first. We can discern three dimensions of potential interest for analysis of fertility: broad socio-economic status; involvement in the cash economy; and involvement in non-familial means of production. There are powerful theoretical grounds for thinking that each of these factors is related to fertility.

The problems of using occupational data in the construction of a convincing index of socio-economic status are well known and exacerbated, in the case of WFS, by the fact that proxy-reports by women are often vague and difficult to code. The coding scheme itself generated controversy in the development phase of WFS. Some members of the Programme Steering Committee strongly urged use of the International Statistical Classification of Occupations (ISCO) developed by the International Labour Organization. Others, including many WFS staff, thought ISCO inappropriate for fertility analysis because, without going to the fifth digit, it did not separate self-employed from other agriculturalists or allow an easy distinction between domestic servants and other related service workers (which was thought to be particularly important for the coding of women's occupation). Furthermore, the imposition of ISCO was impolitic in Latin America which had its own standard classification system, COTA, developed by the Inter-American Statistical Institute. The net result was that a special one-digit WFS classification was used in all surveys, together with three digits of COTA in most of Latin America and three digits of ISCO in most other countries.

It cannot be claimed that the WFS coding system has paid high dividends. Most analysts, including the United Nations Population Division and the WFS itself in its *Cross-National Summaries* series, have used a four category summary of husband's occupation: professional and clerical, sales and service, skilled and unskilled manual, and agricultural. For female occupation, a different four category scheme has been suggested (United Nations 1981b). These broad groupings can be derived easily from ISCO or COTA. To our knowledge, no one has yet used the data on number of employees for the self-employed (who typically comprise one-quarter to a half of all husbands) in definitions of socio-economic status. Though a minority of the self-employed, in the first 19 surveys studied by Singh (1980a), report one or more employees, nevertheless they account for over 10 per cent of the total sample of husbands in 6 countries. The upwards adjustment in socio-economic status for employers would not be entirely trivial, particularly for the problematic sales and service occupations. Here we criticize the WFS for not providing a rationale for the inclusion of items in the core questionnaire nor clear guidelines for their analytic use.

As with the question on number of employees asked about self-employed husbands, the information on mode of payment for family or other employees has been almost entirely neglected in analyses. The major reason is that parallel information was unavailable for the self-employed group. Particularly in the case of self-employed farmers, for whom the issue of cash versus subsistence production is important, this omission was critical; as a result, this datum was totally inadequate as an overall measure of involvement in the cash economy. Perhaps the question was never intended to provide such a measure (again the absence of a clear rationale is regrettable) but merely to refine the somewhat hazy distinction between employees and family workers. If this was the purpose, the question was still of little use. In most surveys, the overwhelming majority of family or other employees were reported by their wives to receive payment in cash, and thus the discriminatory power of this variable was weak.

We come finally to employment status itself, which at least has the merit of availability for the total sample of husbands. In most surveys, the proportion classified as employed by a family member was too small for separate consideration, with the consequence that this group either had to be excluded or amalgamated with the self-employed. As with most other characteristics of husbands, this variable has been largely ignored by analysts, with the exception of one large-scale comparative analysis (Rodríguez and Cleland 1981a). This study showed that in only 1 out of 24 study populations was employment status of the husband significantly related to recent marital fertility, after controls for urban–rural residence, husband's education and occupation; nor were there any significant interactions between employment status and the control variables. Whether this resoundingly negative finding is of theoretical importance, as the authors claim, or the outcome of inadequate measurement or conceptualization need not concern us here. However we must conclude that there are no sound grounds for retaining this item in future fertility surveys, unless accompanied by more detailed information on, for instance, the labour inputs of children, which are often assumed by theorists to be strongly linked to the existence of family enterprises.

In summary, the substantive yield from questions 710–713 of the core questionnaire has been minimal or of such a nature to discourage further interest. While we urge the retention of husband's education and occupation for the purpose of defining, albeit loosely, socio-economic status, the other questions should not be retained in the present form.

As usual in matters of questionnaire content, it is easier to be critical than to be constructive. Can we now suggest items that might be recommended for future surveys, as superior replacements for the items that we have just dismissed? The great restriction in the context of most fertility surveys is the fact that the prime respondent is the wife and not the husband himself.[10] This feature precludes the collection of such potentially interesting variables as regularity and intensity of work, income, and occupational benefits (e.g. pensions). Nevertheless we can make one positive suggestion. In view of the predominantly agricultural nature of many developing countries, the inclusion of a small set of questions on land-ownership is surely justified. The present WFS core allows us to identify self-employed husbands working in the agricultural sector but this is not the precise equivalent of farmers who own, rent or share-crop land. Explicit information on this subject should enhance WFS occupational data, at least from the viewpoint of descriptive accuracy.

Respondent's employment (section 6)

A total of 17 questions is devoted to the topic of female employment, a reflection of the very great theoretical and practical interest in its relationship to fertility. A liberal definition of work, such as to include all productive activities apart from own housework, was used, although this policy was modified in a number of surveys (see appendix B). For employment since first marriage, the following variables were collected: current or most recent occupation; place of work; employment status; mode of payment; recency of work; total number of years worked; and whether worked in the interval between marriage and first birth. For work before marriage, a more restricted subset of items was elicited.

Despite the extensive treatment, certain potentially important characteristics of female employment are missing. The information on the timing of work falls far short of a complete employment history,[11] thus making it difficult for analysts to relate employment to the process of family formation. No data are collected on intensity of work, except for the half-hearted attempt in the 1977 core modifications to classify employment as full-time, part-time or seasonal. Less than half of all surveys implemented this recommendation. No attempt was made to obtain a measure of income or to enquire about child-care arrangements (both obviously relevant to the opportunity costs of childbearing).

Despite these omissions, a considerable wealth of data was collected and there were high hopes in the early stages of the WFS programme that major advances in our understanding of the effect of employment on fertility would be gained. These hopes have not been fulfilled. Though certain country-specific results have been of interest, they have been far from definitive (see Singh 1984b for Caribbean findings and Conning and Marckwardt 1982 for a summary of some Latin American findings). Despite sound exploratory investigation of the various dimensions of female employment (United Nations 1980b; 1982b, ch. 16), few analysts have succeeded in incorporating the information on duration of work[12] or work in the first birth interval into their analytic frameworks.

The most important comparative work on the employment–fertility relationship has concerned contraception rather than fertility itself, because the problems of reciprocal causality are less acute with the former variable (see Chidambaram and Cleland (1981) for a discussion of this problem and a recantation of earlier findings). A multivariate analysis using data from 17 WFS surveys examined the effect of the respondent's current occupation (represented by six categories including no current work) on current use of contraception (United Nations 1981d). Current work was chosen in preference to work at any time since marriage, in the expectation that the relationship would be more clear cut with current status data. Despite this analytic design, a significant effect of employment on contraceptive use, net of demographic controls and wife's education, was found in only eight surveys and the number dropped to four when husband's education and occupation were added as controls. Furthermore, differences, when significant, were small in magnitude and varied in pattern across countries. The analysis was repeated using the wife's employment status since marriage (never worked, family employee or self-employed, employee of non-relative), with even less positive results. The study concludes that 'there is at present no basis for expecting that the size of (occupational) differentials is very large or that occupation is very important in the sense of adding to explained variance, once statistical control is introduced for variables which are causally prior to occupation in most of the countries examined here'.

The instinct of social scientists when faced with an empirical rejection of cherished hypotheses is to blame the adequacy of data or analytic design. By no means do we rule out the possibility of such defects. However, it would be even more irresponsible to ignore the evidence, when appraising the substantive content of the WFS core and especially when recommending future approaches.

Accordingly, we see little justification for retaining the rather full treatment of female employment in future model questionnaires. The 17 questions in the WFS core should be reduced to 4 or 5, perhaps concentrating on the nature of current employment, if any. Questions on employment before marriage should be severely curtailed because the relationship of this topic to age at marriage has proved intractably circular. Interest should be restricted to employment which generates payment in cash or kind and the unsuccessful attempt to broaden the definition of work should be abandoned. WFS's determination to include the measurement of work within the context of the home or the family farm appears to have been motivated more by considerations of social justice than by its likely effect on fertility. At the same time, where special local interest in the link between employment and fertility exists, and there is sufficient female employment to sustain serious study, we recommend that more extensive collection of data be attempted than in the WFS core. For any hope of elucidating this very complex issue, further information on the timing of work and on its financial rewards is probably needed. In retrospect, it is regrettable that WFS did not develop a special module on this subject.

Pregnancy history and breastfeeding (section 2)

As already intimated, section 2 represents the heart of the core questionnaire as it is usually the source of all fertility and childhood mortality information. Pregnancy histories have taken many forms; the variety of measurement procedures and their respective merits and demerits are described by Jemai and Singh in chapter 5 and need not concern us here. This chapter also contains an extensive discussion of the utility of collecting information on foetal losses and stillbirths. We need only repeat the general conclusion that these data appear to have added little to the completeness of live birth reporting or even to infant mortality estimates, which was their original purpose. Their contribution to the accurate dating of live births may be greater but there is no empirical evidence to make an informed judgement. We conclude, therefore, that detailed non-live birth histories, either integrated or separate from the history of live births, should be removed as a 'compulsory' component of future model questionnaires. This recommendation, of course, does not preclude summary questions on the total number of foetal losses or detailed probing of recent inter-live birth intervals where there is some special interest in the subject.

As we emphasized earlier, a major substantive gain has accrued from the presence of questions concerning the length of breastfeeding the last and penultimate child. Much has also been learnt about techniques of analysis. It has emerged clearly that mean or median durations can be estimated as accurately from current status data on proportions of women still breastfeeding the youngest child (in conjunction with dates of recent live births) as from the retrospectively reported durations (Page, Lesthaeghe and Shah 1982; Ferry and Smith 1983). The simple question 'Are you still breastfeeding?' thus represents a parsimonious alternative to the sequence of retrospective questions in the WFS core and can be recommended, unless the survey is pursuing more ambitious analytic objectives, such as the relationship between weaning and mortality. In many countries, it will be of interest to measure the extent to which breast-feeding was initiated. Thus the core question 'Did you ever breastfeed this child?' should be retained, except in societies where it can be confidently assumed that breastfeeding is universal. The merits of further questions at this juncture to ascertain the frequency of nursing in the last 24 hours and whether the child has started taking supplementary food are considerable, though we do not consider them mandatory in a future core questionnaire.

All future fertility surveys would benefit greatly from two extra questions to ascertain whether menstruation and sexual relations have been resumed since the last live birth. As with breastfeeding, these simple questions are adequate for the estimation of aggregate measures of central tendency. The reason for urging the inclusion of the item on the return of menses is, of course, its direct relation to exposure to risk and hence to birth interval length. As for post-natal abstinence, it is now apparent that even in societies such as the Philippines where on average it is short, its effect on fertility may nevertheless be appreciable (Zablan 1984). As will be recalled, this topic was part of the earliest version of the WFS core but was dropped because of its sensitivity. However we believe that both post-partum abstinence, and certainly amenorrhoea, could be included in most future surveys without destroying interview rapport.[13]

Contraceptive knowledge and use (section 3)

The original 1975 version of the core questionnaire contains a very simple section on knowledge and lifetime use of contraceptive methods, in which a question to elicit spontaneously declared knowledge is followed by a prompted list of specific methods. The section was expanded appreciably in the 1977 modifications by the addition of questions on knowledge of supply sources, travelling time to the preferred source and perceived cost of the method. These items were asked for the four main medical or supply methods.

The original major purpose of the knowledge questions was to facilitate sound measurement of use, though knowledge has received some analytic attention in its own right. Particularly in countries where use is low, the long series of method-specific questions appears to be a cumbersome and costly way of ascertaining use. Yet, analyses by Acsádi (1979) and by Vaessen (1981), supported by the results of the Peru re-interview study (O'Muircheartaigh 1984b) prove conclusively that there is no obvious short-cut procedure to the measurement of ever-use and current use of contraception. Unless contraception is painstakingly introduced and defined to the respondent by reading out a list of methods, use will be seriously understated. Thus any future model question-naire cannot circumvent the approach adopted in the WFS (and in the Contra-ceptive Prevalence Surveys), except in those few countries where there is no government interest in family planning and negligible birth control can safely be assumed. There is however evidence that some of the descriptions of the methods can be shortened, even beyond the simplifications recommended in the 1977 Core Modifications, without appreciable danger (Anderson and Cleland 1984).

The data on supply sources have attracted considerable recent analytic attention because of their obvious policy relevance (see Jones 1984 and the refer-ences therein). Our interpretation of the detailed findings may be summarized as follows.

1 Knowledge of supply sources for specific methods is often much lower than awareness of the method itself. As such knowledge may be regarded as a pre-condition of use, it should be retained in future fertility surveys, except in the rapidly diminishing number of countries where contraception is un-important. Knowledge of sources can be added easily to the tabular format of the method-specific knowledge and ever-use questions.

2 Perceived travelling time to specific sources has proved analytically complex and its estimated effects on use appear to be modest, particularly in urban areas, once other factors such as education and desire for another child are controlled. Advances in our understanding[14] of this policy-relevant topic will come from improved 'objective' measures of accessibility, and quality of services, via community data collection, in conjunction with perceived accessibility data from surveys of individuals. Clearly, questions need to be method-specific because accessibility is more important for supply than for clinic methods, and additional information on intention to use and method preference should be sought because these data permit more focused analysis (Cornelius and Novak 1983). But even when these considerations are taken into account, there remains a concern that travelling time *per se* may be a weak surrogate for the perceived inconvenience and cost of obtaining supplies. This may be partially true when contraceptives are available at market centres which are regularly visited for other purposes. We thus conclude that this topic cannot be adequately investigated with a few simple questions and

is therefore better regarded as a module to be highly recommended for all countries with family planning programmes rather than as part of a mandatory core.

3 The data on perceived cost of methods have proved virtually unusable and should be dropped.

A surprising feature of the WFS core is that questions on current use of contraception (or use in the open interval) are separated from data on ever-use and are placed together with the fertility preference data in section 5 after the marriage history (section 4). The main reason for this apparently illogical order was the fear of offending divorced, separated or widowed respondents (and those currently pregnant) by asking them about current use. We are inclined to the view that the fear was exaggerated; in the Contraceptive Prevalence Surveys, questions were asked on current use of all women without apparent ill-effects on rapport and we suspect that well-trained interviewers can overcome any potential embarrassment. If this is so, questions on current use of each method that the respondent has ever tried can conveniently be added to section 3; this approach should be extended to male and female sterilization. These re-arrangements could greatly simplify the introductory set of filters in core section 5. They would also make possible a further improvement in design by allowing Q 523 on intention to use contraception in the future (whose merits will be discussed later) to take its logical place immediately after details of current and ever-use have been established.

There is one further addition that we could make to a revised section 3, namely a question on source of supply of the current method (if any). This addition would greatly enhance the relevance of the contraceptive data in countries with organized provision of family planning services, as it would enable a decomposition of the 'market' into its various component sources.

Marriage history (section 4)

The main interest of WFS in collecting complete marriage or union histories was as a surrogate for exposure to sexual intercourse, which itself is essential for the elucidation of fertility. An important (and unexpected) result to emerge from national reports and more detailed analyses is that exposure time lost by marital dissolution is small in most countries, both at national and subnational levels. The average elapsed time lost in this way between the date of first union and date of interview rarely exceeds 10 per cent. Furthermore dissolution is not an important intervening factor between socio-economic factors and the level of marital fertility (Rodríguez and Cleland 1981a; United Nations 1983c; United Nations 1984). Though there are some important exceptions such as Indonesia, Haiti and Dominican Republic, a complete marriage history need no longer be regarded as an indispensable component of all future fertility surveys in developing countries. In many settings, little will be lost for most fertility analyses in the following more restricted set of questions: current marital status, total number of marriages and date of first marriage. This recommendation is contentious and we accept that opinion will be sharply divided. One telling counter-argument is that the cost of a full marriage history is minimal in societies where dissolution is rare and is justified by its substantive gains where dissolution is common. We are not totally convinced; an analysis by Goldman (1981) indicates that high rates of dissolution can co-exist with little exposure loss because of rapid remarriage; however an analysis by Casterline, Singh, Cleland and Ashurst (1984) estimates a greater fertility-reducing impact of dissolution than of lactational amenorrhoea for nine Caribbean and Latin American countries. Finally, we acknowledge that the WFS approach has yielded a wealth of new information on marital dissolution and remarriage, which is of considerable interest in its own right. In countries where there is interest in this subject and where dissolution is sufficiently common to warrant investigation, then of course a full marriage history is justified.

As a surrogate for sexual exposure, reliance on marriage, albeit liberally defined, has not proved entirely satisfactory. Of 28 surveys analysed by Hobcraft and McDonald (1984), at least one-tenth of recently married women reported a pre-marital birth in six surveys, and in a further six cases at least 10 per cent reported a pre-marital conception. The problem of defining and measuring the onset of exposure to risk is acute; in some African surveys, age at first sexual relations (and age at menarche) has been asked but the reliability of reports must be extremely doubtful. Moreover, in some regions, the issue is fraught with moral and political sensitivity.

In certain societies, the reverse problem may occur; formal marriage may precede consummation (and/or menarche). Though the relevant WFS question 'In what month and year did you and your husband start living together?' was explicitly phrased to minimize this problem, nevertheless it is preferable in these settings to ask separate questions about betrothal, menarche, consummation, and cohabitation. This type of approach was adopted in Bangladesh, Cameroon and Senegal and should perhaps have been more widely employed in the WFS programme. Other suggestions for improved measurement are given in chapter 5. However, successful and precise measurement of the onset of exposure defies standardization and therefore we recommend no changes in this regard to the WFS core questionnaire.

Finally, we note the possibility of indexing subsequent fertility by the entry into motherhood rather than entry into marriage (see for instance Hobcraft, Goldman and Chidambaram 1982). This approach avoids the uncertainty concerning the onset of exposure and benefits from the fact that first birth dates tend to be more reliably reported than marriage dates (O'Muircheartaigh and Marckwardt 1981).

While the issue of the onset of exposure is unamenable to simple solutions, the same is less true of current sexual exposure. Variations in coital frequency across populations and its relationship to marriage duration, age, type of union (particularly the monogamy/polygamy distinction), attainment of grandmotherhood and desire to avoid future childbearing remains one of the least-explored and potentially rewarding topics in fertility analysis. While acknowledging that such questions might be unacceptable in some countries, we would urge the inclusion, wherever possible, of a couple of questions to currently married women on recency of last sexual relations and, where appropriate, on frequency in the last seven days. Only two countries in the WFS programme, Colombia and the Philippines, enquired about frequency in the last week. A slightly larger number of surveys, including these two countries, asked about usual coital frequency. Preliminary analysis suggests that the former question is the preferable approach because it yields more plausible results than the question on usual frequency (Cleland and Kalule-Sabiti 1984).

Fertility regulation (section 5)

Though the core fertility regulation section occupies a total of 31 items (including filters and skip instructions) spread over four pages, only the following eight variables are measured: current method used, if any, including sterilization; method used in the open interval, if any (for non-current users); intention to use contraception in the future (for never-users); desire for another child; preferred sex of next child; additional number of children wanted; total number of children desired; self-reported ability to bear more children (i.e. perceived fecundity). The disparity between the length of this section and the number of resultant variables is, of course, caused by parallel lines of questioning for different categories of respondent. As already noted, the transfer of the contraceptive questions to section 3 would considerably simplify the structure of section 5.

The controversial issue of reproductive preferences is discussed in detail by Lightbourne in chapter 31, and therefore we shall be brief. Our general verdict is that the WFS approach to measurement of this topic is open to appreciable improvement, by deletion of some existing items and by the addition of new questions.

Let us take the deletions first, of which there are five possible candidates: preferred sex of next child; additional number of children wanted; self-reported fecundity; use in the open interval; and intention to use contraception in the future.

Preferences concerning sex of children received scant attention in the core questionnaire, being represented by a single question, although two WFS surveys (Malaysia and Republic of Korea) chose to use the more detailed Coombs-scale approach (Coombs, Coombs and McClelland 1975). Analytic experience, however, suggests that data on preferred sex of the next child are not rewarding beyond a superficial, descriptive interest (Cleland, Verrall and Vaessen 1983). It is better to rely on the classical inferential approach of analysing reproductive attitudes and behaviour by the sex composition of living children, which requires no explicit questioning. In the few but numerically important populations or regions where son-preferences appear to influence behaviour (China, Korea, the

Indian subcontinent and perhaps the Arab world), the Coombs approach could be considered, but not for other regions.

The variable 'additional number of children wanted' should be deleted because it adds little of fresh interest, over and above the information on desire for any more children and the total number desired. When added to number of living children to form a measure of wanted family size, its interpretation is difficult because it combines a factual with an attitudinal component (Ryder 1973). Neither First Country Report authors nor subsequent analysts have made much use of this datum. Furthermore, the question was phrased in the plural ('how many more children do you want to have?') which may account for the heaping of responses at two children at the expense of the category, one child, which has been found in some surveys (Acsádi and Johnson-Acsádi 1983).

WFS's handling of self-reported fecundity has proved to be the most serious error in core section 5. Answers to this question form an important filter; respondents who report themselves infecund are not asked about their future reproductive desires or intentions. We now know that these self-reports are insufficiently reliable to justify their use, especially as a filter. An analysis by Vaessen (1984) demonstrates considerable implausibility when responses are tabulated by the recent history of childbearing. In some surveys, appreciable numbers of younger women with a recent birth inexplicably report themselves unable to bear any further children; the converse phenomenon of older, non-contracepting women with no birth for many years who nevertheless claim to be fecund is more common. The results of WFS post-enumeration surveys (see table 2.2 for Indonesia, Dominican Republic and Lesotho, and Srikantan 1979 for Fiji) confirm the poor measurement of this variable. Its use as a filter by WFS did more harm than good and it should not be retained, but replaced by a question on recency of the last menstrual period, which, in our opinion, is likely to prove a superior measure of fecundity status when analysed in conjunction with the recent fertility and contraceptive history. This datum might also clarify current pregnancy status (it is used for this purpose in some Contraceptive Prevalence Surveys) and would also help in the analysis of information on coital frequency in the previous week.

The information on use of contraception in the open interval has been little used by analysts and should be dropped. Unless accompanied by additional details concerning timing and duration, together with reasons for stopping, it affords little insight into such important topics as contraceptive continuation rates, use-effectiveness or satisfaction with methods.

The question on intention to use contraception in the future was routinely incorporated into Country Reports, as part of the composite variable 'pattern of use'. Subsequently it has been little used by analysts (but see Casterline 1982). Longitudinal studies (e.g. Bhatia 1982) have cast doubt on the predictive validity of responses and we share these reservations. In a number of countries where contraception was well established, implausibly large proportions of young women who had never used contraception professed no intention for future use.

TABLE   2.2

*Cross-classification of respondents according to
answers given in first and second interviews, concerning
self-reported fecundity*

	First interview	
	Fecund or unsure	Infecund
Second interview		
A Dominican Rep.		
Fecund or unsure	338	16
Infecund	21	32
B Indonesia		
Fecund or unsure	259	9
Infecund	22	75
C Lesotho		
Fecund or unsure	340	57
Infecund	18	36

This suggests that respondents may have misinterpreted the time reference to mean use in the near future, rather than at any time in the future. Moreover, there are also implausibly large inter-societal differences; in Pakistan, for instance, the majority of never-users reported a positive intention, compared to small minorities in Bangladesh and Nepal. It would be foolhardy to interpret this difference at face value, as it is unsupported by other circumstantial evidence. Nevertheless, because of the need to obtain sound measures of demand for contraception, we recommend the piloting and pre-testing of alternative versions of the intention to use question, rather than deletion of the item altogether. Furthermore this question should be asked of all non-current users rather than confined to those who have never used any method.

It is of interest to note that the early Contraceptive Prevalence Surveys do not contain a question on intention to use. Instead, reasons for non-use were elicited in the form of an open-ended question. In our view, such direct questions rarely yield trustworthy data because individuals are unwilling or unable to report on their motives. Accordingly we do not recommend this approach. In some later Contraceptive Prevalence Surveys, not only has an intention to use question been employed but preferences for particular methods have been elicited. As this information is relevant for the management of family planning pro-grammes and helpful in elucidating the effect of supply-proximity on use (Cornelius and Novak 1983), it should be seriously considered for future fertility surveys.

We turn now to possible additions, We have already referred to two later, unpublished additions to the core questionnaire, concerning desired timing of the next birth and a check question to confirm that women who report that they want no future children are indeed expressing a desire for a permanent end to reproduction, rather than a postponement. Analytic experience with the latter question is too limited for its firm endorsement, though it is, in principle, worthwhile in view of the great practical interest in measuring the nature and size of the potential demand for contraception and of the evidence adduced by Lightbourne in chapter 31 that spacing considerations influence responses to a hitherto unanticipated extent. This latter factor also lends support to the inclusion of an explicit spacing question in new model questionnaires. There is now abundant evidence, largely from Contraceptive Prevalence Surveys, that the wish to postpone births constitutes an important part of the potential demand for contraception. The main objective would be to classify respondents on a four or five-point scale, ranging from desire for a child as soon as possible at one extreme and desire to terminate childbearing altogether at the other.

The failure of family planning surveys to gauge the salience and intensity of preferences has long attracted criticism, which WFS made no attempt to address, either in the core questionnaire or in any of the modules. Perhaps WFS should have used a two-tier approach to the measurement of total desired family size, to obtain a better idea of the validity of the concept. The spontaneous response would have been recorded in the first part of the question and a probed numerical reply (when not provided spontaneously) in the second part. This remains a priority area for future surveys, but will inevitably require some pilot work before measurement procedures can be recommended with confidence. Similarly, proxy-reporting by respondents on their husbands' preferences, originally considered for the core questionnaire but dropped, may prove a useful addition. A few WFS surveys asked such a question but the experience has not yet been consolidated. Of particular interest in this regard is the Egyptian survey where not only are proxy-reports available but, for a subsample, the husbands' own testimonies.

The fertility regulation module (FRM)

Apart from collecting the same information as core section 5, this module contains a number of additional crucial variables for measuring the efficacy of contraceptive use, fecundability, and the effect of lactation on the ability to conceive. The following four items of information not included in the core section 5 are the underpinning for such analyses: (1) use of contraception, including method, in the last closed interval (or prior to the current pregnancy); (2) whether the pregnancy resulting in the last birth (or current pregnancy) had been wanted; (3) whether the woman had become pregnant while using a contraceptive method, restricted to women who had earlier affirmed that the pregnancy had been wanted; and (4) if the woman had stopped using in the closed interval prior to getting pregnant, or had stopped using in the open interval and is not pregnant, then the reason for stopping use, restricted to women who had wanted (closed interval) or want (open interval) another child.

The restriction of items (3) and (4) to wanted pregnancies was a most unfortunate error. It arose in part because of the conceptual orientation of the module, i.e. the desire to distinguish between 'number' failure and 'timing' failure in the implementation of fertility preferences. The original phrasing of the question on reason for stopping was 'did you stop because you wanted to become pregnant?', which obviously could not be asked of women who had earlier testified that the pregnancy was unwanted. This is an illustration of the danger of designing a questionnaire around a pre-conceived and narrow analytic framework. With the change of this question to an open-ended format 'why did you stop using that method?' in the 1977 modifications to the questionnaire, it would have been possible to redesign the questioning sequence to obtain items (3) and (4) for all contraceptors. Regrettably, this was not done, though such a redesign did find its way into a few country questionnaires. More complete and useful measures of both contraceptive efficacy and reasons for discontinuation could have been obtained but for this oversight.

The WFS tabulation plan for First Country Reports recommended only four tables using these FRM data: two dealing with the wantedness status of the last child, and two with the use of contraception in the last closed interval. Many subsequent studies on fertility preferences incorporate the datum on whether the last child was wanted (see chapter 31). However, the data on contraceptive use and reproductive control have so far received little analytic attention. The major exception is a comparative study of fecundability and extended use-effectiveness of contraceptive methods in five Latin American countries (Goldman, Pebley and Westoff 1982). This study demonstrates both the utility and limitations of the FRM variables. Among the latter are the failure to allow for the possibility of use of more than one method in an interval, and the absence of information on the timing and duration of use.

Only one of the re-interview studies has included any of the four items, so little evidence exists on their test/re-test reliability. It should be noted, however, that worrying inconsistencies exist between reported wantedness of the last pregnancy and the contrast between desired and actual family size (chapter 31). Indeed a case may be made that the contrast approach might provide a more realistic measure of unwanted births than the direct retrospective question, which could be unexpectedly sensitive to unwelcome timing of births. Moreover, it seems likely that the FRM data would have a very low degree of reliability given their retrospective ('before getting pregnant did you want ... ?') and speculative ('did you get pregnant while using ... ?') nature. We do know that items on current fertility preferences are unstable (O'Muircheartaigh and Marckwardt 1981); retrospective preferences must surely be even more so.

Taking into consideration the scant use that has been made of data collected in the module, on the one hand, and their probable unreliability in the developing-world context, on the other, it is difficult to justify the inclusion of these items in their present form in a future model questionnaire. Nevertheless, in countries with widespread contraceptive use and a particular interest in the subjects of fecundability and contraceptive efficacy, it would be most useful to gather even further information, particularly on the timing and duration of contraceptive use in birth intervals. In such cases, the questioning would best be restricted to recent intervals.

2.5 Design of questionnaires

In this section we devote attention to the philosophy underlying the design of the core questionnaire and its related fertility regulation module (FRM); the implications of this philosophy in terms of questionnaire content and size; and the pros and cons of the WFS approach and of alternative approaches. Finally, we make some recommendations concerning the design of future model questionnaires. The related issue of translation is considered in chapter 6.

The design of the WFS core questionnaire and main modules was influenced greatly by the philosophy and traditions underlying social and attitudinal survey-taking in the USA and the UK (e.g. Cannell and Kahn 1953, and Moser and Kalton 1971). Two of the principal premises guiding the work were the following: (1) questionnaires should ideally be administered verbatim with a minimum of ex tempore additions or modifications; and (2) the interests of the interviewer should supersede those of the processor. The need for verbatim questionnaires goes without challenge in attitudinal surveys where the merest variation in inflection or the wording of a question can greatly influence responses (see Schuman and Presser 1981).

Whether verbatim questionnaires are necessary in surveys collecting primarily factual rather than attitudinal data is open to debate. There are, however, examples in the WFS programme of large effects on responses of apparent small deviations or mistakes in the wording of questions. For instance, the unnaturally long periods for which infants are fed exclusively on breast-milk in Egypt and Syria appears to be an artifact of a poorly phrased question which defined supplementary food as a meal in the Arabic translation of the relevant question. In Bangladesh, the deliberate substitution of the word 'soon' for 'sometime' in the question 'do you want another child . . . ?' clearly influenced replies. Experience with a recent linguistic study in the Ivory Coast confirms the common-sense expectation that the advantages of a verbatim over a schedule approach depends on the nature of the question. Straightforward items such as education and sex gain nothing from elaborated questions, whereas more complex issues gain much.

As for catering to the interest of the interviewer rather than the processor, this premise finds justification in the relatively more difficult task of the former. As noted by Moser and Kalton (1971: 304): ' . . . it is the interviewer, rather than the office worker, who has to cope with the schedule under the most difficult circumstances, so it is her convenience that must be given top priority'. Moreover, most errors made at the interview will be undetectable thereafter.

Ultimately, the implication of these premises is to not ask questions that are irrelevant for a given respondent, and to frame relevant questions in such a manner that they are easily understood and are not offensive. This in turn implies the use of skips, filters, alternative wordings, and formalized probes. The WFS core questionnaire is full of these. (For an example of alternative wordings and formalized probes, see core questions 225 and 226 on foetal loss.) The FRM is a particularly extreme example of adapting the questioning to specific character-istics of the respondents: based on such considerations as the marital status, contraceptive history, perceived fecundity and pregnancy status of the respon-dent, the interviewer is directed to one of five streams, differentiated by the colour of the pages. As a result of the use of these design features, the question-naire contains many more questions than would be put to any one respondent. The core questionnaire in conjunction with the FRM (in replacement of section 5) covers 30 pages and a total of 174 questions, assuming four live births but no pregnancy losses and no previous marriages. Yet any given woman would typically be asked only about 80 of these 174 questions. The exact number of questions is dependent upon such biographical characteristics as the number of children she has had, her pregnancy losses, her marriage history, her work history, and the extent of her contraceptive knowledge and use.

To study this issue of questionnaire length in greater detail, let us create a 'traditional' and a 'modern' woman. In both cases they have no pregnancy losses and are once-married and currently married. The 'traditional' woman has had six live births, is fecund and non-pregnant, has never used contraception and has never worked. The 'modern' woman has had three live births, is fecund and non-preg-nant, has used contraception in both the last closed and open intervals, and worked both before and since marriage. These two women would each be asked exactly 83 questions in the combined core and FRM. A tabulation of representative coun-try questionnaires is set out in table 2.3. It can be seen that countries generally

TABLE   2.3

Questions asked as proportion of total questions

Country	Total questions	Traditional woman		Modern woman	
	Number	Number	%	Number	%
Malaysia	329	144	44	191	58
Trinidad and Tobago	229	121	53	123	54
Peru	226	98	43	108	48
Kenya	201	124	62	124	62
Syria	196	110	56	113	58
Average	236	119	50	132	56
Core + FRM	174	83	48	83	48

added to the core material, but that the percentage of total questions actually asked of typical respondents did not vary appreciably from the core design.

Much of the 'wastage' of questions derives, of course, from the FRM. Of the total of 76 questions (excluding filters), no woman is ever asked more than 13 in this module. Hence, of the total wastage of 91 (174–83) questions, 63 (76–13), or nearly 70 per cent is attributable to the FRM. It is on these grounds that the design of the FRM may be criticized. But it is clear that, in general, the rest of the questionnaire is fairly efficient in terms of the ratio of questions asked to total questions.

Let us consider some alternatives to the strategy employed in the design of the FRM. The FOTCAF module (on factors other than contraception affecting fertility) is one such alternative as it also focuses on the open and last closed interval and was used in Africa instead of the FRM. Here, much less segregation and streaming is involved than in the FRM, there are no coloured pages, and a much higher ratio of questions asked to total questions is achieved for the average respondent. Another alternative, designed by Verma and national staff, is section 5 of the questionnaire used in Turkey. It obtains precisely the same information as the FRM in 7 pages (rather than 13) and 30 questions (rather than 76). But aside from reducing the bulk of the questionnaire (and the related costs of paper and printing), how good are these alternatives from the interviewer's standpoint? The interviewer's task is easiest when she can proceed question by question, without having to check back to earlier information nor skip forward. It is the prevalence of back-referenced filters and forward skips which defines the degree of difficulty of a questionnaire. A comparison of the FRM with FOTCAF and the Turkish FRM is most revealing (table 2.4).

TABLE   2.4

Relative difficulty of certain modules

	FRM	FOTCAF	Turkish FRM
(a) Back-referenced filters	20	23	15
(b) Questions with skips[a]	18	26	15
(c) Total questions + filters	96	76	45
(d) Relative difficulty: (a + b)/c	.396	.645	.667

[a] Other than to end of section.

Clearly, these alternatives to the FRM are unsatisfactory from the interviewer's standpoint. And here the processor's interest happens to coincide with the interviewer's. The FOTCAF module has provided the processor with severe problems because of the large number of skip and filter errors that have needed correction (see chapter 18). In contrast, the FRM, while creating difficulties at the later variable-formation and rectangularization stage (see chapter 20) has proved no more difficult to clean than other sections of the questionnaire. Hence, from the perspective of design rather than content, it is difficult to fault the fertility regulation module.

This having been said, we would not advocate replication of the FRM in any future international standardized survey programme. As noted in earlier sections of this paper, WFS erred on the side of being overly cautious about putting potentially embarrassing or irrelevant questions to respondents. Questions on past and current use of contraception need not be restricted by the particular marital status or perceived fecundity status of a respondent, nor need questions concerning future plans or desires relating to contraception and fertility. Well-trained interviewers should be able to overcome possible resentment or embarrassment of asking irrelevant questions, not least by blaming the designer of the questionnaire! Although the details are beyond the scope of the present chapter, it is fairly easy to design a section which obtains approximately the same information as sections 3 and 5 and the FRM in much less space, and without the concomitant back-referenced filters and forward skips which have plagued the FOTCAF module.

Even with these simplifications, however, some back-referenced filters are unavoidable in a fertility questionnaire, because of the many logical inter-relationships between topics. It might facilitate the interviewer's task if key filtering characteristics, such as current marital and pregnancy status, are recorded, when first ascertained, on a special flap for ease of reference. This arrangement would obviate the need for laborious page-turning and is well worth trying in future surveys. Further simplification, this time from the data processing side, would be achieved by not coding the filters.

On the more general issue of the merits of a verbatim questionnaire versus a schedule-type questionnaire, there is little hard evidence, though some will be forthcoming from experiments in Ivory Coast and the Philippines. Interviewers who are experienced and capable tend to memorize questions, and hence deal with a verbatim questionnaire in much the same manner as they would a schedule, maintaining dialogue and eye-contact with the respondent. Interviewers who are less capable probably need the comfort of precisely worded questions provided by the verbatim questionnaire. Tape-recordings have revealed that much of the dialogue taking place during an interview consists of irrelevant answers by respondents and of gentle and often not-so-gentle (and only sometimes non-directive) probing by interviewers (see, for example, Thompson, Ali and Casterline 1982). Under such circumstances the precise format of the questionnaire is less than critical. What is indicated is ever more and better training of interviewers.

We would not radically alter the emphasis placed by WFS design procedures on the needs of interviewers. Some concessions can, however, be made to the processor. The approach used by the WFS for recording responses involved the interviewer ticking or circling numbered boxes, and the later transcription to empty boxes in the right margin by the editor or coder. This was a middle road between the use of separate coding sheets (as in connection with the household schedule) and a fully pre-coded questionnaire. The choice was deliberate and cautious, though in retrospect wrong. It was felt that the questionnaires would in any event pass through the stages of field editing, office editing and machine editing, and that the marginal cost of transcribing, on average, some ten numbers to empty boxes on each page would be low. Evidence now accumulating (see Pullum, Özsever and Harpham 1984) indicates that WFS put excessive emphasis on editing. While field editing is still essential, only cursory structural checks need be undertaken in the office prior to the machine edit.[15] The process of transcription by coders inevitably introduced some errors.[16] Hence, our recommendation for future surveys is to use fully pre-coded questionnaires where interviewers record responses, and receive skip instructions, in the margin. Experience with the Rwanda Fertility Survey (Otto 1983) has shown that the system is workable and not an especial inconvenience for interviewers: the overriding consideration.

2.6 Summary and recommendations

Great care was taken in the development of the contents of the WFS core household schedule and questionnaire to ensure that the data collected would be useful in a variety of national settings and of reasonable reliability. In broad terms the questionnaire has stood the test of time well. The amount of information that has proved to be analytically worthless is rather small, we suspect, by comparison with most other detailed surveys. Its main strength lies in demographic description and, in this regard, the inclusion of complete maternity histories has been fully vindicated. Perhaps the greatest achievement of WFS has been to demonstrate that single-round retrospective surveys can yield reliable estimates of fertility and childhood mortality, provided that they are carried out to high technical and managerial standards. This represents a major shift away from the belief, prevalent a decade ago, that longitudinal designs or dual-record systems were necessary for the collection of trustworthy data on vital events in the Third World.

By the criterion of contribution to an explanation of fertility levels and change, the contents of the core are inadequate. The lack of social, economic or cultural variables has been noted by many commentators and the analytic experience with the limited range of available information has been disappointing, particularly in the case of female employment. However, as argued earlier, remedies are not immediately obvious. In terms of practical relevance to government or other family planning programmes, the core material is also deficient. This is largely a reflection of the aims of the programme, which were scientific rather than applied in their emphasis.

Though any core or model questionnaire has severe drawbacks when applied in diverse settings, the need for such models will persist. The reason is not so much the desire for cross-national comparability of findings, though this aspect has been crucial to WFS's contribution to knowledge, but stems from considerations of economy and efficiency of future surveys. The case for a well-designed and tested model to act as a starting point in the construction of particular national questionnaires seems to us to be overwhelmingly strong.

In view of this need, what recommendations can now be made towards the development of a new model? Based on our critique of the WFS core, the way ahead is clear. What is required is a shorter, streamlined version of the WFS core, stripped of those items that have been found inessential for demographic description and analysis. This compression will have the advantage of allowing greater opportunity for additions in the form of small constellations of questions dealing in more detail with core topics or the incorporation of sub-questionnaires, or modules, in which extra topics can be investigated. In this way, flexibility and sensitivity to national circumstances can be achieved in the content of future surveys, without sacrificing the advantages offered by a pre-designed core of essential items.

Specific recommendations have been made in section 4 of this paper. They are summarized below in terms of deletions, changes and additions to the existing WFS core. We emphasize that recommendations concerning precise techniques of measurement of demographic variables are to be found in chapter 5.

Deletions

1   details of current and childhood residence (Q 101–106, 708)

2   non-live birth history (Q 229–233)

3   former marriage history (Q 409–412)

4   contraceptive use in the open interval (Q 507–508)

5   self-reported fecundity (Q 509)

6   preference for sex of next child (Q 223/515/518)

7   additional number of children wanted (Q 519/521)

8   most aspects of female work history (Q 606, 609, 610, 612, 614, 616, 617)

9   most aspects of male employment (Q 710–713)

10   travel time and cost of methods (S 3, S 4 in 1977 core modifications)

11   FRM module

Changes

1   replace retrospective questions on breastfeeding the last two children (Q 217–220) with two questions to ascertain whether the last child was ever fed at the breast and whether he/she has yet been weaned

2   redesign question on intention to use contraception

Additions

1 resumption of sexual relations since last birth

2 resumption of regular menstruation since last birth

3 recency of last menstruation

4 recency and current frequency of sexual relations (two questions)

5 source of current method of contraception

6 desired postponement of next birth

7 land ownership of agriculturalists (two questions)

The list clearly represents an appreciable shortening of the current core questionnaire, with the additional advantage of eliminating two separate retrospective event histories, which would simplify both interviewer training and processing of the data. The greatly abbreviated set of female employment questions could be integrated into section 1 on the respondent's background, thus reducing the number of major sections from seven to six. Further reductions in the structural complexity of the questionnaire would accrue from the recommended shift of the contraceptive items from section 5 to section 3 where the bulk of contraceptive knowledge and use data is ascertained, and by the elimination of self-reported fecundity as a filter.

The remaining core questions, together with the modest list of recommended additions, do represent, we believe, a major improvement over the UN Short List of 1969 described as 'indispensible for any fertility investigation' and over the existing WFS core. We emphasize that this proposed new core is based almost exclusively on WFS experience and does not contain any radically new or imaginative approaches. However we make no apologies because model questionnaires designed for use in many different settings should be conservative in nature and, like the original WFS core, should not deviate from topics and questions that have been thoroughly tried and tested.

The scope for additions to this new proposed core is considerable. A range of topics springs to mind: health care of infants and children; breastfeeding patterns and their relationship to amenorrhoea; the schooling of children and associated financial costs; aspirations for acquisition of modern consumer goods; perceived and objective accessibility to contraceptive methods; timing, duration and discontinuation of contraceptive practice and the relationship to successful reproductive control; the intensity and salience of preferences for family size. The range of potentially rewarding additions is very wide and the choice should depend on particular national characteristics.

Finally, we would stress again a point made earlier in this chapter, namely the need for a greater investment in the development of questionnaires. WFS itself did little more than pre-testing and its only truly pioneering effort was the FOTCAF module. We believe that major improvements to the substantive yield of national fertility surveys will only come from intensive work to refine the measurement of often elusive concepts.

Appendix A
Questionnaires for low fertility countries

In this appendix we discuss briefly the core questionnaire for low fertility countries. The plans for a comparative study of fertility in countries affiliated with the United Nations Economic Commission for Europe (ECE) antedate the World Fertility Survey by several years. In 1967, the Division of Social Affairs of the ECE established a Working Group on Social Demography, consisting of eminent European demographers. The Working Group held several meetings between 1967 and 1970 devoted to a review of current European demographic problems and the preparation of a model questionnaire for fertility and family planning inquiries. In 1971 the decision was taken to concentrate their work on the fertility surveys then taking place in several countries of the region, and to undertake a comparative study incorporating the results of those national inquiries. This effort resulted in the publication, in 1976, of a monograph, entitled 'Fertility and Family Planning in Europe Around 1970: A Comparative Analysis of Twelve National Surveys' (UN 1976b). This study incorporated data from surveys taken during the period 1966–72.

Meanwhile, the decision was taken by the ECE and its Working Group to affiliate loosely with the programme of the World Fertility Survey. Their decision was that there should be compatibility in the data collected for developed and developing countries. A draft core questionnaire for developed countries (hereafter referred to as Mark II) was prepared in Geneva in October 1973 by a WFS staff member and a consultant, in co-ordination with the ECE Secretariat, using as points of departure three documents: the IUSSP/UN 1970 manual on variables and questionnaire; the questionnaire developed by the ECE Working Group in 1969; and the then current draft (number 3) of the WFS questionnaire for developing countries. Mark II was translated into French and Russian, and then presented to the Conference of European Statisticians in January 1974. Based on the comments made during this meeting and on comments received from WFS consultants, a second draft was prepared by WFS staff in April 1974. This was pre-tested in June in 15 areas of the United Kingdom by interviewers of the Social Survey Division of the Office of Population Censuses and Surveys. From this experience, a third draft of Mark II was published in September 1974 and distributed to interested parties.

Comments on the third draft were received from several people; these comments, in addition to the concomitant developments in the version of the questionnaire for the developing countries, formed the basis on which the WFS staff were able to finalize and publish the definitive version of Mark II in February 1975. Several months later, a module on family size preferences was prepared and published by the ECE Secretariat. These materials formed the basic documentation for the new round of comparative fertility surveys in Europe and the USA. Between 1975 and 1980 surveys were carried out in 20 developed countries, namely: Belgium, Bulgaria, Czechoslovakia, Denmark, Finland, France, Great Britain, Hungary, Israel, Italy, Japan, Netherlands, Norway, Poland,

Romania, Spain, Sweden, Switzerland, USA and Yugoslavia (WFS 1985: app. 4).

As already noted, one of the chief considerations in the preparation of a model questionnaire for the developed ECE countries was the desirability of obtaining data comparable to those being gathered in connection with the WFS programme in developing countries. The question naturally arises of just how comparable they really are.

Throughout the questionnaires, comparable questions are worded identically. The sequencing of the major sections of the questionnaires is the same, as is the sequencing of questions within the sections. Thus, in both, section 1, on the respondent's background, is followed by a maternity (pregnancy) history in section 2. Sections 3 and 4 of Mark II (contraceptive knowledge and past fertility planning, respectively) correspond roughly to section 3 of the developing country version (contraceptive knowledge and use). These are followed in both by a marriage history. Section 6 of Mark II, on current fertility regulation, corresponds to section 5 of the developing country version on fertility regulation. In both questionnaires, the final sections concern the work history of the respondent and the current (last) husband's background.

Probably the most important difference between the two questionnaires is the amount of information collected on fertility planning. Mark II inquires into the planning status of each pregnancy, i.e. contraceptive use in the interval and whether the pregnancy was desired when it occurred, later, or was unwanted. The questionnaire for developing countries asks only for birth control in the open interval. (The fertility regulation module, used by most developing countries, adds birth control in the last closed birth interval.) Another difference between the two is that Mark II requests information both on children wanted and children expected and on the desired length of inter-pregnancy intervals. The version for developing countries only queries the number of children wanted.

The principal differences in respect to explanatory variables occurred in the section on work history and husband's background. The developing country version inquires whether the woman worked between marriage and birth of the first child, but not specifically during any subsequent birth intervals as is the case with Mark II, which asks about work between the first two pregnancies and between the last two pregnancies. It also ascertains the woman's income, where she worked and her intentions about future work. In addition, Mark II provides for information on husband's birth date, current work status, work status during the past 12 months, place and industry of employment and monthly income. The questionnaire for developing countries does not include such questions.

The content of the questionnaires actually utilized in the developed country surveys varied greatly. Only two countries stuck closely to the WFS/ECE recommendations and covered no other major topics. Significantly, neither of these two, Bulgaria and Spain, had conducted any previous national fertility survey. For a diversity of reasons, most countries added other topics to the questionnaire. Some emphasized housing and child care arrangements, and the respondent's time budget. Others added sections on sexual behaviour, communication between partners, the division of household tasks, and the meaning of having children. In others, the questionnaire gave considerable attention to the formation of the couple's relationship and to the couple's housing and economic circumstances at that time. Some surveys covered selected background topics in considerably greater detail than does Mark II. Evidently, the general character of each individual country questionnaire was largely determined by the particular policy interests of the country and the priorities established for the use of the resources allocated to the project (Berent, Jones and Siddiqui 1982).

The coverage of topics recommended by the WFS and the ECE was generally good as regards items on the respondent's and husband's background characteristics, on their work histories, and on the wife's pregnancy history. But there was less than universal coverage of items on fertility regulation and on family size preferences and expectations. However, all countries did ask for the contraceptive method currently being used and for expected number of children. The coverage of 32 recommended topics for the ECE/WFS comparative study is summarized in the table A1[17] taken from the report by Berent, Jones and Siddiqui (1982). The main conclusion is that there is considerably greater comparability among questionnaires in this 1977 (approximately) round of European surveys than in the earlier 1970 round, and that this is in large measure due to the initiative taken by the ECE to collaborate with the programme of the World Fertility Survey.

Appendix B
Major country-specific deviations from the core questionnaire

Sections 1 (respondent's background), 2 (maternity history), and 7 (husband's background) of the WFS core questionnaire were implemented in developing country surveys with few appreciable amendments or omissions. Greater variability is apparent for other sections and these are described below. The appendix draws heavily on material presented in Singh (1984a).

Contraception

The following information is collected by the core questionnaire on contraceptive knowledge and use by ever-married women: spontaneous knowledge of methods; method-by-method probed knowledge; method-by-method probed use; and for currently married, non-pregnant women, current use of a method or, if not using, use in the interval since last birth.

Two countries, Mauritania and Pakistan, did not use the method-by-method specific probe questions for quite distinct reasons: in Mauritania, for reasons of political sensitivity; in Pakistan, for fear that the probing would lead to an overestimate of knowledge. The likely outcome in both cases is, in fact, an underestimate of levels of both knowledge and use (see Vaessen 1981). Nepal omitted the probes for four methods: other female scientific, douche, rhythm and withdrawal. Malaysia omitted the probe on douche, Senegal that on withdrawal, and seven countries that on abstinence (Cameroon, Tunisia, Portugal, Dominican Republic, Mexico, Paraguay and Venezuela). Injections, not mentioned in the core, were added to the list of probed methods in 23 countries. All countries obtained information on current use and method, and all but one (Fiji, which pre-dated finalization of the core) on use in the interval since last birth.

Marriage history

It was recognized that the core section on marriage would require modifications in countries where non-legal or informal unions were prevalent; where single women were interviewed; and where polygamy was significant. To the extent that such modifications do not affect the comparability of the core information required by the WFS, they are not the subject of comment here.

A complete marriage (or union) history was obtained in all WFS country surveys except one: Nepal. Complete information was obtained about current marital status in Nepal, but no questions were asked about previous marriages. The justification given (though not backed by evidence) was that divorce was unknown and that the remarriage of widows was very rare.

The Caribbean variant of the marriage history used a special partners–relationships table to accommodate the existence of more than one type of union with a particular partner. This table was used in Guyana, Haiti, Jamaica and Trinidad and Tobago. Women who had ever been in union were classified as married, common law, visiting and not currently in union. In Haiti, an interesting feature was the explicit linking of each reported child to a father specified in the marriage history. However, though the information collected on relationships and the dates of events in the history for these four countries was much more detailed than in the core questionnaire, the manner in which a union ended (i.e. widowhood, separation or divorce) was not recorded.

Fertility regulation

The core questionnaire obtains the following information on fertility preferences: the desire for more children, including the number of additional children wanted; and the total number of children desired by the respondent.

The base population for the question on desire for more children is ordinarily women who are contracepting, or who are pregnant, or who do not respond negatively to a question on capacity to have more children. This base was widened slightly in a few countries, which presents no problems of cross-national comparability. However a serious non-comparability arises in the case of Cameroon, where the base was severely reduced to include only pregnant women; those under age 25 who had never been pregnant; and women under 25 with only one live birth or those under 30 with two live births. The net result was that only 40 per cent of currently married, fecund women were asked the relevant question. A typing error in Senegal resulted in the restriction of the question on desire for more children to currently pregnant women. A decision in Bangladesh brought about severe incomparability: the core question is 'Do

TABLE A1

Coverage in the country questionnaires of basic topics recommended by WFS and ECE and relevant to the ECE/WFS Comparative Study

Country	Respondent's and family's background							
	Current residence	Childhood residence	Age	Wife's education	Religion	Husband's education	Husband's occupation	Family income
Belgium	X	X	X	X	X	X	X	X
Bulgaria	X	X	X	X		X	X	X
Czechoslovakia	X	X	X	X				X
Denmark	X		X	X		X	X	X
Finland	X	X	X	X		X	X	X
France	X	X	X	X	X	X	X	X
Great Britain			X	X	X	X	X	
Hungary	X	X	X	X		X	X	X
Italy	X	X	X	X	X	X	X	
Netherlands	X	X	X	X	X	X	X	X
Norway	X	X	X	X		X	X	X
Poland	X	X	X	X		X	X	X
Portugal	X	X	X	X	X	X	X	X
Romania	X	X	X	X		X	X	X
Spain	X	X	X	X	X	X	X	X
USA		X	X	X	X	X	X	
Yugoslavia	X		X	X			X	X

	Marriage history		Pregnancy history				
	Current status	Date of first marriage	Number of live births	Dates of live births	Number of pregnancies	Whether currently pregnant	Number of induced abortions
Belgium	X	X	X	X	X	X	X
Bulgaria	X	X	X	X	X	X	X
Czechoslovakia	X	X	X	X	X	X	X[a]
Denmark	X		X	X		X	
Finland	X	X	X	X	X	X	
France	X	X	X	X	X	X	X[a]
Great Britain	X	X	X	X	X	X	X
Hungary	X	X	X	X	X	X	X
Italy	X	X	X	X	X	X	X
Netherlands	X	X	X	X	X	X	
Norway	X	X	X	X	X	X	X
Poland	X	X	X	X	X	X	X
Portugal	X	X	X	X	X	X	
Romania	X	X	X	X	X	X	
Spain	X	X	X	X	X	X	
USA	X	X	X	X	X	X	X
Yugoslavia	X	X	X	X	X	X	X

[a] Refers only to the period since abortion was legalized in the country.

Table A1 continued overleaf

Table A1 continued

Country	Fertility regulation				Fecundity of couple	Surgical sterilization	Attitude towards abortion
	Unwanted fertility	Methods known	Methods ever used	Methods used currently			
Belgium	X	X	X	X	X		
Bulgaria		X		X	X	X	
Czechoslavakia	X	X		X			
Denmark		X	X	X	X		X
Finland		X	X	X	X		
France	X		X	X	X	X	
Great Britain	X		X	X	X	X	X
Hungary	X	X	X	X	X	X	
Italy		X	X	X	X	X	
Netherlands	X	X	X	X	X	X	
Norway			X	X	X		X
Poland	X	X	X	X	X		X
Portugal	X	X	X	X	X	X	
Romania	X	X	X	X	X		
Spain	X	X	X	X	X	X	
USA	X	X	X	X	X	X	
Yugoslavia		X		X	X		X

	Family size preferences and expectations									
	Ideal number	Number wanted at marriage	Number would now choose	Second preference	Number expected	Motivations	Current work status	Work since marriage	Occupation	Earnings
Belgium	X	X			X	X	X	X	X	X
Bulgaria	X	X	X		X	X	X	X	X	X
Czechoslovakia	X	X			X	X	X	X	X	
Denmark	X		X	X	X		X	X	X	X
Finland	X	X	X		X	X	X	X	X	X
France	X			X	X	X	X	X	X	X
Great Britain	X		X	X	X		X	X	X	
Hungary	X	X	X		X		X	X	X	
Italy	X	X	X	X	X		X	X	X	
Netherlands	X		X	X	X	X	X	X	X	X
Norway	X	X	X	X	X	X	X	X	X	X
Poland	X	X	X	X	X	X	X	X	X	X
Portugal	X	X	X	X	X		X	X	X	X
Romania	X	X	X		X	X	X	X	X	X
Spain	X	X	X	X	X		X	X	X	
USA	X	X	X	X	X		X	X	X	X
Yugoslavia	X	X			X	X	X	X	X	

you want to have another child sometime?'; in Bangladesh the word 'soon' replaced 'sometime', thereby narrowing the respondent's frame of reference. The question on the number of additional children wanted was not used in Portugal or Fiji; instead the only question asked was how many children in all they wanted. (Fiji pre-dated the core, and Portugal adopted the Mark II variant.)

The core question on desired family size reads as follows: 'If you could choose exactly the number of children to have in your whole life, how many children would that be?' All but four countries asked the question as recommended of all ever-married women, or, in some cases, of a wider population. Once again, Cameroon chose to restrict the base population to an incomprehensible mix of women similar to that mentioned earlier. The Fiji version was 'How many children in all do you really want?' Pakistan went for 'ideal' size: 'In your opinion how many children should a married couple have?' And Malaysia chose to ask: 'If you were just married and could have just the number of children you want, how many children would you want to have by the time you reach age 50?' None of these three variations is strictly comparable with the core question used in all other countries.

Work history

At the start of section 6 of the core, a lengthy statement defining work is read out to emphasize that any employment, even work on the family farm, or unpaid work, is considered to be work: 'As you know, many women work – I mean aside from doing their own housework. Some take up jobs for which they are paid in cash or kind. Others sell things, or have a small business, or work on the family farm'. Following this definition,[18] women are asked whether they are working at the present time.

Only 26 countries used this definition exactly as recommended. Most of the departures involved de-emphasizing unpaid family work. Some countries went to the extreme of defining work as employment for pay or profit (Ghana), or cash (Bangladesh), or money (Fiji), or a wage or salary (Lesotho and Kenya). This undoubtedly introduces a major non-comparability with other countries. Three countries (Colombia, Costa Rica and Peru) used the following variation, 'As you know, women work, apart from housework, at jobs for which they receive payment in cash or in kind. Are you currently working?'. This is a simplification of the core description, but with no explicit mention of the family farm. Is this likely to make it incomparable? Indirect evidence from Peru would indicate not. Of women who had worked since marriage, 32 per cent indicated that it was work on the family farm. And of women who worked before marriage, fully 36 per cent did so without pay. Probably of more importance than the textual statement that is read to respondents is the actual training of interviewers as to what type of work is relevant, and the amount of probing utilized. It is no coincidence that a large portion of the Peruvian field staff had extensive prior experience as interviewers in labour force surveys.

Notes

1. For an inventory of such surveys conducted between 1960 and 1973, see Duncan (1973), Baum, Dopkowski, Duncan and Gardiner (1974) and Population Council (1970).
2. The work was done during the years 1965-7 and was published at Ann Arbor, Michigan in June 1967. Copies are available from the IUSSP, rue des Augustines, 34, 4000 Liège, Belgium. It was also released as United Nations Document E/CN.9/212.
3. The IUSSP Committee developed three lists of variables, a short list, a core list and an expanded list. The questionnaire is companion to the core list.
4. This was a fruitful time for model fertility questionnaires. Two other such questionnaires were published in 1970 (Population Council 1970 and Bogue 1970). Both were more oriented to family planning than was the IUSSP/UN model.
5. Other pilots and pre-tests were concluded in Zaire, Ghana, India and Malaysia in 1974 and 1975 but these were more concerned with additions to the core questionnaire or with practical problems of fertility surveys in particular regions.
6. Of course, those 42 countries were self-selected and it may be argued that the known core contents may have deterred other countries from participation in the programme. However, only one participant (Chile) withdrew after an initial commitment because of the substantive nature of the survey.
7. Even without these questions, usual household residents can be distinguished from visitors from household schedule data.
8. For an attempt to improve the measurement of rural–urban migration, see the WFS Nigerian questionnaire.
9. The evidence from the Indonesian and Dominican Republic re-interview surveys suggests a satisfactory level of consistent reporting: over 90 per cent in both cases.
10. The additional possibilities in surveys where both spouses are interviewed are beyond the scope of this paper.
11. A complete history was seriously considered by the TAC but rejected because its length would imbalance the questionnaire content.
12. For an exception see Mason and Palan (1981).
13. As with most recommendations, there are bound to be exceptional cases where the analytic return will be predictably low, as for instance in certain Islamic countries where post-partum abstinence only lasts '40 days'.
14. We note that accessibility to services is one of the few fertility determinants which is amenable to experimental testing. The potential of this approach (see for example Phillips, Stinson, Bhatia, Rahman and Chakraborty 1982) far exceeds the likely contribution of cross-sectional surveys.
15. Preliminary results from a special experiment in the Ivory Coast suggest that the total number of errors found at the machine editing stage is influenced to a rather minor degree by whether questionnaires were subjected to prior office editing.
16. For instance, in the Malaysian survey an average of 3.8 transcription errors were made per questionnaire (Palan 1983).
17. Portugal (which is included in this table) is defined by the United Nations as a developing country and was therefore one of the 42 countries whose survey received direct assistance from the London office of WFS.
18. For an alternative to this cumbersome definition, see the Benin Questionnaire.

3

Additions to the Core Questionnaires

Susheela Singh

3.1 Introduction

Even while the WFS questionnaire instruments were being designed, it became clear that a division into core material which was common to all countries and additional optional topics would be necessary. The concept of such a split may not have originated with this project, but its appropriateness for this series of surveys in widely differing cultures was quickly realized. In order to facilitate comparative analysis, but, equally important, to make technical assistance economical, efficient and feasible (given the large number of countries expected to participate), some degree of standardization in the instruments was a basic requirement. The core questionnaire represented the minimum amount of comparable data that countries were expected to obtain. But this would be balanced by a choice of subsets of questions, or 'modules' on a number of supplementary topics, to meet particular needs. These modules would also be more or less standardized and be designed to be easily incorporated into the core household schedule and an individual questionnaire. They would deal with two kinds of fertility determinants in more detail than the core questionnaires: those which affect fertility directly (the so-called proximate or intermediate variables) and the more fundamental socio-economic explanatory variables. However, the division between common core and supplementary material was not achieved easily; the early drafts of the core questionnaire contained several topics which, during the lengthy process of evaluation and revision, were relegated to modules. In addition, as explained below, modules could not be devised successfully for all initially selected topics.

While countries were expected to use the core individual and household questionnaires with only minor changes, use of modules was optional. This principle was stressed from the outset by the Technical Advisory Committee (TAC), along with the idea that a module would only be offered to a country if it was evident that it would contribute to the understanding of fertility in that country. However, as thinking on these subjects became clearer, and following the experience of the early surveys, it was evident by 1975 that certain modules should not simply be left as 'optional' but should be strongly recommended for certain countries in the light of their social and demographic circumstances. Thus the sixth meeting of the TAC in September 1975 shifted the emphasis away from the principle of free choice and recommended that, where appropriate, WFS should encourage countries to adopt one or more of four high-priority modules: fertility regulation, abortion, family planning and factors other than contraception affecting fertility. Countries would still make the final decision, however, and the wide variation in the actual use of modules, as well as the fact that countries felt free to use only parts of modules, testifies to their ultimate freedom of choice.

In this chapter we describe the development of modules, touch briefly on their contents and discuss their actual use by countries. In addition, we evaluate the role of the WFS in the choice of modules by countries, the appropriateness of the choices that were made, and the completeness of coverage of substantive topics by the modules.

Apart from providing modules on certain topics, WFS understood and accepted that countries might have unique areas of interest on which questions might be appropriately devised. We will examine use of country-specific questions to assess the extent to which the principle of encouraging such additions was realized.

3.2 Selection of module topics and their development

The essential criterion for choosing module topics was that they should deal with determinants of fertility. This restriction was inherent in the nature of the surveys themselves, whose scope had in turn been defined by the interests of donor agencies and the academic community. A second equally important condition was that the variables should be measurable and offer a reasonable prospect of yielding reliable and useful results. Thirdly, at least in the initial set of module topics considered if not in that finally developed, WFS intended to achieve comprehensive coverage of the potentially important determinants of fertility.

The lack of a single accepted theoretical framework made the choice of topics very difficult. The range of topics, shown below, represents an attempt to meet the needs of competing frameworks. The second criterion, that modules should be reasonably certain of yielding results, restricted choice. Because some desirable topics (inheritance, kinship, modernism, mortality–fertility interrelationships) were inherently difficult ones or varied so much from culture to culture, no standard set of questions was successfully devised. This meant that the third intention, comprehensive coverage, was not realized.

The list of modules proposed at the second TAC meeting in October 1973 was:

1	Abortion	9	Local hospital and clinical services
2	Community factors	10	Kinship
3	Economic factors	11	Mortality
4	Family planning	12	Miscellaneous questions
5	Fecundability	13	Modernism
6	Housing	14	Marital history (including polygamy)
7	Inheritance	15	Factors other than contraception
8	Advantages and disadvantages of children		affecting fertility (FOTCAF)

In addition, WFS was requested to explore the feasibility of a module on psychological factors affecting fertility, and at a later meeting modules on nutritional status and fertility regulation were considered. Some modules were eventually combined: hospital family planning services at the individual level were included in family planning, and those at the community level in the community variables module; costs and benefits of children was subsumed under economic variables. In addition the marital history became incorporated into the core questionnaire, but no standard set of questions on polygamy was prepared.

In the process of finalizing the core questionnaire, the more detailed questions on fertility regulation were extracted and made into a module (see chapter 2). The suggested module on housing was subsumed into questions on housing and household possessions usually included in the household survey, or into the community and economic modules. Meanwhile, in the process of reviewing the mortality module, designed as an extension of the household schedule, a new module on the effect of mortality on fertility was proposed.

With this large workload, the fourth TAC meeting (May 1974) found it necessary to assign priorities to modules, but had to revise these priorities at later meetings (WFS 1975a). By the sixth meeting in September 1975 the first-priority modules, some already completed and others nearing completion, were:

Abortion
Family planning
Fertility regulation
Factors other than contraception affecting fertility (FOTCAF)
Community-level variables

Second-priority modules were general mortality and economic variables. By this time all other suggested modules had either been discontinued or left as background papers, to be further developed only when countries requested their use, as discussed below.

The seven first- and second-priority modules, which were completed in a form in which they could be easily incorporated into the core instruments, went through a fairly long process of evaluation before finalization. Comments from the first six TAC meetings, other external reviewers and WFS staff were taken into account; the experience of prior surveys and the early WFS surveys, as well as pre-tests on specific modules, were also used in the finalization process. However, they did not pass through the same extensive consultative process used for the core instruments, since they were intended as advisory documents which might themselves require substantial adaptation to suit particular countries. The pre-tests carried out are shown in table 3.1.

Although a community factors questionnaire was not pre-tested before finalization, it made use of the experience of earlier field studies in the Republic of Korea, Nigeria, Pakistan, Taiwan and Thailand. In general, pre-testing was quite thorough, especially in view of the fact that the modules (except FOTCAF) were derived from similar approaches that had already been used in previous surveys.

TABLE   3.1

Pre-testing of various modules

Module	Place	Date	Sample size
Family planning	Bombay, India	1975	102
	Bombay, India[a]	1976	271
	Panama City, Panama[a]	1976	300
	Ankara, Turkey[a]	1976	260
Factors other than contraception affecting fertility (FOTCAF)	Zaire Pilot Survey	1974	762
	Kuala Lumpur, Malaysia	1975	107
	Ghana Pilot Study[b]	1975	643
Influence of mortality on fertility	Cayagan de Oro City, Philippines	1975	101

[a] Not a full module pre-test, but a special pre-test focused on the subject of contraceptive accessiblity and also including questions on knowledge and use of abortion and the 'menstrual regulation' method (see chapter 2 for further details).
[b] A full-scale national pilot survey, including this module.

In addition, each country would be pre-testing its own questionnaire, thus providing a further check.

Of the seven modules which finally became part of WFS's basic documentation, four were focused specifically on the proximate or intermediate fertility determinants:

1 *Fertility regulation module.* This module, which is an expanded version of section 5 of the core questionnaire, was created because of the decision to include only a minimal number of questions on the subject in the core questionnaire (see chapter 2 for further details).

2 *Family planning module.* This module could be substituted for sections 3 and 5 of the core questionnaire. In addition to information gathered by section 3 and the fertility regulation module, it obtains the following information: knowledge of, and visits to, places where family planning advice and supplies may be obtained; the parity at which contraception was started and with which method; approval/disapproval of contraception by never-users; reason for discontinuation of last contraceptive method; source of contraceptive supply and its adequacy. The module was not intended as a vehicle for comprehensive evaluation of a national family planning programme, but could supply some basic information on the success of certain aspects of such a programme. Countries varied more in the implementation of this module than in most others, partly reflecting the variability of family planning

programmes and policies; this has caused problems in comparative analysis (Jones 1984).

3 *Factors other than contraception affecting fertility module (FOTCAF).* Fertility levels are determined not only by the use or non-use of contraception, but also by a host of other 'intermediate' variables causally situated between fertility and the underlying socio-economic and cultural milieu. This module supplemented the core questionnaire by gathering information on age at menarche, menstruation, temporary separation of the marriage partners, frequency of sexual intercourse, the timing of breast-milk supplementation, post-partum amenorrhoea, post-partum abstinence, terminal abstinence, menopause, and respondent's weight and height. However, because it was structured as a collection of submodules, it was possible for countries to choose some subsections only. This was in fact often done, the sections on weight and height and sexual intercourse being those most frequently omitted.

4 *Abortion module.* This consisted of questions to be appended to section 2 (maternity history) and section 3 (contraceptive knowledge and use) of the core questionnaire. The appendage to section 2 was designed to ascertain the mode of termination (spontaneous, induced) of reported abortions. The questions added to section 3 had two purposes: to probe, in the context of contraceptive use, whether the respondent had ever resorted to induced abortion; and to measure the attitudinal climate with respect to the use of induced abortion. The module was not recommended for use in countries in which anti-abortion laws are rigorously enforced or where abortion is a very sensitive subject. It was, however, strongly recommended for all other countries.

The fifth module, general mortality, was designed specifically for countries with deficient vital statistics which might therefore wish to measure adult mortality as well as fertility and childhood mortality. This module was part of the extended household schedule and obtained information on deaths of household members in the 24 months preceding the interview, survival of first spouse, survival of parents, whether the person being interviewed is an eldest living offspring, and survival of offspring of ever-married women. Infant, child and adult mortality may be estimated from this information.

Only two modules, those on economic factors and community factors, dealt with socio-economic determinants of fertility. However, the economic module contained three separate sets of questions. These three submodules dealt with family income, asset holding, and economic costs and benefits of children. The income and assets modules provide measures of the family's economic position. The costs and benefits module attempted to assess the net contribution of children to the family's income, and their effect on the opportunity cost of mother's employment. The expectation is that where their net contribution is greater, fertility will be higher and families will prefer larger numbers of children;

also, where their effect on women's work participation is low — child care is free or easily provided — then women's fertility preferences will be unaffected, other things being equal. In terms of specification of actual questions, these submodules, published as WFS Occasional Papers nos. 11 and 12, lie between the ready-to-use modules and background papers.

While the economic modules related to the individual woman or household, the community module dealt with characteristics common to all the persons living in a community, such as presence or absence of a hospital or school. Among the topics covered in this module were transportation and communication facilities; health levels and facilities; family planning facilities and prevalence; education; agricultural and/or industrial development levels. The collection of community-level data was a supplementary investigation to the main survey; it was usually carried out at the same time as the main survey but required the interviewing of community leaders, the consulting of reference works, and/or simple observation of the community itself. This module required special adaptation wherever used.

A number of modules were never finalized: kinship, inheritance, effect of mortality on fertility, modernism, fertility regulation methods and nutritional status. Part of the reason for these failures was that WFS was not in a position to experiment with uncertain or difficult topics. Modules had to be recommended to large numbers of countries and therefore their quality and robustness needed to be reasonably assured. Thus failure to finalize modules was due mainly to the fact that they dealt with inherently difficult topics, or with topics on which no standard set of questions could be devised or agreed upon.

In the case of the module on the effect of mortality on fertility, whose objective was to study whether the reproductive behaviour of women is affected by their experience and/or expectation of child mortality, its rejection was based on the results of a pre-test in the Philippines which found that several of the key questions were too sensitive to administer.

The proposed module on nutritional status of women was taken as far as creating a list of possible anthropometric and clinical measurements, but the decision was then made not to proceed because of the expense and difficulty of obtaining the data and because of disagreement over the relevance of this factor as a determinant of fertility.

The proposed kinship module included separate sets of questions on the wife's and the husband's relatives, whether any parents lived with them, whether other relatives lived in the same town or village, and if so which ones and the frequency of contact. Only one question was asked about the past — whether the respondent had lived with relatives for one or more years. The main thrust of the inheritance module was to ask about the type of land ownership and whether land could be passed on to children when parents died (separately for land that was being farmed, land that someone else farmed for the couple, and land that no one farmed). Although some revision of the kinship and inheritance module drafts was done by the TAC, by 1975 the decision was taken to leave them as loosely structured background documents containing examples and suggestions but not a final set of recommended questions. This was because of the difficulties of constructing standard modules given the wide cultural variations in inheritance and kinship structure.

The World Health Organization proposed a set of questions entitled 'Acceptability of fertility regulation methods', covering knowledge about the biology of pregnancy and the menstrual cycle, responsibility for contraception, and questions on the advantages and disadvantages of the pill, injection and IUD. The fourth TAC, which reviewed this proposal in May 1974, had strong reservations about the module, based on both technical and operational considerations; it was left that the possibility of co-operation with WHO would be explored, but no further action was taken.

The module on modernism was proposed from the earliest TAC meeting and was expected to include questions on the role and status of women. A document was prepared (eventually published as *WFS Occasional Papers* no. 14) which defined modernism and demonstrated its relevance to fertility by citing questions and findings from surveys carried out in Ankara and Mexico City. However, although this report served as a guide to countries, it was not developed further into an easily used set of recommended questions.

While the intermediate demographic and biological variables that directly influence fertility were adequately covered by the individual core questionnaire and its supplementary modules, the same cannot be said about the broad area of the ultimate determinants of fertility, the economic and cultural factors. Relegating some modules to the status of background documents (kinship, inheritance, modernism, and to some extent the economic variables modules also) greatly reduced the likelihood of countries requesting them or of WFS staff recommending them. Although the economic and community-level modules together with the background papers cover a wide range of fertility determinants, it is evident that they do not cover all possible factors. Perhaps one of the more important gaps is the lack of time-related data, e.g. on migration, on work and income and on the provision of services and facilities (in the community variables module). Apart from these possible measures of social and economic mobility, there was also no attempt to measure generational mobility, that is to obtain even a small amount of data on the socio-economic status of parents of the respondent or husband. An important aspect of the costs and benefits of children that was insufficiently emphasized was school attendance; attitudes to the education of children were questioned but not the actual behaviour.

It has been stressed that the main aim of WFS was to measure fertility and its direct determinants, and given this deliberate focus, the lack of socio-economic data is to some extent understandable. Nevertheless, it can be argued that more should have been done to widen the areas covered, and also in taking a more positive attitude in recommending that countries should cover some of these areas where appropriate.

3.3 Use of modules in WFS surveys

The relevance of modules depended on the socio-cultural circumstances of a country and on the existing availability of data, or other surveys in progress. But one unavoidable limiting factor, even where several modules might have been useful, was the need not to overload the questionnaire and extend the interview to an unmanageable length. The fertility regulation, family planning and abortion modules were appropriate for countries where contraceptive use was already substantial and where fertility decline had probably started. However, as table 3.2 shows, only 11 countries used most of the family planning module and several which could have beneficially used it did not do so — Sri Lanka, Fiji, Indonesia, Republic of Korea, Malaysia, Thailand, Ecuador, Peru, Dominican Republic, Panama, Guyana and Jamaica. However, three of these (Indonesia, Republic of Korea and Malaysia) did ask some questions, a few of which were similar to those of the module. Conversely, the family planning module was administered in a few countries (Ghana, Sudan and Nepal) where contraceptive practice proved to be too low to permit fruitful analysis of the data.

The number of countries which used most of the abortion module was even smaller — eight — although the most important element, the birth history question on whether foetal losses of under seven months gestation were deliberately aborted, was asked by as many as 14 countries, including all except one of the eight countries labelled 'most' in table 3.2. Again, this module was relevant to several countries, in the Americas especially, which did not use it. However, given the general opinion that women would be unwilling to answer these questions and would therefore under-report such events, as well as the illegality (or at least unacceptability) of abortion in many countries, it is understandable that relatively few countries agreed to include them.

Use of the fertility regulation module was more widespread, perhaps mainly because it was printed alongside the core questionnaire with the recommendation that it be used in *most* countries. As shown in table 3.2, 24 countries used some or most of these questions. In sub-Saharan Africa, however, it was never used, being replaced by the more appropriate FOTCAF module. We may note only a few cases which probably would have benefited from using the module but did not do so — Tunisia, Thailand, Mexico, and Trinidad and Tobago.

The FOTCAF module was designed for countries with low contraceptive use, where fertility was mainly or substantially controlled by biological and cultural factors (such as length of the period of fecundability, marriage patterns, frequency of intercourse, and duration of breastfeeding, amenorrhoea and abstinence). Since the module was rather long, it was divided into clearly defined sections in the expectation that countries might choose to use some sections only. Generally, it was employed by countries with low contraceptive use, as expected. All African and Middle Eastern countries and Bangladesh used at least some questions; and two other countries where contraceptive use was moderately high but where the FOTCAF variables still had substantial impact also used at least some — the Philippines and Haiti. However, some important partial

TABLE 3.2

Use of modules and/or extra questions on module topics in specified surveys

Country	Fertility regulation	Family planning	Abortion	Factors other than contraception	Mortality	Community[f]	Income	Economic assets	Costs and benefits[f]	Aspects of modernism[a]
Africa										
Benin	–	Few	Few	Most	Some	–	–	–	–	–
Cameroon	–	–	Few	Most	Some	Some	–	Few	–	Some
Ghana	–	Most	Few	Most	–	Some	–	Few	–	–
Ivory Coast[d]	–	Few	Few	Most	–	Some	–	–	–	Some
Kenya	–	Some	Few	Most	Most	Some	–	–	–	–
Lesotho	–	Few	–	Most	–	–	–	–	–	Some
Nigeria	–	Few	Few	Some	Some[e]	Some	–	Few	–	–
Senegal	–	–	–	Some	–	–	–	–	–	–
Egypt[d]	Most	Most	Few	Some	–	Some	Some[c]	–	Some[b]	Some[c]
Mauritania	–	–	–	Most	Most	Some	–	Few	–	Few
Morocco	Most	Most	–	–	Most	Some	–	Few	–	Some
Sudan (North)	–	Most	–	Most	Most	–	–	–	–	Some
Tunisia	–	Some	Most	Most	–	–	–	–	–	–
Asia and Pacific										
Iran[d]	Most	–	–	–	Most	–	–	Few	–	–
Jordan	Most	Few	Some	Few	Most	Some	–	Few	–	Some
Syria	–	–	Some	Most	–	Some	Some	–	Some	Some
Turkey	Most	Most	Some	Few	Most	–	–	Few	–	Some
Yemen AR	–	–	–	Most	Most	–	–	–	–	–
Bangladesh	Most	–	Most	Some	–	Some	–	Some	Some	Few
Nepal	Some	Most	Some	Few	–	–	–	–	–	–
Pakistan	–	Some	Some	–	–	Some	–	Some	–	–
Sri Lanka	Most	Few	Few	–	–	–	–	Some	–	Some

Fiji	Some	Few	—	Few	—	—	Few
Indonesia	Most	Some	Some	—	—	—	—
Korea, Rep. of	Most	Some	Some	Few	Most	Some	Few
Malaysia	Some	Some	Most	—	—	Some	Some
Philippines	Most	Most	Most	Most	—	Some	Few
Thailand[d]	—	—	—	—	Some	Some[b]	Some[c]
Americas							
Colombia	Most	Most	Most	Few	—	—	—
Ecuador	Most	Few	Few	Few	—	Some	Some
Paraguay	Most	Most	Few	Few	—	—	—
Peru	Most	Few	Few	Few	Some	Some	Few
Venezuela	Most	Most	—	—	—	—	—
Costa Rica	Most	Most	Most	Few	—	Some	Few
Dominican Rep.	Most	Few	—	Few	—	—	Some
Mexico	—	Some	Few	—	Some	Some	Few
Panama	Most	Few	Most	—	—	Some	Some
Guyana	Most	—	—	Some	—	—	Few
Haiti	—	Few	Few	—	—	Some	Few
Jamaica	Most	—	—	—	Some	Some	Some
Trinidad & Tobago	—	Some	Most	—	Some	Some	Some
Europe							
Portugal	Most	Some	—	—	Some	—	Some

a Countries with 'some' asked about both the possession of modern objects and household amenities (water, toilet, lighting); countries with 'few' asked about one of these two topics only.
b From husbands survey, done separately; in the case of Egypt, from both individual and husbands surveys.
c From an expanded household economic survey, done separately.
d These countries also carried out a husbands survey.
e In the multi-round survey attached to the household survey.
f 'Some' indicates use of these modules but a wide range in topics covered and extensiveness of coverage.

omissions must be noted. Mauritania omitted post-partum abstinence, and Senegal did not include either post-partum amenorrhoea or abstinence. Where the Muslim precept of 40 days of abstinence after the birth is followed by most women, this factor is not an important determinant of birth interval length, however, and this may explain its omission in Mauritania. Perhaps more significantly, several Asian countries with long breastfeeding durations, and in some cases with traditions of abstinence and periodic separations, either did not ask any FOTCAF questions (Pakistan, Sri Lanka, Indonesia and Thailand) or did not use important sections of the FOTCAF module (Bangladesh, Nepal and Fiji). But these were all early surveys, pre-dating the final version of the FOTCAF module. The subset of questions on frequency of sexual intercourse, a sensitive subject on which the quality of data obtained is uncertain, was understandably omitted by all but a few countries (Benin, Cameroon, Ghana, Ivory Coast, Kenya, Nigeria, Philippines and Colombia), and not all of these asked the full set.

The general WFS policy was to discourage use of the fertility survey as a means of obtaining information unrelated to fertility. The mortality module was the sole exception to this principle. The general mortality module, designed to be an expansion of the household schedule, was intended for use by countries to measure in particular adult mortality, usually because of inadequate vital statistics. Only eight countries used most of the module, mainly in North Africa and the Middle East, although Lesotho and the Republic of Korea also did so. Only a few other countries made partial use of the module, and it would doubtless be true to say that several other countries, especially in Africa and Asia, could have profitably used it. This underutilization no doubt reflects national preferences, but the cost of an enlarged household sample, which use of the module was thought to require, was doubtless an important factor.

The community variables module had low priority in the early stages of the development of the questionnaires, but at the sixth TAC meeting in September 1975 the decision to relegate the inheritance and kinship drafts to the status of research modules led to greater priority being given to community variables. It was hoped that information on these two subjects could be gained through the community variables module and the household schedule. Discussion of the family planning module also stressed the need for information at the community level. As a result, although the experimental nature of the community variables module was recognized, it was moved into the first-priority group, and was therefore to be recommended as highly as the four modules that dealt with intermediate demographic variables. Given the late entry of this module, it is not surprising that only 17 countries used it. Nevertheless, several African countries with fieldwork beyond 1976 did not use it, and it might also have been useful in these largely rural countries.

The module was designed for rural areas only. Although it might have been useful to apply it to urban communities, fine subdivision of large urban centres would have been necessary, and this was not done in the only two countries which used it in urban areas (Cameroon and Mexico).

As table 3.2 shows, use of the economic modules was not widespread. It was even more restricted than appears here, because the more frequent situation was to ask one or two questions, not the full recommended set. Of the nine countries which asked at least one question on income, only Venezuela, Turkey, Republic of Korea, Malaysia, Thailand and Trinidad and Tobago obtained the income of the whole household, and only Thailand and Trinidad and Tobago used a set of questions similar to those recommended in the module. Two countries which carried out an extended household economic survey (Egypt and Thailand) would also have obtained detailed data on income for all household members who worked. Some questions on the costs and benefits of children were asked in only eight countries, and a few of these restricted questions to child care only. In the case of assets, the five countries labelled 'some' in table 3.2 asked about both agricultural assets and one or more of the following: materials used to build the dwelling, tenancy status and number of rooms used by the household. The 11 countries labelled 'few' did not ask about agricultural assets, but only about one or more characteristics of the dwelling. However, a larger number of countries (25) shown under the column 'aspects of modernism' asked about the possession of one or more of the following: modern objects, water, electricity and toilet facilities — items that are covered in both the economic variables and modernism monographs and which are recommended in the 'core' household schedule.

Obtaining accurate data on income is well known to be very difficult, as well as being a sensitive issue, and this may have influenced countries against including it; but the other topics were not problematic in this sense. The collection of income data from female respondents rather than through a separate husbands survey (as in Thailand) may have been seen as a prohibitive difficulty. Nevertheless, the household interview could have been the vehicle for such questions (as in the case of Turkey, for example). A second problem affecting questions on income and costs and benefits of children was that of integrating them into the core questionnaire: unlike other modules, these were not written up with precise instructions on where they should be inserted. A further constraint was that the sets of questions (particularly on costs and benefits) were extensive, which required that countries choose subsets, therefore reducing the chances of the modules being used. The fact that questions on housing and possession of modern objects were simple, easy to incorporate and familiar explains their more widespread use.

3.4   Assessment of module content

It is beyond the scope of this chapter to attempt a full evaluation of the utility of each module. However, it may be useful to cite the sources of such evaluations where they exist and mention some of the major conclusions. The content of several modules is discussed in this volume.

Chapter 2 provides a critique of the fertility regulation module; the main conclusion is that the absence of information on the precise timing and duration of contraceptive use severely limited analysis of the effectiveness of fertility regulation measures. A study which makes extensive use of the most controversial variable, the wantedness of the last birth, may be found in chapter 31.

As mentioned earlier, the FOTCAF module has received extensive analytical attention and formed the subject of a specially convened workshop in London. Several country-specific analyses may be found in the WFS *Scientific Reports* series. The proximate determinants of fertility also form the subject of chapter 30 and a methodological paper on FOTCAF was presented at an IUSSP/WFS seminar in 1984 (Page, Cleland and Hobcraft 1984). It is clear that the major contribution of this module has been the information gathered on the post-partum variables – breastfeeding, amenorrhoea and sexual abstinence. By comparison, attempts to measure the start and end of reproductive life, temporary spousal separation and fecundability have not proved very successful.

The mortality module has also received adequate attention by analysts, including a comprehensive multinational study (Blacker, Fernández and Timæus 1984). The lessons for future surveys are clearly summarized in chapter 4 and there is no need to repeat them here.

Community-level data were initially neglected, both because the few early studies found disappointingly few relationships with fertility behaviour and because of the failure to construct files which were amenable to analysis. This neglect was later partly remedied through a WFS workshop. A synthesis of WFS experience in the measurement and analysis of community variables may be found in chapter 33. Perhaps the main lesson is that effects of community characteristics on infant and child mortality can be more readily discerned than effects on fertility or contraceptive use.

As with the community-level module, the family planning module received rather little analytic attention in the earlier phase of WFS, partly because the relevant variables were not needed for the main country reports and were omitted from data files. Interest has focused on the perceived availability and accessibility of sources of family planning supplies, which, as explained in chapter 2, became part of the mandatory core in 1977. A comprehensive assessment of this and related topics (e.g. mode of transport to sources, convenience of travel) may be found in Jones (1984). By comparison, other information collected in this module such as approval of family planning and reasons for discontinuation of methods has been underutilized.

WFS experience with the abortion module has confirmed that induced abortions are severely under-reported in interview surveys. The definitive analysis of this subject (Casterline and Ashurst 1984) shows that the reported level of induced abortion is trivially small except in the Republic of Korea and Tunisia, where the proportion of all pregnancies in the preceding five years that terminated in induced abortion was 24 and 4 per cent respectively. Even in these two countries, however, induced abortions are substantially under-reported. Further evidence from the Venezuelan survey suggests that a detailed month-by-month probing of the recent past does not overcome the reluctance of respondents to report induced abortions (Gaslonde and Carrasco 1982). The conclusion is clear: the abortion module proved to be of very limited utility.

There remains the economic modules, about which little can be said. As already explained, most countries used these modules in a partial and fragmented manner and there has so far been no attempt to gather together this disparate experience.

3.5 Husbands survey

The original intention of WFS was to develop and finalize a questionnaire for husbands surveys. However, although a draft was prepared and made available as a Technical Paper, it was never published. Only four countries had a husbands survey: Egypt, Iran, Ivory Coast and Thailand. Two of these have published results from their surveys, and Ivory Coast, the most recent of this group, will eventually analyse these data. The Iranian survey is a special case, since data processing itself was interrupted by the revolution in 1979.

The sample for husbands surveys is limited to husbands of currently married women, and even among these, a subselection may be necessary to cut costs. The three completed surveys had the following samples:

Country	Ever-married women	Husbands
Egypt	8788	2312
Ivory Coast	5764	506
Thailand	3820	2967

Although only the husbands of currently married women could be interviewed, it is doubtful whether this resulted in a biased sample.

Interviewing husbands directly, in addition to the obvious advantages (of being the best means of collecting data on economic questions, providing more accurate data on husbands' characteristics, and enabling cross-checking and therefore improvement of the quality of data on other areas), has proved to yield other unexpected gains. Husbands' responses on contraception, especially the male methods, are invaluable. In addition, the results from the Egyptian survey showed that husbands' fertility preferences were substantially different from those of wives, and more closely linked to use of contraception. This was much less true in the case of Thailand, suggesting that for questions of this kind the use of a husbands survey is more crucial in strongly patriarchal than in more egalitarian socieities.

3.6 Review of country-specific additions

Apart from using the modules designed by WFS, countries were free to include questions on other topics of interest, and WFS staff could also suggest country-specific questions relevant to a particular country. The additions discussed here go beyond the inclusion of country-specific background variables such as ethnicity and religion, which were in any case recommended in the core questionnaire (see Singh 1984a for details of country-specific additions).

The topic of maternal and child health was one favoured by several countries. Although questions varied substantially from country to country, as many as 12 countries covered the topic: five in Latin America and seven in Africa. In the later African surveys, in particular, maternal and child health questions were added because the FOTCAF module provided an ideal framework. By then the usefulness and quality of childhood mortality data were apparent, and these questions could be very relevant to the study of childhood mortality. The topics include ante- and post-natal care, and medical attention at childbirth as well as questions on curative and preventative care of the infant.

A second topic on which a large number of countries made changes or additions was nuptiality. The need for some variation in countries' treatment of the section on marriage was foreseen in the core questionnaire, and WFS staff were partly responsible for suggesting and helping to design alternatives to the core questions. Two of the main areas where the section was adapted to suit local needs were the Caribbean, to cover changes in union type with the same partner, and in some African countries, to cover polygamous marriages or to distinguish between the different types of unions as in Ivory Coast.

Some additions directly related to fertility may also be noted. Four countries asked about employment in birth intervals other than the first, which was included in the core questionnaire — Philippines, Portugal, Sri Lanka and Thailand. Mexico alone asked about the husband's work at the beginning of marriage, using the usual set of questions applied to the current or most recent job. Two Latin American countries (Dominican Republic and Venezuela) obtained detailed exposure information, month by month for the year before interview, in a section called 'Sexual relations history of the last year'.

Additions on topics already covered by the core were also made. Six countries used substantially expanded questions on preferences — Republic of Korea and Malaysia on the preferred family size and sex composition, Egypt and Fiji on husband's preferences, Nigeria on husband's and mother-in-law's preferences and Portugal on the reasons for wanting or not wanting more children. Countries with a separate husbands survey typically also obtained information on husband's preferences for children (Egypt, Iran, Ivory Coast and Thailand). As many as 16 countries used at least one question on the subject of spacing of children, typically ascertaining whether the next child was wanted soon or not for several years. A similar question had been included in the early drafts of the core questionnaire but was dropped in the process of revision; however, it was eventually incorporated as a modification to the core questionnaire about halfway through the WFS programme. A few countries asked general questions on the nearest source of family planning supplies instead of the recommended method-specific questions. However, this was probably because the module was not finalized until 1975 and the early versions did not include method-specific questions. Several countries added questions on problems with obtaining family planning supplies and a few added questions on problems with methods themselves. A few countries asked about the source of knowledge about family planning. Finally, Sudan alone asked individual women about circumcision, while Ivory Coast asked general questions on the practice of female circumcision in the community questionnaire.

Topics which were of particular interest to countries and which may have little bearing on fertility behaviour were added in a few instances: for example, Panama asked about cervical cancer detection, while five countries asked questions on the subject of unemployment of women. Morocco included an extended series of questions on use and accessibility of health services and on vaccination, some in the household and some in the individual questionnaire. Seven countries asked some questions on employment of all members of the household who were above some given minimum age, occasionally including children as well as adults. Within the household schedule, Turkey obtained a migration history of all members over eight years of age for the past eight years while Mexico and Cameroon obtained a lifetime migration history for the individual woman respondent. A few other countries also asked at least one question relating to migration.

These are the substantial changes and additions, but many cases of smaller adaptations also occurred, although they are too numerous to list here. The question of whether countries analysed these additions sufficiently to justify the extra costs must be raised. Some cases of exceptionally useful and heavily analysed additional questions are easily found — the sexual relations history, the union and partnership data in the Caribbean, and some of the preference data. Many of the countries with data on polygamy have either not completed or not started their detailed analysis, but it is clear that this too will be a heavily analysed topic. The information on maternal and child health has certainly proved useful to countries and has been the subject of a comparative analysis. The extra household data on work and migration and added questions on work or unemployment in the individual questionnaire have not been used in many cases, however, and, in general, it is fair to conclude that much country-specific material still remains unexploited.

3.7 Conclusions

Modules were developed to provide countries with flexibility in the topics they covered, given the basic requirement that they must use a comparable core questionnaire. In addition, the original purpose was to design modules to cover all the important explanatory variables determining fertility. Although a commendable effort was made to meet this goal, with a wide range of topics being considered in the early stages of questionnaire design, the resulting set of completed, ready-to-use modules was heavily focused on the intermediate demographic variables, with relatively little coverage of the socio-economic, institutional and cultural factors that ultimately influence fertility. This was the most important gap in the coverage of the modules. The pressure of time and staff resources was only one reason for this limitation: the difficulty of designing effective and generalizable modules on some topics was a more important explanation. A stopgap solution was to give certain draft modules, which were either published as WFS *Occasional Papers* or left as drafts, the status of background papers, meaning that they would be developed into usable form only when requested by countries. This solution did not work very well, however, as their low use shows.

Given that some provision for covering the social, economic and cultural factors was made through suggestions and examples of questions in the WFS *Occasional Papers* (nos. 8, 9, 11, 12 and 14) and through draft modules, why was the inclusion of these topics in surveys so low? One immediate response is that more work and decision-making was needed to formulate a module from these sources than to administer the ready-made modules. Staff within countries may not have been able to do this alone, and staff from WFS also may either not have been sufficiently experienced, may not have considered that the co-ordinator's role included this type of work, or may have had too little time to render the amount of assistance necessary to draft sections of questionnaires.

For reasons such as these, WFS co-ordinators did not generally encourage inclusion of these more difficult topics. The only useful suggestions for increasing the use of questions on social, economic and cultural factors are: to develop more precise sets of questions, perhaps including alternative versions for some regionally specific topics; to bring in specialists on particular topics or areas, as needed, for individual countries; and to put a great deal more effort and time in pre-testing new country-specific questions.

A further question that must be raised is whether the data which were actually collected were fully utilized. Certainly at the level of the Country Reports, the large set of standard tables allowed little room or time for flexibility in including country-specific or module data. In addition, in the case of some modules, omission was due to the slowness of WFS in providing data-processing support by developing recoded variables. The absence of recode instructions and tabulation plans for some modules may itself have discouraged use of these modules. It is difficult to see how this kind of lag could have been avoided, given the way in which the organization had to develop. Some areas of data have been especially useful and well exploited, for example on nuptiality and many of the FOTCAF topics. Family planning and abortion module data have also been used by some countries, but not as extensively as the other two. Community-level data and data on economic factors as well as many of the country-specific additions are only beginning to be exploited, however.

4

Estimation of Fertility and Mortality from WFS Household Surveys

Ian Timæus

4.1 Introduction

Household surveys formed an integral part of all the WFS studies conducted in developing countries. Their main purpose was to list all household members and to collect sufficient information about their characteristics to identify those women who were eligible for interview in the individual surveys. Such listings also provide the denominators required for the calculation of demographic statistics relating to the whole population. WFS staff developed a standard household schedule to be used for the collection of this information. It included a group of essential questions to be asked in all countries. These dealt with the name, relationship to the household head, residence (*de jure* and, usually, *de facto*), sex, age and marital status of each household member. It also included recommended questions about characteristics of households and their members that may relate to fertility. These concerned the educational attainment of each household member, housing conditions and the possession of modern consumer durables. Information was obtained in about half the surveys on each of these topics and, in addition, a minority of household surveys collected data about other characteristics of household heads. A detailed description of the contents of the household schedules is given by Singh (1984a) and an assessment of the core schedule is provided in chapter 2.

From the outset, the household surveys were designed to fulfil additional aims. One of these was the collection of information about the fertility of a larger sample of women than could be interviewed using the detailed individual questionnaire. This was intended to enable countries that lacked good vital statistics to obtain more precise measures of current fertility levels and differentials than would be yielded by the individual survey. An expanded household schedule that included questions about women's lifetime fertility and most recent birth was developed for use in such countries. Data were also obtained that can be used to estimate child mortality. The second major extension to the core household schedule was a mortality module that consisted of a number of questions that can be used for the direct and indirect estimation of adult mortality. About a third of the WFS studies included a household survey that enumerated an enlarged sample. All of these enquired about fertility and all but two used some or all of the mortality module questions; a few other household surveys also asked questions about adult mortality.

As this outline of their contents has indicated, the household surveys conducted as part of the WFS are very diverse. At one extreme, there are surveys that asked only those questions essential for the identification of women eligible for individual interview. At the other extreme, there are surveys that enumerated an enlarged sample and included many additional questions about fertility, mortality and the background characteristics of households and their members. It is difficult to measure the additional costs involved in conducting such household surveys. They were, however, certainly substantial. Moreover, a comparative assessment of the quality of the fertility and mortality estimates obtained from the WFS household and individual surveys might prove useful to those designing further demographic enquiries. Studies of much of the other data collected in the household surveys have been published elsewhere. In particular Kabir (1980) and Zoughlami and Allsopp (1985) present detailed tabulations describing the age, sex, marital, educational and household structures of the populations surveyed while use of the information on household characteristics is illustrated and discussed in Casterline (ed.) (1985). This chapter, therefore, concentrates on the enlarged-sample household surveys, on fertility and on child and adult mortality. In the following sections these topics are considered in turn and the conclusion contains a more general review of the household surveys and the lessons to be learnt from them.

4.2   The expanded household surveys

The main reason for enumerating enlarged household survey samples was to increase the precision with which WFS studies could measure current fertility. The primary objective informing the design of the individual surveys and the core questionnaire was the investigation of behaviour and attitudes affecting fertility and their socio-economic and cultural correlates. Collecting data on such subjects involves a lengthy and detailed interview. The WFS and its advisors were aware, however, that WFS surveys would frequently be conducted in countries lacking such essential and basic information as reliable estimates of the level of fertility. To reduce the sampling errors of estimates of fertility in the year before a survey to acceptable levels requires a sample of some 20 000 households (United Nations 1974). This is several times greater than the size of the sample it was thought practical to cover in the individual surveys. Household surveys which enumerated a sample between two and four times the size of that required for the individual survey were proposed as the solution to this dilemma.

In the event, thirteen of the developing countries that participated in the WFS enumerated an enlarged household survey sample. They include Cameroon and Lesotho in sub-Saharan Africa; Mauritania, Morocco and Sudan in North Africa; and Jordan, Syria and Yemen AR in West Asia. Of the other Asian countries, only the Republic of Korea conducted such a household survey. In Latin America the approach was adopted by Colombia and Venezuela in South America and by the Dominican Republic and Mexico in the Caribbean and

Central America. Most of these surveys used the expanded household schedule. In Venezuela and Mexico, however, the main reason for enlarging the household survey sample was to ensure that almost all the individual survey subsample, which consisted of every second eligible woman, came from different households. Venezuela used only some of the expanded household schedule questions while in the Mexican survey the schedule asked only about births in the household during the preceding year. The expanded schedule was also used in the pilot survey conducted in Fiji. However, because the fertility questions were immediately repeated in the individual interviews, little was learnt from their use. Subsequently they were only used when an enlarged sample was enumerated, with the exceptions that births during the previous year were asked about in the Philippines and that the fertility of women who were ineligible for individual interview was enquired about in some of the Latin American surveys.

There were eight countries in which the WFS study was integrated into a more extensive programme of survey research. In most countries this provided a listing of households or dwellings. The WFS then conducted a household survey that listed household members and identified eligible women in a subsample of households or dwellings (see chapter 13). However, in Benin and Senegal, eligible women were identified in enumerations that formed part of a separate multi-round study, which removed the need for a further WFS household survey. These enumerations can be thought of as equivalent to the enlarged-sample household surveys. However, as few results are yet available from the Benin survey and the Senegal survey was in many ways incompatible with other WFS studies, they are not considered in detail here.

With the exception of Venezuela, where coding and processing of the data were subject to prolonged delay, estimates of current fertility levels based on the household surveys were included in the First Country Reports of all countries that collected the relevant information. However, it is clear that whether or not an enlarged-sample household survey was conducted depended on the interest of participating countries as much as on the need for data on current fertility. A survey or census-based estimate of fertility for 1970 or later already existed for several of the countries that conducted such a survey while in Mexico and Venezuela birth registration data, although imperfect, provide useful information on current fertility levels. In contrast, many countries for which no reliable national estimate of the level of fertility exists decided not to use the expanded household schedule.

From the outset it was realized that the costs involved in enumerating an enlarged household survey sample would be appreciable. Conducting such a survey may mean that a separate operation to list households or dwellings can be avoided. However, such lists can be compiled comparatively cheaply (see chapter 10). When the decision to use them was taken, it was believed that conducting enlarged-sample household surveys to obtain more precise estimates of current fertility would cost less than enlarging the individual surveys. Not only is the household interview shorter, but the need for callbacks is reduced as any adult respondent, and not just women in the reproductive age range, can be interviewed. While this is undoubtedly true and is supported by the analysis of costs in chapter 10, the savings involved are probably smaller than expected. This is because the WFS was not choosing between a household and an individual survey but conducting both. Some of the costs of conducting a survey are affected only slightly by the size of the sample. The obvious exception is the cost of the fieldwork itself but, if a household is to be visited and an interview conducted anyway, the additional costs involved in administering a detailed questionnaire like that used in the individual survey are fairly small. Similarly, it can be argued that the costs of processing and analysis are lower for household surveys than for fertility surveys. However, the WFS was inevitably involved in both operations in all countries. Increasing the size and complexity of the household files may have added nearly as much to costs as would have increasing the size of the individual files.

A further factor underlying the decision to use an expanded household schedule to estimate current fertility levels was the existence of a fairly well-tried methodology for collecting and analysing the relevant data. It had been adopted increasingly in demographic surveys and censuses in the 1960s and early 1970s. Even if the data were imperfect, methods for evaluating and adjusting them to yield acceptable estimates already existed. In contrast, although it was hoped that the individual surveys would yield better quality data, in particular because their design eliminated reporting by proxies and because the interviews were to be conducted by women (Marckwardt 1975), this remained uncertain. At the start of the WFS, methods for evaluating and adjusting birth-history data were relatively undeveloped and untried. Since then P/F and other techniques have been extended to them. What is more, their application has suggested that the birth histories obtained in most WFS surveys are reasonably accurate for at least the few years before the survey. This finding throws severe doubt on the need for large-sample surveys to estimate current fertility levels and differentials. The effective sample size used to calculate the measures can be increased instead by using several years' exposure and births. Thus Little (1982) has shown that fertility rates calculated from WFS individual survey data for a three- or five-year period are sufficiently precise for most purposes at both a national and a subnational level.

At the time of the design of the WFS programme, it was hoped to combine the household and individual survey data to obtain a two-phase estimate of fertility (WFS 1975c). Such estimates would benefit from both the greater precision of the household surveys and the greater reliability of the individual surveys. We believe, however, that the large-sample survey data have never been used in this way. This is largely because the data obtained in the two surveys about those women who were interviewed in both were seldom collected independently of each other. Of course, in future surveys where they were, two-phase estimates could be obtained.

In retrospect then it seems difficult to justify conducting enlarged-sample household surveys as part of the WFS programme of research. On the other hand, conducting household surveys instead of individual surveys to achieve the limited objectives of measuring fertility levels, trends and differentials certainly would result in substantial savings. As early as 1975 Marckwardt suggested:

Perhaps the best justification for conditional recommendation of the expanded household schedule is that it enables the WFS to enhance our knowledge of the best and least expensive way of collecting information on human fertility.

In this respect, the implications of the preliminary results of a number of WFS studies were considered by Chidambaram, Cleland and Verma (1980). Moreover a detailed study of the Colombia National Fertility Survey contains a wealth of material of relevance to this issue (Hobcraft 1980). In this chapter, we use the data collected in all thirteen enlarged-sample household surveys and a comparison of these results with those obtained in the corresponding individual surveys to examine it further.

4.3   Lifetime fertility

The questions on lifetime fertility recommended by the WFS for inclusion in the expanded household schedule enquired separately about the numbers of male and female children ever born who were living at home, were living elsewhere and had died. As a check, a further question asked about the total number of live births. Eleven of the twelve enlarged-sample household surveys that asked about women's lifetime fertility used these questions and in Venezuela only the total number of live births was ascertained. This disaggregated approach to obtaining the information adds seven columns to the household schedule and has three aims. First, it provides information on child mortality and on differentials in mortality by sex. This alone is probably sufficient to justify its use. Secondly, it is intended to minimize the omission of children from the reports. Its success at this is hard to assess within the context of the WFS. Thirdly, it provides useful information for data evaluation since omission of births is often concentrated among births of one sex or those that have died. However, the large sampling errors of sex ratios mean that only severe errors in the data can be detected in this way.

These questions about fertility differ greatly from those used to obtain the individual survey birth histories. The latter enquired in detail about the date of birth, sex and survival of each child. However, there are other important differences between the methodologies of the two surveys that probably affect the quality of the data. First, in the household surveys information about a woman's fertility was often obtained from another member of the household. In the individual surveys the woman herself was always interviewed. Secondly, the household surveys collected the information on a schedule that included only a brief question at the head of each column while, for the individual surveys, detailed questions were translated into the language(s) used for the interviews. Thirdly, about half the enlarged-sample household surveys used different teams of interviewers, usually men, from those used for the individual survey. Interpretation of differences between the results of the household and individual surveys is therefore difficult. The effect on reporting errors of a number of methodological differences, together with any differences in the ability of the two groups of interviewers, are conflated. Moreover, discrepancies between the aggregate results of the two surveys will also stem from sampling errors and any coverage biases in the individual survey samples.

Household and individual survey-based estimates of the mean number of children ever born according to women's age group are presented in table 4.1. In the Arab countries, Republic of Korea and, for the individual survey, Lesotho and Mauritania, the data exclude any children born to single women. The impact of this on the estimates is slight (see chapter 11). Despite the very different approaches used to collect the household and individual survey data, the results of the two series of surveys are very similar. In general, coverage of births is as complete in the household survey as in the individual survey. Information on Yemen AR is the single exception. Apart from the estimates for Yemen AR and for the youngest age group, almost all the pairs of indices differ by less than 5 per cent. Moreover, there is no overall pattern of divergence between the results of the two surveys although within a few countries small but consistent differences in one or the other direction are apparent. The reported mean parities agree fairly well even for women in their forties, the group who are thought most likely to omit births from their responses. In Cameroon, Morocco and Jordan older women did report slightly fewer children on average in the household survey. In contrast in Lesotho, Sudan, Syria and Dominican Republic they reported slightly more.

In Yemen AR substantially fewer births were reported in the household survey. Yet responses in the two surveys agree for 97 per cent of the matched sample of women. The discrepancy stems almost entirely from reports in the household survey about women who were not interviewed individually. In Yemen AR this part of the household survey was conducted by male interviewers, whereas in other households the individual survey interviewer also completed the household schedule. The household survey teams clearly obtained very incomplete data. However, the extent to which poor training and supervision, proxy reporting or other factors are responsible is unclear. Certainly similar problems were not experienced in other countries that used different, and usually male, interviewers for the household survey.

In table 4.2 the mean parities according to age reported in the WFS household surveys are compared with equivalent estimates from censuses and national surveys conducted earlier in the 1970s. Such data are available for seven countries and were collected using broadly the same approach as that adopted in the WFS household surveys. Despite this, women over the age of 30 or 35 reported substantially fewer children on average in all the earlier enquiries except that in the

TABLE 4.1

Mean number of children ever born, WFS household (HH)
and individual (I) surveys

Country	Source	Current age						
		15–19	20–24	25–29	30–34	35–39	40–44	45–49
Cameroon	HH	0.53	1.79	3.02	4.19	4.83	5.10	5.10
	I	0.41	1.63	3.00	4.16	4.87	5.20	5.18
Lesotho[b]	HH	0.16	1.15	2.37	3.67	4.63	5.26	5.54
	I	0.19	1.27	2.50	3.90	4.66	5.08	5.40
Mauritania[b]	HH	0.36	1.60	3.21	4.66	5.67	5.94	6.24
	I	0.38	1.65	3.39	4.77	5.68	5.84	6.01
Morocco[a,b]	HH	0.12	1.10	2.73	4.61	6.06	6.56	6.70
	I	0.17	1.22	2.86	4.77	6.08	7.07	7.06
Sudan (North)[a,b]	HH	0.17	1.36	3.11	4.80	5.65	6.17	6.24
	I	0.15	1.38	3.02	4.75	5.75	5.91	5.98
Jordan[a,b]	HH	0.18	1.55	3.60	5.66	7.26	8.16	8.39
	I	0.17	1.57	3.71	5.68	7.12	8.44	8.71
Syria[a,b]	HH	0.18	1.26	3.02	5.02	6.52	7.50	7.97
	I	0.20	1.30	3.06	4.82	6.26	7.28	7.69
Yemen AR[a,b]	HH	0.34	1.46	2.93	4.26	5.53	5.79	6.07
	I	0.43	1.67	3.24	4.95	6.01	6.45	7.03
Korea, Rep. of[a,b]	HH	0.02	0.45	1.81	3.31	4.36	5.10	5.74
	I	0.02	0.46	1.84	3.32	4.36	5.10	5.73
Colombia	HH	0.17	1.11	2.46	3.92	5.27	6.33	6.60
	I	0.17	1.10	2.44	4.05	5.04	6.08	6.74
Venezuela	HH	0.18	1.07	2.43	3.82	5.08	5.79	6.09
	I	0.19	1.14	2.45	3.90	5.04	6.12	—
Dominican Rep.	HH	0.23	1.43	3.13	4.72	6.38	6.69	6.89
	I	0.21	1.34	3.04	4.62	6.35	6.43	6.53

[a] The household survey data exclude births to single women.
[b] The individual survey data exclude births to single women.

Republic of Korea. The high standard of training and fieldwork insisted on by the WFS may have produced substantial improvements in the coverage of births. Moreover, they appear essential for the collection of useful data on the lifetime fertility of older women. This evidence, combined with the comparison between

TABLE　4.2

Mean number of children ever born,
WFS household surveys (HH) and earlier enquiries

Country	Source	Current age						
		15–19	20–24	25–29	30–34	35–39	40–44	45–49
Lesotho	1977 HH	0.2	1.2	2.4	3.7	4.6	5.3	5.5
	1976 census	0.2	1.1	2.1	3.4	4.2	4.6	4.7
Sudan	1978 HH	0.8	2.1	3.5	5.0	5.8	6.3	6.3
(North)[a]	1973 census	0.4	1.8	3.4	4.6	5.3	5.1	5.0
Jordan	1976 HH	0.2	1.6	3.6	5.7	7.3	8.2	8.4
	1972 survey	0.2	1.7	4.0	5.9	7.2	7.6	7.2
Syria	1978 HH	0.2	1.3	3.0	5.0	6.5	7.5	8.0
	1976 census	0.2	1.2	3.0	4.7	6.3	7.1	7.5
Korea,	1974 HH	0.0	0.5	1.8	3.3	4.4	5.1	5.7
Rep. of	1970 census	0.0	0.4	1.9	3.5	4.5	5.3	5.6
Colombia	1976 HH	0.2	1.1	2.5	3.9	5.3	6.3	6.6
	1973 census	0.1	1.0	2.4	3.9	5.0	5.8	6.0
Dominican	1975 HH	0.2	1.4	3.1	4.7	6.4	6.7	6.9
Rep.	1970 census	0.2	1.6	3.3	4.6	5.6	5.8	6.0

[a] For ever-married women only.

the household and individual survey data, suggests strongly that the quality of interviewers and supervisors, rather than details of survey and questionnaire design, are the key factors affecting the accuracy with which demographic data of this type are collected.

Detailed comparison at an individual level of reports about the fertility of the same women in the two surveys enables the analysis of the consistency of response and its correlates. In particular, it can be used to disentangle, at least partially, the effects of proxy reporting in the household surveys and of biases in the individual survey samples from those of other types of error in the data. However, such comparisons are only useful if the two sets of data were collected independently. In Sudan, Syria, Yemen AR, Republic of Korea, Mexico and Venezuela they were not. The two forms were usually completed by the same interviewers in the course of a single visit to the household concerned. In Lesotho, Morocco and Jordan fieldwork for the two surveys was conducted completely separately. Unfortunately, it has not been possible to match the data from the two surveys in any of these countries. However, in Cameroon, Mauritania, Colombia and Dominican Republic, while fieldwork for the two surveys was carried out as a single operation, the two forms were usually completed on separate visits to the households. Therefore the two sets of data can be considered more or less independent in the relevant sense. Moreover in each country the information on at least 99 per cent of the women interviewed in the individual survey could be matched with that collected in the household survey.

In table 4.3, we examine the consistency of reporting on numbers of children ever born in the surveys. The evidence from Colombia has been discussed by Hobcraft (1980). Although the results agree closely at the aggregate level, considerable discrepancies exist in the reports about individual women. These increase with the women's age. In all four studies, even when they answered the questions themselves on both occasions, less than 90 per cent of women aged 35 or over reported the same parity twice. Moreover in Mauritania reports are far less consistent; they agree for only 61.5 per cent of all women. As the data from Cameroon are almost as consistent as those from the two Latin American countries, it seems likely that problems with fieldwork, rather than the inability of Mauritania's population to supply such information, are responsible. Hobcraft observed that, in Colombia, household survey reports by proxies about older women were far less consistent with those obtained in the individual survey than reports by the women themselves. Moreover the proxies tended to report fewer births than were recorded in the individual survey. This suggests that the individual survey data are more reliable. While the same pattern can be observed in the Dominican Republic, in the two African studies there is little difference in the consistency of reporting between these groups. Moreover in Cameroon there is no evidence of a downwards bias in reports made by proxies. Perhaps when levels of education among women are very low, their husbands are just as able to answer fertility questions posed in demographic surveys. More generally, many of the inconsistencies may represent response variability that has little to do with the details of the questionnaire or fieldwork procedures. Unfortunately none of these countries conducted post-enumeration surveys. But, to take four published examples, in Indonesia, Peru, Fiji and Bangladesh between 8 and 20 per cent of women reported different parities in the main survey and post-enumeration survey although detailed birth histories were collected from the women themselves on both occasions (O'Muircheartaigh and Marckwardt 1981). The basic problem is that an appreciable minority of older women find it difficult to report their parity accurately whatever method is used to obtain the information.

A surprising feature of the data presented in table 4.3 is that women who reported on themselves in the household surveys tended to report more children than they did later in the more detailed individual surveys. In the Latin American studies the difference is small but in Cameroon and Mauritania it is appreciable and also applies to at least the younger women reported on by proxies in the household survey. In part this probably reflects omissions in the individual survey because of fatigue on the part of the interviewer or respondent or because of an unwillingness to answer detailed questions about children who have died (Blacker and Brass 1979). In addition, faulty inclusion of stillbirths and adopted

Colombia

15–19	0.3	99.6	0.1	1.8	97.3	0.9
20–24	1.1	96.9	2.0	1.0	98.3	0.7
25–29	2.7	92.3	5.0	2.2	96.5	1.3
30–34	5.3	87.0	7.6	2.8	95.1	2.1
35–39	6.6	80.3	13.1	6.4	90.1	3.5
40–44	7.9	79.5	12.6	6.6	88.2	5.2
45–49	12.1	71.6	16.4	6.6	89.0	4.4

Dominican Rep.

15–19	0.0	99.3	0.7	1.7	98.0	0.3
20–24	2.5	94.1	3.4	2.8	95.1	2.1
25–29	4.9	91.2	3.9	4.0	91.9	4.0
30–34	6.3	89.4	4.3	4.3	92.1	3.6
35–39	11.9	70.1	17.9	5.4	88.8	5.8
40–44	2.7	78.4	18.9	9.8	82.5	7.7
45–49	15.6	71.1	13.3	5.6	89.3	5.1

children as a woman's own live births in the household survey are almost certainly important factors. Table 4.4 reveals that women who reported fewer children in the individual survey were far more likely than other women to report still-births. Up to one in three of them may have reported such a stillbirth to be a dead child in the household survey.

Inconsistencies between the aggregate estimates from the household and individual surveys might also be produced by biases in the individual survey subsamples. For example, evaluation of the Lesotho Fertility Survey suggested that high-parity women in their forties were under-represented because inter-viewers enumerated them as aged 50 or more in the phase two household screen-ing so as to reduce their workload (Timæus and Balasubramanian 1984). The household survey reports from four countries can be used to examine this possibility and table 4.5 compares the lifetime fertility of the subsample of women interviewed in the individual survey with that of the other women. One cannot distinguish between the effects of selection of a biased subsample and of fertility-related non-response. Moreover, differences between the two sets of estimates will reflect sampling errors and possibly to some extent, even in these countries, revision of the household survey reports subsequent to the individual interview. Nevertheless in the Dominican Republic at least there is evidence of substantial bias in the individual survey subsample. Women of relatively low parity were more likely to be interviewed in depth than other women enumerated in the household survey. To some extent this is compensated for in the estimates in table 4.1 because respondents tended to report more births in the individual survey. Moreover in Mauritania the individual survey seems to be biased some-what in the opposite direction. Up to the age of 40, women who completed the detailed questionnaire tend to have had relatively large numbers of births. In contrast to these two studies, in Cameroon and Colombia any bias in the indi-vidual survey subsamples in this respect is trivial.

4.4 Current fertility

Evaluation of the estimates of current fertility obtained from the enlarged-sample household surveys is particularly important because such rates were the principal objective of these surveys. The questions that WFS recommended for the collection of these data asked about the date at which women's most recent birth occurred and about the child's sex and whether it was still alive. As with the questions on lifetime fertility, this approach is intended to minimize the omission of children that have died, to provide information on child mor-tality and to provide evidence for evaluation of the data. However, because a fairly small number of births is involved, the estimated sex ratios at birth and of dead children are subject to very large sampling errors. Therefore, the question on the sex of the child is only of limited value. The schedule used in Dominican Republic enquired only about the date of the most recent birth. Moreover, as has already been mentioned, Mexico did not use these questions

TABLE 4.4

Mean number of stillbirths in the individual survey
according to relative numbers of dead children reported
in the household and individual surveys

Age	More dead in household	Same in both	More dead in individual
Mauritania			
15–19	0.067	0.009	0.000
20–24	0.094	0.015	0.029
25–29	0.089	0.055	0.020
30–34	0.097	0.040	0.060
35–39	0.113	0.048	0.028
40–44	0.076	0.014	0.013
45–49	0.159	0.018	0.069
Cameroon			
15–19	0.111	0.004	0.046
20–24	0.265	0.017	0.047
25–29	0.319	0.032	0.022
30–34	0.240	0.024	0.037
35–39	0.356	0.033	0.016
40–44	0.409	0.048	0.008
45–49	0.346	0.048	0.098
50–54	0.383	0.089	0.394
Colombia			
15–19	0.250	0.002	0.000
20–24	0.333	0.004	0.000
25–29	0.467	0.027	0.000
30–34	0.333	0.027	0.067
35–39	0.482	0.025	0.048
40–44	0.130	0.037	0.091
45–49	0.419	0.048	0.000
Dominican Rep.			
15–19	0.200	0.010	0.000
20–24	0.600	0.020	0.000
25–29	0.273	0.043	0.000
30–34	0.500	0.046	0.000
35–39	0.667	0.130	0.158
40–44	0.643	0.064	0.143
45–49	0.286	0.097	0.626

either but asked instead about births in the household during the previous year.

Age-specific and total fertility rates calculated from the births reported in the year before the household and corresponding individual surveys are shown in table 4.6. The age-specific fertility rates reported in the individual surveys in

TABLE 4.5
Mean parities of individual interviewees and
once-reported women according to
the household survey

Age	Individual interviewees	Once-reported women[a]
Mauritania[b]		
15–19	0.45	0.33
20–24	1.87	1.51
25–29	3.59	3.10
30–34	5.10	4.53
35–39	5.89	5.60
40–44	5.83	5.96
45–49	5.95	6.32
Cameroon		
15–19	0.45	0.54
20–24	1.60	1.81
25–29	2.95	3.00
30–34	4.11	4.17
35–39	4.87	4.77
40–44	5.14	5.03
45–49	5.13	5.05
Colombia		
15–19	0.17	0.17
20–24	1.12	1.10
25–29	2.43	2.48
30–34	3.97	3.88
35–39	5.16	5.35
40–44	6.24	6.40
45–49	6.75	6.50
Dominican Rep.		
15–19	0.24	0.22
20–24	1.32	1.43
25–29	2.97	3.13
30–34	4.60	4.74
35–39	6.09	6.42
40–44	6.13	6.84
45–49	6.12	7.14

[a] Adjusted where necessary using household or individual survey weights (Hobcraft 1980).

[b] Proportions of women remaining single estimated from the household survey.

particular are subject to quite large sampling errors. Despite this, most of the pairs of estimates agree fairly well. In eleven of the thirteen studies the total fertility rates obtained from the two surveys differ by less than 10 per cent. The exceptions are Sudan, where the household survey estimate is 15 per cent lower than the individual, and Yemen AR, where it is 21 per cent lower. Moreover, in all the studies except Yemen AR, the two surveys indicate similar age patterns of fertility. They agree upon the timing of the peak of the fertility distribution and the relatively high teenage fertility found in Cameroon and Mauritania and the relatively high fertility at ages 30–34 typical of the Arab countries are apparent in both sources. The individual survey estimates for Yemen AR indicate an implausible level and pattern of fertility. This appears to result from a combination of sampling and dating errors. Using data for the last three years, the estimated total fertility rate drops to 8.9 and the fertility rate for 30–34 year old women to 281 per 1,000.

A striking feature of the estimates in table 4.6 is that, except in Venezuela, the household surveys always yield a lower total fertility rate than the individual surveys. One possible explanation of this is that women omit to report a recent birth that has died – thereby representing their penultimate child as their most recent one – more often in the household surveys. However, if omissions were generally more common in the household surveys, this would have been apparent in the data on lifetime fertility. Most household surveys did not distinguish multiple births and a few women failed to answer this question. Probably a more important explanation of the discrepancy lies in dating errors of the type discussed by Potter (1977). The birth-history questions work towards the present and tend to compress too many events into the recent past. In contrast, the question on the date of the most recent birth in the household survey may encourage respondents to shift it further into the past. Potter emphasizes that data for the last few years will usually be fairly accurate. However, two small biases operating in opposite directions might produce the discrepancies observed in the total fertility rates. In general one might expect dates to have been collected with more care in the individual surveys. Even if they were, Goldman and Westoff (1980) found that, in a number of them, fertility rates based on births in the last year were too high. This stemmed partly from heaping of births on dates exactly one year before the interview but also from shifting of the dates of recent births towards the present. On the other hand, there is evidence from other surveys that the recent dates of birth obtained in the birth histories may tend to be shifted backwards (Blacker and Brass 1979).

In table 4.7 we examine the consistency of reporting on the date of women's most recent live birth in the four matched studies that collected the household and individual survey data separately. The table refers to all such births, not just to those occurring in the last year. Moreover, some of the dates recorded in the individual survey will have been imputed and should not be expected to agree exactly with those obtained in the household survey. As with the data on lifetime fertility, reporting is far less consistent in Mauritania than in the Latin

TABLE 4.6

Age-specific and total fertility rates calculated from births in the previous year, WFS household (HH) and individual (I) surveys (per 1000)

Country	Source	Current age							TFR
		15–19	20–24	25–29	30–34	35–39	40–44	45–49	
Cameroon	HH	171	286	256	212	145	76	41	5.94
	I	156	304	284	248	179	90	48	6.55
Lesotho[b]	HH	76	280	280	220	166	75	38	5.68
	I	67	293	289	242	186	87	26	5.95
Mauritania[b]	HH	160	266	272	239	166	68	30	6.01
	I	143	267	296	244	235	99	21	6.53
Morocco[a,b]	HH	49	208	242	220	178	82	39	5.10
	I	73	253	272	240	164	99	22	5.62
Sudan (North)[a,b]	HH	55	224	274	250	174	62	41	5.40
	I	63	240	316	280	217	86	67	6.34
Jordan[a,b]	HH	71	300	367	332	240	112	47	7.35
	I	63	312	401	331	260	103	39	7.55
Syria[a,b]	HH	75	255	319	303	236	141	41	6.85
	I	93	278	344	308	270	167	45	7.53
Yemen AR[a,b]	HH	116	334	364	327	247	145	77	8.05
	I	187	381	359	434	338	203	130	10.16

Korea, Rep. of[a,b]	HH	11	159	276	164	74	29	3	3.58
	I	10	141	304	172	79	37	7	3.75
Colombia	HH	72	213	203	175	134	57	20	4.37
	I	63	204	209	182	136	76	25	4.48
Venezuela	HH	85	208	216	167	130	56	22	4.42
	I	97	226	209	172	97	70	—	4.35
Dominican Rep.	HH	94	233	232	170	143	41	15	4.64
	I	102	258	254	193	153	63	22	5.22
Mexico	HH	77	243	255	217	172	80	16	5.29
	I	80	273	259	223	184	70	21	5.55

[a] The household survey data exclude births to single women.
[b] The individual survey data exclude births to single women.

TABLE 4.7

Per cent distribution according to consistency of reporting on the date of women's most recent live birth, household and individual surveys

Age	Proxy-reported in household survey					Self-reported in household survey				
	Later in household		Same in both	Later in individual		Later in household		Same in both	Later in individual	
	≥ 1 year	< 1 year		< 1 year	≥ 1 year	≥ 1 year	< 1 year		< 1 year	≥ 1 year
Mauritania										
15–19	8.3	38.3	16.7	27.5	9.2	5.4	34.9	11.6	37.2	10.9
20–24	11.4	33.7	13.6	33.2	8.2	8.3	30.6	19.2	34.5	7.4
25–29	12.1	24.2	16.8	40.3	6.7	10.7	33.7	12.6	33.7	9.2
30–34	15.8	25.7	7.9	36.6	13.9	19.5	33.3	8.0	32.2	6.9
35–39	31.1	28.4	6.8	20.3	13.5	18.2	33.1	13.2	26.4	9.1
40–44	34.8	13.0	13.0	17.4	21.7	25.0	21.4	8.9	30.4	14.3
45–49	28.6	19.0	4.8	19.0	28.6	31.3	25.0	9.4	21.9	12.5
Cameroon										
15–19	1.9	7.7	67.3	6.2	16.9	2.3	10.5	68.6	7.0	11.6
20–24	2.6	7.4	64.1	7.1	18.9	2.9	4.4	72.6	6.5	13.5
25–29	2.1	7.4	58.5	5.4	26.6	3.0	5.7	68.6	5.4	17.2
30–34	2.6	6.9	51.3	5.3	33.9	3.7	8.8	60.0	6.5	20.9
35–39	2.5	6.7	49.9	6.7	34.3	5.2	5.2	48.3	5.8	35.5
40–44	5.5	7.2	44.4	7.2	35.7	2.9	5.8	51.1	2.9	37.4
45–49	7.0	5.5	34.8	6.0	46.8	8.5	4.3	38.3	4.3	44.7
50–54	5.6	3.7	34.6	4.7	51.4	12.3	0.0	35.1	3.5	49.1

Colombia

15–19	6.7	6.7	71.1	11.1	4.4	2.7	1.8	89.3	2.7	3.6
20–24	3.6	11.6	72.5	4.3	8.0	2.8	3.5	83.9	6.6	3.1
25–29	7.5	13.4	64.2	6.7	8.2	2.4	4.6	81.0	5.2	6.7
30–34	11.0	7.7	61.5	5.5	14.3	3.4	5.7	78.9	6.9	5.1
35–39	13.3	6.7	54.4	14.4	11.1	5.4	5.9	73.3	6.9	8.6
40–44	11.3	8.2	44.3	13.4	22.7	7.5	6.5	67.3	7.5	11.2
45–49	10.8	7.5	55.9	16.1	9.7	9.7	3.3	63.6	8.6	14.9

Dominican Rep.

15–19	0.0	17.4	69.6	8.7	4.3	0.0	5.1	83.7	7.1	4.1
20–24	4.4	16.2	63.2	11.8	4.4	4.9	6.5	76.5	8.5	3.6
25–29	5.2	3.4	69.0	10.3	12.1	3.9	4.2	82.2	6.8	2.9
30–34	0.0	24.1	51.7	10.3	13.8	3.4	6.8	80.0	5.7	4.2
35–39	8.6	20.7	44.8	13.8	12.1	5.0	6.5	73.7	9.5	5.3
40–44	6.5	16.1	61.3	6.5	9.7	7.6	4.1	64.0	12.2	12.2
45–49	18.8	15.6	53.1	6.3	6.3	9.7	6.5	64.9	10.4	8.4

American countries, while in Cameroon it is of intermediate quality. In the Latin American countries, reports supplied by proxies in the household survey are far less consistent with the individual survey data than reports by the women themselves, although in the two African countries this differential is less marked. In Colombia slightly more distant dates tend to be reported in the household survey, especially by older women and proxies (Hobcraft 1980). A similar pattern prevails in Cameroon where a high proportion of women reported a date of birth in the individual survey that was exactly one year later than that recorded in the household survey. These findings are consistent with the kind of reporting errors that we have suggested might explain the discrepancies between the estimates of the level of fertility yielded by the two surveys. In the Dominican Republic and Mauritania, however, the opposite pattern of inconsistency prevails. Women tend to report earlier dates for their most recent live birth in the individual survey.

Detailed assessment of each of the sets of birth-history data would be needed to determine whether the household or the individual survey estimates of current fertility are generally more accurate. Such a task is outside the scope of this chapter. However, it may be possible to undertake it once a complete series of evaluation reports becomes available. If the tendency for proxies to report too close or distant a date for women's most recent birth in the household surveys is widespread, one would expect rates based on the individual surveys to be generally more reliable. Further insights into the quality of the household survey data can be gained through comparing them with the data on lifetime fertility by means of P/F ratios (Brass 1975). In the absence of fertility change, serious biases in the dating of women's most recent birth will be revealed by ratios greater or less than unity. Moreover, it is sometimes possible to produce adjusted estimates of current fertility, using these ratios, that correct for dating errors.

In table 4.8 P/F ratios are presented for each of the household surveys. On this basis, the surveys can be divided into three groups. First, in the Republic of Korea and the Latin American countries the ratios are dominated by the effects of fertility decline. They rise rapidly with age and are of limited use for the evaluation of the current fertility data. In Cameroon, Lesotho and Mauritania the ratios are somewhat erratic, suggesting that age reporting and other errors have a substantial effect on the estimates. In addition, in Cameroon they decline steadily across the three older age groups revealing that appreciable numbers of births are omitted from the reports about lifetime fertility or that fertility has increased. However, for these countries there is no clear evidence of bias in the estimates of current fertility of the type that would be indicated if the ratios for 20–34 year old women were consistently greater or less than unity. In the five remaining surveys, all of which were conducted in Arab countries, such differences do exist. They suggest that the dates of women's most recent births tend to be shifted away from the time of the survey. On this basis the current level of fertility appears to be underestimated by a factor varying between 15 per cent in Syria and 40 per cent or more in Sudan. The data on Yemen AR appear to be

TABLE 4.8

*P/F ratios comparing the information on lifetime fertility with
that on recent fertility, WFS household surveys*

Country	Current age						
	15–19	20–24	25–29	30–34	35–39	40–44	45–49
Cameroon	1.35	1.05	0.98	0.99	0.95	0.92	0.87
Lesotho	1.04	0.97	0.90	0.95	0.96	0.99	0.98
Mauritania	1.16	0.93	1.07	1.11	1.06	1.02	1.00
Morocco	1.24	1.32	1.36	1.46	1.46	1.39	1.33
Sudan (North)	1.55	1.51	1.41	1.35	1.23	1.23	1.17
Jordan	1.28	1.30	1.22	1.20	1.19	1.19	1.15
Syria	1.14	1.15	1.16	1.20	1.19	1.18	1.17
Yemen AR	1.36	0.96	0.87	0.84	0.86	0.79	0.76
Korea, Rep. of	3.09	1.04	1.06	1.20	1.33	1.45	1.61
Colombia	1.11	1.13	1.21	1.32	1.41	1.52	1.52
Venezuela	0.97	1.04	1.14	1.25	1.34	1.38	1.39
Dominican Rep.	0.93	1.14	1.27	1.38	1.51	1.47	1.47

exceptional. However, comparison with the individual survey revealed that the household survey data for this country underestimate the lifetime fertility of young, as well as older, women. Allowance for this suggests that they also underestimate the level of current fertility by 10–15 per cent.

If the household survey estimates of the total fertility rate are adjusted upwards to the degree indicated by the P/F ratios, the resulting figures are, in all cases, higher than those obtained from the individual surveys. Thus it appears that respondents in Arab countries tend to report too distant a date of birth for young children, or in other words to exaggerate their children's ages, whatever the method of data collection. However the individual survey data are less affected or are subject to compensating biases. In Syria and Yemen AR the discrepancy between the revised household survey estimates and those from the individual survey is quite small – less than half a birth – but in the three other countries it is substantial, between one and two births in all three surveys. In Sudan, analysis of the birth histories confirms that they tend to underestimate the level of current fertility (Department of Statistics, Khartoum 1982). However, in Morocco and Jordan such analyses suggest that the P/F ratios are somewhat misleading (Abdel-Aziz 1983). These countries have experienced appreciable fertility decline recently, partly as a result of a rise in the average age of women at marriage. This tends to inflate the P/F ratios. The individual survey rates are at most very slightly downwardly biased and, while the household survey estimates probably underestimate current fertility, they do so by no more than 10 per cent. A more detailed analysis of the household survey data that used the relational Gompertz model to examine changes in the age pattern of fertility (Zaba 1981) would probably reveal that fertility decline had occurred in these countries and indicate that upward adjustment of the fertility estimates using the P/F ratios was inappropriate. In general, well-conducted household surveys are able to provide acceptable measures of current fertility even if fertility is declining or the data are subject to dating errors. However, when fertility decline and biases in the reporting of dates of birth occur in combination, they perform less well.

Further information both on the recent level of fertility and on trends in fertility during the 15 years before the survey can be obtained by applying own children analysis to the household survey data (United Nations 1983b). Such estimates can be made for countries that used the short household schedule as well as those that used the expanded schedule. Retherford and Alam (1984) have compared such estimates with those obtained from the individual survey birth histories in eight countries: Dominican Republic, Indonesia, Kenya, Republic of Korea, Nepal, Pakistan, Sri Lanka and Syria. They believe that, except perhaps in Kenya, adjustment of the household survey responses to match those collected in the individual survey was uncommon. In some countries the single-year own children estimates of fertility oscillate more violently than those from the individual surveys. However what is more striking is the generally similar level of and trend in fertility indicated by the two sources. This applies not only to overall fertility but also to the fertility rates estimated for each five-year age group. This does not necessarily imply that both sources are accurate. As the authors point out, they suffer from similar errors in the estimation of the age, and therefore the date of birth, of children. It does imply that household surveys, as well as surveys that collect birth histories, can be used to study fertility trends. Their main limitation is that detailed internal evaluation of the quality of the estimates cannot be carried out.

4.5   Child mortality

Questions on lifetime fertility that ask separately about living and dead children also provide information on child mortality. Tabulations of the proportion of women's children that have died according to their ages can be produced from the responses, and indirect estimates of the level and trend of child mortality can be derived from these tabulations. Such data are available from the eleven expanded household surveys that used the disaggregated questions to ask about lifetime fertility.

Such proportions, together with equivalent estimates derived from the individual survey birth histories, are shown in table 4.9. As might be expected, bearing in mind the consistency of the estimates of total numbers of children ever born, the estimates from the two surveys are similar in most countries. In the Republic of Korea and Colombia the agreement is particularly close. Yemen AR is again exceptional; according to the household survey, lower proportions of the women's children have died than is indicated by the individual survey. Under-reporting of parity was common in this household survey and it is children who have died that were omitted most often. What is most surprising about the estimates

TABLE 4.9

Proportion of women's children that have died,
WFS household (HH) and individual (I) surveys

Country	Source	Current age						
		15–19	20–24	25–29	30–34	35–39	40–44	45–49
Cameroon	HH	0.166	0.161	0.193	0.223	0.258	0.283	0.310
	I	0.170	0.148	0.179	0.205	0.232	0.258	0.289
Lesotho	HH	0.126	0.140	0.169	0.192	0.192	0.227	0.245
	I	0.098	0.149	0.156	0.188	0.185	0.200	0.233
Mauritania	HH	0.163	0.154	0.182	0.201	0.212	0.243	0.246
	I	0.152	0.157	0.182	0.176	0.190	0.246	0.261
Morocco	HH	0.142	0.161	0.157	0.173	0.195	0.202	0.227
	I	0.132	0.137	0.149	0.150	0.179	0.201	0.238
Sudan	HH	0.150	0.136	0.134	0.153	0.152	0.183	0.173
(North)	I	0.154	0.160	0.124	0.142	0.154	0.166	0.187
Jordan	HH	0.087	0.091	0.094	0.114	0.140	0.174	0.208
	I	0.085	0.080	0.086	0.094	0.153	0.166	0.170
Syria	HH	0.077	0.083	0.086	0.102	0.112	0.139	0.168
	I	0.079	0.081	0.083	0.094	0.105	0.130	0.144
Yemen AR	HH	0.196	0.191	0.221	0.250	0.276	0.313	0.316
	I	0.217	0.210	0.238	0.283	0.291	0.329	0.349
Korea,	HH	0.060	0.046	0.048	0.067	0.092	0.118	0.176
Rep. of	I	0.077	0.042	0.046	0.070	0.092	0.130	0.190
Colombia	HH	0.087	0.088	0.096	0.104	0.131	0.151	0.170
	I	0.105	0.087	0.094	0.101	0.130	0.145	0.172
Dominican	HH	0.113	0.125	0.124	0.141	0.155	0.161	0.154
Rep.	I	0.090	0.115	0.122	0.133	0.148	0.165	0.150

in table 4.9 is that in the other eight studies consistently higher proportions of children are reported to have died in the household survey. In Cameroon, Lesotho, Morocco, Jordan, Syria and Dominican Republic this is true of at least six of the seven age groups. In Mauritania and Sudan the evidence is almost as clearcut. The discrepancies are greatest in Jordan where on average the household survey figures are about 15 per cent higher than those from the individual survey. In the other countries most of the household survey-based estimates are 0–10 per cent higher than those obtained from the birth-history data.

Table 4.10 examines the consistency of reporting on numbers of children that

TABLE   4.10

Per cent distribution according to consistency of reporting on children
that have died, household and individual surveys

Age	Proxy-reported in household survey			Self-reported in household survey		
	More in household	Same in both	More in individual	More in household	Same in both	More in individual
Mauritania						
15–19	4.6	91.9	3.6	6.4	91.3	2.3
20–24	8.6	83.1	8.3	9.9	81.8	8.2
25–29	12.9	74.7	12.4	13.2	73.8	13.0
30–34	23.8	63.8	12.4	23.4	63.4	13.2
35–39	27.2	60.3	12.6	22.3	64.1	13.5
40–44	17.0	59.1	23.9	20.2	64.1	15.7
45–49	19.1	60.6	20.2	22.3	60.4	17.3
Cameroon						
15–19	0.7	98.6	0.7	1.0	97.2	1.7
20–24	2.8	94.0	3.1	1.7	97.1	1.2
25–29	3.7	93.0	3.3	5.7	90.8	3.5
30–34	6.1	89.9	4.0	5.4	93.7	0.9
35–39	7.6	87.1	5.3	8.1	88.2	3.7
40–44	7.6	84.7	7.8	6.3	87.3	6.3
45–49	8.4	82.6	8.9	10.6	85.7	3.7
50–54	11.4	85.2	3.4	10.3	87.3	2.4

Colombia

Age						
15–19	0.0	99.9	0.1	0.7	98.6	0.7
20–24	0.2	98.7	1.1	0.8	99.0	0.2
25–29	1.5	95.4	3.1	1.9	96.7	1.4
30–34	3.8	90.8	5.3	2.1	96.1	1.7
35–39	5.0	86.8	8.3	4.4	93.4	2.2
40–44	5.6	89.6	4.8	4.3	91.6	4.1
45–49	8.0	79.6	12.4	5.9	91.0	3.1

Dominican Rep.

Age						
15–19	0.0	99.3	0.7	1.4	98.6	0.0
20–24	1.0	97.0	2.0	1.4	97.7	0.9
25–29	1.0	95.0	4.0	2.5	94.5	2.9
30–34	4.3	91.5	4.3	3.6	94.3	2.2
35–39	7.5	79.1	13.4	4.4	92.4	3.3
40–44	0.0	86.5	13.5	6.7	88.6	4.7
45–49	4.5	90.9	4.5	2.3	94.9	2.8

have died in those studies in which the data from the two surveys have been matched but were collected independently. The reports agree more closely than those on the total numbers of children ever born, implying that discrepancies are not restricted to this group of births but are also found in reports about living children. Moreover the inconsistencies follow the pattern already observed in table 4.3: they increase with age; they are much more common in Mauritania; and, in the two Latin American surveys, they are associated with proxy reporting in the household survey. As was revealed by table 4.4, a partial explanation of why a lower proportion of children were reported to have died in the individual surveys in at least these four countries is that in the household surveys stillbirths were often reported to be children that had died. In addition, as we have already suggested, children who died at young ages may tend to be omitted during completion of the lengthy individual interview. It is possible that respondents are willing to report how many of their children have died when asked a simple question in the household survey but not to discuss them in the detail required to complete the birth histories. Table 4.10 confirms that, while there was probably some omission of dead children in the household survey reports, in particular in those made by proxies about older women, more women reported a lower number of children in the individual surveys than revised their responses upwards, presumably for the reasons outlined.

Another explanation of why lower proportions of children were reported to have died in the individual surveys might be that there were biases in the subsamples of women who were interviewed in them. This possibility is examined in table 4.11. In Cameroon such biases are clearly important; women who had lost a high proportion of their children were less likely than other women to be interviewed individually. There is also slight evidence of this in Dominican Republic. Table 4.5 revealed that the individual survey sample in that country was strongly biased towards low-parity women. These results suggest that women with many dead children were nearly as likely to be omitted from it as those with many living children. In Mauritania the opposite bias is apparent. Women with a high proportion of children that have died are over-represented in the individual survey sample. However the effect of this on the aggregate estimates is outweighed by the tendency for women to report fewer dead children relative to living ones compared with the household survey.

The birth histories collected in the individual surveys include the date of birth of each child and the age at death of those that have died. From this information, estimates of the level and trend in infant and child mortality can be calculated directly. By applying indirect methods, similar estimates can be obtained from proportions of children that have died. On the basis of model distributions, the data are adjusted to allow for the timing of fertility and to convert them into conventional mortality indices (Brass 1975). Information on the different five-year cohorts of women can be used to estimate mortality trends (Brass 1982). In figure 4.1 household and individual survey estimates of the probability of death by age five are compared. Unlike, for example, the infant mortality rate, the

TABLE 4.11

*Proportions of individual interviewees' and
once-reported women's children that have died
according to the household survey*

Age	Individual interviewees	Once-reported women[a]
Mauritania		
15–19	0.152	0.169
20–24	0.164	0.150
25–29	0.194	0.178
30–34	0.212	0.197
35–39	0.227	0.208
40–44	0.244	0.242
45–49	0.265	0.241
Cameroon		
15–19	0.174	0.166
20–24	0.155	0.156
25–29	0.185	0.194
30–34	0.212	0.226
35–39	0.238	0.264
40–44	0.259	0.288
45–49	0.297	0.313
Dominican Rep.		
15–19	0.100	0.116
20–24	0.119	0.128
25–29	0.126	0.123
30–34	0.135	0.147
35–39	0.150	0.158
40–44	0.169	0.161
45–49	0.147	0.155

[a] Adjusted where necessary using household or individual weights (Hobcraft 1980).

probability of death by age five is affected relatively little by dating errors in the birth histories or by differences between the pattern of mortality assumed during indirect estimation and that actually prevailing. Both series of estimates are somewhat biased because the mortality of children is associated with the age of their mothers. The more distant direct estimates are based on data that do not include any births to older women. Although relatively few in number, such children typically experience higher mortality than those of younger women. In contrast the more recent indirect estimates are based on births to young women. The first point, in particular, which is obtained from the proportion of 20-24 year old women's children that have died, is visibly biased upwards in nearly half these

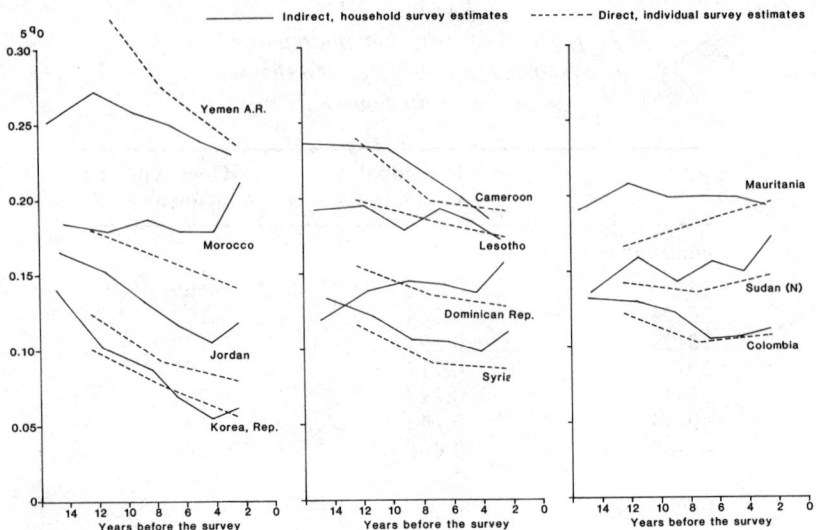

FIG. 4.1 Trends in the probability of death by age five ($_5q_0$), household and individual surveys

surveys as a result of the high mortality experienced by the children of very young mothers.

Agreement between the two series of estimates shown in figure 4.1 varies from the extremely good in the Republic of Korea to the rather poor in Yemen AR, Morocco, Jordan and Mauritania. On the whole the figures are rather close and even in the latter countries the two sources do not indicate widely different levels of mortality. As one would expect from the proportions shown in table 4.9, the household survey data indicate higher levels of child mortality than the individual survey data. The obvious exception is Yemen AR where lower proportions of children were reported to have died in the household survey. However, what is most impressive about these estimates is the generally close agreement between the two surveys about the trend in mortality over time. This extends even to those countries like Yemen AR, Jordan and, to a lesser degree, Sudan and Syria where they indicate rather different levels of child mortality. Only in Morocco and Mauritania do the two sets of estimates indicate rather different trends in child mortality. The direct and indirect measures are calculated in very different ways and the fact that they agree closely in nine of these eleven countries suggests that in general both approaches provide useful information about the speed of declines in child mortality as well as about mortality levels.

The question about the survival of the most recent live birth could also be used to estimate child mortality. It can yield direct measures of the probability of death by different ages and is potentially of great value. However in past applications it has often produced implausibly low estimates largely because interviewers fail to put the question (Blacker 1984; Hill 1981). As a result, little

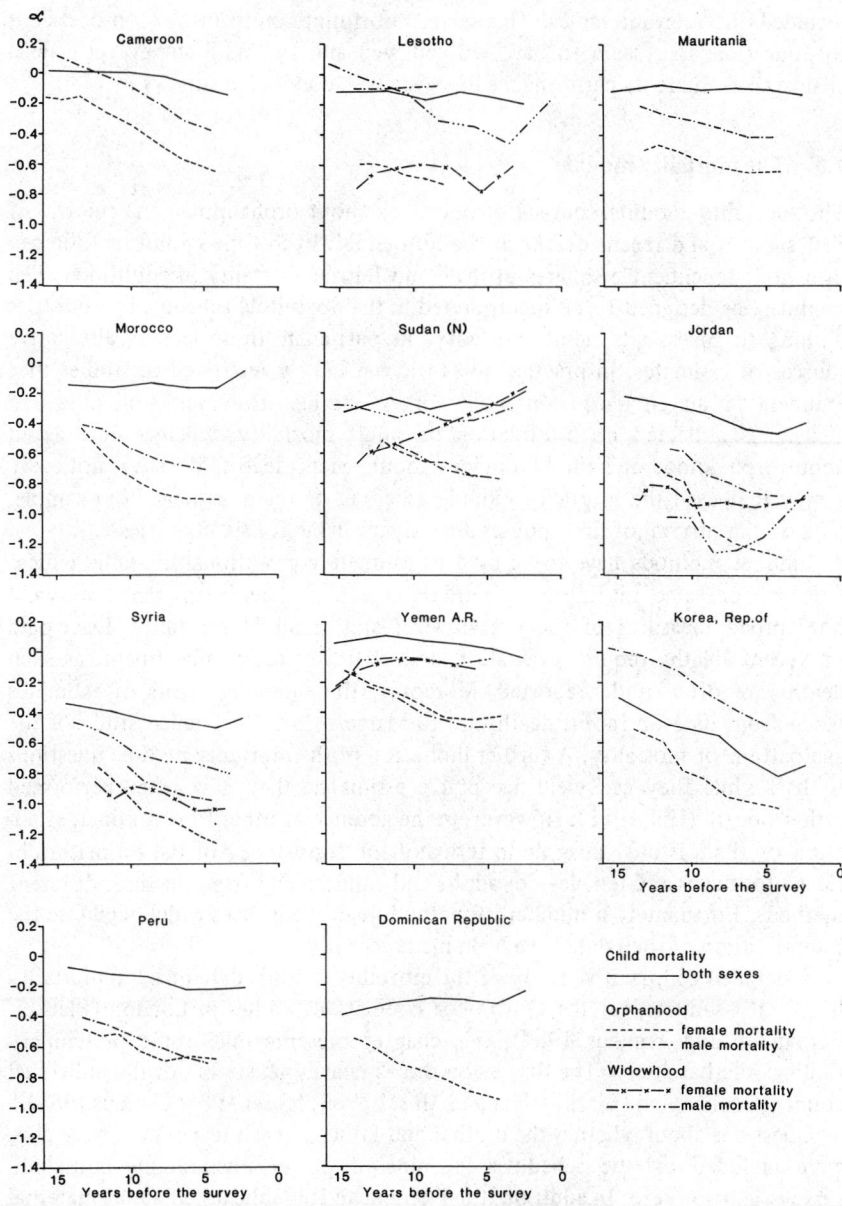

FIG. 4.2 Trends in the level of adult mortality (α) according to orphanhood and widow-hood

use has been made of this information and the First Country Reports have not included the relevant tables. This is an unfortunate omission for, on occasion, the question does seem to have worked well and the WFS surveys provide a chance to evaluate its performance in eleven well-conducted surveys.

4.6   The mortality module

The mortality module consists of questions about orphanhood, the survival of first spouses and recent deaths in the household. Each type of information can provide independent estimates of male and female mortality in adulthood. The module was designed to be incorporated in the household schedule by countries wishing to investigate adult mortality, in particular those lacking alternative sources of estimates. In practice, use of it was largely restricted to studies that enumerated an enlarged household survey sample. However, Colombia and Venezuela collected no information on adult mortality, whereas Peru asked about orphanhood and the Philippines about recent deaths. Moreover not every survey that used the mortality module asked all of the questions. For example, data on the survival of first spouses are only available for six countries.

Indirect methods have to be used to estimate conventional life-table indices from responses to the mortality module questions. This means that they yield only broad measures of the overall level and trend in mortality. Even data on recent deaths require evaluation and, in many cases, adjustment, as such deaths are often under-reported. Moreover, the sampling errors of estimates made from data on recent deaths are too large to permit detailed study of the age pattern of mortality. A further limitation of the mortality module questions is that, while they can yield acceptable estimates, they have often performed rather poorly (Hill 1981). However, in the absence of other types of data, evaluation of them is only possible in terms of the consistency of the estimates obtained for males and females, for adults and children and from the three different methods. Fortunately a number of methodological advances which facilitate the interpretation of such data have been made recently.

A detailed comparative study of the mortality module data on adult mortality has been conducted at the Centre for Population Studies in London (Blacker, Fernández and Timæus 1984); this chapter presents only some preliminary findings of that study. The discussion draws heavily on studies of the individual countries concerned (Blacker, Hill and Moser 1983; Moser 1985; Timæus 1984).[1]

Questions about whether the mother and father of each respondent were alive were included on the schedules for nine of the enlarged-sample household surveys and for Peru. In addition, the Dominican Republic asked about maternal orphanhood alone. In combination with information on the timing of fertility, a series of estimates of the level of adult mortality can be obtained from such data (United Nations 1983b). As with the child mortality data, information on different cohorts of respondents can be used to measure the underlying trend in mortality over time (Brass and Bamgboye 1981). Such estimates are presented in figure 4.2, together with those obtained from the household survey data on child mortality and on widowhood. The level of mortality is expressed in terms of α, the level parameter of the logit relational system of model life tables based on the General Standard. High values of α indicate heavy mortality (Brass 1971).

The pattern of the estimates varies greatly between the different countries and is difficult to summarize. In Peru, Sudan and Yemen AR the orphanhood-based estimates indicate similar levels of mortality among adult men and women while in the other countries they suggest that males experience much heavier mortality than females. This probably means that too many living fathers are reported in the former three countries. The widowhood-based estimates of adult male mortality confirm this in Sudan and Yemen AR and in Yemen AR they also suggest that the orphanhood data underestimate female mortality. Further-more they suggest that the paternal orphanhood question also underestimates male mortality in Syria. In most of the countries the orphanhood data yield relatively lighter mortality estimates than the child mortality data. In Lesotho, however, adult male mortality is apparently similar in level to child mortality for the two sexes combined, while in the Republic of Korea it is considerably heavier. Turning to mortality trends, we find that in Lesotho both sets of orphanhood-based estimates, together with the estimates of child mortality, reveal little mortality decline. In the Republic of Korea, all three sets of indices document very rapid falls in mortality. In all the other countries the data on maternal and paternal orphanhood agree fairly well but suggest a more rapid decline in the level of mortality than is indicated by the child mortality data or, where they exist, the widowhood data. In some of the the countries the discrepancy is slight but in Dominican Republic, Morocco and Cameroon it is very substantial. Part of the problem may arise from the use of inappropriate models of mortality to make these estimates. Experimentation with a new technique developed by Brass (1983), that takes into account the relative levels of adult and child mortality, has yielded more consistent estimates for countries such as Peru and Syria. Moreover, orphanhood data from an early survey conducted in Cameroon tend to confirm that a very rapid decline in adult mortality from exceptionally high levels has occurred there while in Morocco and the Dominican Republic it is the absence of any decline in child mortality that seems implausible. On the other hand, it seems unlikely that adult mortality in Jordan and Syria has fallen to the very low level indicated by these estimates and evidence from successive surveys in countries not considered here reveals that the steep declines in mortality indicated by orphanhood data are often spurious. Thus, to take an overall view, the question on maternal orphanhood seems to have provided useful information in all of these surveys except that in Yemen AR. However, in a few countries the results may indicate an exaggerated decline in the mortality of adult women. The paternal orphanhood question has also worked well, as far as we can determine, in the majority of the surveys. But in about a third of these studies it substantially underestimates adult male mortality.

The mortality module also included two further questions relating to orphanhood. These were intended to identify whether the respondent was the eldest living child of their father and of their mother. They were used by eight countries. If the answers to these questions could be trusted, they could be used to eliminate multiple reporting of the same parents by different children. It seems likely that an individual's fertility and subsequent age at death are correlated. Thus multiple reporting introduces a bias into orphanhood-based estimates of mortality. Unfortunately the additional questions are of little use since too many respondents report themselves to be their parents' eldest living child. For example, in Jordan only 15 639 women claimed to have one or more living children whereas 16 737 respondents claimed that they were their mother's eldest living child.

Indirect estimates of the level and trend in male and female adult mortality can be obtained from data on the survival of the first spouses of the ever-married by allowing for the timing of first marriages (United Nations 1983b). Because data on the first spouse are needed, they can only be collected using special questions in addition to the usual ones on marital status. Six WFS household surveys used them but the Moroccan data have not yet been analysed. The standard mortality module incorporated an unfortunate fault in its design. Respondents were only asked explicitly about the survival of their first spouse if they had been married more than once. Therefore the information required is unavailable for respondents who are currently divorced and have been married only once. Fortunately this group is usually fairly small and the divorced seem unlikely to have ex-spouses whose mortality differs very greatly from that of the population in general.

Returning to figure 4.2, we see that the performance of the widowhood questions seems to have been very mixed. As implied by the discussion of the orphanhood data, in Syria, Sudan and Yemen AR the reports about women's spouses provide very plausible estimates of adult male mortality. However in Jordan these data are useless while in Lesotho they contradict all other evidence and suggest that adult male mortality has declined rapidly. Men's reports about the survival of their first wives also appear to vary in their accuracy. In Lesotho, Syria and Jordan they agree broadly with the orphanhood-based estimates of the level of adult female mortality. Interestingly in the latter two countries they suggest that recent falls in female mortality have been slower than the orphanhood data indicate and are therefore more in accordance with the other evidence. The same applies in Yemen AR, where they also provide evidence that adult female mortality is much heavier than the orphanhood data suggest and are probably to be preferred on these grounds alone. On the other hand, in Sudan the men's reports indicate that female mortality has been rising rapidly and cannot be believed. Thus, overall, although the data obtained are sometimes of little use, the widowhood questions are often of value even in countries that experience high rates of divorce and remarriage, as do most of those considered here. In particular, if the orphanhood- and widowhood-based estimates agree fairly well, the analyst of mortality data can come to much firmer conclusions than if only the orphanhood questions have been asked.

Questions on recent deaths in the household were included on the schedule for ten of the enlarged-sample household surveys. They asked about the age, sex and date of death of those who had died. However, in Mexico only the numbers of deaths, and not the characteristics of those who had died, were coded, meaning that no worthwhile analysis of the data can be attempted. The recommended questions enquired about all deaths in the last 24 months but Cameroon and Mexico asked about the last 12 months only. Examination of the data from the surveys in Lesotho, Mauritania, Jordan and Republic of Korea has revealed that, typically, there is no discernable trend in the numbers of deaths reported by month for the year before the survey, that there is substantial heaping on the date 12 months before the interview and that the number of deaths reported at earlier dates tails off rapidly. This suggests that asking about the previous 24 months is to be preferred. It makes this kind of evaluation possible and avoids problems of the heaping of deaths just inside or outside of the reference period. However, depending on the results of such evaluation, it will usually be best to analyse only the data on the last 12 months.

It is seldom possible to accept data on recent deaths at face value. They are often under-reported and, in particular, the information on young children is usually very incomplete. Moreover, exaggeration of the ages and ages at death of the elderly means that these data are seldom of much value. If conditions are favourable, the completeness with which adult deaths are reported can be assessed by means of the Growth Balance method and related techniques (United Nations 1983b). However, migration and age misreporting often make it impossible to apply them.

To turn to the surveys for which data are available, in Sudan and Yemen AR so few deaths were reported that it was not worth even trying to apply such methods of evaluation and adjustment. In Lesotho and Jordan use of them was attempted, but errors of the type mentioned above meant that no firm conclusions could be drawn. The same is true of Cameroon, Mauritania and Morocco. However, in these three countries it was clear that little more than 50 per cent of deaths can have been reported although it was impossible to measure the deficit precisely. For Syria, the First Country Report concluded that about a third of adult male deaths were being omitted but failed to arrive at an equivalent figure for female deaths. Finally, in the Republic of Korea the Growth Balance method worked well. It suggested that virtually all adult deaths were being reported.

Mortality rates calculated from recent deaths data have large sampling errors even when they have been collected from samples of the size used for the expanded household surveys. One way to smooth the estimates and compare them with the indirect estimates of adult mortality is to calculate the probability of surviving from age 25 to age 60 from the rates and to convert it to the equivalent value of α. It is usually assumed that, unless they can be adjusted using the Growth Balance method, retrospective reports about deaths are of little use (Committee on Population and Demography 1981b; Blacker, Hill and Moser 1983). However, for this study, the level of mortality was estimated for Lesotho and Jordan, assuming reporting to be complete, as well as for the Republic of Korea and for Syrian males. The results are very encouraging. In Lesotho one obtains an α of -0.62 for females and -0.06 for males, indicating slightly heavier mortality in 1976-7 than is obtained by extrapolating the orphanhood estimates. In the Republic of Korea, the estimates of α are -1.03 for females and -0.39 for males, again indicating rather heavier mortality, especially for men, than the trend in the orphanhood data would suggest prevailed in the year before the survey. The same is also true of the estimate of -0.56 for males in Jordan. However, that of -1.26 for females indicates a very low level of adult mortality. It falls in line with the trend of the orphanhood-based estimates but indicates much lighter mortality than is obtained from extrapolating the modest decline in female mortality that the widowhood estimates suggest occurred. Finally, adjusting the number of male deaths upwards by 45 per cent in Syria produces an α of -0.58, representing much heavier mortality than one would expect on the basis of the results of the other questions. It therefore seems likely that deaths in the central years of adulthood were fairly completely reported in Lesotho and Jordan as well as in the Republic of Korea. Moreover, the reporting of deaths in Syria was perhaps more complete than was initially concluded. It appears that data on recent deaths can provide useful estimates of adult mortality even when the Growth Balance method cannot be applied to them.

4.7   Conclusions

The discussion in this chapter has three inter-related themes. First, it is concerned with the appraisal of the methodology and content of the WFS household surveys. Secondly, it suggests further analyses of the data obtained which merit attention and, thirdly, it considers some of the implications of the results of these surveys for future demographic survey research. Two questions are of central importance. First, what additions to the household schedule beyond the essential questions used to identify women eligible for individual interview were worth while? Secondly, and related to the first question in practice if not in principle, was conducting household surveys that enumerated an enlarged sample worth while? The main reason for asking additional questions and enumerating an enlarged sample in a minority of WFS household surveys was to obtain fertility and mortality estimates. To assess the value of this, we have considered the quality of the estimates that can be produced.

In general the enlarged-sample household surveys appear to have produced rather good estimates of current fertility levels, of mean parities and of levels and trends in child mortality. On the whole they agree well with those from the corresponding individual surveys and probably approach the same quality.

The notable exception is the survey in Yemen AR, where the teams of male interviewers who conducted most of the household survey enumeration appear to have collected very incomplete and inaccurate information.

Of course, the household survey data suffer from certain limitations. They lack the detail of birth histories and, when fertility is declining, the information about it may be difficult to interpret. Moreover, such data cannot be used to study the proximate determinants of fertility or the age pattern of, and demographic differentials in, child mortality. One difference between their methodology and that of the individual surveys that adversely affects the quality of the data obtained in some of the household surveys is reporting by proxies. However, from the limited information available from the WFS and other sources, this appears to be far less of a problem than is response variance affecting all methods of data collection. Furthermore, the individual surveys seem to have been prone to appreciable biases stemming from non-coverage and non-response, although in the few countries for which we can examine this problem no consistent pattern emerges. Not all household surveys and censuses have collected data on fertility and mortality of the quality of those obtained by the WFS. The WFS gave particular emphasis to the training of interviewers and supervisors and this seems to have paid large benefits.

Although the enlarged-sample household surveys have fulfilled their intended function very well, we believe that it was a mistake to conduct them within the framework of the WFS programme of research. In retrospect, it is apparent that the concern about sample sizes that led to the proposal to conduct such surveys was somewhat misplaced. The detailed birth-history data are generally of a high quality and, by aggregating the data for several years, can be used to obtain sufficiently precise estimates of current fertility levels and differentials. Moreover, they are an extremely rich source of information about infant and child mortality. Thus the expenditure involved in the large-sample household surveys has produced little in the way of additional substantive findings. Only households whose female members were to be interviewed in the individual survey should have been enumerated in the household surveys and the fertility questions should have been omitted from the schedules.

Such a decision would have limited the possibilities for the collection of data about adult mortality on the household schedule. Questions about recent deaths are only useful if data are to be obtained from a large sample of households. Although they have yielded acceptable estimates of mortality in some countries, these questions have performed very poorly in others. They cannot on their own be viewed as justifying the expense of the large-sample surveys. There is no reason why the widowhood questions could not have been included on the schedule for household surveys of the type recommended here. However, the available evidence suggests that the method is of most value for the measurement of adult male mortality and an alternative procedure would be to ask only about the survival of women's first husbands in the individual survey. In Jordan such a question provided more plausible estimates of adult male mortality than any of the other sources of data (Blacker, Hill and Moser 1983). As far as orphanhood is concerned the questions about whether or not the respondent was their parents' eldest living child do not seem to be worth asking. The remaining two questions about the survival of the parents are simple and occupy little space on the schedule. Although they do not always yield acceptable estimates, they seem well worth including, especially as in most countries alternative sources of data do not exist. Indeed it seems unfortunate that more of the countries that participated in the WFS did not choose to follow the example of Peru and use these questions, even if they did not adopt the other possible extensions to the core household schedule.

Without doubt much of the potential of the WFS household survey data remains to be exploited. One reason is that cleaning and standardization of the data files has not reached the standards applied to the individual surveys. Another is that most First Country Reports have contained only a very limited selection of tables based on the household survey. As far as fertility and mortality data are concerned, it seems most important to analyse the data on the survival of the most recent birth. Matching of the household and individual files has also proceeded rather slowly and it is unfortunate that the WFS did not devote greater efforts to ensuring that this would be possible for every study. Once matched files are readily available, more use will probably be made of the information about the structure and other characteristics of households that was collected in the household surveys.

As regards implications for future survey research, the WFS experience strongly suggests that well-conducted household surveys will usually provide acceptable estimates of the levels, trends and patterns of fertility and of the levels and trends in child mortality. Questions about adult mortality do not always perform well but experience with other approaches to the collection of data on this topic has also been mixed (Committee on Population and Demography 1981b). Given that, for reasons that remain partially unclear, each of the orphanhood, widowhood and recent deaths series of questions may or may not yield acceptable estimates of male and of female mortality, it seems important to ask them all whenever this is possible. Fertility surveys are more expensive to conduct and to analyse. However they provide much more detailed information about fertility and child mortality and can also be used to study certain of their determinants. Some of this information could also be collected in a modified form of household survey although to do this it would probably be necessary to interview the women themselves. If this is to be done, it seems worth while to collect birth histories.

Note

1. The author also wishes to acknowledge the contributions made by C. Callum, F. Juárez and O. Kim to this section.

5

Question Design for Demographic Events

Hédi Jemai
Susheela Singh

5.1 Introduction

The measurement of such central demographic concerns as age, parity and marriage have long been a source of interest, even of controversy. In this chapter, we review the evidence of WFS regarding measurement of such variables.[1]

Our aim is to determine, as far as possible, what types of question are most likely to yield reliable data on specific demographic events, for particular populations being surveyed. Apart from general design issues discussed in other chapters, fertility surveys involve special problems of demographic measurement: the purpose of this paper is to document and critically review the different approaches taken by WFS surveys in measuring these particular events or subjects. Although careful and intensive training of interviewers, which was emphasized by WFS, is essential for collecting high quality data, training cannot overcome bad question design or incorrect question content.

We face an important restriction: as the WFS mandate precluded major methodological field experiments, the assessment of different techniques and questions has to be based largely on subjective experience and judgement. Nevertheless, whenever possible, empirical evidence will also be used in evaluating questions. In addition we will draw heavily on evaluations of data quality, both comparative reviews (Chidambaram, Cleland and Verma 1980; Goldman, Rutstein and Singh 1985) as well as reports on specific countries (see WFS *Scientific Reports* series). Finally, on certain issues, special attention will be paid to a few surveys which obtained and preserved more information of a kind that is relevant for this assessment.

First we will discuss age reporting in the household survey, then dating of the respondent's birth, then birth histories, and finally, questions on marital status and the dating of marriages.

5.2 Obtaining age in the household survey

WFS surveys consist of two interviews. The household interview is carried out first, to obtain some basic data on each household member, at the same time yielding the information necessary to select women who are eligible for the individual interview. Data on age, education and marital status of household members are needed to supply the base population for rates, although they are also useful in their own right. The usual recommendation is that the head of the household should be the informant but, in his absence, any adult member can supply the information.

Age reporting in the household survey is important, for two main reasons: first, the quality of age data in the household survey will indirectly affect any analyses that use the household population distribution as the base for rates; and secondly, age obtained in the household can directly affect results in the individual survey, if this information is transferred to the individual questionnaire, or if the recorded age is biased to exclude some eligible women from the survey.

Evaluations of specific surveys (see WFS *Scientific Reports* series) show that the quality of age reporting in WFS household surveys was an improvement over other recent sources, censuses or surveys, in a fair number of cases. Age distributions are smoother and indices of heaping lower for the WFS household surveys, especially in African and Middle Eastern countries. Moreover this improvement is generally greater for women than for men. In addition, non-response to the question on age was quite low — less than one per cent in all cases, and often only a fraction of one per cent. This is true whatever the mode of questioning used to obtain age. Given all the other intervening factors, we cannot directly relate question format to variations in data quality, but nevertheless we find that some forms of question are better than others, and that the type of household survey is related to differences in reporting quality, as will be discussed later.

Question format

In their household schedule most (28) countries obtained age alone, not requiring date of birth in addition nor even allowing it as an option. Among these the wording of the question varied in precision:

Question type	Use
How old is he/she?	16 countries, mainly in Africa, Middle East and Asia.
How old is he/she (in completed years)?	8 countries, mainly in Latin America.
How old was he/she at his/her last birthday?	4 countries, mainly in the Caribbean.

Although instructions during training always stressed that it was age in completed years which had to be obtained, it has been the experience of WFS co-ordinators and country survey personnel that interviewers tend to forget or misuse instructions specified in manuals and training, if the questionnaire itself does not carry a brief reminder. Thus the second question, with the reminder '(in completed years)' is to be preferred over the first question. The third question, although even more precise, will be limited to those countries where the birthday has some social and cultural recognition as an event to be celebrated, or where the date of birth is generally known.

Clearly even reminders on questionnaires will not have the desired effect in especially difficult interviewing situations. Despite this contrary indication, we recommend that whenever age is asked (in the household schedule or in the individual questionnaire to obtain respondent's, husband's or children's ages) the phrase 'completed years' should be added, in brackets, as a reminder to the interviewer.

Although the date of birth would have been the preferred form of obtaining this information, it was not generally chosen, partly because the approach chosen for the household interview was a quasi-schedule, leaving the details of probing to the interviewer, and partly because of the belief that date of birth takes longer than age to ascertain, and that proxy-reporting of date of birth is not easy. However, some countries (Benin, Cameroon, Ghana, Kenya, Nigeria, Senegal, Bangladesh, Sri Lanka, Republic of Korea, Malaysia, Philippines, Thailand) included a question on date of birth; in all cases except Cameroon, Senegal and Bangladesh, age was also asked, either for all persons or for those whose date of birth was not known (see table 5.1). In most of these countries dates were obtained for the majority of household members. Where both items were asked, the usual approach was to instruct the interviewer to resolve any inconsistency in the field, and correct the data by amending the original answer(s). This approach was unfortunate, since it not only increased the work of the interviewer but it also destroyed some possibly useful information which would have allowed comparison and evaluation of the reliability of the two types of source, as we will see later in the case of Tunisia. It is quite likely that, in an unknown proportion of cases, age was in fact given and converted to a calendar year, particularly where both items were asked for all members, since the interviewer probably felt an obligation to record both items.[2] These problems could have been avoided as shown below in our recommendations.

Because of the importance of obtaining good quality household data on age, which has become evident from its impact on analysis of individual data, we recommend that the typical approach used in the WFS programme be replaced with a somewhat more detailed specification of questions, roughly similar to the appproach used for the respondent's date of birth in the individual questionnaire. The interviewer should first obtain any available official documents, and use those which are known to be reliable to record the date of birth. This approach is especially recommended where accurate birth registration is common (e.g. over 25 per cent) but would be helpful even if coverage is lower. (Ewbank 1981 reached the same recommendation.) Results from documents can be recorded in the same space as the results of a subsequent direct question on date of birth, if availability of a document is also recorded. Where no document is available, a direct question on the date of birth should then be asked and the response fully recorded for both parts of the question (month and year). If no response is obtained a code 99 should be entered. Regardless of information obtained so far

TABLE 5.1

Use of certain questions and techniques for dating events, in 41 WFS surveys

Country	Household survey		Individual survey			Non-live pregnancies dating[c]		Use of event chart	Use of conversion chart	Eligibility for individual survey	
	Age	Date of birth	Respondent's date of birth		Type of birth history[b]						
			Date	Age[a]		(A)	(B)			Age	Marital status[d]
Africa											
Benin	✓**		✓	A	B	X	✓	✓		15–49	ALL
Cameroon		✓	✓	A	C1	✓	X*	X	X	15–54	ALL
Ghana	✓		✓	A	B	✓	✓	X	X	15–49	ALL
Ivory Coast	✓	X	✓	A	C1	✓	X*	✓	X	15–49	ALL
Kenya	✓	✓	✓	A	B	✓	✓	X	X	15–50	ALL
Lesotho	✓	X	✓	A	B	✓	✓	✓	X	15–50	EM
Nigeria	✓	✓	✓	A	B	X	✓	✓	X	15–49	ALL
Senegal	✓**		✓	X	C3	✓	X*	✓	X	15–49	ALL
Egypt	✓	X	✓	A	C2	✓	✓	✓	X	–49	EM
Mauritania	✓	X	✓	A	C2	✓	✓	✓	X	12–50	EM
Morocco	✓	X	✓	B	B	✓	✓	✓	X	15–50	ALL
Sudan (North)	✓	X	✓	A	B	✓	✓	✓	X	–50	EM
Tunisia	✓	X	✓	A	B	✓	✓	X	X	15–49	EM
Asia and Pacific											
Jordan	✓	X	✓	B	A	X	✓	✓	X	15–49	EM
Syria	✓	X	✓	B	C1	✓	✓	✓	X	–49	EM
Turkey	✓	✓[e]	✓	A	B	✓	✓	✓	X	–49	EM
Yemen AR	✓	X	✓	A	B	✓	✓	X	X	–50	EM

										Age	
Bangladesh	**	✓	✓	B	C2	✓	✓	X	X	–49	EM[f]
Nepal	✓	X	✓	B	B	✓	✓	X	✓	15–49	EM
Pakistan	✓	X	✓	B	A	✓	✓	X	X	–50	EM
Sri Lanka	✓	✓	✓	B	A	✓	✓	X	X	–49	EM
Fiji	✓	X	✓	A	A	X	✓	X	X	15–49	EM
Indonesia	✓	X	✓	B	B	✓	✓	✓	X	10–50	EM
Korea, Rep. of	✓	✓	✓	A	B	✓	✓	✓	✓	–50	EM
Malaysia	✓	✓	✓	B	B	✓	✓	X	✓	–49	EM
Philippines	✓	✓	✓	A	D1	✓	✓	X	X	15–49	EM
Thailand	✓	✓	✓	B	A	✓	✓	X	X	–49	EM
Americas											
Colombia	✓	X	✓	A	A	✓	✓	X	X	15–49	ALL
Ecuador	✓	X	✓	A	A	✓	✓	X	X	15–49	ALL
Paraguay	✓	X	✓	A	D2	✓	✓	X	X	15–49	ALL
Peru	✓	X	✓	A	A	✓	✓	X	X	15–49	EM
Venezuela	✓	X	✓	A	D2	✓	✓	X	X	15–44	ALL
Costa Rica	✓	X	✓	A	A	✓	✓	X	X	20–49	ALL
Dominican Rep.	✓	X	✓	A	D2	✓	X*	X	X	15–49	ALL
Mexico	✓	X	✓	A	D2	✓	X*	X	X	20–49[g]	ALL
Panama	✓	X	✓	B	A	✓	✓	X	X	20–49	ALL
Guyana	✓	X	✓	B	C1	✓	X*	X	X	15–49[h]	ALL
Haiti	✓	X	✓	A	C3	✓	X*	X	X	15–49	ALL
Jamaica	✓	X	✓	B	C1	✓	X*	X	X	15–49[h]	ALL
Trinidad & Tobago	✓	X	✓	B	C1	✓	X*	X	X	15–49[h]	ALL
Europe											
Portugal	✓	X	✓	A	B	✓	X*	X	X	15–49	EM

(key to Table 5.1 overleaf)

Key to table 5.1

√ Obtained information.
X Not asked.
X* Not asked, but could be obtained from date of termination.
** Asked as a probe, if date unknown.
a A = age asked of all women; B = age asked only if respondent did not know date of birth.
b A = core questionnaire; B = table integrated, but first all live births, then non-live births for each birth interval;
   C(1) = fully integrated pregnancy history – total number of pregnancies obtained, and questioned sequentially;
   C(2) = alternating live birth, then non-live pregnancies in that interval; C(3) = C(1), except reverse chronological order for questions on birth;
   D(1) and D(2) = segmented histories = first all living children, then all dead children, then all non-live pregnancies (sometimes split into two groups), but all entered in one physical table in approximate chronological order.
c Column A shows if the actual date of termination was asked, while column B shows whether the interval within which the non-live pregnancy occurred was also asked.
d ALL = all women; EM = ever-married women only. EM includes informal unions, where these are common.
e Year only, not month.
f Consummated marriages.
g Plus all women aged 15–19 who had had a live birth or been in a union.
h Excluding full-time schoolgirls aged 15–19.
Source: Susheela Singh (1984). Comparability of Questionnaires in Forty-one WFS Surveys. *WFS Comparative Studies* no. 32.

from a document or the direct question on date of birth, age in completed years should then be asked for all members. Any discrepancies between year of birth and age should be reconciled and the interviewer's estimate recorded in a separate location. The code 99 and a use of separate location should prevent any deduction of missing information by the interviewer.

The layout would be as shown in figure 5.1:

Document obtained		Calendar date of birth	Age in completed years	If discrepancy: Interviewer's estimate of age (in completed years)
Yes	1	Month —— 99	—— 99 (years)	—— (years)
No	2	Year —— 99		
Yes	1	Month —— 99	—— 99 (years)	—— (years)
No	2	Year —— 99		

FIG. 5.1 Recommended layout for age questioning in household survey

This approach would clearly take some more space and time than that typically adopted in the WFS programme. However, we think that the crucial importance of obtaining the best possible estimate of age, as well as the fact that the results from WFS surveys contained many defects, justifies the extra effort of attempting to obtain better data on age. This detailed approach is most justified for females in the age range 10–55, because this group is crucial both for eligibility and for use as a base population. If there is any likelihood of transferring the ages of children to the individual interview, this approach would also be preferred for children.

Three African countries used a completely different approach from the usual one. Ghana and Kenya used detailed probes in the household interview to obtain the date of birth or age of women over the age of 10, and then transferred this best estimate to the individual interview.[3] This was done on the principle that the time-consuming process of obtaining a good estimate should not be repeated. Senegal went further, and not only developed a specific procedure for obtaining the year of birth of all women,[4] but also used the age–event chart[5] in the household interview, for all women, obtaining dates of births and marriages, specially as a means of improving dating of the woman's birth. The quality of household data in Senegal was very good, compared to other sub-Saharan African surveys (Goldman, Rutstein and Singh 1985) suggesting that the extra effort spent was worthwhile. The results for Kenya were not as positive, however, since comparison of age data of the WFS household survey and that of the larger survey (NDS), which formed the frame for the WFS sample, showed about the same degree of heaping on ages 0 and 5, even though the NDS used no special efforts in probing, and their interviewers were trained for a shorter time duration.

Transfer of women out of the margins (15-19 and 45-50) of the eligible age range was also substantial (see chapter 24). Ghana, where a similar approach of intensive probing in the household interview was used, had somewhat better reporting than the census, but it was no better for women, who were the ones probed, than for men. Transfer of 45-49 year olds into the 50-54 age group, partly because of the inevitable heaping on age 50, and partly by interviewers to minimize their workload, also occurred.

While these approaches may not be suitable for all countries, the principle that accurate measurement of age requires greater care than a single question is a generally applicable one. The use of an event chart in the household survey is, however, questionable, and especially so in the case of Senegal, where this was even done for an extended sample. Although Senegal found it a useful approach (especially since the WFS survey was part of a multi-round survey) and in fact the quality of data obtained was very good, we would not recommend this time-consuming approach for general use.

Biases in selecting eligible women

The most serious type of age-reporting errors in WFS household surveys concerns the transference of females at the marginal ages (15-19, 45-49) into younger and older age groups, respectively, thus preventing them from falling into the age range which defined eligibility for the individual interview. This problem was observed in both extended and non-extended household samples but was less serious at the lower end of the age range in the extended surveys (see chapter 24). One of the major implications of these biases, which have been observed in many WFS surveys, is that data for the 45-49 age group should be used only with great care. Yet information on this group is important for the analysis of fertility trends, and some attempt should be made to improve its quality.

One solution is to expand the eligible age range, at least at the upper end, to 54, omitting the 50-54 group in analysis: age-transfer will probably still occur, but in this case it will be from the 50-54 into the 55-59 age group, leaving the 45-49 age group relatively unaffected. The cost of this solution is relatively small, since it is the time spent in contacting the household that is the major determinant of interviewer productivity and extra interviews in selected house-holds do not depress the interviewing rate appreciably. The Cameroon experience, where 54 was the upper age limit, also supports this suggestion: exclusion of women at the upper end of the eligibility range mainly affected the 50-54 age group, with the result that data for the 45-49 group were usable. It is diffi-cult to suggest any solution for transference from the 15-19 to the 10-14 age group, other than improving procedures for obtaining date of birth/age in the household survey. One possibly useful approach, for ever-married samples, is to have no lower age limit, simply including all ever-married females up to some maximum age.

Extended and non-extended household surveys

Checking of the consistency between date/age data from the household and from the individual surveys showed some interesting and suggestive differences between these two types of survey (see table 5.2). The very high level of consistency (97–98 per cent) found in some cases even at single years of age where there was no subselection of women, suggests that transference of information from the household to the individual interview (or vice versa) is common. In contrast consistency in single years of age was only moderate (61–67 per cent) in three cases of extended samples, even though the same interviewers were used, though consistency in five-year age groups, as expected, was higher (88–89 per cent). One other non-extended sample (Indonesia) had only moderately high consistency (about 80 per cent) in single years, but still much higher than the extended samples.

The case of Tunisia lends support to the recommendation for separate recording of date, age and the reconciled estimate, because the relatively low consistency of the single-year comparison of household and individual reports on age show that contamination of individual interview data by household data was very low, even though the two operations were not independent. These results support the earlier argument that it may be better to record age and date of birth separately and not to correct either, but to have the final reconciled estimate in a third location.

5.3 Obtaining respondent's age in the individual interview

In general, more effort was devoted to obtaining the respondent's date of birth in the individual than the household survey: usually the date of birth was asked first, and if this was not known, the age was then obtained or estimated. However, as for age in the household interview, documents were asked for only in a few countries, and even in these cases, use of documents was not always recorded. A fair proportion of countries obtained both age and year for each woman, and in a few cases age was asked in a totally separate location from date of birth, in an attempt to obtain an independent estimate. This is probably a useful practice, since interviewers are much less likely to remember or refer back to the household schedule when they are in a later section of the individual questionnaire.

An experiment in Tunisia supports this argument and allows further useful conclusions. The questionnaire was designed to enable evaluation of the accuracy of age and date reporting. This was especially interesting because of the very high coverage of vital registration (almost 100 per cent since 1975 for births) in the country and the accuracy of registering years for birth certificates at least since 1956, the year of independence. The aim of the experiment was to measure the degree of discrepancy between the actual age (obtained from a birth certificate) and the respondents' perception or declaration of their own age or date of birth.

TABLE 5.2

Consistency in age reporting between household and individual surveys depending on type of household survey, and question format

Country	Household survey Type[a]	Nature of question Age only	Nature of question Date and age	Individual survey: Per cent distribution according to mode of reporting Month and year	Year only	Age	Per cent with consistent ages Single years	Per cent with consistent ages 5-year age group
Colombia	Ex	x		97.0	3.0	–	61.3	88.7
Dominican Rep.	Ex	x		85.9	14.1	–	64.5	87.7
Mexico	Ex	x		100.0[b]	–	–	67.1	–
Tunisia	Not Ex	x		88.2	11.8	99.0[c]	66.3	–
Indonesia	Not Ex	x		22.3	11.2	66.5	80.8	93.4
Malaysia	Not Ex		x	57.0	43.0	–	97.3	–
Philippines	Not Ex		x	97.3	2.5	0.2	–	98.0
Trinidad & Tobago	Not Ex	x		98.3		1.7	97.9	99.7
Peru	Not Ex	x		94.7	5.3	–	98.0	99.0

a Type of household survey: 'extended' means that a larger sample was used, with a subselection of households being used to yield eligible women for the individual interview. 'Not-extended' refers to a survey in which the number of households in the sample was limited to those needed to yield the desired number of women for the individual survey.

b Data on mode of reporting were not preserved after date imputation.

c Age was asked of all women, at a separate point in the interview, regardless of whether a calendar date had already been obtained.

In the first section of the questionnaire women were asked for their birth certificates, and the month and year of birth was taken from this; if no certificate could be supplied, the month and year were directly asked. Almost all women gave their date of birth, with or without document. Later in the interview, all women were also asked their age, and interviewers were instructed not to reconcile any inconsistencies when recording the reported age. Finally, at the end of the interview, a reconciliation or best estimate was reached for women who did not provide a birth certificate. This methodological experiment makes it possible to compare women's reporting of their own age with information on the calendar year of birth, either with a document or without.

The distribution of women by single years of age, for the different reporting subgroups, is shown in figure 5.2. This shows that women with a birth certificate report their age more precisely than those without. Even so, these self-reports are much more heaped than ages calculated from the document itself. Interestingly, even for women who did not have a document, information on calendar year of birth was less heaped than reporting of age directly. It would seem that a direct question on age gives the least accurate information, and that use of documents improves the quality of the data substantially, although the extent of improvement will depend on each country. Finally, Tunisia's experience shows

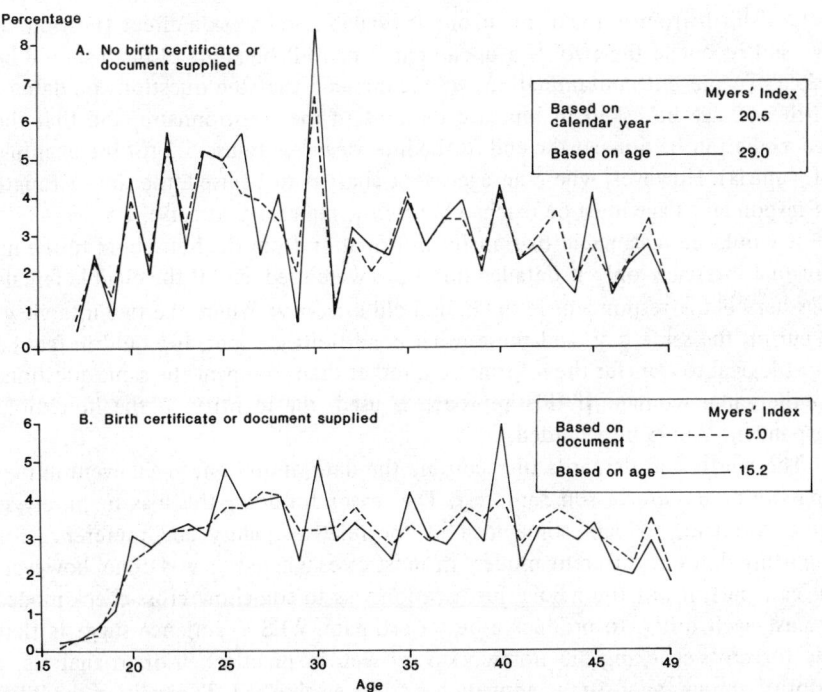

FIG. 5.2 Distribution of respondents by single years of age, according to the form of reporting their date of birth (Tunisia)

that the technique of using separate locations in the interview for date of birth, age, and the final reconciliation, and training of interviewers to avoid contamination of each item by the others, was possible to implement and succeeded in its aims.

The failure to incorporate use of documents into the WFS questionnaire itself (e.g. birth certificates, or identity cards) is also striking. Such documents are a reliable source in many countries, and will increasingly become so, although, given each country's circumstances, special restrictions can be made if necessary. For instance, in Senegal, certificates after a certain year were known to be accurate, and therefore only these were accepted. An advisable precaution in using documentary sources would be to include a direct question on age, and to probe and reconcile the two answers if they differed by more than some minimum amount. One advantage in using and separately recording documents is to obtain some measure of the functioning of vital registration systems. This can be a very useful input into the country's data collection system.

Age reporting in individual surveys shows the usual problems of heaping on preferred digits, as well as some transference between age groups, although these defects are generally much less severe than in the household surveys. We would recommend that a similar approach to that suggested for the household survey be used in the individual interview; that is, the interviewer should first record the date of birth from a document if one is available, then ask a direct question on age and reconcile the two. If a document is unavailable, date of birth should be asked. To prevent contamination, we recommend that the questions on date of birth and age be asked in separate sections of the questionnaire, and that the reconciliation be done at the end of the interview (see figure 5.2 for the example of Tunisia). However, where an age–event chart is to be used, the final estimate of respondent's age must be reached before the maternity history.

It would be reasonable to transfer information from the household to the individual interview only if detailed questions were used, and if the eligible female was herself the respondent in the household interview. Where the two interviews occur on the same day, and these other conditions are met, it would in fact be most logical to transfer the information, rather than to repeat the same questions to the same woman. If this approach is used, the identity of the household respondent should be recorded.

The merits and demerits of recording the date of any one given event in two or more modes are of some interest. The reason for doing this may be purely as an experiment, to gain some idea of the relative quality and preference for reporting dates in different modes. In most cases where this was done, however, at least part, if not the whole, justification was to somehow cross-check modes against each other, to produce a better estimate. WFS experience suggests that use for cross-checking did not work very well in practice. Prior to analysis, a priority among inconsistent answers has to be established. Typically in the WFS programme, date of birth wherever available was assigned priority, and self-reported age was used only when the calendar year of birth was missing, since it

proved impossible to devise any sensible rules for reconciling two or more estimates that differed substantially. It is almost as problematic for such a process
to be carried out in manual editing. The most reasonable approach would seem
to be the resolution of any differences during the interview itself: it is the interviewer who will be best able to judge, from the manner in which different
answers are given, and from all the other information at hand, which is the best
estimate of the date of the event. Most countries which used multiple modes
restricted themselves to two, e.g. date and age for the respondent's birth, date
and years ago (= age of the child) for children's births, and date and duration
for marriages. A few countries did resolve differences in the field, but usually
did not record the interviewer's estimate in a separate location. When no resolution was achieved in the field, priority was usually given to calendar dates, and
no attempt was made to reconcile the two estimates.

The Cameroon survey was exceptional in its use of multiple modes of recording. In the case of respondent's birth, the calendar date, a document, and age
were asked in different locations, and no attempt was made by the interviewer
to reconcile these answers. In the case of dates of pregnancies, four modes were
used. The calendar date was first asked and, if this was not known, three other
modes were obtained in all cases: how long ago the event occurred, the mother's
age at that time and the duration of the interval between pregnancies. This
multiple recording without resolution in the field created severe editing and
analysis problems, because of substantial discrepancies between the different
estimates, without any compensating increase in the reliability of the data. The
lesson is clear; unless clear guidelines can be established for reconciling discrepant
estimates of the same variable, little purpose is served by leaving these estimates
on data files, where they complicate rather than clarify analysis.

5.4 Birth and pregnancy histories

One of the most important aspects of WFS surveys was the collection of dates of
birth, sex, survival status and date or age at death for all live births. The richness
of the information on levels and trends in both fertility and mortality, yielded
from use of a full birth history, confirms that the decision was a good one. While
the overall approach is to be recommended, some details of the core questionnaire's approach can, however, be improved. This section draws upon an earlier
paper on WFS data collection techniques and problems (Scott and Singh 1981).

Evaluations of data quality have found the usual problems associated with
retrospective birth histories, e.g. displacement of births, typically resulting in
heaping at the period 5-14 years before the survey, and some omission of births,
especially for the oldest age group. In addition, the occurrence of various biases,
e.g. heaping on rounded calendar years, or historically important years, or use of
a systematic birth interval duration (e.g. 2, 2½ or 3 years), has been observed.
Such defects are difficult to avoid where dates of births are not used in day-to-
day circumstances. It is nevertheless still necessary and useful to examine the

techniques of data collection which were used by WFS surveys, with the aim of identifying those which worked well and those which failed (see Goldman, Rutstein and Singh 1985; Chidambaram, Cleland and Verma 1980; and evaluation reports on individual countries).

The usual format in the WFS programme was to precede the birth history by a set of five questions on number of sons and daughters living with the respondent and living away from home and the number of children who have died, in order to obtain the total number of children ever born. Some modifications were tried out to shorten the series (e.g. referring only to children, not boys and girls separately) and secondly, for all-women samples, to separate out never-pregnant women first. However the possible problem of adopted children was ignored. Any discrepancy between the numbers thus given and those listed in the birth history was reconciled by further probing. This set of questions has generally been found useful, as an introduction to asking detailed questions on each birth, and for this reason it should be retained. It would moreover appear that the birth history added only a few extra births to the number obtained by these questions. However the possibility still exists that interviewers corrected these numbers after the birth history, and the extent of this is unknown.

While WFS individual survey data cannot give conclusive evidence on this point, other research, comparing a household measure of parity (obtained by a similar set of summary questions) and parity from the birth history of the individual survey, found almost no difference between the two (chapter 4; Hobcraft 1980). There is thus no evidence that parity can be measured more accurately by a sequential listing of births, than by a short set of summary questions on the number of children ever born.

Structure of the maternity history

The more crucial part of this section of the questionnaire is the birth history itself. The originally recommended approach was to use two separate tables, the first for all live births, and the second for all other pregnancies that did not result in a live birth (see figure 5.3). In practice this approach was used by only a minority of countries, while the majority preferred differently structured histories. We will discuss these different types of maternity histories first, and then consider the problems of obtaining dates of live births.

Variations from the recommended format of two separate tables were developed in an attempt to improve reporting of both live and non-live births. Use of a single table, on which all pregnancy terminations were entered, was a common element in all the variations (see figure 5.4). The intention was to improve dating of live births by probing for non-live births, dating these events within an interval at least, even if an exact date of termination was unavailable. At the same time a unified sequence would make long gaps more easily apparent, and these could then be probed for omitted events. Finally, transference from non-live birth status into the sequence of live births (as a result of the special probe on signs of life) would be easier on an integrated history table than with two separate tables.

FIG. 5.3 Extracts from *WFS Basic Documentation* no. 1, Core Questionnaires

BIRTH HISTORY

220. INTERVIEWER: FIRST ENTER NAMES AND SEX OF ALL CHILDREN IN 221, STARTING WITH THE FIRST BORN. CHECK TOTAL WITH 211. THEN COMPLETE 222-226 FOR EACH CHILD.
NEXT, ASK 227-233 FOR EACH INTERVAL (UP TO LAST BIRTH), USING NAMES OF CHILDREN.
FINALLY, GO ON TO 233. PREFACE 221 WITH: Now I want to ask you some questions about each of your (SUM) births. Please give me the names of each of your children, including any who have died, starting with the first child you had.

BIRTH NUMBER	221. NAME	222. SEX	223. In what month and year was (NAME) born? IF DK, ASK: How many years ago?	224. (EXCEPT FOR FIRST BIRTH) How many years and months after the birth of your previous child was (NAME) born?	225. Is (NAME) alive?	226. IF DEAD: How long did (he/she) live? (OBTAIN COMPLETED YEARS AND MONTHS)
01		BOY ☐ 1 GIRL ☐ 2	MONTH ___ YEAR 19 ___ YRS. AGO		YES ☐ 1 NO ☐ 2	COMPLETED YRS. COMPLETED MOS.
02		BOY ☐ 1 GIRL ☐ 2	MONTH ___ YEAR 19 ___ YRS. AGO	COMPLETED YEARS COMPLETED MONTHS	YES ☐ 1 NO ☐ 2	COMPLETED YRS. COMPLETED MOS.
03		BOY ☐ 1 GIRL ☐ 2	MONTH ___ YEAR 19 ___ YRS. AGO	COMPLETED YEARS COMPLETED MONTHS	YES ☐ 1 NO ☐ 2	COMPLETED YRS. COMPLETED MOS.
04		BOY ☐ 1 GIRL ☐ 2	MONTH ___ YEAR 19 ___ YRS. AGO	COMPLETED YEARS COMPLETED MONTHS	YES ☐ 1 NO ☐ 2	COMPLETED YRS. COMPLETED MOS.

OTHER PREGNANCIES

ASK 228-232 FOR EACH PREGNANCY IN THE INTERVAL.
(IF MORE THAN TWO PREGNANCIES IN AN INTERVAL, USE SPACE AT END OF TABLE AND SPECIFY INTERVAL.)

INTERVAL Use names where possible (TO BE USED FOR 227)	227. During the period (INTERVAL) did you have any miscarriage, abortion, or still birth? IF YES: How many?	228. In what month and year did this pregnancy end?	229. How many months did this pregnancy last?	230. IF 6 MONTHS OR LESS (OR DK): Did you or a doctor or someone else do anything to end that pregnancy early?	231. IF 7 MONTHS OR MORE: Did that baby cry or show any sign of life after it was born?	232. IF "YES" TO 231: Was that a boy or a girl?
BEFORE YOUR FIRST BIRTH	YES ☐ → (NUMBER) NO ☐	MONTH ___ YEAR 19 ___	MOS. ___ 6 OR LESS (OR DK) ☐ 7 OR MORE ☐	YES ☐ 1 NO ☐ 2	YES ☐ NO ☐	BOY ☐ GIRL ☐
BETWEEN YOUR 1st AND 2nd BIRTHS	YES ☐ → (NUMBER) NO ☐	MONTH ___ YEAR 19 ___	MOS. ___ 6 OR LESS (OR DK) ☐ 7 OR MORE ☐	YES ☐ 1 NO ☐ 2	YES ☐ NO ☐	BOY ☐ GIRL ☐
BETWEEN YOUR 2nd AND 3rd BIRTHS	YES ☐ → (NUMBER) NO ☐	MONTH ___ YEAR 19 ___	MOS. ___ 6 OR LESS (OR DK) ☐ 7 OR MORE ☐	YES ☐ 1 NO ☐ 2	YES ☐ NO ☐	BOY ☐ GIRL ☐
BETWEEN YOUR 3rd AND 4th BIRTHS	YES ☐ → (NUMBER) NO ☐	MONTH ___ YEAR 19 ___	MOS. ___ 6 OR LESS (OR DK) ☐ 7 OR MORE ☐	YES ☐ 1 NO ☐ 2	YES ☐ NO ☐	BOY ☐ GIRL ☐

6.

FIG. 5.4 Extracts from *Turkish Fertility Survey 1978: First Report* vol. 1

The most common variation on the core format was to integrate the recording of other pregnancies with that of live births, probing each live-birth interval for other pregnancies and entering all events in a single table. This integration was done by different means, however. The most common method was to collect data on all live births first and then probe each interval for non-live pregnancies. Another alternative was to ask about all living children, then all dead children, then all stillbirths and finally all miscarriages and abortions, with a back-up probe for all intervals of some minimum length, the minimum varying between countries. A third method was to use a pregnancy history rather than a birth history, asking about the first to the last pregnancy in sequence, at the same time determining the outcome of each. A fourth approach was to obtain live births, but to probe each birth interval for other pregnancies as soon as that interval was identified.

It is difficult to evaluate the relative success of the different approaches from the available evidence. While coverage of foetal losses may be considered one possible measure of success, this measure is influenced by factors other than the technique of questioning, not least of them being true variations in the rate of abortion (spontaneous and induced). Coverage of 'other pregnancies', measured as the rate per 1000 fertile pregnancies, does show that most surveys obtained a rate of 60 per 1000, or higher (Casterline and Ashurst 1984). The biological minimum for spontaneous abortions and stillbirths beyond the second month of pregnancy is 120 per 1000 but half of this occurs in the third month alone (Bongaarts and Potter 1983). Losses in the first eight weeks and some losses in the third month may not be observed and therefore not reported, suggesting that coverage of spontaneous losses in the surveys was reasonable, but the extent of understatement of induced abortions is unknown.

Some general statements based on WFS experience can be made. The opinion of staff who have used both the separated and the integrated approaches is that the integrated is better since it usually provides more accurate placement of 'other pregnancies'. This in itself would improve the dating and coverage of live births. Secondly, most countries which used an integrated structure preferred obtaining a history of live births and then adding in 'other pregnancies' for each interval, rather than asking for a chronological history of all pregnancies. This was justified either on cultural grounds or because it was believed that a woman would naturally think in terms of her live births rather than in terms of her pregnancies. In addition the chronological pregnancy history, as compared with the interval method, loses the advantage of better recording of live birth dates (except for imputation). This is due to the structure of the pregnancy history which obtains the total number of pregnancies at the beginning of the history and proceeds chronologically with each pregnancy with no probes on intervals (see figure 5.5). By comparison, the integrated pregnancy history probes each birth interval for other pregnancies and uses this information to check the accuracy of dates of live births.

The use of a 'segmented' history by a few Latin American countries and the

PREGNANCY HISTORY

213. Think back to your .... pregnancy, did it result in a Live birth-LB Still-birth-SB or was it not completed - NB	214. If LB: In what month and year was this child born? IF NOT a LB ask: In what month and year did this pregnancy end? IF DON'T KNOW ASK HOW MANY YRS. AGO?	215. Was it a boy or a girl?	216. Is this child still living?	217. What is/was his/her name	218. IF DEAD ASK: In what month and year did the child die? IF D.K. ASK HOW MANY YRS. AGO?	219. How many months did that pregnancy last?	1 - 13 IDENTIFICATION
			IF A LIVE-BIRTH ASK:				

FIG. 5.5 Extract from *Jamaica Fertility Survey 1975/76: Country Report* vol. 1

INTERVIEWER: CHECK QUESTION 212 TO MAKE SURE THAT YOU HAVE RECORDED THE INFORMATION ABOUT EVERY PREGNANCY:

Philippines (all living children, then all dead children, then all miscarriages (split into two groups, sometimes)) may be queried, since it makes the interviewer's checking of the consistency of dates of all live births and other pregnancies somewhat difficult, and it partly loses the advantage of a chronological sequence which may assist the respondent in dating events.

These variations in structure arose chiefly because of the aim of collecting the best possible data on live births. The original reason for including questions on non-live births had been simply as a means of detecting omitted live births that died soon after birth, and which were therefore supposed to have a high probability of being forgotten. The question, 'did the baby cry or show any other sign of life after it was born?' was asked in regard to all stillbirths, in order to cover live births which might otherwise be missed. If this is considered to be the sole or the primary reason for asking about non-live births, then the results suggest that there was no need for these probes. Several countries did not use the question at all, but, among those which did, the number of live births discovered was in all cases less than 0.1 per cent of total number of pregnancies. These results have two alternative interpretations: either the question was unsuccessful in obtaining positive answers even where children had shown signs of life, or the history tables were successful in obtaining most live births in the first place. In either case, the question as it stands has not added a significant amount of information, and would seem unnecessary.

However, the advantage of the inclusion of non-live births in improving the dating of live births, both during the interview and later, in the process of machine imputation, cannot be ignored. Thus this may still be a useful approach, in countries where obtaining dates is especially difficult, and where in the absence of probes about non-live births the tendency to report the same interval duration may be even stronger than what is already believed to exist. The feasibility of including questions on induced abortions would have to be decided on a country-specific basis. A second reason for collecting this information is its substantive importance in countries where induced abortion is known or believed to be significant.

The possibility of improving dating in the field definitely exists, both in the case where probing occurs after all live births are dated, and where probing occurs after each birth is entered, as long as interviewers are trained to use the dates and intervals between non-live births as a check on dates of live births. We therefore recommend probe and change in the latter when necessary. If non-live pregnancies are to be used solely as an aid for dating live births, we recommend that only intervals, not the actual dates, of these events should be used. We base this recommendation on the fact that dates of non-live births are likely to be inaccurate (because of the difficulty of remembering these dates) and consequently will complicate the interviewing process.

The alternatives of proceeding chronologically in the history, beginning with the first event, or going backwards, beginning with the most recent event, were also considered carefully. Almost all countries chose the chronological order, again because it was believed to be closer to the woman's mental framework. Haiti and Senegal used the reverse approach, partly because of the advantage that this method was expected to have in producing better dating of the two most recent births, a result that would be especially useful for estimating current fertility.

These two countries do not allow any evaluation of the merits of the backward approach; however a few suggestive results were found by other studies. A Bangladesh tape-recording study found that interviewer performance declined as the birth history proceeds: there was an increasing tendency to accept approximate answers in the form of child's age or number of years since birth, in the face of the respondent's inability to give quick answers (Thompson, Ali and Casterline 1982). Balancing this finding, we see that the last birth is usually recalled with greater accuracy, because of the recency of the event (Chidambaram and Sathar 1984). An experimental study in Bangladesh, using each approach, forward and backward, on half of the sample, found slight advantages for the backward approach (Becker and Mahmud 1984). The proportion of events correctly placed in time was the same for both approaches, and although the forward approach had slightly more missed live births, missed births were rare, and this was therefore not so important. However the backward form had the advantage of a more symmetric distribution of misreporting errors, which was reflected in more accurate fertility rates for the period 10–14 years before survey. Finally, another small experimental study on university students in the United States on the names of teachers from Grades 1–12 found that backward-oriented search was more successful and efficient, and that the probability of recalling an item from autobiographical memory is primarily a function of recency (Whitten and Leonard 1981).

Our recommendation is to use only a live birth history, without any questions on non-live births, in countries where dates are relatively easy to obtain and accurate, but where, in addition, induced abortion is unimportant. However when either or both of these two conditions are not met, serious consideration should be given to inclusion of questions on non-live births, not as a means of detecting missed live births, but either to help with dating live births, or to obtain a measure of the incidence of induced abortion. Where the decision is to cover non-live births, use of some form of integrated history would be preferable to use of two separate tables.

Techniques for obtaining dates in the birth history

The questions used to obtain the dates of events in the history table varied among countries. The recommended core questions were 'in what month and year did ... occur?' and if the year was unknown, then 'how many years ago ...?' To obtain the age at death of children who died, the core question was 'for how long did the child live?' For both events most countries used the core questions, but some countries also added other probes, while aids to dating, such as event charts, were used in some cases.

In attempting to evaluate the success of the different questioning techniques we encounter the same problems as with date of birth of the respondent. It is not the questions alone that are at issue, but the importance of dates in the society, which influences the level of knowledge of dates. However, on the basis of the varied experience of the WFS countries, we make some suggestions about the techniques which were tried out.

In obtaining dates of live births, we would suggest, even more so than for other events, that documents (typically the birth certificate) be consulted, and backed up with the recording of age, with any discrepancy being resolved by the interviewer in a separate location. If birth certificates are known to be reliable, the recording of age may be limited to cases where no certificate is available, both in the instance when date of birth is given, and necessarily so if date is not known. While use of a third location will not prevent contamination by interviewers (e.g. interviewer calculating age instead of asking it), it will certainly limit the amount of manipulation of the data that the interviewer can achieve. It is striking that so few countries considered this a worthwhile approach. Presumably, with increasing modernization, registration of births will become more common and reliable. We recognize that registration is of doubtful quality in many countries, but still think that with appropriate rules (e.g. as in Senegal, where, after 1960, birth certificates are reliable in the whole country, but within certain urban centres they are reliable even before that year) this can be an extremely useful tool. Separate recording of the use of documents is also to be recommended, partly to allow analysis of data quality, and partly as an objective check on the vital registration system.

Date of birth with years ago or age as a probe would be the alternative if no document is available. Intervals between events should be the last resort, since there is a well-known tendency to give uniform intervals, 2, 2.5 or 3 years, rather than exact interval durations. However, whenever age is used the need to specify completed years is especially important because of the common tendency to confuse completed ($5.0-5.9 = 5$) with rounded years ($4.5-5.5 = 5$) and projected years ($4.1-5.0 = 5$). The article by Chidambaram and Pullum (1981) shows that in the extreme case, where a high proportion of birth dates were imputed, and an increasing proportion going back in time, incorrect interpretation of reported rounded years as complete years for dating of children's births in the individual interview affected the measurement of fertility by displacing births six months closer to the interview. In the same country, Bangladesh, a study of tape-recordings of interviews shows that interviewers did not try to obtain completed years, even though this was specified in training and on the questionnaire itself (Thompson, Ali and Casterline 1982).

In obtaining and recording the age at death, care should be taken to record the exact age, in months and years, and *not* to lose this detail by recording the information in groups, e.g. less than one year, 1-2 years, and so on. A further minor point is that experience suggests that it is better to obtain the name of a child first, then ask questions, because this makes it clear which child is being asked about, rather than, as in the original core questionnaire, referring to 'your first birth', 'your second birth' and so on, until it was ascertained that the child was still alive. The care taken to avoid upsetting the respondent by obtaining names of children who died seems to be excessive and unnecessary in most cultures.

In some countries additional techniques were used, such as the age-event chart, the historical calendar, and conversion charts. The conversion chart is used for the birth history and consists of a visual representation of calendar years in the form of rows, together with information which allows the interviewer to convert answers given in other time-scales to the desired calendar scale (see figure 5.6). The conversion chart does have the advantage shared by the age-event chart of calibrating all dates on a single scale, thereby allowing quick checking of consistency. The ordinary birth history allows events to be recorded in either calendar or 'years ago' format, making subsequent checking very difficult.

The other two types of aid were used not only for dating births of children, but for all other events as well. However the main aim of the age-event chart and conversion charts was to assist with dating births, pregnancies and marriages. WFS experience with historical calendars, or lists of events and their corresponding dates, has not been good. It is difficult to find any group of events which are commonly known, even if the lists are varied among regions; in developing countries, awareness of political or national events, even important ones, tends to be low. Another disadvantage is that when interviewers probe, using specific events and dates, this in itself will probably bias the respondent towards reporting these dates (see also Ewbank 1981; Scott and Sabagh 1970). In contrast, experience with the age-event chart has generally been very good: as a visual summary of the vital events in the woman's life it facilitates the checking of consistency of dates of events, and in probing where inconsistencies or large unexpected gaps occur. Various designs have been used, and in general all the continuous charts seem to work equally well. The technique is sufficiently uncommon to require some explanation. The chart generally takes the form of a horseshoe-shaped curve, or occasionally a circle, with calendar years and the equivalent number of years ago printed along the curve. Historical events may also be indicated next to the appropriate year as a further aid in probing. Events in the woman's life, starting with her date of birth, then the dates of her children's births, and the dates of her marriages are all entered on this chart which is appended to the back of the questionnaire. (See figures 5.7–5.10.) The interviewer then has a clear visual image of the events and can quickly evaluate their consistency. Further, implausibly long or short intervals between events become clearly apparent and can then be probed. Finally, the systematic presentation of information in the chart helps to clarify confusions arising from what is often a chaotic set of responses, for example answers containing a mixture of dates, intervals and years ago. One design that gave some problems was that used in Nigeria, where a rectangular shape rather than a smooth curve was used, causing a break in the chart which confused interviewers (see figure 5.9). Nigeria did have a useful innovation as well; the interviewer was instructed to enter, on the event chart, the points at which the respondent was aged 5, 10, 15, 20, etc, thereby providing not just the usual two types of time-scale, but also a third, respondent's age.

The event chart does have two disadvantages, however, which are not present with a birth history conversion chart. The fact that information must be copied from the event chart to the questionnaire during the interview itself takes time and can disrupt rapport. It also introduces a source of error. Errors in transcription can be serious if, for example, the names of recent births are incorrectly copied, since many other questions use the last closed and open intervals, referring to names of children to identify these intervals. One possible solution to minimize errors in transference is to design the event chart on an extendable flap which is completely visible during the process of transferring. Another disadvantage shared by both the age–event chart and the birth history conversion chart is that they do not record the format in which dates are supplied by the respondent. This information is of methodological interest and could be retained by adding an extra column to the maternity history, specifying the format of dating. The many advantages of charts outweigh this minor possible disadvantage, however.

Conversion charts, specifically designed for the birth history, were used in Nepal, Malaysia and the Republic of Korea. The simplest form of this chart is to have two adjacent columns, one with calendar years and the other with the equivalent number of years ago for the last 50 years. Nepal and the Republic of Korea added a third column, the Nepalese calendar year and the Chinese animal year, respectively, while the Republic of Korea alone added a fourth column, the age of the respondent at the time of the birth, which was entered by the interviewer for each respondent. The advantage of this type of chart is easy conversion from any mode to the coded mode, the Western calendar year. A further advantage of this arrangement is to make the length of intervals obvious at a glance to the interviewer, thereby facilitating the probing of intervals for missed pregnancies or abortions. In this respect the method can be seen as a variation of the event chart since it contains the three forms of date reporting (years ago, mother's age at each calendar year, and calendar year). The disadvantage of the conversion chart, relative to an age–event chart, is that births are not seen in the perspective of other events (e.g. marriages), to enable better consistency checking of events against each other and therefore better estimation of dates.

The conversion chart is useful where more than one calendar system is in use (e.g. Chinese or Nepalese calendars). It was particularly suitable in the Republic of Korea, given a situation where accurate dating was common, but with a high prevalence of non-live pregnancies, some of which would be missed if the interviewer were not aware of the length of intervals. Malaysia also used this approach and found it useful, although there were minor problems with the layout of the table.

From this discussion of the advantages and disadvantages of the different aids for dating events, we can see that the usefulness of each type depends on the

DATA COLLECTION INSTRUMENTS

LIVE BIRTH CHART (1947–1956): PLOT ON EVENTS CHART

KOREAN AGE OF CHILD	ANIMAL YEAR OF BIRTH	217. KOREAN AGE OF MOTHER (TRANSCRIBE FROM EVENTS CHART)	218. In what year was your (first, second,...) child born? (FIX CALENDAR YEAR BY ASKING R'S AGE, CHILD'S AGE AND ANIMAL YEAR)	219. In what month and day was your (first, second,...) child born?	IF MONTH GIVEN 220. Is that solar or lunar calendar?	IF LUNAR 221. Was that a leap month?	IF MONTH DK 222. In what season was your (first, second,...) child born?	223. Was the child a boy or a girl?	224. Is that child still living?	IF LIVING 225. What is that child's name?	226. In what year did that child die? (IF NECESSARY) How old were you then? (RECORD CALENDAR YEAR)	IF DIED 227. In what month and day did that child die?	IF MONTH GIVEN 228. Is that solar or lunar calendar?	IF MONTH DK 229. Was that a leap month?	230. In what season did he/she die?	231. Did you feed this child at the breast?	IF B'ST FEEDING 232. For how many months? (ENTER "STILL" IF STILL BREAST FEEDING)	233. NUMBER BIRTH ORDER AND DRAW A WAVY LINE THROUGH CORRESPONDING ROWS ON OPPOSITE PAGE	SOLAR CALENDAR YEAR
		217	218	219	220	221	222	223	224	225	226	227	228	229	230	231	232	233	
28 BOAR			1947																1947
27 RAT			1948																1948
26 OX			1949																1949
25 TIGER			1950																1950
24 HARE			1951																1951
23 DRAGON			1952																1952
22 SNAKE			1953																1953
21 HORSE			1954																1954
20 RAM			1955																1955
19 MONKEY			1956																1956

FIG. 5.6 Korea – Conversion chart

NONFERTILE PREGNANCY CHART (1947-1956): PLOT ON EVENTS CHART

SOLAR CALENDAR YEAR	234. KOREAN AGE OF MOTHER (TRANSCRIBE FROM 217 OR EVENTS CHART)	ASK FOR EACH INTERVAL BETWEEN LIVE BIRTHS												SOLAR CALENDAR YEAR
		235. Were there any (other) times you were pregnant, even for only one or two months (before your first child, between your first and second child,...after your last child)? (IF YES, ASK 236-245. IF NO, SKIP TO 245.)	ASK FOR EACH PREGNANCY INTERVAL											
			236. In what year did the (1st, 2nd...) such pregnancy end? (IF NECESSARY:) How old were you then? (RECORD CALENDAR YEAR)	237. In what month did the pregnancy end?	IF MONTH GIVEN	IF MONTH DK	IF 7TH MONTH OR LATER	IF 6TH MONTH OR EARLIER	243. Did you or a doctor or someone else do anything to end that pregnancy early-by induced abortion?	244. Was there any other pregnancy (before your 1st child, between your 1st and 2nd child,...after your last child)? (IF YES, REPEAT 236-244, IF NO, PROBE 245.)	245. In this period, did you or a doctor or someone else do anything to end (a. another) pregnancy early by induced abortion? IF YES, REPEAT 236-241, 243-244. IF NO, ASK 235 FOR NEXT INTERVAL, IF ANY.	246. CORRECT LIVE BIRTH ORDER AS NEEDED (BRACKET MULTIPLE BIRTHS)	247. NUMBER PREGNANCIES (INCL. CURRENT PREG. COUNT MULT. BIRTH AS ONE)	
					238. Is that solar or lunar calendar?	239. Was that a leap month?	240. In what season was that?	241. In what month of pregnancy did it end?	242. Did that baby cry or show any other sign of life? (IF YES GO BACK TO 223-233 FOR LIVE BIRTH IN APPROPRIATE ROW. THEN, BE SURE TO PROBE 244-245.)					
	234	235	236	237	238	239	240	241	242	243	244	245	246	247
1947		YES NO							YES NO	YES NO	YES NO	YES NO			1947
1948		YES NO							YES NO	YES NO	YES NO	YES NO			1948
1949		YES NO							YES NO	YES NO	YES NO	YES NO			1949
1950		YES NO							YES NO	YES NO	YES NO	YES NO			1950
1951		YES NO							YES NO	YES NO	YES NO	YES NO			1951
1952		YES NO							YES NO	YES NO	YES NO	YES NO			1952
1953		YES NO							YES NO	YES NO	YES NO	YES NO			1953
1954		YES NO							YES NO	YES NO	YES NO	YES NO			1954
1955		YES NO							YES NO	YES NO	YES NO	YES NO			1955
1956		YES NO							YES NO	YES NO	YES NO	YES NO			1956

FIG. 5.6 continued

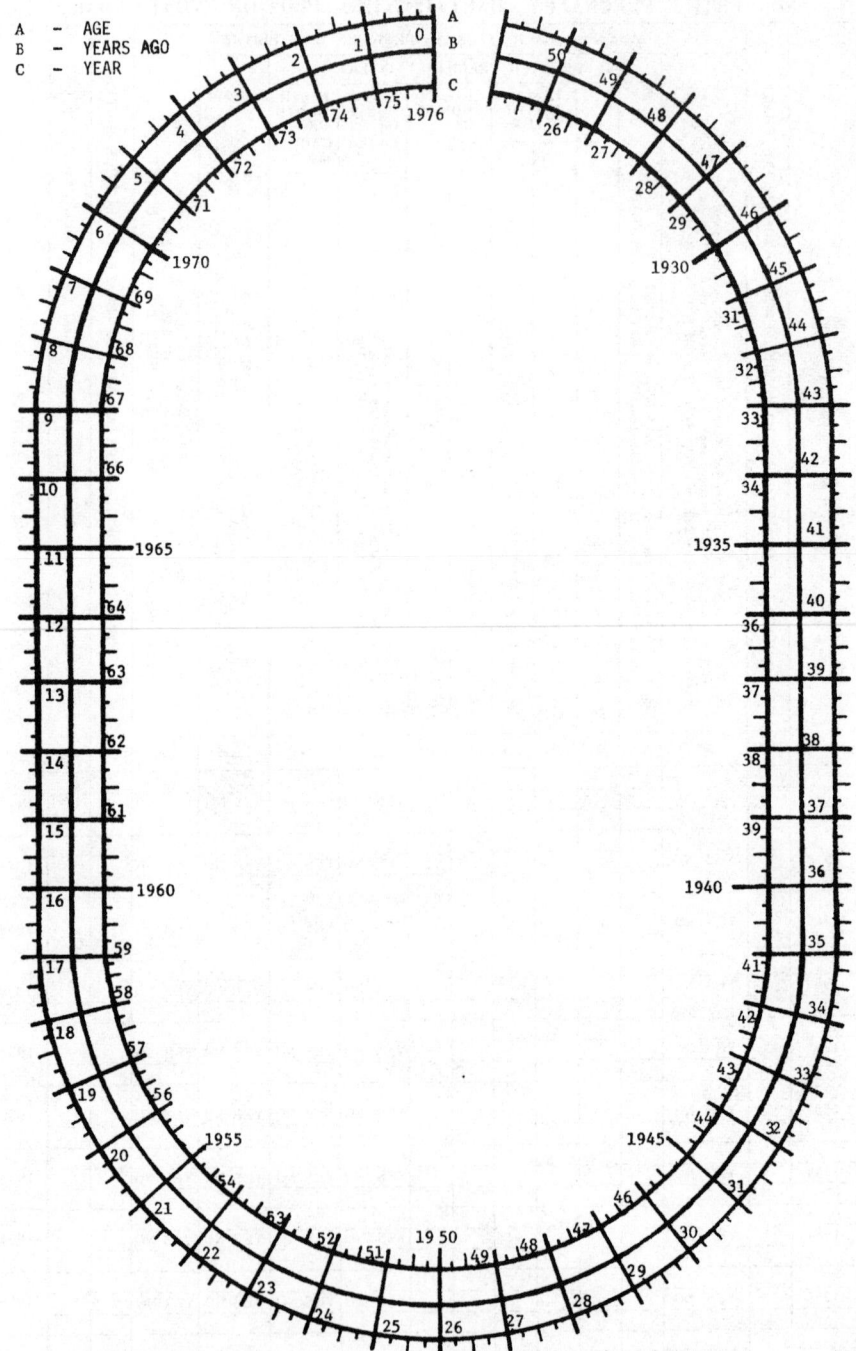

FIG. 5.7 Indonesia – Age–event chart

M – Mariage de l'enquetêé
FM – Fin de mariage de l'enquetêé
DN – Naissance de l'enquetêé
NE – Naissance de l'enfant

زؤ: تاريخ زواج المستجيبة
نم: نهاية زواج المستجيبة
مم: تاريخ ميلاد المستجيبة
مرو: تاريخ ميلاد الولد

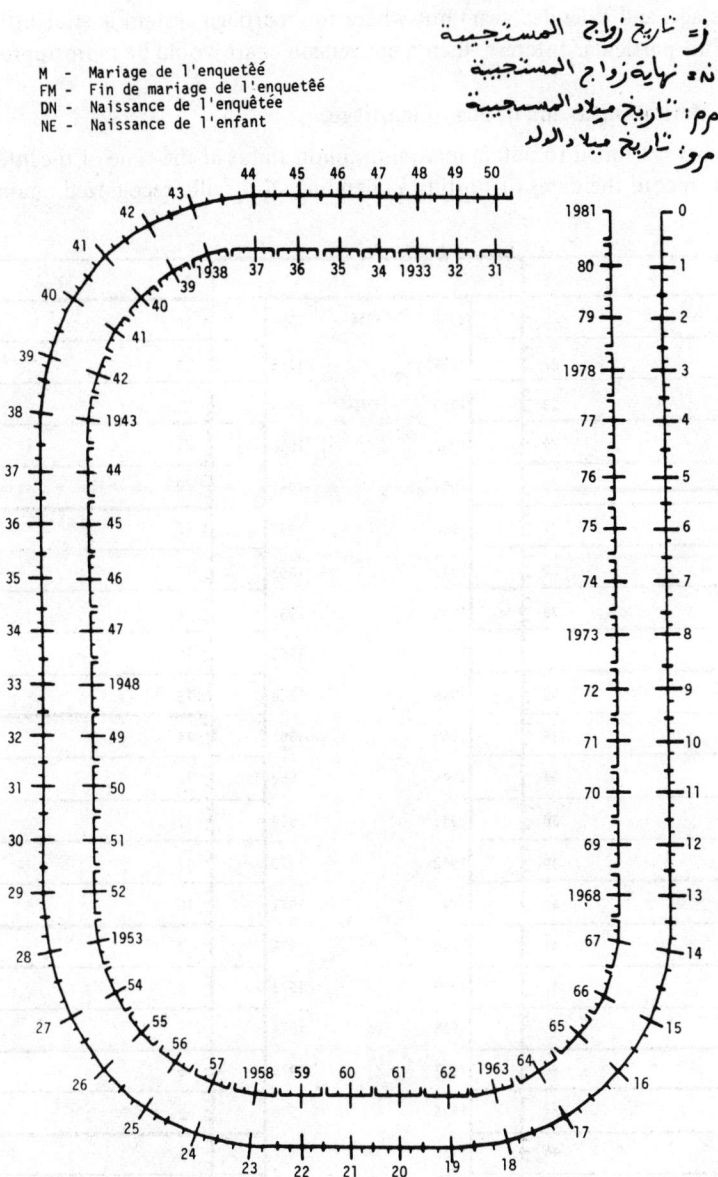

FIG. 5.8 Mauritania – Age–event chart

particular situation of each country. When reporting of dates is generally bad, and where marriage histories are complex or of special interest, an age-event chart is highly recommended. It will improve the dating of both marriages and pregnancies. Where knowledge of dates is good, but dates are likely to be reported in different types of calendars (e.g. Chinese and Western) or in different forms (years ago and calendar year) but where the marriage system is straightforward or of no particular interest, then a conversion chart would be more appropriate.

5.5 Marital status and dating of marriage

WFS surveys aimed to obtain marital or union status at the time of the interview, and to record the dates of starting and ending all socially recognized unions. The

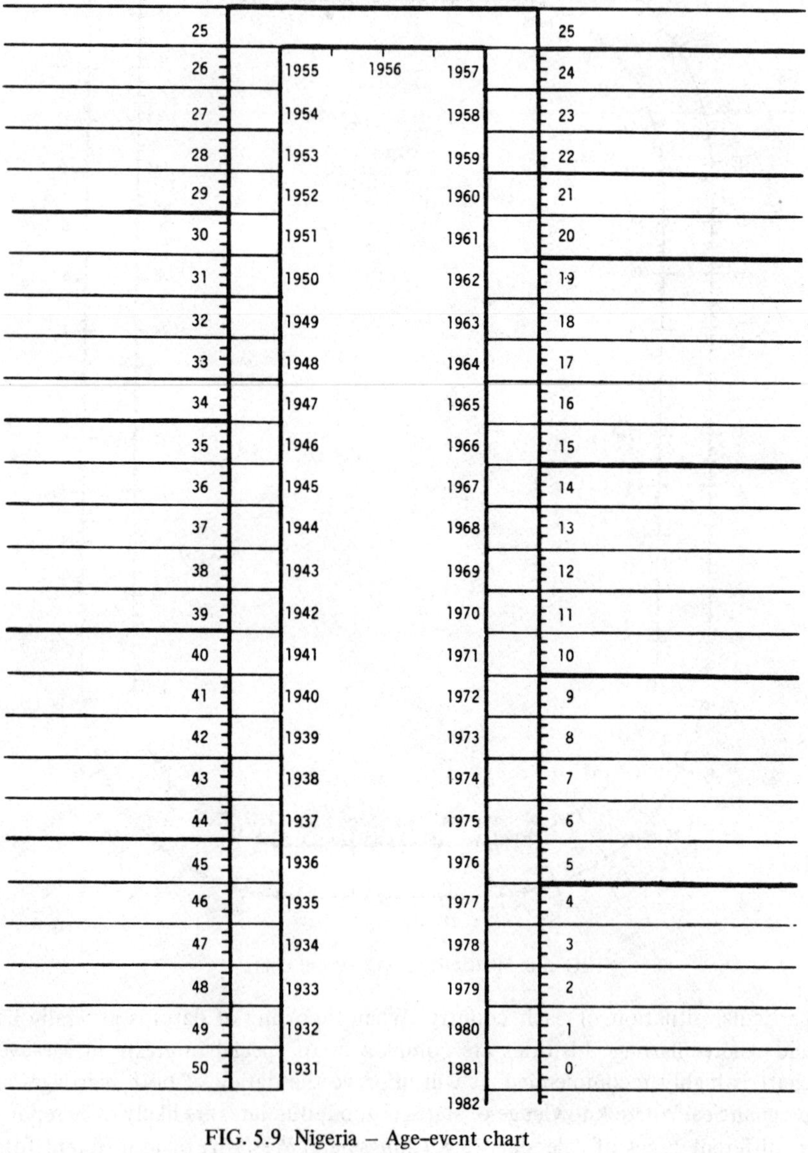

25				25
26	1955	1956	1957	24
27	1954		1958	23
28	1953		1959	22
29	1952		1960	21
30	1951		1961	20
31	1950		1962	19
32	1949		1963	18
33	1948		1964	17
34	1947		1965	16
35	1946		1966	15
36	1945		1967	14
37	1944		1968	13
38	1943		1969	12
39	1942		1970	11
40	1941		1971	10
41	1940		1972	9
42	1939		1973	8
43	1938		1974	7
44	1937		1975	6
45	1936		1976	5
46	1935		1977	4
47	1934		1978	3
48	1933		1979	2
49	1932		1980	1
50	1931		1981	0
			1982	

FIG. 5.9 Nigeria – Age–event chart

generally accepted definitions or names of unions current in each society were used by these surveys. Thus, in effect, socially recognized unions were recorded, but, as individual women interpreted the questions and expressions, some variations in what was considered to be a particular type of union must have been introduced. In many countries, especially in Asia, North Africa and the Middle East, this issue does not arise, because marriage is essentially formal and unambiguous.

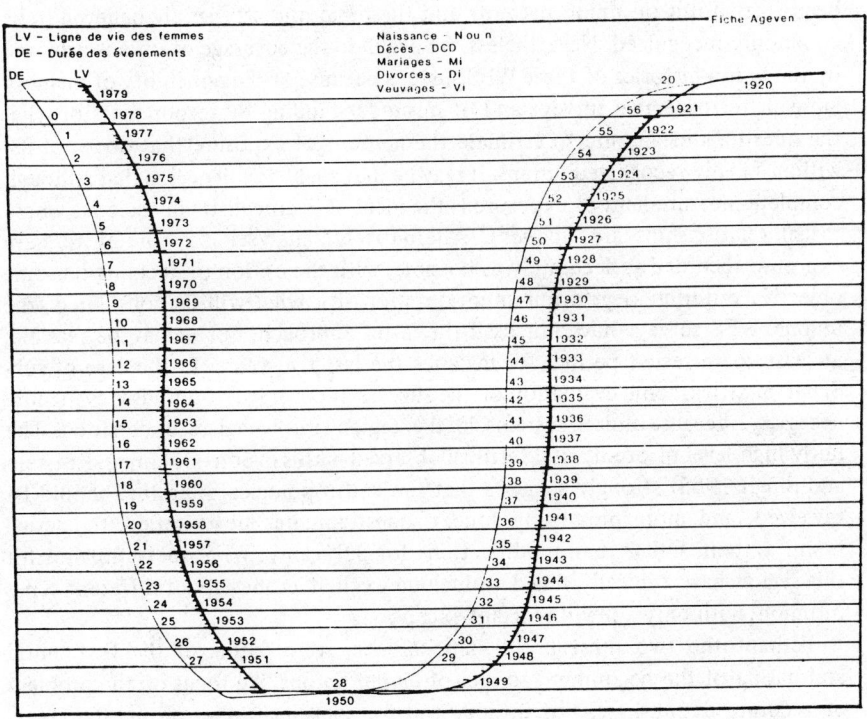

FIG. 5.10 Senegal – Age-event chart

However it is of crucial importance in Latin America, the Caribbean and sub-Saharan Africa, where informal and consensual unions are common. These non-legalized unions are important because not only do a substantial proportion of the population enter them for lengthy durations, but childbearing within these unions is frequently as high as, and occasionally higher than, that within legal marriage. Thus, if exposure to the risk of pregnancy is to be accurately estimated, time spent in both formal and informal unions must be obtained.

In the case of the Caribbean and Latin America, a fair amount of research has been carried out on union patterns and the basic union types are believed to be commonly recognized. Nevertheless, we evaluate the coverage of unions achieved by the union histories of these WFS surveys because of the possibility of memory lapse in retrospective surveys and of misunderstanding by respondents of what the questions mean, and to estimate the amount of exposure that does not fall within socially recognized unions. It may be that analysts will decide that although complete measurement of exposure is the ideal, it is unrealistic in societies where casual relationships are frequent. Alternatively, analysts may prefer to have exposure recorded as accurately as possible, with the option of deciding on some objective criterion (e.g. a minimum duration) for what will be considered true unions. WFS surveys have not used the latter approach, but it may be feasible, at least for a recent period, for instance the last five years. In the case of sub-Saharan Africa, some evaluation of the success in coverage of unions is even more necessary, because union systems in the region are even less understood. The fairly high level of pre-marital fertility observed in this region (Goldman, Rutstein and Singh 1985) strongly suggests that the anthropological literature should be reviewed, and more pre-testing done, if questionnaires are to reflect the actual union system. Other than modifications for polygamy, WFS questionnaires for this region have typically failed to include explicit probes about different types of union, with only a few important exceptions.

Perhaps the two most problematic aspects were dating of the first union and dating of the beginning and end of earlier unions. We focus on the problem of accurate dating here, but in addition, we consider probes on marital status and the special topic of polygamy.

Dating the first union

The definition of union or marriage itself influenced the date obtained. The aim of WFS surveys was to obtain the date of first sexual exposure within a union. Where legal/customary marriage was the primary type of union, the difficulty was to ensure that the date of consummation, and not the date of the formal ceremony, was obtained. Where consensual or common law or visiting unions were common, the date of the earliest union was the desired measure, and it was important to probe even currently married women about the date when their sexual relationship began, rather than obtaining the date of their legal marriage. In those societies where informal unions were common, the age at first sexual intercourse would have been an additional useful point in measuring the beginning of exposure, because casual relationships which may not be considered to be a union, or which may be with a partner other than the partner of the first union, would be otherwise omitted.

Although countries had in common the intention of obtaining at least the date of first exposure within a union, very different approaches were used to achieve this aim. In the case of societies where legal/customary marriage was essentially the only form of union, and where a formal ceremony might precede or postdate the beginning of cohabitation, the best approach for avoiding confusion is to obtain either both dates, or one date and the duration of the gap before or after it. Only Bangladesh, Tunisia and the Philippines took this approach, and the results showed that it was very useful; 21 per cent of women in Bangladesh started cohabiting only after an appreciable period following the marriage ceremony, with an average delay of 22 months; in the Philippines 15.5 per cent of couples started living together before marriage, and their average period of pre-marital cohabitation was 8.5 months, while another 1 per cent began to live together after marriage, with an average delay of 6 months. In the case of Tunisia 35.8 per cent of couples had no delay between formal ceremony and cohabitation while 57.3 per cent started living together on average 15 months after the ceremony, and 6.9 per cent legalized their union after a period of cohabitation. More typically, only one date was obtained, the intention being to obtain the date of cohabitation. Other countries where the problem could arise, in Asia, the Middle East and North Africa, asked for the date of the consummation ceremony, or used a term which translates as 'living together', rather than the marriage ceremony itself. While this is a reasonable approach, it is less certain to avoid confusion than if both dates are obtained.

In countries where legal/customary marriage is not the only type of union, and where other types of union are equally recognized and could be of equally long duration, probing for the date of the first union should take a different form. Not only should women in marital unions be probed about the existence of an informal pre-marital union with their current partner, but probes should also be included about informal unions with partners other than the partner in the union reported as the first. Finally, the date of first sexual intercourse would be a helpful additional piece of information.

Probing for the date of the first relationship may best be done in the form of a set of questions coming after current status is established, but separate from the union history. This was done in Ivory Coast as follows:

1 Current status established.

2 How many times married.

3 If more than once, questions then phrased in terms of 'your first union' rather than 'your union'.

4 If marriage, date of marriage obtained (special probing for customary marriages, which may involve a delay in the start of cohabitation).

5 Probing civil marriages and customary marriages where cohabitation began at the date of the marriage about whether lived together before marriage.

6 Probing everyone, including those in a 'union libre' about whether had sexual relations with their (first) husband before living together.

This detailed probing showed that about one-quarter of women had customary marriages with a later date of consummation, about 10 per cent of ever-in-union women started living with their partners before the date of marriage, and about one-quarter of all ever-in-union women had sexual relations with their partner before starting to live together. A direct implication of these additional probes is their effect in reducing the proportion of 'pre-union' births. In the case of Ivory Coast, 20 per cent of first births occurred before the date of the first union as declared by women, but probing for the date of consummation reduced this to 12 per cent, and it was further reduced to 8 per cent when the date of first sexual relations with the first partner was obtained.

Even in the Ivory Coast survey, some further probing would have been desirable concerning unions with partners other than the one with whom the first union was formed. The existence of some pre-union births, even after the date of first sexual relations with the first partner was established, supports this suggestion. It should be recognized, however, that in a sexually free society, even if all unions/partnerships are recorded, some out-of-union births will be unavoidable.

Typically, most countries in Africa and Latin America used a much less thorough approach in probing for the date of first exposure. In both regions, the phrase 'begin to live together' was used in dating both the current union and earlier unions in the union history, and, in Latin America, consensual unions were recognized in coding type of union. However most countries used no additional probes on living together before marriage or casual relationships before the first union or marriage. A few partial exceptions exist; e.g. Benin and Cameroon obtained the date of first intercourse separately, Nigeria asked interviewers to probe to make sure that the date given as the start of unions/marriages was the date when sexual relations began, and Mexico probed women in married unions about whether they started living together before the date of marriage, and recorded both dates.

Four Caribbean countries used a very different approach from that of the core to allow for a wide definition of unions, including one or more types of non-cohabiting unions. Although these countries probed thoroughly for current exposure status, and ascertained whether the woman had *ever* been in each type of union, there was no specific probing on the reported date of the first union to ascertain whether, for example, a woman reporting the first union as married had been in a common law or visiting union before. In addition, there was no probing about possible unions preceding that reported as the first. One result of this failure to probe heavily for the first sexual relationship, as well as failure to ask for the date of first intercourse in most of the sub-Saharan African and Latin American/Caribbean countries is that the proportion of pre-union births is frequently about 10 per cent, and occasionally as high as 15–20 per cent, while the proportion of pre-union conceptions is even higher (see Goldman, Rutstein and Singh 1985). These results strongly imply a need for additional probing, following the approach of Ivory Coast.

Retrospective dating of marriages and dissolutions

Accurate dating of periods of exposure over the respondent's lifetime was a second aim of the marriage history. The percentage of time which is spent outside unions after the first marriage is usually between 10 and 15 per cent at the national level: this is not an insignificant amount of time lost, and moreover, it would vary much more among individual women, thereby becoming a significant factor in analyses which use the individual as the unit. It can become a particularly important factor if much of this time is lost early in the reproductive period, when its effect on fertility is greater. Correct dating of the beginning and end of unions is important if this factor is to be a useful input into analysis.

A few pieces of evidence available on this subject suggest that some gaps in the coverage of unions still exist. In Haiti, Jamaica and Trinidad and Tobago the mean number of unions by age groups stabilized above age 35 (Tardieu 1984; Singh 1982; Hunte 1983). In the Dominican Republic, Ecuador and Paraguay, a small decline in the mean above age 45 was found, a trend which strongly suggests that older women omitted some unions (Guzmán 1980; Herrera de Rivadeneira 1984; Schoemaker 1984). In addition, in an analysis of 28 countries, comparison of Bongaarts's indices of marriage based on exposure during the five-year period before interview and on current marital status, suggests either that dissolution of unions was under-reported in the last five years by about 5 per cent on average, or that current status reports omit some women currently in union: the first seems the more likely explanation (Casterline, Singh, Cleland and Ashurst 1984). Finally, fertility outside reported unions, during the five years before survey, was estimated at about 7 per cent in Haiti and among non-Indians in Trinidad and Tobago and Guyana, but was as high as 11 per cent in Jamaica even with extensive categories of union types identified (Lightbourne and Singh 1982 for Guyana and Jamaica, and our estimates for Haiti and Trinidad and Tobago).

Apart from problems of accurate recall of dates in the past, particularly where informal unions are concerned, another possible reason for inadequate coverage of unions is the definition of unions being used. Generally, most countries limited the definition of a union to one that involved living together, and where non-cohabiting unions were recognized, the implication of some degree of stability in the union was contained in the definition, e.g. the use of the phrase 'a steady partner' in the English-speaking Caribbean. In societies where informal unions occur, and where dissolution of unions is at a moderately high level, it is in any case to be expected that a proportion of conceptions and births will occur in the period between unions. Nevertheless, it is also likely that unions of a more temporary or casual nature than those allowed for by the usual definitions exist.

One approach to dealing with this situation is to link the union and birth histories, either by combining them literally, or by obtaining the name of fathers of children in a separate birth history, and probing in the union history for fathers who are not reported as partners. This approach was used by Haiti, where the name was obtained of the father of each pregnancy in the birth history, and the name of each partner, in the union history, as well as the names of children for that partner. The intention was that the interviewer should interrelate this information for probing, but in practice, apparently, this was often not done. Nevertheless, Haiti has negligible pre-union fertility, unlike other countries with informal unions; however the percentage of births in the five years before interview which occured outside unions (7 per cent), was about the same as that of some other Caribbean countries, although it was less than that of Jamaica (11 per cent). It is likely that the separation of the two histories made cross-referencing difficult. An integrated table covering both births and marriages would make this approach more feasible, and may well be worth considering for some societies especially for the recent period.

Use of probes in obtaining dates of marriage

Apart from the general issue of defining what is to be measured, the form of questions and the use of probes to obtain dates is very important. The original core questionnaire did not specifically provide probes for cases where a calendar date was not known: the month and year alone were asked. This was presumably done with the intention of countries adding their own probes, where this was considered necessary. Indeed, several of the earlier countries did add detailed probing for dates, even before the 1977 'Modifications to the Core Questionnaires' recommended some probes: age, if the date of beginning union was unknown, and duration of union if the date of dissolution was unknown.

Although several countries used no probes at all, and in these cases the interviewer and respondent together estimated a year, it would be preferable to have the information recorded in the form in which it was reported, rather than require the interviewer, under the pressure of conducting the interview, to convert age at time of event, years ago or durations into calendar years, unless an age-event chart is used. Provision of space in the questionnaire for recording information in at least two possible forms, if not specification of all possible probes, would seem desirable, especially where it is already known or expected that obtaining dates will be problematic. This would avoid the situation where interviewers sometimes enter two different types of answer (e.g. in Nigeria, calendar year and years ago) in the same place because separate spaces had not been provided. The event chart is also clearly a useful aid for dating of marriages, because it allows easy checking of the consistency of the other events against marriages, and use of other events to help in the estimation of dates of marriage.

The high proportions of women who did not give a calendar year for marriages/unions, seen for some countries where this information was recorded, strongly supports the need to probe for dates (see Chidambaram and Sathar 1984).

Examination of cases where more than one probe was used showed that substantial proportions of women respond to each consecutive probe, and in the case of Benin, where a final code of 'don't know' was allowed, almost 5 per cent of women still were unable to answer after calendar date, age and duration were asked.

While the use of two or even three consecutive probes for 'don't know' cases is clearly useful, obtaining several measures of the same event for each woman is obviously excessive. While it allows the possibility of cross-checking dates, some ranking of types of answer ultimately will have to be used to decide on a single value where inconsistent results are obtained, and this ranking may just as well be introduced in the questions. Thus, it seems that, unless multiple recording of dates is being done for a special experimental purpose, it may be simpler to use alternative forms of dating only as probes for 'don't knows'.

Probes on current marital status

Probes on current marital status were used by most countries which had all-women samples. Typically, the countries which used all-women samples were characterized by the existence of informal unions. In such samples it is possible for women to report themselves as never in any union, or currently not in a union, even though they are actually in an informal union, because they consider that the interviewer may not be interested in recording these types of union. Single women can be asked whether they had lived with someone before (or had a union before) and if so, whether they were currently living with someone. A third possible question is either to ascertain the age at first intercourse separately from questions on marriages/unions, or to ask single women who had never lived with anyone whether they had ever had sexual relations. In addition to probing single women about their exposure status, a few countries also asked women who were currently separated, widowed or divorced, whether they were currently living with someone.

The results of using these probes, in a few African and Latin American countries, is shown in table 5.3. The usefulness of the probes varies widely. In three cases a substantial number of women who would otherwise have been incorrectly classified as never in union or not currently in union were detected by the added probes (Ivory Coast, Costa Rica and Panama), and in one case (Cameroon), where about half of all never-married women had had sexual intercourse, probes on union status, had they been used, might have found that some of these women had been in unions also. However in all other countries (8 out of the 12 which used one or more of these probes), the number of women found to be incorrectly classified was very small, usually under ten.

These results suggest that there is a place for probes in some countries. Their failure in other countries may be due to differences in the interviewers' training in the use of these questions and awareness of their importance. Alternatively, differences in marriage/union systems between countries could have produced a genuine difference in the need to use these questions: informal unions or

TABLE 5.3

Results of probing women who are either never married or not currently married

Country	Single Living with someone now?	Lived with someone before?	Sep/Wid/Div Living with someone now?	Had sexual relations though never in a union
Benin	7/452	4/452	21/133	NA
Cameroon	NA	NA	NA	406/827
Ghana	0/1179	NA	8/517	NA
Ivory Coast	141/1004	89/1004	86/346	NA
Kenya	1/869	9/869	NA	NA
Senegal	7/522	2/522	9/180	56/522[a]
Costa Rica	27/1007	82/1007	31/376	257/1007
Panama	20/555	37/555	52/531	68/555
Mexico	NA	0/1055	NA	NA
Dominican Rep.	NA	4/862	NA	NA
Venezuela	NA	0/1645	NA	NA

Note: The left hand figure denotes the number of women who gave a positive response to the probe, while the right hand figure shows the total number of women who were asked the probe.

[a] 56 single women had one or more children. Number who had sexual relations is probably higher.

pre-marital relationships may not exist or women may have had no hesitation in reporting those unions in answer to the initial question on current union status. It is worth noting, however, that the Latin American countries with low levels of positive response to probes asked only one of the four possible probes, and it is possible that inclusion of more of these probes could have obtained different results. While it is possible, in societies where extra-marital fertility is high, that these probes will introduce some pressure on women to answer yes, it is still worth while to use these probes to maximize coverage. Moreover it is easy for analysts to omit unions shorter than some minimum duration, since the duration of all unions will be recorded. In conclusion we recommend that all countries where informal unions occur with some frequency should take these results into consideration when designing further surveys, especially for those countries with similar marriage/union systems. In addition, all such countries should seriously consider including a question on the age at first intercourse for all women.

Probe on the status of currently married women

The core questionnaire included a check question probing all women who said they were currently married, primarily in order to see whether they were in fact permanently separated. Women were asked if their husband ordinarily lived in their household, and if not, whether he was away for the time being, or whether they had stopped living together for good. Most countries followed this question sequence exactly as recommended. The results, shown in table 5.4 for surveys where this information is readily accessible, suggest that the questions were not justified for the reason they were used, that is, to identify women who report that they are currently married while actually separated. Where the core questions were used as recommended, the number of such women who were located was negligible: 0 in five cases, under 10 in seven cases, under 20 in ten cases and slightly over 20 in two other cases.

However, the first question in the sequence, whether the husband was resident in the same household, obtained a significantly high level of response; usually about 5 per cent of currently married women were temporarily separated, and in a few countries as many as 20 per cent of women (in Lesotho, 33 per cent) were in this situation. While these separations may be of relatively short duration, it is also possible that some proportion of these women may prefer to report a separation as temporary, when it is of substantial duration and likely to end in permanent separation, because they hope to save the union or marriage. We should recall that the first question asks whether the husband 'ordinarily' lives in the household, not whether he is away at the time of interview: it seems that these reported separations are therefore unlikely to be very short-term absences. These results do show, however, that a significant level of separation exists in most countries, and some probing may be therefore necessary. An objective approach to measuring separation may be better: a currently married woman could be asked whether her husband is living in the household at the time of the

TABLE 5.4

Results of the probe questions on the status of currently married women

Country	Husband lives in same household	Sep. households, sees him regularly	Temporarily separated	Union ended	Total number currently married
Africa					
Benin	3104	277	69	11	3450
Cameroon	5728	—	325	10	6053
Ghana	3140	1078	208	4	4426
Ivory Coast	4193	413	36	0	4642
Kenya	4566	121[a]	993	13	5680
Lesotho	1940	—	1211	9	3151
Senegal	2922	361	—	16	3283
Mauritania	2298	—	603	6	2901
Morocco	3453	—	227	15	3680
Sudan (North)	2630	—	226	0	2856
Asia and Pacific					
Syria	4239	—	73	0	4312
Yemen AR	1960	—	490[b]	0	2450
Bangladesh	5484	—	266	22	5750
Sri Lanka	6052	—	129	14	6181
Indonesia	7739	—	235	10	7974
Malaysia	5473	—	333	NA	5806
Philippines[c]	5958	—	728	1	6686

Americas

Colombia	2775	—	52	15	2827
Peru	4785	—	256	18	5041
Venezuela	2101	—	179	0	2280
Costa Rica	2545	—	81	8	2626
Dominican Rep.	1739	—	45	24	1784
Mexico	5537	—	103	3	5640
Panama	2517	—	134	1	2651
Guyana	2298	—	—	216[d]	2298
Jamaica	882	—	—	81[d]	882
Trinidad & Tobago	1892	—	—	201[d]	1892

Europe

Portugal	4750	—	143	19	4893

[a] In Kenya, the code is 'staying with you at the moment', i.e. a temporary relationship, but not involving separate households.

[b] 406 living abroad: 84 temporarily separated, living in the country.

[c] Question asked of all women currently married, non-pregnant and having resumed sexual relations since last pregnancy (if any).

[d] Only married women were asked, and all who were not currently living together were considered to be separated. Common law wives and visiting women were omitted.

interview or visiting her regularly (in the case of the Caribbean and in African polygamous unions), and if not, how long he has been absent. Data analysts could then decide how to make use of the reported durations of absence. An additional question could be asked on the reason for the separation. Some measurement of separations, perhaps more detailed, is mandatory in countries where as many as 10 per cent or more of currently married women are separated at the time of the survey. However it is also likely to prove useful in the average case where 4–5 per cent of women are separated, especially if these women are concentrated at the younger, more fecund ages, which could well be the case when separations are caused by a search for employment.

These probe questions also bring into focus the need for allowing for the situation in some African countries where the couple live in separate households. Depending on the type of household structure, this type of living situation may make questions on frequency of intercourse even more useful. Where the 'separation' is simply an artefact of the WFS's type of definition of household, and couples live in the same housing compound, this may not be an important factor. But if separate households implies living in different compounds (as for example among polygamous wives in some parts of Nigeria), then this could be an important factor. These results suggest that there is a definite need for better recording of the living arrangements in these societies.

Polygamy

When the questionnaire instruments were originally being designed, the idea of developing a module on polygamy was considered. However no module was produced, and each country took its own preferred approach. This could have resulted in poor decisions and non-comparable data between countries. In general, however, countries opted for the same questions, the number of co-wives (all nine countries which included the topic) and the rank of the respondent among the wives (seven of the nine countries). Two unfortunate omissions occurred; rank was not asked in Ghana, and in Senegal rank of married women only was asked, not rank of women in consensual unions. Two of the latest surveys, in Benin and Nigeria, went further and obtained the number of co-wives in each earlier union, which may be a useful addition for future surveys. It is not clear that a special module is required, since the questions are few and simple; however the existence of a standard set might have avoided the two omissions described above.

5.6   Summary and recommendations

This chapter has examined WFS practice in the questions and techniques for measurement of the main demographic events covered by these fertility surveys: age in the household and individual surveys, the retrospective birth or pregnancy history, and nuptiality, both current and past. While greater field efforts will generally bring better results, a fundamental limitation should not be forgotten, namely dates of events can only be reported if they are known, and this knowledge depends upon whether the events and their dates are significant and memorable. Where a substantial proportion of the population can only report rough estimates of dates, the most useful solution may well be that the interviewer should flag such events, which would make possible special adjustments in analysis. Although usable histories of births and marriages have proved to be possible to collect, the range in completeness of date reporting among countries must be borne in mind in any analysis. While imputation of dates is possible, given the interlinked nature of the birth history, this should not be allowed to conceal the fact that in several countries only half or less of births were dated exactly. Within these basic limitations, however, it is nevertheless worth while to work towards improvement of questions and fieldwork procedures.Despite the fact that a great deal of effort went into the initial design of the core questionnaire, and into subsequent country-specific modifications, the evidence of this assessment shows that many deficiencies in the data resulted from question design.

In obtaining age, it is clear that the low quality of household data is partially due to the insufficient emphasis placed on designing the relevant questions, as compared to the individual survey. This is seen in the fact that only 12 countries asked date of birth for household members while all countries did so in their individual surveys. However in both the household and individual surveys better question design is necessary to improve the quality of data collected and to avoid interviewer effects such as misuse of instructions, transference of data and unrecorded reconciliation of inconsistencies. The use of the full birth history and the results obtained by the WFS approach is probably the major and most important WFS contribution to fertility surveys. The technique of the integrated birth and pregnancy history table has given good results both on coverage and dating. It is difficult to evaluate exactly the relative success of the different variations (segment, intervals or chronological approach) of this technique. However, its superiority over the recommended format of two separate tables is an undisputed fact. The age-event chart technique has been found useful for increasing both consistency and accuracy of the retrospective data. In contrast to this success the detailed set of questions on non-live births has failed to fulfil its original purpose (better coverage of live births) and therefore should be reconsidered.

The analytical utility of a full history is its ability to describe levels and trends in fertility in a life-cycle or cohort approach. While the history has now been shown to be workable it should not be forgotten that it is a demanding technique, and for different analytical purposes less demanding approaches may be more suitable. For simply measuring the current situation, in regard to the impact of proximate determinants on fertility, a shorter period may be sufficient, for instance 1–5 years before interview. For family planning programme needs, these more restricted fertility measures may be sufficient.

WFS surveys used a very wide definition of 'marriage', including all informal unions. This proved successful in Latin America and the Caribbean, where typologies of union types already existed and were well known. However, in Africa, where the standard marriage history section was used for most countries, because of the lack of appropriate typologies and also because of failure to exploit existing anthropological and sociological knowledge on nuptiality, this was clearly an inappropriate decision. The type of union or marriage system itself influenced the questions which were used to obtain marital status and the dates of unions. Thus, use of probe questions improved reporting of the date of the first union, current marital status and consequently measurement of exposure. Nevertheless it is clear from the results obtained that problems in the definitions of unions and in question design continue to exist (e.g. confusion between the date of formal marriage and the date of consummation, failure to probe for unions of brief duration, especially before the first reported union, and failure to recognize explicitly types of union other than formal marriage in most African countries as was done in the Caribbean). Again, as in the case of the birth history, although the marriage history has proved to be feasible to collect, it may not always be necessary. The date of first cohabitation may be sufficient for the purposes of some surveys, for example.

It is unfortunate that, in the absence of experimental research, we cannot make conclusive recommendations. However we think that many of the above-mentioned problems can be solved by improvements in the design of questions. Therefore we make the following recommendations, recognizing that their relevance and feasibility will depend on the particular circumstances of each country.

Recommendations

1 More effort should be spent on obtaining a good estimate of age in the household interview, preferably for all members, but at least for women who could be in the eligibility range, e.g. 10–55.

   We suggest that consultation of documents should be written into the questionnaire, with rules about their use tailored to suit each country's own situation. The alternative would be date of birth and age, with reconciliation of differences by the interviewer occurring in a third location. We also suggest that the phrase 'in completed years' should be printed on the questionnaire, as a reminder to the interviewer of what is to be obtained or estimated. Where thorough questioning of this kind is used, and the respondent is the eligible woman herself, then the age/date of birth can be transferred to the individual questionnaire. A similar set of questions is recommended in the individual questionnaire, for cases where the woman was not the household respondent.

2 Biases in the selection of individual respondents from the household interview are common. The marital status bias can be handled by including single women in the individual survey, perhaps with a special short questionnaire. This would also have the extremely valuable advantage of simplifying the analysis of fertility and nuptiality data. The bias at the upper end of the age

range, in the age group 45–49 can be dealt with either by making the selection of women from the household survey independent of the interviewers for the individual survey, or by expanding eligibility to 50–54. The second step is to be recommended for in-depth fertility surveys, when past trends are of interest. For surveys focusing on the current situation, the 45–49 age group contributes little and therefore errors in coverage are less important.

3 The use of the birth history should be continued where an in-depth survey is being carried out. Where the quality of dating events is known to be poor, or where there is substantive interest in the level of foetal wastage or induced abortion, then an integrated history is recommended, rather than the addition of a separate non-live birth table. If non-live births are being obtained as an aid in dating live births, then duration of the pregnancy and the birth interval in which it occurred are all that is needed. The maternity history, asked in reverse chronological order, may have a slight advantage over the more common or chronological mode. Again, we recommend, even more strongly than for obtaining the ages of adults, that consultation of documents be written into the birth history. The importance of obtaining the exact age at death, in months and years, and not losing this detail by grouping ages, is stressed.

Aids in dating events are recommended in some situations. An age–event chart should be used wherever dating events is difficult, and perhaps where knowledge of dates is good but an informal union system exists. The birth history conversion chart is useful where knowledge of dates is high but dates may be reported in two or more calendar (or other) forms.

4 Probing on current and past marital status for all-women samples is highly recommended. The probe on separation status of currently married women did not seem useful for the reasons it was designed, but revealed a moderate to high level of separation in many countries. We suggest that consideration should be given to establishing the duration of current separation of women who are nevertheless actually married.

Dating of the first union in countries where either cohabitation occurs before marriage, or consummation occurs after a formal marriage, needs special probing. We suggest that the dates of each event should be obtained, or one date and the duration to the next, as the surest way of avoiding the possibility of confusing the two. Despite all efforts made so far, some improvements in probing for the date of the first relationship can still be made in societies where informal unions are common. Apart from added probes, the age–event chart may assist in coverage and dating of unions, by allowing a visual consistency check of dates of unions and births. Another possibility is to have an integrated union and birth history.

The marriage/union history should be kept as part of the questionnaire except in cases where the aim of a survey is limited to current status description for planning or programmatic needs. Information on marriage and union patterns and changes in these over time is important in its own right (e.g. for legal and social welfare matters); but in addtion, changes in exposure will be increasingly important as an explanatory factor in fertility change, as modernization increases. It would be a great advantage to be able to study trends by combining WFS surveys with any future studies. Moreover, it is worth maintaining the history even where there is little dissolution, for purposes of comparability since, in such countries, little interviewing time will be lost on this section.

Finally, especially for African countries, design of the section on marriage should make use of existing anthropological and sociological material on nuptiality.

5 This chapter shows that experimental research is crucial if we are to improve survey methodology in general and question design and content in particular. Experimental studies can be carried out with little extra cost, if they are incorporated into the pre-test or into the main survey, and are therefore to be recommended.

Notes

1. We will not be looking at the measurement of some factors (breastfeeding, amenorrhoea, coital frequency, infecundity and contraceptive use) which have been discussed in other papers. See Vaessen (1984), Ferry and Smith (1983), Cleland and Kalule-Sabiti (1984), Laing (forthcoming), and Page, Cleland and Hobcraft (1984).
2. Senegal was a special case where only the year of birth was recorded. That this was largely obtained by converting age to a calendar year can be inferred from the fact that a month was recorded for only 27 per cent of household members.
3. Date of birth was asked first, and age was also obtained for everyone, with inconsistencies of over one year being probed and resolved. If date and age were not known, documents were then requested, and if those were unavailable, a historical calendar was used to help estimate age. This list was used in conjunction with other data such as age and number of children or age at marriage, to reach an estimate. Other household members could also be consulted and in the last resort, personal appearance was used to make an estimate.
4. The date of birth was asked, and confirmed with documents (for those born after 1960, if they were not residents of the four large cities, and for all persons resident in these cities). Where documents were not available or not acceptable, reported year or age was cross-checked with probes from a historical calendar, or for women over age 12, by use of an age-event chart.
5. See section 5.4 for a discussion of age-event charts.

6

Translation of Questionnaires into Local Languages

Martin Vaessen
Chris Scott
Jane Verrall
Sidiki Coulibaly

6.1 Introduction

This chapter examines some of the linguistic problems affecting data collection through face-to-face interviewing, with special attention to the problems presented by multilingual countries.

We take as a starting assumption that every interview should be conducted in the native language of the respondent. This objective can be achieved in three ways:

1 Through the use of a local language questionnaire

2 Through on-the-spot translation by the interviewer

3 Through the use of an interpreter.

This chapter discusses the relative merits of options 1 and 2 on the basis of information collected by the WFS. Option 3 is, for obvious reasons, rejected out of hand as a *main* method of data collection.

6.2 Background

The problem

All countries have at least one official language. However, in many countries this language is more a vehicle for use by the bureaucracy and the educational system than a means of daily communication among ordinary people. In some countries literally scores of different languages are spoken (Ware 1977). The problem is particularly acute in Africa but it is also serious in much of Asia. In many cases low participation in educational programmes has contributed to the maintenance of local languages as the prime, or only, means of everyday communication. As a result of this situation, in multilingual countries the official language is often unusable as a vehicle of communication with the masses, in part or all of the country. The need to interview respondents in their native language is therefore clear.

Given this situation, any nationwide data collection effort must deal with the problem of how to ensure that the meaning of each question is correctly conveyed in all languages used. If the wrong question is asked, the interpretation of the data is vitiated. If the meaning is not exactly the same in all the languages, it is impossible to be sure that differences and differentials observed reflect reality rather than being artifacts of translation.

In deciding between on-the-spot translation by the interviewer and local language questionnaires, the major issue is therefore which of these two methods best ensures that the intended meaning of the questions is preserved in all languages.

As early as 1975 the WFS conducted pilot surveys in Zaire and Ghana in which the linguistic issue received special attention. Some interviews conducted through on-the-spot translation by the interviewer were tape-recorded and analysed. The main conclusion can be summed up by quoting from the report on the Ghana pilot (Gaisie and Gyepi-Garbrah 1976): 'There was a tendency among the interviewers using the English version of the questionnaire to paraphrase some of the questions to such an extent that almost invariably the actual meaning of the questions was partially or completely distorted. The majority of them were also guilty of skipping long introductions to questions and also of omitting an important part or parts of a question or questions when translation was done simultaneously with the delivery of the questionnaire.' Essentially similar conclusions were reported from Zaire, where some specific translation errors were noted.[1]

The Ghana pilot also provided some detailed insight into the problems of designing verbatim local language questionnaires. Some specific issues pinpointed were:

1 Difficulty of translating the concept 'household' in any of the three languages tested (Ewe, Asante-Twi and Dagbani).

2 Difficulty in translating terms to do with sexual issues or menstruation, due to the need to avoid direct reference or mention, which would be socially insulting or offensive.

3 Difficulty of referring to death and pregnancy. These terms have to be paraphrased by using locally accepted expressions.

The basic message emanating from this African experience was that: 'Knowledge of local variations of a particular language and certain idioms is therefore one of the important attributes that a translator should possess in addition to his ability to speak the language fluently and also write it very well' (Gaisie and Gyepi-Garbrah 1976).

It is important to note that whatever the mode of interviewing finally selected, survey execution in multilingual countries will always be a difficult task. Whether on-the-spot translation by the interviewer or local language questionnaires are used, the problem will always remain of matching the right interviewer with the right respondent. First, interviewers are needed who can handle the different languages to be used. They should therefore be recruited from among native speakers of each of these languages. If important educational differences exist between language groups, this in turn may pose training problems and result ultimately in different quality interviewers. Supervision also poses a major problem since supervisors cannot generally handle all the languages their interviewers may have to deal with. In some countries dispersion of language groups over the country presents almost insuperable problems with interview assignments.

It is therefore fair to say that the logistic problems of interviewing in a multilingual setting are just as demanding as the purely linguistic considerations. Finally, the logistic problems are aggravated where a specific timetable and budget have been set for the field operation which take no account of the language issue.

WFS policy

From the outset the WFS recognized the problems involved in questionnaire translation. Core questionnaires were produced in London in English, French, Spanish and Arabic. The comparability of these questionnaires was ensured through thorough discussion and office testing and, in the case of Spanish, through a pre-test in Colombia. In all cases where these variants were used there was always insistence on a pre-test to ensure that necessary local variations were incorporated in the questionnaire and were understood.

Concerning local languages different from the four WFS languages, the WFS insisted on translation and back-translation by two different linguists, ending up with a reconciliation of any differences, and also a field pre-test. Based on the results of the Zaire and Ghana pilot surveys the WFS policy was that, as far as possible, interviews in the local languages were to be conducted on the basis of a verbatim version of the questionnaire in these local languages by interviewers who were native speakers of each of the languages involved.

In many countries the main languages to be used could be easily established, but in others this was a more hazardous task.[2] The WFS advocated that, as a general rule, at least 80 per cent of the interviews should be conducted on the basis of verbatim questionnaires. In some countries this rule came into conflict with another rule of thumb which advised against the preparation of a language version likely to cover less than 10 per cent of the sample.

This policy regarding the use of local languages resulted in 16 out of the 42 WFS countries using more than one language version of the questionnaire. The situation is summarized in table 6.1.

In the following sections we will deal with two main issues: first, is the use of local language questionnaires in multilingual countries really worth the effort, and second, to what extent did fieldwork problems affect the proper execution of surveys in multilingual countries?

Concerning the first issue, the WFS realized some time ago that little relevant information was available in its programme apart from the limited material from the Ghana and Zaire pilots. This realization was intensified by the need to keep on convincing countries that local language questionnaires were a necessity for a

TABLE   6.1

Number of language versions of questionnaire, by countries

No. of language versions used	Countries
1	26 countries[a]
2	Bangladesh, Malaysia
3	Fiji, Nepal, Sri Lanka
4	Mauritania, Senegal
5	Pakistan, Peru
7	Benin, Nigeria
9	Philippines
10	Ghana
11	Ivory Coast, Kenya
14	Cameroon
	(Total: 42 countries)

[a] Includes Sudan (North) and Indonesia, which used only one printed version but also used trained interviewers in oral versions of other languages, three in Sudan and four in Indonesia.

successful survey. Many countries had previously relied solely on the interviewer to put the right question to the respondent by on-the-spot translation and improvisation. It was therefore difficult to convince some of the need for translated and printed questionnaire versions for each major language group. To allow a detailed assessment of the issue it was decided to carry out two experiments, one in the Ivory Coast[3] and one in the Philippines,[4] specially designed to evaluate the use of verbatim local language versions of the questionnaire.

On the logistics of dealing with different language versions of the questionnaire, detailed information is available from a number of WFS surveys.

6.3   Experiments in Ivory Coast and Philippines[5]

Method

The general features of both experiments can be briefly described as follows. In each location three languages were used,[6] one international and two local. A special questionnaire was prepared for the experiments. Some questions were taken from WFS surveys but many were selected from other surveys on topics unconnected with fertility, and some were made up in order to test specific points of interest. The questionnaires in the two countries differed considerably, and there was never any intention of comparing the performance of the two countries' fieldworkers.

Translation of the international into the local languages at this stage was achieved through the earlier described procedure of translation and back-translation and reconciliation of any differences.

The data collection aspect of the experiments consisted in the *sequential* execution of three series of interviews:

1 in the international language;
2 from the international into the local language through on-the-spot translation by the interviewer;
3 in the local language through the use of verbatim local language questionnaires.[7]

Two groups of 10–12 interviewers carried out the experiment in each country. All interviewers were fluent in the international language and half each were fluent in one of the two local languages.

Interviewers were trained during a period of about a week and were given verbal instruction in the translation of the international language questionnaire after having completed the initial series of interviews in that language.

A choice had to be made between (1) use of different interviewers for the different experiments and (2) use of the same interviewers. Both options presented problems. With option (1), any difference found could be attributed to chance allocation of more competent interviewers to one method than to another. This ambiguity could be eliminated only through the use of a very large sample of interviewers – perhaps 100 or more. Option (2) on the other hand would introduce the problem of contamination: interviewers having used one method might be influenced by that experience in applying a subsequent method. This could not be eliminated, but by arranging the tasks in the order mentioned above the effect might be minimized. After careful consideration, option (2) was preferred.

Another difficult choice was whether to analyse *responses* or *interviewer behaviour*. At first sight it may seem obvious that the first option is preferable; after all, it is the survey response that concerns us and, if the interviewer makes a mistake that does not affect the response, then no harm is done. Nevertheless, after careful reflection this option was rejected, for three reasons. First, to analyse responses would certainly have required a much larger experiment; second, even so, one could not expect to identify more than a fraction of the errors;[8] and third, any method of identifying errors would have to be statistical in nature and would not reveal in any precise way what had gone wrong with each question. It was therefore decided to base the experiment on the *analysis of tape recordings of interviewers' performance*. Obviously this decision led to its own problems, both practical and interpretative.

The two groups of interviewers were required to execute a total of 132 tape-recorded interviews, two for each interviewer for each of the five types (A–E) of interview involved, resulting in the interviews noted in the table on page 178.

Each interviewer did from five to ten interviews before starting to record, to allow development of reasonably stable interviewing habits. This applied to each of the five types of interviews separately. Since respondents played no role in the study, except to lend realism to the survey, there was no sampling.

Questionnaire	Language of interview		
language	International	Local 1	Local 2
International	44 (A)	22 (B)	22 (C)
Local 1		22 (D)	
Local 2			22 (E)

Interviewers were simply required to find someone who spoke fluently the language required.

In both locations the 132 tape-recorded interviews were transcribed locally. The Ivory Coast data were then coded in London, while the Philippines data were coded in Manila by personnel of the Population Institute, according to guidelines provided by the WFS on the basis of the Ivory Coast experience. Coding consisted of assigning an *error type* to each error found in the transcription in relation to the verbatim questionnaire. The following were the coded error types:

1 Small change of wording, meaning preserved

2 One response picked out or suggested

3 Alternatives not (or not all) read out

4 Large change of wording, meaning preserved

5 Change of meaning

6 Qualifying phrase omitted or changed

7 Introduction to section omitted.

The comparison of interviewer error rates by type of interview will be used to throw light on the translation issues as follows:

Types A, B, C   Baseline information for the estimation of the effect of change of language of interview when the language of the instrument remains unchanged.

Types A vs B and A vs C   How far do interviewers make translation errors?

Types B vs D and C vs E   How far are translation errors reduced by the use of verbatim questionnaire?

Problems of analysis

The coded error type is the main unit of analysis. Coding of errors proved to be the most difficult aspect of the experiments in both countries. As three different languages were used it was not possible to have a single person code all the errors. Typically at least two people were required to do this, one for each local language. Differences in criteria may well therefore have slipped in. By limiting the analysis to groups of errors most of these differences should however be eliminated, especially as far as major errors are concerned. There was generally little argument in any language about whether the question had been fully asked and the correct meaning maintained. Differences of opinion, wherever they could be identified, centred mostly on whether or not there had been a major change or a minor change of wording, without the meaning of the questions being affected.

Another problem is posed by the limited number of interviews of each type and the consequent problem of interpreting small differences.

Preliminary results

The results presented here are preliminary and a more detailed analysis is in preparation. For the purposes of this chapter the results will be presented on a highly aggregated basis, giving special emphasis to those errors which affect the quality of the data. Results are presented as the number of errors per 100 questionnaires, to facilitate dealing with small numbers, but it should be borne in mind that the number of questionnaires is small (see above). Each questionnaire contains from 60 to 70 questions. The basic statistics are presented in table 6.2.

The following are some examples of specific errors.

1 *Error types 1–4, examples:*

(a) What is your age?	instead of:	How old are you?
(b) Are you married?	instead of:	Are you married, widowed, divorced or separated?
(c) Where did you live most of the time during your childhood, in A or in B?	instead of:	Where did you live most of the time during your childhood, in A, B or C?
(d) For how many months? (after response that she did breastfeed the child)	instead of:	For how many months altogether did you breastfeed the child?

2 *Error type 5, examples:*

— Were you in Abidjan last year?	instead of:	Did you live in Abidjan a year ago?
— Do you go to the market to buy things?	instead of:	Did you buy anything in the market?
— In which month and year did you breastfeed the child?	instead of:	For how many months altogether did you breastfeed that child?

3 *Error type 6, examples:*

— How often have you been to *the* market in the last four weeks?	instead of:	How often have you been to *that* market in the last four weeks?
— Can you read?	instead of:	Can you read, say, a newspaper or letter?
— Have you ever given birth to a child who later died?	instead of:	Have you ever given birth to a child who later died, even one who lived for only a short time?

TABLE 6.2

Number of errors per 100 questionnaires by type of error and type of interview; by country

Country	Type of error	Type of interview				
		French to:			Baoule to Baoule	Dioula to Dioula
		French	Baoule	Dioula		
Ivory Coast:	Errors not affecting the meaning of the questions (1–4)	173	255	351	445	162
	Change of meaning (5)	33	532	361	91	94
	Qualifying phrase omitted or changed (6)	13	132	156	59	61
	Introduction to section omitted (7)	8	36	83	9	–
		English to:			Tagalog to Tagalog	Cebuano to Cebuano
		English	Tagalog	Cebuano		
Philippines:	Errors not affecting the meaning of the questions (1–4)	1086	2444	1600	927	719
	Change of meaning (5)	68	290	132	95	68
	Qualifying phrase omitted or changed (6)	93	886	1700	423	818
	Introduction to section omitted (7)	36	73	64	55	27

Before proceeding further it should be said that under no circumstances can the aggregate Ivory Coast and Philippines data be compared. The reasons for this are threefold: (1) different questionnaires were used in the two countries; (2) more stringent coding criteria were followed in the Philippines; (3) different quality interviewers were employed in the two locations. We also stress again that the errors are detected solely through comparison of the transcribed tape recording of the interviewer's words with the questions as printed on the questionnaire.

For all experiments and in both countries, the errors committed by the interviewers increase considerably when they are required to translate questions impromptu in the field. This is also true for all types of error. However major mistakes, such as a change of meaning or the omission of a qualifying phrase, increase much more markedly than minor errors not affecting the meaning of the questions. The latter are in any case more frequent than the other errors in any type of interview (except Cebuano to Cebuano).

The verbatim questionnaire in the local language always (except for errors not affecting the meaning of the question in Baoule to Baoule) gave error rates *between* those observed in the interviews in the international language and on-the-spot translation, being always higher than the former and lower than the latter. The seeming anomaly that verbatim interviews in international languages gave less errors than verbatim interviews in the local languages requires an explanation. It may be plausibly attributed to interviewers' lack of familiarity with the local languages in written form. Some interviewers are likely to have experienced real difficulty in reading those languages.

Compared to the impromptu translation, the local language variant of the questionnaire yielded in all cases a reduction by 50 per cent or more in the number of cases of change of meaning and omission of the qualifying phrase.

Due to the consistency of results over types of interview and countries, there remains little doubt that the use of verbatim local language versions of the questionnaire results in considerably less interviewer error than the use of on-the-spot translation by the interviewers. This is particularly true for major errors such as a change of meaning or the omission of a qualifying phrase.

One of the issues which will be stressed in the forthcoming reports on the experiments is that some types of questions hardly ever give rise to any serious error while other types are almost always problematic. Here are some examples:

Easy:
— Is that child still alive?
— Are you pregnant now?
— Are you using the pill now?

Difficult:
— A year ago, how many adults aged 15 and over, including yourself, were living in your house?
— How many children under 15 altogether?
— Do you have any daughters living with you now?
— (Aside from your own children) how many (other) boys and girls under 15 are living here with you?

— How long did it take you to get to the market on that last visit?

— Did you live in Abidjan a year ago?

A point to bear in mind is that in both the Ivory Coast and the Philippines the two local languages selected for the experiment are the most widely spoken. They were mainly selected for practical considerations, such as to avoid travel outside the capital city and the problematic recruitment of interviewers. Whenever less common languages are to be used the problems seen so far will no doubt be much more severe. It will be more difficult to recruit native speakers of those languages as interviewers and there will be less familiarity with the language in written form.

An important incidental observation in the Ivory Coast experiment was the difficulty of selecting interviewers with the required linguistic competence. The procedure was to advertise for applications and to filter applicants through two consecutive written tests, the second of which was concerned solely with linguistic ability in the designated language. This was followed by a personal interview by senior staff possessing a knowledge of the language concerned. Despite these precautions, at least two of the 22 interviewers were ultimately found (by the transcribers of the tape-recorded interviews) to speak the designated language so badly that they were frequently misunderstood by respondents. The problem arises particularly in relation to lingua franca languages, which are often popularly spoken in a version very different from that used by their native speakers. In such cases it may be inappropriate to select interviewers who are native speakers. Yet if one departs from the principle of native speaker interviewers there is real difficulty in checking the candidates' claims to linguistic competence. A further problem is that a selection interview with the candidate carried out by a professional linguist is liable to lead to emphasis on criteria such as linguistic 'purity' which have no relevance to the survey task.

A final observation is worth noting. It is sometimes argued against verbatim questionnaires that they cannot be used in a village culture where people like to chat and gossip and approach questions in a devious manner. The tape recordings clearly disprove this belief. Many of the questions — indeed most — were asked by almost all interviewers exactly as written and were evidently understood. (Even more would have been if they had been better drafted.) There can be no reasonable doubt that verbatim questionnaires are feasible.

6.4 Logistic problems in using verbatim language questionnaires in multilingual countries

Nature of the problem

In the preceding section a strong case has been made for the use of verbatim local language questionnaires, based on evidence that more accurate questioning is achieved by that procedure than through on-the-spot translation by the interviewer. The mere adoption of the former system does not, however, guarantee that interviews are carried out in the correct language if fieldwork organization and monitoring are deficient. Any language version of the questionnaire needs corresponding interviewers, native speakers of each language. Previous to the fieldwork, estimates must therefore be made of the languages likely to be needed and the number of interviews to be carried out in each. Such estimates should be based on the projected sample size and the actual distribution of the sample over linguistic regions of the country.

These estimates, once produced, will give rise to a number of questions. First, is the number of interviews to be carried out in a given language sufficient to keep the necessary interviewer(s) occupied for enough time to justify the training costs?

Second, is the geographical distribution of interviews in a given language consistent with the team approach? For example, the total number of interviews in a particular language may be only enough to require a single interviewer but may be entirely concentrated in one cluster.

These and other considerations led the WFS to recommend that any language version to be printed should cover at least 10 per cent of the total sample. Calculating on the basis of a low sample size of 4000, this would mean at least 400 interviews, which at three interviews a day would imply 133 interviewer-days, or about six interviewer-months. It would thus require three interviewers working for at least two months.

When we examine the number of interviews actually performed in each language in WFS countries we find numerous cases which fall far short of this minimum. (For details see appendix A.) For instance: in Benin only 106 interviews were done in Ditamari; in Cameroon only 20 were done in Kaka, only 114 in Matakam, 46 in Medumba and around 90 each in Duala, Bassa and Bamun; in Ghana only 30 interviews were done in Hausa and Nzema and 49 in Kasem; in the Ivory Coast only 87 in Gouro and Yacouba and 123 in Attie; in Mauritania only 121 in Wolof; in Senegal only 84 in Serer; in Pakistan only six in Baluchi; and in the Philippines only 119 in Pampango. Questionnaire versions were produced in all of these languages.

Kenya had the best distribution of languages, with a minimum of 164 in Mijikenda and hardly any interviews in languages for which there was no printed questionnaire version.

These figures reveal all too clearly the serious problems which must have been faced in most of the multilingual countries. Two conclusions seem inescapable. First, there was a reluctance by interviewers to use the less common languages, to the extent that many interviews were certainly conducted in a language other than the mother tongue of the respondent, even where an appropriate questionnaire version existed. Second, many interviewers must have interviewed in more than one language.

In many countries the geographical distribution of languages is simple: each large area has its language and very few persons are found in the area who do not speak that language fluently. Where this situation prevails, the languages of field-work are known in advance with reasonable precision and the logistic problems should be fairly easy to handle. In Africa, and particularly in West Africa, the situation is often more complex. In some countries (Cameroon is an extreme example) fragmentation is such that one cannot know, without conducting a specific study for the purpose, what languages one will find in a given selected area unit. In circumstances such as these only a first-class organization and a highly disciplined field force can ensure a correct matching of interviewers to respondents. One has only to ask what is likely to happen when an interviewer, knowing only language A and lingua franca B, encounters a respondent knowing only her native language C but possessing a smattering of B. An interview conducted falteringly in language B, with many misunderstandings, will be the inevitable result unless strong discipline has been enforced on the field force from the outset.

Evaluation

In a number of WFS surveys arrangements were made to collect linguistic information which makes it possible to calculate in detail the logistics of multi-lingual fieldwork. For Benin, Ghana, Kenya and Senegal it is possible to compare the language of the questionnaire with the language of interview. Also in these countries, with the exception of Kenya, it is known whether an interpreter was used in the interview.

The data are summarized in table 6.3. This table shows (column 1) that in Benin and Ghana only two-thirds of the interviews were carried out in the lan-guage of the questionnaire, without an interpreter. In Kenya and Senegal the figure was considerably higher, around 80 per cent.

Column (2) represents an anomaly: although the questionnaire language was used for interview an interpreter was employed. This could mean either that the interviewer selected a questionnaire which she could not use (perhaps asking the interpreter to read from it) or that she misinterpreted the question and recorded the language which she herself used instead of that used between the interpreter and the respondent.

Of the remaining interviews, the majority were carried out in a language for which a questionnaire version existed, yet that version was not used. The remainder were carried out in some other language for which there was no questionnaire.

Columns (2), (3) and (4) together represent interviews marred by assignment problems. Here the language is one for which provision was made in the survey plan, yet the wrong document was used and (in the case of columns (2) and (4) at least) the wrong interviewer was sent.

The fact that an interview is carried out in the language of the questionnaire does not guarantee that it was executed in the native language of the respondent. Thus not all the entries in column (1) necessarily represent correct assignments.

To shed light on this issue the language of interview was compared to the

TABLE 6.3

Per cent distribution of interviews according to interview and questionnaire language and use of interpreter. Four countries

Country	Interview in language of questionnaire		Interview in other language for which a questionnaire version existed		Interview in language not among questionnaire versions		Total
	Without interpreter (1)	With interpreter[a] (2)	Without interpreter (3)	With interpreter[a] (4)	Without interpreter (5)	With interpreter[a] (6)	
Benin	66	10	6	4	7	7	100
Ghana	65	2	22	2	8	1	100
Kenya	78		22		0		100
Senegal	80	1	4	10	2	3	100

[a] Where an interpreter was used the term 'language of interview' becomes ambiguous and interviewers are inclined to report the language used by *them*. In Benin and Senegal an attempt was made to clarify the question with a view to obtaining the language used between the interpreter and the respondent, but it is possible that some interviewers still misunderstood.

ethnic group of the respondent in those cases where the language of the questionnaire was the same as the language of interview. For Benin and Senegal this
could be done for all language versions. The results are shown in table 6.4.

TABLE 6.4

*Among interviews carried out in a given language,
the percentage in which respondent's ethnic group
corresponds to that language (interviews conducted
in language of questionnaire)*

Benin		Senegal	
Adja	93	Wolof	60
Fon	66	Poular	87
Yoruba	29	Mandingue	63
Dendi	40	Serer	95
Bariba	75	Total	63
Ditamari	82		
Total	61		

It is remarkable to see from this table that less than half of the Yoruba and
Dendi interviews in Benin were obtained from respondents of Yoruba and Dendi
ethnicity. Less surprisingly, only about two-thirds of the Fon and Wolof interviews corresponded to the Fon and Wolof ethnicity; no doubt this reflects the
widespread use of these languages as lingua franca. In Mandingue also, only about
two-thirds of the interviews were obtained from respondents of the Mandingue
ethnicity. The explanation of the low Yoruba, Dendi and Mandingue figures is
that these languages were used to obtain interviews from ethnic groups for which
no questionnaire version had been prepared. This happened with 64 per cent of
interviews in Yoruba, 49 per cent in Dendi and 27 per cent in Mandingue.

The counterpart of table 6.4 is table 6.5, in which the per cent distribution of
language of interview is given for ethnic groups. The data in this table clearly
reflect the importance of Wolof as a lingua franca in Senegal and, to a lesser
extent, Fon in Benin.

Overall, only 41 and 50 per cent of interviews respectively were carried out in
Benin and Senegal in the language of the questionnaire and with respondents for
whom that was their native language, without the use of interpreters.

It can thus be stated that in Benin 45 per cent (100–41–7–7) of interviews
were negatively affected by fieldwork logistics, while the equivalent figure in
Senegal was also 45 per cent (100–50–2–3).

For Ghana and Kenya comparable calculations are not at present possible. A
comparison between the interviews in a particular language and the number of
respondents of the corresponding ethnicity shows, however, that the problem is
similar across countries. A few examples are given in table 6.6.

TABLE   6.5

*Per cent distribution of language of interview by ethnic group (interviews
where questionnaire language was the same as interview language)*

Benin

Ethnicity	Language of interview						
	Adja	Fon	Yoruba	Dendi	Bariba	Ditamari	French
Adja	88	11					
Fon		89					11
Yoruba		18	53		10		19
Dendi		6		86	4		4
Bariba				6	90		3
Ditamari					6	87	6

Senegal

Ethnicity	Language of interview			
	Wolof	Poular	Mandingue	Serer
Wolof	100			
Poular	57	42		
Mandingue	40		59	
Serer	88			12

6.5   Discussion

Undoubtedly the fieldwork problems in multilingual countries are massive. The
fact that in Benin and Senegal the right respondent could be matched with the
right questionnaire in only 55 per cent of the interviews in a survey whose
organization paid more than usual attention to linguistic aspects gives some idea
of the magnitude of the problem

We have mentioned in section 6.3 the difficulties that were encountered in
the Ivory Coast experiment in establishing the linguistic competence of interviewers in languages other than their mother tongue. It is clearly desirable that
interviewers should, as far as possible, interview only in their native language.
Regrettably we have no data on the number of cases in which this ideal was
achieved. This additional assignment problem must be set aside in the present
study as an unknown factor, but certainly one that can only aggravate the
difficulties already identified.

How can the assignment problem be handled more efficiently? It is obvious
enough that better planning is necessary, but the problems are formidable. Even
if one knew exactly which language had to be used in every household of the
sample, one would not necessarily be able to deliver the right interviewer to the
right household in all cases. In countries of extreme linguistic fragmentation an

TABLE   6.6

*Examples of discrepancy between interview language
and respondent's mother tongue*

Country	Language	No. of interviews	No. in ethnic group
Ghana	Fante	623	102
	Ewe	609	434
Kenya	Kikuyu	1732	2008
	Kamba	741	980
	Luhya	948	1191
	Luo	989	1421
	Mijikenda	164	424

ideal solution may be unattainable. Nevertheless it is clear that, in countries where the language is not immediately predictable from a knowledge of the geographical location, the first requirement is a linguistic reconnaissance of the sample to identify the languages that will be encountered in each cluster. This could be accomplished at the time of the mapping, segmentation or listing operations in each sample area, provided these are completed about three months before the fieldwork is due to begin. The information collected must be centralized and rapidly analysed.

The first and most urgent problem will then be to identify the languages for which a questionnaire version is to be made. With this decision taken, work can begin on the translations. (Clearly in most multilingual countries the major languages can be identified from common knowledge, and translation of these can begin without awaiting the linguistic reconnaissance.) Perhaps as much as two months will be needed for translation, back-translation, reconciliation, typing, verification and reproduction, and this interval must be fitted in before interviewer training begins.

The second step is to identify the mix of languages for which interviewers must be recruited and to proceed with the recruitment.

The third and most difficult step is to prepare a unified plan specifying team composition and transport. This will require careful study of all the information obtained.

However, it is important to recognize that the prime problem lies not with the questionnaire but with the assignment of interviewers to respondents. The problem of questionnaires is far simpler. Once an interviewer's linguistic capabilities have been identified it is sufficient to ensure that she is sent into the field accompanied by the questionnaires she is competent to use, in numbers somewhat in excess of the amount of interviews she is expected to perform. One significant consequence of this is that the logistic problems we have identified do *not* result from the decision to use different language versions of the questionnaire. The problem of assignment must be present in any survey among a multilingual population. The WFS has been unique only in collecting the data which bring the problem to light. Moreover, if the WFS surveys, whose procedures bring the problem specifically to the attention of the survey organizers in the countries, nevertheless experienced such massive failures in interviewer assignment, it is plausible to suppose that other surveys conducted in comparable multilingual countries have typically concealed even more serious assignment deficiencies.

Thus the linguistic reconnaissance, followed by the systematic preparation of a field plan covering team composition and transport, should be considered an essential procedure for any survey in a multilingual country, whether or not different language versions of the questionnaire are used.

Finally a word should be said about the cost of preparing language versions. While the task is troublesome, there is no reason why it should be very costly. Only the translators' fees and the typists' wages are involved on the personnel side. The main cost is likely to be the increased number of questionnaire copies required to cover the uncertainty in the numbers of interviews in each language — a margin whose size will depend on the specific linguistic situation of each country.

In our view these costs are well worth the demonstrated improvement in interviewers' performance. As for the complexities of organization required in a multilingual survey, these problems are present whether or not translated questionnaires are used, and the only option is whether to face them or brush them under the carpet.

Notes

1. *Examples*: 'Do you know any method of slowing down or stopping a pregnancy?', instead of 'Do you know any method of delaying or preventing a pregnancy?' 'Did you work after you were married?', instead of 'Have you worked since you were married?'
2. In three countries (Cameroon, Ivory Coast and Haiti) WFS sponsored a special study to examine this and related linguistic issues before the survey. One of these has been published (Ware 1977).
3. Executed with the Ivory Coast Direction de la Statistique with a grant from the UK Overseas Development Administration in 1983.
4. Executed with the Population Institute of the Philippines in 1983.
5. A detailed report on each of these experiments is under preparation.
6. French, Dioula and Baoule in the Ivory Coast; English, Tagalog and Cebuano in the Philippines.
7. The experiments also included tests comparing a schedule with the verbatim questionnaire. This part of the research is not reported here.
8. The question 'Did you give birth in the last 12 months?' should yield approximately the same response distribution as 'Did you give birth last year?', since both refer to 12-month periods. Yet a survey designer who wished to ask the former could not be unconcerned to learn that fieldworkers were asking the latter.

Appendix A-Number of interviews by language of interview and country

Benin		Cameroon		Ghana	
French	247	French	1417	Asante Twi	3261
Adja	401	English	66	Fante	623
Fon	1703	Pidgin	1632	Nzema	31
Yoruba	355	Fulfulde	1932	Ga	333
Dendi	244	Matakam	114	Dangbe	116
Bariba	418	Arabe choa[a]	143	Ewe	609
Ditamari	106	Kaka	20	Dagbani	186
Goun[a]	130	Eton[a]	158	Hausa	30
Waama[a]	48	Ewondo	723	Kasem	49
Yom[a]	84	Bulu[a]	114	English	287
Other[a]	282	Fang[a]	119	Other[a]	538
Total	4018	Duala	92	Not stated	62
		Bassa	91	Total	6125
		Bamun	104		
		Medumba	46		
		Dschang	187		
		Gomala	142		
		Other[a]	521		
		Not stated	508		
		Total	8129		

[a] No questionnaire versions in these languages.

Ivory Coast[b]		Kenya		Mauritania	
French	1791	Kikuyu	1732	Hassania	2021
Attie	123	Kamba	741	Poular	949
Baoule	896	UC Swahili	670	Soninke	235
Bete	130	DC Swahili	958	Wolof	121
Dioula	2047	Luhya	948	French	155
Gouro	87	Kalenjin	513	Other[a]	10
Guere	162	Luo	989	Total	3491
Koulango	178	Mijikenda	164		
Senoufo	125	Meru	507		
Yacouba	87	Kisii	436		
More[a]	70	English	275		
Wobe[a]	3	Other[a]	34		
Dida[a]	15	Not stated	133		
Abe Lag[a]	13	Total	8100		
Peul[a]	8				
Other[a]	15				
Not stated	14				
Total	5764				

[a] No questionnaire versions prepared.
[b] No interviews in Mossi, which was one of the questionnaire versions.

Senegal		Indonesia		Malaysia	
Wolof	2881	Bahasa	2138	Bahasa	3599
Poular	630	Javanese[a]	4447	Hokkien[a]	837
Mandingue	200	Sundanese[a]	1468	Cantonese[a]	746
Serer	84	Maduranese[a]	339	Mandarin[b]	180
Dioula[a]	57	Balinese[a]	855	Other Chinese[a]	220
Other[a]	132	Other[a]	1	Tamil[b]	518
Total	3984	Not stated	119	English	231
		Total	9367	Other[a]	7
				Not stated	30
				Total	6368

Pakistan		Philippines	
Urdu	438	Tagalog	2992
Punjabi	3461	Cebuano	3026
Pushto	343	Ilocano	677
Sindi	699	Hiligaynon	1196
Baluchi	6	Bicol	449
Barahi[a]	5	Samar–Leyte	330
Total	4952	Pampango	119
		Pangasinan	130
		Maranao[a]	73
		Magindanao[a]	28
		Tansog[a]	35
		English	92
		Others[a]	121
		Total	9268

[a] No questionnaire versions prepared.
[b] 'Unofficial' translations prepared for use by interviewers.

PART III

Management, Design and Cost

7

Management of National Surveys

Martin Vaessen
Chris Scott

7.1 Introduction

In this chapter we examine the experience of the World Fertility Survey regarding survey management at the national level. The objective is to draw attention to common pitfalls in survey management and to give practical recommendations for overcoming them. The WFS made recommendations to participant countries about management procedures through its 'Survey Organization Manual' (WFS 1975e) and more directly during technical assistance visits to countries, in particular the survey design visit. Our attempt in this chapter to draw attention to deficiencies of management could be construed as criticism either of WFS procedures or of local management. However, criticism is not our primary intention; rather our aim is to assist future survey work by pinpointing commonly encountered problems and suggesting possible solutions.

7.2 The national executing agency

Participation in the WFS was essentially open to all countries. All requests from applicants were seriously considered and almost all were accepted. The very few exceptions were countries in which the survey did not appear feasible or for which funds could not be secured. As a result, the countries which joined the WFS represent a wide range of expertise in survey work.

When a request for participation was received by the WFS the first step was to approach the funding agencies for a positive indication regarding the likely availability of funds. A preliminary visit by a senior WFS staff member of about one week's duration was then arranged. The objectives of this visit were: to assess the degree of interest in a WFS survey, to determine what other programmes in the population field were ongoing or planned, to find out whether an appropriate sampling frame would be available, to evaluate the suitability of the requesting institution to carry out the survey, and to reach a provisional agreement regarding the survey's timing.

The WFS Survey Organization Manual states: 'In principle the WFS is prepared to negotiate a survey with any legitimate governmental or non-governmental organization. The actual choice of organization is determined on a case by case basis and the WFS, expecting that the country will share the goal of achieving high quality data, weighs heavily the recommendations of interested scholars

and officials from the country, discussing the matter with all concerned.' In practice, things hardly ever happened this way: the statement ignores the political
realities behind a bid for a WFS survey. The request for participation normally
came from a government institution; even if it became apparent during a preliminary visit that some other institution was better suited to carry out the survey,
it was extremely difficult to pass over the requesting institution. Furthermore,
the ISI had decided in advance to work for preference with national statistical
offices, whose directors were all *ex officio* members of the ISI. Through prior
communications from the ISI, it was generally these directors who were the first
to become aware of the WFS programme and who initiated the national requests
for participation. Thus, as it turned out, most of the WFS surveys (26) were
carried out by the national statistical office alone, while in a further seven cases
the statistical office collaborated with one or more other institutions. Table 7.1
gives details.

Nearly all of the agencies which carried out WFS surveys were fully governmental in status. A few were semi-autonomous but only one was wholly outside
the government system, and even this one collaborated with the statistical office.
The choice of a government agency has the overwhelming advantage of ensuring
official commitment to the survey, a benefit felt both during the execution of
the survey and when the results are offered for use by policy-makers.

National statistical offices had many advantages as executing agencies for the
survey. In the majority of countries they were the agency with the greatest
experience of conducting surveys, so that they were able to provide experienced
staff for most operations. Often they had regional field offices, which could
provide field staff and sometimes even vehicles. Usually they were the only
organization which could provide a sampling frame (sometimes even a master
sample), so that even where some other agency was to be used the survey often
had to seek the collaboration of the statistical office in providing the sampling
frame. As to data processing, they often possessed coding and data-entry staff
and nearly always had their own computer. Their main weakness was at the
analysis stage: most national statistical offices are primarily data collection
agencies and, particularly in developing countries, have only one or two subject
matter specialists even for such important fields as demography (for a more
detailed discussion of this particular problem see chapter 21). Moreover, the
greater experience of the statistical office compared with other, generally smaller,
offices proved to be in some respects a disadvantage. Older or more experienced
offices tended to be less flexible both in adopting new field techniques and in
the recruitment of supplementary staff. In several cases they were visibly
hampered by bureaucratic procedures.

There is in fact some evidence that other agencies might do as well as or better
than statistical offices, if delay in the conclusion of the survey operations is
taken as the criterion. Of the nine countries where the survey was done without
involvement of the statistical office, five managed to conclude operations within
12 months after the projected termination date. Only in one of the 24 countries[1]

TABLE 7.1

Distribution of WFS countries according to type of executing agencies, by region

	Africa	Asia and Pacific	Middle East	Latin America	Caribbean	Europe	Total
National Statistical Office	8	4	4	5	4	1	26
National Statistical Office & other	1	4	0	2	0	0	7
Ministry of Health	1	2	0	2	0	0	5
Other[a]	2	1	1	0	0	0	4
Total	12	11	5	9	4	1	42

[a] These are: the semi-autonomous National Family Planning Office in Tunisia, the National Population Bureau in Nigeria, the Population Planning Council of Pakistan and Hacettepe University in Turkey.

where the survey was carried out solely by the statistical office, and in two out of the seven countries where the statistical office collaborated with another institution, was this result achieved.

Moreover, in each of the four main regions, Africa, Asia–Pacific, Latin America, Middle East, the survey with the smallest overrun in the timetable was done outside the statistical office.[2] However, the record is not uniformly in one direction. Two countries with large overruns did their survey outside the statistical office: the prime reason in one case (Tunisia, 52 months overrun) was the lack of data processing capability in the executing agency, which led to the whole of the data processing work being passed to a commercial firm, and in the other (Morocco, 31 months overrun) the Health Ministry's legitimate interest in health-related data, which led to the priority processing of the household survey.

Impressions collected from WFS staff suggest that agencies other than the statistical office were often more open towards active external assistance or advice. This may have been in part because they did not have the necessary experience or facilities for managing all stages of the survey on their own. This in turn led to major inputs by the WFS or consultants, especially in the data processing stage. Further, for the statistical offices the fertility survey was never more than one activity among many, while for many of the other offices it became their dominant activity over a long period. That the statistical office is not always the only agency capable of conducting a national survey has also been demonstrated in over 15 countries by the contraceptive prevalence surveys; most of these, and particularly those in Latin America, were executed by ministries of health or family planning associations.[3]

It would, however, be a mistake to conclude that most of the surveys conducted by statistical offices could have been done more expeditiously by some other agency. What the results point to is that it is possible for an organization with limited survey experience or organizational infrastructure to conclude a survey successfully and speedily as long as sufficient technical assistance is provided and accepted. The WFS experience also suggests that experienced agencies like the statistical office cannot necessarily guarantee success without major technical assistance inputs or drastic changes in their planning and/or implementation procedures.

7.3   The survey plan

Once participation of a country had been agreed, the WFS sent out a survey design team, consisting generally of two or three senior staff. Their task, during a two-week mission, was to collaborate with the national staff in drawing up a detailed survey plan. This would include the survey timetable, the sample size, the budget, the assignment of local staff and a rough scheduling of WFS technical assistance. All of this was embodied in a detailed project proposal document which was then used as the basis for a funding request to one of the agencies.

From the start of work to the publication of the report, the planned survey durations averaged 23 months, with a range from 16 to 33 months (for details see chapter 9). Inevitably, assumptions had to be made about circumstances that would prevail up to three years in the future, and in particular about the future availability of personnel.

The survey plan was intended not simply as a project request document but also as a realistic operational directive. How far did it serve the latter purpose? Obviously, the survey characteristics and the externally funded sector of the survey budget were taken very seriously; they were rightly seen as defining the essentials of the contractual agreement between the country and the funding agency. Much the same applied to the detailed arrangements for the central operational stage, the fieldwork: the number of interviewers and supervisors, the duration of their training, the number of vehicles — all of these were indeed rigorously determined by the project plan. But when one turns to other features of the plan the project document was apparently much less firmly based on detailed planning or commitment and gave more scope for deviations.

Frequently the timetable of the survey could not be adhered to. Once slippage started the agreed timetable inevitably began to lose credibility. A plan that has slipped by several months begins to be ignored, the more so if the remaining stages are not planned in sufficient detail. Unless it is formally updated, management style will tend to shift from following the plan to pushing ahead 'as fast as we can'. In this situation most WFS country co-ordinators repeatedly introduced short-term plan revisions; others seem to have felt that such repeated reminders that slippage was occurring would be more demoralizing than constructive. WFS had no policy on this; the matter was left in the hands of the co-ordinator, whose personal knowledge of the situation and individuals involved may indeed have made him or her the best judge. For a fuller discussion of the reasons for slippage, see chapter 9.

Assignment of staff was another area in which the initial plan, though seen at first as prescriptive, tended in some countries to lose its influence progressively as the survey advanced. WFS attempted to prevent this by having key staff designated by name in the survey document. The government was thus led to make a formal commitment as to the availability of key staff. It seems highly probable that this strategy contributed to the stabilization of survey staff, and the principle appears a useful one for future international projects. Nevertheless its success was very far from complete, as will be seen in a later section. The problem is that the reasons for staff mobility either are seen by the countries as very pressing, reflecting real unexpected changes in circumstances or priorities, or are wholly decided by the individual in question. When such a change of circumstances or priorities occurs governments may feel obliged, however reluctantly, to review their commitments.

It would, however, be wrong to say that all staffing problems were caused by staff mobility. Even where staff were nominated in the project request, often they were not in fact assigned to the project at the stage they were needed. Timetable slippage, of course, would make this more likely.

A different kind of problem sometimes arose with the more junior staff grades, such as coders, editors, punchers. Here there seems to have been a tendency to regard the numbers of staff specified in the plan as less binding than the numbers of field staff — perhaps because a longer interval had elapsed since the plan was drawn up, or perhaps because these functions did not seem to require the same urgency as the fieldwork. There was also, in some cases, pressure from already employed staff to be allowed to stay on longer, with a reduction in the planned new recruitment. Very often this staff was paid by the country contribution and the number committed during the design stage could frequently not be found at the time when needed. Whatever the reason, in many cases these grades were ultimately provided in smaller numbers than planned.

Finally, a word must be said here about the 'national contribution' to the survey budget. This was largely a notional figure, covering such items as rent of premises, computer time and salaries (or apportionments of salaries) of permanent staff who would be paid in any case, whether or not the survey was taking place (see chapter 10 for further details). The funding agencies, wishing to be assured of the country commitment, wanted to show a substantial country contribution and this was taken to mean, in most cases, at least 25 per cent of the budget. Many WFS co-ordinators report that this guideline had little effect beyond causing some figures to be re-estimated to a higher level. However, others reported cases in which it had a negative effect, either through inciting countries to commit additional personnel in the planning document who could not in fact be made available, or through preventing the recruitment of outside personnel to do essential work for which no qualified permanent staff were available, simply because outside recruits would have to be paid from the international contribution. Whichever response occurred, the attempt to maintain a minimum national contribution proved to be dysfunctional in terms of management. In this context it should be pointed out that many countries eventually contributed much more than had been actually budgeted. Once operations were underway, many people were drawn into the project without having figured in the original budget. This was partly caused by the substantial timetable overrun which occurred in most countries.

Judged by the straightforward criterion of eventual performance, the survey plans contained in WFS project documents must be regarded as highly unrealistic. Mean planned survey duration was 23 months; mean actual duration was over four years. Instances of personnel assignments specified in the plan which were never made in reality are very frequent. Cases abound of countries unable to complete data processing work, yet with no sign in the plan that the capability to complete this stage needed to be supplied.

When actual events deviate from the plan there are three possible explanations. (1) Planning may have been defective: that is, insufficient effort may have been made to specify the operations to be carried out and the resources required. (2) The plan may have been ignored by those taking operational decisions. (3) The course of events may have been influenced by factors that were unpredictable when the plan was drawn up. We believe that each of these explanations accounts for part of the problem in the case of the WFS survey design documents. Defect in the plan itself is the dominating factor in the data processing phase, and this is discussed more fully in the next section. Lack of attention to the plan has already been discussed above: it affected some aspects more than others. Unpredictability in the planning environment is a problem characteristic of most countries but more so of the developing ones; it is particularly acute in the area of professional staff deployment, and this is examined more fully in a later section. Whatever the causes, there is no doubt that planning can be tightened by several means: first, by obtaining explicit staff commitments in advance; second, by going beyond merely formal commitments or promises and insisting on direct communication with the person to be committed in the plan (as well as his/her current superior); third, by frequent review of the plan and reconfirmation of commitments. An essential requirement is that the planners are able to specify in detail the nature of the operations foreseen and of the resources required for their implementation.

7.4   Technical assistance

It is not realistic to discuss survey management at the local level without taking into account the technical assistance provided by the WFS. Technical assistance was an integral part of the survey plan in that countries were promised all the assistance they needed to complete the different survey stages. It goes without saying that this implied a level of technical assistance which would ensure the execution of the survey according to the survey plan.

WFS technical assistance was typically provided by a country co-ordinator and a data processing co-ordinator, assisted where necessary by other WFS staff or consultants. Details of the WFS technical assistance philosophy and execution are provided in chapter 8. For the purpose of this chapter we shall only discuss briefly the link between WFS technical assistance and survey management.

An important part of the WFS assistance was provided through detailed basic documentation describing all stages of the survey, their work requirements and advice on how to implement them.[4] This documentation is in the main based on the Core Questionnaire. Adaptation to the country-specific requirements could involve considerable work, in particular the specification of edits, recodes and tabulations followed by the programming and execution of all of these. In general, all this was left to the countries. Country staff were thus faced with the problem of adapting the procedures prescribed by the WFS to take into account country-specific requirements, which often proved to be a very difficult task.

Even in the cases where problems were recognized early on, any technical assistance schedule conceived at the beginning of the project had to be modified continuously due to changing circumstances. As a consequence, the opportune assignment of technical assistance visits among WFS staff became more and more problematic, especially as the number of countries participating in the project grew considerably and continuously. A circular relationship between delays and technical assistance therefore developed in some cases: delay led to the need for more technical assistance, which led to problems in providing this assistance and thus to more delays. Ultimately, therefore, the WFS frequently had to take full charge of the final recoding and tabulation stages in London (albeit with the collaboration of local programmers in most cases). Earlier-mentioned problems of personnel availability played, of course, a major role in creating this situation.

7.5   Data processing: a special case

In the earlier phases of WFS surveys it is possible to regard timetable slippage as a measure of managerial inefficiency at the local level. In the case of the data processing stage of the surveys, this is less so. The dominating fact about the planning for this stage is that for a long period — perhaps the first four years of its existence — the WFS itself did not have a clear picture of the work that would be undertaken in the data processing of the surveys. The Survey Organization Manual, produced in its first (working) version in January 1976, contains only the shortest possible mention of machine editing (p. 51), with no indication that the goal was to be a completely error-free tape. Recoding and variable construction receive no mention at all and tabulation, though mentioned in headings, is not once discussed as a processing problem. Even the Editing and Coding Manual was not produced in its first version until September 1976, while the first draft of the Data Processing Guidelines was produced in 1977. By the end of that year 30 countries had already enrolled in the WFS programme. Meanwhile survey design documents were being produced which were in many cases totally unrealistic and which largely ignored the implications of the work programme that was destined to be imposed on the country once the WFS data processing co-ordinator made his first visit, typically several months after completion of the design document.

Over and above the shortcomings of WFS, many local factors also played a major role in making data processing the most difficult stage in nearly all surveys. Some of the major factors were: the unavailability of qualified programmers at the local level, inadequate computer access, incompatibility of local hardware with WFS software, insufficient commitment of the survey director during this stage, insufficient numbers of correction staff following the machine editing, lack of continuity in programming work, etc.

A detailed description of the data processing procedures and problems can be found in chapter 18. Here we will merely highlight some of the issues which have arisen at the local level.

That qualified programmers were unavailable when needed does not necessarily mean that they were non-existent in the executing agency. In many cases they existed but were scarce, so that they had to spread their services over many different projects. When this happened the problem was often aggravated by vaguely defined and part-time assignments and by inadequate liaison between the survey director and the data processing department. Programmers are still a scarce commodity in many countries and are often involved in too many projects at the same time, with the consequence that delays occur in most of these projects. In the case of the WFS the problem was frequently worsened by the inability of the survey director to co-ordinate directly with the programmer, either through a lack of knowledge of programming requirements on his part or a lack of communication with the data processing director. This in turn led to insufficient computer access and lack of full-time programmer commitment. It is clear that the planning of the programming side was frequently seriously deficient, with work starting too late, often only after the end of fieldwork, and unclear staff assignments. Maybe one of the lessons to be learned is that the WFS should have advocated the inclusion of the chief of data processing as a deputy director for the survey. Another clear implication is that programming operations should start as soon as possible: that is, once the questionnaire is finalized. If this is done, planning of the programming stages will also become considerably easier because staff assignments will become effective much nearer to the time of the design visit.

7.6 Management structure

The WFS Survey Organization Manual provided an example of an organizational chart appropriate for a WFS survey. At the head of the organization appears the National Director (annotated 'sometimes only nominal') and immediately under him the Survey Director (marked 'full-time'). The National Director was specified as a post in 33 of the 42 survey design documents and named in 30; the Survey Director (or 'Technical Director' in many countries) was specified as a post in 37 and named in 31.

In the majority of WFS surveys the National Director was the director of the national statistical office. As such he was, clearly, in no position to take charge of the day-to-day management of the survey. Logically, his inclusion in the survey design document and in the specimen organization chart was inappropriate. It is the Survey Director who must take charge of the survey. Of course he has a hierarchical superior to whom he must report, but in any given country their relationship will already be defined and there seems nothing to be gained by representing this superior officer as part of the survey organization. On the contrary there appear to have been cases where this led to bottlenecks, because adequate powers had not been delegated to the Survey Director.

Nevertheless, there seem to be substantial differences between countries in this respect. WFS staff found that where organization was strongly hierarchical in character the National Director seemed to be needed in order to ensure adequate decision-making. There were also instances where the nomination of a National Director helped to raise support for the project. This issue should therefore be decided on a country-to-country basis, bearing in mind the effect on survey execution and management.

The Survey Director was in many cases the chief of the demography division in the national statistical office. Often this division was small and had a number of regular duties which could not be set aside. As a result, the requirement that the Survey Director work full time on the survey was not always realistic. In several instances this problem led to serious delays. It accounts for many of the cases in which WFS co-ordinators reported that work in the countries only seemed to advance during their visits.

The WFS Survey Organization Manual also suggested that some countries might wish to appoint a Co-ordinating or Advisory Committee, particularly where more than one organization was involved in the survey. Nineteen countries appear to have appointed such a committee (if one is to judge from the intention expressed in the design document). Such committees may smooth co-operation between different national bodies, defusing potential conflicts and in particular facilitating the ultimate acceptance of the findings. On the other hand, WFS experience suggests that their continued involvement beyond the survey and questionnaire design stages is likely to be counterproductive. Once the design is fixed, the Survey Director should be free to organize the work with the minimum of interference.

7.7   Professional staff assignment

Undoubtedly the greatest managerial problem faced by countries in implementing WFS surveys was the shortage of adequately qualified staff, and its direct consequence, the high mobility of existing staff.

The shortage is not absolute. With the possible exception of computer programmers, most developing countries possess, somewhere, individuals qualified for any given survey specialization. However, in many cases suitably qualified professionals are not available within the organization executing the survey. When this happens, the problems begin at the survey design stage. Somehow or other such a person must be identified and written into the plan. Various options are therefore examined at the time of the design visit.

First, can a suitable person be found elsewhere within the government service and transferred, or loaned, to the executing agency? This solution is rarely feasible. If the national statistical office is executing the survey and does not possess anyone with the necessary qualification it is unlikely that any other government office will; while if another office is executing the survey it is unlikely that the statistical office will agree to sacrifice its own capability by transferring one of its staff (although there were occasions when this did happen).

Second, can a national be found outside the government service, for example in a university? This solution is often impracticable. In many countries there are administrative obstacles to bringing outsiders temporarily into the civil service at a professional level, even if such a person can be found.

In practice the solution ultimately adopted usually was to make do with existing underqualified staff and to attempt to upgrade them through technical assistance support from WFS headquarters. In extreme cases WFS recruited a resident adviser to stay for an extended period in the country. These solutions, though no doubt the best available, are unsatisfactory, if only because the capability of the assigned staff member(s) is uncertain at the time when the commitment is made.

Added to these problems is that of the high job mobility characteristic of an administration in which skilled personnel are in short supply. The problem begins with the survey director himself. Only 28 of the 41 WFS countries completed the drafting of the report under the same survey director as the one who was in charge at the fieldwork stage.[5] If the problem is serious with the survey director, it is worse with the other specialists whose relationship to the survey is less crucial. The chance of identifying an appropriately qualified report writer, for example, at the time of the survey design visit and finding him or her available on schedule two years later may well be less than 50 per cent. Several WFS surveys suffered major delays due to mobility of staff. Prime examples are Venezuela and Ecuador; for both countries report printing was held up by more than one year for no other reason than the departure of the national and survey directors.

Such experience emphasizes the need for obtaining advance commitment of personnel assignments as well as for periodic reconfirmation of such commitments. Other lessons learned are the importance of bringing data processing and analysis staff into close association with the survey work from the early stages and, finally, the advantages of implementing the whole survey quickly.

7.8   Monitoring and supervision

A key role of management is supervision, and nowhere is this more important than in the management of surveys. Only by constant monitoring of the diverse operations which go to make up a survey can a manager be certain that they are being conducted in accordance with the original design.

Such monitoring requires two conditions of the survey director and other senior staff: they must be willing to spend time visiting survey teams on the ground, not just around the office but in the villages and the slums, and they must be willing to keep contact with, and personally check from time to time, all of the tasks, however lowly, that go to make up the survey operations. A successful survey director cannot stay all the time in his office, he cannot monitor performance by calling people in and questioning them, and he cannot hope to control a survey simply by giving orders.

A simple but key measure is the provision of a clearly defined survey office within the executing agency. This should accommodate at a minimum all the key personnel, and if possible the coders, editors and correctors. It should also house the questionnaires and other survey documentation. Dispersal of such functions throughout a large building, most of which is used for other things, or worse, in separate locations, is a sure recipe for loose organization and weak morale, discouraging wholehearted commitment and efficient co-operation.

These principles, applicable to all surveys, are especially important in developing countries. In the WFS experience, many survey directors understood them but others did not. Others again accepted them in theory but were genuinely too busy with administrative work or other duties to find time for such supervisory work.

7.9   Incentives for operational staff

There are in principle three ways of paying personnel assigned to carry out a specific phase of the survey operations (such as interviewers, coders, editors): by piece work, by time work, or by lump sum. In the case of interviewers, experience accumulated from surveys all over the world has led to a broad consensus in favour of time working. The danger that this might give interviewers an incentive to work unnecessarily slowly is countered by the fact that many interviewers are discontented in the field and wish to return home as soon as possible. It is also countered by meticulous planning of the field operation. However, when one turns to office operations the same approach can easily lead to serious problems. If coders and editors are obtained not by secondment from permanent staff but from the labour market, with unemployment threatening as soon as a job is completed, then payment by time worked may offer a strong incentive to work slowly, especially where supervision is weak or non-existent. If existing staff are paid a bonus to perform the work for the survey a similar situation may arise. There is no doubt that this factor played a part in some WFS surveys. To quote from one mission report by a WFS country co-ordinator: 'Things are being done very slowly: I am sure that it does not escape the notice of anyone concerned that the slower they work the longer their salaries will continue to flow'.

The need to adopt a payment system which encourages efficient working is a fundamental of good management. The issue should be examined explicitly at the survey design stage and a firm decision committed to writing in the design document. The adoption of any particular payment system, however, in no way replaces the need for close supervision and co-ordination of all stages of the survey.

7.10   Practical recommendations

In this section we offer some practical recommendations for the management of surveys, based on the WFS experience.

1 The choice of national executing agency should be based on its perceived capability to carry out the job within reasonable time and budget constraints. A major criterion influencing the choice should be the degree of availability of full-time qualified staff for the project.

2 The survey plan should be established in great detail. As far as possible all key staff should be named in the project document, but only after it has been

established that they will be effectively available for the task and have committed themselves to it.

3 Regular assessment of staff availability should be one of the continuing tasks of the survey director. Prompt action should be taken to find replacements as soon as it becomes clear that assigned staff will not become available. For junior staff, such as interviewers and coders, replacement staff should be provided for by training a small surplus. (In some cases replacements might be found to do the job which is keeping the assigned staff member from working on the survey.)

4 Assignment of staff financed by external funds should be realistic and not motivated by the desire to maximize the external contribution. Similarly, assignment made under the country contribution should be realistic and not based on the need to show a high rate of national participation.

5 The survey plan should be reviewed regularly, preferably every two months, to ensure that the survey director keeps fully informed of progress and problems, and in particular of staffing needs.

6 Technical assistance cannot be standardized but should take into account the particular country needs and the survey plan. All efforts should be geared towards maintaining the planned timetable.

7 The country's, or executing agency's, data processing capabilities, covering available hardware, software and manpower, should be the basis for the planning of the data processing stage and in particular for the planning of technical assistance.

8 The local chief of computing should if possible be nominated in the survey plan as the person in charge of processing the survey.

9 Local data processors should be trained in the procedures needed to process a WFS survey before actual survey processing begins. Budgeting provision should be made for this.

10 The computer specialists should be directly involved in the key phases of survey preparation. In particular, the questionnaire draft should be examined by them before its finalization and they should participate in the work of preparing the questionnaire flow chart, the edit specifications and the recode specifications. Firm plans should be made well in advance covering the arrangements for coding and data entry.

11 Programming should start immediately after the final questionnaire has been produced.

12 Ideally, the survey director will be in charge of all aspects of the survey, including finance and administration. The nomination of a part-time national director may therefore become less necessary. It is highly desirable that the survey director be committed full-time.

13 If essential survey staff cannot be found in the executing agency it is preferable to recruit from outside the agency rather than making do with underqualified or part-time staff.

14 Other things being equal, speedy execution of the survey tends to minimize most of the problems arising from staff mobility, shifting priorities and loss of morale.

15 The survey director should actively supervise all the operations. Delegation of tasks without maintaining personal supervision should be strongly discouraged.

16 An identifiable survey office accommodating all the key personnel and functions should be established within the executing agency.

17 The question of incentives for operational staff should be examined only from the viewpoint of their effect on the survey execution. Payment schemes that discourage speedy execution should not be applied.

Notes

1. Iran and Fiji excluded due to imprecision in actual or projected termination date.
2. The countries concerned were: Nigeria, Nepal, Dominican Republic and Turkey.
3. Contraceptive Prevalence Surveys: A New Source of Family Planning Data. *Population Reports*, Series M No. 5, 1981.
4. This basic documentation consisted of: the Core Questionnaires, the Survey Organization Sampling, Training, Interviewers', Supervisors' and Editing and Coding Manuals, and the Data Processing and Tabulation Guidelines.
5. Iran excluded because report was never completed.

8

Technical Assistance and Co-ordination

Martin Vaessen
Hédi Jemai

8.1 Scope of the chapter

The objective of this chapter is to describe and evaluate the technical assistance given by the WFS in the collection, processing and analysis of data from 41 fertility surveys.[1] Discussion of this topic should assist international survey organizations in planning and executing future surveys and in fixing their own patterns and levels of staffing.

First a detailed description of the WFS technical assistance philosophy will be given. This will be complemented by a description of the different types and configurations of technical assistance employed by the WFS. A detailed analysis of the frequency and amount of technical assistance then follows. The chapter ends with specific conclusions concerning the amount and type of technical assistance provided by the WFS, in the light of the required speed and quality of the survey operations.

8.2 Central strategy

Originally it was envisaged that the WFS London headquarters would employ 'five full-time experts in sampling, questionnaire construction, survey research techniques, electronic data processing and fertility research. In addition to this core staff, some eight to twelve consultants will be made readily available for individual assignments and a much larger roster of short-term consultants provided as the WFS programme develops'.[2] Thus, in the early stages, the WFS was seen as less centralized than it was to become. In the event, most of the technical assistance to countries was provided by WFS central staff, while consultants were used mainly at headquarters. Headquarters staff grew fairly continuously over the years in response to the data collection, processing and analysis needs generated by the project.

Among the numerous reasons for this departure from the original plan, the following may be identified:

1 Technical assistance requirements turned out to be more demanding than originally envisaged, making it desirable to use full-time staff rather than consultants.

2 The standardized nature of the project made it relatively inefficient to recruit short-term consultants.

3   It soon became apparent that the only way the experiences in varying countries could flow together effectively and feed back into the programme was by staff contact, which required a central headquarters.

4   The survey in each country was a fairly long process and the lessons learned during technical assistance visits needed to be passed immediately to the person providing the next input. Consultants could not guarantee this.

5   Most technical assistance visits were multi-purpose, dealing with a variety of issues (except perhaps in the area of data processing). This made it difficult to delegate a particular task to a consultant.

6   Suitable consultants were insufficiently available at the times needed.

Rather than providing in-country technical assistance, consultants were therefore used for development purposes, in-depth analysis of data and specialized projects. The exceptions to this were cases where consultants were recruited as resident advisers, and the special case of the Caribbean, where a regional co-ordinating team was charged with most of the technical assistance to a number of surveys in that region from its base in Port of Spain. These atypical forms of technical assistance are considered separately in section 3.

Thus the WFS organization provided most of its technical assistance through frequent visits of its central staff to participating countries, typically two to three weeks in duration. Time spent in London by this staff was dedicated, especially in the earlier years of the programme, to follow-up of problems encountered in the field, to the development of the core documentation, and in later years, to technical assistance provided to visiting survey staff at WFS London headquarters.

In our view the benefits of centralization were considerable. On issues ranging from budgeting to general survey design, sampling, fieldwork, coding and editing, and especially data processing, the interchange of ideas and improvements among the central staff on the basis of their country experience made a huge contribution to the effectiveness of the whole project.

The centralized staff arrangement also assisted the WFS aim of maintaining maximum comparability of data between countries. This required a substantial degree of standardization of instruments and procedures over countries. With any other mode of technical assistance, it is unlikely that this aim could have been achieved to the extent that it was. Ultimately it was the participating countries which benefited from this accumulated experience in the sense that difficulties and mistakes occurring in one survey could be avoided in the others.

Another advantage of centralization was that it allowed technical assistance to be provided quickly, without the need to await the availability of the appropriate consultant. Furthermore, central staff members were seldom involved in one country only: combination of visits was therefore possible and this in turn allowed short-term monitoring visits without significantly increasing travel costs.

Given that technical assistance was to be provided mainly by WFS central staff, how was the work to be organized? It soon became apparent that overall responsibility for a given country survey within the London headquarters needed to be held by one person. Otherwise, continuity of approach could not be guaranteed and conflicting advice might be given. Also, co-ordination and planning would become more difficult were involvement in a survey to be spread over too many staff. The approach finally adopted was to nominate a staff member experienced in survey design and data collection as co-ordinator for each country. This country co-ordinator was to be responsible for all the survey issues concerning the assigned country and would in general provide or arrange all the required technical assistance.

It was recognized, however, that the data processing skills of the country co-ordinators were usually not sufficient to enable them to provide all the assistance which was required at this stage of survey execution. Therefore, for each country, a data processing co-ordinator was also nominated. This co-ordinator was to take the primary responsibility for data processing in collaboration with, and under the guidance of, the country co-ordinator. This arrangement was not applied to the first ten or so countries, because it took some time for the need to become apparent.

As a further rule it was established that a certain degree of interchange between country co-ordinators was desirable in order to ensure uniform quality of work and avoid dependence on only one person. For this purpose a second co-ordinator was also named.

The system of country co-ordinators seems to have worked well, except for a few mishaps concerning particular countries and co-ordinators. In retrospect it is quite clear that effective collaboration with local counterparts is considerably easier if involvement of central staff is restricted to a few individuals. This reduces problems of co-ordination between technical assistance staff, besides being more conducive to the growth of a relationship of mutual trust and collaboration with the local counterparts. Despite the potential danger of a relaxation of work standards, the balance of advantage seems to favour this arrangement.

Frequency of technical assistance visits

At the time of the survey design visit, a minimum of technical assistance visits was normally specified in the project document. There would typically be at least nine visits, corresponding to the main stages of the survey: preparation of questionnaires and manuals, sample design and implementation, training of supervisors, pre-test and questionnaire finalization, training for main fieldwork, fieldwork, coding and editing, machine editing, and tabulation and report writing. These scheduled visits would total from about 15 to 30 or more weeks of technical assistance, according to the perceived needs of the country at the time of the design visit.

Taken together, these visits would typically involve at least three people from London central staff: the country co-ordinator, a sampling expert, the data processing co-ordinator and, possibly, a training specialist. The project document also stated that the WFS would provide technical assistance if and when required at times other than those scheduled in the agreement. The entire approach towards technical assistance was flexible and aimed at responding to any needs which might arise in the course of the survey, irrespective of any prior agreement. However, it is possible that this philosophy may be partly to blame for the excessive amount of technical assistance provided to some countries. Technical assistance by the WFS was often seen as an obligation and countries frequently did not hesitate to call on WFS assistance every time a problem presented itself, even if it should have been solved by the local staff without any difficulty.

Besides technical assistance in the strict sense, there was the area of *survey monitoring*. In order to keep informed about the progress and problems of the surveys, many visits by WFS central staff were made with the sole initial purpose of monitoring progress. Such visits were usually short and generally made when en route to another assignment. These shorter visits were necessitated in part by deficient telephone or mail communications but it was also considered extremely important to provide a regular presence of central staff in the participating countries.

Nature of technical assistance

From the outset the WFS took the position that all the survey activities should be carried out by local personnel, with the collaboration, where required, of WFS staff and consultants. WFS staff was seen more in a monitoring than executive role. Long visits were therefore discouraged. However, the nature and amount of technical assistance provided to countries varied quite widely. In some countries the WFS played a much more active role than in others, in order to compensate for the shortage of qualified local staff.

Where a heavy involvement of WFS staff in survey execution was thought necessary, every effort was made to avoid imposing this assistance on the country. Co-ordinators worked towards a position of partnership with the local survey team. In such cases, care had to be taken to ensure that all activities carried the endorsement of the survey director and were in line with his/her guidelines. In other countries the WFS staff worked mostly in a monitoring and advisory role, as sufficient local staff was available to execute the work properly.

Both in the designation of country co-ordinators and in their activities in the countries, the WFS tried to ensure that its staff was acceptable to the local counterparts and technically competent. There were only a few cases when a change of country co-ordinator was necessary due to poor working relations with local counterparts.

Technical assistance documentation

The emphasis planned from the beginning by the WFS on comparability of the data between countries led naturally to the development of a core questionnaire and supporting documentation. This documentation consisted of draft manuals for interviewers and supervisors, coding and editing manuals and detailed instructions for machine editing, recoding and tabulation. In addition, manuals on sampling, training and survey organization were also provided.

The core documentation constituted a major part of the central WFS technical assistance, as it contained the description of all procedures and problems related to the execution of a WFS survey. The conversion of the core documentation to country-specific documents required only the adaptation to the local situation, leaving the main body of the instructions and procedures generally intact. This in turn facilitated technical assistance, for which the survey documentation was always the guiding light.

The advantages of preparing this core documentation were manifold and can be summarized as follows:

1 The documentation helped to ensure comparability between countries.

2 It reduced the amount of work needed at the country level.

3 It provided solutions for a variety of problems likely to arise at the local level.

4 Unlike technical assistance, it was always instantly accessible to the country staff.

5 It was of substantial help for the planning and costing of the surveys.

6 More widely, it provided each country with a set of model documents and procedures likely to prove useful in the design of other surveys. At the same time it provided valuable training material for use in Third World teaching institutions.

Among the possible disadvantages associated with this core documentation are the following:

1 It may have made the survey too mechanical and thereby sapped initiative.

2 It strait-jacketed certain procedures, sometimes to the dislike of local survey staff.

3 The necessary adaptation to local conditions was sometimes overlooked and led to neglect of important issues.

4 In particular, questions added locally to the core questionnaire often did not receive sufficient attention during data processing and analysis.

On balance, however, there can be no doubt that the WFS core documentation performed its function admirably. It is difficult to imagine a better way of encouraging high standards of work and comparability of results between countries. The main drawback was undoubtedly that questions added locally were not always sufficiently analysed and incorporated in the country reports due to the failure to create the necessary recoding and tabulation instructions. Prompt adaptation of all data processing documentation as soon as the question-naire had been finalized should have overcome this problem. Regrettably this did not always occur.

8.3   Supplementary forms of technical assistance

Resident advisers

In certain countries it became apparent during the planning stage that there was a very serious lack of qualified staff available. It was considered therefore that the WFS should have a permanent representative in these countries in order to reinforce the survey team and to give continuous technical assistance. In such cases, and after consultation with the local executing agency, the WFS nominated a resident adviser to work full time in the country for a prolonged period. There were nine countries in which a resident adviser was used: Bangladesh, Cameroon, Dominican Republic, Fiji, Haiti, Kenya, Mauritania, Morocco and Sudan, with periods of residence varying from 12 months for Bangladesh to 42 months for Mauritania. In three of the countries, Dominican Republic, Fiji and Kenya, the decision to employ such an adviser was partly influenced by the fact that a suitable person was already *in situ*.

There were also three instances where the data processing technical assistance was supplemented by the use of a resident adviser. This happened in Ivory Coast, Lesotho and Senegal for six, six and thirteen months respectively. Provision of these data processing resident advisers was not planned at the outset but decided upon as an emergency measure to ensure that proper processing of the data took place in the country.

With the exception of the Dominican Republic, none of the countries where a resident adviser was used did a notably quick survey. This is not surprising, given the initial reasons for assigning a resident adviser. Moreover, as is now well known, the main delays in completion took place at the data processing and report writing stages; with the exception of Kenya and Mauritania, the resident advisers were mostly involved in the preparation and fieldwork stages of the survey. This was particularly the case in Cameroon and Bangladesh; in the remaining countries they did participate to some extent in the data processing, but were withdrawn before the report was finalized.

The use of resident advisers is certainly to be recommended when it is apparent that local manpower or organization is insufficient to bring a survey to a successful and speedy end. However, resident advisers should not be withdrawn at the end of the fieldwork but retained for the whole of the survey period. Much of the work to be done after fieldwork requires a heavy input of organization and supervision; where these are not available for fieldwork it is unlikely they will be available at later stages.

An alternative to resident advisers would be larger technical assistance missions or even a team-oriented technical assistance approach with the team actually taking charge of the tasks at hand, if local commitment or manpower are insufficient.

United Nations liaison officers

One of the co-operative agreements between the WFS and the United Nations provided for the UN to appoint regional liaison officers for the WFS surveys.

Their functions were to monitor country participation and participate in survey design visits, help provide technical assistance where appropriate and stimulate the use of the survey results in governmental programmes and second-stage analysis. In fact, liaison officers were only made available in Latin America and Asia, from mid-1976. The Latin American liaison officer provided substantial technical assistance to a number of countries, while for Asia such technical assistance was mainly concentrated on second-stage analysis.

Regional co-ordinator

In one case only the WFS adopted a totally regionalized approach. To cover Guyana, Jamaica and Trinidad and Tobago, the WFS set up a regional office in Port of Spain headed by a regional co-ordinator. This arrangement was established because it was believed that the particular Caribbean situation, requiring substantial amendments to the core questionnaire because of the complex systems of marital union, could best be handled by a local expert. Two other Caribbean countries, Haiti and Dominican Republic, were assisted from London due to the linguistic constraints of the Caribbean co-ordinator. In the three English-speaking countries, the Caribbean office provided most of the technical assistance, although WFS monitoring visits still took place. The WFS central office also played the major role in providing technical assistance during the data processing stages of the surveys.

A regional co-ordinator was also appointed for a limited period for the Arab countries and was based in Cairo.

Visits to London

One of the ways in which the WFS provided technical assistance was through working visits of nationals to the central office in London, especially during the data processing and report writing stages. This mechanism was used to ensure full-time commitment of local staff, easy access to a computer and the opportunity to involve several WFS staff in the work without incurring substantial travel and subsistence costs. Other visits to London took place in the earlier stages of the surveys for discussion of questionnaire content and operational issues.

Data processing visits to London took place from the following countries: Benin, Cameroon, Bangladesh, Morocco, Senegal, Sudan, Portugal, Syria, Turkey and Yemen AR. Report writing visits involved Benin, Cameroon, Ghana, Ivory Coast, Lesotho, Morocco, Nigeria, Senegal, Sudan, Republic of Korea, Malaysia, Nepal, Thailand, Haiti, Portugal, Mexico and Yemen AR. A total of 134 national survey personnel came to WFS for working and training visits for a total duration of 206 person months, 117 of which were spent in workshops (see below).

Inter-country assistance

In a few instances the WFS arranged for survey executives of participating countries to provide assistance to other countries. The following such visits took place: from Malaysia to Sri Lanka and from Ghana to Nigeria for interviewer training; from Benin to Ivory Coast for survey organization; from Cameroon to Ivory Coast for a linguistic study and selection of languages; and from Senegal to Cameroon for training and survey organization. In Panama a one-week meeting was arranged for survey staff from Colombia, Costa Rica, Panama and Dominican Republic to enable the first three countries to profit from the experience of the last before their fieldwork began.

Although in principle inter-country assistance seemed desirable, there were several practical problems. First, assistance to another country reduced the survey manpower resources in the country providing the assistance. Secondly, lack of knowledge of the overall picture might lead to advice being given that was not in line with WFS norms. Thus there was a need for a WFS presence during such visits.

Consultants

WFS also provided technical assistance through the use of short-term consultants. This happened particularly during the sampling and data processing stages. Sampling consultancies were provided in Egypt, Colombia, Lesotho, Sudan and Venezuela.

All Latin American surveys benefited from the technical assistance provided by the Latin American Demographic Centre (CELADE) during the data processing stage of their surveys. With the exceptions of Mexico and Colombia, CELADE provided the bulk of technical assistance input during data processing. The United States Bureau of the Census provided substantial input during the tabulation stages of the surveys in the Dominican Republic and Malaysia. Consultancies by individuals were arranged frequently during the report writing stages of the surveys, in particular in Bangladesh, Benin, Cameroon, Ecuador, Jordan, Republic of Korea, Mauritania, Morocco, Sri Lanka, Syria and Venezuela.

Workshops

One of the main means adopted by the WFS for training and further analysis purposes was the use of multi-national workshops. WFS organized workshops at the London headquarters and in some of the regions and also gave substantial technical assistance during several workshops organized by outside organizations. Most of the workshops lasted for at least three months. Typically, one participant came from each of 4–6 countries. Each worked on his/her own data but all tackled essentially the same problem. The opportunity to exchange experience between students facing similar difficulties provided an exceptionally profitable training situation, while the prospect of producing a published report on a matter of national interest was an effective incentive.

The main thrust of the workshops organized in London was towards the evaluation of the survey data quality. Seven evaluation workshops were held in all, each with a duration of three months, and attended by representatives of 26 countries. Further workshops in London concerned the analysis of the FOTCAF module, and community factors in infant and child mortality, each also of three months' duration and each attended by representatives of six countries.

One evaluation workshop was held in Santiago, Chile, attended by representatives of three countries and executed with the collaboration of the Catholic University of Santiago. Further regional workshops where the WFS provided considerable input were held in Bombay, Bangkok (three), Santiago and Honolulu. WFS also provided assistance in the conduct of data processing workshops in Addis Ababa, Cairo and Dakar.

Among the many advantages of the workshop approach the following deserve special mention: the possibility of combining an effective training programme with genuinely useful work; the virtual certainty that participants will work full-time on the assigned project; a high level of interchange of ideas between participants; the learning by participants of new data processing and analysis skills.

The only obvious disadvantage is that it is necessary to take participants out of their work environment for a prolonged period. This can adversely affect other projects. However, on balance it is more likely that the increased skill and commitment of participants will ultimately benefit most other projects in which they may later be involved.

8.4   Volume of technical assistance

This section summarizes the amount of technical assistance that the WFS has provided to participating countries over the years. The assistance given by WFS staff will be divided into that provided in-country and at WFS headquarters. Assistance through the use of resident advisers, UN liaison officers and consultants will each be dealt with separately. Finally, the total technical assistance provided to each country will be presented.

Only technical assistance rendered from the preliminary stage to the completion of the First Country Report is considered in this section. Assistance for further analysis is not taken into account due to the widely varying importance of second-stage analysis in the 41 countries concerned. This in turn is partly due to the different completion dates of the First Country Report. Some countries finished their report just before this paper was drafted, while others did so as early as 1976. Consequently some had considerable time for further analysis projects while others did not. Comparison of technical assistance between regions and/or countries would therefore be biased if assistance for further analysis were taken into account.

In-country technical assistance

The breakdown of in-country technical assistance by region and source is provided in table 8.1. On average 325 working person-days were spent by WFS headquarters staff on in-country technical assistance per country. This rises to 528 days when work by resident advisers, consultants, etc. is included.

TABLE 8.1

Number of days of in-country technical assistance by source and region and mean number of visits and assistance days per region

Region	No. of countries	Source						Means per country		
		WFS staff	Resident advisers	UN liaison officers	Consult- ants	CELADE	Total	WFS staff		Total days all sources
								No. of days	No. of visits	
Africa	12	5 227	3 795	–	605	–	9 627	436	32	802
Asia/Pacific	10	3 268	275	–	11	–	3 554	327	20	355
Latin America	9	1 435	218	252	65	906	2 876	159	16	320
Caribbean	4	907	1 849[a]	–	160	–	2 916	227	16	729
Middle East	5	2 219	–	–	179	–	2 398	444	34	480
Europe	1	266	–	–	–	–	266	266	33	266
Total	41	13 322	6 137	252	1 020	906	21 637	325	24	528

[a] Caribbean regional co-ordinator's time included in this count.

In-country technical assistance required on average 24 visits per country by WFS staff.

The region which received most support from WFS headquarters staff per country was the Middle East (444 days), followed by Africa (436 days), Asia and Pacific (327 days), Europe (266 days), Caribbean (227 days) and Latin America (159 days). Eight of the twelve countries in Africa had a resident adviser (either for general purposes or for data processing only) for periods ranging from six months to four years. In Asia and Pacific only Bangladesh and Fiji had resident advisers, in Latin America only the Dominican Republic and in the Caribbean Haiti. The English-speaking Caribbean surveys were however co-ordinated by the Caribbean co-ordinator's office, an arrangement approaching that of the resident adviser. The very low WFS headquarters assistance to Latin America is partly due to the fact that most of the data processing for this region was handled by CELADE (Latin American Demographic Centre).

If all sources of in-country assistance are considered together, African countries received by far the largest input (802 days per country), followed by the Caribbean (729 days), the Middle East (480 days), Asia and Pacific (355 days), Latin America (320 days) and Europe (266 days).

The above count of technical assistance days, based on WFS payment records, includes time spent in travel. It also includes weekend days for visiting staff but not for resident advisers. Table 8.2 gives the figures after excluding travel time. For each trip we have deducted two travel days for all regions except Europe (Portugal) where we deducted only one day per trip for each WFS staff trip. These adjustments do not affect the pattern of results, but the two sets of figures are useful for different purposes.

TABLE 8.2

Mean number of in-country technical assistance days by source and region, adjusted to exclude travel time

Region	Source	
	WFS staff	All in-country assistance
Africa	372	730
Asia/Pacific	287	340
Latin America	127	287
Caribbean	195	698
Middle East	376	412
Europe	233	233
Total	278	484

Note: Weekend days included for visiting personnel but not for resident advisers.

Table 8.3 presents the mean number of in-country WFS headquarters staff days by region and activity (unadjusted for travel time). The table shows that by far the largest amount of in-country assistance was given during the data processing stage and particularly during machine editing. This is in line with the fact that this stage lasted the longest in most countries and presented the most problems (see chapter 9).

In-country assistance with report writing was generally low. This is largely because countries needing substantial assistance in this area usually sent a staff member to do the work in London. The assistance given by the WFS staff in such cases is not included in the in-country figures (but see next section).

Training of field staff and the pre-test are two more areas in which substantial assistance was provided. This was to be expected given the WFS policy on the length of the training courses (three weeks for interviewers) and the need for a WFS presence during these stages.

Technical assistance in London

London time spent on survey activities until the production of the First Country Report is presented in table 8.4. These data were derived from the daily time sheets completed once a month by WFS professional staff and consultants. Each day of work attributed to a *specific country survey* in such a sheet is counted in the total. If 'technical assistance' is imagined in terms of advice given to local staff by an international expert, then the figures given here have a much wider connotation. Two broad categories of activity may be identified outside this narrow definition which account for a high proportion of the working days. First is the category of *back-up work for country visits*. Before any trip the staff member has to brief himself and make various travel arrangements, often involving writing of letters. After the trip he writes a report and perhaps further letters. Assuming that such activities account for 3 days per trip, then they amount to roughly 20 per cent of the London time spent on country-specific work. The second, and more important, category is that of *production work*. Although this is assistance, it is not the same as the giving of advice. It was predominant in the areas of data processing and report preparation. Much of the programming and execution of recoding and tabulation were performed by WFS staff in London. (For example, all of the sampling error computations were done in London.) Several of the country reports were largely written, at least in the first draft, by WFS staff in London. Many were printed in the UK and where this was done there was a very substantial input of editing work by the WFS editors. Further, the report summaries were a WFS responsibility and were normally produced entirely by WFS staff or consultants. All these activities are included in the London total. The remaining country-specific work done in London corresponds more closely to the concept of technical assistance in the narrower sense: support and assistance given to visiting country staff. As far as possible such staff were brought to London to participate in the production activities of the types listed above. (Note, however, that assistance given through the workshops is

TABLE 8.3

WFS staff in-country technical assistance by activity and region (mean days per country)

Region	Preliminary	Survey design	Preparatory	Sample design	Fieldwork for sampling	Pre-test	Training	Fieldwork
Africa	11.7	43.6	28.8	15.0	14.4	43.2	47.4	28.5
Asia/Pacific	10.4	27.1	17.3	10.0	13.7	29.8	38.2	28.5
Latin America	5.3	22.7	10.9	9.1	7.4	14.4	13.9	3.1
Caribbean	1.5	29.0	–	13.5	14.5	20.5	22.8	21.0
Middle East	10.6	60.8	12.6	16.0	21.4	52.2	33.4	16.2
Europe	–	24.0	12.0	14.0	7.0	7.0	6.0	30.0

Region	Supplementary studies	Editing, coding, punching	Data processing assessment	Machine edit	Recoding	Tabulation	Sampling errors	Country report
Africa	3.3	16.3	13.4	125.0	23.0	16.2	1.2	8.0
Asia/Pacific	14.5	23.7	8.2	39.8	18.2	21.5	–	38.4
Latin America	–	10.4	0.4	21.4	6.1	14.9	1.8	17.6
Caribbean	4.8	6.0	11.3	52.3	–	22.0	–	19.8
Middle East	2.0	27.6	14.8	123.2	10.6	21.8	–	20.4
Europe	–	–	11.0	120.0	24.0	6.0	–	5.0

TABLE 8.4

Number of days of survey-specific work by WFS staff and consultants in London, classified by activity and region

Region	Preliminary	Survey design	Preparatory	Sample design	Fieldwork for sampling	Pre-test	Training	Fieldwork
Africa	30	61	322	138	37	310	49	21
Asia/Pacific	–	–	–	–	1	8	2	3
Latin America	1	1	6	5	–	4	–	1
Caribbean	–	–	–	1	10	13	–	6
Middle East	12	22	117	26	2	120	–	–
Europe	–	4	4	3	–	10	–	3
Grand total	43	88	449	173	50	465	51	34

Region	Editing, coding, punching	Data processing assessment	Machine edit	Recoding	Tabulation	Sampling errors	Country report	Total
Africa	120	79	878	1 102	954	195	1 378	5 674
Asia/Pacific	7	–	89	207	292	142	669	1 420
Latin America	17	–	43	230	173	146	231	858
Caribbean	14	–	169	223	409	50	150	1 045
Middle East	88	7	532	279	471	121	734	2 531
Europe	1	6	26	44	86	7	48	242
Grand Total	247	92	1 737	2 085	2 385	661	3 210	11 770

excluded from the total, which covers only the period up to completion of the First Report.)

One more word of caution is needed. London time accounting was not started until January 1975 and even then no activity codes were used at first. Consequently, information is missing for the earlier stages of the earlier surveys, and this means especially those in Asia and Pacific and Latin America.

Despite these shortcomings, table 8.4 shows clearly that most of the London work was spent on data processing; about 60 per cent in the cases of the Middle East and Africa and 80 per cent in the Caribbean. For Latin America and Asia and Pacific the proportion was probably around 60 per cent, though the figures are incomplete.

The London data processing assistance covered many different activities, ranging from the development of machine edit specifications and recode specifications to the actual machine editing and correction and the production of country report tabulations. A further 25 per cent of the in-London total is accounted for by country report work.

Summary of technical assistance

The final total count of all technical assistance provided by the WFS up to the production of country reports is provided in table 8.5. The table specifies for each country the adjusted days of in-country WFS assistance, assistance by resident advisers, consultants and UN liaison officers and time spent in London on the country survey activities, including the time which could not be allocated to a specific survey stage for the purposes of table 8.4. Overall, the WFS programme provided an average of 826 days of technical assistance per country. Assistance varied however considerably as follows: Africa 1210 days per country, Caribbean 1006 days, Middle East 927 days, Asia and Pacific 679 days, Europe 478 days and Latin America 405 days.

Countries which received most assistance were those with resident advisers. Nevertheless countries without resident advisers generally needed a considerable input of assistance; among these the highest figure was recorded for Nigeria, followed by Egypt and Yemen AR. Least assistance was rendered to Colombia; the main reason for this was that data processing was handled locally and efficiently with a minimum of WFS input and no involvement of CELADE.

Totalling all technical assistance (in the broad sense) up to completion of the First Country Report, 34 per cent was spent in-country by WFS staff, 24 per cent was taken up by resident advisers, consultants and UN liaison officers, while 42 per cent was accounted for by work at the London headquarters of WFS.

If technical assistance given after completion of the First Country Report were to be considered, the total would rise very substantially, with a relatively greater weighting for the London component due to the extensive workshop programme. In this connection it is worth recording that the average number of working days spent by national staff at WFS headquarters was 110 per country;

TABLE 8.5

Number of technical assistance days by source, location and country

	In-country[a]		London	Total
	WFS staff	Other		
Africa				
Benin	364	–	482	846
Cameroon[b]	399	713	587	1 699
Ghana	472	–	504	976
Ivory Coast[c]	401	302	373	1 076
Kenya[b]	280	774	259	1 313
Lesotho[c]	234	125	757	1 116
Mauritania[b]	353	882	489	1 724
Morocco[b]	275	537	396	1 208
Nigeria	517	47	712	1 276
Senegal[c]	351	281	216	848
Sudan (North)[b]	455	639	465	1 559
Tunisia	366	–	516	882
Total	4 467	4 300	5 756	14 523
Mean	372	358	480	1 210
Asia and Pacific				
Bangladesh[b]	412	275	676	1 363
Fiji	155	255	754	1 164
Indonesia	347	–	463	810
Korea, Rep. of	378	–	289	667
Malaysia	224	–	128	352
Nepal	155	–	242	397
Pakistan	230	–	238	468
Philippines	384	–	136	520
Sri Lanka	363	–	329	692
Thailand	226	–	134	360
Total	2 874	530	3 389	6 793
Mean	287	53	339	679
Latin America				
Colombia	141	30	91	262
Costa Rica	124	148	97	369
Dominican Rep.[b]	126	306	149	581
Ecuador	91	235	128	454
Mexico	166	32	147	345
Panama	135	200	84	419
Paraguay	152	132	137	421
Peru	162	75	89	326
Venezuela	54	283	135	472
Total	1 151	1 441	1 057	3 649
Mean	128	160	117	405

Table 8.5 continued

	In-country[a]		London	Total
	WFS staff	Other		
Caribbean				
Guyana	157	422	160	739
Haiti[b]	441	743	676	1 860
Jamaica	83	422	245	750
Trinidad & Tobago	102	422	151	675
Total	783	2 009	1 232	4 024
Mean	196	502	308	1 006
Middle East				
Egypt	481	73	572	1 126
Jordan	282	68	626	976
Syria	262	38	677	977
Turkey	348	–	107	455
Yemen AR	510	–	593	1 103
Total	1 883	179	2 575	4 637
Mean	377	36	515	927
Europe				
Portugal	232	–	246	478
Overall total	11 390	8 459	14 255	34 104
Overall mean	278	206	348	832

[a] Excludes travel. Includes weekends for visiting personnel but not for resident advisers.
[b] Countries with general resident adviser.
[c] Countries with data processing resident adviser.

the greater part of this is accounted for by the workshops and falls in the period after completion of the First Country Report.

8.5   Conclusions and recommendations

Calculated on the basis of 220 effective working days per year, the WFS surveys received an average of 2.2 person-years of in-country assistance. This figure should be seen in the light of the planned and achieved mean survey durations: 2 years and 4½ years respectively.

Data processing work absorbed a high percentage of this input, while report writing accounts for most of the remainder. These findings are consistent with the observation, made repeatedly in this volume, that these two areas of survey activity present the most serious problems in the countries. Essentially this was due to the greater complexity of the operations involved and the lesser country experience in these two domains.

In organizing its technical assistance, WFS consciously adopted a policy of maximal flexibility. The aim was to respond to any need for assistance as soon as it became apparent. Although a provisional programme of assistance was planned in advance for each country, it was always assumed that a major part of the assistance given would take the form of trouble-shooting — that is, quick response to unforeseen problems with a minimum of formality. Further, the cost of technical assistance was not included in the country budget, and indeed was never seen by national officers. There is no doubt that the countries themselves appreciated this policy; WFS staff repeatedly received compliments on the speed and informality of the organization's response to requests, often accompanied by a favourable comparison with the older agencies.

Unfortunately the very attractions of this policy tended to undermine the longer-term objectives of technical assistance. The easier it is to obtain assistance, the greater the incentive for a national office to turn to the outside agency for the solution of its problems and to reduce the scale of its own effort in proportion. For an office desperately short of competent staff, it is no more than rational to concentrate the available skills on those areas where no external assistance is on offer. Thus the free supply of technical assistance created its own demand. As a consequence one saw in many countries minimal involvement by local staff in the WFS survey and minimal local activity in the intervals between WFS staff visits. Inevitably this syndrome was particularly acute during the long-drawn-out data processing and report stages.

The problem was aggravated by what, in these authors' view, was a serious misjudgement of the potential of routine work for enhancing country capability. The WFS committees, in particular, urged the policy of leaving to the local office all but the most technically demanding tasks: everything that *could* be done by local staff *should* be done by them. This policy assumed that the basic constraints on the completion of survey work in a developing country statistical unit were nothing more than a lack of technical know-how and that the sole duty of external assistance was to remedy this deficiency. Yet this is unrealistic in at least two respects. First, the areas in which WFS surveys met the longest delays, and which, by that pragmatic definition, may reasonably be called the most 'difficult' for the countries, did not require any very sophisticated know-how. Above all, the editing and correction process, which often continued for many months, could be fully understood within a few weeks. The remaining months of work contributed nothing to the achievement of country capability but much to the sapping of enthusiasm. Secondly, the view that technical know-how constitutes the major bottleneck overlooks the existence of a more crucial constraint: in almost every national office professional staff is insufficient in number, or in productivity, to undertake the full work plan which has been assigned to the unit. There are, quite simply, too many things to be done. The result is that once a project appears to be bogging down in a mass of detailed and uninteresting tasks, local professional staff tend to turn their attention to other equally pressing but more interesting work.

The clear implication here is the primary importance of maintaining *speed* in the survey processing. Once the operations begin to slow down, interest will flag, morale droop and attention turn to other matters.

We therefore advocate a crash approach to survey processing. We recommend that, for the major stages of data processing in a survey, the supporting agency should send a team sufficient in numbers and capacity to undertake the work themselves. While local staff should be encouraged to play as active a role as possible, this factor should not be allowed to limit the speed of progress. The overriding aim should be to get the work done in the shortest possible time. Such a policy was adopted in a few of the later WFS surveys. It may be thought high-handed but experience shows that it maintains the interest and enthusiasm of local staff simply because it is seen as effective. In our view the experience of such a dynamic approach does more to enhance local capability than the traditional strategy of minimum intervention.

A possible format for such a crash programme, applicable perhaps for the report writing phase as well, is that of the *in-country workshop*. This allows the work to be spread among all available personnel and encourages co-operation while making the training aspect explicit.

We turn now to some other issues discussed here. The use of resident advisers seems to have been necessary, yet the heavy additional input which was needed even when a resident adviser was present must raise doubts as to whether the best use was made of the advisers' time. In some cases, perhaps, better results could have been achieved by using two resident advisers consecutively, changing over (with some overlap) as work moved into the data processing phase.

Similar doubts arise about the decision to set up the Caribbean co-ordinator's office. In the three countries concerned, 50 per cent of technical assistance was still given by London-based staff and the total was inordinately high for a group of countries at a relatively high level of development. One obvious reason for this was the absence of any data processing expertise in the co-ordinator's office.

Finally, the high levels of technical assistance input found in the WFS country projects must be seen as a consequence of the exceptionally ambitious data processing and reporting requirements imposed by WFS. Whether these standards were set unnecessarily high is discussed elsewhere in this volume, notably in chapters 18 and 21, and in Pullum, Özsever and Harpham (1984). There is little doubt that in a future survey external assistance could be reduced if these authors' recommendations, as well as our own, were implemented.

Notes

1. Iran excluded, since WFS was involved only at the earlier stages of the survey.
2. WFS Project Proposal, 15 August 1972.

9

Survey Timing

Chris Scott
Martin Vaessen

9.1 Introduction

This chapter examines problems of timing encountered in WFS surveys. Timing actually achieved is considered in relation both to the planned timetables of the individual surveys and to more subjective norms of what seems, in retrospect, 'reasonable'. The primary purpose is descriptive, but we also devote some discussion to the question of the *causes* of the discrepancies observed between plans and performance. In the areas of data processing and report writing these issues are examined more fully in chapter 18. In the present chapter, therefore, relatively more attention is given to the earlier survey phases.

9.2 Duration of survey stages

In this section we report the durations of the country surveys and of their various operational stages. In the next section we compare these achieved durations with the planned durations as contained in the survey plans.

Identification of clear-cut survey stages is not entirely straightforward. The simplest procedure is to identify certain moments in the life of the survey — such as the start of the pre-test, the end of the main fieldwork, completion of the first report — and to define the stages as the periods between such moments. The stages are then non-overlapping and without gaps by definition and this simplifies the presentation. A second approach is to identify *operations* — such as coding, programming, etc. — and to record the start and finish of each. Though more meaningful, this leads to overlapping durations, and sometimes to empty periods, with consequent problems of presentation and greater difficulty in obtaining precise data. The first approach turns out to be adequate for a broad description and is used in the present section. Table 9.1 shows the selected points and stages with their definitions. Note that the short names given to the stages are provided for convenience only and do not always correspond exactly to the activities taking place during the stage. The *end* of a survey is, of course, open and for this reason stage 6, Further analysis, is not covered in our figures and tables.

Figure 9.1 shows the durations achieved by 41 countries for the different stages. The countries are lined up according to the *median date of interview*; this has been done so that the extension of the bars on the right shows the effective

TABLE   9.1
Definition of survey stages

Stages	Events	Definitions
	Design visit(s)	
1 Preliminary	Start of operations	Normally the moment of funding approval but may be earlier
2 Preparatory	Start of pre-test	Start of fieldwork for first pre-test
3 Fieldwork	Start of fieldwork	First calendar month in which number of individual interviews achieved exceeds 1 per cent of final total
4 Data processing	End of fieldwork	Last calendar month in which number of individual interviews achieved exceeds 1 per cent of final total
	Tabulation	Production of first usable set of standard tables from woman's file
5 Report	Report to printer	Submission to printer of first (main) country report. If spread over a period, date of submitting last of main tables
6 Further analysis	Publication	Publication of first (main) country report. If spread over a period date of release of volume of tables
	Open	

average delay in making the data available after their collection. In addition to the stages defined above, the figure shows the design visit(s) and the publication date of the first (main) report.

Table 9.2 shows the regional averages, by operational stage.

Table 9.3 gives the quartile distribution of the durations across countries. This serves as an indicator of the amount of inter-country variation.

These tables also show the *total* durations according to two different definitions: first the sum of the five stages, i.e. the duration from the start of operations to the submission of the report for printing; second the time from the design visit to publication of the report.

The most striking feature of these results is the enormously long time spent

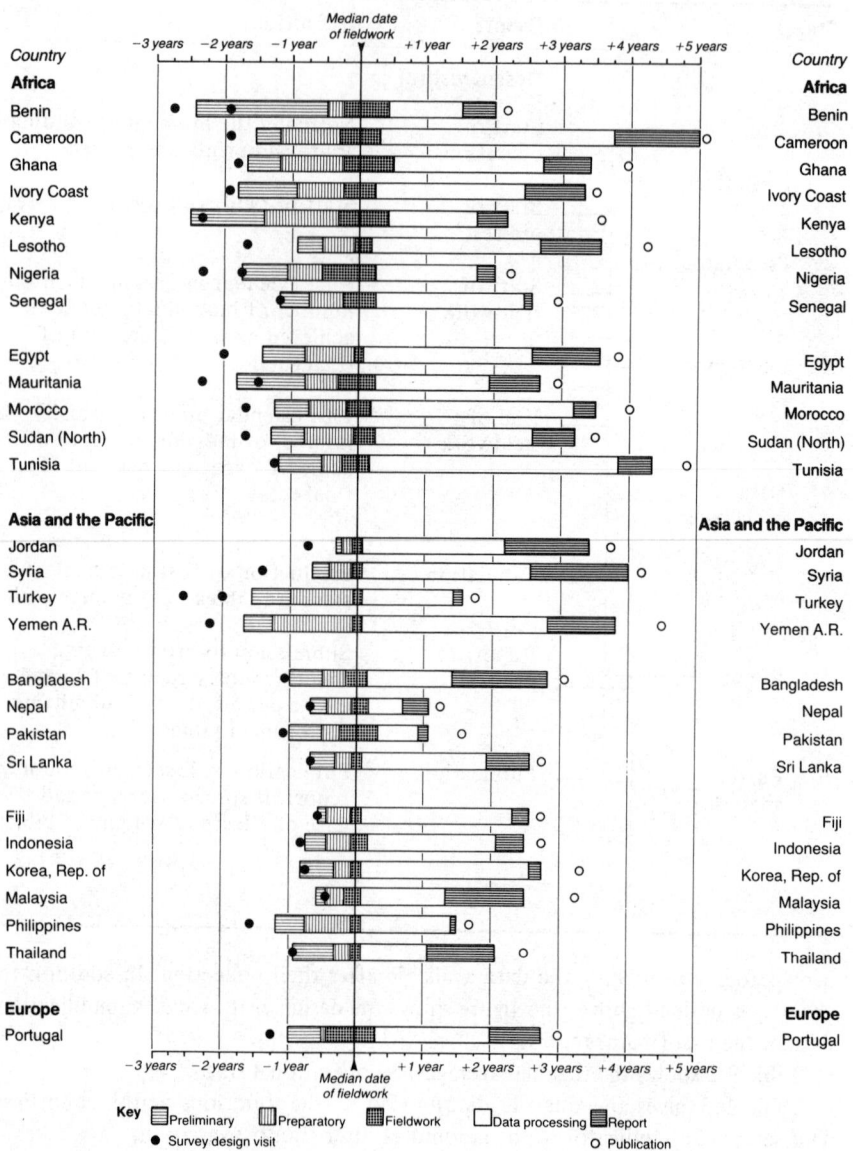

FIG. 9.1 Duration of survey stages

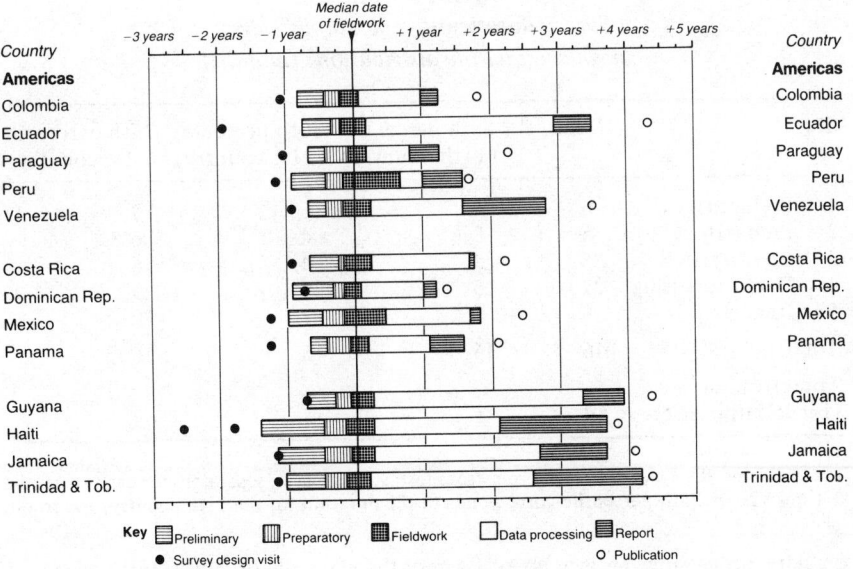

FIG. 9.1 continued

TABLE 9.2

Mean survey duration by operational stage; regional averages (months)

Stage		All[a] countries (n = 41)	Africa (n = 12)	Asia and Pacific (n = 10)	Carib- bean (n = 4)	Latin America (n = 9)	Middle East (n = 5)
1	Preliminary	6	9	5	8	5	5
2	Preparatory	5	7	4	4	3	8
3	Fieldwork	5	7	3	4	5	2
4	Data processing	22	27	17	29	14	27
5	Report	8	7	7	14	5	12
Total 1–5 (Range)		46 (21–79)	57 (45–79)	36 (21–46)	60 (56–63)	32 (23–51)	53 (38–66)
Total from design visit to publication[b]		54	66	40	67	43	65

[a] Portugal included here, although not appearing in regional breakdown.
[b] If more than one design visit occurred, only the last is considered.

TABLE 9.3

Survey duration by operational stage;
mean and quartile distribution[a] (months)

Stage	Mean	25th percentile (11th country)	50th percentile (21st country)	75th percentile (31st country)
1 Preliminary	6	4	6	7
2 Preparatory	5	3	4	6
3 Fieldwork	5	3	4	6
4 Data processing	22	15	22	29
5 Report	8	3	7	12
Total 1–5	46	36	45	56
Total from design visit to publication	54	41	53	67

[a] Placing the 41 countries in order from fastest to slowest, separately for each stage, the 1st quartile or 25th percentile corresponds to the duration for the 11th country, and so on.

on data processing, an average of 22 months. This phase consistently accounts for close to half of the total operational duration. Nor is this simply due to a few exceptional countries: 75 per cent of the countries took more than 15 months with this phase. Even Latin America, with the best performance among the regions, averaged 14 months.

Also striking is the length of time spent in the report-writing stage — an average of eight months. Here there is a wider variation between countries: while in each of the other stages the 75th percentile is always close to double the 25th, for the report stage this ratio is 4:1.

9.3 Achieved versus planned durations

In this section we compare achieved durations for the different stages with the durations contained in the project plan drawn up at the time of the survey design visit.

In order to bring out salient features of the data we introduce some modifications in the schema used in the preceding section. Stages 1 and 2 are now combined into a phase which we treat as a whole. Stage 4, Data processing, is divided into three operational activities, as follows:

4.1 Data preparation and entry — Office editing, coding, punching

4.2 Machine editing — Includes manual correction of errors detected by machine editing. Excludes work on specifying and programming editing rules

4.3 Tabulation — Interval between end of 4.2 and start of 5.

Here the substages 4.1 and 4.2 depart from the earlier methodology in that they are defined in terms of the operations conducted. Thus they may overlap with each other and/or with stage 3 (fieldwork), or alternatively there may be gaps during which no work is done on the survey. With the third substage, 4.3, we return to the earlier system. These adjustments are designed to allow the maximum of meaningful analysis from the available information. Finally we introduce the new stage 'report printing', which is simply the period between the submission of the report to the printer and its publication.

Table 9.4 shows the mean planned and achieved durations, by stage, together with the slippage for each stage and the cumulative slippage suffered up to the end of each stage counting from the start of work. Planned durations are taken from the project documents prepared at the survey design visit. If the document was revised before operations started, the revised timetable is used; otherwise no revisions are considered.

TABLE   9.4
Slippage in survey timetables (months)[a]

Stage	Mean duration			Cumulative slippage by end of stage
	Planned	Actual	Difference	
Operations prior to fieldwork	9.0	11.4	2.4	2.4
Fieldwork	3.6	4.5	0.9	3.3
Data preparation and entry[b]	4.7	7.9	3.2	6.4
Machine editing[b]	2.6	11.0	8.4	14.3
Tabulation	2.3	6.7	4.4	18.7
Report	3.2	8.1	4.9	23.6
Report printing	1.7	4.9	3.2	26.8
Total	24.0	51.0	27.0	

[a] Covers 41 countries.
[b] Stages defined in terms of operations performed, allowing possible overlapping and gaps between stages. In these cases cumulative slippage in the last column may differ from the cumulated third column.

Table 9.5 shows the same data on planned duration and on cumulative slippage at end of stage, broken down by region. (The achieved durations are available from table 9.2.)

Up to the report completion, the tables show an average cumulative slippage of two years, varying regionally from 11 months in Latin America to 39 months in the Caribbean. About two-thirds of this slippage occurs during the data processing stages, and among these the machine editing stage makes much the largest contribution, accounting on its own for about one-third of the total operational slippage.

TABLE 9.5

Slippage in survey timetables, by region (months)[a]

Stage	Africa (n = 12)		Asia & Pacific (n = 10)		Caribbean (n = 4)		Latin America (n = 9)		Middle East (n = 5)	
	Planned duration	Cumulative slippage	Planned duration	Cumulative slippage	Planned duration	Cumulative slippage	Planned duration	Cumulative slippage	Planned duration	Cumulative slippage
Operations prior to fieldwork	11.5	4.6	7.9	0.6	9.5	2.6	6.9	0.8	9.3	3.3
Fieldwork	4.9	6.3	3.0	0.7	2.1	4.3	3.4	2.1	3.4	2.1
Data preparation and entry[b]	6.4	11.1	3.8	2.8	3.4	3.9	4.2	3.1	4.9	9.3
Machine editing[b]	4.0	21.0	2.5	6.3	1.5	22.3	1.7	6.9	2.3	20.9
Tabulation	2.8	26.1	2.3	11.3	1.8	28.3	2.0	10.8	2.2	22.7
Report	2.6	31.0	2.3	15.9	3.2	39.3	4.7	11.4	4.0	30.5
Report printing	2.0	34.5	1.4	18.6	1.3	41.7	1.4	16.4	2.5	31.7

a Covers 40 countries, Portugal excluded.
b Stages defined in terms of operations performed, allowing possible overlapping and gaps between stages.

The overall level of slippage may appear alarming at first sight. However, caution is needed in drawing inferences from discrepancies found between plan and performance. When achievement falls short of the plan it is usual to speak of slippage, a term that implies that the performance is at fault. Yet it is just as possible that the plan was at fault. A plan is based on partial information and, in particular, on prediction; but not all problems can be foreseen. Unforeseen problems may create a discrepancy between the plan and the performance; but it may be that, had the problem been foreseen, an adjustment would have been made to the plan rather than an attempt made to improve performance. Moreover, a plan is not merely a prediction, it is also to some extent an incitement. It seems reasonable, therefore, to adopt a plan that is somewhat more optimistic than the most objective prediction available. This means that some degree of 'slippage' is most often to be expected.

For all these reasons, precise comparisons between plans and performances should not be taken too literally. Such comparisons provide a useful management tool but hardly a reliable means of measuring deficiencies in performance. Nevertheless, when large discrepancies are found it must be concluded that something is seriously amiss. Even if the fault is with the plan, a very large error implies an alarming lack of realism on the part of the planner.

The above basic data on timing and slippage form the essential background to the discussion in the remainder of this chapter on causes and consequences.

9.4 Timing and slippage according to the survey stages

Introduction

In this section we examine more closely the operations involved at each stage of the survey and attempt to describe the way in which the timetable is drawn up and how slippage arises.

Preliminary and preparatory stages

This phase covers the period up to the start of the main fieldwork. The main operations to be executed during these stages are described below.

1 *Planning.* A detailed plan of the survey operations is drawn up, showing the timetable, the numbers and grades of personnel involved, equipment needs, and costs. The plan includes identification of the main topics of the questionnaire, including any use of the WFS modules, specification of the sample size and sampling frame, the arrangements for training of fieldworkers and for their supervision and transport in the field, the set-up for office coding and editing, the objectives as regards machine editing and tabulation and the corresponding manpower, software and hardware requirements, the personnel responsible for writing the report, and the arrangements for its printing and dissemination. It includes a description of the organizational structure for the survey and the names of the key personnel. There will also be an estimate of

technical assistance needs. Most of this planning work is completed by the end of the survey design visit.

2 *Adaptation of questionnaires and manuals.* The household and individual questionnaires, based on the WFS core and modules, are adapted to specific country needs (typically about two weeks' work). Translations are made into relevant local languages, and back-translations are made independently as a check. About one month is generally allowed for this translation work and if several languages are involved these are treated simultaneously by separate teams. Finalization of the questionnaires involves careful layout work and typing, and as much as one month may be allowed for this. Typically some method of rapid reproduction (stencil or photocopy) is used to produce the few hundred copies needed for the pre-test. Drafting of interviewers' and supervisors' manuals, based on WFS models and adapted to the country questionnaire, starts as soon as the content of the questionnaires has been fixed, and the manuals are usually ready for the pre-test by the time the questionnaires have been reproduced.

3 *Pre-test.* Meanwhile, field personnel for the pre-test are identified and recruited so that the pre-test training can begin as soon as the documents are ready. Typically such training lasts two weeks and the pre-test itself runs for a further one or two weeks.

4 *Finalization of instruments.* Review of the pre-test results generally leads to some modifications of the instruments. These are now finalized and sent for printing – often a considerably longer process than that used for the pre-test documents.

5 *Sampling.* The various operations under this head can start at any time and need to be completed by the time of the main fieldwork. They seldom constitute a bottleneck. They include sample design, selection of areas, mapping/ segmentation, listing of dwellings/households, selection of dwellings/households. The last, or last two, of these operations may be included in the main fieldwork.

6 *Other preparatory work.* While awaiting the printing of the final instruments, interviewers are identified or recruited, the training course is prepared and the final arrangements are made for the fieldwork. During this period, or not long afterwards, specification of the machine edits should be completed and programming of these should begin.

7 *Training.* Field supervisors are generally trained by means of the pre-test, but often this arrangement has not been able to cater for the number of supervisors required and in that case a two weeks supervisors' training course is typically arranged. Interviewers are generally trained for three weeks.

Essentially, the first part of the survey timetable is worked out by putting together the above operations, each with a plausible estimate of elapsed time required, and allowing for overlap. Typically this leads to an estimated interval of 8-10 months from the start of the design visit to the end of training. In countries with limited experience or very scant resources of manpower, some allowance – say perhaps a month – is often made for unforeseen contingencies. It often happens that the start of fieldwork is constrained by climatic or other factors (see below), thus fixing the end point of the period we are considering.

By and large, as we see from tables 9.2, 9.3 and 9.4, although stages 1 and 2 vary somewhat in duration between countries, few countries slip very far behind their timetable at this period of the survey. A variety of factors favour efficient implementation during this time: the project is new and morale is high; though some of the operations are technically complex (questionnaire design, sample design) these are individually of short duration and do not threaten the momentum of the project's progress. Perhaps the most important factor is that once the date of the start of fieldwork has been determined a commitment is made involving substantial resources and personnel, and this in itself exercises a strong forward pull on the preceding operations, making delay unacceptable. Regrettably, in most cases this forward momentum is not destined to last for very much longer than the end of fieldwork.

Slippage does, indeed, sometimes occur at these early stages even if it is less common than later. Several countries (Turkey, Haiti, Morocco) reconsidered after the first design visit to the extent that the whole project was dropped for a period, or work was passed to a different executing agency, and in such cases a second design visit was generally necessary. But once work began there were only two or three countries (mainly those with very limited professional manpower – Benin, Cameroon, Guyana are examples) which did not move swiftly and on schedule through to the fieldwork stage. It should be noted that slippage prior to the fieldwork stage does not affect the ultimate value of the data; it may create organizational problems for the executing agency but in the long run no lasting harm is done. The worst experience during these early stages is slippage *between the end of training and the start of fieldwork*. This occurred in only three countries, Guyana, Morocco and Nigeria, and in two of these was due to high-level intervention. Obviously such an occurrence seriously threatens the quality of interviews and the efficacy of training, making some period of retraining generally necessary.

Fieldwork stage

For most survey activities it can reasonably be argued that the faster they are carried out the better. In the case of fieldwork the situation is more complex: there are arguments in favour of drawing it out over a long period. Moreover the fieldwork duration is a variable under the direct control of the survey planner: by doubling the number of fieldworkers, for example, he can (approximately) halve the duration. The planner has therefore to face a direct choice: how much time should he allow for the fieldwork and (the counterpart question) how many fieldworkers should be allocated?

The arguments in favour of short duration (and a large field force) are as follows:[1]

1 The results can become available sooner

2 The results are likely to be more up-to-date when produced

3 There is less chance of conflict with climatic constraints

4 There is less chance of conflict with cultural constraints – Ramadan, Christmas, vacation periods, etc.

5 Dropout of field staff is minimized

6 Fall in work standards due to fatigue is minimized

7 The larger total field force may offer greater flexibility in allocation of interviewers to meet linguistic or ethnic requirements

8 Finally, it sometimes happens that there are resource availability constraints, such as limited availability of vehicles or of staff obtained on loan, or the need to release staff for the next survey, and these may in themselves force the options regarding length of fieldwork.

Since fieldwork duration is in any case generally short in comparison with other survey operations, arguments 1 and 2 above are of minor significance. Regarding arguments 6 and 7, there is evidence from the study of interviewer attrition in WFS surveys (see chapter 16) which suggests that in many countries any extension of fieldwork beyond three months leads to heavy dropout of field staff as well as a fall in the quality of work. It is possible, however, that the effects observed are a function of *unforeseen prolongation* of fieldwork rather than a *long duration* as such and that they would be eliminated if interviewers were told at the time of their recruitment how long they should expect to work.

Turning to the arguments in favour of a long duration, essentially these are the arguments for a smaller field force. They are as follows:

1 Ease of recruitment of fieldworkers

2 Possibility of employing stricter selection criteria and thus recruiting better quality interviewers

3 Ease of training

4 Ease of control in the field

5 Fewer vehicles required

6 Smaller training costs relative to those for fieldwork.

The third argument is particularly important, since if the number of trainees exceeds about 20 it becomes desirable to divide them into two classes. This doubles the requirement for trainers and for classrooms; it also raises the problem of ensuring consistency between the two training groups. In some WFS surveys there have been as many as four training classes. For certain countries the fifth argument has been decisive: there has been an upper limit on the number of vehicles obtainable (though not on the duration of their availability) and this has imposed a firm constraint on the speed of fieldwork.

The argument for a longer fieldwork duration becomes stronger where the professional staff of the survey are very small in number. In general, a larger organization will tend to arrange for a more rapid field operation.

Figure 9.1 and table 9.2 show that field durations in the WFS ranged from about two to seven months, with few exceptions, and tended to be longer in Africa. In general, work was completed approximately on schedule. In three cases (Ghana, Nigeria and Peru) very long durations are shown and these were far in excess of plans: they were due to total stoppages of work due to external causes.

Some of the advantages of a short duration can be achieved while employing *at any given moment* only a small field force by carrying out the fieldwork in waves. This approach was adopted in Kenya. The country was divided into three regions which were surveyed consecutively; fieldwork lasted two and a half months in each region and three training courses were given at two and a half month intervals. This type of arrangement is particularly attractive where language differences between the regions would in any case necessitate a different group of fieldworkers for each region.

Data processing stage

We have already drawn attention to the fact that the data processing phase accounted for half of the total operational duration of the average WFS survey and two-thirds of the final slippage in relation to the initial timetable. The crucial problem of timing in relation to this phase is examined in detail in chapter 18 by Otto and Rattenbury. In this section we shall attempt little more than to summarize that discussion. Aspects of the problem — notably WFS's own contribution to the deficiencies in the survey plans — are also discussed by Vaessen and Scott in chapter 7 and we shall draw on that chapter also.

It has been pointed out earlier that discrepancies between planned and actual timetables cannot automatically be attributed to tardy implementation: there is also the possibility of unrealistic planning. This consideration is particularly relevant in the case of the data processing phase. Vaessen and Scott mention that several — perhaps as many as half — of the survey plans were produced before firm decisions had been taken by WFS defining the operations which were supposed to constitute the standard data processing plan for a WFS survey. Further, actual experience of data processing for WFS surveys hardly began to feed back to the London headquarters before 1976. At this point 19 countries (including nearly all of the ultimate participants in Asia and in the Caribbean) had already completed their survey plan under the guidance of WFS staff. Thus these plans were made largely in the dark. Nevertheless, the plans made were actually generous in relation to the duration suggested by Otto and Rattenbury as 'reasonable estimates' for the work that had to be done: they allow on average seven months between the end of fieldwork and the completion of the main tabulations, while Otto and Rattenbury suggest 24 weeks. Since the actual average duration was 22 months, it is clear that much more went wrong than mere unrealistic planning.

The main causes cited by Otto and Rattenbury for excessive time spent in the data processing phase may be listed as follows:

1 Editing/coding not started until fieldwork completed

2 Insufficient numbers of coders and/or data entry workers

3 Editing software not ready when needed. A variety of reasons are mentioned:
   (a) Software mistakenly thought to be ready
   (b) Delayed by job changes
   (c) Delayed by specifications produced too late
   (d) Delayed by inadequate computer access for testing
   (e) Deficient software (Concor contained unsuspected bugs)
   (f) Magnitude of task underestimated (in relation to available staff)

4 Problems with hardware:
   (a) Electricity cuts
   (b) Air conditioning failures
   (c) Computer failures
   (d) System software not functioning
   (e) Other applications had priority
   (f) Limited working hours

5 Shortage of supplies; long delays in obtaining supplies

6 Poor quality work at the field, coding, data entry or correction stages

7 Insufficient staff for correction work (or high level required for this work not foreseen)

8 Lack of involvement by survey director

9 Delayed access to competent technical trouble-shooter

10 Excessive perfectionism.

The number and variety of problems cited here is striking — and discouraging to anyone seeking a simple solution. (Yet even this list is not exhaustive: the authors can recall from their own experience more than one country in which the main cause of delay was none of those mentioned above.) Some, but not all, of the problems might be resolved if a survey director with sufficient authority tackled them with sufficient energy and intelligence, and this subset might be regarded therefore as essentially 'management' problems. But even here, the technical nature of the data processing operation tends to encourage the development of specialist enclaves, resisting the authority of a generalist survey director and tending to nullify any efforts he may make to monitor progress and foresee bottlenecks. Outside this area there are the diverse problems characteristic of the developing country environment — electricity and equipment failures, shortage of supplies, bureaucratic delays, instability of job assignments — and these are largely beyond the control of any civil servant in the national statistical office.

One solution which might radically reduce the time spent on survey data processing would be to reduce the objectives themselves. Essentially this means relaxing the editing requirements and cutting the number of tables. The first option is explored by Pullum, Özsever and Harpham (1984) and the second in chapter 21 of this volume. In both cases it becomes clear that important savings can indeed be achieved without drastic loss in the value of the final product.

Report writing

As we have seen, the duration of this phase varies more from one country to another than any other stage of the survey. Obviously the work depends above all on the individual capacity of the professional worker(s) involved. Unlike the other stages, there are few *managerial* problems here. (There are, all the same, two such problems where slow reactions have led to delays: the advance assignment of the necessary personnel, and the decision to start work on the descriptive chapters of the report well in advance of the arrival of the tables.) This is also an area in which the magnitude of the WFS contribution has varied greatly between countries and this in turn has affected the speed of working.

Delays at this stage are, once again, discussed in fuller detail in chapter 21. The authors note the disappointing performance of several (but not all) countries and suggest that 'interpretation and concise presentation of results is plainly a weakness of many statistical offices in developing countries and contrasts with their general capability in data collection'. They add: 'We believe that this area is badly neglected in training programmes and that the consequences are, and will continue to be, serious'.

But it was also WFS experience that other countries were able to supply a highly competent author who wrote quickly and effectively once relieved of the burdens of his local duties. In several cases such persons spent a period at the London headquarters to undertake the main report-writing task.

One further warning should be made before we come to the main conclusions and recommendations. Surveys are highly complex operations, Many different activities are involved. Different types of documents and equipment have to be prepared or obtained and brought together at the right time. People at different levels and in different places have to co-operate. Field staff have to be moved about the country on dates that cannot be accurately predicted. The skills involved range from psychology to mathematics, accounting to computer programming, typing to driving. The consequence of all this variety is a correspondingly wide range of things that can go wrong. WFS surveys have overrun their timetables in the countries not simply because local or expatriate staff have sometimes been inefficient, but as a consequence of a wide range of one-off mishaps — electricity cuts in one country, change of government policy in another, a strike in another, an equipment failure here a resignation there. In an international operation a new dimension is added which offers further opportunities for failure: headquarters staff may move, financial crisis may hit a funding agency, the international mails may lose a key document or tape, and of course international personnel, like others, are sometimes inefficieñt. The conclusion is that no *general* explanation for cost overruns and slippage exists, and no *general* measure to reduce them will guarantee a faultless performance. Despite this reservation there are undoubtedly important areas in which some of the delays could have been avoided if organization of the surveys had been better.

9.5   Conclusions and recommendations

The scheduling of operations and the prevention of slippage are, essentially, responsibilities of management. They depend above all on two of the basic management functions: *planning* and *monitoring*. In a general way, therefore, the first recommendation must be for a strengthening of these two activities, namely:

Greater *realism* and greater *care* in operational planning.

More *active* and more *detailed* monitoring of operations.

The first of these implies, specifically, detailed consideration of what operations are going to be carried out, identification of the resources which will be required — both people and things — and an assessment of how long each process will take, with due allowance for interactions (some operations can overlap, some cannot be started until others have been completed). Monitoring requires meticulous and personal attention to project activities in course, constant attention to detail and unflagging alertness for signs of breakdown.

These requirements are unlikely to be met unless the managerial staff feel a strong personal commitment to the success of the project.

Slippage may be defined as the discrepancy between the planned and achieved durations. Examination of actual survey timetables shows far wider variation in the achieved than the planned durations. While unrealistic forecasting certainly contributed to slippage, there is little doubt that the main source is to be found in deficiencies of implementation.

We turn now to specific recommendations designed to reduce timetable overruns.

1   *Availability of qualified personnel*

A crucial problem for countries participating in the WFS was to provide the personnel required. This showed itself in two ways. First, needed qualified personnel were not always supplied; this applies particularly to the data processing stages of the work. Second, appropriate personnel, even where supplied, were often not made available full time.

In addition to the obvious drawbacks of understaffing, a subsidiary consequence of part-time assignments was often observed: unclear definition of responsibilities. In the situation found in most developing country agencies, overloaded with numerous responsibilities and seriously understaffed, it may be unrealistic to expect full-time assignment of senior staff to one survey for periods of a year or more. Nevertheless, the division and assignment of responsibilities should always be kept clear and should be effectively taken up by those to whom they are assigned. It is possibly in this area that the root of much of the slippage can be found.

Among the various survey stages, that of *fieldwork* was observed to be the least subject to delay. One contributory cause of this was perhaps unexpected: the wide use of temporary personnel at this stage. The duration for which such temporary workers are available is often strictly limited and this fact puts pressure on the permanent survey staff to keep to the timetable and meet commitments in order to maintain the availability of the temporary staff.

2 *Office organization*

Even when staffing issues seemed to be settled, the office organization often contributed negatively to survey execution. Few countries established survey offices, within or outside the executing agency, where all staff working on the survey were physically brought together. In many WFS surveys staff assigned to the project stayed in their existing offices, often far removed from each other. Coders, editors and correctors were frequently housed a long way away from their supervisors. This system of organization undoubtedly contributed to: deficient implementation of responsibilities, lack of supervision, lack of team spirit, lack of project identification and so forth.

3 *Data processing*

The survey stage during which most slippage occurred was data processing. Especially in the early years of the project this could be blamed in part on optimistic estimation by WFS staff of the time needed for this stage, and this in turn was partly caused by the fact that the full implications of the variable construction and tabulation requirements were not as yet defined.

For many countries these delays were, however, caused mainly by other factors. Data processing operations were typically started too late. As a result, programs were not fully ready when the data became available, either for machine editing or tabulation. Early and continuous involvement of programming staff is absolutely essential to achieve better performance during this stage.

Machine editing of the data was where the most extreme data processing delays built up. Aside from the above-mentioned deficiencies in the programming operation, the most important source of delay here was the inadequacy, either in number or in quality, of the machine editing clerks or 'correctors'. Typically, the correctors used did not have sufficient training in the mechanics of the questionnaire and the survey objectives. Only correctors who had been previously trained as supervisors or interviewers should have been used. In many cases too few correctors were used (only two in one particular country and generally no more than five). Monotony of work then became unavoidable and performance became extremely inefficient. Sufficient personnel should have been scheduled to complete this stage in no more than two months, or at most three.

4 *Report writing*

As with data processing, report writing suffered from delays in starting and from a lack of experienced personnel. The latter was aggravated by the specific and rather demanding format and content of the reports required by the WFS. In many countries the drafting of such an extensive report constituted something of an innovation and had seldom been attempted by the personnel assigned to the WFS survey. Notwithstanding this, an earlier start to the report drafting could have reduced some of the most substantial overruns which countries finally suffered during this stage.

5 *General*

Aside from some of the hardware and software problems discussed by Otto and Rattenbury with respect to the data processing of WFS surveys, it seems that most timing problems of survey execution could be overcome by tighter management and supervision. This can, of course, only be effective if the survey plans are realistic and if availability of personnel can be maintained as established in the plan.

Although many factors have contributed, most of the major delays have been due to deficient management and insufficient commitment, sometimes aggravated by deficient technical assistance. It is in these areas that positive intervention is likely to contribute most to the achievement of future survey timetables.

Note

1. Note that these arguments apply to a survey in which there is no large seasonal factor. Many economic and agricultural surveys require that data collection be spread over the whole year.

10

Survey Costs

John Cleland
Jane Verrall

10.1 Introduction

Less is known about costs than about any other feature of developing country surveys. The reasons for this neglect are not difficult to locate. They include the sensitivity of financial data, the problems of defining and measuring various types of cost, such as overheads and depreciation, and the practical difficulty of maintaining cost records of sufficient reliability to sustain serious analysis. As a result, documentation of sample surveys often omits any mention of this subject or includes expenditure figures that vary so widely between apparently similar surveys that the underlying accountancy principles must be different (see the UN series 'Sample Surveys of Current Interest'). The discussion of costs of data collection by the US National Academy of Sciences (Committee on Population and Demography 1981b) is symptomatic of the difficulties. While a systematic list of cost determinants is assembled, no attempt is made to present or analyse actual expenditures.

As a major international survey programme, WFS is well placed to remedy this gap in our knowledge of surveys and indeed has an obligation to report on the costs of its activities. The purposes of presenting WFS cost data in this chapter are both retrospective and prospective. In terms of past performance we wish to provide at least the evidence on which can be based a broad assessment of the consistency of WFS expenditure with its major objectives and achievements and the overall cost-efficiency of the programme. This objective can only be partially fulfilled because of lack of comparable financial data for alternative approaches. In terms of future surveys, we wish to present information that will be useful both to international donors and national organizations in planning and costing. Of particular relevance here is the identification of possible ways of reducing future costs without jeopardizing the quality of results. This second objective is more easily realized and we believe that this chapter will be helpful in the planning of future similar surveys.

The approach is essentially descriptive. As will become clear, the available data are insufficiently detailed to permit a statistical analysis of the determinants of cost. Moreover these determinants are numerous and often idiosyncratic in nature; any statistical model of costs would need to be so complex that its utility would be doubtful.

We begin by describing the source of the data and their limitations. The main section presents in-country expenditure by the major components or survey stages for the 30 surveys whose expenditure was completed by mid-1983. In later sections, a brief discussion of cost-efficiency is given, a comparison of initial budgets with final expenditure is presented and finally the costs of technical assistance are introduced.

10.2   Source and Limitations of the Data

It is helpful to divide the financing of WFS surveys into three types: funds or resources contributed by the country itself; funds contributed by one of the three external funding agencies (UNFPA, USAID, UKODA) for expenditure within the country; and funds for technical assistance to specific surveys in the form of the salaries and expenses of WFS staff, consultants, and long-term advisers. In this and the following sections, attention will be concentrated exclusively on the first two types. The costs of technical assistance and co-ordination will be discussed in section 10.6.

To understand the nature of in-country survey expenditure figures, we must first describe the budgeting process. Survey budgets were negotiated at the survey design visit by one of the ISI/WFS contract officers, in consultation with local staff and WFS staff. The agreed budget formed part of the project agreement, which was subsequently submitted to the funding agency concerned for its consideration and approval. Thus, in financial planning, WFS acted as a broker between recipient and donor, though, as we shall see, a broker with considerable influence and powers.

The WFS project was fortunate in having no rigid and externally imposed constraints in its financing of individual surveys. No upper cost ceiling was fixed, and indeed survey budgets varied widely. The approach adopted by WFS was that budgets should faithfully reflect the work plan, should accord as closely as possible with existing host government pay scales and subsistence allowances, should be sufficiently detailed to permit thorough appraisal and should exclude substantial capital expenditure on vehicles, computers and such-like or on long-term overseas training which could not be justified by the needs of one survey. The latter restriction was an important one, because it implied a narrow concentration on the execution of a single survey, leaving to other development projects the task of long-term enhancement of local capability.

Nor were there any pre-determined rules concerning the division of costs between the country and the external agency. Rather there was an unwritten understanding that the country would contribute the time of its regular staff and its facilities and that these components, if costed realistically, would amount to at least one-quarter of the total budget. Generally, then, the country contribution was made in kind and could be met within the normal operating budget of the executive institution, usually the statistical office. This arrangement avoided the need for a budgetary application by the statistical office to central government funds and concomitant long delays in starting the survey.

The costing of contributions in kind, for instance depreciation of vehicles or notional rental charges for use of accommodation or computer, was to some extent arbitrary. This feature carries important implications for the analysis of costs, because it largely invalidates inter-survey comparisons of the countries' own expenditures on their surveys. There are however a few exceptions to the prevailing pattern of contributions made exclusively in kind; some survey organizations asked for and received from central government funds increments to their normal budgets for the fertility survey. There are also wide variations in the types of cost met by countries. For instance, some paid the travel and sub-sistence expenses incurred by their senior staff during fieldwork and the running costs of vehicles. In other countries, these costs were met from external funds.

An example of a budget summary is shown in figure 10.1 and a page from a detailed budget in figure 10.2. Both have been extracted from a project agreement. Figure 10.1 depicts the major heads and sub-heads used in WFS budgeting, while figure 10.2 illustrates the level of detail contained in most project agreements. Budgets were always calculated and expressed in the local currency, though the summary also contained equivalent figures in US dollars at the contemporary exchange rate for USAID or UNFPA-funded surveys or in pounds sterling for UKODA-funded surveys. In a number of countries, subsequent currency fluctuations necessitated revision of the dollar or sterling budget, on the principle that the funding agency's obligation was incurred in terms of the local currency.

In addition to drawing up and agreeing survey budgets as illustrated in figures 10.1 and 10.2, the ISI/WFS contract officer used the survey work plan to compile a monthly cash flow chart which showed the anticipated monthly expenditure by sub-head. This detailed breakdown was used to devise an approximate schedule of financial instalments from the funding agency to the country and in addition was intended to serve as a financial planning tool for the local executing agency.

Once the project agreement had been approved by the funding agency (such approval was nearly always forthcoming without further negotiation) and the first instalment of money made, the executive institution was obliged to comply with a pre-arranged system of financial monitoring. For surveys funded by USAID or UKODA, financial control and disbursement were delegated to ISI. For UNFPA-funded surveys, the local United Nations Development Programme office held financial responsibility, though copies of financial reports were sent to ISI and some offices requested ISI confirmation of satisfactory progress before releasing further funds. Either way, the local survey office was expected to submit monthly statements on a form which showed cumulative expenditure, expenditure last month, expected expenditure next month and overall balance of the externally contributed budget separately for about 15 subheads. (See figure 10.3 for an example.)

The completion and submission of the monthly form shown in figure 10.3 was an obligation and failure to comply occasionally resulted in the postponement of further financial instalments, and even to a temporary cessation of survey

COMPONENT	TOTAL BUDGET			1978		1979		1980	
	Country contribut.	Contribution ISI		Contribution ISI		Contribution ISI		Contribution ISI	
	Country currency	Country currency	US$	Country currency	US$	Country currency	US$	Country currency	US$
PROJECT PERSONNEL									
Administrative Personnel	869,000	1,023,000	8,119	279,000	2,214	558,000	4,429	186,000	1,476
National Technical Personnel	5,404,000	4,398,000	34,905	1,285,000	10,198	2,461,000	19,532	652,000	5,175
Training and Pre-Test		1,639,650	13,013	392,250	3,113	1,247,400	9,900		
Field Work-sample		952,000	7,556	952,000	7,556				
Field Work-Survey		11,022,000	87,476			11,022,000	87,476		
Data Proc. Preparation		1,250,500	9,924			1,250,500	9,924		
COMPONENT TOTAL	6,273,000	20,285,150	160,993	2,908,250	23,081	16,538,900	131,261	838,000	6,651
EQUIPMENT									
Expendable		359,000	2,849	359,000	2,849				
Non-Expendable		69,000	548	69,000	584				
Computer Rental		882,000	7,000			882,000	7,000		
Other Equipment Rental									
Rental of Premises	1,650,000								
COMPONENT TOTAL	1,650,000	1,310,000	10,397	428,000	3,397	882,000	7,000		
MISCELLANEOUS									
Operation of Vehicles	1,070,000	916,400	7,273	450,000	3,571	446,400	3,702		
Printing Costs	108,000	929,000	7,373	929,000	7,373	80,000	635	177,000	1,405
Sundry	100,000	267,000	2,119	10,000	79				
COMPONENT TOTAL	1,278,000	2,112,400	16,765	1,389,000	11,023	546,400	4,337	177,000	1,405
GRAND TOTAL	9,201,000	23,707,550	188,155	4,725,250	37,501	17,967,300	142,598	1,015,000	8,056
GRAND TOTAL	9,201,000		73,024						
TOTAL COUNTRY-ISI		32,908,550	261,179						

DATE OF COMPILATION   20 February, 1978

RATE OF EXCHANGE   126 units of currency = 1 US$

FIG. 10.1 Budget summary

CHAPTER IV. PROJECT BUDGET

		Total survey costs				Annual survey costs					
		COUNTRY	CONTR	WFS/UNFPA		1980		1981		1982	
Description	No	m/m	N	m/m	N	m/m	N	m/m	N	m/m	N
91											
(a) Pre-test and training											
PRE-TEST I - Training (Editors)											
Night Allow: (20x14 days xN10)	20	-	-	9.3	2,800	-	-	9.3	2,800	-	-
Travel: (20x1000 km x (0.1N)	-	-	-	-	2,000	-	-	-	2,000	-	-
Field work											
N/Allow:(15x6 days x N10)	15	-	-	3	900	-	-	3.0	900	-	-
(b) PRE-TEST II - Training											
N/Allow:(20x 14 x N10)	20	-	-	9.3	2,800	-	-	9.3	2,800	-	-
Travel:(20 x 100 Km x (0.1N)	-	-	-	-	2,000	-	-	-	2,000	-	-
Fieldwork											
N/Allow:(15 x 6 days x N10)	15	-	-	3.0	900	-	-	3.0	900	-	-
PRE-TEST I & II DRIVERS: (Sal)											
(6 x 7 days at N107 p.m.)	6	1.5	148	-	-	-	-	-	-	-	-
PRE-TEST: Sub-total	76	1.5	148	24.6	11,400	-	-	24.6	11,400	-	-
(c) Main field work training											
Superv. (39 x 15 dys x N10) (N/All)	39	-	-	9.5	5,850	-	-	19.5	5,850	-	-
-do- (30 x 21 " x N10) (")	30	-	-	21	6,300	-	-	21	6,300	-	-
Fld Edit (30 x 36 x N10) (")	30	-	-	36	10,800	-	-	36	10,800	-	-
Inter: (156 x 21 dys x N10 (")	156	-	-	109.5	32,760	-	-	109.5	32,760	-	-
(255 x 1000 km x (0.1N) (Travel)	-	-	-	-	22,500	-	-	-	22,500	-	-
(Sup 39 Edit 30, Int. 156)	-	-	-	-	-	-	-	-	-	-	-
Fld edit (30 x 1.25mxN202.4) (Sal)	30	-	-	-	-	-	-	-	-	-	-
Drivers (6x7 dys at N107 p.m.)	6	1.5	148	45	7,590	-	-	45	7,590	-	-
Main field work training sub-total	291	1.5	148	231	85,800	-	-	231	85,800	-	-
(d) Editors/Coders - Training allow											
(20 x 3 dys x N45) " "	20	-	1,654	2	300	-	-	2	300	-	-
Verifiers (20x10 dys at N165.4pm)	20	10	-	-	-	-	-	-	-	-	-
Sub-total	40	10	1,654	2	300	-	-	2	300	-	-

FIG. 10.2   Illustrative page from a survey budget

FORM D   (Expressed in 000s: Local currency: Rate _____ = US$) _

Code for UNFPA	DESCRIPTION	COUNTRY CONTRIB.	WFS FUND CONTRIB.	EXPENDITURE - WFS/FUND CONTRIBUTION ONLY				GRANT BALANCE End	Latest est. Project WFS share	Expected Final Surplus/ deficit
				End Prev. Month 197	Current Month 197	Ext. Next Month 197	Total end next month 197	197		
		MM	MM	MM	MM	MM	MM	MM		
		—	a	b	c	d	e=b+c+d	F = a-e	g	h= a-g
10	PROJECT PERSONNEL									
13	Admin. support staff									
16 90	National techn. staff									
16 91	Training and Pretest									
16 92	Fieldwork - sample									
16 93	Fieldwork - survey									
16 94	Data process. Prep.									
19	COMPONENT TOTAL									
40	EQUIPMENT									
41	Expendable									
42	Non-expendable									
42 51	Computer rental									
42 97	Other equip. rental									
43 51	Rental of premises									
49	COMPONENT TOTAL									
50	MISCELLANEOUS									
51	Operation of vehicles									
52	Printing/Report costs									
53	Sundry									
05	Contingency element									
59	COMPONENT TOTAL									
99	TOTALS - LOCAL CURR.									
99	TOTALS - US$									

PAYMENT SCHEDULE IN AGREEMENT

Date	Loc. Cur. 000	US$000s

AMOUNTS RECEIVED

Date	L.C.000s	US$000s

TOTALS

COMMENTS ON MAIN ACTIVITIES INVOLVING EXPENDITURE

CASH REQUIREMENTS

	LOCAL CURRENCY
Cash at hand end current month	
cash required before	197

SIGNATURE DIRECTOR: Country/Project:
Date:

FIG. 10.3   The monthly expenditure report

activities. In addition to this form, countries were requested, but not obliged, to complete and remit a more detailed monthly form, which gave a finer breakdown of budget subheads and included not only expenditure figures for the externally funded activities but also expenditure from the countries' own funds. Justification for this further form was two-fold: first, it allowed the local institution to monitor its expenditure very closely and thus provided a high degree of financial control; and secondly, it was intended to permit WFS to undertake detailed cost analyses of surveys. However, as perhaps is inevitable with any reporting system that requires painstaking effort and is not compulsory, only a minority of countries routinely used and dispatched this more detailed form. This failure further erodes the validity of expenditure data from the countries' own resources. In most cases, the sole information on locally contributed expenditure is the original budget and any deviation from this forecast will remain unrecorded.

The budgets for WFS surveys were not rigidly enforced. Countries were permitted to transfer funds within reason from one sub-head to another within the major categories of expenditure. Transfers across major categories required the authorization of the funding agency but this was usually granted. Revisions of the overall budget were also made in many of the 41 surveys. These revisions required a new formal agreement between funding agency and executive institution. Their nature and causes are discussed briefly in section 10.5.

At the end of each USAID and UKODA-funded survey, an audit of survey expenditure was conducted, either by a commercial accountancy firm or by a government audit department. The major purpose of this audit, which formed part of the original contract, was to act as a deterrent against mishandling of funds. Once the money had actually been disbursed, there was little that donor agencies could do to recover funds that had been expended in an unauthorized manner. In any case, rather few such instances were uncovered by the audits. Audits were rarely carried out for UNFPA-funded surveys.

The cost data, presented in the following section of this chapter, are derived from the monthly financial reporting forms though use will also be made of the budgets themselves. The reliability of these costs or expenditures is thus a critical issue which should be considered before presentation of the data themselves. Unfortunately, no precise answer to the question of reliability can be given. No doubt there have been instances where costs have been exaggerated and concealed by 'creative' bookkeeping. More commonly, however, the true costs have been understated. Survey organizations when faced with the exhaustion of external funds for a particular activity, may have preferred to remedy the deficit out of their own resources rather than request a budget revision. Such unbudgeted use of local funds usually remains unrecorded. These two tendencies, exaggerated and understated expenditure, exert contrary and, to some extent, compensating biases.

Expenditure figures become progressively less reliable with the extent of disaggregation into subheads. Though initial budgets were precisely detailed, expenditures were often reported in broader categories. In order to retain a degree of specificity in our presentation of costs, frequent resort has been necessary to the distribution of broad expenditure heads to subheads, using the proportionate breakdown in the budget.

Contract officers, who not only drew up the survey budgets but had the responsibility of monitoring USAID and UKODA-funded surveys, have a good though subjective impression of the relative quality of the financial reports from different countries. In order to gauge whether defects in reporting introduced large systematic biases, we compared key expenditure indicators for reliably reported surveys with those rated as less reliable. The results of this comparison are shown in table 10.1.

On average the 12 surveys rated as unreliable cost more (US$254 000 at 1975 prices) than the 18 surveys rated as reliable (US$208 000). However this difference is not caused by over-expenditure of the agreed budget; the ratios of actual to budgeted expenditure are similar in the two groups both for total and externally contributed costs. In terms of the relative costs of different components of the survey, the two groups show a similar profile. In each, fieldwork accounts for about one-third of total costs and central staff for about one-fifth. Our general conclusion from the evidence of table 10.1 is that inaccuracies in the financial data have not distorted in any gross manner the pattern of expenditure and we shall thus proceed to present information for all 30 surveys.

To compare the costs of 30 surveys spread both geographically and over time, a common unit of value is needed. We chose 1975 US dollars as this common unit and converted all survey budgets and expenditures to this unit in the following way. The simplifying assumption was first made that all survey expenditure took place in the calendar year when the bulk of the main fieldwork occurred. Survey expenditures in local currency were then converted to a 1975 base by using the consumer price index for each country published in the International Financial Statistical Year-book. Finally we used the appropriate mid-1975 US dollar: local currency exchange rate to bring all financial figures to the common unit.

When expressed in 1975 US dollars, the average cost of the 30 surveys was $226 000. What does this imply at 1984 prices and exchange rates? By using the consumer price index up until 1983 (where available) and 1983 dollar exchange rates, and extrapolating to 1984, we can estimate that the 1975 cost of $226 000 is equivalent to about $300 000 at 1984 prices, a difference of 31 per cent. Note that the figure of $300 000 does not take into account the large rise in the value of the US dollar against most other currencies that occurred in 1984 itself, because our 1984 cost estimate is extrapolated from earlier trends in prices and exchange rates.

We admit that both the 1975 cost estimates, and the 1984 equivalent, are very approximate, being based on the assumption that survey costs (dominated by salaries and subsistence allowances) follow closely the trend in consumer prices. Obviously there are instances, particularly in the short term, where this relationship is far from close. However there is, to our knowledge, no

TABLE 10.1

Cost comparisons of reliably and less reliably reported surveys[a]

	Central staff	Pre-test and training	Sample preparation	Fieldwork	Data processing	Printing	Equipment and miscellaneous	Total
A Total costs								
Percentage of expenditure								
Reliable	23.20	6.17	4.05	36.10	10.86	9.78	9.84	100.00
Unreliable	19.05	5.11	7.90	34.03	11.32	11.23	11.36	100.00
1975 US $								
Reliable	48 139	12 795	8 409	74 904	22 531	20 295	20 431	207 504
Unreliable	48 321	12 974	20 054	86 329	28 720	28 479	28 814	253 691
Ratio expenditure/budget								
Reliable	1.01	2.17	1.94	1.11	1.26	2.42	1.18	1.12
Unreliable	0.97	2.26	1.15	1.20	1.27	3.87	1.91	1.10
B External costs								
Percentage of expenditure								
Reliable	12.93	7.11	3.73	46.39	10.23	12.24	7.37	100.00
Unreliable	9.23	7.31	3.31	46.79	11.01	11.96	10.39	100.00
1975 US $								
Reliable	18 093	9 956	5 220	64 927	14 319	17 128	10 316	139 959
Unreliable	15 541	12 312	5 573	78 780	18 547	20 133	17 492	168 378
Ratio expenditure/budget								
Reliable	0.96	2.10	1.66	1.10	1.42	2.37	1.25	1.16
Unreliable	1.00	2.27	1.03	1.24	1.45	3.65	3.14	1.21

[a] Based on a rating by ISI/WFS contract officers of quality of financial reporting: 18 surveys rated 'reliable', 12 'unreliable'.

other feasible way of converting survey costs to a common unit with greater precision.

10.3   A description of survey costs

In this section, we describe survey costs, starting with an overview of in-country expenditure (expressed in 1975 US dollars) for the 30 surveys whose expenditure was complete by mid-1983. On average, these surveys cost $226 000, of which exactly one-third was contributed by the country, the rest being supplied by one of the three donors, USAID, UNFPA or UKODA (see table 10.2). The range of total costs is wide, from just under $100 000 to nearly half a million dollars; this variability is more pronounced for the national than for the external contribution, but it should be recalled that national expenditure figures are relatively unreliable and arbitrary.

The average costs of the 30 surveys are disaggregated by major expenditure head in table 10.3. The main fieldwork phase is by far the biggest item, costing an average of $79 000, or 36 per cent of the total expenditure. The next most costly item is salaries and allowances of central staff, representing one-fifth of the total. The other five heads account for only between 5 and 12 per cent each.

The allocations of country and external contributions contrast markedly. On average, nearly two-thirds of the cost of central staff salaries and over half the cost of sample preparation were paid for by countries themselves. For all other items, over 50 per cent of expenses were met from external funds, particularly for fieldwork (89 per cent) and pre-test and training (85 per cent). Altogether, nearly 60 per cent of external funds went to support operational costs in the field. We suspect that this proportion is exceptionally high, as most forms of external aid concentrate on external inputs rather than local costs. We turn now to look more closely at each of the seven major expenditure heads in turn.

Central staff

Salaries and allowances of central staff[1] are an appreciable component of survey costs, being second only to fieldwork among the seven major budget heads. For the 30 surveys analysed in this paper, an average of $48 000 was spent in this way, representing a fifth of total expenditure. Despite their importance, the reliability of these financial data is insufficient to sustain detailed investigation, because the bulk of expenditure was met by the participating country, typically in form of salaries of full-time staff of the implementing organization. During budget negotiations, estimates of the staff input that would be required for survey execution were made and costed. But accurate recording of actual head-quarters staff time devoted to survey work was rarely attempted. In common with most government institutions, few statistical offices employ a system of projectized staff time-sheets, which can be the only reliable source of true staff costs. Hence the expenditure figures represent estimates made in the survey contract and bear only a tenuous link to subsequent reality. It is even difficult

TABLE 10.2

In-country survey costs, by source of funds[a] (1975 US$ 000s)

	Total	Country	External	Country as percentage of total
Africa				
Kenya	202	101	101	50
Lesotho	97	26	71	27
Senegal	484	110	374	23
Sudan (North)	368	121	247	33
Tunisia	242	59	183	24
Asia and Pacific				
Jordan	158	42	116	27
Syria	192	50	142	26
Turkey	228	86	142	38
Bangladesh	192	22	170	11
Nepal	107	17	90	16
Pakistan	241	82	159	34
Sri Lanka	185	82	103	44
Indonesia	175	46	129	26
Korea, Rep. of	365	121	244	33
Malaysia	453	305	148	67
Philippines	203	51	152	25
Thailand	346	150	196	43
Americas				
Colombia	234	51	183	22
Paraguay	141	46	95	33
Peru	187	36	151	19
Venezuela	212	119	93	56
Costa Rica	155	48	107	31
Dominican Rep.	196	32	164	16
Mexico	286	112	174	39
Panama	187	50	137	27
Guyana	185	51	134	28
Haiti	144	21	123	15
Jamaica	259	76	183	29
Trinidad & Tobago	177	81	96	46
Europe				
Portugal	175	44	131	25
Average	226	75	151	33

[a] Excludes costs of technical assistance.

TABLE 10.3

Average costs of surveys, by source of funds and major category

Source	Central staff	Pre-test and training	Sample preparation	Fieldwork	Data processing	Printing	Equipment and miscellaneous	Total
A Percentage of expenditure								
Total	21	6	5	36	11	11	10	100
Country	46	3	6	12	10	8	15	100
External	11	7	4	46	11	13	8	100
B 1975 US$ 000s								
Total	48	13	13	79	25	24	24	226
Country	31	2	8	9	9	5	11	75
External	17	11	5	70	16	19	13	151

to judge whether these budget estimates are in general higher or lower than the costs of staff time which were actually incurred. In certain instances, staff inputs may have been inflated to increase the national contribution to the initial survey budget; conversely, there were undoubtedly many occasions when the involvement of permanent statistical office staff was much more prolonged, due to slippage of the survey timetable, or more intense than originally envisaged.

In view of these difficulties, attention should focus on the external funding component in tables 10.4 and 10.5. This was generally modest, amounting to less than 10 per cent of external funds in half of these 30 surveys and less than $20 000 in 22 surveys. There is no clear regional pattern to the minority of surveys where greater external support was given. In some surveys, the relatively high cost is attributed to high subsistence rates which could not be met from the regular funds of the organization; in others, extra staff had to be recruited for the duration of the survey. Table 10.5 indicates that these staff were more often needed for administration (particularly, accountants or accounts clerks) and secretarial services than for technical work. This reflects the special requirements of the survey, both in the form of the separate accounting and regular financial reporting required by the funding agencies and in the number of survey documents that needed high quality typing and reproduction.

Pre-test and training

All WFS surveys conducted a pre-test of the questionnaire prior to finalization for the main interviewing phase. Some countries, particularly multi-lingual ones, had two or even three separate pre-tests of different versions of the questionnaire. Typically a pre-test involved five to ten interviewers who were trained for one week and who interviewed for one or two weeks (see chapter 14 for further details). In many surveys, these pre-test interviewers later became supervisors for the main survey.

The main training phase immediately preceded the fieldwork and was usually conducted in two phases. In the first phase, personnel destined to become team supervisors or field editors were trained for two weeks.[2] In the second phase, which lasted for three weeks, interviewers were trained by senior staff with the assistance of supervisors. Typically, salaries and some form of subsistence allowance were payable to trainees, although these amounts were sometimes less than those payable during fieldwork itself.

Pre-test and training, on average, account for only 6 per cent, or $13 000, of total survey expenditure. The major portion of this sum ($11 000) was met from external funds. Further details are provided in tables 10.6 and 10.7. The latter table shows that the majority of expenditure is attributable to training rather than pre-testing. The unspecified 'other' category includes hire of training premises and other similar miscellaneous expenditure.

One feature of table 10.6 is more surprising. There are a small number of countries where the costs of pre-test and training were exceptionally high; in three cases, these stages of the survey account for 15 per cent or more of the total

TABLE 10.4

Distribution of the surveys according to proportionate and absolute costs of central staff

Source	<10	10–19	20–29	30–39	40–49	50–59	60–69	70–79	80–89	90 +	Total
A Percentage of expenditure											
Total	2	14	8	5	1	0	0	0	0	0	30
Country	0	2	7	4	6	3	3	2	1	2	30
External	16	9	5	0	0	0	0	0	0	0	30
B 1975 US$ 000s											
Total	1	3	2	7	5	6	2	2	0	2	30
Country	1	10	6	6	2	3	0	1	0	1	20
External	11	11	4	2	1	0	0	1	0	0	30

TABLE 10.5

Breakdown of average central staff costs (1975 US$)

Source	Total	Director(s)	Technical support	Adminis-tration	Consult-ants	Other[a]
Total	48 211	14 155	17 459	12 748	431	3 418
Country	31 139	11 197	12 308	6 472	121	1 041
External	17 072	2 958	5 151	6 276	310	2 377

[a] Includes travel and subsistence, not allocated in the budget to specific grades, and insurance, social security payments etc.

external contribution and six cases where the total cost exceeded $20 000. As these figures are relatively reliable, we can pursue the analysis at the individual country level by presenting, in table 10.8, further details in an attempt to discern the reason for the high cost of training or pre-testing in a few countries.

Two countries are clearly maverick in terms of training or pre-test costs: Indonesia and Philippines. In both cases, training accounts for nearly one-quarter of the whole budget and the ratio of training to fieldwork costs is very high. Training and pre-test costs also tend to be high in the Caribbean both as a proportion of the total budget and in relation to fieldwork. Conversely, costs of training tend to be lower in Latin America than in other regions.

One obvious possible explanation for these variations concerns the overall survey design. In each survey a decision had to be made concerning the trade-off between the size of the interviewing force and length of fieldwork. (See chapters 9 and 16 for further discussion of this point). Could the high training/

TABLE 10.6

Distribution of the surveys according to proportionate and absolute costs of pre-test and training

Source							
A Percentage of expenditure							
	< 1	1–4	5–9	10–14	15–19	20–24	25 +	Total
Total	2	15	9	2	1	1	0	30
Country	20	3	4	2	1	0	0	30
External	1	12	9	5	2	0	1	30
B 1975 US$ 000s							
	< 1	1–4	5–9	10–14	15–19	20–24	25 +	Total
Total	1	7	7	5	4	3	3	30
Country	19	7	2	2	0	0	0	30
External	1	9	7	5	4	2	2	30

TABLE   10.7
Breakdown of average pre-test and training costs (1975 US$)

Source	Pre-test			
	Total	Supervisors	Interviewers	Drivers, transport, other
Total	2 352	726	1 445	181
Country	226	131	65	30
External	2 126	595	1 380	151

Source	Training				
	Total	Supervisors	Interviewers	Instructors	Other
Total	10 513	3 239	5 993	295	986
Country	1 741	727	675	90	249
External	8 772	2 512	5 318	205	737

pre-test costs in Indonesia, Philippines and the Caribbean simply be the result of decisions to train large numbers of interviewers and conduct the fieldwork in a short space of time, thereby raising training costs both absolutely and relative to fieldwork? The figures in table 10.8 show that this is not the reason. When the relationship between training effort and fieldwork is expressed as the planned number of field interviews per person-day of training, the surveys with high training costs are not out of line with other surveys.

A country-by-country appraisal of training and pre-test budgets and expenditure shows that a combination of different factors is responsible. Training costs in Indonesia and the Philippines were high because both conducted four separate regional training sessions with high salary, subsistence, travel and rental costs. In Haiti costs were high because the pre-test was much larger than usual and performed a dual purpose: to pre-test the fertility survey questionnaire and to yield substantive results for a Ministry of Health project. In Jamaica, also, three separate small pre-tests were conducted. In Latin America, training costs were low because of a greater success in retaining pre-test interviewers to act as main survey supervisors, thereby obviating the need for a separate supervisor training.

In conclusion, there are no general lessons to be learnt from the minority of countries with high pre-test or training costs. Furthermore, the preceding paragraphs should not be allowed to obscure the fact that expenditure in the majority of surveys on this component was modest in both absolute and relative terms, particularly in Latin America, where survey organizations exercised a higher level of cost-efficiency than most surveys in other regions.

Sample preparation

WFS's sampling strategy and its implementation are discussed in chapters 12 and

TABLE 10.8

Survey-specific information on pre-test and training costs

	Pre-test and training costs as a percentage of total survey expenditure	Number of planned individual interviews per person-day of training
Africa		
Kenya	9.58	5.17
Lesotho	0.51	5.26
Senegal	4.76	10.08
Sudan (North)	8.75	2.09
Tunisia	4.19	5.22
Asia and Pacific		
Bangladesh	2.56	2.49
Nepal	10.90	2.94
Pakistan	0.80	7.65
Sri Lanka	5.64	5.26
Indonesia	22.92	4.41
Korea, Rep. of	4.28	1.97
Malaysia	2.19	5.04
Philippines	18.14	3.27
Thailand	2.85	5.88
Americas		
Colombia	1.92	3.89
Paraguay	2.54	4.55
Peru	1.71	4.01
Venezuela	2.66	7.21
Costa Rica	5.26	4.75
Dominican Rep.	2.45	2.58
Mexico	2.20	5.19
Panama	3.38	5.00
Guyana	8.30	4.10
Haiti	9.91	5.50
Jamaica	9.39	3.07
Trinidad & Tobago	9.37	4.04
Europe		
Portugal	2.68	4.66

13. A detailed analysis of the sample coverage achieved in the WFS programme may also be found in Marckwardt (1984). In view of the great determination of the project to use strict probability samples and up-to-date sampling frames, it is at first sight surprising to see the inexpensiveness of this stage of the survey. On

average, the costs of sample preparation comprise only five per cent of total survey costs, amounting to $13 000, of which $8000 was contributed by the country.[3] As shown in table 10.10, the salaries and expenses of staff who carried out the listing of households or dwellings is the dominant cost, amounting on average to nearly $10 000 out of the $13 000. The sub-component 'sampling' refers to the salaries of local sampling statisticians or cartographers and cost, on average, only $2000. Field mapping and segmentation of selected sample areas was usually combined with listing and the costs cannot therefore be separated from those of listing.

TABLE　10.9

Distribution of the surveys according to proportionate and absolute costs of sample preparation

Source								
A Percentage of expenditure								
	< 1	1–4	5–9	10–14	15–19	20–24	24 +	Total
Total	7	9	12	0	1	0	1	30
Country	16	5	1	3	1	2	2	30
External	12	8	8	1	0	1	0	30
B 1975 US$ 000s								
	< 1	1–4	5–9	10–14	15–19	20–24	25 +	Total
Total	6	5	4	6	6	0	3	30
Country	16	5	3	2	2	0	2	30
External	11	7	7	2	2	0	1	30

Although on average the costs of sample preparation were low, there are a number of exceptions (table 10.9). Both the low average and the exceptions can be explained by variations in survey design. In 8 of the 30 surveys, the WFS survey was based on a previous household or dwelling frame. For these surveys (see column 1(a) of table 10.11), the external contribution to sample preparation

TABLE　10.10

Breakdown of average sample preparation costs (1975 US$)

Source	Total	Listing	Sampling[a]	Transport
Total	13 067	9 794	2 116	1 157
Country	7 706	6 512	734	460
External	5 361	3 282	1 382	697

[a]　This category comprises the salaries and allowances of local sampling experts and cartographers.

TABLE   10.11

Average sample preparation costs for different types of survey design (1975 US$)

Source	Survey design	
	1 (a) No separate listing operation (8 surveys)[a]	1 (b) Listing costs subsumed in main fieldwork (3 surveys)
Total	7 442	5 242
Country	6 105	2 661
External	1 337	2 581
	2 Separate listing operation (15 surveys)	3 Listing costs include costs of expanded household survey (3 surveys)
Total	10 679	20 410
Country	3 909	2 731
External	6 770	17 679

[a]   The exceptional case of Malaysia has been excluded. In this survey, the huge sum of $115 385 was included in the country contribution to the budget, as representing the value of a master frame of dwellings.

costs is understandably low, amounting to an average of only $1300. The relatively high average country contribution for this group is explained by the need to update the frame, as for instance in Mexico and in Trinidad and Tobago.

The second group, comprising Republic of Korea, Colombia and Venezuela, is similar to the first, in that listing costs are not included under sample preparation. In these three surveys, an expanded household sample also performed the function of listing for the individual survey. As both household and individual surveys were conducted by the same interviewing teams in a single visit to each area, their respective costs cannot be separated and have been included under main fieldwork. For this small group of surveys, the average cost of sample preparation amounts to $5242 of which approximately half came from external funds.

The third and largest group, comprising 15 of the 30 surveys, required a separate listing operation. (Three of these countries – Sudan, Syria and Dominican Republic – also used an expanded household sample but nevertheless conducted a separate prior listing). In this circumstance, the average sample preparation cost was $10 679, two-thirds of which came from external funds. This seems to be a modest sum in relation to the average expenditure of $79 000 spent on the main fieldwork in view of the fact that the distribution of areas is the same for both field operations and that listing usually covered two to three times as many dwellings or households as the main interviewing phase. Indeed a general conclusion from the WFS experience (see Marckwardt 1984 and chapter 13) is that WFS did not allocate sufficient resources to the supervision and quality control of cartographic and listing work in the field. These cost figures for surveys with a separate listing operation tend to support this assertion.

In the remaining three surveys (Lesotho, Jordan and Senegal), an expanded household survey performed the function of the listing operation for the individual survey, but this fieldwork was conducted separately from the individual survey and we have chosen to include the costs under listing rather than under main fieldwork. For this small group of surveys, the total costs of sample preparation, including the conduct of a large household survey, amount to $20 410 on average, of which $17 679 was contributed externally.

Two main points emerge from a comparison of the different types of survey, portrayed in table 10.11. First, the existence of a prior frame of households or dwellings reduced the listing costs by about $5000 on average. This sum is modest partly because the costs of preparing a frame were not large and because many pre-existing frames required expenditure on updating. Secondly, the additional costs of an expanded household survey appear to have been approximately $10 000. This estimate is based only on those three surveys where the household survey was conducted as a separate operation. It is dangerous to generalize from such a small number of surveys, but for these at least costs were modest in comparison with the costs of the individual survey.

Main fieldwork

The main fieldwork phase is the largest component of total survey costs; on average, $79 000 was spent on fieldwork of which $70 000 came from external funds. This latter sum amounts to nearly half of the total external contribution. The distribution of the 30 surveys according to the proportionate and absolute costs of fieldwork is given in table 10.12. The modest level of expenditure by countries themselves is clearly evident; in 22 surveys the sum contributed from domestic funds amounted to less than $10 000 and in only one case did it exceed $30 000. In absolute terms, the foreign contribution was very variable, but, as a proportion of total external funds, the distribution is much more clustered round a pronounced mode of 50–60 per cent. Clearly fieldwork costs are correlated with other costs.

Table 10.13 provides a breakdown of average fieldwork costs into its major components. In broad terms, the salaries and subsistence of interviewers comprise half the costs, those of team supervisors and editors one-quarter of the costs and transport (mainly vehicle running costs, vehicle depreciation and remuneration of drivers) a further quarter. The costs of other components are trivial by comparison.

In budgeting fieldwork, the WFS practice was to pay a fixed subsistence sum

TABLE 10.12

Distribution of the surveys according to proportionate and absolute costs of fieldwork

Source	<10	10–19	20–29	30–39	40–49	50–59	60–69	70–79	80–89	90 +	Total
A Percentage of expenditure											
Total	0	0	6	12	10	1	1	0	0	0	30
Country	13	10	3	4	0	0	0	0	0	0	30
External	0	0	1	8	6	10	2	2	1	0	30
B 1975 US$ 000s											
Total	0	0	0	3	4	5	2	7	0	9	30
Country	22	4	3	0	1	0	0	0	0	0	30
External	0	0	1	4	4	5	4	5	2	5	30

TABLE 10.13

Breakdown of average fieldwork costs (1975 US$)

Source	Total	Supervisors and Field Editors	Interviewers	Drivers	Vehicles	Technical supervision	Other
Total	79 474	17 707	39 133	3 998	14 800	1 510	2 326
Country	9 006	2 814	1 869	1 039	2 657	275	352
External	70 468	14 893	37 264	2 959	12 143	1 235	1 974

per person-day of fieldwork, using established government rates wherever possible. The alternative system of reimbursement against receipted expenditure is
an extremely time-consuming method of meeting costs and, of course, is open to
abuse. For these reasons it was discouraged. Under the fixed daily allowance
system interviewing teams were free to lodge and feed wherever they wished.
Typically they were also able to live cheaply in the rural areas, often staying in
the village schools or private houses.

In order to provide an idea of the budgeted cost per interviewer-day (salary
plus subsistence) we present below groupings of surveys expressing the budget
sums in 1975 US dollars:

Budgeted cost (salary plus subsistence)
per interviewer-day in the field.

$15 +	Venezuela, Dominican Republic, Costa Rica, Panama, Jordan, Korea (Rep.).
$10–14.9	Colombia, Paraguay.
$ 5– 9.9	Malaysia, Jamaica, Kenya, Sudan (North), Senegal, Portugal, Peru, Indonesia, Trinidad and Tobago, Tunisia, Turkey.
<$5	Sri Lanka, Thailand, Haiti, Philippines, Guyana, Nepal, Pakistan, Lesotho, Syria, Bangladesh, Mexico.

On average, interviewers in these 30 surveys received a daily sum of $8, at
1975 prices and exchange rates. As can be seen above, the range is considerable,
from over $15 per day in six surveys to under $5 per day in eleven surveys. In
general, the level of daily payments corresponds to the average per capita income
of the countries, though there are a number of exceptions which reflect unusual
government regulations or customs concerning their employees.

These unit costs can be used to calculate indirectly the productivity of interviewers, as measured by the number of successful individual interviews per day.
By dividing the total expenditure on interviewers' salaries and subsistence during
the main fieldwork by the unit cost, we arrive at an estimate of the number of
paid interviewer-days. This estimate assumes that the salaries and subsistence
levels agreed in the budget were implemented without change, an assumption
which does not hold true for all 30 surveys but is sufficiently valid for our purposes. Finally, interviewer productivity per paid day is estimated by dividing the
total achieved sample of individual female respondents[4] by the number of paid
interviewer-days.

The average interviewer productivity estimated from budget and expenditure
figures is 0.97 completed individual interviews per paid interviewer-day. This
figure may appear exceedingly low but this impression would be to some extent
mistaken. The total number of paid interviewer-days includes: official rest days,
particularly weekends; days of sickness; days of inactivity caused by floods,
public disturbance, transport breakdown and a host of other reasons; and days
spent travelling between clusters. Further discussion of these aspects of field-

work may be found in chapter 15: here it suffices to say that a rate of about one interview per paid day is consistent with a productivity of two to three completed interviews per day actually spent interviewing. This performance rate is approximately that expected in the WFS programme and assumed in the budget. As we shall see later, most countries did not exceed the budget sum allocated for the main field phase. Below we present groups of surveys according to estimated interviewer productivity:

Estimated number of
completed individual
interviews per paid
interviewer-day

1.50 +	Paraguay, Colombia[a].
1.30–1.49	Venezuela[a], Jordan, Sri Lanka, Costa Rica.
1.00–1.29	Indonesia, Malaysia, Lesotho, Syria[a], Senegal, Bangladesh, Dominican Republic[a], Trinidad and Tobago, Tunisia, Pakistan, Nepal.
0.80–0.99	Turkey, Mexico[a], Haiti.
0.60–0.79	Jamaica, Portugal, Korea (Rep.)[a], Guyana,
<0.50	Philippines, Peru, Thailand[b], Kenya, Panama, Sudan (North)[a].

[a] Interviewer-days include work on expanded household survey
[b] Interviewing includes subsample of husbands

This display possesses several interesting features. It is remarkable that a number of surveys in which the costs include interviewing an expanded household sample (typically two to three times larger than the individual sample) nevertheless record a high productivity in terms of individual interviews. This achievement suggests that the critical determinants of fieldwork productivity are travel between and within clusters rather than the number of units to be interviewed. Distance between clusters can be reduced by the introduction of multiple area stages of selection, but it has been argued convincingly in chapter 12 that, when interviewing teams are provided with vehicles, distance between clusters is only weakly related to travel time. Travel time within clusters is affected by the intra-cluster sampling density. Surveys which used an enlarged household sample typically enumerated all dwellings or households within each selected cluster (i.e. compact cluster sampling) and it is perhaps this feature that offsets the greater interviewing burden and accounts for the surprisingly high field productivity in Colombia, Venezuela, Syria and the Dominican Republic. However, this hypothesis is not confirmed by the correlation between productivity and sampling density within clusters for all surveys without an expanded household survey. This correlation is in the expected direction — the higher the density, the higher the productivity — but is not statistically significant.

A further tentative generalization concerns the low productivity of Jamaica and Guyana which are among the small minority of WFS surveys which did not use the team approach to fieldwork, but instead arranged for interviewers to work individually using public transport. It is sometimes assumed the team approach is inherently less efficient than the individual approach, because some team members may be forced into inactivity while others complete their assignments. Any such tendency would be particularly pronounced during the last day of fieldwork in a cluster. The WFS experience with individualized fieldwork is too limited to allow a convincing comparison of the two strategies but nevertheless suggests that any inherent inefficiency of teams may be compensated by greater morale and better transport.

In other respects, the distribution of surveys according to estimated fieldwork productivity does not contain any general lessons. Most of the low productivity cases can be explained by the intervention of external factors such as the temporary cessation of fieldwork due to lack of funds (Peru), floods and linguistic problems (Kenya), a large number of vacant dwellings (Portugal), or an expectedly low achieved individual sample due to age misreporting on the household schedule (Panama). Conversely, the high achieving surveys generally had good morale and good logistical support, or an easily accessible population (Paraguay, Costa Rica, Jordan, Sri Lanka).

Finally it is of interest to examine in slightly more detail the transport costs of the main fieldwork. On average this expenditure (mainly on running costs of vehicles, and salaries and allowances of drivers) amounted to almost one-third of total fieldwork costs. As indicated below, there was considerable variability across surveys in this proportion:

*Transport as a
percentage of Total
Main Fieldwork Costs*

50% +	Lesotho, Pakistan, Nepal, Bangladesh.
40–49%	Jordan, Senegal.
30–39%	Haiti, Paraguay, Peru, Tunisia, Costa Rica, Guyana, Thailand.
20–29%	Sudan (North), Mexico, Syria.
10–19%	Indonesia, Kenya, Dominican Republic, Colombia, Panama.
<10%	Sri Lanka, Korea (Rep.), Turkey, Malaysia, Portugal, Venezuela, Philippines, Jamaica, Trinidad and Tobago.

It is difficult to interpret the distribution because the expenditure figures on transport are less reliable than those relating to wages and subsistence rates of fieldworkers. For instance in both Malaysia and Philippines, where the provision of vehicles was a local contribution, it is likely that the true running costs have been underestimated. Among the surveys where the travel component was very high is the exceptional case of Nepal where helicopters were used to drop teams in place at the start of fieldwork and for some monitoring visits. The other three surveys (Lesotho, Pakistan and Bangladesh) where transport amounted to one-half of the total main fieldwork expenditure are characterized by low salary and subsistence levels which have inflated the relative transport costs.

At the outset of this sub-section on main fieldwork, the great variability of costs between surveys was mentioned. The reasons for this variability are now clearer. There is a wide range in: travel costs; budgeted daily salary and subsistence levels, reflecting differences in living standards and government regulations; interviewer productivity per day, reflecting a complex interplay of survey design factors, external factors such as geography, climate and language, and managerial and logistical factors, many of which defy quantification. The variability in these components far exceeds variability in sample sizes, which explains the lack of relationship between size and field costs.

This variability in costs is best summarized by the familiar measure, field cost per completed interview. For all 30 surveys, this average cost is $17, with a range from about $5 to over $25. Further details are shown below:

Main fieldwork cost
per completed individual
interview

$20.0 +	Senegal, Sudan (North), Korea (Rep.)[a], Thailand[b], Dominican Republic[a], Venezuela[a], Mexico[a].
$15.0–19.9	Tunisia, Pakistan, Portugal, Syria[a], Panama, Jamaica, Turkey.
$10.0–14.9	Colombia[a], Costa Rica, Jordan, Peru, Haiti, Malaysia, Guyana, Kenya, Trinidad and Tobago, Nepal.
<$10.0	Lesotho, Bangladesh, Paraguay, Philippines, Indonesia, Sri Lanka.

[a] Costs of an expanded household survey are included
[b] Costs of a husbands survey are included

These fieldwork costs per completed individual interview are presumably much higher than costs for most other government-conducted surveys in developing countries. But to condemn WFS as over-expensive from such a comparison would be facile. Most other surveys collect far less information from much larger samples; fieldworkers require less training and supervision; and the reliability of the data is typically lower than that of most WFS surveys.

Data processing

The data processing phase of WFS surveys covers processing activities from receipt of completed questionnaires at the survey headquarters to the production of a large set of tabulations for the main report. It includes: an office or clerical editing operation; a coding stage; entry of data onto a computer-readable medium; the programming, testing and running of extensive edit checks and subsequent clerical correction of detected errors and updating of files; the construction of a recode or analysis file; and the running of the tabulations. These steps were usually performed in the country (see chapter 18 for further details), though they required very substantial technical assistance from WFS staff on site and in London (see chapter 8). The only aspect of data processing that was routinely performed at WFS headquarters was the computation of sampling errors.

On average, expenditure on data processing activities amounted to $25 000 (or 11 per cent of total expenditure) of which $16 000 was contributed by the external funding agencies. This level of expenditure is probably an underestimate. Data processing of WFS surveys usually took much longer than planned and was more demanding in manpower than anticipated. It is therefore likely that the country contribution, particularly in the form of salaries for programmers and clerical grades, was in many cases higher than the expenditure figures suggest.

Bearing in mind these reservations, a further impression of data processing expenditure is provided in tables 10.14 and 10.15. On average, data entry was very cheap, amounting to only $2800. The low figures for the salaries of computer programming staff should not be taken seriously, nor can cost of computer time or rental. Many organizations processed the survey on their own machine, thus making it difficult to budget a realistic cost.

Printing

WFS surveys imposed a heavy printing burden. The individual questionnaire was frequently 40 or more pages in length and, in an appreciable number of surveys, had to be produced in more than one linguistic version. The main survey reports were voluminous, typically comprising over 100 pages of text together with several hundred pages of tabulations. In the latter half of the WFS programme, most reports were issued in two separate volumes. Furthermore large numbers of these reports were needed for international circulation by ISI. The length of the questionnaire, the insistence on linguistic variants and the whole style of reporting the results made printing costs much higher in WFS surveys than is typical in other surveys. The questionnaire, produced in-country in almost every case, also entailed a heavy cost in paper, sometimes exceeding the cost of production. This is included in the 'printing' total. On average $24 000 (or 11 per cent of total expenditure) was spent on printing, of which $18 000 was provided from external funds. A further breakdown of costs is shown in tables 10.16 and 10.17 but no further comment is needed.

Equipment and miscellaneous expenses

As mentioned earlier, the mandate given to WFS by its funding agencies precluded in most instances the provision of major items of equipment such as vehicles or computers. It was argued that upgrading of developing country statistical offices in this way should remain the responsibility of other foreign aid programmes. WFS expenditure should be strictly related to the narrower and more immediate goal of executing a single survey.

This limitation was an important one, because lack of vehicles represents a serious constraint on the activities of many developing country organizations,

TABLE 10.14

Distribution of the surveys according to proportionate and absolute costs of data processing

A Percentage of expenditure

Source	<10	10-19	20-29	30-39	40-49	50-59	60-69	70-79	80-89	90 +	Total
Total	16	11	3	0	0	0	0	0	0	0	30
Country	19	6	4	1	0	0	0	0	0	0	30
External	17	9	3	1	0	0	0	0	0	0	30

B 1975 US$ 000s

Source	<10	10-19	20-29	30-39	40-49	50-59	60-69	70-79	80-89	90 +	Total
Total	2	12	9	5	0	0	1	0	0	1	30
Country	22	4	3	0	0	0	1	0	0	0	30
External	10	13	4	2	0	1	0	0	0	0	30

TABLE 10.15

Breakdown of average data processing costs (1975 US$)

Source	Total	Training and supervisory	Coders	Editors	Data entry staff	Programming staff	Computer rental and other
Total	25 006	872	5 115	4 555	2 814	3 197	8 453
Country	8 996	392	1 677	1 439	672	1 779	3 037
External	16 010	480	3 438	3 116	2 142	1 418	5 416

TABLE 10.16

Distribution of the surveys according to proportionate and absolute costs of printing

Source	<10	10–19	20–29	30–39	40–49	50–59	60–69	70–79	80–89	90 +	Total
A Percentage of expenditure											
Total	15	11	4	0	0	0	0	0	0	0	30
Country	22	5	2	0	1	0	0	0	0	0	30
External	14	11	3	2	0	0	0	0	0	0	30
B 1975 US$ 000s											
Total	5	9	9	4	1	1	0	0	0	1	30
Country	26	3	1	0	0	0	0	0	0	0	30
External	8	11	7	2	0	1	0	0	1	0	30

TABLE 10.17

Breakdown of average printing costs (1975 US$)

Source	Total	Manuals and questionnaires	Report
Total	23 568	8 450	15 118
Country	5 238	1 451	3 787
External	18 330	6 999	11 331

and WFS surveys, with their emphasis on mobile interviewing teams, relied heavily on the availability of vehicles in good running condition. In extreme conditions, new vehicles were occasionally provided by the funding agency, though these donations typically came from other sources of funds and did not comprise part of the survey budget. In some other countries, provision was made in the survey budget for the purchase of spare parts and more commonly still the cost of renting vehicles was met from survey funds. However these items are shown under fieldwork costs as part of the transport component.

WFS was however allowed to provide smaller items of equipment, either expendable (e.g. office stationery, cassette batteries) or non-expendable (e.g. interviewer kits, typewriters, office furniture, cassette recorders, calculators). As indicated in table 10.19, about $5000 on average was contributed from external funds towards the cost of expendable items and about $3000 towards non-expendable equipment.

Two other types of expenditure are included under the heading of Equipment and Miscellaneous. Rental of office accommodation was usually a notional cost contributed by the local organization and the sum of $5474 shown in table 10.19 should be regarded as arbitrary. Finally, there is a truly miscellaneous category which includes such items as telephone and postal costs, and costs of publicity. On average, $3600 was spent from external funds on such items.

10.4 Cost-efficiency

In the previous section the in-country costs of 30 WFS surveys have been described. At this juncture two questions need to be raised. Firstly, without changing in any regard the design of surveys, can ways be identified by which savings could have been made? Secondly, could the design of surveys have been made more cost-effective, without jeopardizing the quality and usefulness of results?

In response to the first question, our judgement is that there is only one clear way of achieving a substantial reduction in costs without changing survey design, namely by an increase in interviewer productivity. It is the opinion of many WFS staff that productivity in the field (which as we saw earlier was on average

TABLE 10.18

Distribution of the surveys according to proportionate and absolute costs of equipment and miscellaneous items

Source	<10	10–19	20–29	30–39	40–49	50–59	60–69	70–79	80–89	90 +	Total
A Percentage of expenditure											
Total	16	13	1	0	0	0	0	0	0	0	30
Country	12	10	4	3	1	0	0	0	0	0	30
External	23	5	2	0	0	0	0	0	0	0	30
B 1975 US$ 000s											
Total	7	10	4	2	5	1	1	0	0	0	30
Country	19	7	1	2	0	1	0	0	0	0	30
External	17	7	2	2	1	1	0	0	0	0	30

TABLE 10.19

Breakdown of average equipment and miscellaneous costs
(1975 US$)

Source	Total	Expendable	Non-expendable	Rental	Other
Total	23 784	6 781	4 551	5 474	6 978
Country	10 598	1 632	1 598	4 003	3 365
External	13 186	5 149	2 953	1 471	3 613

one interview per paid day) could have been increased by greater pressure on interviewers and greater efficiency. In budgeting surveys, WFS set rather modest standards for the interviewing rate and these goals became a self-fulfilling prophecy. If fieldwork was expected to last, say, three months, there was usually no incentive 'for interviewing teams to complete the work in a shorter time, because the prospect for most of them was a return to unemployment.

Most of the fieldwork costs are in a direct proportion to the number of person-days in the field and thus any increase in productivity would have a major effect on total field costs. For instance an increase of 25 per cent in completed interviews per elapsed day would have reduced the external contribution to total survey expenditure by about 10 per cent. In comparison, improvements in the efficiency of other aspects of survey implementation would bring about much more modest cost decreases.

An answer to the second question concerning the cost-efficiency of WFS survey designs is much more complex and requires subjective judgement concerning the trade-off between costs and quality. In suggesting ways in which the design of fertility surveys of the WFS type could be changed we rely heavily on the conclusions of other chapters in this volume. We suggest below five ways in which the design of future surveys could be made cheaper without, we believe, any offsetting effects on the results.

1 Make questionnaires shorter and less complex (see chapter 2). This would reduce paper, printing and data processing costs and perhaps allow a reduction in the length of interviewer training.

2 Increase the size of cluster takes (see chapter 12) and increase the density of sampling within the selected clusters.

3 Eliminate the clerical or office editing stage but introduce combined data entry editing using interactive video terminals (see chapters 18 and 19). Although 'this strategy would increase the costs of data entry, it would decrease the costs of programming time and clerical updating procedures.

4 Adopt a less perfectionist attitude to error detection and reconciliation (see chapters 18 and 19).

5 Reduce the number of tabulations and publish only the more relevant ones (see chapter 21).

It is impossible to be precise about the cost implications of these suggested design changes but our calculations imply that, together with an improvement in fieldwork productivity that was described earlier, cost reductions of 15 to 25 per cent could be achieved without any appreciable losses in data quality or precision.

10.5 Budgeting versus expenditure

Survey budgets formed part of the survey agreement which was submitted to funding agencies for approval. As mentioned earlier, a degree of flexibility in budget implementation was allowed. Transfers from one sub-head to another needed no prior approval and transfers across major heads were usually granted without difficulty. Increases in the total amount of the external contribution, however, required formal application and negotiation of a revised budget which had to be approved by the funding agency. A comparison of the initial budget with the final expenditure, both expressed in 1975 US dollars, gives some idea of the extent of unanticipated expenditure. It should be stressed that the data are inadequate for a full analysis of this topic. Many countries, when faced with an exhaustion of external funds, chose to supplement from their own sources rather than seek extra external funds. Such occurrences are often unrecorded. Moreover, instances of under-expenditure are usually concealed, because of the widely accepted belief that donors do not expect to receive back unspent money, provided that the task, or contract, has been successfully completed.

Despite these inadequacies, the figures in table 10.20 are of interest. On average, actual total expenditure exceeded the initial budget by 16 per cent. In 16 of the 30 surveys, the difference is less than 10 per cent, including six cases of slight under-expenditure. In four surveys, expenditure exceeded the initial budget by 10–19 per cent, while in a further ten cases, over-expenditure reached a level of 20 per cent or more. As might be expected, the ratio of expenditure to budget is higher when attention is confined to the external contribution, being 1.23 as opposed to 1.16 for the total.

In many instances, deviation from the initial budget was caused by factors beyond the control of ISI or the local survey organization, such as currency changes or inflation. The expression of both budgets and expenditures in 1975 dollars does not fully overcome these problems because of the simplifying assumption that all expenditure occurred in the year when the main fieldwork was conducted. Expenditure on the later phases, particularly data processing and printing, often occurred several years after fieldwork and are therefore subject to the twin influences of inflation and currency change. This may partly explain the fact that over-expenditure is most pronounced for data processing and printing of reports; but another and probably more important cause is the failure to provide realistic budgets for these components. Particularly in the early stages of the programme, WFS staff did not anticipate the length of time and local staff effort that would be needed for data cleaning and

TABLE 10.20

Average ratios (unweighted) of actual expenditures to
initial budgets (both expressed in 1975 US$) for 30 surveys

	Total (external plus country contribution)	External only
Total	1.16	1.23
Central staff	1.00	1.01
Pre-test and training	1.06	1.05
Sample preparation	1.27	1.17
Fieldwork	1.14	1.15
Data processing	1.27	1.48
Printing	3.00	2.84
Equipment and miscellaneous	1.47	1.32

tabulation, nor did they foresee the huge size of country reports and the consequently high printing costs.

Over-expenditure on other survey components is modest by comparison, being 14 per cent, for instance, for the main fieldwork which, as we saw above, is the most expensive item. Table 10.20 contains evidence that countries spent more on sample preparation and equipment than they had planned. Finally the apparent accuracy of central staff budgets cannot be taken seriously, as survey organizations rarely kept accurate records of staff time devoted to the survey.

Perhaps the main lesson from this brief comparison of budgets and actual expenditures is the need to budget for contingencies (which was not permitted in the case of WFS survey budgets). Budgeting for WFS surveys was very detailed and was carried out by very experienced staff. Nevertheless some degree of over-expenditure occurred in most surveys and this will undoubtedly continue to happen in future operations of this type. It could be argued that a stricter attitude by donors, perhaps a declaration that the agreed budget (in local currency) would not be supplemented in any circumstances, might have resulted in tighter financial control and discipline by local survey organizations and an even greater willingness to remedy deficits from their own funds. No doubt this would have happened to some extent. But it is clear that some surveys would have collapsed. A number of WFS surveys halted completely when external funds were delayed for some reason or pending a budget re-negotiation. The major achievement of the WFS in bringing to successful completion all 41 externally funded surveys is due in no small measure to the flexibility of the funding agencies with regard to expenditure.

10.6 Costs of technical assistance and co-ordination

So far the discussion of costs has been confined to the in-country component, whether contributed locally or externally. In this section we consider the costs of technical assistance in the form of visits by WFS staff to the country, back-up work in London of a survey-specific nature and the contributions of resident advisers and short-term consultants.

Technical assistance and the limitations of the numerical information on this subject are discussed in detail in chapter 8. In particular, the reader is reminded that these activities are defined broadly to include technical contributions which cannot be regarded as assistance. The approach in this chapter is simply to express in financial terms, using 1975 dollars, the total person-days of assistance spent in-country and the person-days worked at WFS headquarters on specific surveys up to the completion of the country report. This conversion is highly arbitrary and is intended to be no more than a crude indicator of the costs of technical assistance. At 1975 prices, we have costed each person-day worked in-country at $250 and each person-day worked in London at $150. The higher cost of in-country work reflects the additional expenses of subsistence and air travel. Both figures are set to take into account not just the base salaries and fringe benefits of the professional staff but also support or overhead costs, such as rental, telephone and secretarial expenses at WFS headquarters.

The costs of technical assistance to specific surveys (excluding all work on analysis and archiving after the completion of the country report), when calculated in the manner outlined above, are shown in column 2 of table 10.21. On average, each survey received $153 000 (at 1975 prices) worth of technical assistance or input, with a range from $56 000 to $397 000. Some of the reasons for this wide variation have already been explained in chapter 8 and, at this juncture, we need only stress that the presence of a long-term resident adviser accounts for the very high estimated costs in certain surveys.

The addition of total in-country expenditure (from table 10.2) to the costs of technical assistance provides an estimate of the total cost of each survey, which is shown in column 3. The total cost of the majority of surveys lies in the range of $250 000 to $500 000. The exceptions are Kenya, Senegal, Sudan, Republic of Korea, Malaysia and Haiti where costs exceeded half a million dollars, and Nepal, Paraguay and Costa Rica where costs were less than one-quarter of a million. The average total cost for the 30 surveys analysed here is about $380 000.

This average figure of $380 000 includes the country's own contribution. If this sum is subtracted, we reach an estimate that the average external cost of each survey was just over $3000 000. Details are shown in column 4.

The two final columns of table 10.21 show technical assistance costs as a percentage of total survey costs and as a percentage of all externally contributed costs. On average technical assistance accounts for about 40 per cent of the estimated total cost of each survey but 50 per cent of the total external contribution.

These expenditure figures raise a number of questions. For instance, were WFS surveys excessively expensive relative to their achievements? Can the amount and cost of technical assistance be justified? Unfortunately, the dearth of reliable information on the costs of other surveys in developing countries

precludes firm answers. The generous level of funding of the whole WFS programme is in no doubt. Nor can there be much doubt that individual surveys
were generously funded. Moreover, technical assistance was provided on a lavish
scale with an emphasis on high quality work but with little regard to costs.
Whether these features have resulted in excessive cost or whether the high
costs are entirely justified by the achievements (and their wider impact on
developing country survey-taking) is a delicate matter of judgement, that will
not be attempted here.

10.7 Summary

This chapter has been descriptive rather than analytical because of the inherent
limitations of the data. Nevertheless such is the paucity of information concerning the costs of developing country surveys that even this simple portrayal of the
major cost components of fertility surveys conducted under the auspices of WFS
should be useful in the planning of future surveys.

WFS survey costs fall into three main categories: the contribution of the
country; externally contributed funds for in-country survey execution; and the
costs of technical assistance in the broadest sense. When these three components
are summed, the average total cost of 30 surveys is estimated to be very approximately US$380 000 at 1975 exchange rates and prices. The equivalent 1984
cost is roughly $500 000. Of the three components, the country's own contri-
bution is the smallest, amounting to about 20 per cent of the whole. The other
two components, are approximately equal in financial terms, each comprising
about 40 per cent of the total expenditure.

Because the technical assistance offered under the WFS programme is so unusual in scale and nature, reflecting to a large extent the cross-national character
of the project, the disaggregation of in-country costs is more useful for future
survey work than technical assistance costs. By far the largest component of
these in-country costs was the main fieldwork phase which accounted for 36
per cent of total expenditure. Interviewers' salaries and subsistence comprise
approximately half of fieldwork costs, with the costs of supervision and transport each amounting to about one-quarter. These proportions underline the exceptionally close supervision of WFS fieldwork and the dependence on vehicles.

The costs of the central staff, including administrators, typists and clerks is
the next largest component, accounting for 21 per cent of total in-country
costs. By comparison other aspects of the survey were relatively inexpensive:
data processing (11 per cent), printing (11 per cent), equipment and miscellaneous (10 per cent), pre-test and training (6 per cent) and sample preparation
(5 per cent).

WFS surveys are said to be very expensive, though in the lack of comparable data for other complex surveys it is difficult to substantiate this assertion.
However, with hindsight, it may prove possible to reduce in-country costs of
future similar surveys by about 25 per cent without jeopardizing the quality and

TABLE 10.21

Comparison of in-country and technical assistance costs

	Total in-country costs	Estimated total technical assistance costs	Total costs (col 1 + col 2)	Total external contribution	Technical assistance costs as percentage of total costs (col 2 ÷ col 3)	Technical assistance costs as percentage of total external contribution (col 2 ÷ col 4)
	(1)	(2)	(3)	(4)	(5)	(6)
Africa						
Kenya	202	302	504	403	60	75
Lesotho	97	203	300	274	68	74
Senegal	484	190	674	564	28	34
Sudan (North)	368	343	711	590	48	58
Tunisia	242	169	411	352	41	48
Asia and Pacific						
Jordan	158	181	339	297	53	61
Syria	192	176	368	318	48	55
Turkey	228	103	331	245	31	42
Bangladesh	192	273	465	443	59	62
Nepal	107	75	182	165	41	45
Pakistan	241	93	334	252	28	37
Sri Lanka	185	231	416	334	56	69

Indonesia	175	156	331	285	47	55
Korea, Rep. of	365	138	503	382	27	36
Malaysia	453	75	528	223	14	34
Philippines	203	116	319	268	36	43
Thailand	346	77	423	273	18	28
Americas						
Colombia	234	56	290	239	19	23
Paraguay	141	91	232	186	39	49
Peru	187	72	259	223	28	32
Venezuela	212	104	316	197	33	53
Costa Rica	155	82	237	189	35	43
Dominican Rep.	196	130	326	294	40	44
Mexico	286	71	357	245	20	29
Panama	187	96	283	233	34	41
Guyana	185	169	354	303	48	56
Haiti	144	397	541	520	73	76
Jamaica	259	163	422	346	39	47
Trinidad & Tobago	177	154	331	250	47	62
Europe						
Portugal	175	95	270	226	35	42
Average	226	153	379	304	40	50

usefulness of the data. This reduction could be achieved by improved interviewer productivity (itself partly a function of stricter management and partly of change in sample design), by streamlining data collection instruments and data processing procedures and by cutting down the size of reports.

Notes

1. This item excludes specialist sampling and computer programming staff (whose costs are included in the appropriate heads) but includes administrative, clerical, secretarial and manual grades as well as most technical grades. It also includes the travelling and subsistence expenses of headquarters staff.
2. Even in surveys where pre-test interviewers were retained as supervisors, an additional supervisor training was sometimes necessary both to train new recruits and to explain fully their supervisory duties.
3. The average country contribution includes the exceptional case of Malaysia where the sum of $115 385 was included in the budget as representing the value of a master sample frame. See table 10.11 for analysis which excludes Malaysia.
4. This measure of production is chosen because the major focus of WFS surveys was the individual survey. However, it is not an ideal measure because it does not take into account the number of households or dwellings that had to be enumerated. For countries which used an expanded household sample and conducted the household and individual survey in a single integrated field operation, this measure understates productivity relative to other countries.

11

Sample Size and Survey Domain

Chris Scott
Trudy Harpham

11.1 Introduction

Survey design has to meet two types of requirements: those imposed from out-side the survey and those arising from the need for internal efficiency in the survey operations. It is convenient to refer to them as exogenous and endogenous. Exogenous requirements arise from the objectives of the survey and from the resources available for its implementation. The most important among them are the sample size and the definition of the study population, and these are the subjects of this chapter. Endogenous requirements determine such cost-efficiency issues as cluster size or stratification; often they involve balancing one advantage against another, sometimes allowing solution in terms of a formal optimization procedure. Such issues, generally referred to as sample design, are treated in chapter 12 of the present volume.

11.2 World representation

In the early days of the WFS there was much discussion about the selection of countries and the allocation of the world sample among them. However, as the WFS moved nearer to the real world it soon became clear that this was not a real issue. It was not diplomatically possible for the WFS staff to pick and choose among applicant countries. Essentially the WFS had to be available to all applicants. Moreover, national sovereignty required that the countries themselves take the initiative in proposing participation. Since the countries were expected to make a substantial contribution of resources to the survey an obvious consequence was that the WFS operation within any country had to be of value in its own right to that country. This consideration alone was enough to rule out the possibility that the WFS programme might be based on a world sample distributed in proportion to each country's population. Inevitably, the WFS became a set of self-contained national surveys covering a largely self-selected sample of countries.

Notably absent from the list of WFS participants were the two largest countries, China and India, as well as Brazil and the USSR. Together these four countries account for 46 per cent of the world's population. (If they are set aside, WFS covered about 71 per cent of the population of the rest of the world.) China in fact requested participation in the WFS programme in 1981, but this came too late in the agencies' plans for WFS funding. However, the

ISI's International Statistical Institute Research Centre is under contract to assist the Chinese Government with surveys based on WFS in the years to come. The absence of India and Brazil from the list is explained in part by the number of fertility surveys already carried out in these countries; moreover they already had large statistical agencies and did not feel the need for international assistance in this area.

While cross-national comparative analysis was an important objective of WFS, the estimation of world totals has very little practical significance and never played a significant role among WFS objectives.

11.3   Sample size and coverage

Ideally, sample size should be decided by considering the objectives on the one hand and the available resources on the other. We now examine these in turn.

The objectives bear on the sample size essentially because they impose a certain level of *required precision* in relation to the findings. One aspect of this is sampling precision. Since sampling precision increases (approximately) in proportion to the square root of sample size, a minimum sample size is necessary to achieve any stated precision. In nearly all surveys the complete sample is more than enough to meet any likely requirements as regards sampling precision, but this constraint begins to bite as we look at small subgroups of the sample, for example in the individual cells of a cross-tabulation. Thus the factor determining minimum sample size is likely to be the permissible error in the smaller cells of the most detailed cross-tabulations. Conversely, if sample size is regarded as fixed, then this determines the degree to which meaningful cross-tabulation can be achieved.

On the resource side one has to consider human resources, or capability, and financial resources. (In principle financial resources can be used to buy human resources, but in practice the human resources may not be available.) Human resources affect sample size in that a large survey is more difficult to manage efficiently. If the sample increases too far, control is likely to be lost and data quality will suffer. Thus non-sampling error tends to increase with sample size, counterbalancing the trend found with sampling error – though this effect is uncertain in magnitude and unpredictable. The financial constraint is more clear-cut. The costs of the more expensive survey operations are essentially proportional to the sample size. This is true of fieldwork (assuming a given cluster 'take'), coding, editing, machine time and paper for questionnaires; it is not true of design and planning work, programming or report writing, but these are relatively inexpensive operations.

In the WFS a complicating factor was that external funding was offered for most of the former group of operations, so that the amount of funds received by a country would increase with the sample size. As a result, planning of the sample size often took the form of a negotiation, with the countries feeling that it was in their interest to press for the largest sample feasible. In addition, national survey staff were sometimes influenced by the question of the sample size in neighbouring, or comparable, countries; thus, some kind of equity had to be preserved.

In these complex circumstances there could be no fully rational basis for allocating resources between countries. However, the following factors were clearly relevant and were taken into account in the decisions on sample size:

1 A minimum was set at 2000 women, to allow sufficiently detailed tabulation. In the event, no country's sample fell below 2500.

2 A maximum was set at approximately 10 000 women, in order to limit the organizational burden and also to preserve an approximate equity between countries.

3 Within these limits larger samples were admitted:
   — for countries with larger populations (on the grounds that they would need more detailed geographical breakdowns)
   — for countries with greater ethnic or regional heterogeneity
   — for countries which had already done a similar survey and could argue that a primary reason for repeating the survey was to allow more detailed analyses, requiring a larger sample.

Table 11.1 shows the sample sizes for the household survey and the survey of individual women for all WFS developing country surveys.

It might be supposed that in an assessment of the WFS programme one should be able to answer the question 'Were the samples of WFS surveys large enough for the needs of analysis — or alternatively, were they larger than necessary?' After consultation with some of the most active analysts of WFS data we incline to the view that this question cannot be fruitfully posed. Most analysts adopt a mode of procedure that is, to some extent at least, interactive rather than being based on a prior plan established in full detail before the data are examined. Sooner or later in their work they come up against sample size limitations, and when that happens the sample appears 'too small' to them. Often their reaction is to group together some categories of a variable; the sample then becomes 'large enough' for this modified analysis plan. If a larger sample were to be used the specific constraint encountered would be relaxed, but only to be replaced by another as soon as the analyst, raising his bid, meets a new sample size limitation. The demand for detailed analysis is, for practical purposes, infinite: in the absence of sample size constraints it expands without limit — generally along a dimension of increasing sophistication in the case of explanatory analysis, or increasing disaggregation in the case of descriptive analysis.

It follows that no sample size is ever analytically adequate. The relevant question is not that of adequacy for some undefined analytic 'needs' but adequacy to sustain analyses useful enough to justify the expenditure of the resources which occurred. This important but immensely complex question depends on an evaluation of the total output of the WFS programme. It would take us far beyond the scope of this chapter.

TABLE   11.1

Sample size for household survey and women's survey

Country	National population (thousands) 1981[a]	Target coverage (%)[b]	Number of households selected	Number of women selected[c]
Africa				
Benin	3 640	100	20 816	4 163
Cameroon	8 650	100	35 324	9 390
Ghana	12 063	100	6 791	7 183
Ivory Coast	8 298	100	4 387	7 800
Kenya	17 148	95	10 763	10 232
Lesotho	1 374	100	20 333	4 106[e]
Nigeria	79 680	100	9 361	10 996
Senegal	5 811	100	193 032[d]	4 495
Egypt	19 590	100	10 596	9 827[e]
Mauritania	1 681	70	15 041	3 852[e]
Morocco	20 971	99	19 352	6 639
Sudan (North)	18 901	70	13 921	3 708[e]
Tunisia	6 513	100	5 988	5 077[e]
Asia and Pacific				
Jordan	3 364	71	15 067	3 898[e]
Syria	9 331	100	15 287	4 841[e]
Turkey	46 375	100	6 393	5 929[e]
Yemen AR	5 940	94	14 364	2 694[e]
Bangladesh	90 693	100	6 145	6 980[e]
Iran	39 320	100	6 113	5 500[e]
Nepal	14 617	98	5 976	6 398[e]
Pakistan	89 416	93	5 246	5 401[e]
Sri Lanka	15 109	100	8 834	7 667[e]
Fiji	641	96	5 388	5 555[e]
Indonesia	159 520	67	10 504	9 687[e]
Korea, Rep. of	39 110	99	21 248	5 810[e]
Malaysia	14 415	85	8 103	6 654[e]
Philippines	50 525	95	14 747	11 122[e]
Thailand	48 125	100	4 518	4 204[e]
Americas				
Colombia	26 355	99	9 999	5 931
Ecuador	8 275	96	6 979	8 545
Paraguay	3 269	94	4 627	5 552
Peru	18 119	100	8 949	7 336[e]
Venezuela	16 156	98	8 200	4 500

Table 11.1 continued

Country	National population (thousands) 1981[a]	Target coverage (%)[b]	Number of households selected	Number of women selected[c]
Americas (cont.)				
Costa Rica	2 266	97	4 724	4 530
Dominican Rep.	6 095	100	12 069	3 556
Mexico	71 814	100	15 551	9 121
Panama	1 940	90	5 214	4 150
Guyana	903	90	4 668	5 114
Haiti	5 954	100	3 720	4 399
Jamaica	2 220	100	5 579	4 001
Trinidad & Tobago	1 185	100	4 973	4 868
Europe				
Portugal	9 908	100	15 115	7 720[e]

[a]   *Source:* United Nations, *World Population Prospects*, 1981.
[b]   Per cent of whole country's population represented by the sample.

[c]   Selected women = $\dfrac{\text{No. of identified women} \times \text{No. of selected households}}{\text{No. of successfully interviewed households}}$

[d]   Number of persons. The household was not used as a unit in the Senegal survey.
[e]   Women's sample covered ever-married women only.

Despite the difficulty of identifying clear analytic requirements as to sample size there is one related feature of the samples which was indeed tailored rather directly to user requirements. In several WFS countries a specific geographical sector (usually the urban sector) was deliberately oversampled in order to ensure an adequate sample for analysis within the sector concerned. For fuller details, see chapter 13 of this volume.

Finally, turning to the question of the geographical coverage of the sample, in principle the WFS was supposed to cover a sample representative of the whole of each country. Table 11.1 shows how far this principle was implemented in practice. In most cases the exclusion of certain small domains was justified by their inaccessibility, and of some of the larger regions by political considerations (Jordan West Bank, for example). In Malaysia the exclusion of the eastern region, and in Sudan the exclusion of the south, were due essentially to the special character of these regions and it was hoped to cover them in later surveys — though in fact these have not so far taken place. In Indonesia the limitation to Java and Bali was decided by the Government, supported by the funding agency, and seems to have been motivated also by the relative difficulty and expense of access.

11.4   The study population — criteria and cut-offs

A fertility survey is concerned, by definition, with women who are subject to the risk of childbearing. WFS took this to imply physiological age limits of 15–49 years. Minor variations occurred in these limits in some surveys and these will be discussed later in this section. A more important issue is that of the cultural constraints relating childbearing to marital status in many countries. Such constraints affect childbearing but they also affect interviewing; WFS assumed that these two effects would be closely correlated. It was accepted from the beginning that in most or all of the countries of Asia, the Middle East and North Africa cultural norms would make it impossible to ask never-married women about their own fertility or use of contraception; but it was also assumed that in these same countries such women's fertility and contraceptive use would be negligible. Since most of the individual questionnaire was concerned with questions on fertility, contraception or marital history it was decided that, in the regions mentioned, never-married women should not be put through the individual interview. They were thus excluded not only from the sensitive questions but also from the questions on age, residence, affiliation, education and occupation (except in so far as these were covered by the household interview) as well as the semi-sensitive topics of contraceptive knowledge and family-size preferences.

Application of the age and marital status criteria to filter ineligible women out of the individual interview was based on the household interview, at which all household members were listed together with their main demographic characteristics. In most countries education was also included in the household questionnaire.

Table 11.2 gives details of the eligibility criteria for the household and individual surveys and of the main items of information collected in the former.

We turn now from description of procedures to their evaluation. Were the criteria that were used to define the study population for the individual interview the most appropriate? We discuss here the marital status and age criteria only. The third main criterion, residence, was determined essentially by efficiency requirements and is discussed in chapter 12. A fourth criterion, nationality, was often applied. Most countries excluded non-nationals. In Africa, where nationality is often difficult to determine, many countries excluded only foreigners of non-African nationalities.

Although the reasons for applying cut-offs to limit the scope of the individual sample were simple — essentially they were to avoid the cost of interviewing women who would not have any current or recent fertility to report — the implications of such cut-offs are complex. To evaluate the policy that was adopted we need first to consider the following questions.

1 Was the assumption correct that fertility was negligible among the women excluded?

2 Was there significant substantive information other than on current fertility, for example on contraception, that the women could have given?

3 Was there significant *background* information other than on current fertility, for example on education, that was needed on the excluded women in order to allow study of differentials affecting the substantive variables?

4 If any of this information was needed, could it have been picked up through the household survey?

We now address each of these questions. Note that age and marital status will always be obtained in the household interview. For this reason these variables are not considered in this part of the discussion.

Was fertility negligible among the women excluded?

We look first at the lower age limit. In two countries an age limit lower than 15 was used for questions on children ever born in the household schedule. Table 11.3 gives the relevant results.

Information is also available for all countries by tracing back the maternity history to the period when the respondent was under 15.

Table 11.4 shows the number of births reported by respondents to have occurred when they were under 15 as a percentage of those reported to have occurred when they were 15-19, during the period 5-9 years before the survey. The table covers 15 countries selected for broad regional representation.[1]

The age group 15-19 itself accounts for no more than 10 per cent of total fertility in most countries. It is clear therefore that a negligible amount of fertility reporting has been lost by the exclusion of the under 15s, except perhaps in Bangladesh. (In the latter country, women under 15 were not in fact excluded from the individual survey, which was based on an ever-married sample with no lower age limit.) During negotiations with countries on survey design, WFS often encountered pressure to lower the age limit on the grounds that there was a significant number of mothers under 15. The figures in table 11.4 provide useful evidence on this issue.

As to the upper age limit, it is sufficient to note that the age-specific fertility rates for the age group 45-49 average 0.015 in the first 19 countries analysed (Hanenberg 1980). This means that only 1.7 per cent of the total fertility rate (which averages 4.3 children per woman) is accounted for by this age group. Clearly, no significant current fertility has been lost through the cut-off after age 49.

Turning to the marital status cut-off, we have data for three countries which excluded never-married women from the individual interview but included questions on fertility for them in the household interview. Table 11.5 gives the relevant data from the household survey.

These data suggest that in the younger age groups the exclusion of never-married women did sometimes lead to omission of a small, but not negligible, amount of fertility. It is important to note, however, that these three countries are not typical of those which used ever-married samples; on the contrary, the

TABLE 11.2

Eligibility criteria for household and individual interviews and content of the household questionniare

Country	Eligibility criteria			Content of household schedule[b]						
	House-hold survey	Individual survey		Marital status	Affiliation[c]	Education	Employment	Fertility	Mortality	Possessions
	F = de facto; J = de jure	Marital status. A = all; EM = ever married[a]	Age limits							
Africa										
Benin	F,J	A	15–49	X	X	—	—	X	X	—
Cameroon	F,J	A	15–54	X	X	X	X	X	X	X
Ghana	F,J	A	15–49	—	—	—	—	—	—	—
Ivory Coast	F,J	A	15–50	X	X	—	—	—	—	X
Kenya	F,J	A	15–50	—	—	—	—	—	—	—
Lesotho	F,J	EM	15–49	X	—	X	—	X	X	—
Nigeria	F,J	A	15–49	—	—	—	—	—	—	X
Senegal	F,J	A	15–49	X	—	—	—	—	X	—
Egypt	J	EM	–49	X	X	X	—	X	X	X
Mauritania	F,J	EM	12–50	X	X	—	—	X	X	—
Morocco	F,J	A	15–50	X	—	X	—	X	X	X
Sudan (North)	F,J	EM	–50	X	X	X	X	—	—	X
Tunisia	F,J	EM	15–49	X	—	X	—	—	—	—

Asia and Pacific

Country										
Jordan	F,J	F	EM	15–49	X	X	–	X	X	X
Syria	F,J	F	EM	–49	X	X	–	X	X	X
Turkey	J	J	EM	–49	X	–	X	X	–	–
Yemen AR	F,J	F	EM	–50	X	X	–	X	X	X^g
Bangladesh	F,J	F	EM	–49	X	X	–	X	–	–
Nepal	F,J	F	EM	15–49	X	–	–	–	–	–
Pakistan	F,J	F	EM	–50	X	X	–	X	–	–
Sri Lanka	F,J	F	EM	–49	X	–	–	–	–	X
Fiji	F,J	F	EM	15–49	X	X	–	–	X	X
Indonesia	J	J	EM	–49	X	–	–	X	–	–
Korea, Rep. of	F,J	F	EM	–49	X	X	–	–	–	X
Malaysia	F,J	F	EM	–49	X	X	–	X	X	X
Philippines	J	J	EM	15–49	X	X	–	X	–	–
Thailand	F,J	F	EM	–49	X	–	–	X	–	X

Americas

Country										
Colombia	F,J	F	A	15–49	X	X	X	X	–	–
Ecuador	J	J	A	15–49	X	X	X	X	X	X
Paraguay	F	F	A	15–49	X	X	–	X	–	–
Peru	F,J	F	EM	15–49	X	X	X	X	–	–
Venezuela	J	J	A	15–44	X	X	–	X	–	–
Costa Rica	J	J	A	20–49	X	X	–	X	–	–
Dominican Rep.	F,J	F	A	15–49	X	X	X	X	–	–
Mexico	J	J	A	$30–49^e$	X	–	–	–	X	X^g
Panama	F,J	F	A	20–49	X	X	–	X	–	X

Table 11.2 continued overleaf

Table 11.2 continued

Country	Eligibility criteria			Content of household schedule[b]						
	Household survey — F = de facto; J = de jure	Individual survey — Marital status. A = all; EM = ever married[a]	Age limits	Marital status	Affiliation[c]	Education	Employment	Fertility	Mortality	Possessions
Americas (cont.)										
Guyana	J[f]	J	A[d]	14–49	–	–	–	–	–	–	X
Haiti	F,J	F	A[d]	15–49	X	–	X	–	–	–	–
Jamaica	F,J	J	A[d]	15–49	–	–	–	–	–	–	–
Trinidad & Tobago	J	J	A[d]	15–49	–	–	–	–	–	–	X
Europe										
Portugal	F,J	F	EM	15–49	X	–	X	–	–	–	X

a   Definition of 'married' was adapted to local institutions with objective of approximating to sexual union.

b   In addition to the items cited, the following were included in all surveys: name, relationship, sex, age and the residence information needed for determination of eligibility for individual interview. A few countries also asked some other items. X = Yes; – = No.
In most cases where a topic was covered using non-standard questions a 'yes' is counted. For fuller details see Singh (1984a).

c   Ethnic, linguistic, religious or racial affiliation.

d   Full-time schoolgirls exluded.

e   Plus all women aged 15–19 who had had a live birth or been in a union.

f   Added qualification of at least one daily meal normally taken in household.

g   From individual interview.

TABLE 11.3

Children ever born, by respondent's age,
in Cameroon and Mauritania

Age of respondent	Cameroon		Mauritania	
	Mean	n	Mean	n
11	0.006	1 659	NA	
12	0.008	1 911	0.010	1 205
13	0.028	1 717	0.014	957
14	0.042	1 854	0.066	810
15	0.092	1 496	0.128	1 268
16	0.209	1 380	0.190	878
17	0.390	1 391	0.396	767
18	0.704	2 467	0.563	1 065
19	1.094	1 561	0.637	596
20–49	3.761	31 144	3.953	14 884

Note: NA: not asked; n: number of women.

above data are available for them precisely because they were borderline cases in which the question *could* be asked. It remains highly plausible to suppose that no useful data could have been obtained by attempting to ask unmarried women about their fertility in nearly all of the remaining countries. (Possible exceptions might be Thailand and the Philippines.) The data of table 11.5 do, however, suggest that the decision to exclude never-married women from the fertility questions of the individual questionnaire should be made only where there is strong reason. In the three countries of table 11.5 it would have been better to include them.

Were other substantive data excluded by the cut-off?
Here we consider contraceptive use and knowledge, fertility preferences, and past fertility.

Questions on contraception and preferences were never asked in the household schedule so that we have no direct evidence from the ever-married sample countries as to whether information could have been obtained from never-married women. (We do know that never-married women in Latin America reported negligible use of contraception in every survey.) It seems highly probable that any attempt to broaden the age limits and marital status cut-off for contraceptive use questions would be both unwelcome and largely fruitless in most of the countries concerned (though the borderline countries already mentioned might be exceptions.) Possibly, for what it is worth, a few more countries could have been pressed to allow questions on *contraceptive knowledge* to be put to never-married women, and no doubt a few more still would have agreed to allow *family size preference* questions. It is uncertain whether the latter would be of substantive value where the question would inevitably require the respondent to

TABLE 11.4

*Births below 15 as percentage of
births 15–19, occurring 5–9 years
before the survey*

Country	Per cent
Ghana	5.8
Kenya	7.3
Senegal	5.5
Egypt	4.9
Morocco	3.8
Syria	5.0
Bangladesh	17.5
Pakistan	4.7
Indonesia	7.6
Korea, Rep. of	0.0
Thailand	1.7
Paraguay	1.9
Venezuela	3.3
Mexico	5.5
Jamaica	5.5

project her preferences forward to an as yet uncertain, or even totally imaginary, marriage. Indeed, among the 12 WFS countries in which these questions were asked of all women, the data for never-married respondents do not appear to have been analysed. In short, for none of these substantive questions is there a strong case for including never-married women in the sample in the countries where they were excluded (except perhaps in the borderline countries), nor for an alteration in the age limits.

As regards *past fertility*, the question arises only in relation to the upper age cut-off. The group 45–49 has provided useful data contributing to evidence on fertility trends, particularly where comparisons have been attempted between the periods 5–9 and 10–14 years before the survey. Is there a case for extending this capability by including the 50–54 age group in future surveys? A counter-argument would be that most of those countries which are likely to undertake a survey in the future will have already undertaken a survey in the WFS round and the cohort in question will have been surveyed during that operation. Essentially the issue is one of priorities. The 50–54 age group undoubtedly have interesting information to give on past fertility if one can afford the cost of collecting it. We return to this question later.

Did the cut-offs exclude significant background population data?[2]

Computation of rates requires a knowledge of the population at risk. Clearly the truncated population of the individual survey does not contain the information

TABLE 11.5

Percentage of all reported live births which are reported by
never-married respondents, by current age of respondent:
Fiji, Lesotho, Peru; household survey data

Current age of respondent	Fiji		Lesotho		Peru	
	%NM	CEB % by NM mothers	% NM	CEB % by NM mothers	% NM	CEB % by NM mothers
15–19	87	17.4	67	9.4	86	5.4
20–24	33	4.2	16	3.3	48	4.0
25–29	9	1.6	7	2.6	23	2.1
30–34	4	0.5	5	1.8	11	1.0
35–39	3	1.0	3	1.2	8	1.0
40–44	2	0.3	2	0.6	5	0.3
45–49	1	0.4	2	1.1	5	0.5

Notes:
% NM: percentage of never-married women;
CEB: children ever born.
In Lesotho 7 per cent of cases failed to respond on the parity question. Nearly all of these were never married. They have been assigned zero parity for the present analysis.

required for estimation of rates, including differential rates, in the general female population. In particular, for the ever-married women samples we do not have, within the individual sample, the necessary information on the population at risk even for the limited age range 15–49. The problem arises most acutely in relation to age-at-marriage differentials. To estimate, for example, the educational differentials in age at first marriage it is necessary to know the distribution of the educational variable for never-married as well as ever-married women.

Can the missing information be supplied by the household survey?

For full exploitation of the material in the Core Individual Questionnaire one would need background data on age, residence (childhood and current), education and literacy, religious and/or ethnic affiliation and employment for all women aged 15–49. This is missing for never-married women in the individual survey for countries using ever-married samples. Table 11.2 gives information on how much of this information is available in the household surveys. Generally, current residence, education and some kind of affiliation variable are available more often than not. In a future survey childhood residence and literacy could easily be added if there were sufficient interest in them. Employment perhaps presents the only serious problem. Apart from the not very informative question 'whether or not currently working', only six countries in the WFS asked questions on economic activity or occupation in their household survey and only two of these (Tunisia and Turkey) are among the group of countries whose individual sample is restricted to ever-married women. For the remaining countries with ever-married women's samples occupational differentials would not be available. Unfortunately occupation, as is well known, presents difficulties of data collection and coding which are not negligible; certainly it would not be admissible to have to ask the whole household schedule sample (including men) the occupation question simply to obtain the information for never-married women. Therefore if this variable is worth pursuing the question must be asked specifically of never-married women, and this almost certainly by person-to-person questioning. This amounts to including such women in the individual interview sample.

The alternative of obtaining the required background information on never-married women from the census might occasionally be considered, but in general it would be rare to find data from that source that were both up to date and collected on a comparable basis.

We turn now to the rather more complex question of the effect of the cut-off on the estimation of the variables which are themselves used for defining the cut-off — namely, age in all countries and marital status in about half. Information for these variables was obtained twice: once in the household survey, with a view to operating the cut-off, and again in the individual interview for the purpose of data analysis. It is this double collection that raises the problems. There are in fact three issues to be considered:

1 The interviewer's knowledge that a cut-off is to be applied may lead her to distort the response, presumably in order to reduce her subsequent workload. Such a distortion would affect the household data directly, and the individual data indirectly by biasing the sample of women interviewed.

2 The use of a cut-off based on an unreliable variable (i.e. one which may give a different value each time it is measured) will in general lead to a distortion in the curtailed population, that is, in the *individual* survey data.

3 We have to consider whether the *response quality* in the two successive enquiries is the same.

We shall examine these problems in turn.

Distortion in the household response due to interviewer's knowledge that a cut-off is planned

Examination of the age–sex distribution from the household schedule around the cut-off ages (generally 15 and 49) has been a feature of every country's survey evaluation report. The results are summarized in chapter 24. Interpretation is not straightforward since other age distortions are certainly present and some of these operate differentially according to sex. There are wide differences between the countries but in many cases the distortion of present concern is clearly visible.

The clearest evidence comes from countries in which two separate household surveys were carried out, the second on a subsample of the first, and only the second of which was used for selection of women with a view to individual interview. (The latter was carried out immediately after the second household survey by the same interviewer.) In table 11.6 we compare the sex ratios on either side of the cut-off for two such pairs of surveys. By focusing on the sex ratios we introduce the male population as a control, eliminating general age biases affecting the population as a whole.[3]

TABLE   11.6
Sex ratios in independent and dependent household surveys in nested samples

Country	Type of household survey[a]	Age groups			
		10–14	15–19	45–49	50–54
Indonesia[b]	I	–	–	105	95
	D	–	–	114	79
Kenya[b]	I	100	94	98	85
	D	93	105	102	87
Lesotho	I	–	–	98	84
	D	–	–	114	63

  [a]   I = independent. No operational link with the second household survey or the individual survey.
       D = dependent. Survey data used to identify women for the subsequent individual survey, carried out by the same interviewers at the same visit to the household.
  [b]   Eligibility for individual survey includes *age 50* in Indonesia and Kenya.
  Note: The individual samples in Indonesia and Lesotho covered ever-married women only. The lower age cut-off is therefore irrelevant for the present analysis.

In Kenya there is a substantial difference at the lower age cut-off and a small one at the upper. In Lesotho, where only the upper cut-off is relevant, the effect is extreme. All the differences between the two types of survey are in the direction corresponding to the exclusion of women from the individual sample. In Lesotho it would appear that more than one-third of the women in the 45–49 age group were reported 50–54 as a result of the cut-off, while a further 15 per cent were omitted altogether.

Such an effect was foreseen in the WFS Manual on Sample Design (p. 220). However, it was considered excessively wasteful of resources to insist on two independent field forces, one for the household survey and one for the individual, except in the surveys which used a specially enlarged household sample (all three independent cases in our analysis are in the latter category).[4] It was partly as a defence against this source of error that the upper age limit was set as high as 49. The group 45–49 was intended to act as a buffer, leaving the more significant 40–44 group hopefully unaffected by the existence of a cut-off. In a sense this strategy clearly succeeded, but it replaced one problem with another.

The availability of data for the 45–49 group created a new demand for its analysis — and with that demand, the need for a new buffer group still higher. In fact the 45–49 group has been quoted with the younger ages in all routine analyses and in some cases has played an important role, as we have already mentioned. There is thus, by now, quite a strong case for including the 50–54 age group in the individual survey.

In a few countries in which age reporting was known to be particularly poor the eligibility criterion was extended to cover age 50 in the hope of minimizing losses due to heaping on 50. Examination of the results for these countries shows clearly that this strategy did reduce heaping on 50; however, the data show too much variability to enable us to assess the more crucial issue, namely, whether the numbers lost to the 45–49 age group through age overstatement were reduced.

Evidence of the kind quoted previously is not available regarding possible distortion in the marital status information. In most countries where a marital status cut-off was applied it seems implausible to suppose that many women currently married would be recorded as never married. On the other hand, one could imagine easily enough that a widowed or divorced woman, particularly in a younger age group, might be reported as never married. Thus one should not assume that this kind of distortion never occurred.

Before leaving this subject let us note again that the distortions discussed above, which directly affect the household response, will also affect the individual sample data by removing from the sample some women who are close to the cut-off age, or perhaps whose marital status is widowed, divorced or separated.

Bias due to unreliability in the cut-off

When a cut-off is operated on a variable that includes a random error component, distortion in the resulting distribution is inevitable. For example, if we accept for the individual interview only women reported over 15 in the household schedule, there will be errors in both directions:

Some women under 15 will be wrongly reported over 15 and accepted.

Some women over 15 will be wrongly reported under 15 and rejected.

At the individual interview a second age determination is made. Those in the first group above may now be correctly reported; however, those in the second group get no chance for a second report. If the second interview's data are now used as the basis for analysis, then women who are in fact just above 15 are given two separate chances of disappearing from the sample, while those just below 15 will get only one chance of being brought in. These effects will not compensate and there will be a definite discontinuity, with a deficit of persons just inside the cut-off boundaries. This effect is quite distinct from age-heaping or motivated distortion.

If p is the proportion of different responses when a question is repeated, then assuming that successive responses are independent, that the error distribution is symmetrical and that the age distribution is locally flat, it is easily shown that the expected loss in a borderline category due to the process we have described is simply p, to the first order of approximation. Further, at the second age determination a proportion equal to p of an age (or age group) will be reported as just outside the acceptance range. If the two age determinations have different values of p, then in both of the statements made above p will be replaced by $(p_1 + p_2)/2$. We ignore terms in $p_1 p_2$. In the WFS standard recode tapes out-of-range cases in the individual interview are supposed to have been treated as falling within the borderline admissible category. Thus the WFS procedure corrects the error to a first approximation.[5]

In practice, the independence of the two relevant age determinations can never be assumed in any WFS survey. In the first place, in most surveys the household interview on which the age and marital status filters were based was carried out by an interviewer who herself went straight on to do the individual interview. One cannot expect an independent response in such circumstances. It is probably unrealistic even to expect the interviewer to *try* for an independent response; she is much more likely to copy down the earlier response blindly. But secondly, even if separate interviewers were used for the two operations, as occurred in two WFS countries (Benin and Senegal), it is inevitable that the individual interviewers know that they have been handed a list of women who are supposed to be between 15 and 49. It would be unreasonable to suppose that their age determination around the critical ages was unaffected by this knowledge. In fact, the number of out-of-range cases recorded in the standard recode tapes is very small in all countries and generally negligible.

While these facts do create problems regarding the quality of the age response, they actually reduce the significance of the problem we are considering here. Where interviewers simply accepted the household survey age determination without attempting to improve it in the individual survey, then the bias we are considering will not occur. On the other hand, where they made a new determination and the WFS rule of retaining any interviewed out-of-range women in the sample was applied, then the bias is approximately corrected.

We therefore suggest that the problem of a statistical bias created by the use of a cut-off based on an unreliably measured variable is of minor significance in the WFS.

Response quality in the household and individual surveys

Several features of the questionnaires and field procedures lead one to expect a higher response quality in the individual survey.[6] First, the household survey allowed proxy responses. Second, the individual survey often asked age, and always marital status, through a more elaborate sequence of questions than the household survey. Third, the individual survey provided numerous cross-checks whose use by interviewers, field editors and office editors was encouraged. Fourth, in some countries the household interviews were carried out by separate, male interviewers who generally had a much briefer training than the female interviewers. In many others, however, the two determinations are virtually identical, presumably due to contamination in one or other direction.

Most of the features mentioned above which imply the superiority of the individual survey age determination could in principle, and at a cost, be incorporated into the household survey. One could insist on person-to-person interviewing for adult women; on production of birth certificates where available; on use of well-trained interviewers.[7] On the other hand, cross-checks with the birth history and other elaborate question sequences will never be feasible in the household survey — though it seems unlikely that these often lead to significant corrections to an adult woman's age in practice. Thus the option is available of an improved age determination before the cut-off, at additional cost. It should be noted, however, that if this were adopted one could not ask the same interviewer to repeat the age questioning in the individual interview. The only practical procedure, if the same interviewer is used, would be to copy the initial determination into the individual questionnaire.

There is also the option of using different field staff for the initial age determination on which selection is based (normally the household survey) and the individual interview. This should practically eliminate age distortion in the individual sample due to selection, besides improving the final age estimate. Unfortunately it would be much more expensive, besides being cumbersome in the field.

We have now discussed the numerous technical issues involved in the fixing of cut-offs for the individual sample. Before drawing conclusions it remains to examine the costs that would be involved in any change.

Table 11.7 shows, for a range of countries, the increase in sample size that would be involved in extending the sample to include women aged 50–54, or girls aged 14, relative to a standard 15–49. Data come from the household schedule tables (First Country Reports).

Note that many of the figures will have been inflated by age distortions. In practice, it would probably be safe to assume an increase of not more than 7 per cent were the group 50–54 to be added, and 6 per cent were the 14-year-olds included.

Table 11.8 shows, for the WFS *ever-married women* samples, the per cent increase that would be involved in extending to an *all women 15–49* base.

We have also examined how many of such never-married women would be found in a household already containing a currently eligible woman. The tabulation is difficult and has been carried out for only a few countries. The results, expressed as a percentage of never-married women 15–49, are:

Indonesia	79%	Philippines	61%
Malaysia	77%	Syria	76%
Nepal	79%	Thailand	72%

TABLE 11.7

*Size of supplementary age groups of potential
interest, as per cent of all women aged 15–49*

Country	Females aged 50–54	Females aged 14
Cameroon	7	5
Ghana	10	5
Kenya	7	8
Lesotho	7	6
Egypt	7	6
Tunisia	9	6
Jordan	5	7
Turkey	9	6
Bangladesh	5	6
Sri Lanka	6	5
Indonesia	10	5
Philippines	8	6
Colombia	6	6
Paraguay	7	—
Mexico	7	6
Haiti	11	6

Note: Base of percentage is all women 15–49 even where
this is not the WFS individual base.
Source: Household surveys, WFS.

These figures would be relevant only if one were considering a method of sampling women which involved identifying eligible women in one visit and interviewing them in another, a procedure that was adopted in only a few of the WFS surveys. In countries using the more normal WFS procedure a second visit for interviewing the women (after the household interview visit) will be necessary only in the event of a callback. WFS data on callbacks are of dubious validity for most countries. However, if we limit ourselves to countries in which the proportion of successful visits recorded as callbacks exceeded 5 per cent (in order to exclude clearly unreliable data), and at the same time to countries with samples covering all women aged 15–49, we find, for ten countries,[8] an average of 11 per cent of callbacks among all successful interviews, with the same figure for never-married as ever-married women (although the countries show considerable individual variation).

In summary, the inclusion of never-married women would not impose any exceptional burden beyond the obvious one of increasing the sample size in the

TABLE   11.8

Per cent increase in WFS samples if never-married women 15–49 were added (countries with ever-married women samples only)

Country	Never-married 15–49 as % of ever-married 15–49
Lesotho	26
Mauritania	26
Egypt	40
Sudan (North)	39
Tunisia	70
Jordan	44
Syria	49
Turkey	35
Yemen AR	11
Bangladesh	10
Nepal	11
Pakistan	26
Sri Lanka	66
Fiji	46
Indonesia	32
Korea, Rep. of	61
Malaysia	53
Thailand	53
Peru	59
Portugal	51

proportions shown in table 11.8. If the usual WFS field arrangement is adopted, the number of additional visits would be negligible, except in a few countries with exceptionally late age at marriage.

11.5   Conclusions and recommendations

We summarize below the findings of this discussion on the eligibility criteria for the individual interview, before attempting a conclusion.

1 The age cut-offs did not cut off any significant quantum of current fertility.

2 The marital status filter did cut off significant fertility in three countries where its application does not seem to have been really necessary in terms of cultural constraints. In countries where these constraints were strong we have no evidence but it seems very unlikely that any useful information on current fertility for never-married women could have been obtained even if such fertility existed.

3 The lower age cut-off causes no loss of useful information on other topics.

4 The upper age cut-off causes loss of some useful information on past fertility.

5 The never-married cut-off causes loss of significant background information. Most of this could be easily supplied through the household survey in a future survey (and much of it was, in WFS surveys). An exception is the area of employment. These questions are complex and difficult to code and not well suited to the household schedule.

6 The age cut-offs can substantially distort age reporting in the household schedule and distort the age distribution of the sample filtered through to the individual interview. We do not know whether an analogous distortion occurs on marital status due to the never-married filter, but it is at least possible that there may be some loss of widowed and divorced women from this source.

7 Statistical bias due to operation of a double cut-off on an unreliably measured variable can probably be avoided to a sufficient approximation by ensuring that anomalous (out-of-range) data are retained in the individual survey data file. They should then be treated by analysts as if they belonged to the age, or age group, just inside the boundary.

8 The option is available of improving the age determination at the household interview, at increased cost, through use of methods normally only employed in the individual interview.

9 Compared with a standard sample of 15–49, addition of the age group 50–54 would imply an increase of about 7 per cent in the sample, and addition of the age 14 would imply an increase of about 6 per cent.

10 In countries currently restricting their individual sample to ever-married women, inclusion of never-married women would increase the sample by amounts which vary widely from country to country – from 10 per cent in Bangladesh to 70 per cent in Tunisia. In the normal WFS fieldwork arrangement this will not involve visiting any more households and the number of additional callbacks will usually be negligible.

Before making recommendations, a brief discussion is needed on the conceptual issue. What does it mean to say that a specific group, such as never-married women, is 'part of the individual sample'? The term could be understood at several different levels, referring for example to:

1 Whether the specified women are to be interviewed with the same questionnaire as other women.

2 Whether they are to be interviewed personally, like other women in the individual sample, or merely by proxy as in the household schedule.

3 Whether they are to appear on the same data file.

4 Whether they are to be regarded by the survey organizers as belonging to the main data set.

Examining these issues in turn, the first is little more than a trivial logistic matter. Whatever the document used as questionnaire, the sequence of questions would clearly be different for never-married women, who will necessarily be filtered through a different route. If the sequence for never-married women is short enough, it will be worth using a distinct questionnaire. The problem is a practical one of fieldwork logistics.

The second issue, proxy versus personal interview, is more substantial. It has to be decided as a function of the questions to be asked and the precision required.

The third, the data file, is a technical issue independent of the others. With current technology it is still a considerable advantage to have a simple rectangularized file for all women who are ever likely to be included in one analysis. The waste of disk or tape space is not very significant.

The fourth issue, at first sight the vaguest, is perhaps the most important. Experience shows that the attention paid to a subgroup such as never-married women during processing, analysis, archiving and dissemination may depend to a remarkable extent on the way in which this group is seen, subjectively, by those who specify the computer programs, tabulation plans and other analytic strategies. If the group is perceived as part of the survey sample, it is likely to be fully processed and archived; if not, it will tend to be pushed aside, overlooked, or handled with less care and rigour than other parts of the data file. However irrational it may appear, this subjective factor seems to be of crucial importance.

These four issues therefore need to be distinguished, in addition to the central issue of what questions to ask in the survey, for any specific group.

Our main recommendation is that the survey sample, or data set, should represent all women between the cut-off ages. Though data on never-married women are much less often needed by analysts, when they *are* needed it is an overwhelming advantage that they be available on the same basis, and from the same physical source, as the rest of the sample. They should therefore be included in the same data file.

Where factors affecting marriage and age at marriage are of special interest in the survey a personal interview with never-married women is desirable. Otherwise analytic interest in these women seems to be small; there appears to be little demand for substantive information on such topics as family planning knowledge and use, or family size preferences. However, it is essential that the full range of background ('independent') variables be obtained for such women. It is suggested that a proxy interview using the household schedule would generally be adequate for the purpose.

The age limits 15–49 appear in general appropriate. Where there is a special interest in past trends in fertility, there is a case for extension to age 54.

Notes

1. The countries were selected before obtaining the data.
2. The special case of age as a background variable will be considered later.

3. There are, of course, sex-specific age biases. However, these are somewhat less pronounced. Our data show that there is indeed some reduction in variance to be achieved by studying sex ratios rather than numbers of females.

4. A similar distortion due to motivated bias in sample selection was, however, regarded as too serious to be risked: the WFS Manual was explicit in rejecting any system of 'sampling as you go' by interviewers.

5. We make the further assumption here that the incidence of displacement across *two* categories is of order p^2 and therefore negligible.

6. Though, as shown in chapter 4 by Timaeus, the reporting of lifetime fertility in household surveys appears more or less equal in quality to that achieved in individual surveys.

7. Some surveys adopted this approach. See for instance the household questionnaire used in Kenya.

8. Cameroon, Colombia, Ecuador, Ghana, Guyana, Haiti, Ivory Coast, Jamaica, Kenya, Trinidad and Tobago. Countries averaged with equal weight.

PART IV

Sampling and Data Collection

12

Sample Design

Chris Scott
Trudy Harpham

12.1 The WFS sampling strategy

The WFS made no conscious attempt to standardize sample design, since the possibility of comparing results across countries does not depend on the surveys having similar sample designs. WFS did, however, produce a 'Manual on Sample Design' (WFS 1975c) which outlined a general strategy for the design of WFS samples.

The strategy postulates as a basic condition the use of strict probability sampling – that is, probabilities known (or knowable) and non-zero for every unit in the sample. Constraints on coverage have been mentioned in chapter 11. One further general constraint should be mentioned. Before starting work on a specific WFS sample design two questions were always asked: first whether or not an existing sample for a current or recent survey could provide a suitable sample for the proposed fertility survey, possibly by subsampling either at the area, dwelling, household or individual stage, and secondly whether the sampling work for the fertility survey could be applied to provide a sample for other surveys. In about one-third of cases one or other of these questions was answered in the affirmative and it follows that, in all such cases, the sample design was substantially affected by factors that had nothing to do with the WFS project. Some of the more deviant WFS sample designs are explained in this way.

With regard to the strategy itself, the first step is to seek a sampling frame of area units whose boundaries are reasonably well defined and whose individual population sizes are as small as possible. These are called the 'basic area units' (BAUs). In some countries the BAUs may be large, in others small. Whatever their size, they form a convenient starting point for designing the sample because, in the hierarchy of sampling stages, they mark the point beyond which sampling operations have to move out of the office and into the field. The BAUs may be first-stage units, intermediate units, or ultimate-stage units; this remains to be decided.

The second step is to decide at what stage the sampling process is to move from area demarcation to listing (of dwellings or households). This decision determines the lowest stage of area sampling, the 'ultimate area unit' (UAU).

If the desired size of the UAUs is consistently and substantially smaller than that of the BAUs, we need a segmentation operation, to create UAUs; to economize effort, this is done only in the selected BAUs. Otherwise, the BAU itself is adopted as UAU. Whichever the case, we plan to list all dwellings, or all households, in the selected UAUs. From these we select a sample of households for the individual survey, the number selected being roughly constant and called the cluster 'take', and in these selected households we interview all women meeting the criteria for interview.

The third decision is to fix the average cluster take. In most cases this was between 20 and 50 households, and in most cases if we then take all women eligible for interview in each selected household this will give approximately the same figure in terms of individual women. Since the total sample size is by this time fixed, we know the number of UAUs to be selected. Typically the figure fell between 100 and 300.

For the fourth decision we backtrack to the BAUs and ask whether there is a case for introducing a stage of sampling before the BAU. Any additional sampling stage may be justified for two reasons: to reduce travel costs by clustering the sample, or to reduce the amount of work in sampling frame creation for later sampling stages. The latter consideration is ruled out in the present case, since by definition we already have a sampling frame for BAUs. Hence the issue reduces to that of cutting travel costs by clustering the sample BAUs. Bearing in mind, among other things, that in developing countries long distance travel is in general proportionately cheaper than short distance, it was judged that this factor would be negligible in most countries. Thus in most WFS samples either the BAU or the UAU was the primary sampling unit.

Explicit stratification was introduced at the first stage only and was based on geographic criteria. Implicit stratification was obtained by systematic selection at all sampling stages. In a few cases stratification was also introduced at the first stage in order to allow different sampling rates to be used in different domains — typically an increase in the sampling rate for the urban sector, but also occasionally differences between regions. This strategy may be appropriate where some domain of analytic interest is so small in the population that a very small sample would be obtained if the sampling fraction were constant throughout; in such a case one may, for example, double the sampling rate for that domain in order to ensure adequate sampling precision for its estimates. Of course this creates a 'biased' sample and, when making estimates for the whole country, the bias has to be corrected by appropriate reweighting. The technique is well known to sampling statisticians. Occasionally stratification was also introduced in WFS samples because of the need for a difference in sample design between the urban and rural sectors; for example, in several cases a single stage of area sampling was used in the urban sector but two stages in the rural.

Finally, in most WFS samples the area sampling units were selected with probability proportional to size and, within each selected UAU, the dwellings or households for the individual survey were selected with probability inversely proportional to the UAU selection probability; when these two probabilities are multiplied together the variations therefore cancel. Thus this design yields constant selection probability for households — a 'self-weighting' sample. In such cases 'size' is measured in terms of census population, or census households, or some very rough measure based on these. The more accurate the size measure, the more nearly fixed will be the resulting take per UAU; however the self-weighting character of the sample does not depend on the accuracy of the size measures.

The above strategy was applied in nearly all WFS countries and was found to stand up very well to the test of practice. Indeed, standardization went further than expected in that the most recent population census was found to constitute a suitable area sampling frame in almost every country and usually the census enumeration districts (EDs) were adopted as the BAUs. In most cases further segmentation was required, at least for the majority of the EDs. At the other extreme, there were often some EDs which were unacceptably small and which had to be combined with neighbouring EDs before sampling. Finally, in most cases the EDs also constituted the first stage of sampling.

One variant of this design was particularly attractive where the household questionnaire was to be used at the stage of listing of households in order to collect substantive demographic information, because this variant yields a self-weighting sample for both the household and the individual survey. The procedure involves first fixing a standard segment size — typically around 500 census population. For each ED in the country the number of segments to be made was then determined by dividing the ED population by 500 and rounding. Let this number be s_i for the i-th ED. (For example, assuming a standard segment size of 500, of an ED of 600 census population would be given an s_i of 1, while an ED of 900 would be given $s_i = 2$.) The EDs were then selected with probability proportional to s_i. The segments were created, usually by a field operation, in the selected EDs only, taking care to create exactly the number already fixed, namely s_i, in each case. In each such ED the segments were numbered and one was selected at random with equal probability $1/s_i$. This procedure is exactly equivalent to a single-stage sample of segments. The household survey covers all the households in the segment and a fixed fraction of these is selected for the individual survey. Thus both surveys have self-weighting samples.

It is clear from the above description of the general WFS sampling strategy that several technical issues were settled in a fairly arbitrary manner simply because evidence was lacking and *some* decision had to be taken. Now that the surveys have been completed it is possible to evaluate the decisions that were made in terms of the results obtained. In the rest of this chapter we attempt such evaluations for several of the main sample features: stratification; the number of stages; segmentation and the choice of UAU size; the size and constancy of the take within UAUs; and the structural relationship between the household and individual surveys.

Fuller details of the designs actually adopted in WFS surveys, and of their implementation, will be found in chapter 13.

12.2   Stratification

Stratification means dividing up the population into subgroups or strata and selecting the sample separately in each stratum. This guarantees that each stratum receives the sample size planned for it: without stratification the over-all sample is planned but the way the sample distributes between subgroups is left to chance. The essential objective of stratification is reduction in sampling error.

Stratification makes it possible to vary the sampling fraction in different strata. If advance knowledge is available on the population variance in the different strata this strategy can be used to increase sampling efficiency, and if knowledge is also available on cost variations of survey work in the different strata it can further be used to increase the cost-efficiency of the sample. These circumstances rarely exist in developing countries. Apart from some cases in which sampling rates were varied between the urban and rural sectors, and one or two others in which the rate was augmented in some domain of special interest, most WFS samples made use of fixed overall sampling rates throughout and were self-weighting.

However, even with constant sampling rates stratification in general has the effect of reducing sampling error. It is this effect that we examine here. The reduction occurs in so far as the strata correspond to real differences in the population in terms of the variables under study. For example, if the northern region has higher fertility than the south then stratifying by north versus south will reduce the sampling error for the estimate of national fertility.

Systematic sampling (selection at fixed intervals from a list) has a similar effect to stratification provided the list is in some meaningful order, since it ensures an even distribution of the sample over the list. The variable that orders the list plays the role of the stratifying criterion. For purposes of sampling error computation, it is usual to regard the list as divided into implicit strata in such a way that each pair of selected units falls into one such stratum.

In WFS samples, with few exceptions, only geographical stratification was used and in most cases these were implicit strata — that is, the area units were selected by systematic sampling. Such stratification has its greatest effect on sampling efficiency when it is done at the first stage of sampling. The extent to which first-stage geographical stratification contributed to the sampling efficiency of WFS samples was examined by Verma, Scott and O'Muircheartaigh (1980) and we summarize their main conclusions below.

We begin by defining sampling efficiency. In the absence of stratification the most efficient sample is a fully random one. For this reason the random sample (single-stage, unstratified, equal probability) is used as a standard and we measure a sample's efficiency by comparing its sampling error to that of a random sample of the same size. The ratio of these two sampling errors is termed *deft* — the design factor for the sample and variable concerned. If deft = 1 the actual sample is fully efficient; if deft = 2 then its sampling standard error is twice that of a random sample of the same size. Inefficiency is usually caused by the clustering of the sample, i.e. multi-stage sampling, and it can be reduced by stratification. Thus we wish to examine the effect of stratification in reducing deft.

Verma, Scott and O'Muircheartaigh (1980) analysed six WFS surveys and computed defts for 38 variables in each survey.[1] A sample's efficiency depends on the variable studied: for variables whose distribution in the population is highly clustered the loss of efficiency due to clustered sampling will tend to be greater. Contraceptive knowledge, for example, tends to be highly clustered in the population and so questions on this tend to have high deft values, whereas fertility variables tend to be well spread out over the population and hence have low defts. Thus, from the point of view of sampling efficiency, it makes sense to group variables according to their subject matter. In order to condense a large amount of material we have used such a grouping in table 12.1, which presents average deft values for a number of variables in each subject matter group. For each group and each country we show two quantities: the average deft for the actual stratified sample, and the estimated percentage reduction in deft that was achieved by the first-stage stratification used.

Gains in efficiency due to the stratification actually used range in most cases between 5 and 25 per cent. Note that a given gain in efficiency implies approximately twice as much gain in terms of sample size — for example, achievement of a 10 per cent reduction in sampling error by increasing the sample would require roughly a 20 per cent increase in sample size; the table shows that such a gain can be expected (almost free of cost) by simple geographical stratification.

Before practical conclusions are drawn, however, there is another important factor to be considered. The table relates to sampling errors for the whole national sample; but such sampling errors are nearly always very small and in general negligible compared with non-sampling errors. Where sampling error really begins to constrain the analyst is in the smaller subclasses of the sample. Such subclasses are of two kinds (with many intermediate cases): cross-classes, which are well distributed across clusters, and segregated classes, which are concentrated in a few clusters. Age groups are an example of a cross-class, while occupation groups tend towards the segregated end of the spectrum, and regions are totally segregated. The above analysis was extended to investigate two selected subclasses: one cross-class (age group 25–34) and one small mixed class (husband's education, secondary level or higher). Results, averaged over all variables, are shown in table 12.2. The comparable bottom line of table 12.1 is reproduced for comparison. Since the size of the subclass is likely to affect its behaviour, this is also shown (column C). Though now somewhat smaller, the gains due to stratification are still in most cases appreciable.

In the first three countries the area sampling was multi-stage while in the last three it was single-stage. When multi-stage sampling is used the first-stage units are likely to be large and the number selected will be small. Thailand is an extreme case: the first-stage units, the *changwat* or provinces, had average populations of half a million and only 37 were selected. It is not surprising that the efficiency of such a sampling stage can be greatly improved by stratification. For

TABLE 12.1
Sampling efficiency and stratification: whole sample

Variable group	Number of variables[a]	Thailand rural		Colombia rural		Nepal		Indonesia		Bangladesh		Guyana	
		(A)	(B)	(A)	(B)	(A)	(B)	(A)	(B)	(A)	(B)	(A)	(B)
Nuptiality	7	1.26	18	1.40	23	1.90	5	1.45	8	1.22	5	1.16	15
Fertility	11	1.34	25	1.33	15	1.92	0	1.41	13	1.12	8	1.02	6
Fertility preferences	6	1.35	24	1.26	10	2.76	13	1.55	8	1.20	11	1.13	4
Contraceptive knowledge	4	2.54	18	3.05	7	3.21	10	2.44	21	1.65	22	1.51	3
Contraceptive use	10	2.30	22	2.24	6	2.23	−9	1.70	21	1.31	12	1.24	7
All	38	1.66	22	1.75	12	2.32	6	1.62	15	1.26	11	1.17	7

(A) Mean deft for actual sample.
(B) Estimated per cent reduction in deft due to first-stage stratification.
a Not all of these were used for every country. For specification of variables and other details, see Verma, Scott and O'Muircheartaigh (1980).

TABLE 12.2

Sampling efficiency and stratification: selected subclasses (average over all variables in table 12.1)

Subclass	Thailand rural			Colombia rural			Nepal			Indonesia			Bangladesh			Guyana		
	(A)	(B)	(C)	(A)	(B)	(C)	(A)	(B)	(C)	(A)	(B)	(C)	(A)	(B)	(C)	(A)	(B)	(C)
Age 25–34	1.31	20	30	1.31	10	27	1.68	7	34	1.37	11	32	1.13	8	29	1.08	5	34
Husband's education, secondary or higher	0.94	4	4	0.98	8	6	1.11	8	6	1.51	9	32	1.14	5	20	1.07	1	16
Whole sample	1.66	22	100	1.75	12	100	2.32	6	100	1.62	15	100	1.26	11	100	1.17	7	100

(A) Mean deft for actual sample.
(B) Estimated per cent reduction in deft due to first-stage stratification.
(C) Per cent size of subclass in the survey population.

the more typical single-stage samples, and for the subclasses (which is where sampling error really matters), the efficiency gain contributed by stratification seems to have been about 5–10 per cent. This is still not negligible. Considering the ease with which geographical stratification can be carried out, it must be regarded as obligatory in surveys of the WFS type.

It has been suggested that WFS should have made more use of stratification and, in particular, should have attempted to stratify in terms of the intensity of the family planning programme in different localities. The conditions necessary for this to be profitable would be:

1 There must be an active family planning programme which is having an impact on fertility behaviour;
2 There must be available data making it possible to distinguish areas where the programme activity is more intense (or better still, more successful);
3 This geographical information must be at a level more detailed than that of the stratification which would be planned anyway, or at least not included in the latter; and
4 It must be possible to interpret the geographical information in terms of the sampling frame that will be used.

There might be half a dozen developing countries where all these conditions are fulfilled and it is probably a justified criticism that WFS should have looked more closely at this. In addition, some countries collect basic fertility data in their censuses and it may be that a closer look at these data would have led to improved stratification – although here again it seems rather unlikely that real differences in fertility could be identified in this way at a geographical level not already taken into account by the stratification used in WFS surveys. In future fertility surveys it would be worth examining the variation of fertility between clusters in the WFS survey in the country concerned to see whether any variable which could be useful for stratification can be identified at the cluster level.

12.3 Multi-stage sampling

In this section we consider the effects of introducing area sampling stages before the BAU. Stages introduced below the BAU are considered in section 12.4. Before coming to the substance of the discussion, however, we must deal with an issue of terminology.

A sampling stage is essentially a level in a hierarchically structured sample. Suppose we select a sample of districts and within each selected district we select a sample of villages, so that the two stages of sampling are the district and the village. If we select two or more villages per district then the village sample will be to some degree clustered by the introduction of the district sampling stage. However, if we select only one village per district it will generally be true that the district stage has no clustering effect on the village sample; we may reach a sample no different from a single-stage sample of villages. In such cases (which are quite common) the initial sampling of districts is done, not to cluster the selected villages in groups, but to reduce the amount of work in mapping or listing villages; essentially the district here serves as a kind of address to help us to identify the selected village, rather than influencing the actual choice of village.

A sampling stage which does not have the effect of clustering the next stage, is called a notional stage. The amount of work saved by a notional stage may be trivial or it may be very considerable, but in any case it does not affect the sample design, nor the sampling error. Stages which have the effect of clustering the next stage sample are called effective stages. In this section we consider only effective stages and their impact on sampling error and costs.

As we have seen, most WFS samples have used only one effective area stage although Verma, Scott and O'Muircheartaigh (1980) identified three WFS surveys with more than one effective area stage (Thailand with three, Colombia and Nepal with two) and carried out an analysis similar to that described above to examine the effect on the sampling error of introducing additional stages above the BAU. Table 12.3 gives the main results for the same set of variables as table 12.1 (column (A) is the same in both tables). The table compares deft for the actual sample (shown in column (A)) with an estimate of deft for a single sampling stage based on the lowest area stage actually used. The increase due to multi-stage sampling is shown as a percentage in column (B).

The table reveals very substantial losses in sampling efficiency due to multi-area-stage sampling. But once again before drawing practical conclusions we look at the effect in subclasses. Table 12.4 is analogous to table 12.2. Interest

TABLE   12.3
Sampling efficiency and multiple area sampling stages:
whole sample

Variable group	Thailand rural		Colombia rural		Nepal rural	
	(A)	(B)	(A)	(B)	(A)	(B)
Nuptiality	1.26	15	1.40	32	1.90	27
Fertility	1.34	9	1.33	31	1.92	40
Fertility preferences	1.35	13	1.26	21	2.76	40
Contraceptive knowledge	2.54	33	3.05	133	3.21	32
Contraceptive use	2.30	29	2.24	100	2.23	29
All	1.66	20	1.75	61	2.32	36

(A) Mean deft for actual sample.
(B) Estimated per cent increase in deft due to multi-stage area sampling.

TABLE 12.4

Sampling efficiency and multiple area sampling stages:
selected subclasses (average over all variables in table 12.3)

Subclass	Thailand rural			Colombia rural			Nepal		
	(A)	(B)	(C)	(A)	(B)	(C)	(A)	(B)	(C)
Age 25–24	1.31	10	30	1.31	24	27	1.68	24	34
Husband's education									
secondary or higher	0.94	0	4	0.98	−4	6	1.11	6	6
Whole sample	1.66	20	100	1.75	61	100	2.32	36	100

(A) Mean deft for actual sample.
(B) Estimated per cent increase in deft due to multi-stage area sampling.
(C) Per cent size of subclass in the survey population.

centres primarily on column **(B)**. The age cross-class still shows serious losses of sampling efficiency, though smaller than in the whole sample. The education subclass, probably because of its very small size, remains efficiently sampled even with the multi-stage designs used, so that in this case there has been no serious loss of efficiency.

The loss in efficiency due to multi-stage sampling must be weighed against any saving in costs. Since we are considering stages above the BAU, by definition the sampling frames already exist and there is no saving to be considered in terms of frame construction. The potential saving is in terms of transport of field teams: if the area units are clustered, teams should have less far to travel in moving from one unit to another. The WFS Manual on Sample Design suggested (p. 55) that this effect was likely to be negligible. We have looked for evidence bearing on this from WFS records of surveys.

We consider first Ghana as an example. The rural sample in the Ghana Fertility Survey consists of 192 clusters. For the argument that follows we regard them as points rather than areas. If 192 points are distributed evenly in a square grid over the whole surface of Ghana (238 537 sq. km.) the distance between neighbouring points will be $\sqrt{(238\,537/192)} = 35$ km.[2] We obtained a plot of the actual sample clusters on a map of Ghana and measured the average distance between each point and its nearest neighbour, omitting urban clusters. It came to 14 km. (The clusters were selected in Ghana by systematic sampling with explicit stratification by region.) The figure of 35 km. is based on hypothetical 'area clusters' uniformly distributed while the observed figure of 14 km. is based on real population clusters randomly selected. The ratio 14/35 represents the effect of random selection together with the natural clustering of the population.

All of these distances are 'as the crow flies'. We now want to look at them 'as the Land Rover travels'. Unfortunately, for Ghana we have a plot of clusters on a map but we do not have odometer readings; in Ivory Coast we have odometer readings but no map of clusters. To make use of the evidence of both countries involves rather contorted reasoning.

In Ivory Coast we have records showing the odometer reading at the time of arriving in and leaving each cluster. We first eliminate all journeys which start or end at Abidjan, the survey headquarters, and journeys between urban clusters. The mean distance travelled is then 83 km. between clusters. This mean is much influenced by a small number of very long distances and it is possible that these do not truly represent between-cluster travel. If we eliminate all figures above 150 km we reach a mean of 65 km.

In the Ivory Coast rural sample there were 109 clusters selected in a single sampling stage. The 'theoretical' distance between neighbours if these points were distributed in a square grid over the country would be $\sqrt{(332\ 463/109)} = 54$ km. This figure is about 50 per cent larger than that for Ghana. If the population is distributed in a pattern similar to that in Ghana (the countries are neighbours and have comparable ecological and ethnic profiles, at least in the rural sector) we might expect to find the same random selection and population clustering effects. Applying the same ratio 14/35 to the Ivory Coast figure of 54 km. we arrive at an estimated straight-line distance between neighbouring rural sample clusters in Ivory Coast of 22 km. Whether the true distance travelled was 65 km. or 83 km. it is clearly very much greater than the straight-line distance. There is no need to speculate here on the reasons for this discrepancy: the Ivory Coast fieldwork was carried out under close supervision by senior staff and notably strong discipline, but there are many good reasons why survey cars do not always take the direct route between clusters, and, of course, there will be many cases in which the most direct route is much longer than the linear distance. Whatever the explanation, these calculations serve to suggest that the straight-line distance between neighbouring clusters is unlikely to be closely correlated with the travel cost in a typical developing country of modest size. As for the time factor, the distances are so small that, once again, they seem unlikely to be a crucial factor in determining the time interval between the end of work in one cluster and the start in the next. Moreover the correlations will be further attenuated by the fact that long distances are travelled on better roads, where costs per kilometre are lower.

Finally we may note that vehicle costs for travel between clusters account for only 9 per cent of total field costs in the Ivory Coast rural sector. Wage costs covering time spent in travelling between clusters are more significant, at 20 per cent, but even together these times do not reach 30 per cent of the fieldwork budget.

These data tend to support the argument of the WFS Manual of Sample Design that the introduction of sampling stages above the BAU would produce negligible savings except perhaps in large countries. Returning to the data on sampling efficiency, if we adopt the first line of table 12.4, column (B), as an indicator, we can expect an efficiency loss within the range of 10–25 per cent through the introduction of multiple area stages. Since sampling error is roughly proportional to the square root of sample size, which itself is roughly proportional to operational costs, it follows that such costs would have to be reduced by 20–35 per cent to compensate for the lost efficiency. It appears most unlikely that the clustering of the BAUs would achieve a saving of this order, unless perhaps in the largest countries.

How far is this conclusion specific to the WFS design and how far can it be generalized to quite different surveys? The findings that the combined effect of random selection and the population distribution leads to a natural clustering, which greatly reduces the distance between neighbouring clusters in a sample of the human population; that road distance actually travelled is only tenuously linked to linear distance in a survey in a developing country of small-to-average size; and the known fact that in developing countries long distance travel is much cheaper per kilometre than short, all argue against expecting any substantial saving on transport costs through the introduction of an additional prior sampling stage in any survey except in larger countries. Even with a field organization using isolated enumerators, each resident in a sample village and visited periodically by a supervisor who lives within range of all of his team of enumerators, it is difficult to see that the conclusion would be different, unless the sampling density were very much lower. Briefly, if, as in the Ghana Fertility Survey, sample clusters are separated by only 14 km., one cannot expect to gain much in transport costs by pushing them still closer.

However, one reservation should be made before generalizing too widely. It may happen that the type of area unit chosen to serve as the BAU (typically the census ED) does not have sufficiently well-defined boundaries to justify its use for this purpose without a prior re-mapping operation. To confine such re-mapping to the BAUs selected in the sample introduces a risk of bias, yet to re-map all the BAUs in the country would be impossibly expensive. In this situation a higher stage of sampling, based on a larger unit whose boundaries are securely known, may be introduced for the sole purpose of reducing the volume of re-mapping work. This situation would depart from the assumptions we have made above and our conclusions would not apply to it. Even so, the costs would be high and such a procedure could hardly be acceptable for anything but a master sample, designed for use in several surveys.

12.4 Segmentation

In section 12.1 we defined the basic area unit (BAU) as the smallest type of area unit for which there already exists a sampling frame. In most WFS samples this has been the census enumeration district or ED. For convenience we shall assume in this section that it is always the ED.

Having selected our sample of EDs we have two options:

1 List all dwellings or households in the selected EDs, with a view to sampling from the list;

2 Create a further stage of area sampling by dividing the EDs into segments and selecting one (or more) in each ED.

varied the size of segments; we could then examine how homogeneity varies with segment size. Such an experiment would have been difficult to organize and was in fact never seriously considered in the WFS. It might have been simpler to require listers to locate each dwelling on a map, in terms of its ID, and to use this map to create pseudo-segments of any desired size within the actual UAU. Since the survey sample is spread over the whole UAU such pseudo-segments could be identified on the data file. The only limitation is that the method allows one to investigate homogeneity for area units smaller than the UAU but not larger; however, by studying several countries, including some with relatively large UAUs, much useful information would certainly be obtained. Such a study was envisaged more than once in the WFS but was never implemented; its requirements in terms of staff resources were simply too high. Another possibility would have been to compare variance within segments with variance within whole EDs, which are on average a good deal larger than segments. However, for this purpose WFS would have needed to select at least two segments per ED and this was never done. Finally the possibility of analysing homogeneity of area units in terms of naturally occurring variations in UAU size was also considered, but was rejected simply because of the likelihood of these variations being themselves linked to factors related to homogeneity, thus concealing the effect of interest. In summary, regrettably we do not have data from the WFS relating the degree of homogeneity within area units to their population size.

A second effect of segmentation on sampling efficiency concerns the loss of control over the size of the area units in the sampling process. When area units are selected with equal probability one factor contributing to sampling error is the variation in population size of the units. (The reason is easily understood in the following terms. Suppose we select one-tenth of all areas. If the areas are all equal in population size then this will yield one-tenth of the population. But if the areas vary in size the fraction of the population selected will in general deviate from one-tenth; this unpredictable variation will be reflected in a higher sampling error.) This source of sampling error can be eliminated by sampling the units with probability proportional to size. The varying probabilities 'take care of' the variations in size. In practice, exact size is not known; we only have measures of size and the more accurate the measure, the greater the reduction in sampling error. Essentially the gain in efficiency depends on the correlation we are able to achieve between our selection probabilities and the size of the units (see section 12.7 below). Alternatively, if we select units with equal probability, efficiency depends on the extent to which we are able to achieve units of constant size. Compared with listing, segmentation is certain to reduce this efficiency: we cannot hope to create segments of exactly equal size, nor can we exactly estimate the size of the segments created (except by counting the households they contain, but in that case we are back to a complete listing of the ED). By contrast, if listing is used instead of segmentation then the sampling fraction is known almost exactly; to return to our earlier example, if we select one dwelling in ten then we will obtain approximately one-tenth of the population.

If we knew how much segment sizes varied around their predicted sizes we could determine the importance of additional sampling error due to uncontrolled segment size. Unfortunately the actual variation in segment size reflects another factor which confuses the picture, namely uncertainty in the ED size. The EDs are themselves selected with probability proportional to measures of size; if any ED is larger than expected, the required number of segments created in it will also be larger than expected. The latter deviation is not due to segmentation; it would arise anyway even if we replaced segmentation by complete listing. Once again, WFS could have eliminated this factor by selecting two or more segments per ED. But as we have said, WFS did not do this because it would have meant a less efficient sample. Once again, the needs of research conflicted with the needs of survey execution and, in the WFS, the latter had to be given priority. Thus we have no data from the WFS bearing on this issue.

Non-sampling error

We have already noted that segmentation requires more skill than listing and so is more subject to error. Furthermore, segmentation offers additional scope for error just because it is an additional operation. (Listing, by contrast, has to be done anyway; the only issue is more listing or less listing.) In general, segmentation becomes more difficult the smaller the segments to be made, because more detailed mapping is required. Moreover mapping only works well when physical features – roads, rivers, fences, etc. – can be used as boundaries to define the areas. This means that it is difficult to make clear maps of very small areas containing only a few houses. The WFS Manual on Sample Design suggests, as a reasonable and practical rule at least for rural areas, that one should aim for areas corresponding to the smallest natural population groupings – villages in most places. This is a sensible policy, it was argued, first because it is above all the attempt to draw boundaries within villages that causes difficulties and, secondly, because the use of a natural social unit eases the task of the field-workers in getting the co-operation of the local people. In most of Africa and Latin America a unit size of 400–1000 people (say 100–200 households) would be large enough to include most villages, but in much of Asia the size would have to be considerably bigger than this.

Conclusion

As we have seen, WFS operations, though constantly using segmentation, did not throw any significant light on the optimal parameters for segmentation. Since there is good reason to suppose that segmentation is profitable, it is likely to be carried out in future surveys; it is therefore obviously desirable to investigate empirically the parameters involved. The necessary design modifications for such investigation within a survey have been described above. Inevitably they have some cost implications and they would marginally reduce the efficiency for the survey vehicle concerned. Yet in the long run such basic methodological work would pay off and should be regarded as an essential feature of future surveys by survey designers.

12.5 Choice of cluster take

Nature of the cluster take option

In a clustered sample with a single area stage, the sample design consists of a sample of area units, or clusters, and within each such unit selected, a sample of households (or persons). The issue to be addressed in this section concerns a simple option, almost always available to the sample designer: whether to select a small number of clusters and many households in each, or a large number of clusters and a few households in each. Before coming to the main issue we mention some points of terminology, as well as some basic simplifying assumptions.

Some writers use the term 'cluster' to refer to the area unit, some to the sample of households selected from that unit. For the former, the number of households selected per area unit is called the 'cluster take'; for the latter, the 'cluster size'. In certain samples the survey covers all of the households in each area unit. In this case ('compact cluster sampling') the distinction between cluster take and cluster size disappears, for either group of writers. We shall align ourselves with the first group. Thus we shall use the term 'cluster' for the whole unit and the 'take' for the selected sample in the cluster. Normally we do not assume compact cluster sampling, although most of our conclusions will also apply to that special case.

We also assume for simplicity a single stage of area sampling without stratification. The effect of multi-stage sampling at the area stage has already been discussed in section 12.3. The effect of area stratification is ignored, but another way of looking at this is that our conclusions refer to the situation within any one area stratum.

Formulation of the problem

The trade-off between the extra cost and the reduced sampling error as the cluster take is made smaller is a traditional problem in sampling theory and nothing very original will be said about it here.[3] We shall briefly sketch the theory, then move on to its practical application.

The trade-off arises because of the contrasting behaviour of costs and sampling error as the cluster take is reduced, and the number of clusters increases, for a given total sample size. Obviously, costs increase because interviewers have to travel more often, thus interrupting their productive work of interviewing, and because costs like mapping and listing increase with the increased number of clusters. On the other hand, sampling error is reduced, because the sample becomes more widespread over the survey population. The latter effect arises essentially because neighbours show a statistical tendency to resemble each other more than people who live far apart. Thus if one interviews people living in one place they tend to give the same answers; more information is obtained if one interviews a more widespread sample. To compute an optimal cluster take one needs to quantify the contrasting effects of cost and sampling error in terms of mathematical models. We will look at these in turn.

The classical model for fieldwork costs in clustered sampling supposes that the total cost C can be broken down into two components, one representing the cost C_2 per interview within a cluster, the other the cost C_1 of the non-interviewing work incurred per cluster independently of the take, such as mapping, listing, travelling between clusters, arranging local accommodation, etc. We write:

$$C = mC_1 + mbC_2 \tag{1}$$

where m is the number of clusters selected and b is the cluster take, i.e. number of interviews per cluster (replaced by $\bar{b}$ if this varies). An overhead term C_0 is sometimes mentioned but is omitted here as it has no effect on the discussion which follows.

In the sampling error model, the key parameter is the intraclass correlation, ρ. Essentially this measures the homogeneity within clusters, that is, the degree to which people in the same cluster resemble one another. If $\rho = 1$ then everyone in any given cluster gives the same response. If $\rho = 0$ then there is no clustering effect, so that people who live in one cluster are no more likely to resemble each other than people in different clusters. More exactly, ρ measures the between-cluster variance as a proportion of the total between- and within-cluster variance. Obviously this parameter varies according to the variable considered. It tends to be relatively high for highly clustered characteristics, such as age or measures of fertility or nuptiality. Sampling error variance V for an unstratified unweighted clustered sample with constant take b is estimated by the function:

$$V = \frac{S^2}{mb} \{ 1 + (\bar{b} - 1)\rho \} \tag{2}$$

where S^2 is the population variance of the variable under consideration.

Taken over the whole sample, sampling error is usually sufficiently small to be negligible compared with other, non-sampling errors. However, sampling error increases as the sample size decreases, and thus becomes important in the smaller subclasses of the population. In section 12.2, we introduced the distinction between cross-classes and segregated classes. This is again crucial when we come to consider how sampling error is affected as we move from the whole sample to subclasses of the sample.

Suppose that subclass s represents a proportion M_s of the population. It is clear that, in the case of a cross-class, formula (2) must be modified by replacing b by $M_s b$. We assume here that the cross-class appears with exactly equal relative frequency in every cluster; in practice there will be random variation, but the effect of this is small compared with the accuracy with which we are concerned. On the other hand, in the case of a segregated subclass, formula (2) must be modified by replacing m by M_sm, with no change in b. This time we assume that the cluster take does not vary between the segregated subclass concerned and the rest of the population.

We shall also assume that ρ remains the same for the subclass as for the whole population. There is some empirical evidence to support this generalization (Verma, Scott and O'Muircheartaigh 1980). We now have all the elements required for the choice of optimal cluster take b.

The mathematical solution

To compute optimal b we eliminate m between (1) and (2) and compute minimal V for varying b; all other quantities are kept constant.

Differentiating V with respect to b and equating the derivative to zero, we easily find that:

$$b^2_{opt} = \frac{C_1}{C_2} \cdot \frac{1-\rho}{\rho} \tag{3}$$

$$\doteq \frac{C_1}{C_2} \cdot \frac{1}{\rho} \tag{3'}$$

representing the cluster size which gives minimum variance for given total cost. (Computing minimal cost for given variance yields the same solution.)

For full cross-classes (M_sb subclass elements selected in every cluster) we obtain:

$$b^2_{opt} = \frac{C_1}{C_2} \cdot \frac{1}{M_s} \cdot \frac{1-\rho}{\rho} \tag{4}$$

For full segregated classes (subclass exists in M_sm clusters only) formula (3) applies with no change.

In practice, the principal use of sampling errors in surveys is in testing differences between subclasses. Empirical evidence based on a fairly wide range of variables in four WFS countries (Verma, Scott and O'Muircheartaigh 1980) indicates that, in the case of cross-classes, ρ for differences is generally much smaller, typically less than one-third of the values for the subclasses concerned. This implies values of b_{opt} at least twice as large as the optimum computed from (4). For segregated subclasses the reduction is much smaller and the increase in b_{opt} compared with (3) is generally no greater than 10 per cent.

Practical implications

In practice, values of ρ, even when cited as 'large', are always far below 1. Table 12.5, extracted from Verma, Scott and O'Muircheartaigh (1980), shows median values of ρ for five groups of variables in 12 WFS surveys. Hardly any exceed 0.1. One consequence of this is that the optimum for b is very broad. For example, if $\rho = 0.04$, the average value in the table, and if $C_1/C_2 = 40$, a cluster take of even double the optimum (that is, 62 instead of 31) would yield a

TABLE 12.5

Median roh by variable group and country[a]

	Mexico	Peru	Jamaica	Indonesia	Sri Lanka	Thailand	Guyana	Nepal	Colombia	Bangladesh	Fiji	Costa Rica	All
Nuptiality	0.03	0.01	0.04	0.02	0.02	0.01	0.02	0.02	0.01	0.01	0.02	0.01	0.02
Fertility	0.06	0.04	0.03	0.02	0.03	0.01	0.05	0.02	0.00	0.01	0.00	0.02	0.025
Preferences	0.03	0.05	0.07	0.05	0.03	0.02	0.03	0.05	0.01	0.02	0.02	0.00	0.03
Knowledge	0.17	0.14	0.09	0.14	0.07	0.08	0.08	0.05	0.05	0.06	0.04	0.01	0.08
Use	0.11	0.09	0.04	0.06	0.07	0.06	0.03	0.03	0.04	0.03	0.02	0.02	0.05
All variables[b]	0.07	0.05	0.05	0.05	0.05	0.04	0.03	0.03	0.02	0.02	0.02	0.01	0.04

[a] If formula (2) is applied to an obtained sample without any restriction regarding stratification or weighting, then solving for ρ yields a 'synthetic' measure called 'roh' by Kish (1975). Values in the table relate to this roh, which thus takes account not only of clustering but also of stratification and weighting. In the present cases roh is a close approximation to ρ. Professor D. Holt, in the discussion of this paper at the WFS 1984 Symposium, suggested that, with wide variations in b between clusters, the mean b would be better replaced by $\Sigma b^2_i / \Sigma b_i$ in formula (2). We agree that this would be an improvement. Regrettably existing time constraints have not allowed us to recompute roh on this basis.
[b] Average of median values. Countries arranged according to last row.

sampling error ($\sqrt{V}$ computed from (2)) only 6 per cent higher for the same total cost or 25 per cent higher for the same total sample size. For a cross-class the optimum is both higher and broader; for example, with a cross-class of size $M_s = 0.2$ and the remaining assumptions as above, the optimum cluster take becomes 69, and if one used double this take the resulting increase in sampling error would be 5.6 per cent for the same total cost or 17 per cent for the same total sample. It follows that, in fixing the cluster take as as to minimize sampling error per unit cost, we need to think only in orders of magnitude; precise values of the parameters are not needed. This is fortunate because on the one hand the cost parameters are difficult to estimate with precision and on the other the sampling error parameters vary quite widely according to the survey variables with which we are concerned – the optimal cluster take for fertility, for example, would be substantially larger than for the more clustered variable contraceptive knowledge.

Evidence on cost parameters is available from the WFS survey in Ivory Coast, where careful records of travel times and distances were kept. (Regrettably there is no other survey for which such information is available and relevant.)[4] These data enable estimates to be made of field costs for the rural sector in a way which distinguishes costs 'between' clusters (including mapping and listing) from those affected only by the size of the sample within clusters (thus, including interviewing but excluding listing). The ratio C_1/C_2 comes to 42. In Ivory Coast the listing operation was combined with both mapping and segmentation and all this has been included in C_1. Thus the figure may be somewhat above the norm.[5]

Thus, for the cost ratio C_1/C_2 we adopt as a plausible range of values: 30, 40, 50. For values of ρ we consider 0.01, 0.02, 0.05, 0.10. Table 12.6 shows values of b_{opt} for these ranges, computed from (3). Note that, since the number of women qualifying for a fertility interview varies in different developing countries between 0.8 and 1.2 per household, it would not be unreasonable to regard b as measuring the number of women as well as the number of households.

TABLE　12.6
Optimal cluster take (households per cluster)

Cost ratio C_1/C_2	Intraclass correlation			
	0.01	0.02	0.05	0.10
30	54	38	24	16
40	63	44	28	19
50	70	49	31	21

We have already mentioned that sampling errors for the whole sample are generally of negligible magnitude compared with non-sampling errors. It is only within relatively small subclasses that the sampling error begins to dominate. Referring to the discussion in section 12.3 above, if we consider subclasses consisting of only one-fifth of the population ($M_s = 0.2$), then for a cross-class the above optimal cluster takes would be multiplied by $M_s^{-1/2}$, i.e. more than doubled, while for cross-class differences they would be roughly doubled again. On the other hand, for segregated classes, as well as differences between segregated classes, the values in the table hold approximately. It is clear that the situation is dominated by the sampling error requirements for segregated classes and in particular for variables which are highly clustered in the population, such as contraceptive knowledge and use. If we can satisfy the requirements for these, the sample will be sufficient (albeit over-generous) for the other cases.

Segregated classes are, above all, geographical classes. In a fertility survey one cannot hope to present useful data for more than about five such domains. It could be argued that urban–rural differentials are usually so marked that they do not often depend for their assessment on having a low sampling error. More important from the sampling error standpoint are the regional comparisons, which will dominate the sample design if they are to be studied. The position can be seen very simply by noting that the requirement to make comparisons between domains implies a sample with many clusters in each domain; for a given total sample, many clusters implies small clusters, therefore such comparisons require relatively small clusters.

It is not possible to give a single recommended cluster size because the figure depends on the objectives and, in particular, two aspects of the objectives:

1 The importance of family planning variables.
2 The importance of inter-regional comparison within the country.

If these objectives are considered crucial then they will dominate the sample design and lead to a cluster size of around 20–25; as far as the other variables are concerned this will waste money. If less priority is given to the above objectives, and more, for example, to obtaining accurate data on fertility and its social and demographic correlates, then the optimum cluster take will be larger, probably 50 at least. Assuming the value $C_1/C_2 = 40$, then for a given total sample size the decision to adopt a cluster take of 20 instead of 50 will imply a 67 per cent increase in field costs (excluding overheads and training).

The urban case

In the urban sector, the costs C_1 associated with the cluster as such (and not with the interviewing within the cluster) are proportionately lower. First, there is no real equivalent to the cost of moving the team to a new cluster. When work is finished in one cluster the team can reassemble the next day in a different cluster of the same town with no additional cost. Secondly, listing is in many cases cheaper because there is often a convenient system of dwelling numbering already in existence and moreover the dwellings are closer together. Thirdly, mapping and segmentation are clearly easier: in many cases good maps already exist. Still favouring a reduction in the ratio C_1/C_2 is the fact that interviewing is more difficult in town: there are more not-at-homes and refusals and people are, generally, less-co-operative. Perhaps the only urban-rural difference operating the other way is the fact that interviewers in town spend less time walking from one interview to another. It is unlikely that this balances the other effects mentioned.

If the ratio C_1/C_2 is lower in towns then the optimum cluster take is smaller for the urban sector. In several WFS samples the sampling probabilities in the urban sector were increased at the area stage and reduced at the household stage (leaving overall probability unchanged), relative to the rural sector, to allow for this effect. Such a modification clearly seems desirable.

Generalization to other surveys

While the above methodology is widely applicable, the parameters themselves will vary between topics and surveys. Scott (1967) has quoted for African surveys values of ρ as high as 0.1 for employment variables and values of C_1/C_2 as high as 200 in demographic surveys. Where enumerators reside for long periods within the sample area unit, as in many agricultural surveys, there are likely to be times when they are effectively unemployed and the value C_2 becomes zero for any new survey topic. Thus before fixing the cluster size an examination of the specific circumstances of the planned fieldwork, with a view to preparation of survey-specific estimates of the parameters, is required. Such a procedure seems to be rarely attempted.

12.6 PPS sampling and constancy of the cluster take

Description of the problem

In section 12.1 we described a sampling strategy frequently used in WFS surveys, namely selection of ultimate area units (UAUs) with probability proportional to size (PPS) followed by listing of households or dwellings[6] and selection among these with a probability inversely proportional to the UAU selection probability. Here the probabilities at the two stages vary in opposite directions and when multiplied together yield a constant, implying a self-weighting sample.

The strategy has a further advantage. Let M_i be the number of households in the i-th UAU. Then the first-stage probabilities, being proportional to the size M_i, are given by:

$$p_{1i} = k_1 M_i \tag{5}$$

where k_1 is constant.

The second-stage probabilities are:

$$p_{2i} = k_2/p_{1i}$$
$$= \frac{k_2}{k_1} \cdot \frac{1}{M_i} \tag{6}$$

These results follow directly from the design as described. When a selection probability of p_{2i} is applied to a list of M_i households, the number of households selected will be $p_{2i}M_i$. Equation (6) shows that this will be constant. Thus the cluster take is constant. This presents a significant practical advantage in the organization of fieldwork.

In practice, this simple model needs modification because in most cases we do not know M_i, the number of households, accurately before selecting the areas. In developing countries in particular the only source of information on the UAU size M_i is likely to be the census. This may be out of date or inaccurate, or there may be a discrepancy between the census UAU and the sample UAU due to mapping uncertainties. So in selecting with PPS we have only estimated sizes, M'_i, say. Thus M_i must be replaced by M'_i in equations (5) and (6), assuming we still select the households in the same way. It is easily seen that the cluster take $p_{2i}M_i$ now becomes proportional to M_i/M'_i instead of being constant, where M_i still means the true size of unit i.

Error or outdatedness of the census is not the only source of uncontrolled variation in cluster takes. In addition, it often happens that census data on the number of households are not available and we have to make do with the population numbers. Use of such substitute data further increases the ultimate variation in the cluster take. Furthermore, in the WFS at least, the main survey is not one of households but of women. In most WFS surveys all eligible women were interviewed in each selected household. But the number of such women varies from one household to another. Thus, even if the number of households selected were constant the number of women selected would not be. Finally, non-response – households or women who are absent or who refuse – provides a further source of variation in the final cluster takes.

In this section we examine the variations in the cluster take in WFS samples and ask how far the PPS self-weighting design (PPS-SW) succeeded in suppressing them, comparing its success in this respect with what could have been achieved by other possible strategies. In this connection we consider two specific alternative strategies which we call, for brevity, fixed probability (FP) and fixed take (FT). In the FP strategy, we select area units (AUs) with equal probability, make a list of households, select from among them with constant probability in all UAUs, and interview every eligible woman in the selected households. In the FT strategy, we select UAUs with PPS and list the dwellings or households, then select always a fixed number of these and interview every eligible woman in each. Of course the FT strategy eliminates variation in cluster take totally at the household level, though leaving a small residual variation at the level of women interviewed due to the varying number of women per household. In compensation the method requires weights to be introduced. The weights are in fact the same as the cluster takes in the PPS-SW design.

We shall measure variation, whether in cluster takes or weights, in terms of the coefficient of variation (CV), i.e. the ratio of the standard deviation to the mean. The important property of this measure is that it is independent of scale, so that $CV(x) = CV(kx)$, where k is any constant.

In the FP strategy, since we are always taking a fixed fraction of the M_i households, the CV of the cluster take is the same as the CV of the UAU size, i.e. $CV(M_i)$. In summary, we have the following:

Strategy	Cluster take (households)	Variation in cluster take at household level	Variation in weights
(1)	(2)	(3)	(4)
PPS–SW	$K_1 \, M_i/M'_i$	$CV(M_i/M'_i)$	0
FP	$K_2 \, M_i$	$CV(M_i)$	0
FT	K_3	0	$CV(M_i/M'_i)$

where the Ks are constants. This section is concerned essentially with columns (3) and (4). If measures of size were perfect then M'_i would be equal to M_i and the first entry in column (3) would be zero. If the measures of size bore no relation to reality, then the first entry in column (3) would be no smaller than the second. The weights which arise in the FT design (column (4)) have the same CV as that of the cluster takes in the PPS-SW design.

Before examining the cluster take in terms of the number of households selected, it is more relevant to look first at the CVs of the actually achieved cluster takes, in terms of women successfully interviewed. Having examined these in relation to the sample designs for a number of countries we shall attempt to trace through the specific sources of cluster take variation in a selected country.

Variation in achieved cluster take

The number of women successfully interviewed per cluster is readily available from the standard data tapes (though at the time of writing several countries still lack full cluster identification). For the present purpose we wish to examine how the variation in this cluster take is affected by PPS selection. We therefore classify countries according to whether the ultimate area units (UAUs) are represented in the sample with equal probability or with probability proportional to size. It is also of interest to know whether the UAUs were units that already existed before the survey or whether they were created specifically for the survey in a segmentation operation. Table 12.7 presents the available data. Since urban and rural cluster takes often differ markedly, we have separated these domains in all cases, as well as any other domains known to us in which the planned cluster take was different. With these precautions it is believed that the sampling parameters (the ks in equations (1) and (2)) are indeed constant throughout the whole of each domain cited.[7]

TABLE   12.7

Coefficient of variation of cluster take (women successfully interviewed
per UAU), by type of sample

UAUs represented with equal probability			UAUs represented with PPS		
Country and domain U = Urban R = Rural	UAUs pre-existing units[a]	UAUs created for the survey[a]	Country and domain		
	(1)	(2)			(3)
Benin U		0.603	Colombia	U	0.550
R		0.625		R	0.642
Egypt U	0.350		Costa Rica[b]	U	0.427
Jamaica U	0.821			R	0.346
R	0.589		Egypt	R	0.223
Korea, Rep. of U		0.735	Fiji	U	0.551
R		0.396		R	0.307
Mauritania U	0.532		Ghana	U	0.607
R	0.457			R	0.542
Senegal U		0.313	Haiti	U	0.633
R		0.310		R	0.546
			Pakistan	U	0.457
				R	0.351
			Panama	U	0.594
				R	0.416
			Portugal	U	0.403
				R	0.587
			Tunisia	U	0.385
				R	0.450

[a]   Two operations are often performed on a pre-existing sampling frame before it is used for selection: combining of exceptionally small units and splitting of large units. If only the former was done we have retained the country in the first column. If splitting (segmentation) was done, we have counted the country in the second column.

[b]   Urban areas outside Central Valley are classified R.

Ideally, the CVs in column 3 should be zero, and in any case they should be less than those on the left. There is no sign of such a tendency (compare columns (1) and (2) with (3)). This suggests that the attempt to use PPS sampling to reduce the variation in cluster take achieved very little: unless one makes the implausible assumption that the decision to use PPS sampling resulted from the prior observation of a high CV among UAUs, it appears that the same objective could have been approached equally closely by combining and splitting units in an existing frame and selecting them with equal probability.

More surprisingly, the CV does not seem to be much higher even when a frame of pre-existing units was used without any attempt at segmentation (compare columns (1) and (3)). However, this conclusion is based on too few cases to be secure.

One advantage of PPS sampling is that it 'controls' for the effect of variation in UAU size – that is, it eliminates the contribution that this variation makes to the sampling error. Does this finding imply that, in the cases cited, PPS selection failed also in this objective? In fact this inference cannot be made without examining the variation in the cluster take within the strata of the sample design, including the implicit strata. It is quite possible that PPS selection did reduce cluster take variation within small strata even though it has not done so over larger domains, and if that is so it should also have reduced the survey sampling error. We hope to examine this in a later study.

Sources of variation in the cluster take

In this section we examine the variations in the variables which together determine cluster size, with a view to estimating the contribution made by these different sources to the final variation. Figure 12.1 shows schematically the chain of variables involved. Fiji is presented as an illustrative example; the analysis will be repeated for other countries in due course.

We start at the top with a certain degree of variation among the UAUs. The

		CV of cluster totals[a]	
		Sample	Universe
1st Stage	Census population	0.349	0.367
	Listed population	0.483	0.447
	Listed households	0.494	0.453
SELECTION			
2nd Stage	Households selected	0.375	
	Households interviewed	0.383	
	Women in interviewed households	0.421	
	Women interviewed	0.417	

[a] The distribution in the sample and the estimated distribution in the universe differ because the sample is selected with unequal probabilities in the first stage. The universe estimates are based on the sample, re-weighted to take account of the selection probabilities.

FIG. 12.1   Steps in the selection of a PPS sample: Fiji

first variable is the one used as the basis for PPS selection. In the ideal case the variables in the top half of the diagram would be perfectly correlated and have identical CVs; the selection with inverse PPS would then cancel the variation perfectly and we would get CV = 0 at the top of the second half, which would then, ideally, be maintained through the last three steps. The column of CVs shows what happens in practice. The selection cancels only part of the variation, and increases are contributed by each step (except the last, in which the extent of selection occurring is negligible). The reduction due to PPS and inverse PPS sampling is quite modest and is in fact more than offset by these various other distortions. In the case of Fiji no segmentation was used; the UAUs were census EDs. If these had been selected with equal probability instead of PPS, the column of CVs in the lower half of the table would have started with 0.453 instead of 0.375. Clearly this implies some loss of control (increase in CV) over the size of the ultimate take. However, in practice the realistic alternative to the PPS design is not equal probability selection of EDs, but segmentation of EDs followed by equal overall probability selection of segments. It is certainly reasonable to expect that this would substantially reduce the figure against 'listed households' in the column headed 'universe' well below the value of 0.453 shown for the existing sample. If it were to fall below 0.375, one could expect a final take more nearly constant than with the existing sample.

Figure 12.2 shows more clearly what happens at each stage. Here we show the correlation coefficients between the variables concerned. Every value less than 1 represents a loss of precision. It is seen immediately that the main contributor to the variance is the gap between the census population and the listed population. The correlations which cover two or more steps, such as the value 0.93 between households selected and women identified, could also be estimated by multiplying together the individual steps, in this example the value 0.98 between households selected and households interviewed and the value 0.94 between households interviewed and women identified. The resulting figure is given in parentheses: it is again 0.93. The fact that this agrees with the first estimate demonstrates that the two processes are independent: that is to say, the variation due to household non-response acts independently of that due to the varying number of women found per interviewed household. The figures in parentheses are seen to be in every case very close to the corresponding unparenthesized figure, showing that all of these effects act essentially independently.

The fixed take option

As we have seen, in the conditions of developing countries in which there is no means of estimating accurately the current number of households in individual UAUs, the fixed take (FT) design is not compatible with self-weighting. The introduction of cluster-specific weights has a number of disadvantages.

First, the weights will increase the sampling error. Assuming that the weights are uncorrelated with the survey variable (which is a reasonable assumption for

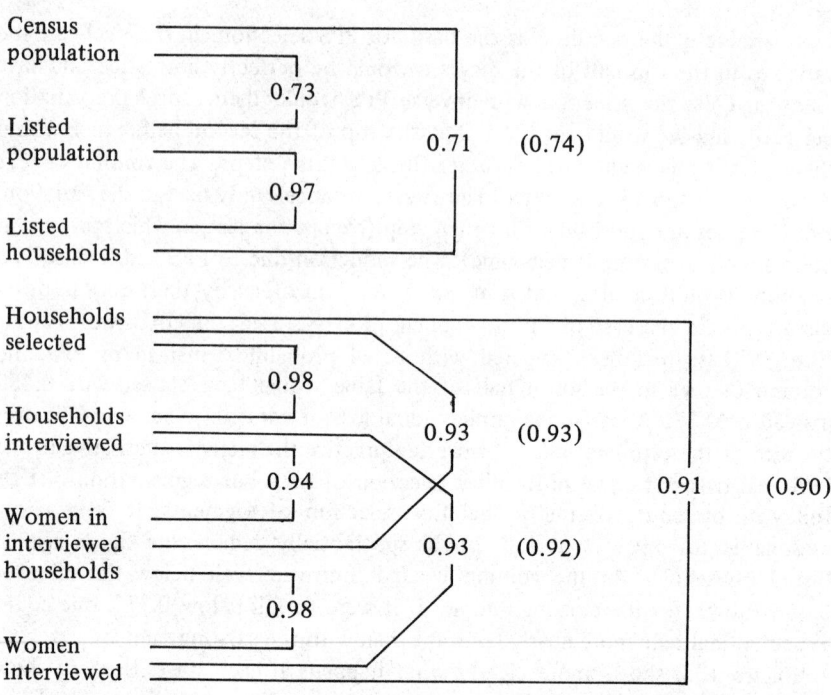

FIG. 12.2 Correlation between steps in selection of PPS sample: Fiji (product-moment correlations between cluster totals)

weights arising in this way) then the sampling variance is increased by a proportionate amount $(CV)^2$. As we have seen, a typical figure for the CV of the weights in an FT sample would be 0.46. This implies an error variance increase of 20 per cent, and this would also be roughly the increase in field costs necessary to maintain the same sampling error.

Secondly, the weights have to be computed and retained in the memory of the organization until needed. Their presence on the data tape has to be communicated to the user who then has to decide whether and how to use them. While these requirements may sound banal the experience of the WFS has been that they amount to a very serious argument in favour of self-weighting samples. Even the problem of discovering whether a given table or analysis was based on weighted or unweighted data has on more than one occasion caused wasted effort and expenditure which would have been better employed on more constructive work.

Thirdly, the weights present problems for the analyst. Some analyses (such as significance tests) may be more appropriately conducted on unweighted data, while others, in particular estimation of descriptive parameters (such as regression coefficients) require weighted data. Yet the two may normally be conducted in the same operation.

While these arguments tell against the FT option there are practical arguments in its favour. The advantage of knowing in advance the exact sample size in every area is very substantial, in terms of both cost and organization. Moreover, with a fixed take of women stipulated in advance the interviewers no longer have an incentive to bias their estimates of age or other variables determining eligibility for interview in such a way as to reduce the number of women who have to be interviewed. Note, on the other hand, that in the FT design we have described it is only the household sample size that is fixed: the individual sample will still vary due to the varying number of women per household. This nullifies the second advantage and, to some extent, the first. A truly fixed take in terms of women could only be achieved if the listing of households also yielded a listing of women; except where an XHS survey is planned this would be an expensive additional requirement. Moreover, although it is true that fixing the number of women per cluster removes the interviewer's motivation to reduce the number of women interviewed, it still leaves a motive for the main age distortion that seems to have been observed. It is still in the interviewer's interest to reduce the special burden of interviewing *older* women by estimating their age above the limit for interview.

Finally the FT design requires a more complex sampling procedure, and one which should be carried out in the field if long delays, with accompanying sample losses, are to be avoided. In most countries the educational standard of field supervisors should, however, be adequate to the task.

It appears to us that the balance of arguments still favours the self-weighting design. However, the advantages of the FT design are not negligible and in our view it would be useful to accumulate more experience on this option, if countries wish to do so, especially in a situation where a listing of persons will in any case be included in the household listing.

One more 'fixed take' option is worth discussing here. Many surveys in developing countries have been carried out without a listing operation and without the use of any prior list. The procedure has generally been to select localities with PPS in the census and have interviewers carry out a fixed number of interviews in each locality, using either a compact cluster centred on some randomly determined point, or selection at intervals during some kind of random walk. Such methods have been widely used in quick and cheap surveys designed to estimate prevalence rates for diseases, and in some cases family planning use. Comparing this with the FT option we have described, two problems are seen. First the method of selection, however ingeniously devised, can never be sure of giving an equal chance of selection to everyone in the locality as long as there is no sampling frame. (How, for example, can one be sure of giving equal chances to those living in hamlets away from the main village?) Second, the method provides no means for obtaining the weights which are required for an FT sample. We have seen that such a sample, if properly weighted, is likely to be about 20 per cent less efficient (more costly) than a self-weighting sample. In other words, one could just as well choose a self-weighting design with a 20 per cent smaller sample and use the money saved to carry out a proper listing operation (which typically costs 15-20 per cent of total field costs). Compared with this option, therefore, the popular no-listing design is no cheaper and contains unknown biases in the final-stage selection.

In summary, if a cheaper survey is required it is more efficient to reduce the sample size than to cut out the listing operation.

12.7 From households to individuals

Introduction

A key feature of the structure and design of the WFS surveys was the organizational relationship between three main operations: the listing of households/ dwellings, the listing of persons, and the individual interview. This aspect of the survey structure was discussed at length in the WFS Manual on Sample Design, which was written before any WFS experience had accumulated. The matter is reconsidered here as the structure of the survey involves important design decisions. In this chapter we have avoided discussion of the implementation of sample designs as this can be found in chapter 13. However, in discussing survey structure issues of design and implementation are inextricably woven; therefore the present section includes details of how countries implemented this aspect of survey design. The discussion is inevitably complex because of the multiple relationships involved. We begin by defining the meaning and purpose of the operations.

Definitions

Listing of households/dwellings.[8] The primary purpose of this operation was to provide a sampling frame from which a sample of households was selected for interview of their individual women. It is important to distinguish the case of a pure listing operation from a combined listing and data collection operation. The former proceeds rapidly: no interview is necessary and the fieldworker can list between 20 and 50 households in a day, depending on whether the habitat is dispersed or concentrated. If substantive data collection is combined with the listing, an interview will be involved and one cannot normally expect to achieve much more than 10 per day.

Listing of persons. This is a listing of household members with the aim of identifying women eligible for the individual interview. The listing of persons is done with the use of the shorter household schedule or the extended household schedule.

Shorter household schedule (SHS). This provides a list of all household members by age, sex, relationship to household head and, in some cases, marital status. Its purposes are as a document for the listing of persons and to provide base data for computation of demographic rates.

Extended household schedule (XHS). This includes the same information as the

SHS but asks in addition, for each woman of childbearing age, the number, survival and sex of children ever born and the date, survival and sex of the last live birth. Answers to these questions provide estimates of recent fertility and child mortality. For these measures, a large sample is required covering at least three times as many households as those containing the women's sample. The need for such large-sample fertility data arose when a country had neither a good civil registration system nor a recent demographic survey or census which could provide the same type of data.[9]

Some countries had an enlarged household sample and used an XHS, not for substantive reasons, but to obtain an appropriate number of women at the final stage of selection. In these cases (Mexico, Venezuela, Colombia and Dominican Republic) the household sample was only approximately twice as large as the individual sample (see chapter 11) and the household schedule was not always fully extended to collect information on fertility.

We first examine countries which used an extended household schedule (XHS) as defined above. Figure 12.3 provides a categorization of all the forms of survey structure used by WFS. Categories A, B, C, and the special case of Yemen AR (E) involve the use of an XHS.

Method	First visit to area			Second visit to area
A	XHS→SF→IQ			
B	XHS ⟶	SO	⟶	SHS→IQ
C	LISTHH ⟶	SO	⟶	XHS→SF→IQ
D	LISTHH ⟶	SO	⟶	SHS→IQ
E OTHERS:				
Nepal	SHS→IQ			
Nigeria	LISTHH→SF→SHS→IQ			
	↗ XHS⟶IQ			
Yemen AR	SO			
	↘ XHS			

XHS	=	extended household schedule.
SHS	=	shorter household schedule.
IQ	=	individual questionnaire.
SF	=	sampling in the field.
SO	=	sampling in the office (headquarters).
LISTHH	=	listing of households/dwellings.

FIG. 12.3   Categorization of the survey structures used by WFS

A country which requires XHS data on a large sample may seek to achieve this economically by using the XHS for the listing of households. If this is done then the same operation may serve as a listing of persons provided that the sampling can be done quickly and that the individual survey is executed after a short interval, before the list of persons has gone out of date. This is method A in figure 12.3. The same team may do the XHS and individual questionnaires (IQ) or two separate teams may go approximately simultaneously to each cluster, one for the XHS and the other for the IQ. Table 12.8 lists the countries which used this method A and indicates whether the same or different interviewers were used for the two operations. Method B was used in countries where the two surveys (XHS and IQ) were separated by more than a few weeks. In these cases the XHS could provide a frame of households but not of persons for the IQ. Household members had to be re-listed immediately before the individual interview by use of the SHS. The re-listing in these cases was confined to households selected for the IQ. Whenever this method was used different interviewers completed the XHS and the IQ.

Some countries preferred to avoid the need for updating by keeping the listing of households/dwellings quite separate from the listing of persons. Accordingly, in method C a listing of households/dwellings (in practice usually dwellings) was completed during the first visit to the area. In the second visit the XHS was employed for the listing of persons and was followed by the individual interview. Countries adopting this method inserted a further stage of sampling between the listing of households/dwellings and the XHS. This sampling in the office was necessary because the number of households contained in the selected ultimate area units was larger than the number needed for the XHS.

Countries employing method C organized the second field visit in slightly different ways. In the Dominican Republic the XHS operation was completed in the cluster before undertaking the final sample selection and starting the individual interviews. In Mexico, Syria and Venezuela the individual interview immediately followed the XHS interview in each household. As women were the sampling units in Mexico and Venezuela, this meant that it was necessary for interviewers to select the sample as they went along. In these cases specially designed sheets were used to avoid systematic bias in the selection procedure. In Sudan, two teams, one male, one female, were sent to each area unit. The female team visited the households selected for the individual interview and used the XHS followed immediately by the individual interview. The male team visited the remaining households and used the XHS. If the team of women finished first, they helped out the team of men with the XHS. Thus both teams stayed together in each area unit.

We now turn to method D which was used by most of the WFS countries. This is the survey structure normally used in the absence of an XHS. All households or dwellings within the selected UAUs were listed in the first visit to the area unit. In the second visit interviewers conducted a short household interview to list persons and identify women eligible for the individual interview. The two interviews covered the same sample base and were conducted in a given sample household by the same interviewer, usually during a single visit to the household.

The last category, E, covers three special cases: Nepal, Nigeria and Yemen AR. These have in common the feature that a single visit was made to each area but each country used a unique survey structure. Nepal used compact cluster

TABLE 12.8

Survey structure used by WFS countries (see figure 12.3)

Method A		Method B	Method C		Method D	Method E
Interviewers: Same	Different	Different interviewers	Interviewers: Same	Different	Same interviewers	Same interviewers
Cameroon	Benin	Indonesia[a]	Dominican Rep.[b]	Sudan (North)[c]	Bangladesh	Nepal[e]
Colombia	Senegal	Jordan	Mexico[a]		Costa Rica	Nigeria[f]
Korea, Rep. of	Mauritania	Kenya[a]	Syria		Ecuador	Yemen AR[g]
		Lesotho	Venezuela[a]		Egypt	
		Morocco			Fijid	
		Thailand[a]			Ghana	
					Guyana	
					Haiti	
					Ivory Coast	
					Jamaica	
					Malaysia[a]	
					Pakistan	
					Panama	
					Paraguay	

Method E (continued): Peru[a], Philippines, Portugal, Sri Lanka, Trinidad & Tobago[a], Tunisia, Turkey[a]

a Listing of households from an earlier survey.
b The XHS was completed in the cluster before selection of women and the start of the individual interviews.
c Female team visited selected households and did XHS and IQ. Male team visited remaining households and did XHS.
d The extended household schedule (XHS) was used instead of the SHS, but only in the sample of households which had been selected for the survey of individual women.
e No household listing. Compact cluster sampling with SHS used on all households.
f Listing of households by supervisor of interviewing teams.
g SHS used on a separate sample from XHS.

Notes: (i) Women, not households, were selected at the final stage in: Colombia, Dominican Republic, Mauritania, Mexico, Senegal, and Venezuela.
(ii) 'Same' or 'different' interviewers refers to personnel used for the XHS and IQ in methods A to C and Yemen AR; SHS and IQ in method D, Nepal and Nigeria.

sampling (no listing or sampling of households); interviewers used the SHS for listing of persons and went on immediately to the individual interview. In Nigeria the listing and selection of households was performed by the supervisor of the interviewing team on arrival in the area unit. In Yemen AR each area unit was divided into four segments; in three of these the XHS was used for all households by a team of male interviewers, while in the fourth a team of female interviewers was sent with instructions to use the XHS in all households followed immediately in each household by interview of eligible women.

Evaluation

Discussions of the advantages and disadvantages of some of these methods can be found in Scott and Singh (1981) and Verma (1981). Here, we summarize previous discussions and assess each method in turn.

It is clearly more economical to combine the two operations into a single visit to the sample area (methods A and E) and the problem of communication between the lister and the interviewer (how does the lister tell the interviewer where a given household is to be found?) is resolved. However, if the same interviewers are used there is some loss of control, with a more than usually direct incentive to the interviewer to miss out households and eligible women. In this method, also, the female interviewers do all the work; this means that they are retained in the field for a relatively long period. Many countries noted high drop-out rates for female interviewers and for this reason any system which prolongs the fieldwork period for the female personnel must be viewed with caution. Method A with different interviewers for the XHS and IQ (Benin and Senegal) provides the best possible control against cheating but introduces a serious logistical problem: the two teams have to work at the same pace if one of them is not to experience idle time. In Senegal such detailed co-ordination of the teams' speed of work was found difficult to achieve efficiently. Benin attempted to tackle this problem by allowing more flexibility in the timing of the two teams' movements and providing for an update of the list of individual women by the IQ interviewer. Even more serious, compared with other methods, twice as many cars are needed (or alternatively, if the number of cars is kept fixed the duration of the survey fieldwork has to be doubled).

It is organizationally simpler to keep the two operations separate and have the IQ follow the XHS after several weeks (method B). The two operations can then share the same vehicles and other facilities, and sample selection can be done in the office during the intervening period. In fact, different sets of interviewers can be used for the two: many organizations are in a better position to use their regular staff for the XHS even when (female) interviewers have to be specially recruited for the IQ. Method B also offers the small advantage of a data quality evaluation through a consistency check of the XHS against the individual survey. However, the obvious disadvantage of B is the need to re-list household members for the selection of eligible women.

Combining the two operations into a single visit to the household (method C with the exception of the Dominican Republic) can be economical but destroys the independence of the two data sets. However, this method avoids the need for an updating operation. If households form the sampling units for the IQ (as in Sudan and Syria), sample selection can be done in the office or in the field before the interview. This is also possible if areas form the sampling units, as in Yemen AR. If women are the sampling units (Dominican Republic, Mexico, Venezuela), sampling in the field is necessary. Sampling in these cases can be done most economically by interviewers 'sampling as they go', i.e. doing the XHS, making a selection of women and then doing the IQ all in one visit to the household. This was the method used in Mexico and Venezuela, which adopted careful precautions against motivated selection. A more reliable, though more expensive, method is for the interviewers to complete the XHS, return to the field office where the supervisor selects the sample, and then return to the households to do the IQ. This was the method employed in the Dominican Republic.

Where the XHS was not required, method D was adopted almost universally; the exceptions were Nepal and Nigeria. The main objection to the Nepal solution is sampling inefficiency. In Nigeria the main problem was undercoverage of households due to unsupervised and hurried listing.

It is interesting to see how far these various problems and their solutions were foreseen by the WFS Manual on Sample Design. Chapter 7 of the publication appears to have correctly anticipated most of the considerations which affected the designs ultimately adopted and which are described above. Nevertheless, in the light of today's greater experience the discussion now appears unrealistic in one important respect: it overestimates the potentiality of the household schedule as an instrument for the listing of households. This mis-emphasis arises from two sources. On the one hand the manual assumes, as did the early WFS planners, that the XHS survey would prove the norm. (Witness the fact that we have called the XHS the WFS Core Household Schedule.) In reality only 18 of the 42 surveys used this type of household survey.[10] On the other, it assumes that there will be countries in which the concept of a 'household' will be so ill-defined that its use as a sampling unit will be feasible only if the actual membership of each household is reported as a means of identification. The latter implies that the listing of households must involve a listing of persons. If there is to be an XHS this is easily arranged: the XHS can serve both purposes simultaneously. This is method A, which was adopted in fact by only six countries. If there is to be no XHS, the WFS Manual on Sample Design suggested the possible use of the SHS as an instrument for listing of households. This expensive design was not adopted by any WFS country. Thus, when it came to the point, the designers of the country surveys were less impressed by the problem of an uncertain household definition than by the arguments (mainly logistic) cited earlier against method A or, in the absence of an XHS requirement, by the cost argument.

We believe now that the rejection of the SHS as an instrument for the listing of households was probably correct. However there is a worrying lack of evidence about the extent of error due to ambiguous household definition. In West Africa in particular it is at least possible that there may have been serious coverage error from this source in those countries (Ghana, Ivory Coast, Nigeria) in which the XHS was not used. Such countries would be well advised to investigate this problem next time they plan a survey involving the listing and sampling of dwellings or households.

Residence criteria for eligibility

Another feature of the link between the household and individual surveys was the choice of residence criteria for inclusion in the sample. The choice is between a *de jure* and *de facto* coverage definition. The *de jure* population consists of the household members, whether present or absent; *de facto* coverage includes all those present, whether members or not, but excludes those absent. This choice has to be made for the household survey and the individual survey. Details of the choices that countries made concerning residence criteria in the household and individual surveys are presented in table 11.2 of the present volume. Here we discuss factors affecting that choice.

Since the individual questionnaire requires an interview with the woman herself, the *de facto* definition was generally recommended for this. However, presence at the time of the interviewer's visit could not be accepted as a criterion: this would have automatically excluded callbacks, and women who go out to work would in many cases have been omitted, with an obvious bias. It was suggested that a respondent be classified as present if she spent 'last night' in the household. It was realized that even this would result in some bias (against short-term visitors) and WFS recommended that the household schedule should cover both the *de facto* and *de jure* populations, i.e. household members, whether present or absent, plus visitors who spent 'last night' in the household. It was considered that this procedure, by removing the decision on eligibility from the interviewer, provided less motivation for biased reporting of residential status. However, the coverage of both *de facto* and *de jure* populations on the household schedule causes certain problems at the analysis stage. A household file containing both populations is, in total, analytically meaningless. The analyst should select one or the other population. Unfortunately, this is not always done. An option which solves this problem is to include only one of the populations in the final processed data tape. The loss of information would appear to be trivial.

A special problem arises when there is a long time interval between the household interview and the individual interview. We saw in figure 12.3 that in some countries these two questionnaires were completed at two different visits while in others they constituted a single interview. If they are separated, the question arises whether *de facto* for the second (individual) interview relates to the same 'last night' as the first (household) interview, or whether it relates only to the night before the second interview. The longer the interval between the listing of persons and the time when it is used for the individual interview, the more favourable is the *de jure* coverage for households compared with *de facto*. In practice, if the interval between listing of households and the individual interview could not be kept short, an updating exercise was performed immediately before the individual survey (method B in figure 12.3). In this case the household schedule completed in the first visit should be the recommended *de facto* and *de jure*. As there is an updating operation the individual interview can cover the *de facto* population, with the reference date for the *de facto* definition in this case being the night before the first successful call for this updating visit.

12.8 Summary and conclusions

1 The WFS recommended sample design strategy, based on census enumeration districts with segmentation of larger units, has proved workable in practice and is still recommended.

2 Stratification based on geographical criteria is likely to yield substantial benefits. It would be desirable in any future fertility survey to examine between-cluster variation found in the national WFS surveys with a view to identifying appropriate variables for further stratification.

3 Except in the larger countries, the use of more than one effective stage of area sampling would be likely to increase the sampling error more than could be compensated by any reduction in costs.

4 Segmentation within census enumeration districts is almost certainly desirable but resources have not been available to estimate optimal segment size. There is an urgent need for such information and we have indicated some appropriate studies which could be carried out at a modest cost.

5 The optimal cluster take depends on the survey parameters in a calculable way but depends also on the variable studied. When a survey is planned the parameters should be estimated and a decision taken on priorities among the survey variables.

6 In most countries, the self-weighting design using first-stage sample selection with probability proportional to size achieves little success in reducing variations in interviewer workloads. The combination of small areas and segmentation of large ones, with fixed probability selection at each stage, is likely to be just as effective in this respect.

7 On balance, the self-weighting design is preferable to the fixed take design. However, there are some serious arguments for the latter, particularly where a listing of persons is planned in any case as part of the household listing; there is a case for gaining more experience with this option. On the other hand, the fixed take without listing is not a viable option; it would be more efficient to achieve the equivalent saving by retaining listing but cutting sample size.

8 At the last stage (households and women), assuming that interview with an extended household sample is not planned the optimal procedure appears to be:

(a) listing of dwellings or households;

(b) sample selection;

(c) return to the selected households for listing of persons, followed immediately by

(d) interview of any eligible women.

However this arrangement carries with it the risk of motivated age distortion by the interviewer near the cut-off boundary.

9   If interview with an extended household sample is planned the options are more complex and the choice depends on assessment of such factors as the duration for which interviewers can be retained, the preferred location for the sampling operation for dwellings/households, the elapsed interval to be allowed between the listing of dwellings/households and the individual interview, and the need for independence between the household and individual interviews.

10 The WFS recommendation to collect data for both *de jure* and *de facto* populations in the household survey and *de facto* alone in the individual survey seems optimal. However, careful attention is then needed by analysts to avoid using the complete household file, which without selection of one or other population is meaningless. It seems preferable to include only one of the populations in the final processed data tape.

Notes

1   Some of the variables were omitted for some of the surveys because of small numbers of cases in the categories.

2   The 'best' packing (hexagonal) corresponds to a slightly higher figure, by the factor $\sqrt{(2/\sqrt{3})}$, which works out at 38 km.

3   We are grateful to Alan Sunter for suggesting the (very straightforward) extension to the case of sampling error for subclasses. The rest of the discussion follows that in Scott (1978).

4   Nigeria also collected information of the same kind but the special circumstances of the fieldwork in Nigeria preclude generalization to other countries.

5   Samples for countries collecting substantive data from a larger sample during the listing operation (the XHS countries of section 12.7 below) cannot be evaluated in the same way. Optimization for them will depend on assumptions about relative costs of sampling error to the data user for the household and individual surveys.

6   For simplicity we drop the qualifying 'or dwelling' after 'household' throughout this section. It should always be understood.

7   There may remain, however, variations due to rounding. Where explicit strata are used with only two or three clusters selected in each, such variations could be substantial in their effect on the resulting cluster take. This type of design was not common in WFS surveys, where most small strata were implicit.

8   We deliberately avoid the term 'household listing' because of its ambiguous interpretation – either as listing of households or as listing of household members.

9   The extended household schedule was in almost every case used with an extended household sample, and vice versa. The single exception was Fiji, which used the extended schedule on a limited sample; we classify Fiji in table 12.8 with the countries using the SHS.

10 Reasons for this are reviewed in chapter 4.

13

Sample Implementation

Trudy Harpham
Chris Scott

13.1 Introduction

The technical aspects of sample design are discussed in the previous chapter. The objective of this chapter is to provide a critical account of the implementation of sample designs by WFS. It documents the basic characteristics of the 42 WFS samples, examines the nature and the problems of the sampling frames used, discusses the implementation of the segmentation and listing procedures, presents the achieved response rates and discusses some common errors in implementing sample designs. Finally, some specific recommendations are made on the documentation of sample designs.

13.2 Characteristics of the WFS samples

A discussion of the WFS sample sizes can be found in chapter 11. In the present chapter we first turn our attention to the allocation of the sample between different sampling domains. The straightforward solution would have been to apply the same sampling rates to all domains. The WFS 'Manual on Sample Design' (WFS 1975c) recommended the adoption of this solution as normal, or as a starting point, to be set aside only after very careful justification. Departure from proportionate allocation may be justified (1) because domains differ in population variances and survey costs, so that it is optimal to oversample the more variable domains and undersample the more expensive ones, or (2) because for the smaller domains more precise estimates are required than would be obtained with proportionate allocation.

Table 13.1 shows that there has been a preference for proportionate allocation in WFS surveys; in fact, 27 out of the 42 samples are fully self-weighting, at least for the women's survey. Of the remaining 15 countries, and considering only the women's survey, two had such small deviations that they were self-weighting for practical purposes (Nepal and Trinidad and Tobago), nine countries were oversampled in the urban sector or other small domains, three had more elaborate sets of weights (Philippines, Sri Lanka and Indonesia), and one (Nigeria) was non-self-weighting. The latter occurred because there was a large uncertainty regarding total population size; in such circumstances a fixed take per ultimate area unit seemed advisable to ensure achievement of the overall target sample size. Table 13.1 also notes that in Cameroon, Kenya, Nigeria, Jordan and Yemen

TABLE 13.1
Sample weighting

Country	Design		Domain weights
	Household sample	Individual sample	
Africa			
Benin	SW	SW	.
Cameroon	SW-D[a]	SW-D[a]	East : U : R = 4 : 2 : 1
Ghana	SW	SW	.
Ivory Coast	Non-SW	SW	
Kenya	Non-SW[a]	SW-D[a]	U : R = 2 : 1
Lesotho	Non-SW	SW	
Nigeria	Non-SW[a]	Non-SW[a]	.
Senegal	SW	SW	.
Egypt	SW	SW	.
Mauritania	SW-D	SW-D	River and urban : other = 2 : 1
Morocco	SW	SW	.
Sudan (North)	SW-D	SW-D	U : R = 2 : 1
Tunisia	SW	SW	.
Asia and Pacific			
Jordan	SW-D[a]	SW-D[a]	Range mainly 1–3
Syria	SW	SW	.
Turkey	SW	SW	.
Yemen AR	SW-D[a]	SW-D[a]	U : R = 2 : 1
Bangladesh	SW-D	SW-D	U : R = 7 : 2
Iran	SW	SW	.
Nepal	Approx. SW	Approx. SW	.
Pakistan	SW-D	SW-D	U : R = 2 : 1
Sri Lanka	SW-D	SW-D	Range mainly 1–2
Fiji	SW	SW	.
Indonesia	Approx. SW-D	Approx. SW-D	Range mainly 1–6
Korea, Rep. of	SW	SW	.
Malaysia	SW	SW	.
Philippines	SW-D	SW-D	5 : 4 : 3 : 2
Thailand	SW	SW	.
Americas			
Colombia	Non-SW	SW	.
Ecuador	SW	SW	.
Paraguay	SW	SW	.
Peru	SW-D	SW-D	Oriente : rest = 4 : 1
Venezuela	SW	SW	.

Table 13.1 continued

Country	Design		Domain weights
	Household sample	Individual sample	
Americas (cont.)			
Costa Rica	SW	SW	·
Dominican Rep.	SW	SW	·
Mexico	SW	SW	·
Panama	SW	SW	·
Guyana	SW	SW	·
Haiti	SW-D	SW-D	Small towns : rest = 2 : 1
Jamaica	SW	SW	·
Trinidad & Tobago	Approx. SW	Approx. SW	·
Europe			
Portugal	SW	SW	·

[a] External weights were applied to adjust errors of sample implementation.
Notes: SW = fully self-weighting; SW-D = self-weighting within domains; Non-SW = non-self-weighting.

AR external weights were introduced in an attempt to compensate for errors in sample selection and implementation.

It is notable that the majority of WFS countries avoided the difficulties caused by the use of weighting. Elimination of weights saves trouble in many ways: weights have to be computed, retained for a period, then used in programming and tabulation; their presence must be communicated to the data tape user; and finally, both weighted and unweighted sample frequencies need to be shown in the published tables if they differ appreciably. It can be convincingly argued that significance tests should be carried out on an unweighted basis. Yet when the parameters of the relationships involved are estimated — generally in the course of the same analysis — they need to be correctly weighted if they are to be meaningful.

Other basic characteristics of the 42 WFS samples are presented in table 13.2. Perhaps the first impression given by the table is the wide range of variation in WFS samples. A notable feature is the frequency of designs using a single effective area stage (column 2).[1] In 24 countries the area sample was single stage throughout and in 11 others it was single stage in the urban sector.

The wide variation in household sample sizes (column 3) is largely explained by the presence or absence of a household sample deliberately expanded in order to collect fertility and mortality data with enhanced sampling precision. Wherever columns (3) and (4) differ widely, such an operation was present. Table 13.2 forms the basis of the following discussion of sampling frames, segmentation and listing, and response rates.

TABLE 13.2

Characteristics of the WFS samples

Country	Domain (1)	No. of effective area stages[a] (2)	Size of selected sample — Household survey (3)	Size of selected sample — Individual survey[b] (4)	No. of area units selected[c] — Effective PSUs (5)	No. of area units selected[c] — UAUs (6)	Mean population of selected units[d] — Effective PSUs (7)	Mean population of selected units[d] — UAUs (8)	No. of women selected per selected unit — PSUs[e] (9)	No. of women selected per selected unit — UAUs[f] (10)	Final-stage sampling interval[g] (11)
Africa											
Benin		2	20 816	4 163	248	322	1 200	390	16.8	12.9	5
Cameroon	U	1	35 324	9 390	67	*	450	*	73.9	35.2	4
	R	2			60	200	78 000	770			
Ghana		1	6 791	7 183	300	*	78 000	*	23.9	*	3.5
Ivory Coast	Major towns	1	4 387	7 800	118	*	420	*	12.5	*	11
	Other towns	2			63	183	240	96	26.0	8.9	3[h]
	Rural	1			109	*	8 000	*	45.6	*	2
Kenya	U	1	10 763	10 232	80	*	343	*	73.1	51.7	2.5
	R	2			60	118	400	960			
Lesotho		1	20 333	4 106	100	*	40 000	*	41.1		4
Nigeria		1	9 361	10 996	248	*	1 000	*	44.3		2
Senegal		1	193 032[i]	4 495	358	*	500	*	12.6		9
Egypt	U	2	10 596	9 827	92	184	510	⋯	49.1	33.7	8
	R	1			108	*	44 000	*			
Mauritania		1	15 041	3 852	101	*	3 600	*	38.1	*	4
Morocco		1	19 352	6 639	280	*	850	*	23.7	*	3
Sudan (North)		1	13 921	3 708	144	*	400	*	25.8	*	5
Tunisia		1	5 988	5 077	255	*	700	*	19.9	*	2.5

Table 13.2 (continued)

Region / Country	Stratum	Design									
Asia and Pacific											
Jordan	Towns and large villages	2 }	15 067	3 898	11 }	50 }	...	400 }	20.1	16.7	4
	Other	1 }			183 }			1 100 }			
Syria	U	2 }	15 287	4 841	84 }	157	12 600	*	28.1	19.8	10
	R	1 }			88 }		1 100				
Turkey		1	6 393	5 929	215	*	550	*	27.6	*	3
Yemen AR		1	14 364	2 694	88	*	220	*	56.8	*	1
Bangladesh		1	6 145	6 980	240	*	1 900	*	29.1	*	13
Iran		1	6 113	5 500	250	*	350	*	22.0	*	3
Nepal	U	1 }	5 976	6 398	7 }	95	200 000	290	160.0	62.7	1
	R	2 }			33 }						
Pakistan		1	5 246	5 401	326	*	2 200	*	16.6	*	25
Sri Lanka		1	8 834	7 667	750	*	260	*	10.2	*	4
Fiji		1	5 388	5 555	100	*	1 400	*	55.5	*	4
Indonesia	Rural Yogyakarta	2 }	10 504	9 687	10 }	30 }	750	*	25.8	24.5	62
	Rest	1 }	21 248	5 810	366 }		500	*	18.2	*	4.5
Korea, Rep. of		1	8 103	6 654	319	*	10 000	*	76.5	*	21
Malaysia		1	14 747	11 122	87	*	960	*	15.0	*	8
Philippines		1			742 }	*	800	*			
Thailand	U	1 }	4 518	4 204	33 }	234	500 000	690 }	60.7	15.7	75
	R	3			37 }						
Americas											
Colombia	U	1^m }	9 999	5 931	370 }	*	60	*	14.6	5.9	2.5
	R	2 }			35 }	630	970	50 }	3.9	*	2
Ecuador	U	1^n	6 979	8 545	238	*	300	*	3.9	*	2
Paraguay	U	1^m }	4 627	5 552	100 }	240 }	...	290	39.7	16.3	5
	Rest	2 }			40 }						
Peru	U	1^m }	8 949	7 336	410	1 424	7 000	240	16.6	*	8
	R	2 }									
Venezuela		1	8 200	4 500	480	*	225	*	9.4	*	5.5

Table 13.2 continued overleaf

Table 13.2 continued

Country	Domain	No. of effective area stages[a]	Size of selected sample		No. of area units selected[c]		Mean population of selected units[d]		No. of women selected per selected unit		Final-stage sampling interval[g]
			Household survey	Individual survey[b]	Effective PSUs	UAUs	Effective PSUs	UAUs	PSUs[e]	UAUs[f]	
(1)		(2)	(3)	(4)	(5)	(6)	(7)	(8)	(9)	(10)	(11)
Americas (cont.)											
Costa Rica	U	1[p]	} 4 724	4 530	{ 262	*	490	*	15.7	13.3	6
	R	2			26	78	13 500	} 410			
Dominican Rep.	U	2[m]	} 12 069	3 556	26	553 }	19 000 {	135 }	136.8	5.3	4
	R	3[m]				112		870			
Mexico	U	2[m]	} 15 551	9 188	182	2 280	...	230	50.5	4.0	14
	R	3									
Panama	U	1[q]	} 5 214	4 150	{ 354	* }	...	135	10.2	9.0	3
	R	2			54	108					
Guyana		1	4 668	5 114	200	*	700	*	25.6	*	6
Haiti		1	3 720	4 399	111	*	810	*	39.6	*	5
Jamaica		1	5 579	4 001	428	*	520	*	9.3	*	10
Trinidad & Tobago		1	4 973	4 868	648	*	900	*	7.5	*	25
Europe											
Portugal	U	2	} 15 115	7 720	318	*	255	*	24.3	*	2
	R	1									

a In certain samples a sampling stage was introduced for the sole purpose of easing the task of creating or identifying the area units of the subsequent stage. Where such a notional stage has no clustering effect on the next sampling stage, it has been disregarded altogether in this table.

b Estimated number of individual respondents who would have been eligible for selection if all selected *households* had been successfully interviewed, estimated by the formula:

$$\frac{\text{No. of identified women} \times \text{No. of selected households}}{\text{No. of successfully interviewed households}}.$$

Procedure probably overestimates the selected sample size because in reality a proportion of the 'households' categorized as not successfully interviewed were probably non-existent.

c PSU = primary sampling unit (first area sampling stage);
  UAU = ultimate area unit (last area sampling stage).
d Number of persons per unit averaged over the sample.
e Column (9) equals (4)/(5). The achieved sample size per PSU differs from this quantity due to non-response.
f Column (10) equals (4)/(6).
g Ratio of final-stage units (households or women) *listed* to number *selected* in the sample UAUs.
h Households in the listing with more than 20 members were included with certainty (no sampling).
i Number of persons. The 'household' was not used as a unit in the Senegal survey.
j Number of households from which the women were selected.
k Area unit size 890 for household interview.
m Actual distinction was between self-representing and non-self-representing areas. These roughly correspond to urban and rural.
n Metropolitan Asunción.
p One-stage in all urban areas plus rural Central Valley. Two-stage in rural areas outside Central Valley.
q One-stage in all urban plus rural parts of metropolitan Panama. Two-stage in all other areas.

Notes: (1) U = urban; R = rural.
       (2) *: In cases of single-stage area sampling, PSUs were the UAUs and therefore the numbers were the same.
       (3) . . . = data not available.

13.3   Sampling frames

The choice of a sample design depends above all on the availability of suitable sampling frames, that is, lists of units from which a sample can be selected. The units with which WFS was concerned were areas, dwellings or households, and individuals. At each of these levels a sampling frame, or list, either did or did not already exist. If it did not exist, a list had to be constructed.

The WFS Manual on Sample Design listed the characteristics which are required of a good sampling frame as follows: the frame should be exhaustive, non-repetitive and up-to-date, and units should be unambiguously demarcated and traceable. WFS advised against any use of lists of individuals except those that are made by the survey fieldworkers themselves. The use of existing lists of households was also discouraged with the possible exception of a list drawn from a very recent census or other survey. Moreover, it was pointed out that in developing countries even a census often does not provide a satisfactory household sampling frame: addresses are generally inadequate and the fieldwork is often of poor quality, with the consequence that households cannot be identified. Another, earlier survey may supply an acceptable sampling frame if the time interval is short, but this assumes that its sample design is compatible with the objectives and field procedures of the fertility survey.

Another possibility was the use of dwelling sampling frames as a substitute for household sampling frames. Although dwelling sampling frames are considerably more durable than lists of households in developing countries, they are likely to exist in urban areas only. Moreover, dwelling lists in any country are likely to be incomplete because of recent housing developments and structural changes or changes from non-residential to dwelling use. In most developing countries dwelling listings would have a useful lifetime of a year or two. Where listings are essentially linear — that is, where dwellings are numbered or are lined up along streets or roads — their lifetime can be extended by use of the half-open interval method (see WFS Manual on Sample Design, p. 25). This was used in several of the Latin American surveys of WFS. However, in most WFS countries a special listing operation, either of dwellings or households, was considered necessary.

In the event, eight of the WFS surveys used a large sample of dwellings or households from a recently completed demographic or other household survey. In eight others an existing sample of area units (but not of dwellings or households) was used. Table 13.3 identifies the surveys or master samples these 16 countries used.

Countries which used an existing sample from another survey experienced various problems. Inadequate documentation of the prior sample sometimes caused difficulties. For example, in the 1979 Ivory Coast Fertility Survey it was originally planned that the sample for the rural and small town sectors should be based on the sample for the Multi-Round Demographic Survey of 1978. That survey had included a segmentation operation, followed by a survey of all households in each selected segment. It was intended to use the latter as the listing for

TABLE 13.3
Details of WFS samples which were based on a prior survey
or master sample

Country	Name of prior survey or master sample	Area stage (A) or area and listing stage (A, L) used
Africa		
Benin[a]	Multi-Round Demographic Survey	A, L
Ivory Coast	National Multi-Round Demographic Survey	Rural only: A
Kenya	National Multi-Purpose Area Sample	Urban: A Rural: A, L
Nigeria	National Demographic Sample Survey	A
Tunisia	Employment Survey	A
Asia and Pacific		
Indonesia[a]	Intercensal Population Survey (SUPAS 1)	A, L
Malaysia	Household Expenditure Survey	A, L[b]
Thailand	Survey of Population Change	A, L
Turkey	National Demographic Survey	A, L
Americas		
Colombia	Ministry of Health master sample	A
Haiti	1971 sample census	Rural only: A
Mexico	National Household Survey	A, L[b]
Peru	OTEMO master sample	A, L
Trinidad & Tobago	Continuous Sample Survey of Population	A
Venezuela	National Household Survey	A
Europe		
Portugal	National master sample	A

[a] In these cases the 'prior' survey was closely associated with the fertility survey, the two operations being planned together and executed by the same national office.
[b] In these cases the prior survey provided not a complete listing for each area but a sample from the listing.

the fertility survey. However, it was later discovered that rigorous selection probabilities for the segments were unobtainable. As a result, it was necessary to go back to the sample of first-stage units and carry out a new segmentation and a new listing. The change of plan delayed the survey for several months and extra costs were incurred.

In Haiti, the fertility survey (1978) used a sample of area units from the sample census which was performed in rural areas in 1971, the original sampling frame being the census of 1950. Many of the maps were discovered to be out of date or incomplete, and aerial photographs had to be used for urban areas which had no cartographic records. In Kenya, gross coverage errors were discovered in the master sample which had to be corrected by province-level weighting at the analysis stage. Recency as well as adequacy of documentation is therefore another problem in the use of existing sampling frames. Nevertheless, the sharing of sampling frames between surveys results in savings in cost. It is notable that this was possible with 16 of the 42 WFS surveys.

In the absence of an existing master sample, the WFS sampling strategy was to examine the available area sampling frames to seek the smallest category of area units for which there existed, or could easily be constructed, a sampling frame with boundaries of the units reasonably well defined (WFS Manual on Sample Design). In this context it is striking that, in 37 of the 42 countries, census enumeration districts (EDs) could be used as one stage in the area sample design. If we exclude countries for which areas or lists were provided by another survey the proportion becomes 25 out of 26 countries. (The exception is Dominican Republic, which used material from the malaria eradication campaign.) Of course, the available census units often fell short of the ideal: units sometimes varied greatly in size, requiring splitting of large ones and combining of small ones; there were often inaccuracies in maps and difficulties in boundary identification; supplementary data such as population size were occasionally seriously out of date; or the units were too large to be directly used for the selection of households and individuals. However, the cases of Nigeria and Morocco demonstrate that WFS's solutions to such problems can be of long-term use to the country. The Nigeria Fertility Survey (NFS 1982) selected a subsample from the 111 835 enumeration areas (EAs) originally defined for the 1973 census (the census itself was never published). Unfortunately, the descriptions of the EAs suffered from errors such as double coverage, omission, inadequate description and internal inconsistencies where written boundary descriptions and sketch maps did not concur. There was also the problem that the EA descriptions were nearly 10 years old. It was decided to re-map the 250 EAs selected for the NFS and a cartographer's manual and training were supplied by WFS to this end. The manual, control procedures and organizational arrangements used for the NFS are currently being employed to systematically map every EA in preparation for the next Nigerian census. In Morocco, ten-year-old census maps were being used for the fertility survey. It was acknowledged that during the previous ten years Morocco had experienced high growth rates and rapid urbanization. Areas which were most likely to have been affected by such developments (such as cities and areas flooded by dam construction) were pinpointed and the appropriate EDs were re-mapped. Such mapping updates were of direct use for the next census.

The fact that WFS was able to use census EDs whenever necessary and managed to employ prior sampling frames in so many countries is encouraging. The work of the United Nations Statistical Office and, in particular, the National

Household Survey Capability Programme will perhaps ensure that such frames will be of higher quality and available in more countries in the future.

13.4   Segmentation

In the previous section we noted that in most WFS surveys the ED was the smallest type of area unit for which a sampling frame already existed. (The WFS Manual on Sample Design gave the name 'basic area unit' (BAU) to such a unit.) Having selected a sample of EDs, there are two options:

1 We can create a further stage of area sampling by dividing the EDs into segments and selecting one (or more) in each ED;
2 We can list all dwellings or households in the selected EDs, with a view to sampling from the list.

The listing procedure of (2) is discussed in the following section. The first option is termed *segmentation*. A discussion of the advantages and disadvantages of segmenting basic area units in order to reduce listing was presented in section 12.4 of chapter 12. In this section we discuss what happened in practice in WFS.

Table 13.4 gives details of segmentation in countries which did not use a household/dwelling list from a previous survey or master sample. The table also excludes Iran, for which we have only limited information. Of the remaining 32 countries, 23 used segmentation in some form. Referring back to table 13.2, which provides details of the characteristics of the WFS samples, we are able to examine how segmentation affected the size (as measured by mean population) of the ultimate area units (UAUs). Three of the nine countries which used no segmentation ended up with excessively large UAUs in terms of population: Bangladesh, Pakistan and Fiji had UAU mean populations of 1900, 2200 and 1400 respectively. The only country which had larger UAUs was Malaysia, which used areas and lists from an expenditure survey. Two other countries which did not use segmentation (Colombia and Venezuela) inherited suitably sized area units from previous surveys. Sri Lanka, Guyana and Jamaica are relatively small countries whose enumeration districts were not excessively large.

The WFS Manual on Sample Design recommends segments of size 500–1000 persons. Looking at the mean population of UAUs (columns 7/8 of table 13.2), it is evident that, on the whole, the 23 countries which used segmentation followed this recommendation. Of the countries which used segmentation, Lesotho and Syria had the largest UAUs: 1000 and 1100 mean population per sample UAU respectively. The recommended lower limit to segment size was based primarily on the need to avoid very small segment sizes in order to reduce errors in mapping. (See the previous chapter for a discussion of this non-sampling error.) We do not have any direct evidence bearing on the significance of such errors.

The last column of table 13.2 shows the density of sampling at the final sampling stage (selection of households from the listings). Where the density is low a relatively large amount of listing has been done. This will be either because the

TABLE 13.4

Details of segmentation of basic area units (BAUs)

Details of selective segmentation

Segments made in:				No segmentation
All BAUs	Larger BAUs only	Urban BAUs only	Large rural BAUs only	
(1)	(2)	(3)	(4)	(5)
Morocco	Cameroon	Jordan[a]	Egypt	Bangladesh
Sudan (North)	Ghana	Syria	Paraguay	Nepal
Portugal	Ivory Coast	Yemen AR	Costa Rica	Pakistan
	Lesotho		Dominican Rep.	Sri Lanka
	Nigeria		Panama	Fiji
	Senegal			Colombia
	Mauritania			Venezuela
	Tunisia			Guyana
	Korea, Rep. of			Jamaica
	Philippines			
	Ecuador			
	Haiti			

[a] Segmentation performed in towns and large villages only

Details of field operations for segmentation

No fieldwork used for segmentation	Segmentation combined with listing	Segmentation combined with mapping	Separate field operation
(1)	(2)	(3)	(4)
Korea, Rep. of	Ivory Coast	Cameroon	Ghana
Philippines	Morocco	Nigeria	Lesotho
	Sudan (North)	Senegal	Egypt
	Ecuador	Yemen AR	Tunisia
	Paraguay		Syria
	Costa Rica		Haiti
	Dominican Rep.		
	Panama		
	Portugal		

Note: Even if a field operation was required for only a small proportion of BAUs, the country is included in columns (2)–(4) above. Information not available for Jordan and Mauritania.

UAUs are large or because the 'take' within each is unusually small. Most cases fall between a density of 1/2 and 1/6. Some of the lower densities arise where a sample was borrowed from another survey. Where the whole listing was borrowed the normal need to economize in listing was absent so that there was less motive for segmentation; where only a sample from the listing was borrowed this may have limited the available take per cluster (as happened in Mexico). In Pakistan and Bangladesh, the last-stage density is low because the UAU is unusually large; it seems likely that further segmentation would have been more efficient here.

We now examine in more detail how segmentation was employed in different countries. Table 13.4 shows that 21 of the 24 countries which used segmentation did so selectively in certain types of BAUs. For example, in Egypt, Paraguay, Costa Rica, Dominican Republic and Panama, segmentation was only used in larger, rural BAUs. Several other countries segmented only the larger BAUs, but in both the rural and urban sectors. Syria and Yemen AR segmented only urban BAUs.

Haiti provides an example of selective segmentation. In that country, 60 out of a total of 111 BAUs were segmented with a breakdown as follows: 43 out of 46 urban BAUs; 7 out of 10 semi-urban BAUs; and 10 out of 55 rural BAUs.

Table 13.4 also provides further details of the segmentation procedures. If recent and sufficiently detailed maps of BAUs are available then segmentation can be done in the office and the cost of segmentation becomes minimal. This is rarely the case in developing countries and only two of the WFS countries did not see any need for fieldwork to implement segmentation, namely the Republic of Korea and the Philippines. If fieldwork is involved, then we must distinguish between those cases where a special field operation was performed for the segmentation and the countries which integrated the listing and segmentation procedures. Segmentation was done in conjunction with listing in nine of the countries which required fieldwork for segmentation. In a further four countries (Cameroon, Nigeria, Senegal and Yemen AR) the segmentation was performed at the same time as a substantial updating of maps. Clearly, segmentation requires some form of mapping but in some of these countries an updating of maps would probably have been necessary before the survey could begin, even if segmentation was not required.

If segmentation is confounded with listing and/or mapping, we cannot hope to calculate the marginal cost of segmentation though it is likely to be small. As an example of segmentation combined with mapping, details of the Senegal operation are given here. In Senegal, the size of a segment was set at 500 population, i.e. there was no segmentation if an enumeration district did not exceed approximately 750 persons. Enumeration districts were selected with probability proportional to the number of segments they had theoretically been assigned. Fieldworkers then only had to materialize segments in the EDs which had been selected in the office. Seven teams visited the selected enumeration districts and updated the maps which had been used in the office to split the enumeration districts into segments. At the same time the number of compounds was noted in order to obtain a better estimate of the size of each segment. The field teams also delimited the segment because the maps were not sufficiently detailed to do this very well in the office. So, although the segmentation was a field operation separate from the listing or interviewing in Senegal it may be regarded as a by-product of another necessary activity, that of improving the maps.

It was noted above that segmentation was combined with listing in half of the countries which required fieldwork for segmentation. However, the countries that combined the two operations (for example Costa Rica, Ecuador, Ivory Coast, Panama, Paraguay and Portugal) generally had to segment only a few, large BAUs. A separate field operation was therefore not justified as segmentation could quite easily be incorporated into the listing process without incurring extra travel costs.

In countries where a large proportion of BAUs are to be segmented it appears that a separate segmentation operation is preferable due to the complexity of the operation, the different skills required and the time involved. For example, Ghana and Haiti segmented 75 and 54 per cent of selected BAUs respectively and separated segmentation from listing. Both countries used 36 person-months for the segmentation and Ghana then needed 32 person-months for listing and Haiti 9 person-months. Sample preparation (map-checking, segmentation and listing) in both countries constituted 17 per cent of total fieldwork costs, which was slightly higher than average WFS sample preparation costs. Another reason for separating segmentation and listing operations, if substantial segmentation is required, is that the process of listing is complex. Indeed, listing was often not as simple or straightforward as WFS sometimes imagined it would be. The problems associated with the listing operation are discussed below.

13.5 Listing

Strictly speaking, two listing operations were performed in the majority of WFS surveys: the listing of households or dwellings in order to obtain a sampling frame from which the households to be interviewed were selected, and the listing of persons for the individual interview. The *household/dwelling listing* will be discussed first; it is this that the term 'listing operation' usually refers to.

As with segmentation, the household listing operation rarely consisted of a separate field operation. We have already noted that segmentation was performed during the same field operation as the listing in nine countries (table 13.4). In some countries listing was combined with an updating of maps; in others it was combined with the interviewing operation. Of the eight countries (Benin, Indonesia, Kenya, Malaysia, Mexico, Peru, Thailand and Turkey) which used a prior survey or master sample for a list of dwellings or households, only Thailand and Turkey undertook a special field operation to update their existing lists.

Listing was combined with the interviewing field operation in several countries. This usually happened when an extended household schedule (XHS) was used. The XHS was designed primarily to collect fertility and mortality data on a large sample (for further details of the XHS see chapter 4). However, it also contains all the information necessary for the listing of persons and selection of eligible women and may therefore replace the listing of households/dwellings and the listing of persons. The following countries replaced the listing operation in this way: Cameroon, Lesotho, Senegal, Mauritania, Morocco, Jordan, Yemen AR, Republic of Korea and Colombia. Although listing (XHS) and interviewing were done during the same field operation in the latter countries, the structure and organization of the two operations varied (see chapter 12). For example, in Senegal, two separate teams went simultaneously to each cluster, one for the listing (with the XHS) and the other for the women's interviews. In other countries the same team performed both operations but with separate visits to the household.

Some countries which used the XHS preferred to keep the listing of households quite separate from the listing of persons. This avoids the need for updating the list of persons if there is a long interval between the XHS and the women's interview. In these countries (e.g. Sudan, Syria and Venezuela) a separate household listing was done. The XHS was then used for the listing of persons and was followed immediately by the women's interview.

Nepal and Nigeria were special cases. Nepal used a single-visit arrangement with compact cluster sampling. There was therefore no listing or sampling of households. In Nigeria, the supervisor of the interviewing team was responsible for the household listing.

Table 13.5 gives details of the listing operation for those countries which did not combine listing and interviewing in the same visit to the cluster. However, many of these countries performed another operation with the listing. For example, Ivory Coast, Sudan, Ecuador, Paraguay, Costa Rica, Dominican Republic and Panama carried out the listing immediately after segmentation in each area. The organization of listing differed appreciably between countries. For example, Costa Rica, Dominican Republic and Panama used few listers but extended listing over several months, while Sri Lanka and the Philippines had a more intensive operation using more listers. The duration of listing shown in table 13.5 is intended as an approximate guide only. Information on the time that individual listers worked during the elapsed period of time is unavailable. For example, in Guyana the 60 listers worked part-time, without supervision, for a duration of 2.5 months. In such cases no useful figures on work rates can be produced. However, we examine below two case studies where listing was not combined with segmentation, mapping or interviewing and for which we have good data.

In *Egypt*, 25 teams of listers were supervised by five regional co-ordinators. (In many countries the listing supervisors were regional officers who did not go into the field.) Supervisors and listers received a one-week training course. A total of 112 239 dwellings were listed in 50 working days. It follows that 44 dwellings were listed per person-day. This is a reasonable work rate bearing in mind that listers in Egypt only had to chalk a serial number on each dwelling without making contact with the residents.

In *Ghana*, there were nine listing teams, each consisting of one supervisor and five listers. Listing in northern Ghana was undertaken from 4–31 October 1978

TABLE 13.5
Details of listing

	No. of supervisors	No. of listers	Duration of complete listing operation (approx.)
Africa			
Ghana	9	45	3 months
Ivory Coast	R: 3	27	1 month
	U: 4	16	3 months
Egypt	5	50	2 months
Sudan (North) (XHS)	34	144	3 months
Tunisia	5	18	2 months
Asia and Pacific			
Syria (XHS)	25	50	1.5 months
Bangladesh	6	32	U: 2 weeks
			R: 1 month
Pakistan	10	1–4 per district	8 months
Sri Lanka	22	220	1 month
Fiji	12	100	11 days
Philippines	13	403	1 month
Americas			
Ecuador	3	12	2.5 months
Paraguay	1	4	4 months
Costa Rica	1	4	5 months
Dominican Rep. (XHS)	1	5	2 months
Panama	0	4	2 months
Guyana	0	60	2.5 months
Haiti	2	9	1 month
Jamaica	0	60	1 month
Trinidad & Tobago	8	14	7 months

Note: XIS = countries which used an extended household schedule but listed households during a field operation separate from the XHS.

and in southern Ghana from 27 November 1978 to 10 January 1979. Each lister was responsible for listing all households in approximately six enumeration areas within a period of 21 days (15 working days). Supervisors and listers received five days' training. 7500 households were listed, giving a work rate of 11 households per lister-day. The difference between the work rates for Egypt and Ghana reflects in part the greater amount of work required of the Ghanaian listers. They noted the name of the head of household, the size of the household and the main language spoken by members of the household.

The cost of listing thus depends crucially on whether it is necessary to contact someone in each dwelling/household or whether the listing can be done without this. If there is a good address system, or if dwellings are arranged in a simple way (e.g. on each side of the road in single file, or in a rectangular grid), or if the village chief has a list of all the households, then listing may require no more than a brief visit to the area. In an intermediate case, it may be necessary to affix stickers or chalk a number on every dwelling — this was the case in Egypt. But in other cases, and probably the majority of cases in developing countries, listing will require contact with a household member, either to obtain permission to affix a sticker or to obtain clear identification of the unit listed. In this case listing is a costly operation and, as we have seen in the case of Ghana, a lister may not cover more than 12 households per day. Clearly, in these circumstances it is best to reduce, as far as possible, the size of the UAUs by segmentation.

The definition of the household/dwelling listing units utilized in WFS surveys varied along a continuum from purely social to purely structural units. The 'dwelling' was the favoured listing unit in the Latin American surveys. Here, we use the term 'dwelling' as broadly as possible to mean any identifiable, structural unit of habitation which could be used for listing and sampling. Several Asian countries, for example Bangladesh, Republic of Korea and Philippines, used households as their listing units. In other Asian and most African surveys, a system was used that can be regarded either as a dwelling or a household list: the list appears on paper to be one of households but the survey interviewers who are the eventual users of the list are instructed that, in the event that the named household has moved away, they are to accept the household which has moved in to replace it. Such a list can be regarded as a dwelling list, with the dwellings identified by the name of the current occupant — in effect, the household name serves as a sort of address for identifying the dwelling. In principle, the distinction between a dwelling list and a household list is that the former should include dwellings which are unoccupied at the time of listing; however, if the time interval between the listing operation and the survey interviews is quite short — not more than a few weeks — one can reasonably ignore this requirement as an expensive refinement unlikely to have any significant effect. In the latter event, the distinction between a dwelling list and a household list disappears, and the above system can be regarded either way. On the other hand, if the time interval between listing and survey is long this issue has to be faced. If the list is now regarded as a household list there is a danger of serious bias through failure to cover recently formed households; if it is regarded as a dwelling list the corresponding bias can be avoided by including empty dwellings in the listing.

Assuming that nearly all dwellings contain only one household and nearly all households occupy only one dwelling, the situation can be summarized easily in the following recommendations:

1 If an address system is available, then list dwellings, identifying them by their address.

2 If an address system is not available, then *either* (2a) construct such a system by affixing stickers or painting numbers beside doors or showing locations on a sketch-map, *or* (2b) identify the dwellings in terms of the name of their occupant (household head). In the latter case, interviewers should be instructed to accept whatever household is occupying the selected dwelling at the time of the interview.

3 If the time interval between listing and interviewing is greater than a few weeks, then unoccupied dwellings should be included in the listing.

The above statements amount to recommending a dwelling listing in all cases. However, if method 2b is used and if empty dwellings are not included, the method could be regarded as a household listing with a rule for substitution — indeed, fieldworkers are likely to find it easier to view the procedure in this way. In view of the ambiguity noted, it is not feasible to classify all listings as either dwelling listings or household listings: while some are unambiguous, others can be regarded either way.

The conventional notion of a 'household' proved to be inappropriate in several West African countries, especially Ivory Coast and Senegal. In the latter two countries, compounds (French: *concessions*) are a common form of dwelling organization, where a chief ('head of household') may live with a number of wives, children, grandchildren, etc., who sleep in different huts within a compound. The problem is that in these cases the standard definition of household crosses dwelling units. This has resulted in very large 'households'. Kabir (1980) presented the per cent distribution of households according to *de jure* household size for Asian and Latin American countries in the WFS. The percentage of households with 20 or more members ranged from zero (all Latin American countries) to 2.6 (Malaysia). In Ivory Coast, 4.2 per cent of households had 20 or more members (the largest household in the sample had 72 members). In Senegal, the problem of very large 'households' was foreseen and as a result the sample design was based on the selection of women, not households; thus *concessions* did not cause problems at the sampling stage. However, surveys which are interested in household characteristics and relationships, or household budget surveys, will usually need the household as an analytical unit. In any case, countries which have compounds or *concessions* need to pay special attention to the problems of defining the listing unit.

Most WFS countries which used a true household listing (i.e. a household listing which ignored vacant dwellings and permitted no substitution) succeeded in limiting the time between listing and interviewing to an extremely short (three days for the Republic of Korea) or moderate (an average of four months in Bangladesh) duration. The exception is the Philippines, where the time lag was nine months and many of the households listed could not be found at the interviewing stage. Marckwardt (1984) gives details of the response and data distortions introduced by this delay.

Another problem associated with the household or dwelling listing operation is that of coverage. An error in coverage occurs when a unit in the population which should have been included is omitted from the sample, or, less commonly, when some unit which has not been selected in the sample is erroneously included. There is evidence of undercoverage in WFS surveys (see Marckwardt 1984) which is related to the household/dwelling listing in so far as boundary problems and incomplete listing cause errors. The quality of the basic cartographic material available in the country may affect the degree of coverage errors.

In Kenya, a post-survey field checking operation was performed and confirmed that 'faulty sample implementation in the field leading to wrong identification of some cluster boundaries, as well as incomplete household listing and structure numbering are the major causes of under-coverage' (Kenya Fertility Survey, First Report, p. 31). In Dominican Republic an initial listing/mapping operation lacked supervision. Interviewers experienced difficulties in locating households so a re-mapping was performed in selected UAUs. In urban areas it was discovered that households at the backs of blocks, and dwellings near the boundary, had been omitted and dwellings were wrongly located on the maps. To give an example of the original undercoverage, four *municipios* had an initial listing of 1925 households; after checking, this increased to 2389, reflecting a 19.4 per cent omission rate. Similar mistakes were discovered in rural areas: here the main problems were underenumeration of mountainous regions, with omission of dwellings which were not clearly visible from the road or which were located a long way from the road. Occasionally overenumeration was caused by listers including kitchens which separated dwellings. Lack of supervision and lack of training were seen as the main reasons for the poor quality of the initial operation.

In two other surveys where gross undercoverage demonstrably occurred (Cameroon and Nigeria), the initial listing task was assigned to field supervisors who operated largely on their own without any systematic supervision of their work. There seems to be a real risk of gross omission in this kind of organization. Certainly, future data collection projects of the WFS type would benefit from greater attention to monitoring the household/dwelling listing operation. In WFS surveys the operation was typically left in the hands of local field staff, with little central supervision, and used a variety of manpower for the listing (for example secondary school children in Fiji, teachers in Ghana). Minimal control was exercised over the operation, in the belief that it was a simple and straight-forward task.

Even with efficient supervision of the listing, problems of undercoverage may still be experienced. One possible source of undercoverage may be disagreement between lister and interviewer on household demarcation. If two groups of people live in association so that there is ambiguity as to whether they constitute two households or one, the lister may regard them as one household (or one dwelling) and the interviewer may regard them as two. (Note that these distortions would reflect the natural bias of both lister and interviewer if they wished to minimize their workload.) If the dwelling or household is identified by the name of the head, then the ambiguity may go unnoticed and the interviewer may simply not interview the second group. As a protection against this error, in some countries the lister was asked to include an estimate of household size against each household. Unfortunately we have no evidence as to whether this method is effective or how common this household definition error may be.

Use of the half-open interval method has already been mentioned as a device for prolonging the life of a dwelling list. The method is also valuable because it gives a second chance to correct listing errors: omissions by the lister can be rectified by the interviewer. In Peru and Ecuador, where the method was used, the numbers of dwellings which it added to the sample were 7.5 and 3.5 per cent respectively of the numbers originally listed. In the case of Peru a master listing was used which was in places up to four years old. In Ecuador the fertility survey carried out its own listing, and interviewing came four months afterwards (interval between median dates).

The *listing of persons* can also create coverage errors. A basic feature of the individual women's sample was that the respondents had to be selected on the basis of the individual's characteristics, which were identified during the listing of persons. The listing of persons and the selection and interviewing of women typically took place during a single visit to the household and were carried out by the same interviewer. A degree of coverage error was caused by misreporting of age and/or marital status information on women in the household. Such coverage errors tended in the direction of classifying eligible women as ineligible (see chapters 11 and 24). In some surveys there is evidence of omission of women from household member listings. This tendency of interviewers to misrecord characteristics of household members so as to reduce their individual workload is likely to be a particular problem in countries where interviewers have to guess the respondent's age. Supervisors should be trained to be aware of bias due to the respondent's age being pushed out of the eligible age range. Interviewers might be encouraged to ask for birth certificates or other documentation when determining ages or, preferably, to insist upon person-to-person interviews.

13.6 Response rates

Obtaining a response from the final sample unit, however defined, may be seen as the final task in implementing the survey design. Response rates for the household interviews are presented in table 13.6. The rates are first given (column 3) in terms of the number of households successfully interviewed expressed as a percentage of the number selected. (The number selected can be found in table 13.2.) Next, the response rates are given as a percentage of the households *found* (column 4). This represents the number of households selected less the number recorded as 'Not a dwelling' or 'Not found'.

The response rates for the individual survey and overall response rates are presented in table 13.7. Two estimates of the overall response rate are provided: estimate A based on households *selected* and estimate B based on households *found*. Marckwardt (1984) suggests that the former is likely to be a better estimate for true household samples and the latter for true dwelling samples.

Marckwardt (1984) discusses WFS response rates in detail and examines the reasons for non-response. Here, we limit ourselves to a comparison across countries. As there were only a few WFS countries which used a true household sample, we examine the response rates that are based on located or 'found' units. Examining the household response rates (column (4) of table 13.6), we can see that if Portugal is excluded (the only European country), response rates were over 85 per cent in all 35 countries for which we have data and above 95 per cent in 26. Response rates for the individual interview were also generally very high. Looking at column (3) in table 13.7, we can see that response rates were above 90 per cent in all but 3 of the 38 countries for which data are available and above 95 per cent in 25 countries.

The overall response rates based on 'found' households (column (5) of table 13.7) are above 90 per cent in 24 of the 35 countries for which data are available and above 95 per cent in eight countries.

13.7   Some useful statistics for sample design

The sample designer for a fertility survey needs a variety of information about households and the distribution among them of women eligible for the individual interview. A collection of such data is presented in table 13.8.

Comparison of columns (2) and (3) shows an almost universal excess of households with absent members over households with visitors. For a closed population correctly represented by the sample the number of absent household members should equal the number of visitors. Some of the more extreme anomalies may be explained by external temporary migration (Lesotho) or nomadism (Mauritania), but the widespread nature of the phenomenon strongly suggests an error of coverage. It also emphasizes the difficulty of achieving a consistent household definition in most countries.

Columns (4)–(15) provide information on the distribution among households of the two populations used in the WFS individual interviews, namely *women aged 15–49* in columns (4)–(9) and *ever-married women aged 15–49* in columns (10)–(15). Both the mean per person and the mean per household will be of use to the sample designer. For illustrative purposes we have shown the mean per person in column (9) and the mean per household in column (15). (The former can be converted into the latter by multiplying by the household size, column (1).) The particular interest of the mean per person in column (9) is its high degree of constancy; a figure of 0.225 could be assumed anywhere with very little risk of serious error.

13.8   Conceptual errors in sample implementation

Problems in the implementation of sample designs are not limited to practical difficulties; there also occur from time to time difficulties of *understanding*

TABLE 13.6

Response rates for the household survey

Country	Number[a] found	Successfully interviewed		
		Number	As % of selected[b]	As % of number found
	(1)	(2)	(3)	(4)
Africa				
Benin	–	20 030	–	–
Cameroon	40 392	37 870	–	93.8
Ghana	6 127	6 016	88.6	98.2
Ivory Coast	3 852	3 754	85.3	97.5
Kenya	9 576	8 891	82.6	92.8
Lesotho	18 297	18 244	89.7	99.7
Nigeria	9 236	8 624	92.1	93.4
Senegal	193 032[c]	–	–	–
Egypt	10 343	10 079	95.1	97.4
Mauritania	15 041	14 827	–	98.6
Morocco	17 702	17 125	88.5	96.7
Sudan (North)	12 639	12 028	86.5	95.2
Tunisia	5 959	5 735	95.8	93.0
Asia and Pacific				
Jordan	–	14 490	96.2	–
Syria	15 257	14 670	96.0	96.2
Yemen AR	13 495	13 255	92.3	98.2
Bangladesh	5 960	5 853	95.2	98.2
Nepal	5 976	5 655	94.6	94.8
Pakistan	4 929	4 901	93.4	99.4
Sri Lanka	8 173	8 149	92.3	99.7
Fiji	5 200	4 901	91.0	94.2
Indonesia	10 504	10 156	–	96.7
Korea, Rep. of	21 248	20 932	–	98.5
Malaysia	7 770	7 755	95.7	99.8
Philippines	12 939	12 742	86.4	98.5
Thailand	4 358	4 301	95.2	98.7
Americas				
Colombia	–	9 796	98.0	–
Ecuador	6 053	5 825	83.5	96.2
Paraguay	4 218	4 030	87.1	95.5
Peru	7 688	7 395	82.6	96.2
Venezuela	8 834	8 560	–	96.9
Costa Rica	4 317	4 244	89.8	98.3
Dominican Rep.	11 526	10 921	90.5	94.7
Mexico	13 620	13 080	84.1	96.0
Panama	4 805	4 771	91.5	99.3

Table 13.6 continued

Country	Number[a] found	Successfully interviewed		
		Number	As % of selected[b]	As % of number found
	(1)	(2)	(3)	(4)
Americas (cont.)				
Guyana	4 541	4 433	95.0	97.6
Haiti	3 356	3 008	80.9	89.6
Jamaica	4 968	4 613	82.7	92.9
Trinidad & Tobago	4 768	4 583	92.2	96.1
Europe				
Portugal	13 586	10 888	72.0	80.1

Notes: Figures in columns (1) and (2) are derived from Marckwardt (1984) (where a different definition of coverage was used).
– Figures not available.

[a]   Represents number selected less numbers recorded as 'Not a dwelling' or 'Not found', at the stage of the household interview; includes household residences identified although household members absent.
  [b]   Selected number of households can be found in column (3) of table 13.2.
  [c]   Number of persons; the 'household' was not used as a unit in the Senegal survey.

which can lead to significant distortion of the design when it is put into effect. One of these in particular arose so frequently in the WFS experience that we believe it will be a public service to bring it into the open. In most cases the error was discovered in time for it to be rectified, but in two surveys the discovery came too late and the only solution was a retrospective adjustment which left the sample not strictly probabilistic.

The problem arises when a sample of area units is selected with probability proportional to size (PPS) and this is followed by a stage of sampling with probability inversely proportional to that used at the first stage. In such designs the variations in the two sets of probabilities cancel and we arrive at a self-weighting sample. For simplicity we shall assume here just two stages of sampling. Thus, at the first stage, primary sampling units (PSUs) are selected with PPS, while at the second stage the selection is with inverse PPS, where S (= size) means the *size of the PSU* at both stages. There are two slightly different cases.

The first case relates to a sample design in which it is decided to break up the PSUs into area segments of approximately standard size and it is these that constitute the second-stage sampling unit. If S_i is the number of segments to be created in the i-th PSU, the numbers S_i are computed by dividing the PSU population (obtained from the census) by the standard segment size and rounding to

TABLE   13.7
Response rates for the individual survey

Country	Eligible respondents identified[a]	Successfully interviewed			
		Number	Individual survey response rate[b]	Overall response rate[c]	
				A	B
	(1)	(2)	(3)	(4)	(5)
Africa					
Benin	–	4 018	–	96.5	–
Cameroon	9 137	8 219	90.0	87.5	84.3
Ghana	6 363	6 125	96.3	85.3	94.5
Ivory Coast	6 785	5 764	85.0	72.4	82.8
Kenya	8 452	8 100	95.8	79.2	89.0
Lesotho	3 684	3 603	97.8	87.7	97.5
Nigeria	10 130	9 727	96.0	88.5	89.7
Senegal	4 441	3 985	89.7	–	–
Egypt	8 974	8 788	97.9	89.4	95.4
Mauritania	3 852	3 504	91.0	–	89.7
Morocco	5 875	5 801	98.7	87.4	95.5
Sudan (North)	3 204	3 115	97.2	84.0	92.5
Tunisia	4 432	4 123	93.0	81.2	89.5
Asia and Pacific					
Jordan	3 750	3 612	96.3	92.6	–
Syria	4 646	4 487	96.6	92.7	92.9
Yemen AR	2 808	2 605	92.8	85.6	91.1
Bangladesh	6 648	6 513	98.0	93.3	96.2
Nepal	6 065	5 940	97.9	92.8	92.7
Pakistan	5 046	4 996	99.0	92.5	98.4
Sri Lanka	6 854	6 812	99.4	88.8	99.1
Fiji	5 055	4 928	97.5	88.7	80.1
Indonesia	9 367	9 155	97.7	94.5	94.5
Korea, Rep. of	5 724	5 430	94.9	93.5	93.5
Malaysia	6 368	6 316	99.2	94.9	99.0
Philippines	9 609	9 268	96.5	83.3	95.0
Thailand	4 002	3 778	94.9	89.9	93.2
Americas					
Colombia	5 685	5 378	94.6	90.7	–
Ecuador	7 135	6 797	95.3	79.5	91.7
Paraguay	4 836	4 622	95.6	83.2	91.3
Peru	6 062	5 640	93.0	79.6	89.5
Venezuela	4 836	4 361	93.1	–	87.4

Table 13.7 continued

Country	Eligible respondents identified[a]	Successfully interviewed			
		Number	Individual survey response rate[b]	Overall response rate[c]	
				A	B
	(1)	(2)	(3)	(4)	(5)
Americas (cont.)					
Costa Rica	4 070	3 935	96.7	86.9	95.0
Dominican Rep.	3 218	3 115	96.8	87.6	91.7
Mexico	7 672	7 310	95.3	80.1	91.5
Panama	3 797	3 701	97.5	89.2	96.8
Guyana	4 858	4 642	95.6	90.8	93.3
Haiti	3 557	3 365	94.6	76.5	84.8
Jamaica	3 308	3 096	93.6	77.4	86.9
Trinidad & Tobago	4 486	4 359	97.2	89.5	93.4
Europe					
Portugal	5 561	5 148	92.6	66.7	74.2

[a] Persons eligible for the individual interview listed in those households which were successfully interviewed.

[b] (2)/(1) × 100.

[c] Estimate A: (3) × $\dfrac{\text{Interviewed households}}{\text{Selected households}}$. Estimate B: (3) × $\dfrac{\text{Interviewed households}}{\text{Found households}}$

Note: – Figures not available.

the nearest whole number. At this stage the segments are purely hypothetical. (In Latin American countries such imaginary segments are often called 'measures of size'.) PSUs are now selected with probability proportional to S_i. Thus:

$$\text{1st-stage probability } p_{1i} = kS_i \tag{1}$$

where k is a constant. The imaginary segments are now mapped as real areas in the selected PSUs and the second stage consists of the selection of one segment with equal probability among the S_i segments existing in the i-th PSU. Thus:

$$\text{2nd-stage probability } p_{2i} = 1/S_i. \tag{2}$$

The *overall* probability is the product of the first-stage and second-stage probabilities:

$$p = p_{1i} \times p_{2i} = k. \tag{3}$$

Since this is constant, the sample is self-weighting.

In many countries the work of segmentation will involve field visits to the sample PSUs and at this time it is frequently observed that a PSU has a population

TABLE 13.8

Household size, absent members, visitors, women aged 15–49 and ever-married women 15–49
(Data from household interview)

Country	Households			Women aged 15–49						Ever-married women aged 15–49					
	Mean h/h size (de jure)	% with 1+ members absent	% with 1+ visitor present	% households with:					Mean no. per person	% households with:					Mean no. per h/h
				0	1	2	3	4+		0	1	2	3	4+	
	(1)	(2)	(3)	(4)	(5)	(6)	(7)	(8)	(9)	(10)	(11)	(12)	(13)	(14)	(15)
Africa															
Cameroon	4.7	13	8	30	47	15	5	3	0.22	34	51	11	3	1	0.87
Ghana	4.7	3	1	29	49	15	5	3	0.22	–	–	–	–	–	–
Ivory Coast	8.0	24	13	19	38	21	11	12	0.22	23	43	19	8	8	1.45
Kenya	5.2	18	8	28	52	15	4	2	0.19	–	–	–	–	–	–
Lesotho	4.8	48	16	21	56	17	5	2	0.23	26	63	9	1	0	0.86
Nigeria	5.8	21	2	14	54	20	7	5	0.24	20	63	12	3	2	1.04
Egypt	5.3	–	–	15	58	18	7	2	0.23	21	70	7	1	0	0.89
Mauritania	5.6	12	2	19	52	19	7	3	0.22	25	59	13	3	1	0.99
Morocco	6.1	2	1	12	53	22	9	4	0.23	17	69	12	2	1	1.00
Sudan (North)	5.5	21	3	16	59	16	6	3	0.22	22	70	7	1	0	0.88
Tunisia	5.7	13	3	14	56	19	8	3	0.23	27	71	2	0	0	0.76
Asia and Pacific															
Jordan	6.8	11	5	8	62	19	8	3	0.20	13	80	6	1	0	0.95
Syria	6.6	9	2	10	60	19	8	3	0.21	17	76	6	1	0	0.91
Turkey	5.3	–	–	14	58	21	6	2	0.24	19	71	9	1	0	0.93
Yemen AR	6.0	5	1	11	62	19	6	2	0.21	12	67	16	4	1	1.15

Bangladesh	6.0	21	11	9	66	25[1]	—	—	0.21	9	71	20[1]	—	—	1.15
Nepal	5.4	24	11	11	62	20	6	2	0.23	13	67	16	4	1	1.14
Pakistan	6.3	24	10	11	59	20	7	3	0.21	14	70	13	3	1	1.06
Sri Lanka[2]	5.9	15	3	12	51	23	10	5	0.25	22	70	7	1	0	0.86
Fiji	6.5	25	13	7	55	23	10	5	0.23	14	74	10	2	1	1.02
Indonesia	4.8	—	—	14	65	17	4	1	0.24	18	74	8	1	0	0.92
Korea, Rep. of	4.9	6	4	14	59	19	6	2	0.25	25	74	2	0	0	0.77
Malaysia	5.9	14	3	16	50	21	9	4	0.23	24	67	8	1	1	0.89
Philippines	5.7	—	—	15	56	19	8	4	0.23	28	69	3	0	0	0.75
Thailand	5.9	2	3	9	58	22	9	3	0.24	18	73	8	1	0	0.92
Americas															
Colombia	5.6	17	7	15	55	19	7	4	0.24	28	67	4	0	0	0.77
Ecuador	5.4	—	—	17	56	18	6	3	0.23	29	65	6	1	0	0.79
Peru	5.4	14	6	19	53	19	7	3	0.23	29	65	5	1	0	0.77
Venezuela	5.9	—	—	13	49	23	9	5	0.24	22	65	11	1	0	0.94
Costa Rica	5.4	—	—	15	55	20	7	3	0.24	28	67	4	1	0	0.77
Dominican Rep.	5.3	19	11	19	55	26[1]	—	—	0.23	24	67	9[1]	1	—	0.87
Mexico	5.6	—	—	15	59	17	7	3	0.22	24	70	6	1	0	0.83
Panama	4.9	5	6	27	50	16	6	1	0.21	36	58	6	1	0	0.72
Guyana	5.4	—	—	20	53	16	7	3	0.22	—	—	—	—	—	—
Haiti	4.8	8	5	24	50	17	6	3	0.23	34	56	9	1	0	0.78
Trinidad & Tobago	4.7	—	—	28	47	15	6	3	0.24	—	—	—	—	—	—
Europe															
Portugal	3.4	10	3	39	47	11	3	1	0.23	49	49	1	0	0	0.52

[1] Percentage of households with two or more women.

[2] Women in unconsummated marriages excluded from 'ever-married' category.

Notes: — Not available. In addition, no data are available for Benin, Senegal, Iran, Paraguay and Jamaica.

different from that which was used in computing S_i (whether due to error or because people have moved). The mistake with which we are concerned consists of *adjusting S_i to take account of this discrepancy*. Exactly equivalent to this is the error of instructing the segmentation workers to make segments of *standard size*, when they should be told to make exactly *the pre-calculated number S_i* of segments in the i-th PSU. This is a mistake because it changes S_i in equation (2) but not in (1). Equation (1) cannot be changed because p_{1i} represents the probability of a selection which has already been made. If we wanted to change p_{1i} we should have to change the selection itself, and it is too late for that.

In summary, even if the S_i is based on a population figure known to be wrong it cannot be changed once the selection of PSUs has been made. The use of an incorrect population figure does not invalidate equation (3) and so does not invalidate the self-weighting assumption.

The second case is similar but relates to a sample design in which the second stage is the household. After selecting PSUs with PPS, a household listing operation is carried out in the selected PSUs and a sample of households is selected in each PSU with inverse PPS. Suppose that the 'size' used for PPS selection at the first stage was the number of census households, H_i. Then:

$$p_{1i} = k_1 H_i. \tag{1$'$}$$

Then we need a second-stage selection with inverse PPS, so that

$$p_{2i} = k_2/H_i. \tag{2$'$}$$

This will give an overall probability:

$$p = p_{1i} \times p_{2i} = k_1 k_2 \tag{3$'$}$$

which is constant, so ensuring self-weighting.

The error occurs when, in the course of the household listing, it is observed that the figure H_i is no longer correct and an attempt is made to correct it in computing the second-stage sampling fraction from (2$'$). Unfortunately H_i cannot be corrected in equation (1$'$) since the sampling of PSUs has already been done. If it is corrected in (2$'$) but not in (1$'$) this will vitiate (3$'$), so that the sample is no longer self-weighting.

Other errors observed less frequently may be mentioned briefly.

1 An attempt is sometimes made to adjust the stratification retrospectively after selection. In particular, if urban areas are given a different weight in selection and an area is observed to have been misclassified as urban or rural during the fieldwork, an attempt is sometimes made to readjust the sampling after selection to correct the error. This is unnecessary. If desired, the unit in question can be reclassified for analytic purposes while still retaining the sampling weight which was used in its selection. This involves defining two distinct urban/rural variables, one relating to the sampling process, the other to be used for analysis. This was done in some WFS surveys and is fully acceptable.

2 In systematic PPS selection the sizes n_j of units are cumulated to give a series
of values

$$c_i = \sum_{j=1}^{i} n_j.$$

Selection is then made by starting with a random number and adding a fixed
interval repeatedly, yielding a sequence of numbers. Let t be one such number.
Which area unit does t select? The correct answer is:

t selects the first area whose
value c_i exceeds (or equals) t.

In one survey the mistake (corrected just in time) was made of having t select
the area whose c_i fell *closest* to t.

3 In some cases the *random number* for starting the PPS selection was confused
with the *fixed interval* and the former was used where the latter should have
been.

13.9   Sample documentation

Although a thorough documentation of the sample design and its implementation was recommended by WFS very few countries paid sufficient attention to
this. Such documentation can be produced easily at the time of the sampling
operations but becomes progressively more difficult to supply as time passes.

The information required is, essentially, the complete specification of the
sample in terms of the number of units selected, with their selection probabilities,
in every explicit stratum and at every sampling stage. The numbers *existing* in the
frame are also required at the first area stage (number of PSUs in each stratum)
and the last stage (number of households listed in each UAU) as well as the
numbers of interviews attempted and achieved in each UAU. Where systematic
selection is used, information is needed on the ordering of the units in the frame
prior to selection. The ID numbering system used in the final record needs to be
related on the one hand to the order of selection and on the other to any independent ID system (such as census ED numbers) which may be in current use
and of potential relevance as a supplementary data source; these relationships
may be reported either by including the alternative IDs in the data file or by
providing a separate file showing the correspondence between the two (or more)
systems. Finally, for any domain within which the sample is self-weighting, the
overall sampling fraction for the final units (households or individuals) should
be reported.

Provision of all this information may appear an arduous chore but in fact
every one of these items serves a specific analytic need and each has been used
in one or more studies carried out by WFS. We give below some examples of
such uses.

1 Selection probabilities are needed for computation of weights. Even if the ultimate sample is self-weighting, there may be supplementary data available at the level of a sampling stage which is not self-weighting, or checks with independent data sources may be made at such levels, or subsequent surveys may be linked at such levels. For these reasons the probabilities are needed at all sampling stages.

2 Information on stratification and on systematic selection is needed in considerable detail for the computation of sampling errors. Such computation often proceeds by the retrospective creation of implicit strata by grouping the selected units in pairs. For this purpose one needs to know the ordering of the frame and how this order is represented in the survey ID system, as well as the presence of any breaks in the ordering such as occur at the boundaries of explicit strata. It is not uncommon that the area frame is reordered before selection in order to improve implicit stratification; it is also common to renumber the survey clusters before starting data processing. Any such rearrangement threatens the validity of the process by which sample units selected consecutively are paired together to represent implicit strata, unless the reordering is fully documented.

3 The number of units existing in the frame may be needed at the first area sampling stage in order to use the finite population correction $(M-m)/(M-1)$ in estimation of sampling error.

4 The number of units listed is of value in estimation of cost parameters and for monitoring sample implementation.

5 Numbers of respondents selected and successfully interviewed are needed for computation of response rates (and possible corrective weighting).

6 Recording of alternative IDs which relate the sample units to other data sources will be of value when such sources are used for checking or for improved estimation.

7 Overall sampling fractions are needed for raising to national totals, whether for direct reporting purposes or for checking against census or other national data.

Information of the kind mentioned above is obtained at three stages: when selecting the sample, at the field stage, and after production of the final data tape, but at all three stages the information must be given in terms of the same list of selected area units. Experience shows that this requirement for co-ordinated record-keeping over different survey stages is not easily fulfilled by survey offices which are understaffed and whose activities are typically dominated by the need to handle urgent practical problems before it is too late.

In some cases a survey sample is based on a master sample, or at least on a sample selected for a prior survey. Where this is so the information required may not be directly available. Conversely, the current survey sample may be used later by future surveys. There is thus a long-term obligation to provide detailed sample documentation in the interests of future users.

Finally, mention should be made of an additional problem which WFS frequently encountered. Unforeseen problems of field implementation are common in any country; these have to be dealt with urgently and are rarely documented. Special efforts are needed to ensure that such problems are described, together with the solutions adopted, and to note any departures from the initial sample design.

13.10   Conclusions

This chapter has reviewed WFS experience in the implementation of sample designs. The basic characteristics of the 42 WFS samples are documented and recommendations for future similar surveys in developing countries are made.

The chapter points to some of the problems experienced by WFS countries which based their sampling on an existing sample of dwellings/households or area units from previous surveys. Although the sharing of sampling frames between surveys results in savings in cost, it is important not to take for granted the adequacy of cartographic records and listing documentation. Unexpected problems may cause timetable slippage and fieldwork delays.

The degree of difficulty experienced by the 37 WFS countries which used census enumeration districts depended on the recency of the last census. Work carried out to overcome such problems may be of use to the country after an *ad hoc* survey such as WFS by assisting future census or survey operations.

In general, WFS countries used a separate segmentation operation when a large number of BAUs needed dividing. Segmentation was performed in conjunction with listing in nine of the 20 countries which required fieldwork for segmentation. In a further four countries the segmentation was performed at the same time as a substantial updating of maps.

The distinction between dwelling and household listing units is discussed in the light of the importance of the timing of listing and interviewing. As the time lag between the two operations increases, a pure household listing becomes progressively more prone to non-response bias. If a delay between listing and interviewing is inevitable, then a dwelling listing is desirable and vacant dwellings should be included. Provided the latter condition is observed, the dwelling listing may be represented to the fieldworkers as a household listing together with a substitution rule requiring that a household moving out be replaced by the new household moving in to the same dwelling.

Listing of households or dwellings, and to a lesser extent mapping, were not always given the attention they required in WFS surveys. There is widespread evidence of undercoverage, in some cases severe. Better training of listers is desirable, but above all better supervision of listing work in the field. The largest coverage deficits occurred where listing was carried out by the field supervisor in each team and there was no systematic supervision of his work.

One of the most important conclusions to emerge, which is relevant to all survey work in developing countries, is that it was found feasible to conduct surveys based on strict probability samples in all the WFS countries. The data on such a large number of recent sample designs, each national in scope, with details of how the samples were implemented, represent a rich and perhaps unique source which will hopefully be of use to designers of future samples in developing countries.

Note

1. For definition of 'effective' versus 'notional' stages, see section 12.3 of chapter 12.

14

Recruitment of Field Staff, Pre-test and Training

Jane Verrall

14.1 Introduction

In this chapter three important aspects of WFS surveys are described and discussed: recruitment of field staff; the pre-test; and training of field staff. The reason for linking the topic of pre-testing to those of recruitment and training is that the pre-test played an important educational or training role. This was true for senior local staff, because the pre-test often provided their first practical experience of female interviewers and the use of complex, verbatim questionnaires. Moreover, in most Latin American and some other surveys, the pre-test performed the dual role of evaluating instruments and of training staff who would later become field supervisors during the main interviewing phase.

14.2 Female interviewers: assumptions and implications

WFS staff argued that the many delicate and personal questions in the core questionnaire necessitated the use of female interviewers. Respondents would be embarrassed if these questions were asked by men and their husbands might object or insist on being present. Refusals to participate in the survey, or the possible contaminating effect of the presence of other people, might seriously affect the results of the survey. Other possible advantages of using female interviewers included the greater availability of unemployed, educated women, and their greater conscientiousness.

Country survey staff were sometimes sceptical about the feasibility of using female survey staff. In contrast to developed countries, most permanent field staff in developing countries are male and were therefore available at low extra cost for the fertility survey. There was, in general, little experience in using female interviewers and there was a tendency to believe that women would not be able to work away from home. It was maintained that female candidates of the educational level required would not accept the hardship of field conditions and that they would need chaperoning, which might create personal and social problems. If older women were recruited, their husbands might object to their long absence from home, but younger females would be unacceptable to older respondents. There was generally less resistance to the use of females in South America and East Asia, perhaps because in these regions there was more experience of female staff. The use of female interviewers was not innovative in most countries. As discussed in chapter 37, 17 of the 23 WFS countries which replied to a postal questionnaire claimed to have had experience of female field staff before participation in the WFS programme; in the remaining six countries, the practice was introduced after participation in the programme and continues, and in no country has the practice been discontinued.

In parts of West Africa, while there was no opposition to the use of females, it was considered unnecessary. In Ghana, for example, it was felt that respondents could speak more freely to males than to females because they would be afraid that the women would gossip. In view of this, early in the WFS programme a pilot survey was carried out in Ghana to test this assumption among other things. The pilot survey was designed as other pre-test surveys but with the interviews randomly assigned to male and female interviewers. The sex of the interviewer had no effect on co-operation in the survey and refusal rates were negligible. Yet 53 per cent of the respondents (all female, of course) reported preferring women interviewers, 18 per cent preferred male interviewers and 29 per cent did not mind whether they were interviewed by men or women. In the fertility survey, however, there was a deficiency of females with the necessary language capabilities, and since the pilot had shown that respondents had no great objection to being interviewed by males, the field force was made up of 62 males and 16 females.

Similarly, previous fertility surveys in western Nigeria suggested that male interviewers might be preferable because the respondents were less suspicious of them and felt less threatened. The pre-test confirmed the suitability of male interviewers, but senior Nigerian staff preferred females and, for the main survey, very few male interviewers were used.

Apart from Ghana, Nepal was the only other survey where substantial numbers of male interviewers were employed. The reason was essentially one of expediency. Not only was it difficult to recruit sufficient numbers of women but the field conditions in the higher altitude parts of the country were considered too harsh for females. Subsequent family planning surveys in Nepal have also had to rely largely on a male field force. Doubts have been expressed about the validity of the data but it is not known whether the apparent under-reporting of contraceptive knowledge and use is related to the sex of interviewers.

Since supervisory tasks included re-interviewing and observing interviews for quality control purposes, WFS also recommended that both the team supervisor and the team editor should be female. In 12 of the 42 surveys all of the supervisors were female, in 21 surveys more than 50 per cent of the supervisors were female and in only nine were less than 50 per cent female. Where male supervisors were used, they took responsibility for the organizational and editing aspects of supervision leaving the female editor free to supervise the interviewing process.

Initial scepticism about the sex of interviewers was largely confounded by experience in the field. The success of the fieldwork proved that women could cope with the hardships, and the problems anticipated by some country staff were not realized. This is illustrated in chapter 16 by the low dropout rates of interviewers in most WFS surveys, regardless of culture or region. It is worth noting, however, that interviewing with females does not necessarily mean that the respondent will be able to answer questions in complete privacy. As described in chapter 17, other members of the household or visitors, including men, were often present during the interview.

The major disadvantages of the policy of using a female field force were those of recruitment and cost. Most countries were not able to draw on a pool of staff because most of their existing staff were male. This meant that field staff had to be specially recruited or transferred from somewhere else in the executing agency. Special recruitment brings its own problems. Novice interviewers need relatively long periods of training. More interviewers than required have to be recruited to enable selection of the most suitable candidates. More emphasis has to be placed on the use of formally translated, verbatim questionnaires. Fieldwork has to be kept short to avoid problems arising from the use of temporary staff. Further, the use of *ad hoc*, specially recruited female interviewing staff seriously limits any contribution of WFS towards the building of a permanent survey machinery. Of course these objections remain valid only as long as countries maintain an all-male regular field force.

On balance WFS's policy regarding the sex of interviewers was probably correct. Male interviewers may well perform as well as female interviewers in collecting straightforward background information and data on births and deaths. Indeed this contention is supported by the comparison in chapter 4 of household survey results (where the interviewing was done by men in such surveys as Jordan and Lesotho) with those from the individual survey. But in most cultures it is likely that the quality of information on contraception and sexual matters would have been jeopardized by the use of male interviewers.

14.3 Recruitment of field staff

Field staff were recruited either from government agencies or on the open market by means of advertisement. External recruitment was hampered because applicants were looking for permanent jobs, whereas the survey only offered employment for an average of five to six months, including the training period. While recruitment on the open market has the advantage of greater flexibility in fixing conditions of employment and pay levels, there was no appreciable unemployed pool of literate women in some countries. Problems were also encountered with those hired internally. For instance, staff were not always available full time or they were prone to stop work to fulfil other duties. Such dropouts pose less of a problem when fieldwork is short. There was a need for supervisors to be older and have more authority and experience. Typically they were recruited internally, a policy that should aid institutionalization. Overall, about 70 per cent of the countries in the programme specially recruited their field staff, rather than seconding government employees.

Staff recruited on the open market came from a diversity of backgrounds, though in many countries preference was given to candidates with training in social or community work, midwifery, family planning or teaching. Students were used in a number of surveys, particularly in Latin America. For example, third-year students from the Home Economics and Nutrition Studies Department were employed in Turkey, and their training formed part of their study course. In most surveys, interviewers tended to be young and single. Despite a preference in many places for older, married women, in practice recruitment was governed by the characteristics of women willing and available to do survey work.

When recruitment was done from within the government service, WFS recommended that staff from other government departments be formally seconded to the survey office because they generally had to work harder and for longer hours, sometimes without adequate overtime payments, than in their normal jobs. Some problems were encountered with the use of government staff, especially if they had already received some training. For example, the candidate supervisors in the Philippines were reluctant to join in formalized training because they had been used to 'briefings'. Written tests were also a departure from their usual routine and were therefore not taken seriously. There was a general lack of motivation because they had been assigned without the option to decline. These problems were especially rife among the older, more established staff.

WFS recommended screening twice the number of candidates required for training and that the number admitted for training should be 20 per cent more than the number that would eventually be required for fieldwork. There were several reasons for this recommendation. First, some trainees would be lost during the course of training as they became aware of the hardships involved in the task. Secondly, a surplus would permit the use of selection tests both at initial screening and at the end of training to ensure a high standard of ability in the staff employed. In the event, 24 countries trained more applicant supervisors than needed and 28 countries trained more applicant interviewers than needed. On the average 1.26 interviewers completed training for every one who took part in the fieldwork (see table 14.2). This ratio is inflated by the practice in some surveys of including in the interviewer training staff who were destined to become office editors or coders.

For the field staff, WFS recommended that candidates have some higher education beyond secondary school, be willing to stay away from home for fairly long periods of time and have a commitment to work for the whole survey period. In addition, the supervisors should be of an age and maturity to command respect, and be of a higher educational ability than the interviewers. WFS recommended selection procedures as a means of raising the quality of the group. Most countries accepted this recommendation, though some were reluctant, especially where recruitment was internal, so they compromised by keeping the weakest for office duties such as coding. The selection process included a series of interviews with the survey director and his staff, and a test. The tests varied in complexity. Some simply collected information on the candidate herself to assess her form-filling ability, while others consisted of complicated questionnaires that tested numeracy and comprehension. While these procedures are certainly indispensable, where there were a large number of candidates, there were a few cases where other considerations dominated the selection procedure, for example, linguistic ability and, as in Nepal, physical fitness. In the Ivory Coast, candidates were examined on their knowledge of languages. There were not enough candidates of sufficient quality with the necessary language abilities, and recruitment had to be extended. Similarly in Benin, there were not enough candidates who spoke Adja; a fresh recruitment drive was necessary and a supplementary training course was organized. In Yemen AR, a shortage of educated women was overcome by offering high salaries and scheduling the fieldwork during the long school vacation, so that teachers were available.

The countries' attitudes to the retention of these highly trained field staff were varied. In some, the staff were absorbed into the permanent staff of the executing agency. In others, lists were given to relevant agencies. Some were employed to work in subsequent surveys, as in the Dominican Republic, where the second-round fertility survey used almost all the personnel from the first. In a survey of participating developing countries (response rate of about 60 per cent), just over half reported such retention of staff.

The main lesson from WFS experience is that it is possible to find female recruits in sufficient numbers and of sufficient calibre for national surveys in almost all settings. In view of the low educational levels for the female populations of some WFS countries (e.g. Mauritania, Yemen AR) this is a surprising conclusion. As regards the mode of recruitment, few generalizations can be made. It is clear that the most appropriate tactic depends entirely on the local situation.

14.4   The pre-test

The pre-test forms an essential function in any survey, that of testing out instruments and procedures. Within the context of the WFS, the pre-test served a slightly wider role. The function and objectives of the WFS pre-test were clearly set out in the WFS 'Training Manual' (WFS 1976b). In brief they were:

to test the questionnaire and other documents

to measure respondent receptivity to the survey

to collect information on the operating characteristics of the interview and evaluate survey procedures

to contribute to the training of supervisors and senior staff.

In order to fulfil these objectives, the WFS pre-test was envisaged as a miniature version of the full-scale survey reflecting its organization, its respondents, the expected quality of the field staff and field conditions; its primary purpose was to identify various possible sources of trouble.

The pre-tests were conducted in selected areas, avoiding sample areas where known. WFS recommended a minimum of 100 pre-test interviews but the need for testing out different language versions of the questionnaire often led to many more interviews. Only three countries conducted 100 or less household interviews, 19 countries were in the range 101–200, 10 in the range 201–300 and 10 countries did over 300 household interviews. For the individual interviews, six countries produced 100 or less, 20 countries were in the range 101–200, eight in the range 201–300 and eight countries did over 300 interviews. The largest number of pre-test interviews were in Africa where languages are most diverse (see table 14.1).

The pre-test sample did not aim to be roughly representative although some attempt was made to include the main variations likely to be met in the survey environment. The pre-test was usually conducted in one urban and one rural cluster but sometimes other factors were also taken into account. For instance, in Guyana an area where mining predominated was also sampled. In Indonesia both Muslim and Hindu populations were sampled. In Jordan a sample of Bedouins was included and in Ecuador the socio-economic structure was taken into account along with the mountain and coastal regions. Occasionally a separate pre-test was conducted where the long version of the household schedule was to be used, or several separate pre-tests for different language versions of the questionnaire, for example in Kenya and Morocco. This, of course, contributed to higher pre-test sample sizes.

The pre-test was evaluated by discussion between fieldworkers and senior staff, by using pre-test information sheets, by the use of tape recordings (to detect interview problems) and by examination of the results through looking at hand tabulations of single-variable marginals. The pre-test information sheets represented a formalized approach to the informal debriefings between fieldworkers and senior staff, and were used in many countries. In Colombia, for example, they were incorporated into the pre-test questionnaire.

Fieldworkers were asked specifically to report on difficulties with or comments on the following aspects of the pre-test: locating the household, introducing the interviewer to the respondent, privacy during the interview, working conditions, degree of co-operation, embarrassment or resistance on certain sections of the questionnaire, age reporting, wording of the questions, the layout of the questionnaire and the duration of the interview.

Tape recording of interviews during the pre-test was used as a supplement to direct observation of the interviews. Recordings were used to improve interviewer performance, to detect problems in questionnaire design and clarity of wording, especially with respect to country-specific (non-core) items, and to estimate the success of the translation and show up any over-sophisticated language. In fact the use of tape recording in the interview situation won acceptance as a result of its proven value during the pre-test.

One of the stated aims of the pre-test was to test the questionnaire and supporting documents. The WFS core questionnaire (and to a lesser extent the modules) was both standardized and thoroughly evaluated, so for this purpose the pre-test in the context of the WFS was less important than in other surveys. Nevertheless, 14 countries made major changes to the questionnaire as a result of the pre-test and there were many minor modifications in other countries. As expected, most of the problems concerned non-core items which were being tested for the first time.

All countries reported difficulties with event dating. This had been foreseen, but the pre-test enabled the survey staff to gauge the extent of the problem. This had a direct effect on the identification of the survey population, age being one of the criteria for eligibility for the survey. The pre-test also threw light on ambiguities in the definition of the other survey criteria, for example, how precisely membership of the household was defined and the criteria by which women were judged eligible for the individual interview.

Fiji was a special case. It had the status of pilot survey for the whole WFS programme and was thus essentially testing the core questionnaire. As a result, considerable changes were made to the questionnaire after the pre-test. Ideally the new version should have been pre-tested again, but there was no time to do so before the scheduled start of the fieldwork. Colombia had the additional responsibility for testing the survey instruction manuals in their first translation into Spanish, and Jordan tested the first translation into Arabic. Evidence from the Fiji pilot suggested the need for the translation of the questionnaire into two major languages (Fijian and Hindustani). The spontaneous translation used by the interviewers in the field tended to vary the precise meanings of the questions. This evidence supported the WFS view that verbatim questionnaires were necessary to ensure reliability in data collection, and that such questionnaires should be thoroughly pre-tested (see chapter 6).

A typical problem with language translation was that the translation turned out to be too formal, as in Thailand and Bangladesh, for example. In Egypt too, classical Arabic had to be replaced by colloquial Arabic. In Paraguay there had been an initial reluctance to using a written form of Guaraní because the official language of the country is Spanish. The pre-test proved the feasibility of using Guaraní, and although the survey questionnaires were printed in Spanish, a Guaraní translation of the questions was issued and frequently used in the fertility survey. In the Philippines, the pre-test showed up inconsistencies in different translations which had been produced by the two executing agencies responsible for the survey.

Some countries experienced problems with 'sensitive' questions. For example, questions on abortion could not be used in Sri Lanka where abortion is illegal. In Bangladesh the marriage history had to be relocated before the pregnancy history to avoid the embarrassment of asking widowed or divorced women the question 'Are you now pregnant?'. The questions on abortion were also moved to the end of the questionnaire, so that the whole interview would not be jeopardized by a refusal to a question too early on. In Nepal the question on number of times married was not tolerated but the pre-test showed

TABLE 14.1
Pre-test sample sizes

Country	Sample size	
	Households	Individuals
Africa		
Benin	400	350
Cameroon[a]	840	475
Ghana	300	300
Ivory Coast	190	228
Kenya[b]	616	713
Lesotho	71	71
Mauritania	120	100
Morocco	247	171
Nigeria[c]	400	400
Senegal	315	130
Sudan (North)	218	189
Tunisia	190	176
Asia and Pacific		
Bangladesh	245	245
Fiji	200	200
Indonesia	276	276
Iran	100	100
Korea, Rep. of	50	110
Malaysia	120	100
Nepal	175	193
Pakistan[d]	200	200
Philippines	251	251
Sri Lanka	167	160
Thailand		
Women	150	150
Husbands	1000	1000
Caribbean		
Guyana	280	280
Haiti	750	750
Jamaica[e]	216	297
Trinidad & Tobago	118	150
Europe		
Portugal	200	100
Latin America		
Colombia	159	58
Costa Rica	150	150
Dominican Rep.	304	105
Ecuador	300	250
Mexico	400	200
Panama	180	120

Table 14.1 continued

Country	Sample size	
	Households	Individuals
Latin America (continued)		
Paraguay	160	200
Peru	350	350
Venezuela	112	112
Middle East		
Egypt[f]		
Women	439	357
Economic and		
husbands	181	177
Economic	167	–
Jordan	193	152
Syria	128	128
Turkey	200	200
Yemen AR	268	310

[a] Cameroon – two pre-tests: first for seven languages including English and French (50 women's interviews in each language); second for five more languages (25 women's interviews in each).

[b] Kenya – two pre-tests: first for four languages; second for six languages.

[c] Nigeria – three pre-tests: in Kaduna, Anambra and Oyo states in four languages, Ibo, Hausa, Yoruba, Fulfulde.

[d] Pakistan – four pre-tests covering four main languages.

[e] Jamaica – three successive pre-tests testing different versions of the questionnaire.

[f] Egypt – three pre-tests: one for Women survey; one for Economic and Husbands survey; and one for Economic survey.

a need for the inclusion of a probe on date of consummation for early marriages.

In Mauritania the pre-test coincided with the application of the Islamic law. Unfortunately, this influenced the respondents' perceptions of the section on contraceptive methods. In this section, respondents are asked for spontaneous knowledge of methods, and, for those methods not mentioned, a brief description is given as an aid to recall. During the Mauritanian pre-test, respondents saw this either as an incitement to corruption or as a way for the government to check up on 'bad women'. The problems this caused were so great as to necessitate the total withdrawal of all method descriptions and in the main survey the respondents were only asked for spontaneous knowledge of traditional and modern methods.

In some cases the country-adapted questionnaires simply proved too long and cumbersome. The best solution was to drop the least important questions, the usual victims being country-specific additions to the questionnaires. For example,

Republic of Korea had to drop or reduce questions on migration, induced abortion, contraceptive supply and kinship. Morocco dropped some sociological questions.

Rewording of questions was often necessary where attitudinal questions and other non-core items had been included. In Jamaica a response rate of as little as 33.4 per cent on questions on the costs and benefits of raising children in an early pre-test was attributed to the fact that attitudinal questions had precipitated resistance on the part of the respondents. These questions were refined in two subsequent pre-tests. The Republic of Korea also had to reword the attitudinal questions in the section on fertility preferences. In other cases re-arrangement of the questions was sufficient. In Nepal this was done for questions in the family planning module to allow more probing on knowledge and use of contraception. However, Turkey dropped the husbands survey as a result of the pre-test, but put extra questions on the household schedule, and Syria added questions on education.

Some countries reported difficulties with the administration of the two separate histories of live births and non-live births. They found that data collection was easier and more reliable if they put the two sets of questions together in one integrated pregnancy history. Examples were Nepal and Syria.

One problem was peculiar to the Caribbean region. The marriage history as defined in the core questionnaire was unsuitable for the Caribbean society. A completely new section had to be designed to take into account the more varied and fluid nature of cohabitation and consensual unions. Two alternative versions were tested by the WFS Caribbean office in a special pre-test in Trinidad and Tobago. This was done by interviewing the same respondents twice, first with one version and then with the other, varying the order over respondents. The final version, an amalgam of both, was used in Trinidad and Tobago, Guyana and Jamaica, and a modified version was used in Haiti.

The various changes in the questionnaires had to be incorporated, coding boxes and skip instructions had to be thoroughly checked and the various survey instruction manuals had to be revised before training of field staff could begin. The more languages used for the survey, the more changes had to be made and the longer the time needed for the preparation of documents. Finally, the pre-test was also useful for the development of coding frames, and was used as a source of material to train editors and coders.

The pre-test provided a valuable opportunity for evaluating the reception both of the survey as a whole and of the individual interview in particular. The WFS has been remarkable for its high response rates and this was also true in the pre-test, except in a few cases where possible future difficulties were made obvious. Kenya is a case in point: some areas showed a high degree of non-co-operation and lack of tolerance for what they regarded as unnecessary, foolish or repetitive questions. Field staff found that if they convinced the local dignitaries of the need for the survey, their help was invaluable in persuading the respondent to co-operate. This was so in many other surveys as well. Other countries experienced different kinds of problems. In Sudan and Syria, the respondents would not allow tape recording during the pre-test.

The pre-test also permitted countries to make more realistic estimates of the daily work rate. For example, in Ecuador, the survey staff planned on three or four interviews per day but this was raised to four to five interviews per day as a result of the pre-test experience. The pattern of work adopted by the field staff also affects the successful completion of work. Field staff in general were expected to work during the evenings or at any time when they were most likely to find respondents available for interview. In Ecuador, it was found that keeping to the usual working week would be too restricting in the field, so it was planned to finish all interviews in a cluster before allowing the field staff to take a break.

Local village chiefs were very helpful in ascertaining when respondents were most likely to be available for interview and the likelihood of obtaining confidentiality. The feasibility of the sampling procedures adopted could also be tested at the same time. The pre-test also sometimes gave useful information for the planning and organization of the fieldwork. Information on the adequacy of survey procedures, documentation and quality of translation were fed back into the survey plan which was corrected or improved before the start of the fertility survey.

The pre-test was designed as a mini-survey essentially to provide an opportunity for testing the survey procedures. However, this 'dry run' served another important purpose, that of giving a psychological impetus to the preparation of the survey as a whole. It identified areas where improvements could be made in the planned survey procedures and gave the senior staff an idea of what conditions would really be like in the field. It also provided field experience for the supervisors. It underlined the need for the inclusion of plenty of practice interviews during training because the performance of the pre-test interviewers in many cases was inadequate. Apart from showing where wording had to be modified, the taped interviews pinpointed what needed to be emphasized in training. It highlighted areas where the interviewers had most difficulties and indicated whether this was due to poor pre-test training or to the inherent complexity of the interviewing task. The familiarization of the survey staff with the questionnaires and documentation proved invaluable during training.

The pre-test questionnaires were sometimes useful for the development of the data processing components of the survey, although their utility was limited. The pre-test could provide realistic data for the construction of data files which could then be used to test programs being developed to process the data from the survey. This, of course, was not possible where considerable changes had been made to the pre-test questionnaire. In Haiti, the pre-test was designed as a complete, though small, survey which was fully processed to provide needed information for a development aid project in the local area concerned. But even here the processing itself did not feed back into the main survey. It is probably true to say that the WFS did not make full use of the completed pre-test questionnaires as an input to data processing development. However to have done this would have involved additional office work when the rest of the staff were engaged in the main fieldwork, and this would have made additional managerial demands.

14.5   Training of field supervisors and interviewers

Training is the key to quality data. WFS accordingly insisted that training of field staff should be long, thorough and, where possible, centralized to ensure uniform standards. The countries participating in the WFS programme needed to be convinced of the necessity for special training. WFS advocated three weeks of training for the interviewers, although local staff often did not see the need for this because they had made do with much less for other surveys. Interviewer capability was often taken for granted, although the existing training facilities were likely to be inadequate.

For the supervisors, the WFS recommended a two-week preparatory course including field practice, administrative duties, fieldwork planning and evaluation of interviewers' work, to be followed by participation in the interviewer training. The interviewer training was carried out partly in the classroom but also there was great emphasis on fieldwork practice. The classwork covered the background of the survey, the role of the fieldwork staff in the survey, detailed explanations of the questionnaire and practical aspects of the survey organization.

Most Latin American countries (and also Senegal) used the pre-test for training all their supervisory staff. There is little doubt that this is the best possible method. The remaining 32 countries did so for some supervisors only: their small pre-test sample size did not permit training all supervisors in this way. Their supervisors were trained immediately before their participation in the interviewer training. Those countries which adopted this method did so because their supervisory staff had to be specially recruited and it would have been uneconomical to retain their services over the period (often several months) between pre-test and training. Further, when this period was particularly long, experience would be lost with time. WFS recommended using whichever method was suitable for the conditions prevailing in any particular country.

The modal length of supervisor training was between 10 and 14 working days (26 countries). Seven countries trained the supervisors for more than 14 days. At the other extreme, in nine countries the supervisors received between five and nine days of training, but among these were countries that had given some training before the pre-test (see table 14.2).

Although the supervisors were supposed to be good interviewers, there was not so much emphasis on their field practice interviews. The supervisor training mainly consisted of supervisory duties: how to allocate interviews and monitor fieldwork. Great emphasis was placed on training in quality control. The course covered field practice, administrative duties (materials, expenses, payments), planning fieldwork (division of work, order of work, expected duration of work), evaluation of interviewers' work (tape-recording, spot checking, re-interviewing, callbacks, editing of questionnaires and interviewer debriefing) and control of fieldwork (identification of the sample, verification of correct sample implementation, control sheets and dealing with non-response).

Most countries followed WFS recommendations for interviewer training. Fifteen countries gave 10–15 days' interviewer training, 23 gave 16–20 days and four gave 21–25 days. Those countries which gave less than the recommended three weeks were restricted by the fieldwork timing. In Jordan, one region was susceptible to seasonal migration and a team of interviewers had to be sent there in advance of the main field force. These interviewers were given one week of very intensive training before going into the field; the other teams received the usual amount of training. Where there was a large number of trainees, for example in Jamaica, they were split into ability groups and trained separately, with the trainers alternating between groups. The interviewer training covered the background to the survey, an explanation of the questionnaire and practice interviews, a lecture on the physiology of reproduction and contraceptive methods, the organization of fieldwork and interviewer responsibilities and implementation of the sample.

Training was centralized in or near to the survey headquarters in 34 countries in the programme. Local centres were set up for training in the other eight countries, three in Africa, four in Asia and Pacific and one in Latin America. The main reason for decentralizing the training was the variations in language within the country. For example in Cameroon, where languages are particularly diverse, there would have been great difficulty in finding respondents for practice interviews representative of all the languages used in the survey if training had been centralized in one place. In Pakistan too, there were problems in finding enough Pushto, Sindhi and Baluchi speakers although Urdu and Punjabi speakers were plentiful. Decentralization also reduced the cost of transporting trainees, particularly in larger countries. Some countries phased their regional training so that training, and subsequently fieldwork, started at different times in different regions with different sets of interviewers. For example in Kenya, there were three training courses at two and half-month intervals. One great advantage of this approach was in the allocation of headquarters staff: all were able to participate fully at each training session. In 26 countries there was one language version of the questionnaire, five countries had two or three versions and seven countries between four and nine, and there were ten or more versions in four countries. One difficulty encountered with regional training centres was that of maintaining consistency in the instruction given throughout all training centres. WFS stressed the importance of identical instruction, and recommended the rotation of trainers, to ensure uniformity.

The training was conducted mainly by the survey director and his junior staff, assisted by visiting WFS personnel. The junior staff had been involved in the survey preparation and the development of questionnaires and were quite familiar with the survey procedures. The same survey staff had also been responsible for

TABLE 14.2
Training of fieldworkers

Country	Supervisors/field editors				Interviewers				Number of tape-recorders
	Number of trainees			Duration of course (working days)[a]	Location of courses	Number of trainees		Duration of course (working days)	
	At start of course	Completing course				At start of course	Completing course[b]		
		Total	Of which female						
Africa									
Benin	16	16	8	14	Cotonou	32	32	21	10
Cameroon	50	30	15	13	Buea, Yaounde, Douala, Garoua	150	75	25	8
Ghana	26	22	5	9	Medina	65	56[c]	15	5
Ivory Coast	30	20	10	16.5	Abidjan	45	30	16.5	10
Kenya	15	12	9	13	Nairobi	94	85	18.5	6
Lesotho									
HH	d	6	—	—	Maseru	60	54	20	8
Ind.	17	17	9	10	Maseru	39	39	20	8
Mauritania	19	16	8	19	Nouakchott	40	36	20	8
Morocco									
HH	13	10	—	12	Rabat	50	40	11	—
Ind.	28	20	—	12	Rabat	40	32	16.5	8
Nigeria	12	12	5	14	Enugu	40	38	13	6
	20	20	11	15	Ibadan	66	53[e]	15	8
	16	16	8	13	Kaduna	79	43[e]	15	—

Senegal								
HH	11	11	–	12	Dakar	55	55	12	–
Ind.	8	8	4	8	Dakar	24	20	18	4
Sudan (North)	13	13	–	6	Khartoum / Port Sudan	102	90	18	–
					El Fashir				
Tunisia	18	12	6	11	Tunis	40	24	19	6
Asia and Pacific								
Bangladesh	30	24	12	11	Dhaka	85	55	23	10
Fiji	24	23	23	10	Suva / Lautoka / Labasa	75	67	15	5
Indonesia	28	22	6	12	Bali / Jogyakarta / East Java	146	110	12	20
Iran	16	16	8	17	Tehran	68	48	17	–
Korea, Rep. of	22	21	5	5	Seoul	135	130	18	5
Malaysia	15	15	9	13	Kuala Lumpur	73	73	18	5
Nepal	17	17	3	6	Janakpur / Pokhara	80	80[f]	20	6
Pakistan	10	10	–	10	Lahore	38	33	18	10
Philippines	36	36	32	10	Manila / Cebu City / Cagayan de Oro / Baguio	216	180	21	36
Sri Lanka	19	19	19	12	Colombo	71	71	15	6
Thailand	20	20	20	4	Bangkok	60	60	10	10

Table 14.2 continued overleaf

Table 14.2 continued

Country	Supervisors/field editors				Interviewers				Number of tape-recorders
	Number of trainees			Duration of course (working days)[a]	Location of courses	Number of trainees		Duration of course (working days)	
	At start of course	Completing course				At start of course	Completing course[b]		
		Total	Of which female						
Caribbean									
Guyana	36	36	32	12	Georgetown	86	83	12	5
Haiti	15	12	6	7	Port au Prince	40	24	11	6
Jamaica	11	7	7	10	Kingston	84	67	20	10
Trinidad & Tobago	12	11	11	20	Port of Spain	56	40	20	6
Europe									
Portugal	8	8	8	15	Lisbon	85[g]	75[g]	15	8
Latin America									
Colombia	27	12	6	12	Bogotá	48	36	20	6
Costa Rica	12	7	7	12	San José	40	21	18	6
Dominican Rep.	20	10	10	12	Santo Domingo	60	30	17	6
Ecuador	12	9	9	12	Quito / Guayaquil / Cuenca	38	30	12	12
Mexico	20	11	11	12	Mexico City	65	36	20	6

Panama	10	10	10	10	Panama City	35	30	20	6
Paraguay	19	10	12	12	Asunción	40	30	19h	6
Peru	23	12	12	15	Lima	56	36	15	6
Venezuela	17	10	5	15	Caracas	20	19	15	5
Middle East									
Egypt	39	39	–	10	Cairo	150	130i	19	25
Jordan	20	16	8	12	Amman	63	42	17	8
Syria	34	34	17	6	Damascus	100	62	12	–
Turkey	27	27	16	14	Ankara	79	55	14	5
Yemen AR									
HH	16	10	–	6	Sana'a	60	42	6	–
Ind.	12	12	12	6	Sana'a	75	48	12	–

a　In some countries only a few days' specific supervisor training were given but in addition candidates attended interviewers' training, and in most cases had also acted as interviewers during the pre-test.
b　In several countries some trainees who successfully completed the course were assigned as field editors. Thus, figures in this column do not necessarily correspond to the number of interviewers in the field.
c　Of which 45 were male.
d　Recruited from interviewers.
e　Fieldwork did not start until nine months after the training. The field staff were disbanded and a refresher course was conducted later.
f　Of which 53 were male.
g　Includes 35 candidates recruited for second phase of training needed to replace supervisors and interviewers who left when fieldwork was extended.
h　Half days.
i　Including 25 allocated as field editors.

the supervision of the pre-test. The WFS co-ordinator briefed them before the start of training and participated in the training itself. This participation was sometimes hampered by the lack of knowledge of the local language. Experts were brought in for specialist lectures. The participation of the junior staff was very important, since they would provide support for the survey director throughout the survey. However, the workload for them proved to be very heavy because in all countries the preparation for the fieldwork was concurrent with the training. Their responsibilities included classroom work, evaluation of trainees' performance and organization of practice interviews in the field. WFS felt it necessary to give extensive technical assistance during the training phase of operations, as shown in table 14.3. Mean WFS staff days in-country for the pre-test and training were 8.8 per cent and 9.2 per cent respectively of all WFS in-country technical assistance given throughout the survey.

TABLE   14.3

Mean WFS staff days in-country during pre-test and training

Region	No. of countries	Pre-test days	%	Training days	%	Total days	%
Africa	12	43.2	9.4	47.4	10.3	460.8	100.0
Asia and Pacific	11	29.8	7.8	39.2	10.3	382.4	100.0
Caribbean	4	20.5	7.8	22.8	8.7	263.0	100.0
Europe	1	7.0	2.5	7.0	2.5	277.0	100.0
Latin America	9	14.4	7.9	13.9	7.6	183.1	100.0
Middle East	5	52.2	10.9	33.4	7.0	477.6	100.0
Total	42	30.9	8.8	32.1	9.2	350.4	100.0

In some of the earlier surveys there was a misunderstanding about who would conduct the training. The countries supposed that WFS would take the responsibility for training and consequently did not brief their trainers adequately; they were not prepared for lectures, and gave candidates' questions answers which were contrary to instructions given in the manuals. However, there was always a WFS staff member present during training, so all such problems were dealt with as soon as they arose.

All countries, except one, invited a guest speaker from the medical profession to lecture on reproductive physiology and contraceptive practice. (The exception was Morocco where the trainees were nurses and special training was not considered necessary; trainees were issued with a two-page note describing the various family planning methods.) These lectures were very popular and provided light relief during the theoretical part of the training. Some of the lecturers illustrated their talks with films, slides or demonstration packs used in family planning clinics.

In order to balance the theoretical content of training, the WFS paid great attention to practical work both in the classroom and out. Initially the candidate interviewers needed practice in reading aloud to overcome shyness and to give them the confidence to conduct interviews successfully in the field. The role-playing exercises and demonstration interviews advocated by WFS proved to be very valuable in this respect. They were used in all surveys. Demonstration interviews which increased in complexity as the candidates progressed through the course were given by the trainers. Where possible, female volunteers, usually culled from the offices of the executive agency, were also used, especially towards the end of training, when the trainees had already gained a little experience. The demonstrations given by the trainers were based on imaginary case histories, designed to illustrate teaching points, whereas the demonstrations given by the volunteers represented a more realistic situation. Some of the more advanced case histories were taken from pre-test questionnaires. Special practice was given in the use of the translated versions of the questionnaire, especially in reading aloud, role-playing and demonstration interviews.

For the role-playing exercises, the interviewers would form groups of three, one acting as the respondent, one as the interviewer and one as an observer offering criticism and advice. These roles were rotated in order to give all of the interviewers sufficient practice. The observer role was frequently played by the supervisors who had the experience of the pre-test behind them. The role-playing exercises were particularly useful where several languages were to be used in the survey, especially where free translation in the field would be required.

Pre-prepared visual aids were recommended but not used in all countries — they were not used in Benin, Mexico or Sri Lanka, for example — mainly due to lack of facilities. Blackboards were always available and were used extensively, although they were very time-consuming to use when large sections of the questionnaire had to be reproduced. Where large blow-ups of difficult sections of the questionnaire were available, as in the earlier surveys, they were found especially useful for the household schedule and the various tables in the individual questionnaire. Several countries reported that the interviewers found the household schedule more difficult to understand than the individual questionnaire. With the tabular presentation of the schedule the interviewer needs more initiative to adapt the questions to the situation. In the individual questionnaire the interviewer simply has to read verbatim questions. Video was also used in one country (Republic of Korea) but the sound quality was poor and the videos could only be used to illustrate the interview situation.

Tape-recordings were used extensively during the practical training sessions, especially during demonstrations and role-playing interviews. Their use permitted illustration of difficult sections of the questionnaire and encouraged class-room discussion. Both problem areas and good work could be highlighted in this way. Tape-recordings were also intended for use in quality control in the field and were introduced during training to familiarize interviewers with their use. This early introduction to tape-recording made it easier for the interviewers to accept the various quality control methods as a routine procedure.

Unfortunately the use of tape-recordings puts a heavy evaluatory load on the senior staff.

Field practice is undoubtedly the most important part of training. Non-sample areas for the practice interviews were to be identified before training started. WFS recommended ten practice interviews, to be highly supervised, with individual counselling. Candidates were sent out in twos, one interviewer to conduct the interview and the other to supervise and give critical comment after the interview. Typically the interviewers came back to the office with many problems during the first few days. Apart from being given individual instruction, the interviewers attended regular intensive debriefing during the fieldwork practice.

WFS provided three core documents to assist with the pre-test and training phase of the survey. They were the training manual (designed as a guideline to the organization and conduct of recruitment, pre-testing and training) and the supervisors' and interviewers' instruction manuals, for country adaptation.

The training manual provided essential support for those responsible for the training, for, although a member of the WFS central staff was always present during training, in many cases the survey staff had to complete the preparation unaided. The manual was comprehensive and was an invaluable source of information, especially with regard to the timing of the many and varied operations leading up to recruitment and training.

The supervisors' and interviewers' instructions described briefly the roles and duties of the field staff but consisted essentially of detailed explanations of the survey questions. The country survey staff were responsible for adapting these instructions to the country questionnaire and learned much in the process, quickly becoming familiar with the questionnaire. These instructions were used as a basis for course work and the trainees were expected to become well acquainted with the contents. It might be said that the instructions were too detailed and the constant reference to them during the training course did at times become somewhat tedious. However, the extensive elaboration of the questions is to some extent justified since the instructions formed part of the field staff equipment and were used as reference manuals to solve problems of definition occurring in the field. In this way, uniformity of question interpretation was assured even when the interviewing teams were spread across the country during the fieldwork period.

Of the 42 countries, six translated the supervisors' manual into the major national language (Indonesia, Iran, Republic of Korea, Thailand, Portugal and Turkey). The same countries, along with Nepal and Bangladesh, also translated the interviewers' manual into the major national language. The remaining countries used an international language for both manuals and Sri Lanka produced manuals in both an international and national language. Countries were advised to provide ample copies of all questionnaires, interviewers' and supervisors' manuals and control sheets. However, one common problem was the lack of time between the pre-test and main survey training. During this period the questionnaire had to be revised, and supporting documentation adapted. There were frequent delays at this stage because the questionnaires were not ready in time to be used during training. Problems also occurred at this stage when there were many language versions of the questionnaire. For example, in Ghana, some of the translations were unavailable for training altogether and the survey director was obliged to visit and brief his regional teams on their particular language versions of the questionnaire.

Some countries administered formal assessment tests during the course of training to stress the importance of dedicated work and also to ensure that the training was following the right direction. The importance of feedback from these tests was recognized and acted upon. Formal tests were given in all countries at the end of training, to form a basis for selection of the most suitable candidates. Individual performance record sheets were also kept during the course of training and practice interviews were marked. WFS had recommended two tests, after one week and one at the end of training.

There is no doubt that the extensive training as recommended by WFS provided substantial benefits in the quality of data collection, albeit an expensive enterprise. The three weeks recommended by WFS seemed to be a suitable period of training but perhaps the distribution of the formal course work and practical work could be re-organized. Too much attention paid to reading manuals is boring and counter-productive. The course work, although necessary, should be kept to a minimum, and demonstration interviews and role-playing introduced as early as possible in the course. Practice interviews in the field were most valuable, and the ten such interviews recommended by WFS could be considerably increased to great advantage. The training manual and the supervisors' and interviewers' instruction manuals contain much information useful to other surveys. However, because of time constraints, there were not always sufficient copies of this documentation, and of questionnaires, in particular, during training. The various techniques, such as role-playing and demonstration interviews, employed by WFS were extremely useful and easily adaptable to other survey situations.

15

Fieldwork

John Cleland
Chris Scott
Trudy Harpham

15.1 Introduction

The intention of this chapter is to describe briefly the main features of WFS's fieldwork strategy and to illustrate the practical problems with a few examples. Some aspects of this subject are discussed elsewhere and will not be repeated here. The logistical problems of multilingual surveys and the use of interpreters has been covered in chapter 6. A detailed analysis of callbacks on households and individuals to obtain an interview may be found in Marckwardt (1984) and response rates are documented in chapter 13. Other specialized aspects of field-work are analysed in the succeeding chapters which examine the effect of field-work duration on attrition of field staff and quality of response (chapter 16) and characteristics of the individual interview itself (chapter 17). In addition, detailed accounts of the practical problems encountered in the Fiji and Dominican Republic surveys may be found in Sahib, Navunisaravi, Chandra and Cleland (1975) and Ramírez, Tactuk, Hardy and Vaessen (1976); a similar unpublished report for the Ivory Coast has been prepared.

This chapter will focus on the team approach to fieldwork, logistical aspects, productivity, quality control and field editing. WFS was precluded by its mandate from conducting more than a few methodological experiments. This restriction applies with particular force to fieldwork and consequently there is little evidence by which to assess the efficacy of WFS procedures or to contrast one approach with another. Our account is thus more descriptive than evaluative in tone.

Perhaps the most remarkable feature of the main fieldwork phase in the 42 WFS surveys is that it was successfully completed in all cases. Despite a host of practical problems (climatic, political, financial, linguistic), there was no survey in which fieldwork had to be abandoned once it was underway. In view of the national nature of nearly all the samples, the use of female interviewing teams and the delicate nature of the subject matter, this is a remarkable achievement and says much for the determination of local survey staff and the momentum of the whole WFS programme.

15.2 The team approach

The characteristic which distinguishes most clearly WFS surveys from the majority of nationwide surveys in developing countries is the use of small, mobile female teams for the fieldwork. The reasons for preferring women to men have been outlined in chapter 14. The team approach was an equally fundamental feature of WFS strategy. There are a number of reasons for insisting upon teams for fieldwork in rural areas. Such an arrangement makes efficient use of vehicles, provides a measure of security for staff, permits constant supervision and facilitates communication with headquarters personnel. In metropolitan areas these advantages scarcely apply; here staff can usually return their completed work to a central office each day and live at home.

All but three surveys organized their fieldworkers into teams, at least for the rural sample. The exceptions were the three English-speaking Caribbean countries, with compact populations and good public transport. In these circumstances it was considered more cost-efficient to employ part-time interviewers working individually but visited regularly by supervisors — essentially the system used in developed countries.

A second feature which distinguishes the WFS from most other surveys is the emphasis on constant supervision and checking of fieldwork. As shown in table 15.1, the typical team comprised four or five interviewers, one supervisor and one editor, plus a vehicle and driver. This is an exceptionally low ratio of interviewers to higher level staff. The carrying capacity of the vehicle was the main determinant of team size. Most vehicles cannot accommodate more than six passengers , with their personal baggage and survey supplies.

Some important deviations from this model or typical team can be noted from the table. The ratio of interviewers to supervisory staff tended to be higher in Latin America than in other regions. This is partly because three surveys in this region (Costa Rica, Ecuador and Panama) had only one supervisor per team, who combined the roles of editor and supervisor. In these three surveys, and in Fiji and Sri Lanka, the typical team consisted of three (four in Sri Lanka) interviewers and a single supervisor. The interviewer:supervisor ratio was also invariably higher for the household surveys, where these were conducted separately from the individual survey. As the household schedules were much shorter than the questionnaires used in the individual surveys, less intensive supervision was considered justifiable.

The first column of table 15.1 reflects the fact that many surveys did not make a clear distinction between supervisors and field editors. The original intention explained in the WFS 'Supervisors' Instructions' (WFS 1975d) was that the supervisor would be in overall charge and hold responsibility for transport, accommodation, liaison with local authorities, location of selected clusters, collection of community data, assignment of work, record-keeping and general discipline. This person could be male or female, depending upon local conditions. The field editor was required to be female,[1] and was responsible for quality control of interviewing (which implies an ability to conduct re-interviews) and for editing of completed questionnaires. Clearly these two task definitions overlap and, in surveys or teams where both supervisory grades were female, the distinction was not always made, particularly in the Latin American surveys.

TABLE 15.1

Numbers and organization of field personnel

Country	Number of			Number of interviewers per supervisor/field editor	Number of teams	Transport (rural)
	Supervisors	Field editors	Interviewers			
Africa						
Benin	8	8	32	2.0	8	Cars, mobylettes
Cameroon	15	15	75	2.5	15	Landrovers, cars
Ghana	22		56[a]	2.5	10	Landrovers, cars
Ivory Coast[b]	10	10	30	1.5	10	Cars
Kenya[c]	34		85	2.5	17	Landrovers, cars
Lesotho						
HH	6	–	54	9.0	6	Cars, horses
Ind.	16		39	2.4	8	
Nigeria	30	30	128	2.1	30	Landrovers, boats
Senegal						
HH	11	–	55	5.0	11	Landrovers, cars
Ind.	8		20	2.5	4	
Egypt	25	25	94	1.8	25	Cars, jeeps, minibuses
Mauritania						
HH	4		16	4.0	4	Landrovers, cars
Ind.	8	8	32	2.0	8	
Morocco						
HH	8	–	40	5.0	8	Landrovers, cars
Ind.	8	3	32	2.0	8	
Sudan (North)	18	18	72	2.0	18	Landrovers, cars
Tunisia	12	–	24	2.0	6	Cars

Asia and Pacific

							Means of transport
Jordan							
HH	12		—	48	4.0	12 ⎱	Cars
Ind.	8		8	36	2.3	8 ⎰	
Syria	17		17	62	1.8	15	Cars
Turkey	13		13	55	2.3	13	Public, cars
Yemen AR							
HH	8		8	42	2.6	8 ⎱	Cars
Ind.	12		12	48	2.0	12 ⎰	
Bangladesh	12		12	55	2.3	12	Minibuses, landrovers, boats, motor launches, planes
Iran	17	16		40	2.5	8	Minibuses
Nepal	10		15	65	2.0	17[e]	Helicopters, cars
Pakistan		19	6	27	1.7	9	Public, landrovers
Sri Lanka				71	3.7	15	Public, jeeps, cars
Fiji	23		[d]	67	2.9	22	Buses, boats, cars,
Indonesia	22		22	88	2.0	22	Public
Korea, Rep. of	21		21	109	2.6	21	Public
Malaysia	15		8	59	2.6	4	Minibuses, cars
Philippines	36		36	144	2.0	36	Public and official
Thailand							
Women	10		10	60	3.0	10 ⎱	Landrovers
Husbands		35		70	2.0	35 ⎰	

Americas

Colombia	6		6	36	3.0	6	Public, jeeps
Ecuador	10			30	3.0	10	Cars
Paraguay	12			30	2.5		Cars
Peru	12			36	3.0	6[f]	Public, jeeps
Venezuela	10			19	1.9	5	Jeeps

Table 15.1 continued overleaf

Table 15.1 continued

Country	Number of		Interviewers	Number of interviewers per supervisor/ field editor	Number of teams	Transport (rural)
	Supervisors	Field editors				
Americas (cont.)						
Costa Rica	7		21	3.0	7	Public, cars
Dominican Rep.	6	6	29	2.4	6	Public, cars
Mexico	6	6	36	3.0	6	Cars
Panama	10		30	3.0	10	Public, jeeps
Guyana	35		80	2.3	Not used	Public
Haiti	12		24	2.0	6	Jeeps
Jamaica	12	12	52	2.2	Not used	Public
Trinidad & Tobago	11		40	3.6	Not used	Public, cars
Europe						
Portugal	8	—	40	5.0	8	Public, cars

a   Of which 45 were male.
b   Fieldwork carried out in two stages: (1) Abidjan and Bouake; (2) the rest of the country.
c   Survey was conducted in three consecutive phases in different areas, each taking 2.5 months, using the same supervisors but new interviewers for each phase. Personnel figures summed given here are total figures for all three phases.
d   Field editing done by senior staff.
e   Ten of the 17 teams were all-male.
f   Six teams operated during the first two stages of fieldwork but in the third and fourth stages smaller teams with four interviewers each were formed

Note: For countries where no distinction could be made between supervisors and field editors, the figure has been entered between the two columns.

Conversely, in countries where it was thought desirable that the team leader should be a man, the distinction between supervisor and editor carried operational force (because men were considered unsuitable for interviewing women on contraceptive and sexual matters) and was usually retained.

The feasibility of the approach used in some Latin American and other surveys, namely a small team with a single supervisor, depends upon the local cultural need for male leadership. Where such a need exists, the WFS system of dual leadership is essential if regular quality .control by re-interviewing and spot-checks is to be carried out. Where such a need does not exist, a single female supervisor represents a viable alternative, but is it preferable? The answer to this question depends upon two factors: the cost and availability of vehicles and the size of cluster takes. When vehicles are readily available at moderate cost and cluster takes are small, it is probably more efficient to use small teams with a single supervisor in each, because there is less likelihood of field staff being forced into inactivity while their colleagues finish off a few remaining interviews in a cluster before moving to the next selected area. This advantage of a small team diminishes as cluster takes become larger. When vehicles are scarce and running costs are high (and as shown in chapter 10, transport costs on average account for one-third of total fieldwork costs), the small-team model becomes more expensive than large teams with two supervisors, simply because more vehicles are required to complete the same workload in the same timespan.

While there is room for argument about the precise size and composition of teams, there can be little doubt that the concept of field teams was correct. However, they are not without their own particular problems. As already mentioned, a team approach is difficult to implement in metropolitan areas. For instance, in both Manila and Accra — and there are no doubt many other examples — senior staff discovered that the team structure had collapsed with the result that no effective supervision or editing was taking place. The ability of supervisors to enforce discipline was a constant worry in both urban and rural areas. When a group is in close contact for long periods, sharing the same food, sleeping quarters and transport, it is often difficult for any individual to impose his or her authority or to check and criticize the work of others. In more egalitarian societies when the personality of the supervisor or editor was not strong, the team hierarchy tended to collapse and standards of quality control to deteriorate.

The reverse problem also occurred. A strong supervisor who fails to grasp the technical requirements of the survey or to accept the need for high standards can ruin the work of a whole team. In Pakistan one supervisor was dismissed because of his counter-productive attitude and in Central Luzon province of the Philippines a supervisor lost the entire work from two clusters, which resulted in a complete reorganization of fieldwork in that province. In general, the poor performance of certain teams can be attributed to the inadequacies of the supervisor.

15.3   Logistics

In this section we describe the main logistical aspects of fieldwork: transport, accommodation and communication. As mentioned earlier, the team approach to fieldwork assumes the availability of a vehicle or other means of team transport, yet WFS itself was precluded from providing new vehicles for the survey. Thus a crucial issue at the survey design stage was to establish whether the executing agency possessed sufficient transport for teams and, if not, how the deficit could be overcome. The problems were often acute. In the poorer developing countries, the mobility afforded by a vehicle is a rare, greatly treasured and stoutly defended privilege. It can be seen from the number of teams in table 15.1 that typically six to twelve vehicles were required for the interviewing teams, in addition to the smaller number needed for senior staff to monitor progress. In many countries this demand for vehicles exceeded the fleet at the disposal of the statistical office and sufficient numbers had to be found elsewhere. On occasion survey funds were used to repair defunct vehicles and in at least one case spare parts had to be specially imported. More commonly, other government departments and provincial or regional administrative offices were persuaded to release a vehicle or two for the duration of fieldwork, on condition that all running costs were met from survey funds. In some UNFPA-funded surveys, vehicles were acquired from other similarly funded projects whose transport needs were less urgent. In other countries, vehicles were rented from a central government pool or from commercial companies.

By this variety of means, sufficient vehicles — landrovers, jeeps or minibuses — were found for the start of fieldwork but there were few surveys where subsequent breakdowns did not impede progress. To hold reserve vehicles for these emergencies is obviously desirable but proved to be a luxury rarely achieved. Teams had little choice but to sit idle while repairs were carried out.

Road vehicles were supplemented by other means of transport where necessary. Boats had to be hired in Bangladesh, Fiji and south-eastern Nigeria. Horses were used in Lesotho, and in Nepal helicopters were hired to place some of the teams at the start of fieldwork and later on to supervise progress.

The recommended WFS policy concerning subsistence and accommodation of field teams was essentially one of expedience. In most surveys staff were paid a fixed daily subsistence allowance and were left to find their own accommodation. This arrangement had the great advantage of administrative simplicity. The alternative of reimbursement against receipted expenditure would have been a bureaucratic nightmare, by comparison, and would have increased costs because of the inevitable tendency to spend up to the permitted ceiling. Furthermore, the fixed daily allowance was usually popular because it enabled staff to save money by exercising strict economy.

In some countries bedrolls or sleeping mats were provided out of survey funds but, more typically, interviewers provided their own sleeping gear. Similarly in a few instances cooking utensils were supplied to each team but more often field staff were expected to make their own arrangements.

Our general impression is that field staff did not often experience great problems in finding accommodation, food or water, though occasionally access to drinking water was cited as a problem. They either shared rooms in cheap hotels, slept in schools or community centres or were housed by private individuals. Often they were helped in securing suitable accommodation by district officials or village heads whose co-operation had been requested earlier by post, by radio messages or by personal visits. Indeed in many countries advance notice to local authorities was essential to ensure co-operation and failure to give it had serious consequences. Thus in Nepal a group of 30 households refused to be interviewed because they had not been officially informed of the survey. In one Nigerian cluster a team took five days to persuade a village chief to allow women to be interviewed. In the Dominican Republic illegal squatters were only persuaded to co-operate following the mediation of the local municipal authorities and in Mexico one rural community refused to participate in the survey, on the grounds that previous government surveys had brought no tangible benefit. This latter complaint was perhaps the commonest barrier to co-operation. Where communities are dependent on government decisions for vital facilities such as schools, health centres, irrigation and roads, it is understandable that resentment against apparent government inactivity may be strong and that resistance to government-sponsored surveys (with no visible benefits) may be initially high. However, as the high overall response rates indicate, these problems were nearly always overcome by tact and patience, occasionally backed by the intervention of more senior survey officials.

Apart from transport and accommodation, communication between field teams and senior survey staff is another vital logistical factor. The difficulties of achieving this varied greatly between surveys, depending upon the adequacy of telephone and postal systems, the road system, dispersion of population and nature of the terrain. At the beginning of fieldwork, teams were usually given a rough itinerary, or order in which selected clusters were to be visited, together with maps and lists of selected dwellings or households, but strict adherence to a predetermined timetable was impossible. As a consequence, senior staff had to have a good communication system to know the location of a team at any particular time. A number of devices were used in the attempt to achieve this. Some countries organized their fieldwork regionally with roving regional supervisors who could act as a communication channel. Others requested team supervisors to telephone or cable at pre-set times. Frequently, rendezvous were arranged so that senior staff could meet teams and discuss progress. Varying degrees of success were met. At worst, teams working in inaccessible parts of the country 'disappeared' for a couple of weeks. More frequently, imperfect communications led to temporary shortages of new questionnaires, delays in the dispatch of completed questionnaires to headquarters and interruptions in the payment of subsistence allowances or salaries.

In many countries fieldwork was undoubtedly arduous. Though transport was provided, accommodation and food were often spartan, the climate tiresome and distances to be walked within selected clusters long. Moreover, the interviewers, whatever their family background, were educated women, usually accustomed to the relative luxuries of urban life. In some surveys, harmful effects of these conditions on morale were anticipated and special efforts made to alleviate them. Thus in Peru, teams alternated between work in the rural areas and work in the capital, Lima; and in Mauritania certain teams periodically returned to the capital for the less demanding task of coding, before returning to the field. In several other surveys, teams were allowed one week's paid leave in mid-fieldwork, so that they could return home. In most surveys, however, no such special arrangements were made; instead teams were allowed to organize the pace of work according to their own convenience, within the overall constraint that fieldwork be finished within the predetermined number of weeks. Very often, interviewers found it efficient to work at weekends and official holidays and in the evenings, when respondents were more likely to be at home. In compensation, they rested on days when the rest of the population were at work and during the midday heat.

15.4 Productivity

Analysis of survey cost data (see chapter 10) implies an average of about one completed individual interview per paid interviewer-day in the field. This apparently low productivity is consistent with the (admittedly modest) rate assumed in WFS survey budgets. For costing of surveys it was assumed that an interviewer should be able to complete two to three households (schedule plus individual questionnaire) per day actually spent interviewing, but that a high proportion of elapsed time in the field would be spent travelling between clusters, resting or in other unproductive activities.

The data presented in chapter 10 suggested a wide range in interviewing rates among surveys, from over 1.5 to less than 0.5 interviews per paid day. Because of the high cost of the main fieldwork, it would be of great interest to examine the determinants of productivity and thus identify ways in which improvements could be made in future surveys.

These determinants are of two types: those that reflect design decisions and which can be quantified, at least in principle; and unquantifiable factors, unrelated to design, such as management and morale and the impact of external forces such as floods or public disturbances. Among the former are included: length of the questionnaire, policies regarding callbacks and response rates, the distance between clusters, the geographic compactness of clusters, the sampling density within clusters and the size of cluster takes.

Proper investigation of all these factors requires extremely detailed record-keeping in the form of team diaries and individual interviewer work records. This type of record-keeping was only attempted in two surveys, Nigeria and Ivory Coast; despite the limited nature of the evidence these two surveys provide a revealing contrast. The Ivory Coast survey records a high productivity – 2.1

interviews per elapsed day;[2] for Nigeria the rate was 1.0, which is probably close to the average for all WFS surveys. The difference between the two lies not in the intra-cluster productivity but in the time taken between finishing one cluster and starting work on the next. For Nigeria this mean inter-cluster interval is 4.5 days and the median 2.4. For the Ivory Coast, the mean is less than one. For Nigeria about 40 per cent of elapsed time was spent between clusters, while for the Ivory Coast only about 20 per cent was spent in this way. Distance between clusters cannot account for this huge disparity, nor were transport arrangements markedly different between the two surveys.

The Ivory Coast fieldwork was undoubtedly extremely efficient by comparison with the Nigerian survey, where local conditions are more difficult. But it would certainly be incorrect to attribute the entire difference in inter-cluster time to efficiency. The Nigerian fieldwork spanned the Christmas holiday when all field-work temporarily came to a halt. Difficulties of communication in Nigeria resulted in occasional shortage of supplies and lack of vehicles. These factors all contributed to the long inter-cluster gaps and to the lowering of the interviewing rate per elapsed day but yet cannot be attributed to laziness of the field staff or to ineffective survey management.

Nigeria is by no means exceptional in suffering disruptions to the orderly progress of fieldwork. Flooding brought a temporary halt to work in Kenya, Ghana, Pakistan and other countries. Political disturbance had the same effect in the Philippines, while in Ghana a political coup and a currency reform in the fieldwork period caused major delays. Among other disruptive factors were petrol rationing (particularly in the mid-1970s due to the increase in the price of oil), vehicle accidents, and temporary lack of funds. The general lesson is that serious disruptions in developing country surveys of the WFS type are the norm rather than the exception, and while it is impossible to quantify their effect on productivity, it is a major one.

The detailed documentation of fieldwork in the Ivory Coast and Nigeria is interesting in other ways. While there is no significant correlation between team size and productivity in Nigeria, there is a significant negative correlation in the Ivory Coast. This evidence, though slender and inconclusive, supports the commonsense expectation that operational efficiency is less easy to achieve with large teams than with small ones. Perhaps of greater importance is the significant correlation for both surveys between the size of cluster takes and productivity. The reasons for this relationship are made clearer by Marckwardt's (1984) analysis of callbacks. As can be seen from table 15.2, the number of successfully completed interviews usually declines in the last day or so of work in a cluster. This is partly a selection effect, whereby the less accessible and less contactable households are left to the end. It also reflects the difficulty of ensuring pro-ductive employment of all team members when there is only a small residue of households or individuals to be interviewed. Larger cluster takes imply relatively less interviewer time spent on these small residues and thus greater average productivity.

TABLE 15.2

Distribution of interviews and proportion callbacks by serial day in cluster

	Per cent distribution of interviews					Per cent of interviews achieved on callback				
	PE	CR	GH	PH	TH	PE	CR	GH	PH	TH
Two-day clusters										
Day 1	—	37	63	63	74	—	0	0	3	7
Day 2	—	63	37	37	26	—	9	3	16	44
Total	—	100	100	100	100	—	6	1	7	17
n	—	198	1248	1761	1516					
Three-day clusters										
Day 1	36	44	39	41	47	7	0	1	3	7
Day 2	35	33	45	36	39	5	3	3	11	23
Day 3	29	23	16	23	14	18	10	8	19	70
Total	100	100	100	100	100	10	3	3	9	22
n	171	215	1320	3467	625					
Four-day clusters										
Day 1	28	44	26	26	39	1	0	0	4	5
Day 2	32	10	36	31	35	3	0	5	10	9
Day 3	26	23	25	26	16	3	3	6	20	38
Day 4	14	23	13	17	10	14	10	12	26	58
Total	100	100	100	100	100	4	3	5	14	17
n	332	151	884	2006	385					

Five-day clusters

Day 1	22	10	18	—	27	—	0	2	2	7	—
Day 2	24	25	24	—	23	—	16	4	2	12	—
Day 3	32	30	25	—	23	—	6	2	7	29	—
Day 4	16	28	18	—	15	—	10	3	10	36	—
Day 5	6	7	15	—	12	—	17	31	8	44	—
Total	100	100	100	—	100	—	8	5	6	22	—
n	202	423	712	—	943	—					

Six-day clusters

Day 1	31	—	16	—	23	—	2	—	12	22	—
Day 2	29	—	17	—	22	—	0	—	6	30	—
Day 3	9	—	14	—	16	—	6	—	12	36	—
Day 4	15	—	25	—	16	—	4	—	5	38	—
Day 5	10	—	20	—	11	—	19	—	13	49	—
Day 6	6	—	8	—	12	—	21	—	16	61	—
Total	100	—	100	—	100	—	6	—	10	36	—
n	165	—	392	—	387	—					

Source: Marckwardt (1984).

Country key: PE = Peru; CR = Costa Rica; GH = Ghana; PH = Philippines; TH = Thailand.

It is also clear that productivity could be enhanced by accepting a lower response rate. If, for instance, team supervisors had been instructed not to remain for a further day in a cluster once the response rate had reached, say, 85 per cent, considerable increments in productivity could have been achieved. However, Marckwardt advances convincing evidence that this strategy would have introduced a non-trivial bias, because the characteristics of 'difficult to interview' households and women are appreciably different from 'easy to interview' ones. No doubt other means of accelerating the workrate such as allowing substitutes for households that are unoccupied at the first visit are even more dangerous in terms of potential bias.

15.5   Quality control

In the years before the WFS programme, surprisingly little attention was given within the demographic community to the problem of improving the quality of survey data at the point of collection. During this period much ingenuity was devoted to the development of analytic methods for adjusting defective data. To some demographers such methods must have seemed to offer the possibility of controlling a messy situation without getting dirty: there was no need to clean up the fieldwork if, instead, one could subsequently clean up the data in the office. Among the survey specialists a parallel development was taking place: emphasis was being put on the adoption of new data collection methodologies — the dual record system, the multi-round survey — rather than on the improvement of the traditional single-round retrospective survey. Some even went so far as to criticize any attempt to improve ordinary data collection as futile.[3]

The WFS committees and headquarters staff in no way shared this view and a decision was made to break sharply with the trend described. Thus the manuals defining WFS procedures give particular attention to the training of fieldworkers and the quality control of their operations.

The institution of a three-week training period was the first important measure in this direction; this has been discussed in chapter 14. The second was the use of verbatim questionnaires, translated into local languages, discussed in chapters 2 and 6. The third was the adoption of the team method of organizing fieldwork, reviewed in section 15.2 above, together with the inclusion within the team of a field editor with the specific duty of checking each day's work as soon as possible after its completion. This arrangement made it possible to feed back to interviewers information on their errors within 24 hours. In the best cases the influence of the team as a social group, together with the evidence of concern and interest in the work implicit in the editor's rapid reaction to error, provided a strong psychological basis for high quality performance by interviewers.

Obviously a field editor's document check can detect only certain types of errors: questions omitted, skip errors, simple inconsistencies. The WFS field manuals provide for four other means of quality control by team supervisor or editor: spot-checks, re-interviewing, listening to interviews, and tape-recording.

The purpose of spot-checking by the supervisory staff was to verify that the correct households and the correct (eligible) women had been interviewed. A fraction (to be specified in each country) of households was to be selected in advance for such checking and supervisors were instructed to add in any other doubtful cases. Female supervisors or field editors were further required to re-interview a minimum number (specified in each country) of respondents as a check on the responses, again including in addition any cases in which the initial interview raised doubts. Typically, such re-interviews involved the re-asking of a subset of questions rather than a re-administration of the entire questionnaire. These checks were to be made more frequently in the first and last weeks of the survey.

Finally, interviewers were required to tape-record a sample of interviews. Generally one tape-recorder was provided for every two teams. Their use was stressed during the first week or two of fieldwork. However, listening to tapes consumes a great deal of supervisory time and this check was not generally continued after the initial period.

In the best surveys, teams held a meeting at the end of each day's work, under the guidance of their supervisors, to discuss the results, the problems encountered, the errors noted and the progress made. A tape-recording of one of the day's interviews might be played and discussed, providing a combination of instruction and entertainment which could do much to maintain morale.

Were these measures actually implemented and did they contribute significantly to an improvement in data quality in WFS surveys?

On the question of implementation, the answer depends on the particular quality-control measure under consideration. Undoubtedly field editing was routinely, if not uniformly, carried out. Moreover, in a few surveys, special editing forms (extracts from the questionnaire designed to reveal inconsistencies and errors) were completed in the first fortnight of fieldwork in order to inculcate high quality-control standards. In Nigeria, editors were required to complete a short extract of each questionnaire which performed the dual purpose of an editing aid and a summary of key results which were processed and formed the basis of a quick preliminary report. Headquarters staff also spent much of their time in the field scrutinizing completed questionnaires for systematic errors.

The efficacy of field editing is more doubtful. The amount of time and effort involved at the machine-editing stage (see chapter 18) implies that a large proportion of errors remained undetected. The reason for this is clear. The checking of a complex questionnaire, often amounting to 40 pages or more, is boring but demands a high level of concentration. Such a combination can rarely be sustained for long periods and undoubtedly many editors lapsed into giving questionnaires a mere cursory glance. Furthermore, a wide range of skills are needed in order to edit properly. Most interviewer mistakes are obvious and consist of failures to follow the routine patterns of the questionnaire. With concentration these can be detected, and often remedied, with relative ease. But other types of error, involving inconsistency between different answers, are much more difficult to spot and some require considerable detective ability. A typical example is a combination of respondent's current age and the reported date of the first live birth which implies an impossibly young age at motherhood. Such inconsistencies often remained undetected in the field.

Despite these inherent limitations of the field-editing process, it would be foolhardy to advocate discontinuing this practice in future surveys. Misunderstanding of instructions by interviewers can be disastrous if not spotted and corrected early in fieldwork. WFS's editing strategy must have radically reduced such occurrences. However the designers of future surveys have an obligation to try to make editing less boring and more effective. A more widespread use of summary extracts might be a step in this direction. Even better would be the introduction of an addendum to the questionnaire to act as a self-editing guide to be completed by interviewers immediately after the end of the interview. This arrangement would have the advantage of allowing inconsistencies to be resolved with the respondent without the need for a revisit. Looking further ahead, machine editing using micro-computers in the field would make human editing obsolete (see chapter 19).

The other forms of quality control — spot-checking, re-interviewing, observation of interviews and use of tape-recorders — were much less frequently implemented than editing. Hard evidence is limited to two surveys where the use of these checks was recorded on the questionnaire and preserved on files. In Ghana, apparently only 3.3 per cent of interviews were spot-checked, 1.3 per cent observed and 0.2 per cent tape-recorded. In Nigeria, 2.5 per cent were re-interviewed and 1.1 per cent taped, though an unrealistically high level of spot-checking (37 per cent) was reported. It is likely that supervisory staff in Nigeria confused spot-checking with editing. In other surveys, precise figures are unavailable but it is our general impression that these quality-control checks were not commonly implemented. Revisits to a household are never popular either with field staff or with respondents. Furthermore, in countries where dates of events and ages frequently have to be estimated, discrepancies between first and second interview results cannot be readily interpreted. Yet another factor militating against revisits was mentioned earlier; in a closely knit team, it is difficult for supervisors to play the role of inquisitor, with its imputation of dishonesty by colleagues.

A few surveys, notably that in Bangladesh, made good use of tape-recorders, but they were not widely used for quality-control purposes. Apart from troubles with maintenance and batteries, listening to a tape-recording is a time-consuming process, and extraneous noise often interferes with the audibility of question and answer.

In summary, these quality-control measures involving revisiting households or listening to live or recorded interviews proved too difficult to implement on the recommended scale. It may be argued that the mere possibility of such checks acted as a deterrent against dishonest or shoddy work. However, internalized standards and the example of team colleagues (i.e. the team culture) were probably more important determinants of quality of work than the implementation or threat of these checks.

Earlier in this section we asked whether the extensive array of WFS quality-enhancement and quality-control measures contributed significantly to an improvement of data quality, compared to other data collection projects. At least a partial answer may be found in chapter 24. In general terms, the high quality of WFS data has surprised most demographers, and it is fair to claim that they are considerably more reliable than data from most other similar sources.

Notes

1. The few exceptions are noted in chapter 14.
2. The concept of elapsed day is close to that of paid day. Note that the Ivory Coast and Nigerian surveys were too recent to be included in the cost analysis of chapter 10.
3. K. Krotki stigmatized the WFS effort in this direction as amounting to no more than the 'Try harder!' strategy. (ISI Warsaw Conference 1977, discussion.)

16

Fieldwork Duration

Trudy Harpham

16.1 Introduction

This chapter examines the effect of fieldwork duration on other aspects of the fieldwork. While chapter 9 examines the timing and slippage of survey operations, including fieldwork, the present chapter looks at some of the repercussions of long fieldwork periods, namely, interviewer attrition and response decay.

Chapter 9 presents the arguments for and against a short duration of fieldwork which involves the use of a large field force. The arguments in favour of a *long* duration are essentially the arguments for a smaller field force, i.e. ease of recruitment of fieldworkers, ease of training, ease of control in the field and fewer vehicles required. Table 9.1 shows that field durations in the WFS ranged from about two to seven months, with few exceptions, and tended to be longer in Africa. The following two sections focus on two possible disadvantages of long fieldwork durations.

16.2 Interviewer attrition in WFS

Throughout the experience of the WFS the view was taken that it would be preferable to use female interviewers as some delicate and personal questions were to be asked of female respondents. Although most countries accepted this principle (Ghana and Nepal were the only countries to use some male interviewers), some national survey organizations were uneasy about the use of female staff in the field:

It was argued that women with the necessary education would not readily accept the hardship involved in fieldwork, that women would need chaperoning and finally that younger women interviewers would be unacceptable to older respondents while older women interviewers would generally be married and their husbands would object to their long absence from home, and this would lead to dropout. (Scott and Singh 1981)

It is now evident that, of these misgivings, only the fear of dropout, or attrition, was justified as many countries experienced high rates of attrition. Although it is not always possible to provide specific reasons for observed attrition rates it is possible to examine how the rates vary between countries and to consider the implications for future surveys.

The repercussions of such attrition are manifold, but can usually be measured in terms of cost of a survey. The cost of training interviewers constituted, on average, 16 per cent of the total cost of fieldwork in a country. If an interviewer drops out, the cost of training that individual is lost and extra costs are incurred in either training replacements or lengthening the fieldwork period. Use of replacements involves either initially training a surplus to constitute a reserve, or arranging a second training course when the need for replacements becomes apparent. In the latter case it is unlikely that the replacements will be given such intensive training as original interviewers and there may be a loss of data quality. If fieldwork is extended with a reduced personnel there may be reduced efficiency due to imbalance of vehicle/supervisor/interviewer ratios.

It is possible that observed attrition is a function of *unforeseen* prolonging of fieldwork rather than of a long *planned* duration and that it would be eliminated if interviewers were told at the time of their recruitment how long they should expect to work. Another consideration is whether existing government staff were used to carry out the fieldwork or whether special recruitment took place. Both procedures have their shortcomings: existing staff may drop out knowing that their jobs and salaries are secure, while specially recruited staff may be available only for a certain time and delays or changes on the timetable may cause major dropout. With the above considerations in mind, table 16.1 provides the projected and actual completion dates of fieldwork and indicates whether interviewers were specially recruited or government employees. Details are given for 19 countries which had sufficient data for the analysis of attrition rates.

In this chapter 'attrition' refers to unplanned dropouts. Although individual dropouts may have had idiosyncratic reasons for leaving the survey (for example, pregnancy, discord within a team, taking up other work, dismissal), there were a few instances of 'mass attrition' when problems were encountered in the survey as a whole and several interviewers did not return to work after a temporary halt in fieldwork. As such delays were unexpected, the consequent loss of personnel has been included in the attrition rate. Planned dropouts, for example, whole teams transferring to office editing or coding, or interviewers being promoted to supervisors, are, as far as possible, excluded. Although the promotion of an interviewer to supervisor reflects supervisor attrition, the present focus is upon interviewer attrition. Replacement interviewers are also excluded from the calculation of attrition and are examined separately.

The analysis of attrition rates addresses two distinct but related questions. First, by a certain stage of fieldwork what level of attrition is likely to have been reached? For example, what proportion of interviewers will have been lost by the start of the last month of fieldwork? Secondly, what are the monthly probabilities of attrition? For example, is attrition higher in the first or last months of a survey? Figure 16.1 shows diagrammatically an 'interviewers diary' with each line representing one interviewer and table 16.2 demonstrates how the cumulative attrition rates and monthly probabilities of attrition are subsequently calculated.

The date of dropout is taken as the day following the interviewer's last successful interview. If an interviewer stops work before the last month of fieldwork

TABLE 16.1

*Mode of recruitment of interviewers and planned versus
actual completion dates of fieldwork*

Country	Mode of recruitment[a] (1)	Planned end of fieldwork (2)	Actual end of fieldwork (3)	Overrun (months) (4)
Bangladesh (BD)	SR	March 76	March 76	0
Colombia (CO)	SR	July 76	August 76	1
Costa Rica (CR)	SR	Sept 76	Nov 76	2
Dominican Rep. (DR)	SR	June 75	July 75	1
Ghana (GH)	GE	May 79	March 80	10
Guyana (GY)	SR[b]	June 75	August 75	2
Haiti (HT)	SR	Aug 77	Dec 77	4
Jordan (JO)	SR and GE	Sept 76	Sept 76	0
Kenya (KE)	SR	March 78	April 78	1
Lesotho (LS)	SR	Sept 77	Oct 77	1
Malaysia (MY)	SR	Nov 74	Nov 74	0
Mexico (MX)	SR	Dec 76	Feb 77	2
Pakistan (PK)	SR	May 75	Sept 75	4
Panama (PA)	SR	Jan 76	March 76	2
Peru (PE)	SR	Nov 77	June 78	7
Paraguay (PY)	SR	April 79	May 79	1
Senegal (SN)	SR	Sept 78	Oct 78	1
Syria (SY)	SR and GE	July 78	Aug 78	1
Venezuela (VE)	SR	May 77	Aug 77	3

[a] SR = specially recruited; GE = government employees.
[b] Interviewers worked part-time.

it is assumed that she has dropped out, unless she belongs to a team whose other members have also stopped work, in which case the team is presumed to have completed their work. Wherever possible teams are identified on the diagrammatic representation of attrition rates.

Figures 16.2 (Africa and Asia) and 16.3 (Latin America and Caribbean) show the cumulative attrition rates by completed month of fieldwork for the 19 countries, and figure 16.4 is a scatter plot of the duration of fieldwork against the final cumulative attrition. Although the attrition rates vary a great deal, each country may be assigned to one of four groups exhibiting different patterns.

Syria, Malaysia, Colombia, Panama and Dominican Republic have relatively short fieldwork periods (three months or less) and achieve low final attrition rates (under 20 per cent). Kenya is also included in this group as fieldwork in this country was divided into three short cycles using different interviewers for each stage, so attrition rates follow a similar pattern, as shown in figure 16.5. Figures 16.6 (Colombia) and 16.7 (Panama) show the typical pattern of attrition in this group which averages 13 per cent by the final month of fieldwork. Note

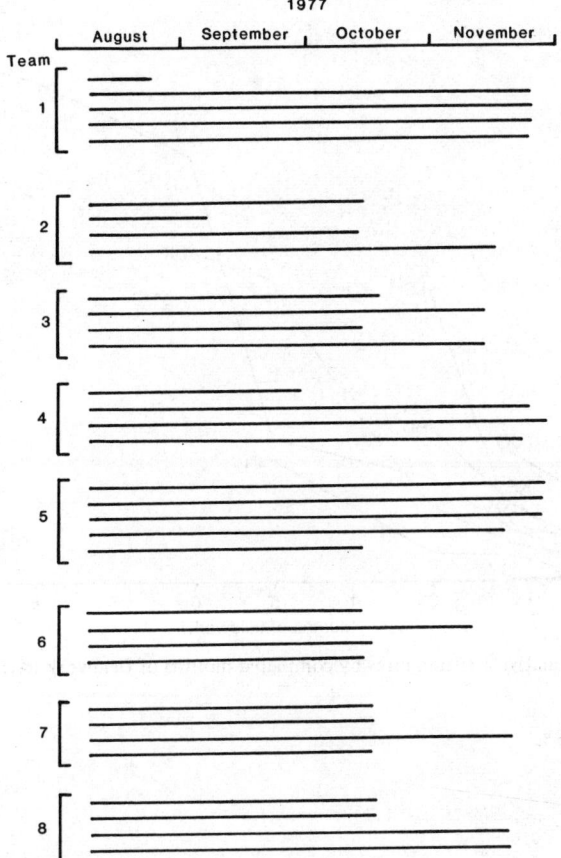

FIG. 16.1 Diagrammatic representation of interviewer attrition in Lesotho

TABLE   16.2

Cumulative attrition and monthly probabilities of attrition: Lesotho

Month[a]	No. of interviewers at start of month	Dropout during month	Probability of attrition $(3)/(2)\times100$	Cumulative dropout by end of month	Cumulative attrition rate $(5)/(2)\times100$
(1)	(2)	(3)	(4)	(5)	(6)
1	34	2	5.9	2	5.9
2	32	1	3.1	3	8.8
3	31	13	41.9	16	47.1

[a] From fieldwork starting date.

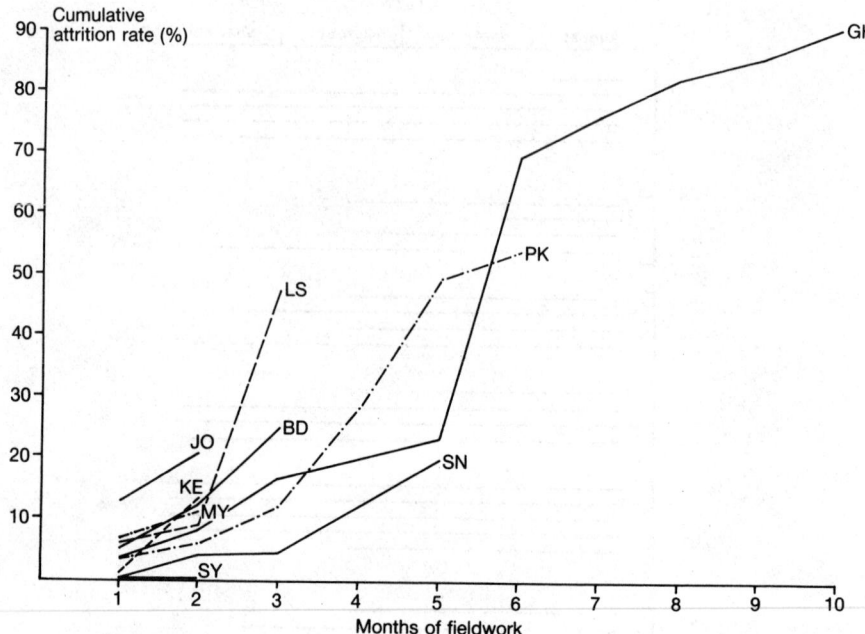

FIG. 16.2 Cumulative attrition rates by completed months of fieldwork (Africa and Asia)

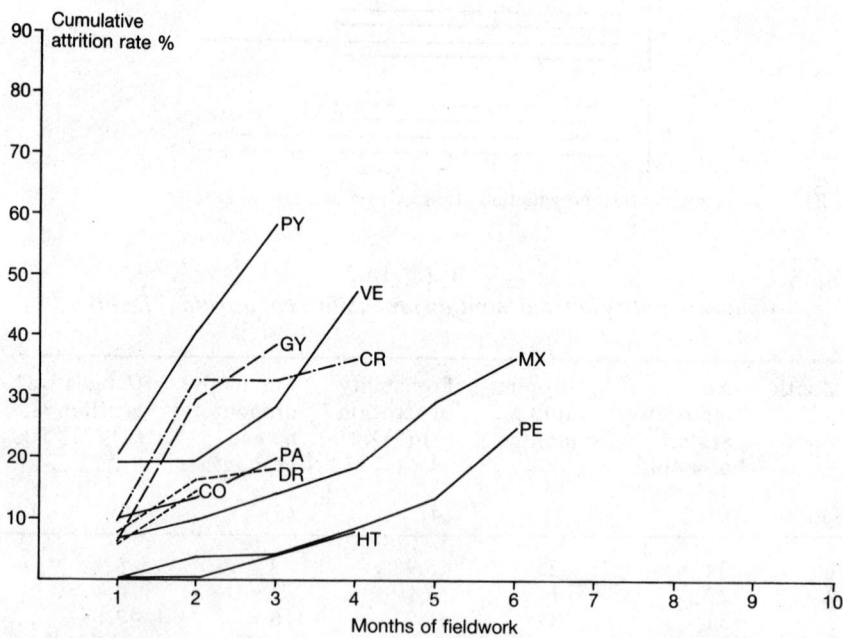

FIG. 16.3 Cumulative attrition rates by completed months of fieldwork (Latin America and the Caribbean)

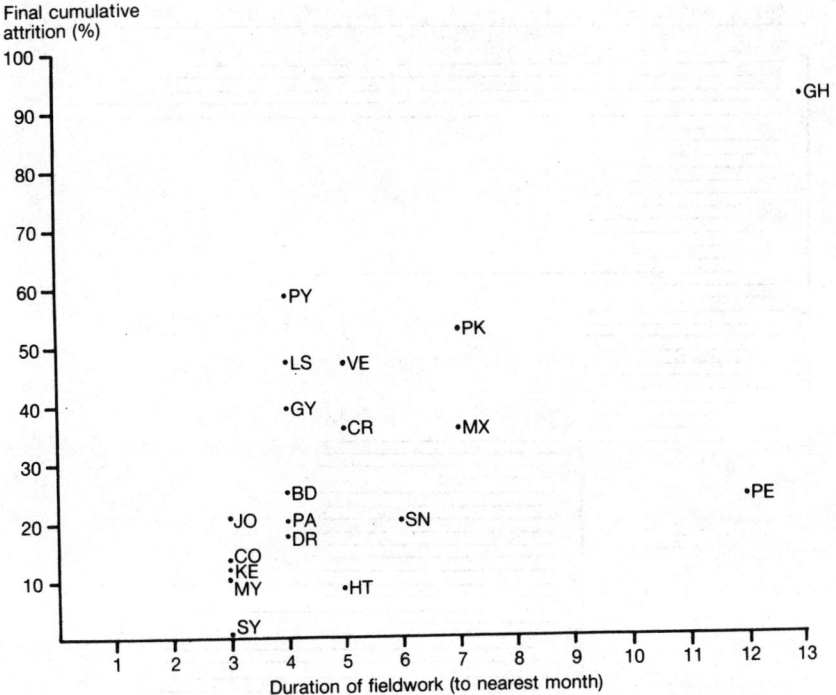

FIG. 16.4 Duration of fieldwork and final cumulative attrition

that teams 7 and 9 in Panama completed work early and are not included in the calculation of attrition.

The second group — Paraguay, Lesotho, Guyana, Bangladesh and Jordan — is also characterized by short fieldwork periods but all these countries have final attrition rates greater than 20 per cent and an average of 38 per cent. The extraordinarily high attrition in Paraguay was partly due to a whole team being dismissed due to the poor performance of one of its members. The dismissal of this team is represented in figure 16.8 by the six interviewers who simultaneously ceased work at the end of February. The attrition pattern of Lesotho is shown in figure 16.1 which demonstrates that many interviewers failed to resume work after a delay in fieldwork in late October due to difficulties in travelling to isolated regions of the country. Problems in Bangladesh are explained as follows in the First Country Report (1975):

The difficult circumstances in which teams had to work, in a social milieu in which females lead secluded lives, led to personal problems for some of the interviewers particularly for those who had left young children in Dacca. The interphase re-visits to Dacca helped somewhat, but their long absences and other uncertainties in the field led to a rather high drop out rate of 20–25 per cent during the fieldwork. (Population and Family Planning Division 1978)

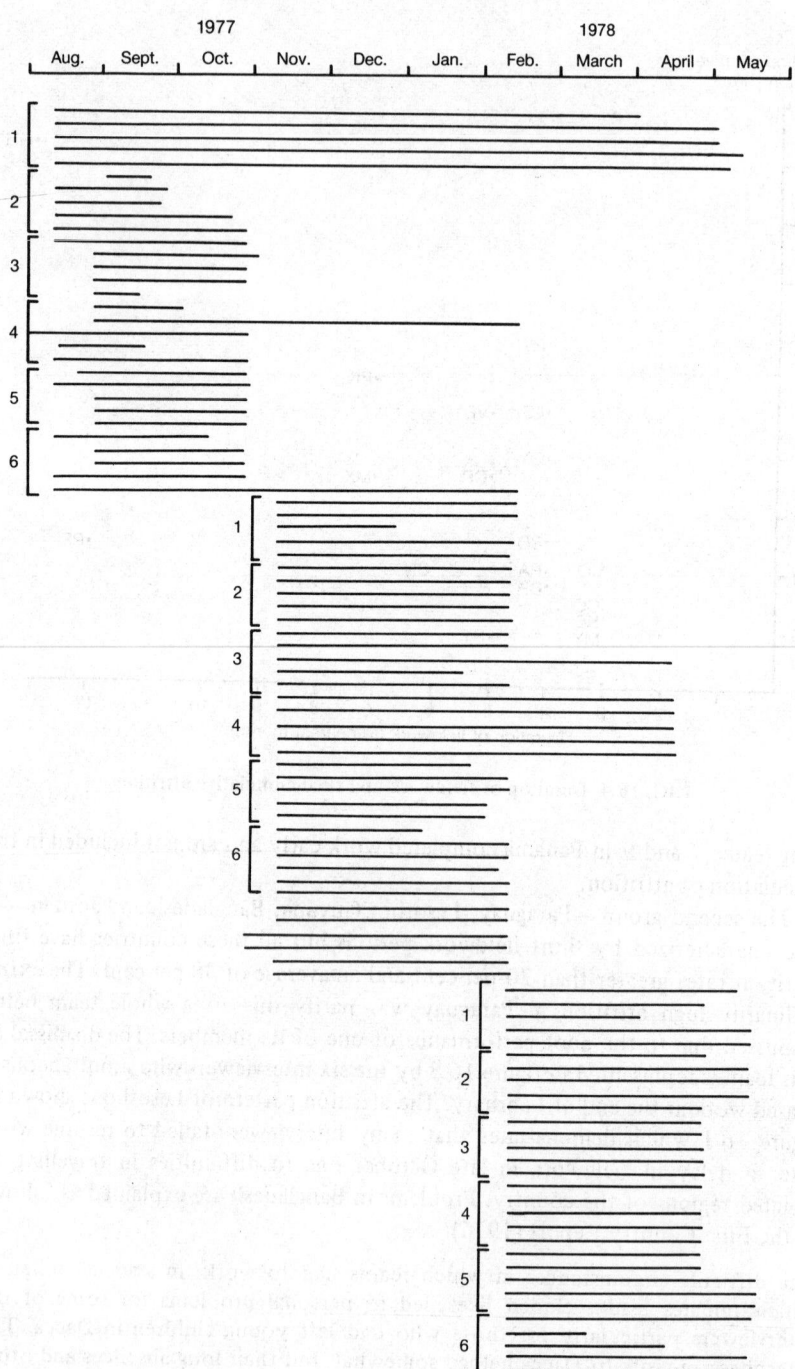

FIG. 16.5 Diagrammatic representation of attrition in Kenya

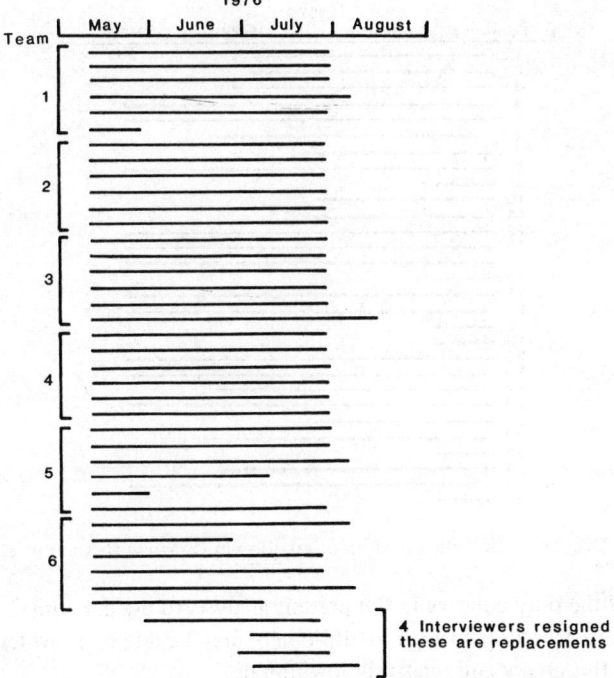

FIG. 16.6 Diagrammatic representation of attrition in Colombia

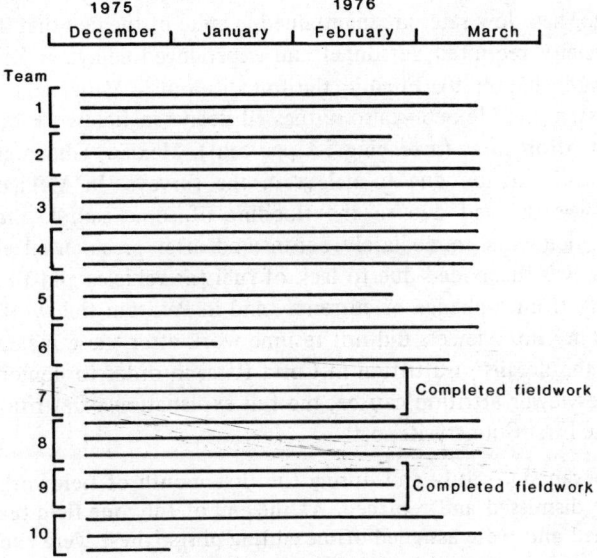

FIG. 16.7 Diagrammatic representation of attrition in Panama

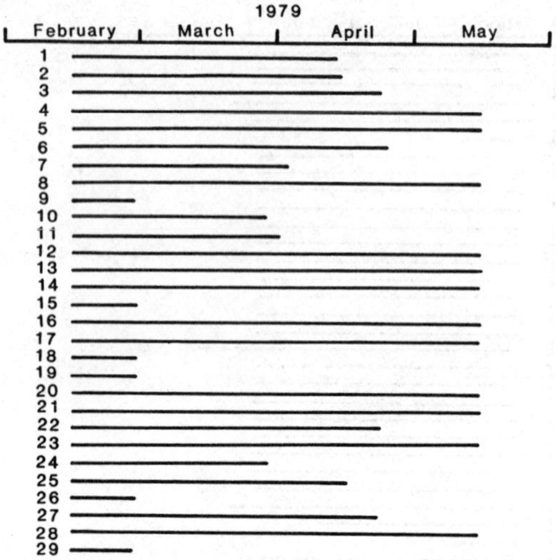

FIG. 16.8 Diagrammatic representation of attrition in Paraguay (teams not identifiable)

Guyana was the only country in the present analysis to use part-time interviewers with no team structure, so high attrition here may be due to a low level of commitment to the survey and relatively low morale.

In contrast to the two previous groups, the third group of countries — Haiti, Senegal and Peru — has long fieldwork periods, averaging five months, but maintains low attrition rates with an average of only 8 per cent by the final month of interviewing. These low rates are maintained in spite of the fact that the countries all used specially recruited personnel and experienced delays in fieldwork (see table 16.1 and chapter 9). Finally, the fourth group — Venezuela, Costa Rica, Ghana, Pakistan and Mexico — also witnessed delays in fieldwork but have very high final attrition rates (averaging 53 per cent). Mexico, Ghana and Pakistan suffered 'mass' attrition due to delays in the surveys. In Mexico fieldwork completion was delayed due to the flooding of some sample areas and the cessation of fieldwork immediately before and after presidential elections. In Ghana, work was suspended due to lack of fuel for vehicles and financial difficulties arising from a change of currency, and in Pakistan fieldwork halted for Ramadan. Many interviewers did not resume work after these incidents. Figure 16.9 shows the details of attrition in Costa Rica, in order to demonstrate how complex interviewer attrition can be; the full explanation of attrition is quoted here from the First Country Report:

Fieldwork began on 7 July and during the first month of fieldwork two interviewers were dismissed and replaced. At the end of July one field team dropped out as planned and were assigned office editing posts [these were excluded from the attrition rates but are shown in figure 16.9]. By mid-August there were five teams consisting of seventeen interviewers and six supervisors, and one supervisor

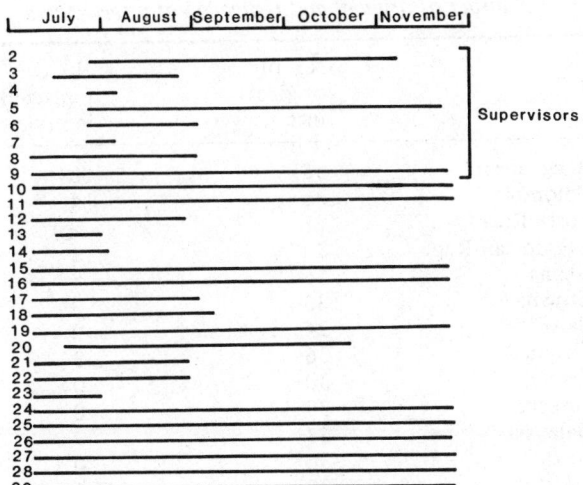

FIG. 16.9 Diagrammatic representation of attrition in Costa Rica (teams not identifiable)

and one interviewer had resigned. Towards the end of fieldwork one of the best qualified interviewers was promoted to supervisor and three supervisors and five interviewers were dismissed leaving eleven interviewers to complete the fieldwork. (Dirección General de Estadística y Censos 1978).

This description and figure 16.9 show that there were two replacement interviewers during the Costa Rica survey. The need for replacement interviewers can be an important consequence of interviewer attrition and the numbers of original and replacement interviewers are given in table 16.3.

There is no direct relationship between the final attrition rate in a country and the number of replacements used because approximately half of the countries chose not to replace lost interviewers. Also, the decision to replace dropouts depends at which stage of the survey attrition occurs. In general, if attrition occurs towards the end of fieldwork the remaining interviewers will be required to undertake extra work to complete the fieldwork. The Bangladesh First Country Report gives that particular country's response to attrition in some detail:

This [high attrition] rate was not altogether unexpected and to an extent we were able to plan for it. First, we had formed a reserve team — who filled in the vacancies. Second, until the first computer batch-edit printout was available, we could use the quality control teams. Third, we recruited female coders on condition that they should be prepared, if necessary, to interview. Thus there was never an actual shortage of interviewers. (Population and Family Planning Division 1978)

These details explain the high number (18) of 'replacements' in table 16.3 and demonstrate that replacement was easy in Bangladesh as reserve interviewers were

TABLE   16.3

Number of original and replacement interviewers

	No. of original interviewers	No. of replacement interviewers
Bangladesh	55	18
Colombia	36	4
Costa Rica	21	2
Dominican Rep.	29	2
Ghana	56	8
Guyana	35	0
Haiti	24	0
Jordan	36	2
Kenya	30[a]	0
Lesotho	39	0
Malaysia	51	9
Mexico	36	0
Pakistan	27	3
Panama	30	0
Paraguay	16	0
Peru	36	4
Senegal	20	0
Syria	62	0
Venezuela	19	0

[a]   For each phase of fieldwork.

trained at the beginning of fieldwork. If countries choose to replace dropouts and have not previously trained extra personnel the costs of the survey may be substantially increased in terms of technical assistance for training, and in terms of the quality of data since in this situation replacement interviewers rarely receive the same degree of training as original interviewers.

The need for replacements is partly determined by the stage at which attrition is most severe during fieldwork. In order to discover if attrition tends to occur at specific stages of fieldwork the monthly probabilities of attrition were examined. Table 16.4, which shows monthly probabilities of attrition by month and by country, demonstrates that monthly probabilities generally rise as the length of fieldwork is increased, from 4.5 per cent in the first month to 22 per cent in the sixth month.

Using these monthly probabilities of attrition the extra number of days needed to complete fieldwork, if no replacements were used, may be calculated. Let us suppose we need 10 000 interviews completed. If we assume that each interviewer completes three interviews each working day, we could choose between 60 interviewers working for three months (assuming 20 working days per month) or 30 interviewers for six months. With a short fieldwork period an extension of 6.6 working days is needed, whereas 50 extra working days are required if a long fieldwork duration is selected.

TABLE 16.4

Monthly probabilities of attrition by month and by country

Country	Month of fieldwork										Average[a]
	1	2	3	4	5	6	7	8	9	10	
Bangladesh	5.3	7.5	12.2								8.3
Colombia	5.5	8.8									7.2
Costa Rica	9.1	25.0	0	6.6							10.2
Dominican Rep.	6.9	7.4	4.0								-6.1
Ghana	3.6	3.8	9.8	4.4	4.5	59.5	23.2	23.1	10.0	50.0	20.2
Guyana	6.5	24.1	13.6								14.7
Haiti	0	0	4.2	4.3							2.1
Jordan	12.5	9.5									11.0
Kenya[b]	1.1	13.0									7.1
Lesotho	5.9	3.1	41.9								17.0
Malaysia	6.9	4.4									5.7
Mexico	7.1	2.6	5.3	2.8	14.3	10.0					7.0
Pakistan	2.9	3.0	6.3	20.0	29.0	5.9					10.7
Panama	10.0	3.7	7.7								7.1
Paraguay	20.7	26.0	29.4								25.4
Peru	0	2.7	0	5.5	5.8	12.5					4.4
Senegal	0	4.0	0	8.3	9.1						4.3
Syria	0	0									0
Venezuela	19.0	0	11.8	26.7							14.4
Average over month[a]	4.5	7.8	9.6	9.8	12.5	22.0					

[a] Unweighted average of the probabilities.
[b] Averaged over three separate phases of fieldwork.

To summarize, it may be noted that in the WFS experience, which is essentially confined to female interviewers, a 5–8 per cent attrition rate can be expected by the end of the first month of fieldwork. If a survey has a fieldwork period of three months the total rate may be kept down to 20 per cent. Monthly attrition rates generally rise as the length of surveys increases, so surveys lasting longer than three months experience heavy final attrition rates. The longer the planned fieldwork period (given standard work rates per day), the greater the effect of attrition on the total duration of fieldwork. Finally, attrition is exacerbated by any temporary suspension of fieldwork or other incidents which delay the completion date and extend the duration of fieldwork.

In future similar surveys it would be prudent to allow for a 10 per cent monthly interview attrition rate for the first three to four months of fieldwork and to expect a higher rate thereafter. It should also be realized that any delay in fieldwork is likely to result in mass attrition.

16.3   Interviewer errors

In addition to the costs in interviewer attrition rates which long fieldwork periods may incur, further indirect costs may result from variations in interviewer behaviour which will affect the quality of responses obtained.

Various characteristics of a survey have previously been acknowledged as factors which can cause response errors attributable to the interviewer. Interviewer errors such as differential probing and partial cheating have been linked to the structure of the questionnaire, interviewer instructions and even the place of interview. However, there has been little work on examining how duration of fieldwork affects interviewer response errors. A brief analysis of interviewer errors in WFS surveys which had long fieldwork durations is given below.

It may be supposed that, during an extended fieldwork period, interviewer behaviour may have various effects upon the quality of the data. First, there may well be a learning effect. WFS always laid great emphasis on the importance of field editing all questionnaires, and for this reason every fieldwork team had a field editor. If the feedback from the editor to interviewer is good, then the quality of data may improve with time as the interviewer learns not to repeat mistakes which have been detected by the field editor. Secondly, an expectation effect may develop through time. This may lead to a modification of the interviewer's behaviour and tend to cause any minority responses to be less commonly reported. For example, after a respondent declared knowledge of a certain number of contraceptive methods in the response to an open question, the WFS interviewer was required to probe for knowledge and use of every individual method which had not yet been mentioned. In countries where knowledge of few contraceptive methods is elicited, for example in certain African countries, the interviewer may tire of working through such a list when she believes that she knows that the normal response will be negative. In this manner, the minority response could be further attenuated by the failure of interviewers to administer the relevant questions properly.

A third hypothesis is that a general decay of effort may have an effect upon the quality of data. This is most likely to occur with questions which require detailed probing and where such effort is relatively unrewarding. An example of a variable which may be susceptible to such an effect is the number of non-live births. In most surveys, for every interval between live births in the birth-history section of the questionnaire the interviewer must probe for the occurrence of non-live births (i.e. miscarriages, induced abortions or stillbirths). Interviewers may feel that repeated, intensive probing on such a sensitive and emotional issue is difficult and fails to elicit any information; as a result they begin to omit such probing. Unfortunately, the reporting of such sensitive items is liable to serious omission if detailed probing does not occur in every interview; it is indeed clear that the number of non-live births in WFS surveys was under-reported. Another example of a variable which might be particularly affected by an attrition of effort is desired family size. In many African countries, when asked about desired family size, women often give a non-numerical response such as 'the number of children I have is decided by God'. It often requires probing on the part of the interviewer to obtain a numerical response and the effort put in to getting such response may decline over time.

In the analysis which follows, six variables were chosen which were derived from questions that were highly sensitive, demanding in terms of interviewer time, required careful probing or elicited minority responses. They are: percentage of dead children, number of non-live births, number of spontaneously known contraceptive methods, number of contraceptive methods known after probing, percentage of non-numerical responses to the question on desired family size, and age of respondent. The latter was examined in terms of the percentage of answers 'heaped' on the ages of 20, 30 or 40 years. The extent of such rounding effects is likely to reflect the degree of probing by the interviewer. As WFS fieldwork periods varied from two to fourteen months, the six countries with longest fieldwork durations, Cameroon, Ghana, Haiti, Mexico, Peru and Senegal were selected. The six selected variables were tabulated by month of survey for each of the six countries. In all analyses, the data were disaggregated into rural and urban areas.

At this point, possible confounding effects of two factors need to be discussed. First, interviewer attrition with consequent replacement of interviewers may tend to obscure response decay. This is because those interviewers who drop out for various reasons, including dismissal, could well be the worst interviewers. If such dropouts were not replaced, the quality of response might appear to improve once they had left. Alternatively, if replacements are employed, response quality might decrease due to the limited training that replacements sometimes receive. As the countries examined in the present study did not use many replacements it is perhaps only the former effect that is likely to be significant; thus any *improvement* in response quality over time should be viewed with caution as a possible artifact of dropout. Another possible confounding effect is that certain areas tend to be left until the end of fieldwork. Such 'peripheral' areas may exhibit idiosyncratic characteristics in the data; for example, outlying remote rural areas may experience more non-live births, a limited knowledge of contraception and so on. This geographical selectivity over time is partially compensated for by disaggregating the analysis into rural and urban areas.

The number of non-live births and the number of contraceptive methods known after probing were the only variables which exhibited a distinct trend in certain countries. Figure 16.10 shows the average number of non-live births by month of fieldwork in Cameroon, Ghana and Haiti. The number of women interviewed each month in these countries is given in table 16.5. It appears that, in these countries, interviewers may have become increasingly reluctant to ask sensitive questions about wasted pregnancies or gradually probed less when asking women if there had been other pregnancies apart from live births. Such findings correspond with those of Thompson, Ali and Casterline (1982) who analysed tape-recorded interviews from the Bangladesh Fertility Survey and emphasized that for all but the lowest parity women the pregnancy history was the most time-consuming section of the interview. It was found that as the fieldwork progressed, interviewers evolved methods of dating pregnancies which increasingly diverged from the format provided in the questionnaire. It is reasonable to surmise that the interviewers adopted these methods as a response to their frustrating experiences when following the requested questioning procedure (Thompson, Ali and Casterline 1982).

Figure 16.11 shows the number of contraceptive methods known after probing by months of fieldwork in Haiti and Cameroon, the two countries where there was a distinct trend for the number of contraceptive methods known after probing to decrease during the survey period. The trends in urban and rural Cameroon are not so distinct and do not involve such a wide range of values as the trends in Haiti. In the latter case the number of contraceptive methods known after probing ranges from 4.5 in the first month of the survey to 1.8 in the last month of the survey in urban Haiti, and decreases from 3.0 to 1.2 in rural Haiti. These figures suggest that the interviewers were possibly probing less on this question as the survey progressed.

The two variables which exhibited a trend of response decay in certain countries both required *repeated* probing. It appears that interviewers come to expect certain responses and consequently feel that intensive, repeated probing is futile. Where probing is only required once in a question, for example to a non-numerical response to the question on desired family size, it appears that interviewers are consistent in their behaviour over time, and no response decay is evident.

Although only some of the countries analysed experienced response decay and then only with certain variables, the risk of a fall in the quality of data collected over a long period of time is certainly one disadvantage of a long fieldwork duration.

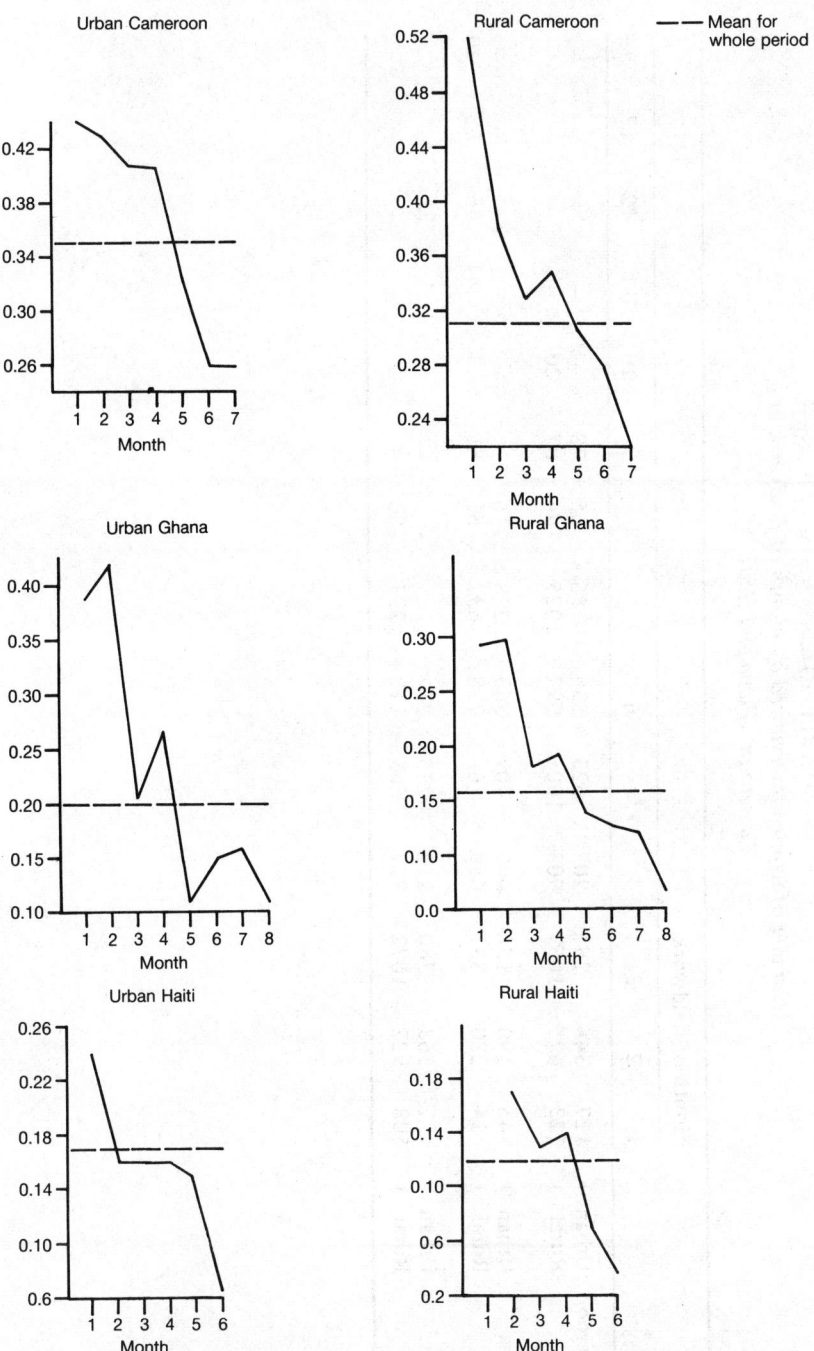

Note: Data exclude last months of fieldwork which were limited to specific areas.

FIG. 16.10. Average number of non-live births per woman, by month of fieldwork in Cameroon, Ghana and Haiti

TABLE 16.5

Number of women interviewed by month of fieldwork in Cameroon, Ghana and Haiti

		Month of fieldwork													
		1	2	3	4	5	6	7	8	9	10	11	12	13	14
Cameroon	Urban	127	346	262	207	523	539	56	65	78	—	—	—	—	—
	Rural	123	675	1057	903	1005	997	1025	124	87	20	—	—	—	—
Ghana	Urban	45	190	158	400	409	363	298	216	—	—	—	—	—	—
	Rural	14	280	331	689	768	778	632	61	81	23	241	46	62	40
Haiti	Urban	7	563	780	222	265	257	—	—	—	—	—	—	—	—
	Rural	508	922	1072	927	563	119	237	86	—	—	—	—	—	—

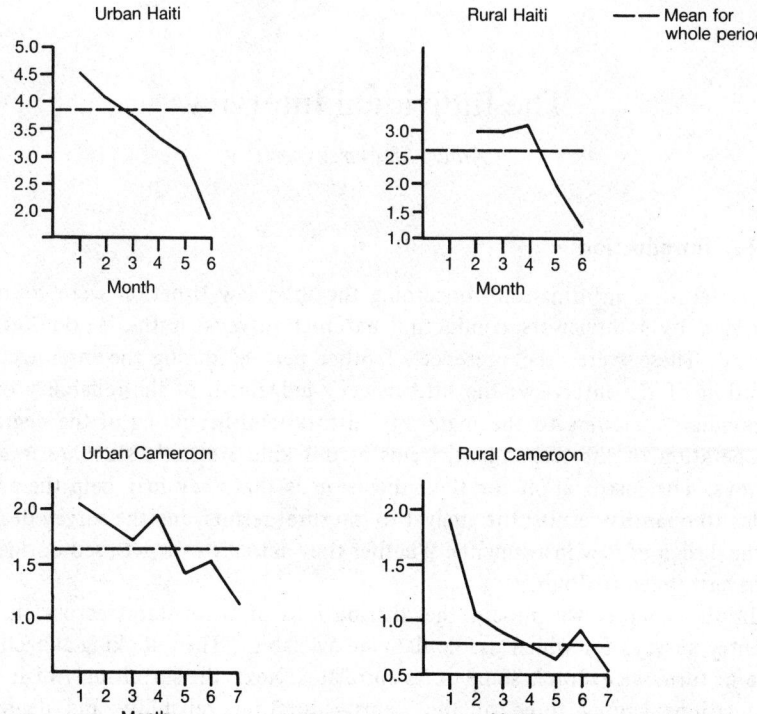

FIG. 16.11. Number of contraceptive methods known after probing, by month of fieldwork in Haiti and Cameroon

16.4 Conclusions

If a survey has a relatively short fieldwork period, say three months, and suffers no temporary suspension or other incidents which delay the completion date, interviewer attrition may be kept down to 20 per cent. In future similar surveys to WFS, it would be prudent to allow for a 10 per cent monthly interview attrition rate for the first three to four months of fieldwork and to expect a higher rate thereafter.

In the analysis of response decay it was reassuring to find that there was no evidence of decay for the two most important variables, namely dead children and age. Although it has been shown that decay is not inevitable, the risk of a fall in the quality of data collected over a long period of time is certainly one disadvantage of a long fieldwork duration.

17

The Individual Interview

Albert M. Marckwardt

17.1   Introduction

Four items of information concerning the interview situation were routinely recorded by interviewers conducting national surveys in the World Fertility Survey. These were: the presence of other persons during the interview; the duration of the interview; the interviewer's judgement of the reliability of the respondent's answers to the maternity history; and her rating of the degree of co-operation of the respondent. Items of this kind are fairly standard in social surveys. The justification for their inclusion is that they may help the editor-coder to quantify results; the analyst to interpret results; and the survey designer in the design of new instruments. Whether they actually ever get used in this way is, at best, open to doubt.

In this chapter we present the distributions of these items across all WFS country surveys for which usable data are available.[1] Then, looking at each variable in turn, we examine some of its correlates. Next, the surprisingly high inter-correlations among three of the items – duration, reliability and degree of co-operation – are examined. Finally, a brief look is taken at the utility of subjective interviewers' assessments in predicting objective measures of response reliability; for this purpose, some results from the WFS response errors project are examined.

17.2   Presence of other persons during the interview

Interviewers in social surveys are generally encouraged to try to interview respondents in private, on the assumption that privacy encourages more complete, truthful and accurate reporting. In the case of fertility surveys, the presence of others is assumed to affect detrimentally responses to both attitudinal items, such as desire for another child, and 'sensitive' behavioural items, such as contraception, abortion and sexual intercourse. The best interviewing situation has long been presumed to be one in which a relaxed air of confidentiality between interviewer and respondent is established (Cannell and Kahn 1953). This is reflected in the strict instructions given to interviewers in WFS surveys:

It is very important that the individual interview be done privately and that all the questions are answered by the respondent herself. The presence of other persons during the interview may make the woman embarrassed and influence some of her answers. Explain to her that some of the questions are private and confidential and ask her where is the best place for privacy (e.g. a verandah, a corner of the main room, a bedroom, or a kitchen). If another adult does not take the hint and leave you alone with the woman, you will have to use tact and ingenuity to attempt to get the respondent by herself . . .

Sometimes you may have to visit the house again at a different time, or make a special effort to seek the permission of some other members of the household, before you can approach the respondent. (WFS 1975b, p. 21.)

As a standard item in the WFS questionnaires, interviewers were asked to record the presence of others, usually at two separate points during the interview (point A, normally between the sections on maternity history and family planning; point B, normally between the sections on union history and fertility regulation). The item has five categories, coded in an ascending geometric order so that multiple categories can be ticked:

NO OTHERS	0
CHILDREN UNDER 10	1
HUSBAND	2
OTHER MALES	4
OTHER FEMALES	8

When summed at the coding stage, each combination of one or more categories assumes a unique value.

Privacy across countries

Information on the presence of others at the two points during the interview is presented in table 17.1. For the sake of convenience, the full distributions (16 categories) are not shown, but rather are summarized in terms of the original categories, and hence, add up to more than 100 per cent. Three notable features emerge from an examination of the table.

First, interviewers were generally not very successful in conducting unaccompanied interviews. In fewer than one-quarter of the countries were as many as three-quarters of the interviews conducted in private. Interviewers appear to have been particularly successful at isolating the respondents in Cameroon, Colombia, Ecuador and Paraguay, where over 80 per cent of interviews were unaccompanied. At the opposite extreme, in Tunisia and Nepal fewer than 20 per cent of interviews were held privately. To the extent that generalization according to continent is possible, greater privacy appears to have been achieved in the Americas than in Asia and the Pacific. The results from Africa are heterogeneous and defy easy generalization.

A second feature of note is that for most countries the category 'no others present' increases in size from point A to point B. This indicates increasing privacy as the interview proceeds, and suggests that interviewers were responsive to a suggestion contained in their instructions: 'Yet another way is to satisfy the curiosity of the other [third] person by reading out the early questions, then saying something like "So now you have heard a few questions, can you leave us to ourselves for a little while?"' (WFS 1975b, p. 21). Sizeable increases in privacy as the interview proceeded were registered in Sri Lanka, Thailand, Peru, Dominican Republic, Mexico and Guyana.

A third aspect of the table is the seeming implausibility of the variations it reports, that is to say, the presence of so many improbable differences between culturally similar or geographically adjacent countries. Examples abound: Ghana and Ivory Coast, Jordan and Syria, Peru and Ecuador, and Guyana and Trinidad and Tobago. These differences suggest the presence of survey-specific effects, presumably reflecting differential emphasis placed upon the necessity of obtaining privacy during the interviewers' training period. A heavy emphasis may have had two effects: to actually inspire interviewers to achieve privacy, on the one hand; or to encourage them to tick the 'no others present' box even if complete privacy was not achieved, on the other. We do not wish to imply actual dishonesty on the part of interviewers. In certain circumstances there may be considerable ambiguity about whether others are 'present' or not, particularly if they are just within earshot. To the extent that lesser or greater emphasis was placed by supervisors on the necessity of obtaining privacy, interviewers would be either less tempted or more tempted to interpret such ambiguity in their favour. For this reason, many of the large between-country differences in table 17.1 may not represent any objective situation.

Correlates of the presence of others

In examining the correlates of the presence of others here and the effect that the presence of others has on responses in the next section, we draw heavily upon Casterline and Chidambaram (1984). In a careful and detailed study, they examined data from 24 WFS surveys. Using multivariate analysis techniques, they investigated sequentially the correlates of the presence of 'someone', of the husband, and of other adult females, respectively. Perhaps their most interesting finding was the extent to which the correlates of the various 'presence' categories differed. In most countries, 'someone' had larger numbers of significant correlates than the two smaller, more specific categories. Generally, the presence of someone was negatively correlated with age, positively correlated with the number of living children, negatively correlated with years of education, and positively correlated with having a husband who worked in the agricultural sector.

The variable which best predicted the presence of the husband during the interview was whether or not he worked in agriculture, presumably because family farmers work close to their homes during the day, when interviews were normally conducted. The predictive power of the remaining three variables (age, living children and education) was much less in connection with 'husband' than with 'someone', and the directions of the relationships were often reversed.

The variable showing the strongest and most consistent effect across countries on the presence of other females was education, and the relationship was negative. Age was also frequently associated with the presence of other females, often negatively but sometimes in a curvilinear fashion.

TABLE 17.1

Privacy of interview; presence of others at two points in the interview

Country	Percentage of interviews at which other persons were present									
	Point A[a]					Point B[a]				
	No others	Husband	Other males 10+	Females 10+	Children <10	No others	Husband	Other males 10+	Females 10+	Children <10
Africa										
Benin	36.2	14.4	18.1	34.7	43.0	..... not recorded				
Cameroon	82.1	1.4	0.7	11.0	5.1	82.7	1.6	0.6	11.0	4.3
Ghana	38.0	22.5	16.5	32.9	37.5	78.5	2.4	1.4	12.5	6.6
Ivory Coast	76.4	2.7	1.7	13.1	7.6	..... not recorded				
Kenya	..... not recorded					47.7	3.4	6.0	31.5	32.1
Lesotho	69.3	1.4	2.3	15.2	15.5	72.4	1.3	1.8	13.2	14.0
Senegal	39.8	11.1	15.3	26.0	33.7	38.6	11.4	16.4	26.9	34.4
Egypt	79.2	2.8	1.2	8.7	11.6	77.8	2.6	1.4	8.4	13.4
Mauritania	50.7	4.4	3.9	23.1	32.8	50.1	4.9	4.5	24.2	32.9
Morocco	24.0	7.5	13.2	59.7	34.9	21.6	8.5	15.6	60.4	35.6
Sudan (North)	57.6	1.6	0.6	14.7	26.3	58.5	2.2	0.8	15.8	23.8
Tunisia	..... not recorded					16.5	12.1	9.4	54.9	59.5
Asia and Pacific										
Jordan	24.3	3.9	3.7	47.7	46.9	..... not recorded				
Syria	50.0	5.2	2.4	28.0	22.5	50.8	4.7	1.9	27.2	22.9
Yemen AR	29.7	5.2	5.6	39.0	34.6	33.0	5.6	5.7	37.9	32.2

Table 17.1 continued overleaf

Table 17.1 continued

Percentage of interviews at which other persons were present

Country	Point A[a]					Point B[a]				
	No others	Husband	Other males 10+	Females 10+	Children <10	No others	Husband	Other males 10+	Females 10+	Children <10
Bangladesh	18.4	....not recorded....[b]		[b]	50.8	45.8	3.4	3.7	33.3	33.5
Nepal	52.9	23.6		37.8	20.3	19.9	23.0	22.4	40.6	47.9
Pakistan	56.9	4.1	2.7	18.5	26.4	55.5	2.5	1.7	36.5	18.2
Sri Lanka		6.1	3.0			66.4	4.4	1.8	14.2	21.3
Indonesia	27.7	26.1	23.2	23.7	33.2	27.3	26.4	23.3	24.0	31.9
Korea, Rep. of	39.8	6.0	4.3	18.9	42.3	45.0	5.1	3.7	19.1	38.1
Philippines	45.5	11.1	7.8	29.4	22.7	49.0	10.9	7.3	27.8	20.7
Thailand	32.5	16.2	13.0	32.4	40.5	40.9	12.1	6.9	28.7	36.3
Americas										
Colombia	80.1	2.0	2.3	9.4	11.0	83.0	1.7	2.0	8.6	8.9
Ecuador	81.9	3.8	1.5	6.1	9.1	84.4	3.3	1.5	5.1	7.5
Paraguay	85.5	2.0	0.6	4.3	8.0	85.5	2.5	0.5	3.0	8.9
Peru	42.5	14.1	8.8	24.3	31.0	50.1	12.4	7.6	22.5	25.4
Venezuela	46.7	3.5	7.1	31.3	27.4	51.3	3.5	5.4	28.5	24.8
Costa Rica	67.1	3.9	3.5	14.8	18.1	67.3	5.1	2.2	13.4	17.9
Dominican Rep.	70.4	2.9	2.8	9.1	20.9	79.4	2.2	0.3	8.0	14.7
Mexico	45.4	8.4	5.5	24.9	33.5	58.4	6.5	2.8	20.5	22.9
Panama	55.5	4.6	4.4	12.5	31.5	57.6	4.4	3.7	9.6	32.1

Guyana	58.9	6.5	2.5	16.8	22.9	70.6	5.5	1.6	9.2	18.4
Haiti	74.5	3.5	5.2	10.0	12.0	81.7	3.2	3.5	5.4	9.6
Jamaica	54.0	5.3	3.3	21.2	26.1	59.3	5.7	3.0	16.5	25.4
Trinidad & Tobago	75.6	3.6	2.0	10.9	12.0	77.5	3.8	1.5	7.7	12.7
Europe										
Portugal	65.7	7.6	2.2	14.5	17.8	. . . . . . not recorded				

[a] 'Presence of others' was usually recorded at two points during the interview. Point A was in most cases after section 2 (the birth history), and point B after section 4 (the marriage history). The women eligible for classification varied from country to country, and within countries, from point A to point B. For example, in some countries, never-pregnant women were skipped over the classification at the end of section 2; and in many countries, never-married women were excluded before calculating the percentages.

[b] Data given as follows:

    Father-in-law or mother-in-law: 9.4 per cent
    Other males (adult):   20.5 per cent
    Other females (adult):   37.5 per cent

Note: In Fiji, interviewers were asked to note, at the end of the interview, whether the husband or other adult had been present during the interview. The results:

    Husband present: 6.5 per cent
    Other adult present: 15.0 per cent

Casterline and Chidambaram, in summarizing their findings, drew special attention to education as being the one variable most consistently related to the presence of others at the interview. They speculated that one effect of education is to raise the status of the respondent in relation to that of other household members, especially that of the husband and of other relatives, particularly female. It is this increased status and independence which a respondent can draw upon to gain privacy when asked to do so by the interviewer.

In examining the correlates of variables describing the interview situation in this chapter, we will restrict our attention to eight countries, one from each of the subregions of the developing world. This restriction is deliberate and is due to the sheer number of computations required, on the one hand, and to the fact that for many countries data on one or more of the relevant items are missing. The eight countries are Ivory Coast (CI), Morocco (MA), Yemen AR (YE), Pakistan (PK), Philippines (PH), Peru (PE), Costa Rica (CR) and Guyana (GY). They are not meant to be representative of the regions wherein they lie, but can be considered to represent a cross-section of WFS experience. Throughout this chapter the statistical model used is that of Multiple Classification Analysis (MCA) (see Andrews, Morgan and Sonquist 1969), regardless of whether the underlying distribution of a given dependent variable is binary, ordinal or interval. While this is a preferred statistical approach only for those variables whose underlying distributions are interval, the model does produce fairly robust results for other variables. Again, this is for ease of computation, considering the bulk of the data involved. The model is additive and essentially the same as the analysis of variance. The beta coefficients, italicized in the tables, show the relative importance of the selected predictors in their joint explanation of the dependent variable. An F-test has been used to compute their statistical significance (and we have indicated those which are significant at the 5 per cent level). The adjusted deviations for each category of each predictor are deviations from the overall mean of the dependent variable; the weighted sum of the deviations for each predictor is zero. These deviations are the same as the coefficients derived from multiple regression using dummy variables. The values R^2 at the foot of each table show the proportion of the variance in the dependent variable which is accounted for; they should not be interpreted as multiple correlations where the dependent variable is binary or contains very few levels.

In table 17.2 we have chosen to synthesize the approach taken by Casterline and Chidambaram (1981) and to look at the correlates of simply the presence of another adult during the interview. To homogenize as much as possible the relative risks of having someone present, the population is restricted to currently married women. Data relate to reported presence at point A. Once again, tremendous cross-national variability is evident: from 17 per cent accompanied interviews in the Ivory Coast to 66 per cent in Morocco. The table corroborates earlier findings on the importance of the respondent's educational level in enhancing the interviewer's chances of achieving privacy: this is the one variable that is powerfully and consistently related to the presence of another adult. The adjusted betas range from a low of 0.04 in the case of Yemen AR to a high of 0.21 for Peru. The coefficients for Peru tell us that, taking into account the other variables included in the model, the net effect of not having had any formal education at all is to increase the overall proportion of accompanied interviews by 12.9 per cent, while the net effect of having had 7 or more years of schooling is to reduce it by 13.6 per cent. Hence, the adjusted proportions of interviews at which other adults were present are 51.9 per cent for women with no education (39.0 + 12.9), and 25.4 per cent for women with 7 or more years of education (39.0 -13.6).

The only other variable included in the model which appears to have generally consistent and significant explanatory effects is whether or not the respondent's husband is a farmer. Casterline and Chidambaram found this variable to be the best predictor of the presence of the husband during the interview. Hence it is not suprising that it also predicts the presence of *any* adult. Tabulations not presented here reveal that the reversal in sign of the coefficients for Yemen AR and the Philippines is due to the fact that having a farmer as a husband is strongly and negatively related to the presence of other females in these countries, and to the fact that females are more commonly present at the interview than are husbands.

Our findings would seem to reconfirm that the correlates of the different categories of 'others' differ. Children are more likely to be present at the interview if the respondent has had many children; the husband is more likely to be present if he is a farmer. The one commonality, already discussed in detail, is the positive effect that education has on the probability of obtaining an interview in privacy.

Effects of the presence of others on responses

We have already noted that the presence of third persons is assumed to have a detrimental effect on the quality of responses given by the respondent. Casterline and Chidambaram (1984) found that reported knowledge and use of contraception '. . . tend to be five to eight percentage points lower, net of other factors, when a husband or another adult female is present during the interview . . .' (p. 34). But they hastened to add that this effect is not proof of the existence of actual reporting error, because the '. . . same [unmeasured] social factors which affect the respondent's roles within her family [i.e. her status] . . . probably influence her contraceptive behaviour as well . . .'.

In an attempt to explore further the possible effects of the presence of others on responses given to 'sensitive' questions, we have looked at the reporting of pregnancy losses. In table 17.3 the presence of 'someone' during the interview is entered into the model along with educational level, age, urban–rural residence, and the number of fertile pregnancies. (According to WFS convention, this latter variable is defined as the number of pregnancies a woman has had which have resulted in a live birth, plus the current pregnancy if the woman is pregnant.) As might be expected, the number of pregnancy losses reported increases with age

TABLE 17.2
Presence of another adult; betas and adjusted deviations

	CI^a	MA	YE	PK	PH	PE	CR	GY
Mean (per cent)	17.1	66.2	44.3	40.6	40.1	39.0	20.4	23.0
Age	0.05^b	0.04	0.05	0.01	0.04^b	0.06^b	0.04	0.05
15–24	− 1.0	+ 2.8	+ 3.7	+ 0.7	+ 0.1	+ 0.4	− 1.8^c	+ 3.7
25–34	− 1.7	− 2.3	− 0.3	+ 0.1	− 2.1	− 3.0	+ 0.2	− 2.0
35–44	+ 3.0	+ 0.2	− 1.4	− 1.0	+ 0.7	+ 0.8	+ 2.3	− 1.0
45 +	+ 3.1	+ 1.1	− 5.0	+ 0.8	+ 4.5	+ 6.6		+ 0.9
Living children	0.01	0.03	0.06	0.04	0.01	0.04	0.06^b	0.08^b
0–3	+ 0.3	− 1.5	+ 2.4	+ 2.2	+ 0.4	+ 1.9	+ 0.3	− 1.7
4–6	− 0.5	+ 0.8	− 3.4	− 1.7	− 0.3	− 1.5	− 2.6	− 1.8
7–9	− 0.6	+ 1.4	− 4.0	− 3.3	− 0.2	− 2.9	+ 0.3	+ 6.8
10 +	+ 2.3	+ 4.5	+ 8.5	− 0.9	− 0.6	− 1.0	+ 7.8	+ 7.7
Wife's education	0.06^b	0.07^b	0.04	0.06^b	0.08^b	0.21^b	0.10^b	0.10^b
None	+ 1.0	+ 0.9	+ 0.1	+ 0.8	+14.9	+12.9	+ 4.4	+17.4
Low	− 4.1	− 2.5	− 7.2	− 2.8	+ 2.8	+ 3.4	+ 0.1	+ 2.6
Medium	− 7.3	−19.1	—	− 1.0	− 0.6	− 7.8	− 4.1	+ 0.4
High	− 3.1	—	—	−11.5	− 2.8	−13.6	− 7.5	− 3.9
Difference in education	0.05^b	0.01	0.05	0.05^b	0.01	0.04	0.02	0.04
Wife more	− 1.7	+ 1.7	—	−13.1	+ 0.1	+ 1.5	+ 1.7	+ 0.1
Same	− 0.9	− 0.2	+ 0.1	+ 1.7	− 0.4	+ 1.7	− 0.4	− 1.2
Husband more	+ 3.2	+ 0.5	− 2.4	− 2.0	+ 1.0	− 2.2	− 0.6	+ 3.0

Husband a farmer	0.05^b	0.12^b	0.04^b	0.08^b	0.03^b	0.09^b	0.00	0.06^b
No	− 1.9	− 4.5	+ 1.7	− 3.2	+ 1.4	− 3.8	− 0.1	− 1.4
Yes	+ 1.6	+ 6.6	− 2.9	+ 5.0	− 2.0	+ 5.5	+ 0.3	+ 4.7
R^2	0.013	0.025	0.014	0.019	0.009	0.070	0.018	0.033

a See page 440 of text for explanation of country abbreviations.
b Variable significant at the 5 per cent level.
c Age groupings 20–29, 30–39, 40–49.
Note: The coding of the education variable is generally 0, 1–3, 4–6 and 7 +; for Morocco it truncates at 4 +; for Yemen AR at 1 +; and for Philippines and Costa Rica the coding is 0–3, 4–6, 7–9, and 10 +.

TABLE 17.3

Number of pregnancy losses reported (per 100 women); betas and adjusted deviations

	CI[a]	MA	YE	PK	PH	PE	CR	GY
Mean	41.6	28.1	29.4	34.8	40.1	34.6	57.1	70.7
Education	*0.06*[b]	*0.02*	*0.01*	*0.04*	*0.02*	*0.04*	*0.08*[b]	*0.09*[b]
None	− 1.0	− 0.4	− 0.1	− 0.8	− 1.6	− 3.9	13.1	20.5
Low	− 0.1	1.9	3.0	5.7	0.2	0.1	− 4.2	13.2
Medium	− 1.5	6.9	–	− 2.0	1.7	0.0	− 10.8	5.9
High	20.7	–	–	11.4	− 1.2	5.3	− 9.9	− 14.5
Age	*0.25*[b]	*0.14*[b]	*0.14*[b]	*0.14*[b]	*0.16*[b]	*0.15*[b]	*0.12*[b]	*0.19*[b]
15–24	− 21.2	− 13.2	− 9.7	− 15.7	− 16.8	− 14.0	− 14.6[c]	− 30.1
25–34	− 1.3	− 4.2	− 1.4	1.5	− 8.1	− 6.7	1.0	− 6.5
35–44	25.4	9.6	11.4	12.7	9.5	12.9	20.6	32.0
45+	35.8	14.3	20.8	9.9	19.3	13.6		30.6
Area	*0.06*[b]	*0.08*[b]	*0.03*	*0.03*	*0.02*	*0.09*[b]	*0.01*	*0.04*[b]
Urban	5.8	6.9	6.3	2.7	1.5	5.0	1.2	7.1
Rural	− 3.6	− 4.3	− 0.8	− 1.6	− 1.5	− 8.9	− 1.4	− 4.1
Fertile pregnancies	*0.06*[b]	*0.10*[b]	*0.19*[b]	*0.07*[b]	*0.11*[b]	*0.12*[b]	*0.21*[b]	*0.06*[b]
0	9.5	− 14.0	− 16.8	− 10.8	− 5.6	− 3.4	− 14.4	0.6
1–3	1.4	− 4.0	− 7.7	− 3.4	− 7.4	− 9.8	− 18.4	− 5.0
4–6	0.2	0.6	0.6	4.2	0.6	4.8	1.7	2.4
7–9	− 5.7	7.4	23.2	4.1	7.9	6.2	41.3	6.4
10+	− 13.5	11.4	23.4	5.8	21.8	19.1	44.0	25.6

Presence	0.03^b	0.03	0.03	0.01	0.00	0.01	0.00	0.01
No one	1.6	− 3.3	− 3.3	− 0.7	0.2	0.6	− 0.4	0.7
Someone	− 4.9	1.0	1.4	0.8	− 0.2	− 0.4	0.7	− 0.9
R^2	0.053	0.052	0.089	0.039	0.053	0.058	0.113	0.077

a   See page 440 of text for explanation of country abbreviations.
b   Variable significant at the 5 per cent level.
c   Age groupings 20–29, 30–39, 40–49.
Note: The coding of the education variable is generally 0, 1–3, 4–6 and 7 +; for Morocco it truncates at 4 +; for Yemen AR at 1 +; and for Philippines and Costa Rica the coding is 0–3, 4–6, 7–9, and 10 +.

and with the number of fertile pregnancies, and is greater in urban than rural areas. The effects of education are generally not significant. Most importantly, the presence of a third person during the interview appears to have no effect at all on the reporting of pregnancy losses.

In so far as Casterline and Chidambaram established a relationship between the reporting of contraceptive use and the presence of others, and since this could be obscuring the relationship with reported pregnancy losses, the ever-use of contraception is introduced into the model in table 17.4, while the number of fertile pregnancies is retained as a covariate. (The SPSS version of MCA permits the use of a maximum of five predictor variables.) The most interesting outcome of this exercise is the revelation of a significant and positive relationship between the ever-use of efficient methods of contraception and the number of pregnancy losses reported. This cross-national association lends credence to the hypothesis that the experience of an unwanted pregnancy will lead a woman to abort it, and to adopt thereafter the use of efficient contraceptives to prevent further pregnancies. But, once again, the presence of another person during the interview appears to bear no relation to the reporting of pregnancy losses.

In searching for other possibly 'sensitive' topics, we have noted the question asked of single women in Panama and Costa Rica, 'Have you ever had sexual intercourse with a man?'. After introducing controls for age, education, urban-rural residence and employment status, we surprisingly found a statistically significant and *positive* association between the presence of others and reports of sexual activity (table not shown). The presence of other females was particularly associated with reported sexual activity. But once again it is unfortunately impossible to disentangle whether the 'presence of others' influenced responses (i.e. bragging), or was simply a manifestation of the social gregariousness of the respondent, which in turn would presumably be not unrelated to her sexual gregariousness. In any event, while significant, the effects of the 'presence' variable were small in comparison with the effects of the other variables included in the model.

In tables 17.5 and 17.6 we complement the Casterline and Chidambaram analysis of the current use of contraception over our selected subsample of eight countries, first for the presence of 'someone', then for the presence of a male (other than the husband). They reported significant effects for the presence of the husband or of another adult male. Looking more closely at their tables, however, it appears that in only 10 of the 19 countries studied was the effect detected at the 5 per cent significance level. In our own analysis, two of the eight countries showed a significant effect for the presence of 'someone' but none for the presence of a male. It is clear that the effects are not found universally.

17.3   Duration of the interview

An item of information routinely recorded on the cover page of the individual questionnaire was the duration, in minutes, of the interview. Interviewers were normally instructed to record the time at the start and at the conclusion of the interview, and to work out the interview duration. In some countries the presumption was that all interviewers would have a watch in working condition. (The author's observation, based on experience in half a dozen countries, was that many interviewers did not own a watch.) In other countries watches were supplied or interviewers were instructed to obtain one. But other difficulties sometimes arose. In one country the differencing of starting and ending times was performed by the computer but no allowance was made for cases where an interview was initially left incomplete and only completed on the next visit, perhaps a day or more later. In some countries 'successful' interviews of only one or two minutes are not uncommonly reported. In others the number of 'not stated' durations is excessive. For these reasons, seven countries whose data seem unacceptably aberrant have been deleted from the dataset of 36 countries for which the data exist on the standard tape at the time of writing.

Interview duration across countries

Information on the duration of the individual interview for 29 countries is presented in table 17.7. For reasons of comparability, only data for ever-married women are tabulated. One aspect of the data is the tremendous heaping at five-minute intervals: in most countries over 95 per cent of the recorded durations were in multiples of 5. The most striking feature of table 17.7 is the great dispersion in the mean duration across countries: from less than 25 minutes in Costa Rica to 56 minutes in the Republic of Korea. While the overall average is approximately 35 minutes, six of the 29 countries lie outside the range of 25–45 minutes.

Factors affecting interview duration

An aspect of table 17.7 not mentioned so far is the within-country variation in the duration of interviews. The distribution of duration generally follows that of the normal curve, as might be expected. Women with few births or marriages to report can be interviewed very quickly, while those with long histories must be dealt with slowly and patiently. The Philippines, for example, with a mean reported interview duration of 52 minutes, had one of the longest questionnaires, asking approximately 180 questions of the average woman, while at the other extreme Peru, with a mean duration of 30 minutes, asked the average woman only 103 questions. The average of three or four questions per minute appears to hold quite well over a number of countries.

Some of the factors which influence the duration of interviews are examined in table 17.8. The variable having the greatest impact, as would be expected, is the number of births that a woman has had, with beta values generally around 0.30. The number of unions she reports is also significantly and positively related to interview duration. Education, when taken alone, is usually strongly and negatively correlated with duration. Even after adjusting for the other variables in the model, it is significantly and negatively related to duration in

TABLE 17.4

Number of pregnancy losses reported (per 100 women); betas and adjusted deviations (fertile pregnancies as a covariate)

	CI[a]	MA	YE	PK	PH	PE	CR	GY
Mean	41.6	28.1	29.4	34.8	40.1	34.6	57.1	70.7
Education	*0.03*	*0.02*	*0.01*	*0.03*	*0.02*	*0.02*	*0.09*[b]	*0.09*[b]
None	− 0.1	− 0.5	− 0.1	− 0.6	0.4	0.8	14.6	22.2
Low	− 1.1	1.9	3.3	5.0	0.8	1.9	− 4.7	14.2
Medium	− 4.3	7.6	—	− 2.7	1.7	1.2	−11.8	5.8
High	9.9	—	—	9.2	− 1.9	0.2	−11.1	−14.9
Age	*0.26*[b]	*0.13*[b]	*0.13*[b]	*0.15*[b]	*0.16*[b]	*0.14*[b]	*0.14*[b]	*0.19*[b]
15–24	−22.7	−12.1	− 8.3	−16.2	−15.5	−12.2	−16.5[c]	−27.9
25–34	− 0.5	− 4.1	− 2.1	2.2	− 8.8	− 7.1	1.1	− 9.2
35–44	26.5	9.0	10.9	12.2	9.2	11.9	23.1	32.2
45 +	36.8	13.2	18.8	9.8	20.5	14.0	—	32.7
Area	*0.05*[b]	*0.08*[b]	*0.02*	*0.02*	*0.01*	*0.07*[b]	*0.00*	*0.04*[b]
Urban	4.9	7.0	3.7	2.1	1.1	3.8	0.5	6.4
Rural	− 3.1	− 4.4	− 0.5	− 1.3	− 1.1	− 6.7	− 0.5	− 3.7
Ever-use	*0.10*[b]	*0.02*	*0.04*	*0.04*[b]	*0.05*[b]	*0.11*[b]	*0.06*[b]	*0.04*[b]
Never	1.5	− 0.2	− 0.4	− 1.1	− 3.2	− 6.0	−13.8	− 5.2
Inefficient	− 2.4	− 8.0	−11.8	− 1.5	− 3.7	− 0.7	− 1.8	− 5.8
Efficient	47.1	1.3	14.6	10.3	4.3	14.3	3.7	6.4

Presence	0.03^b	0.03	0.03	0.01	0.00	0.01	0.00	0.01
No one	1.5	− 3.2	− 3.2	− 0.8	0.3	0.5	− 0.3	0.9
Someone	− 4.7	1.0	1.4	0.9	− 0.2	− 0.3	0.6	− 1.2
R^2	0.061	0.053	0.092	0.039	0.056	0.067	0.113	0.078

a   See page 440 of text for explanation of country abbreviations.
b   Variable significant at the 5 per cent level.
c   Age groupings 20–29, 30–39, 40–49.

Note: The coding of the education variable is generally 0, 1–3, 4–6 and 7 +; for Morocco it truncates at 4 +; for Yemen AR at 1 +; and for Philippines and Costa Rica the coding is 0–3, 4–6, 7–9, and 10 +.

TABLE 17.5

Current use of contraception (per 100 exposed women); betas and adjusted deviations

	CI[a]	MA	YE	PK	PH	PE	CR	GY
Mean (per cent)	3.8	29.6	2.0	8.6	51.4	40.5	78.2	37.9
Education	0.21[b]	0.21[b]	0.16[b]	0.17[b]	0.23[b]	0.29[b]	0.11[b]	0.13[b]
None	− 1.4	− 3.7	− 0.1	− 1.7	−31.7	−17.1	− 6.6	− 7.3
Low	0.7	23.9	5.0	6.2	−14.1	− 6.7	2.1	4.0
Medium	4.2	25.1	—	4.0	− 2.2	6.8	3.4	4.6
High	17.2	—	—	17.6	11.8	20.8	5.8	8.4
Age	0.02	0.05	0.03	0.12[b]	0.06[b]	0.10[b]	0.09[b]	0.10[b]
15–24	− 0.4	3.5	− 0.3	− 3.6	− 3.9	− 8.7	− 2.2[c]	− 5.3
25–34	0.5	− 1.5	0.0	− 0.3	1.5	2.3	1.8	5.4
35–44	− 0.1	0.6	0.8	3.7	1.7	3.5	− 7.0	0.9
45–49	0.6	3.4	− 0.6	8.3	− 8.1	− 0.1		− 8.8
Area	0.03	0.32[b]	0.23[b]	0.16[b]	0.10[b]	0.21[b]	0.07[b]	0.07[b]
Urban	0.8	18.4	9.3	5.8	5.0	7.5	2.9	4.4
Rural	− 0.5	−11.5	1.1	3.4	5.2	−14.0	3.1	2.5
Fertile pregnancies	0.04	0.23[b]	0.11[b]	0.12[b]	0.21[b]	0.10[b]	0.23[b]	0.23[b]
0	− 1.6	−20.5	− 1.7	− 6.0	−46.4	−24.6	−43.1	−18.6
1–2	− 0.4	− 9.3	− 0.6	− 2.9	− 7.3	− 1.7	− 2.8	− 9.8
3–4	0.6	− 3.6	0.4	0.5	4.8	4.5	2.9	− 1.8
5–8	0.3	9.2	0.3	3.7	6.0	0.6	6.3	13.3
9 +	0.8	13.9	4.5	1.9	2.3	1.9	3.5	12.4

Presence	0.02	0.03	0.05	0.04[b]	0.00	0.07[b]	0.01	0.00
No one	0.2	2.6	1.0	1.1	− 0.2	3.9	0.3	− 0.2
Someone	− 0.5	− 0.8	− 0.4	− 1.1	0.1	− 2.9	− 0.6	0.2
R^2	0.051	0.237	0.105	0.117	0.120	0.220	0.067	0.057

a   See page 440 of text for explanation of country abbreviations.
b   Variable significant at the 5 per cent level.
c   Age groupings 20–29, 30–39, 40–49.
Note: The coding of the education variable is generally 0, 1–3, 4–6, and 7 +; for Morocco it truncates at 4 +; for Yemen AR at 1 +; and for Philippines and Costa Rica the coding is 0–3, 4–6, 7–9, and 10 +.

TABLE 17.6

Current use of contraception (per 100 exposed women); betas and adjusted deviations

	CI[a]	MA	YE	PK	PH	PE	CR	GY
Mean (per cent)	3.8	29.6	2.0	8.6	51.4	40.5	78.2	37.8
Education	0.22[b]	0.21[b]	0.16[b]	0.17[b]	0.23[b]	0.30[b]	0.12[b]	0.13[b]
None	− 1.4	− 3.8	− 0.1	− 1.7	−31.5	−17.8	− 6.7	− 6.8
Low	0.8	24.0	4.9	6.3	−14.1	− 6.8	2.1	3.5
Medium	4.2	26.3	—	4.0	− 2.2	7.2	3.5	4.6
High	17.3	—	—	17.8	11.7	21.4	5.9	8.2
Age	0.02	0.05	0.03	0.12[b]	0.06[b]	0.10[b]	0.09[b]	0.11[b]
15–24	− 0.5	3.3	− 0.3	− 3.6	− 3.9	− 9.2	− 2.2[c]	− 5.3
25–34	0.5	− 1.5	0.0	− 0.3	1.4	2.2	1.9	5.5
35–44	− 0.1	− 0.6	0.9	3.7	1.7	3.8		0.9
45–49	0.6	− 3.1	− 0.4	8.4	− 8.1	0.4	− 7.0	− 9.0
Area	0.03	0.32[b]	0.23[b]	0.16[b]	0.10[b]	0.22[b]	0.07[b]	0.07[b]
Urban	0.8	18.4	9.4	5.8	5.0	7.7	2.9	4.4
Rural	− 0.5	−11.6	− 1.1	− 3.4	− 5.2	−14.4	− 3.0	− 2.5
Fertile pregnancies	0.03	0.23[b]	0.10[b]	0.12[b]	0.21[b]	0.10[b]	0.23[b]	0.24[b]
0	− 1.5	−20.3	− 1.6	− 5.9	−46.4	−24.3	−43.0	−19.1
1–2	− 0.4	− 9.2	− 0.6	− 2.8	− 7.3	− 1.3	− 2.7	− 9.8
3–4	0.7	− 3.5	0.3	0.5	4.8	4.6	2.9	− 1.6
5–8	0.3	9.1	0.2	3.6	6.0	0.4	6.3	13.5
9 +	0.8	13.9	4.4	1.8	2.3	− 2.4	3.4	12.6

Presence	0.01	0.01	0.02	0.02	0.01	0.00	0.01	0.01
No male[d]	0.0	− 0.1	0.1	0.1	0.2	0.0	− 0.1	− 0.1
Male[d]	1.0	0.6	− 0.9	− 2.6	− 2.0	− 0.1	2.1	3.9
R^2	0.051	0.237	0.103	0.116	0.120	0.215	0.067	0.059

a See page 440 of text for explanation of country abbreviations.
b Variable significant at the 5 per cent level.
c Age groupings 20–29, 30–39, 40–49.
d Male other than husband.

Note: The coding of the education variable is generally 0, 1–3, 4–6 and 7 +; for Morocco it truncates at 4 +; for Yemen AR at 1 +; and for Philippines and Costa Rica the coding is 0–3, 4–6, 7–9, and 10 +.

TABLE 17.7

Duration of the individual interview: per cent distribution of ever-married women only

Country	15 mins. or less	20–30 mins.	35–45 mins.	50–60 mins.	65–75 mins.	80 mins. or more	Not stated	Mean mins.	Number of interviews (100 per cent)
Africa									
Benin	16.4	37.1	20.5	8.8	3.8	6.2	7.2	34.6	3577
Ghana	5.2	26.0	24.9	27.7	7.2	8.2	0.8	46.8	4943
Ivory Coast	6.3	35.1	34.4	13.3	3.8	2.0	5.2	36.9	4990
Kenya	9.2	50.2	25.6	10.2	2.3	2.0	0.5	33.8	6241
Egypt	3.3	38.0	29.7	25.1	2.7	0.4	0.8	40.6	8788
Morocco	22.0	57.5	14.0	4.7	1.0	0.3	0.5	27.1	4105
Sudan (North)	16.3	54.3	16.8	9.0	1.3	2.4	0.0	31.3	3115
Asia and Pacific									
Syria	16.6	56.6	10.0	7.8	5.7	3.2	0.1	33.1	4487
Bangladesh	0.4	8.9	23.6	38.3	15.5	10.5	2.8	55.4	6504
Pakistan	12.9	61.1	21.5	3.3	0.6	0.5	0.0	29.2	4952
Sri Lanka	0.4	13.3	34.7	29.6	14.1	7.7	0.1	52.7	6810
Fiji	2.3	34.3	38.9	17.9	3.3	2.4	1.1	40.1	4928
Indonesia	1.5	37.0	46.6	11.9	2.2	0.8	0.2	37.0	9155
Korea, Rep. of	1.1	6.7	27.2	33.3	18.9	12.4	0.4	56.1	5430
Philippines	0.0	10.0	37.8	34.3	9.3	8.7	0.0	51.6	9268
Thailand	19.8	61.4	15.8	2.2	0.4	0.1	0.3	25.4	3820

Americas									
Colombia	7.1	61.1	24.5	4.8	0.8	0.5	1.1	30.7	3302
Ecuador	23.9	58.7	14.4	2.5	0.2	0.1	0.2	25.0	4408
Paraguay	5.6	57.6	30.6	3.8	0.4	0.1	1.9	31.4	2997
Peru	9.8	61.8	22.7	4.3	0.5	0.2	0.7	29.6	5640
Venezuela	15.8	59.3	19.1	4.1	0.8	0.3	0.6	29.0	2716
Costa Rica	26.3	54.4	14.7	3.0	0.6	0.2	0.8	24.8	3037
Dominican Rep.	7.4	54.5	26.2	8.9	2.0	0.6	0.4	32.2	2257
Mexico	7.3	51.3	29.7	9.0	2.1	0.7	0.0	32.4	6255
Panama	18.9	64.1	14.1	2.1	0.6	0.0	0.2	25.4	3203
Guyana	14.0	58.4	20.6	3.2	0.0	3.4	0.3	26.9	3616
Jamaica	3.2	34.8	29.8	20.5	5.1	4.8	1.8	42.7	2766
Trinidad & Tobago	3.3	47.3	36.0	10.7	1.9	0.7	0.0	34.7	3468
Europe									
Portugal	19.2	64.2	13.3	2.4	0.4	0.1	0.4	25.6	5148

Notes:

(i) For the sake of comparability between surveys, data are confined to interviews with ever-married women.

(ii) Because of heavy heaping, durations were rounded to the nearest 5 minutes during processing. Thus, for example, '15 mins or less' means ⩽17 mins; and '20–30 mins' means 18–32 mins.

TABLE 17.8

Length of interview (minutes); betas and adjusted deviations

	CI[a]	MA	PK	PH	PE	CR	GY
Mean (per cent)	36.9	27.1	29.2	51.6	29.6	24.8	26.9
Unions	*0.09*[b]	*0.09*[b]	*0.05*[b]	*0.03*[b]	*0.09*[b]	*0.08*[b]	*0.13*[b]
1	− 0.7	− 0.4	− 0.1	− 0.1	− 0.3	− 0.3	− 1.0
2	+ 2.2	+ 1.9	+ 2.6	+ 1.4	+ 1.9	+ 2.6	+ 0.6
3 +	+ 5.5	+ 4.6	+ 4.8	+ 7.4	+ 4.0	+ 4.8	+ 2.5
Births	*0.32*[b]	*0.32*[b]	*0.38*[b]	*0.16*[b]	*0.21*[b]	*0.29*[b]	*0.31*[b]
0	− 9.3	− 7.8	− 5.9	− 5.3	− 5.1	− 6.3	− 4.5
1–3	− 2.3	− 2.3	− 3.1	− 2.2	− 1.7	− 1.6	− 1.5
4–6	+ 2.4	+ 1.8	+ 1.9	+ 1.2	+ 0.6	+ 0.6	+ 1.0
7–9	+ 6.1	+ 3.9	+ 4.4	+ 1.8	+ 2.1	+ 2.0	+ 3.2
10 +	+10.3	+ 4.3	+ 8.2	+ 6.0	+ 4.4	+ 7.8	+ 7.8
Education	*0.09*[b]	*0.09*[b]	*0.05*[b]	*0.11*[b]	*0.12*[b]	*0.04*	*0.09*[b]
None	− 0.5	− 0.4	+ 0.2	+ 6.4	+ 1.8	+ 0.2	+ 1.2
Low	+ 0.7	+ 2.1	− 1.5	+ 1.5	− 0.4	− 0.3	+ 0.8
Medium	+ 1.9	+ 4.1	− 0.9	− 0.5	− 0.8	+ 1.1	+ 0.6
High	+ 5.6	—	− 1.8	− 1.1	− 1.1	− 0.3	− 1.1

Work	*0.03*	*0.08*[b]	*0.01*	*0.06*[b]	*0.10*[b]	*0.14*[b]	*0.06*[b]
None	+ 1.2	− 0.5	+ 0.1	− 1.2	− 2.1	− 2.4	− 0.7
Before or after marriage	− 0.2	+ 2.3	− 0.3	+ 0.7	+ 0.1	− 0.1	+ 0.1
Before and after marriage	− 0.2	+ 0.1	− 0.2	+ 0.7	+ 0.7	+ 1.8	+ 0.7
Presence of others	*0.08*[b]	*0.03*	*0.03*	*0.07*[b]	*0.03*	*0.10*[b]	*0.00*
No one	− 0.7	+ 0.4	− 0.2	− 1.0	− 0.4	− 0.7	0.0
Someone	+ 2.2	− 0.1	+ 0.2	+ 0.7	+ 0.3	+ 1.4	0.0
R^2	0.124	0.113	0.154	0.053	0.109	0.128	0.146

[a] See page 440 of text for explanation of country abbreviations.
[b] Variable significant at the 5 per cent level.
Note: The coding of the education variable is generally 0, 1–3, 4–6 and 7 +; for Morocco it truncates at 4 +; and for Philippines and Costa Rica the coding is 0–3, 4–6, 7–9, and 10 +.

four of the seven countries. The interesting exceptions are the Ivory Coast and Morocco. Perhaps in these countries the interviewers are so excited when they come across an educated woman that they linger to chat after completing the interview.

The work experience of the respondents, i.e. never, before or after marriage, or both before and after marriage, is only weakly associated with interview duration; it is statistically significant in only five of the seven countries. Of even less importance is whether or not someone else is present during the interview. But in the three countries where this variable has a significant effect, the presence of others can add up to three minutes to the length of interviews.

Perhaps the best way of summing up the effects noted in table 17.8 is to characterize women as being easy, difficult or very difficult to interview in terms of the lengths of their respective histories. Such a presentation is given in table 17.9. In general, women with long histories take about 20 minutes longer to interview than women with little history to report. It should be kept in mind, however, that with these variables we have explained, on average, only about 10 per cent of the variance in duration. A large amount of the variance is undoubtedly attributable to interviewer effects, a subject beyond the scope of this chapter.

17.4   Interviewer's judgement of the reliability of fertility data

After completing section 2 of the questionnaire, which deals with the maternity history, the interviewer was requested to tick a box representing her judgement of the reliability of the information given by the respondent. The guidelines given to interviewers were specific:

If the respondent was able to answer most of the questions with ease and directly, if dates (months and years) of all the births and pregnancies were obtained without difficulty . . . and if you did not correct any totals . . . tick the box for GOOD . . . .

On the other hand, if you had to do considerable probing for determination of the dates of births and pregnancies, or if you had to correct the [totals] . . . and, in general, if you had the impression that the respondent was not herself sure of many answers she gave, tick the POOR box. Occasionally you may come to the conclusion that the respondent is not properly telling the truth: in that case also tick the POOR box. For other cases, where a moderate amount of probing or correcting of answers was required, tick the FAIR box. (WFS 1975b, p. 57.)

Certainly most, if not all, of the locally adapted interviewers' manuals cited these instructions virtually verbatim.

Reliability across countries

The distribution of the interviewers' ratings of the reliability of the maternity history information is presented for 32 countries in table 17.10. In most countries the rating of 'good' far exceeded the alternatives. Indeed, in some of the

TABLE   17.9

Length of interview (minutes) adjusted[a] for marriage, fertility and work history

	CI[b]	MA	PK	PH	PE	CR	GY
Overall average	36.9	27.1	29.2	51.6	29.6	24.8	26.9
Easy[c] interview	28.1	18.4	23.2	45.0	26.2	15.8	20.7
Difficult[c] interview	41.2	33.1	33.6	54.9	32.2	28.0	28.7
Very difficult[c] interview	52.4	36.1	42.1	65.6	38.6	39.1	37.9

[a] Based on the adjusted deviations presented in table 17.8.
[b] See page 440 of text for explanation of country abbreviations.
[c] Easy: 1 marriage, no children, never worked.
Difficult: 2 marriages, 4–6 children, worked either before or after marriage.
Very difficult: 3 + marriages, 10 + children, worked both before and after marriage.

Latin American countries there is virtually no variance to examine. The exceptions, where the 'fair' category was more frequently selected than 'good', tend to concur with what we know about data quality from other sources. Thus, that fair ratings should outnumber good in Mauritania, Morocco, Tunisia, Nepal and Pakistan is of little surprise. What is surprising is the paucity of good ratings in Indonesia and, above all, the Republic of Korea. Clearly, the criteria used by interviewers to judge reliability, despite rather explicit instructions, varied from country to country, and undoubtedly from interviewer to interviewer within countries.

Correlates of reliability

Not unexpectedly, the interviewer's judgement of the reliability of the maternity history information is strongly related to the level of respondent's education (table 17.11). In all of the selected countries but Yemen AR, the relationship is highly significant, with beta values ranging from 0.12 for Costa Rica to 0.33 for Peru. The reliability rating is also a function of the number of pregnancies women have had: women with more pregnancies in their history are given lower reliability ratings, once again excepting Yemen AR. Clearly, the complexity of a maternity history is a function both of the number of events that must be recorded, and of how far back in time they occurred. Hence, age and number of pregnancies are, in a sense, competing in the multivariate analysis of reliability. Age is of statistical significance for five of the eight countries.

In four countries, women residing in urban areas were given significantly higher reliability ratings than their rural counterparts, net of the other variables included in the model. This perhaps represents some sort of interviewer prejudice: most interviewers in most countries were city women.

TABLE 17.10

Interviewer's judgement of the reliability of the information on fertility: per cent distribution

	Good	Fair	Poor	Not stated	Base no. of interviews[a] (100 per cent)
Africa					
Cameroon	62.1	27.9	2.2	7.8	7595
Ivory Coast	67.9	29.6	2.5	0.0	5710
Lesotho	67.0	28.9	3.3	0.8	3603
Senegal	85.0	13.7	0.8	0.5	3985
Egypt	72.3	24.9	1.9	0.9	8788
Mauritania	43.7	52.9	3.2	0.2	3477
Morocco	31.0	64.0	2.8	2.2	4105
Sudan (North)	66.8	31.5	1.5	0.2	3114
Tunisia	49.2	43.2	6.7	0.9	3814
Asia and Pacific					
Jordan	60.5	35.4	3.7	0.4	3612
Syria	73.8	23.5	2.7	0.0	4487
Yemen AR	55.5	38.5	5.5	0.5	2605
Nepal	37.9	60.2	1.6	0.3	5940
Pakistan	11.3	81.1	7.5	0.1	4952
Sri Lanka	59.1	39.7	1.2	0.0	6810
Indonesia	24.5	63.4	12.0	0.1	9155
Korea, Rep. of	30.4	65.6	3.5	0.5	5430
Philippines	71.9	26.0	2.1	0.0	9268
Thailand	82.6	16.6	0.8	0.0	3820

Americas					
Colombia	92.5	6.3	1.1	0.1	5378
Ecuador	94.4	5.2	0.4	0.0	6797
Paraguay	98.2	1.5	0.2	0.1	4622
Peru	77.8	19.1	3.1	0.0	5640
Venezuela	97.3	2.3	0.4	0.0	4361
Costa Rica	88.2	9.8	1.9	0.1	3935
Dominican Rep.	87.0	10.9	1.9	0.2	2126
Mexico	89.7	8.6	1.7	0.0	7310
Panama	89.1	9.8	1.1	0.0	3701
Guyana	85.2	12.9	1.1	0.8	4642
Haiti	71.1	26.7	2.2	0.0	3350
Jamaica	84.4	13.5	1.4	0.7	3096
Trinidad & Tobago	94.0	5.0	1.0	0.0	4355

[a] In some countries the base excludes never-pregnant or childless women.

TABLE 17.11

Interviewer's judgement of reliability of responses in the maternity history[a]; betas and adjusted deviations

	CI[b]	MA	YE	PK	PH	PE	CR	GY
Mean	2.64	2.29	2.50	2.05	2.71	2.75	2.84	2.83
Education	*0.15*[c]	*0.18*[c]	*0.04*	*0.27*[c]	*0.21*[c]	*0.33*[c]	*0.12*[c]	*0.14*[c]
None	−0.03	−0.03	0.00	−0.04	−0.33	−0.25	−0.07	−0.24
Low	0.07	0.19	0.16	0.13	−0.12	0.05	0.03	−0.06
Medium	0.19	0.37	—	0.15	0.02	0.12	0.06	0.01
High	0.23	—	—	0.45	0.09	0.14	0.05	0.03
Age	*0.03*	*0.07*[c]	*0.11*[c]	*0.11*[c]	*0.03*	*0.14*[c]	*0.02*	*0.09*[c]
15–24	0.01	0.04	0.08	0.07	−0.02	0.07	0.00[d]	0.01
25–34	0.00	0.02	−0.02	0.00	0.01	0.04	0.00	0.04
35–44	−0.02	−0.02	−0.04	−0.05	0.01	−0.03	0.01	−0.03
45 +	−0.04	−0.07	−0.14	−0.07	−0.03	−0.15		−0.08
Area	*0.02*	*0.09*[c]	*0.07*[c]	*0.04*[c]	*0.01*	*0.01*	*0.05*[c]	*0.02*
Urban	0.01	0.06	0.11	0.03	0.00	0.00	0.02	0.01
Rural	−0.01	−0.04	−0.01	−0.02	0.00	−0.01	−0.02	−0.01
Pregnancies	*0.06*[c]	*0.13*[c]	*0.05*	*0.17*[c]	*0.08*[c]	*0.05*[c]	*0.23*[c]	*0.10*[c]
0	0.06	0.15	0.04	0.16	0.05	0.04	0.10	0.02
1–3	0.03	0.04	−0.04	0.05	0.04	0.02	0.07	0.04
4–6	−0.01	−0.04	0.00	−0.02	0.01	0.01	0.03	0.00
7 +	−0.04	−0.06	0.03	−0.09	−0.06	−0.04	−0.16	−0.06

Presence	0.15^c	0.01	0.09^c	0.04^c	0.09^c	0.09^c	0.04^c	0.10^c
No one	0.04	0.01	0.08	0.02	0.05	0.05	0.01	0.03
Someone	– 0.14	0.00	– 0.03	– 0.02	– 0.04	– 0.04	– 0.03	– 0.04
R^2	0.063	0.090	0.027	0.169	0.076	0.194	0.110	0.077

[a] Scored 1 = poor, 2 = average, 3 = good.
[b] See page 440 of text for explanation of country abbreviations.
[c] Variable significant at the 5 per cent level.
[d] Age groupings 20–29, 30–39, 40–49.

Note: The coding of the education variable is generally 0, 1–3, 4–6, and 7 +; for Morocco it truncates at 4 +; for Yemen AR at 1 +; and for Philippines and Costa Rica the coding is 0–3, 4–6, 7–9, and 10 +.

Perhaps the most interesting correlate of the reliability rating is the presence of other persons during the interview. Even though we could find no evidence that the presence of others affected the reporting of pregnancy losses (or, for that matter, of live births, in unpublished tabulations), this factor stands out as clearly related to the interviewer's perception of the reliability of the responses to the maternity history. We may surmise that either the presence of others influences the interviewer's perception of the respondent or that others tend to be called in when the interviewer encounters difficulty in obtaining answers from the respondent. For seven of the eight countries interviewers gave significantly lower reliability ratings to women they were unable to interview privately.

17.5   Interviewer's rating of the co-operation of the respondent

The last page of WFS questionnaires was reserved for the interviewer's comments; it was to be filled in after completion of the interview, and after having departed from the respondent's home. The first item on this page, and the only one which was routinely coded, was a rating of the respondent's degree of co-operation. The interviewer was asked to tick one of four boxes, labelled 'bad', 'fair', 'good', 'very good'. This was intended as a completely subjective rating, and no guidelines were offered as to when to tick which box.

Degree of co-operation across countries

In most countries the modal category chosen by interviewers in describing respondents' co-operation was 'good' (table 17.12). However, there are exceptions which run in both directions. In Kenya, Mexico and Haiti the rating most often given was 'very good'. On the other hand, among countries using all four categories, 'fair' was the most commonly selected rating in Benin, Mauritania, Morocco, Nepal and Pakistan. The Indonesian interviewers were the harshest critics of their respondents: in their three-point scale, cases of bad co-operation amounted to 10 per cent.

It was noted above that the item on degree of co-operation was generally the only coded item on the last page of the questionnaire. Keypunchers often overlooked it and, just as frequently, little effort at recuperation of these data was made at the data-cleaning stage. This is the reason for the relatively high frequency of 'not stated' codes. Particularly notable in this regard are Cameroon, Colombia and Guyana. Steps were taken in some of the later WFS surveys to remedy this problem by placing the coding box on the penultimate page.

Correlates of co-operation

Those variables which are correlates of duration of the interview and of the reliability of the maternity history — education, age, area of residence, number of live births (or fertile pregnancies or total pregnancies), and the presence of others during the interview — prove to be correlates of the degree of co-operation.

Since the degree of co-operation is the interviewer's last entry in the question-naire, it seems logical to suspect that it would not be independent of her earlier assessments of the reliability of the maternity history, the presence of other people, and the elapsed time since the start of the interview. The data presented in table 17.13 confirm this.

By far the single best predictor of the interviewer's rating of the degree of co-operation of the respondent is her earlier rating of the reliability of the maternity history. The beta values range from 0.32 for Pakistan to 0.76 for Yemen AR. Once 'reliability' has been introduced into the model, only two other variables retain a significant and consistent relationship with 'co-operation'. These are education and the duration of the interview, in the expected directions: better educated women and those who were interviewed quickly got the highest ratings on 'degree of co-operation'.

17.6 Inter-relationships between co-operation, reliability and duration

The inter-relationships discovered in section 17.5 are further explored in table 17.14, which presents the rank-order correlation matrix of five variables for the eight countries: degree of co-operation, level of education, duration of interview, judged reliability of the maternity history, and the number of live births. From a substantive standpoint the matrix presents no 'surprises, since most of the re-lationships have already been examined. The truly remarkable aspect of the table is the cross-national consistency in the signs and the approximate magnitudes of the coefficients. In the whole set of 80 rank-order correlation coefficients there is only one sign reversal (education and duration in Morocco, as noted earlier).

What emerges from this and earlier tables is that interviewers have less trouble interviewing educated women, and this is only in part a function of the fact that such women are generally younger, have fewer births and are therefore easier and quicker to interview.

17.7 Interviewers' assessment and objective response reliability

Are interviewers' ratings of the reliability and the degree of co-operation of respondents simply a function of personal preferences unrelated to any objective criteria, or are they of some value in predicting response reliability? It would normally be impossible to answer this question with data from a single-round survey. Fortunately, the WFS was able to undertake studies of response variance in three countries, thanks to a grant from the International Development Research Centre (IDRC) of Canada. These studies involved two elements: first, re-interviews with a subsample of respondents to the main survey, under the same essential survey conditions; and, secondly, random allocation of workloads among interviewers in each team for the main survey, with systematic rotation for the re-interviews. This design permits estimation of four components of the total variance: simple sampling variance, correlated sampling variance (due to

TABLE 17.12

Interviewer's judgement of degree of co-operation during the individual interview

Country	Bad	Fair	Good	Very good	Not stated	Number of interviews (100 per cent)
Africa						
Benin	1.7	56.2	32.4	8.3	1.4	4018
Cameroon	1.2	21.1	47.7	12.3	17.7	8219
Ghana	0.4	17.7	56.7	23.1	2.2	6125
Ivory Coast	2.0	26.2	67.2	3.2	1.5	5764
Kenya	1.0	10.4	38.6	47.2	2.7	8093
Lesotho	2.7	27.8	53.5	15.7	0.3	3603
Senegal	0.7	12.4	76.3	3.9	6.7	3985
Egypt	2.2	24.2	55.4	17.3	0.9	8788
Mauritania	2.4	48.3	22.9	25.3	1.1	3500
Morocco	1.9	47.8	41.6	4.9	3.8	5800
Sudan (North)	1.4	24.3	37.6	33.5	3.3	3114
Tunisia	4.9	36.3	47.0	11.7	0.0	4123
Asia and Pacific						
Jordan	3.3	23.1	42.5	29.1	2.0	3612
Syria	2.7	19.8	59.5	17.9	0.0	4487
Yemen AR	5.9	34.0	46.1	11.2	2.9	2605
Bangladesh	3.6	41.9	43.3	10.0	1.2	6504
Nepal	1.6	46.8	45.3	4.2	2.1	5940
Pakistan	3.2	53.8	39.5	3.2	0.2	4952

				not used		
Indonesia	10.2	68.3	20.9		0.6	9155
Korea, Rep. of	3.5	19.8	49.2	24.4	3.1	5430
Malaysia	2.0	28.2	61.3	8.4	0.1	6321
Philippines	1.0	29.2	61.5	8.4	0.0	9268
Thailand	0.9	10.9	61.2	26.9	0.0	3820
Americas						
Colombia	0.9	9.1	53.3	23.9	12.8	5378
Ecuador	0.6	5.3	47.6	46.5	0.0	6797
Paraguay	0.2	4.5	62.4	31.2	1.8	4622
Peru	1.5	18.1	54.6	24.9	0.9	5640
Venezuela	0.4	5.3	69.4	24.8	0.2	4361
Costa Rica	1.8	11.5	56.6	29.6	0.6	3935
Dominican Rep.	0.4	5.3	53.0	39.5	1.9	3115
Mexico	2.1	9.1	38.3	50.5	0.0	7310
Panama	0.7	10.6	71.0	17.5	0.1	3701
Guyana	0.4	9.3	36.9	29.8	23.6	3616
Haiti	0.5	13.1	39.2	46.4	0.8	3350
Europe						
Portugal	1.2	17.0	64.4	17.4	0.0	5148

TABLE 17.13

Interviewer's judgement of degree of co-operation[a]; betas and adjusted deviations

	CI[b]	MA	YE	PK	PH	PE	CR	GY
Mean	2.73	2.43	2.69	2.42	2.79	3.04	3.15	3.26
Area	*0.03[c]*	*0.09[c]*	*0.01*	*0.03*	*0.05[c]*	*0.03[c]*	*0.05[c]*	*0.13[c]*
Urban	− 0.02	+ 0.07	+ 0.03	+ 0.03	− 0.03	+ 0.01	+ 0.03	− 0.12
Rural	+ 0.01	− 0.04	0.00	− 0.02	+ 0.03	− 0.02	− 0.04	+ 0.07
Education	*0.07[c]*	*0.07[c]*	*0.03*	*0.12[c]*	*0.08[c]*	*0.13[c]*	*0.10[c]*	*0.07[c]*
None	− 0.02	− 0.01	0.00	− 0.03	− 0.10	− 0.12	− 0.09	− 0.04
Low	+ 0.06	+ 0.09	+ 0.14	+ 0.12	− 0.05	− 0.02	+ 0.01	− 0.12
Medium	+ 0.04	+ 0.16	—	+ 0.06	− 0.02	+ 0.07	+ 0.05	+ 0.03
High	+ 0.11	—	—	+ 0.28	+ 0.06	+ 0.12	+ 0.10	+ 0.01
Length of interview	*0.07[c]*	*0.06[c]*	*0.02*	*0.04[c]*	*0.03[c]*	*0.08[c]*	*0.08[c]*	*0.07[c]*
<18 minutes	+ 0.06	+ 0.04	+ 0.01	+ 0.03	+ 0.03	+ 0.13	+ 0.06	+ 0.08
18–32	+ 0.03	+ 0.01	− 0.01	+ 0.01	+ 0.01	+ 0.01	− 0.03	+ 0.01
33–47	− 0.02	− 0.06	− 0.02	− 0.04	− 0.01	− 0.08	− 0.05	− 0.06
48 +	− 0.07	− 0.07	− 0.10	− 0.05	− 0.02	− 0.04	− 0.19	− 0.08
Reliability	*0.64[c]*	*0.54[c]*	*0.76[c]*	*0.32[c]*	*0.50[c]*	*0.48[c]*	*0.46[c]*	*0.39[c]*
Poor	− 1.12	− 0.80	− 1.45	− 0.53	− 0.81	− 1.08	− 1.38	− 1.21
Fair	− 0.44	− 0.18	− 0.49	− 0.01	− 0.47	− 0.54	− 0.71	− 0.55
Good	+ 0.23	+ 0.45	+ 0.47	+ 0.38	+ 0.19	+ 0.17	+ 0.11	+ 0.11

Presence	0.06^c	0.01	0.03	0.08^c	0.03^c	0.05^c	0.07^c	0.04^c
No one	+ 0.02	− 0.01	+ 0.03	+ 0.04	+ 0.01	+ 0.04	− 0.03	+ 0.02
Someone	− 0.06	0.00	− 0.02	− 0.04	− 0.01	− 0.03	+ 0.07	− 0.03
R^2	0.467	0.351	0.599	0.166	0.278	0.350	0.275	0.188

a Scored 1 = bad; 2 = average; 3 = good; 4 = very good.
b See page 440 of text for explanation of country abbreviations.
c Variable significant at the 5 per cent level.

Note: The coding of the education variable is generally 0, 1–3, 4–6, and 7+; for Morocco it truncates at 4+; for Yemen AR at 1+; and for Philippines and Costa Rica the coding is 0–3, 4–6, 7–9, and 10+.

TABLE 17.14

First order inter-correlations among education, live births, degree of co-operation, reliability of responses and duration of interview

	CI[a]	MA	YE	PK	PH	PE	CR	GY
COOP/RELIAB	+ 0.67	+ 0.58	+ 0.77	+ 0.37	+ 0.52	+ 0.56	+ 0.51	+ 0.40
COOP/EDUC	+ 0.20	+ 0.23	+ 0.08	+ 0.23	+ 0.18	+ 0.35	+ 0.22	+ 0.10
COOP/BIRTHS	− 0.12	− 0.12	− 0.03	− 0.11	− 0.07	− 0.14	− 0.19	− 0.01
COOP/DUR	− 0.19	− 0.06	—	− 0.12	− 0.11	− 0.23	− 0.19	− 0.13
RELIAB/EDUC	+ 0.20	+ 0.25	+ 0.07	+ 0.31	+ 0.24	+ 0.37	+ 0.22	+ 0.21
RELIAB/BIRTHS	− 0.13	− 0.18	− 0.05	− 0.22	− 0.14	− 0.26	− 0.29	− 0.16
RELIAB/DUR	− 0.15	− 0.05	—	− 0.22	− 0.15	− 0.25	− 0.23	− 0.15
EDUC/BIRTHS	− 0.26	− 0.15	− 0.08	− 0.12	− 0.28	− 0.39	− 0.40	− 0.43
EDUC/DUR	− 0.12	+ 0.04	—	− 0.09	− 0.14	− 0.21	− 0.11	− 0.18
BIRTHS/DUR	+ 0.45	+ 0.29	—	+ 0.39	+ 0.18	+ 0.26	+ 0.29	+ 0.34
R^2 predicting COOP	0.463	0.345	0.599	0.162	0.276	0.352	0.280	0.177

[a] See page 440 of text for explanation of country abbreviations.

Notes:

(i)   COOP   = rated degree of co-operation (bad, fair, good, very good).
(ii)   EDUC   = scaled years of education (usually 0, 1–3, 4–6, 7+).
(iii) DUR   = scaled length of interview (usually 0–17, 18–32, 33–47, 48 +).
(iv)   RELIAB = rated reliability of answers in maternity history (poor, fair, good).
(vi)   BIRTHS = scaled number of live births (0, 1–3, 4–6, 7–9, 10 +).

clustering), simple response variance, and correlated response variance (i.e. interviewer effects). Full details are contained in O'Muircheartaigh (1982).

For the present purpose we are interested in examining the extent to which an interviewer's assessments of respondents are reflected in the magnitudes of response variations between the initial interview and the re-interview. For this purpose, we use the absolute value of the difference between the responses obtained from the two interviews for each woman as a measure of response error. The magnitude is thus the difference in units (months, years, births) between the responses at the first and second interviews. The interviewer's assessments are taken from the first interview. Results from Peru, Lesotho and the Dominican Republic are presented in table 17.15.

A very clear pattern emerges: with the exception of only two of the 30 instances, there is a perfect rank-order correlation between the interviewers' assessments and the magnitude of the response deviations. While the 'poor' categories are generally very small, the middle categories are also effective in identifying a group with high response variability. The differences between categories are generally highly significant, the level of statistical significance being less than 0.001 for most comparisons. The two variables, 'reliability' and 'co-operation' appear to do equally well in differentiating between respondents. This, of course, is not unrelated to the high correlations we have encountered between these two items across eight countries.

The results in table 17.15 answer the question we posed at the start of this concluding section: interviewers' assessments are of value in predicting response reliability. However, a word of caution is appropriate here. Although the differences are large, and are of both statistical and substantive significance, the proportion of the total variability in the response deviations which they explain is generally small.

Note

1. Data for the first two variables, presence of others and interview duration, have been presented and briefly discussed for the then available countries by Scott and Singh (1981).

TABLE 17.15

Magnitude of response deviations[a] cross-tabulated by interviewers' assessments for Peru, Lesotho and Dominican Republic.

Country and variable	Reliability of birth history			Average	Degree of co-operation[b]		
	Good	Fair	Poor		Very good/good	Good/fair	Fair/poor
Peru[c]							
Children ever born	0.12	0.28	0.76	0.17	0.09	0.15	0.34
Month of last birth	3.52	7.97	10.63	4.60	1.81	4.39	8.51
Current age	0.58	0.95	1.31	0.67	0.30	0.65	1.10
Age at first union	1.20	1.76	2.19	1.34	0.93	1.36	1.67
First birth interval	13.60	24.00	25.42	15.95	10.00	15.68	23.67
(No. of cases)	(932)	(223)	(42)	(1197)	(280)	(667)	(237)
Lesotho[d]							
Children ever born	0.32	0.46	1.00	0.36	0.30	0.53	1.32
Month of last birth	5.97	9.43	26.83	6.85	5.97	11.02	10.79
Current age	1.04	2.05	1.50	1.24	1.07	1.65	4.78
Age at first union	1.16	1.63	2.00	1.26	1.18	1.44	3.03
First birth interval	7.31	14.06	66.96	9.33	7.87	10.29	64.20
(No. of cases)	(486)	(115)	(8)	(609)	(499)	(97)	(12)

Dominican Republic[e]

Children ever born	0.07	0.22	0.71	0.09	0.04	0.09	0.28
Month of last birth	4.27	5.06	11.33	4.37	2.40	3.80	19.66
Current age	0.69	1.84	1.86	0.79	0.62	0.68	2.40
Age at first union	1.29	2.07	6.71	1.39	1.16	1.32	2.97
First birth interval	9.95	21.38	31.50	10.88	8.80	10.80	21.94
(No. of cases)	(707)	(68)	(7)	(796)	(281)	(455)	(60)

a   Mean of absolute difference between responses at two interviews.

b   In all three countries the categories were very good, good, fair, poor. They have been collapsed into three. For Peru and the Dominican Republic the fair and poor categories were combined; for Lesotho the very good and good categories were combined.

c   *Source:* O'Muircheartaigh (1984b).

d   *Source:* O'Muircheartaigh (1984a).

e   *Source:* Unpublished tabulations.

PART V
Data Processing

18

WFS Data Processing Strategy

James Otto
Judith Rattenbury

18.1 Introduction and background

The development of mechanized data processing (DP) equipment and techniques has been connected with statistical applications since the late 19th century, when tabulating equipment was designed to process the 1890 population census of the United States. Since 1950, when one of the first commercial computers was installed at the US Bureau of the Census, the use of computers to process and analyse data collected by surveys and censuses has increased rapidly. Today computers are an integral part of most statistical applications. Yet the potential of computers has often raised expectations that were not realized. There are many reasons for this: the over-optimism of computer enthusiasts; the fundamental differences between human and machine processing; the slow progress in developing appropriate software; and the need for mutual understanding between developers and users of data processing systems for software to be effective.

This chapter discusses the data processing activities of an international survey conducted in 42 countries between 1974 and 1984. It starts by stating what was achieved and what were some of the major shortcomings. The components of the data processing task and the conditions under which it had to be performed in terms of hardware, software and the resources are then described. We then discuss possible alternative strategies that could have been used and describe and assess the approach actually followed.

Finally we summarize some of the lessons learned, drawing the distinction between processing data for a one-off survey versus a repeated data collection, and between a survey resulting in a single report and one whose data are to be used for extensive secondary analysis.

18.2 Achievements and failures: a synopsis

In order to place the detailed appraisal in perspective, we start by summarizing those achievements and shortcomings of the WFS which may be attributed partly or wholly to the data processing component of the programme.

All developing countries participating in the programme (except Iran) successfully produced detailed reports on their data (the First Country Reports). In addition, all countries prepared, checked, cleaned and documented micro-level data files (for the households and the individual women) both in the original questionnaire format and in a form more suitable for analysis (the standard recode). These data files not only made it possible to carry out the analysis for the First Country Reports but have since, with the countries' permission, been widely distributed and used for further analysis around the world. Over 1300 data sets were distributed to outside institutions for at least 600 research projects during the lifetime of the WFS.

Apart from these concrete products, WFS contributed to general survey data methods by publishing suggested procedures (the 'Editing and Coding Manual' (WFS 1976a) and the 'Data Processing Guidelines' (WFS 1980a)), by recommending, obtaining and setting up in local installations some existing computer software and by developing new software useful for both specific WFS purposes and also general survey processing.

Help in institution building or training was achieved by insisting, wherever possible, that work be done in-country by local staff and occasionally by bringing local staff to the London headquarters to expose them to a more active computing environment. In 37 of the 41 countries all data checking and cleaning was done in-country using local hardware and staff. In 21, *all* data processing up to the production of working versions of the tables for the First Country Report was done locally. In the remaining 20, tables were produced at the Centro Latinoamericano de Demografía (CELADE) offices in Chile or Costa Rica or at the WFS London headquarters to expedite the work. Fourteen national computer staff had the opportunity to work at CELADE or at the London headquarters for two to four weeks, either while writing programs to be used in the country or during the variable-construction/tabulation phase of the work when tables were produced outside the country.

In addition to the on-the-job training for computing staff, many statisticians/ demographers participated in data analysis workshops (in Bangkok, Honolulu, London and Santiago) and learned to use a computer through data analysis software packages (mainly SPSS). Individual national researchers working on second-stage analysis projects also received computer training at the London headquarters and through special courses held in Senegal and Egypt.

However, in spite of these achievements, there were problems and shortcomings in data processing. Although data were cleaned and tabulations eventually produced for all countries, the cost in terms of elapsed time and heavy technical assistance was considerable (see chapters 8 and 9). There was little scope for upgrading a national government's computing hardware (this was not in the WFS brief) or staff (owing to high turnover) and by no means all countries benefited from the acquisition of software that could be used for other surveys. The goal of completing all work in-country was not achieved to the extent that should have been possible.

18.3   The WFS data processing task

Data processing in the WFS context was taken to mean all steps performed once the data had been collected on questionnaires in the field and returned to the local survey office, up to and including production of the tables to be used for the principal report on the findings and for the preparation of standardized individual-level data files for further analysis. As the project evolved, these steps became roughly identified as follows:

1 data preparation
   — office editing
   — coding
   — data entry

2 machine editing
   — structure checking
   — consistency editing
   — date editing and imputation

3 analysis
   — variable construction
   — tabulation
   — sampling error estimation

4 archive
   — documenting and standardizing data files.

Except for the special treatment of dates, this is a typical sequence of procedures used in processing data from any survey. We will confine ourselves here to a brief description of each. Before doing that, it is necessary to take a look at the basic data collection instruments — the WFS questionnaires.

The core questionnaire set has at least three levels of information: household, household members and eligible women. The amount of information varies at each level. For example, the number of members in a household or the number of births or marriages of an individual respondent vary, while within the individual questionnaires, questions and even entire sections can be omitted depending on the respondent's characteristics. Community questionnaires, an economic module and separate surveys of husbands were also used in some countries. The resulting data structure is complex and this has important implications for data processing.

The individual core questionnaire had 160 basic questions plus up to 210 more for the histories — births, other pregnancies and marriages. Since every country except one used at least one of the standard extra modules, the actual total number of possible questions in the individual questionnaire was over 400 although in general any specific respondent answered only a fraction of this number (see chapter 2).

Although the substantive content of the questionnaire was much the same, the form of recording and coding, the order of questions, the skips, etc. made each questionnaire into a country-specific data collection instrument.

In carrying out the data processing, the basic objectives were to produce computerized data files which corresponded to the data collected in the field as accurately as possible, followed by the tabulations necessary for the first report; the work was to be done as far as possible in-country making use of local staff and hardware.

Data processing starts with the manual operations of data preparation. Editing of data is initially done in the field, but additional office editing is also recommended in order to eliminate easily recognizable inconsistencies in the data before transfer to the computer. A coding operation is then required to ensure that all responses are recorded as codes, normally numeric, and written into fixed positions on forms that can be used for data entry (these forms can be separate coding sheets or else the original questionnaires). The data entry step then transforms the information into a machine-readable medium so that it can be processed by computer.

At the different stages of data preparation errors are introduced by the respondent, interviewer, coding clerk or data entry operator. Attempts can be made to minimize the possibility of errors at each step of a survey: the questionnaire is designed with great care; interviewers are thoroughly trained and carefully supervised; completed questionnaires are scrutinized in the field and the survey office; data entry is verified by repeating the entire process, comparing the results and resolving differences. Yet errors still avoid detection and because the computer processes the data last, it has to handle the accumulation of all possible errors.

For WFS surveys it was assumed[1] from the start that all identifiable inconsistencies would be detected and resolved and that this process of data cleaning or validation would be achieved by the classical method of:

1 Prior specification of a set of consistency rules written by someone familiar with the questionnaire;

2 Use of a computer and suitable program to locate and print all the responses in the data file which violate the rules;

3 Resolution of errors by reference to the original questionnaire or, in extreme cases, re-interview of the respondent or an 'educated guess' by someone with specialist knowledge;

4 Coding of corrections and their processing by another computer program which creates an updated or corrected version of the data file; and

5 Repetition of steps 2, 3 and 4 until all inconsistencies are removed.

It is not always necessary to correct all errors or inconsistencies; in fact some may be intentionally retained to allow the comparison of alternative analytical techniques. However, all significant errors should at least be detected, their presence documented and explicit procedures used to treat them at each subsequent processing step. Some errors can also be reconciled automatically (i.e. by a computer program) by specifying rules or statistical procedures to be applied to each. This is known as imputation. It can be effective (and necessary) when there is a substantial amount of incomplete or inconsistent data that is either impossible or too expensive to correct manually. The WFS only used this technique for imputation of missing date information.

The complexity of the WFS questionnaire and the emphasis on producing high quality data required an extensive set of validation checks comprising the 'machine editing' which was separated into three stages: a structure and completeness check, a range and consistency check for individual responses and a special check on all dates.

The structure check confirms that the correct amount and type of information is present at all levels. The presence of all necessary records is verified by preparing summaries of the number of households, household members, and individual questionnaires in the raw data file to be compared with statistics recorded during the fieldwork.

The validation of the questionnaire starts with checking that each response has a value within the range permitted for the question. Responses are then checked for internal consistency. The consistency checks are of two types: skip/filter and internal consistency checks. The desire to pose each question with wording appropriate for the particular circumstances of the respondent means that the sequence and number of questions vary from respondent to respondent. It is then necessary to verify that only the appropriate questions are completed, and those questions that should be skipped are blank. The WFS questionnaire contained a large number of skip/filter questions (the basic core questionnaire had 80). Finally, whenever variables are related or if there is redundant information in a questionnaire, the appropriate variables can be checked for consistency. Simple examples from the WFS questionnaire include the relationship between literacy and education, date of birth and date of marriage, and knowledge and use of each contraceptive method.

The dating of events is critical for the establishment of demographic variables, like age, date and duration of marriage or intervals between births, so an extensive set of consistency checks for the dates of events was recommended. In the final editing steps, imputation was carried out for genuinely missing date information, in particular missing months or calendar dates.

At the analysis stage, three distinct steps are performed: recoding, tabulation and sampling error estimation. Recoding of the raw data is done to construct the variables needed for the tabulations and at the same time to convert the data to a standard format to simplify further national and cross-national analysis.

A standard tabulation plan, called 'Guidelines for Country Report No. 1' (WFS 1977a) prescribed the form and contents of the primary report from WFS surveys. The report has two parts: chapters of text describing the survey background, methodology and results; and the tables. The majority of the tables are cross-tabulations showing counts, percentages, means and ratios classified by standard demographic and socio-economic characteristics of the respondent. Sampling errors were produced for key variables.

The data processing operations described above are not independent. They must be studied and methods developed to make efficient and appropriate use of human and machine processing abilities and to satisfy the overall requirements — the system design.

The questionnaire affects every data processing operation, so the system design evolves with the questionnaire. The system requirements are defined by the questionnaire, but likewise, the questionnaire should reflect the capabilities of the intended data processing system. Implementation of the individual system components is done in parallel with other survey operations, but each component must be installed, tested and ready for use before it is required, or the resulting delays will affect the processing of the data.

In order to implement data processing systems and ensure that the data could be processed, there were several requirements from the point of view of the WFS headquarters. First, a detailed outline of the recommended data processing steps was needed as a reference document. This would be adapted by the individual countries to reflect their questionnaire and their tabulation plan. Secondly, it was necessary to locate and acquire suitable software which could be implemented on the local hardware and could perform all the computer steps outlined in the basic document. Thirdly, technical assistance was required both to assist with the system design specifications and software implementation and also to monitor progress during the execution phases of the data processing. Finally, a headquarters activity was needed as a back-up to the technical assistance for the development and testing of software tools, for developing standards for and then supporting the distribution of data in the archive and for supporting data analysis activities both through workshops and individual research projects.

18.4   The computing environment (hardware, liveware and software)

One of the principal policies of WFS was that as much work as possible was to be done in the countries. In addition, the decision was taken to use the computer normally available to the institution carrying out the survey, whatever it might be. The data processing environment has a considerable effect on the data processing system, so we will take a brief look at the data processing facilities used for the survey processing. Tables 18.1, 18.2 and 18.3 show characteristics of the computers used, by country and region. Although IBM is the principal manufacturer, the range of hardware runs from the very small (including some micro-computers) to quite large. Half the machines fit into the medium-size category (128–511K bytes of memory), but a third are in the small computer category (less than 128K bytes). More importantly, many of the machines are old and use operating systems considered to be obsolete. The agency operating the computer varies although many are government organizations, notably the statistics office or finance ministry. Almost all the systems have tape and disc drives. Keypunches or key to tape and disc are the usual data entry equipment,

TABLE 18.1
Primary computer manufacturer by region

	IBM	ICL	UNIVAC	NCR	HB	Burr	Micro	None	Total
Africa	8	1			2		1		12
Asia/Pacific	7	2						1	10
Caribbean	2	1					1		4
Latin America	7		1					1	9
Middle East	2	1		2		1			6
Europe			1						1
Total	26	5	2	2	2	1	2	2	42

TABLE 18.2
Primary computer size by region

	Small < 128K	Medium 128–511K	Large 512K +	None	Total
Africa	4	4	4		12
Asia/Pacific	3	5	1	1	10
Caribbean	3	1			4
Latin America		8		1	9
Middle East	3	1	2		6
Europe		1			1
Total	13	20	7	2	42

TABLE 18.3
Primary computer agency by region

	Type of organization running computer						Controlled by survey executing agency		
	Stats. Office	Pop. Office	Cent. Gov.	Univ.	Priv.	None	Yes	No	Total
Africa	3	2	6		1		4	8	12
Asia/Pacific	5	1	2	1		1	6	4	10
Caribbean	2		1		1		2	2	4
Latin America	3	1	3		1	1	4	5	9
Middle East	4		1	1			5	1	6
Europe			1				0	1	1
Total	17	4	14	2	3	2	21	21	42

with the exception of a few countries where the data were keyed directly into the computer system.

The computer is usually used for a mixture of administrative and statistical applications, although the administrative applications (payroll, government accounting, etc.) normally receive priority in the use of the computer and the systems and programming staff. Information about computer personnel is limited, but staff usually consists of a small number of junior civil servants, several more senior civil servants in managerial positions and possibly some expatriate advisers. The majority of the staff are university graduates with 0–4 years on-the-job training, experience in one or two applications, and knowledge of a high-level programming language, usually Cobol. Civil servants are often poorly paid and since there is strong demand from the private sector for people with data processing experience, there can be rapid turnover. The few experienced, competent people available are engaged for the most part in the day-to-day struggle to keep the installation operating and are not available for additional assignments. If statistical applications are important, some of the staff may have attended a training course, such as those conducted by the International Statistical Programs Center (ISPC) of the US Bureau of the Census.

There are other aspects of the computing environment which are specific to developing countries. A mainframe computer demands a fairly antiseptic environment and often imposes requirements that stretch the local infrastructure to its limits. In particular, a regular electricity supply and a high level of air-conditioning are essential for a third-generation computer. Even when back-up facilities, such as in-house generators and special air-conditioning units are available, these impose additional burdens for regular maintenance, fuel, etc. In many countries fairly frequent breakdowns of over a week were not uncommon and in the particular extreme case of Nigeria, the computer was effectively out of action for over a year due to a combination of air-conditioner, electricity and computer hardware failures. Basic computer supplies, such as punchcards, paper and magnetic tapes, can be difficult to obtain. For example, in Ghana a combination of import restrictions and lack of in-country supplies resulted in a stoppage of data entry until cards were specially shipped from London. Even more critical is the lack of spare parts and qualified personnel for computer maintenance and repairs. Likewise, the lack of experienced systems engineers on the computer manufacturer's local staff means that the manufacturer-supplied system software is out of date and technical information difficult to obtain. Working hours may be short and further curtailed because of security or financial problems. The 24-hour service provided by many computer centres in developed countries is the exception rather than the rule. In many countries, especially in Africa, only one shift was worked. In addition, the productivity of the computer staff can be adversely affected by the problems of low pay, low staff morale, and consequent frequent changes of personnel.

Access to the computer is a problem, even when a survey executing agency has its own, because there are standard cyclical applications done on a monthly or annual basis which will have priority over a special purpose survey. If the computer is located in a different agency then access becomes more difficult and is sometimes only obtained by carefully developing and maintaining a good working relationship with the computing facility. This requires tact, psychology, public relations and management skills, qualities that are difficult to find any- where. Low priority given to the survey processing affected many countries. In Panama, for example, the payroll took all computer resources for one week in every month.

The computer being used was under the direct control of the national survey director in only 19 of the 40 countries where a local computer was used. In only 15 was access no problem, i.e. there were no excessive delays due to breakdowns or conflicting priorities, and computer runs were generally obtained the same day as requested.

It had not been envisaged originally that the London headquarters would need its own computer since it had naïvely been assumed that all computing work would be done in the countries. The exception would only be for Fiji for which a service bureau in London would be used. As more and more preparatory work for data processing technical assistance was done in London, and increasing demands for preliminary tabulations of some data were made, the cost of using the service bureau became exorbitant and it was decided that a computer should be purchased for London. After some searching a mini-computer, the HP3000, was chosen and installed in 1978. It was initially used for the preparation of software and other materials connected with country data processing activities. Later, as the other stages of the project developed, it became more heavily used for analytical purposes, for handling the growing data archive and for helping finish country data processing work, especially tabulations. It also made possible the conduct of several successful data analysis workshops.

It was clearly necessary to have a headquarters computer. However, some of the software problems encountered were due to hardware incompatibilities and all procedures developed in London badly needed testing on the type of com- puters available in the countries. Although the WFS continued to use service bureaux for this purpose it did not make enough effort to set up arrangements with suitable computer installations in London which offered the same configur- ations as were being used in the countries.

Software is an essential element for any data processing system. Although there has been a continuous increase in the capabilities of computer hardware, and a dramatic decrease in its cost, the methods used for creating software have developed more slowly, so that today software is the major component of the cost of data processing applications.

If programming staff are available, software can theoretically be developed by the organization requiring it, otherwise it must be purchased outright or commissioned from another source. Tailor-made programs, whether written locally or externally, require detailed specification and sufficient time must be allowed for their development. The use of external sources demands particularly well-defined specifications and requires close co-ordination to ensure that the final product meets them. General-purpose programs must be carefully evaluated to determine that they:

— provide the necessary functions and can accommodate the data structures of the application
— fit the configuration of the target computer
— have been thoroughly tested and used in other installations
— provide a user language and documentation suitable for the intended audience
— are easy to install and maintain
— interface with other programs or packages used within the organization.

Software already available in local installations was usually limited to one or two language compilers, for example Cobol and Fortran, and a few utility programs for such tasks as copying and sorting files. In 24 countries, the tabulation package Cocents was available but not necessarily in use, and in some of these, and additional countries, another general-purpose statistical data analysis or tabulation package such as Osiris, SPSS, TPL was installed. Thus very few countries had any software at all for the data cleaning activity but over half had, in theory, some software for generating tables although not necessarily any staff who knew how to use it.

It is generally agreed that the most critical element in making any data processing system work is the human factor and, for a survey, the most critical person is the survey director. If this person does not have the right qualities, then every stage of the survey, but in particular the data processing where keeping up momentum is imperative for a speedy termination, suffers. What are the right qualities? Given some experience of survey work, then the most important quality is dedication. That is, a real interest in the survey, its objectives and results and the attendant ability to motivate others. Also essential is a knowledge of the meaning and goals of data processing. This does not mean programming skills but rather a knowledge of how to specify tasks unambiguously and completely and how to interpret output from the computer. Given a motivated survey director, the other people necessary for carrying out the data processing work are:

— office editors
— coders
— data entry staff
— person to specify data processing requirements (editing/coding manual, machine edit, recode and tabulation specifications)
— system design/programming staff
— staff for reconciling data inconsistencies
— supervisor for execution of machine editing.

In most countries these staff were, in principle, already available within the government organization carrying out the survey. In some cases editors, coders

and data entry staff were specially recruited. By and large, staff for data preparation were already experienced or were relatively easily trained for the project.
Suitably experienced people for the other four categories were harder to locate.

A large part of the data processing work, in particular the computer-related
part but sometimes the whole job, was normally delegated to a separate group,
e.g. a separately administered computer centre or a specialized group within the
statistics office. Here, experienced staff were extremely scarce and usually heavily
overcommitted, free to do no more than give occasional supervision to junior
staff. The junior staff often simply did not have the skills or experience to work
on their own nor the professional maturity to communicate adequately with the
survey team. When it came to computer editing, the team of correctors was in
many cases inadequate both in size but more importantly in level of training –
this is a job which requires more experience than coding. Finally, a supervisor
was needed during the execution of the computer editing to see that computer
jobs were run, error reconciliations carried out and data updates prepared, etc. in
an orderly way. The person necessary here required skills encompassing a knowledge of the survey content, an understanding of the system being used, and the
ability to interpret the computer output and to submit jobs to the computer.
Such a person rarely existed.

18.5   The options

The WFS job concerned a survey to be repeated in many different countries
(initially forecast as 20, eventually 42). One could imagine two approaches for
handling the data processing for such a project: at the one extreme, a totally
standard data collection instrument, a totally standard set of tabulations to be
produced and a purpose-built set of software to accomplish all prescribed data
checking, variable creation and tabulation; at the other extreme, a completely
laissez-faire approach with each country designing its own questionnaire, given
overall guidance as to its content, and proceeding with the processing of the
data as it thought fit. Some of the goals of the WFS restricted this continuum.
Gathering data relevant to individual countries' national needs meant that the
data collection instrument could not be completely standardized. On the other
hand, the goal of producing data suitable for cross-national comparisons implied
initially (when it was not known whether micro-data files would be released by
countries) producing a comprehensive set of standard tables, and later, as data
were released, data files containing standard variables. The goal of institutionalization also placed some constraints on the types of strategy used, particularly
during the computer processing. For example, development of completely
WFS-specific software was not desirable as it would not have been usable for
other surveys.

When a survey is to be repeated only once or twice, then the question of
standardization of methods is not critical. But in the WFS context of over 40

repetitions, it was of prime importance both to ensure standard products and to reduce the technical assistance cost.

We will begin with the data collection instrument since decisions made in this regard have a direct effect on data processing strategy and also on data processing speed. With a totally standardized instrument, a completely tailor-made software system could be developed and applied directly to each repeat survey. The design and layout of the questionnaire also affect the options available, especially with respect to data preparation. The options here relate to ease for the interviewer versus ease for data processing. Questionnaires may be completely precoded in such a way that the interviewers enter the information into boxes or circle codes which will subsequently be used directly for data entry, largely eliminating the coding step; or answers to questions on the questionnaire may be transferred to special forms during a totally separate coding exercise; or as a compromise, separate coding may be carried out but into boxes preprinted on the questionnaires themselves (the WFS approach). It is generally agreed that transcription of codes is a boring and error-prone operation. On the other hand, bulky questionnaires with only one or two items of possible information scattered on the page and, as in the case of WFS, many blank pages for parts of the questionnaire skipped for particular respondents, are difficult to handle and very error-prone at the data entry stage.

Data entry is the step required to get information into machine-readable form. There were really no options on how this should be done since it was assumed that the equipment available to the office carrying out the survey would be used. In the majority of cases this was punch card equipment but diskettes and magnetic tapes were also used and in two cases data were entered directly on to the main computer's discs. Alternative methods of data entry such as direct reading of questionnaires or mark sensing devices require special coding forms but were in any case not considered since the equipment was not available.

Let us now turn to the computer processing. There are two aspects here: *what* is to be done and *how* it is to be done. The 'what' was laid down as part of WFS philosophy — all data were to be fully cleaned and a standard set of tables was to be produced. Later in the project a standard data file containing a set of well specified variables was added to the requirements. The 'what' was completely defined as far as the end product was concerned although there was some flexibility as to the exact edit checks to be made on the data.

The 'how' raises more options. At the prescriptive end of the scale one would design a total system to cover all variations of the implementation of the survey and provide associated software to execute this system. Each survey would then be *required* to use the provided system and associated software, making only changes necessary to accommodate country-specific items in the questionnaire. Of course the more standard the questionnaire, the better this approach works.

At the *laissez-faire* end, a survey-specific system would be designed for each survey and software would be written as necessary, making use of any software already available at the institution. This approach has some potential advantages. Software can be written which exactly fits both the needs of the particular survey and those of the computer hardware. If problems arise in the software, the authors are at hand to fix it. These points do not seem very convincing from the point of view of a limited headquarters staff giving technical assistance to 40 countries unless one assumes skilled human resources available with no other work to do in every institution.

The advantages of the prescriptive approach as far as they do not conflict with the 'institutionalization' goal seem overwhelming. After the effort needed for the initial set up, the resources for implementing each survey become marginal and there is the additional assurance that all surveys are processed to the same standard. For the software to support this approach there are three basic alternatives:

— use available packages
— develop a new package
— develop tailor-made software for local adaptation.

In 1974 there were several generally available packages (Osiris and PSTAT are two examples) which could have been used for the entire WFS task and many more that were suitable for the tabulation step. There were also many programs in use at specific institutions but the dangers of using such a one-institution product are discussed below with respect to Concor.

These packages were not ideal and did not necessarily do exactly the functions envisaged. However, DP steps can be restructured to fit the package so that the desired results are still achieved. Having designed the data processing system around the capabilities of the particular package, complete sets of control parameters to achieve all steps can be set up for processing a basic questionnaire. A single technical assistance mission of six to eight weeks can then be used to install the package, give general training to as many people as possible, help local staff adapt the core questionnaire, test all steps and train survey staff in the interpretation of the computer printouts. There were two major snags to this approach: finding a package that could do the task and making it run on a variety of computers.

As far as choosing a package is concerned, it should be said that use of packages sometimes requires looking at a problem in a different way and only a person experienced with that package can do this. What was missing in the early WFS days was a person on the staff who had detailed knowledge of and commitment to a particular package with the skill to design the data processing steps to make use of its components. Although the selection would have depended on a particular person's predilection, the *commitment* to a particular selection is often more important than the theoretically 'best' solution.

The prescriptive strategy outlined above is basically the one which has been used successfully in a somewhat similar multinational project being sponsored by UNESCO: ICSOPRU (International Comparative Study on Organization and

Performance of Research Units). Countries in this project are required to use the Osiris package for all data validation and management processes and a set of standard procedures which make use of fixed programs from this package has been set up for them to follow. This has not only ensured that data from all countries are cleaned to exactly the same standards but has also resulted in edited data with preliminary results being available two or three months after the data were collected. The quantity of data is admittedly smaller and the countries so far participating reasonably self-sufficient but the results are none the less impressive. The technical assistance input consists of a two-week training in Osiris and a complete set of control cards for performing all required steps which merely require some slight local modification. One proviso is necessary however: in all cases the UNESCO secretariat staff found inconsistencies in country-edited data when the same procedures were applied at the headquarters and at least a year elapsed in reconciling final errors through communication with the country before the data were suitable for archiving.

There is no existing package that can cope with all survey data processing for all computers. However, if a reasonably small package is selected which runs on the major target computer and is written mainly in a language available on most computers, then there are various ways to overcome the hardware problem. Perhaps the most attractive would be to commission the adaptation to the required computers. Another solution would be to insist on locating a local compatible computer if the normal one used by the survey executing agency is not suitable. Lastly, several different packages could be selected covering the different computers. The last solution would require considerably more breadth of experience for the staff giving technical assistance. The UNESCO project described above, having selected the IBM OS specific package Osiris, opted for the second solution and required the executing agency to locate a suitable computer.

The second possible strategy for providing software was to develop new portable programs, limited in scope to satisfy the data editing and analysis needs of the WFS but general enough to be usable for other surveys. Writing a new package was considered but never got off the ground, perhaps because the writing of a relatively general-purpose editing system is an extremely complicated task (after all, no one seems to have done it yet). However, it is an attractive alternative. If the design had been limited to strictly WFS needs, it is estimated that a six person-year input plus generous access to a variety of computers for testing would have been required early in the project (1974/75). The advantages would have been a headquarters staff who were dedicated to the software and who were in an excellent position to implement and promote it in the countries, and a package that could possibly be used later for other projects in the countries. But it would have been a risky undertaking. Software projects are notorious for their over-runs.

The third alternative was to fix the system design and provide well documented sample programs to go with it for in-country adaptation. If the questionnaire is completely standard, then no adaption is required. This approach requires much less input at the beginning to develop the prototypes (say two person-years) and implementation on different computers is simpler. However, more input in the countries for programming and testing is needed, requiring skills not necessarily available. In addition, at the end of the day, nothing is left for use with other data. Thus, although this solution might well result in a more streamlined system with printouts more oriented to the task at hand, it requires more input from technical assistance missions including good access to local computers during the testing phase and does not contribute to the 'institutionalization' goal.

These three software alternatives are concerned with what could have been planned in 1974. Ten years on, technology has advanced considerably, making other options available. Most of these advances have been in hardware — small computers are available at a fraction of the price of the mainframe computers normally found in government statistical offices. Not only are they cheaper but they can be used in much less controlled environments requiring relatively little air-conditioning. This advance has made it feasible for a single project to have its own computer which in turn theoretically solves the problem of computer access. Having a dedicated computer also makes possible a different overall system design which eliminates some of the classical steps. For example, it is possible to code data directly into the computer with checks being performed at the entry stage. If the staff doing the coding/data entry are knowledgeable, then they could do the reconciliation immediately. Alternatively the batch of errors accumulated on one day could be dealt with the following day. In either case there is much more intense contact with the data as soon as they arrive from the field. The result of the data entry operation will be a clean file ready for analysis. This strategy is not dependent on the use of micro-computers but does depend on computer facilities, including terminals, being continuously available for a period of, say, three or four months which is not usually the case on a large central computer. The strategy is presented here as being a hope for the future. The hardware exists. A generalized data entry/editing system has yet to be launched and flexible tabulation/data analysis software is not yet available. Future prospects are discussed further in chapter 19.

Limited local computing experience can be supported by technical assistance. This can be thought of as the provision of manuals, documents, software, etc. or as the physical presence of a person to assist local staff in their preparation. Options here range from placing a resident expert in the country for the length of time needed to accomplish all preparation and execution of the data processing, to a single short mission to set up and train local staff to use a system totally prepared abroad. The latter option implies no local involvement in the system design and software preparation.

18.6 The approach chosen by WFS

The original strategies proposed by the WFS fell somewhere between the standardized/prescribed and free approaches discussed above and were outlined in the 'Survey Organization Manual' (WFS 1975e). For example, the content of the main tables was fixed but the *form* of the data collection instrument was not.

A core set of questions was always to be included with possible slight adaptations and country-specific additions either in the body of the questionnaire or at the end. Thus the content of the questionnaire was standardized to the extent that it had a minimum set of core questions. As far as the layout was concerned, the ease of interview argument won the day and interviewers recorded responses in the body of the questionnaire. A separate coding operation to transfer responses to special coding boxes printed on one side of each page of the questionnaire was then carried out in almost all countries. In some cases, the birth-history data were transferred to special coding sheets and, in many, information from the household schedule was also coded on to separate forms. Judging by the wide variety of formats used in the questionnaires there was no concerted attempt to make sure that a standard basic questionnaire structure (e.g. the allocation of parts of the questionnaires to a particular card type) was enforced.

Office editing was carried out before coding and was intended to verify all responses but in particular to check that the skips had been correctly followed. The editing rules were outlined in the WFS Editing and Coding Manual and were adapted for each country. The coding part of the same manual gives guidelines on how to code yes/no questions or non-response and so on, but specifically was not a coding manual. Thus a totally new coding manual was written from scratch by each country.

The Editing and Coding Manual was the only basic document originally envisaged concerning data processing (apart from the tables) and was intended to cover both office and computerized editing. To quote the Survey Organization Manual: '. . . since each country's questionnaire is an individual adaptation of WFS documentation, it is impossible to prepare generalized instructions for coding and editing.' It then goes on to say that WFS would provide general guidelines and a generalized computer program for editing of data. This was not only wishful thinking, since no such program existed at the time, but worse, hopelessly oversimplified the task by not addressing at all the problem of the necessary system design and detailed specification for the job, nor the organization of carrying out the computer editing. A committee of experts was, however, set to work to locate suitable software.

Meanwhile the processing of the first few surveys was carried out on an *ad hoc* basis following no overall guidelines and in general using specially written software as the need arose. The data from the Fiji survey were processed in London with the intention of documenting carefully all steps performed so that the same techniques could be used for future surveys. Unfortunately, although the data were duly processed, the documentation exercise was not achieved. For the next two surveys (Thailand and Malaysia) the data processing work was contracted out to ISPC (US Bureau of the Census). Again, although the work was done satisfactorily, no record was kept of the procedures and no general software or experience was passed on to help in future surveys. By the middle of 1975 it was realized that a more general strategy was essential and a new senior-level member of staff was recruited at the WFS headquarters.

There were now two separate problems. The first was to outline in detail the computerized data processing steps to be performed, in other words, to perform the systems analysis for the job. The second was to find suitable software to accomplish the steps.

The overall objectives and policies of WFS suggested that special software would be needed. The work was to be done in the countries on an initially unknown range of computers. Something was to be left behind to help in processing future surveys, and very limited skilled human resources were expected to be available in some countries. As a result, much of the early data processing effort was devoted to the search for 'universal' validation and tabulation packages that could be used in all surveys.

At the time of the search, most software for data validation had been developed by institutions for specific computers, often requiring quite a large computer; in addition such software was not widely distributed. An example was Canedit, an extremely general editing package developed by Statistics Canada. On the other hand, where the software was more generally available it was not sophisticated enough to handle the large number of variables and the comprehensive editing for the WFS surveys. An example here was Unedit, a small program with limited facilities, developed at the United Nations Statistical Office.

After more than six months of searching and an abortive attempt to commission a package specially oriented to the WFS, selection was made of Concor, a data validation tool being developed by CELADE in Santiago. Unfortunately it was limited to IBM 360/370 computers, but it was easy to use, allowed enough flexibility for the kinds of edit checks envisaged and was usable on relatively small computers under both the common IBM operating systems (OS and DOS).

Concor is a compiler for a language which allows the user to define the questionnaire, the data validation checks and the error messages to be printed when errors are detected. It also has facilities for recoding and automatic correction. However, when originally selected, it was not fully developed or tested and its documentation was inadequate. WFS headquarters assumed responsibility for the testing, documentation, distribution and installation of Concor for the countries in the programme. This proved to be a major undertaking as Concor was incomplete, difficult to modify and required extensive testing and debugging before it was suitable for general use. In addition, it initially required substantial work to fit local installations and often failed mysteriously because of these modifications or because of errors in the user-prepared specifications. This caused delays in processing and led to lack of confidence in the package. These problems were overcome eventually as Concor developed and WFS gained experience with its use. It was primarily used for range, skip, and consistency checking and, in Latin America, for some structure checking and recoding.

As far as tabulation software is concerned, there was theoretically more choice. The requirement for something available on small and varied computers and the additional requirement to produce printout for direct photo-reproduction led to the choice of Cocents. Cocents is a general tabulation package developed by ISPC (US Bureau of the Census). It had already been installed in many developing countries for tabulating census data, was well tested and documented and there were many programmers already familiar with it. The disadvantages of Cocents are that it uses a command language more appropriate for programmers than end-users and it has very primitive facilities for data definition. The table specifications require great detail and once written can be difficult to modify.

At its September 1975 meeting, the Technical Advisory Committee (TAC) was alerted to the fact that data processing was proving much more difficult than had been foreseen with most countries requiring extensive assistance. The committee was also told that the search for the perfect software had not been totally successful but that Concor had finally been selected to aid with the data editing and Cocents for the tabulations. Work was under way to make Concor reasonably robust and suitable for distribution.

As far as software was concerned, WFS thus started out with the limited software already installed in the countries together with the tabulation package Cocents which could be installed on practically any computer and by 1976 the data editing package Concor for IBM 360/370 computers. It was recognized that this would not be sufficient.

In spite of these decisions and in spite of the increasing number of data processing specialists recruited for the headquarters (six by mid-1976) data processing problems in the countries continued to be acute with the headquarters staff spending all their time reacting to emergencies rather than setting up general systems and standards.

At the next TAC meeting in August 1976, a preliminary version of a new basic document 'DP guidelines', which laid down in descriptive terms the detail of the recommended DP steps, was presented. The definitive version was finally published in 1980 (WFS 1980a). At the same meeting, a strong recommendation was given to the WFS to seek necessary funds and take the lead in getting one or two of the principal survey processing packages miniaturized and portable. This was never done. Rather, over the next four years, a series of *ad hoc* solutions gradually merged into a reasonably coherent system that was used for the later countries. These are discussed below.

As early surveys were processed and the data processing requirements became more clearly defined, programs were written to supplement Concor and Cocents and to provide functions that were not otherwise available or were unique to WFS. These programs were modified from survey to survey and some were eventually generalized. This approach provided programs for data file updating, for marginal frequency distributions and for data validation when a package was not available. Concor was not suitable for structure checking so several different methods were tried. Tailor-made programs were used for the early surveys, but were difficult to write because of the complexity of the questionnaire and inexperience of the programmers involved. Later, two general structure checking programs developed by WFS headquarters were tried and rejected because of their complexity and inefficiency. Structure errors detected during later stages of processing caused difficulties which were overcome by including simple structure checks in all programs that processed the raw data file. This led to the technique of developing a basic structure check program that could be extended to provide other functions.

After the date imputation requirements were determined, a program was developed employing standard date editing and imputation procedures. This program evolved through several versions and the final version, DEIR (Date Editing, Imputation and Recoding), incorporates construction of the date dependent variables used for analysis with the date editing and imputation procedure. Variations in data structure and content of the questionnaire are handled by writing a survey-specific program to convert the date information in the birth and marriage histories to a standard format. The editing procedures are controlled by user-specified parameters which define the type of information available and establish values used to check the dates for consistency. Similarly, but much later, a method was developed for producing recode programs more quickly and accurately. This program, called Codbox, which generates Cobol code from users' recode specifications, was only installed in three countries but helped in producing standard recode data files in London for some of the later countries and for the archive files.

The strategy regarding tabulation was different. First, the 'Guidelines for Country Report No. 1' (WFS 1977a) outlined in detail the tables to be produced. Secondly, software to do the work was already installed in many countries and it was known that Cocents could be installed in nearly all the rest. To overcome the difficulties of using Cocents, WFS developed a program to generate Cocents commands from table specifications expressed in a more natural way. This 'Cocents Generator' (Cocgen) was then made available along with standard libraries of table headings and specifications in machine-readable form, suitable for producing the recommended tables. Each country merely had to make minor modifications to these standard libraries to produce their tables, providing they had previously constructed a standard data file containing at minimum the variables used in the tables.

Although Cocents (or a similar tabulation package already in use in the country) took care of most of the tabulation work required for First Country Reports, one special program was eventually developed to assist in computing fertility rates (Fertrate).

Finally, the need to include sampling errors of selected variables in the standard tables of the First Country Report was realized early. There were no package programs that could handle the multi-stage, clustered samples used in most WFS surveys, so a program was developed by an outside agency according to WFS specifications. This program, called Clusters, permits the calculation of sampling errors from complex sample designs. After substantial modification by the WFS staff, it was used for all WFS surveys. It has been distributed to many other government statistical offices because it provides a frequently needed function not commonly available in tabulation and data analysis packages.

Software requirements then were met by using the two selected packages (Concor, Cocents), software already available at installations (e.g. SPSS, TPL, Corrector), installation utilities for sorting, copying, listing, etc. programs developed for specific WFS requirements (Update, DEIR, Cocgen, Fertrate, Clusters) and filling the gaps with survey-specific programs written locally or at WFS headquarters. Table 18.4 shows the software used for the nine main functions eventually identified and table 18.5 shows approximately the number of countries which made use of each. This approach evolved over the first six years of the WFS and required considerably more resources than was envisaged. Because the processing requirements were not well defined at the beginning of the project but emerged as surveys were conducted, the headquarters data processing staff was forced to divide its time between active surveys and software development, to the detriment of both.

TABLE 18.4

Data processing functions and software used by WFS countries

Structure checking	Special
Range checking	Concor, Range, special
Consistency checking	Concor, special
File updating	Update, Corrector, local utility, special
Date imputation	DEIR, CELADE date imputation, special
Frequency distribution	SPSS, Osiris, MARG, special
Variable construction (recoding)	Concor, Codbox, special
Tabulations	Cocents, Cocgen, SPSS, TPL, Osiris, Minitab
Sampling errors	Clusters

'Special' means that a one-off program was written for each country.

TABLE 18.5

Software products used in-country for WFS data processing

Non-WFS programs	No. of countries	WFS programs	No. of countries
Cocents	20	Cocgen	12
TPL	2	MARG	5
SPSS	10	DEIR	18
Osiris	2	Codbox	2
Concor (Assembler)	18	Range	3
Corrector	6	Update	11
Minitab (Chicago)	2	Clusters	2

In 1981, realizing the extent of the software problem and in response originally to needs of the London office, some integrated software was developed based on a machine-readable codebook (the WFS dictionary) as the means of providing data definition. This development still took second place to work on individual country surveys but resulted in a relatively portable package comprising range checking, frequency distributions, data subsetting, listing, file match merging, and links to a variety of statistical packages. From this work came the idea of describing the original questionnaire in a machine-readable form at the start of a survey and using this to generate all necessary software automatically. This was discussed at some length and seemed full of promise but was not achieved in the lifetime of the WFS project.

As far as the *execution* of the data processing was concerned, WFS generally followed the practice of the particular local institution. The office editing, coding and data entry jobs were well understood and caused no problem. Some attempt was made to encourage overlap of these stages with each other and also with the fieldwork where this was of more than two months' duration. This was not often done in practice because of lack of resources, especially for supervision.

For the computerized editing, WFS recommended that a team of correctors be available although this was not always foreseen in the earlier project documents. Otherwise the organization of the work again tended to be left to the local staff, often a separate data processing group.

In all but four countries, data editing was carried out locally (table 18.6). Of these four, editing runs for Fiji and Haiti were done on a computer in London and printouts sent to the countries for local error reconciliation. In the case of the Dominican Republic and Nigeria, coding sheets were taken to Costa Rica and London respectively where all computer runs and error reconciliations were carried out with the help of national staff. For the variable construction and tabulation phases, increased pressure to get out results and lack of local computer resources led to the outside production of tables for half the countries, mainly in London or Santiago. In nearly all cases, however, a national representative came to the centre to assist and in many some preliminary trial tables had previously been produced locally.

Early policy stated that technical assistance would be provided for implementing software and for producing tables but that provision of general training in computer techniques was not a major objective (WFS Survey Organization Manual). Perhaps partly because it was not foreseen that the WFS headquarters would put major efforts into this activity, technical assistance for the first few surveys was contracted out and a special arrangement was also set up with CELADE to provide all computer support for the participating Latin American countries. Later, when it was realized that data processing was a major problem, a special DP co-ordinator was assigned by WFS to each country to work with the country co-ordinator.

The overall technical assistance strategy was to arrange short visits to get

TABLE 18.6

*Distribution of countries processing data in-country and
outside by region*

	Validation done in country	Validation done outside	Working tables in country	Working tables outside
Africa	11	1	2	10
Asia	9	1	5	5
Caribbean	3	1	3	1
Latin America	8	1	6	3
Middle East	5	0	4	1
Europe	1	0	1	0
Total	37	4	21	20

individual activities started, on the assumption that full-time local staff would be assigned to carry out the necessary design and programming work and supervise its execution. A resident (for 6–12 months) data processing adviser was used in four countries. The assistance was intended for:

— assessment of computing, software and personnel resources
— system design and planning, including specification of the software to be used or written
— installation of, and training in, already available software
— verification of locally written software
— assistance during data validation
— assistance in producing standard tabulations.

The first four of these tasks were essentially preparations for the data processing, designing the processing system and programming. The last two tasks were concerned with execution — actually doing the data processing. The distinction between preparation and execution was, however, never clearly made. The tendency was for the survey director to consider data processing (preparation and execution) from the end of coding up until the appearance of tabulations as the entire responsibility of the computer staff. The computer staff on the other hand saw their role as preparing software but not as supervisors of the execution. This attitude in the countries tended to be mirrored at the London headquarters. Thus, by and large, the people providing technical assistance for data processing were computer people with skills and interests relating to the development and installation of computer software. They often lacked the experience of working on data and of managing the execution of a large-scale data processing operation.

18.7   Factors affecting data processing time

The difficulty of the processing phase and hence of producing fast results was not fully appreciated at the beginning of the project. Rather, it was assumed that a report would be available within a year of fieldwork. In reality, it took two years or longer to produce the First Country Report for more than half of the surveys and most of this time was spent in trying to process the data. Since the utility of the data, particularly for planning and policy-making purposes, deteriorates quickly, there was concern about the length of time required for data processing.

The factors which influence the amount of time required for survey data processing can best be studied by looking at the optimal conditions for rapid progress. These are:

1 enough trained coding and data entry staff and overlapping of data preparation with the fieldwork
2 accurate specifications for data validation, variable construction and tabulations, compiled as soon as the questionnaire is ready by the survey director and programmer together and fully understood by both
3 software installed and fully tested before needed for production runs
4 access to a computer whenever needed, e.g. two-hour turnaround for tests, one-day turnaround for production jobs
5 sufficient computing supplies (cards, paper, tapes etc.)
6 not more than 10 per cent error rate (questionnaires with one or more errors) in coding, data entry or corrections
7 comprehensible error messages output by validation programs and easy-to-prepare transactions for updating computer records
8 enough trained 'correction' staff for reconciling errors during data validation
9 full-time survey director involvement throughout all data processing stages
10 access to a skilled programmer for problem solving during the data validation
11 acceptance of less than perfection in tabulation style.

For each of the main steps described in section 18.3, it is estimated that under these optimal conditions the following numbers of 'production' computer runs and elapsed times would be reasonable estimates for a WFS-style survey:

	Number of computer runs	Elapsed weeks
Coding and data entry	–	4 (from end of fieldwork)
Structure editing	2	3
Consistency editing	3	5
Date editing	3	5
Variable construction	3	2
Main tables	3	5
Total	14	24

This timetable assumes overlap only of data preparation with fieldwork.

The complexity of the questionnaire and the number of respondents will affect the number of people required during data preparation and validation in order to keep to this timetable. It is not possible to reduce the elapsed time by much, given the constraint of waiting for a computer run before being able to start on the next step. However, for a survey with few cases or relatively few errors to correct, the elapsed time could be reduced by a few weeks. It is also possible, with careful organization and control, to start validating data as soon as they are entered. This is another way of reducing time.

What are the effects on the 'ideal' timetable of about six months if the above conditions are not met?

Sufficient coders and data entry staff

Office editing, coding and data entry can be overlapped with each other and with the fieldwork. As soon as the first batch of questionnaires comes back from the field, it can enter this data preparation stage. One week after starting the editing, coding can start and one week later data entry can start. In principle, therefore, all data preparation could be finished a maximum of one month after the end of fieldwork. This was originally planned in nearly all the WFS surveys but only achieved in five. Two main reasons are found: insufficient staff to supervise fieldwork and data preparation at the same time and too few coders or data entry operators. Given an estimate of four months to achieve the data preparation, we lose three months by not overlapping and possibly another four months by having insufficient staff. In some countries it was desirable to use field staff for subsequent coding and editing. In such cases there should be enough trained staff but three months is nevertheless lost because of lack of overlap.

Data processing preparation (specifications and software)

Over half the countries started data validation more than two months after fieldwork finished and six of these more than a month after data entry was complete. In most countries, especially those with relatively large samples and where coding and data entry were to be prolonged, it had been the intention to start data validation as soon as a reasonably sized batch was ready. This was done in most cases but the overlap was only in the last week or two of data entry and probably made no difference to the eventual total time. Sometimes there was a deliberate decision not to overlap so as to avoid the confusion of dealing with batches or because staff were not available for the error reconciliation. However, trip reports from headquarters staff indicate that in the majority of cases the delay was caused because the software for the validation was not operational in time. If the software is not ready for the first phase, then it is unlikely to be ready at any stage. A six-week break in production before each of five stages gives an extra 30 weeks in total elapsed time.

Why was software not always ready? First, we have the situation where everybody thinks it is ready. When production day arrives it is found that, when the programmers said the program was tested, they had meant that it had no syntax errors and not that a series of tests on a number of cases had been satisfactorily carried out. There are variations on this theme: the program has been run on test cases but when it is used on the real data fails because some eventualities have not been tested; the program checks for things it should not be checking or prints errors for things which are not errors; error messages are printed correctly but are incomprehensible to anyone but the programmer. All point to the same solution – properly designed tests and a thorough checking of test results by the person responsible for the survey, e.g. the survey director, *before* the production runs start.

Secondly, we have the case where the software is known to be not ready. This can happen for a variety of reasons: no specifications in time, bad estimation of time needed, staff mobility, inexperienced or incompetent staff, no computer time available for testing, etc. In the case of the WFS there was a particular additional factor where it had been decided to use Concor. Early countries suffered from errors in this package and from lack of expertise in knowing how to work around them.

Computer access

At least half the countries reported continual problems with access to hardware for one or more of the following reasons:

— electricity cuts
— air-conditioner failures
— computer component failures
— system software not functioning
— other applications with higher priority
— limited working hours.

Even if enough lead time had been set aside so that, in spite of these problems, software was ready in time, the problems still had a serious effect on the actual data processing. If, in general, there is an average turnaround of one week instead of the ideal one day for each of the scheduled 14 production runs, 14 weeks are added to the total elapsed time.

Supplies

Running out of supplies (cards, paper, tapes, etc.) in many developing countries means delays while a source is found. This can add several extra weeks to the data preparation or data processing.

Quality of fieldwork, coding, data entry, corrections

The number of inconsistencies in the data has a direct effect on the resources needed for data validation. In WFS surveys in most countries, practically every questionnaire had at least one error to be corrected. Badly formulated or mispunched corrections during data validation are particularly time consuming because they imply additional computer runs. It is particularly important that the error messages printed by validation programs and the format of the correction records are simple to understand if new errors are not to be introduced. If the number of validation runs is increased from eight to 16, and average turnaround on the computer is one week, eight weeks for computer access are added and perhaps another 16 weeks for additional reconciliations.

Sufficient correction staff

The time taken for data validation in WFS surveys is perhaps where most concern has been focused. The policy was to check for and reconcile all detectable inconsistencies in the data, whether they were caused by mistakes in the field, in coding or data entry. In early surveys the need for trained correctors was not realized and not budgeted for. This omission was rectified, but the number and quality of people needed were still underestimated. Correctors need the same kind of knowledge of the questionnaire as the interviewers but rarely received that kind of training. The countries where reconciliation went quickly were by and large where professional staff did the work themselves, usually with a mixture of WFS headquarters and country personnel or where the field supervisors or interviewers were used.

To give some idea of the delays that can be caused, suppose you can count on one person reconciling errors in 40 questionnaires per day and you have 4000 questionnaires with errors. Doing a reconciliation pass in two weeks would require 10 correctors. If you reduce the number of correctors to five and each one only corrects 20 questionnaires per day, then you quadruple the total reconciliation time, i.e. 13 weeks become 52. The achieved production rate in many WFS countries was in fact even lower than this. At one stage it was reported from Haiti for example that there were only three correctors working at a collective rate of five questionnaires per day.

Survey director involvement

The lack of involvement of the survey director (or similarly qualified and responsible person) in the preparation of specifications needed for data validation, variable construction and tabulation leads to delays in the software preparation stage. During the production stage full involvement is even more critical, both for motivating the coding and correction staff and for immediate resolution of any questions arising. In two countries the survey directors departed completely (Tunisia to USAID, Cameroon to the UN) and were never fully replaced. Lack of presence will slow the work down or even cause a complete halt. As a conservative estimate, one must then double the data validation time (an additional 13 weeks) and add half a week for each of, say, eight temporary halts waiting for instructions.

Presence of technical trouble-shooter

Theoretically, once production runs for validation start, there should be no more need for a computing expert. However, even if programs have been exceptionally well tested, there will be surprises and unforeseen technical problems during the processing. For as long as it takes to solve the problem, work may be stopped. Suppose that it takes three weeks to get a technical solution to a malfunctioning computer program and such problems arise four times during the processing, then 12 weeks are added to the elapsed time.

In the analysis and tabulation phases, the close involvement of the survey director with the programmer is again critical. It was rare that the tables were carefully checked when initially produced. Errors were only discovered several months later while the report was being written. This necessitated going back to correct variable construction specifications and rerunning tables, often a lengthy business, especially if the programming staff had since been assigned to a different project. This cleaning up work was in many cases carried out at the London headquarters. A delay of 4-12 weeks can be caused by this lack of co-ordination.

Perfectionism

One final cause of delays is unnecessary perfectionism. What is unnecessary is to a certain extent a value judgement which will vary among different people. However it seems reasonably clear that a few unclassified cases (less than 0.5 per cent), small spelling mistakes in titles and to some extent the layout of the final tables are really not important. The policy of producing camera-ready tables directly from the computer, while undeniably the most sensible to avoid introducing errors through retyping, in some cases led to several months' delay in the publication of results while small errors were corrected and tables rerun several times in a bid for perfection.

The figures below show in summary what can happen to the data processing schedule when the ideal conditions do not obtain, taking a fairly conservative 'extra time needed' for the failure of each. If, for a given survey, all these happen, it can be seen that our reasonable estimate of six months from end of fieldwork to tabulation becomes six months *plus* over three years.

Departure from ideal conditions	Possible extra elapsed weeks
Insufficient entry stations/operators and non-overlap with fieldwork	28
Software not ready	30
One-week computer turnaround during production	14
Lack of supplies	6
Insufficient or poorly motivated correction staff	39
Bad original data, bad keypunching, bad corrections	26
Lack of substantive and technical problem-solvers when needed	12

(cont.)

Departure from ideal conditons	Possible extra elapsed weeks
Lack of substantive assistance during variable construction and table building	8
Misplaced perfectionism	10
Total	173

18.8   Appraisal of WFS data processing strategies

This appraisal does not concern itself with the final products *per se* which, as already has been stated, were produced to a high quality in all countries, but rather with the cost and time for producing them.

We start by looking at the form of the data collection instrument. The desire to make life as easy as possible for the interviewers led to a complicated series of skips in order to pose questions in exactly the correct words for each respondent. The repercussions of this during the data processing were enormous. Apart from the sheer bulk of the questionnaires and the attendant difficulty in their handling, substantial data checking was necessary to ascertain that the right questions had been asked of each respondent. The total number of possible questions was greatly increased and so was the number of checks and possible error messages. Greater attempts should have been made to simplify the questionnaire. The decision, for the same reason of interviewer convenience, that interviewer's entries would not be used directly for computer entry but rather transferred to separate coding boxes printed on the questionnaire meant another delay and introduction of transcription errors. The questionnaire could have been designed to eliminate the coding step (except for a few verbal responses such as occupation) without impairing interviewer convenience.

Finally, the decision to allow country adaptation of the core questionnaire was obviously correct but it could have been done in such a way as to preserve the essential *form* of the data. For example, standard questions could have been left with standard question numbers, the same sections of the questionnaire could have been coded on the same card types, etc. This would have greatly simplified the adaptations to the core questionnaire versions of the edit specifications and the structure-checking software.

Given that extensive field editing and computerized editing were carried out, office editing may have been an unnecessary step. An experiment comparing non-office edited and office edited data was carried out in the Ivory Coast in an attempt to evaluate the efficacy of office editing. The preliminary results seem to indicate that office editing did not reduce the amount of computer editing required. Coding and data entry caused no particular problems but could have been greatly simplified by more attention to the questionnaire format, as we have seen.

The main problems seem to have occurred in the computerized editing of the data, first in the design of the steps and the implementation of the necessary software and secondly during the execution.

The fact that a basic document giving guidelines for this process was not originally envisaged gives some insight into why problems were encountered. By the time this was rectified and some guidelines were produced in late 1976, design for a number of surveys had already taken place, each one in an *ad hoc* fashion. Moreover, the 1976 guidelines still did not give a clear design of the exact steps to be performed and the exact programs that would be required. The document containing this more prescriptive statement did not appear in published form until 1980 and even then the design was never strictly adhered to. In view of the reasonably standard questionnaire, it would certainly have been possible to design a system much earlier and enforce its application. This would have ensured that each country started out with a foolproof system, that people giving technical assistance were working to a common scheme and that all software needs were clearly defined. It would have in no way diminished the institutionalization goal, but enhanced it by providing a well-thought-out model applicable to other projects. It would also have discouraged wild deviations in questionnaire format in that the system placed certain constraints on the data structure.

The lack of a coherent system design in some ways caused the lack of software. The search for software was launched with the idea of finding general software for editing without being precise about the actual capabilities needed (structure checking, consistency checking, updating, file merging, listing, copying, recoding, frequency distributions, etc.). The search ended with the selection of Concor. This was not ideal in that it was only usable on IBM 360/370 computers and it did not have facilities for all required steps. In addition, as was discovered belatedly, it was not fully debugged. To fill the gaps left by Concor, other software was gradually developed so that the system design laid down in the final DP guidelines could be followed.

The resources required to make Concor an acceptable package and to develop the WFS-specific software show the difficulties inherent in developing generalized software. Even a little generality complicates program logic. Moreover, the need for a suitable user language, testing and documentation increases with the size of the intended audience. Programs with a limited audience can survive with little documentation and a primitive user language, particularly if the program's author is available for consultation. When a program or package is intended for wider distribution, it must function correctly in all circumstances; documentation must be complete and understandable to everyone from the systems programmers responsible for its installation to the eventual end-users; and the user language must be well designed and easy to use. These additional requirements make the development of generalized programs a more complex process perhaps to the order of ten to one. The fact that Concor, seemingly an ideal tool except for its IBM restriction, was by no means successful for earlier countries teaches the lesson that a package developed and used successfully by a single institution is not necessarily suitable for general distribution. The combination of errors in the software and the lack of experience in the use of Concor of WFS headquarters staff led to some very unfortunate delays. On the other hand CELADE personnel, well used to Concor and its foibles, helped process some of the Latin American surveys in record time. In spite of early problems, the final vindication for the installation of Concor is that it is indeed a useful tool and it is known to have been effectively used for post-WFS surveys in several countries (Cameroon, Tunisia, Dominican Republic, Sri Lanka, for example).

Thus, ultimately Concor was useful. Its application would have been much more effective if complete Concor programs for carrying out the various edit steps on the core questionnaire had been written, tested and distributed along with the package. If the country questionnaire did not deviate too much from the core, then the work necessary to adapt existing well written Concor programs would have been minimal. Instead, each country that used Concor started from scratch, took 4–12 weeks to write and test the programs and needed extensive technical assistance.

Even with Concor and the various supplementary programs eventually provided by WFS, some programming was needed in each country. It had been assumed that programming staff would be available for this. However, experienced computer programmers were rarely allocated full time to the survey and expectations of how much local staff would be able to do were in general not realistic.

In nearly all countries there was a continual battle to get software working and not nearly enough effort was put into setting up a streamlined operation for the actual data processing, especially during the editing phase. Worse, the execution sometimes was begun with insufficiently tested programs or programs written to incorrect specifications.

The tabulations required the prior construction of variables (recoding) based on the original questionnaire data. The decision to build a separate analysis or 'recode' file rather than doing *ad hoc* variable recoding as the tables were produced was wise. It ensured that a permanent record was kept of the variables used in the tables and enabled extensive checks on the recoding to be made (both programming and specification errors were very common at the first pass) before using the variables for analysis. A more detailed evaluation of the recoding step can be found in chapter 20. This extra step took time (between one and six months) but greatly simplified the production of tables for two reasons: first, the variables in the recode file were standardized so that standard control cards for producing the tables for each country could be prepared and, secondly, the need for *ad hoc* construction of variables while producing tables was largely eliminated. The method for producing the recode file, which consisted of preparing detailed specifications and then writing a country-specific program, was, however, error prone and time consuming. The development of the Codbox program, which allows entry of the specifications into the computer and then converts them into a Cobol program, improved the situation but it was used only by very few countries and still required accurate specifications. Again, given a more standard and simpler questionnaire, adaptation of a standard set of specifications would have been relatively trivial.

A much more prescriptive stance to the tabulation phase was taken from the start, both as regards the content of the tables and the software to produce them. Once Cocgen and the associated libraries for producing the standard tables had been prepared (early 1977), the adaptation by the country was simple and quick.

Apart from the original lack of planning and the abortive search for the perfect software, there were two other factors which led to the piecemeal nature of the software used. One of these was the desire to allow countries to design the system and choose the methods they were going to use, rather than prescribe from outside. The other was the decision to use the hardware normally used by the executing agency; this meant that the type of hardware was unknown until after the design mission to a country, which in many cases did not occur until the late 1970s. It was difficult to envisage developing a standard system for an unknown set of miscellaneous computers. However, the lack of a standard system design to perform all WFS data processing tasks and a single well-tested set of programs and control statements for using these programs even by the end of the project was a major factor contributing to the length of time taken for data processing. It was perhaps an error of judgement not to commit substantial resources (of the order of six person-years) at the start of the project to set up such a system and provide software to fulfil it. And it was a further failure not to have seriously reconsidered existing policies even as late as 1977 when many countries were still collecting data.

A major problem in the execution of the data processing was the lack of supervision during the computerized editing or the failure to identify a person responsible for following the work. All too often, survey directors handed over all responsibility to a separate data processing outfit and expected tabulations to appear miraculously a few weeks later with no further involvement on their part. This was serious at the program preparation stage (for example, the specifications for the edit checks and recode were often not verified by the substantive staff) and even more serious at the execution stage. There, it was critical that staff were motivated and that the cycle of error reconciliation, punching of updates, computer file updating and rechecking be kept moving. This chain was, however, often broken because no one took responsibility for the whole operation. In some ways, the WFS strategy of appointing a data processing co-ordinator exacerbated the situation since this person usually did not have the experience or authority to insist on substantive involvement in the management of the work. Technical assistance in the data processing area was, by and large, in software preparation, and the WFS staff were recruited with that in mind. If these people had demonstrated management skills and knowledge of survey practice, then they would have been better able to bridge the gap between the substantive and data processing tasks. A better and more lasting approach would have been to train a key person from the survey team to understand the data editing system and the printouts from the programs (with the same training being given to the WFS country co-ordinators where necessary). Apart from the inadequate management there was also a shortage of good 'correctors' for many surveys. The number required and the training level required were generally underestimated.

Production of working tables usually went quite smoothly *provided* that the data editing and variable construction jobs had been done thoroughly. The proviso is important. There are indications that incomplete editing does not appreciably affect analytical results (Pullum, Özsever and Harpham 1984). However it must be stressed that data analysis (including recoding) is greatly simplified if the data are consistent. Delays in producing tables were always the result of inconsistencies in the recode data file caused by original data inconsistencies, recoding specifications or programming errors.

The technical assistance strategy of short visits to initiate activities and monitor progress was not satisfactory. There were repeated complaints from those giving technical assistance that nothing had been done since their previous visit. This complaint came both during the preparation stage and during the data processing execution. It was due to both the lack of an easy-to-implement standard data processing system and the shortage of experienced and motivated local staff. The art of good technical assistance is to get the recipients to do the job themselves. When there is pressure to finish quickly or when there appears to be no one available to do the work, there is always the temptation for the donors to do the work themselves. Unless they complete everything, this can in fact hinder rather than help. For example, to save time, data editing specifications were prepared in London and taken to the country and explained; however, because no local person had been involved in thinking them through, there was no commitment to them and no way of modifying them when problems arose. Similarly, WFS staff wrote programs and left them for completion and testing; again, lack of involvement in the design or writing ensured that the necessary additional work was not done once the WFS staff member had left.

Given the circumstances, two long visits of between three and four months would have been preferable: the first to complete all software writing and implementation connected with the data entry and editing phase, including setting up the execution phase and monitoring the first pass of all steps on live data; the second to prepare software and execute the analysis phase (date imputation, variable construction and tabulations).

Instead, up to 14 separate visits of two to three weeks were made to a country for assistance in software preparation and data processing execution, and the total number of weeks varied from six to over 40. This was not only more costly but prolonged the elapsed time considerably.

In no country were all the conditions laid out in section 18.7 fulfilled. As a general rule the most important determinant of adequate software preparation was the experience of the people involved. During execution, if there was reasonable access to the computer and if the software functioned correctly, the most important factors were the experience and motivation of the correction staff and the administrative arrangements for the work.

Tables 18.7, 18.8 and 18.9 show times required for data processing by region. Table 18.7 gives the time taken to get 'clean' data, measured from the *end* of the fieldwork. In some countries this represents the total time taken for office editing, coding, data entry and machine editing. In others, particularly where the fieldwork was drawn out over a long period, there was some overlapping of activities so that some of the data processing started earlier. Table 18.8 looks at the time from the *start* of fieldwork to the end of tabulation and table 18.9 shows how much of the data processing time was spent in constructing variables and producing working tables once the validation was complete. Thus, on average, countries took 14 months after the end of fieldwork to obtain clean data and a further six months to produce a working version of the tables. These times reflect certain characteristics of WFS surveys, in particular the desire to produce high quality data suitable for sophisticated demographic analysis and international distribution, but in general are not significantly different from the time required for other similar surveys.

Regional differences are evident in the data cleaning (table 18.7): Asia and Latin America were much more successful than other areas. In Latin American countries, technical assistance was usually provided by CELADE whose staff made use of Concor and their own update program Corrector for the majority of the work. They were fully committed to the use of Concor, were aware of its limitations and were able to circumvent them. They often prepared material in advance of visiting the country. In addition, both the survey director and the WFS country co-ordinator were generally involved during data processing. This then is an example of using a standardized, prescriptive methodology with good supervision. In Asia, the situation was different and varied among countries. In some, outside organizations (e.g. US Bureau of the Census/ISPC) provided extensive technical assistance using their own established techniques; in others, experienced personnel were available who were able to do the work without too much external assistance and computer time was freely available; in a few, the original work was done in a fairly rough and ready fashion which ensured quick initial results but meant that extensive work was required during the data archiving phase.

By contrast, in the other regions many factors contributed to the slow processing, the most noticeable being unreliable or inaccessible hardware, complete delegation of data processing to a separate uncommitted and often inexperienced data processing group, and great difficulty in motivating staff. One country, Mauritania, is worth identifying separately as a special case. Here all data entry and most of the data cleaning was carried out on a micro-computer. This involved heavy initial technical assistance for the software development since all software had to be developed from scratch and there were no local computer staff. However, compared with many countries, the execution went very smoothly. The reason for this was partly that the computer was more or

TABLE 18.7

Distribution of countries by elapsed time (months) from end of fieldwork to end of validation, by region[a]

	Months for data validation						Range	Mean	Median	N
	1-6	7-12	13-18	19-24	25-30	31-40				
Africa	—	3	3	2	2	1	8-39.5	19.5	16.5	11
Asia & Pacific	4	1	4	1	—	—	1.5-16	9	8	9
Caribbean	4	1	1	1	1	—	10-26	18	18	4
Latin America	4	4	1	1	—	—	0-13	6.5	7	9
Middle East	—	—	1	1	3	—	14-28	22.5	25	5
Europe	—	—	1	—	—	—	15.5	15.5	15.5	1
Total	8	9	11	4	6	1	0-39.5	14	13	39

[a] Excluding Iran, Nigeria and Fiji.

TABLE 18.8

Distribution of countries by elapsed time (months) from start of fieldwork to end of tabulation, by region[a]

	Months from start of fieldwork to first tables								Range	Mean	Median	N
	1-12	13-18	19-24	25-30	31-36	37-42	43-48	48 +				
Africa	—	—	1	2	5	1	—	2	21-49	34.5	32.5	11
Asia & Pacific	1	3	3	1	1	—	—	—	9-32	19	18.5	9
Caribbean	—	—	—	—	1	2	1	—	34.5-43	39.5	40	4
Latin America	1	4	3	—	1	—	—	—	11.5-36	18.5	14	9
Middle East	—	—	1	1	3	—	—	—	20-35	29	31	5
Europe	—	—	—	1	—	—	—	—	29	29	29	1
Total	2	7	8	5	11	3	1	2	9-49	27	27.5	39

[a] Excluding Iran, Nigeria and Fiji.

TABLE 18.9

Distribution of countries by time taken (in months) for variable construction and production of working version of tables, by region[a]

	Months for variable construction and tables				Range	Mean	Median	N
	1-3	4-6	7-12	13-18				
Africa	3	4	2	2	2-14	6	6	11
Asia & Pacific	2	5	2	1	3-15	6.5	6.5	10
Caribbean	–	1	3	–	6-9	7.5	7.5	4
Latin America	4	3	1	1	1-17	6	6	9
Middle East	1	4	–	–	2-6	4	4	5
Europe	–	1	–	–	5	5	5	1
Total	10	18	8	4	1-17	6	6	40

[a] Excluding Iran and Nigeria.

less dedicated to the project but much more important was the excellent control and administration of the work by a key substantive staff member of the project who was thoroughly familiar with the data processing steps to be performed.

There were no significant regional differences in the time taken to produce a working version of the main tables (table 18.9). This is partly because for half the countries, and especially for those where use of the computer had proved particularly difficult, the work was done outside, at the WFS headquarters or at CELADE in Chile or, in two cases, at institutions in the USA. In theory, therefore, the work was done in good, reasonably constant, computing environments. The mean and median-time of six months seems long but was required to resolve obvious errors in the data revealed only when tables were produced.

The goal of carrying out all work locally using local resources was achieved admirably for the data validation. Only in the four countries discussed in section 18.6 was the hardware unable to cope. The WFS was not so successful at the tabulation stage and data for half the countries were moved to other centres. In Latin America, this was mainly because an efficient system for doing the work existed at CELADE and would have been impossible to implement locally. Money and time constraints dictated that this system be used. In the other regions, the bottleneck was not so much the actual tables but rather the variable construction and the interaction between the two. Technical assistance staff found it difficult to achieve accurate recoding specifications, an accurate computer program, careful checking of the tables and the repeated iterations necessary, where access to the computer was often limited and where the enthusiasm for the survey had long since worn off.

We end this appraisal by summarizing the areas where WFS could have performed better without jeopardizing its goals:

1   more care in questionnaire design, particularly with respect to layout and keeping standard parts standard

2   complete prescription of data processing design and associated software

3   provision of a complete set of software and associated control statements for processing the core questionnaire for minimal local adaptation

4   insistence on survey director (or designate) involvement throughout data processing

5   better training for technical assistance staff and local staff (substantive and computer oriented) in the DP system being used and in the interpretation of computer printouts

6   longer technical assistance missions

7   imparting a greater realization that delays in report production reduce the whole value of the survey findings.

18.9   Conclusions and recommendations

This chapter has described what was meant by data processing in the WFS project and how strategies evolved to do this work in terms of the hardware, software and people available. The necessity for some of the data processing has been questioned, in particular with respect to the perfectionist approach in data validation and in tabulation. This aspect is discussed in more detail in other chapters. Given the overall policy of reconciling all data inconsistencies and producing camera-ready tabulations, we have enquired how the job could have been done at less cost and in less time while at the same time adhering to the goals of:

— good quality data
— internationally comparable data available for secondary analysis
— institutionalization
— work to be done in-country using local equipment and personnel.

The differences between processing a one-off survey with a single report and processing 42 similar surveys and leaving data in a well-documented form for secondary analysis are undoubtedly enormous. Although data from a one-off survey can be processed without much preparation, coping with problems as they arise, this strategy is clearly unacceptable for a survey that is to be repeated over 40 times. It is also unacceptable if results are to be published and data subsequently made widely available for extensive further analysis. In these circumstances published results must tally with the archived data, which means that annoying inconsistencies cannot be concealed or so easily dealt with on a table-by-table *ad hoc* basis. When both a repeated survey *and* secondary analysis of data are required, then standards for the methods and results of data processing must be laid down. And if standards are to be laid down, then they must be fully specified before embarking on the project. The main shortcoming of the WFS in this area was that this was not done until very late.

Designing a standard system means identifying all the necessary software components, locating or developing them, then setting up all the detailed control language for testing the entire system on the basic questionnaire· envisaged. Adaptation to individual surveys will only be necessary to accommodate minor changes in the questionnaire and, possibly, hardware differences.

If such a prescriptive system is to be effective, then all technical assistance personnel, both those who are to install it and give training and those substantive staff who are going to help with the execution, must be thoroughly trained and committed to its use.

Where institutionalization, as well as efficacy, is a goal then the software components used in the system should be reasonably general and preferably, but not necessarily, from a reputable package. But it is important to stress that provision of software is not sufficient. The system design defining how the components are to be used, together with a well-tested set of jobs for processing the basic questionnaire, are essential.

Having such a prescribed, tested system would largely avoid the delays encountered in WFS data processing due to software not being ready in time or not functioning correctly, and this is especially important when human resources are scarce.

The second recommendation concerns the design of the data collection instrument for such a project. Computers can, in theory, be made to process anything. However a data collection instrument designed with interviewer convenience as the main criterion may result in difficulties in processing. If timely results are required, then data processing convenience is as important as interviewer convenience. The system design for data processing must be carried out in conjunction with questionnaire design. Modifications to the questionnaire should be made in such a way that they be accommodated within the system design.

Thirdly, even if system specification and software for data processing are in perfect order, smooth execution depends on good management, supervision and motivation. A criticism of the WFS strategy is the lack of distinction drawn between system design and software preparation tasks on the one hand and the *execution* of data processing on the other. It is the authors' clear belief that responsibility for the latter should be in the hands of the survey director (or his deputy) and never delegated to a person with no other involvement in the survey. Given this belief, some training may be required and this should be foreseen in the survey planning.

We should mention here technological advances. Experiments have been under way in several institutions in recent years in the design of systems which eliminate nearly all the data processing steps. In such systems, coding staff code data directly into the computer, and structure, range and consistency checks are performed simultaneously. As such systems, in combination with relatively cheap hardware, become generally available, real improvements will become possible in the time necessary for data processing. In order to make use of this new technology, survey projects would be well advised to build in a budget item for a hardware/software system with enough terminals for on-line coding. Even though this would be a capital investment not always accepted by donors, it could lead to large savings in often scarce skilled human resources as well as more timely results. It should, however, be stressed that use of new technology does not diminish the need for control and administration seen to be such an important factor in the WFS experience.

Finally, it should be said that the WFS in general underestimated the complexity of and practical problems associated with the data processing task. There was at first only a limited amount of specialist experience of using general-purpose software for processing survey data among the staff. Until 1976 there were never more than four people coping with the day-to-day problems of processing country surveys while at the same time searching for software and setting up standard methods, the first always taking precedence. This inexperience was also reflected in overly optimistic time estimates for data processing in nearly all the survey project documents. Computers make possible more sophisticated methods and more rigorous standards but do not necessarily simplify the basic task of checking data and producing tabulations.

Note

1. The validity of this assumption is analysed by Pullum, Özsever and Harpham (1984) and not discussed here.

19

The Prospects for Survey Data Processing in Developing Countries

Andrew Westlake
Beverley Rowe
Trevor Croft
Bob Thompson

19.1   Introduction

This chapter builds on the experience gained at WFS in the conduct of 42 fertility surveys in developing countries. With one exception, it has been possible to produce for each survey a substantial volume of basic tabulations together with a high quality, standardized, well-documented data file suitable for further analysis (see chapter 20). The data files are documented with machine-readable data dictionaries (see Rowe 1983), which are in turn supported by dictionary processing software which provides descriptions of the data to analysis programs and interfaces the data to general packages such as SPSS. These facilities have greatly aided the further analysis of data from the WFS surveys, which has proceeded very smoothly, whether in the host countries, at WFS in London or at other centres.

However, this achievement has not been without cost. In chapter 18, there are catalogued the sources of delay which have attended the data processing (DP) phase of many of the WFS surveys. Table 18.8 shows that the time from the start of fieldwork to the production of tables for the First Country Report ranged from nine months to over four years, with an average in excess of two years, and in many cases even these unsatisfactory timetables were achieved only with the input of substantial technical support from the WFS central staff. Experience suggests that such delays are common but that 12 months is a reasonable target (and 18 months an upper limit) for this work.

Most of the delays arose from:

1 early problems with the availability and production of specifications and the corresponding programs
2 poor access to facilities (over which the survey organization had inadequate control)
3 the policy of correcting errors allowed into the data in the early stages.

In themselves, these delays represent a substantial cost to the survey organization (see Pullum, Özsever and Harpham 1984); overall, these costs are compounded by the costs of technical support.

In this chapter we address, in particular, the need to improve the efficiency with which demographic surveys can be processed in developing countries, thus reducing the cost and the time taken to produce results, without compromising quality, and the need for procedures that suit survey offices in developing countries and improve their capability for future surveys. These considerations conflict to a certain extent because a survey operation will lose efficiency if it does not fit in with the organization and practices of the office. On the other hand, where these practices are clearly deficient, the general capability of the office will be enhanced if better procedures can be established.

We address these problems particularly in the context of the conduct of repeated surveys of similar type where the ability to reuse relevant work from previous surveys is required. This applies to co-ordinated international surveys of the WFS type and to repeated surveys within a country. We are not so concerned with *ad hoc* surveys, although many of our proposals will aid these also.

19.2   New technology

Hardware

Ten years ago most of the survey offices in developing countries were using small expensive batch computer systems, perhaps belonging to some other office. Since that time the cost of computing has fallen dramatically, first through the development of interactive services using mini-computers and now with the advent of desk-top micro-computers. These provide better access and more storage than the old computers at a fraction of the price, and models currently appearing offer comparable processing power. These new machines are cheap because they use the cheap new technology of processor and memory chips, and because of the development of new cheap, fixed and flexible disc technology. Some machines are now also sufficiently small to be truly portable, hand-held computers.

Various other hardware technologies have advanced in step: keyboards, screens and printers. Of much interest is the recent introduction of printers based on laser technology, which promise at reasonable cost a device for high speed, high quality output of both text and graphics. For the first time this gives (with word processing software) a cheap solution to the problems of the production of reports and documents, both as masters for reproduction and for the direct production of short runs.

Software

Software development has improved through the techniques of software engineering. Design support, other software tools and the newer structured languages make software production quicker and more reliable. Database systems have improved access to complex data structures and have separated programs from the structure of the data they process. Data dictionary systems characterize the abstraction of formalizable components of software, and indicate the general increase of awareness of the value of formalization and structure in the production of maintainable and reliable software. Macro-systems and code generators can minimize the repetitive and detailed work of code production.

In the area of packaged software, the availability of statistical software has changed out of all recognition over the last decade. SPSS became widely available and was followed by an increasing number of more modern or more specialized packages (P-Stat, SAS, BMDP, Package-X, Genstat, Minitab, Glim, etc.) on mainframe and mini-computers. Micro-computers have brought their own revolution to software in the form of word processing, spreadsheets and graphics, all designed to bring usable computing power to the novice who does not have specialized computing skills.

19.3 Management

New hardware and software technology has allowed people to change. Managers have become more familiar with computers and computing processes through better software, clearer designs and formalized control procedures. Computer specialists have become more productive and more attuned to the needs of the users, and the users have multiplied as computer systems and software have become easier to use.

People, however, remain the key to the successful execution of any project. Without the enthusiastic commitment of both management and staff, any project can slip into delay and apathy; with that commitment even old technology can be made to function efficiently.

From the very beginning, WFS recognized that DP would present problems and early working groups were concerned with the choice of software for tabulation and data checking. However, this approach reflected the belief that survey processing is straightforward and just requires the selection of appropriate software. The result was a failure to address from the outset the systems analysis required for a fully defined survey DP system. Instead of the development of a coherent system, WFS proceeded with reactive development of *ad hoc* improvements, without even a central computer until 1978 (see section 18.6). It was five years before the DP problems were seriously tackled with the appointment to WFS management of someone with experience and skills in survey processing. The core documentation produced by WFS shows similar imbalance. Detailed (and necessary) documents on the questionnaire, on sample design, on training interviewers, supervisors and coders and on the tabulations to form the principal report all appeared between 1975 and 1977. Guidelines for data processing were not finalized until 1980.

Similar imbalance existed in the organization conducting surveys in the countries. Computing is a relatively new skill, rarely possessed by people in senior management positions, who are not able to supervise it effectively. The corollary is that those with computing skills do not have the general management experience needed to take an overall view of DP and so are not able to help keep it under control. Frequently this leads to tension and polarization and to complaints about unreasonableness from both sides.

For management to function effectively it must exercise control, and to do this it must have information. General discussion of the mechanisms by which control can be exercised are beyond the scope of this chapter, since they apply equally to all areas of survey conduct. However, we do feel that some formal work is needed for this aspect of management, building on the analysis in chapter 18. Whatever mechanism is chosen as appropriate in a particular situation, whether weekly review meetings, project targets and slippage triggers, or other more or less formal systems, this control mechanism must have information through which to exercise control.

The management of areas (such as DP) in which managers lack experience presents particular requirements for information. Usually a review of progress and completion is sufficient, but with complex problems it is even more important to have information about the tasks themselves: what they are, how they interact, what resources they need, and so on. This information is the subject matter for systems analysis. It can be used to construct a systems plan, that is, a detailed description of all the tasks to be performed.

With such a plan of the data processing operation, the tactics for the execution of the project can be decided by informed agreement between management and DP staff. The plan details the tasks to be performed and helps to ensure completeness. With detailed tasks grouped into larger blocks, management has a framework within which to exercise control. The plan may exist simply on paper, but greater flexibility will obtain if it is maintained as a file on the computer, whether simply for editing and updating or for more formal processing.

Production of the information for the plan is itself a skilled and time-consuming task. It can be simplified through the use of prototype descriptions from other projects (presumably produced by more skilled people) and (if stored on the computer) through the use of software to control the description, producing reports about the structure and implications of the plan and highlighting inconsistencies or omissions. The need for this type of plan was recognized by the WFS (see section 18.3), and resulted in the preparation of the WFS Data Processing Guidelines (WFS 1980a) from which such a plan can be derived.

In chapter 18 it is stated: 'The data processing operations . . . are not independent. They must be studied and methods developed to make efficient and appropriate use of human and machine processing abilities and to satisfy the overall requirements — the system design.' For a future co-ordinated international project we propose the production of two sets of guidelines and a detailed manual. The guidelines for DP management would be written for managers not experienced in DP and would list and explain all the tasks in the DP phase of the project, concentrating on their problems and relationships. Data processing guidelines would be written for the DP staff and would cover all the details of the processing for each task and introduce the software to be used for the processing. This would be in addition to the documentation of the software. Finally a DP manual would be prepared for each survey and contain the explicit instructions about how the processing is to proceed and the detailed specifications for each task. This manual should be produced as part of the preparation for the survey, but in a co-ordinated project a prototype would be available as a model for modification.

This structure for documentation was included in an early proposal for the WFS DP guidelines but not implemented. The final version contains components of all of the three parts, but their lack of separation has made the WFS Data Processing Guidelines difficult for anyone to use. With these documents, management will be in a position to formulate a data processing plan. Whether this need be done in a formal way would depend on the general level of skill of the staff and on the complexity of the particular survey, but the tools for this formalization certainly exist.

Project evaluation and review techniques (PERT) have existed for many years and are widely used in industry for the management of complex projects. Recently there has been a move to introduce related aids into the field of computer system design, for example the UK government initiatives with the Structured Systems Analysis and Design Methodology proposals, and as an adjunct to the developing data dictionary systems. Some of these techniques are intended for control purposes, others to help system design, but they are all closely related. We believe that the management of the DP process can be substantially improved through this type of approach. Its implementation, however, requires the development or discovery of suitable portable software and the elaboration of a complete prototype and guidelines.

We do not advocate the use of a fully computer-based management and control system. That is beyond our remit, and anyway we do not think it a particularly practical approach for use in the current environment in survey organizations. Rather, we propose the use of software to aid the development of a plan which will then be used as a (static) aid to inform management about the process to be controlled.

19.4   Points of attack

The data processing delays in the WFS surveys are largely accounted for by the time spent in checking the data. This time can be reduced in four ways.

1 Increase data quality in the field by reducing errors from the respondent and the interviewer;

2 Combine data entry with some data editing so as to detect errors introduced at entry, to resolve errors coming from the field and generally to reduce record handling;

3 Ensure that all programs needed for data handling are written more quickly and more reliably; and

4 Develop a reasonable and practical strategy for the detection and resolution of errors.

Fieldwork

The procedures used in the field by WFS proved fairly good, and while improvement is always possible it is not expected that very much can be gained in this way without disproportionate expense. Only significant new techniques can help: portable computers provide two such possibilities. Each interviewing team can be equipped with a computer to enter each day's interviews as they go along. This allows immediate checking of the structure and consistency and means that there is a real possibility of taking up problems with the respondent. Alternatively, interviewers can be issued with hand-held devices to capture data direct. Either, or some combination, of these approaches raises chances for more error-free data, sooner and at lower cost. However, such systems must be carefully examined since their failure results in disaster and delays far worse than those experienced with more traditional approaches.

Data entry

The combining of some data editing with data entry is already happening and can be developed further. It also raises problems. Based on conventional unit record equipment (card punches), data entry is straightforward and has the same characteristics everywhere. Programmed devices depend on the availability of suitable software to drive them and such software is complex. If it is late or unreliable, the resulting delays will be more serious than those WFS encountered in batch checking. If we rely on *ad hoc* software being prepared for each survey, or even adapted from prototypes, we can say for certain that there will be some disasters. It is vital that general, data-driven programs be available. If this problem can be overcome then the enormous advantage of combining data entry with data checking/editing can be realized: the great bulk of questionnaires need be handled only once. After data entry there must still be a run through all the records to carry out a final check and this will mean that some of the original forms must be extracted and consulted, but far fewer than would normally be the case.

Getting better computer programs

The WFS experience was that there are difficulties in producing *ad hoc* the programs needed in a survey operation. The reasons for this are set out in chapter 18: they include high staff turnover, poor motivation and lack of facilities (access to hardware, etc.). Staff of sufficient calibre has generally been available for survey design, fieldwork operations and analysis, but not for data processing. Even general programs (e.g. Concor) that need parameter input may not necessarily solve these problems. The answer is to establish a systematic way of describing data, preferably one which is also a useful form of documentation for all those involved in the survey, and then develop programs which can automatically read that description and carry out specified operations such as data entry, data checking and even certain types of tabulation. WFS has already done a great deal of work on developing such software and it has proved very useful.

Strategies for errors

It has been suggested (Pullum, Özsever and Harpham 1984) that it is not necessary to eliminate all inconsistencies from survey data as their effect is simply to inflate the variance by a small amount. The cost function for error correction rises very steeply and this had a real effect in making WFS surveys more expensive and less timely. However, this view does not allow for the fact that programs that operate on a particular dataset may have built into them assumptions about the format of the file and the relations between the variables. If these assumptions are violated, the program may fail, possibly after considerable time on the computer. The resulting delays can be very costly and frustrating. The cost function looks very different. The problem can be avoided partly by making programs better able to handle exceptions without crashing and partly by eliminating the inconsistencies. This does not, however, have to involve reference back to the source documents but can be done by procedures to force consistency. In the simplest case this can be done by use of special codes.

For errors which do not affect program running, we propose that an appropriate strategy is to detect and document such errors so that a decision can be made about whether further correction is necessary and so that information is available to subsequent data users about the quality and limitations of the data. Serious errors which cannot be resolved can be removed by suitable insertion of missing value codes.

19.5 The way ahead

Before too long, it will be possible to use hand-held computers in the field to present the questions for the interviewer to ask, to accept and validate the responses and to allow review and updating of inconsistent responses. We do not anticipate that such a system will become routine within the next five years for several reasons. First, suitable hardware does not yet exist. At present hand-held machines have neither adequate display facilities nor the capability to run the necessary programs. However, the latest models come close to these requirements and general interest will ensure that suitable machines will become available. In time the price will fall enough to make the purchase of a machine for each interviewer a possibility. Secondly, the logistic and organizational load involved in mounting such a system rule it out at present in most developing countries. This will change as the general level of communications and other facilities improve in countries, and as survey offices gain more skill and experience in organizing the efficient execution of survey processing operations. Finally, software development is needed to produce the programs to present and accept the questions (see section 19.6). In addition, we are convinced that such systems should not be attempted in developing countries until they have been shown to work well in developed countries. There will, of course, be additional problems to solve in the developing countries, but there is no reason to carry out experimental work there when it can be done under less demanding conditions elsewhere.

While waiting for conditions to change there are limited actions we can take to prepare the ground. The speed or direction of hardware development is such that survey specialists must just wait and observe developments. There can be a specific commitment to training as an input to organizational skill, based on model procedures. The major input need is to identify and develop the software needed for such a system. At this stage we can identify the following requirements:

1 The construction of a question database for each survey. The best way to do this would be through an interactive questionnaire design aid, building on a prototype questionnaire and able to display and validate the general structure and detailed form of the questionnaire.

2 Software which uses information in the question database to prepare the program to be used in the hand-held computer. This generator software runs on a larger computer. The generated program used on the field computer must be able to present questions, accept and validate responses, follow the skip pattern for the respondent and allow the interviewer to review and update responses when inconsistencies are detected.

3 A link from the question database to the software to be used for tabulation and analysis. We are confident that such software will develop adequately as a result of pressures from other users.

19.6 Software for intelligent data entry

Data entry and checking is a complex task. The software to be used must be flexible in its application to different surveys, must provide the keyer with an environment tailored to the survey and to the entry and correction operations, and must provide the supervisors with appropriate controls and reports. We feel that the software should work through a link to a question database from which most of the entry and checking specifications can be extracted without substantial programming. An alternative approach has been proposed in which there is no attempt to use general-purpose software but instead high-quality, well-designed prototype programs are developed which are modified to the specific form required for each survey. The disadvantage of this is that it requires skilled programmers in each survey office and gives no aid to ensuring the detailed integrity of the final programs. There is also a problem with surveys that depart significantly from the prototype. However, some similar development of model programs will certainly be needed to provide the basis for generated programs.

Proprietary data entry software is an obvious first source to examine, but we suspect that this will not be very fruitful. Certainly the data entry facilities in most micro database software seem deficient in that they are ill adapted to the the style and context of survey processing. Moreover, if better programs exist, we suspect that they will not be widely available or portable. A second source is in packages for data management in related fields. Computer-aided telephone interviewing (CATI) systems are clearly relevant, as are systems for other sorts of survey or trials, such as the Compact package for the management of data from cancer trials at present under development at the Brompton Hospital in London. A third possibility is to build on the experience gained at WFS with the WFS data dictionary system, as this is a form of question database.

The software must support data entry using traditional operators who know nothing of the questionnaire and must detect and allow them to correct their own errors. It must support data entry by coders and editors who are trained to correct errors on the questionnaire, and it must support the correction of values at an updating stage. It must allow values which violate logical checks to be left in the data file, and must allow a section of the questionnaire to be abandoned if structural errors are found. It must produce a report for an editor or supervisor detailing any problems or errors remaining in each questionnaire, and must produce error statistics by question, keyer and interviewer to detect systematic errors.

More detailed requirements for the software and some possible strategies for implementation are discussed in appendix A.

19.7 Impact on the survey office in the developing country

To achieve a long-term improvement in the capabilities of the survey office in a developing country we must have a commitment to education and enhancement in the short term. So the execution of the survey processing should use procedures which, though innovative, can be retained for future use by the office and so should not impose unsustainable strains on the office structure and organization. This implies that there cannot be a single optimal method for processing, usable in all circumstances, since quite clearly it will be better to use procedures which take longer if they are easier to organize in a particular office.

Hardware facilities

Where a survey office has access to a good interactive computing facility this must be used for the survey processing, with the implication that any software which we propose must be portable across the range of machines in use. Where no such facility is available, appropriate computing power should be provided for processing the survey and as an enhancement to the general capabilities of the office. With the widespread availability of micro-computers it is not unreasonable to consider the installation of suitable machines for a substantial number of surveys. Where the facility is to be the sole computing resource for the whole of the survey processing (from data entry to tabulation and analysis) it must have the following capabilities:

1 Fortran and Cobol compilers and the ability to run large programs, including some widely available tabulation and analysis programs.

2 Support for multiple users for data entry (at least four) and enough power to avoid delays to users.

3 Storage for the full data for the survey (say 25 Mb of storage).

4 Enough power to allow timely completion of tabulation and analysis runs on the complete survey file, say a maximum of one hour for the completion of a single two-way table on the whole survey file of about 5 Mb.

5 Standard format tapes for program and data interchange.

The present generation of super-micros (for example, those based on the Motorola 68000 chip) can provide all of these facilities at a cost of some $20-$30 000. An alternative would be a small network of smaller machines (say the IBM PC) sharing a fixed disc system, though this would barely meet our last two requirements and perhaps some of the others. If the survey office has access to a good batch service it might be reasonable to run the interactive data entry and the batch tabulation phases on different systems provided good data interchange is possible, and provided the additional load of supporting the use of two systems is acceptable to the office.

Software

Hardware is by itself no solution to computing problems. Software systems are needed which allow skilled computing staff to work more productively and which allow appropriate tasks to be performed by staff without specific computing skills.

It has long been recognized that package programs provide an efficient way of accessing certain classes of algorithms. Thus a statistical package gives access to statistical computations without the need to program the details of these processes. The data dictionary concept extends the idea of abstraction to the description of the data file, thus allowing a variety of programs efficient access to fixed characteristics of the data, in much the same way as a package gives access to the fixed aspects of algorithms.

Package software is often large and unwieldy and difficult to use when machine resources are limited. This problem can be overcome by the use of generators, which produce programs tailored to the problem and the resources available. There is further discussion of these programs in the appendix.

The production of specifications for package software can involve a substantial overhead as the facilities of the package are learnt. In a co-ordinated survey much can be gained by producing prototype specifications which demonstrate the application of the package to the type of survey and which just need modification to encompass specific details. In repeated surveys of a similar kind the specifications from previous projects can act as a model for modification for the next one.

Overall, the greatest benefit of packages comes from the fact that they can take care of computing details not central to the task to be executed and allow users to concentrate on the subject matter components of the task. Not all packages achieve this, but many do. For the survey office this reduces dependence on highly skilled staff (though some specialists are still needed) and allows many of the tasks to be set up and controlled by the general survey staff.

19.8 Documentation

However reliable, clever or competent software may be, its value is substantially reduced if it lacks documentation of matching quality. For some reason, readability is not given high priority for technical documentation. This is a mistake. Even the driest technical data are better taken in by the reader if presented clearly and in an interesting manner. Unfortunately, DP staff are not known for their literacy, but this can be overcome to some extent by training and encouragement. Employment of technical editors can help, too. If the reader understands better, fewer mistakes are made. We should therefore judge software documentation by the normal standards of good English.

That the documentation should be comprehensive and pedantically accurate goes without saying. The key difficulty here is to keep the software and its accompanying documentation in step. Techniques are developing to make this more automatic. The development of dictionary-driven software, described at length in the appendix, is partly motivated by just this consideration. Even with such methods, though, the problem must be taken seriously from the top and from the start, and good management is crucial if this is to happen.

A readable, accurate document is no use if its existence is little known. A total scheme of indexing and classification, within which each document can be placed, must be developed. This should go along with a set of documentation standards, house rules and rules covering the administration of documents, in particular page dating and page versioning.

In fact everything said here applies with equal force to the documentation of all phases of a survey programme. It would be hoped that detailed proposals for computing documentation could be fitted into a comprehensive structure that would apply to the entire project.

19.9 Conclusion

By far the most urgent problem in survey DP is to ensure the timely execution of the processes from the achievement of completed questionnaires to the production of a clean raw data file. The main cause of delays has been the separation of the entry of data from the detection and correction of errors which is required by a batch-oriented system. The solution is to combine error detection with data entry in an intelligent, interactive data entry program. This could possibly be incorporated in a hand-held computer operated by an interviewer. Such a program removes the need for a separate updating program as all such facilities would be needed during entry.

A second source of delay has been in the production of the programs to be used for processing the data, from machine editing through to preparation of a final data file for tabulation and analysis. Intelligent data entry will reduce the number of programs but the entry program will be much more complicated than those produced in the past, and we will still need a program for restructuring the raw data to a form convenient for analysis. As in other areas we can overcome this production problem by the use of general-purpose software (which will need to be found or developed) driven by a machine-readable version of the questionnaire (a dictionary or question database). This must handle the link between the data and the tabulation and analysis phases of the survey processing, as well as data entry.

Appendix A

In this appendix we present various further details which expand on the general points raised in the main part of the paper.

A1   The content of a question database

The WFS data dictionary is no more than a machine-readable codebook, containing the physical locations and labels for variables and with ranges, special values and labels for code values. A data dictionary which is a full question database must be able to store all the following physical and logical characteristics of the survey. The package called 'The Research Machine' comes close to providing all these, but is not yet available on anything smaller than a DEC VAX minicomputer.

1 Characteristics of each question:
   - Full text of the question, with additional prompting text if appropriate.
   - Specification of the type and size of answer expected.
   - List of special answers allowed (don't know, up to God, etc.).
   - Ranges for numeric answers with both unfeasible and impossible limits.
   - Text of answers for coded questions, with code values.
   - Layout specifications for printing or display of the question and its answer.
   - Short forms of questions and answers (labels), perhaps linked to specific uses (e.g. with SPSS).
2 Structuring questions into a questionnaire:
   - Flow of questions, sequences, skips following particular answers, unconditional skips.
   - Repetition of questions for multiple response (which methods have you used?) or repeated questions (birth and marriage histories, have you ever heard of method . . . ?).
   - Internal variables constructed from responses, for inclusion with raw data (number of entries in a history) or for use in filters (skip next section if not 'exposed').

- Internal consistency specifications, e.g. sequencing of event dates, comparison of stated age and date of birth.
3 Joint specification of questionnaires:
- Identification of (key) fields which link questionnaires, e.g. household identification number and household member number to link individual questionnaire with members in household questionnaire.
4 Physical storage of data:
- Layout and organization of master file into which data are input.
- Specification and layout of files created from the master file (selection of variables, construction and reorganization of variables; cf. internal variables).

Constructing the complete dictionary is equivalent to performing an analysis of the data structure. The dictionary should be supported by a checking program which provides reports about completeness and consistency. Other support programs may prove desirable. For example it would be natural to add a facility to design the record layouts needed from the specifications of the variables to be collected, i.e. to construct a physical representation of the data from its logical structure.

A2   Algorithms for office data entry

We identify three different classes of answer to a question, corresponding to three different states:

1 Real answers from the respondent, which include special answers such as don't know.
2 Inapplicable questions which are skipped as the result of real answers to earlier questions.
3 Questions not (yet) answered. Initially all questions are in this state, and in the surveys under consideration all questions become either real answers or inapplicable as entry proceeds. In a more general situation one might want to allow questions to remain unanswered, as in a medical survey where laboratory results are expected later for a patient and will be added when available. This could also happen if we allow the input of incomplete questionnaires or the abandonment of parts of a questionnaire with structural errors.

These states could be represented by special values of the questions (e.g. blanks for not answered, 9s for inapplicable). A better approach is to have a separate flag for the state of each question. The state concept could then be extended to filters and checks, and include information about the acceptability of a value.

Initial data entry

At the start of entry for a respondent the program should log the identification of the individual and, if feasible, check the identification number in a list of selected households or eligible respondents.

For each question the program will prompt (see below) and accept a value, which will be checked for size, structure and range, appropriate to the type of answer expected. If a problem is found, the value can be re-entered, or the bad value accepted and a record entered by the program in a log of problems. If the value results in a skip, all questions down to the next one to be asked are set to the inapplicable value. The evaluation of internal variables and filters and consistency checks are performed after accepting the answer to one question and before prompting for the next. Incorrect skipping is a major cause of editing problems, so we cannot allow into the data file bad values for questions which cause skipping. There will be an option to abandon any section of the questionnaire with structural problems and to restart entry at the next unconditional question, leaving the editor or supervisor to review the questionnaire and resolve the problem.

Consistency checks

The message produced for an inconsistency must show the values of all constituent questions, and the user must be able to update any value (as discussed below) or proceed, leaving an entry in the error log. The checks should be placed immediately after the last constituent question for evaluation after that question has been entered. Alternatively, the checks could be written separately but with explicit identification of all the constituent questions. Then the program could automatically apply the check when all the components have been answered, or whenever any one is altered.

Updating facilities

These can be invoked both during initial data entry and at a later stage to resolve previous errors. Updating will be performed by the same routines as data entry since most of the requirements are the same. There will be a facility to jump to any question, either a jump back during data entry, or a jump to the question to be updated once the records for an individual have been located. We also need a facility to display the values of any set of questions as an aid to deciding on the cause of a problem. Alteration of the value of a specific question will be the same as data entry for the question, except that a value will already exist which can be displayed before the new value is accepted and could be left unaltered.

The major problem with updating is that of ensuring the correctness of the skip structure for an individual as values are altered, since the user can jump around the questions in an arbitrary way.

Prompting for values

The different amounts of information desired will depend on the skill and experience of the users and the nature of the questions. At least three different levels of prompting will be provided. The fullest level will display the name and label of the question, the type and size of value expected, and any other relevant information such as any specified code values and labels. For the next level the name and label of the variable should be enough, and for experienced users a list of the question names up to the next jump point will be sufficient, allowing the questions in a sequence to be answered on one line. This typing ahead should be allowed as a general facility, whatever the level of prompting. The user should be able to ask for a repeat prompt at the next level of information, perhaps by typing ?. In the long term it will certainly be advantageous to make use of screen handling facilities for data entry, but this can perhaps best be viewed as just another aspect of prompting.

Difficult types of question

The repeated questions or series of questions such as contraceptive knowledge and use for each method or the birth or other histories present some extra problems. The existence of such structures in the question database should automatically generate a data entry loop. For the loop over all methods this will be sufficient, but for a history there is the additional problem of knowing when to stop expecting entries. This could be handled explicitly in the question database by inserting a question at the end of each entry to ask whether there are more entries. Alternatively such a question could be generated automatically, or the number of entries could be taken from an earlier explicit question, although this method is not very reliable.

Quality control

Statistical quality control procedures should be established to check for errors which cannot be detected by the data entry software (i.e. feasible but incorrect values, or unreasonable resolution of problems). A suitable procedure would be to re-enter independently (with a different operator) a random sample of questionnaires from each batch. The data entry program would have to recognize this situation, and after the second entry of the sample was complete would compare the two versions. If too many discrepancies are found the whole of the batch would be re-entered and all discrepancies passed to the supervisor. It is important that the discrepancies are resolved by the supervisor, not by either of the people involved in data entry. If an acceptable level of difference is found this information is recorded, leading to an estimate of the rate of undetected keying errors in the whole data set.

A3   Presentation of questions on a hand-held computer

The essential difference between this and office data entry is the absence of the physical questionnaire on paper, both for presentation of the questions and for organizing the responses.

Question presentation will proceed as for office data entry except that the full form of the question (and any prompts) to ask the respondent must be presented to the interviewer. Checking, review and correction can proceed as before, except that the respondent can be asked to confirm answers and resolve inconsistencies (if she can). Facilities to review answers (and the speed of this presentation) will be very important in the absence of a written copy.

The looping questions discussed above are even more difficult in the field. With a paper questionnaire they can be organized into a tabular form, whereas a presentation program must be able to present the questions in the correct sequence. This might involve accepting a list of methods, looping over each method in this list to ask about use, and then looping over all methods not mentioned (perhaps in random order) to prompt about knowledge and use. This can obviously be done, but it will not be simple to represent this structure in a general way in the question database.

An even more futuristic alternative to the hand-held computer is the intelligent clipboard. Here a paper questionnaire will be used, but placed on a pressure-sensitive board which will detect, record and check the answers as they are written by the interviewer.

A4   Statistical and tabulation software

Spreadsheet programs (essentially calculator systems based on tables) are one of the great successes of micro-computers. In parallel, a large number of more traditional statistical packages have been produced, mostly of rather dubious quality. Some of the well-established mainframe packages are moving on to smaller machines, with SPSS, SAS, P-Stat, Minitab, Glim and others appearing on the IBM PC/XT and similar machines. The intense activity in this area indicates that good facilities will be available as we need them: we shall just have to seek them out.

Some newer systems (such as Knowledge-man) integrate a spreadsheet facility with a database and a programming language for both, and so offer a programmable tabulation system. Rather like the Cocents generator, it is possible to write a set of basic spreadsheet programs for common types of table which produce detailed, decorated tables with totals, percentages and means (as required) and full labelling from simple tables of counts produced by the database. The tables can then be edited by hand and incorporated into documents using word-processing facilities. This approach follows a discernible trend in tabulation software in which the formation of tables is separated from their manipulation into presentation form.

Some of the micro packages are being moved on to super micros in order to use greater computer power for larger datasets. The Unix operating system is extremely widespread on these larger machines and so provides a standard for compatibility and portability, and a meeting ground with the larger systems which have moved down from mainframe computers.

The development of tabulation software

The software used for the main tabulation phase of a large survey should have the following capabilities:

1 Produce camera-ready output of appropriate standard.

2 Produce tables in languages other than English, certainly French and Spanish and preferably also Arabic.

3 Operate reasonably efficiently on the large volume of tables needed for such a report.

4 Support easy use of prototype tabulation specifications where there are standard or previous survey specifications available.

5 Take advantage in the specifications of the similarity of many of the table structures and content.

6 Allow reasonably easy specification of additional tables.

These requirements rule out packages like SPSS which do not have table manipulation and presentation facilities. Other statistical packages (P-Stat, SAS, Sir) could produce the required tables, if available. WFS used the package Cocents with a specially written pre-processor (Cocgen) for most of the main reports produced both in countries and at WFS headquarters. However, while the concepts and structure of the software are novel and appropriate, the combination is rather old-fashioned and not particularly easy to use for additional tables.

We are hopeful that suitable tabulation software will become available in the micro market. If this does not happen we suggest the development of a system built round spreadsheet tabulation software, taking advantage of its facilities to:

— calculate marginal totals, percentages, means, etc. from tables of counts
— flexibly label and decorate a table
— interface with word-processing software for integrating tables with reports.

However, performing these operations individually by hand for each table in a large report is an impossible task, especially if we take the practical view that many tables will be subject to revision and reformation. In addition, there is the heavy processing task of producing the tables of counts for input to the spreadsheet.

A system which takes the best characteristics of the Cocents/Cocgen system and implements them in a more practical and user-oriented way is needed. The following components are required:

1 A simple tabulation program which will efficiently produce undecorated tables of counts and means. These tables will include identification of the variables used for their construction and of the selection rules for inclusion of respondents, but will not be labelled for presentation. Such a program can readily be written (and would be dictionary driven) if it cannot be found.

2 A database package which allows these undecorated tables to be stored as entries, so that we can construct a library of tables, updated as tables are revised.

3 A spreadsheet package which can be programmed in a reasonably general way to extract tables from the table library, operate on these basic tables in a small number of predefined ways to produce margins, percentages, etc. (like the seven basic table structures supported in Cocgen), and then access the dictionary and a library of titling information to decorate the resulting table. This would constitute a draft version of the final tables (with most of the decorative work done) which could then be further modified by hand for any final details.

4 Word-processing software which can access these final tables and incorporate them into the body of a report, or organize the main body of tables and produce a list of contents, etc.

The crucial component here is the spreadsheet with sufficient programmability to support the preparation of a generalized table production system. Such software certainly exists: an example is the product Knowledge-man, which runs under the MS-DOS operating system and which in addition has an integrated database system, has links to word-processing software, is available in a number of languages (not just English) and will shortly be available under Unix.

A5   Comparison of driven and generated software

We have mentioned both dictionary-driven and dictionary-generated software, and it is perhaps useful to highlight the distinction between these two types of software.

A dictionary-driven program performs useful work (such as tabulation or data management) and reads the dictionary to obtain information needed to control or simplify these operations (such as the locations of variables and the labels which describe a variable). Examples are the WFS programs Subsets, Combiner, Range and Freqs, all of which use the WFS data dictionary to obtain information about variables in a file. Details of these programs will be found in the WFS 'Software User's Manual' (WFS 1984).

In contrast, a dictionary-generated program requires two phases. First, a dictionary-driven program is used, not to do work on the data but rather to create (generate) a program which is specific to the data described by the dictionary. Only when this second program is run is the work actually done on the data. The tabulation program Cocents, Corrector from CELADE and the WFS program Codbox are all examples of generators, though none of these is essentially based on a dictionary.

Generator programs are actually very common, though not many are linked to a dictionary. A compiler is one example. It reads instructions (written in a high-level language) and converts these into a form which can be executed (usually assembler or machine code). The WFSPSS interface with SPSS is a dictionary-based generator, in that the dictionary-driven program WFSPSS generates a proper SPSS program using instructions from the user and information about variables from a dictionary. The actual work is done by SPSS using the generated instructions. The Cocents system as used by WFS for tabulation is a multi-stage generator. We first run the Cocgen program, which draws on a library of table descriptions (a type of dictionary) and parameters to generate instructions for Cocents, which in turn uses these to generate a Cobol program, which is then compiled and executed to form the tables. The Codbox recode program is another generator which writes Cobol code, this time for use in a restructuring program.

The essential distinction is that a dictionary-driven program is general and can be used with any dataset which can be described by a dictionary, whereas a program produced by a generator is specific to the dataset described by a particular dictionary.

Dictionary-generated software offers many advantages over dictionary-driven programs. These are listed below. However, in the short term it will be possible to gain significant advantage by building on the existing WFS experience, utilizing the portable dictionary-based software tools to produce a dictionary-driven data entry program. This will give time to acquire or develop the experience needed to produce a good generator system.

1 General-purpose programs are usually large as they have to carry the overhead of understanding and interpreting the user's instructions (and the dictionary) in addition to the code for performing the functions of the program. A generator program will have to carry this load, but the generated program, being specific to a task, can be much more compact.

2 If a generated program is used repeatedly it avoids the inefficiency of repeated interpretation and dictionary processing, and if it is compiled it will usually be much more efficient than an interpretative driven program.

3 The target machine for a generated program does not have to be the same as the machine on which the generator is run, so it is possible to support a system where the generator is run on a larger machine to create programs to be run on small machines which could not accommodate the generator (or a dictionary-driven program).

4 If the generator works from model programs it can be much easier to alter the system to generate codes for a new environment than it would be to alter the driven programs. Indeed, it is not unreasonable to consider the development of facilities for generating programs in completely different languages, whereas to convert a driven program to another language is practically unthinkable.

5 A generator can have the facility to pass code (e.g. Fortran) straight through to the generated program, giving great flexibility. As a last resort it is always possible to edit the generated code, perhaps to access facilities not supported by the generator or in dire emergencies.

6 Finally, because the production of generated code is controlled by the generator, we can ensure that the generated program adheres to high standards of

coding and structure and can incorporate features (such as the automatic validity checking of Codbox) which would be boring or inconvenient or uneconomical when writing programs by hand and under pressure of time.

There are, of course, some disadvantages of a system based on generators. These include:

1 The more complex structure of a generator system can be confusing for novice users.

2 Any significant change in the dictionary structure requires the rerunning of the system to regenerate the programs.

3 The generator program cannot interact with the data since it does not process it.

In any system there will be a mix of dictionary-driven programs which carry out their task immediately and dictionary-driven programs which generate a further program to do the work. Some applications are clearly very suitable for one style, some for the other. However, there are also applications and situations where both styles could be suitable. Where possible it may be best to supply both.

A6   A programme of development work

We suggest that one of the first tasks for any future international project of comparable surveys should be the production of a suitably co-ordinated suite of software for the processing of the surveys. The following proposals form a possible outline for such a process.

Preliminary phase

This phase is devoted to a review of the different strategies to be pursued, considering, in particular:

1 Micro-computer based data entry with proprietary software, backed up with mainframe processing for tabulations and analysis.

2 Use of existing general-purpose data entry/management software portable across super-mini and larger computers.

3 Development of the WFS data dictionary system for dictionary-driven data entry, followed by development of a generator system based on a redesigned question database.

4 Proceeding directly to a new questionnaire design system with question database and generator programs.

As already indicated we are confident that the third strategy will give the best combination of short- and long-term benefits, and assume this in our discussion of the later phases.

Phase 1

This will provide a usable dictionary-driven survey processing system based on the existing WFS data dictionary, in three steps.

Step 1 involves the design of extensions to the WFS dictionary structure and their implementation in the support routines: skip and occurrence information (simple), filter and other internal variables and consistency rules (less simple).

Step 2 involves work to complete the set of dictionary-driven programs for batch processing begun by WFS. The existing programs for range checking, marginals and updating will be retained and new programs are needed for structure, skip and consistency checking. If the new surveys are similar in structure to those of WFS, date editing can be performed with the program DEIR, using Codbox to create the extract file. Otherwise the development of a more general date editing facility must be brought forward from phase 2 and linked with the consistency check system. This step will ensure that processing can proceed even for pilot studies in the early months of the project, and will provide a back-up system if later stages are delayed.

Step 3 produces a new dictionary-driven data entry program, integrating necessary checks and including review and updating facilities. Some proposed details of this program have already been discussed.

By the end of this phase much of the substantial programming load associated with a survey will have been eliminated. Processing will be carried out on-line with batch back-up as necessary. The programs used will be driven by the data dictionary and so will be consistent, ready on time and free from errors. It will be possible to offer a fully integrated on-line data entry system to survey organizations with adequate on-line computing facilities, eliminating the repetitive, iterative correction process and ensuring consistent, structurally sound data.

Phase 2

The second phase of the project develops a system for generating programs for performing intelligent data entry in the survey office, to replace the dictionary-driven program developed in phase 1 and to provide greater flexibility in the choice of machine to be used for data entry. During the project additional manpower must be invested in resolving problems revealed by field experience with the system and in implementing generation into other target languages. For example, if a particularly suitable micro-computer package for data entry is discovered it might prove valuable to generate the data description instructions which this needs.

The design of a new form of data dictionary is the next step. We must change in our view of the dictionary so that it is a database of questions and a description of the data structure of a questionnaire, rather than of a file. Files can be described, but merely as physical representations of the structure.

Following initial analysis we expect the generator system to develop as a set of modules for generating the different components for the entry program (reading values, structural, range, skip checks, etc.) plus a system for integrating these generated components into a complete program using a model outline. This approach will give the flexibility to use the generators to build both an integrated intelligent data entry program and also stand-alone batch programs, whichever is more appropriate in a particular situation. The content of these two types of program is essentially the same, the modules just being inserted into different program outlines. In this way we can also allow choice over the amount of checking done and over the error correction processes to be used to be integrated into the data entry program.

A new date editing module will be needed to replace the WFS program DEIR, with general rules for expressing relationships between dates, and generating codes for inclusion with the other components. This could be done as part of the general system of consistency checks, but recent work on processing event histories (Westlake 1984) might provide an alternative approach.

Code generators have already been used by WFS (e.g. Codbox, Cocgen and Cocents, Command Writing System), and some very sophisticated generation tools are becoming available in commercial software markets (e.g. the Delta macro-processor and Cobol code generator). On the basis of current experience, we expect the generator programs to be written in Fortran (as an extension of the existing set of portable dictionary-driven programs). The choice for the initial generated target language probably lies between Fortran (as the language of the generators) and Cobol (which is perhaps more easily generated).

Phase 3

Phase 3 extends the use of the new data dictionary to support questionnaire design and production and allows the extension of the generator system to produce the question presentation programs which will be needed for field data entry.

The full logical structure of the questionnaire will be extended by the addition of the full text of the questions to allow the dictionary system to be used for the design of the questionnaire (see e.g. Questmast, The Research Machine). With appropriate text processing facilities this leads to the production of the questionnaire itself. This material is also needed for use in the question presentation program.

The generator system will be extended to encompass question presentation: much of this will come directly from the data entry system developed in phase 2, but there are several serious complications associated with the absence of a physical questionnaire on which the responses are recorded, for example the contraceptive knowledge and use questions. If suitable hand-held machines are not yet available the program will have to be developed initially for an office machine with appropriate facilities and characteristics.

Manpower requirements

The diagram below summarizes the input which we think would be needed to undertake this development work. Using two high-class programmers, familiar with dictionary and generator systems and experienced in the development of portable programs, we believe that the work can be accomplished over a period of three years.

```
Phase
     Step  ...Year  1... ...Year  2... ...Year 3...  Activity
Preliminary . . .                                    Review and report
   1   1   . . .                                     Extend dictionary
       2   . . . . . .                               Batch programs
       3   . . . . : . . .                           On-line data entry
   2            . . . : : : : : : : : : : . . . . . . . . . . . . . .  Generator system
   3                          . . . ? ——————— ?      Field system
```

Each dot (.) represents one man-month of work

A7   Sources of software items mentioned in the text

WFS software

Cocgen, Codbox, Corrector, Subsetter, Range, Freqs are all described in the WFS 'Software User's Manual' (WFS 1984).

Other software

Concor	International Statistical Program Center US Bureau of the Census Washington, DC 20233, USA
P-Stat	P-Stat Inc PO Box AH Princeton NJ 08544, USA
SAS	SAS Institute Inc Box 8000 Cary NC 27511-8000, USA
BMDP	BMDP Statistical Software Inc Suite 202 1964 Westwood Boulevard Los Angeles CA 90025, USA
Package-X	ICL 12 Crown Street Reading RG1 2HD UK

Genstat	Statistical Program Co-ordinator
	Nag Central Office
	256 Banbury Road
	Oxford OX2 7DE
	UK
Minitab	Marketing
	Minitab Data Analysis Software
	1124 Edgehill Drive
	Madison
	WI 53705, USA
Glim	Statistical Program Co-ordinator
	Nag Central Office
	256 Banbury Road
	Oxford OX2 7DE
	UK
SPSS	SPSS Inc
	Suite 3300
	444 North Michigan Avenue
	Chicago
	IL 60611, USA
Sir	Sir Inc
	PO Box 1404
	Evanston
	IL 60204, USA
Knowledge-man	Micro Data Base Systems Inc
	PO Box 248
	Lafayette
	IL 47902, USA
The Research Machine	Donovan Data Systems Inc
	666 Fifth Avenue
	New York
	NY 10103, USA
Compact	MRC Chest Diseases Unit
	Brompton Hospital
	Fulham Road
	London, SW3 6HP
	UK
Questmast	Centre for Educational Sociology
	7 Buccleugh Place
	Edinburgh
	UK

20

Construction of Analysis Files

Beverley Rowe
Trevor Croft

20.1 Introduction

Standardized data files are one of the hallmarks of WFS. Positively, they have simplified and so extended access to WFS data, particularly by less experienced users. Negatively, the standardization has held up some researchers and has been expensive. A description of the genesis and development of the standard file must therefore form part of any assessment of WFS.

The main type of dataset distributed by the WFS Archive contains the information collected from the interviewed individual women and is in a format described as a 'Standard Recode (SR) file'. Most of this chapter is about SR files. However, at the end we shall look briefly at problems of standardization with other types of data.

20.2 The reason for a derived or recoded file

Questionnaires adapted from the WFS core are complex, and machine-readable transcriptions of them are marked by the same complexity.

All WFS questionnaires contain history tables in which are collected the subject's marital and reproductive experience, the latter sometimes in two tables, one for live births and one for non-live births. Some questionnaires include other tables, e.g. describing the contraceptive history. These tables demonstrate one of the classic dilemmas of form design: in order to allow for a few large cases they must be too big for most cases. For instance, the Kenya questionnaire provides for fifteen pregnancies although the median is three and the upper quartile is six. It is normal practice in creating a computer record from these tables to enter only as many pregnancies as occurred. The alternative allows for the highest number found in the sample and creates empty lines for the 99 per cent or more respondents who had fewer births, marriages or whatever. Since this second approach is wasteful of data entry time, cards and disc space, it is usually avoided.

However, the economical approach has the disadvantage that it creates a record inherently variable in length and so non-rectangular; non-rectangular files cannot be used with most existing general computer software (although this situation is changing). This, then, is the first source of complexity.

The history tables present a further difficulty. As almost any analytic process based on them is concerned with dates, missing or inconsistent dates render such analyses at best difficult and at worst impossible. But missing or partial dating is endemic in retrospective surveys. Missing dates affect other parts of the questionnaire too, but it is in the tables that the problem is acute. To overcome this, it was WFS practice to impute missing dates, a process discussed more fully below and critically appraised in chapter 26.

It is possible to create a new version of the original file with these revised dates incorporated. They do not thus constitute a strong argument in themselves for a newly structured file. However, if such a file can be argued for on other grounds then it is attractive to add the imputed dates to a rectangular, derived file, while still holding an original file, non-rectangular and with unimputed dates. In any case, these tables and their date structures are the next source of complexity.

Missing dates are part of the more general problem of incomplete, missing or inconsistent data. It has been WFS policy to minimize this problem by extensive editing. Naturally, there is no reason why the data revisions cannot be carried out on a new version of the raw data, and most are. But the point of transfer to a restructured file is a natural one for carrying out certain types of update, particularly those of a systematic nature.

Most of the WFS surveys in Asia and Latin America used the fertility regulation module. This is not the place for a substantive critique of this module but it has created difficulties for data processing. The module collects an essentially constant set of data from each respondent. However, the subject's biographical status either requires variations in the wording of questions which are in fact addressed to the same end or makes some information otiose. Thus, questions about the open interval are not relevant to pregnant women; a widow should not be asked about future fertility. The module therefore divides the subjects into five main groups based on combinations of marital status, contraceptive history, fecundity and whether currently pregnant or not. Any given interview used one of five sub-questionnaires and these are of different structures and lengths. For example, questions 529, 535, 557, 559, 564, 566, 585 and 590 in the core questionnaire all solicit the same item of information (method used in the last closed birth interval) but each addresses a different subgroup of respondents. Bringing these together within one variable is a helpful simplification. Hence arises a second source of non-rectangularity and further complexity.

The reduction of the fertility regulation module could have been done as part of the manual coding. WFS policy was to take data straight from the questionnaire as far as possible and use the computer to sort it out later. Experience with such complex coding, in general, suggests that this policy was right. The problem, to the extent that there is one, lies partly in the basic design of the module and partly in underestimating the difficulty of carrying out the chosen policy.

Even a questionaire designed to generate a rectangular data processing record might be of limited use as there are important variables not addressed by a single question. For example, the encoding of a woman's pattern of contraceptive use (V645 in the SR file) brings together information from many places in the questionnaire. It is cumbersome to construct this variable for every analysis. Secondary variables are also needed to summarize information from history tables. Thus, V224 in the SR (sons born before or within the first five years of marriage) is awkward or impossible to derive using table-producing systems such as SPSS or Cocents. (With the latter, in particular, deriving new variables is clumsy in any case and this is the system used to produce most of the tables in WFS reports.) Furthermore, some variables, particularly those concerned with sampling design or those included in the household schedule, may not be present in the original questionnaire at all.

From four separate directions, then — processing of history tables, imputation of missing dates, compression of the fertility regulation module and the need for secondary variables — we see that the WFS raw data files are not suitable for normal analytic or computer use. Systems like Sir now accommodate erratic data formats, but we deal here with the software climate of the 1970s, and in developing countries.

After data cleaning and editing are completed, therefore, a recoded data file is created from which the tabulations for the First Country Report can be produced. This embodies rectangular history tables, considerably padded in most records, but unavoidable if a rectangular file is needed. The questions in the fertility regulation module are collapsed into one set of variables. Finally, all the derived variables needed at the table-forming and analysis stages are produced. However, standardization across countries is not a necessary feature of such a file.

The virtues of these derived, recoded files are:

— rectangularization
— systematically edited dates
— reassembly of divergent lines of interviewing
— construction of secondary variables.

All this is difficult to achieve with a file that reflects the format of the raw data.

Non-standard recoded (RE) files of this sort were produced for Bangladesh, Costa Rica, Fiji, Guyana, Jamaica, Kenya, Republic of Korea, Malaysia, Mexico, Nepal, Pakistan, Panama, Peru, Sri Lanka, Trinidad and Tobago and Venezuela. RE files were much easier to handle than the raw data files from which they derived. Furthermore, as more countries became available, various comparative projects were undertaken based on WFS data. The original RE files were easier to use for this than the raw data files would have been. However, new problems occurred.

A typical RE file contains up to 200 variables. The derivation of each from the original questionnaire had to be specified in detail, a skilled and lengthy task. A computer program was then prepared to realize this specification, another skilful and lengthy task. Such a program reveals errors and inconsistencies caused by faults in the specification or data errors not detected in the original editing. To get rid of them can take a long time. Nor was this the only problem with RE files.

The recoded variables were geared to the Country Report. This did not entail the inclusion of other data items that were in the questionnaire but not analysed in the reports. Although provision was made for country-specific variables, there were almost always items omitted. This caused inconvenience and delays in subsequent analysis. The danger of not carrying primary data over to derived files was one of the early lessons of the WFS experience.

The recode programs were complex. New errors were introduced into the data by software and many of these went undetected. Efforts were made to check them but that came later.

Finally, the complex specification often left the analysts feeling rather remote from the data. This is considered further in section 20.6.

20.3   The form and content of Standard Recode datasets

The RE files were not standard across countries. For instance, respondent's date of birth is called V402 in the Guyana RE, but V426 in the Indonesia RE. In many cases, the specification for a country is based on that for a previous country (thus, date of birth is also V426 for Mexico) but there is no simple way of knowing this.

Such borrowing saved time, both in preparing the specification and in using the data, and more time would be saved were all data files recoded to a standard format. This is why the SR format was introduced in 1978.

The standard recode format, then, satisfies the need for a rectangular analysis file, and at the same time incorporates all recoded variables used in the recommended standard tables in the First Country Report.

The recommended tables do not furnish all the material needed for a specific Country Report, nor does a report necessarily review all variables in the questionnaire. So if an SR is to be comprehensive, non-standard variables must be included; the original SR design therefore allowed for two major sections, one standard, the other country-specific.

The standard section is a set of variables each with fixed location, length, name, definition and structure. If a variable cannot be formed for a particular SR, it is not omitted but given a constant dummy value (equivalent to 'not applicable'). The standard section breaks into divisions grouping related variables.

Table 20.1 sets out the standard section. Variables are named by a three-digit number preceded by 'V', with the first digit after 'V' serving to group variables (except in the union or birth histories, where variable names follow a different convention). Thus, all variables about contraception start 'V6. .'.

A prominent feature of the standard section is that all variables, except some in the union and birth tables, occupy an even number of locations. This feature is not imposed on any other section (except that dates coded by century months always occupy four positions, wherever they come).

The country-specific section is a set of variables usually named by 'S' and a number. In later SRs these numbers reflect the grouping of variables in the standard section. For example, country-specific variables about family planning may be named S601, and so on.

TABLE 20.1
Contents of the standard section of the
Standard Recode files

---

0 Base data

V000–V006	Identification and sample structure
V007–V012	Reference dates and respondent's age

1 Union data

Union history	Details of each union
V101–V108	Marital status
V109–V113	Age at union
V114–V123	Marital duration

2–5 Fertility

Birth history	Details of each birth
V201–V206	Other pregnancies
V207–V212	Cumulative fertility
V213–V222	Living children
V223–V227	Period fertility
V228–V236	Birth intervals
V301–V306	Breastfeeding
V401–V407	Exposure status
V501–V513	Fertility preferences

6 Family planning

V601–V617	Knowledge of contraception
V618–V634	Ever-use of contraception
V635–V639	Current use of contraception
V640–V645	Pattern of use of contraception

7–9 Background data

V701–V713	Respondent's background
V801–V805	Partner's background
V901–V907	Characteristics of the interview

After finalizing the SR format, WFS was asked to include certain extra variables routinely in all SR files. It was undesirable to change the standard section because of changes to documentation and because the fixed location of the V variables makes change difficult. It was recommended that certain 'standard' S variables be created (see WFS 'Data Processing Guidelines' (WFS 1980a) p. 200). When the need for yet more standard variables arose, a new section was devised with X variables (X = 'Extra standard'). These are defined like V variables, with an important difference: they are not assigned fixed locations, so that in SRs for which a particular X variable is not defined there is no dummy entry as there is with V variables. It also renders the section more flexible: further variables may be defined and inserted later at appropriate points.

The original plan for SR files specified that data based on the WFS modules should also be represented by standard variables. The modules have had varying histories in this respect.

The fertility regulation module was defined so early and used so widely, apart from the African surveys, that it is virtually part of the core questionnaire. It is mostly represented in the standard section, which has alternative specifications for variables whose structure is affected by the presence or absence of the module. Items not covered by the V variables are all represented by X variables.

The small abortion module was early translated into a set of recommended S variables, later transformed to X variables.

More work was called for by the module on factors other than contraception affecting fertility (FOTCAF). A new section was created, with variables named by 'F' and a number. This section has fixed locations and follows the standard section when present. It is virtually part of the core questionnaire for the later surveys, particularly those in Africa.

The family planning module had the most miscellaneous treatment. Its variables had no standard definition for a long time, though widely used, and its contents were variously assigned to S variables. Later, the module was represented as a set of X variables, so that in the most recent SR files the information from this module has a more uniform appearance.

Finally, all surveys collect data on non-live births. These do not appear in the birth history. They are therefore usually included in a table of their own.

20.4   Support files and documentation

Introduction

SR datasets are thus far easier to use than the original files in questionnaire format and have been requested some five times more frequently by non-WFS users. When dispatched to them, an SR dataset is bolstered by an extensive information structure.

The distribution tape itself contains other machine-readable files. There is a data dictionary, a complete set of marginals for all variables in the file and a complete description of the dataset in terms of SPSS control cards.

Also with the tape comes a booklet (the 'data document'), which can run to 100 pages or more, specifically written for each SR file. It is not normal practice to issue questionnaires and coding manuals with SR files, though questionnaires are always printed in the Country Reports and so are available. In any case, either of these, or any other relevant information, such as the detailed recoding specifications, are available on request from ISI.

Printed documentation

The specially written *data document* gives all the information needed in normal use. It opens with a description of the organizational and methodological background:

— executing agency or agencies
— sampling and population coverage
— fieldwork
— editing and other office procedures
— data processing.

An explanation follows of the various files accompanying the dataset (dictionary, marginals, SPSS control cards), particular attention being given to the dictionary.

The heart of the document is a set of notes about the variables. This is not comprehensive; the complete specification of the file is provided by the dictionary, which always appears as an appendix to the document as well as on the tape as a machine-readable file. These notes flesh out the rather skeletal dictionary and identify variables which deviate from standard, variables changed from previous versions of the data and known deficiencies still present in the data. Apart from the dictionary, which is always appended, there may be other appendices. For example, appendix B for the Colombia SR lists the full occupation coding, which is far too long to be included in the dictionary.

If it is necessary to know precisely how a variable is formed, then the data document may not be enough. Reference may be had to the full *specification* prepared by the country specialist as a guide to the programmer. The paradigm of these is the specifications in appendix II (part 3) of the WFS Data Processing Guidelines. Sometimes these are based on the output from a special computer program, Codbox (see below). Unfortunately, printed specifications are not available for all countries.

To settle particularly tricky problems, the *questionnaires, coding manuals* and other office documentation are available. The archives contain a mass of material — memos, letters, reports — which may be needed for special examination.

Machine-readable files

The dictionary. Data dictionaries have been a recommended way of describing datasets for some 15 years. They have been developed for files of survey data in several applications: probably Osiris is the best known survey/statistical system making heavy use of a dictionary.

WFS started to use data dictionaries in 1978. They furnish machine-readable documentation for programs but they are also designed to be referred to by people. Like all functional compromises, the WFS dictionary is not ideal for either humans or machines, but any loss is more than compensated for by the advantage of everything being in one place. It is a fundamental of data processing that two versions of the same information will diverge. The discipline of preparing file descriptions for software is valuable anyway. Software does not forgive gaps or errors; the accuracy required by a computer system is a real gain for human users.

Figure 20.1 shows an extract from the dictionary for the Nepal SR. Each variable is described by a formal name ('V401') as well as a 30-character label ('Husband or wife sterilized'): two-level variable naming like this will be familiar to users of statistical packages. The numbers between the name and the label give the location, width and range of the variable together with an indication of

```
V305  507   2   1   12   88   99   Length breastfed <12 grps>
                                     1   Did not breastfeed
                                     2   0-2
                                     3   3-5
                                     4   6
                                     5   7-8
                                     6   9-11
                                     7   12
                                     8   13-17
                                     9   18
                                    10   19-23
                                    11   24
                                    12   25+
                                    88   No closed interval
                                    99   Not stated
V306  509   2   0    1               CI  >32 and child lived >23
                                     0   No
                                     1   Yes
```

Group 4

—Exposure status

```
V401  511   2   1   4   Husband or wife sterilized
                         1   Wife contraceptive
                         2   Husband
                         3   Wife not contracep
                         4   Other cases
V402  513   2   1   5   Exposure status
                         1   Pregnant
                         2   Not married
                         3   Sterilized
                         4   Not fecund
                         5   Fecund
V403  515   2   0   1   Married and fecund
                         0   No
                         1   Yes
V404  517   2   0   1   Exposed                           V403
V405  519   2   0   1   Exposed, not strlzed, 1+birth     V403
V406  521   2   0   1   Curr married and not pregnant     V403
V407  523   2   0   1   Ever married not pregnant         V403
```

FIG. 20.1   Extract from Nepal SR dictionary

values for residual classes (inapplicable, not stated, etc.). The main entry for a variable is followed by labels for the individual codes or values of the variable.

Dictionaries include information bearing on the dictionary's provenance, the overall parameters of the file, a brief description of the dictionary format itself and guidance on bibliographic citation for the dataset.

There is provision for a concise description of information represented in table format (birth histories, for example) and, although this is not relevant to the rectangularized SR files, the dictionary format also allows for complex file structures. For francophone countries, the dictionary is available in French. It is not available in Spanish or Arabic.

Marginals. The machine-readable file of marginals is produced with SPSS. A semi-automatic procedure has been devised to do this: a set of SR marginals needs seven separate computer runs. Marginal files created after 1981 are more strictly formatted. The marginals are given for each variable in the file, except for the history variables. Here a full tabulation is done for the first event (union, birth, etc.) but information about subsequent events is coalesced using the SPSS MULT RESPONSE command. Where the records in the file have a variable weight, there will be two marginals files, one weighted, one unweighted.

SPSS control cards. In addition to the WFS dictionary, a description of the dataset is supplied in the form of SPSS control cards. This is not usable directly as the number of variables exceeds the normal limits for SPSS. However, it is far easier to extract a subset from this description than to compose one from scratch.

20.5 The Standard Recode file and its creation

From 1978 onwards, all First Country Reports were prepared direct from an SR file. Also, to facilitate comparative studies, datasets for which RE files had been produced were reworked into an SR file. The existence of the SR format encouraged the development of a range of simplifying techniques.

Recoding instructions

The WFS style of recoding instructions allows the demographer to specify the transposition of data from an original file to the SR file without needing to know how to program. Recoding instructions are embodied in box diagrams which set out rules by which new variables are constructed from old ones, and the value to be assigned for each condition. As an example, we look at V635 (current method of contraception) (figure 20.2). This has code 0 for non-current users, 1–15 for methods (or 99 for not stated) and 88 for respondents not asked the question (the non-exposed). The basic information is in core Q505 ('What method are you using?'). But for compatibility with other questions we first remove the contraceptively sterilized (V401 = 1 or 2), the non-exposed (V402 ≠ 5) and also filter on the preliminary Q504 ('Are you or your husband currently . . .?'). We

V635 *if*				*then*
V401 = 1				9
V401 = 2				10
V401 = 3 or 4	V402 ≠ 5			88
	V402 = 5	Q504 = 1		Q505
		Q504 ≠ 1		0

FIG. 20.2. Recoding instructions for V635 (current method of contraception)

can now specify V635, with the conditions on the left ('if') and the resulting value of V635 on the right ('then'). The conditions are evaluated from the top until a match is found.

The diagram can be translated by a programmer to produce, say, a Cobol program:

```
IF V401 = 1 THEN MOVE 9 TO V635
ELSE IF V401 = 2 THEN MOVE 10 TO V635
    ELSE IF V401 = 3 OR 4
        THEN IF V402 NOT = 5 THEN MOVE 88 TO V635
        ELSE IF V402 = 5
            THEN IF Q504 = 1 THEN MOVE Q505 to V635
            ELSE IF Q504 NOT = I THEN MOVE 0 TO V635
```

Several techniques evolved to check that recoding instructions are correct. An examination of frequency distributions reveals values of output variables not in the expected range, checks the consistency of the recoded variables by comparison of their distributions for particular values with that implied in the recoding instructions and, finally, checks the consistency of the recoded variables with the raw data variables from which they are created.

Manual recoding of a small number of cases shows how the calculated values compare with those produced by the program and thus identifies unexpected conditions not handled by the recoding instructions.

Cross-tabulation checks the construction of recoded variables in terms of other recoded variables. This particular form of checking was greatly extended and standardized later; it is discussed below.

Codbox

Whenever any of these methods of checking indicates mistakes, both the recode program and the recode specifications must be changed so that when recoding is completed the specifications properly document the resulting file. In practice, though, the specifications become out of date and corrections are made to the program but not the specifications.

The program Codbox both solves this problem and simplifies programming. Codbox processes a specification written in the form of box diagrams rather as shown above. These can be entered directly by the demographer. It creates a tidily boxed listing of the specification, suitable for documentation, and generates appropriate program statements, usually in Cobol. This means that only the input to Codbox has to be modified when an error is found, while the final specification must exactly document the recoded file. The programmer's task is obviously reduced. (See WFS 'Software User's Manual' (WFS 1984) section 12.)

Imputation

The imputation of imperfect, missing or contradictory dates called for standard software. This was refined and improved over several years leading up to the creation of DEIR (Date Edit and Imputation Recode Program). This edits the birth and union histories, imputing dates where necessary. The input file to DEIR is created by a questionnaire-specific program which extracts the history information and related data from the original raw data file and rectangularizes it.

Date imputation is possible because the period within which an offending date may lie is constrained. For example, if a respondent had a third live birth in February 1965 and a fifth in December 1967, then a missing date for a fourth live birth probably lies after October 1965 and before March 1967. Within this range a date is selected, usually at random (although midpoint imputation is possible). Any other available relevant information can be used as well; we need not go into detail here but merely point out that such a procedure is reasonable and necessary and consider what should happen to these imputed dates.

The file created by DEIR is the first part of an SR file and the construction of the event tables and the table-related variables is completely standardized.

In some of the later WFS surveys, particularly those in Africa, the module on factors other than contraception affecting fertility (FOTCAF) was used. The questions in this module relate to pregnancy intervals whereas the comparable questions in non-FOTCAF questionnaires are in terms of birth intervals. There is also a lot of date information which is not found in non-FOTCAF surveys. DEIR was therefore enlarged as FDEIR for use with FOTCAF surveys. FDEIR does everything DEIR does but in addition edits the non-live pregnancy table and FOTCAF module dates, creates the original Standard Recode variables in terms of birth intervals from the data given in terms of pregnancy intervals and produces a set of special FOTCAF variables (F variables) appended to the V variables, along with a non-live pregnancy history and other variables which are difficult to construct otherwise. (See WFS Software User's Manual section 13.)

Cross-checks system

Even with these tools, the quality of the SR files varied dramatically from survey to survey. A system of cross-checks was created to avoid this. The system is a set of SPSS cross-tabulations plus a set of Fortran programs and it ensures that an SR file is correctly constructed. The output from the SPSS runs is automatically compared with a set of standard templates. Cells in the cross-tabulations which have entries where no entries appear on the templates are shown as errors.

For example, we may refer back to V635. If we examine figure 20.2 we can draw a chart like this:

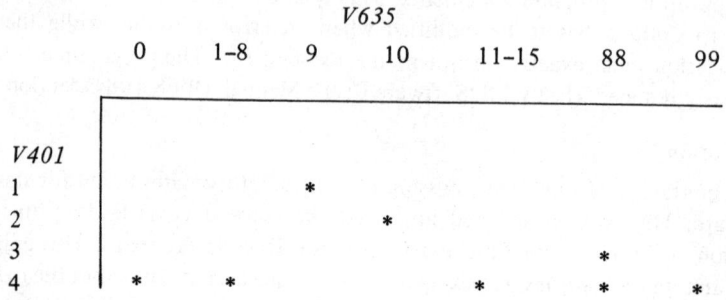

The distribution of stars shows which cells within a cross-tabulation of V401 and V635 can contain a non-zero value. So if we find cases where V401 = 1 and V635 = 0, then we know that a mistake has been made.

For certain checks, particularly those of the internal consistency of the histories, SPSS is clumsy so Fortran programs are used. (See WFS Data Archive Handbook section 4.)

By iterative refinement of the recoding specifications, using all of the tools discussed, the final SR files are produced to a high standard of consistency.

20.6 Evaluation of the SR format

The concept of a standardized file is sound and makes all WFS analysis easier, in particular regional and comparative studies. But the format chosen is not necessarily the best.

The inclusion of *all* variables recommended for the country report, though attractive as a documentary record, leads to redundancy. Less than half the V variables are derived from the raw data, the rest being derived from other V variables. The effect is to increase the length of an SR file by some 25 per cent. It is true that this standardization increases the standardization of reports and reduces errors. But other ways of achieving this could have been found. For example, given a really standard but simple file, a program could have been developed that expanded it precisely for reports and this could have been used for all countries.

Some derived variables are directly useful to the analyst, particularly those that summarize the union and birth histories, as these are tedious or even imposs-ible to derive within systems such as SPSS. But age at first marriage — derivable from the union history without iteration — hardly needs to be represented by four variables differing only by the grouping factor. There are many such examples. The increase in utility is not a full recompense for extra space.

The more complex derived variables also have drawbacks. Some have analytical assumptions built into them that could confuse or lead to their being disregarded and therefore wasting more space. For example, V306 ('Whether closed interval exceeds 32 months and child survived at least 24 months') was intended to isolate a group of infants whose breastfeeding was not restricted by either a succeeding pregnancy or their own death. This was to be used as a denominator for breastfeeding differentials. However, results of an analysis on this subgroup can give rise to a distorted picture if extrapolated to the population, as women are differentially selected for inclusion in it. It would not seem to be of any other, general, use. This is partly a criticism of the basic structure of the WFS tabulation plan but, as these variables are enshrined in the SR files, their continued use could be said to be condoned. Often the complexity of the specifications can itself be confusing. For example, many of the FOTCAF variables are difficult to comprehend, particularly by the time they have been broken down by other variables.

While some variables are over-represented by repeated recoding, some are overly compressed, with loss of detail. For instance, women were asked about family size preferences. Many answered in terms of a range but this has been summarized by a rounded-down midpoint. The original data are rarely added as country-specific variables, yet to some analysts the nature of the ranges is significant.

More table-derived variables would be useful. For example, it is fiddly to get at the data for current marriage, last birth and penultimate birth (particularly the births, as allowance must be made for multiple last births). It would be sensible to have the data for these as secondary variables as well as in the tables.

The orientation towards the standard country reports caused the neglect of other variables. Thus, for Malaysia, over 100 variables were later extracted that were not in the SR file. The cost of redoing many SRs in order to ensure that all data from the original questionnaires had been included was substantial. Even as late as 1982, all the questions in the *core* questionnaire had not been allowed for.

Ironing out the complexities of the fertility regulation module is one of the main reasons for having a separate standardized file. It is also one of the most costly and complex parts of creating the SR. This is not the place to evaluate the attempt to give interviewers a simple sequence of exact questions. It can be said, however, that in terms of clerical coding, computer checking and programming effort, this module has been enormously expensive in manpower and computer time.

Another complicating factor has been the allocation of variables to fixed locations. The relaxing of this provision for the X variables has allowed flexibility and organic growth. Within WFS, software has been developed that used the machine-readable dictionaries and so permits the user to refer to variables by name without worrying where they are located; the loss of fixed locations would be a nuisance to those not having access to such software. Nevertheless, it would be a gain to be able to add variables within the framework of the V variables as this would reduce the need for country-specific variables.

The allocation of an even number of locations to all V variables, probably based on a confused understanding of computer needs, was, to say the least, strange and wasteful. Over 170 variables use one position more than necessary, increasing the size of the standard section by about 25 per cent and tying up over three megabytes of computer storage if all WFS SR files are on-line.

These criticisms do not detract from the value of having a standard file. The evidence for this is anecdotal but it is worth quoting one analyst's subjective assessment. The data processing for a particular comparative study took him three weeks. Using non-standard WFS files he estimated it could have taken a year. This contrast is a criticism of the complexity of the non-standard files but does suggest that the standard files justify their existence. Up to the time of writing there have been over 200 comparative projects on WFS data. Even if processing time on all these were reduced by a factor of four (an underestimate), the cost of producing the SR files would seem to be reasonable.

SR files cannot be produced without help from a programmer. WFS programmers usually built up considerable knowledge of how the surveys were done and why, but they were not demographers or statisticians. As a result, decisions may have been made in developing an SR file which should have been referred to the country specialist but, for a variety of reasons, were made by the programmer. Some of these decisions could be questioned.

There is a further criticism which calls into question not aspects of SR files but their very existence. It has been suggested that they distance the careless analyst from the important special conditions that apply in each country. For instance, unthinking use of V306 (see above) without regard to the reasons why different groups of women have short intervals could invalidate some cross-country comparisons. But bad research is not obviated by being made more difficult; on the contrary. Denying analysts standard files forces them to waste more time wrestling with clumsy data formats so the likelihood of shoddy research is increased. Good roads help criminals get away but they also help law-abiding citizens to go about their business.

It was late in the history of WFS before a serious difficulty with SR files was felt. By the middle of 1983 WFS had distributed over 1000 datasets to some 300 sites. Responsible management of such a pool of data needs careful record-keeping. It is also important that all users of a particular dataset are aware of further developments of it. The result was increasing expense associated with updating SR files because of the extensive user base and the high standards of validation, support and documentation which were established. All the activities arising from creation of a new SR were labour-intensive:

— programming the new variables, correction or whatever
— file validation (cross-checks, etc.)

- new dictionary
- new marginals
- new SPSS file
- archiving
- new descriptive document
- notification to external users
- distribution of new tapes.

Yet, at the point when the first 40 SR files were ready, more than three-quarters required further work before they could be called definitive. Once the end of the project neared, such a massive programme of work became difficult. To overcome this problem, supplementary standard (SS) files were devised. These contain an appropriate selection of:

- corrections to SR variables
- items from the original data omitted from the SR
- extra recoded variables.

(The last includes, in particular, a set of four variables used in all the WFS cross-national summaries.)

Could a standard format closer to that of the raw data have been developed? Certainly, the answer is 'yes', with less derived variables and items ordered more as in the core questionnaire. On the other hand, many of the derived variables are extremely useful and non-trivial to construct (consider V212, V633 and V645), while the fertility regulation module almost by itself makes raw data files unusable and forces the analyst away from any format based on them. There would, with such a format, then be a problem of the location in the record of the derived variables. If they are located among the questions with which they are most associated in content, then the association with the original structure is broken. If they are added at the end, then associated items may be widely separated in the file. Fortunately, we do not have to resolve that dilemma here.

20.7 Standardization of other files

Household files

WFS surveys always include a household survey as well as a survey of individual women. These are often substantial. The survey in Cameroon has information on over 200 000 household members. In some cases, they represent one of the best sources of information on the population.

The files are set up as *household* files. Each case has a record with household-level data. This is followed by a set of household member subrecords. In 1980 transformed versions of these files were produced. The unit of analysis became the *household member*.

That creates a problem with the household-level data, if a conventional rectangular record format is to be used. For these household member (HM) files, the policy was adopted of appending the household data to each member record.

The HM files were not edited beyond any editing already done in the countries. All variables in the WFS core household schedule were given standard names but codes were not standardized. They may be called semi-standardized.

The success of the SR files for the individual data created a demand for fully standardized household member (SM) files. A format was specified in 1982 but work on creating these files is still incomplete.

The household files are diverse and vary greatly in size. The SM format is therefore more like X variables than V variables: fixed names, labels, code structure and order but not fixed locations. This means that variables which cannot be formed are omitted and that new variables can be fitted into the schema, thus avoiding variables that must be defined country-specifically because they do not fit into the schema.

Basic editing of the files is important. Even with SR files, the further elimination of discrepancies was valuable. With SM files it is particularly important to have a coherent and consistent household structure as many of the derived variables in the SM files are across and inter-record summaries. Bad data lead to clumsy analyses. Comprehensive editing is therefore regarded as part of the project.

The derived variables are kept to a minimum. Virtually no within-member recodes are specified. All the new variables are ones which can only be created by summing across records or linking to other records.

Other files

The only other data that might have lent themselves to standardization were the community-level files. No work was done on these. The issue of standardization hardly arises with the few husbands survey files or the post-enumeration surveys.

PART VI

Data Evaluation, Analysis and Archiving

21

The Main Country Report

John Cleland
Mary-Beth Weinberger
J. R. Rele

21.1 Development of the strategy

Ironically, WFS, in so many other respects a model of scientific rectitude, committed the classic error of designing its measurement instruments before defining analytical objectives and substance. It was not until early 1974, when the Core Questionnaire for high-fertility countries was nearing its final state, that serious attention was paid to the planning of analysis. However, this error was not as grave as it sounds, because the results of similar surveys to those of the WFS programme were well known to the designers of WFS instruments. Furthermore, the contents of the questionnaire were dictated primarily by descriptive aims and required no elaborate theoretical rationale.

It was soon realized that the presentation and analysis of results from national surveys could not be accomplished in a single report without unacceptable delays in publication. Instead a two-phase reporting strategy was envisaged. The first report would contain a brief description of the national setting, a full account of the survey methodology and a presentation of the preliminary results. Further analysis of the data using more refined statistical and demographic techniques would be postponed for a second report or reports.

The major forum for discussion of the nature of the first or main country report was a specially convened Seminar on Tabulation and Analysis of Survey Data, held in London in September 1974 and attended by 21 demographers and statisticians. Reflecting the determination of WFS to unite demographic and statistical methods, equal weight was given to both disciplines, though our main concern in this chapter lies with the former.

The demographers at this seminar were presented with two radically different analytic schemes. The first, prepared by Pullum (then of the University of California at Davis) and Freedman, of the University of Michigan, was dubbed the classical approach, because it focused on conventional measures of lifetime fertility and consisted largely of cross-classifications of proportions and means, following the traditional demographic style. The second, prepared by Ryder, of Princeton University, proposed a much more ambitious and complete reconstruction of marriage and maternity careers of cohorts, based on the retrospective histories. Among the advantages of this scheme, it was argued, were that it overcame many problems of censoring and bias; made maximum use of the available data; rightly regarded reproduction as a sequential process usually starting with marriage; addressed the central issue of the timing of fertility in addition to the quantum; and permitted the integration of the intermediate variables such as reproductive intentions and control and breastfeeding into a single coherent framework.

Ryder's ideas received considerable support, notably from Hauser and Brass, but they were deemed too demanding of data quality and data processing skills, too untested and unfamiliar for WFS endorsement as a model for a first report. Though a partial and modified version of his original recommendations was eventually published as a *WFS Technical Bulletin* (Ryder 1982), and though the essence of his scheme was later successfully implemented (e.g. Rodríguez and Hobcraft 1980), the fact that some 10 years after the original suggestion the full Ryder approach has not been applied to any WFS data set validates the correctness of these original apprehensions.

The Pullum/Freedman tabulation plan, based on the Core Questionnaire for ever-married women, was adopted, albeit with reservations from some quarters, as an appropriate model for the first phase of analysis. It consisted of five main sections (shown in the upper panel of table 21.1) comprising a total of 171 tables. Over the subsequent nine months minor changes were made and three appendices added. The latter contained modifications and a short set of extra tables for surveys using the Fertility Regulation Module, recommended tabulations from the household schedule derived from a paper prepared by Brass for the 1974 seminar, and a limited set of tabulations for exploitation of the birth histories, originally proposed by Lee-Jay Cho at the same seminar. In June 1975, the Guidelines for the Country Report No. 1 were produced and disseminated (eventually being published as WFS 1977a).

After the experience of the first few country reports, these Guidelines underwent one major revision which expanded the total number of recommended tabulations from 220 to 308 without changing the essential nature of the earlier version. This large increase in size (see table 21.1) was the inevitable consequence of attempting to meet the multitudinous and conflicting interests of many individuals. In such circumstances, it proved easier to expand than to impose difficult choices. This final version of the Guidelines was published in April 1977. Apart from a detailed and precise description of each table, the document contains a suggested outline for the text of the report, lists the variables needed for constructing the tables (see table 21.2), and devotes 20 pages to a rationale for recommended tabulations and to hints on interpretation of findings. The document must rank among the most meticulously prepared survey tabulation plans ever written.

21.2   Criteria for appraisal

The central objective of this chapter is to appraise both the basic strategy and detailed recommendations of WFS with regard to country reports and the way

TABLE 21.1

Number of tables in the tabulation plan for the First Country Report

		Sept. 1974 version	June 1975 version	April 1977 version
Section				
Nuptiality		31	26	47
Fertility		44	43	63
Preferences		38	39	44
Contraception		37	37	54
Contraception in relation to preferences		21	15	27
Subtotal		171	160	235
Appendix I	Fertility Regulation	NA	4	4
Appendix II	Household Schedule	NA	50	54
Appendix III	Birth History	NA	6	6
Appendix IV	Additions and Modifications for All-Women Samples	NA	NA	9
Total		171	220	308

in which these recommendations were actually implemented by countries. Choice of the most appropriate criteria for this evaluation is difficult. Like most large enterprises, WFS was faced with varied and sometimes conflicting priorities and pressures and had to try to meet the different needs of national and international audiences. Clearly, one consideration was to produce quick, policy-relevant results which could be widely disseminated among non-demographers, particularly within participating countries. A very different and yet equally compelling aim was the achievement of a detailed description and a greater scientific understanding of the process of reproduction in particular countries. A third central aim, enshrined in the WFS mandate, was to produce results that would be comparable across countries. Among other criteria might be included the self-imposed obligation that WFS procedures should be models of excellence for countries to follow in subsequent similar surveys. Yet another is the potential utility of main reports as a secondary research resource. Finally, it is necessary to appraise the nature and scope of main reports, both in the context of the need to accomplish most of the work in participating countries and in that of the wider scheme of analysis.

There is no clear-cut way of reconciling the diverse goals enumerated in the preceding paragraph. Indeed, an awareness of the incompatibility of the aims is essential to an understanding of the whole WFS programme. However, we shall attempt in the sections that follow to make explicit the standards by which we judge, in the full knowledge that the application of different criteria will imply different conclusions.

TABLE 21.2

Major demographic and attitudinal variables^a used in First Country Report tabulations of the individual survey

Section of report	Dependent variables	Demographic and attitudinal classifying variables
1 Nuptiality and exposure status	* Age at first marriage	Age
	* Status of first marriage	Duration of marriage, Age at marriage
	* Number of marriages	Duration of marriage, Age at marriage
	* Whether remarried	Duration of marriage
	* Percentage of time spent married	Age, Age at marriage
	* Current marital status	Duration of marriage, Age at marriage
	* Exposure status	Age, Duration of marriage, Number of living children, Age at marriage
2 Fertility	* Fertility early in marriage	Duration of marriage, Age at marriage
	* Children ever born	Age, Duration of marriage, Age at marriage
	Number of living children	Age, Duration of marriage, Children ever born
	* Children born last 5 years	Age, Age at marriage, Number of living children ^{b}
	Currently pregnant?	Age, Age at marriage, Number of living children
3 Fertility preferences	* Wants no more children	Age, Duration of marriage, Number of living children
	* Additional number wanted	Age, Duration of marriage, Number of living children (sons, daughters)
	Last birth wanted?^{c}	Age, Duration of marriage, Number of living children
	* Total children desired	Age, Duration of marriage, Age at marriage, Number of living children (sons, daughters)
	Preferred sex of next child	Living sons, daughters, Age, Duration of marriage

4 Contraceptive knowledge and use

* Breastfeeding, last inter-birth interval — Age, Children ever born
* Knowledge of contraception — Age, Number of living children
* Ever-use of contraception — Age, Number of living children
* Current use of contraception — Age, Number of living children (sons, daughters), Duration of marriage

* Pattern of contraceptive use — Age, Duration of marriage, Exposure status, Age at marriage, Number of living children

5 Contraception related to fertility preferences

  Knowledge of contraception — Age, Whether more children wanted, Desired versus actual family size

  Current use (any method) — Number of living children, Whether more children wanted

* Current use (efficient method)[d] — Duration of marriage, Age at marriage, Age, Number of living children

* Pattern of contraceptive use — Age, Whether more children wanted, Desired versus actual family size

---

a Variables for a few tables dealing with open and last closed birth intervals, sex of recent births and childhood mortality are omitted.
b Number five years ago.
c Countries which used the Fertility Regulation Module.
d Use of efficient method among women who want no more children, and percentage of exposed women who both want no more children and are using an efficient method.
Note: * Tabulated by socio-economic background variables.

21.3   The nature and scope of First Country Reports

The most fundamental question that can be asked is whether comprehensive general reports of the type recommended by WFS were needed at all. In this regard, it is interesting to compare the reporting strategy of the low-fertility developed countries which participated in the WFS programme. While some chose to issue a major report containing both methodology and preliminary findings, more countries (e.g. France, Norway, Belgium, Denmark, Israel, Netherlands) published the findings in a series of monographs or articles on particular topics. Monographs of the sort issued in some developed countries are not the only alternative to a single report. It would have been possible to publish a sequence of documents similar to the individual sections of the WFS reporting scheme. In our opinion, the adoption of this latter policy for developing countries would have been an error of judgement. The benefits of a single report integrating the methodology of the survey, reproduction of the complete questionnaire, description of variables and preliminary results outweigh the undoubted attractions and flexibility of a fragmented or serial reporting style. A coherent overall view of a survey is greatly facilitated by an integrated presentation of methodology and findings. Of equal importance is the fact that it can represent the harvesting of an appreciable portion of the total analytic yield of a survey. As WFS was well aware, survey organizations, especially in developing countries, frequently fail to publish any results at all, or only report a small fraction of the potential of their enquiries. It is to the credit of the WFS programme that all developing countries (except Iran) have published comprehensive results. It is doubtful whether this record could have been achieved under a more protracted reporting strategy. Reporting in a series of publications would have encouraged coding and processing of subsets of the data, one at a time. WFS could not have provided on-site technical assistance over long periods and consequently some of the data might have remained unprocessed.

Accepting the principle of a general report, we turn now to consider the major alternative forms that it could have taken. WFS faced decisions regarding its analytic complexity, from exclusive reliance on cross-tabulations at one end of the spectrum to extensive use of statistical and demographic techniques at the other. As already intimated, the tabular approach was chosen and there is no attempt in the Guidelines, or in most of the actual reports, to carry the analysis beyond straightforward cross-classifications of proportions and means (except for the use of standardization). Despite the drawback that a reliance on tabulations inevitably gives a proliferation of figures, this policy was correct in its context. Data processing, analysis and report writing had rightly been seen as the prime responsibility of participating countries themselves. The unfamiliarity of many statistical office staff with analytical techniques and lack of suitable hardware and software precluded the timely production of technically complex reports without considerable further inputs of technical assistance or the involvement of other organizations. Furthermore, it is desirable that more complex analysis be preceded by an evaluation of data quality, itself a lengthy process.

Hence the appropriate strategy was to have straightforward and relatively standardized First Country Reports.

The other major choice concerned the scope of the report. Should it be confined to 20–30 key tables or, at the other extreme, should it pursue the tabular approach to the fullest reasonable extent? In recommending a tabulation plan of 308 tables, WFS's policy corresponded more closely to the latter than to the former policy. There were several reasons for this. In 1974 and 1975, the willingness of countries to make available their data files for further in-depth analysis and for cross-national comparison was uncertain. Hence, a comprehensive and detailed set of tables was needed, as a safeguard against subsequent unavailability of the primary data. There was also a fear that countries would lose interest in the data as soon as the first report was completed, a factor that militated in favour of a substantial initial product. Experience has shown that this fear was justified in some countries but not at all in others.

However justifiable the decision to prepare such a lengthy tabulation plan may have been at the time, it proved extremely costly and damaging. The recommendation to produce a First Country Report based on such a large and detailed set of cross-tabulations, involving the creation of many complex variables from the raw data, in conjunction with the decision that all data cleaning should be done before tabulation, doomed WFS's original aspirations for reports to be published within six months of fieldwork completion. The actual mean elapsed time between the end of fieldwork and dispatch of the complete report to the printer was about 20 months. Further details may be found in chapter 9. While much of this delay can be attributed to the cleaning process (which undoubtedly facilitated secondary analysis), the creation of an extensive set of variables from the raw data and running of tables in a form suitable for direct photographic printing were inevitably time-consuming. Furthermore, the assimilation and written summarization of such a large volume of tabular material took at least two months and, in the case of inexperienced authors, much longer. Considerable printing time has also to be added.

With the wisdom of hindsight, it is clear that WFS should have opted for a much smaller, quick-release report of key findings prior to the preparation of a more comprehensive general report. This preliminary publication should have been based on a handful of simple variables and on no more than 30 tables, derived if necessary from unedited data.[1] Most of the immediate policy interest in the output of WFS-type surveys can be met by standard measures of lifetime and current fertility, method-specific use of contraception and source of supply, age at first marriage, some indication of fertility preferences and childhood mortality, disaggregated by such factors as region, urban–rural residence and education. With the possible exceptions of age at marriage and mortality, these items can be easily extracted from questionnaires or from raw data files for priority attention and are amenable to simple tabulation. Some countries, on their own initiative, produced preliminary results of this nature for local management needs and, in the final stages of the programme, this approach was officially adopted by WFS for the surveys in Benin, Mauritania and Nigeria. Moreover there was little detrimental effect on the subsequent production of a comprehensive main report, and, even if there had been delays, the consequences would not have been so grave. WFS fears that the issue of a preliminary report might erode interest in later reports may have been exaggerated, but it is difficult to generalize from the limited experience of the last few surveys. Certainly, any expansion of a preliminary report beyond the limited scope outlined above would tend to erode motivation for a main report.

Quite apart from the inevitable delay in publication, the sheer scale of the recommended tabulations in the Country Report No. 1 Guidelines had the additional, unfortunate and largely unintended consequence of fostering formidably large publications. The early reports were typically 500 pages in length and the later ones grew further (to between 700 and 1000 pages), in response to the increasing incorporation of non-core material. To handle this size of publication, most later reports were split into two volumes, one containing text and appendices and the other comprising the detailed tabulations. Quite apart from the implications for cost of printing and distribution, we suspect that the size of the reports deterred readership and thus reduced the diffusion of findings. The need to index the detailed tables in an attractive, clear and concise manner was overlooked and this exacerbated the problem. Particularly within countries, however, these large volumes may remain useful reference sources for some time.

We mentioned above that this consequence was unintended because the authors of the Guidelines expected participating countries, with the advice of WFS staff, to be highly selective in the publication of tables, deleting those of minor interest. Rejected tables could still be made available on request. Why did this process of elimination not happen to any appreciable extent? We suggest that the prime reason was that it required time, skill and judgement, which are always in short supply. It is easier to publish everything than to make a multitude of awkward decisions. Once this example had been set by the early countries with the encouragement of WFS country co-ordinators, the rest followed automatically.

21.4   Standardization of report contents and use of modules

Standardization of tabulation has major advantages: it reduces the cost of producing reports, particularly through standardized software, and helps speed their publication, and it ensures that the international comparability built into the questionnaires is not lost when the results appear. However, standardization can be carried to such an extreme that matters of importance within particular countries are ignored and topics of little local interest receive the 'standard' amount of attention. The degree of standardization in national reports has elicited occasional but scathing criticism (e.g. Caldwell 1980).

Besides the expectation, mentioned above, that uninteresting tables would be omitted, the Guidelines for Country Report No. 1 envisaged that countries would add tabulations covering other topics (see pp. 1-3, 16-17, 23) and also anticipated that categories of variables would be altered to suit local conditions. At the same time, it was expected that reports would include a substantial proportion of the tables outlined in the Guidelines.

No report included all tables exactly as outlined in the Guidelines. There were numerous, if usually minor, differences in the categories of demographic variables and in base populations, and some tables (usually a small number) were omitted from many reports (Singh 1980b). Some countries also added a few tables to sections 1-5 (outlined in table 21.2) or increased the amount of detail, distinguishing, for example, between spontaneous and probed knowledge of contraceptive methods. Generally, though, sections 1-5 of the tabulations appeared in a form close to that recommended.

Many countries added variables of local interest to the recommended set of socio-economic characteristics and a few produced extensive results for major regions or ethnic groups. Sometimes a standard background variable was omitted, generally because it was not relevant for the country or because nearly all respondents fell into a single category. Many reports used a reduced set of three or four background characteristics for some tables and a larger set for others. Also, some reports added a new set of tables, showing interrelationships of the background variables.

The household and birth history sections frequently did not follow the Guidelines. In the early survey reports, birth history tables were usually left out, partly because appropriate computer software was not yet readily available. A few reports contained no household tables and others printed only the age-sex by marital status distribution for the whole country. Although the reason for omitting some tables may have been because they were judged as poorly designed or of too narrow a focus for a general report, they were rarely replaced by others of greater relevance.

The incorporation of information from modules depended in part on which modules were used. Some tables based on the fertility regulation module, which were included in the Guidelines from the start, typically appeared. Results from the module on factors other than contraception affecting fertility (FOTCAF) were also extensively reported. By contrast, the family planning, economic, and abortion modules and other country-specific questions were often omitted entirely. Results from the community module, which was actually a separate survey, were never mentioned, though with careful planning these data could have been added to the individual files and/or tabulated separately. There were some items from each of the other modules that merited at least a brief presentation, if only to indicate their potential for more detailed study.

The erratic coverage of the modules was partly a consequence of the failure of WFS to develop a recommended set of variables or tables for each module, itself a reflection of the classic error of designing questionnaires before deciding upon analytic aims and substance. The omission of module data from the earlier recode files had the serious consequence of retarding subsequent analysis. In particular, the family planning and abortion modules have become the least utilized components of the total substantive content of surveys, and the attention received by other country-specific questions is even poorer.[2] This mistake was not repeated for the FOTCAF module and as a result these data figure prominently both in country reports and in specialized analyses. This experience emphasizes the dangers, expressed earlier, of serial processing.

A benign sort of departure from the Guidelines was the tendency, as time went on, to supplement inadequacies in the recommended tables with other tabulations shown only in the text. It was primarily the treatment of period fertility and, later on, childhood mortality that benefited in this way. In general, topics that were not covered well in the Guidelines were also discussed very superficially, or not at all, in the reports.

It is important to ask why the Guidelines appear to have limited the reports in undesirable ways, and to consider whether the WFS experience bears on problems that future surveys will share. One possibility which would not necessarily apply to other surveys is that the sheer volume of standard tables discouraged survey personnel from making the reports even longer. Another is that WFS staff, who were often involved in producing tables and writing reports, were insensitive to local needs.

While each of these may have been involved in some instances, the main problem appears to have been the difficulty of designing new tables under pressure of time, rather than the neglect of issues of local concern. Some of the weak features of most reports concern topics that are relevant everywhere, important enough to have merited a few more pages even in an already voluminous report and suitable for standard tabulation – infant and child mortality, for instance. While it is relatively easy to add more panels to predesigned tables that are already being produced for other background variables, it is more difficult to design a completely new set of tables to deal succinctly with dependent variables that are country-specific or that, like infant mortality, were neglected in the Guidelines.

Certainly, once the data are ready for tabulation it is hard to plan major revisions to a standard set of tables because of the pressure to produce a report as quickly as possible. This sort of pressure is not peculiar to WFS. The optimum strategy involves both advance planning of tabulation and the retention of flexibility until the initial results have been screened. In practice, this is hard to achieve. If the person(s) who are to write the report have not been appointed and involved in early stages of planning, no one may feel any responsibility for revising a standard set of tables until it is too late.

21.5   Critique of the tabulation guidelines

We have already discussed the analytic philosophy and overall scope of the 'Guidelines for Country Report No. 1' (WFS 1977a) and referred to the implementation of the recommendations by individual countries. In this section we consider more closely the nature and style of the tabulation plan and, in the light of experience, its defects and the potential for improvement. This is not merely an exercise in retrospective criticism. It is probable that all the WFS basic documentation will be used as reference points for future fertility surveys, and it is thus of practical importance to reveal inadequacies and identify possible improvements.

Balance between substantive topics

The relegation of full birth history tabulations to an appendix in the Guidelines and the related absence of any conventional estimates of period fertility from nearly all the earlier country reports is the most striking defect of WFS reporting strategy. The majority of participating countries lacked a good vital registration system and needed above all else an estimate of the level of current fertility. Such an estimate, in conjunction with reasonable assumptions about the growth rate and migration, could provide an approximate estimate of the crude death rate and, by comparison with earlier estimates, a preliminary indication of fertility change. Yet, amidst the myriad of more esoteric descriptive detail, this crucial figure was missing.

The omission reflected a deep ambivalence of WFS and its advisers towards the utility of small retrospective surveys for demographic estimation. Demographers, accustomed to working with censuses or large household samples, assumed that vital rates could not be derived from sample sizes of 5000 women with sufficient sampling precision to be useful. The main purpose of WFS individual surveys, it was argued, was to elucidate fertility determinants rather than to estimate rates. If vital rates were needed, then countries should opt for an enlarged household sample containing summary fertility and mortality questions. In the event, 16 of the 42 countries did exercise this option and in these cases current fertility levels, based on the traditional measure of date of last birth, were usually presented in the main report. Many countries such as Nepal, however, sorely lacking reliable recent estimates of the level of fertility, were not among this minority group.

The concern with sampling precision was unwarranted because it was based on the unnecessary assumption of single-year rates. If aggregated from births and exposure over three- or five-year periods, fertility rates can be estimated from moderate sample sizes with adequate precision, not only at the national but also at the subnational level (Little 1982).

A more justifiable reluctance to place much emphasis on exploitation of the retrospective histories in the main report stemmed from uncertainty about the quality of data and fears of publishing incorrect rates, coupled with lack of a suitable technology for cleaning, imputing and tabulating the data.[3] Concern for data quality, which was heavily influenced by contemporary opinion that dual-record or longitudinal designs were necessary to obtain reliable vital event data in developing countries, led to the view that the First Country Report should avoid the presentation of findings on levels and trends of fertility or childhood mortality until the data had been thoroughly evaluated.[4] Subsequent experience (summarized in chapter 24) indicates that the caution concerning the estimation of fertility trends was justified, but current fertility levels based on the five years preceding the survey have usually not been seriously biased. The lack of suitable technology constituted a powerful argument for pressing ahead with the First Country Report and avoiding the delays inherent in processing the history data. As a result, the recode or analysis file for the earlier surveys did not even contain the full event histories.

Regrettably, this policy of cautious self-denial was not observed consistently within the tabulation plan itself. Tabulations of the interval between marriage and first birth, number of births in the first five years of marriage, births in the five years preceding the survey, lengths of open and last closed interval, and proportion of exposure time lost by marital dissolution are all derived from the retrospective histories and a few of them (particularly the first birth interval) are extremely sensitive to completeness and accuracy of event dating. In retrospect, it seems absurd that this ambivalent and partial use of the birth histories should have resulted in extensive investigation of the tempo of early marital fertility, for instance, but a failure to include total or marital fertility rates for the period immediately prior to the survey. The implicit reason appears to have been that possible defects in these unfamiliar measures would not matter as much as the publication of incorrect estimates of current fertility. Thus excessive caution, combined with bad advice and a failure to understand the priorities of participating countries, were to blame.

This defect in the initial strategy was quickly remedied. Indeed, most of the early Latin American surveys produced an estimate of current fertility in their reports. By 1978, WFS had developed software for processing retrospective histories and the full history data were routinely transferred to the recode files. Increasingly, country reports contained various types of fertility rates derived from the retrospective data and typically discussed the level of current fertility. Serious analysis of trends, however, was rarely attempted within the First Country Report.

The presentation of childhood mortality in First Country Reports also benefited greatly from the increased ability and willingness to exploit the maternity histories. Additional impetus has been provided by a growing awareness of the high quality of WFS mortality data. In the Guidelines, this topic was covered cursorily in a single table. Most reports issued since 1979 have greatly expanded investigation to include preliminary information on levels and differentials. In most later reports, an entire chapter is devoted to a discussion of mortality.

A further defect of the initial 1975 version of the Guidelines, though less striking or important than the neglect of period fertility, was the failure to amend the tabulation plan for all-women samples. This had unfortunate consequences for the early Latin American survey reports which were based exclusively on the ever-married portions of the samples. In particular, the topic of age at first marriage, which can be investigated much more adequately with an unrestricted sample, suffered. This defect was remedied in the final 1977 Guidelines by an appendix specifying additional tables.

So far we have concentrated on errors of omission in the tabulation plan. It is also important to identify topics that received excessive emphasis. A content analysis of four country reports (Paraguay, Philippines, Senegal and Syria) shows that the detailed tables which were referred to or summarized in the text account for only 60 per cent of the total number of pages devoted to detailed tables. Though tabulations not exploited in one report may be analysed in another, it is nevertheless possible to pinpoint four areas in which the amount of detail was excessive for a general, preliminary report and which, as a consequence, were underutilized in the text.

The first of these topics is marital dissolution and remarriage, on which the Guidelines specify 28 tables, implying 20-50 pages of figures, depending on the printing style. Though we acknowledge that the WFS programme has generated a uniquely rich array of data on this topic, such detail was excessive for First Country Reports and should have been delayed for later analysis by more appropriate life-table techniques. Subsequent analytical experience has shown that marital stability is not a major source of fertility variation either between or within countries (with a few important exceptions, such as Indonesia), which further reinforces the view that greater economy of presentation should have been exercised.

A further example of excessive detail in the nuptiality section is the set of eight tables (1.6.1-1.6.3) concerning current exposure status. The rationale for their inclusion was that they defined the sample bases (e.g. 'exposed' and 'currently married fecund' for tabulation of current use and preferences, respectively) for many other tables. However, the utility of this function was limited[5] and the variable itself was too cumbersome for succinct analysis in its own right.

In our judgement, too much detail was also provided on fertility preferences in section 3 of the tabulation plan. The problem here was the existence of three closely related dependent variables: desire for another child, additional numer of children wanted and total desired family size. All three were subjected to equally detailed cross-classification, resulting in repetitive description but little additional insight. The obvious solution in this instance would have been to curtail severely the tabulations of additional number of children wanted (3.2.1-3.2.5).

The volume of tabular material was also formidably large in section 4 on contraception. The main culprit was the set of 16 tables (4.5.1-4.5.6) dealing with the variable 'pattern of contraceptive use'. A further eight tables (5.3.1-5.3.3) on the same topic were included in section 5. Rather like exposure status, the 'pattern of use' variable attempted to summarize a number of characteristics in a single classification. The main new ingredient was the information on intentions to use in the future, which could have been presented much more briefly as an item in its own right. The bulk of these tables greatly exceeded their value as a summary of contraceptive status.

A severe pruning of the four topics discussed above (marital dissolution, exposure status, additional number of children wanted, pattern of use) would have removed about 50 tables from the core tabulation plan with only a minor loss of useful information.

In conclusion, the tabulation plan would have been more balanced, and more useful, if it had contained less detail on certain aspects of nuptiality, fertility preferences and contraception but more information on current fertility and childhood mortality.

Household tabulations

The Guidelines outlined tables showing the age, sex and marital status distribution of the total population by single year of age; tables showing the distribution of the adult population by various characteristics such as region and urban-rural residence; a number of tables that were to be classified by the latter characteristics; a comparison of wives' and husbands' ages; seven tables dealing with the special information gathered in some surveys about parity and date of last birth; and tabulations required for 'own-children' estimates of fertility (Cho 1973; United Nations 1983b). Including those that were to be produced for the total population and by background characteristics, 54 tables were recommended. In practice, many fewer were printed.

Tables from the household survey that would have been useful but were rarely given because they were not covered in the Guidelines include the age–sex by marital status distribution of the entire population for a few important characteristics (region, urban-rural residence and education) and tables showing household size and composition (as in Kabir 1980). For some other topics, such as timing of the most recent birth, the Guidelines called for excessive detail.

The tabulations needed for own-children estimates of fertility were never published. We differ among ourselves as to whether the own-children table for the total population would have added enough information to have justified the difficulty of producing it. Such a tabulation, with various adjustment factors, permits calculation of age-specific fertility rates for the 10–15 years preceding the survey, based on ages of mothers and children living together in households. As far as the WFS is concerned, this adds relatively little, since the maternity histories supply rates which are very probably of superior quality. Still, it is of some interest to know whether rates from the two sources agree, and own-children estimates do supply some new information: they provide fertility rates for the higher reproductive ages for periods in the past, rates that are missing from the maternity histories because of restrictions on the current age of women interviewed. This addition is most likely to be of practical value in countries with seriously deficient vital registration but in which age misstatement is not very severe, conditions that are met by some but certainly not all of the countries that participated in WFS.

Choice of demographic controls

Table 21.2 shows the major dependent variables and demographic controls employed in sections 1–5 of the tabulations. Most tables included age or marriage duration as a classifying variable. Many dependent variables were cross-classified by two, and a few by three, demographic variables. The starred dependent variables in table 21.2 were also tabulated by social characteristics, along with one or two demographic controls.

As the elaboration of control variables adds to the volume of tables, it should be asked whether all this detail is useful. The main questions about the two key control variables, age and marriage duration, are whether one was clearly superior to the other, and whether it was necessary to have so many tables produced once with an age and again with a duration control.

Age is usually a good control variable because it is strongly related to the physiological capacity for reproduction, and because age-specific tabulations are more likely than duration-specific ones to be useful for comparisons with other data sources. In addition, because age was a criterion for sample eligibility, data for women of longer marriage durations (25 or 30 years) suffer a severe selection bias, as they are necessarily based on those who married atypically early.

Marriage duration usually provides a better approximation of 'length of exposure' than does age, so that a duration control may be desirable for examining socio-economic differences in the incidence of marital disruption or levels of fertility early in marriage. The end of childbearing, however, is more clearly identified by reference to age. This suggests that it was justifiable to produce some of the fertility tabulations by both age and duration, and both types of tables were usually drawn upon in drafting the reports. In addition, both age- and duration-specific tabulations of parity and surviving children can be used for indirect estimates of fertility and child mortality. In general, the use of both age and duration in the Guidelines for fertility tabulation was correct, but was excessive for analysis of preferences and contraception, where age-specific tables alone would have sufficed.

The other major control variables – age at marriage (mainly sections 1 and 2) and number of living children (mainly sections 3–5) – were usually employed along with age or duration. Were so many tables with two or more controls needed, and were the combinations of variables well chosen?

Differentials according to demographic characteristics are often of interest in themselves. For instance, it was appropriate to show differentials in fertility and marital disruption by age at marriage and essential to examine differentials in preferences and contraception according to family size. However, the utility of tabulating exposure status in section 1 and current or recent fertility in section 2 by number of living children is more debatable. Even less convincing is the need to cross-classify preferences and contraception in sections 3, 4 and 5 by age at marriage (tables 3.3.6, 4.5.2 and 5.2.2). The extra detail provided by these atypical controls was not much used in the reports or elsewhere, and, with a couple of possible exceptions, the information was of insufficient relevance to include in a general report.

Base populations

In considering the subsamples on which tabulations were based, the two main issues are whether refined bases were a significant improvement over cruder ones, and whether anything was gained by repeating some tables for different bases.

Sometimes bases were restricted in order to cope with censoring biases. For instance, the age-at-marriage distribution of young women is incomplete, 'censored' by the interview, so that the observed mean marriage age for young women cannot sensibly be compared to that for older cohorts. The solution adopted in the reports has its own costs. In the case of marriage age, where the base was 'women aged 25 or more who married at less than age 25', estimates for older women were deliberately biased downward in order that means could be compared across cohorts, and the experience of the youngest women was ignored. This problem can be overcome for all-women samples by tabulating the cumulative proportion of birth cohorts of women married by certain ages, and for ever-married samples use of the household survey proportions single in conjunction with individual survey data is a preferable approach to that recommended in the Guidelines. Most later reports made this improvement.

A more successful example of the use of a restricted sample base to obtain unbiased inter-cohort comparisons is the treatment of early marital fertility. The dependent variables are restricted to events up to the fifth year of marriage and the problem of censoring overcome by discarding data for women who had been married less than five years.

This policy of restricting tabulations to a segment of experience shared by all cohorts represented in the tabulations was not uniformly applied. Most obviously, all the tabulations of parity and most of those on marital dissolution and remarriage, whether by birth or marriage cohort, make no attempt to avoid censoring and therefore suffer from a confounding of life-cycle and cohort effects. Of course, there were also dependent variables, such as contraception and breastfeeding, on which little or no reconstruction of past experience was attempted in the questionnaire. For these topics, no disentangling of cohort and life-cycle phenomena was possible.

In other instances, restrictions were placed on table bases, in accordance with the demographic principle that events of interest should be related as closely as possible to exposure to risk. For some topics, the sample base was limited by collection procedures. For instance, many of the fertility preference findings were based on currently married fecund women because only this category of respondent was asked the relevant questions. Most tables showing current contraceptive use are based on currently married, non-pregnant women who report themselves as fecund, the rationale being that these 'exposed' women are the only ones for whom it is reasonable to expect current use. However, there is a dependency, over time, between the amount of contraceptive practice and the proportion pregnant (and probably the level of perceived infecundity as well), which makes it arguable whether any benefits from the precise definition of exposure outweigh selection biases. Inspection of tables using alternate bases suggests that the choice of base does not have much effect on the size of differentials in contraceptive practice according to rural–urban residence or education. This being so, any gain in refinement from the 'exposed' base must be weighed against the loss of comparability with other published sources, which have usually employed currently married women as the base. The arguments against restricted bases are strengthened when the criteria of restriction are poorly measured, as in the case of current pregnancy or self-reported infecundity.

Perhaps the most complex and unsuccessful table base concerns the restriction of the tabulations of breastfeeding in the last closed interval (4.1.3–4.1.5) to women whose penultimate child survived at least two years and whose last closed interval exceeded 32 months. Though the intention is clear, namely to restrict attention to women at risk of voluntary weaning at any time in the 24 months following delivery, problems of selectivity and reciprocal causality render these data almost uninterpretable. Subsequently, greatly improved methods of measuring breastfeeding durations evolved (Ferry 1981); Page, Lesthaeghe and Shah 1982).

Refined bases are difficult to construct and prone to error. Unless there is something important to be gained from the extra work, it is best to use simple bases when planning a report that ought to be produced quickly. The exposed base, for example, was occasionally constructed incorrectly. Limitation of the base to women *continuously* married in the last five years, when examining births in that period, was also a clear case of over-refinement and made extra demands on data processing. It would have been much simpler to base the data on women who first married at least five years ago and, in the light of subsequent analysis, we know that the results would have been much the same (Rodríguez and Cleland 1981a).

Sections 2–4 contain pairs of tables identical except for relatively small differences in the base population – currently married as opposed to ever married, for example. Apart from a few of the tables dealing with achieved fertility, the contrasts between values for alternate bases are not of much substantive interest, and the reports rarely referred to both members of such a pair of tables. Discussions of fertility preferences focused mainly on currently married, or currently married fecund women, even in surveys where unmarried women were asked about preferences. When questions about preferences and contraception are directed to all women, it might be best to publish a table for each major variable to show mean values by age and marital status, and then to concentrate in other tables on currently married women.

Use of socio-economic variables

In the Guidelines for Country Report No. 1 countries are urged to tabulate some key dependent variables by four socio-economic factors: wife's education, rural–urban residence, wife's lifetime pattern of work and husband's occupation. Three other factors (childhood type of place of residence, husband's education and ownership of consumer durables) are mentioned as possible candidates for inclusion but are assigned lower priority. In addition, it was recommended that region of residence, religion and ethnic group be added to the list of socio-economic characteristics wherever appropriate.

The majority of countries implemented these recommendations faithfully. The four priority variables were nearly always included, as were regional, religious and ethnic classifications where relevant. Occasionally husband's education was added, but ownership of consumer durables was rarely used, largely because these data were collected during the household survey and were not available on the individual data files. Thus the typical report used about six background variables which were applied in 22 instances, generating a total of 132 tables. In all but one instance, the background variables were introduced singly, the exception being an examination of parity where the cross-classification is bivariate (table 2.2.7).

Was the choice and definition of background factors optimal? Were they applied to the most appropriate substantive topics? Was the overall volume of material on socio-economic differentials justifiable?

There can be little argument about the desirability of disaggregating results by wife's education and residence,[6] both of which are major correlates of demographic behaviour and in the mainstream of demographic enquiry. Similarly, regional, ethnic and religious breakdowns are usually of sufficient descriptive interest to justify priority treatment in the First Country Report. Indeed, in large heterogeneous countries, disaggregation by region of all major topics is desirable. The merit of adding husband's occupation is more debatable, both because of intractable difficulties in attaching precise meanings to broad occupational categories and because its association with residence and wife's education further complicates interpretation. The net effect tends to be a proliferation of descriptive detail which is only of minor interest.

The last of the four standard background variables concerns female labour force participation. The WFS Core Questionnaire devotes a whole section to this topic and there was a range of variables from which to choose for tabulation purposes. The decision was to concentrate on the timing of work and summarize this information in a six-category classification according to whether the respondent worked before and/or after marriage, and/or whether she was currently working.

In retrospect, the timing of work variable proved unsatisfactory because of its failure to distinguish different types of activity, with their vastly divergent social, economic and demographic implications. It is clear now that a simpler variable distinguishing the three types of employment status since marriage would have yielded a greater analytic return. But in our judgement, the wisest strategy would have been to postpone investigation of this topic until after the First Country Report. The complexities of the inter-relationships between reproductive behaviour and employment have proved testing even for elaborate multivariate analysis and are unamenable to simple cross-tabulation.

The deletion of husband's occupation and wife's work pattern from the tabulation plan eliminates 44 tables. Further reductions could be achieved by omitting some of the material on socio-economic differentials in marital dissolution, exposure status, parity distribution (table 2.2.5), additional number of children wanted and pattern of contraceptive use, resulting in the loss of a further 30 or so tables. Finally, we regard the bivariable tabulation of parity in table 2.2.7, which comprises an extensive set of 15 subtables, as unsatisfactory. Multivariate analysis of socio-economic effects is not best pursued by a standardized tabular approach and quickly results in an overwhelming volume of material. Few country report authors were able to derive much of interest from any of these tables.

Conclusions

The major defect of the tabulation plan was its prolixity, which had severe implications for speed and cost of report publication. In the preceding pages, we have suggested a number of ways in which the total output of tables could have been reduced by at least 30 per cent without serious loss of useful information. A related defect was the dependence of certain tables on the construction of exceedingly complex variables, which made heavy demands on the internal consistency of the raw data and on data processing skills. Together with the perfectionist policy towards editing, these two features indicate that WFS had a totally unrealistic view of the amount of work involved which doomed the important objective of producing quick results. The most serious omission from the original plan was neglecting conventional measures of period fertility and mortality. For many countries these are the items of greater interest and we now know that the survey estimates were generally of good quality.

Inevitably the discussion has focused on defects, but these should not be allowed to overshadow the substantial merits of the tabulation plan. In many regards it was so comprehensive and skilfully designed that it was definitive, in the sense that further analysis could add little of substantive importance. In surveys where the birth history data subsequently proved too poor to sustain serious investigation of fertility trends or family formation, it appears to us that most major findings (with the exception of mortality, breastfeeding and material contained in modules) are already contained in the First Country Report.

21.6 Sampling errors

A distinctive feature of WFS main reports is the routine inclusion of information on sampling errors of key estimates for a range of demographic and social subclasses and subpopulations. There is no doubt that the WFS programme has created 'the largest, most valuable set of data ever assembled on sampling errors' (Kish 1980) and that major advances in our knowledge of the sampling efficiency of developing country surveys have resulted (Verma, Scott and O'Muircheartaigh 1980). As part of the methodological description, the merit of including sampling errors in country reports is unquestioned. However, our main concern in this chapter lies with their contribution to the interpretation of substantive findings.

WFS devoted considerable resources of skilled manpower to the computation of sampling errors and their presentation in an appendix of the country reports. With few exceptions, the work was done in London using the specially developed package, Clusters (Verma and Pearce 1978). Despite this investment, the authors of the reports have rarely made any reference in the text to the sampling precision of the results that they discuss or to the statistical significance of differences. Even when they have been used in the text (e.g. Syria, Sudan, Nepal), references are few in number and rarely contribute incisively to the discussion.

One major cause of the neglect of sampling errors was the simple fact that they were sometimes computed after completion of the analysis and report drafting. But even when errors were available in time, several factors militated against their use Unlike, for instance, most agricultural surveys, which are used to measure or predict the absolute magnitude of crop yields at the national level and where the precision of estimates is vital, WFS reports contain few estimates for which standard errors are of comparable interest. Among these few is the proportion using contraception, particularly when similar estimates are available for other surveys. It is also important to know the precision of estimates of current age-specific fertility rates, but the precise methodology for computing errors for these rates from WFS files was elaborated only late in the programme (Little 1982). For most other dependent variables in country reports, precision was not a matter of practical importance. This is particularly true of attitudinal and other variables which are highly sensitive to response error.

The standard errors of differences between subclass estimates are potentially much more useful for authors of country reports because a great part of the discussion focuses on differences between cohorts or between socio-economic and other classes. The difficulty here lies in the large number of comparisons. In practice it was not feasible either to compute errors for all differences of substantive interest or, had this been done, to have made sensible use of the material. Inevitably analysts searched for consistent patterns in the cross-classified data and drew their conclusions accordingly, with little attention to questions of statistical significance.

Perhaps the information on sampling errors might have been exploited more fully had they been presented differently. In the Indonesian and Turkish reports, tables are provided by which standard errors of differences in 25 key variables can be derived for any pair of subclasses by simple interpolation based on the sample sizes of the two subclasses. Though these errors are only an approximation, they are of much greater use to the analyst, who requires general applicability rather than a limited number of exact errors. Several other country reports provide the formulae by which errors can be approximated but do not take the additional step, like Indonesia and Turkey, of generating easily used reference tables.

A radically different way of increasing the utility of standard errors would be to integrate error computation into the analytical process. This would involve the calculation of the statistical significance of differences, selected by the author on the grounds of their special interest or their critical role in the network of evidence. Such flexibility requires considerable skill, collaboration between demographer and statistician, and ideal access to software and computer time, conditions rarely fulfilled in the preparation of reports.

We conclude that the routine incorporation of substantial sets of sampling errors in country reports, though admirable in principle, paid disappointingly few dividends for the reports themselves. The chief benefits will accrue to future surveys from the better understanding of sampling efficiency. The major justification for their routine inclusion was that this policy ensured that the efficiency of samples could later be compared in a cross-national context. Had the initial effort not been made, it is doubtful whether details of sample designs would have been documented with sufficient care to permit error computation several years after the completion of respective surveys.

The WFS experience raises a general point about the difficulty of incorporating standard errors into the analysis and discussion of broad-ranging descriptive reports covering many relationships of potential interest. Though it is impractical to calculate, certainly to publish, precise errors for all relationships that might be examined, the analyst needs a rough sense of sampling error as a safeguard against naïve interpretation of small differences. Difficult and incompletely resolved statistical problems are involved in deriving a small set of approximate errors that are easy to apply and that at the same time provide a sound basis for interpretation in such reports. Yet, with further study of the wealth of sampling information from WFS, it may be possible to evolve a standard set of error approximations for future fertility surveys with three parameters: degree of sample clustering, nature of the variable and size of subclasses.

21.7 Use of tabulations as a research resource

The main justification for running such a large volume of tables at the first stage of analysis was the belief that the data would be used for further study, both for national and cross-national purposes. As a resource for secondary analysis, the standard set of tables had some shortcomings. The most serious was the failure in some of the earlier reports to publish mean parities and family sizes to more than one decimal place, thereby preventing the application of indirect techniques to estimate childhood mortality and fertility. Other shortcomings which detracted from the utility of First Country Reports for further national analysis were the reluctance to include ungrouped data (which provide additional flexibility to the analyst, but at the expense of large additions to the volume of tabular material), the use of unconventional table bases, thus preventing comparison with other published findings, and the omission from the earlier reports of detailed arrays of birth history data and the concomitant lack of conventional fertility rates.

As raw material for cross-national analysis the published data contained minor but annoying differences between reports, with the result that certain countries had to be omitted or extra tabulations run. Though complete standardization would not have served country needs, the inevitable lack of uniformity in specifying background variables, such as education, further eroded the potential for cross-national work.

The actual use made of country reports for further analysis is difficult to assess because of the unknown amount of work by national and international organizations for in-house purposes. In terms of published analyses, however, use of country reports has been very meagre. Very few national analyses have relied upon data contained in country reports and comparative work is largely confined to a series of reports by the Population Reference Bureau (e.g. Durch 1980; Kent 1981; Mamlouk 1982; Kent and Larson 1982; Curtin 1982), two monographs of the United Nations (United Nations 1980a, 1981c) and a few papers presented in the 1980 WFS Conference. The prime reason is not the inherent limitations of published tables mentioned in the preceding paragraph, but the widespread availability of computer data files, which permitted much more scope to the analyst. The excellent data file documentation and standardization by the WFS archive section further facilitated use of the files themselves. A subsidiary factor is the *Cross-National Summaries* series, produced and published by WFS.

The widespread use of WFS data files is a welcome departure from initial expectations. The generosity of participating countries in making available their data files and giving hundreds of researchers, both from developing and developed countries, the opportunity to work with primary data is to be applauded. The unfortunate by-product, namely the severe underutilization of published country report tables relative to the effort and expense of their preparation, is a small price to pay.

21.8   Report writing and dissemination of findings

The writing of the First Country Report was primarily the responsibility of national staff, but in an appreciable number of instances this final phase was accomplished partly or wholly by WFS personnel or consultants. There are a number of reasons for this. Mobility of staff was undoubtedly a factor: analysis of results typically occurred one and a half years after the end of fieldwork, by which time nationals involved in the earlier stages of the survey had sometimes left the organization or transferred to other duties, leaving a vacuum at the report-writing stage. Outside Latin America and the Caribbean, language was a second important barrier. Nearly all Asian, Middle Eastern and African statistical reports are published in English or French and this policy was followed for WFS reports. Writing in a language other than one's mother tongue is rarely easy and this problem surfaced frequently in the WFS programme. However, even when language was not an acute problem, the performance of national staff was often disappointing. Perhaps daunted by the volume of material to be assimilated or insufficiently confident that they could match the high standards expected of them, several survey organizations exhibited a marked reluctance to write their own reports or made only unacceptably slow progress. Though the circumstances may have been unfavourable in some respects, interpretation and concise presentation of results is plainly a weakness of many statistical offices in developing countries and contrasts with their general capability in data collection.

Indeed, many statistical offices, in developed and developing countries alike, have traditionally seen their mission as primarily the collection and publication of data, and not the writing of interpretative reports. This strategy may serve for presentation of censuses and routine statistical series, but complex sample surveys, with their intricate detail and varied content, require an initial analysis and summary in order to make the most important results accessible. We believe that this area is badly neglected in training programmes and that the consequences are, and will continue to be, serious.

WFS often faced a dilemma in the writing of reports. While it was clearly desirable that the staff of participating countries themselves should be fully involved in all aspects of the work, WFS was also committed to high standards and speed of execution. Where these considerations conflicted, WFS usually opted for the latter objective and in effect took over prime responsibility for report-writing and preparation in London or in the participating country. There has been some criticism that reports written by non-nationals are insensitive to the local context. We can discern little difference in this respect between reports drafted by nationals and non-nationals and thus regard this criticism as invalid. No doubt the discussion of findings in WFS reports often fails to take sufficient account of other evidence and exhibits apparent ignorance of social and cultural institutions. But such sensitivity of interpretation is not easily achieved and is rarely exhibited by government statistical offices. Inadequacies cannot be attributed to the role played by foreign authors.

We turn now to a consideration of the dissemination of the results contained in country reports. As this topic is examined in detail in chapter 37, we shall be brief. From the beginning, WFS realized that the main reports would be too long, detailed and specialized to reach a wide audience. Accordingly, a *Summary of Findings* series was initiated, in which the major findings of each survey were described in a 10-20 page document prepared by WFS staff. Rather later, beginning in 1978, WFS took the further step of encouraging countries to hold national meetings shortly after publication of the main report, at which the results could be presented and their policy implications discussed by a mixture of academics, civil servants and politicians.

In our view, these national meetings proved to be a cost-effective means of creating interest and awareness of results among key individuals and institutions. Moreover, wider dissemination was often achieved by mass media coverage of the meetings. In contrast, the published summaries, though both necessary and admirable in concept, probably failed in one of their main purposes, namely to reach beyond the narrow scientific community of statisticians and demographers. We suspect that their style never broke sufficiently free from the strictly scientific to capture the interest and understanding of intelligent lay-people. They were unable to transcend the limitation of the main report with regard to insensitivity to local context and policy relevance. Insufficient attention was paid to visual presentation of results or the eradication of technical terminology. While accepting that the communication of scientific findings to a lay audience is a highly specialized skill, we conclude that WFS made too little effort in this direction. The record of national statistical offices is also weak in this regard. Kenya was one of the few participating countries to make a serious attempt to disseminate the main findings, through the periodical *Social Perspectives*, published by the Central Bureau of Statistics.

Results themselves, when attractively presented, can and should be of widespread interest; but their implications for practical policy are probably of greater concern. With few exceptions, neither the main report nor the summaries spell out the practical implications of the survey results. This absence largely reflects the determination of WFS to confine its programme to purely scientific objectives and to avoid the more controversial matters of population policies and programmes. Underlying this position was an awareness that there is an ill-defined boundary, easy to cross, between pointing out practical implications and appearing to prescribe social policy. In our opinion, this stance was correct and is largely responsible for WFS's unblemished reputation for scientific objectivity. Nevertheless it left a void, in that no systematic attempts, apart from the national meetings, were made to identify the items of particular relevance to government policies or programmes or to convey these to the appropriate institutions. Perhaps WFS's funding agencies could have taken a more active interest but, as with the communication of findings, this is a much more difficult process than is usually acknowledged as it requires an understanding of the results themselves, an intimate knowledge of existing policies and programmes and a sense of financial and political feasibility. Nevertheless it is regrettable that WFS did not do more to encourage countries to exploit survey findings in this way.

21.9 General conclusions and recommendations

In conclusion, we believe that WFS was correct in recommending a comprehensive general report, containing a detailed description of survey methodology and instruments and a discussion of preliminary findings, based on straightforward tabulations. However, the delays associated with the production of reports of the size implied by WFS Guidelines should have been anticipated, and the harmful consequences largely averted by the issue of a short quick-release report comprising the main findings of potential policy interest prior to the detailed general report. Such preliminary reports should be based on a dozen or so variables and contain a maximum of 30 tables.

Undoubtedly the tabulation plan was too ambitious in size. We estimate that the number of tables could have been reduced by at least 30 per cent without serious loss by a judicious pruning of substantive topics, demographic controls and background variables. The justification for this prolixity was greatly weakened by the availability of the primary data for further analysis. As a result, little use has been made of tables subsequent to the preliminary analysis in country reports themselves. The unfortunate consequences of excessive size were made more serious because national and WFS staff exercised insufficient selectivity in the choice of tables for publication, resulting in formidably large and costly reports of 500–1000 pages.

Within the limitations of a cross-tabular approach, the tabulation plan was skilfully designed to avoid most of the potential pitfalls arising from censoring and selectivity. Nor are we convinced by those who have argued against the degree of international standardization implicit in such a detailed plan. The alternative, an *ad hoc* set of tables for each survey, would have been vastly more expensive in terms of technical assistance and taken longer to produce, without any guarantee of superiority over the standardized approach.

Among the major technical flaws of the plan was the self-indulgent use of certain extremely complex variables which were not essential at the initial phase of reporting and which hampered processing. Its deeply divided attitude towards the retrospective history data was perhaps the most serious defect, and the related failure to realize the over-riding importance of current fertility and mortality estimations constitutes the most grave error of judgement. We hasten to add that this last error was quickly remedied. With the additional material on fertility and mortality rates contained in most later reports, and bearing in mind the criticism and suggestions detailed above, we believe that the WFS tabulation plan represents an extremely useful compendium for future fertility survey reports.

WFS's experience in the actual interpretation of data and report-drafting points to a widespread weakness of statistical offices, which contrasts starkly with their overall competence in data collection. Dissemination of findings and their relevance to policy in a comprehensible and attractive way was rarely accomplished in a satisfactory manner and here WFS itself was partly at fault. However, national meetings proved to be an effective way of publicizing results.

Many recommendations for future surveys are implicit in the criticisms that we have made of WFS reporting procedures. Below, we summarize the lessons learned by WFS in the form of general but explicit recommendations. Of course, the optimum policy depends critically on the precise objectives of any future survey and the resources available. In framing a set of recommendations, we have in mind a fertility survey similar in content to WFS surveys, with the same broad mixture of policy and scientific aims, but we have made no *a priori* assumptions about available human resources.

One of our most emphatic recommendations is for a short preliminary report which should be available for release within six months of the end of fieldwork. The main purpose of this report would be to extract and disseminate the key findings of policy relevance before they become outdated. A brief non-technical summary of the results should also be prepared, either for inclusion in the preliminary report or for release as a companion document; a non-demographer, perhaps someone with journalistic experience, should participate in the drafting.

Following this report, major decisions have to be made concerning the next phase of reporting. Should the report(s) rely on current and lifetime measures or should a start be made at this stage to analyse the marital and maternity careers of cohorts and to examine trends? Should the report(s) be restricted to straight-forward cross-classification of proportions, means and rates or should more refined demographic and statistical techniques be applied? Should there be one general report or a series dealing with the major substantive topics? The choices plainly depend in part upon the availability of skilled analysts and access to suitable computer hardware and software, but it is important that explicit choices be made.

The inclusion in the main report(s) of various types of fertility and mortality rates brings great benefits, and we strongly recommend that they be presented whenever this is feasible. Cohort–period specific rates permit an initial assessment of data quality, while the more conventional age–period specific rates allow comparison with other sources. The computer programs developed at WFS to calculate rates and to allocate missing dates should prove useful for other surveys, provided the requirements for rate calculations are taken into account during planning and data coding and editing.

With respect to the number and analytic complexity of reports we anticipate that, in the circumstances of many statistical offices in developing countries, the WFS strategy of a single general report based on straightforward tabulations, with a tentative but specific outline prepared in advance, will still represent the wisest course of action. Production of a series of reports risks loss of the coherent overview that a general report provides. And, while a serial reporting strategy allows greater flexibility, it is also likely to take longer, particularly if refined techniques are applied, and runs the risk of loss of commitment. Only rarely can statistical offices of developing countries devote the time and command the skills necessary for the compilation of a series of analytically complex reports. Typically, such work is better left to university departments or research institutes. If this diagnosis is accepted, then the WFS Guidelines for Country Report No. 1, amended and reduced in size in the ways that we have suggested, should be of great value in planning the nature and scope of future reports.

Notes

1. In the light of recent evidence that machine editing of data makes little difference to the substantive results (Pullum, Özsever and Harpham 1984), it is now possible to recommend the use of unedited data for release of preliminary findings.

2. The neglect of country-specific items extended to further analysis, and much information gathered in WFS surveys is still unexploited.
3. Though retrospective histories had been processed before WFS, notably by CELADE, the procedures usually involved an elaborate coding exercise. Furthermore, no acceptable way of handling missing or incomplete dates had been evolved. See Bogue and Bogue (1970) for an early approach to processing pregnancy histories.
4. There were also hopes that routine methods of checking data reliability could be derived which would permit the safe incorporation of vital rates into the First Country Report.
5. The age detail was insufficient to convert many of the current contraceptive use data to a base equivalent to those used in other tables. The inclusion of divorced and widowed women in the pregnant category also prevented the precise calculation and cross-checking of table bases and so further detracted from the main purpose of these tables.
6. A finer gradation of urban–rural residence should have been more widely used as there are often sizeable differences between the largest cities and smaller urban areas (Lightbourne 1980).

22

Country-Specific Analysis

V. C. Chidambaram
Trudy Harpham
Thomas W. Pullum

22.1 Introduction

One of the commonest criticisms of survey researchers is that they never fully analyse their data. Thanks to the farsightedness of the WFS funding agencies, to the liberality of participating countries in releasing their data and to the inclinations of the WFS staff, this criticism cannot be directed at the WFS programme. Indeed, the list of achievements in this regard is an impressive one, and includes:

- the publication of 41 main country reports plus summaries;
- the organization of 27 national meetings to discuss findings;
- over 600 country-specific in-depth studies, many of which have been published;
- the holding of 19 analysis workshops in which 172 participants from 55 developing countries received training;
- detailed evaluations of the quality of demographic data for 40 surveys;
- the publication of 11 technical bulletins and 12 illustrative analyses;
- over 200 cross-national studies, many of which have been published.

The purpose of this chapter is to provide a historical account and overview of WFS policies and achievements concerning country-specific analysis, following the publication of the main country report, which was discussed in the previous chapter.

22.2 Beginnings

As is evident from the statement of Kendall at the 1974 WFS Seminar on Tabulation and Analysis (WFS 1974), the initial WFS policy was to follow the First Country Report by a second more detailed and in-depth study which would undertake causal analysis through multivariate and other techniques. However, in agreement with the funding agencies the project document for each survey, which contained detailed descriptions of various activities, stopped with the First Country Report, leaving an open-ended analysis phase defined by a vaguely worded indication that further analysis was both desired and needed.

At this early stage there was a general lack of commitment to analysis beyond the first report, and indeed no resources were earmarked for this activity by the funding agencies until at least 1978. The Analysis Division in the WFS Professional Centre was itself only established in 1976 and, until then, the responsibility for further analysis was shared equally among the professional staff. Among some of the staff, both in WFS and in the countries, there was and remained little enthusiasm for further analysis. They were sceptical of the relevance of sophisticated analysis to the needs of policy-makers, particularly in view of the amount of resources and time needed to carry the analytical work out. The main support and demand for analysis came from the academic community. It was against this background that WFS began its analysis activities, its policy being largely moulded through experience as the project progressed. We will now describe the developments as they occurred and identify the main components of this aspect of WFS work.

Encouraged by the rewarding experience of preparing 'Guidelines for Country Report No. 1' (WFS 1977a), WFS started work on the preparation of a similar document for the so-called second report, which was to be analytic in nature, explaining and illustrating the use of more refined demographic and statistical techniques of analysis in a multivariate context. A preliminary document running into hundreds of pages was prepared with the assistance of a consultant. It soon became clear that such a document was too large to be of practical use to any specific country, yet too short to explain fully the whole range of analytical methods and issues. There was (and still is) no single accepted framework for fertility analysis applicable to all countries; many research hypotheses have to be very country-specific. The national priorities for further analysis themselves varied across countries and had to be decided by national policy needs. Furthermore, analytic techniques were to a large extent decided by the nature of the preliminary findings and quality of the data, which again were expected to vary across countries. There were also complex issues regarding the choice of the unit of analysis, measures of fertility to be used, lack of explanatory variables in the surveys, limitation of conventional multiple regresssion techniques, and a host of other related problems. After much discussion, the WFS Technical Advisory Committee (TAC) recommended in 1975 that the idea of a single second report be abandoned, and instead suggested preparation of a smaller document which would outline a general strategy for fertility analysis, to be supplemented by a series of *Technical Bulletins* to assist researchers. In 1976 an Analysis Division headed by an assistant director was established and this marked the beginning of the WFS programme of analysis. In January 1977 a small group of experts met in London to discuss co-ordination and implementation of analysis, and on the basis of their recommendations WFS prepared a policy statement on the analysis of WFS data. This smaller document, entitled 'Strategies for the Analysis of WFS Data', was eventually published in 1977 in the *Basic Documentation* series (WFS 1977c), but it was too general to be of much use to countries.

22.3   Technical bulletins

The main object of the WFS *Technical Bulletins* series was to demonstrate the usefulness as well as the pitfalls of certain commonly used techniques of analysis.

Wherever possible these bulletins also tried to illustrate the applicability of the particular method using real data from a country survey. Originally a set of nine topics was selected, of which only five were published in this series – Statistical Problems, Path Analysis, Standardization, Fertility Measures and Generalized Linear Models – the first one appearing in 1976. Of the remaining four, one on the own-children method was never completed and the other three (Evaluation of Birth History Data, Birth Intervals and Analysis of Maternity Histories) were published elsewhere, as they turned out to be more akin to country case studies than to methodological texts. Later the following topics were added: Life-Table Techniques, Coale Nuptiality Model, Progressive Fertility Analysis, Linear Models, Sampling Errors of Rates, and Estimation and Presentation of Sampling Errors. Selection of these topics was guided by analysts' needs in the context of WFS efforts to implement the programme of further analysis desired by the participating countries. Some of them are innovative; others attempt to demonstrate the applicability of well-known techniques to the analysis of fertility survey data. All of them have been well received, not only by the country analysts but also by many teaching and academic institutions all over the world. These technical bulletins have made an important contribution to WFS efforts to increase analytical skills in the developing world.

22.4   Recommended topics for analysis

Towards the end of 1976, the national directors of the surveys which had completed fieldwork were requested to identify possible topics for further analysis and their needs for implementation. It was hoped that the responses would help WFS to estimate the potential demand for technical assistance in this context and to prepare a work plan for each country. However, the responses indicated that most of the countries expected further guidance from WFS in the identification of topics. To meet this need, WFS prepared a document entitled 'Selected Topics for Further Analysis of WFS Data' (WFS 1977b), the purpose of which was not to provide a comprehensive list of possible areas but rather to identify topics relevant to many countries. A list of 32 topics under seven major areas – fertility levels and trends, nuptiality and fertility, contraception and fertility, factors other than contraception affecting fertility, fertility preferences, socio-economic factors and fertility, and other demographic variables – with a brief commentary on each topic was prepared and widely circulated. However, this initiative still elicited little response from countries.

22.5   Illustrative analyses

In 1977 the WFS Programme Steering Committee, in the light of the limited progress in analysis beyond the first report, came to the conclusion that WFS should provide further guidelines to the countries in the form of 'illustrative analyses' on selected important topics. These studies, using available country data, were to be published in monograph form and would serve the participating countries as examples of possible research. Acting upon this, WFS prepared and implemented a plan for illustrative analysis on 12 selected topics, most of which were believed to be of top priority and of great interest to every participating country. It was envisaged that each study should include a brief literature review summarizing important developments in the subjects studied and a clear statement of the substantive and methodological approach to the data from the country concerned, but with emphasis on the general applicability of the analysis. The studies were allocated among WFS staff and outside consultants for implementation and were to be carried out in close collaboration with, and preferably with the active participation of, national staff of the countries concerned, whose data were used. The countries participating were Bangladesh, Colombia, Panama, Pakistan, Sri Lanka and Thailand. In this task the WFS was assisted by an *ad hoc* Advisory Committee appointed in consultation with the IUSSP consisting of Ansley Coale (chairman), Mercedes Concepción, Henri Leridon and representatives of UNFPA and USAID.

Recognizing the urgency of providing the guidelines for data analysis, WFS prepared a plan in late 1977 with the over-ambitious target of completing the 12 studies during 1978. In the event, funding was approved only by late 1978, and with other problems and delays in selection of researchers, procurement of country approval, review of documents, etc., only two reports were published in 1979, another five in 1980, three in 1981 and the last two in 1982.[1]

How far did these 12 studies help participating countries? Probably not much. Many of the reports came too late to be of use for at least half of them. Even for the remaining countries, analysts did not always find the reports 'illustrative' enough. Some were too complicated for easy replication. Of the twelve, only four had some kind of local collaboration, the remaining eight being carried out by 'foreigners' as far as the countries were concerned. No doubt they are first-class research documents with a high level of methodological sophistication, and they have received nothing but praise from the academic community. But the majority of them did not carry 'illustrative' appeal in the countries, probably because their authors used the report as a medium for experiment and then to promulgate their preferred line of research, and some even to propagate a particular philosophical orientation, all in the context of the situation in a selected country chosen in advance by the WFS. The mission which evaluated WFS in 1980 also expressed disappointment with the substantive yield of some of these analyses.

22.6 Workshops

In 1978, while the planning of the illustrative analyses was in course, the WFS Analysis Division started debating the possibility and usefulness of additional activities, namely national meetings and workshops. These later proved to be most effective and productive means for stimulating interest in and implementing the further analysis programme in the countries. We will first discuss workshops.

In the regional meetings held in Bangkok and in Mexico in 1977, many of the national survey directors voiced strong support for the idea of holding regional workshops on analysis of their survey data. In the absence of direct relevant experience, there was considerable scepticism about this activity even among a section of the WFS staff, particularly because of the large amount of time and cost that would be demanded by the workshops at a time when WFS itself was experiencing heavy financial constraints. Moreover, there was little consensus about the topics to be covered. But open debates and frank criticisms were daily phenomena at WFS headquarters, and there was always willingness to try new approaches. As a first step, WFS collaborated with UNESCAP in organizing a regional workshop on Techniques of Analysis of WFS Data at the International Institute for Population Studies in Bombay during 27 November-8 December 1978. Twenty-five participants from 12 countries attended the workshop supported by UNFPA. The programme covered lectures on 17 topics followed by practical work using WFS data (WFS 1980b). From the comments made by the participants at the completion of the workshop, it was clear that such short-term programmes covering a multitude of topics were not very effective because there was not enough time to discuss any topic in detail. Having learned from this experience, WFS decided to organize three-month workshops, each preferably covering a particular topic. The first such workshop was held in London in July-October 1978 on the theme of data quality evaluation with participation from four countries. The results were so encouraging that the workshop approach became an integral part of the WFS analysis programme with full support from the Programme Steering Committee (PSC) and the funding agencies. The additional cost of such workshops in London was met from the separate finance allocated by USAID for analysis, while UNFPA financed such activities through the Regional Commissions.

WFS organized ten workshops (nine in London and one in Santiago), of which seven were devoted to evaluation of data, one to analysis of data from the FOTCAF module, one to community determinants of infant and child mortality and one to further analysis of the Ghana Fertility Survey. In addition, WFS supported and actively participated in the following workshops held at regional and national institutions:

Organizer	Theme	No. of participants
ESCAP, Bangkok	Application of Multivariate Techniques to the Analysis of WFS Data	11
CELADE, Santiago	In-depth Research and Training Seminar	8
EWPI, Honolulu	WFS Working Group; emphasis on unmet need for contraception	14

(*cont.*)

Organizer	Theme	No. of participants
ECA, Addis Ababa	Use of SPSS Package	5
CAPMAS, Cairo	Use of SPSS Package	20
Direction de la Statistique, Dakar	Use of SPSS Package	8
ESCAP, Bangkok	Multivariate Analysis of Nuptiality and Fertility from WFS Survey Data	10
RIPS, Accra	Estimation of Fertility and Mortality in Africa	40

These workshops played a significant role in the analysis of WFS data. They provided perhaps the best means for increasing national capability in analytical skills and at the same time ensured completion of the research projects in a relatively short period. In the workshop environment participants had the unique opportunity of discussion with, and receiving assistance from, WFS staff and consultants with a wide variety of skills. In addition, they were able to compare and exchange experiences with fellow participants, thereby improving the quality of the work. During the period of the workshop the participants were free from their regular duties at home base and hence were able to concentrate full time on the project without any interruptions; only in this way could they have completed the work in a period of three months. They also benefited from efficient computer services, often not readily accessible in many of the developing countries. Finally, the financial and human resources which would be required for meeting the same objectives by organizing the projects separately in each country would much exceed those needed for the workshop approach. This is amply demonstrated by the achievements in the past six years. A total of 172 researchers from 55 countries participated (a few attended more than once) in 18 workshops and produced over 50 research reports of good quality.

22.7 National meetings

The technical bulletins, list of selected topics, illustrative analyses and workshops constituted the main means of achieving WFS's objective of assisting the countries in further analysis. But they alone could not generate sufficient initiative or enthusiasm within the countries, in spite of the expressed commitment to carry out detailed national analyses. In fact, the absence of local skills or guidelines was not the major obstacle in the translation of such commitment into action in the countries. There were other issues — of operation, motivation, communication and organization:

1 In many countries, the survey staff were transferred to other jobs within the country or joined international organizations even before the completion of the First County Report, leaving no one specifically responsible for the organization and implementation of the analysis.

2 The national organization which carried out the data collection did not necessarily have the capability, or even the interest, for further analysis. There was therefore the need to enlist the collaboration of other research organizations, universities and government departments, which was not easy in many countries.

3 Institutional possessiveness over data within the national executing agencies and professional rivalry occasionally created unnecessary delays in access to data even among national researchers.

4 The WFS policy required, rightly, that the analysis be carried out in the country by local researchers as far as possible.

5 Essential information about the national survey and the results from the first report were not adequately disseminated even among those potentially interested and involved in further analysis.

6 The topics for analysis were determined by national needs and policy, while the analytical methods to be used largely depended on the quality and nature of the data collected. Almost all countries required an appropriate forum of interested researchers to discuss the relevant issues.

It was against this background that WFS decided to experiment with the idea of holding two-day meetings in Nepal and Sri Lanka in 1979. The main objectives of the meetings were to:

— disseminate information about the survey and its main findings
— discuss the policy implications of the findings
— stimulate interest in further analysis among national researchers and policy-makers
— obtain feedback on the priority topics to be analysed.

The meetings in both countries turned out to be very successful and thereafter WFS encouraged countries to organize similar meetings and provided limited financial support to meet any additional cost. A total of 27 countries organized national meetings within the WFS context. Most of them devoted the two-day meeting largely to discussion of the fertility survey and its results, while in a few cases the survey formed one important component of a meeting dealing with the broader theme of population and development, as in Lesotho, Malaysia and Sudan for example. All of the meetings, however, were initiated within the WFS context, and with very few exceptions were attended by high-ranking policy-makers, officials from government ministries, academic researchers and visiting demographers. The opening sessions were generally honoured by the presence of a senior minister or a representative of the head of state, which naturally helped to attract publicity. Invariably the meeting and the results from the fertility survey were covered by the local media.

The impact of the national meetings varied between countries. It is only fair to admit that there were a few countries where the meetings lacked sufficient support and recognition from the high ranks of government and had been organized primarily in response to pressure from WFS. Barring those few, all the remaining meetings made significant impact on the government, researchers and even the public. The officials outside the executing agency were made to realize what the survey offered; clear ideas for second-stage analysis were formulated in some countries; the quality of the survey was critically examined in many of the meetings; and the policy implications of the survey findings were invariably discussed. In addition to the discussion of fertility and population issues, in at least three countries the meeting was considered to be an appropriate occasion to announce important national decisions, such as the establishment of a national population commission or the adoption of a population policy. In general, the meetings made useful and significant contributions to the achievement of WFS objectives in analysis of data. In fact, the national director of the survey in Trinidad and Tobago found the meeting, the first of its kind in the country, so useful that he recommended that the Central Statistical Office should organize similar ones for every major project.

22.8 Achievements

The foregoing account depicts the essential elements of the WFS policy on national analysis and how this evolved over time. At this juncture the reader may ask the question, 'How successful was the policy?'. Here one should look at both the qualitative and the quantitative aspects of the achievements regarding country-specific further analysis. In the present section we will discuss the latter aspect, as the former is considered in later chapters.

The analyses that are referred to below are country-specific, post-First Country Report projects. They include, for example, workshop projects, illustrative analyses, evaluations, theses and technical bulletins. Country-specific studies are those based on one or at most two countries. (See chapter 23 for an assessment of comparative analyses.) The projects may be completed or under way. The analysts may be of any nationality.

As the last WFS Annual Report included projects only through 1982, all countries were invited in mid-1984 to update the list of projects that appeared in that publication. It was emphasized that if no response was received the 1982 list would be treated as complete. A third of the countries took this opportunity to provide information about new and completed projects.

At the time of writing, WFS had information about 680 national analysis projects which were completed or under way. Table 22.1 allows us to examine the initiation of the projects.

TABLE 22.1
Initiation of national analyses

Category	Origin	Number	Per cent
A	Country initiated	243	36
B	WFS initiated	35	5
C	Other	248	36
D	Theses	137	20
	Not known	17	3
Total		680	100

A Projects initiated by survey staff in the country whether funded by WFS or by other means.

B Projects initiated by WFS with the concurrence of the country for the purposes of illustrative analysis, technical bulletins or other methodological work.

C Projects initiated by staff of other organizations either in the country or elsewhere.

D Work done by university students (usually nationals of the country) leading to a thesis for a Master's or Ph.D. degree.

As can be seen, the projects initiated by WFS constitute only five per cent of the projects undertaken, implying that interest in the surveys was widespread among the agencies and researchers. This small core of WFS-initiated projects may well have stimulated the larger number of country-initiated analyses, and it is also believed that the preparation of standard recode files and of illustrative analyses greatly facilitated the non-WFS projects. Of the 680 projects, 26 involved two countries. In the analysis of projects by country below, such projects are counted twice, one for each country.

Over half of the 680 national analyses had, at the time of writing, been published. (This does not include master's or doctoral theses.) Table 22.2 shows the form of publication for these 357 analyses.

Nearly a quarter of the published analyses were institutions' in-house publications, but 31 per cent of the papers appeared in periodicals or as essays in published volumes. WFS supported the publication of 22 per cent of the analyses.

Table 22.3 shows that every WFS country except Iran has produced at least one national analysis project. The table reflects the timing of the WFS surveys, since the Asian countries, which were surveyed first, have the most projects while the more recent African surveys generally have fewer. The exceptions in Africa are Kenya and Senegal. Kenya was the first African survey to be finished and had a resident adviser who encouraged much work to be completed in Nairobi. Senegal received special assistance for national analyses from the Institut National d'Etudes Démographiques (INED), Paris, and quickly produced ten.

Many of the Asian countries have more than 20 national analyses. Sri Lanka has had 54 projects, but over 40 of these were done outside the country,

TABLE 22.2

Form of publication of national analyses

	Number	Per cent
WFS Scientific Reports	67	19
WFS Occasional Papers	11	3
Demographic periodicals	69	19
Economic/development periodicals	8	2
Institution in-house (excluding WFS)	85	24
Papers submitted to conferences/seminars	70	20
Papers in books	37	10
Other	10	3
Total	357	100

including a number of WFS illustrative analyses. Pakistan, Philippines, Syria and Ghana had WFS analysis volumes which were collections of national analysis papers. It is hoped that further analysis results from Egypt will also be published in book form.

The Pakistan First Report was published before the WFS Guidelines for Country Report No. 1 were finalized and therefore had certain limitations. For this reason and 'in order to ensure increased training opportunities for the local researchers and also to prevent misuse of the data by foreigners, the Government decided that PFS data should be released for further analysis only if a Pakistan national was involved in the work' (Alam and Dinesen 1984). Six of the Pakistan analyses were presented as background papers for the 1980 WFS Conference and were then published in book form. The Philippines published an analysis volume after the National Census and Statistics Office and the University of the Philippines Population Institute implemented a comprehensive programme for national analysis. Out of all the Asian countries, Yemen AR has the least number of projects, which may reflect the recency of the completion of this survey.

In Latin America the reasons for the large numbers of analyses are similar to those above. Colombia, for example, was used in many illustrative analyses and Haiti had a long-term resident adviser who produced many papers. A few Latin American countries completed only a small number of projects, as suitable nationals could not commit sufficient time to such work.

Although some WFS countries have not yet produced many national analyses it must be emphasized that new projects will be undertaken in many countries, especially the recently surveyed African states. Indeed, the continued funding of the WFS archive will ensure continued availability of the data files. But even the current average of over 15 national analyses per WFS country seems a successful aspect of the WFS enterprise.

Equally as important as the number of projects is the choice of topics. Each project was classified using the categorization in table 22.4. Many projects

TABLE 22.3

National analysis projects by country and region (number of projects in parentheses followed by First Country Report publication year)

No. of projects	Africa	Asia and Pacific	Latin America and Caribbean
20 +	Kenya (35) 1980/1	Sri Lanka (54) 1978 Bangladesh (47) 1979 Korea, Rep. of (44) 1978 Malaysia (40) 1978 Pakistan (37) 1977	Philippines (33) 1979 Thailand (31) 1977 Egypt (29) 1983 Indonesia (28) 1979 Jordan (28) 1980 Nepal (24) 1977	Colombia (30) 1978 Haiti (23) 1981
10–19	Senegal (18) 1981	Fiji (18) 1976 Turkey (17) 1980 Syria (11) 1982		Dominican Rep. (19) 1976 Mexico (18) 1979 Costa Rica (16) 1978 Peru'(13) 1979 Jamaica (12) 1979 Trinidad & Tobago (12) 1981 Guyana (11) 1979
1–9	Lesotho (9) 1981 Cameroon (8) 1983 Ghana (6) 1983 Sudan (North) (6) 1982 Mauritania (4) 1984 Benin (2) 1984 Ivory Coast (1) 1984 Morocco (1) 1984 Nigeria (1) 1984 Tunisia (1) 1983	Yemen AR (2) 1984		Panama (8) 1978 Ecuador (3) 1984 Paraguay (3) 1981 Venezuela (2) 1980/2
Total	92	443		170

Note: Portugal had one project

TABLE 22.4
Classification and distribution of topics

Label	Title	No. of projects
CONT	Contraception (e.g. use levels, trends, factors affecting use, accessibility and supply, knowledge, unmet need)	87
EVAL	Evaluation (e.g. birth and marriage histories, mortality data)	64
FERT-L	Fertility levels and trends .	77
FERT-LF	Effects of fertility on labour force	29
FERT-SE	Relationships between social and economic factors and fertility	58
FERT-COM	Relationships between community-level variables and fertility	17
FERT-HH	Relationship between household structure and fertility	14
FERT-RES	Effects of residence and migration on fertility	21
FERT-INT	Effects of intermediate variables on fertility	38
FERT-NUPT	Effects of nuptiality on fertility	31
FERT-MORT	Effects of infant mortality on fertility	24
FERT-TIME	Birth interval analysis; birth spacing/timing	36
FERT-MISC	Miscellaneous fertility studies	17
PREFS	Fertility preferences	24
LACT	Levels, trends and factors affecting breastfeeding	15
METH	Development of new methodologies; response errors; sampling studies	34
MORT	Levels, trends and factors affecting foetal, infant, child and adult mortality	73
NUPT	Levels, patterns, trends and factors affecting age at first marriage	44
POLICY	Studies which explicitly address policy issues	19
MISC	Miscellaneous	39

involved two distinct topics and a few involved three or four. Because of this each project was allowed up to four topic classifications and each topic is treated as distinct in the discussion below.

The overall distribution of topics is given in table 22.4. The five most popular are contraception, fertility levels and trends, mortality, evaluation of data quality, and socio-economic factors affecting fertility. It is natural that contraception and fertility levels are the most widely studied topics, of course, as these receive great attention in the WFS core questionnaire and were the primary focus of the surveys. Perhaps the amount of use made of the WFS mortality data was not anticipated, but the reports of infant and child deaths in the birth histories were generally found to be of much better quality than had been expected. Nearly every country performed an evaluation of its data, thus accounting for the large number of papers on this topic. Analyses concentrating on socio-economic factors and fertility have made good use of the background variables collected in the questionnaire.

Substantive topics occupy the top nine places in table 22.4, while 5 per cent of the projects were methodological. Policy issues were the main focus of only 3 per cent of projects, although many, if not most, of the substantive papers probably had implications for family planning and health programmes. Table 22.5 breaks down topics by region. The distribution of topics within regions is remarkably similar to the overall distribution of topics. There are some anomalies which are noted in the table. Africa has more than the average number of papers on the evaluation of data and the effects of nuptiality, mortality and residence on fertility. As methodological studies tend to be done well after the survey, African countries generally have not yet had time to produce many methodological analyses. There is also a lack of papers examining nuptiality *per se*. It is expected that such gaps in the coverage of topics in Africa will be filled in the near future. Latin America has a particularly large number of papers on fertility levels and trends, a subject of great interest to researchers examining the demographic transition in Latin America. The few studies of the effects of nuptiality on fertility in Latin America may reflect the fact that there is much fertility outside marriage (i.e. in informal unions which are difficult to measure) and that marriage is therefore not regarded as an important intermediate variable affecting fertility. An exception to this generalization is found in the four Caribbean surveys, which made a special effort to record all types of union, informal and formal, and where detailed analyses of these data were performed.

Any assessment of the lessons learned from this experience with a view to formulating a policy for analysis in future survey activities should also recognize two important aspects of WFS strategy which have not yet been mentioned.

First was the WFS commitment to a scientific evaluation of the quality of demographic data of each survey. The decision to achieve this formidable goal was motivated by four main factors:

1 The pressure from leading demographers such as Brass and Coale who, based on their past experience, repeatedly expressed their doubts about the quality of the data generated by the WFS.

2 Scientific curiosity: the desire to find out whether the expensive and elaborate methods of data collection employed by WFS had really paid dividends.

3 The need to estimate as accurately as possible the current levels and trends of

TABLE 22.5
Percentage distribution of topics by region

Topic	Africa (%)	Asia (%)	Latin America (%)	Total (%)
CONT	9	12	11	11
FERT–L	8	9	14 (+)	10
MORT	11	9	10	10
EVAL	12 (+)	7	9	8
FERT–SE	6	9	7	8
NUPT	1 (–)	6	8	6
MISC	6	5	6	5
FERT–INT	4	5	4	5
FERT–TIME	6	5	3	5
METH	2 (–)	5	5	5
FERT–NUPT	7 (+)	5	1 (–)	4
FERT–LF	2	3	6	4
FERT–MORT	6 (+)	2	4	3
PREFS	3	4	2	3
FERT–RES	7 (+)	2	2	3
POLICY	2	3	3	3
FERT–MISC	4	2	3	2
FERT–COM	4	2	1	2
LACT	1	3	1	2
FERT–HH	0	2	2	2
	100	100	100	100

Notes: (+) indicates that the region percentage is more than 2 points higher than the percentage over all countries; (–) indicates that the region percentage is more than 2 points less than the percentage over all countries.
See table 22.4 for full explanation of topic titles.

fertility in the countries, which in turn are dependent on the quality of the demographic data collected.

4 The consensus that all datasets should be evaluated prior to, and as an aid to, substantive analysis following the First Country Report.

In response to these factors, WFS commissioned Brass and Coale themselves to evaluate the WFS data from two early surveys (Bangladesh and Nepal) and to provide guidelines for such evaluation exercises. The advent of the workshop approach around the same time resulted in the choice of 'evaluation' as the major theme for the workshops. As a result, the WFS achieved what was thought to be impossible – evaluation of data from 40 surveys out of the 41 for which a First Country Report was published.[2] This scientific evaluation helped to generate confidence in the data by identifying any weaknesses and to stimulate an interest in further analysis.

Second was the question of finance for analysis. The most significant and important development was the decision by one of the funding agencies (USAID) to earmark a specific sum solely for the support of further analysis, with priority for national analysis. This very much quickened progress, as it was possible for the WFS to follow the promotional efforts with firm commitment of assistance whenever it was needed. Out of the 680 national projects noted earlier, WFS through its special USAID funds provided financial support to 85 including most of the evaluation reports. All but five of these projects have been successfully completed with the publication of a final report. This experience demonstrates the need for, and the benefits from, earmarking separate funds for analysis which would not compete with the needs in other areas of the project.

22.9   Conclusions

This chapter has given a frank account of the evolution and achievements of WFS policy on national analysis and reporting. This is by no means an assessment of the policy itself, though the authors have not refrained from quoting statistics of WFS accomplishment nor from making, at times, critical observations.

To sum up, the WFS policy on national analysis which emerged over the years was based on a strategy designed to ensure maximum possible analytical exploitation and utilization of the valuable data by *bona fide* national and international researchers, with the principal commitment to meet the needs of the participating countries which provided the primary data and to whom those data belong. The sheer number of country-specific analyses completed or under way suggests that the policy has been sucessful. Indeed, the emergence of WFS as a major analytical centre, as opposed to a data collection exercise, is one of the more surprising features of the programme. Quite apart from the value of the results themselves, WFS has been able to introduce scores of developing country demographers and statisticians to new techniques of data processing and analysis which should prove useful to their future careers and to the enhancement of country capabilities.

Notes

1. These are published as nos. 4, 5, 9, 10, 12, 13, 15, 16, 17, 25, 37 and 39 in the *WFS Scientific Reports* series.
2. One dataset not evaluated is that of the survey in Panama.

23

Multi-Country Analysis

Cynthia B. Lloyd

23.1 Introduction

Demographic analysis based on a comparison of national experiences has had a long and distinguished history in the population field. The theory of the demographic transition and its various modifications, which still forms the general framework within which much current multinational demographic analysis is formulated, was developed from comparative studies of the demographic experiences of different countries using very imperfect historical data. In the early post-war period, several leading demographic institutions were set up which, because of their institutional mandates, have provided strong support within the field for cross-national comparative analysis. The first of these was the United Nations Population Division which, since its inception in 1946, has had the function within the United Nations Secretariat of informing the Secretary-General and various United Nations legislative bodies of demographic developments from a global perspective and of assisting governments and the international community in dealing with population issues. In fulfilling that commitment, the Population Division has developed various methodologies designed to overcome the obstacles presented by the scarcity and poor quality of demographic data for much of the world and has published a series of global comparative studies of demographic phenomena. The other major institution is the International Union for the Scientific Study of Population (IUSSP) which, through its various committees, has served as a catalyst in stimulating comparative analysis within the various subdisciplines of demography.[1]

The establishment of the World Fertility Survey programme in 1972 marked a critical turning point for the field of comparative demographic analysis. One of the programme's three major objectives was the collection of internationally comparable survey data on fertility and its proximate determinants – an ambitious objective which has, by and large, been met. The resulting datasets which have become available to the international community for analysis provide the opportunity to study and compare in depth the multiple dimensions (i.e. period, cohort and cross-section) of demographic relationships in a way never before (and maybe never again) possible. The scope of the data has provided many opportunities for methodological and analytical breakthroughs but, at the same time, the sheer extent of the information to be digested has also forced analytical compromises in the interest of digestable output and has inevitably increased the risk of interpretational errors as country idiosyncracies are overlooked.

In the assessment which follows, four major aspects of multinational analysis as they relate to the WFS experience will be discussed. First, the history of the institutional participation in comparative analysis is reviewed. Secondly, the comparability of the WFS data itself is discussed. Thirdly, we consider analytical methodologies and finally the major pieces of research which have made or are expected to make a contribution to the field of multinational analysis are reviewed with respect to the nature of their contributions. The details of the findings themselves can be found in the publications cited and in some of the other chapters in this volume and, therefore, there is no attempt to summarize them here. However, it should be emphasized that the assessment of research findings at this stage is very premature because the majority of the comparative work based on WFS findings has yet to be published. In addition, it is not yet known how many countries might undertake second-round WFS-type surveys on their own initiative, thus adding still further to the potential and complexity of multinational analysis.

23.2 Institutional involvement

Early on in the WFS programme, even before any data were available for analysis, strategies for the comparative analysis of WFS data were discussed at various international fora. In 1975, the first meeting of the IUSSP Committee on Comparative Analysis of Fertility discussed guidelines for the comparative analysis of WFS data. Attention was primarily directed to the data that would be forthcoming in the published First Country Reports since, at that time, plans had not been formulated to make standard data tapes available for further analysis.

In mid-1977, the United Nations Population Division organized the first meeting of the United Nations Working Group on Comparative Analysis, designed to develop a comparative research programme for the United Nations system, including all the population units of the Regional Commissions as well as interested Specialized Agencies.[2] A minimum research programme was agreed upon comprising 17 topics which would involve an analysis of the data from the first 20 WFS countries, with the Regional Commissions and the Population Division undertaking parallel analyses. This was seen as the first phase of a two-phase project, the final output of which would be a complete analysis of all participating countries. The design of the final study would be based on the lessons learned from the first phase of analysis.[3]

By mid-1978, the WFS had built up an efficient data processing section and by early 1979, the process of developing standard recode tapes with accompanying data dictionaries and other documentation was in full swing. A fuller account may be found in chapter 20. Various research organizations wrote to WFS and to countries requesting permission to release tapes for purposes of comparative analysis. As explained in chapter 27, some countries provided general release but others adopted more restrictive policies.[4] The availability of standard data tapes vastly expanded the possibilities for comparative analysis.

With the availability of the standard recode tapes beginning in 1979, comparative analysis of the data could get under way. Heightened interest in this area of work prompted WFS to host an expert group meeting on the methodology of comparative fertility studies in London in August 1979. This group included representatives from most of the institutions which have, to date, played a significant role in the comparative analysis of WFS data. These include the WFS itself, the United Nations, University of Michigan, Princeton University Office of Population Research, East-West Population Institute, and the IUSSP Committee on Comparative Analysis of Fertility. The WFS was also encouraged to pursue its plans to publish a series of comparative tabulations on the major demographic variables of interest.

The *Cross-National Summaries* series published by the WFS, the first of which became available at the time of the 1980 WFS London Conference, provided 'comparable' tabulations for a series of demographic topics as well as guides to the comparability of the questionnaires, the surveys, the First Country Reports and the background variables. These summaries have become an invaluable reference tool in the design of more detailed and sophisticated comparative analysis.

At the time of formal termination of the WFS programme in 1984, full comparative analysis of WFS data, including all major regions, was only just beginning because many of the African data tapes had only recently become available to the research community. The final round of Cross-National Summaries based on all the countries had yet to be issued and the main publication planned by the United Nations Population Division, summarizing the major findings for 40 countries, is not scheduled for completion until mid-1986 (United Nations forthcoming, b). Thus, at the time of writing, the data are beginning to reach their full potential for multinational analysis both from the point of view of data availability but also in terms of available documentation.

Indeed, with hindsight, it is easy to understand, but nonetheless disappointing to realize, that the funding for comparative research programmes such as those named above, which sprang up in response to the anticipated availability of WFS data, had a life roughly congruent with the WFS. Thus, in many cases, research studies had to be finalized before many of the errors in the early data tapes were detected and corrected, before standardization procedures were revised and perfected, before complete data documentation was available and before the quality of the data had been fully evaluated. Research funding for multinational analysis of WFS findings is diminishing just at the time when such research could be most efficiently and effectively undertaken, particularly in the case of Africa where the data may hold the greatest potential for new insights. Funding agencies and international policy-makers are understandably impatient for results and it is indeed true that, even in their very incomplete form, the results which have already emerged from WFS comparative analysis have played a very influential role in policy discussions[5] and international funding decisions.[6] Nonetheless, multinational analysis based on 40 micro-datasets is time-consuming and expensive, and without further financial support it is unlikely that research institutions will be able to exploit the full potential of the WFS data for multinational analysis.

23.3   Comparability of data

The ultimate value of conclusions drawn from multinational analysis depends on the underlying comparability of the data on which the analyses are based. To the extent that non-comparabilities exist, the successful design of multinational research and its subsequent interpretation rests on a full understanding of inter-country differences in the data. While the goal of collecting comparable data was, by and large, met by the WFS, non-comparabilities are nonetheless present in the data. Some of these could have been reduced or even eliminated through more careful design of the sample[7] but many were unavoidable and stem from basic differences in the underlying populations which are reflected by culture, institutions and levels of development. For these reasons, the meaning of the phrase 'data comparability' is potentially confusing as it can mean very different things in different contexts.

The comparability of WFS data results from a complex interaction between characteristics of the country setting and characteristics of the survey design.

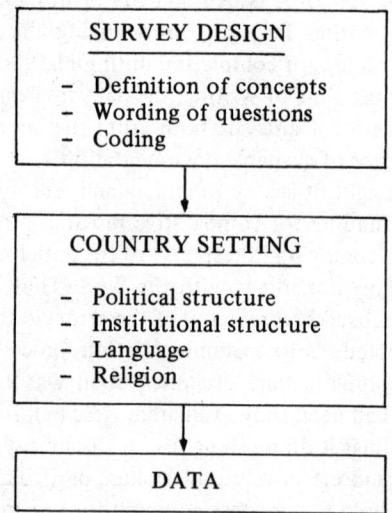

FIG. 23.1. Characteristics of the survey design and the country setting which can influence comparability of the data

Figure 23.1 shows the essential characteristics of the survey design and the country setting, both of which can influence the resulting comparability of the data. Only when the country settings are very similar and the design and the implementation of the surveys have been identical can the resulting data be fully comparable. While this was essentially achieved for certain subsets of surveys in neighbouring countries which have similar historical and cultural traditions, the picture is considerably more complex when all the survey data are examined together.

The high degree of overall comparability between different surveys is the direct result of a carefully designed core questionnaire based on certain essential underlying concepts which was developed before countries were asked to participate. While countries were not asked to follow the structure and wording of the core questionnaire exactly, it was expected that they would want to collect all the data specified in the core while maintaining reasonable comparability with both other WFS surveys and any earlier fertility surveys of their own. Appendix B of chapter 2 summarizes the major deviations from the recommended core. The availability of special modules (see chapter 3) allowed countries to pursue topics of special interest as supplements to the core. This minimized structural changes in the design of individual countries' questionnaires and preserved the integrity of the core elements of the survey. The availability of standard modules on particular topics provided a useful tool for reconciling country concerns and data comparability in many cases.

The preparation of a standard recode tape with common variable names, numbers and value labels for each survey eliminated a whole layer of non-comparabilities — such as differences that existed between countries in the sequence or wording of questions — from the analysts' concern. By the end of the WFS, it was expected that all standard recode tapes would have a uniform format not just with respect to all the variables derived from the core questionnaire but also with respect to those from the modules. Early recode files did not include the responses to all core questions (e.g. work history) and did not always use standard coding (e.g. one-digit occupational groups) but almost all have now been revised to conform to a standard format. Thus, although certain topics have been difficult to handle in a comprehensive framework in previous years, this is not expected to remain a problem.

While greatly facilitating the work of the scholar interested in multinational analysis, the standard recode tapes do sometimes obscure remaining non-comparabilities by giving common names and value labels to variables which are not, in fact, the same. A careful reading of the data documentation does reveal some of the most significant of these non-comparabilities (i.e. those which stem from differences in questionnaire design), but others are more subtle and require a thorough knowledge of a country's culture and institutions, as well as information on the imputation of dates, the base populations to which certain questions were addressed, the use of probes, the order of questions, etc. In the discussion which follows, the major types of incomparabilities which are present in the data are briefly summarized in order to facilitate the work of those who may wish to embark on any multinational analysis using these data in the future. More specific details on some of these aspects can be found in certain WFS Cross-National Summaries (Singh and Platridis 1980; Singh 1980a; Singh 1980b; Singh 1980c).

Even when concepts are clear and questions are worded identically, non-comparabilities can arise if the completeness and accuracy of the responses are influenced by cultural traditions and education. Accurate date reporting is an example of such a problem. An in-depth United Nations study of the comparative quality of recent fertility estimates based on WFS data reviewed systematically the accuracy of date reporting with respect to date of the respondent's birth, date of first marriage and the birth history (United Nations 1983a). It is clear that certain problems with date reporting, familiar to demographers from previous survey experiences, have recurred in certain WFS surveys and in some cases are specific to a region or culture. Some of the types of date misreporting that appear to have recurred in several surveys include the apparent reluctance of Latin American women to report ages over 40; the apparent tendency of interviewers to guess age as some function of parity; the apparent tendency of women to under-report or misdate the births of children born between one and two years before the survey; and the tendency of older women to omit or postdate their earliest births.

Similar problems recurred in the reporting of breastfeeding duration, which in most countries shows marked heaping at six-month intervals. The extent of such heaping varies widely across countries and appears to depend not only on variations in the accuracy of reporting across countries but also on differences between countries in the true duration of breastfeeding and in the definition of weaning (Ferry 1981). However, the recent development of methodologies of measuring the average breastfeeding durations for groups of women from current status data (which is assumed to be accurately and comparably reported) reduces significantly the importance of these problems (Mosley, Werner and Becker 1982; Page, Lesthaeghe and Shah 1982; Ferry and Smith 1983).

In certain cases where such non-comparabilities in reporting can be anticipated in advance, the questionnaire itself can be adapted in such a way as to remove some of these difficulties. For example, the decision to have an open-ended question on knowledge of contraception followed by method-specific probes proved particularly effective and substantially increased the comparability of contraceptive prevalence estimates for countries using both types of questions (Vaessen 1981). In the more complex case of marital unions, the WFS chose to allow the definition of union status to vary from country to country in the interests of measuring more comparably across countries the dates and duration of each respondent's periods of regular exposure to the risk of conception. This involved adapting the definition of union to the country setting while still preserving the distinction between legal and other forms of union. While the resulting data probably provide a reasonably comparable approach to the measurement of time spent in socially recognized unions across countries,[8] the existence of non-trivial amounts of extra-union fertility in certain countries (United Nations 1983c) suggests that the concept of sexual exposure is not comparably measured across countries; but this may indeed not even be a desirable goal.

While the concept of sexual exposure is at least potentially measurable, a woman's actual fecundity status is not, because in many cases it is unknown even to the individual woman herself. Nonetheless, it has been important in fertility analysis because it has been used to refine the concept of 'exposure' so that contraceptive prevalence can be assessed in relationship to those genuinely at risk of a pregnancy. In the WFS, fecundity status was established from the respondent's response to the question 'As far as you know, is it physically possible for you and your husband to have a child, supposing you wanted one?', and in most countries questionnaire design and coding were reasonably comparable. Those using contraception at the time of interview (as well as those who were pregnant) were assumed to be fecund and not asked the question. In addition, those responding 'Don't know' were coded as fecund. Because contraceptive users are assumed to be fecund, it is not surprising that self-reported infecundity is relatively low in societies with high rates of contraceptive use because contraceptive users have no way to assess their current fecundity status (Vaessen 1984). While improvements in the measurement of fecundity could be made in the case of non-users through the use of more objective measures (such as the length of the open interval), rapidly changing levels of contraceptive use in many countries will continuously increase the proportion of the population for which no objective measure is available. For these reasons, analysis of contraceptive use from WFS data has increasingly been based on a more internationally comparable measure of exposure (i.e. currently married women).

The desire to test demographic transition theories led the survey designers to include a set of background variables comprising, among others, questions on place of residence (both current and childhood), years of education (and literacy) and the respondent's work history both before and after marriage, as well as information on husband's education and work status. In the case of residence, the measurement of type of place was constrained by a country's usual definition of city, town and rural area as specified in the census and thus the criteria for differentiating rural from urban areas varied widely among countries according to such factors as the socio-economic characteristics of place, the administrative function and its population size (Singh 1980a). Nonetheless, while type of place is not comparable across countries, it does measure some kind of continuum within each country. In order to enhance the comparability of the place of residence variable, the WFS has provided users of the standard recode tapes with the means to develop a new variable which will distinguish major urban from other urban and rural areas using various criteria for determining major urban (including the capital city regardless of size, any city of over a million inhabitants, and roughly half of the urban population). By assuming that modernity and size are reasonably correlated within each country, urban–rural differentials can be compared across countries in the context of some general index of urbanization for each country.

Education is also bounded by country-specific definitions and institutions, and levels, grades and content vary substantially across countries. To provide comparability with respect to at least one dimension of education, the WFS chose to measure years of schooling. This variable — years of education — was actually constructed out of the responses to two questions which were not asked in the same way in all countries, i.e. 'What level of education did you attain?' and 'How many years did you achieve at that level?'. Thus, the years of education variable constructed for the standard recode tapes was based on knowledge of the local education systems of WFS staff and country co-ordinators. In some countries, such as Mauritania, there were two different educational tracks (Western style or Koranic) which were weighted differently in arriving at total years. In addition, it must be remembered that because of rapid changes in the educational systems in some countries, women of different ages who have the same recorded number of years of education may have experienced very different types and intensities of schooling. When cross-tabulating years of education by literacy, it can be seen that there is an enormous variation between countries in the percentages literate of those respondents with 1–3 years of education, suggesting that underlying variations in other dimensions of education such as content, quality and intensity of schooling may be important factors in the link between education and literacy.

One of the most challenging aspects of the questionnaire was its work history for women. Unfortunately, despite considerable discussion and 17 core questions designed to probe many dimensions of the variable, this section of the interview was ultimately unsuccessful in capturing a uniform concept of work across countries. To introduce the subject of work the following definition was proposed in the core questionnaire: 'As you know, many women work — I mean aside from doing their own housework. Some take up jobs for which they are paid in cash or kind. Others sell things, or have a small business, or work on the family farm. Are you doing any such work at the present time?' Such a definition represented a bold step forward from the point of view of inclusiveness in that work in the informal sector and non-cash work were implicitly included. However, by not setting a minimum number of hours for inclusion or providing women with a guide as to what would be considered sufficient for inclusion, it is unclear how women interpreted this question. The word 'work', when translated into different languages, may have subtly different meanings which would be hard to transcend without very precise guidelines and locally appropriate examples. In addition, only 26 out of 40 countries used the recommended wording (United Nations 1985b). The result was that in Pakistan work on the family farm was omitted and in Ghana, Bangladesh, Fiji, Kenya and Lesotho work was restricted to paid in cash or salaried work only, depending on the country. Variations between countries in the concept of work occurred not only because certain countries deviated from the recommended definition of work as worded in the core questionnaire but also because the definition itself left room for ambiguity. This ambiguity was often resolved in the field by the interviewers themselves in ways that are unknown but are likely to have been heavily coloured by their own culture-bound definitions of work, as well as by their previous experience.[9] This is assumed because instructions to the interviewers often did not clarify the concept as described in the core questionnaire. The result of all these factors is that the proportion of women currently working varies across countries in ways which are not always expected when such factors as level of development, religion (i.e. Muslim or other) and percentage in agriculture are taken into account (United Nations 1985b). Thus, in the case of the work variables, the resulting non-comparabilities stem from many causes, some having to do with the characteristics of the country setting and some with the design and implementation of the survey.

While the measurement of work is complex, particularly in developing societies, it is at least a characteristic of women that is potentially observable, whereas their fertility preferences are not. All women in the sample, with only a few exceptions, were asked 'If you could choose exactly the number of children to have in your whole life, how many children would that be?'. While interviewers were encouraged to press for a number, the results of that process are not fully apparent in the standard recode tape because, where a range was reported, a number was imputed (Lightbourne and MacDonald 1982). Because the context within which such a question should be interpreted was not made clear either in the question or in the interviewers' instructions (i.e. whether to assume a healthy body, a co-operative husband and an unlimited budget or a more realistic scenario), there was not only wide scope for individual interpretation but also the possibility of systematic cross-country differences in interpretation. Not surprisingly, in certain African countries (Ghana, Kenya, Senegal, Sudan) and in Bangladesh 10–30 per cent of women gave non-numerical answers. Even where most women were urged to provide a number, the interpretation is in doubt.

This detailed discussion of non-comparabilities is not designed to deter the analyst from undertaking comparative analysis but only to elucidate remaining problems in such a way as to facilitate the design of workable studies and to assist in the interpretation of results. Many of the incomparabilities present in the WFS data were unavoidable, since they stem from differences in culture, institutions and levels of development. However, the comparability of future surveys could be enhanced still further with the experience now gained through familiarizing interviewers with some of the conceptual problems discussed, as well as some of the common pitfalls.

23.4   Methodology of analysis

In a typology of comparative analysis, Hobcraft (1981) identified four major types of approach which are distinguished by the degree of sophistication of their statistical treatment of within-country variables and between-country variables. This typology is reproduced in figure 23.2.

In Hobcraft's terminology, the word 'model' refers to multivariate statistical

Type	Treatment of	
	Within-country variables	Between-country variables
1 Comparative description	Descriptive	Descriptive
2 Replicated models	Model	Descriptive
3 Aggregated models	Descriptive	Model
4 Multi-level models (or micro-macro models)	Model	Model

Source: Hobcraft (1981).

FIG. 23.2. Hobcraft's typology of cross-national comparative analysis

models which may or may not be based on theoretical models of behaviour. If this typology of statistical approaches is accompanied by a typology of theoretical approaches it is possible to assess the level(s) of analysis best suited to answer particular questions. Then the quality of the data available, their comparability and the level at which they were collected (i.e. individual, areal, national) can determine what statistical techniques are possible and suitable.

Multinational analysis can contribute to advancing theoretical models of individual reproductive behaviour as well as to more general theories of societal change, such as the theory of the demographic transition. While the development of causal models is problematic given the cross-sectional nature of the data, the rich descriptive material can provide a basis for reassessing existing theories and developing new theoretical hypotheses. In addition, a multinational approach can be a useful framework for exploring two different kinds of theoretical questions. First, the general applicability of certain simple reproductive models which are hypothesized to be universal in scope — Bongaarts' (1978) proximate determinants model, for example — can be tested using comparable data from widely different country settings. Economic models of individual decision-making would also fit into this category. Such models are called 'universal' because the theories on which they are based would predict no intercountry differences in parameter estimates unless theoretical concepts were not adequately measured by the available data, the data were not comparably measured across countries, or the theoretical model was not correctly specified. Some but not all the components of the Easterlin synthesis framework would fit into this category (Easterlin and Crimmins 1982). The second major type of theoretical question that can be addressed with multinational analysis concerns the effect of different country settings on fertility differentials or on differentials in its proximate determinants.[10] Here the implicit or explicit question is usually to assess to what extent culture on the one hand and policy on the other can intervene to alter the relationship between socio-economic development and fertility as it was conceived in the theory of the demographic transition. In this case, intercountry differences in aggregate-level data or in parameter estimates based on individual-level data are assumed to relate to macro-country characteristics because the direction of socio-economic policy and the level of family planning programme effort are dependent to an important degree on the decisions of national governments; but obviously such differences could also arise due to non-comparabilities in the data.

Before the advent of the WFS programme, multinational analysis in the demographic field had to rely on data drawn from different sources which, although based on similar methods of data collection (i.e. census, survey, vital registration), and possibly certain international guidelines (United Nations 1969), were nonetheless collected entirely independently and sometimes for different purposes. The methodologies developed and adapted for multinational analysis were, therefore, constrained by the non-comparabilities inherent in the available data. Nonetheless, most of the methodologies currently in use are firmly based on the experience of the past.

In the past 20 years, a great deal of multinational analysis has been based on census data and has focused on the description and the explanation of fertility differences at the macro-level (see, for example, United Nations 1977a). Statistical models at the macro-level, designed to explain intercountry differences in fertility rates at a point in time, have a long tradition. Multivariate analysis is used to measure the relationship between various aggregate measures of economic development and socio-cultural setting (as the 'independent' variables) and some crude measures of fertility (as the 'dependent' variables) with each country representing one sample point. Well-known examples of such studies include those by Adelman (1963), Russett et al. (1964) and Friedlander and Silver (1967). More recently the increasing availability of trend data has permitted a significant expansion of this statistical approach to measure the impact of changes in these social and economic aggregates, including policy variables on fertility change (Mauldin and Berelson 1978; Cutright 1983; Mauldin and Lapham 1984).

In the early 1960s, heightened interest in fertility and family planning, spurred by the acceleration in population growth, led to the widespread recognition that a full understanding of demographic processes required data at the individual level. During this period a distinctive type of fertility survey known as the KAP (knowledge, attitudes and practice) survey developed. Although these surveys varied in terms of the degree of emphasis they placed on fertility versus strictly contraceptive practice, the survey methods and the types of questions used were remarkably consistent. This may seem surprising given the variety of countries and organizations that sponsored KAP surveys but it is likely that the recommendations and model questionnaires developed by the Population Council (1970) and IUSSP in collaboration with the United Nations (1969) were an important contributory factor to the many similarities between these surveys. While these data were primarily designed for within-country analysis of reproductive processes at the individual level they were also used as the basis of a few multinational analyses in which micro-level statistical relationships using descriptive as well as multivariate techniques were replicated and findings compared across countries (United Nations 1976b; 1979a).

The anticipation of 40 more or less comparable fertility surveys stimulated the thinking of demographers interested in multinational analysis and even before the data were fully available, new strategies of analysis to exploit the full potential of the data were being discussed (Hobcraft 1981). Although a great deal of the WFS comparative analysis is still being processed at the time of writing, it is nevertheless possible to identify the major approaches used so far and to make some preliminary assessments of their relative merits.

With the exception of multi-level statistical models which require the appli-cation of multivariate statistical techniques at both the macro- and micro-level, all the other methodologies described by Hobcraft (1981) in his typology (figure 23.2), that is, comparative description, replicated models and aggregate models, were already in use for comparative analysis before the availability of multiple WFS datasets. To date, most of the comparative analysis of WFS data falls in the category of replicated statistical models which involve multivariate statistical analysis of the individual datasets and a display of estimated parameters or adjusted means for a selected group of countries. No attempts, or only rather informal attempts, to use differences in country-level characteristics to explain country differences in results have been made. Ultimately, from the point of view of comparative analysis, such studies are primarily descriptive because, al-though the comparability and high quality of the data have permitted the use of even more sophisticated statistical techniques at the micro-level, no universal models of individual fertility behaviour were being tested. However, in many of these studies, there is at least some implicit acceptance of the theory of the demographic transition which underlies the discussion and presentation of coun-try differentials. Much useful information, with important policy implications, has emerged from many of these studies; a good example is the comparative work at the Office of Population Research, Princeton University on unwanted fertility and unmet need for family planning (see e.g. Westoff and Pebley 1981).

Some comparative studies have been undertaken to test 'universal' models of reproductive behaviour (Hobcraft and Casterline 1983; Singh, Casterline and Cleland 1985; Hobcraft and McDonald 1984). However, economic models have not been widely attempted because the WFS did not include in its core question-naire all the variables that would be required to test the full model and it was never intended that it should. More of the comparative work that has been done to date has attempted to use some information on the country setting to explain cross-country differences in findings but only the work at the Population Studies Center, University of Michigan has attempted to use multivariate statistical tech-niques to model the macro-level relationship between the range of parameter estimates derived at the micro-level (Entwisle, Hermalin and Mason 1982; Entwisle and Mason 1983; Entwisle, Mason and Hermalin 1984). A simpler approach, in which replicated micro-level statistical findings are grouped by country setting variables, has been used by the United Nations (1981d; 1983c;

1983d; 1985b; forthcoming, b) and by several other authors (Rodríguez and Cleland 1981a; Singh, Casterline and Cleland 1985). Here, such variables as socioeconomic development and family planning programme strength are used to focus attention on the importance of social and economic setting without confronting the enormous econometric complexities of using micro-level parameter estimates in macro-level equations. It remains questionable whether underlying macro-level relationships have a quantifiable structure and whether, even if they did, the statistical assumptions necessary to make such estimates are plausible.

23.5 Substantive results

The findings from the multinational analysis of WFS data fall into three broad categories:

1 those which address the extent and range of intercountry differences in demographic variables and their differentials;
2 those which address the applicability of certain theoretical models of the reproductive process at the individual level through the comparison of country-level findings; and
3 those which address the relationship between macro-level differences between countries in culture, economic development and population policy and micro-level reproductive processes.

At the time of writing, the vast majority of research findings fall into the first category and, although some measure of balance between these categories may be achieved in the years to come, this imbalance is not likely to be overcome in the context of WFS data. This is because the WFS questionnaire was atheoretic in its design with the result that neither biological nor economic models can be properly or fully tested with WFS data because information is lacking on key variables in the respective models. While further results derived from multi-level analysis can be expected now that the full range of data are available, the shortcomings of WFS data with respect to the testing of behavioural models also represents a limitation on multi-level analysis.

As a result of the WFS data and the descriptive findings published by the WFS in its *Cross-National Summaries* series, the World Fertility Survey reports published by the Population Reference Bureau[11] and the Minimum Research Programme of the United Nations Working Group on Comparative Analysis (United Nations 1981c; 1981d; 1982c; 1983a; 1983c; 1983d; 1984), there has been a substantial increase in our knowledge of intercountry differences in levels and patterns of fertility and childhood mortality. In addition, the detailed attention to the major proximate determinants of fertility in the core questionnaire has provided much new knowledge on the similarities and differences between countries in patterns of nuptiality, contraceptive use and breastfeeding and their relationship with age patterns of fertility and birth intervals. While WFS findings document the near universality of certain institutions and practices such as marriage (or its social equivalent) and breastfeeding, the practice of contraception, although widely known in most societies outside Africa, varies widely among developing societies. Another important area of new knowledge is related to fertility preferences from which estimates of unwanted fertility and potential fertility decline have been derived. While in none of the developing countries where WFS surveys were conducted do current stated desired family sizes approach replacement fertility, estimates of unwanted fertility derived from fertility preference data imply a significant potential for further fertility decline in Asia and Latin America but almost none in Africa (Westoff 1981; Blanc 1982; Lightbourne 1985) where family size preferences in most countries remain extremely large (i.e. seven or eight children desired).

A variety of measures of unmet need for contraception have also been derived from data on contraceptive use and information on the desire for more children; the estimates vary widely depending on assumptions made. Because WFS did not ask routinely about the desire for spacing births, the value of their estimates for programme administrators is probably limited in most countries. None the less, WFS findings have been important in drawing international attention to the existence of the problem of unmet need, even though its extent is probably underestimated in WFS data. Before the WFS, a United Nations comparative analysis of KAP surveys (United Nations 1979a), which showed many women in a range of societies not using contraception but expressing a desire for no more children, raised doubts about the validity and reliability of expressed preferences because of women's apparently inconsistent behaviour. As a result of the WFS and its more detailed examination of preferences, however, it is more generally accepted that the current demand for family planning services is not being fully met, although some doubts still remain about the appropriate interpretation of women's expressed preferences.

The retrospective birth histories collected by WFS permit cross-country comparisons of fertility decline and infant mortality decline. However, because of non-comparabilities between countries in the quality of date reporting, a full comparative assessment of the quality of the retrospective birth history must be completed before confident comparative statements can be made with respect to such demographic trends. Such a comparative study of WFS fertility estimates published by the United Nations (1983a) and based on the first 20 WFS countries, found that trends could be compared confidently for only 12 of these countries; trends implied by the birth histories for the other eight countries were potentially distorted by reporting errors.

Socio-economic differentials in fertility according to education, residence and work status have been the subject of much research to date. For most countries findings have conformed to the expectations which have emerged from earlier comparative analyses based on a variety of non-comparable studies (see Cochrane 1979; 1983). Because of the number of countries covered and the range of demographic variables for which differentials can be studied, WFS findings add significantly to the range of information available on a comparative basis and document as well the existence of exceptions to almost every expected pattern. The most widely cited of the studies in this genre is Rodríguez and Cleland (1981a) in which a complex multivariate model is developed in order to assess the relative contributions of the key socio-economic variables to fertility differentials, using an additive approach in which the order in which variables are introduced into the model is based on considerations of causal ordering. The multivariate procedures are replicated for each country and the findings compared. While claims were made at the time that this represented a major step forward in the understanding of fertility determinants, particularly with respect to women's work (Cleland and Rodríguez 1980; Rodríguez and Cleland 1981b), it has subsequently been recognized that, even with a sophisticated statistical modelling procedure, such findings can only result in a more careful and systematic description of the factors associated with fertility differentials but cannot deduce causal relationships (Chidambaram and Cleland 1981). This is particularly disappointing in the case of the women's work variables because substantial effort was devoted to the collection of a work history.[12] Nonetheless, much more is known than previously about intercountry differences in patterns of work and how they vary with fertility and contraceptive use (United Nations 1982b, ch. 16; 1985b).

Multinational analysis based on WFS data to test models of the reproductive process has been notably successful. After extensive testing with WFS data, Bongaarts' (1978) proximate determinants model has been found to be a useful, although imperfect, way of relating the major intermediate variables with fertility (Singh, Casterline and Cleland 1985). In Bongaarts' model, the four intermediate variables (i.e. proportions married, contraceptive prevalence and effectiveness, the incidence of abortion and the duration of post-partum infecundability) are hypothesized to explain cross-country variations in actual fertility levels. Because comparative data on the prevalence of abortion are lacking, comparative studies of the model using WFS data had to rely on assessing the role of the other three factors in fertility variation. The detailed comparative findings which have emerged from this analysis with respect to the variations in the relative contributions to levels of fertility of the different proximate determinants in different societies and socio-economic subgroups has substantially broadened our knowledge of the major intermediate variables affecting fertility and the inter-relationships between them. For the future, the analysis potentially lays the base for further theoretical development not only with respect to the reproductive process itself but also with respect to the channels through which psychological, social and economic factors may operate on fertility. It is also likely to lead to further empirical probing in order to identify more precisely some of the major sources of unexplained variation.

Other models of the reproductive process have also been tested using WFS data, in particular on the determinants of birth interval length and the pace of reproduction (Hobcraft and Casterline 1983; Hobcraft and McDonald 1984). Some provocative and surprising findings have emerged from these analyses which will force demographers to re-examine closely former assumptions about the effect of achieved parity on subsequent reproductive behaviour. Findings suggest that cross-national variations in fertility control seem to be captured better by age than by duration of marriage. In addition, parity does not appear to have an independent effect on the probability that a woman will have a higher order birth once age at first birth and socio-economic characteristics have been controlled. At this stage, the results of these analyses are very preliminary and have not been tested on all the countries, but their implications are potentially important and should be reassessed when other data become available.

Because no universal theory guided the selection of variables included in the core questionnaire and thus crucial economic variables were omitted, no real possibility exists for testing economic models of reproductive processes in a comparative context. Even the results from the testing of Easterlin's hybrid model (Easterlin and Crimmins 1982; United Nations 1985a) have been disappointing because of the lack of correspondence between actual variables and theoretical concepts.

The other major area where comparative analysis of WFS data has the potential to make a major contribution to our understanding of country differences is multilevel analysis. This includes all research which attempts to explain inter-country differences in findings through variations in key macro-characteristics such as culture, policy implementation and socio-economic development. While many studies tend to conclude with some observations with respect to the pattern of findings as they relate to a country's stage in the demographic transition (e.g. Singh, Casterline and Cleland 1985; Rodríguez and Cleland 1981a), only two current major comparative research projects based on WFS data use a systematic approach to relating country setting variables to micro-level findings based on multivariate statistical procedures (Entwisle and Mason 1983; United Nations forthcoming b).

In addition to its statistical complexity, the Michigan study (Entwisle and Mason 1983) has two important features which distinguish it from other comparative studies. First, it is based on a comprehensive micro-model of determinants of the fertility process at its three major phases: fertility onset, early family building and later fertility.[13] From this model, hypotheses were developed about functional form and coefficient signs of the relationship between children ever born and its exogeneous predictors: respondent's education and childhood residence. Secondly, the theory of the demographic transition has led to hypotheses on the way in which the estimated micro-coefficients should vary according to certain key macro-variables: e.g. family planning programme strength and gross national product (GNP) per capita. Thus, the effect of macro-characteristics such as GNP depends not only on the level of GNP but also on the educational and residential distribution within the country as well as interactions between educational and residential composition and the macro-variables. Results from the analysis at this point are preliminary and interpretation is complex. However, it appears that the findings generally support the hypothesis of the authors that micro socio-economic effects on fertility tend to travel from positive to negative as development proceeds and that at all levels of GNP, increased programme effort tends to dampen fertility differentials. One of the most important findings is the evidence of interactions between programme strength and development levels. The findings imply that countries with low development and no programme effort have positive micro socio-economic fertility differentials which become negative if either development or programme strength are achieved independently. However, these negative differentials are moderated when both development and strong programme activity are present simultaneously.

The United Nations study (forthcoming b), currently in preparation, is more wide-ranging in scope than the Michigan research project because not only are fertility patterns examined in depth but also all the major proximate determinants are being analysed individually and the particular effects of education, residence and women's work highlighted separately. While the approach to the analysis of the micro-relationships will be more descriptive and not model based, the findings with respect to each and every variable will be analysed systematically according to three important dimensions of country setting: region, socio-economic development and programme strength. Rather than building an elaborate statistical structure, findings will be ordered according to major groupings of countries with each of the 40 WFS countries assigned to one of three or four major groups depending on their rankings according to each country setting variable. Group averages of demographic variables or multivariate statistical coefficients will then be compared in order to focus on the major ways in which intercountry patterns can be summarized. This simpler approach is nonetheless systematic and is based on the view that the measurement of actual numerical effects for the macro-variables is neither theoretically nor statistically advisable given the small size of our sample (40 countries), the ensuing econometric complexity of the models to be estimated (i.e. the error structure of a regression in which the dependent variable is an estimated coefficient) and the infancy of the theory on the nature and processes underlying multilevel relationships, all of which raise questions about the selection of appropriate macro-variables and our ability to measure such relationships. In addition, it is not at all clear that the findings of a negative relationship between family size preferences, for example, and family planning programme strength (United Nations forthcoming b) necessarily implies anything about the impact of programmes on desired family size. Instead, it is entirely plausible that countries with relatively low preferred family sizes will implement relatively strong and active programmes in response to the resulting demand for services. Policy implementation is not always the determinant of behaviour but often the result of changes in behaviour (Lloyd 1974) and the disentangling of these mutual effects is not always statistically possible.

23.6   Implications for the future

Despite the atheoretic approach that was used to design the WFS core questionnaire, findings from the WFS may none the less form the basis for modifications and improvements in existing reproductive models and in transition theory. Cleland's (1985) reassessment of demographic transition theory based on a thorough review of the literature emerging from WFS data marks the beginning of a potentially promising new phase in the comparative analysis of WFS data. However, time may be needed to gain sufficient distance from the intensive analysis and assessment before the full implications of WFS findings for our knowledge of demographic processes can be adequately assessed. Indeed, two major projects (University of Michigan and United Nations) of WFS comparative analysis have yet to complete their work.

It is unlikely that any international survey programme will be launched in the foreseeable future with comparability of data as one of its primary goals. Thus the knowledge that has been achieved from the comparative analysis of WFS data will form an essential baseline against which to assess demographic trends within countries as they conduct future national surveys. It will be interesting to compare the within-country trends implied by future surveys to the multinational cross-sectional relationships and trends implied by the retro-spective birth histories which have emerged from the WFS. Not only will such comparisons shed new light on demographic processes but they will also high-light the strengths and weaknesses of different methods of survey design and different modes of analysis.

In conclusion, it must be emphasized that multinational analysis of the data was the only phase of the WFS programme that was not largely completed at the time of this assessment. Therefore, many of the statements made, particularly those relating to research findings, may appear incomplete or incorrect in a few years time. Given the potential locked within the 41 multidimensional datasets (and the household data which have yet to be fully released in a standardized format), it is hoped that further multinational analysis will be forthcoming even after the current wave of projects is completed.

Notes

1. The IUSSP was founded in 1928 as a federation of national committees and was re-constituted in 1947 as an association of individual scholars.
2. These included the World Health Organization, the International Labour Organization and UNESCO.
3. One major difficulty with this research design turned out to be that only one and some-times two African countries were available for the first phase of the analysis and, thus, the African demographic experience could not be fully taken account of in designing the final study.
4. By April 1984, 18 participating countries had provided general release of their data for comparative analysis while access to the other 25 tapes required clearance from the country in each individual case. Given the United Nations' special relationships with its member states, it had acquired all the WFS tapes but those of Turkey, Nigeria and Iran for the special purposes of its comparative analysis by the time of writing.
5. See for example, the section on fertility and the family in the 1984 Mexico City rec-ommendations for the Further Implementation of the World Population Plan of Action, August 1984.

6. See the US Agency for International Development proposal for a new survey project: Family Health and Demographic Surveys. See chapter 37 for a discussion of the impact on individual country policies.

7. However, in certain cases, modifications in the questionnaire were made deliberately in response to individual country requests and, therefore, were unavoidable.

8. However, such comprehensive definitions of union status in many countries of Latin America and Africa make it sometimes difficult to assess totally the quality of this data, because they cannot be fully compared with census data and data from other surveys.

9. Despite a vague definition of work, the Peruvian survey recorded many women as working in farming, probably because most of interviewers in the Peruvian survey had previous experience as interviewers for a labour-force survey (see chapter 2).

10. We use the word differentials advisedly because without longitudinal data or a second-round survey, it is not possible to test adequately a causal model.

11. The Population Reference Bureau published five reports on WFS findings relating to nuptiality (Durch 1980), breastfeeding (Kent 1981), contraceptive knowledge and use (Mamlouk 1982), fertility preferences (Kent and Larson 1982) and the status of women (Curtin 1982).

12. Unfortunately, the timing of work could not be tied to events in the birth history or in the marriage history subsequent to the date of the first marriage.

13. Later publications are expected to examine other dimensions of the fertility process including age at first birth, use of contraception and fertility at different life-cycle phases. See, for example, Entwisle, Mason and Hermalin (1984).

24
Evaluation of Data Quality[1]

Susheela Singh

24.1   Introduction

That the evaluation of data should be a required step before they can be used is a fundamental premise which few would question. This becomes even more necessary when the data are from retrospective surveys, in the less developed countries. Very early in its development, WFS recognized this need and commissioned research on the techniques of evaluating retrospective fertility surveys. Because this was the first time a large number of such surveys had been carried out in developing countries, knowledge of the particular problems that might arise, and of the techniques for detecting them, was limited. The very existence of this set of surveys, therefore, greatly stimulated the development of methods of evaluating data quality.

WFS's policy was to have an evaluation study done for each survey. Because of the time it took to produce the basic illustrative reports on techniques of evaluation, however, it was not possible to carry out such a study for a few early surveys. In addition, the earlier evaluation reports varied greatly in their coverage even of the basic topics (age, fertility, nuptiality and infant mortality) because it took time for standardization in techniques and coverage to emerge. The six evaluation workshops – the first of which took place in 1979 – which each included between three and five countries, were the principal mechanism for trying out techniques and eventually selecting a battery of essential tests and developing a somewhat standard approach for evaluation reports. They were also the main means of ensuring that these evaluations were performed, although in addition a few were done independently by individual researchers. This report will draw heavily upon the national evaluation reports, but will also use the results of the relevant WFS cross-national summaries, since the latter contain uniform tables for all WFS surveys.

Two further comparative reports which take an overview of WFS data quality have been published. The first in 1980 (Chidambaram, Cleland and Verma) was a preliminary effort, looking for common types of errors, drawing on the illustrative analyses of data quality, on existing evaluation reports and cross-national summary statistics, and covering some 19 countries. The second, published by the United Nations in 1983 concentrated on fertility levels and trends, but also briefly looked at the other main demographic topics. The approach of this report was to carry out national-level evaluations, devoting 8–10 pages per country, and then to summarize these in a comparative chapter. This country-specific approach certainly has some advantages over the wholly comparative one taken here and complements our assessment. Again, however, coverage was limited to about half the WFS surveys, partly because of the availability of data tapes at the time the study was conducted.

Evaluations of data quality should include comparisons with external sources as well as internal consistency checking. External comparisons are needed both at the time of the survey, as a check on current or recent estimates, and over time, to check on trends in the data obtained from the retrospective histories of events used in these surveys. Comparisons were made with census data, typically, for cumulative fertility or marital status comparisons, and with vital statistics for comparisons of recent fertility or mortality estimates. Use of other surveys for external comparison was infrequent. In this chapter, internal evaluations receive more emphasis, however, chiefly because the constraints of time and resources available to produce this assessment precluded the major effort that would have been needed to consult and evaluate all external source data for the 41 countries. We recognize that external comparisons are very compelling, and we include as many of these as possible; although the checking of recent estimates was quite adequate, trend data are covered in less detail. Nevertheless, this chapter has the advantage of summarizing the important internal consistency checks and external comparisons with recent data, for 41 WFS surveys.[2] In addition, this comparative, as opposed to a more country-specific, approach facilitates identification of those errors which are common to a large number of countries, and which may therefore be caused by the common instruments or methodology used by WFS surveys.

This chapter deals with subjects separately, with sections on age reporting, fertility, nuptiality, and infant and child mortality, each covering all countries. This approach has the advantage of being able to reveal parallels or common patterns across countries, but is not the best way to reveal the complete picture in any particular country. The reader who is interested in an in-depth evaluation of particular countries is referred to the WFS evaluation reports in the *Scientific Reports* series (see also WFS 1985, app. 10) and to the very useful country summaries in United Nations (1983a). This split by subject means that an effort has to be made to accommodate interactions between different subjects. The interaction of age misreporting with fertility and nuptiality measures are the two most important such areas, and we include discussion of these in the fertility and nuptiality sections, respectively. In addition, we discuss below the basic types of errors which can occur in retrospective surveys.

24.2 Types of errors

A few general types of error may be recognized. The first is omission of events by the respondent (e.g. live births or unions) or of individuals (e.g. members of the household or eligible respondents from the individual survey). The second important type of error is misreporting of dates of events (e.g. age of household members or of the respondent, dates of children's births and deaths, and dates of starting and ending marriages). If such misreporting is not random but systematic, it will produce biases. Thus, while omission is a fundamental problem, misreporting of dates will only become a serious issue when it produces biases, or displaces events in particular directions. These two types of errors are, to some extent, to be expected because the data are derived from retrospective surveys and depend upon the recall of events and dates of events in the past, sometimes in the distant past. Moreover, they will be exaggerated among populations where low levels of modernization imply that knowledge of dates of vital events is of little relevance, and where there is no other cultural emphasis on knowledge of dates to counterbalance this.

A further source of error is in sample implementation. Although all possible precautions are taken to design representative samples, errors may still arise, and these are very difficult to detect, although comparison with external data can show up this type of defect. Undercoverage of WFS samples is discussed in chapter 13. The fact that only surviving women can be included in the sample may itself produce an unavoidable bias in analysis of earlier periods.

Yet another source of error lies in the questions themselves: if they are poorly worded, or if insufficient probing is allowed for, or if mistranslations occur, the data obtained may not be that intended. Chapters 5 and 6 deal with these issues in detail. Even the manner in which recording and coding of information is done can result in unforeseen errors. Often these kinds of mistakes are only learned by trial and error. A final potential source of error in dating is imputation. The imputation programme which was specially developed for use by WFS has proved very useful, in general. However, its correct use depends on knowledge of the form of reporting which is common in a given society (reporting in rounded, completed or projected years) and the wrong assumption can cause errors where the percentage of imputed dates is high and varying over time, as in Bangladesh (Chidambaram and Pullum 1981). Although simulation experiments described in chapter 26 show that imputation made less difference to general substantive conclusions than to quantitative results, it seems that any overly uniform approach to imputation does not accurately mimic reproductive behaviour in the real world, and it would be advisable to switch to an imputation algorithm that more nearly reflects real reproductive behaviour to avoid the introduction of systematic bias.

Our approach is to apply a battery of tests to identify common errors in the data. These fall into two basic types: internal consistency tests and validation of WFS data against external sources. Although a further mechanism for evaluation (post-enumeration surveys) exists, we do not deal with this, since it is covered elsewhere (MacDonald, Simpson and Whitfield 1978; O'Muircheartaigh 1982; 1984a; 1984b; Paita 1984; Srikantan 1979). We do not attempt to explain why these errors occurred in any depth and will proceed by summarizing the results of each of the four main sections (age reporting, fertility, nuptiality and infant mortality) of Goldman, Rutstein and Singh (1985).

24.3 Age reporting

The correct determination of age is crucial for the analysis and understanding of practically all demographic phenomena: it is used implicitly or explicitly in most calculations of levels, trends, effects and correlations. Ascertaining the respondent's age incorrectly can and usually will bias estimates of fertility, nuptiality and mortality levels and trends as well as the analysis of any other characteristics that change with age or which have been determined by reference to age. Particularly disastrous biases can occur if age has been estimated by the use of the variable which is to be the subject of the analysis, for example, a study of parity by age when some women have had their ages estimated on the basis of the number of children they have. While these points apply mainly to age as obtained in the individual interview, age in the household survey is crucial for ever-married samples because it determines the denominator for fertility and nuptiality analyses. In addition, since age obtained in the household survey is used to determine eligibility for the individual interview, it is important for both all-women and ever-married samples. We will look at the reporting of age in both the household and individual surveys.

It should not be surprising that in many societies, knowledge of exact date of birth is hazy, and therefore is probably less well reported than other events in a person's life. In societies where the registration of births is not common, or where no particular importance is placed on the knowledge of age, a person will probably have neither reliable documentary evidence nor a firm basis on which to increment age as the years pass. It is likely that in these situations, current age or date of birth is required only when dealing with official matters and rarely, if ever, in daily life. For a woman, the situation is likely to be compounded by her low education and social status; frequently, either her husband or her father represents her in official matters.

It is at the household interview that the first report of age is obtained for all household members. Since any adult could have provided the information, proxy reports of age occurred for many eligible respondents, possibly introducing error. Note, however, that in the three countries with evidence on proxy reporting, such reporting seems only slightly less consistent than self-reporting. Furthermore, when the interviewer had to estimate current age on the basis of physical appearance or the milestones reached in the person's life, it is likely that such appearances and milestones will be related to the phenomena under study and thus bias the results. In many cases, an estimate of an eligible respondent's age will be based on the number of children she has borne, or the age of the oldest or the youngest of her children. Evidence from the tape-recorded interviews in Bangladesh (Thompson, Ali and Casterline 1982) shows that many women's ages were estimated by taking the age of their oldest child, adding one year and then adding the common age at marriage of 15 years. Where the age of an apparently fecund woman is not known, interviewers are likely to place her in the middle of the fertile age range, usually between ages 25 and 40. From evidence presented below and from other studies, it appears that such a centralizing tendency did occur in many surveys.

In order to detect errors in data, we must in general make comparisons. The standard against which we compare our data for internal consistency checks will be other individual items of the same dataset and *a priori* notions of distributions and their 'smoothness' or lack thereof. For external checks, we can compare distributions of independent datasets, such as other surveys, censuses or registration statistics. There is a third category of quasi-independent checks. For WFS work this would include comparisons made between the individual survey data and the household schedule data and comparisons with models, such as stable populations, model life tables, model nuptiality schedules, and so on. In this section we look at internal and external consistency checks for age reporting in the household survey and internal tests for the individual survey data.

Age reporting in the household interview

As an indication of the likelihood that age is well reported, Myers' index and the United Nations' combined index are used to measure conformity to expected age structures. Myers' index measures discrepancy from smooth trends of five-year age-sex groupings. Nine countries have values exceeding 60 on the UN index, indicating very poor reporting of the age-sex structure: Pakistan, Cameroon, Sudan, Panama, Benin, Ghana, Fiji, Ivory Coast and Trinidad and Tobago, in decreasing order. Large-scale international migration and a large population living outside households can raise the value of the index, and this may contribute to the high values in the case of Trinidad and Tobago, and possibly Ghana, but not the other cases listed above. Only five countries, Syria, Thailand, Peru, Mexico and Jamaica, have index values of less than 30, and all are above 20, indicating some distortion of the age-sex structure.

In the country-specific evaluation reports, most household age distributions have been compared with either censuses or other surveys. In general, when compared with the external data, the household distributions show either the same or a somewhat reduced tendency towards digit preference. Apart from heaping, misreporting of age groups is about the same in the household survey as in previous censuses or surveys, except around the upper age limit of eligibility for the individual survey, where it is worse for females in many of the household surveys.

Using the UN index to compare the household survey age-group distributions with an external data source, we find that only Egypt, Lesotho (large household survey), Morocco and Nepal are definitely less distorted than the external source, while 20 countries are definitely more distorted. Most of this extra distortion is from two sources: the boundary effect and the deficit of men. The deficit of men, particularly at ages 20–49, also occurs in many of the external sources, but is not as prevalent as in the household surveys. Because of the nature of the household surveys, institutions which primarily house men in these ages were not covered. In addition, the emphasis on identifying respondents for the individual survey may have led interviewers to regard men as less important; in particular, they may not have wanted to return to a single-person male household to conduct the household interview.

One important criterion for selecting women for the individual interview was age. Most countries had 49 as the upper age limit, while a few had age 50, Cameroon had 54 and Venezuela had 44. The lower age limit in most countries was 15 years; however, several countries which included only ever-married women used no lower age boundary and some used 10 or 12 years. Costa Rica and Panama used 20 years as the lower age limit for eligibility and the Caribbean countries of Guyana, Jamaica and Trinidad and Tobago excluded from eligibility women aged 15-19 who were full-time students.

As age was used as a criterion for eligibility in all WFS surveys, the erroneous report of age on the household schedule of women near the boundaries leads to biases due to the exclusion of potentially eligible women. In order to estimate the amount of exclusion, age and sex ratios were calculated for the five-year age groups straddling the boundary ages. If women have been displaced from cohorts just inside the boundaries to cohorts immediately outside, the age ratio for the former will be low and the sex ratio will be high; the reverse will be true for the cohorts just outside the boundaries.

Almost all surveys show exclusion of women at the upper age limit of eligibility: out of the 39 surveys with data,[1] only seven (Benin, Colombia, Costa Rica, Dominican Republic, Morocco, Peru and Malaysia), with indices of 10 or less, show little evidence of this upper boundary effect. Ten show a moderate effect, with indices of 11-33 (Egypt, Jordan, Kenya, Republic of Korea, Mexico, Mauritania, Paraguay, Sudan, Thailand and Venezuela), while in 18 others the effect is strong to very strong. Conversely, in four countries (Bangladesh, Pakistan, Sri Lanka and Syria) there is evidence of a shift *into* the eligible age range, very strong in Pakistan and quite strong in Sri Lanka and Bangladesh.

There are several indications that the reason for this transference is that the interviewer deliberately did so in order to reduce the effort she would have to make to interview older women, who are less educated and have longer birth histories. The fact that the 'boundary effect' also occurs strongly in both Cameroon, with an upper age limit of 54, and in Venezuela, with a limit of 44, is strong circumstantial evidence that the error is largely due to the interviewers' bias. The experience of Lesotho, where the 'maxi-household' survey did not show this anomaly, but where the 'mini-household' survey, from which women were selected, did show a strong boundary effect, also supports our argument (Timæus and Balasubramanian 1984).

Sex ratios at the upper boundary also indicate that in most countries the transfer over the boundary has been selective for women. In 27 countries, sex ratios are more than five points lower for the age group just above the boundary than for the group just below. Only six countries, Bangladesh, Benin, Morocco, Pakistan, Sri Lanka and Syria, show higher sex ratios for the older age group, indicating an inward shift of women; however, in two of these six countries, Benin and Morocco, the *age* ratios operate in the opposite direction.

The misreporting of age at the lower boundary appears to occur much less frequently than at the upper boundary. In only seven countries, Bangladesh, Benin, Costa Rica, Ghana, Kenya, Nepal and Panama, is the age ratio for the group just inside the boundary less than 90. The largest transfer out of the eligible ages has occurred in Kenya, followed by Costa Rica and Panama, the only two countries where the lower limit was 20 years of age.

A more refined index, combining the upper and lower boundary effects allowed classification of countries by the degree of the boundary effect:

Little effect: Dominican Republic, Peru, Colombia, Malaysia, Benin, Syria, Sudan, Republic of Korea, Thailand (9 countries)

Some effect: Mexico, Egypt, Venezuela, Morocco, Jordan, Paraguay, Costa Rica (7 countries)

Strong effect: Bangladesh, Ecuador, Philippines, Nepal, Kenya, Sri Lanka, Tunisia, Trinidad and Tobago, Senegal, Turkey, Portugal, Mauritania (12 countries)

Very strong effect: Yemen AR, Jamaica, Indonesia, Ghana, Fiji, Lesotho, Haiti, Ivory Coast, Pakistan, Panama, Cameroon (11 countries)

The interesting feature of this display is that no strong ordering of countries by region or general educational level is apparent. This in turn suggests that the motivation of the interviewers and the intensity and nature of supervision is an important determinant of age shifting across eligibility boundaries.

Age reporting in the individual interview

The core individual questionnaire obtained the respondent's age by asking, 'In what month and year were you born?' (Q 107) and if she did not know, the interviewer was to ask, 'How old are you?' (Q 108). The interviewer was instructed to 'record the best estimate'. Subsequently, the core individual questionnaire was modified to ask age in all cases, in the form of 'How old are you?', as well as the date of birth. The recommendation was that it was very important to collect both pieces of information, although the question on age could be asked after the birth history. Both the interviewers' and supervisors' instructions stress the importance of checking the consistency of dates of events and ages (during the interview, by the interviewer), specifically to assure that the respondent was at least 12 years old when she had her first live birth, first pregnancy or entered her first marital union. If a woman was found to be below the age limit for eligibility (or never married for ever-married surveys), the interviewer was to mark the questionnaire 'Ineligible'.

Most countries followed the recommended procedures. However, in countries where ages and dates were thought to be difficult to obtain, they were recorded on an age-event chart. These were, in fact, used in Benin, Ivory Coast, Nigeria, Senegal, Egypt, Mauritania, Morocco, and Sudan in Africa, and in Indonesia, Republic of Korea, Jordan, Syria, Turkey and Yemen AR in Asia. Conversion charts were used in Republic of Korea, Malaysia and Nepal. In Ghana, Kenya,

Mauritania, and Senegal especially extensive probing was used and in some surveys historical calendars were tried. These measurement techniques are described in chapter 5.

Month and year of birth were given by over half the respondents in only three of 12 African surveys, and in only seven of 13 Asian surveys, but in all 13 American surveys, month and year were given by over 80 per cent of respondents (Chidambaram and Sathar 1984). The authors show that complete reporting of respondents' birth date is positively related to urbanization, and education, and negatively to age.

Myers' and Whipple's indices were calculated for the ever-married populations between the ages of 20 and 49. These indices show the extent of heaping on preferred digits, for example on ages ending in 0 and 5. We classified countries as good, acceptable and unacceptable on each, then produced the following joint classification:

Good on both indices:	Thailand, Philippines, Venezuela, Portugal, Tunisia, Costa Rica, Fiji, Malaysia, Republic of Korea, Panama (10 countries)
Good on one, acceptable on the other:	Jamaica, Peru, Mexico, Paraguay, Trinidad and Tobago (5 countries)
Acceptable on both indices:	Senegal, Bangladesh, Colombia, Guyana, Lesotho, Ecuador, Sri Lanka, Ivory Coast (8 countries)
Acceptable on one only, not the other:	Syria, Pakistan, Dominican Republic, Benin, Morocco, Turkey (6 countries)
Unacceptable on both indices:	Indonesia, Kenya, Ghana, Haiti, Egypt, Cameroon, Jordan, Nepal, Mauritania, Sudan, Yemen AR (11 countries)

If rounding or heaping of the kind measured by Myers' and Whipple's indices were random, the bias should disappear when grouped ages are used. We looked at five-year age groups, and again made use of age ratios for the analysis. The problem of ever-married samples was solved by using proportions ever married from the household to estimate the size of the whole age group. Thus the method does not purely evaluate individual survey data, but, since many analyses use all-women estimates, the approach is justified. We expect the proportions to decrease consistently, as age increases, in the absence of real variations due to factors such as wars, famines and migrations.

We found anomalous patterns in many countries. Using an index based on the age ratios, we find that although 11 countries had poor data by this test, they are not all the same as those found unacceptable for heaping. Six countries which had unacceptably high heaping indices have acceptable five-year distributions (Ghana, Jordan, Egypt, Cameroon, Mauritania and Indonesia) while a few countries with acceptable heaping indices have unacceptable five-year age distributions (Bangladesh, Paraguay, Senegal and Lesotho).

Countries which are unacceptable in both are Nepal, Dominican Republic, Haiti, Yemen AR, Kenya and Sudan.

A closer analysis was made to determine which age groups were deficient or excessive. Eleven countries had no problematic five-year age groups or only had a deficiency in the oldest or youngest group (Ghana, Egypt, Tunisia, Fiji, Philippines, Ecuador, Venezuela, Costa Rica, Mexico, Jamaica and Portugal). All other countries had more serious problems, either with excessive groups only (Thailand, Guyana), or deficient groups only (Mauritania, Morocco, Syria, Nepal, Indonesia, Colombia, Peru), while the remaining 20 countries had both types of anomalous age groups. A common error was that the 45–49 group was deficient, and also that the 30–34 group was deficient. In contrast the 25–29 cohort was much more likely to be inflated than deflated in size.

In conclusion, satisfactory determination of the date of birth or age of adult women still appears to be beyond our grasp in many developing countries. In view of the careful questionnaire design, including the use of aids such as age-event charts and prolonged training of field staff, this is a disappointing result, for which there is no obvious remedy.

24.4   Fertility

Date reporting

In this section we concentrate exclusively on the quality of individual survey data, as household survey estimates are discussed in chapter 4. As a preliminary step in the evaluation of fertility data, the proportion of births for which actual months and years were reported is considered. It is assumed that dates are more accurate when month and year are supplied, rather than the calendar year only or number of years ago or when any other form of determination is used. Reporting is more complete in Latin America and less complete in Africa and Asia, although for a few countries the actual form in which dates were given is no longer available, either because of editing at an earlier stage or because the type of birth history or the form of recording ensured that all responses were converted to calendar years. Among countries where the information survived, the worst cases are Bangladesh, Benin, Mauritania and Yemen AR. In these countries, as in all others, the date of the last birth was in general reported with higher frequency than dates of earlier births, reiterating the problem of recall being related to recency of events.

Omission of live births

Without the existence of reliable external data sources, there are no easy methods for estimating the level of omission of births in WFS surveys. The techniques used can, in certain circumstances, point out *substantial* omissions, but do not indicate the severity of the omission nor the presence of less severe misreporting.

One straightforward test is to examine the mean number of children ever born by age: in the absence of fertility increases in the past, and of omission, it should continuously increase with age. The expected pattern was found for all countries except Mauritania, Morocco, Bangladesh, Pakistan and Indonesia, where the lower mean number of live births for 45-49 year olds compared to the 40-44 age group suggests that either the oldest cohort has not reported all of its births, or that transference of more fecund 45-49 year olds into the 50-54 age group occurred in the household interview, or both.

Comparison of survey results on mean parity with an external source also provides a minimal test of coverage of live births: if survey estimates are the same as or higher than the external source, then survey coverage is at least as good, as, or better than, the external source. Even in this situation, however, some omission could have occurred but not have been detected by this test. Reconstruction of mean parity from the survey for the same year as the external source did not show any cases where survey coverage was worse: in a few cases agreement was very close and in several cases, especially for older age groups, the surveys achieved substantially better coverage.

Sex ratios at birth, by time periods, were examined to see whether older women failed to report all of their female children (or female deaths) in distant periods before the survey. Although high sampling errors associated with sex ratios makes this a hazardous task, it seems that this type of error occurred in Mauritania, Sudan, Bangladesh and Pakistan (table 24.1).

TABLE 24.1

Sex ratios at birth (males per 100 females)

	Years before the survey						
	0–4	5–9	10–14	15–19	20–24	25–29	30–34
Mauritania	109	113	108	111	120	128	(118)
Sudan (N)	109	99	109	103	109	139	(189)
Bangladesh	101	105	104	102	112	120	127
Pakistan	106	105	111	110	115	124	(138)

Note: Parentheses indicate fewer than 100 female births.

In the absence of rising infant and child mortality, the percentage of children ever born who have died should increase with the age of the mother, because the offspring of older women have had more exposure to the risk of dying. (An exception is the 15-19 age group because the children of teenage mothers have a high risk of death.) With only a few exceptions, the expected pattern is found. While this observed absence of irregularities shows that the data are not severely distorted, it is still possible that omission of infant deaths occurred.

Examination of reported parity by single-year age cohorts for Nepal revealed omission which did not show up in the mean parities of five-year age groups. Heaped ages 35, 40 and 45 had lower fertility than neighbouring ages, presumably because women who give rounded ages (i.e. probably do not know their age) are more likely to omit live births.

In general, tests for omission of live births did not disclose any surveys with severe problems, and WFS surveys achieved better coverage than external sources. While these are comforting results, we must remember that these are minimal tests of data quality: the surveys may be as good as, or better than, external sources, but we' have no absolute means of checking on the completeness of coverage itself. In addition, the absence of irregularities may not necessarily indicate accuracy, although it is a reason for having more trust in the data.

Displacement of dates of birth

Misreporting of dates of births is due mainly to the difficulty of recalling events in the past, but is exaggerated where knowledge of these dates is in any case poor. Thus it is worse among older women or among women with several children or for early births, which are further back in time. Recent births are likely to be dated more accurately, even by older women, simply because of the recency of the events, but also because errors would produce relatively large age misstatements of young children. A typical form of displacement is that births are moved forward, closer to the date of the survey. Combined with accurate reporting in the recent past, this would result in a concentration of births in the period 5-15 years before interview, resulting in an apparent rise in fertility in earlier periods, followed by a decline in more recent periods, i.e. the 'Potter effect' (Potter 1977). Where a real decline also occurred, this pattern will exaggerate the real trend. While this is a commonly observed pattern of misreporting, it should not be forgotten that several countries have also experienced true increases in fecundity and fertility since the 1940s (Collver 1965; Lesthaeghe 1984; Mati, Hatimy and Gebbie 1971; Roberts 1975; Sukdeo 1973; Singh 1982; Tekse 1967; WHO 1975).

Under the 'Potter effect', median age at first birth for cohorts aged 20-24 to 45-49 will exhibit an unexpected trend, typically a decline from the oldest age group to younger age groups. If no such displacement occurs, the expected pattern would be for age at first birth to remain stable or to rise at younger ages, especially if a recent fertility decline has taken place. About half of all countries show the acceptable pattern of a recent increase in the age at first birth. However, in addition, two-thirds indicate a higher age at first birth for the 45-49 cohort than for the next oldest one or two cohorts. For example, in Kenya the pattern is:

Age cohort	30-34	35-39	40-44	45-49
Median age at first birth	18.6	18.8	19.5	20.4

In some countries only the oldest cohort is distorted, but in several countries two or three older cohorts are affected. The reasons for these implausible patterns are misreporting of the age at first birth, misreporting of the age of the respondent or omission of some early births.

Examination of cumulative fertility at successive ages for the three oldest cohorts reinforces the findings from trends in the median age at first birth. In the majority of WFS surveys, women aged 45-49 have fewer births by a specified age than do women aged 40-44; and in some cases women aged 40-44 have fewer than women aged 35-39.

For example, in the case of Tunisia, the pattern is as shown in table 24.2.

TABLE 24.2
Mean number of children ever born: Tunisia

Cohort	At age			
	20-24	25-29	30-34	35-39
45-49	1.10	2.74	4.46	5.84
40-44	1.30	2.91	4.50	5.69
35-39	1.38	3.06	4.55	5.70

In Tunisia, the difference in births was 'made up' by age 35-39, as it was in many other surveys (e.g. Egypt, Syria, Thailand and most Latin American countries) indicating that displacement but not omission of births has occurred. In some countries these differences persist even at older ages. If we assume that the level of fertility has not risen in the past, then the persistence of differences at older ages indicates both omission of births and misreporting of dates of birth. This is evident in Benin, Cameroon, Ivory Coast, Kenya, Lesotho, Morocco, Sudan, Yemen AR, Bangladesh, Nepal, Pakistan, Indonesia, Haiti, and to a lesser extent in the Philippines, Dominican Republic, Jamaica and Mexico. Misreporting of the age of the respondent can also contribute to the patterns observed. In addition, real rises in fertility, which have been documented in countries where major problems of primary and secondary sterility had existed, would mimic the misreporting pattern.

A serious consequence of this type of displacement is either to concentrate births in an intermediate period, producing an apparent rise in fertility from the earliest periods, and a recent fertility decline where none occurred, or to exaggerate real trends. Where a real decline has occurred, however, it is not always possible to detect over-reporting of births for a particular period. The pattern in cumulative fertility up to age 30-34 was examined for the four most recent five-year periods, for evidence of anomalies. Although firm conclusions should be based on detailed analysis of all period-cohort rates, these data indicate the existence of misreporting in five African, four Asian and Middle Eastern and two Latin American countries. For example, low fertility values are found in periods more than ten years ago in Cameroon, Ivory Coast and Yemen AR, and more than 15 years ago in Kenya and Bangladesh. A few of the worst examples demonstrate the problem (see table 24.3), but most countries have much less severe anomalies than these.

TABLE   24.3
Cumulative fertility up to age 30–34

Country	Years before the survey			
	0–4	5–9	10–14	15–19
Kenya	5.2	5.5	5.7	5.1
Mauritania	4.2	4.9	4.6	4.2
Sudan (N)	3.9	4.9	4.7	4.3
Bangladesh	4.5	6.2	6.0	5.2

Estimates of recent fertility

The level of current fertility is one of the most important pieces of information collected by WFS surveys. While some countries may show incorrect trends in earlier periods, it is even more relevant to evaluate the accuracy of fertility estimates obtained for the five-year period immediately before interview. One useful technique is comparison of the TFRs based on estimated cohort-period fertility rates from the survey with recent estimates from external sources. Two main types of results emerged from these comparisons. First, for 14 of the 25 countries with available external estimates, WFS survey estimates agree closely with external estimates; and secondly, for nine countries, external estimates were too low to provide any useful estimation of the reliability of WFS estimates. In the remaining two countries (Pakistan and Venezuela), the comparable external estimate was slightly higher than the survey estimate. An encouraging finding is the reliability of recent fertility estimates in two cases where trends for earlier periods were distorted (Kenya and Nepal).

A second technique used to evaluate recent fertility estimates is the P/F ratio, an internal consistency test which, unlike the first technique, could be applied to all countries. P/F ratios compare reported cumulative fertility with a synthetic cohort estimate of cumulative fertility, based on fertility rates for the most recent five-year period. This may be done for age or duration (of marriage or motherhood) groups. Motherhood duration P/F ratios have the advantage of being less distorted by changes in fertility which arise from a changing age at first birth. P/F ratios should be near unity, in the absence of fertility change or reporting errors. Deviations from 1.0 which are the same at all ages or durations may reflect reference period error for a particular period and could provide an adjustment factor for reported fertility rates. Declining P/F ratios by age usually indicate omission of births by older women, while increasing ratios often indicate a true fertility decline (Brass and Coale 1968; Hobcraft, Goldman and Chidambaram 1982). We examine here age and motherhood duration P/F ratios.

The results show plausible P/F ratios for most durations of motherhood, for several countries where no decline in marital fertility is believed to have occurred. These countries include several which had distorted fertility trends in periods before the survey — Benin, Ivory Coast, Kenya, Mauritania, Sudan, Syria, Yemen AR, Nepal and Pakistan. This result suggests that these surveys probably had good reporting of births at least for the most recent five-year period. In addition, the expected pattern of increasing ratios with age and duration for countries where age at marriage/first birth has risen and fertility has declined, is also observed.

Some anomalies were found for older cohorts in a few countries when P/F ratios for age groups were examined, however, which suggests omission of births. Such omission had already been indicated by other tests in Cameroon, Lesotho, Kenya, Mauritania, Sudan, Yemen AR, Bangladesh and Nepal. As an illustration, the results for Cameroon are shown in table 24.4.

TABLE   24.4

P/F ratios by age group and motherhood duration — Cameroon

	Age groups					
	20–24	25–29	30–34	35–39	40–44	45–49
P/F ratios	0.99	0.97	0.96	0.92	0.88	0.82

	Years since first birth				
	5–9	10–14	15–19	20–24	25–29
P/F ratios	1.01	1.02	1.01	1.00	1.03

The absence of distortion for motherhood P/F ratios is probably due to a selection bias for women at higher durations — since the upper age limit in most WFS samples is 49, women at high marriage durations must have married at young ages and probably are selected for high fertility.

Although these two techniques by and large indicate that WFS fertility estimates for the five years before the survey are usually of good quality, this does not mean that rates for a shorter period (e.g. one year) before the survey are equally reliable. The very high sampling error for single-year rates (Little 1982), and the finding that in more than half of 15 surveys analysed more births were recorded in the past year than in the preceding year before survey (Goldman and Westoff 1980), suggests that rates for the most recent one-year period should not be used. However, estimates based on the last two or the last three years before survey are much more accurate than the single-year rates (Goldman and Westoff 1980; Hanenberg 1980). Five-year rates have the advantage of further reducing sampling error as well as of minimizing age or date misstatement.

Other types of errors in birth histories

Detailed evaluation reports have found errors of a different nature in some surveys. In large part, they concern the effect of age-reporting errors on fertility estimates. For example, in the Dominican Republic, parity for the 35–39 age group was too high, because of selective transference of high-parity women from neighbouring age groups; in addition, under-reporting of births by those over age 40 (due both to omission of births and age-reporting errors, including exclusion of high-parity 45–49 year olds from the individual interview) resulted in spurious trends before the survey (Guzmán 1980). Errors of this type also occurred in Turkey, Nepal, Haiti, Senegal and Pakistan.

An analysis of Egyptian data concluded that overstatement of the age of young women, especially those reported to be 15–19, caused an apparent recent decline in marital fertility at young ages and an apparent recent increase in the age at marriage (Coale forthcoming). Age overstatement for teenagers, especially those who have reached puberty, are married, or have a child, occurs frequently in South Asia and Africa (United Nations 1976a). This type of error may have occurred in WFS surveys in Fiji, Philippines, Sri Lanka and Thailand as indicated by widening differences between WFS and external estimates of fertility for 15–19 year olds for successive periods in the past (Makinson 1984). If women reported as 15–19 are in fact younger in both external sources and WFS surveys, then estimates will yield greater discrepancies in earlier, as opposed to more recent, periods because WFS-based estimates for earlier periods are based on increasingly older age groups, most of which have better age reporting. Age misreporting of 15–19 year olds, even if it happens only in the household survey, is a serious error for surveys with ever-married individual samples, because the household population forms the denominator for fertility rates.

24.5   Nuptiality

WFS surveys collected data on two main aspects of nuptiality, current marital status and retrospective marriage histories. Each of these can suffer from specific types of error, which have different effects on data analysis. A classic problem in the reporting of current marital (or union) status is that of formerly married women classified as single or never married. This is important where surveys cover ever-married women only, since omission of these women can bias overall fertility estimates as well as estimates of the amount of time spent exposed to the risk of pregnancy. The main potential problem with retrospective marriage histories is misreporting of the dates of marriages or unions, most importantly the date of the first union. This issue is the main focus of this section. Its chief impact is on analyses of age at first marriage or union, and on analyses of marital fertility rates which are based on time spent exposed by ever-married women.

We evaluate the quality of nuptiality data against an objective but ideal criterion, that is, the recording of all sexual exposure. In fact this was not the intention of most WFS surveys: their aim was to obtain dates of all socially recognized unions. This discrepancy between the concept of total exposure and time spent in recognized unions concerns societies where informal sexual relationships exist; in such societies some proportion of births occurring outside of recognized unions must be accepted as reality rather than a problem of data quality. Although we do not know what this proportion is, we use information on premarital births as a check on quality, because its variation across countries in the same region, or across age groups in the same country, may identify countries or groups with especially poor reporting. This issue is crucial in evaluating the quality of nuptiality data, and because it arises only in some regions and cultures, our measures of this reporting problem may seem culture-bound. However it is inevitable that countries where informal sexual relationships occur will have greater difficulties in obtaining high-quality data on nuptiality, and it is desirable that indicators of data quality should reflect this basic difference in the quality of data on this topic.

Date reporting

As in the case of dates of births of children, we looked at a measure of the completeness of reporting, in this case, the proportion reporting at least the calendar year for the date of the first union. Allowing for the fact that this already included imputation in several Latin American countries, we find that African and Middle Eastern countries usually had 70-90 per cent reporting a calendar year, whereas three Asian countries (Bangladesh, Nepal and Indonesia) and one Caribbean country (Jamaica) had very low proportions reporting the year of first union.

Indices of heaping on rounded calendar and duration years (values ending in digits 0 and 5 in both cases) were calculated. Substantial heaping for duration was found in five out of the 12 African countries, in Yemen AR and in Nepal. Calendar year heaping was noticeable in Lesotho, in five Asian countries, and in all Latin American and Caribbean countries. The absence of any heaping in a few countries known to have poor reporting may be explained if reporting of age at first union was the alternative to a calendar date, since our indices do not reflect heaping on preferred ages. Heaping in the Americas is largely due to the common occurrence of various types of informal unions, especially as the first union, which no doubt affects accurate recall.

Marital status: household and individual surveys

Analysts of surveys with ever-married women samples, who were able to check the consistency of married, widowed, divorced and separated statuses only, but by definition not the single status, generally found a very high level of consistency between the household and the individual interview. For the few all-women samples in which this comparison was made, slightly higher proportions ever married (Cameroon, Senegal and Venezuela) or a small shift towards consensual unions, away from married and single (Dominican Republic) were found in the individual survey. In contrast, lower proportions ever in union in the individual survey were reported for Haiti. Although differences are in general small, the results suggest that ever-married samples are likely to suffer from exclusion of a small proportion of formerly married women who are classified as single in the household survey.

Comparison of the age at first birth and the age at first marriage

It has been suggested that the age at first birth, rather than age at first marriage, may be a more reliable point from which to measure exposure, especially where informal unions are common, because of the difficulty of accurately dating the first union. The trend across cohorts in the median ages for these two points are examined here for their relative reliability, to see whether the difference between the two is acceptable. We also look at the overall proportion with a negative first birth interval to evaluate the reporting of the age at first marriage.

As we may have expected, sub-Saharan Africa and the Americas have quite high proportions with negative first birth intervals, countries with 10 per cent or more being Benin, Cameroon, Ivory Coast, Kenya, Colombia, Ecuador, Paraguay, Peru, Costa Rica and Jamaica. This high incidence of negative first birth intervals probably implies some omission of early unions, but in these societies some proportion of births does occur from brief non-cohabiting relationships which may not be considered a union, either by the woman or by some minimum objective criterion.

A rise in the median age at first union or no change, from older to younger cohorts, are plausible. A U-shaped pattern or continuous decline are much less acceptable trends. The same expectations apply to the age at first birth, except that the U-shaped pattern is somewhat more plausible, given the possibility of improvements in health and fecundity over time, with increased modernization. The results showed acceptable trends of continuous rise or stability in the age at first union for under half of all countries (15 out of 40 countries), mainly in Asia. The majority of African and American countries have U-shaped trends, which suggest omission or misdating of the first union by older women.

The cases in table 24.5, for example, illustrate the common patterns.

TABLE 24.5

Patterns of median age at first union, by age groups

	Pattern	Median age at first union					
		20–24	25–29	30–34	35–39	40–44	45–49
Kenya	U-shaped	18.5	18.1	17.5	17.5	17.7	18.5
Senegal	U-shaped	16.7	16.3	15.6	15.6	15.6	16.1
Sudan (N)	Irregular	18.6	17.0	15.7	16.2	15.9	16.2
Colombia	U-shaped	21.0	20.7	20.2	19.8	20.7	20.9
Mexico	U-shaped	20.4	20.1	19.7	19.6	19.3	20.0
Malaysia	Rise	21.8	20.9	19.4	18.1	17.9	16.9

Alternatively, the unexpected findings can be partly explained if the exclusion of some 45-49 year olds from the individual survey was selective of women who married at young ages (as it appears to be for high fertility women). Evidence to suggest that reporting error by older women is an important contributing cause is found in the fact that older cohorts 'make up' their low proportion ever married at young ages (e.g. under age 20) by older ages. This pattern was found in several Latin American and African countries which also had implausible trends in the median age at first marriage. An example of this 'making up' pattern, for Senegal, is shown in table 24.6.

TABLE   24.6

Percentages ever married by exact ages, by age cohorts

Age	Age cohorts			
	30-34	35-39	40-44	45-49
17	73	72	68	64
19	86	85	82	80
21	94	93	92	91
23	96	96	96	95

We expect that the age at first birth will be better reported because the high incidence of premarital births suggests that the two sets of events were independently recorded: i.e., interviewers did not typically estimate the age at first union from the age at first birth. Nevertheless, the results show that 15 countries with U-shaped trends in the age at first union still had U-shaped trends in the age at first birth, while stability was observed for 10 other cases with different types of trends. Moreover, 13 cases changed from more acceptable trends in the age at first birth (continuous rise or no change or U-shaped) to less acceptable trends in the age at first marriage (U-shaped, irregular or continuous decline). The lack of change for the majority of countries with a U-shaped trend in age at first union is striking.

We conclude that either both measures suffer from reporting problems, or the consistency in estimated trends for both measures indicates a real pattern. For example, displacement of both the date of first marriage and the date of first birth of older cohorts, combined with a recent rise in both, could cause the U-shaped pattern in both measures (15 countries had this combination). The same errors could also produce the combination of an apparently stable trend in the age at first marriage and a U-shaped trend in the age at first birth, if displacement cancels out a real rise in the age at marriage.

These results, however, do not strongly suggest that the age at first birth is a more reliable measure of the start of exposure than the age at first marriage. This does not negate other reasons for preferring reports of age at first birth, such as the greater plausibility of the U-shaped pattern for the measure, the apparent independence of reporting of the two items, and the likelihood of omission of short first unions, especially by older women, for whom the event would have taken place 20 or more years before. We stress that these tests detected few reporting problems for the Asian and Pacific countries which form the majority of the 16 countries which showed little or no error.

Comparison of survey and external sources

Evaluation reports typically compare both the proportion ever married and distribution by marital status with an external source. We looked only at proportions ever married, for the external source closest to the survey date. In all cases, comparisons were made using survey proportions reconstructed to the date of the external source.

The typical pattern observed is that WFS surveys find higher proportions ever married than do the external sources. The difference between the two (averaged across age groups) is positive (survey higher) in all but four cases where small negative differences occur. Four Latin American countries show a large average difference (8-13 per cent), while the Caribbean countries show quite large differences when all unions are considered, because censuses omit some informal union types which the surveys cover (see evaluation reports for the Caribbean surveys). The more typical difference is positive, but smaller, however: 3-5 per cent in 13 countries, mainly in the Americas and Africa, and 0-2 per cent in slightly under half of the 37 countries covered here, mainly those in Asia. The improvements in Latin American and Caribbean WFS surveys as compared with external sources are notable, emphasizing the success of the surveys in their use of a wider definition of unions.

The problem of greater discrepancies arising for comparisons with external sources further back in time, discussed in section 24.4 for fertility, can also affect nuptiality data. Since these increasing discrepancies are due to age-reporting errors for younger women, especially those aged 15-19, we can rely on the retrospective data of older women for proportions ever married at younger ages in earlier periods of time, more than on external sources. Given our reservations in the previous section about data for older women, this reliance would not usually extend beyond age 35-39 or 40-44.

The average per cent difference between the two sources for the two youngest age groups (15-24) was compared with the average per cent difference at all ages, as a means of checking on the possibility that the sources mainly differed at these young ages. Only four countries showed a difference of 4 per cent or more between the two averages. Two of these cases did have an eight-year gap between the two sources, but on the other hand, five other surveys with equally long gaps did not show large discrepancies between the two sources for the two youngest age groups. However, the evaluation reports which compared at least two external sources (usually at about 5 and 15 years before the surveys) found a greater discrepancy at young ages for the earlier period, compared to the later period, lending some support to the occurrence of age-reporting errors for young married women (see evaluation reports for Mexico, Peru and Philippines).

In conclusion, WFS surveys appear to have collected information on age at first union which is considerably better than that collected in most previous surveys or censuses. This is a reflection of the liberal definition of union used by WFS. However, the appreciable proportions of women in Latin America and Africa who reported births before their first union indicates the extreme difficulty of measuring sexual exposure by means of a surrogate. For many surveys, trends in age at first union were implausible, implying omission or displacement of such unions by older women. Finally we should mention one aspect of nuptiality that has not been covered in this chapter, namely dissolution and remarriage. So far major defects in these data have not been reported (Smith 1981a; Goldman 1981; Smith, Carrasco and McDonald 1984).

24.6   Infant and child mortality

To produce estimates of infant and child mortality, the dates of birth for all children and ages at death for dead children are required. The WFS birth histories do provide such information, although estimates made from them may be biased.

There are no definitive tests of quality for other aspects of the data, except where complete vital registration occurs, which is not the case for most of the less developed countries covered by the WFS. In fact, many countries lack any national direct estimates of infant and child mortality apart from the WFS. Comparisons with vital statistics can be made, however, to show gross errors, since lower estimates from the survey would undoubtedly mean that the data are deficient. Because of this general absence of external data, internal consistency checks become especially useful. These divide into two groups: those derived from basic data and those based on the estimated mortality rates. For the basic data we are limited to checking the plausibility of the pattern of births through time and the reporting of age at death. In order to check the estimates of mortality, we can examine the plausibility of age patterns, trends over time and differentials according to sex, age of mother at birth, parity, education, type of area of residence, and so on. Only the most deficient data are likely to produce implausible patterns and so these checks are not conclusive. Furthermore, an implausible result, such as a rise in mortality over time or higher urban than rural mortality, may be real.

Internal checks applied to the WFS data

The percentage of deaths for which the age, either in years or months, was missing was examined. Reported ages at death were maintained in an ungrouped format for only 29 countries. In 24 of the 29 countries, less than 2 per cent of the deaths were missing both year and month of age at death. In Benin, Lesotho and Haiti about 6 per cent were missing; in Ghana about 5 per cent; and in Mauritania about 4 per cent. Cameroon is the most extreme case of partial reporting: 40 per cent of deaths lacked data on months, but had the age at death in completed years, because of the questionnaire design. In Fiji and Tunisia, about 10 per cent of the deaths have missing data codes for months; this is also the case for 8 per cent in Portugal and 4 per cent in Senegal and Yemen AR. We suspect that much of this incomplete reporting is due to women reporting age of death in years and either not being asked, or not knowing exactly how many months longer the child lived.

We would expect that deaths that occurred longer ago would be more subject to missing age at death and in general this was found to be true, although the effect is not very strong. Four countries, however, show more missing data for later born children: Mauritania, Tunisia, Yemen AR and Jamaica. This pattern may be a warning sign of omission of earlier deaths.

For most countries with ungrouped ages at death we looked at the extent of heaping on certain ages at death. We classified countries on the basis of the percentage of deaths at 0-60 months that occurred at months 6, 12, 18, 24, 30 and 36:

Less than 10%	:	Republic of Korea, Trinidad and Tobago, Portugal
10-19%	:	Nepal, Philippines, Guyana, Jamaica, Fiji
20-29%	:	Ivory Coast, Kenya, Lesotho, Senegal, Jordan, Malaysia, Haiti, Bangladesh
30-39%	:	Benin, Ghana, Egypt, Morocco, Sudan, Tunisia, Yemen AR
40% and above	:	Mauritania

Heaping on month 12 is especially crucial for the estimation of infant mortality rates. Ten countries have more than 10 per cent of deaths in months 0 to 30 occurring at month 12: Benin, Ivory Coast, Egypt, Mauritania, Morocco, Sudan, Tunisia, Jordan, Syria, and Yemen AR.

Age pattern of mortality

The most likely children to be omitted, it is thought, are those who die soon after birth. We therefore examined the proportion of infant mortality that is neo-natal. A low percentage of neo-natal deaths does not necessarily indicate omission, but may mean that neo-natal deaths were understated and post-neo-natal overstated. Also a decrease in the proportion of neo-natal deaths from earlier time periods would in general occur if mortality were higher at those times, so judgement must be cautious.

Only three countries, Syria, Malaysia and Philippines, show suspiciously low levels of neo-natal mortality in the most recent five-year period and one, Trinidad and Tobago, shows a very high level. As both Malaysia and the Philippines asked for date of death (rather than age), misstatements of dates rather than omission is probably the cause of the low neo-natal mortality rates. Further information on the age patterns of mortality is given in chapter 32.

A number of countries, however, show substantial decreases in the proportion of infant deaths that are neo-natal in earlier periods. In eight cases, this occurs during the 15-19 year period before interview, or earlier (Kenya, Jordan,

Republic of Korea, Philippines, Thailand, Colombia, Peru and Panama). In a few cases, the 10–14 year period also shows this pattern (Syria, Nepal, Costa Rica and Trinidad and Tobago). Only in Turkey and Malaysia does this trend occur as recently as the 5–9 year period before interview. In Haiti the proportion declines consistently from recent to earlier periods, which is difficult to explain.

Sex differentials in mortality

It is suspected that a strong preference for children of one sex may lead to differential omission of the less preferred sex. Therefore, a study of sex differentials in mortality could reveal omission. The West model life tables at levels 7 and 22 have ratios of male to female infant mortality rates of 117 and 136 respectively. Since these levels are likely to encompass the rates in WFS surveys, we will use these as limits to the normal range. Interpretation must be careful, however, since the presumed direction of preference may have the opposite effect in reporting. For example, greater care may be given to boys, but a greater reluctance to disclose such deaths may also occur. We must also be careful to distinguish omission from the effects of sampling errors.

Only one country, Portugal, has a ratio above 140 that would indicate omission of girls who died. However, several countries have ratios below 110: in Africa, Cameroon (107), Lesotho (106), Morocco (106), and Tunisia (102); in Asia, Nepal (103), Pakistan (105), Jordan (85), Syria (92), and Thailand (108); in the Americas, Peru (105), Paraguay (103), and Panama (109). These findings support the argument of greater care being given to boys, resulting in lower than expected mortality for them, in these countries. This differential child care rather than sex-selective omission is the more likely explanation for these unexpected low ratios.

Mortality by birth order and by age of mother at birth

The pattern of infant and child mortality according to order of birth and age of mother is usually described as a 'J' or a 'U'; as order and age rise, mortality first falls and then rises. These patterns can be disturbed by omission. In fact, it is thought that first-born children and children of young mothers, especially those born a while before the survey, are more likely to have been omitted.

For infant mortality in the period 0–4 years before the survey, 17 countries have lower or about the same mortality for first births as for second and third births, but no countries show lower mortality for births to mothers at less than 20 years of age than at 20–29, although for Lesotho, Philippines and Jamaica the differences are small. The explanation seems to lie in the effect of birth intervals, since first births are not affected by the presence of a previously born child and therefore have a comparative advantage (Hobcraft, McDonald and Rutstein 1983).

Trends in mortality

We looked at mortality levels for time periods in the past (restricted to children whose mothers were 20–29 years old at their birth). Several countries show substantial rises in the most recent period in mortality under age five: Mauritania (23 point rise), Bangladesh (22), Pakistan (15), Paraguay (10), Guyana (10). Of these, only Mauritania, Bangladesh, and Pakistan also show an increase in neo-natal rates. The reasons for these recent upward trends are not clear. In some countries they may be genuine, but data errors may also have occurred. Over-reporting of recent deaths appears intuitively unlikely but overstatement of the ages of surviving children may have biased upwards mortality rates by deflating the denominators. This combination of an understatement of recent fertility but overstatement of recent childhood mortality has almost certainly occurred in Pakistan where evidence from a more recent fertility survey has proved invaluable in distinguishing error from genuine trend (Sathar forthcoming). A similar phenomenon may have occurred in the Egypt survey, where the infant mortality rate of 132 is considered in some quarters to be excessively high, while recent fertility may be underestimated (Coale forthcoming).

However, only four countries, Senegal, Lesotho, Paraguay and Costa Rica, show lower rates at 15-19 years before the survey than at 10-14 years before. Nevertheless, we should be careful in concluding that mortality always declines and that any deviation is due to omission or other error. A study of mortality estimates from a second fertility survey in the Dominican Republic showed the same calendar pattern of mortality as the earlier survey (Hobcraft and Rodríguez 1982a), a pattern that had previously been thought to be the result of omission (Guzmán 1980). In general, the observed trends in childhood mortality from WFS surveys are remarkably plausible.

Comparison with indirect estimates from household data

The proportions dead of children according to current age of mother from 11 household surveys are compared with those derived from the individual survey in chapter 4. Only in the Republic of Korea and Colombia are the proportions very close. In Yemen AR the proportions are much lower and in the other eight countries the proportions are higher in the household survey.

There appears to be no consistent explanation of the differences. When in-direct estimates from the household survey data are compared with direct esti-mates for mortality under the age of five, on the whole, the figures are rather close, but in Yemen AR, Morocco, and Mauritania the trends diverge and in Mauritania the household trends appear more plausible (the household data show a small decline, while the individual data show a substantial rise).

External comparisons with vital statistics

Comparisons with the rates from the United Nations Demographic Yearbooks, made by Rutstein (1983), have shown that the direct estimates of mortality from the birth histories are as high as or higher than vital statistics. The principal differences lie in the neo-natal rates, which, except for the countries that asked date of death, are substantially higher than those of the vital statistics. A detailed comparison of WFS and external estimates may be found in chapter 32.

Summary

Some surveys indicate deficiencies on several of the checks used to assess the quality of mortality data. The countries affected are Egypt, Fiji, Indonesia, Lesotho, Mauritania, Paraguay, Philippines, Sudan, Syria, Tunisia, and Yemen AR. However, several factors should be stressed:

1 Practically all surveys showed discrepancies on at least one test.

2 The evaluation reports have shown that most of the serious errors of omission occur more than 15 years before the survey, when truncation by maternal age also begins to seriously affect the data.

3 Comparisons with vital statistics and other external sources show that the data on mortality collected by the WFS are by far the best such data for most countries, including most of those in the list above.

24.7 Conclusions

Beyond the details of evaluating each individual topic, it would be helpful to be able to make some general statements about the quality of WFS survey data. The major questions of interest are: how did the surveys perform relative to external sources? is any grouping of countries according to data quality possible? are current estimates accurate? and, are data on trends over the past 15–20 years usable?

On the question of comparable quality with external sources, survey results were usually found to be better, with one exception. In coverage of live births and infant and child deaths, as well as in the recording of exposure within unions, the surveys did better than external sources. In the case of informal unions in societies where they are common, the surveys achieved considerably better coverage than external sources. However, surveys were not as successful in obtaining high-quality data on age: digit preference was the same or lower in WFS household surveys compared to censuses or other sources but the UN age index showed that about half of WFS household surveys were more distorted than the external source. In comparison, age reporting by respondents in the individual survey was better, but we do not usually have a comparison with external sources for this restricted age range.

It will come as no surprise that the countries with most problems in data quality are mainly African; but in addition, a few countries from the South Asian and American regions also had poor results. Using only age reporting and fertility results to rank countries, we find that seven countries had severe problems on both – Kenya, Lesotho, Sudan, Yemen AR, Bangladesh, Nepal and Haiti. Three countries had severe problems on one and some problems with the other of these two main topics (Benin, Cameroon and Dominican Republic). A further two countries had marked problems principally with age reporting, (Senegal and Paraguay) while five others revealed anomalies, mainly with fertility (Ivory Coast, Morocco, Mauritania, Pakistan and Indonesia). Finally the age group 45-49 is biased for one or more substantive topic for the majority of countries.

Current estimates of fertility and of infant and child mortality are of good quality in the majority of countries, often superior to estimates from vital statistics and other external sources. However, rates based on single calendar years are not to be recommended because of the high sampling variation. Rates for the last five years are reasonable, and even two- or three-year rates can be used, but a tendency for heaping of births in the year preceding the survey has been observed.

The acquisition of reliable fertility trends for a 15-20 year period before the survey was one of the major potential benefits of using a complete birth history. However one type of reporting error that commonly occurred in such histories was event displacement, particularly in the form of a shift by older women of distant births towards the survey date. In more than half of all surveys (mainly in Latin America and some parts of Asia), such displacement is minor and produces distortions only in the earliest periods. Thus, for these countries, trends for the past 15-20 years can be used without difficulty. However, in a number of surveys (mainly in Africa and in South Asia), spurious trends were found for the most recent 10 or 15 years, because of event displacement alone or the combination of displacement and age misstatement. These reporting errors are evident in the form of a trend of rising fertility, from the earliest periods, up to the 5-9 or 10-14 years period before the survey, followed by constant rates or a small decline. One qualification to the general conclusion that such a trend is evidence of reporting errors is that some countries or parts of countries have in fact experienced a true increase in fertility: thus, especially in the case of African countries, part of the observed trend, though probably not all of it, may be real (Lesthaeghe 1984).

WFS's decision in the early 1970s to apply the retrospective birth history in surveys of developing countries was an innovation at the time. A large part of the demographic world was very sceptical of the possibility of success of this demanding technique for collecting fertility information, in countries where any data collection was difficult. This was especially true of specialists in techniques of indirect estimation. However, the decision has been vindicated by the quality of the results obtained and their richness, in all but a few countries – this has now been recognized by some previous sceptics (e.g. Preston 1985). In the few most problematic countries, it is possible that the history should have been replaced by a simpler approach. The high quality of the trend data on infant and child mortality was a further unexpected outcome of the use of retrospective histories.

Perhaps because of fears about the quality of data that would be produced by WFS surveys, the organization was guided by its Programme Steering Committee into putting resources first into the development of the methodology of evaluation, and then its application to each survey. Proceeding in this direction was both necessary and useful. However, ultimately, the stress in the national evaluation reports fell on the application of a number of detailed tests or checks on quality, instead of being placed on reaching a final series of best estimates. It is hoped that, as one of the goals of future evaluations of surveys' data, more emphasis will be put on the production of a set of preferred estimates.

Notes

1. This chapter represents a summary of the material in N. Goldman, S. O. Rutstein and S. Singh (1985). Assessment of the Quality of Data in 41 WFS Surveys: a Comparative Approach. *WFS Comparative Studies* no. 44.
2. Excluding Iran whose data were not available for evaluation.
3. Guyana did not record single years of age in the household survey, and Nigerian results were not available at the time this section was prepared.

25

Analytical Methodology

Thomas W. Pullum

25.1 Introduction

Research methodology is a very general topic which encompasses all phases of the sequence leading from the formulation of research questions to the development of responses to those questions. In the context of the World Fertility Survey, the research objectives were to estimate levels of fertility, fertility preferences, the intermediate variables or proximate determinants such as marital exposure, breastfeeding and contraception, and to relate these variables to each other and to their socio-economic determinants or correlates. The development of the survey instrument, the selection of the sample in each country, the fieldwork, the data processing and the reduction of the data to statistical and demographic measures are all parts of the general methodology of WFS and are reviewed in various chapters in this volume.

In this chapter the term 'analytical methodology' will refer to the final phase in the sequence described above. It consists of the statistical and demographic procedures by which WFS or similar cross-sectional survey data can be manipulated to provide parameter estimates, descriptive statistics, test statistics, etc., which motivated the research from the start. From the beginning, a subsidiary objective of WFS was to contribute to the development of such procedures. One role of analytic methods is to compensate for inadequacies in the basic data as research questions develop which were not originally envisaged. Hence this phase of the overall methodology has the possibility of refining and developing the utility of the data even after the data collection has been completed.

Early in its existence WFS developed a standard tabulation plan and a First Country Report, with a standard format, which was to be prepared for each survey. These are described in chapter 21. It is generally agreed that these reports became rather stylized and rarely went beyond a discussion of the core tables. If WFS had gone no further in its ambitions than the First Country Report, as it might well have done, then this particular assessment would be short indeed. Rather, the following mechanisms were developed to promote further use of WFS data, and it is their implications for analytic methods which will concern us.

First, the notion of advanced or 'second-stage' analysis evolved, to focus on specific advanced research questions for each country. This was to be followed by comparative analyses as soon as several countries had passed the stage of the First Country Report. This programme was planned with substantive concerns in mind, but it was a natural stimulus to the development of new methods of analysis.

Second, in order to facilitate more advanced analyses, WFS central staff or consultants prepared two parallel series of publications: technical bulletins and illustrative analyses. The technical reports dealt with specific methods of analysis which could be quite broadly applied. They were intended to convey the potential value of techniques such as path analysis, the general linear model and life tables, etc. They usually included several examples of such uses and were frequently accompanied by computer software. The illustrative analyses had the complementary task of presenting research on specific topics such as fertility trends, fertility preferences, breastfeeding, etc., but using a variety of advanced techniques. They appeared in the WFS *Scientific Reports* series.

Third, central staff or consultants conducted second-stage analyses of WFS data which were related to WFS-sponsored conferences or workshops and were sometimes published in professional journals. Some of these analyses contributed to the development of analytical methods, either as their primary objective or as a by-product. And fourth, stimulated by the availability of WFS data, but without direct WFS support, independent researchers around the world have advanced the state of analytic models.

This chapter will attempt to summarize, integrate and appraise these developments, placing emphasis upon those which were made directly by WFS staff or with WFS support. We wish to describe the influence WFS has had upon analytic methods, but will not attempt to determine what was done that would not have been done if WFS had never existed. Even without WFS, there would undoubtedly have been several large-scale fertility surveys around the world during the past decade. Even if WFS had never existed as an organization, its staff and contractors would presumably have been active under other auspices. The conclusions will speculate on how the role of WFS was enhanced by certain aspects of its mandate and structure, and how this role might have been enhanced further, but we shall not conjecture what might have happened without the existence of WFS.

The major development in demographic methodology in the past decade has been a shift from aggregates to individuals as the units of analysis. Many factors have contributed to this trend, some of them extending back over two or more decades. They include the widespread access to public use samples from US censuses beginning with the 1960 census; large fertility and demographic sample surveys following World War II but particularly during the 1960s; the improvements in computing hardware and software; and parallel developments in applied statistics with their dissemination into population study through training programmes and collaborative research. It is arguable that the concomitant sophistication of demographic theories and interpretations has been more a consequence than a cause of the greater sophistication of analytic methods. Within this very general type of development, WFS will be shown to have been a powerful force from approximately 1977, when the first major methodological papers began to appear and the first datasets began to be available, up until the present. Presumably this legacy will continue, particularly through the data archives, for several years to come.

In assessing the role of WFS, this chapter will focus on the refinement and application of multivariate techniques for individual-level or multi-level data. In the discussions of standard procedures, it is assumed that the fundamental techniques were originated by applied statisticians and biostatisticians. This point is generally made quite clearly in the work to which we shall refer. As it is not our objective to extend this review to the literature outside WFS, these origins will not generally be described in any detail. Similarly, the review will not extend to research outside the immediate WFS sphere which has benefited by these advances.

As a part of the overall assessment of WFS, this chapter supplements several others and is in turn supplemented by them. Thus, other chapters deal with the substantive findings of WFS; here, at the risk of appearing sterile, but in order to minimize the overall redundancy, we will be limited to methods and will largely ignore the empirical findings which are of interest to a larger audience. With regard to demographic methodology, in particular the analysis of birth histories, this author believes that WFS has made or inspired several valuable contributions which will be ignored here. These include improvements in P/F ratio methods, the measurement of sample selection biases, and others. These contributions are sufficiently important that they have been documented elsewhere (e.g. Hobcraft, Goldman and Chidambaram 1982; Marckwardt 1984), and further papers are in preparation. There have been many advances in evaluating the quality of data, some of which are described in chapter 24. Another major contribution, due to a group at the University of Michigan, has been in the comparative analysis of surveys, in which statistics from several surveys are themselves treated as data and are summarized with statistical models (see chapter 23 for further discussion). The omission of these topics and others should certainly not be interpreted as a minimization of their importance. On the contrary, in the cases just cited it means that they are so important that they are treated elsewhere in more detail than is possible here. Thus, the present chapter may appear to some readers to be slanted towards certain analytic methods; the reason is that it is simply part of a volume which is intended as a whole to be quite comprehensive.

Another important limitation of this appraisal is that we will not be able to compare the new procedures with simpler and pre-existing alternatives. Ideally, a new procedure should be assessed in terms of criteria such as relative ease of computation, statistical efficiency, responsiveness to theoretical issues and interpretability. Perhaps most importantly, can we learn more about how the world works from a new approach than we can from a pre-existing alternative? Although we accept the importance of this question, we do not have the resources or time to attempt to answer it, and unfortunately it is one which the authors of new procedures almost never even ask of themselves.

The first part of this assessment will present some major developments which pertain to the techniques of general linear models and life tables or hazard models.

These developments carry over to a wide range of applications. The second part will examine some specific substantive applications. This division is somewhat arbitrary; the first part will also include some applications in order to facilitate the presentation.

25.2 Major frameworks

The following section will briefly describe some work on generalized linear models which cuts across several topics. The section on life tables and hazard models will provide a much lengthier exposition of that class of models on the assumption that they are less familiar to the readers of this chapter.

The general linear model

Additive linear models are the core of statistical methodology in the social sciences, but only comparatively recently have they become commonplace in population research. As stated in section 25.1, it is only in recent years that the individual has been regarded as a proper unit of analysis within demography, with a consequent adaptation of multivariate statistical models appropriate for such a unit. WFS promoted this development in several ways, motivated initially by the first project director, Maurice Kendall.

An outstanding developer and expositor of multivariate methods, Kendall strongly believed that WFS should construct bridges between statistical and demographic methodology. In addition to writing the first technical bulletin, on statistical issues such as multi-collinearity (Kendall 1976), he co-authored the second in that series, on path analysis and model building (Kendall and O'Muircheartaigh 1977). Like most of the technical bulletins after the first, this provided several examples from WFS surveys, with interpretations in relation to a substantive topic.

Three subsequent technical bulletins dealt with the same issues of quantifying the effects of predictors upon dependent variables while holding control variables constant. No. 3, by Pullum (1978), presented test factor standardization as a simple alternative to multiple classification analysis when computing facilities are restricted. The theoretical linkages between these techniques were discussed by Little and Pullum (1979). The most general and most important technical bulletins on the subject are those by Little (1978, 1980), which are supplemented by a conference paper (Little 1981). We shall briefly review the main features of these three papers. As with virtually all the material being reviewed in this assessment, their contribution lies in adapting more general pre-existing statistical methods to cross-sectional demographic survey data. The methods themselves are not new, but their adaptation to demographic purposes is frequently ingenious.

Little shows how the framework of the general linear model can be applied to a very wide range of situations. There is generally a dependent variable which is expressed as a fitted value plus a residual or error term for each unit in a sample. The fitted value is a linear combination of predictor variables, which may be at any level of measurement and may include products or other interaction terms. The residual terms are minimized in the sense that the sum of squares of residuals is minimized during the estimation of the coefficients. Depending upon the distribution of the error terms about zero, the sum to be minimized may differentially weight the terms.

In the analysis of contingency tables, the formal statement of a model can be similar to the above, with the dependent variable replaced by the log of an expected frequency or by the log of the ratio of two categories of a categorical dependent variable. However, these models analyse interdependence and have quite a different error structure from regression-type models, in which only the dependent variable is subject to error, despite their superficial resemblance. In such a situation, the maximum likelihood and least squares estimation procedures differ.

Although it is widely known that multiple regression, analysis of variance, multiple classification analysis, analysis of covariance, contingency table analysis and logit regression are all part of a single framework, and in fact can all be estimated by a single computer package (Glim), Little's three papers (1978, 1980, 1981), totalling nearly 200 pages in length, provide a unique integration and specificity of application. They emphasize, on the one hand, the exploratory character of data analysis as developed by John Tukey, and on the other hand, the importance of a sensitivity to substantive theory or knowledge, which leads to a choice of transformations, the inclusion of interaction terms and the specification of error distributions. For example, Little considers the appropriateness of log transformations of children ever born and argues for interactions between marital duration and the predictors in models for children ever born. (These models will be described elsewhere in this chapter.) He shows that when a predictor or control variable is inherently an interval-level variable — as in the case of age or marital duration or years of education — but has non-linear effects, then it may be better to categorize that variable than to enter it in polynomial form. He also illustrates the importance of censoring and selection effects, urges careful checking for interaction terms, and shows how the analysis of variance can be used in survey analysis more than it usually is.

These papers will be discussed further in connection with some of the specialized topics in section 25.3.

Life tables and hazard models

One of the greatest areas of expansion in demographic methods in recent years has centred upon the basic model of the life table. Outside WFS, a major direction of growth has been towards multi-state and multi-dimensional life tables, with both increments and decrements. The closely related topic of event history analysis has also seen major recent advances. Because of the character of its data base, WFS has only participated indirectly in these particular developments, but it has taken a leading role in another major direction of growth, described as life tables with covariates or hazard models.

This section will describe the general characteristics of life-table methods as used within WFS. Most of the features to be described here can be extended to other kinds of event histories. Features which are quite specific to certain applications, such as birth intervals or breastfeeding or infant mortality, will be given under those headings.

A technical bulletin on the basic model of the life table was prepared by Smith (1980b). At approximately the same time, a paper by Hobcraft and Rodríguez (1985) discussed general features but with specific relevance to birth history analysis. These papers, and others mentioned below, are excellent guides to the use and interpretation of life tables and hazard models. We shall simply select some highlights from them.

Censoring. All of the work has been with discrete intervals of time and age. At issue is whether or not an event will occur during a specific interval of time after some initiating event, and what are the covariates or determinants of the timing of that event. Time is marked off in successive intervals following the starting event. The intervals can be, for example, three months each, or a year each, or a mixture. The starting event can occur long before the interview or just shortly before, and as a result women differ in the duration of their exposure to the risk of closing the interval, i.e. experiencing the subsequent event which is of interest.

Some women will still be at risk of the event at the date of the interview, i.e. their exposure will be censored by the interview. The treatment of such cases is problematic and several alternatives may be found in the current literature. Suppose, for example, that one is interested in the proportion of women who have a second birth during the three-month interval 12–14 months following the first birth. There are four types of women in the survey: (1) women who had never experienced a first birth, or had their first birth less than 12 months before the survey, and were therefore never at risk of the event in the specified interval; (2) women who had their first birth between 12 and 14 months before the survey and are currently in the specified interval; (3) women who had their first birth more than 14 months before the survey and in fact had a second birth during the specified 12–14 month interval; and (4) women with the same exposure as (3) but *not* having a birth in the interval. Initially, it was WFS practice to ignore women or intervals of types (1) and (2). The probability of closing the interval at the specified duration was then estimated as the ratio of the frequency of (3) to the frequency of (3) and (4) combined. Thus, both exposure and events were ignored if the woman did not experience full exposure. The same principle extended to other kinds of demographic histories and events besides births.

Any estimation procedure would omit women of type (1), but some would include women of type (2), allowing them to contribute to the numerator of the estimate if they had an event in the incomplete interval and to the denominator to the degree that they were exposed (if the degree of exposure is not known, it is sometimes assumed to be half of the interval). Such contributions have always been allowed in the WFS estimation of central fertility rates, for example (as in Alam and Cleland 1981). However, life-table probabilities can be biased by such inclusions, particularly if there are trends in the continuous-time forces within the interval. The cost of such an approach, in terms of omitted cases of type (2), will be proportional to the length of the interval in question. And the longer the interval, the greater the chance of trends within it. WFS abandoned its earlier approach as too purist and wasteful of data: women and intervals of type (2) are now included. At present, bias is minimized by using duration intervals which are as short as possible.

Selectivity. A more pernicious type of censoring produces selectivity. Consider, for example, the probability in the previous illustration of having a second birth within 12-14 months of the previous birth. Many of the women of type (1), who do not contribute to the estimate in any way, will in fact eventually have a second birth, which may or may not be in the specified interval of duration. The omitted women in (1) will tend to be systematically different from women of the other types. Thus, the censoring of event histories by the interview, whose timing is an accident so far as the history itself is concerned, will systematically select for women with shorter intervals, earlier starting events, more events, and so on.

WFS was concerned with this issue, and generally followed a procedure again described by Hobcraft and Rodríguez (1985). This is the use of controls or stratification on the variables which are believed to manifest the selectivity. For example, the second birth interval will be weighted towards women who married early or who had their first birth early, since they will be under-represented in the omitted (1) category. One can stratify the sample on the basis of the woman's age at first marriage or age at first birth, preparing separate life tables and summary statistics for each stratum. The summary statistics can then be averaged across strata, with weights which correspond to the relative sizes of strata in some standard population which has been observed throughout its reproductive career. Thus if the strata are for ages less than 15, 15-19, 20-24 and 25 or more at first birth, then four life tables would be prepared and the median length of interval calculated for each. These four medians would be averaged with weights derived elsewhere. The weights in this example could come from the women aged 25 or more at the date of interview, for example (in a population which had most of its first births by age 25), for whom one could calculate the proportion of first births occurring before age 15, at ages 15-19, 20-24 and 25 or more. An alternative approach would be to control for age at marriage in a hazard model.

Hobcraft and Rodríguez (1985) give another example of selection which is specific to WFS data and is more serious than expected. WFS obtained details about breastfeeding for the two most recent births. If these two birth intervals are analysed with a period restriction – e.g. looking just at rates of closure of the last two intervals within the five years preceding the survey – then there is a bias towards slower rates of closure. The reason is that women who have short intervals will tend to have more than two intervals (open or closed) in the preceding five years; and since two intervals at most will be counted, there will be an under-representation of short intervals. This bias would actually be reduced if the period of coverage were shortened, e.g. to the two or three years preceding the survey.

Measures of the pace of events. Several WFS-related papers, beginning with Hobcraft and Rodríguez (1985) and Rodríguez and Hobcraft (1980), have used the quintum and trimean as summaries of the survival or waiting time distributions of successive events. The quintum is defined for birth intervals; it is the fitted proportion of intervals which will be closed within 60 months (five years) after they have begun. It is empirically rare for an interval to be closed after five years, and it is sometimes assumed that a woman who has been exposed and not using contraception for five years without a live birth is sterile (or her partner is sterile). The quintum for a specific birth order is only a slight underestimate of a parity progression ratio, even in a contracepting population. In other applications, a similar measure of closure could be defined.

The trimean derives from Tukey's methods of exploratory data analysis (Tukey 1971). Of the fitted intervals which are closed in 60 months or less, let $Q1$, $Q2$ and $Q3$ be the durations by which 25, 50 and 75 per cent of them have been closed (quartiles). Then the trimean T is defined by $T = (Q1 + 2Q2 + Q3)/4$. The range, $Q3-Q1$, can be used as a measure of dispersion. If the force of decrement is a constant, then all linear combinations of $Q1$, $Q2$ and $Q3$, and also the quintum, are simply functions of that parameter. In general, of course, the force of decrement is *not* a constant, and WFS has found that the quintum, trimean and range all include information which the others lack.

Hazard models. With hazard models, also described as life tables with covariates, it is not necessary to subdivide the population and prepare separate life tables within each category of a predictor. Rather, the log hazard function, which for the usual life table is treated as a constant within each interval of duration, can be expressed as a linear combination of terms which are specific for the interval and also for the characteristics of the respondent, such as age and socio-economic status, or of the preceding event, such as the date when it occurred. A pooling of all cases for the estimation of the influence of these characteristics is statistically efficient in the same sense that multiple regression is preferable to a comparison of category means.

The basic statistical model was originated by Cox (1972), whose influential work was followed by several refinements and biostatistical applications. Demographic applications lagged by several years, despite an awareness by many statistically oriented demographers of the great potential of these models. The factors which impeded the more rapid diffusion of hazard models into demography were less a matter of intellectual receptivity than of the sheer technical difficulties of implementation. First, computer software was either not generally available or difficult to use. Now, appropriate packages include Glim, Rates, LOGLIN, and even subprograms of SPSS and BMDP. Second, the preparation of data for these models was seen as, and in fact was, a formidable task. In order to produce statistically stable estimates, large data files were needed, with proportionately high costs of data preparation, imputation of missing dates, recoding, and so on.

WFS activities in both promoting and facilitating the demographic application of hazard models may be viewed as exemplary of its role more generally. WFS staff or consultants, and the existence of high-quality Standard Recode files, have been instrumental in several recent developments. Two papers which use hazard models for the comparative analysis of birth interval lengths are by Trussell, Martin, Feldman, Concepción and Noor Laily Abu Bakar (1984) and Rodríguez, Hobcraft, McDonald, Menken, and Trussell (1984).

Two other papers are by Gilks (1984) on birth history analysis and Trussell and Hammerslough (1983) on infant and child mortality. Several other papers using hazard models have appeared very recently, typically emanating from Princeton, but they will not be discussed here.

The paper by Trussell and Hammerslough (1983) includes an excellent description of the logic of hazard models and of maximum likelihood methods for estimating their parameters. We shall not go into detail on these models, partly because of that paper's accessibility (the other three mentioned above were at the time of writing unpublished). It may be useful, however, to state the most general form of these models. Let k serve as the index of duration categories in which an individual may or may not close the interval. In our continuing example of birth intervals, duration 12–14 months after the first birth is a duration category for having a second birth. Let the index i serve to identify an individual (here a woman) with a vector X_i of characteristics. The conditional probability that a specified event which has not yet occurred will occur in interval k for woman i is the risk or hazard, r_{ik}. The general model states that the risk can be factored into components or, equivalently, that its logarithm can be expressed as a sum of effects as follows:

$$\ln(r_{ik}) = a_k + X_i'b + W_{ik}'c + Y_i'd_k + Z_{ik}'e_k.$$

This form is given in Trussell et al. (1983). Here a_k is a scalar, specific to the duration interval but not the woman which would be the force of decrement for all women if covariates were not employed. All other terms are column vectors. X_i was defined above and its coefficient vector, b, consists of effect parameters to be estimated. These parameters do not vary across duration categories. For example, one might hypothesize that an extra year of schooling will add the same amount (presumably a negative amount) to the log hazard in every interval of duration. The $Y_i'd_k$ term, by contrast, allows for a change in the effect of education from one duration to the next.

The $W_{ik}'c$ term refers to the use of covariates with differ across women and across durations. Examples would be the labour force activity of the woman during successive birth intervals, duration of breastfeeding within a birth interval, etc. Although the variables may change during the event history, the coefficients for them are not allowed to change. For example, labour force activity during the duration 12-14 months may be hypothesized to have the same effect within that duration that labour force activity during duration 15-17 months would have upon that duration. The final term in the general model, $Z_{ik}'e_k$, would allow both variables and effects to change from one duration interval to the next. Hypotheses about the nature of effects can be tested by comparing simpler models with more complicated ones.

When such models are applied to fertility analysis, an interval is initiated by a birth and terminated by another birth. In the study of infant and child mortality, the starting event is the same but the terminating event is the death of the child. In the study of breastfeeding, the interval is once again started by a birth, and it is closed by the termination of breastfeeding. All of these applications are somewhat different. Birth intervals have a minimum length of about seven months; only a fraction of births end in child deaths; breastfeeding can have duration zero and is certain to terminate eventually, whereas other kinds of intervals may never close. The covariates of theoretical or empirical interest will also vary from one application to another. However, the basic estimation procedures, summary measures and appropriate software are the same for all applications. Later sections of this chapter will consider several uses of these models in some detail.

It may be noted that hazard models are a special case of rate models, which encompass an even broader variety of demographic applications. The response variable is binary (yes/no) in a hazard model, and simply describes whether an event did or did not occur in a unit of time. In a rate model, multiple events can occur in the numerator, and there can be a denominator which reflects exposure to risk. Otherwise, there is close correspondence between the two types of models.

25.3   Major areas of application

Models of fertility counts

At the individual level, cumulative fertility, the number of children born to a woman by particular age or marital duration, had only rarely been taken as the dependent variable prior to WFS. When it was used, some of its basic defining properties were usually overlooked. In particular, the number of children born up to some specified age or marital duration is a non-negative, monotonically non-decreasing count, and its relationship to age and marital duration is obviously non-linear.

Several WFS-related papers have attempted to model various counts of births in a demographically meaningful way. Using somewhat different forms of the general linear model, they generally agree on these points:

1 The number of children born in an interval of time or age is a non-linear function of the level of age or marital duration.

2 Duration of marriage or of motherhood (time since first birth) are the preferred demographic controls, although age sometimes has an additional effect.

3 An additive model which includes substantive predictors, such as years of education, should also include interaction terms between that variable and duration. The monotonically increasing effect of duration implies that the additive effect of education, say, must be different at different levels of duration.

4 The dependent variable, number of children born in an interval of exposure, should be refined by dividing it by the length of exposure. This gives a standardized dependent measure, the individual-level analogue of a rate.

5 Each case should be assigned a weight which is proportional to the amount of exposure.

The first two points pre-date WFS, of course, but the last three appear to be specific contributions of WFS, appearing in different forms in two papers from the 1980 Conference, one by Little (1981) and one by Rodríguez and Cleland (1981a), and also in a paper by Little and Perera (1981).

Little (1981, p. 206) specifically proposes two equivalent functional forms along these lines. For an individual woman, let y be her parity, d her marital duration and x her level of education.

In one of Little's models,

$$\hat{y} = b_0 d + b_1 d^2 + b_2 dx + b_3 d^2 x. \tag{1}$$

Note that duration is a factor in each term on the right-hand side; when $d = 0$, then $y = 0$, as it should. Births before marriage need not pose a problem. It is exposure, rather than formal marriage, which is involved here, and if a birth precedes formal marriage, one can then backdate the initiation of exposure to nine months or a year prior to the first birth. Moreover, in this functional form, the increment produced by an increase in education will depend on the level of duration. The variance about the fitted regression line is assumed to be proportional to duration, a simple modification of a Poisson error structure.

The second and essentially equivalent model proposed by Little (1981, p. 206) involves a division of each term in (1) by d. Defining $z = y/d$, the individual-level analogue of a rate, the model becomes

$$\hat{z} = b_0 + b_1 d + b_2 x + b_3 dx. \tag{2}$$

The variance of the errors around this line is assumed to be inversely proportional to d, and the least-squares line will be fitted with weights proportional to d.

One may note, although Little does not explicitly do so, that the apparently additive model (2) can be factorized as follows, with an appropriate linkage between the 'a', 'c' and 'b' coefficients:

$$\hat{z} = (a_0 + a_1 d)(c_0 + c_1 x). \tag{3}$$

This multiplicative form may better show how (2) is analogous to models for rates, which are best motivated in multiplicative form or equivalently in additive form in logarithms. It is difficult to employ multiplicative forms at the individual level, because of women with no children (the log of zero is undefined); an additive model in logs of parities cannot include such women without adjustments such as the addition of 0.5 to y. Yet (2) is capable of being fitted to all parities, including parity zero. The form of (3) suggests how additional covariates might be added into the model multiplicatively, if such a feature is considered to be desirable.

A related alternative version of the same basic model was used by Rodríguez and Cleland (1981a) in a comparative study of socio-economic differentials in fertility. Their model does not treat cumulative fertility as the dependent variable, but rather the number of children during the most recent five years born to women married at least 2.5 years at the date of the survey. This measurement is used to construct a synthetic total marital duration rate, TMDR. In a real marriage cohort, the TMDR is the mean cumulative fertility after 25 years (or some comparable length) of marital duration (as used in Alam and Cleland 1981). The synthetic measure for the preceding five years of observed births is developed as follows. For each woman, let y be her number of births during the five-year interval and e the amount of her marital exposure during this interval — usually five years, but less if she was married in the first 2.5 years of the interval, experienced a marital disruption, etc. Then $z = y/e$ will correspond, at the individual level, to a marital fertility rate for the most recent five years. Let d be years of marital duration for the woman at the midpoint of the interval — i.e. 2.5 years into the interval for most women. The assumption is made that z can be fitted acceptably with a quadratic function:

$$\hat{z} = b_0 + b_1 d + b_2 d^2. \tag{4}$$

In making this fit, each case is weighted in proportion to e. Also, in order to avoid the collinearity of d and d^2, the fitted regression line is actually

$$\hat{z} = c_0 + c_1(d-12.5) + c_2(d-12.5)^2 \tag{4'}$$

with appropriate linkages between the 'b' and 'c' coefficients. However, the simpler form (4) will be used in this exposition.

Empirically, the fit is quite good; z is basically a monotonically declining function of d, with a slight downward concavity ($b_2 > 0$). Regarding z as a function of d, and integrating to some upper limit D, the synthetic cumulative fertility up to duration D is therefore:

$$F(D) = b_0 D + b_1 D^2/2 + b_2 D^3/3. \tag{5}$$

$D = 25$ corresponds to cumulative fertility after 25 years of marriage.

This format can be extended to include other controls, such as age at marriage, and other predictors, such as education. If, say, years of education is represented by x, then (4) will become

$$\hat{z} = b_0 + b_1 d + b_2 d^2 + b_3 x + b_4 x d + b_5 x d^2 \qquad (6)$$

Note that with proper definitions of the 'a' and 'c' coefficients, (6) can be re-written in multiplicative form as

$$\hat{z} = (a_0 + a_1 d + a_2 d^2)(c_0 + c_1 x) \qquad (7)$$

that is, as the product of a quadratic term in duration d and a linear term in years of education x. The integral of (6) or of (7), evaluated at final duration D and at a specific level of education x = X, is therefore

$$F(D,X) = b_0 D + b_1 D^2/2 + b_2 D^3/3 + b_3 XD + b_4 XD^2/2 + b_5 XD^3/3. \qquad (8)$$

By inserting a specific X into this equation (and D = 25), one obtains a synthetic measure which can be calculated and compared for different values of X and in different data sets. Rodríguez and Cleland (1981a) proceed in this way in their comparative analysis, using many different predictors and interaction terms.

This synthetic fertility model marks an advance in the analysis of current fertility. It provides an interpretable summary measure of current fertility which can be calculated with regression procedures. However, in an effort to replicate it for another purpose, the present author had some difficulties which may be mentioned. First, the quadratic form (4) will decrease monotonically until it reaches a minimum; beyond that point it will unrealistically begin to increase. Moreover, the function will either be positive for all durations or there will be an interval of d for which f(d) is negative; both of these alternatives are unrealistic. The estimates F produced by (5) and (8) are quite sensitive to the choice of D and can behave implausibly in the neighbourhood of a large value such as D = 25. An alternative to the functional form (4) with an asymptote of zero as d increases would be preferable. Second, and related to this point, late-marrying categories of women will empirically cease reproduction well before a duration of 25 years. Rodríguez and Cleland (1981a) include a control for age at marriage, and in the integration they set it equal to the mean age at marriage within the predictor category. But because of the non-asymptotic functional form (4), a high value of D will lead to inconsistencies for a late-marrying group. Third and finally, this model has an undesirable proliferation of interaction terms as the number of predictors increases, a situation which may be impossible to avoid.

These reservations are relatively minor. With some refinements, this basic model could see many applications.

Controlling fertility for the major demographic variables: age, period and cohort analyses

Under this general heading we shall describe a few analyses which have included combinations of age, period and cohort identifications, particularly in an effort to describe or to control for changes over time. Thus, some studies of fertility have specifically concerned change in recent years, controlling for age or marital duration. Others have regarded time and period variation more as a reporting bias to be purged from the data.

An excellent study of differentials in cumulative fertility in Sri Lanka is due to Little and Perera (1981). Their approach is innovative in two ways: in the definition of the dependent variable and in their particular use of multiple regression to identify socio-economic differentials. Six interrelated measures of fertility were used, based on the marital duration of a respondent at the date of the survey and on her marital duration at the date of childbirth. These six measures are the cumulative fertility of three different marital duration cohorts: women married 0-9 years, 10-19 years and 20 or more years. Each woman in the youngest cohort yields one measure: cumulative fertility to the date of interview. The second cohort yields two measures: cumulative fertility during the first ten years of duration and subsequent fertility to the date of interview. Finally, three measures come from the third cohort: the number of children born in years 0-9, the number in years 10-19, and the number ever born, which is the sum of the latter two plus any births after 20 completed years of marriage.

These measures are calculated at the individual level; each but the last one is then divided by the woman's months of exposure to the interval in question, and then multiplied by 120, the maximum possible exposure. In other words, these dependent variables are inflated to their implied value after ten years of exposure. Any woman with less than a year of exposure to an interval is omitted. Table 25.1 from Little and Perera (1981, p. 17) gives the means of these six individual measures for Sri Lanka as a whole. In these and other aggregate measures, each woman is weighted in proportion to her months of exposure.

TABLE 25.1

Mean fertility, by marriage duration and marriage cohort: Sri Lanka

Measure	Marriage cohort		
	0-9	10-19	20 +
Births 0-9 (BM0-9)	3.57	3.36	3.50
Births 10-19 (BM10-19)	–	1.97	2.40
Children ever born (CEB)	–	–	6.37

The individual-level measures can be used for summary statistics within socio-economic groups, or they can be taken as dependent variables in multiple regressions or other versions of the general linear model. Little and Perera present several such multiple regressions, beginning with terms for the effect of age at marriage, AGFM. The control for AGFM is made with a quadratic function expressed in terms of deviations about the mean for each cohort. In other words, the regressions for the third marriage cohort (20+ years), for which the mean age at marriage is 16.9 years, include the term (AGFM-16.9) and its square. The advantage of using these two forms instead of simply AGFM and its square is that the latter pair are highly correlated, a circumstance which decreases the numerical accuracy of estimating procedures. Also, coefficients in polynomial forms are more interpretable if expressed as the impact of a deviation from the mean value. Socio-economic variables, such as education and region of residence, are then added in sequence. They are included in the regressions as sets of binary variables if categorical, and then converted to deviations from means by the usual procedures. In this way, for each dependent measure and each predictor, one can compute effects which are (1) unadjusted for other variables, (2) adjusted for age at marriage, and (3) adjusted for all other covariates.

The Little and Perera technique can be regarded equally as a way of detecting and describing socio-economic differentials in marital fertility and as a tool for detecting fertility trends. All three cohorts, for example, use as a dependent variable the births in years 0–9 of marriage. If the cohorts are compared, then we have descriptions of early marital fertility in years 0–9 before the survey, 10–19 years before and 20 or more years before. Similarly, the second and third cohorts may be compared for fertility during durations 10–19 after marriage. Leaving aside issues of reporting errors, these comparisons are potentially central to the study of trends in levels and differentials.

A second major method for articulating age, period and cohort variation appears in a paper by Hobcraft and Casterline (1983). They define six intervals as pertinent to fertility at the individual level. These may be indicated diagrammatically by the four events in the following life line:

1 --------------- 2 -------------------- 3 ----------------- 4
Woman's birth   Marriage or first birth   Later birth event   Interview

The six possible intervals between these four points are as follows:

1–3 AGE (age at birth)
3–4 PER (period since childbirth)
1–4 BCO (birth cohort = age)
2–4 MCO (marriage or motherhood cohort)
1–2 AGM (age at marriage or motherhood)
2–3 MDR (marriage or motherhood duration at childbirth)

These definitions conform to the usage of 'cohort' and 'period' by WFS. 'Cohort' refers to the woman's age at the survey; 'period' refers to the length of time by which the event (childbirth) preceded the survey.

If subsets of three terms from this list of six are examined, certain triples will be found to contain a redundancy. For example, if AGE and PER are known for a specific woman and birth event, then BCO is implied. (If the intervals from points 1–3 and 3–4 are known, then the interval from 1 to 4 is known.) Hobcraft and Casterline select a set of three terms which is free of such redundancies: AGE, PER and MDR. The case for using these three intervals rather than some others with the same linear independence (e.g. AGM, PER and MDR) is made on substantive and statistical grounds.

The statistical model for estimating the coefficients which describe variations in fertility by age, period and duration is as follows:

$$\ln(\hat{B}) = \ln(W) + GM + AGE + PER + MDR.$$

This notation omits subscripts for the three effects, for simplicity, but has a clear interpretation. B is the total number of births and W is the total amount of exposure observed in the sample for a specific combination of AGE, PER and MDR. B is the fitted or expected number of births. AGE, PER and MDR are treated as categorical variables. Typically, AGE is defined with intervals 15-19, 20-24, ..., 45-49; and PER and MDR have intervals 0-4, 5-9, ..., 25+. A modification by Hobcraft and Casterline is to centre the age intervals on 15, 20, ..., 45 and the duration intervals on 0, 5, ..., 25. If, say, there are seven intervals of AGE, and six each of PER and MDR, then there are $7 \times 6 \times 6 = 252$ combinations, but many of these are impossible (e.g. low age and high marital duration) and others are missing from the sample (e.g. distant periods and late age or marital duration). Through the retrospective birth histories, each woman contributes births and marital exposure to a subset of these cells. The model is stated in additive form, with logarithms taken of B and W, but if both sides are exponentiated, it is clear that the ratio of births to exposure — which is, of course, an age-period-duration specific fertility rate — is being expressed as a product of a main effect and effects for the age, period and duration categories. In the additive form of the model, the constant term is labelled GM (but it is not the grand mean), and the three sets of coefficients are constrained to be contrasts, with the age group centred on 25 years of age, the period 0-4 years before the survey, and the duration group centred on five years. An alternative parameterization would take GM to be the overall level (when the parameters are exponentiated) and the other effects would be required to add to zero in each set, i.e. to be expressed as deviations from GM. In fitting the model, a Poisson error distribution is assumed, and estimation is done with the computer program Glim. The model can be extended by incorporating interaction terms, whose significance can be tested hierarchically.

Models fairly similar to the above can be traced back ten years or so, in a tradition which will not be cited here, although the present author has contributed to it. The Hobcraft and Casterline approach has several novel features which merit its inclusion in this assessment. First, the model brings together age, period and duration in a single model. It had earlier been demonstrated by Page (1977) that age and duration each contains information that the other lacks, but it has been difficult to include both in the same model because of their strong correlation. Hobcraft and Casterline minimize this issue by categorizing both variables. Second, these controls for demographic effects are applied to data from the birth histories of cross-sectional fertility surveys. Previous applications have been to vital statistics data.

A third novel feature of this approach, not indicated thus far, is that two alternative definitions of duration are used. In addition to years since marriage, the usual definition, parallel use is made of years since first birth, termed duration of motherhood. A choice between the two is partly a matter of theoretical reasoning and partly a matter of empirical evidence. Hobcraft and Casterline do not conclude unequivocally that either definition is superior to the other, but for most countries in their comparative analysis the empirical evidence, as gauged by greater regularity of coefficients, favours duration of motherhood as the control. Probably the major drawback of this alternative definition, however, is that it begs the question of fitting the first birth in the series. First births are a rather high proportion of all the births in a survey – at least a third of them – and if they are omitted, then any model can be expected to improve in some ways. To be complete, a companion model should be developed to fit the distribution of first births across combinations of age and period, with exposure derived from the household survey, which includes both married and unmarried women. A companion model of this sort is more important when duration is measured from the first birth than when it is measured from an extraneous though related event, the woman's date of first marriage.

Hobcraft and Casterline use the model mainly to compare the age and duration effects computed for a set of nine countries, with some breakdowns by educational group. The age and duration effects may be regarded as purged of the period variation, so to speak, in the same sense that partial regression coefficients may be interpreted as controlled for variation in other variables (indeed, the present model, like multiple regression, is a species of the general linear model). By the same token, although this interpretation is not exploited by Hobcraft and Casterline, the period effects may be regarded as purged of age and duration effects, and used for the description and analysis of trends in the quantum of fertility. This interpretation of the adjustment in purging of effects requires that the underlying relationship is additive.

Note that this model requires data from the birth histories of individual women, but is nevertheless presented as an aggregate-level model. It uses individual-level data to compute contributions to the numerators and denominators of a three-dimensional array of fertility rates. In this sense it differs from the MCA-type models of Little described above, but it is fundamentally the same in the sense that fertility is proportional to exposure and also to sets of effects representing other identifications.

A third paper to be discussed here is by Gilks (1984). In many ways it is a companion to the paper by Hobcraft and Casterline but it uses hazard models. Gilks takes as his dependent variable not the number of births occurring in an interval of exposure, but the length of a birth interval specific for other demographic characteristics of the interval and of the woman. We shall not repeat the earlier description of hazard models, except to state that the log of the probability of closing the interval in a specific interval of duration is expressed as a linear combination of predictors and controls. Gilks uses the birth histories from the same nine surveys as Hobcraft and Casterline, and attempts to describe the tempo of childbearing with intervals drawn from the following sequence:

```
1 --------- 2 ------- 3 --------- 4 --------- 5 --------- 6 ----------- 7
Woman's    First     First  ...  Previous    Previous    Birth    ...  Survey
birth      union     birth       birth       birth       event of
           or first              but one                 interest
           marriage
```

In this sequence, point 6 is a specific birth of interest. Point 5 refers to the immediately preceding birth and point 4 is the birth just before that one. Date of first union and date of first birth are distinguished. Gilks defines ten intervals of interest from this sequence. Note that some of these intervals are referred to as dates, following the WFS convention that a period is identified by time before the survey. The definitions are modified in obvious ways if the birth of interest is the first or second birth, etc.

2-3 FBI (first birth interval, from first union to first birth)
4-5 PBI (length of previous birth interval)
3-5 Divided by the number of birth intervals it includes
     ABI (average birth interval, excluding FBI)
1-3 FBA (age at first birth)
1-5 PBA (age at previous birth)
1-2 FMA (age at first union)
3-7 FBD (date of first birth)
5-7 PBD (date of previous birth)
2-7 FMD (date of first union)
1-7 DBD (date of woman's own birth)

The dependent variable is derived from the interval 5–6. A hazard model is developed which appears to be optimal across the nine countries:

$$\ln\lambda(t) = \mu(t) + \alpha(t)\ln(\text{PBI}) + \beta(t)\text{PBA} + \eta\text{BOR} + \gamma\text{PBD} + \theta\text{BOR.PBD}.$$

(As given by Gilks, a substantive predictor, education, is also included, without any interaction terms.)

Here, BOR is the birth order of the event and $\ln\lambda(t)$ is the log hazard, i.e. the log of the probability of closing the interval after duration t. $\mu(t)$, $\alpha(t)$ and $\beta(t)$ are coefficients which vary for different durations; η, γ and θ are constants. The model differs from that of Trussell and Hammerslough (1983) described earlier, because duration is continuous rather than categorical. It is developed partly through empirical stepwise selection procedures, but it is also guided by careful demographic considerations. The auto-regressive term, $\ln(\text{PBI})$, is stated as a logarithm, thereby in the same scale as the dependent measure. PBA and PBD, the woman's age when the interval in question began and the period of time when the interval began, are equivalent to AGE and PER in the quantum model of Hobcraft and Casterline (1983). The role of duration (MDR) in their model would be taken here by the interval from points 2 (or 3) to 5. However, rather than including such an interval, Gilks uses BOR, the woman's parity at the beginning of the interval, as a demographically more interpretable indicator of the stage in the family-building process. The effects of birth order (BOR) and period (PBD) are not assumed to vary by the length of the interval in question, but to interact; that is, the impact of being at a specific birth order varies according to the date at which the interval began. Several alternatives to this basic model are estimated, including in some cases the proximate determinants of contraceptive use and breastfeeding in the interval. These, of course, have time-varying effects.

The fourth and final approach to be reviewed very briefly in this section is set out in a technical bulletin by Ryder (1982). The approach, labelled 'progressive fertility analysis', provides an integration of themes which Ryder has long promulgated as central to fertility analysis: the lifetime importance of cohort identification, because of the shared experiences and norms of persons who were born or who married at about the same time; and the value of representing child-bearing as a cumulative or sequential progression through successive family sizes. Cohort and parity are more socially interpretable dimensions of family building than is biological age, the usual index of vital registration systems.

Ryder's analytic method is illustrated with hypothetical data, and some doubt about its feasibility and usefulness must remain pending a full-scale application to actual survey data. A somewhat similar model by Feeney (1983) has been applied to non-WFS data, with promising results. The drawbacks in the method are in its data requirements — especially in its need for a very large survey if the measures are to be statistically stable.

The method is built upon a four-dimensional progression probability, $q(x,y, e,k)$, indexed by parity x, duration y since entry into parity x, age e at entry into parity x, and birth cohort k. These probabilities of moving to parity $x + 1$, or closing the open birth interval, within each combination of y, e and k, and for each possible value of x, are combined to yield both real and synthetic life-table measures. Some of the marginal rates, for example with aggregation over x, are also described by Ryder.

This framework is in many ways isomorphic to that of Gilks, with the following linkages between Gilks' preferred model and the set of rates developed by Ryder. (1) y or t is the length of the open interval; (2) x or BOR is parity at the beginning of the interval; (3) e or PBA is age at the beginning of the interval; (4) k or OBD identifies the cohort. Gilks' model does not specifically include OBD, but it does include PBD and PBA, and since OBD = PBD + PBA, it takes account of all four of Ryder's dimensions.

To pursue the differences a little further, Ryder has conceptualized a framework but he has not proposed a model in the statistical sense, nor does he claim to have done so. Gilks has taken the same basic variables, tested their significance in a hazard model, and fitted that model to a log transformation of the same four-dimensional array as Ryder. In addition, Gilks has included an auto-regressive term, the length of the preceding birth interval, and uses a technique which can include additional individual-level covariates such as years or level of education. In our view, there is a valuable complementarity of conceptual and applied strengths in these two contributions.

Fertility preferences

This assessment deals primarily with methods related to actual fertility and to a lesser degree with the proximate determinants and with child mortality. A related area of contributions should not be overlooked: the interpretation of WFS data on fertility preferences. Several researchers connected with WFS have attempted to construct synthetic measures of desired family size using the following pieces of information: current parity or current number of living children; whether or not another child was wanted; and whether or not the last child was wanted. WFS surveys included a question specifically on ideal or desired family size, but it has been argued that the question demands excessive abstraction by the respondent. The two simple dichotomies about the next child and the last child, specific for each parity, are more immediate and may offer less opportunity for rationalization of children already born but not wanted at the time. These questions certainly have their own weaknesses. The stated desire for another child is elicited without any time reference. There is undoubtedly also some tendency to state that the last child was wanted at the time the woman became pregnant, even though it was not.

A synthetic measure derived from the above information must apply the logic of the life table to parity progression. Family building is treated as analogous to ageing, and the above information must be manipulated to construct 'survival' probabilities, specific for each family size, and then the usual summary measures of a life table, primarily the synthetic mean family size, which is analogous to the expected age at death or the life expectancy of a life table. This basic analogy is not new, and efforts were made by Udry and by Lightbourne (before the latter joined the WFS staff) and by Pullum, using the Sri Lanka Fertility Survey. Spurred by the inadequacies of the above approaches, Rodríguez and Trussell (1981) proposed a technique which will be described here. (See their paper for descriptions and citations of earlier approaches.)

The basic problem is to estimate the parity progression ratio P_i for each parity i, that is, the conditional probability of progressing from i to the next higher parity, implied by the above attitudinal information. The ratio P_i is fully analogous to the familiar $1-q_x$ of a life table. The ratio for the synthetic population is taken to be equal to M_i/L_i, where L_i is the number of women with i or more children who want i or more, and M_i is the number of such women who want $i + 1$ or more..The issue is how to estimate L_i and M_i.

In describing the Rodríguez and Trussell method, we shall modify their notation to simplify the presentation. Let N_i be the observed number of women in the sample who actually have i children or more. Then, at each specific parity i, let a_i be the number who want to stop at i (in other words, wanted their last child but not another); let b_i be the number who wanted to stop before i (that is, did not want their last child), although we do not know how far back they wanted to stop. and let m_i be the number who want more.

M_i is calculated easily as $M_i = \sum_{j=i}^{k} m_j$, where k is the highest observed parity. All of these women want more than i children. L_i is harder to estimate because we do not know where women classified as b_i would have preferred to stop. The proposed estimate of L_i is $N_i - b_i - (\sum_{j=i-1}^{k} b_j)b_i/ (a_i + b_i)$. Here, N_i is reduced by those women who did not want to have i or more children. Of the women with exactly i children, we know (if we can trust the responses, an issue which will remain moot) b_i wanted fewer than i. Out of the b_j women at each higher parity who wanted fewer than j, it is somewhat arbitrarily assumed that a fraction $b_i/(a_i + b_i)$ wanted fewer than i and the remaining fraction wanted something between i and j-1.

Rodríguez and Trussell demonstrate some desirable properties of the synthetic distributions thus generated, encompassing the range from full implementation of preferences to complete lack of implementation. In this writer's view, the estimates of L_i tend to be too low because $b_i/(a_i + b_i)$ is too high a ratio to apply to all parties above i in the manner just described. As a result, the (synthetic) mean desired family size may tend to be too large. However, the basic approach developed by these authors is better motivated than preceding ones, and has the potential for useful applications and further refinements. Lightbourne (chapter 31) shows, with extensive simulations of family building under varying degrees of implementation of preferences, that his synthetic estimate $M_i/(N_i-N_{i+1})$ is an effective lower bound on the desired mean, for which the Rodríguez-Trussell estimate serves as an upper bound. (Note that N_i-N_{i+1} is simply the number of women with exactly i children, and M_i divided by this is the proportion who want to continue.) Lightbourne terminates the summation when the denominator falls below 15 cases or the proportion falls below 0.10. His estimate and the Rodríguez-Trussell estimate do indeed seem to bracket other plausible alternatives.

Another cross-sectional estimate of desired family size is the 'wanted TFR', proposed by Westoff (1981) and also described by Lightbourne in chapter 31. This, or a 'wanted CBR', can be calculated from the births in, say, the three years before the survey, by omitting from the recent birth history any births which can be inferred to be unwanted. These will include any in excess of the desired family size. If the last birth was stated to be unwanted at the time, then it can be omitted too. This measure is an effort to estimate what the TFR (or CBR) would be if preferences could be implemented. It falls somewhat short of this goal because of timing errors; that is, some of the recent births were wanted but wanted later, causing an upward bias. Lightbourne gives several applications of these measures.

Models of marital status

Marital status is pertinent to the study of fertility because in most countries the great bulk of childbearing occurs to currently married women. The standard tabulation plan and country report deal with age at first marriage, and the incidence of marital dissolution and remarriage, because of their relevance to fertility. One of the central tasks in the study of fertility trends is the allocation between changes in marital exposure and changes in marital fertility.

Some WFS-related analyses have been conducted with the various aspects of marital exposure as the object of study, not just as determinants of fertility. Three of these will be considered here, two from the *Scientific Reports* and one from the *Technical Bulletins* series.

The first, by Smith (1981a), is an application, at least in part, of the life-table methodology described in Smith (1980b). Much of the analysis is very straightforward. Using the marriage histories from a survey of ever-married women, the conditional probability of divorce during year of duration d, given that a woman was married at the beginning of that year, is calculated as the following ratio. First, women married less than a full d years ago are excluded from the calculation. Second, the denominator of the ratio consists of all women who were still in their first marriage at the beginning of year d. Third, the numerator consists of those women (from the denominator) who were divorced during that year. These probabilities can be manipulated in the usual way to calculate the life-table proportions divorced by duration d. Similar life tables can be prepared for widowhood and for the sum of widowhood and divorce. Using the entire sample in this way, let $1-_1q_{i-1}$ be the probability that a marriage ended between duration i-1 and duration i. (We have modified Smith's notation to simplify this exposition.)

Smith then proposes a novel procedure for including covariates. His approach serves much the same function as hazard models, with less computational complexity. He does not establish a formal linkage with hazard models, although such a linkage would be useful; the simpler methods could perhaps be acceptable for exploration or selection leading to a hazard formulation.

Let the individual-level analogue of $1-_1q_{i-1}$ consist of a binary variable y_i, which is 0 if the first marriage ended between exact durations i-1 and i, and 1 if it continued. If a woman lacked full exposure to the interval, then she is dropped. Thus the expectation of y_i is $1-_1q_{i-1}$, and the difference $z_i = y_i-(1-_1q_{i-1})$ is the deviation from this expectation. Smith regresses z_i on a set of regressor values x_{ji}, which can vary across durations i, using regression coefficients b_j which do not vary across durations. That is, $z_i = \sum b_j x_{ji}$. Smith obtains interpretable results and the method merits further consideration.

An illustrative analysis by Trussell (1980) and a *Technical Bulletin* by Rodríguez and Trussell (1980) are essentially companion pieces and will be described together. Both papers deal with methods for fitting, smoothing and parameterizing distributions of age at first marriage. This distribution is usually computed by bringing together the survey of ever-married women and the household survey (except for countries which had all-women surveys), and is usually expressed as the cumulative proportion of women in a birth cohort who are ever married by age x. Under a synthetic cohort interpretation, the distribution can be prepared from household data alone, because the data give a woman's age and marital status although not her age at first marriage.

The work of Coale on this distribution is well known (Coale and McNeil 1972). It may be remarked here that he noted an extraordinary regularity across countries and dates in the distribution of age at first marriage. He found that observed distributions could be fitted well as a transformation of a standard distribution derived from first marriage frequencies in Swedish data for 1865–69. Three indices were involved in the transformation: c, the proportion eventually marrying; k, the initial age at which an appreciable number of women marry; and a, a measure of the central age at marriage but not a standard one such as the mean, median or mode. The two papers by Rodríguez and Trussell mark a substantial improvement in the interpretability and applicability of Coale's model, by replacing a and k with the mean μ and standard deviation σ of the age at marriage, and by developing a procedure which produces maximum likelihood estimates of μ, σ and c. (Obviously, these three parameters are interrelated. The value of c is not known for younger cohorts, and it must be estimated along with μ and σ.) The previous methods for estimating c, k and a, originally suggested by Coale, were quite sensitive to the rather poorly defined k, and were statistically inefficient.

Rodríguez and Trussell prepared a computer program, called Nuptial, which produces parameter estimates and fitted values. They applied this program to fit the age at first birth using the same standard schedules as for nuptiality. Elsewhere we have noted the evidence that age at first birth can serve as a starting point for motherhood or family building, with some advantages over age at first marriage. It is thus of interest that attempts to describe age at first birth as a transformation of the basic nuptiality schedule have been quite sucessful. Rodríguez and Trussell also show that the mean interval between marriage and first birth can be estimated simply as the difference between the means of the marriage and first birth fitted distributions.

Breastfeeding

Since the mid 1970s there has been an extraordinary increase in the importance attached to breastfeeding. Demographic interest has centred upon the fact that prolonged breastfeeding tends to lengthen substantially the interval of postpartum amenorrhoea, and thereby the interval to a subsequent birth. There is also interest in the action of breastfeeding in promoting child health and reducing mortality.

There is good reason to believe that WFS was a stimulus to this line of research and was, in turn, quite clearly responsive to the interests of demographers outside WFS. The core questionnaire obtained information about the breastfeeding of the two most recent births. A more general set of questions was prepared for the so-called Factors Other Than Contraception Affecting Fertility (FOTCAF) module. This module was prepared in co-operation with Leridon and Cantrelle and was mainly used in the African participating countries. At this point it appears not to have produced new analytic methods, and our discussion will be restricted to the basic breastfeeding information yielded by the core questionnaire.

The principal analytic advances regarding the impact of breastfeeding on fertility are contained in a scientific report by Page, Lesthaeghe and Shah (1982), which uses data from the Pakistan Fertility Survey. This illustrative analysis is based partly on Smith's technical bulletin on general methods of life-table analysis (1980b) and on a subsequent paper by J. W. McDonald (1981) which dealt specifically with breastfeeding life tables but never appeared in published form.

Although the basic methods used by Page, Lesthaeghe and Shah, such as life-table analysis to overcome censoring, hazard models and logit regression, are not formally advanced by their paper, there is nevertheless an exemplary application of these methods in a new way, setting a new standard for research on breast-feeding. Some of the more important of these applications will be singled out.

The authors note the implications of selecting just the open interval, or the open and closed intervals, or all intervals, for different kinds of censoring. They distinguish between the woman and the child as alternative units of analysis, and indicate the weighting procedures that allow a shift from one to the other.

Breastfeeding can legitimately have a duration of zero, if the child is born alive but almost immediately dies or if the infant is fed exclusively with powdered milk. Since a duration of zero is impossible with most other demographic event histories, Page, Lesthaeghe and Shah show how to handle such cases. Basically, they are ignored in the life-table calculations but are added or weighted back into the 'survivorship' distribution, expected duration of breastfeeding, and so on.

One of the major recommendations in their analysis is that current status information on breastfeeding should take the place of retrospective statements about earlier periods of breastfeeding. The term 'current status', of course, refers to whether the woman is or is not breastfeeding her youngest child at the date of the survey, according to the age of that child. This information is far more reliable than the retrospective variety and is also as up-to-date as possible. McDonald (1981) has described the procedures by which current status information may be used to construct life tables. He deals with the apparent major obstacle to the use of current status data, in that the observed proportion of children who are currently being breastfed in a cross-section need not decline monotonically with the age of the child, even though a cohort interpretation would of course require this to be the case. McDonald introduces from bio-statistics an algorithm for imposing monotonicity on the observed proportions. There are many potential applications of such a procedure to other types of current status data. For further refinements see Diamond, McDonald and Shah (1984).

If retrospective rather than just current information is used, perhaps because it will dramatically increase the effective case base, then Page, Lesthaeghe and Shah (1982) suggest several ways to compensate for its lesser quality. Due to the pronounced heaping of reported durations on certain months such as 6, 12, 18, 24, and so on, the authors recommend that intervals be centred on months 3, 6, 9, etc., and have a width of three months. This approach will largely overcome the upward bias which would occur if each interval began with a multiple of three months. Three other ways of smoothing these irregular distributions are also suggested. The first is a three-month weighted moving average of the original data; the second is a three-month moving median. Neither of these methods guarantees that the estimated proportion of women still breastfeeding at duration d will decline monotonically, however. The third procedure for smoothing the data does have this desirable property: the relational logit transformation. Lesthaeghe and Page earlier developed a 'standard' distribution for the duration of breastfeeding. This is applied to the Pakistan data through a two-parameter relational logit transformation, with an excellent fit. The two parameters of the transformation are helpful for comparing subgroups within the population.

Two multivariate procedures for describing differentials are also used, for greater statistical efficiency than a simple comparison of the parameters of the relational logit as just described. A binary variable, whether or not the mother was still breastfeeding a child at duration d, is regressed upon the following groups of variables: (1) d, d^2 and d^3; (2) age of the mother at the beginning of the interval and socio-economic predictors; and (3) interactions between all the terms in (1) and all the terms in (2). The three variables d, d^2 and d^3 are actually replaced by three orthogonal polynomials in d in order to eliminate collinearity; children who died before two years of age are eliminated; and only births in the 40 months before the interview are included.

In our view, this regression of a binary dependent variable upon a cubic in d and a host of interaction terms is not well motivated and the interpretation of its coefficients is difficult. With the authors, we prefer the logit regression approach which they also undertake. In their logit regression, age is the only demographic control. Parity and marital duration are omitted; period is implicit in the restriction to births in the past 40 months. Results are not presented in terms of coefficients, but in terms of fitted proportions still breastfeeding at durations of 12, 18, 24 and 30 months since childbirth, within combinations of age and predictors (all variables are expressed in categories). The authors note that a hazard model could serve the same purpose.

One of the most useful features of several of the illustrative analyses, and particularly this one, is the presentation of alternative methods varying in their difficulty and in the severity of their assumptions. This is especially useful when there have been very few advanced analyses of the topic under discussion, and guidelines are needed for the intelligent adaptation of complex general methods.

An integrated model of the proximate determinants

A recent reconceptualization by Hobcraft and Little (1984) of Bongaarts' model for the proximate determinants exemplifies the translation by WFS of aggregate methods down to the level of the individual. It is possible that this particular development, whose ramifications are yet to be fully explored, will prove to be one of the most useful methods for future analysis of fertility surveys. The method to be described here rests heavily on earlier work by Bongaarts and by Gaslonde (Gaslonde and Carrasco 1982). Those linkages will not be given here in any detail because they are clearly indicated by Hobcraft and Little (1984). This summary will concentrate on the main conceptual features of the method, keeping the notation to a minimum and simplifying it where necessary.

The well-known decomposition by Bongaarts (1978) serves the function of allocating to the various intermediate variables or proximate determinants the 'shortfall' in the fertility of an aggregate, relative to its potential maximum. The maximum is reduced in proportion to the person-years spent in the unmarried (unexposed) state, the level of contraceptive use, the extended post-partum amenorrhoea due to prolonged lactation, and the use of induced abortion. Although other factors could be included, these four are generally the most important. The factors which represent these proximate determinants can be calculated from an aggregate observed in a cross-section – for example, from the proportions currently married, currently using contraception, currently breastfeeding by age of child – and, for the case of abortion, by the fraction of conceptions in some interval of time which have ended in an abortion. The indices are conditional, i.e. are hierarchically ordered, such that all women are in the denominator of the married index, only married women are in the denominator of the contraceptive index, and so on. The indices can be calculated for different populations or sub-populations to show how different groups use different mechanisms to suppress their fertility below its potential maximum, which is never actually observed.

The individual-level form of the model replaces cross-sectional counts with allocation of time by individuals, a rather common type of translation (in either direction) in demography, but one which is new in this context. Thus, an interval of time such as one year or five years is selected (three years is claimed to be optimal), and within that interval the proportions of time spent in each of several states are calculated. Seven exhaustive and mutually exclusive states are defined, and the proportions of time spent in each of them are $d(m)$, never married; $d(u)$, ever married but not currently in a union; $d(c)$, in union but contracepting; $d(i)$, post-partum infecund; $d(1)$, lactationally infecund; $d(p)$, pregnant; and $d(f)$, the residual proportion of time at risk of conceiving. Because of the definition of $d(f)$, these proportions will add to unity. These individual proportions can be obtained from the birth history, marital history, and questions about contraception, breastfeeding and amenorrhoea. The time interval of observation (e.g. three years) can be backdated to exclude the twelve months immediately prior to the date of the survey. This exclusion can be useful in order to avoid an underestimate of the proportion of time in the pregnant state. The pregnant state is then determined wholly by working back from a birth, with no use of self-reports on a current pregnancy. Pregnancies which ended in a non-live birth can also be included, although such pregnancy terminations are seriously under-reported. Note that abortion is not included explicitly in this model, except as a pregnancy outcome recorded in the pregnancy history. Of course, data which meet the full requirements of the model rarely exist, and available data must be adapted with strong assumptions.

The fertility rate for a group of women, or the mean number of births per woman in an interval of a year, is proportional to the average fraction of time that a woman in a group was pregnant, because there will be one live birth for every nine months spent in a viable pregnancy. Thus a formal linkage between the proportion of time pregnant and the proportion of time spent in other states is equivalent to a linkage between the aggregate proportions defined by Bongaarts. Hobcraft and Little actually propose two decompositions, one multiplicative and the other additive. The additive form is an identity drawn from the condition that the proportions must add to unity: $F = P \{1-d(m)-d(u)-d(c)-d(1)\}$, where $F = (12/9)d(p)$ is the observed individual-level 'fertility rate' and $P = (12/9)d(p)/\{d(p) + d(i) + d(f)\}$ is the 'potential fertility rate' which would be observed for the woman if the proximate effects all acted to maximize her fertility, i.e. if $d(m)$, $d(u)$, $d(c)$ and $d(1)$ were all zero. The multiplicative form which is more closely analogous to the Bongaarts decomposition is $F = PC(m)C(u|m)C(c|mu)C(1|muc)$, with F and P defined as above and the other indices defined by:

$$C(m) \quad = \quad 1-d(m),$$
$$C(u|m) \quad = \quad \{1-d(m)-d(u)\}/C(m),$$
$$C(c|mu) \quad = \quad \{1-d(m)-d(u)-d(c)\}/C(u|m), \text{ and}$$
$$C(1|muc) \quad = \quad \{1-d(m)-d(u)-d(c)-d(1)\}/C(c|mu).$$

(To repeat, there is not a strict correspondence between our notation and that in the original paper.) These terms are all conditional upon the order of effects. The potential fertility, P, can be calculated by dividing F by the other terms on the right-hand side of the above equations.

Hobcraft and Little apply this approach to data from the Dominican Republic survey in two different ways. The first is quite parallel to that developed by Bongaarts. Using the average values of F and the C proportions within education and residence categories, they calculate the potential fertility P in each group and link it to F by a sequence of proportionate reductions. In so far as the terms are comparable, there is good correspondence with the Bongaarts coefficients.

Second, strictly at the individual level, F and P are taken as the dependent variables in regressions on age, education, region and type of place of residence. Since these four independent variables are employed in categorical form, the results are presented in MCA format. P is regarded as an adjusted value of F, net of the effects of the measured proximate determinants. That is, the potential fertility P describes what an individual woman's fertility would be if variation in the intermediate variables were controlled; the coefficients from the latter regression express the 'direct' (as contrasted with 'indirect') effects of these covariates. The coefficients from the regression of F on the other variables may be described as 'total' effects. It may be mentioned that if all the proximate determinants could be measured and included in the model, then variations in P should be due entirely to variations in biological fecundity. The model described above falls short of this goal because it excludes some variables, such as frequency of intercourse, measures others imperfectly, and is limited to a relatively short period of observation of the woman. The authors prefer the additive to the multiplicative decomposition because it is not conditional upon the order of the terms — except in the sense that ambiguous cases must still be resolved in some way. For example, if a woman is both breastfeeding and contracepting at the same time, then she is classified as breastfeeding.

Hobcraft and Little indicate, but do not actually demonstrate, that a full causal model could be estimated at the level of the individual. In such a model, the proximate determinants would be regressed upon the predictors, and F could be regressed upon all the prior variables, with some restrictions on the coefficients for the proximate determinants. The potential for such modelling seems promising.

Infant and child mortality

One of the major unexpected strengths of the World Fertility Survey has been in the measurement of infant and child mortality. This topic was incorporated in the birth history primarily for the purpose of eliciting births which had resulted in early deaths. However, the responses have been of sufficient quality to generate analyses of mortality in its own right. We shall focus here on only one paper, by Hobcraft, McDonald and Rutstein (1983), which applies hazard models to the basic question: what is the impact of child spacing on mortality? Because their approach seems to be original, it will be discussed in some detail.

Although it is not a theoretical necessity that the predictor variables be categorized for a hazard analysis, it is much easier to work with existing computer programs if they are. For this reason, childspacing is not represented in the obvious way, as the length of the preceding birth interval, but as the number of births in two-year time intervals prior to the birth of the 'index' child. The authors use three intervals: 0-2, 2-4 and 4-6 years (more precisely, 0-23 months, 24-47 months and 48-71 months). As will be seen below, a coding system is used to combine most of the information from the two earliest intervals.

Subsequent birth intervals are measured by a binary variable, whether or not there was a birth 0-18 months or 0-30 months after the index child, the interval depending upon the type of mortality being investigated. Deaths to the index children are analysed in four intervals: the first month (neo-natal), the remainder of the first year (post-neonatal), the second year or deaths while age 1 (toddler), and the third to fifth years or deaths while age 2-4 (child). The subsequent birth interval of 0-18 months is included for toddler mortality, and the subsequent interval of 0-30 months for child mortality. Obviously, subsequent birth intervals are omitted from models for neo-natal and post-neonatal mortality.

The model will be presented in two forms: first, without covariates, and second, with education as an illustrative covariate. Define i, j, k and l as follows:

$i = 0, 1, 2+$ is the number of births 0-2 years before the index child
$j = 0, 1, 2+$ is the number of births 2-4 years before the index child
$k = 0, 1, 2+$ is the number of births 4-6 years before the index child
$l = 0,1$ is the number of births 0-18 (or 0-30) months after the index child.

Two other codes are constructed from i, j and k. The first of these is n, which is 1 if there have been no births at all in the previous six years and 0 otherwise. To a considerable extent, n serves to identify first births. The other code, h, is basically the sum of j and k and gives the number of births 2-6 years before the index child, coded as 0, 1, 2, 3+. Although all of the indices listed here are assigned numerical codes, they are treated as categorical. Index children and deaths to these children are organized into two tables. N_{ijk} is the number of children surviving at the start of the age range (for each of the four kinds of mortality).

Children are excluded if they were not born long enough ago to be observed for the full five years before the survey. D_{ijk} is the subset of those children who died within the interval of age. The model without covariates is $\ln(\hat{D}_{ijk}) = \ln(N_{ijk}) + a + Z_i + S_h + ZS_n$ for neo-natal and post-neonatal mortality and $\ln(\hat{D}_{ijk}) = \ln(N_{ijk}) + a + Z_i + L_l$ for toddler and child mortality.[1] The second form thus eliminates the term ZS_n, which essentially identifies first-born children and becomes statistically insignificant, and replaces it with L_l to identify subsequent births. The reasoning behind this change, of course, is that after a first-born child has survived for a full year, then competition with a later child for nurturance and resources may become problematic. These models were developed through a selection process, and the D and N arrays are presented in terms of i, j and k, even though the indices on the right-hand side are recoded from these three, because in other applications some other recoding might be optimal.

Hobcraft, McDonald and Rutstein (1983) incorporate education as a covariate with an additive term and an interaction term. Specifically, if m = 0, 1-3, 4-6, 7+ denotes the mother's years of education, and if p is a binary index with value 1 if i = 0 and m = 0-3 and value 0 otherwise, then the terms M_m and ZM_p are added to both of the above models. The interaction term ZM_p conveys the probable circumstance that the amount by which increased education will reduce mortality differs by whether the child was or was not preceded by a short interval. Whether this interaction term is statistically significant, and whether the binary index p captures it optimally, are empirical questions which were considered by the authors.

The D and N arrays, which are four-dimensional if education is included and three-dimensional if it is not, are used to test and estimate these models with Glim, assuming a Poisson error structure for the observed counts.

It is not clear to us that the models employed by these authors were specified optimally. The use of birth counts in two-year windows, rather than the lengths of the birth intervals which immediately precede or follow the specified birth, leaves some questions unanswered. In particular, we do not know the effect of marginal increases in lengths of birth intervals, and there is a confounding of interval lengths and close sibling counts. Even so, the method is innovative and the results should be useful.

As is our practice, we shall not present the empirical findings in Hobcraft, McDonald and Rutstein (1983) other than to state that short prior birth intervals appear to have a dramatic effect on child survival in all WFS countries — a stronger effect than any other source of variation.

25.4 Conclusion

This chapter has described a number of accomplishments which can be attributed in large part to the existence of the WFS programme. It may be appropriate to identify some areas, within the purview of this chapter, which have not seen the kinds of advances one might have hoped for.

First, although a great deal of effort went into the evaluation of the quality of WFS data, particularly the birth histories, as described in other chapters, scarcely any attention was paid to the impact of such evaluations upon the analysis. There seems to have been an extraordinary separation between these two activities. In country after country, the analysts either explicitly or implicitly ignored the fact that an evaluation had been done. There appears to be a need for more pointed conclusions from these evaluations, and also for research which will indicate the likely impact of age heaping, memory recall failure, interval distortion, etc., upon demographic and statistical measures.

Second, the same kind of point can be made about sampling error. WFS invested unprecedented levels of resources in the estimation of sampling errors. This effort has been hailed elsewhere as a major achievement. Yet the fact remains that almost no analysts paid any attention at all to the extensive tabulations of sampling errors which appeared in the First Country Report. This situation can be blamed partly on the analysts, but it is also due to the absence of convenient procedures for actually employing these estimates. WFS could have attempted to develop such procedures.

Third, WFS has contributed relatively little to the causal modelling of socioeconomic or background variables, although creative use has been made of the proximate determinants and of demographic 'control' variables as described in the body of this chapter. For the most part, the effects of explanatory variables have been analysed in a rather shallow manner. This author has argued elsewhere, in his own analyses of WFS data, that the cross-sectional nature of the surveys and the rather coarse variables usually available serve to justify such shallow interpretation, and it is possible that nothing elegant could in fact have been done with such data. But perhaps more methodological effort could have been fruitfully expended in this direction.

WFS appears to have made major contributions to analytic methods in the adaptation of linear models to individual-level measures of fertility and of life tables/hazard models to demographic event histories. This chapter has reviewed a range of such applications made by WFS staff and consultants or contractors. It is hoped that this review will have the function of stimulating further applications as well as summarizing, and to some extent integrating, this work.

There have been other kinds of significant contributions — apart from those which, as stated in the introduction, are discussed in other chapters. Two of these will be mentioned briefly. The first is the development of computer software. Some packages, such as Nuptial, have been mentioned already; other exportable programs include Clusters, for the calculation of standard errors, and Fertrate, for the calculation of several kinds of fertility rates. Other procedures described here have also been programmed and could be made generally available. A second type of contribution has been in the presentation of results. Several papers by WFS staff, such as Rodríguez and Cleland (1981a), have been particularly effective in their use of graphics and in the presentation of fitted values rather than estimated coefficients. The importance of such techniques and of software should not be underestimated, because they help to demonstrate the utility of new procedures and may result in a more rapid diffusion of the procedures into general use.

In this admittedly biased author's view, the developments and applications described here are among the most exciting and creative methodological work done by demographers in recent years. In potential value and also in sheer quantity, the contributions of the small group of researchers whose names have repeatedly occurred rank with those of any university-based group in the world. And this review has almost totally bypassed the substantive contributions of the same researchers and of others at WFS whose activity was analytical but not to a major degree methodological.

How did these activities develop within a non-academic setting, in an organization whose mandate was primarily to describe fertility levels and variations in developing countries? This task could ostensibly have been achieved, as mentioned in the introduction, with the First Country Report, or even a less thorough reporting format. Accepting the premise that the methodological innovations described here are valuable for our understanding of fertility and related variables, and do not represent useless sophistication for its own sake, what circumstances led to their development?

It is only possible to answer this question in a speculative and in part a rather personal way, based on this author's extended contact with WFS. Several factors appear to have been conducive to this work, and they will be listed and described briefly.

A stimulating, research-oriented environment had its roots in the highest levels within WFS. The limitation of this chapter to analytic methods as such should not obscure the overall breadth of WFS research, which encompasses many more individuals and topics than are included here. Virtually all of the professional staff were active researchers. Management and administrative activities were kept to a minimum. Work was shared and discussed. One notes particularly the high proportion of papers with joint authorship as an indication of the level of collegiality, communication and research emphasis.

The recruitment of staff and of contractors was auspicious. The importance of this factor must not be underestimated, even though it is very difficult to trace the mechanisms behind it. WFS had the resources to be highly competitive in attracting good staff; its non-profit status and scholarly credentials may have helped; and its location in London was clearly a bonus for staff and visitors. The staff represented a range of complementary skills and, of special relevance to the advances described here, they included statisticians and also demographers with strong statistical backgrounds, who were given the freedom to pursue their own ideas.

Related to the above features was the importance of links with universities and scholars around the world. WFS was sharply distinguished from many other data collection programmes by its emphasis on analysis and its collaboration with university-based researchers. One can easily imagine an alternative scenario in which WFS might have taken a proprietary approach to datasets, opposed rather than initiated joint research projects, workshops and conferences, and in other ways erected obstacles to creative work. On the contrary, however, it is probably fair to say that WFS staff participated openly and equally with population studies centres of the highest standing. Many staff members came to WFS from an academic setting and/or have moved over to one. Related to this point, WFS was able to maintain an independence from its funding sources and had considerable freedom in setting its research priorities.

Two rather more tangible factors were the computing facilities and the publication system. Although the importance of computing facilities and WFS software was not fully recognized until about 1977, they later became major strengths. The existence of fully edited Standard Recode files, a WFS-specific version of SPSS, a fully-supported version of Glim and an efficient in-house computer were conducive to the research described here. Some of the analysis staff were excellent programmers in their own right, a skill which they could freely exercise with the in-house facilities.

The publication programme was also an instrumental factor. As described in the introduction, it helped to define the objectives and the target audiences for WFS activities. The technical bulletins, scientific reports, comparative studies, etc., were not just outlets for research, in the sense that scholarly journals tend to be; they also gave definition to that research. Each series developed from a plan of work. Each publication provided a deadline, albeit flexible, for its authors, as well as a reward through the recognition of authorship.

The factors listed here are rather general and diffuse and are not confined to methodological developments as distinguished from other kinds of research. Yet we suggest that it is ingredients such as these which led to the creativity and productivity of WFS analysts and which may be expected to do the same in future projects of this kind.

Note

1.   The subscripted variables Z, S, ZS and L are binary variables which identify the numbers of births in intervals before and after the birth of the index child.

26

Date Imputation

James Trussell

26.1 Introduction[1]

A primary objective of the World Fertility Survey was to produce high-quality data in standard form and to make those data available as soon as possible. As a corollary to the goal of producing high-quality data, those in the central staff at WFS made every attempt to avoid having variables with missing data codes. The felt, and this belief is shared by many analysts outside WFS, that the convenience of being able to run standard analysis programs without elaborate checks for missing data, especially missing dates of births or marriages, far outweighs the potential bias introduced by imputation or editing. As a consequence, standard recode files have few variables with missing values.

The objective of this chapter is to assess empirically whether this belief, which formed a central strand of WFS's archiving and analysis policy, is correct. The focus is exclusively on the automatic imputation of precise birth dates for children whose dates are not fully reported in the maternity history. Many important WFS analyses are concerned with the timing of successive births. We wish to discover whether the results of these analyses could have been biased by massive imputation of birth dates.

The WFS standard operating procedure for data production was fairly labour-intensive. While the term editing (correction of faulty or inconsistent information) is usually distinguished from imputation (assignment of values to missing observations), this distinction is in practice seldom rigid and seems to have been even less rigid than usual at WFS. Imputation and editing occur in many phases of data production. First, the respondent may impute (guess) the answers to questions of which she is unsure. Secondly, the interviewer may impute answers not supplied by the respondent or may edit inconsistent or obviously defective information. Taped recordings of interviews reveal that the respondent and interviewer may bargain over the correct response (Thompson, Ali and Casterline 1982). A third stage of editing/imputation occurs in the field office, and a fourth (final) stage occurs in the central collection office within the host country, although it was sometimes performed in the WFS central office in London. Thereafter, corrections to the standard recode files were made, when necessary, to correct errors discovered by users.

Given these stages, it is clear that an evaluation of the overall imputation process would be difficult, if not impossible. Much of the information about manual editing and imputation in the field is simply not retrievable. Hence, the only bounded and feasible task is to evaluate the final imputation stage conducted either in the host country or (more rarely) in London. Even this task would be far too expensive, as the following description implies. Once the raw data tape has been assembled, editing/imputation is split into two parts. The first is concerned with *dates*. The WFS-provided computer software package DEIR (date edit, imputation and recode) reads and evaluates all dates (birth, marriage, sterilization).[2] Missing dates are imputed where possible. The output includes a file containing standard recode variables located in positions 17–510 and a detailed list of records with erroneous dates, which are converted into a code 9999 for missing values. These are examined individually by hand and are 'corrected' in the raw data file. DEIR is then run on the new raw data file. This process is repeated until DEIR reports no errors. A more detailed description of DEIR is provided in section 26.2 below.

A second computer program, which is usually tailored to a specific country, produces the other standard recode and country-specific variables. These are then examined for obvious errors, including out-of-range values and missing codes. Practice has varied among surveys, but in general there has been some attempt to resolve errors by examining the original questionnaires. Many times other available information in the questionnaire can be used to form an educated guess for missing or out-of-range values.

We decided from the outset to limit our inquiry to an analysis of the machine imputation of dates by DEIR. To evaluate imputation of other standard recode variables would have required considerable amounts of WFS central staff time. Likewise, we decided to restrict even our limited inquiry, because manual fixing of errors spotted by DEIR also requires considerable time. Hence, birth records produced by DEIR with missing dates were dropped from files produced for subsequent substantive analyses used later in this chapter to assess the effects of imputation.

Our general strategy is as follows. We start from a situation in which all relevant dates are known (though they may be incorrect). Specifically, we use the data from the Republic of Korea Fertility Survey (KFS) because it is the only WFS survey in which month and year of birth was provided for all births in the raw data file. An additional advantage of the KFS is that date reporting appears to be very accurate. We then adopt several strategies for selectively removing some of these dates and then recovering them by imputation. We next assess the effects of imputation by replicating previous multivariate analyses of determinants of birth interval length and infant mortality on both the original 'true' file and the imputed files and comparing results. These two previous analyses have been chosen because of the importance of their substantive conclusions and because they appear to be heavily dependent on the accuracy of birth dating. This study is meant to complement the assessment of machine-editing policies of the World Fertility Survey completed by Pullum, Özsever and Harpham (1984).

26.2 Imputation with DEIR

A full description of DEIR would include minute details that are extremely tedious. Nevertheless, we must provide some of those details here because they bear directly upon our later evaluations. We confine our description to the imputation of dates of birth of children, though similar rules are used to impute other dates. In general, WFS allows births to be dated in four ways. The first attempt is to obtain from the respondent year and month of birth. Sometimes only the year is provided. In either case, this type of information is called Type 1. If not only the month but also the year is unknown, the interviewer is normally instructed to ask either how long ago the birth took place (Type 2 information) or the age of the child at the interview, obviously not asked about children who have died (Type 4). In most surveys, Types 2 and 4 information is recorded in years only, i.e. years ago or age in years. A final source of information in a few surveys, usually collected only if all previous questions fail to elicit answers, is the age of the mother at the time of birth (Type 3 information). Additional information, the interval in months for the previous birth, is sometimes collected and may be employed by DEIR to set constraints on possible birth dates. When using DEIR, the analyst must specify a hierarchy of information type to be used in determining the year and month of birth required for the standard recode tape. WFS practice is usually to accept Type 1 information first. The type specified to be second in priority depends on the wording of the questions for a particular country, but normally would be Type 2 or Type 4. Once this hierarchy is specified, DEIR next constructs a logical range (the lower and upper limits for the date) for each date of birth. This range determines the set of possible birth dates. If month and year are provided, then this range is zero; the last month in which the birth could have occurred is the same as the first, so that the set of possible birth dates includes only one month. If only the year is provided, then the range is 11 months (a set of 12 possible months). Initial logical ranges are calculated in similar fashion for the other data types. For Types 2 and 4, the analyst must specify how 'years ago' or 'age' are to be interpreted. For example, the reported age of a child may be interpreted as completed years (age at *last* birthday), rounded years (age at *nearest* birthday), or projected years (age at *next* birthday). In each case, an initial logical range of 11 months is defined. In the second stage, the initial logical ranges, either 0 months if the month and year of birth are given or 11 months if other data types are used, must be compared to ensure that they are compatible. For example, the user may stipulate that births (except multiple births) be separated by a minimum of m (usually seven) months. Similarly, data on the length of the interval from the previous birth may (if available and desired) be used to place further constraints on the logical range. Likewise, children may not be born after the date of sterilization or after the date of interview or before the date of birth of the previous child (birth order is inferred from the order of the listing in the file) and may be constrained by the analyst not to occur before marriage.

If, after adjustment for all constraints, the logical range is non-negative, then

DEIR imputes the date of birth, with each possible month of birth defined by the final logical range having an equal probability of being selected. On the other hand, if the final logical range is negative or is undefined because *no* information on date of birth is available, then no imputation is performed and a code of 9999 (missing) is given for the date of birth. All such errors are listed. The analyst then examines these by hand and 'corrects' each error. Some errors are the result of obvious transposition of digits; for example, the years of birth of four consecutive children might be given as 53, 55, 75, and 59, where the third date should clearly be *57*, not *75*. Regardless of whether month of birth of the fourth child is given, DEIR will change the date to 9999 in this example, because the fourth birth appears to occur before the third birth. In order to proceed, the analyst would have to correct the third date manually (to *57* from *75*).

26.3   Methods and data

As stated earlier, we decided to limit our evaluation to the stage in which dates are imputed by DEIR. Our next decision was to pick appropriate WFS countries for experimentation. We chose to experiment on the Republic of Korea Fertility Survey, because dates of birth were available on the raw data type for all children in month and year form. A recent Cross-National Summary (Chidambaram and Sathar 1984) provides comparative information for other WFS surveys.[3] Other countries with 100 per cent reporting of month and year of birth are Colombia, Venezuela, Costa Rica and Mexico, but figures for these countries reflect the situation *after* imputation by an *ad hoc* program used before the data were transmitted to London. In contrast, only 11 per cent of birth dates were reported in month/year form in Yemen AR, 11.6 per cent in Mauritania, 12.3 per cent in Bangladesh, and 12.4 per cent in Benin. In most countries, the majority of births had at least a calendar year reported. There are, however, exceptions; the proportion of birth dates imputed from a question on years ago or current age was 85.2 per cent in Bangladesh, 51.1 per cent in Egypt, 43.1 per cent in Indonesia, 37.4 per cent in Nigeria, 25.4 per cent in Morocco, 22.3 per cent in Jordan, and 15.6 per cent in Ivory Coast.

Our strategy for assessing the likely impact of massive imputation of month of birth is to remove artificially the month (and year) of birth and impute the date from the number of years ago that the birth occurred. This number was calculated correctly (based on a completed year's interpretation) from the date of birth of the child before the date was removed. Except for sampling variation due to the fact that imputation is random within a 12-month or somewhat shortened 'window', the following experiments are equivalent in the sense that *month* of birth is imputed from a set (without constraints) of 12 possible months:

1   remove month but keep calendar year → impute calendar month;

2   remove month and year and replace with age at interview (or hypothetical age if the child died) → impute year and month;

3 remove month and year and replace with 'years ago' → impute year and month.

For options 2 and 3, one must specify an interpretation of years ago or age as completed, rounded or projected years. Provided that the *same* interpretation is used in discarding the date and in imputation by DEIR, then options 2 and 3 are truly identical. Option 1 is not identical to the other two because it preserves the number of births in each calendar year. Even on average 2 and 3 will not result in the correct number of births in each *calendar* year because births do not occur uniformly over time. In our own analysis, described below, the reference periods are years before the survey and not calendar years; in this case, options 2 and 3 preserve the correct number of births in each year. We concentrate in the main text on option 3, in which age is 'reported' as completed years so that sensitivity to the wrong interpretation of age or years ago can be assessed as well. Results for option 1 are confined to appendix B.

Next we had to decide which dates were to be discarded and replaced by imputed dates. We settled on four experiments:

1 R33: remove randomly one-third of dates;

2 R67: remove randomly two-thirds of dates;

3 ED: remove dates based on the education of the mother
      no schooling — remove 70 per cent of dates
      1–5 years of schooling — remove 40 per cent of dates
      6+ years of schooling — remove 10 per cent of dates

4 SURV: remove dates based on survival of the child
      died — remove 75 per cent of dates
      survived — remove 25 per cent of dates.

Options R33 and R67 were chosen to see whether more imputation resulted in less precise estimates (described below). Options ED and SURV were chosen because it is well documented that reporting of dates varies with education of the mother and with survival status of the child (Chidambaram and Sathar 1984). Systematic variation in the proportion of birth dates requiring imputation depending on the values of these two variables was also induced for substantive reasons that are described below.

As stated above, we also have the opportunity to assess the error which arises if the analyst chooses the wrong interpretation of answers to 'years ago' or age of the child. It is very unlikely indeed that all women use the same interpretation; even the same woman may report rounded years for one child and completed for another. Hence, whatever interpretation is selected by the user of DEIR, it is almost certain not to be correct for all relevant cases. Those who have prepared WFS standard recode files for the data archive (and hence distribution) have almost always opted for the 'completed years' interpretation.

Chidambaram and Pullum (1981) have shown that in Bangladesh (where 51 per cent of dates were imputed from the 'years ago' question), a change in interpretation from the standard *completed* years to *rounded* years results in a time series of births that is more plausible. Specifically, a decline in the number of births between 1971 and 1972, caused by the war of 1971 and evident when only births with exact date are examined, is replicated only in the sequence based on a 'rounded years' interpretation. This finding, while interesting, provides little evidence on the correct interpretation of 'years ago' in other populations. We here do little to further this meagre knowledge; instead we simply explore how much of a difference the two interpretations make in substantive analyses described below.

Based on the previous discussion, we adopt a convention of identifying each of our Korea standard recode files by the name OPTION.INTERPRETATION. Options are TRUE, R33, R67, ED and SURV. Interpretations are c (completed), r (rounded) or p (projected).

26.4   Substantive analyses employed

We examine the effect of imputation in two substantive analyses performed latterly at WFS as part of the Comparative Studies series. One is an examination of the determinants of birth interval length (Rodríguez, Hobcraft, McDonald, Menken and Trussell 1984) and the other is an attempt to measure the effect of birth spacing on infant and child mortality (Hobcraft, McDonald and Rutstein 1983).

In the birth interval study, the investigators fit a common six-factor model to data from nine countries. They restricted their analysis to intervals begun during the period 1–15 years before the date of the survey. Using a hazard model framework, they modelled the effects on the log of the birth rate as a linear function of six factors: *duration* since the start of the birth interval, *length* of the previous interval, *age* of the woman at the start of the interval, *time period, education* of the woman, and *birth order* of the child that closed the interval (or would if the interval were not censored). In addition, interactions between duration and education and between duration and length of the previous interval are permitted. Only birth intervals of orders three to eight were examined. All factors are categorical, each having three categories, except duration with five. Their substantive results include the finding that length of the previous interval is an important determinant of current interval length, with long prior intervals being associated with long subsequent ones and vice versa. Only in Korea was birth order an important factor. Other factors proved to be important and each operated in the expected way.

Hobcraft, McDonald and Rutstein (1983) employed a probability model to estimate the effect of birth spacing on infant and child mortality in 26 populations. They limited the analysis to children born in the period 5–15 years before the survey in order to eliminate the censoring problem that would arise if more recent births were included. They modelled the log of the probability of death in each of two age intervals (neo-natal, up to one month and post-neonatal, months 1–12) to be a linear function of the number of births 2–6 years before the birth of the index child (S), the number of births 0–2 years before the birth of the index child (Z), and the mother's education (M). In addition, the effects of two interaction terms were estimated: ZS, no births either 0–2 or 2–6 years before the birth of the index child; and ZM, at least one birth 0–2 years earlier for mothers with 4+ years of education. All factors are categorical, with four categories for S (0, 1, 2, 3+), three for Z (0, 1, 2+) and four for M (categories depend on the country). Their main substantive result was a powerful effect of close prior spacing on increasing the risk of death of the index child,[4] which they attribute to competition between the index child and its older sibling(s) for limited resources.

Our procedure is to estimate the models employed in both of these substantive cross-national analyses on each of the Korean datasets that we obtained by discarding some of the dates and then imputing them. We are interested in determining how similar are results of models estimated on the distorted datasets to results of the same models estimated on the TRUE dataset. It must be emphasized that we are not seeking to judge absolute truth. It is very likely that many dates reported in our file labelled TRUE are in fact incorrect, and it is nearly certain that the models that we estimate are not the ones that determine outcomes in the real world. It should also be emphasized that the test we have devised is rather severe, for reasons given below. If we were interested in calculating only fertility rates for particular periods of time in the past, then we would expect the effects of imputation to be less pronounced.

Our expectations are qualitative only. First, we would not expect to find in practice very much variation in the size of estimated standard errors. Secondly, datasets with incorrect interpretations of r or p should produce contaminated parameter estimates (increasingly as we move from c to r to p). Our third expectation is that *any* imputation scheme will yield parameter estimates for the fertility and mortality analyses that are systematically distorted, even when the interpretation of years ago is correct. The reason is that both analyses employ explanatory variables whose values are affected by imputation. The distortion injected into the fertility analysis is most apparent. One of the explanatory variables is the length of the previous interval (LPI). Imputation of dates will result in incorrect classification of LPI for some births, thereby rendering the subsequent birth intervals for the three LPI categories more nearly alike. Such attenuation bias is well understood in the context of regression models and operates equally forcefully here. Imputation of dates will also result in incorrect assignments of current interval length. If we ignore the effect of censoring, we can see that the effect of imputation will be to make the number of births in each duration category more nearly equal. As a consequence, the fertility rates in each category will also be made more nearly equal; hence an attenuation bias in the effects estimates of the duration factor should also be observed.[5] In the mortality analysis, the effects of imputation are more difficult to predict. Clearly, the variables S and Z will be distorted, and we would expect a sort of attenuation bias. But the variables S and Z are clearly not independent, so that moving a birth from the period 0-2 years before the survey to the period 2-6 years before affects both S and Z simultaneously. Hence, we are unable to predict the impact of imputation on the S and Z effects estimates, other than to suspect that there will be distortion. Beyond these general expectations, it is difficult to provide more specific predictions.

Before proceeding to discuss the results, we should pause to consider just how the parameter estimates resulting from various imputation schemes should be compared. Probably the most helpful and reassuring result would be to find that all imputation schemes yielded identical parameter estimates; we could then conclude our chapter with an unqualified finding. For the reasons outlined above, we do not expect such a happy conclusion. The outcome next easiest to interpret would occur if parameter estimates differed but only within a band of uncertainty that would be expected from the attached standard errors. Under these circumstances, careful analysts would reach similar substantive conclusions. Again, we do not expect such a finding. All other outcomes are more difficult to interpret. If parameter estimates differ by amounts far larger than one would expect on the basis of estimated standard errors, then we cannot be sure whether the differences are a result of systematic bias in the imputation scheme or sampling error resulting from imputation. To discover the relative importance of each source of error, we would need to conduct a more elaborate Monte Carlo experiment, wherein multiple observations of a single imputation scheme would give an idea both of sampling variability around the sample mean and of bias (being estimated as the difference between the parameter estimate from the TRUE file and the sample mean of the estimates from the several runs). Due to the tremendous computing resources required, we could not run the same experiment many times. Hence, for each option described earlier, we examine just one realization of the possible outcomes. We are inclined, nevertheless, to attribute variation that does not exhibit a tendency for patterns in the magnitude and sign of the distortions across coefficients to sampling variability.

26.5   Results

In table 26.1 we show the characteristics of our set of standard recode files and of the subfiles created for the birth interval and infant mortality analyses. The percentages of births with date of birth imputed is 0 in the TRUE file, 34 in R33, 66 in R67, 33 in ED and 31 in SURV. The number of birth dates that could not be imputed by DEIR, due to an implied negative logical range, varies across datasets but is never large; the largest number occurs when the projected years ago interpretation is employed erroneously for answers that were given in completed years.

The absence of dates of birth for cases in which DEIR was unable to impute a birth date creates difficulties in preparing the mortality and birth interval subfiles. Ideally, we would have submitted these records to experienced WFS data

TABLE 26.1

Characteristics of Korean standard recode files constructed by discarding dates of birth and then imputing them. The total number of births is 19 400

File	Percentage of births with birth date imputed	No. of births with birth date missing (DEIR unable to impute)	No. of intervals available for birth interval analysis	No. of births available for mortality analysis
TRUE	0	0	10 087	8 874
R33.c	34	4	10 083	8 873
R33.p	33	136	9 908	8 687
R67.c	66	0	10 089	8 873
R67.p	65	168	9 823	8 577
ED.c	33	2	10 085	8 873
ED.r	33	14	10 107	8 871
ED.p	33	117	10 023	8 738
SURV.c	31	0	10 085	8 873
SURV.r	31	24	10 046	8 808
SURV.p	29	239	9 772	8 547

Note: Files are labelled OPTION.INTERPRETATION:.

OPTION designates which birth dates were removed and then imputed:
TRUE = original standard recode file, all birth dates given in month/year form
R33   = one-third of birth dates removed randomly
R67   = two-thirds of birth dates removed randomly
ED   = probability of birth date being removed depends on education of woman:
           (0 years → 70 per cent; 1–5 years → 40 per cent; 6+ years → 10 per cent)
SURV = probability of birth date being removed depends on survival status of child:
           (survived → 25 per cent; died → 75 per cent)

INTERPRETATION of 'years ago' or 'age':
c = completed years (age at last birthday)
r = rounded years (age at nearest birthday)
p = projected years (age at next birthday.

processing staff for resolution. Due to severe constraints on personnel time, this strategy was not possible. The only alternative was to delete records from the analysis subfile when the presence of a missing date would have introduced errors into the dataset. Suppose, for example, that the birth dates of the only three children of a woman in century months $(= 12 \star YR + MO)$ were *9999, 0781* $(= $ Jan. 1965), and *0805* (Jan. 1967). In the mortality analysis, we would have no way of knowing to which category (0-2 years before birth of the second child or 2-6 years before) the birth with missing birth date should be assigned. Likewise, we could not identify the length of the preceding interval for the third birth. The decision to eliminate contaminated records reduces the sample size, as can be seen from table 26.1; the maximum reduction is 4 per cent from SURV.c to SURV.p.[6] By default, therefore, we have introduced potential sample selection bias, which by design in some cases systematically depends on the education of the woman or the survival status of the child. Even with random discards

(R33 and R67), there will be a selection by number of children, with those having many children and thus shorter birth intervals on average being more likely to have at least part of their records deleted from the fertility and mortality analyses. The more obvious bias occurs for the mortality analysis, since dead children will be selectively removed. We have no clear expectation of the magnitude of such bias, but reason that it must be small given the relatively small proportion of cases lost.

Parameter estimates for two versions of models in the birth interval analysis are shown in tables 26.2 and 26.3 and those from the analysis of neo-natal and post-neonatal mortality are shown in tables 26.4 and 26.5. Standard errors corresponding to these parameter estimates are given in tables A1, A2, A3 and A4, respectively. These are confined to an appendix because they will not subsequently be discussed − there is relatively little variation across imputation options and what variation there is does not tend to be systematic; in particular, parameter estimates based on age interpretation p (projected years), with a correspondingly smaller sample size, are not uniformly or predominantly larger.

If we examine table 26.2 and then look at the magnitude of the relevant standard errors (table A1), we quickly realize that the parameter estimates do vary widely across columns, more widely by far than can be explained by the standard errors of the estimates.[7] First, consider just those imputation runs with an age interpretation of completed years (c) that can more reasonably be expected to yield the 'true' parameter estimates in column 1. There is much variation even among these; hence our initial impression is that imputation can lead to quite different parameter estimates, if *different* is interpreted relative to the attached standard error. We hasten to add that the standard error of the estimate is a correct measure of the variation we might expect due to hypothetical repeated observations of the entire sample provided that the model is consistent with the data. But the standard error is not a proper measure of the variation we should expect from imputation. We are interested in the standard error only because it is a measure of uncertainty commonly used by analysts. We also note that parts of the true sample and of each sample generated by each different imputation option are the same, due to the fact that not *all* dates were imputed. If we conducted a similar exercise in which only parts of the sample were discarded and replaced by another subsample, then the expected standard errors would be smaller than those given in the tables. Hence, since the observed deviation between parameter estimates based on 'truth' and an imputation scheme are larger than would be expected on the basis of estimated standard errors, they are even larger when judged relative to the smaller standard errors we would expect when the samples are not independent but in fact partially overlap.

In order to ensure that variability was not caused by an attempt to estimate a model more complicated than the data could reasonably support, we compare the parameter estimates from a main effects model (with 15 fewer or only half as many parameters) in table 26.3. The conclusion is, however, the same; and exactly the same conclusion is reached after scrutiny of parameter estimates for the mortality analyses shown in tables 26.4 and 26.5.

Examination of the main effects model in table 26.3 is far more revealing than scrutiny of the estimates in table 26.2 because effects estimates are always difficult to interpret when there are interaction terms. In table 26.3, we can clearly see the expected attenuation bias in the effects estimates for D and L. Recall that, subject to certain restrictions, DEIR imputes dates randomly from a possible set of 12 months, where each month has an equal probability of being selected. Such a selection procedure will, as argued earlier, have the effect of making birth rates for all duration categories more nearly equal; peaks will be lowered and valleys raised. As a consequence, we should expect the effects estimates of D to be driven towards zero and the constant term (grand mean) to be lowered in absolute value. This pattern is observed in every imputation run in table 26.3. A similar argument has been made about the effects estimates for L. Imputation will cause erroneous assignments to the three length-of-previous-interval categories; as a consequence, the power of this variable will be diluted and the effects estimates driven towards zero. This pattern, too, is observed in all imputation runs. Therefore, we have clear evidence of systematic bias injected into the fertility effects estimates by DEIR. This attenuation bias was predicted from first principles and is clearly displayed in table 26.3.

Attenuation is not evident, for several reasons, in the mortality analyses whose results are shown in tables 26.4 and 26.5. Age at death was not altered by the experiments, so there is no shifting of deaths from one duration category to another similar to the shifting of births in the fertility analysis. Moreover, there were separate mortality models for each duration-of-life category instead of a common model with duration as a covariate similar to that employed in the fertility study. Finally, the variables in the mortality analyses which correspond to the length of the previous interval in the fertility analysis are quite different in concept. It is certain that some 'index' births are assigned to the wrong categories of the Z (number of births 0–2 years before) and S (number of births 2–6 years before) variables, but the effect of such misclassification is not a simple attenuation bias. That some systematic 'distortion is caused by imputation is suggested by the fact that the effects estimates for Z2 are smaller in absolute value in all imputation runs than in the TRUE run.

From quantitative considerations, we must now turn to the question of whether different qualitative conclusions would be reached by analysts having access to only one of the sets of parameter estimates. In essence, we consider here whether analysts would draw different substantive conclusions. We do not ask this question in the literal sense, because different quantitative results will surely imply different substantive conclusions. However, we recognize that each careful analyst probably attaches a greater margin of uncertainty to his or her predictions about the effects of policy changes on fertility or mortality than would be implied by standard errors or goodness-of-fit measures resulting from estimation of a statistical model. In fact, most of us would be happy to be able

TABLE 26.2

Parameter estimates in the birth interval analysis: main effects plus D × L and D × E interactions model

	TRUE	R33.c	R33.p	R67.c	R67.p	ED.c	ED.r	ED.p	SURV.c	SURV.r	SURV.p
GM	-4.601	-4.673	-4.611	-4.812	-4.645	-4.626	-4.564	-4.487	-4.789	-4.737	-4.749
D2	1.256	1.167	0.966	1.324	0.853	1.214	1.034	0.862	1.526	1.189	1.158
D3	2.050	1.863	1.792	2.050	1.612	1.637	1.705	1.486	1.931	2.074	1.913
D4	2.160	2.139	2.021	2.218	2.026	2.047	1.917	1.816	2.339	2.207	2.141
D5	1.780	1.786	1.888	2.083	2.059	1.831	1.872	1.826	1.971	1.935	1.952
B2	-0.237	-0.257	-0.267	-0.255	-0.275	-0.249	-0.230	-0.275	-0.237	-0.258	-0.254
B3	-0.466	-0.485	-0.468	-0.476	-0.487	-0.484	-0.460	-0.477	-0.452	-0.500	-0.484
P2	0.128	0.131	0.051	0.138	0.002	0.144	0.084	-0.032	0.134	0.097	0.057
P3	0.255	0.250	0.218	0.241	0.152	0.263	0.212	0.157	0.256	0.204	0.207
A2	-0.219	-0.169	-0.136	-0.198	-0.117	-0.186	-0.212	-0.114	-0.202	-0.170	-0.121
A3	-0.807	-0.783	-0.780	-0.839	-0.659	-0.764	-0.784	-0.646	-0.808	-0.742	-0.681
L2	-0.770	-0.347	0.199	0.101	0.586	-0.079	0.056	0.430	-0.301	-0.007	0.278
L3	-0.356	0.040	0.668	0.257	0.453	0.032	0.349	0.652	0.064	0.450	0.744
E2	0.009	-0.001	-0.033	-0.166	-0.081	-0.267	-0.326	-0.183	0.072	-0.114	-0.077
D2L2	0.306	0.250	-0.175	-0.114	-0.036	0.011	0.060	-0.069	-0.149	-0.042	-0.436
D2L3	-0.273	-0.538	-0.293	-0.358	0.062	-0.231	-0.420	-0.244	-0.576	-0.491	-0.438
D3L2	0.603	0.350	-0.399	-0.236	-0.615	0.118	-0.061	-0.401	0.312	-0.270	-0.450
D3L3	-0.282	-0.550	-1.035	-0.715	-0.359	-0.326	-0.730	-0.769	-0.359	-1.012	-1.188
D4L2	0.825	0.389	-0.219	-0.003	-0.698	0.080	0.072	-0.413	0.281	0.092	-0.319
D4L3	-0.090	-0.471	-1.083	-0.703	-0.742	-0.439	-0.556	-0.842	-0.544	-0.856	-1.154
D5L2	0.446	0.147	-0.508	-0.421	-0.890	-0.200	-0.298	-0.630	-0.024	-0.244	-0.442
D5L3	-0.380	-0.748	-1.346	-1.036	-1.331	-0.716	-1.209	-1.464	-0.696	-1.165	-1.596
D2E2	-0.131	-0.171	-0.117	0.112	-0.032	0.021	0.178	-0.102	-0.280	0.001	0.004
D3E2	-0.022	0.014	0.085	0.064	0.051	0.374	0.415	0.181	-0.021	0.151	0.066
D4E2	-0.143	-0.085	-0.123	0.101	-0.019	0.229	0.229	0.077	-0.207	-0.008	-0.017
D5E2	-0.149	-0.208	-0.054	0.035	0.036	0.026	0.154	0.015	-0.262	-0.009	-0.056

Notes:

1 All variables are categorical, and the first category of each is omitted:

GM = constant
D = duration (completed months) since last birth: 8–17, 18–23, 24–29, 30–41, 42–59
B = birth order at end of interval: 3, 4–5, 6–8
P = period (completed years before survey): 1–5, 6–10, 11–15
A = age (completed years): 15–24, 25–34, 35–49
L = length of previous interval (completed months): 6–21, 22–41, 42+
E = maternal education (years): 0, 1–5.

2 Files are labelled OPTION.INTERPRETATION:

OPTION designates which birth dates were removed and then imputed:

TRUE = original standard recode file, all birth dates given in month/year form
R33 = one-third of birth dates removed randomly
R67 = two-thirds of birth dates removed randomly
ED = probability of birth date being removed depends on education of woman
     (0 years: 70 per cent; 1–5 years: 40 per cent; 6+ years: 10 per cent)
SURV = probability of birth date being removed depends on survival status of child
       (survived: 25 per cent; died: 75 per cent)

INTERPRETATION of 'years ago' or 'age':

c = completed years (age at last birthday)
r = rounded years (age at nearest birthday)
p = projected years (age at next birthday).

TABLE 26.3

Parameter estimates in the birth interval analysis: main effects model

	TRUE	R33.c	R33.p	R67.c	R67.p	ED.c	ED.r	ED.p	SURV.c	SURV.r	SURV.p
GM	-4.913	-4.754	-4.244	-4.640	-4.203	-4.636	-4.499	-4.130	-4.754	-4.555	-4.320
D2	1.355	1.183	0.746	1.221	0.830	1.185	1.039	0.725	1.234	1.060	0.793
D3	2.397	2.010	1.360	1.799	1.189	1.787	1.666	1.136	2.068	1.771	1.406
D4	2.655	2.288	1.618	2.134	1.451	2.100	1.927	1.410	2.364	2.114	1.689
D5	1.950	1.683	1.273	1.643	1.272	1.585	1.506	1.155	1.738	1.558	1.324
B2	-0.242	-0.258	-0.266	-0.255	-0.275	-0.251	-0.228	-0.270	-0.238	-0.258	-0.255
B3	-0.469	-0.484	-0.461	-0.473	-0.479	-0.482	-0.452	-0.465	-0.451	-0.495	-0.476
P2	0.129	0.130	0.047	0.139	-0.001	0.144	0.084	-0.036	0.134	0.098	0.052
P3	0.257	0.250	0.219	0.241	0.152	0.263	0.214	0.160	0.256	0.207	0.206
A2	-0.215	-0.167	-0.126	-0.195	-0.105	-0.185	-0.210	-0.110	-0.199	-0.167	-0.114
A3	-0.803	-0.783	-0.784	-0.843	-0.662	-0.768	-0.791	-0.658	-0.809	-0.746	-0.687
L2	-0.190	-0.053	-0.081	-0.038	0.038	-0.051	0.024	0.073	-0.139	-0.081	-0.072
L3	-0.578	-0.461	-0.189	-0.395	-0.127	-0.360	-0.281	-0.084	-0.425	-0.363	-0.237
E2	-0.091	-0.083	-0.078	-0.090	-0.074	-0.087	-0.097	-0.136	-0.089	-0.081	-0.076

Notes:

1 All variables are categorical, and the first category of each is omitted:

GM = constant
D = duration (completed months) since last birth: 8–17, 18–23, 24–29, 30–41, 42–59
B = birth order at end of interval: 3, 4–5, 6–8
P = period (completed years before survey): 1–5, 6–10, 11–15
A = age (completed years): 15–24, 25–34, 35–49
L = length of previous interval (completed months): 6–21, 22–41, 42+
E = maternal education (years): 0, 1–5.

2 Files are labelled OPTION.INTERPRETATION:

OPTION designates which birth dates were removed and then imputed:

TRUE = original standard recode file, all birth dates given in month/year form
R33 = one-third of birth dates removed randomly
R67 = two-thirds of birth dates removed randomly
ED = probability of birth date being removed depends on education of woman
(0 years: 70 per cent; 1–5 years: 40 per cent; 6+ years: 10 per cent)
SURV = probability of birth date being removed depends on survival status of child
(survived: 25 per cent; died: 75 per cent)

INTERPRETATION of 'years ago' or 'age':

c = completed years (age at last birthday)
r = rounded years (age at nearest birthday)
p = projected years (age at next birthday).

TABLE 26.4

Parameter estimates in the analysis of neo-natal mortality

	TRUE	R33.c	R33.p	R67.c	R67.p	ED.c	ED.r	ED.p	SURV.c	SURV.r	SURV.p
GM	-3.402	-3.448	-3.483	-3.387	-3.445	-3.450	-3.417	-3.386	-3.356	-3.516	-3.545
Z2	0.594	0.589	0.463	0.183	0.072	0.520	0.458	0.064	0.460	0.491	0.098
Z3	2.069	2.298	1.949	1.578	0.283	2.173	1.851	1.618	1.681	1.785	1.882
S2	-0.559	-0.474	-0.393	-0.496	-0.458	-0.491	-0.706	-0.567	-0.620	-0.365	-0.214
S3	-0.137	-0.085	0.036	-0.059	0.022	-0.144	-0.013	-0.087	-0.264	0.030	-0.004
S4	0.365	0.323	0.151	0.265	0.734	0.150	0.156	0.299	0.417	0.358	0.491
E2	-0.047	-0.034	-0.013	-0.030	-0.092	-0.003	-0.034	0.047	-0.041	-0.044	-0.083
E3	-0.225	-0.164	-0.320	-0.267	-0.356	-0.164	-0.225	-0.271	-0.283	-0.201	-0.256
E4	-0.401	-0.336	-0.495	-0.428	-0.576	-0.351	-0.375	-0.450	-0.492	-0.467	-0.471
ZS	0.559	0.438	0.185	0.676	0.724	0.557	0.543	0.636	0.743	0.417	0.351
ZM	-0.167	-0.337	0.147	0.017	0.016	-0.178	-0.040	0.237	0.025	-0.238	-0.338

TABLE 26.5

Parameter estimates in the analysis of post-neonatal mortality

	TRUE	R33.c	R33.p	R67.c	R67.p	ED.c	ED.r	ED.p	SURV.c	SURV.r	SURV.p
GM	-3.191	-3.166	-3.191	-3.169	-3.261	-3.218	-3.217	-3.352	-3.194	-3.287	-3.321
Z2	-0.314	-0.259	-0.089	-0.114	-0.332	-0.385	-0.415	-0.182	-0.593	-0.531	-0.634
Z3	0.766	0.654	0.173	0.575	0.175	0.643	0.158	0.387	0.307	0.543	0.232
S2	-0.258	-0.330	-0.354	-0.296	-0.428	-0.288	-0.193	-0.207	-0.214	-0.074	-0.048
S3	-0.414	-0.406	-0.380	-0.424	-0.285	-0.333	-0.402	-0.408	-0.330	-0.400	-0.284
S4	-0.063	-0.097	0.017	0.195	-0.014	-0.512	-0.266	-0.386	-1.133	0.122	-0.372
E2	-0.286	-0.280	-0.287	-0.278	-0.177	-0.254	-0.226	-0.216	-0.262	-0.131	-0.176
E3	-0.430	-0.474	-0.436	-0.507	-0.352	-0.399	-0.463	-0.313	-0.460	-0.330	-0.318
E4	-0.780	-0.819	-0.715	-0.869	-0.638	-0.759	-0.757	-0.608	-0.808	-0.730	-0.751
ZS	0.945	0.810	0.622	0.509	0.824	0.955	0.757	0.781	1.040	0.750	0.598
ZM	0.057	0.197	0.025	0.290	0.152	0.096	0.365	-0.047	0.306	0.036	-0.051

Notes to tables 26.4 and 26.5

Notes:

1 All variables are categorical, and the first category of each is omitted:

GM = constant
Z = number of births 0–2 years before birth of index child: 0, 1, 2+
S = number of births 2–6 years before birth of index child: 0, 1, 2, 3+
E = maternal education: 0, 1–3, 4–6, 7+
ZS = Z1 × S1
ZM = (1 – Z1) (E3 + E4).

2 Files are labelled OPTION.INTERPRETATION

OPTION designates which birth dates were removed and then imputed:

TRUE = original standard recode file, all birth dates given in month/year form
R33 = one-third of birth dates removed randomly
R67 = two-thirds of birth dates removed randomly
ED = probability of birth date being removed depends on education of woman
(0 years: 70 per cent; 1–5 years: 40 per cent; 6+ years: 10 per cent)
SURV = probability of birth date being removed depends on survival status of child
(survived: 25 per cent; died: 75 per cent)

INTERPRETATION of 'years ago' or 'age':

c = completed years (age at last birthday)
r = rounded years (age at nearest birthday)
p = projected years (age at next birthday).

to make an accurate prediction of the sign of the effect of a policy change and delighted to be able to distinguish accurately whether the effects would be small or large (even if these concepts are imprecise). When the question is viewed in this way and results are judged by the correspondingly more lenient criterion implied, is imputation innocuous?

The answer to this question appears to be much more encouraging. Interpretation of the interaction effects in table 26.2 is difficult in any event, so we confine our detailed examination to tables 26.3, 26.4 and 26.5. In the main effects birth interval model (table 26.3), we find the same shape of the underlying hazard by duration since the last birth, with a uniform peak in months 30–41. Likewise, we find identical patterns of birth-order effects, with third births occurring more quickly than fourth and fifth births, which in turn occur more quickly than births of orders six to eight. With the exception of R67.p and ED.p, both of which deliberately misinterpret the time location of births to be imputed, rates of childbearing decline as we move closer to the present ($p1 < p2 < p3$). Age effects are strong and in all cases have the expected pattern, with decreased rates of childbearing the older the woman at the start of an interval. The more educated women uniformly exhibit lower fertility. The effects estimates most likely to be interpreted differently, if analysts examined different sets of results, are those for length of the previous interval. Even here it is universally true that a long previous interval exerts a powerful tendency for the subsequent interval to be long. A previous interval of intermediate length should also exert a significantly negative effect relative to a short previous interval, though not so strongly as a long prior interval. This effect estimate is indeed negative in all cases with a correct interpretation c of years ago (or age), but it is significantly so in only one of four cases labelled c. Even with this limitation, it would be difficult not to detect the strong effect of length of previous interval unless the analyst completely misinterpreted the response to the years ago question (here simulated by an interpretation of p instead of c).

Conclusions reached after examination of the mortality analyses are no less strong. The neo-natal results are most consistent. Having two or more births in the two years before the birth of the index child exerts a powerful positive effect on the risk of death (powerful in all cases but R67.p, ED.p and SURV.p). Having only one birth in the period 2–6 years before the birth of the index child is associated with much lower mortality; having two children in the same window also lowers mortality relative to having none, though not by so much as having only one, while having three or more raises death rates significantly. Increased educational attainment is universally and monotonically associated with lower risks of death. Having no births in either the period 0–2 years or the period 2–6 years before the birth of the index child raises mortality of the index child (in most instances the *first* child) by a very large amount (by at least 60 per cent) in every run. The interactive term ZM is insignificant in every case.

The results for three variables — education, the ZS interaction and the ZM interaction — are the same in the analysis of post-neonatal mortality (table 26.5) as in the neo-natal analysis, so that they need not be repeated in detail. Having two births in the window 2-6 years before the birth of the index child is associated with the lowest level of post-neonatal mortality, with the next lowest level produced by having one birth (except for R67.p). The optimal number of births to have in the window 0-2 years before the birth of the index child is one, followed in order by zero and two or more; the effects estimates for Z2 are always negative and those for Z3 always positive, but the magnitudes do vary, especially for age interpretations other than the correct c.

26.6 Summary and conclusion

In this chapter we have evaluated the effects of date imputation in WFS surveys. To do so we assumed that dates reported by the respondent, or at least recorded by the interviewer, are correct. We then systematically removed dates from one survey with 100 per cent of dates reported (the Republic of Korea National Fertility Survey 1974) and recovered them by using the standard WFS imputation package DEIR. We produced a total of ten distorted standard recode files which were to be compared with the original undistorted (and assumed true) file. This set of ten different files differed in two respects. In some runs dates were removed randomly while in others those women with lower education, or those women whose children died, had a higher proportion of their children's birth dates removed and then recovered by imputation. The second respect in which imputation runs differed lies in the interpretation of age. Date of birth was imputed where necessary from the age of the child, given in *completed* years. Though age was recorded as age at last birthday, the analyst never can know whether the respondent calculated age in this way or in rounded years (nearest birthday) or projected years (next birthday). Hence in the runs all three possible interpretations were employed to test sensitivity to incorrect interpretation. In all imputations, date of birth was randomly chosen from a uniform distribution of 12 possible months,[8] since information on a child's age, assumed correct, narrowed the choice to a range of one year.

Once we had the set of one true and ten distorted standard recode files, we next had to consider how to determine the impact of imputation. We decided to use as a test the results from two multivariate analyses performed earlier at WFS as a part of the comparative analysis programme. One of these examined the determinants of birth interval length and the other the effect of previous birth interval on neo-natal and post-neonatal mortality. Hence, we compared the parameter estimates from the birth interval and mortality models estimated for the 'true' standard recode file with those based on the ten files with a lesser or greater extent of imputation. We concluded that the estimates varied much more than the estimated standard errors would imply. We, therefore, reasoned that differences are due to two sources: first, sampling variability due to random imputation; and secondly, systematic distortion introduced by the fact that no imputation scheme can avoid attenuation bias.

We emphasize here that our test is very stringent due to the fact that in our two substantive analyses attenuation bias cannot be avoided. Simpler calculations such as fertility rates by time period are likely to be far less distorted. Indeed, in some cases no distortion whatsoever is introduced. For example, if calendar year of birth is given and only the calendar month is imputed, imputation cannot affect fertility rates calculated for calendar years.

Based on our stringent test, we concluded, nevertheless, that the qualitative interpretation of the results would differ little according to whether the true file or an imputed version were used. The biggest differences occur exactly where expected, in those cases in which systematic bias was injected by imputing birth dates in a range that was one year too early, because age was interpreted (incorrectly) to mean projected years, not completed years. Even in these cases there was surprising consistency of results for most variables.

We close this exercise with several observations which capture what we have learned:

1 Variation in parameter estimates induced merely by sampling variability could be studied further by a simple Monte Carlo experiment in which the same birth dates were imputed several times.

2 If it is found that most of the variation is not due to sampling variability but rather to systematic bias induced by the imputation algorithm, then some consideration should be given to improving imputation by switching from a uniform distribution to one that more nearly reflects real reproductive behaviour. The evidence presented in appendix B suggests that the portion of variation attributable to systematic bias may be substantial. Nevertheless, no algorithm can avoid attenuation bias, so the search for the 'perfect' imputation scheme is illusory. We suspect strongly, however, that imputation schemes that introduce less distortion could be found.

3 When interpreting results, analysts should avoid making distinctions that are too fine. In particular, emphasizing one result because it is barely statistically significant while de-emphasizing another that just fails a significance test is probably a distinction without a real difference. A corollary is well known to most investigators, but worth repeating — big effects are easier to identify than small ones.

A concluding comment, not based on the results examined in this chapter but pertinent nevertheless, is that confidence in a particular finding is considerably strengthened if the result holds for several populations. Hence, the conclusions of Hobcraft, McDonald and Rutstein (1983) regarding the deleterious effect on mortality of short interbirth intervals and of Rodríguez et al. (1984) concerning the effect of previous birth interval length on subsequent interval length are much more powerful because they are based on simultaneous examination of multiple samples.

Notes

1. The project on date imputation would not have been conducted in finite time without the help of several of the WFS central staff. Scott Wallace left the Korea files with sufficient documentation so that I could assemble the relevant programs quickly. Sakina Harji was very helpful in restoring old files and shepherding the runs through a packed queue. Andrew Westlake, as usual, provided technical advice at many stages. Shea Rutstein and John McDonald supplied me with software and documentation for producing the data needed for the substantive analyses. Manny Pasaba and Nuri Özsever generously shared their experience in producing standard recode files. Barbara Vaughan at the Office of Population Research was enormously helpful in producing the final parameter estimates. Noreen Goldman suggested many revisions which improved the clarity of the presentation.
2. For some surveys, a date imputation program written by CELADE was used, while for others imputation programs were specially written. See chapter 18.
3. This summary actually reports the *use* of data in the standard recode files, not their presence in the raw data.
4. They actually estimated two more models, one for toddler (1–2 years) and one for child (2–5 years) mortality. In these they also allowed for an increased risk due to the closely spaced birth of a subsequent child. This risk was also found to be substantial.
5. Imputation can, in principle, result in duration-specific birth rates that are less nearly equal. For example, if the data were generated by an exponential model, then except for sampling error, all duration-specific *rates* would be equal and the *number* of births by duration would decline monotonically. Imputation would make the number of births by duration more nearly equal and would result in estimated birth rates that *rise* with duration. When birth rates (and births) before imputation rise to a peak and then decline, we would expect that imputation would result in estimated rates that are more nearly equal, though clearly pathological cases can be constructed.
6. Some part of the difference between samples with age interpretations of c and p is caused by the tendency for imputations under p to be one year later than those under c. This has the effect of causing the analysis window to include those aged 5–14 under c and 6–15 under p. Since 15 year olds are less numerous than five year olds, the p sample is consequently reduced.
7. When assembling the many computer programs used to create the original birth interval analysis, we did not notice that a change had later been made (but not documented) that resulted in the exclusion of intervals of women with 6+ years of education. Though the outcome is rather less elegant than we would have preferred, comparison across standard recode files is unaffected. The numbers in table 26.1, however, pertain to the excluded intervals as well as the interval *actually* used in the analysis.
8. Except that the range might be narrower if a previous birth precluded some months from consideration.

Appendix A

TABLE A1

Standard errors in the birth interval analysis: main effects plus D × L and D × E interactions model

	TRUE	R33.c	R33.p	R67.c	R67.p	ED.c	ED.r	ED.p	SURV.c	SURV.r	SURV.p
GM	0.174	0.163	0.144	0.165	0.144	0.155	0.151	0.136	0.172	0.166	0.155
D2	0.206	0.193	0.174	0.190	0.176	0.181	0.181	0.166	0.197	0.195	0.182
D3	0.190	0.178	0.156	0.178	0.159	0.173	0.166	0.151	0.190	0.178	0.167
D4	0.187	0.170	0.149	0.172	0.146	0.161	0.158	0.139	0.180	0.173	0.160
D5	0.216	0.193	0.162	0.186	0.155	0.178	0.170	0.148	0.205	0.191	0.174
B2	0.054	0.054	0.053	0.053	0.052	0.054	0.053	0.052	0.054	0.053	0.054
B3	0.061	0.061	0.060	0.061	0.059	0.061	0.060	0.059	0.061	0.061	0.061
P2	0.053	0.053	0.052	0.054	0.051	0.054	0.052	0.050	0.054	0.053	0.053
P3	0.053	0.053	0.051	0.053	0.050	0.053	0.051	0.050	0.053	0.052	0.052
A2	0.058	0.058	0.059	0.057	0.060	0.057	0.059	0.061	0.058	0.058	0.060
A3	0.091	0.091	0.090	0.091	0.088	0.090	0.089	0.089	0.090	0.090	0.090
L2	0.183	0.167	0.144	0.168	0.141	0.160	0.155	0.135	0.177	0.168	0.156
L3	0.229	0.201	0.158	0.201	0.163	0.197	0.179	0.150	0.211	0.192	0.169
E2	0.156	0.135	0.107	0.132	0.103	0.133	0.126	0.102	0.138	0.128	0.112
D2L2	0.226	0.210	0.192	0.205	0.190	0.199	0.198	0.182	0.214	0.211	0.200
D2L3	0.294	0.270	0.214	0.251	0.218	0.250	0.237	0.206	0.266	0.251	0.220
D3L2	0.208	0.193	0.172	0.193	0.174	0.189	0.182	0.167	0.204	0.192	0.183
D3L3	0.266	0.242	0.201	0.238	0.201	0.238	0.220	0.195	0.249	0.232	0.213
D4L2	0.204	0.185	0.163	0.185	0.159	0.177	0.174	0.154	0.194	0.186	0.173
D4L3	0.255	0.225	0.187	0.225	0.187	0.220	0.204	0.176	0.235	0.219	0.196
D5L2	0.234	0.210	0.177	0.202	0.168	0.198	0.188	0.165	0.220	0.206	0.189
D5L3	0.288	0.255	0.206	0.246	0.205	0.243	0.228	0.197	0.264	0.244	0.221

D2E2	0.190	0.171	0.149	0.163	0.141	0.166	0.160	0.142	0.174	0.164	0.153
D3E2	0.171	0.155	0.135	0.154	0.135	0.154	0.147	0.133	0.157	0.149	0.140
D4E2	0.167	0.148	0.125	0.145	0.123	0.146	0.140	0.121	0.151	0.141	0.129
D5E2	0.186	0.168	0.139	0.162	0.133	0.165	0.157	0.134	0.170	0.159	0.145

Notes:

1 All variables are categorical, and the first category of each is omitted:

GM = constant
D = duration (completed months) since last birth: 8–17, 18–23, 24–29, 30–41, 42–59
B = birth order at end of interval: 3, 4–5, 6–8
P = period (completed years before survey): 1–5, 6–10, 11–15
A = age (completed years): 15–24, 25–34, 35–49
L = length of previous interval (completed months): 6–21, 22–41, 42+
E = maternal education (years): 0, 1–5.

2 Files are labelled OPTION. INTERPRETATION:

OPTION designates which birth dates were removed and then imputed:

TRUE = original standard recode file, all birth dates given in month/year form
R33 = one-third of birth dates removed randomly
R67 = two-thirds of birth dates removed randomly
ED = probability of birth date being removed depends on education of woman
 (0 years: 70 per cent; 1–5 years: 40 per cent; 6+ years: 10 per cent)
SURV = probability of birth date being removed depends on survival status of child
 (survived: 25 per cent; died: 75 per cent)

INTERPRETATION of 'years ago' or 'age':

c = completed years (age at last birthday)
r = rounded years (age at nearest birthday)
p = projected years (age at next birthday).

TABLE A2

Standard errors in the birth interval analysis: main effects model

	TRUE	R33.c	R33.p	R67.c	R67.p	ED.c	ED.r	ED.p	SURV.c	SURV.r	SURV.p
GM	0.103	0.095	0.085	0.092	0.083	0.091	0.088	0.082	0.097	0.092	0.087
D2	0.090	0.081	0.070	0.076	0.066	0.076	0.073	0.065	0.082	0.077	0.072
D3	0.082	0.074	0.064	0.072	0.064	0.071	0.068	0.062	0.076	0.070	0.066
D4	0.080	0.071	0.059	0.068	0.058	0.067	0.064	0.056	0.072	0.066	0.061
D5	0.089	0.080	0.066	0.076	0.063	0.076	0.071	0.062	0.081	0.075	0.068
B2	0.054	0.054	0.053	0.053	0.052	0.054	0.053	0.052	0.054	0.053	0.054
B3	0.061	0.061	0.060	0.061	0.059	0.061	0.060	0.059	0.061	0.061	0.061
P2	0.053	0.053	0.052	0.053	0.051	0.053	0.052	0.050	0.054	0.053	0.053
P3	0.053	0.053	0.051	0.053	0.050	0.053	0.051	0.050	0.053	0.052	0.052
A2	0.058	0.058	0.059	0.057	0.061	0.057	0.059	0.061	0.058	0.058	0.060
A3	0.091	0.091	0.090	0.091	0.088	0.090	0.090	0.089	0.090	0.090	0.090
L2	0.053	0.050	0.045	0.047	0.044	0.048	0.047	0.044	0.050	0.048	0.046
L3	0.070	0.067	0.058	0.063	0.055	0.063	0.062	0.056	0.066	0.064	0.059
E2	0.038	0.038	0.038	0.038	0.038	0.038	0.038	0.038	0.038	0.038	0.039

Notes:

1 All variables are categorical, and the first category of each is omitted:

GM = constant
D = duration (completed months) since last birth: 8–17, 18–23, 24–29, 30–41, 42–59
B = birth order at end of interval: 3, 4–5, 6–8
P = period (completed years before survey): 1–5, 6–10, 11–15
A = age (completed years): 15–24, 25–34, 35–49
L = length of previous interval (completed months): 6–21, 22–41, 42+
E = maternal education (years): 0, 1–5.

2 Files are labelled OPTION.INTERPRETATION:

OPTION designates which birth dates were removed and then imputed:

TRUE = original standard recode file, all birth dates given in month/year form
R33 = one-third of birth dates removed randomly
R67 = two-thirds of birth dates removed randomly
ED = probability of birth date being removed depends on education of woman
(0 years: 70 per cent; 1–5 years: 40 per cent; 6+ years: 10 per cent)
SURV = probability of birth date being removed depends on survival status of child
(survived: 25 per cent; died: 75 per cent).

INTERPRETATION of 'years ago' or 'age':

c = completed years (age at last birthday)
r = rounded years (age at nearest birthday)
p = projected years (age at next birthday).

TABLE A3

Standard errors in the analysis of neo-natal mortality

	TRUE	R33.c	R33.p	R67.c	R67.p	ED.c	ED.r	ED.p	SURV.c	SURV.r	SURV.p
GM	0.186	0.187	0.193	0.185	0.192	0.188	0.186	0.184	0.187	0.192	0.198
Z2	0.298	0.300	0.294	0.307	0.328	0.299	0.295	0.308	0.296	0.316	0.357
Z3	0.643	0.583	0.533	0.639	1.043	0.577	0.572	0.573	0.638	0.644	0.608
S2	0.198	0.196	0.205	0.185	0.207	0.195	0.204	0.198	0.199	0.201	0.205
S3	0.184	0.185	0.196	0.185	0.200	0.186	0.183	0.186	0.188	0.191	0.205
S4	0.348	0.362	0.432	0.382	0.352	0.382	0.382	0.364	0.336	0.367	0.368
E2	0.204	0.204	0.210	0.204	0.212	0.204	0.207	0.209	0.204	0.207	0.224
E3	0.175	0.175	0.184	0.176	0.186	0.178	0.178	0.180	0.180	0.176	0.184
E4	0.229	0.229	0.239	0.229	0.252	0.231	0.231	0.235	0.235	0.241	0.252
ZS	0.300	0.302	0.299	0.304	0.334	0.300	0.298	0.309	0.294	0.319	0.368
ZM	0.281	0.283	0.283	0.279	0.295	0.278	0.281	0.288	0.273	0.294	0.343

TABLE A4

Standard errors in the analysis of post-neonatal mortality

	TRUE	R33.c	R33.p	R67.c	R67.p	ED.c	ED.r	ED.p	SURV.c	SURV.r	SURV.p
GM	0.182	0.182	0.182	0.183	0.185	0.183	0.182	0.188	0.183	0.183	0.187
Z2	0.384	0.360	0.329	0.330	-0.350	0.380	0.367	0.356	0.399	0.412	0.425
Z3	1.047	1.042	1.049	1.044	1.046	1.065	1.057	1.023	1.069	1.029	1.081
S2	0.189	0.192	0.192	0.193	0.196	0.190	0.188	0.192	0.189	0.185	0.189
S3	0.194	0.196	0.200	0.201	0.201	0.194	0.200	0.208	0.194	0.200	0.206
S4	0.433	0.433	0.433	0.405	0.470	0.521	0.471	0.518	0.721	0.404	0.521
E2	0.223	0.223	0.227	0.223	0.225	0.223	0.224	0.233	0.223	0.219	0.230
E3	0.173	0.177	0.180	0.179	0.185	0.175	0.176	0.184	0.174	0.172	0.177
E4	0.246	0.248	0.246	0.250	0.251	0.248	0.244	0.252	0.247	0.250	0.260
ZS	0.381	0.355	0.337	0.331	0.352	0.378	0.363	0.361	0.390	0.408	0.430
ZM	0.332	0.317	0.310	0.309	0.312	0.324	0.321	0.321	0.329	0.352	0.382

Notes to tables A3 and A4

Notes:

1 All variables are categorical, and the first category of each is omitted:

GM = constant
Z = number of births 0–2 years before birth of index child: 0, 1, 2+
S = number of births 2–6 years before birth of index child: 0, 1, 2, 3+
E = maternal education: 0, 1–3, 4–6, 7+
ZS = Z1 × S1
ZM = (1 – Z1) (E3 + E4).

2 Files are labelled OPTION.INTERPRETATION:

OPTION designates which birth dates were removed and then imputed:
TRUE = original standard recode file, all birth dates given in month/year form
R33 = one-third of birth dates removed randomly
R67 = two-thirds of birth dates removed randomly
ED = probability of birth date being removed depends on survival status of child
(0 years: 70 per cent; 1–5 years: 40 per cent; 6+ years: 10 per cent)
SURV = probability of birthdate being removed depends on survival status of child
(survived: 25 per cent; died: 75 per cent).

INTERPRETATION of 'years ago' or 'age':

c = completed years (age at last birthday)
r = rounded years (age at nearest birthday)
p = projected years (age at next birthday).

Appendix B

Some further notion of variation in parameter estimates due to sampling variability induced by random imputation can be gleaned by considering experiments in which the calendar year of birth is retained but the month is deleted and recovered by imputation using DEIR. These experiments are similar to those performed earlier in which 'years ago' or 'age' was correctly interpreted as completed years. In fact, the same birth dates for a given option were imputed; the only difference was the logical window initially identified by DEIR. In both cases the window is initially 12 months wide. The results of these additional runs, labelled as options R33, R67, ED, and SURV, are shown in the following tables. No age interpretation is necessary since the logical window was the calendar year of birth.

Results are similar to those obtained earlier, and this similarity strengthens our conviction that a sizeable portion of the differences between the parameters based on files with imputed birth dates and the parameters based on the true file may be due to systematic tendencies rather than random sampling variation. We reach this conclusion by treating R33 and R33.c, R67 and R67.c, ED and ED.c, and SURV and SURV.c as pairs of observations which differ only in the random draws for birth dates. They, of course, do not differ only in this respect, since the logical windows are slightly different, but they are sufficiently alike to give some idea of systematic, as opposed to chance, variation. Suppose we assign a plus (+) if a particular parameter estimate based on TRUE is either higher or lower than both estimates from the two imputed files; we assign a minus (−) otherwise. If all we were observing was sampling variability, we would expect equal numbers of + and −. In the birth interval main effects model, we record 43+ in 56 observations (77 per cent), while in the neo-natal and post-neonatal models the corresponding figures are 30+ in 44 observations (68 per cent) and 30+ in 44 observations (68 per cent). Such patterns could occur by chance less than 5 per cent of the time, as scrutiny of a binomial table will reveal, if the null hypothesis of equally likely outcomes is correct. Examination of table B7, in which + or − indicates that the parameter estimate in a particular run is larger or smaller, respectively, in absolute value than the parameter estimate in the TRUE run, is quite revealing. The uniform pattern of − in the fertility analysis for the variables D and L and the grand mean clearly indicates attenuation bias.

Hence, though a full Monte Carlo experiment is needed to gain a complete picture, the limited information available suggests that the imputation scheme employed by WFS can, in complex multivariate analyses, lead to results that are systematically biased. We have argued, nevertheless, that analysts can overcome such bias through careful interpretation of results.

TABLE B1

Parameter estimates in the birth interval analysis: main effects model

	TRUE	R33	R67	ED	SURV
GM	−4.913	−4.787	−4.669	−4.688	−4.791
D2	1.355	1.244	1.302	1.310	1.342
D3	2.397	2.084	1.788	1.878	2.144
D4	2.655	2.352	2.182	2.199	2.465
D5	1.950	1.763	1.679	1.728	1.831
B2	−0.242	−0.249	−0.260	−0.276	−0.255
B3	−0.469	−0.475	−0.464	−0.501	−0.473
P2	0.129	0.129	0.099	0.119	0.149
P3	0.257	0.266	0.261	0.266	0.282
A2	−0.215	−0.187	−0.206	−0.202	−0.228
A3	−0.803	−0.788	−0.792	−0.799	−0.830
L2	−0.190	−0.095	−0.044	−0.058	−0.158
L3	−0.578	−0.453	−0.381	−0.348	−0.476
E2	−0.091	−0.081	−0.094	−0.093	−0.096

Notes:

1 All variables are categorical, and the first category of each is omitted:

GM = constant
D = duration (completed months) since last birth: 8–17, 18–23, 24–29, 30–41, 42–59
B = birth order at end of interval: 3, 4–5, 6–8
P = period (completed years before survey): 1–5, 6–10, 11–15
A = age (completed years): 15–24, 25–34, 35–49
L = length of previous interval (completed months): 6–21, 22–41, 42+
E = maternal education (years): 0, 1–5.

2 Files are labelled OPTION:

OPTION designates which birth dates were removed and then imputed:
TRUE = original standard recode file, all birth dates given in month/year form
R33 = one-third of birth dates removed randomly
R67 = two-thirds of birth dates removed randomly
ED = probability of birth date being removed depends on education of woman:
(0 years: 70 per cent; 1–5 years: 40 per cent; 6+ years: 10 per cent)
SURV = probability of birth date being removed depends on survival status of child
(survived: 25 per cent; died: 75 per cent).

TABLE B2

Standard errors in the birth interval analysis: main effects model

	TRUE	R33	R67	ED	SURV
GM	0.103	0.097	0.092	0.093	0.098
D2	0.090	0.083	0.077	0.078	0.084
D3	0.082	0.076	0.074	0.074	0.078
D4	0.080	0.073	0.069	0.070	0.075
D5	0.089	0.081	0.077	0.077	0.084
B2	0.054	0.054	0.054	0.053	0.053
B3	0.061	0.061	0.061	0.061	0.061
P2	0.053	0.054	0.054	0.054	0.054
P3	0.053	0.053	0.053	0.053	0.053
A2	0.058	0.058	0.057	0.057	0.057
A3	0.091	0.090	0.089	0.091	0.091
L2	0.053	0.050	0.048	0.048	0.051
L3	0.070	0.067	0.063	0.063	0.066
E2	0.038	0.038	0.038	0.038	0.038

Notes:

1 All variables are categorical, and the first category of each is omitted:

GM = constant
D = duration (completed months) since last birth: 8–17, 18–23, 24–29, 30–41, 42–59
B = birth order at end of interval: 3, 4–5, 6–8
P = period (completed years before survey): 1–5, 6–10, 11–15
A = age (completed years): 15–24, 25–34, 35–49
L = length of previous interval (completed months): 6–21, 22–41, 42+
E = maternal education (years): 0, 1–5.

2 Files are labelled OPTION:

OPTION designates which birth dates were removed and then imputed:
TRUE = original standard recode file, all birth dates given in month/year form
R33 = one-third of birth dates removed randomly
R67 = two-thirds of birth dates removed randomly
ED = probability of birth date being removed depends on education of woman: (0 years: 70 per cent; 1–5 years: 40 per cent; 6+ years: 10 per cent)
SURV = probability of birth date being removed depends on survival status of child (survived: 25 per cent; died: 75 per cent).

TABLE B3
Parameter estimates in the analysis of neo-natal mortality

	TRUE	R33	R67	ED	SURV
GM	− 3.402	− 3.446	− 3.285	− 3.360	− 3.382
Z2	0.594	0.704	0.330	0.371	0.563
Z3	2.069	2.544	2.024	1.909	2.475
S2	− 0.559	− 0.546	− 0.560	− 0.555	− 0.588
S3	− 0.137	− 0.105	− 0.274	− 0.100	− 0.141
S4	0.365	0.393	0.304	0.024	0.133
E2	− 0.047	− 0.037	− 0.066	− 0.009	− 0.044
E3	− 0.225	− 0.158	− 0.367	− 0.259	− 0.235
E4	− 0.401	− 0.353	− 0.533	− 0.432	− 0.487
ZS	0.559	0.369	0.589	0.486	0.495
ZM	− 0.167	− 0.426	0.140	0.003	− 0.103

TABLE B4
Standard errors in the analysis of neo-natal mortality

	TRUE	R33	R67	ED	SURV
GM	0.186	0.188	0.184	0.185	0.186
Z2	0.298	0.294	0.290	0.298	0.294
Z3	0.643	0.497	0.584	0.571	0.493
S2	0.198	0.198	0.196	0.196	0.199
S3	0.184	0.186	0.190	0.183	0.185
S4	0.348	0.347	0.364	0.405	0.383
E2	0.204	0.204	0.203	0.204	0.204
E3	0.175	0.177	0.180	0.176	0.177
E4	0.229	0.232	0.231	0.229	0.235
ZS	0.300	0.299	0.290	0.300	0.296
ZM	0.281	0.283	0.274	0.282	0.279

Notes for tables B3 and B4.

1 All variables are categorical, and the first category of each is omitted:

GM = constant
Z = number of births 0–2 years before birth of index child: 0, 1, 2+
S = number of births 2–6 years before birth of index child: 0, 1, 2, 3+
E = maternal education: 0, 1–3, 4–6, 7+
ZS = Z1 × S1
ZM = (1 − Z1) (E3 + E4).

2 Files are labelled OPTION:

OPTION designates which birth dates were removed and then imputed:
TRUE = original standard recode file, all birth dates given in month/year form
R33 = one-third of birth dates removed randomly
R67 = two-thirds of birth dates removed randomly
ED = probability of birth date being removed depends on education of woman
(0 years: 70 per cent; 1–5 years: 40 per cent; 6+ years: 10 per cent)
SURV = probability of birth date being removed depends on survival status of child
(survived: 25 per cent; died: 75 per cent).

TABLE B5

Parameter estimates in the analysis of post-neonatal mortality

	TRUE	R33	R67	ED	SURV
GM	-3.191	-3.175	-3.207	-3.211	-3.186
Z2	-0.314	-0.164	0.008	-0.175	-0.195
Z3	0.766	0.489	1.074	0.486	0.891
S2	-0.258	-0.406	-0.324	-0.242	-0.414
S3	-0.414	-0.274	-0.335	-0.483	-0.277
S4	-0.063	-0.265	-0.297	0.072	-1.152
E2	-0.286	-0.236	-0.260	-0.254	-0.224
E3	-0.430	-0.464	-0.436	-0.388	-0.445
E4	-0.780	-0.804	-0.784	-0.763	-0.817
ZS	0.945	0.684	0.429	0.697	0.812
ZM	0.057	0.189	0.080	0.049	0.262

Notes:

1 All variables are categorical, and the first category of each is omitted:

GM = constant
Z = number of births 0–2 years before birth of index child: 0, 1, 2+
S = number of births 2–6 years before birth of index child: 0, 1, 2, 3+
E = maternal education: 0, 1–3, 4–6, 7+
ZS = Z1 × S1
ZM = (1 – Z1) (E3 + E4).

2 Files are labelled OPTION:

OPTION designates which birth dates were removed and then imputed:
TRUE = original standard recode file, all birth dates given in month/year form
R33 = one-third of birth dates removed randomly
R67 = two-thirds of birth dates removed randomly
ED = probability of birth date being removed depends on education of woman (0 years: 70 per cent; 1–5 years: 40 per cent; 6+ years: 10 per cent)
SURV = probability of birth date being removed depends on survival status of child (survived: 25 per cent; died: 75 per cent).

TABLE B6

Standard errors in the analysis of post-neonatal mortality

	TRUE	R33	R67	ED	SURV
GM	0.182	0.182	0.185	0.184	0.183
Z2	0.384	0.353	0.335	0.354	0.355
Z3	1.047	1.055	1.039	1.052	1.049
S2	0.189	0.194	0.193	0.189	0.194
S3	0.194	0.192	0.198	0.201	0.190
S4	0.433	0.471	0.516	0.406	0.721
E2	0.223	0.220	0.224	0.224	0.220
E3	0.173	0.176	0.178	0.176	0.177
E4	0.246	0.248	0.249	0.248	0.249
ZS	0.381	0.351	0.339	0.355	0.351
ZM	0.332	0.320	0.318	0.320	0.317

Notes:

1 All variables are categorical, and the first category of each is omitted:

GM = constant
Z   = number of births 0–2 years before birth of index child: 0, 1, 2+
S   = number of births 2–6 years before birth of index child: 0, 1, 2, 3+
E   = maternal education: 0, 1–3, 4–6, 7+
ZS = Z1 × S1
ZM = (1 – Z1) (E3 + E4).

2 Files are labelled OPTION:

OPTION designates which birth dates were removed and then imputed:
TRUE = original standard recode file, all birth dates given in month/year form
R33 = one-third of birth dates removed randomly
R67 = two-thirds of birth dates removed randomly
ED   = probability of birth date being removed depends on education of woman
       (0 years: 70 per cent; 1–5 years: 40 per cent; 6+ years: 10 per cent)
SURV = probability of birth date being removed depends on survival status of child
       (survived: 25 per cent; died: 75 per cent).

TABLE B7

Comparison of estimates from selected runs with those based on the TRUE file

	R33.c	R33	R67.c	R67	ED.c	ED	SURV.c	SURV
Fertility: main effects model[a]								
GM	−	−	−	−	−	−	−	−
D2	−	−	−	−	−	−	−	−
D3	−	−	−	−	−	−	−	−
D4	−	−	−	−	−	−	−	−
D5	−	−	−	−	−	−	−	−
B2	+	+	+	+	+	+	−	+
B3	+	+	+	−	+	+	−	+
P2	−	●	+	−	+	−	+	+
P3	−	+	−	+	+	+	−	+
A2	−	−	−	−	−	−	−	+
A3	−	−	+	−	−	−	+	+
L2	−	−	−	−	−	−	−	−
L3	−	−	−	−	−	−	−	−
E2	−	−	−	+	−	+	−	+
Mortality: neo-natal[b]								
GM	+	+	−	−	+	−	−	−
Z2	−	+	−	−	−	−	−	−
Z3	+	+	−	−	+	−	−	+
S2	−	−	−	+	−	−	+	+
S3	−	−	−	+	+	−	+	+
S4	−	+	−	−	−	−	+	−
E2	−	−	−	+	−	−	−	−
E3	−	−	+	+	−	−	+	+
E4	−	−	+	+	−	+	+	+
ZS	−	−	+	+	−	+	+	−
ZM	+	+	[−]	[−]	+	[−]	[−]	−

Mortality: post-neonatal[c]

GM	−	+	+	+	+	−	−
Z2	+	+	−	+	[−]	−	−
Z3	+	−	−	−	+	−	−
S2	+	−	−	+	+	+	+
S3	−	−	+	−	−	+	−
S4	+	+	[+]	+	−	[+]	+
E2	−	−	−	−	−	−	−
E3	+	+	−	−	+	+	+
E4	+	+	−	−	+	+	+
ZS	−	+	−	+	−	−	−
ZM	+	+	−	+	+	+	+

[a] *Source*: Tables 26.3 and B1.
[b] *Source*: Tables 26.4 and B3.
[c] *Source*: Tables 26.5 and B5.

Note:
+ indicates that absolute value of estimate is higher when compared with TRUE.
− indicates that absolute value of estimate is lower when compared with TRUE.
• indicates that absolute value of estimate is the same when compared with TRUE.
[] indicates that sign of estimate is opposite to that in TRUE.

27

Archiving and Distributing Datasets

Beverley Rowe

27.1 Prologue

The ISI has always accepted that it is the right of the originating countries to make decisions on access to data and within this framework it has tried to negotiate policies which allow data to be exploited by other researchers. Because of the mutual trust established between countries and the ISI, fairly liberal access has been achieved, although this trust is fragile and can easily be broken. The importance of researchers adhering to the conditions laid down cannot be overemphasized if similar arrangements are to be possible for other projects. The data from the WFS will remain a valuable asset for some time and care must be taken to ensure that they will continue to be available. (An editorial postscript on events following the closure of WFS may be found in section 27.8.)

27.2 The distributive function of WFS

WFS has developed as an important source of data for secondary analysis. Distribution started in 1978 and by mid-1984 over 1300 datasets had been shipped by the WFS headquarters to research institutions on behalf of individual countries. Over 800 projects based on WFS data have been identified, of which over 60 per cent are within the original WFS countries. This chapter touches on the problems created by international data distribution, emphasizing the question of how researchers gain access to WFS-derived data which are the property of individual national governments.

All participating developing countries except Iran have, under conditions differing slightly from case to case, accepted the ISI as custodian of their data. At the end of the WFS programme, comprehensive datasets from 40 developing countries had been brought together, constituting a rich source for scientific and policy-oriented analysis. (Turkey agreed to deposit its data in the archive shortly after the end of the WFS project.)

Most government statistical offices have national policies or laws governing data release. Close relations with the developing countries participating in the WFS programme produced policies which allow for more liberal data access than is often the case.

The archive was the last major function of WFS to develop and the demand for WFS data was underestimated. The standardization of the data across countries, in particular, augmented this demand, and WFS did not foresee how far the countries would be prepared to see their data sent out for projects. Had this been realized earlier, the style established for First Country Reports might have been different (see chapter 21).

The WFS project was conceived in response to practical problems and its findings usually command attention. Survey planning, sample design and data collection were carried out to high standards, particularly in view of the operational conditions that often prevailed: lack of sample frames, difficult communications, unfriendly terrain, etc. There is thus a demand for these data and, as an agency for distributing them, WFS had advantages compared to a conventional survey data archive:

1 Most countries agreed to release data, at least for cross-national comparisons, as part of the contract for the survey.

2 There is extensive documentation for each survey.

3 WFS had considerable support from the international demographic and statistical community.

4 Despite difficult patches, WFS was generously financed and it was generally possible to do the job in hand properly.

5. Headquarters staff had a full-time involvement in the project and no other duties to distract them.

6 The data are well defined and relatively standardized.

7 Since the distributing archive grew up as part of the data-originating project, there was strong motivation to present it well and maintain high standards.

However, there are also two negative aspects which cannot be ignored:

1 Operative conditions, local considerations, perfectionism and, in particular, problems with data processing combined to produce delays in finalizing datasets and reports.

2 The standardized data structure required substantial computer programming and processing. This introduced a new type of error — caused by faulty software — into the datasets (a problem which has however now been largely eliminated).

With a large database and extensive international contacts, WFS spent a great deal of time trying to ensure that its administrative procedures were robust. In particular, it established a system of error notification for datasets modelled on systems used by software distributors. The administration of data holdings and their distribution was handled by a database system. This database could be used for examining WFS-based projects from many points of view and included a subject classification which could be used to notify researchers of projects in the same area as their own.

27.3　The scale of the WFS archive

Almost every country in the programme collected at least two datasets — household and full individual interview — because sampling was carried out in two phases: a selection of households within which eligible women were chosen for interview. The samples of individuals vary from 2500 to 10 000 and the household datasets can run to over 100 000 household members. In five countries, the household phase was a non-WFS survey.

The *raw data* from the individual survey is in the same format as the original questionnaire. As this is generally rather complex, there is also the *standard recode*, a rectangularized file, standardized across countries. The household data are held in formats corresponding to the household level and the household member level. For some countries datasets are also available for the community level and for special studies, for example on husbands.

Altogether, by the middle of 1984 the WFS archive included almost 200 datasets from 40 countries and contained the following:

1　the individual data as received from each country after local editing;

2　the individual data, still in questionnaire format, but with further amendments carried out in London;

3　the standardized individual data (standard recode);

4　the original household data;

5　the data on household members;

6　any other sets of data collected, such as community-level variables, husbands survey, economic variables, post-enumeration survey results, and so on;

7　data dictionaries: machine-readable guides to the datasets;

8　specifications and records of decisions made in collecting, processing, correcting and recoding data;

9　data-related documentation including agreements with countries about use of data and research projects for which data have been distributed;

10　records of studies utilizing WFS data;

11　a library and stock of WFS publications.

Thus, all information necessary for the further exploitation and analysis of the survey results is available. There are clean versions for all the available individual datasets. Work on the household datasets is less complete but at least almost all are properly documented and checked.

27.4　Why standard recodes?

Cross-national comparative studies were one of the *raisons d'être* of WFS and the WFS core questionnaire was developed to facilitate them. However, the specific needs of the participating countries naturally took precedence and each used an adapted version of the core questionnaire. This preserved the essence of cross-country comparison because basic variables can still be derived from each survey. But the variations render comparative studies difficult in practice, in terms of the meaning of data items and of their format or structure.

The important data items collected in the histories present another problem. The tables of unions, live births and other pregnancies (and other events) do not lie easily in a computer file because the amount of information about each woman varies a great deal. Countries adopted different strategies but the resulting computer files are nearly all variable in length. This does not suit most standard analysis packages.

Then, there are the questions in the fertility regulation module. These were matched to the characteristics of different classes of women. Typically the schedule branches at this point five or more ways, depending on the respondent's marital status, parity and contraceptive practice. The branches address largely the same matters but with questions suitably selected, phrased and ordered. For the analyst this creates a chore: collating questions that elicit the same information.

To resolve these difficulties, the data for each country were mapped on to a standardized set of variables to form the standard recode (SR). But this is not sufficient to explain fully the format of SR files. The main exposition of WFS surveys is the First Country Reports, substantial works of up to five volumes. Tables in these standardized reports use variables derived from the original data, sometimes by complex paths. Files were constructed which contain all these derived variables. It is these SR files that are made available to analysts.

The production and maintenance of standardized datasets was an elaborate undertaking and the heavy cost fell on central funds. Some of the work was necessary to the production of First Country Reports, but these did not require datasets produced to such a standard. The gain to the demographic community has been very great. Researchers working on single countries have been helped a great deal (by rectangularization if nothing else), but for those doing comparative studies standardization has been vital. Most of the larger studies based on WFS data could not have been done using raw datasets, or even with non-standard rectangularized files.

27.5 The set of distribution files

The tape shipped to satisfy the request for a standard recode carries at least four computer files and may have as many as ten. Some of these relate to SS data (see below) but the rest appertain to the SR file itself. The basic types of files are:

- the dataset
- a data dictionary (or codebook)
- marginals (duplicated if the data contain weights)
- an SPSS data description.

The data file

An SR file falls into sections, usually three or four but in a few cases up to eight, with the variable names in each section starting with the same letter. Generally the rest of the name consists of three digits, e.g. V701.

The main part of the file embraces 167 variables plus the union and birth tables. All have names starting with V (except for the two tables) and range between V000 and V907. The section subdivides on the first digit which represents the 'group' of variables – a subject-matter grouping based on the sections of the Core Questionnaire. Thus all variables in the V600s relate to contraception. All the V variables occur in all SRs. Even where a variable cannot be formed for a country, a dummy value is supplied so that this section has the same structure in all SRs. Many of the variables are binary, dividing the sample into two categories coded 0 and 1. Such variables make up 17 per cent of the section. Most dates in SR files are expressed in century month code (cmc) form. This is the number of months that have passed since 1899, i.e. January 1900 has cmc = 1.

The *table of unions* allows for up to eight unions, each described by four items of information (32 variables). The union history is present in all SR files. The *table of live births* comes between V123 and V201 and allows for 24 births, which has been enough for every country.

Many questionnaires, particularly those in Africa, incorporated a module exploring factors other than contraception affecting fertility (FOTCAF), such as breastfeeding, amenorrhoea and sexual exposure. The answers from this module map on to a set of variables with names starting with F and subdivided by the following digit into four sections, 90 variables in all with names in the range F101 to F411. A few of the surveys have 36 further variables numbered F501 to F536. Fifteen countries have FOTCAF variables. Like the V variables, they have fixed locations, both within their section and relative to the start of the file.

The original definition of the SR format omitted a few variables available from the core questionnaire and many more from modules such as those for abortion and family planning. These have gradually been incorporated as *X (Extra) variables*. X variables are not as standardized as V variables. More importantly, the X section includes only those variables relevant to that survey. Thus, they do not have fixed locations but they are always in a standard order. The first digit following the X subdivides the variables into groups echoing those in the V section. So just as variables starting V6 relate to contraception, so do those starting X6. The number of X variables ranges from none up to 60 or more.

A *table of non-fertile pregnancies* is included in most SRs. It is similar to the birth table, but the number and importance of the variables are different, indeed differ somewhat from country to country.

A section of country-specific variables is the most miscellaneous part of the file. Ideally it should contain everything in the original questionnaire that has not been defined as a V or X variable. All the variables should have names starting with S, with first digit categorizing the variables similarly to the first digit of the V variables.

However, some datasets do not satisfy all these rules:

1 they may not contain all the original data;

2 some were created before X variables were introduced, so material which now goes into the X section is in the S section;

3 names have been created not starting with S;

4 not all the S variables are grouped by the first digit: some are ungrouped, some grouped on other principles.

The data dictionary

An analyst using a file of survey data must know where different items are placed, the range of values to be found and what these values may mean. For example, if respondents have indicated the preferred sex of the next child, the analyst needs to know that the responses appear at position 29 in the data record, that 1 means 'boy', 2 means 'girl' and 3 means 'don't know', while people who did not answer are coded 9. If the question was posed only to pregnant women, then those not asked the question might be coded 8, 'not applicable' (as opposed to 9, which means 'no answer available although question asked'). There may be other codes with special values. Thus, 7 might mean 'could not decide'.

For any variable, then, there may be three classes of values:

— values with a 'real' (substantive) meaning;
— special values;
— a value to indicate 'not applicable'.

All this, and more, information may be gleaned from the questionnaire plus the original coding manual. It is more convenient if both documents are collated and summarized in tables. Such a summary is called a codebook, or dictionary (the words are interchangeable). Where, as with SR files, a data file is restructured to make it more convenient or relevant, the original documentation is of little value: a codebook is not a convenience but a necessity.

Codebooks are for people, but there is much to be said for allowing machines to read them, too. If nothing else, this has the advantages of word-processing. It is hard to keep such technical documentation error-free and up to date, while new errors are often introduced during retyping. Using a computer avoids this. But there is a more important advantage. Once a codebook is machine-readable, and if it is set out in an orderly and systematic way, then computer programs can operate with it directly.

If an analyst wants a program to use certain variables from a data file, a lot of information must be supplied: location in the record, length, coding structure, labelling and so on. But if a program can read a dictionary, then the analyst only has to supply the name of the variable and the program can look up the rest. An example of such a program is WFSPSS which, given variable names from a WFS dictionary, can generate the lines needed by SPSS to pick up and use the variables. Several hundred lines of SPSS can be generated in this way, all of which would have to be typed in by a user without access to such a program.

The dictionary/codebook, therefore, has come to play a vital role in the way WFS datasets are handled. Figure 27.1 shows a typical page of a WFS dictionary. From left to right the columns indicate: variable number; variable name; starting location on the file; length of the variable; the range of valid values; the code used for 'not applicable' cases; special codes; variable and value labels; and a final column indicating that the codes and cases for this variable are the same as for a previously defined variable.

Marginals

The file of frequency distributions on all variables is provided to help researchers plan their analysis and set up computer runs. It is produced using the Frequencies option of SPSS. For variables in tables, full marginals are produced on the first entry and the rest are summarized using the Multresponse option. Where the sampling design requires weighting, both weighted and unweighted marginals are produced.

SPSS control file

The greater part of most SPSS control files is taken up by the full description of the variables. The file provided with each SR contains just such a description for all variables in the dataset. The file is produced by a WFS program, CONVDICT, which translates WFS dictionaries into (among other things) SPSS control statements. Users may be confident that they are syntactically correct, except that the whole dictionary is translated together and this may produce more variables than many versions of SPSS can handle on a single run.

Non-computer information

In addition to these computer files, WFS produced a great wealth of other documentation. All phases of the survey are documented: planning, fieldwork, data editing, table production and so on. Letters, memos and trip reports supplement formal documentation such as contracts, questionnaires and coding manuals. For SR files, a special document is created that describes the file completely; there is, too, an exact specification of all the variables in the file.

Supplementary standard files

The introduction of a new version of an SR file entails a considerable overhead. The standard procedures, while in themselves useful and correct, carried the disadvantage of being time-consuming and expensive, both for WFS London and for data recipients. In the long run it is the archive's intention to create a set of definitive SRs but as a short-term measure a new type of file is in use, the standard supplementary file (SS). These files contain selections of:

1 items from the raw data not carried over to the SR;

```
*  _ _ _ _ _ _ _ _ _ _ _ _ _ _ _ _ _ _ _ _ _ _ _ _ _ _ _ _ _ _ _ _ _ _  *
*                           *** Group 5 ***                             *
*  _ _ _ _ _ _ _ _ _ _ _ _ _ _ _ _ _ _ _ _ _ _ _ _ _ _ _ _ _ _ _ _ _ _  *
*                         Fertility preferences                         *
*  _ _ _ _ _ _ _ _ _ _ _ _ _ _ _ _ _ _ _ _ _ _ _ _ _ _ _ _ _ _ _ _ _ _  *
```

V501	525	2	1	3	88	99	Desire for future birth	
						1	Wants more	
						2	Wants no more	
						3	Undecided	
						88	Not in union, fecund	
						99	Not stated	
V502	527	2	0	1			In union,fecund, wants no more	
						0	No	
						1	Yes	
V503	529	2	0	1			Exposed, wants no more	V502
V504	531	2	0	1			Exposed, wants more	V502
V505	533	2	1	3	88	99	Last pregnancy	
						1	Wanted	
						2	Not wanted	
						3	Undecided	
						88	Never had fert preg	
						99	Not stated	
V506	535	2	0	1	88	99	Last pregnancy unwanted	
						0	No	
						1	Yes	
						88	Never had fert preg	
						99	Not stated	
V507	537	2	0	1	88	99	Prefers next child to be boy	
						0	No	
						1	Yes	
						88	Not applicable	
						99	Not stated	
V508	539	2	0	1	88	99	Prefers next child to be girl	V507
V509	541	2	0	18	88	66	Additional children wanted	
						66	Last not wanted	
						88	Not in union, fecund	
						97	Undecided	
						98	Other answers	
						99	Not stated	
V510	543	2	0	5	88	66	Additional children wanted <5+>	V509
						5	5+	
V511	545	2	0	25		98	Total children desired	
						98	Other answers	
						99	Not stated	
V512	547	2	0	9		98	Total children desired <9+>	V511
						9	9+	
V513	549	2	1	4		99	Number desired: number alive	
						1	Desired < living	
						2	Desired = living	
						3	Desired > living	
						4	Other answers	
						99	Not stated	

FIG. 27.1 Page of WFS dictionary

2 corrected versions of variables in the SR, in particular the sampling variables (V002-V005);

3 versions of the four standard background variables used in the cross-national summaries series.

27.6 The process of distribution

Contracts

WFS surveys were governed by a contract between the relevant government and the ISI. This sets out the plans and schedules for the whole survey and includes a clause on rights to data. The phrasing varies but article XV of the Morocco contract is typical (appendix A). The substance of the clause is:

1 no questionnaires to leave the country;

2 no information to be divulged identifying individuals;

3 a clean data tape to be deposited with ISI;

4 government approval needed for any analysis of the data, except cross-national comparative studies carried out at WFS headquarters;

5 priority of data access to nationals of the country;

6 exchange of information on the use of the data.

Other contracts, for example Bangladesh (appendix A), are simpler, but at least half the contracts are essentially the same as that for Morocco.

Non-contractual authorities

In practice, however, the contract does not specify the distribution policy pursued in London. Between its signing and the availability of the data a fairly long period elapsed during which conditions in the country might change. Ministers, governments, even constitutions, come and go. Certainly, there were changes in the personnel concerned with the survey.

WFS always ensured that those responsible for the survey felt happy about any use of the data. Once the First Country Report had been written, they were invited to define how they wished WFS London to handle their data for further research. In the majority of cases a ruling was given by letter and this became the basis of WFS policy. A typical letter is shown in appendix A.

The background to release

Each survey in the WFS programme is described in the First Country Report and its appearance closed the first phase of analysis. It was generally introduced at a special meeting in the country of interested researchers and government officials, at which a programme of secondary analysis was set up. This programme was based on the local demographic community but might involve overseas institutions, particularly where there were few indigenous demographers. Then, too, the data would often be released to researchers not associated with the country or with the programme of secondary analysis. However, for some countries this was too early, dissemination being postponed until their own nationals had completed their programme of research.

In a few cases a conservative policy is part of national strategy for statistical data. This may be for a number of reasons, all of which must be viewed with respect. For example, countries may have hosted surveys, only to see the data carried off for analysis abroad. This has created a protectionist attitude from which later surveys, such as WFS, have suffered. Sometimes background variables which appear harmless acquire extreme sensitivity. In one country, particular breakdowns were suppressed as they might have had a bearing on political representation and resource allocation; another country realized that strategic information could be calculated from a particular variable.

Preconditions

Before they could receive data, researchers had to satisfy certain conditions. For example, Thailand insisted that those handling its data demonstrate familiarity with the Thai background. A universal qualification has been that researchers must be bona fide scientists. The nature of these conditions has varied from country to country. We may refer to them as *preconditions*, to be satisfied *before* release can be considered.

Some preconditions were laid down explicitly, others became apparent only when embodied in a decision. For example, one country, which operated a notably liberal attitude toward data release, unexpectedly refused a request on the grounds that the proposed study was not original enough. They were quite within their rights to do so but this type of precondition was not usually stated at the outset.

Sometimes the personal attributes of the researcher, unknown to the archivist, could influence the decision. This could even lead to the situation that, whereas being a national of the country is generally a bonus point, it could be counterproductive where there is local inter-institutional disagreement.

Release has often been to institutions rather than individuals. This was particularly striking in the case of a young university lecturer whose application was refused and was only endorsed, after some delay, when re-submitted (at the country's request) under the name of his professor.

Postconditions

Given that the data were available and that the researcher satisfied the preconditions, there was then a set of rules which applied *after* the data were released. These postconditions were set out in an agreement form, one of which had to be signed for each country used by any project using WFS-derived data. These agreement forms are similar for most countries. The researcher undertakes three things:

1   to use the data only for the specified project;

2   not to release the data to any third party without authorization;

3   to supply copies (generally two) of any publications arising from the project.

The WFS agreement form for Sri Lanka in appendix B is typical. An important variation occasionally encountered is a clause insisting that all publications must be sent *in draft* for clearance.

The agreement form is a record that the researcher is committed to the necessary conditions. In a few cases the form fulfilled a further function. The signed form was sent to the country where it was countersigned and returned as a record of its agreement that the data could be distributed. In these cases the form is more elaborate and contains more conditions. An example of this format is Indonesia (appendix B).

The variety of users

The great divide among WFS data users has been between those in the original country and others. Those within the country have tended to look to the survey agency for their data and negotiate their own conditions of release. Many are closely associated with the survey agency anyway. For those outside, negotiations were normally conducted via WFS London. In what follows, in-country researchers are ignored, not because their work on WFS data has been unimportant, but because they do not raise the problems to which we are addressing ourselves.

Expatriate nationals of the country generally occupy a privileged position and some aura of their privilege may fall on those from neighbouring countries or even from developing countries in general. For the rest, the critical distinction is between participants in comparative studies and those involved in single-country studies. The documents in appendix A show comparative projects singled out for more liberal treatment. We talk about projects rather than people as the same researcher may get access for a comparative study but be refused for a non-comparative one. However, the categorization can present problems.

How many countries constitute a comparative study? Two? Three? Four? As a rule of thumb, we have said that a comparative study must cover at least three countries. Again, is it comparative if each country is written up separately? That is particularly tricky: we have tended to rule that each paper is a single-country study and must be treated as a separate project. Since much is already published about WFS surveys, how should we classify a study which uses published sources for four surveys but needs access to the original data for a fifth? Or where all the surveys being used are non-WFS except one? Here is scope for highly theological debate. Fortunately most cases are straightforward.

Certain bodies have had a privileged role in the analysis of WFS data. One is WFS London itself. Its cross-national studies used data from countries to which no general access had been allowed. The other is the Population Division of the

United Nations. This has the commission for the main comparative work on WFS data and has access to the data for almost every country in the programme.

Other UN agencies have been accorded similar privileges, either under the wing of the Population Division or in their own right: ILO, UNESCO, WHO, ESCAP, ECA, ECE. Two UN-sponsored demographic study centres, in Cairo and Accra, have also been granted rather wide-ranging access by some countries to use·data for teaching purposes.

There have been few approaches from profit-making organizations and none have been pursued very far.

On whose authority?

The overriding importance of the distinction between single-country studies on the one hand and comparative studies on the other now comes into focus. The data belong to the country of origin and the right to authorization rests with it. However, half the countries in the WFS gave ISI the privilege of distributing their data for any comparative projects. This simplified the procedure for everyone. For most datasets shipped from London no specific authority was required once ISI saw that the researcher and the project could satisfy the necessary preconditions.

For countries which had not given such clearance, a specific application to the country was prepared. Apart from two countries for which the agreement form acted as an application form, the request was made by letter with a description of the project included or attached.

Most of these requests were promptly and liberally dealt with. There was sometimes a problem in getting a reply, at least within a reasonable time. But even apart from this, there could be a real problem in getting a release: it was by no means always a formality. There were countries, certainly, which virtually never refused and, conversely, countries which almost always refused. These we generally knew about and could advise clients in advance. Some countries, however, authorized some and not others, though even here one could get a fair idea of what to expect.

All non-comparative requests needed specific clearance, whether there was clearance for comparative projects or not, except for Fiji which gave ISI *carte blanche* in distributing its data.

In each country there was a single person with whom contact was maintained. In three-quarters of the cases this was a director of a statistical bureau, either national or within a major ministry, sometimes with some added function ('statistics and censuses', 'statistics and information'). The rest were mostly concerned with population statistics or a family-planning programme. It appears that the officers usually made the decision themselves but sometimes higher consultation occurred, up to cabinet level in one case. Or there might be national policies or laws within which they had to operate. In Jordan, for example, data distribution is governed by Article 3 of the *Jordan Statistics Act* No. 24 (1950).

This is not a static situation: countries change. Almost always change has been in the direction of allowing freer use of the data, although occasionally the reverse is true.

The release

The needs of some users of WFS-based data were met directly by the originating country, particularly where they were nationals, but most data release — including the preceding negotiations — was handled by WFS. WFS, in effect, acted as a broker for the data. The actual process — the steps between thinking up a research project and starting on the data analysis — varied a great deal.

If a user was new to WFS, particularly if from a new institution, it might take one or two exchanges of letters before WFS had sufficient information to proceed. The archive needed to know:

— who was involved in a project;
— what countries' data were needed;
— the arrangements for data security;
— the hardware requirements (tape formats, etc.);
— the subject to be studied.

All this was best supplied using the WFS application form, the content of which is contained in the WFS Data Archive Leaflet reproduced at appendix C. An agreement form had also to be completed for each country. WFS could then send any datasets for which no specific authorization was needed and start negotiations for any that needed authorization from the country.

There were several institutions where the number of users of WFS data warranted the establishment of a local contact who acted as a channel between WFS and the local researchers. The local contact kept all datasets supplied and released them for use only on receipt of written authorization from London. This had advantages to both sides and providing the conditions laid down by the countries were adhered to seemed a sensible arrangement. In fact, our impression is that these conditions are even more likely to be understood and followed under the guidance of these experienced contacts.

A couple of case studies flesh out this sequence, in particular with respect to timing. All dates are the dates on the document, not those of receipt.

1 A researcher in the US wrote on 20 May 1983 requesting data from seven countries. Five of those were on general release and already available at his institution, so an authorization was sent to his local data centre on 6 June for him to have access to the tapes. Letters went to the other two countries on the same day. One replied on 16 June, the other on 21 July. Authorizations were dispatched by WFS on 24 June and 4 August as, again, the datasets were already available. On 16 August the researcher requested further countries. One had embargoed all requests. A letter went to the other on 30 August but no reply has been received at the time of writing.

2 A researcher in Paris wrote on 22 April 1983 requesting the use of data from five countries. He was asked for further information (27 April) and this was

sent on 3 June. He was sent the appropriate agreement forms on 18 June and the datasets for two countries for which there was a general release were dispatched soon after. Letters to the other three countries were also sent on 19 June, with replies on 9 July, 6 August and 16 September. These datasets were sent in two dispatches on 28 August and 16 October.

These two cases are fairly typical. In one case the researcher was able to start work within three weeks of writing to WFS but some of the project requests were still outstanding nearly a year later. In the other, all requests were satisfied but the process took six months.

27.7 A look at the countries (as at mid-1984)

The Asian and Pacific group of countries contains the oldest WFS surveys, with fieldwork ranging from 1974 to 1978 and covering a wide range of release conditions. Fiji was unique in having gone beyond releasing data for comparative studies: WFS could release the Fijian data for any bona fide research. Bangladesh, Pakistan and Sri Lanka gave release for comparative studies and generally endorsed country-specific requests. Nepal also gave a release for comparative studies but did insist on seeing texts in draft before publication. Indonesia and the Republic of Korea liked to vet all requests but in general were happy to release their data. Thailand was prepared to release only to researchers with a detailed knowledge and experience of the Thai background. Malaysia usually agreed to release. The Philippines released to some international agencies but in general was unwilling for other researchers to have its data. Iran was still carrying out data processing; the results are 'being revised in some respects and necessary alterations are being carried out to make it compatible with the aims and achievements of the Islamic Revolution of our people'.

Fieldwork in Latin America was carried out from 1975 to 1979. General release for comparative studies was given by Colombia, Costa Rica, Dominican Republic, Mexico, Panama and Peru. Paraguay vetted all requests but was keen not to restrict distribution. Ecuador was delayed in publishing its First Country Report, so a general policy had yet to be evolved. Venezuela was thought to have given a general release but this was withdrawn.

The Caribbean surveys were in the field between 1975 and 1977. Guyana and Jamaica both gave a general release but Jamaica expected to clear all publications in draft. Haiti and Trinidad and Tobago preferred to vet each application.

The Middle East surveys were later, and were carried out from 1976 to 1980. Syria and Egypt preferred to vet all applications but Jordan distributed widely. Egypt, in fact, restricted release to projects involving Egyptian nationals. Yemen AR had only just published its First Country Report. Turkey was the only country where even WFS London and the UN might not have the data (but see comment in section 27.2 on p. 712 above).

The African countries form the last round of WFS surveys, with fieldwork between 1975 and 1982. Kenya, Lesotho and Cameroon gave a general release for comparative studies. For other African countries, scattered releases were authorized but in general it is too early for clear policies to have emerged.

Portugal gave a general release for comparative studies.

The developed countries are different again. The data from these surveys are not handled by ISI but by a UN agency and no general information on their policies about data release is available.

27.8   Editorial postscript

Previous sections have dealt with the archiving and distribution of datasets during the currency of the WFS programme. In this postscript we briefly describe the fate of the archive since mid-1984.

In recognition of the fact that a strong international demand for WFS data-sets would continue for a number of years, ISI and IUSSP decided in 1984 to create a Dynamic Data Base (DDB), as part of the newly formed ISI Research Centre in The Hague. One of the major functions of the DDB would be to continue the work of the WFS archive. Financial support for this endeavour was provided by USAID. The DDB officially took responsibility for WFS archiving functions in September 1984, though the physical transfer of the data, documentation and equipment from London to The Hague did not take place until early 1985.

The essential procedures of the WFS archive, described above, have been preserved by the DDB. Such continuity was made possible by the appointment of three ex-WFS staff to the DDB.

The DDB has continued to improve the amenability for analysis of WFS data. Particular attention has been paid to the household files which were in a relatively poor state compared to the SR files. The consistency of household data has been improved by further editing and automatic correction. New variables describing household composition have been created and added. Standardization in the ordering and labelling of variables has been imposed, and household variables have been systematically transferred to SR files. By mid-1986, this work had been completed for the 12 African surveys.

More limited improvements have been made to the SR files. For a few surveys, definitive versions were still lacking by the end of the WFS programme and hard-copy documentation was incomplete. These loose ends have been tidied up. More significantly, the SS files are being integrated with the SR files.

With the addition of household variables and community data (where available), the DDB is systematically creating final, fully comprehensive versions of SR files, which had been the ultimate goal of the WFS archive.

Concurrently with these developments, further liberalization of release conditions have been negotiated with a number of countries. At mid-1984, Fiji was the only country to allow automatic release for all bona fide research projects. By mid-1986, Indonesia, Republic of Korea, Thailand, Dominican Republic, Peru, Jordan and Guyana had agreed to a similar policy and it is hoped that this liberalizing trend will continue.

The DDB also assists analysts of WFS data by maintaining and distributing the suite of software developed at the London headquarters (see chapter 18). Many of the programs have been downloaded for use on micro-computers, thereby further increasing their utility. Further demographic analysis programs are being added.

The archiving function of the DDB is not restricted to the inheritance from the WFS project. It has a mandate from ISI and IUSSP to add to its collection files from other similar surveys and to improve their structure, consistency and documentation before making them available. A total of eight developing-country non-WFS fertility survey files have been fully incorporated into the archive and are already available for distribution under conditions agreed with the originators of the data. A number of developed-country WFS files have also been acquired. In collaboration with the Westinghouse Institute for Resource Development work has started on the proper archiving of files from the Contraceptive Prevalence Survey programme. In these ways, the DDB is building upon the expertise and reputation of the London archive and ensuring that the services provided to the research community continue to grow in value.

APPENDIX A. Examples of documents controlling data release

1 Extract from contract for Morocco Fertility Survey (1980)

Article XV: Rights to use and publication of data. The Ministry grants to the Institute and to other regional and international organizations designated by the Institute, access to the data collected, on the following conditions:

a No primary data will be taken out of Morocco without the specific authority of the Ministry.

b No information permitting identification of persons interviewed will be divulged.

c A clean (machine-edited) copy of the magnetic tape, containing all the variables as originally coded, will be handed over to the Institute one month after it has been successfully used in the preparation of tables for Country Report No. 1. The date anticipated for the handing over of the tape is 15 June 1981.

d Except for cross-national comparative studies, no individual or organization, including the Institute, will be permitted to use the tape or any other survey data not published by Morocco, in order to publish them, without the prior written consent of the Ministry with respect to the document.

e Priority for country-specific studies of the Moroccan data will be given to requests originating from Morocco.

It is understood that the Ministry and the Institute will keep each other informed of the use to which the data will be put in accordance with the foregoing articles.

2 *Extract from contract for Bangladesh Fertility Survey (1975-6)*

Article XVI: Right to data and publication. The Government of the People's Republic of Bangladesh grants to the Institute the right to analyse and publish all data procured under this Agreement and to put tabulations on raw data produced under this Agreement in the ISI/WFS data library where they will be available for scientific use of responsible researchers subject to prior approval of ISI/WFS. Copies of all publications should be sent to the Government.

3 *Extract from a letter from Colombia (25.11.79)*

1.1. By agreement, you have generally the right to release data for any specified comparative analysis inter-countries, and there is no need for us to receive here all the requests. We would appreciate it, however, if you would require authors to give due credits, and convey to them our interest in receiving all publications, if possible three copies, one for the library, one for the Socio-Economic Area and one for the Central Offices.

1.2. For any other in-depth analysis for Colombia, we would like to know about requests. There are two alternative situations:

   a That we will not be interested but will welcome any other recognized researcher carrying out as many pieces of research as feasible, and

   b That either we already are in the process of analysing the specific subject or that we will be interested, and again here, we will welcome any co-operative enterprise in which we could help or participate, if financial and other conditions permit . . . .

APPENDIX B. Examples of data release forms

World Fertility Survey **INTERNATIONAL STATISTICAL INSTITUTE** *WFS Project Director:* Halvor Gille 35–37 Grosvenor Gardens, London SW1WOBS · UK *Tel. (01) 828-42 42 · Telex. 919229 isiwfs g ·* *Cable: Fertilis London SW1*	Sri Lanka Fertility Survey (1975) Conditions for release of data

Person(s) requesting data	
Address	
Outline of project (and/or reference to other documents)	
Conditions (as specified by the Government of Sri Lanka)	1. The data shall not be used for any other purpose than the above specific study. 2. The data shall not be handed over to anyone else without prior approval of WFS. 3. Two copies of any publication substantially arising from these data shall be sent to WFS.

I/We undertake to observe these conditions in relation to the above project.

Signed: ——————————————————— ———————————————————

Date: ——————————————————— ———————————————————

World Fertility Survey **INTERNATIONAL STATISTICAL** **INSTITUTE** *WFS Project Director:* Halvor Gille 35–37 Grosvenor Gardens, London SW1WOBS · UK *Tel. (01) 828–42 42 · Telex: 919229 isiwfs g ·* *Cable: Fertilis London SW1*	Indonesia Fertility Survey (1976)
	Conditions for release of data

Person(s) requesting data	
Address	
Outline of project (and/or reference to other documents)	
Conditions (as specified by the Government of Indonesia)	(In the following paragraphs the computer data tape(s) are abbreviated as the tape(s)). The Central Bureau of Statistics, Government of Indonesia, agrees to provide tape(s) of the INDONESIA FERTILITY SURVEY, at cost to the Receiver with the terms and conditions as below. The Receiver agrees to use the tape(s) under the following terms and conditions: a) the Receiver will not make a copy of the tape(s) for use of any other persons or organization; *Cont'd . . . .*

Conditions (as specified by the Government of Indonesia).

b) the Receiver will make use of the tape(s) only for the purpose of research and data analysis so as to gain further understanding about the Indonesian population and so that the highest benefit could be drawn by the Indonesian Government, the Receiver, as well as researchers in the advancement of science;

c) the Receiver will make every effort to include the participation of Indonesian nationals in the analysis of the data;

d) the Receiver agrees to send at least two (2) copies of any report resulting from research using the tape(s) to the Central Bureau of Statistics;

e) for any research paper or report where the main sources of data are drawn exclusively from the tape(s) it is required that approval be obtained from the CBS on the content of the report prior to publication. In such a situation the CBS agrees to send the Comments within 60 days, otherwise it is considered approved. Such research papers or draft papers should be addressed to the Director General of the Central Bureau of Statistics;

f) any other use of the tape(s) deviating from the above terms and conditions can only be undertaken with the prior written approval of the Central Bureau of Statistics. Inquiries should be addressed to the Director General of CBS.

I/We undertake to observe these conditions in relation to the above project.

Signed: _____ _____

Date: _____ _____

APPENDIX C. WFS Data Archive Leaflet

DATA ARCHIVE

INTERNATIONAL STATISTICAL INSTITUTE	**WORLD FERTILITY SURVEY**
Permanent Office · Director: E. Lunenberg	Project Director:
428 Prinses Beatrixlaan, PO Box 950	Halvor Gille
2270 AZ Voorburg	35-37 Grosvenor Gardens
Netherlands	London SW1W 0BS, UK

Introduction

All data collected through the fertility surveys carried out within the WFS programme remain the property of the country concerned. The WFS has been accepted by the participating developing countries as the general custodian of their data. WFS policy is to encourage maximum utilization of ·the data for scientific analysis, while in the interests of the countries safeguarding against any possible misuse. It is therefore necessary for WFS and the users to respect the wishes of the countries and to follow strictly the conditions laid down by them. These conditions vary from country to country. In general they refer to data in the form of individual responses in datasets on magnetic tape or unpublished tabulations.

Status of First Country Report

Countries do not generally agree to release their data until the First Country Report is published. Exceptionally they may do so subject to embargo on any publication until the appearance of the First Country Report.

Nature of studies proposed

There are two main categories of studies for which WFS data are normally requested — country-specific and comparative — and the corresponding conditions for release are different.

Single country studies

Any individual or organization requiring access to the data for analysis based on a single country should obtain specific authorization for the use of data from the country concerned.

Application for such permission may be made direct to the national director of the survey with a copy to WFS headquarters, or may be made to WFS headquarters which will then apply to the country on behalf of the researcher. In either case, the request should be accompanied by a brief and clear description of the research planned. If a researcher requests data for use in more than one project, separate authorization is needed for each project. Direct and active participation of national researchers in the project is highly desirable: most countries tend to give priority to research work carried out by their own nationals.

Studies based on only two countries may also be expected to follow the same procedure.

Cross-national comparative analysis

In the case of research projects involving comparative analysis, some countries have delegated the responsibility for data release to WFS. The status of each country in this respect is indicated in the bi-monthly status report issued by the Data Archive and available on request.

Application forms

For all new projects, an application form must be completed. Copies of this are supplied on request.

Agreement forms

Regardless of whether the research project is single country or comparative, every user is requested by WFS to sign an agreement with respect to each country's data accessed for each project. Agreement forms are supplied by WFS London on request. The conditions for use of the data are set out in the agreement forms. No data will be distributed until a signed agreement has been received by the WFS headquarters; a copy of each agreement is then forwarded to the country concerned. There are three standard requirements which apply in all cases:

- The data are to be used only for the research project described on the agreement form.
- The data shall not be handed over to anyone else without prior approval of WFS.
- Copies of the report arising from the research must be sent to the WFS headquarters for forwarding to the country.

Some countries also require country approval prior to distribution or publication and additional conditions are made by certain countries.

How the data are distributed

All datasets are sent airmail on magnetic tapes. Each is accompanied by a machine-readable dictionary, and frequency distributions. There may also be an SPSS data description (Standard Recode files only). Appropriate documentation will also be sent.

Types of data available

Individual data

These are available in two forms:

- in a standard format across countries (SR data)
- in a format directly reflecting the original questionnaire (IN data).

The SR data are those normally used for analysis.

Household data

These, too, take two forms:

- in a semi-standard form by household member (HM data)
- in a format directly reflecting the original schedule (HH data).

Household data have not to date been as comprehensively checked as the individual data.

Community data, husbands' data, and other datasets

These are available for a few countries only and are not generally available for distribution.

Charges

A charge of US $60 (or UK £30) is made for each dataset dispatched. This covers the magnetic tape, postage and documentation.

World Fertility Survey
INTERNATIONAL STATISTICAL
INSTITUTE
WFS Project Director: Halvor Gille
35–37 Grosvenor Gardens,
London SW1WOBS · UK
Tel. (01) 828–42 42 · Telex. 919229 isiwfs g ·
Cable: Fertilis London SW1

Data Archive

**Application for use
of dataset(s) from
WFS programme.**

This form is intended as a guide. Use extra sheets as necessary

1	Institution/department (full address) (Please note address for invoice, if different.)	
2	Who is primarily responsible for this project, including security of the data? (Usually principal researcher or head of department. Give address if different from (1)).	
3	Names of other people associated with this project and their role. (Give nationality if not that of country of institution, and address if different from (1)).	☐ None
4	WFS datasets to be used that are already available at institution.	
5	Datasets to be used that WFS Archive will have to supply.	
6	Duration of project	Start: Finish:

7	For countries from which clearance must be sought, do you want WFS London to apply on your behalf or do you want to apply direct? Also indicate any other special circumstances affecting this.	
8	For projects leading to an academic qualification (MSc, PhD, etc.), please give details. For other projects, please indicate source of sponsorship, funding or other support.	
9	What sort of publication is envisaged?	
10	*For first application from institution:* Where will the data be kept and what security system will be used for protecting them from unauthorized users? Tape format required:	Tracks: Parity: Labels: Mode: Code: Max blocking: Density:

Date ————————————————————————

Signed————————————————————————

Outline of project.   Continue on blank sheets if necessary.

PART VII

Contribution to Knowledge in Selected Areas

28

Demographic Levels and Trends

John C. Caldwell
Lado T. Ruzicka

28.1 Introduction[1]

When the World Fertility Survey (WFS) was first conceived, it was seen largely as a way of measuring fertility levels and trends, and the impact of fertility control exercised through contraception. Early in its history doubt was expressed as to whether the planned sample sizes could provide trustworthy guides to fertility levels,[2] while shortly afterwards it was argued that retrospective fertility histories were likely to be so biased as to disguise real fertility trends behind spurious ones (Potter 1977). Since then, WFS has produced data and reports on a much wider range of matters. It has also recovered its nerve with regard to fertility trends, while methodologies have been developed which apparently yield reasonably correct estimates of trends for both fertility and infant and child mortality for the past 10 or 15 years.[3] At the same time contraception has been placed in a perspective where it is seen as only one of a range of constraints on fertility.

There has as yet been little attempt to assess the impact of WFS findings on generally accepted views on demographic levels and trends. This chapter attempts to do this with regard to fertility, mortality, nuptiality and lactation, but will not enter the area of fertility determinants, and confines itself to developing countries. We examine both the impact of WFS upon demographic figures with official authorization and its more general contribution to knowledge in these fields. The emphasis is on the contribution made since the WFS Conference in 1980 and we discuss the papers in the three volumes of proceedings (WFS 1981) only in passing. Considerable attention is paid to journal articles which represent publications independent of WFS and of governments and which have been accepted by the usual academic screening procedures.

28.2 The emergence of knowledge

The first WFS survey, in Fiji, was not carried out until 1974, while the First Country Report for that survey was not published until 1976 (Bureau of Statistics 1976). The first significant wave of surveys occurred in 1975 and 1976[4] with First Country Reports beginning to emerge in 1976 and 1977. A significant number of data tapes began to become available from 1976 although Standard Recode Tapes were delayed for another two or three years. Thus, given the lead time necessary to prepare and publish demographic estimates by international agencies, the WFS impact was limited even at the end of the 1970s. This was also true in terms of comparative assessments, as is clear from many of the major contributions to the 1980 Conference where pre-existing knowledge and the WFS plans and strategies formed the bulk of the presentation (Tabah 1980; 1981; Macura 1981; Mauldin 1981).

WFS began its *Occasional Papers* series as early as 1973 and its *Basic Documentation* in 1975. The *Technical Bulletins* followed in 1976, the *Scientific Reports* in 1977 and the *Comparative Studies* in 1980. The earlier publications were methodological and a significant body of analysed findings was not published until 1979. Even then, there was a greater emphasis on contraception than on fertility, while nothing appeared on either nuptiality or mortality until 1980.

Meanwhile, other organizations, usually by collaborative arrangements with WFS, were beginning to publish analyses of the data. Perhaps the clearest publications of all, lucidly written and emphasizing major findings, have been those published by the Population Reference Bureau of Washington. Between 1980 and 1982 five publications covered levels and trends in marriage, breastfeeding, contraception, family-size preferences and the status of women (Durch 1980; Kent 1981; Mamlouk 1982; Kent and Larson 1982; Curtin 1982). In addition Lightbourne, Singh and Green (1982) attempted to chart global childbearing. Even earlier, the Population Reference Bureau was incorporating WFS findings in its widely distributed *Population Data Sheets*.

Meanwhile the United Nations Population Division 'in fulfilment of recommendations by the United Nations Population Commission and with financial support from the United Nations Fund for Population Activities' had begun a series of analyses of WFS data which will prove influential in that the conclusions emerge from the UN secretariat. A preliminary treatment of fertility was published in 1982 (United Nations 1982c), and, building upon this, the more comprehensive *Fertility Levels and Trends as Assessed from Twenty World Fertility Surveys* (United Nations 1983a) and a study of the relationship between fertility and education (United Nations 1983d) both appeared in 1983. The 20 countries covered in the study of levels and trends included in 1975 one-seventh of the world's population and one-fifth of that of the Third World. These populations were heavily concentrated in the tropical Americas, South-East Asia and the countries on the Indian border. However, the assessment concluded that the data from Indonesia, Bangladesh, Pakistan and Nepal were too weak to provide reliable estimates (particularly serious with regard to assessing trends), thus confining the analysis of what was believed to be acceptable data to just under half the populations listed above.

We have examined seven English-language journals which publish in the population field,[5] and have identified 34 major papers analysing WFS data or reporting upon methodologies for doing so. The first papers appeared in 1978, when five were published, while peak publication occurred in 1981, partly as a result of the preparation of analyses for the 1980 WFS Conference in London and the 1981 IUSSP Conference in Manila. Since then, the average annual rate of publication has been at about half the 1981 level, possibly partly because of a desire by journals not to be too dominated by a single source. The first papers were entirely concerned with the inter-relations between desired fertility, contraception and the fertility impact of contraceptive practices, some of the authors being employed by the agencies funding WFS. By 1983 the emphasis was largely on fertility and mortality. Some of the exciting new and slightly peripheral findings (at least in terms of the original objectives) received most attention in 1981: nuptiality and lactation being particular examples. Since 1981 interest in mortality has accelerated. Over the whole period, more than a quarter of the papers have been on the inter-related areas of contraception and desired family size while almost half have been on fertility. The IUSSP Conference in Manila in 1981 (IUSSP 1981) yielded fewer papers employing WFS data than might have been anticipated. The half-dozen major papers employing WFS data concentrated heavily on fertility and its proximate determinants. We make no attempt to assess the contribution of the First Country Reports which have had a very considerable impact within most countries and which form a major source of data for researchers. Nor can we hope to provide a systematic review of 600 or so country-specific analyses that WFS informed us have been completed or are in progress.

28.3 The use of WFS data in authoritative international assessments of demographic levels and trends

Outside the academic field, the real test of WFS is the extent to which estimates based upon its data and analyses are accepted as reliable guides to demographic levels and trends. Some institutional users take a great deal of data straight from WFS publications and note the fact (for instance, the Population Reference Bureau publications).

While preparing this chapter, we wrote to most institutions which issue regular or periodic assessments of demographic measures, asking them to explain (or to provide existing documentation) how data from various sources are employed in producing their estimates and in particular the mechanisms involved to incorporate WFS data and analyses. All replied that their methods were complex and sophisticated and hence that no general principles could be stated. Nor, apparently, is there any routine procedure for dealing with new results from WFS. The only alternative approach is to examine the series that they produce in an attempt to identify discontinuities which might be attributed to WFS information.

In a slightly different category are the programmes of the United Nations Population Division (UNPD). Unlike the WFS, this is treated by the international agencies and by governments as being representative of national governments. Its reassessment of infant mortality levels had a major impact on the *1981 Demographic Yearbook,*[6] which is produced by the United Nations Statistical Office (UNSO), both the UN Population Division and the UN Statistical Office being parts of the United Nations Department of International Economic and Social Affairs. This has not yet been the case with such better known indices as crude birth and death rates where there are more national data and stronger governmental opinions. Changes to date have been piecemeal and often reluctant. However, it is probable that the Population Division assessments — certainly with regard to trends and a little less certainly with regard to levels — will ultimately be accepted.

The 1983 assessment of fertility trends by the Population Division programme (United Nations 1983a) attempted to assess WFS fertility levels by comparing the findings with other available sources. The WFS total fertility rate was over 10 per cent higher than the other data source in Fiji, Guyana and Colombia, while it was more than 10 per cent lower in Bangladesh and 5 per cent lower in Nepal. Such comparisons are important but one could debate their validity as an assessment criterion. More serious disagreement was found when comparing the analyses of population trends for retrospective periods varying between 5 and 12 years obtained by applying the same analytical methods to WFS and other data. In only about half of all cases was there even approximate agreement, demonstrating perhaps that not all the misgivings about the retrospective analysis of trends were unjustified. Indeed, in the cases of Bangladesh, Kenya and Jordan, the trends were in the opposite direction (in Bangladesh WFS implied a decline in the total fertility rate between 1964 and 1973 of 21 per cent compared with a rise of 7 per cent in the other data source, but Bangladesh is a special case for reasons given below). Where both sources agreed upon a decline, WFS found almost treble the rate in Indonesia and close to double in Jamaica and Panama, while the competing source identified a decline fourteen times as steep in Pakistan and three times as steep in the Philippines. The important finding is probably that in these 20 Third World countries both surveys (or WFS alone in the two cases where there was no comparable source) agree that there was significant fertility decline in 15 cases. The disclaimer — a highly significant one — is that the exceptions include the only mainland South Asian, Middle Eastern and African countries analysed. Certainly, by the beginning of the 1970s, fertility was falling generally in East and South-East Asia and in Latin America. However, with regard to Indonesia, the most populous country in these regions (apart from China), there was a major disagreement about the rate, WFS indicating a relatively steep fall (for Java and Bali to which the survey was restricted). The United Nations assessment emphasized changes in marital fertility and discovered contrasting patterns. Marital fertility tended to fall faster with age but this was more marked in Asia than in Latin America and even in the former this pattern is beginning to be modified. Marital fertility still resembles natural fertility in its distribution in Kenya and Nepal and in Pakistan except at the older ages, particularly in urban areas. Bangladesh unexpectedly exhibited marked deviations from natural fertility. The evidence appeared to show that only 15 years before the surveys, namely around 1960, a natural fertility pattern had obtained even in the Republic of Korea, Colombia, Thailand and the Philippines.

Ultimately, the most influential and authoritative series of demographic measures is the United Nations *Demographic Yearbook (DYB)*.[7] With regard to fertility measures, the impact of the World Fertility Survey has as yet been relatively slight. At the time of preparation of the 1981 *Demographic Yearbook* (the most recently published), WFS information was available from 29 countries. The crude birth rate estimated by WFS was reasonably close and led to no readjustment in 20 cases. This was also true of the total fertility rate (TFR) for 24 countries.[8] This is not surprising. Even crude and patchy data can yield reasonably good approximations of single fertility measures. In tropical Africa, where the data were poorest, the series of estimates in the *Demographic Yearbooks* were little changed by the major analytical input represented by the development of the Brass and stable population methods and the analyses published from the Princeton African project (Brass *et al.* 1968). Where WFS indicated considerable discrepancies in the published birth rate, the *DYB* published a figure much closer to the WFS findings shortly after the latter became available in the cases of Colombia, Paraguay, Republic of Korea and Nepal while the rate for Thailand was not altered until several years later. In spite of major discrepancies (for instance a discrepancy of seven points for the Philippines), no adjustment has been carried out for Lesotho, Mexico, Panama or the Philippines. Total fertility rates were changed, apparently in accordance with WFS findings, for Colombia, Mexico, Panama and Thailand. The alteration of the TFR for Thailand was in fact conceded three years earlier than the crude birth rate. It should be emphasized that the UN Statistical Office does not change *DYB* figures without guidance from national governments and the battles for the acceptance of WFS figures are usually fought by (or sometimes within) national statistical offices. When there are conflicts in data, as in Bangladesh, not even a collaborating national statistical office is necessarily convinced of the relative correctness of the WFS estimate.

The WFS fertility histories also provided much better infant mortality estimates than most countries had hitherto possessed (or than had originally been anticipated by WFS). Usually they were much higher than those published in the *DYBs*, often twice the magnitude or greater still. Of 28 estimates in the *DYBs*, their retention on the grounds that they approximated WFS findings can be justified only for five (Trinidad and Tobago, Panama, Turkey, Lesotho and Malaysia). Seven clearly understated estimates (Sri Lanka, Guyana, Jamaica, Costa Rica, Senegal, Sudan and Indonesia) have never been changed. Seven others were altered at various periods after the initial survey, often three to five years later (Mexico, Paraguay, Peru, Venezuela, Jordan, Syria and Republic of Korea). However, the most interesting development was a mass change in the 1981 *Demographic Yearbook*, footnoted, as explained, by a reassessment by the UN Population Division, which moved the levels for eight countries with WFS surveys close to the WFS finding (Philippines, Thailand, Haiti, Colombia, Dominican Republic, Kenya, Bangladesh and Fiji).

During the 1970s the United Nations projections of the world population in the year 2000 slowly fell, but the cause appeared to be largely new assessments for the industrial world and China, with no apparent direct impact from new estimates for countries surveyed by WFS (United Nations 1973; 1977c; 1982a).

The 'Population Data Sheets' published by the Population Reference Bureau are assembled and distributed more quickly than any other estimates. Furthermore, they have no close institutional affiliations to hinder them from changing assessments to agree with data being provided by new sources (although in 1978–81 a contract with the Demographic Section of the Population Office of USAID meant co-operation between that office and the PRB in determining some estimates). We analysed their apparent handling of data from the first 20 surveys. For four countries (Thailand, Philippines, Pakistan and Dominican Republic) PRB moved quickly to accept the birth rate supplied by WFS, while in two cases (Colombia and Republic of Korea) both they and the *DYB* moved quickly at the same time. In other instances, their estimates and those of the *DYB* were already similar to the WFS findings (Sri Lanka, Malaysia, Guyana and Jordan). WFS estimates probably played a role in readjustments for two countries, Fiji and Panama, and seemed to have resulted in estimates averaged with those of the *DYB* in two other cases (Mexico and Indonesia, although the latter case may well include an adjustment for the Outer Islands). In the remaining six countries the *DYB* estimates were clearly preferred to those of the World Fertility Survey (Bangladesh, Nepal, Kenya, Costa Rica, Jamaica and Peru, with Bangladesh the most conspicuous example of a deliberate choice being made).

WFS had greater influence on PRB in the case of its infant mortality rate estimates. Six were immediately accepted (Fiji, Thailand, Republic of Korea, Philippines, Pakistan and, with some delay, Indonesia), while WFS estimates appear to have been influential in modifying four other estimates (Nepal, Colombia, Guyana and Mexico). In two other countries changes were made when the *DYB* changed its estimates in 1981 (Bangladesh and Peru). For four countries the *DYB* estimate was regarded as the most acceptable (Sri Lanka, Jordan, Costa Rica and Jamaica). The most interesting cases are, however, the four countries where the Population Reference Bureau believed that both WFS and *DYB* had underestimated the true infant mortality level (Malaysia, Kenya, Dominican Republic and Panama).

In 1975 and 1980 the World Bank published 'World Tables' (World Bank 1980) which included demographic estimates which apparently approximate the continuing demographic estimates maintained by the Bank. Only the 1980 edition was in a position to include WFS estimates. The World Bank has not been a major consumer of WFS estimates. Only one of its crude birth rate estimates appears to have originated directly with WFS (Kenya), although a few have probably been influenced (Senegal, Philippines, Thailand and Paraguay) and nine are approximate averages of WFS and *DYB* figures (Lesotho, Indonesia, Bangladesh, Nepal, Costa Rica, Dominican Republic, Jamaica, Panama and Peru). The most interesting estimates are those where the Bank appears to have sources quite distinct from the *DYB* or WFS: five where the estimates are clearly lower

(Republic of Korea, Malaysia, Pakistan, Sri Lanka and Mexico) and two where they are markedly higher (Colombia and Trinidad and Tobago). The World Bank's infant mortality rates mostly come direct from the *DYB*. Where they do not, the other sources rarely seem to have been WFS although there may have been some influence in the case of Bangladesh and Thailand. Most of the data on the level of fertility control do not appear to derive from WFS (Thailand may be an exception), while those for only a limited number of countries are drawn from either the Westinghouse Health Systems Contraceptive Prevalence Surveys or the Population Council's *Fact Book* (Nortman and Hofstatter 1980).

The United States Bureau of the Census issued volumes of world demographic estimates in 1977, 1979, and, for populations of over 10 million, in 1981 (US Bureau of the Census 1978; 1980; 1981). Fourteen crude birth rates are available for examination. Four appear to originate with the WFS (Thailand, Turkey, Colombia and Jamaica), one with the *DYB* (Guyana), four to be close to an average of these two sources (Bangladesh, Jordan, Nepal and Peru) and five to differ markedly from both these sources (Kenya, Pakistan, Philippines, Dominican Republic and Mexico). Of the 13 infant mortality rates available for comparison, seven appear to be from WFS analysis (Nepal, Thailand, Turkey, Colombia, Dominican Republic, Guyana and Mexico), one from the *DYB* (Jamaica) and five from completely different sources (Kenya, Bangladesh, Jordan, Philippines and Peru).

To compile its 1980 *Fact Book* (Nortman and Hofstatter 1980), the Population Council published data on the fertility control of married women for 28 countries: four solely from WFS data, six from both WFS data and special Population Council questionnaires, two from both these sources plus the Contraceptive Prevalence Surveys, one from both the first two sources plus a third source, 12 solely from Population Council questionnaires, one solely from Contraceptive Prevalence Surveys and two from both Population Council questionnaires and Contraceptive Prevalence Surveys. The four countries for which WFS data were the sole source were Jamaica, Nepal, Pakistan and Panama. The two countries which had reported WFS findings but where these were not utilized were the Republic of Korea and Mexico.

In 1977 the Assembly of Behavioral and Social Sciences of the (American) National Research Council set up a Committee on Population and Demography to report on demographic levels and trends for a range of countries. The reports on Republic of Korea, Thailand, Bangladesh, Egypt and Colombia made major use of WFS data and frequently treated WFS as the most reliable source (Committee on Population and Demography 1980a; 1980b; 1981a; 1982b; 1982c). The Turkish Study reported that WFS data had become available too late and noted only the total fertility rate (Committee on Population and Demography 1982a), while no WFS survey was carried out for Honduras (Committee on Population and Demography 1980c). A Panel on Fertility Determinants produced studies of the determinants of fertility trends in Thailand and the Republic of Korea (Committee on Population and Demography

1982d; 1982e) which drew heavily on the proximate variables data in the WFS surveys.

As yet, the World Fertility Survey has been used less as the major source of data for international population statistics than many of us associated with its activities would have anticipated. Its lowest level of use has been for fertility estimates, while it has been more frequently employed to provide supposedly the most reliable evidence for infant mortality rates and levels of fertility control. Part of the problem with regard to birth rates is pre-existing assumptions and estimates, especially by national administrations. Nevertheless, other organizations exhibit considerable scepticism of some WFS measures, largely because they clash with the results of other investigations. They point to the relatively small size of WFS samples and to the fact that the level of scientific expertise in the organization was always qualified by the competence and resolve of the collaborators with whom the organization worked. A few WFS findings have received practically no acceptance.

WFS is widely believed to have understated the birth rate and overstated the rate of fertility decline for Bangladesh, Philippines, Thailand, Peru and Haiti. Conversely there is a measure of agreement that it may have overstated the birth rate and underestimated the rate of fertility decline for Panama and, possibly, Turkey. WFS has not led to any internationally accepted birth rate for Pakistan. There is a view that WFS may have understated the infant mortality rate for Nepal and may have overstated it for Sri Lanka, Trinidad and Tobago, and Costa Rica. There is no agreement about any figures for the Philippines or Jamaica. Bangladesh is probably a special case where data analysis may prove very valuable if carried out in terms of its special timing and circumstances. The fieldwork occurred just as a severe famine had temporarily lowered fertility (and raised infant mortality) as data from the International Cholera Research Laboratory's Matlab area showed (Ruzicka and Chowdhury 1978). This produced both a real fertility decline at the time of the survey and an apparently longer-term one through some kind of distortion of the retrospective fertility histories. The use of Bangladesh data for comparative purposes is likely to lead to difficulties.

We believe that the years ahead will not find WFS consolidating these fertility estimates or making a massive contribution to new estimates except where there are few alternative sources, particularly in Africa. Its estimates may be needed more (because of lesser competition) in the areas of infant mortality and levels of contraceptive use – although, already, in the latter field, it has been succeeded by a surprising number of Contraceptive Prevalence Surveys, which are frequently at odds with WFS findings unless such prevalence is increasing unexpectedly rapidly (Morris et al. 1981). The demonstrations of declines in fertility and infant mortality will probably be largely upheld even if the exact rates are not.

However, partial failures in these areas are of no great importance. The World Fertility Survey has made outstanding contributions in three ways. The first is in the advance of standardized fertility survey techniques and in the spread of expertise (although one should not underestimate the drawbacks of standardiz-ation or the rate at which experts disappear). The second is the development of statistical methodology for analysing demographic surveys, especially those built around retrospective histories of demographic events. The third involves the explanation of different fertility levels and different rates of fertility change. The number of major contributions to demographic knowledge is increasing and this is the subject of the second half of this chapter. The emphasis is mainly on the broader academic community and on material published in journals, even though this may do less than justice to the WFS's own publications where many ideas originated.

Even in the area of estimating demographic levels and trends, it is perhaps surprising that WFS estimates were not accepted more generally and more quickly. The sample size was not particularly large, but it was usually of sufficient size for a fairly accurate estimate of national measures such as the birth rate, and sampling errors have always been determined and published. Furthermore, and in contrast to nearly all other sources, its data have been published and its methods fully revealed.

28.4   Contributions to demographic knowledge by subject area

Fertility

From 1980 a series of fertility analyses appeared in the *Scientific Reports* and in the course of the next two years these covered Sri Lanka, Colombia, Dominican Republic and Kenya (Little and Perera 1981; Alam and Cleland 1981; Langford 1982; Hobcraft 1980; Rodríguez and Hobcraft 1980; Hobcraft and Rodríguez 1982a; Mosley, Werner and Becker 1982). At the same time the *Comparative Studies* presented parallel information on an increasing range of countries in terms of different measures of fertility (Hanenberg 1980; Hodgson and Gibbs 1980; Casterline and Trussell 1980; Goldman and Hobcraft 1982; Jones 1982). In an attempt to depart from the measurement of fertility from the time of first marriage, which is often an unsatisfactory measure because of pre-pubescent marriage or pre-marital births, Casterline and Trussell (1980) carried out an analysis using as the alternative starting point the time of first birth. The draw-back to this approach is that, in spite of all the problems involved, there is for most countries a strong association between age at marriage and age at first birth and the most common reason for movement in the latter is change in the former. Furthermore, progress is being made in the study of the determinants of change in the age at marriage.

At the 1980 WFS Conference Rodríguez and Cleland (1981a) presented a multivariate analysis of the socio-economic determinants of marital fertility in 20 countries showing that the work status of the wife (especially if she works in the modern sector of the economy) is an important determinant, while other significant variables are the wife's education (more important than her husband's although the latter is particularly influential in the Middle East and Latin America) and urban residence (especially in Latin America). Husband's occupation is important in Asia while his work status (particularly whether he is working for relatives or non-relatives) is surprisingly nowhere significant. Chidambaram (1981) reported second-stage analysis findings for Pakistan where three-quarters of the fertility decline could be explained by delayed marriage for women, which was particularly common in urban areas (although urban areas exhibited higher marital fertility than rural areas because of reduced duration of lactation). Only female education beyond primary schooling lowered fertility. Breastfeeding was the most powerful determinant of fertility variations, although the existence of other controls was suggested by the fact that fertility was inversely related to the number of sons. The determinants of contraceptive practice were education, occupation and excess fertility.

Goldman and Westoff (1980) published in *Population Studies* an exploration of WFS data for 15 countries to determine whether fertility could be estimated from current pregnancy data. They found that on average such estimates would have to be raised by 13 per cent to yield correct total fertility rates but great variations in the required inflation factor between countries ruled this out as a practicable approach. Hobcraft, Goldman and Chidambaram (1982) and Goldman and Hobcraft (1982) showed how the P/F ratio method could be employed for the screening and evaluation of fertility history data, with considerable emphasis on subgroups of the population, and could be of value for determining fertility trends. In 1983 the *Journal of Biosocial Science* published two papers: Khalifa (1983) applied the Coale-Hill-Trussell (1975) method to the age pattern of fertility in Sudan, while Poston *et al.* (1983) examined childlessness, and showed that, with the significant exception of the Republic of Korea, nearly all Third World childlessness is involuntary (the 6.1 per cent of childless Mexican wives can be divided into 4.9 per cent who may become pregnant, 1.1 per cent infecund, and 0.1 per cent voluntarily sterile).

From 1980, analyses of WFS data to demonstrate or explain fertility trends began to appear in the journals. Potter's earlier demonstration of the possibility of obtaining results which spuriously indicate fertility change (Potter 1977) was confirmed for one type of data by Chidambaram and Pullum (1981) who showed that this might arise from taking the ages of children as substitutes for birth dates. Fernando (1980) and Hirschman (1980) compared WFS surveys with earlier data for Sri Lanka and Malaysia respectively, the former reporting that the WFS survey had indicated a slightly steeper fertility decline than had previously been believed. Lee and Amin (1981) employed Bangladesh WFS data first in comparison with other data to argue that a modest decline in fertility had occurred and secondly to suggest that it could be wholly explained by declining infant and child mortality. At the 1981 IUSSP Manila Conference, Ochoa (1981) presented a paper on fertility decline in Colombia, and Debavalya (1981) one on fertility decline in Thailand, while Srinivasan and Pathak (1981), when discussing the onset of fertility decline, employed some WFS data in their examination and dating of fertility declines in 10 Asian countries. In an important paper, Hobcraft and Rodríguez (1982b) examined what were in effect the only two successive WFS surveys, those in the Dominican Republic in 1975 and 1980. They claimed that the first survey's findings had led to government promotion of sterilization and that the comparison of the two surveys accurately established the extent of the fertility decline (32 per cent over 15 years), a modest but persistent rise in the average age of female marriage, surprising stability in breastfeeding practices and a 20 per cent decline in the infant mortality rate (over the same 15 years as the fertility decline). They concluded: 'We have accounted for the fertility decline in terms of its proximate determinants, with virtually all of it accounted for by increased contraceptive use.'

By contrast, Lieberman (1982), surveying demographic trends in Pakistan for the *Population and Development Review*, found practically no use for WFS data, largely employing alternative sources even though the Pakistan survey was held in 1975. This was also true of an earlier *Population and Development Review* report on Latin America with the exception of fertility control data (Center for Policy Studies 1980). The *Journal of Biosocial Science* published two papers on fertility differentials in South Asia: Yusuf and Retherford (1981) demonstrated for Pakistan that the beginnings of parity-specific birth control are discernible at the older reproductive ages in urban areas, thus indicating the onset of fertility transition, while Gubhaju (1983) showed that father's education was a more important determinant of fertility in Nepal than mother's education (perhaps largely explained by the very small number of educated women). In 1982 the Population Reference Bureau's *Population Bulletin* summarized WFS findings, showing that steep fertility falls had been reported in 16 countries (all in Latin America, Asia and the Pacific), moderate falls in four countries, and no change in eight (all in Africa, South Asia and the Middle East) (Lightbourne, Singh and Green 1982).

Desired family size and contraception

So important was the question of unmet demand for fertility control to those sponsoring WFS that this was the first question analysed from the data. Indeed, five papers appeared in journals in 1978 before any other journal articles had appeared on WFS findings and before WFS had published any of its own findings on the area. Brackett (1978) and Brackett, Ravenholt and Chao (1978), in their analysis of 10 surveys, concluded that a large proportion of women in the Third World do not want any more children and that these women were found in great numbers even among the poor and uneducated and in rural areas. A far more suspect conclusion was that strong family-planning programmes in eight countries explained contraceptive use rates above 30 per cent, while weak programmes were responsible for 2–5 per cent rates of use and no fertility decline. Westoff (1978), employing a measure based on currently married women exposed to the risk of conception who say that they want no more children even though they are not practising contraception, concluded that around half or more of all women in this group in Republic of Korea, Malaysia, Nepal, Pakistan and Thailand were experiencing an unmet need and indeed around one-quarter of all currently married women, both in these countries and in the Dominican Republic, were in this category (a view he has since modified) (Westoff and Pebley 1981). Rodríguez (1978) showed that there was a greater likelihood that women who knew about contraception or who lived near to family-planning services would practise contraception but that the underlying explanation lay largely in education and urban residence. Knodel and Debavalya (1978) employed two earlier national surveys as well as the WFS survey for Thailand to show that over six years contraceptive use had climbed 150 per cent while marital fertility had fallen 20 per cent. They concluded that the impact of the family-planning programme had been decisive and that a decline in fertility preferences had followed an increase in contraception with its accompanying fertility decline, as in Taiwan and Republic of Korea, although there had been two-way interactions and the situation in the country could be understood only in the context of modernizing tastes and attitudes and a specific cultural situation especially with regard to the position of women. By 1979 WFS had published in its *Scientific Reports* illustrative analyses both of births averted by sterilization (Westoff *et al.* 1979) and of the socio-economic determinants of contraceptive use in Thailand (Cleland, Little and Pitaktepsombati 1979). Pullum (1980) examined fertility preferences in Sri Lanka. The *Comparative Studies* series examined contraceptive knowledge (Vaessen 1980), contraceptive practice (Carrasco 1981) and family size preferences (Lightbourne and MacDonald 1982), as well as dealing with urban–rural differentials in contraceptive use (Lightbourne 1980). WFS surveys suggest that before the employment of modern contraception, often associated with family-planning programmes, traditional methods of contraception have been little used.

In *Population Studies*, Rodríguez and Trussell (1981) sounded a note of caution about the interpretation of WFS and other survey data on desired family size, showing that estimates based on parity-specific proportions wanting more children yielded average desired family sizes from Sri Lankan data ranging from 2.17 (employing Pullum's procedure) to 4.4 (employing their own second procedure). Dow and Werner (1981) compared previous survey and WFS data to show that an increase in the knowledge and practice of contraception in Kenya had not reduced fertility, while Tsui *et al.* (1981a) showed that in Republic of Korea, Mexico and Bangladesh the community level of contraceptive availability directly affected the likelihood of current use, net of the effects of community development (measured by number of schools and newspaper circulation), education (wife's), parity and marital duration. In 1982, WFS methods for measuring the impact on fertility of sterilization were employed for two studies of Latin America (Gomez Barrantes and McCarthy 1982; McCarthy 1982a). An interesting study (Park 1983) of the Korean WFS data showed that the strong son preference in that country resulted in significantly higher sex ratios in small families, and for the last born child, as well as a smaller proportion of all-female families than might be anticipated from a random distribution.

The analyses of WFS surveys gave considerable support to the view that, given a suitable cultural context and if introduced at an appropriate time in terms of socio-economic change, family-planning programmes can accelerate or even initiate a fertility decline. Nevertheless, the qualifications suggesting that this is not a necessary consequence will doubtless be underscored as more African surveys are analysed.

Other intermediate variables, especially lactation

WFS has made a distinguished contribution in the area of the proximate determinants of fertility, especially with regard to lactation. A *Comparative Studies* report appeared in 1981 on breastfeeding (Ferry 1981) and this was followed by an illustrative analysis of Pakistan data in the *Scientific Reports* (Page, Lesthaeghe and Shah 1982). Subsequently, a comparative analysis was published of the differentials in breastfeeding durations and patterns in 28 WFS countries by Ferry and Smith (1983). Meanwhile, Jain and Bongaarts (1981) had shown that there was a range of socio-economic determinants of the duration of lactation; surprisingly, however, the sex of the child, the mother's age and parity and whether she had worked exhibited no significant impact. On average each extra month of lactation increased the birth interval by 0.4 months but there were substantial national differences. They drew the conclusion from the lack of association between parity and the duration of lactation that breastfeeding has not traditionally been regarded as a method for limiting family size. By contrast, Akin *et al.* (1981), analysing Sri Lankan data with a complex probit model, demonstrated that lactation was likely to be shorter when women worked away from home; they also showed that educated women were more likely to breastfeed but to do so for shorter durations and that women on the pill were less likely to breastfeed at all. In a very important paper, Jain (1981) demonstrated that the major determinant of fertility differentials between countries is the great diversity in fertility levels of uneducated women and that these are almost entirely explained by differences in duration of lactation and post-partum abstinence. He concluded that even primary schooling brought women out into the world, allowing communication with outside ideas and enhancing their position in the family. WFS demonstrated remarkable national contrasts in lactation. Women in half or more of the countries of Asia and Africa breastfed for at least 18 months, contrary to all countries in Latin America or the Middle East. This alone shows why the contraceptive demand may increase more rapidly in Latin America than in South Asia (Lightbourne, Singh and Green 1982).

In another important paper on education and intermediate variables Bumpass, Rindfuss, Palmore, Concepción and Choi (1982) showed that, although education affects fertility through breastfeeding and contraception, there is a residual impact even after these intermediate variables are taken into account. This can possibly be explained by the efficiency with which contraception is practised. In a paper of great cultural significance, Rindfuss and Morgan (1983) were able to overcome the inability of WFS to secure adequate data on coital frequency[9] by using conception rates to show that a sexual revolution was taking place within the Asian marriage, now confirmed even more vividly for China (Caldwell and Srinivasan 1984) and clearly happening in India too (Srinivasan, Reddy and Raju 1978; Caldwell, Reddy and Caldwell 1984).

Nuptiality

The WFS has provided the opportunity to analyse changing ages at marriage and changing proportions married by age. The *Scientific Reports* presented illustrative analyses of the situation in Colombia (Flórez and Goldman 1980) and Sri Lanka and Thailand (Trussell 1980) while the *Comparative Studies* presented a report on age at first marriage (Smith 1980a), another on differentials in age at first marriage (McCarthy 1982b), and one on cohort analysis (Smith, Shahidullah and Alcantara 1983).

Jones (1981) compared WFS data with earlier information to evaluate marriage change in Malaysia, while Goldman (1981) showed that the high rates of dissolution of unions in Latin America are accompanied by equally high levels of establishing new unions and hence that the total time outside marriage has little effect on fertility. At the 1980 WFS Conference, Concepción (1981) showed that substantial upward movements in the average female age at first marriage were not universal: among countries where that age was low there had been an upward movement in Fiji, Indonesia and Pakistan; and, where it had been higher, continuing rise was recorded for Republic of Korea, Malaysia, Sri Lanka and Panama. Nevertheless, where the marriage age was low, there had apparently been little movement in Bangladesh; while, where it was high, the same was true not only of the Philippines and Thailand, but, more significantly, of nearly all the Latin American countries studied. Thus Latin America might well be in the process of a dramatic family-planning revolution for two reasons: stable age at marriage and relatively short lactation. McDonald, Ruzicka and Caldwell (1981) showed that fertility declines as the age at marriage rises (except during adolescence) but that women marrying later exhibit a partial catch-up effect in that they have higher age-specific fertility rates at all ages. Nor, in a comparison across countries, can age at marriage be employed to predict fertility (presumably because of different lactation durations). Within each educational class, parity, and not marriage duration or age, is the major determinant of contraceptive use. Divorce is selective of women of low fertility. Only in Malaysia and Indonesia does it appear to be on a sufficiently massive scale to depress fertility. By 1982 the apparent movement in female marriage ages over 20 years could be summarized for 20 countries. In only three, all in Asia, had there been an upward movement of three or more years; by contrast there had been a decline in seven countries, of which five were in Latin America (Lightbourne, Singh and Green 1982). Clearly nuptiality was unlikely to be the major engine of fertility transition, although in parts of Asia it is playing a role that will ultimately prove supplementary but has nevertheless been the major element in early fertility declines, first in parts of East and South-East Asia and now in some countries of South Asia.

One of the WFS comparative analyses (Casterline and McDonald 1983) examined in detail the age difference between husband and wife at marriage, and attempted to explain the wide variation across the 22 countries investigated in terms of differences in family systems and the manner in which unions are formed. In societies where it is claimed that females have had a comparatively low status in the family, the median age differences are relatively large (Bangladesh 9.1 years; Sudan 8.4; and Ghana 7.6; by contrast to the Philippines 2.5 years; Costa Rica 3.0; and Mexico 3.0). The situation may be more complex than this, for most social scientists would debate the classification of female status for Ghana, and indeed for all of sub-Saharan Africa, while others would claim that the latter group are essentially following the European pattern. In the African and Asian countries the age difference is largely determined by the male's age at marriage while the age of entry of the females into a union is rather narrowly limited. Hence, when the marriage of the male partner is late, the age difference between partners is much greater (in Bangladesh, from 5.4 years if the groom is under 20 to 20.3 years if he is 32 years old or more; in the Philippines, from 0.6 to 12.2 years and in Mexico from 1.4 to 12.2 years for the same comparisons of age at marriage category). Because it is the male age at marriage that determines the age gap, one could examine the circumstances that determine the arrangement of a son's marriage in each of these societies (and the advantages accruing to parents of having an unmarried young adult son in the household) or one could even lay some stress on the fact that the arrangement of the sons' marriages is still largely intact in the first group of countries but has almost disappeared in the second. The age difference between marriage partners in most countries narrows somewhat with increase in the educational level of either spouse, and with work before marriage by the wife in non-family cash employment. Both variables probably capture the deviant position of the couple relative to the traditional familial system. Little work has been done in the past on marriage dissolution and remarriage in Asian countries (D'Souza 1982 is an exception) in comparison to Latin America and the Caribbean (for instance, Downing and Yaukey 1979; Roberts 1975; 1982). This may change with information now becoming available from WFS data. The illustrative analysis by Smith (1981a), based on Sri Lanka and Thailand, may encourage similar studies elsewhere in South and East Asia. Smith has shown marked differences in the rates of marital dissolution in these countries by age at marriage and education, and less often by religion and work experience of the wife. In both countries the risk of divorce (generally higher in Thailand than in Sri Lanka) exceeded that of widowhood during the first ten years of marriage. Dissolution rates fall markedly with increasing education; the greater stability of marriages at later age also appeared to be largely confined to women with more than primary education. Higher dissolution rates applied to Muslims than to Buddhists in both countries though such differentials became less pronounced (but were still statistically significant) after controlling for educational level, age at marriage and the work status of the respondent before marriage.

Mortality

A comment made four years ago by Paul Demeny at the 1980 Conference that WFS's contribution to demographic knowledge lay not so much in fertility as in infant and child mortality may be an overstatement in terms of quantity of the studies. But WFS has certainly provided high-quality data, which has meant that a diversity of issues can now be investigated with the methodological and analytical tools developed largely since the late 1960s.

In this section we have deliberately focused on the two aspects of infant and child mortality[10] that, in our view, benefited most from the WFS: the investigation of mortality differentials by demographic and socio-economic characteristics of the individuals and their families, and the impact of birth spacing on mortality. Some findings that are reported as exceptions in the subsequent sections may be largely due to quality of the data rather than reflecting reality. Women with no education, for instance, are likely to under-report births and deaths of their children more often than those with some education; misplacement of events in time and misreporting of ages at death may also occur more often among the former. In the following analyses some of the deviant findings for Senegal, Haiti and Pakistan may well have resulted from such data defects. Where the ages of surviving children have been employed partly or wholly to determine the date of birth, then low levels of education of both mother and children can lead to defective data.

Differential mortality. Mortality differentials have always been a difficult area of demographic study as the data have been drawn from two independent sources: census enumeration and death registration, or birth and death registration in the case of infant mortality. Information on the social and economic characteristics of the deceased has been limited (in particular on the birth and death records) and the linking of the records between the two sources was often an arduous task, leaving on occasion an uncomfortable proportion of records for which no corresponding record in the other source was found (UN/WHO 1979).

The development of indirect methods of infant and child mortality estimation, which has resulted from seminal work by Brass in the late 1960s and further extension of his approach during the 1970s, and the development of methodologies for estimating infant and child mortality from birth histories, enhanced the scope of mortality investigation (Hobcraft 1984). In addition, WFS collected information on the socio-economic and cultural characteristics of the families that has not been matched by most of the traditional sources to date. An additional advantage was that – in most instances for the first time – data became available for the countries where either there was no system of vital registration at all or, more often, the system covered only a segment of the national population or failed to register all relevant events or was defective on both scores.

The analysis of differentials in infant and child mortality from the WFS type of data is not without problems which may be unrecognized (P. F. McDonald

1981), but by and large most of them are minor by comparison to the benefits that have accrued.

Of the demographic characteristics of the child or the mother, four have been shown to have a pronounced impact on the chances of the child's survival: the sex of the child, its birth order, mother's age at the time of confinement, and multiplicity of the birth. Their impact has been documented in Rutstein's (1983) comparative analysis. In 27 of the 29 WFS surveys analysed, infant mortality was higher for males than for females (the exceptions were Jordan and Syria). Toddler and childhood mortality ($_1q_1$ and $_3q_2$) was higher for males than females in only about one-half and one-third of the countries respectively. The tendency towards higher female mortality at these ages was particularly strong in parts of Asia: Nepal, Bangladesh, Pakistan, Philippines and Sri Lanka exhibited higher female than male mortality between ages one and two; in all these countries and, in addition, in Thailand and the Republic of Korea, the mortality of children between ages two and five was also higher for females than for males. Only Indonesia and Malaysia proved exceptions over the whole range of childhood, and the Republic of Korea and Thailand in the case of early childhood ($_1q_1$) only.

By age of the mother, infant mortality showed the expected U-shaped pattern with a trough at ages 20–29 and higher levels at ages under 20 (in all instances), and 30–39 (23 out of 29 countries) and 40 and above (26 countries). The U-shaped pattern was less frequent for toddler and later childhood mortality, appearing in only 12 out of 29 countries (but only in three – Lesotho, Sri Lanka and Jordan – for both toddler and later childhood mortality). The U-shaped pattern of infant mortality by birth order was also less uniform: only in 16 countries was infant mortality higher for first-order births than for second- and third-born children, only in 19 was infant mortality higher for fourth- to sixth-order children; and only in four for seventh and higher order children. The U-shaped pattern of toddler mortality was clearly present in only eight countries, and of late childhood mortality in five countries. In most instances, mortality at ages beyond one year rose sharply with birth order; this pattern of excessive mortality of higher order children was particularly marked in the group of countries with an overall moderate level of mortality (with a proportion of live-born children dying before fifth birthday of between 4 and 8 per cent).

Birth order and maternal age are obviously related. The risk of death of children of mothers of the same age varies with birth order: infant mortality is higher for higher birth-order children of young mothers and for low birth-order children of relatively older mothers (Nortman 1974). This relation is difficult to study with retrospective data of the WFS type if infant mortality is declining. The mortality experience of older mothers and of higher order births is more recent whereas a higher proportion of children of younger mothers and of lower order births were exposed to the higher levels of mortality that prevailed in the past (Somoza 1980).

Children from multiple births – twins, triplets, etc. – have a considerably lower chance of surviving than single births. In the WFS surveys, children from multiple births represented 1.8 per cent of all births analysed in Rutstein's study. As an overall average, children from multiple births were more than four times as likely to die during infancy as single births. The increased risk is carried over to early and later childhood, though considerably reduced to about 1.6 times the level prevailing for single births.

All WFS surveys included information on such background characteristics of the respondents as education, current and childhood place of residence, and work history, while husband's characteristics covered education, current and childhood place of residence, and occupation. Several WFS surveys included additional questions on religion, ethnicity, income, and husband's migration. A comparative analysis of infant and child mortality by selected socio-economic characteristics of the parents and families in 28 countries, using the WFS data, was conducted by Hobcraft, McDonald and Rutstein (1984). The existence of social inequalities in the risk of death has long been known, but, until comparatively recently, it was established quantitatively almost exclusively for the low mortality countries with good census and registration data. The WFS data reveal that striking inequalities exist within many populations with moderate and high levels of mortality. 'It is by no means unusual for the ratio between the group with the highest neo-natal mortality and that with the lowest in the same country to be between two and four; for post-neonatal mortality to be between two and five; and for child mortality to be between four and thirty' (Hobcraft, McDonald and Rutstein 1984).

There are two major concerns of comparative analysis: a search for common features and exceptions; and an investigation of the extent to which socio-economic differentials account for variation between countries (Hobcraft 1984). In the study of mortality differentials, Hobcraft, McDonald and Rutstein (1984) found a huge variability in levels of infant (neo-natal, post-neonatal) mortality and child mortality between countries for the children of the most disadvantaged group (rural non-working mothers with no education whose husbands have received no education and work in agriculture). By contrast, for the children of a middle-class group (mothers with seven or more years of education, working outside the home, and having husbands educated also for at least seven years, working in professional or clerical occupations and living in metropolitan areas), levels of mortality were considerably lower, with only three exceptions in neo-natal mortality (Senegal, Lesotho, Trinidad and Tobago), eight exceptions in post-neonatal mortality (Lesotho and Sudan; Haiti, Guyana and Jamaica; Nepal, Bangladesh and Pakistan) and three in childhood mortality (Guyana, Trinidad and Tobago and Nepal). Moreover, the variability of mortality was substantially reduced. The complex of health-related factors that accompanies higher social status appears to be producing a considerable homogeneity in child mortality across a wide range of countries.

The best model to highlight the majority of the variation in infant and child mortality encompassed three factors: mother's education, father's occupation and father's education.

The importance of parental education in reducing the mortality of their children during the first two years of life was a focus of a comparative analysis by Caldwell and McDonald (1981), covering 10 WFS countries. Although the attainment of primary education by the mother significantly reduced the child's mortality, the step from primary to secondary education had a more critical impact on child survival. In most instances, father's education also had a bearing on early childhood mortality independent of that of occupation. The authors suggested that the combined effect of parental education appears to be greater than the effects of the combined income factors and access to health facilities.

The individual country studies investigating infant and child mortality differentials by demographic and socio-economic factors using WFS data are too numerous to be reviewed in detail and they are still increasing. In the Caribbean surveys, where legal marriages were distinguished from other types of union, children born in the former were found to be generally at a lower risk of dying than those born in other types of union or to mothers who, at the time of confinement, were not in a union. A few studies made use of the characteristics of the household (as opposed to those of individuals) in the investigation of differential child survival (Martin, Trussell, Reyes-Salvail and Shah 1983; Conning and Marckwardt 1982). The availability of sanitation and electricity (Philippines), housing conditions, the type of water supply and sewage disposal (Panama) and access to toilet facilities (Sri Lanka, Mexico) appeared to affect the child's chances of surviving the first years of life. There has been, so far, little published exploitation of the WFS surveys that incorporated the community module in the investigation of the effects of the availability of certain health facilities and other amenities on infant and child mortality.[11] In our view, this area of study is important as the fragmentary and widely scattered information appears to suggest that having access to modern facilities – either piped water and sanitation or health-care provision – does not necessarily confer an advantage on all children. Rather, the impact appears to be greater if the parents themselves are prepared, for instance through having some education, to make effective use of them (Ruzicka and Hansluwka 1982).

The effect of birth spacing on infant and child mortality. The deleterious effect of the close spacing of pregnancies and live births has been noted for at least 60 years (Stevenson 1923; Hughes 1923). Despite subsequent investigations of the association between the patterns of pregnancy and birth spacing and the risk of foetal loss, infant death and child death, the causal mechanisms underlying the relationship have remained unclear (Winikoff 1983). Methodological problems and the shortcomings of many earlier studies make the identification of the possible causal factors merely conjectural or doubtful and the comparison of the results difficult or impossible. The roots of the difficulties lie partly in the complexity of the relationship between birth spacing and infant and child health even though, on the surface, it appears to be a rather straightfoward one. Birth intervals are influenced by a number of factors, both biological and behavioural, that themselves are related in a complex fashion to the health risks and chances of child survival. In most studies the data were originally collected for other purposes and, hence, are inadequate for dealing properly with the complexity of the relationship. Such problems, for instance, largely restrict the validity of the findings of the only comparative programme that preceded the World Fertility Survey, namely the study of family formation patterns and health conducted in nine countries under the sponsorship of the World Health Organization (Omran and Standley 1976; 1981).

The WFS data provide an opportunity to enhance the existing knowledge of the spacing–mortality relationship, first, by improving the quality of the analysis by using a more adequate conceptual frame and taking into account the complexity of the relationship through the application of suitable statistical models, and, secondly, by undertaking a series of comparative studies that would use identical definitions and concepts. The analyses of the WFS data will not, and cannot, answer the questions on causality and mechanisms through which the association between childspacing and mortality operate (for instance, maternal depletion, competition for maternal care among closely spaced siblings, and the increased risk of malnutrition of one or both siblings). However, they may provide useful hints for the design of special surveys and investigations.

So far, two comparative studies (Rutstein 1983; Hobcraft, McDonald and Rutstein 1983) have been completed and a few country studies have addressed the problem using WFS data (for Nepal, Thapa and Retherford 1981; Gubhaju 1984; for Pakistan, Cleland and Sathar 1984; for Sri Lanka, Trussell and Hammerslough 1983; and for Colombia, Baldión 1981). The country studies differ in methodological as well as analytical approaches, thus yielding results that are not strictly comparable. Probably the best study so far is, in both aspects, that by Cleland and Sathar.

Rutstein used WFS data for 29 countries to investigate a broader topic of levels and trends and demographic differentials in infant, toddler and child mortality (defined as $_1q_0, _1q_1, _3q_2$ respectively). A section of the study focused on the effect of the preceding interval length, employing three intervals between live births: short (less than 24 months), normal (24–47 months) and long (48 months or more). In addition, mortality rates were examined for a subpopulation of short intervals where the preceding, older sibling survived either until the birth of the index child (younger sibling) or for at least 24 months. This restriction controls for any correlation between the mortality of siblings and the effects of the older child's death on the length of the interval. All births were aggregated, irrespective of mother's age and the index child's birth order. No allowance was made for the possible effect of the declining trend of infant and child mortality on the amount of the differential impact of spacing patterns.

The findings summarized in table 28.1 confirmed higher infant, toddler and child mortality after short intervals than after normal intervals, and a further improvement in survival after long intervals. The survival of the older sibling further improved the chances of the younger (index) child surviving infancy, but did not markedly reduce toddler and child mortality.

TABLE 28.1

Relative levels of infant, toddler, and child mortality by length of time since preceding birth and national mortality level[a]

National level of mortality[a]	Infant $1q_0$				Toddler $1q_1$				Child $3q_2$			
	Less than 24 months		24–47	48+	Less than 24 months		24–47	48+	Less than 24 months		24–47	48+
	All	Surv.			All	Surv.			All	Surv.		
Extremely high (20+ per cent)	167	142	100	66	124	120	100	53	116	122	100	45
Very high (16–20 per cent)	179	155	100	79	179	195	100	72	125	131	100	81
High (12–15 per cent)	163	137	100	71	149	139	100	54	127	126	100	65
Moderate to high (8–12 per cent)	173	154	100	93	154	150	100	76	118	119	100	75
Moderate (4–8 per cent)	192	152	100	106	139	136	100	64	159	165	100	48
All	178	148	100	89	146	142	100	65	134	138	100	62

[a] The national mortality level is determined by the proportion of children dying before their fifth birthday (percentages given in parentheses).

Note: Surv. = only those cases where the preceding sibling lived until the next birth or for at least 24 months.

Source: Rutstein (1983): table 16

Rutstein's analysis is straightforward, using birth histories and calculating directly the respective mortality measures as well as the length of the intervals. In the other comparative analysis based on WFS data, Hobcraft, McDonald and Rutstein (1983) addressed the problem of childspacing effects on mortality by employing a different approach: they counted the number of births in segments of time before and after the birth of the child in question (index child). Hence, they could identify a series of spacing patterns by counting the number of births 2–6 years before the birth of the index child, and less than two years before the index birth. Furthermore, in order to be able to measure the impact on toddler and child mortality, they expanded the spacing patterns by taking into consideration whether a birth occurred subsequent to the index birth within 0–17 months (toddler mortality) or at 18–29 months (child mortality).

The effect of spacing on infant mortality may be gleaned from the following few examples: *well-spaced children*, that is one live birth 2–6 years before the birth of the index child but no live birth 0–2 years before the index birth, exhibited the lowest IMR in the 26 countries studied (less than 75 in 17 and above 100 in only three countries). A *bad spacing in the past* (three live births 2–6 years before the index birth and no live births in the two years preceding the index birth) raised the risk of infant death by 50 per cent or more in eight countries, by 25–49 per cent in 11 countries and by less than 25 per cent in only seven countries. In the first group were Lesotho with an increase of 131 per cent, Thailand 76 per cent, Portugal 74 per cent, and Republic of Korea 69 per cent. In the last group, where the effect of past short spacing was least noticeable, were three countries (Panama, Jamaica and Senegal). A pattern of *reasonable spacing in the past followed by a short interval* (one live birth 2–6 years and one 0–2 years before the index birth) also raised the chances of infant death: by 100 or more per cent in 12 countries, by 50–99 per cent in 12, and by less than 50 per cent in only two countries. The largest increments of infant mortality in this instance were found in Jamaica, Jordan and Syria, and the lowest in Senegal and Malaysia. Finally, the *history of rapid childbearing* (which, of course, could be identified only for births of order five and above) was characterized by three births in the period 2–6 years before the index birth and one birth during the 0–2 years before the index birth. The effects were disastrous: the risk of death of the index child during infancy more than doubled in all but two countries (Malaysia and Senegal which increased by 63 and 43 per cent, respectively), while in a few countries the risk was four times higher than for well-spaced children (Lesotho, Jamaica, Jordan, Syria and Republic of Korea).

The analysis of the effect of spacing on child mortality ($_4q_1$) could be expanded by taking into consideration whether there was a birth within 18 or within 30 months after the index birth or not. The methodological approach also permits the assessment of the mortality of the first live birth according to whether it was followed by another birth within 18 or 30 months or not. In the case of *well-spaced children* (identified as the index birth being preceded by only one live birth 2–6 years earlier, and with no births 0–2 years earlier and 0–18 or

0–30 months later), only one country (Senegal) recorded a probability of dying between ages one and five in excess of 100 per 1000 survivors to age one. In 12 countries it was between 50 and 99 and in the remaining seven countries it was less than 50 (the three lowest recorded levels being for the Philippines with 15; Jordan 20; Syria and Republic of Korea 22). An additional birth within 0–2 years before the index birth increased the baseline probabilities in 19 out of the 20 countries studied (the exception was Senegal). The increase was by at least 50 per cent in 12 of them (this was the case in all Asian countries except Sri Lanka). The highest impact was recorded in Thailand, Jordan and the Philippines where this type of spacing caused child mortality almost to double. An additional birth immediately before or after the index birth (within 0–2 years before or 0–18 or 0–30 months after) increased the risk for the index child in all but one country (Senegal). In most instances the risk was more than double the baseline mortality (in 15 out of 19 countries, once again in nine Asian countries, not including Sri Lanka and in four Latin American countries, but not Haiti). The estimated $_4q_1$ was a staggering 150 or more in six countries (Lesotho, Peru, Ecuador, Nepal, Bangladesh, Indonesia) and between 100 and 149 in nine out of a further 15.

Another important finding of this study was that the increased risk of infant and child mortality from the poor spacing of births was largely independent of the mother's educational level.

The authors issued some caveats concerning the interpretation of their results. Apart from the problems associated with the quality of the data (Senegal is probably the most striking example of most results being out of line), the spacing of births of individual women and the survival chances of these births may be highly correlated. As no attempt was made to control for the survival of the births that might compete with the index child, such an association might well have biased the results. In addition, there was no statistical control in the study design for the maternal age or the birth order of the index child.

The study is particularly interesting in its attempt to examine the *patterns* of childbearing rather than the length of only one of the intervals (preceding interval in most previous studies). It could thus not only incorporate the effect of the single preceding interval but also expand the pattern to the spacing of the next birth following the index birth.

Of the studies examining the impact of childspacing on infant and child mortality in individual countries, that by Cleland and Sathar (1984) is appealing for its careful conceptual design. They used cohort probabilities of death per 1000 children from between one and 15 years before the survey. Cases with incomplete exposure were discarded and only second and higher order births were used in the analysis. The statistical model used was log-linear.

The Pakistan survey provided in many respects an ideal setting for the study of the effects of spacing on mortality. There was no evidence of a major decline in marital fertility over the period under study, or of differentials in marital fertility among various socio-economic strata of the society (defined by spouses' education, region or urban–rural residence). The prevalence of contraceptive use was very low. The study considered the relationship between the length of the preceding interval and (1) survival of the index child, controlling for the survival of the older sibling; (2) the effect of a succession of inadequately spaced births; and (3) the effect of the timing of the subsequent birth. The length of the preceding interval emerged as a strong determinant of child mortality; in the neo-natal period there appeared to be a threshold of about three years, above which no further advantage was conferred on the index child. In post-neonatal and toddler mortality ($_1q_1$), the decline was almost linear as the interval lengthened. Children born after an interval of up to two years were twice as likely to die as those born after four or more years. After age two the relationship between interval length and survival was less strong but still appreciable. These effects persisted in rural as well as urban families, for the children of uneducated as well as educated mothers, for boys as well as girls and in large and small families.

A surprising finding was that the preceding interval effect remained unchanged in magnitude whether or not the older sibling died at an early age (under age two). Unlike the study by Hobcraft, McDonald and Rutstein (1983), the Pakistan data did not show an appreciable worsening of the survival chances of the index child by a succession of inadequately spaced births; the crucial interval was that preceding the birth of the index child.

The effect of the timing of the subsequent birth (for children who were alive at the conception of the next sibling) was studied with respect to toddler and child mortality ($_1q_1$ and $_3q_2$, respectively). Only about 10 per cent of index children who survived the first year of life had a younger sibling who was born within 18 months of the index birth. The early childhood (toddler) mortality of this group was almost twice as high as that for children with longer succeeding intervals. The chances of death were particularly severe where the index child was bounded on both sides by short intervals, a finding similar to that of Hobcraft, McDonald and Rutstein. The mortality of older children ($_3q_2$) was less affected by the spacing of the succeeding birth. Much of the effect on toddler mortality was probably due to premature involuntary weaning of the index child, though there appeared to be a residual effect of spacing as well, independent of the age at weaning.

Judicious use of variables in this study and controls to avoid biases due to the effect of child mortality on the length of the interval rather than vice versa suggest that a repetition of the analytical procedures for other countries would be a fruitful exercise that, by providing comparable results, may help us to identify the likely causal links and mechanisms through which they operate. Individual country studies could pay due attention to social and cultural practices specific to the societies under study, a task difficult to accomplish in a comparative study encompassing 20 or more societies.

Family structure and fertility

One section of the WFS data that has been less studied is the household questionnaire. One reason for this neglect is the limited accessibility of the household data, partly because of the variation in the structuring of the questionnaires among individual countries and partly because of the technical complexity of household reconstitution. The content of the questionnaire and the definition of the household were largely left to each country and its primary use was in the identification of the eligible respondents for the individual interviews. One potential use of the household questionnaire, i.e. the study of adult mortality, at least for some countries, was mentioned above. Of the other possible uses, only the investigation of the relationship between family structure and fertility has appeared as a part of the WFS Illustrative Analyses subseries (Caldwell, Immerwahr and Ruzicka 1982).

The theoretical formulation of the relationship between family type and fertility by Notestein (1945; 1953), Lorimer (1954) and Davis (1955) has not been clearly confirmed by the results of empirical studies (almost all of them based on data from Asia and largely confined to the Indian subcontinent). Most of the studies show either no significant difference between the fertility of women in nuclear and complex families or even slightly higher fertility in nuclear families. Admittedly, most — probably all — of these studies used data collected for other purposes and, hence, are inadequate to test the original hypotheses. In this respect, the WFS data are no exception. In addition to the conceptual problems inherent in the study of the relationship between family type and fertility, WFS data, by their very nature, have at least two further limitations: the definition of the household and the time frame of reference.

The household was defined so that it rarely exceeded one physical housing unit. However, many of the social issues, pressures and relations that are conceptually associated with supports for high fertility may extend beyond the limits of the physical housing unit. There may be, for instance, little difference between living under the same roof and living in adjacent households where common economic interest and mutual obligations are still maintained; and it is, after all, on these grounds that the rural extended family — at least in theory — exerts its influence on the reproductive behaviour of its members.

The time reference problem is of a different nature but equally crucial. Family structure changes over time and there is no certainty that the fertility we measure took place while the couple lived in the present family structure — nuclear or extended as the case may be. The study by Caldwell, Immerwahr and Ruzicka (1982) used WFS data for Sri Lanka and Bangladesh. It highlighted some interesting features of family structure, some of which, in particular in urban Sri Lanka, may have been the result of a housing shortage rather than of intentional or traditional living arrangements. In both Sri Lanka and Bangladesh most couples start married life in their parents' households and only later, often after some children have been born, form their own households. In Bangladesh, newly married couples almost invariably live with the groom's parents while in Sri Lanka such couples are almost equally divided between living with husband's or with wife's parents. In terms of the possession of chattels and, in the rural areas, land ownership, extended family types appeared to be better off than nuclear families.

With regard to fertility, in Sri Lanka, recent fertility (births in the five years preceding the survey) was higher in nuclear than other types of households, after controlling for an array of social and economic variables; in Bangladesh there was no clear indication of any systematic differences. In Sri Lanka the use of contraception by women currently exposed to the risk of pregnancy was less common in the more complex family types than in nuclear families (contrary to the pattern of current fertility). In Bangladesh contraceptive use was lowest in the families where the wife lived in the same household as her mother-in-law.

This form of analysis was followed in Rodríguez (1981), who extended the analysis to Colombia, Indonesia, Jordan and Pakistan. Unfortunately, some of the findings may be misleading because of adherence to the WFS standard classification of households. This fails to distinguish a married couple (with or without children) living on their own from, for instance, a couple continuing to live in the husband's ancestral house with his widowed mother. To classify the latter as a nuclear family is to ignore half a century's work on the sociology of the Asian and African family.

In spite of the limitations mentioned earlier, the study of family structure *per se*, and of marriage formation patterns, current or recent fertility, and contraception in families of various types, should not be completely dismissed. We can see, however, only a limited scope for cross-national comparative studies; the family formation and family structure patterns evolved within the cultural context of a given society may be better understood if the analysis of the WFS data is underpinned by detailed knowledge of the society and its cultural traditions. In addition, the specific question of the effect of family type on fertility (and childbearing limitations) might perhaps be better examined in the societies which are more clearly divided by lifetime residential patterns. Whether family structure determines fertility, or whether fertility determines when families divide may not be answerable from the WFS-type surveys but rather may have to depend on collecting different types of information in specially designed surveys (Caldwell, Immerwahr and Ruzicka 1982).

28.5　Demographic transition

WFS has provided a fascinating snapshot of global demographic transition. In the countries which have already reported their data, substantial fertility decline is usually the case, but this picture will be modified as the data from the later surveys become available. Where we already possess the data, it is clear that these declines have been largely the result of greatly increased fertility control through modern contraception. Indeed, WFS suggests that traditional methods were probably little used within marriage before the onset of fertility transition (although it can be argued that the survey approach is better fitted to securing information about modern than traditional fertility control). Only in specific regions have increases in the age of female marriage made a major contribution to fertility decline. Such a contribution appears to have been greatest in East and South-East

Asia and non-existent in Latin America. Declines in infant and child mortality and increases in the level of female education appear to have been almost universal and both have clearly contributed to fertility transition. WFS has underlined the major role played by breastfeeding. Indeed, most differences in the levels of natural fertility between countries are probably explained by the duration of lactation, supplemented in some areas by post-partum sexual abstinence (Gaisie 1981). In some countries the existence of a traditional group neither appreciably shortening breastfeeding nor practising contraception, an intermediate group reducing lactation but as yet not effectively contracepting, and a modern group well advanced in fertility control results in an inverted U-shaped fertility curve when the analysis is carried out by education or other indices of modernization. At the 1981 IUSSP Conference, Lesthaeghe, Shah and Page (1981) concluded that increasing contraception might largely offset the decline in lactation and post-partum abstinence in Asia and Africa, but not in Latin America. This might very well be true in Africa for years to come and might result in apparent fertility equilibrium followed by substantial fertility declines once abstinence and lactation reach a minimum. It is unlikely to occur in much of Asia where the adoption of contraception is proceeding rapidly in East and South-East Asia and where lactation is changing only slowly in mainland South Asia.

28.6 Conclusion

The World Fertility Survey has made a major contribution to the study of fertility by insisting, so far as was in its power, on standards of excellence in survey work, data processing and analysis. The existence of its fertility histories and lactation data have substantially advanced analytical methodology and will probably continue to do so for some time to come.

WFS has probably not greatly affected estimates of the overall birth rates, death rates or rates of population growth. It almost certainly has made a greater contribution to estimates of infant and child mortality and to the age structure of fertility. For some countries, its estimates of trends in fertility and infant and child mortality will probably be found to be sound, but we suspect that a substantial number will prove to have been quite wide of the mark. Nevertheless, WFS provided important leadership in demonstrating the exact basis of the estimates.

WFS has done more than any other survey to provide material which can lead us to an understanding of the mechanisms which determine specific levels of fertility and the nature (if not the cause) of fertility change. This achievement came about largely because of the creation of a well-endowed, largely independent institution with real standards and a zest for work and with the necessary freedom to hire good staff for both long-term and short-term periods and to contract out analyses. The lesson should be heeded. In spite of the very substantial cost of WFS, its institutional nature seems to provide a model for what will be needed again to examine the major changes in both fertility and mortality that are yet to come in the process of a protracted global demographic transition. It has had great independence and it was this, for instance, which allowed successive modification of the earlier conclusions about the importance of the density of contraceptive outlets or the magnitude of the unmet demand for contraception.

The use of WFS material has hardly begun. Major journal articles date only from about 1981. So far, the majority of papers have been authored by two groups: WFS staff, often in collaboration with others, and university researchers, overwhelmingly from the major universities of the United States. Especially in the latter category there has been increasing justification for the views expressed by Caldwell (1980) that many analysts would lack any real knowledge of the society being examined. It can no longer be said that this is because well-situated foreigners have beaten local groups to the punch. Sadly, there appears to be growing evidence that many Third World countries will not carry out exhaustive analyses of their own WFS surveys. The journals either have very distinct policies or attract a specific clientele. *Demography* has tended to specialize in comparative analyses of many countries by teams who often know little about them (it has been easier to obtain permission to employ tapes for comparative studies). *Population and Development Review* has published little which concentrates largely on WFS, but some of its papers draw on WFS as well as other data. *Population Studies* has included many of the major methodological papers which have been authored or co-authored by WFS staff. Obtaining the maximum future use of WFS material appears to depend largely on independent researchers having increasing unrestricted access to data tapes. Restrictions so far placed on tapes seem to have resulted in surprisingly little prior publication by the nationals involved. Perhaps a maximum three-year limitation from the time of the survey, much like access to governmental archive material, could be instituted. There is some evidence from the most recent journal articles of an increasing trend towards massive comparative surveys at the expense of culturally specific studies, where in the latter case WFS data are placed in an appropriate framework of other social scientific knowledge and other demographic data.

Often the function of WFS, with its mass of data from different countries, has been to confirm or qualify patterns or relationships reported from more culturally specific studies. For instance, Caldwell and McDonald (1981) examined data from 10 WFS surveys to demonstrate modifications in the relative impact on infant and child mortality of mother's and father's education and of different durations of parental education previously reported from a study of a single African city (Caldwell 1979). On other occasions WFS has contributed to a much larger body of information. Mauldin and Berelson (1978) wrote a paper of fundamental importance on the contribution of family-planning programmes to fertility decline, but, although this is a basic WFS focus, very few WFS data seem to have been directly employed (largely, admittedly, because WFS data were only just becoming available).

Finally, we might emphasize a few important points.

The first is that the impression given by WFS has, through no fault of its own, been affected by a major bias arising from the alacrity of countries in certain geographical regions to undertake the first surveys. The majority of analyses so far published have included in their comparative data mostly countries from the tropical Americas and from East and South-East Asia. They have reported anomalous patterns from a minority of countries (usually one or more of Pakistan, Bangladesh, Nepal and Kenya). Indeed, Africa has been represented only by Kenya. But, as data from the other 12 African countries, from four more countries in the Middle East, and from parallel surveys in a range of Indian states[12] become available, these exceptions are likely to prove the rule for Africa and South and South-West Asia, that is four-fifths of the population of the developing world outside Latin America and China. One reason why it is so important that WFS analyses should continue is the necessity of obtaining a more balanced view.

Nevertheless, as data come from more of these countries, the picture of demographic transition and of the impact of family-planning programmes may change and analysts may be less satisfied with one of WFS's basic analytical approaches, fertility histories and birth spacing data. Fieldwork in many parts of Africa and South Asia shows that, where a considerable proportion of both parents and their children have never been to school, both individual fertility histories and the ages of their surviving children are implausible and mutually irreconcilable. This may affect the analysis of fertility and mortality trends and also the analysis of infant and child mortality by birth intervals.

There has been a tendency lately to concentrate more on briefer questionnaires, such as those of the Contraceptive Prevalence Programme, which are cheaper because of their brevity and because they have a less costly central base. This may prove to be a mistake for three reasons. First, a short questionnaire and a briefer period of fieldwork may prevent the survey from being treated seriously by either interviewees or local co-operating bodies. Estimates may easily be wrong. Secondly, WFS experience has shown that it is only the tedious collection of histories and supporting information that can throw sufficient light on what is happening. Thirdly, a central authority of high calibre is needed to keep up standards and to provide continuing help of better quality than can be given even by 'visiting firemen' who come from good institutions but have not been continually immersed in the same kind of undertaking. The WFS surveys were not, of course, without their faults. Most contained far too few questions eliciting social and economic information and national exactness was often sacrificed to international comparability. For few countries do we know even the education provided for each child of the respondent (mainly those who have left home), even though transition theorists have long believed that it might be this economic burden which proves critical in leading to the decision to limit family size. Equally surprising is the lack of a time dimension for the contraceptive information. In order to understand the mechanisms of fertility transition, we need to be able to link fertility histories with contraceptive histories and probably also with histories of household structure.

WFS has already become a major vehicle for graduate education in demography and other disciplines, a point which is sometimes overlooked. It provides good Third World data for students who cannot undertake fieldwork themselves, and this is particularly valuable when students wish to study their own country. However, it would be a tragedy if the availability of WFS data were to lead to a reduction in fieldwork by students or academic staff or if students came to feel that most relevant explanatory data were on the tapes.

For the successor organization of WFS, there appear to us to be several priority areas. The first is necessarily the preservation and accumulation of the archival data, the continued analysis, and the continued provision of data tapes to institutions which can assist with the analysis. The second is to be a living archive where new material, not necessarily of WFS origin, can be added. We suggest that a matter of absolute importance is the development of some kind of collaborative arrangements with Indian governments and institutions which will allow the maximum analysis of Indian state surveys along WFS lines and the production of global analyses and comparative reports which allow this material to be contrasted with that from the WFS and other surveys. The third is the encouragement of new complementary research work in a range of countries, less standardized than WFS, including more social and economic data, and often incorporating non-survey approaches.

Addendum

After this assessment had been completed the November 1983 issue of *Population Studies* became available. Three out of its seven papers were based on WFS data. Tan (1983) examined the impact of grandmother's sexual abstinence on fertility in Nepal, Bangladesh and Sri Lanka, showing that the practice was important in the first two countries and reduced fertility by around one-third of a child. It was possible to show for Bangladesh that contraception was not substituted for terminal abstinence. The practice makes hazardous the interpretation of the Coale–Trussell natural fertility schedule and of the m index of fertility control. In point of fact the proxy actually employed for being a grandmother was living with married children (perhaps a more stringent measure) and that for abstinence was zero fertility. Trussell and Bloom (1983) compared regression analysis with the use of the proportional hazards approach and the employment of a Coale–McNeil standard schedule to estimate the covariates of age at marriage and first birth in Colombia, rejecting the first as biased and sterile but discovering different strengths for the two latter approaches. We dealt with the third paper, by Martin, Trussell, Reyes-Salvail and Shah (1983) on the covariates of child mortality, in the mortality section.

Notes

1. Research assistance on this chapter was provided by Pat Quiggin, Wendy Cosford and Leonie Brown. Valuable comments were received from Michael Bracher, Pat Caldwell, Virginia Josephian, Ann Larson, and Gigi Santow.

2. William Brass at the first technical meeting in The Hague, March 1972.
3. On mortality, see Feeney (1976; 1980); on fertility, see Goldman, Coale and Weinstein (1979), Hobcraft (1980) and Rodríguez and Hobcraft (1980).
4. The following surveys had completed fieldwork by the end of 1976: Bangladesh, Colombia, Costa Rica, Dominican Republic, Fiji, Guyana, Indonesia, Jamaica, Jordan, Republic of Korea, Malaysia, Mexico, Nepal, Pakistan, Panama, Sri Lanka, Thailand and Trinidad and Tobago; 'associate status' surveys in Hong Kong and Martinique and Guadeloupe had also been completed.
5. *Population Studies,* *Demography, Population and Development Review, Journal of Biosocial Science, Studies in Family Planning, International Family Planning Perspectives* and *Family Planning Perspectives*.
6. This was a special project headed by Birgita Bucht, which, although it took WFS data into account, was not part of the Population Division's WFS programme.
7. UNSO data collection is carried out by sending requests for information, including annual questionnaires, to national government statistical offices. The UNSO carries out this function in order to maintain its own database and to supply data to other UN bodies, including the UNPD. It is the official link to the national offices. The UNSO also collects data, but in a more passive way, by looking at official national publications. If the national government statistical office publishes a series of population estimates or vital rates, these can be used. Census results are often taken from publications although census questionnaires are sent as well. In collecting data, under no circumstance is the work of an individual researcher or organization taken as a government figure, unless the government sends it to the UNSO. Neither are the figures taken from other governments. By contrast, in fulfilling its function of analysing and evaluating demographic data, the UNPD uses a variety of sources. They certainly have full access to the UNSO database, but they are not restricted to it. UNPD estimates are not official (i.e. government) figures but are the UN's 'best guess' as to the 'correct' population estimates, vital rates and other demographic indicators. The UNPD publishes its estimates and they appear selectively in UNSO publications as well.

   With the UNSO database described above, the UNSO produces the UN *Demographic Yearbook* (*DYB*) and *Population and Vital Statistics Report Quarterly* (Series A), and supplies data for other UNSO publications such as the *Pocketbook*. As far as possible, these publications, and especially the *DYB* and Series A, present official government statistics. Population estimates and data from vital registration are assessed for quality by the governments providing the data. If no information is forthcoming from the government, the UNSO assumes the data are 'less reliable' and treats them accordingly.

   In brief, in UNSO publications UNPD estimates are used to supplement official data where the latter do not exist and in cases where the latter are considered 'less reliable'. The UNSO tries to present as much official government data as possible but not to mislead the user.

   The choice of whether or not to use UNPD estimates in place of 'less reliable' data varies with the criteria used for any given statistical table. Table 4 in the *DYB* relies more on UNPD estimates than does Series A, which, dealing only with births, deaths, and infant deaths, presents both registered events and corresponding rates as well as estimated rates, including UNPD rates.

   Regarding WFS estimates, they could therefore appear in the *DYB*, having been forwarded by the national statistical office. They would probably, but not necessarily, be accompanied by a footnote giving the source. Alternatively the WFS estimates could be used in making the UNPD estimates, in which case the UNPD estimates would be the same as the WFS figures or at least close. No footnoting with regard to WFS would appear in the *DYB* as UNPD estimates are only identified as such. In our text analysis, we have concentrated on the *DYB*'s table 4, the widely used world summary of vital statistics.
8. The *DYB* publishes gross reproduction rates which we have converted to TFRs for purposes of comparison.
9. Three questions were recommended in the module on factors other than contraception affecting fertility. Only eight countries asked any of these questions, of which six were in Africa (where only one, Kenya, was among the countries with early reports). Else-

where, only the Philippines and Colombia employed the question and there are doubts about the quality of these data.

10. From the complete marital histories collected in all WFS surveys, it is possible, at least in principle, to estimate adult male mortality from widowhood rates. Many household questionnaires include information on deaths of household members in the preceding 12 or 24 months. Some surveys (for instance, Lesotho, Cameroon, Morocco) included questions on orphanhood, widowhood and sibling survival. We do not attempt to review relevant findings in First Country Reports or in the few published analyses.

11. A workshop was held in London in 1983 to explore the relations between infant and child mortality and community characteristics in several less developed countries. Participants came from Bangladesh, Cameroon, Ecuador, Egypt, Ivory Coast and Peru.

12. These include Bihar, Rajasthan, Kerala, Karnataka, Orissa, Maharashtra and Gujarat.

29

Fertility Determinants[1]

Ronald Freedman

Human fertility is determined by a complex bio-social system. Hundreds of articles and reports have been written about relationships in varying parts of that system, based on results from the World Fertility Survey. Most deal with relationships within specific countries, a smaller number compare relationships across countries and a still smaller number try to explain why the relationships vary across countries. That there has been no attempt to use the WFS to describe the reproductive bio-social system as a whole, either in general or for a specific country, is not surprising, since no one has been audacious enough to formulate an appropriate, inclusive theory or model. The WFS did not begin with an explicit general theory and model.

Nevertheless, important relationships in the reproductive system have been studied using WFS data and a large volume of additional analyses will be forthcoming because data from many surveys have only recently become available. Data for all 42 countries will facilitate particularly the work on cross-national analyses, especially since many of the additional countries will be African, which may have rather different patterns from those of other continents.[2]

29.1 Framework

To facilitate discussion, a grouping of variables in the reproductive system is presented in figure 29.1, which does not presume to be an operational dynamic model. The proximate variables stand between fertility and all other preceding variables. They immediately determine fertility, and all other variables act through combinations of them. They can usefully be divided into natural fertility and fertility-control variables; the natural fertility variables (post-partum infecundability and nuptiality) affect fertility, but their level is not deliberately set for this purpose in societies with natural fertility. They determine fertility in the absence of deliberate fertility control. The importance of these natural fertility variables is underscored by Cleland's (1985) conclusion,[3] largely on the basis of WFS data on knowledge and use of contraception, that '. . . the case for asserting that until recently conscious regulation of marital fertility was largely absent from many, if not all, Third World countries is strong though not proven beyond doubt'.

Abortions and contraceptive use are fertility-control variables which are deliberately used to limit family size, although they may also be used for spacing births.

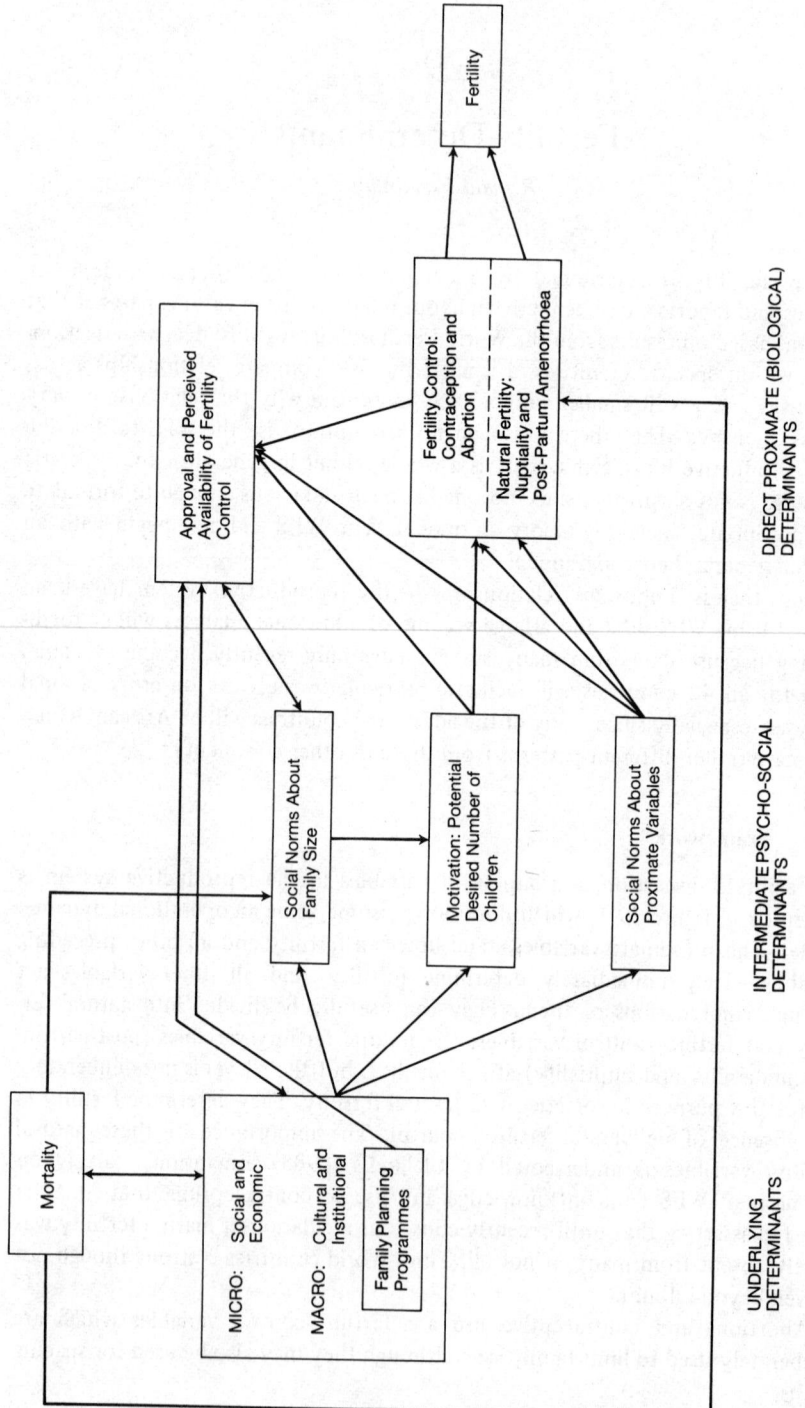

FIG. 29.1 Schema for factors affecting fertility

The motivation to limit family size, social norms about motivations and about the proximate variables themselves, and knowledge about fertility control measures and their perceived costs and benefits come before the proximate variables. Presumably, the motivation to limit family size should be a primary determinant of the use of contraception and abortion.

Behind all of these variables are the ultimate determinants of the motivation to limit fertility, of the proximate determinants, and ultimately of fertility. These background variables include:

1 demographic characteristics of the couple;

2 social and economic characteristics of the couple;

3 characteristics of the institutions and the community, region, and nation;

4 cultural factors related to any part of the reproductive system.

While the discussion of the determinants of fertility is sometimes limited to the direct link between the ultimate socio-economic (SES) or cultural variables and fertility, the increasing attention to the system of intervening links between SES and fertility makes it essential to consider these, too, in evaluating the WFS. Such variables as the measures of motivation to limit family size and the proximate variables are as important as socio-economic variables in determining the total functioning of the reproductive system. They are both dependent on prior socio-economic and demographic determinants and are themselves determinants of succeeding variables in the reproductive system. Many of the most important WFS contributions involve such relationships farther along in the causal chain than the ultimate determinants.

29.2   Fertility, the dependent variable

While fertility is the ultimate dependent variable, WFS data have been used to demonstrate that components of the internal dynamics of fertility — age at first birth and birth intervals — are determinants of fertility and themselves are determined by different cross-national patterns (Rindfuss et al. 1984; Rindfuss, Parnell and Hirschman 1983). The complexity of fertility can, thus, be studied through its elements. In a group of Asian countries, for example, education was found to be important for time of first birth but not for mean birth intervals, while the effects of urbanization were the reverse. The significance of these studies is their demonstration that understanding complex reproductive systems is often facilitated by breaking fertility into the elements through which the prior determinants operate and which, in turn, determine fertility. Another approach is to deal separately with earlier, middle, and later fertility as having differing determinants and consequences (Entwisle, Hermalin and Mason 1982).

Rodríguez, Hobcraft, McDonald, Menken and Trussell (1984) have advanced a theory of birth intervals based on an analysis of nine WFS countries, which is a profound challenge to previous work, because it proposes quite a different view of the sequence of the reproductive process. They conclude that, after the second birth interval, birth order *per se* has little effect on succeeding birth intervals and the probability of advancing to those birth intervals. They write: 'On the contrary, there seems to be an inbuilt momentum to the reproductive process whereby early behaviour and socio-economic differences fundamentally determine the remainder of the childbearing experience.' The length of earlier birth intervals – affected by patterns of breastfeeding, contraception, abortion, and fecundity and other influences – plays a major role. This work leads to serious questions about the effect of target fertility (desired family size) when contrasted with the absence of a birth-order effect. The linking of birth intervals through other behavioural and social variables, rather than by their sequence, suggests to the authors that progress will best be made by taking a holistic view of the reproductive process rather than by studying the correlates of specific birth intervals.

29.3   Proximate determinants

Beginning to quantify the varying effects of the proximate determinants on fertility is, perhaps, the most important achievement in fertility research since the WFS began. For many years the concept of the proximate determinants was available under the name, 'intermediate variables' (Davis and Blake 1956), but only recently has the concept been modelled for empirical analysis. It is a significant advance to be able to estimate the effect of each proximate variable and through them to link the ultimate determinants to fertility.

Significant parts of the primary work of Bongaarts (1982) utilized WFS data. In establishing that age at marriage and lactation amenorrhoea are the principal determinants of natural fertility, Bongaarts has helped to explain the reason for the very large differences in fertility (between moderately and very high fertility) in pre-industrial societies. Hobcraft and Little (1984), in an important advance on Bongaarts' work, moved from aggregate to individual estimation, which permits use of individual data for regression analysis (see also Little and Hobcraft forthcoming).

Application of the complete Bongaarts model to rural–urban and educational subgroups across countries produces important results, only possible now with WFS data (Casterline, Singh, Cleland and Ashurst 1984; Singh, Cleland and Casterline 1985). The results are estimates of how much each proximate variable explains first, inter-country differences between observed and potential fertility and, secondly, variations in fertility between educational and rural–urban subgroups. Despite data limitations, the rich results are too numerous to include here, but some of the most important are:

1 '. . . the movement of the index of infecundability toward increasing fertility as modernization was increased was almost always counterbalanced by contrary movements in the marriage and contraception indices'. There are, however, some exceptions when decreases in breastfeeding probably account for increasing fertility in the early modernization period.

2 Decomposition of educational fertility differences established that differences between the two lowest educational subgroups were mainly due to contraception, while differences between successively higher education strata are increasingly a result of nuptiality and lactation increases. The results for rural-urban groups are less regular, but contraception emerges as the variable which accounts for declining fertility in the process of urbanization.

There is no single set of neat additive monotonic patterns through which the proximate variables affect differential fertility. 'Comparison of these means . . . makes clear what country investigations emphasize more strongly: similar reduction of fertility from unrestricted levels comes about through varying mixes of the proximate determinants.' There are, however, important uniformities for regions, stages of demographic transition, and specific subgroup comparisons which clarify the relations between ultimate determinants, proximate variables, and fertility.

One of the proximate variables – nuptiality – has long been studied by demographers. However, the WFS cross-national data are yielding further substantial results. For example, increasing the age at marriage has little effect on fertility until after age 18 (Chidambaram and Cleland 1981). Marital dissolution has been found to have less effect on fertility than expected, because, in those countries where dissolution is high enough to have a potential effect, remarriage within a short time period is often frequent enough to diminish that potential effect.

For many of the WFS countries, declining fertility partly results from increasing age at marriage. This role of nuptiality in demographic transition differs from that in Western Europe, where changes in marriage patterns did not accompany the major fertility decline which preceded the Second World War.

A United Nations study based on 22 countries found a consistently positive effect of education on age at marriage except in rural subsamples of some countries and in Nepal (United Nations 1983d).

Another study based on 19 WFS countries (McCarthy 1982b) examined the relation between age at marriage and proportions ever marrying, on the one hand, and rural–urban and educational strata, on the other. Women in rural strata married at younger ages than urban women in 17 of the 19 countries, and the difference in rural–urban singulate mean age at marriage was at least two years in 15 of the 19 countries. This is true whether average age at marriage is relatively young or relatively old. In Asia and the Pacific the percentage married by age 45–49 was uniformly high, so there was no rural–urban differential. However, Latin American patterns were different, with a larger percentage still unmarried at 45–49, and larger rural–urban differentials. The more education, the greater the singulate mean age at marriage and the fewer married by age 15–19 in Asia and the Pacific. The relationship is less uniform in Latin America. Since almost all women in Asia and the Pacific marry by age 45–49, there is little difference there by education in the proportion marrying by age 45–49. There is a stronger relationship in Latin America. This study aims at description rather than explanation, so the report has many statements about the specific countries which are exceptions to these generalizations.

Another analysis (Hobcraft and Casterline 1983), based on data for nine countries, indicates that the positive association between age at marriage and age-specific marital fertility can be attributed to a strong marriage-duration effect. There is not yet a comprehensive multivariate analysis of the determinants of age at marriage, which should be a significant result of future WFS analyses.

The emphasis in recent years on breastfeeding as a major immediate determinant of fertility arises largely from the availability of comparable WFS data for many countries (Akin *et al.* 1981; Ferry 1981; Ferry and Smith 1983). These data have indicated large international differences in the duration of breastfeeding and lesser differences in its prevalence. These differences apparently account for much of the large difference in fertility in pre-industrial societies. They also account for part of the fertility differentials between urban–rural and educational strata. In the absence of time series, the role of changing breastfeeding habits on fertility change can only be inferred from cross-section data. Thus, the reversal of fertility in the two lowest educational strata is inferred as due to more rapid decline in breastfeeding in the higher than lower education groups. The relatively low level of breastfeeding in low-fertility countries means that part of the effect of contraceptive practice compensates for the loss of fertility controls as breastfeeding prevalence and duration have decreased. Jain and Bongaarts (1981) estimate from WFS cross-section data that one month less of breastfeeding subtracts 0.4 months from the length of the birth interval.

Urbanization and education of the wife are consistently negatively related to the extent and duration of breastfeeding. Wife's work pattern has a somewhat less consistent effect. Age and parity have a consistent, positive effect. All of these relations vary in degree and sometimes even in direction by country (Ferry and Smith 1983). Understanding more completely the determinants of breastfeeding, like understanding the determinants of fertility, presumably will require better understanding of cross-national differences. Cultural variations in the meaning of the determinant categories and differences in survey procedures, no doubt, account for some of the differences observed.

Fertility declines in the West in the modern period, and recently in many developing countries too, are substantially a result of increasing use of contraception. The WFS has documented the variation in the use of contraception within and between countries. Determinants of fertility increasingly operate through differential use of contraception. An analysis of the determinants of contraceptive use based on 20 countries (United Nations 1981d) found education of either husband or wife to be the most important determinant, with large differentials in most, but not all, countries. However, it is clear that the education of individual women is not always essential, since significant numbers of women with no education used contraception in several countries. Rural–urban differentials were found in all countries except Indonesia. Contraceptive use by women whose husbands worked in agriculture was generally low, although this was not the case in Indonesia. Wife's work was found to have little effect once other variables were controlled.

Once parity is controlled, the relation to contraceptive use of wanting no more children is relatively small, even after allowing for the use of contraception for spacing. This is puzzling, since it is plausible that contraception is used mainly to limit family size. The explanation may be — as some have suggested — that motivation to limit family size is poorly measured in surveys. However, it may also be that, since parity is an important determinant of fertility preferences and motivation, holding it constant minimizes the role of fertility preferences.

Contraceptive differentials appear to be smaller where there are strong family-planning programmes. Further, a United Nations study based on 22 WFS countries (United Nations 1983d) also found that the relationship of education to contraceptive use decreased 'when generalized development had gotten underway'. Also, countries which have large contraceptive differentials on one variable tend to have them for others.

In most of the few countries for which we have relevant data, there is a positive relationship between standard of living or family income and contraceptive use, net of various other socio-economic background variables. This is true for Thailand (Cleland, Little and Pitaktepsombati 1979), Malaysia (Tey and Abdurahman 1981) and Sri Lanka (Immerwahr 1981). Cleland, Little and Pitaktepsombati found that in Thailand there was a significant relationship between standard of living and contraception,[4] net of size of farm and family income, and concluded that the standard of living must capture '. . . dimensions of modernization and community development not measured by other background variables'. In Thailand it was also found that low contraceptive use, as well as high desired family size, was related to perceptions of high utility and low cost of children (Arnold and Pejaranonda 1977). In contrast to all of these studies, an analysis for Indonesia found that, net of other background and demographic factors, couples in the very lowest and very highest standard of living categories used contraception most. Indonesia is perhaps different because its effective family-planning programme has been unusually successful in reaching groups believed to be hard to reach — the poor, the small farmers, and the rural populations — perhaps as a result of its unusually effective administrative pressure at the grass-roots level, which is not found in the other countries considered here (Freedman, Khoo and Supraptilah 1981).

The findings on the determinants of contraceptive use follow a pattern that we see repeatedly for other relationships too — fairly small relationships varying in size and sometimes even in direction between countries.

Understandably, the WFS has contributed little to our knowledge of one important proximate variable — abortion. The WFS was no more successful than other investigations in developing a method of obtaining reliable data on abortion from a survey. The module dealing with abortion was not productive and abortion was not included in the core, since it is illegal in many countries.

29.4   Family size preferences: motivation

The WFS included several measures of desired family size because, either alone or in combination with number of living children, they are indicators of the motivation to have no more children and, therefore, to practise birth control, subject to its cost and physical and psychological availability. In most models of fertility, socio-economic determinants are presumed to affect the proximate determinants and fertility, in large part because they affect how many (additional) children are wanted.

Most measures of fertility preference are more or less indicators of 'pure' demand, since they do not take into account the 'real' circumstances which affect the translation of preferences into behaviour. These circumstances are not only such matters as the economic situation and family health but also how the fertility preferences of the 'significant others' affect the respondents.

The role of preferences as indicated by several measures in cross-national WFS datasets was presented in a synthesis and summary (chapter 31; Lightbourne 1984b; 1984c) at the 1984 WFS Symposium. The results are promising in a number of directions, but were available too late for intensive evaluation here. Nevertheless, important ideas emerge even from a cursory reading of these important Symposium reports when added to several others (Lightbourne 1985; Lightbourne and Singh 1982).

For many years the most important use of preference measures has been to indicate whether significant fertility declines were likely in high-fertility countries. While different measures gave different results, it is clear from the WFS data on unwanted last births that in many less developed countries significant numbers of women want to stop having children. It is likely that more women would understate than overstate the unwantedness of last children. That fertility desires are not unlimited is indicated even in sub-Saharan Africa.

One of the most important WFS results is the finding that postponement of births is a significant part of the fertility preference structure. Lightbourne (chapter 31; 1984b) suggests that models based on first, initial stable preference or, secondly, choices between continuing and stopping childbearing are inferior to a three-stage sequential model 'in which individuals fluctuate between the motives of "have more", "postpone", and "want no more"'. He sees this as often involving a balance between a vague desire for additional children and a contrary desire not to have any more children soon.

Introducing the postponement questions in the later WFS studies has had important consequences. They help, for example, to account for the significant numbers of women in many countries who report that they want more children but also report contraceptive use. Many are probably postponing rather than terminating childbearing. It is also likely that it may explain some other seeming anomalies. For example, some of the women who report that they want no more children may really mean that they want no more children soon. An interesting phenomenon is the significant number of women reporting that they do not want another child soon even though their previous birth was six or more years ago. Unless they have been using contraception or have impaired fecundity, the credibility of such reports is seriously in question.

An important development is the new measures of preference – especially a 'wanted total fertility rate' – adjusting the conventional TFR for unwanted children. Other measures are 'stopping-point synthetic cohort measures'. The reliability and validity of these new measures compared with the conventional preferences measures is discussed but not definitively settled in the recent literature.

While the work on preferences with WFS data represents significant progress, much remains to be done to improve measures and to understand their relation to ultimate determinants, on the one hand, and proximate determinants and fertility, on the other.

As in many other areas, there is a call for longitudinal studies, in this case to improve understanding of why preference statements are unreliable and why they may lack validity, for example, with respect to fecund women who say they want no more children and still fail to use birth control. A WFS-based longitudinal study by Stycos (1984) yielded useful results on how different measures reinforce each other over time. However, such longitudinal studies are unlikely to go far enough when they consist only of the repetition of the same questions. What is needed are investigations of the social and economic circumstances surrounding changing or unchanging statements of fertility preference. This should involve the social, economic and normative circumstances under which preferences are developed, expressed, modified and realized. Further, such longitudinal efforts should include offering contraceptives in attractive ways to women who initially say they want no more children but are not using contraception, followed by intensive interviews with those who do not accept contraception to find the nature of the countervailing forces.

The critics of the preference measures generally take the position that in many less developed countries there is no effective demand for contraception, because there is a traditional social and economic structure which keeps the value of children high and their cost low, so that parents really do not want to limit the number of their children. Further, such an argument frequently states that the supply side is largely irrelevant, since if there is a demand, birth control will be practised with or without a family-planning programme. On the other hand, there is the view that the availability of contraceptive services will increase use at varying levels of demand. The WFS was not primarily intended to resolve this important issue, but some WFS work is relevant.

Tsui (1982) has shown that in Mexico and the rural sector of the Republic of Korea both the perceived and objective availability of contraceptive services is related to contraceptive use, net of the effect of education, occupation, and urban–rural residence.

Rodríguez (1978), studying data from five countries, found that contraceptive use is affected by type of place of residence, education, and perceived availability and accessibility of contraception and that, in addition to a joint effect, each has a net effect. He indicates difficulty in disentangling causal sequences, a normal problem with non-experimental data.

Hermalin, Freedman, Sun and Chang (1979) found that intentions to have more children predicted subsequent fertility better than a large battery of other socio-economic and demographic variables.

Palmore and Concepción (1981) in an analysis based on WFS data for 10 countries found that two of the fertility preference measures had only a modest relation to use of contraception after controls for demographic and socio-economic variables. While they reported that the motivation variables are as highly correlated with contraception as any other variables, a large percentage of women who said that they wanted no more children — varying from 34 per cent in Panama to 93 per cent in Pakistan — were not using contraception. There are also significant numbers of women using contraception (presumably for spacing) although they say they want more children. Wanting no more children is systematically related to contraceptive use in all countries considered in a United Nations study (1981d). The relation of the fertility preference measure to contraception varies across countries. The significance of the motivation variables is sometimes incorrectly diminished by controlling the prior socio-economic and demographic determinants which must operate through motivation (Hermalin 1983). The WFS analyses by no means resolve the issues of the demand and supply situation, but they are useful steps toward a more reasoned and empirically based position.

A United Nations study (1983d) of 22 countries found that education was negatively related to desired fertility in a manner similar to, but somewhat greater than, that found between education and actual fertility.

Recent multivariate studies with larger numbers of countries (chapter 31; Lightbourne 1984b) conclude that, overall, the conventional determinants are much more closely related to actual fertility than to fertility preferences.

The few studies relating economic variables to fertility preferences give varying results. For the Republic of Korea, Kim and Choi (1981) found that such measures as home ownership, rooms per person, or ownership of modern consumer durables have no significant relationship to preferences after adjustment for other variables. Arnold and Pejaranonda (1977) found for Thailand that fertility preferences were negatively related to the perceived utility of children and positively related to their perceived cost. For Egypt (Central Agency for Public Mobilisation and Statistics 1983), desired family size was negatively related to per capita income and expenditure, as well as to ownership of consumer durables, net of other variables. Moreover, aspirations for daughters' education (not sons') — which has cost implications — were negatively related to fertility preferences. Expectations for long-term benefits from children (expectations for co-residence and support in old age) were positively related to fertility preferences, but this was not the case for the short-term benefits from children's labour at a young age.

Easterlin and Crimmins (1982) used the difference between the potential and the desired number of children as a measure of the demand for children and, therefore, of motivation for fertility control to limit fertility in a model of fertility change in several WFS countries. While the relationships are modest, they found their measure of motivation to be related to modernization, on the one hand, and to contraceptive use and fertility, on the other. While this study is handicapped by the fact that the improvised measures are imperfect proxies for the model's concepts, it vindicates the use of desired fertility and other WFS data to test a theoretical model.

29.5 Socio-economic determinants of fertility

The classical demographic studies of the determinants of fertility linked a limited number of demographic and socio-economic variables directly to fertility with little or no reference to the proximate variables or to fertility preferences and motivations which intervene between the ultimate prior determinants and fertility. The WFS core contains only a limited number of such SES determinants: wife's education and her labour-force status or occupation; and husband's education, labour-force status, and occupation. In some cases, ethnic or tribal membership, religion, and region are also included. Some countries did obtain other data by utilizing one or more of the optional modules.

The core variables are familiar in demographic studies based on censuses and large-scale surveys. While it would have been unthinkable not to include these variables, the fact that often little else was included meant that advances in the general knowledge of fertility would have to come mainly from the opportunity for multivariate cross-national and multilevel analyses of the traditional variables. There was little potential for experimenting with other variables in the core, since the questions about fertility and marital histories and the proximate variables were very time-consuming.

The WFS has made an important contribution by providing evidence that the relation between urbanization, socio-economic status, and reproductive behaviour does not uniformly follow the standard patterns conventionally expected in demographic theory. While almost always negative, the relationships vary considerably in degree and occasionally even in direction. Adjusted net relationships between social variables and fertility change differentially by country, region, and stratum with controls for other variables. The size of the relationships is usually quite different regionally even after common controls for other variables. Almost any generalization across countries has exceptions for at least a few countries for which explanations are then sought.

These results may be quite important since studies of differential fertility had become somewhat sterile, consisting increasingly of descriptive statements which did not satisfy the need for the generality or the explanation of the differentials.

The WFS findings make it clear not only that the urbanization and SES relationships vary considerably by country and region but also that the explanation for these differences probably must be sought in the cultural and institutional characteristics of the country and in micro-variables other than the conventional SES. Providing data on the differentials after appropriate controls sets the stage for new approaches to explain the variations in the relationships and to make specific case studies of the deviant cases.

The most comprehensive study of the socio-economic fertility determinants is the multivariate analysis by Rodríguez and Cleland (1981a) based on 27 populations (in 20 countries, with several divided into ethnic strata). Perhaps the most important finding of this important study is that the classical relationships usually studied vary considerably across countries and regions.

For example, the net rural–urban differentials in fertility are relatively large and universal in Latin America. However, they are relatively small in Asia and in some countries do not exist at all. The same factors do not operate in the same way in different countries. Thus, in Thailand controlling employment status and education eliminates the rural–urban fertility differential, although these control factors have no effect on the rural–urban differential in Kenya. So, even with such a supposedly well-established determinant as urbanization, the question is not how the pattern repeats itself but what explains the variation. In this case the authors provide a plausible speculative explanation: Latin American urbanization is older; the more recent Asian modernization may mean that many of its urban residents have rural characteristics.

The United Nations study of 22 countries (1983d) comes to the following conclusions about educational differentials in fertility:

1 differentials were greater in countries with higher levels of development;
2 where there were effective family-planning programmes, educational differentials tended to be smaller, suggesting that the programmes might serve to bring family planning to lower educational strata where it might otherwise have come more slowly;
3 female and male education had a similar relationship to fertility;
4 with more development, the threshold for the education-fertility relationship found at lower educational levels vanished;
5 ethnic group and region were found not to affect the education-fertility relation when gross regional categories were used (e.g. Latin America, Africa) or where ethnic differences were studied in seven countries.

However, the multivariate analysis by Rodríguez and Cleland finds that, on a net basis, the effect of education is less, and less consistent, than often assumed. This is consistent with other recent analyses (Cochrane 1979). They found that, once again, differentials (by wife's education) in Latin America are greater than in Asia and Africa, where the differentials are sometimes quite small. Further, with controls by type of place of residence and husband's education, the relation of wife's education to fertility is not significant for 12 populations and considerably attenuated in the remaining 15. They conclude that differentials in female education reflect, by and large, a general effect for socio-economic status. Their further conclusion that 'the differences that remain after adjustments are not negligible' obviously must refer to a subset of populations and the next question is: why these?

Ogawa (1982) finds that in Indonesia education is positively related to fertility and that the predominantly small-scale farmers have low rather than the expected high fertility. This fits the contraceptive use patterns for Indonesia reported above, with the possibility that the powerful Indonesian family-planning programme and other distinctive cultural aspects of Indonesia are responsible.

Another finding of Rodríguez and Cleland is important not only for its substance but for the interpretation given to it. They find that, after controls, work status of the husband is related to fertility in only one country – Sri Lanka. From this, they conclude that:

This result is quite important because narrowly defined economic theories of fertility place emphasis on the role of kinship in economic organization as sustaining high fertility, while wage employment is conducive to reduction in fertility. This differential doesn't show up in these particular findings.

Before setting aside the possible fertility effects of economic contrasts between kinship-based and secular, impersonal societies, it is desirable to consider whether the WFS questions reflect well these aspects of husband's economic activity in less developed countries, which might affect fertility differentially cross-nationally. The theory is sufficiently important for a negating proof to be a very significant contribution. However, the economic environment which might influence fertility is sufficiently complex that one or a few particular standard questions about occupation and labour-force status may not capture it. Ideally, when the first studies showed no relationship, it would have been desirable to experiment with parallel alternate wordings. However, there was no provision for such experimentation in the WFS. So, the standardization which had so many advantages for the WFS also had its disadvantages.

Rodríguez and Cleland found that wife's work status had a significant effect in 19 of 27 study populations after adjustment for other variables. These results were inconsistent with a finding that there was little net relation of work status and contraceptive use (United Nations 1981d). Chidambaram and Cleland (1981) reconciled the two findings by concluding that for technical reasons response errors probably led to a 'falsely exaggerated impression of the effect of work on fertility'. In a recent review of the evidence, Cleland (1985) asserts that: 'In broad terms WFS findings suggest that participation of women in non-familial work is neither a necessary nor sufficient precondition for fertility decline'. Such a conclusion will undoubtedly be challenged again because of the persistent expectation that some aspects of wife's work should affect fertility if properly conceptualized and measured.

Apart from the data on work status and occupation, there are scattered data on the relation of economic variables to fertility in those WFS studies which added such variables to the core. For example, for Egypt (Central Agency for Public Mobilisation and Statistics 1983) children ever born was found to be negatively related to per capita income, to source of water, and to availability of electricity, net of wife's age and education. Total fertility rates in the previous five years were similarly related to these economic variables. Little and Perera (1981) found that a standard of living index was related negatively to fertility for the second decade of marriage, although the effect was small, especially after controls for age at marriage and education. In Thailand (Institute of Population Studies 1977), family income is negatively related to fertility within three 10-year marriage duration groups. These few studies are rather consistent, but, on the basis of the other variables considered, it is likely that there would be a considerable variation in the relationships for a larger sample of countries.

Rodríguez and Cleland developed a seven-category scale to reflect basic concepts of modernization and demographic transition theory. This is an effort to combine the elements of classical differential fertility analysis variables into a single 'modernization' scale. On an aggregate basis, the unweighted average fertility of the 27 populations does differ monotonically across the seven types, going from 6.9 births for rural agricultural couples, where both husband and wife have no more than low primary education, to 4.2 children at the most modern end. However, the pattern of differentials differs considerably across populations. Within each of the seven types, there are considerable differences in fertility by country. So, broad classifications reflecting multiple demographic transition and modernization concepts differentiate fertility at the broadest aggregation of 27 populations, but there is a relatively weak determination when individual populations are considered as units.

On the basis of WFS data and other studies, household type (extended or nuclear) does not appear to be related to fertility (Cleland 1985; Caldwell, Immerwahr and Ruzicka 1982). However, this is not conclusive, since these analyses have not been able to take into account whether the relatives appropriate for extended co-residence were alive and whether those currently in nuclear households had previously lived in extended arrangements for a significant period of time. One study (Freedman, Chang and Sun 1982) found a modest but significant relationship to desired and actual fertility once these factors were taken into account.

That the relation of the conventional socio-economic determinants to fertility is usually negative is hardly a new finding, of course, although it is an essential beginning. What is more important is that the WFS has the data resources to chart the rather wide variations between countries in the size and pattern of these relationships, especially in comparisons of regions.

The proportion of variance explained in multivariate social science analysis is often modest. As the Rodríguez–Cleland analysis indicates, this WFS-based analysis is not distinguished by a high level of statistical explanation. Considered jointly, the main effects of all the socio-economic variables contribute to R^2 values between 1 and 10 per cent. In this respect, too, the regional effects are notable, with the largest effects found in Latin America and the Caribbean. All the Latin American R^2 values are greater than those of any other country considered.

The reader is referred to a recent review of socio-economic differentials in fertility by Singh and Casterline (1985), which offers a more positive view of the substantive findings on relationships rather than, as here, stressing the importance of the new knowledge of cross-national variability.

29.6   Region and ethnicity as determinants

The role of intra-country region and ethnicity in affecting fertility has not often been treated systematically in cross-national analyses. This is difficult in view of the many diverse methods of delineating region and of demarcating ethnicity. Alam and Cleland (1981) have shown the strong effects of region and ethnicity in differential fertility in Sri Lanka. While such differentials were found in Europe's demographic transition, the European socio-economic differentials in the timing of the fertility decline were not found in Sri Lanka. This led to the observation that the demographic transition does not follow a single pattern. In Malaysia, too, there are much-studied ethnic differentials in fertility. Such differentials found in many countries vary considerably in size. Mosley, Werner and Becker (1982) have systematically related regional and ethnic fertility variations in Kenya to the proximate variables. Zablan (1984) has done a similar exercise for the Philippines. Mosley, Werner and Becker (1982) also suggest that regional variations in fertility may be related to different levels of polygamy. Cleland, Little and Pitaktepsombati (1979) and Freedman, Khoo and Supraptilah (1981) found that region was more strongly related to contraceptive use than any of the socio-economic variables in Thailand and Indonesia respectively. Other country reports also deal with the regional and ethnic effects in their specific situations. Rindfuss, Parnell and Hirschman (1983) have studied the varying role of ethnicity in the relationship between socio-economic status and age at first birth and birth intervals in several South-East Asian countries.

So far, the difficult question of *why* ethnicity has differing effects on fertility in different countries is little discussed in WFS studies or elsewhere — the treatments are almost always descriptive. The UN study of educational differences (United Nations 1983d), in effect, eliminates the problem in one analysis by showing that regional and ethnic differences in the education-fertility relation are due to differences in developmental level. But, where ethnic and regional studies of differential fertility have been done, they generally do not fade away with multivariate controls. The remaining net ethnic or regional effects are generally attributed to 'culture', but, without specific analysis of what it is about culture or region that produces high or low fertility, we may have little more than a name for the problem. However, it is important to identify the ethnic or regional differential to give a direction to future work. The WFS has often done that.

29.7   Community-level determinants

Community-level effects on fertility, contraception, and other aspects of the reproductive system have not yet been shown to be substantial or consistent, but there are exceptions. Generally weak or null results have been reported for analyses of the WFS community-level module for 11 countries, but there are significant relationships in several others.

One community-level analysis found that the availability of contraception at the local community level was related significantly to the use of contraception, net of community development, education, parity, and marital duration (Tsui, Hogan, Teachman and Welti-Chanés 1981a).

An analysis by Tienda (1983) for Peru established that a community development indicator and community education level were significantly related to fertility, net of the individual's education and other appropriate controls.

Using region as the unit for contextual analysis, Lesthaeghe, Vanderhoeft, Becker and Kibet (1983) found that:

The impact of rises in individual levels of female education on life-time fertility (. . . 1965–78) and on the joint fertility-reducing impact of lactational amenorrhoea and contraception (. . . 1974–78) is highly differentiated in Kenya, depending on the contextual levels of education and on the region.

An analysis of the relation of the aggregate intention to use contraception to actual individual use turned out to be significant in two (Thailand and Indonesia) of the five countries studied (Casterline 1981). Casterline also indicated that negative results in the three Latin American countries may arise from the fact that the areal units are less congruent with local units of collective interaction than is the case in the Asian countries.

A WFS seminar in 1983, reviewing these results, agreed that the negative results from many, but not all, community-level studies might result from:

1   inadequate selection and definition of the variables of the module;
2   inadequate methodology in collecting the data in the field specified in detail;
3   inadequate definition of the community;
4   the assumption that the same module could be widely used in different cultural situations;
5   the failure in specific countries to adapt the model to the specific situation;
6   failure to give this module the serious attention given to the core questionnaire in the field (Freedman 1985).

In view of probable inadequacies of some of the community-level data, there was no disposition to give up the proposition that individual fertility is affected by the collective group characteristics, values, and institutions of the effective communities in which rural people live. There is preliminary indication that community-level variables may prove more significant in some of the WFS African studies just becoming available. The positive results in the study by

Tienda became available only after the seminar. There are, in addition, studies by Anker (1977) and by Rosenzweig and Schultz (1982) which show significant community-level effects from other than WFS data.

The evidence just reviewed on WFS determinants taken as a whole does not support very strongly theories which emphasize the primacy of social-structural and economic determinants of fertility. On the basis of such negative evidence and the persistent finding of cultural and regional effects, theories involving the importance of the development and diffusion of new ideas and mental frameworks may have greater appeal. In his review of the possible causes of recent fertility declines, Cleland (1985), taking into account these facts and evidence and arguments not developed here, concludes that:

... taken *en masse* the results are more consistent with an ideational theory of change based on the spread of a new attitude toward family formation and birth control than a structural theory which emphasizes changes in economic roles of family units or of women or children.

While the case for this conclusion is plausible, it is necessarily based mainly on the negation of the principal alternative theory and of observations from other sources, since the WFS did not directly collect data on the ideational elements at issue.

There is, in addition, the fact that, where data on such matters as standard of living, consumer durables, and household amenities were available in WFS studies, in most cases they tended to have a negative relationship to fertility preferences and fertility and a positive relation to contraceptive use. In any case, ideational and economic issues are not cleanly separable. Aspirations for a higher standard of living, for example, are undoubtedly affected by perception of its actual availability and the idea of the value of education is strengthened if those who have it are successful.

29.8 Intra-country relationships

This review has stressed cross-national and comparative analyses, because they are the distinctive result of the WFS and because they are likely to lead to the greatest understanding of fertility determinants. However, the largest body of results are those for each of the 42 individual countries. There are, in the first place, the 41 First Country Reports. These provide for each country very useful descriptive results of the relation between the principal determinants and fertility, fertility preferences, and the principal proximate variables treated by the WFS. In addition, there is an increasing number of multivariate analyses for specific problems in specific countries. These results will be useful in each country. There are many useful country-specific interpretations.

For some countries, these are the first such data available; for others, they can be compared with previous studies. The specific differentials observed can be used for local interpretation and administrative purposes, even if they do not fit a uniform cross-national pattern. The results for each country, however, are likely to be most meaningful when examined on a comparative cross-national basis. Then, it is possible to see how each country conforms to or deviates from a cross-national pattern and to ask the specific question 'why' for specific comparative similarities and differences.

29.9   Multi-level analyses

As we have seen, the relationships of socio-economic determinants to fertility vary considerably between countries. This is usually handled in a descriptive manner: the relationship varies between this and that numerical value with countries L and M low and X and Y high. Usually there is little to indicate why the inter-country variation occurs and why the relationship is low for some countries and high for others. This often makes for dull reading, since it names countries instead of substituting for countries the concepts and variables which might explain their deviant or modal position.

Of course, the mode of analysis is not always so simple, since some explanation is provided by controlling other variables and by considering the relationship within strata of other variables for interaction. However, even after such refinement there remains a great deal of variation. Since the problem being considered is one of cross-national variation in micro-level relationships, presumably a major part of the explanation should come from macro characteristics of the countries.

Such macro-variable explanation of micro-level relationships is the line taken by Entwisle, Hermalin, and Mason in a series of experimental analyses. In the first study, based on only 10 countries (Hermalin and Mason 1980), the authors first showed that the coefficient for the relationship between education and fertility, with a control for marriage duration, had varying negative values and even one positive value. Then, they related these partial coefficients as the dependent variables to a series of characteristics of the countries as explanatory variables. This work is being extended to other problems and to a larger number of countries (Entwisle, Hermalin and Mason 1982; Entwisle and Mason 1983).

Jain (1981), also working with 10 countries, demonstrates that the variation in the micro-based regression for the relation between education and fertility can be explained by the proportion of married women who have no education and the fertility level of such women. The problem is thus shifted to why fertility among uneducated women varies so much between countries.

So far, this kind of work is, necessarily, exploratory and cannot be said yet to have established new, definitive knowledge of determinants. With larger numbers of countries and with more intensive work on both macro- and micro-variables, there is promise for the future. No doubt other approaches to this general problem will be developed. One approach is to try to explain the deviant countries on a case-by-case basis by finding other variables or situations that make them distinctive.

Providing systematic evidence that the relationship of socio-economic and demographic variables to reproductive variables is itself variable is one of the important contributions of the WFS. Finding rather uniform relationships after micro-level controls would have made the study of determinants neat and simple. Establishing the variation that exists is a more realistic approach to the underlying complexity. It also suggests that prescriptions for population policy based on increasing educational levels or women's participation in the labour force, while plausible and appealing, may not always be consistent with the net differentials in specific countries. These relationships are often not as strong or uniform as we had believed.

29.10 The WFS and general fertility theory

The limited number and routine character of the socio-economic variables covered by the WFS has led to criticism that this large enterprise has failed to make as much significant progress as some had hoped it would towards understanding the fundamental social forces determining reproductive patterns. For example, Demeny (1981), referring to the work of Aries, indicates that the WFS did not approach such variables as 'shifts in the status of children within the family' or 'shifting parental aspirations for the children's economic and social status'. He writes that the WFS relies on 'such opaque, if time-honored, variables as urban-rural status, educational status measured by years of school and the like'. Further, he says that, without an adequate theory to explain their meaning and the mechanisms through which they operate, they 'bring no illumination to the causal linkages involved'.

Miró (1981) criticizes the determinants selected because:

1 they are not based on any theory of fertility;
2 they do not provide information for testing competing views of fertility;
3 the variables in the community-level module reflect outmoded modernization ideas and omit questions on the organization of social production, inheritance patterns, differential access to land, the political decision framework, type of family organizations, etc;
4 they do not consider institutional theory or 'at least identifying in a preliminary way the absence, presence, or change of certain institutional forms of cultural patterns, for example, inheritance rules, marriage customs, and the system of local government'.

Such criticisms offer legitimate, but not necessarily practical, suggestions of what is essential for fundamental advances in the theory of fertility in a programme like the WFS. The WFS was not designed to move in these directions. It is not at all certain that it could or should have been. First of all, it is inconceivable that any of the limited number of WFS 'standard' socio-economic determinants could have been deleted in favour of any others, and no one has suggested that. Omitting any of them would have produced an uproar among demographers.

So, it would have been a matter of adding questions and the areas suggested for addition would, in most cases, involve a considerable block of questions — mainly untested. It would, however, have been difficult to add many questions, given the large number already required for the proximate variables and various components of fertility and the few standard SES questions.

The more serious problem is whether questions in the areas suggested by Demeny, Miró, and others have been sufficiently tested to merit standard inclusion in the core required of 42 countries. In retrospect, it seems that some of these topics should have been treated in special modules, if interested scholars could have been commissioned to prepare them. The substantive ideas of the critics have merit, but it is doubtful if they could have been advanced very far through the mechanism of standardized national surveys. (They do not suggest that they could have been.) Insofar as they involve testing a theory of fertility or its components, that might best be done first by a small number of intensive studies — and not necessarily by surveys. Once favourable results are obtained by intensive studies, it might be possible to translate them into a survey format for wider testing.

There is considerable question as to whether such a transfer is possible, but experiments are desirable to test whether such findings as those of Caldwell, Reddy and Caldwell (1982) and Cain (1981) from village studies can be tested in a national survey format. Such experimentation in selected parallel studies might well have been a part of WFS.

A more fundamental question is whether a general theory of fertility determinants exists or where it would come from. Brass suggested at the 1980 WFS Conference that, for fundamental advances in basic fertility theory, we need a Darwin or a Newton of fertility. Such genius does not arise out of contracts or commissions. Certainly, the WFS did not begin with a general fertility theory. However, important middle-level theories and generalizations are emerging out of the work being done with WFS data on important parts of the reproductive system, for example, the work on proximate variables (Casterline, Singh, Cleland and Ashurt 1984) and of birth interval determinants (Rodríguez *et al.* 1984).

Cleland's broad-ranging essay (1985) illustrates how WFS analyses — along with findings from other sources — may be used to advance the discussion of larger theoretical issues.

It is questionable whether a valid *general* theory of fertility is possible without greater knowledge than we have at present of specific sub-relationships within the reproductive system through which ultimate determinants can affect fertility. The WFS has contributed substantially to such essential building blocks of a more general structure.

The standardized format of the WFS did not lend itself to using first-stage results for testing ideas and modifying the next study accordingly. Thus, the null results of the husband's work variable, if perceived early enough, could have been a basis for testing a parallel variant. In retrospect, the opportunity for experimental related studies, suggested early on, might profitably have been followed.

29.11 Summary

Studies based on the WFS data have provided a large body of information for 41 countries on many of the specific relationships which compose the complex bio-social system of reproduction. While the description of determinants and relationships in each country is of great value in itself, the distinctive contribution of the WFS is in placing the values for each country in a cross-national, comparative framework. That process frequently has not found closely comparable patterns cross-nationally. Usually, the finding has been that a relationship varies considerably cross-nationally in degree and sometimes even in direction.

A distinctive contribution of the WFS with respect to ultimate fertility determinants is in charting the variations in the size and pattern of the relationships, while demonstrating again the usual consistency with expectations of the broad directions of relationships.

Many of the most important WFS contributions are concerned with determinants and measures farther along the causal chain than the ultimate determinants. An example is in indicating the value of breaking fertility into components of age at first birth and the length of birth intervals (Rindfuss *et al.* 1984) or into early, middle, and later fertility (Entwisle, Hermalin and Mason 1982). Especially noteworthy is an analysis suggesting that birth intervals past the second are determined by prior experience and socio-economic determinants rather than target fertility (Rodríguez *et al.* 1984).

One of the most important results has been in quantifying the role of the proximate variables between countries and social subgroups. Pioneering work on the cross-national relations between social variables, on the one hand, and the proximate variables and, through them, fertility, on the other, illuminate the path to substantial further progress (Casterline, Singh, Cleland and Ashurst 1984). In particular, for Third World countries the balance of the opposite effects of increasing age at marriage and decreasing breastfeeding helps to explain both the rates of decline (or sometimes increase) in fertility and the character of the differentials. Estimates are available of how much variation in breastfeeding affects fertility. Knowledge and use of contraception tend to be related to fertility, on the one hand, and to demographic and socio-economic determinants, on the other, usually but not always in expected ways, although the relationships are modest and are variable cross-nationally. In addition to quantifying the effect of nuptiality change on fertility declines, the studies have estimated the age at which further postponement of marriage affects fertility (about 18) and have shown that marital dissolution, even when common, has relatively little effect on fertility in the Third World.

How many children respondents want and whether they may have more than they want are related to use of contraception modestly, but as strongly as most other determinants. There is also a modest relation to fertility.

Fertility preference measures, while still imprecise, indicate rather clearly that many couples in high-fertility countries have more children than they want. Further, it appears that fertility desires are not unlimited even in countries of sub-Saharan Africa. The reliability and validity of new preference measures (e.g. wanted total fertility rates and stopping-point synthetic cohort measures) can best be tested in longitudinal studies, but to be useful such studies need to go beyond simple repetition of questions to a study of the social circumstances of changing preferences. There is already evidence that use of contraception is affected by the perceived actual availability of supplies and services.

Wife's and husband's education is related to fertility cross-nationally. However, for wife's education, fertility is often higher for the next to the lowest than for the lowest educational category. The relation of education to fertility becomes attenuated when other socio-economic variables are controlled, so that education may be interpreted as a broad socio-economic indicator. The WFS found that husband's occupation and work status are almost never related to fertility. This has been interpreted as an indication of the weakness of an economic-kinship hypothesis, but such an interpretation based on a specific limited measurement may be premature.

Ethnicity and region have been shown to be significantly related to various aspects of reproduction, but we still have to explain why this is so and attempt to understand inter-country variations.

The essentially null results so far in many, but not all, studies relating community-level variables to various reproductive measures have been disappointing. However, in view of the probability that both the concepts and methodology can be substantially improved and some positive results achieved, a review seminar concluded that it is premature to decide that the collective values and institutions of communities do not affect fertility. Since then, several studies have appeared with positive results.

The ultimate determinants considered in the WFS are those which have been studied for a long time in demography. The distinctive WFS contribution is in giving us for the first time information on the cross-national variations in relationships for a large set of countries. The WFS did not, and probably could not in a single cross-section study, deal with less conventional determinants, which may be quite important.

The WFS has not yet been the basis for a new general theory of fertility. The WFS did not begin with a general theory or the major objective of developing one. Those tasks and that of testing new concepts may be better advanced in a limited number of intensive studies than in highly standardized multi-country studies. The WFS should not be faulted for what lay outside its goals and methodology.

The WFS is, nevertheless, relevant for fertility theory. Many of the specific findings are pertinent to such general questions as the relative role of structural and ideational elements in fertility change, or the role of supply and demand factors in the adoption of contraception. Cleland (1985) has written a stimulating essay on how the WFS relates to larger theoretical issues. In any case, many of the specific relationships illuminated by WFS analyses are probably necessary building blocks for a larger structure of general theory. But no one can predict just when and where major new integrating ideas will emerge.

Currently, large numbers of scholars, including many graduate students, are working on the massive cumulative body of WFS data and analyses. Some of the most significant reports are very recent. The probability of significant results is increasing, because the larger the number of prior significant findings, the greater the probability that they will lead to new ideas.

Notes

1. Much of the work on this chapter was done while I was a Visiting Fellow at the Office of Population Research, Princeton University. It was completed at the Population Studies Center of the University of Michigan. I received helpful suggestions from John Casterline, John Cleland, V. C. Chidambaram, Albert Hermalin, and John Knodel. Responsibility for the chapter is, of course, mine alone.
2. This chapter is necessarily based on papers available to the author before December 1983. The considerable number of new papers, including those for the 1984 WFS Symposium, could not be taken into account. An exception was made for several papers on fertility preferences, since these represented major new materials on an important topic.
3. When this chapter was almost complete, I had the opportunity to read Cleland's excellent paper which drew on some materials and publications not yet fully available to me. I cite some of his observations, although I could not in every case fully examine the evidence on which they are based.
4. Phananiramai (1981) had similar results in another analysis for Thailand.

30

The Proximate Determinants of Fertility

John Hobcraft

30.1 Introduction

It is now just over ten years since the publication in English of two important books on mathematical models for human fertility: these represented the culmination of about 20 years' work (Henry 1972; Sheps and Menken 1973). The late 1960s and early 1970s also saw much activity in microsimulation of fertility. In retrospect, and probably at the time to those involved, what was conspicuously lacking from much of this work was a solid empirical foundation, although numerous investigators struggled valiantly and ingeniously to circumvent this. A major contribution of WFS in the past ten years has been a substantial addition to our knowledge on some of these issues, although this chapter will also demonstrate the patchiness of the coverage on some crucial topics.

As is well known and amply documented, the content of the WFS core questionnaire was determined by very widespread consultation. But it is certain that Ryder and Westoff played a crucial role in the design, thus bringing to bear the fruits of their long involvement with pathbreaking fertility surveys in the US. The key features of the WFS core questionnaire which are of relevance to this review of the proximate determinants of fertility include the birth history, the marriage history, duration of breastfeeding for the two most recent births, current and ever-use of contraception by method and self-reported fecundity status. There was also commonly an attempt to collect information on non-live births and on contraceptive use in the open and last closed interval where the fertility regulation module was used.

A further, decisive contribution to the impact of WFS on our knowledge of proximate determinants came from the module on factors other than contraception affecting fertility (FOTCAF). In 1973, Leridon's valuable review of biometric aspects of fertility was first published (Leridon 1973: see also the revised and expanded English translation, Leridon 1977). This work was a synthesis of information available at that time and is still a valuable reference source. Leridon and Cantrelle were asked to design the FOTCAF module, which constitutes the most innovative contribution from the WFS programme to questionnaire content. This module covers ages at menarche, at first sexual relations and at menopause; duration of post-partum amenorrhoea and abstinence for the last two pregnancies (or births); duration of full breastfeeding as well as partial breastfeeding from the core; temporary separations; menstruation; and coital frequency (rarely included). These constitute a rich array of information which had hitherto only been obtained in small-scale surveys, mainly in West Africa.

In reviewing the contribution of WFS to our knowledge of proximate determinants and fertility, it is important to bear in mind that very little change occurred in the field instruments used after 1977. An exception was the substantial revision of the FOTCAF module for the last few surveys in Africa. Standing as we are in 1984, it is clearly useful to examine once again the issues of measurement and questionnaire content; there is no doubt that the information gained from WFS and the lessons learned from fieldwork and analysis of these data are an important component of such an assessment.

The information collected in fertility surveys should always be determined by the analysis requirements. The opportunity provided by availability of results from WFS to the international research community has generated many lessons about appropriate analysis. WFS has played a direct and major role in the development of appropriate analytic procedures (see chapter 25). In our review of the gains here, we distinguish between analyses concerned with individual proximate determinants and the various attempts to treat all measurable proximate determinants in coherent, integrated frameworks.

During the past decade, and especially since large amounts of comparable data have become available from the WFS programme, there has been a continuing stream of research related to the proximate determinants of fertility. We review some of the key findings in this area and attempt to identify a few emerging topics for research. These include the continuing attempts to integrate the proximate determinants into analyses of socio-economic and cultural correlates of fertility; the related question of how far the proximate determinants have common antecedents; and substitutability of proximate determinants.

30.2 Measurement and analysis of individual proximate determinants

Many individual proximate determinants of fertility are of interest in their own right; but in the context of fertility analysis it is usually important to achieve a balanced and systematic treatment of all relevant or measurable proximate determinants. In this section, though, we concentrate on the building blocks for integrated analysis by considering measurement and analysis of the several proximate determinants in turn. To facilitate discussion we group the proximate determinants under a few key headings, which relate to other organizational principles for discussion of these variables but are unorthodox in a few respects. These headings comprise (1) fecundability, (2) coital frequency, (3) deliberate fecundability reduction and (4) pregnancy outcome.

Fecundability

Our first major grouping covers fecundability, which we define as the monthly probability of recognizable conception, ideally given a reference coital frequency, and in the absence of any deliberate fertility control. Whenever fecundability takes the value zero, we identify women who are infecundable and may be infecund. However, variations in fecundability for fecundable women are almost certainly an important source of both between-woman and within-woman over life-course variability. Unfortunately, measurement of this variability is fraught with difficulty, with the result that much work on proximate determinants fails to treat this source of heterogeneity adequately. We remain unclear as to how much of this variation (both inter- and intra-woman) arises from differences in coital frequency, which we would prefer to treat separately as implied by our unusual inclusion of a reference coital frequency in the definition of fecundability. Undoubtedly some heterogeneity will remain, for example due to differences in the viability of the sperm and ovum, but it would be useful to have an idea of how much, especially with or without an age control.

Inevitably, most attempts to incorporate fecundability into analysis of the proximate determinants fall back upon determination of fecundity status, thus ignoring heterogeneity among the fecundable. Couples can be in the infecundable state for a number of reasons, including primary sterility, not having reached menarche, being menopausal or other secondary sterility, being temporarily infecundable following a pregnancy and being pregnant. The major measurement issues concerned with each of these types of infecundable state are summarized in table 30.1 (the first three and final columns). We shall not repeat or elaborate upon all of these in the text, but will highlight a few points, especially where WFS has provided a firmer base for conclusions.

All WFS surveys included a question on fecundity status of the couple. It was curiously, in retrospect, only asked of non-contracepting couples (currently married non-users), thus restricting its general applicability. The main reason for inclusion of this question was to provide a more precise base for calculation of contraceptive use. Only very rarely has the 'uncertain' response category been preserved on the standard recode file, which is a pity. Undoubtedly, a number of couples believe it unlikely that they could conceive, but nevertheless use contraception as a safety net. It would be useful in future to identify users and non-users of uncertain fecundity status. An assessment of the quality of self-reported fecundity status is given for 28 WFS countries by Vaessen (1984). A comparison is made with behavioural measures of fecundity status for non-contraceptors fully exposed for five years before the survey; those with no live birth or current pregnancy are deemed infecund. Judged by this reference point, which also treats all contraceptors as fecund, the self-reported fecundity-status measures are manifestly deficient. Despite measurement problems, it is clear that inclusion of sterility among the explicitly treated proximate determinants can be of considerable importance for several sub-Saharan African societies (see e.g. Lesthaeghe 1984).

There is universal agreement that WFS has contributed enormously to our knowledge about breastfeeding incidence and duration in the Third World. Among the more important contributions are the documentation of a wide range of differentials by education, age, parity and mother's work status as provided by Ferry and Smith (1983). The availability of data from the WFS has generated a great deal of methodological work on how to analyse breast feeding data, most of which has been carried out under direct WFS auspices (e.g. Ferry 1981; Page, Lesthaeghe and Shah 1982; Ferry and Smith 1983; Akin *et al*. 1981; J. W. McDonald 1981; Smith 1981b). Most would now agree that such analyses require to be restricted to information for a recent period; many have a preference for current status information as being less susceptible to heaping, although Ferry and Smith clearly demonstrate that correct use of duration information gives almost identical results with greater precision; there is now greater sensitivity to the issue of calculations on a per birth or per woman basis and the related length-biased sampling problems. On the other hand, the early WFS emphasis on breastfeeding in the last closed interval is now clearly recognized as biased and the degree of selection involved if births more than five years (perhaps even less) before the survey are included is better appreciated, although some fairly recent analyses are biased in this respect (e.g. Jain and Bongaarts 1981). Methodologically, WFS has a proven clear advance on other surveys, such as the Contraceptive Prevalence Surveys (Anderson and Cleland 1984) and the WHO collaborative study (WHO 1981; see also Leridon and Ferry 1985), although clearly lacking the richness of information provided by the WHO study.

If documentation and analysis of breastfeeding patterns can be counted among the great successes of the WFS programme, what about its relation to other variables? Surprisingly little work has been attempted on its links to mortality using WFS, despite the generally acknowledged substantial contribution to information on mortality. What though of fertility, which is our preoccupation here? First, it is clear that it is not duration of breastfeeding that we require information on for fertility analysis, but the period of post-partum infecundability, which is largely determined by breastfeeding patterns. It is a pity that questions relating to post-partum amenorrhoea were removed from early drafts of the core questionnaire; we have to rely on the FOTCAF module for such information as a consequence (see Leridon and Ferry 1985, for further discussion). However, a number of investigations have used the direct information on breastfeeding in analyses which examine fertility, usually using regression approaches. Thus, Jain and Bongaarts (1981) reached the general conclusion that each three months of breastfeeding extends the birth interval by from one to two months. More sophisticated recent analyses have examined the relationship between breast-feeding status and pregnancy risk at successive birth interval durations using logit or hazards models (e.g. Trussell *et al*. 1984; Palloni forthcoming). Far more commonly, analysts assume a fixed schedule linking mean breastfeeding duration with mean duration of amenorrhoea for conversion purposes and then attribute the estimated mean duration of amenorrhoea (or anovulation) to all women, thus ignoring important heterogeneity problems. If all variation in durations of amenorrhoea were between women (an over-statement), by using actual reported distributions of post-partum amenorrhoea it is a simple matter to show that

TABLE 30.1

Proximate determinants: common surrogates, measurement issues and use in various analytic frameworks

Proximate determinant	Commonly used surrogates	Measurement issues	Use in various analytic frameworks				Other comments
			Bongaarts	Gaslonde	Hobcraft-Little	Mosley, Werner and Becker	
1 *Fecundability*		Virtually impossible to measure, except for groups with zero fecundability – then becomes fecundity status	Assumed constant but heterogeneous for all non-sterile women. Invariant with age or any other subgroup, although can be extended to permit variation	Omitted	Attempt to treat heterogeneity through stratification by early reproductive performance. This yields little gain, except for treatment of sterility	Estimate mean wait to pregnancy. No explicit consideration of heterogeneity	Probably lower in teens and after age 30, although evidence largely circumstantial
Fecundity status		Problematic, especially for contraceptors and those not in sexual relationship	Uses self-reported from outside source	Omitted	Uses endogenous 'objective' measure		Clearly a key source of heterogeneity. Definitely requires explicit treatment
(a) Menarche		Problems of retrospective reporting, although might use current status for some applications. Needed for single women as well as married, as evidence of association with age at marriage in some countries	Omitted as being of no consequence. Could easily be incorporated in sterility patterns by age	Omitted	Omitted but easily incorporated	Omitted	Small role in determining actual fertility, but may cause considerable variation in potential fertility (including 10–14 group)

Measure	Description					
(b) Primary sterility	Unmeasurable for virgins or those without several years of sexual activity, preferably unprotected by contraception. Often only defined for women with at least five years exposure who have had no pregnancy		Omitted	Included by working definition of sterility	Not explicitly treated. Sterility calculated as age, but not parity, specific. These women will bias estimates	Note that the source of sterility may be th[e] husband, who could be changed
(c) Menopause/ secondary sterility	Notoriously difficult to measure. Menopause is a process rather than an event and hence real uncertainty	Uses self-reported fecundity status (q.v.)				
(i) Self-reported fecundity status (for couple) (theoretically includes primary sterility)	Vaessen study shows clear under-reporting. Not usually asked of contraceptors, but theoretically could reasonably be so, especially if uncertain status made clearly available to respondent	Used in more recent publications – defended as being what the couple think, which determines behaviour. Usually takes exogenous estimates, but can endogenize. Not explicit, presumably on same grounds of imprecision as Hobcraft and Little	Omitted	Rejected in favour of 'objective' measure, but easily used. 'Uncertain' category can be maintained as an explicit stratum	Use alternative measure	Note that treatment of contraceptors is problematic: some are almost certainly infertile. Similarly those not in sexual relationship

Table 30.1 continued overleaf

Table 30.1 continued

Proximate determinant	Commonly used surrogates	Measurement issues	Use in various analytic frameworks				Other comments
			Bongaarts	Gaslonde	Hobcraft–Little	Mosley, Werner and Becker	
1 *Fecundability* (cont.)	(ii) 'Objective' measures: e.g. non-contraceptors at risk for x years without pregnancy	Complications include exposure to coitus, temporary infecundity after a birth and non-fertile pregnancies (q.v.)	Not used. At one stage used exogenous set, now rejected in favour of self-reported values	Omitted	Uses internal measure, dependent upon window of observation, which rigorously excludes those not fully at risk. Age dependence. Can use exogenous set for aggregate but not individual analysis. In view of imprecision of measurement, prefer to use as a 'stratification' variable, rather than a separate, explicit PD. Can easily do either	Use seven-year threshold for non-users. Age groups identified. Used as interval-specific measure. Curiously labelled as pregnancy progression ratios	As above
	(d) Post-partum infecundity	Anovulation is strictly required. Needs prospective medical study, including menstruating women, particularly those still breastfeeding					General difficulty of separating lactational component from that which would occur anyway

(i) Post-partum amenorrhoea	Problems of retrospective reporting. Can use current status-type measures, or prevalence/ incidence ratio to get mean. Problems of resumption before or after ovulation. Does breastfeeding still inhibit ovulation after menstruation resumed? Inclusion for non-live births	Simple to incorporate. Ignores heterogeneity. Age variation can be included	Omitted	Simple to incorporate, requires information for whole window of observation. Preferred	Treated, using prevalence incidence estimate of mean	Preferable to have direct information rather than indirect from breastfeeding
(ii) Breast-feeding	As above. Additional complications as a determinant of p-p amenorrhoea (maternal nutrition perhaps exerts weak influence as well). Links to amenorrhoea (or anovulation) present difficulties: variations in frequency and duration of suckling; night feeds; and effects of breastfeeding on ovulation once menstruation resumed. Really a key determinant of a proximate determinant element	Usual procedure converts mean duration to mean duration of amenorrhoea, using aggregate exogenous formula, which takes no account of relative timing of first menstruation and cessation of breastfeeding	Omitted	Presents problems, Use probabilistic conversion which needs improvement and requires exogenous information unless amenorrhoea also available, when direct use is preferred	Not considered	Worth collecting f[or] other reasons, but direct information preferred. If sole source, then info. for non-live births is lacking and need[s] exogenously

Table 30.1 continued overleaf

Table 30.1 continued

Proximate determinant	Commonly used surrogates	Measurement issues	Use in various analytic frameworks				Other comments
			Bongaarts	Gaslonde	Hobcraft-Little	Mosley, Werner and Becker	
1 *Fecundability* (cont.)	(e) Pregnancy (more detail later)	Current status usually severely under-reported, especially for short durations. Outcome of current pregnancy indeterminate. Under-reporting of foetal loss and induced abortion	Infecundity index uses length of live birth pregnancy. Abortion index needs induced abortion reports. Contraceptive index includes an exogenous estimate of pregnancies due to method failures	Explicit treatment	Explicit treatment in full. Also basis of fertility estimates to keep absolutely consistent observation period	Explicit treatment. Non live-birth gestation assumed constant and exogenous. No information on abortion	Easily forgotten as a source of infecundability or zero fecundability. Partly depends upon exact definition
2 *Coital frequency*		Reliability of information is questionable. At best, except in prospective study, can get 'usual frequency' or frequency in last week or month. (See Cleland and Kalule-Sabiti). Usually asked of restricted universe, — which assumes zero frequency for all others (e.g. not in union etc.). Most frameworks concentrate upon surrogate identifiers for zero frequency, as below	Not included. Hard to see how such information could be incorporated	Omitted	Easily incorporated as a stratification variable, which avoids the inherent measurement imprecision. Almost inconceivable to have monthly frequency for extended observation period	Omitted. Not obvious how to incorporate	Probably the major source of apparent heterogeneity in fecundability and thus worthy of explicit treatment.*

Sexual exposure status	Required for all women in reproductive age range for many societies, although degree of exposure (coital frequency or regularity) really also required				A key source of heterogeneity. Cannot be ignored
(a) Union status	Need to widen definitions of marriage. Problems of sexual relations outside stable unions, e.g. visiting unions in Caribbean; of cohabitation between unions; degrees of exposure by type of union for those within a union	All not currently married assumed to have zero coital frequency. Hence problems of pre-union births. Questionable assumption of 50% exposure for visiting unions (see evidence on coital frequency)	Explicit and detailed treatment of absence of sexual relations	Original paper treats being outside a union as equivalent to zero coital frequency. Little and Hobcraft (forthcoming) provides means of estimating the relative "efficacy' of union types (awaits application)	Only analyse marital fertility, hence assume no exposure outside union (a clear mistake for Kenya)	Need to keep time prior to 1st union separate from other spells out of union as determinants probably differ. Easily achieved for Bongaarts, Gaslon? and Hobcraft–Littl?
(b) Permanent separation	Especially relevant between unions. Often a prior element of dissolution of formal unions. Rarely explicitly measured. Cohabitation with different partner	Not explicit, but easily incorporated as not currently married	Explicit	Easily incorporated, otherwise lengthens mean wait and lowers potential fertility	Presumably could exclude from analysis	Of less consequence where union structures are least formal
(c) Temporary absences	Seem to suffer from severe under-reporting, e.g. Lesotho WFS	Awaits developments; depends crucially on other factors	Explicit	As above	? Lengthen estimated wait	Can be important during famines, e.g. Matlab study

Table 30.1 continued overleaf

Table 30.1 continued

Proximate determinant	Commonly used surrogates	Measurement issues	Use in various analytic frameworks				Other comments
			Bongaarts	Gaslonde	Hobcraft–Little	Mosley, Werner and Becker	
2 *Coital frequency* (cont.) *Sexual exposure status* (cont.) (d) *Abstinence*							
	(i) Post-partum	Retrospective reporting; overlap with amenorrhoea, breastfeeding	Incorporated as non-susceptible period in infecundity index, although better kept separate	Omitted	Easily incorporated	Ignored, even though available for Kenya	Can be important
	(ii) Terminal	Possibly under-reported	As contraception	Omitted, but easily included	As above	? As contra-	Not necessarily adopted for contraceptive reasons, e.g. Hindu males
	(iii) Other, e.g. due to illness	Probably under-reported	As contraception	Explicit	As above	?	Perhaps periods of extreme poor nutrition. Seasonal?
3 *Deliberate fecundability reduction or contraception*		Require method-specific use and efficacy. Treatment of overlap with other PDs	Current use; exogenous efficacy. Overlap argued away	History for last year, month by month use. Estimates efficacy. Overlap with fecundity status ignored	Ideally month-by-month use within observation window. If sufficient information available on failures can endogenize contraceptive	Purely descriptive index of per cent currently using	

Table 30.1 continued overleaf

					efficacy; otherwise exogenous. Overlaps treated explicitly
(a) Contraceptive use	Probe required on methods (Vaessen). Usually very poor time reference, except for current use. Current use occurs after births in short period before survey, and thus cannot strictly be linked to the relevant pregnancies. Probably an especially acute problem when use changing very rapidly	Relies on current use with retrospective fertility. Uses equilibrium renewal process results, which may be wrong when use rapidly changing	Only obtains use for non-pregnant, sexually exposed women (probably acceptable)	Detailed history for reference period preferred; otherwise can make heroic assumptions, using use in previous interval, past use in open and current use; or just current use, when similar to Bongaarts.	Current use, but retrospective fertility and sterility estimates
(b) Contraceptive efficacy	Require reduction in fecundability achieved by method. Efficacies for less reliable methods probably highly variable between and within societies. Need detailed episode data for a reference period, with contraceptive failure through pregnancy explicitly identified as a possible reason for end of use episode	Assumes fixed exogenous efficacies	Explicit effort to estimate	Usually assume exogenous efficacies, but can endogenize if episode history data available for window, including method failure. Can probably only be estimated for commoner methods or groups of methods	Omitted A priority area for careful measureme

Table 30.1 continued

Proximate determinant	Commonly used surrogates	Measurement issues	Use in various analytic frameworks				Other comments
			Bongaarts	Gaslonde	Hobcraft–Little	Mosley, Werner and Becker	
4 *Pregnancy by outcome*		General problems include poor reporting of current pregnancy, especially at early durations; outcome of current pregnancy; under-reporting of induced and spontaneous abortions					
(a) Live births		Gestation period — usually assumed fixed. Birth histories fairly successful. Births in last n years? Reference period: conception-related PDs refer to time of conception not birth, which is awkward in periods of rapid change	Fertility estimated from counts of births; reference period problem	Uses counts of births, although perhaps needlessly	A very precise matching of reference periods, using months of pregnancy. Vulnerable to recent pregnancy problems unless window placed appropriately	Early pregnancy recognition is neatly avoided. Fertility estimated from births in last year	
(b) Foetal loss		Problems of under-reporting. Require timing and gestation length. Cause a further conception wait, which complicates analysis. Variable rates with age and socio-economic status (Casterline and Ashurst)	Treated as invariant and exogenous, with two months added to mean wait	Explicit endogenous inclusion. Problem of current pregnancies	Can be incorporated as for induced abortion. Needs two-step procedure to allocate waiting times for non-sterile women with no pregnancy	Exogenous gestation and late foetal loss rates per LB pregnancy. Otherwise analytically sound, except for varying reference periods	

		Explicit attempt to include	Omitted but possibly incorporable
(c) Induced abortion	Notorious under-reporting, particularly of clandestine abortions. Even randomized response procedures fail, although resulting in improvement. All too often omitted because of measurement problem. Further conception wait complicates analysis: is wait up to the conception or after the conception?	Uses Potter's renewal theory, results on births averted. Assumes equilibrium, where-as end effects at higher ages may be acute from sterility onset	in reference period for individual-level analysis. One step suffices for aggregate
			Two-step procedure for allocation of waiting times for non-sterile women with no pregnancy in reference period at individual level. One step suffices for aggregate

* For example, using fecundability estimates in table 2.3 of Bongaarts and Potter (p. 34) but taking 1/f as mean wait, where f is the fecundability (i.e. assuming all heterogeneity among the fecund as being due to coital frequency), we get, for 300 months exposure, the following total potential fertility values (Tp)

Coital frequency (per cycle)	Tp	Mean wait
1	7.3	28.6
2	11.0	14.7
4	14.9	7.7
8	18.0	4.2
12	19.5	2.9
20	20.3	2.3
6.5 with heterogeneity	15.0	7.5

application of the widely used Bongaarts procedure would bias estimates of total fecundity upwards by about half a child with relatively short mean post-partum amenorrhoea of 4.5 months; by about a child for a mean of nine months; and by more than one and a half children with the prolonged amenorrhoea of Bangladesh. Put another way, the three mean durations of post-partum amenorrhoea 4.5, 8.9 and 15.6 months would generate C_is (the fertility-reducing effect of lactational infecundity) of 0.86, 0.73 and 0.59 using Bongaarts' average approach. Taking account of the distribution leads to C_is of 0.89, 0.79 and 0.66 respectively, on the assumption that all variation is between women, which overstates the error from heterogeneity; we here ignore likely errors induced by imprecision of the conversion schedules used to obtain amenorrhoea from breastfeeding. Given that fertility analysts actually require information on post-partum infecundity, it makes sense to collect data on its closest surrogate, post-partum amenorrhoea, in surveys.

We now turn briefly to the links between post-partum amenorrhoea and breastfeeding. As yet, there has been only partial exploitation of the available information, mainly because most surveys including the FOTCAF module were later. Much basic information has been documented in the papers emanating from the WFS workshop on analysis of FOTCAF data (Ferry and Page 1984, the illustrative report; and Alwani and Santow 1986; Fortunat 1984; Gaisie 1984; Mpiti and Kalule-Sabiti 1985; and Zablan 1984). In addition, a WFS cross-national summary brings together summary results on all FOTCAF variables, including the post-partum variables (Singh and Ferry 1984). Of greatest interest in our context is Singh and Ferry's appendix table 11, which examines proportions still amenorrhoeic and still abstaining by months since birth for four categories of breastfeeding status: never breastfed, not now breastfeeding, still breastfeeding with supplementation, and still fully breastfeeding. These findings have been analysed further by Santow and Singh (forthcoming). Table 30.2 gives some summary results on percentages still amenorrhoeic and still abstaining at durations 4–6 and 11–13 months after a birth. Breastfeeding seems to give considerably reduced contraceptive protection in Mauritania, Egypt, Tunisia, Syria and Fiji compared with most other countries. In general, remarkably few past or never-breastfeeders are amenorrhoeic. There is a very strong association between abstinence and whether the child is currently being breastfed, although adequate analysis might control for survival status of the child (death of the child being the main reason for no breastfeeding or early cessation in most of these countries).

There also seem to be strong links between reported menstrual and abstinence status which require pinning down at the individual level. Finally, abstinence is clearly of considerable importance in Benin, Cameroon, Ivory Coast and Lesotho (perhaps absence?), with Ghana and Fiji also reporting substantial levels. Santow and Singh (forthcoming) provide an interesting discussion of these links and make a convincing case that resumption of ovulation can be an important determinant of breastfeeding length, by permitting the next pregnancy to occur. Considerable progress on the methodology of assessing the contraceptive efficacy of · breastfeeding is made by Habicht, Butz, Meyers and DaVanzo (1984).

Our conclusions about post-partum information collected by WFS are as follows. We value the great addition to knowledge, but regret that information on amenorrhoea was not routinely obtained in all countries. We would prefer to have durations of full and partial breastfeeding, of amenorrhoea and of abstinence for all births in, say, the five years preceding the survey, with explicit questions on current status. For analysis, we would stress the difficulties caused by mixing censoring and duration information on standard recode files: it would be far better to give duration in months for all cases and provide (an) additional variable(s) indicating censoring by interview or by child death; the addition of explicit records identifying the relevant birth dates would again simplify analysis a great deal. Such additions and modifications are being made to WFS standard recode files. We hope future surveys will learn these lessons, but achieve WFS's high standards of data cleaning, documentation and, especially, availability for secondary analysis.

We close this subsection by returning to the estimation of fecundability. Direct measurement of fecundability or of related mean waits to conception is fraught with difficulty. Nevertheless, fragmentary results from analysis of WFS data do exist. First and simplest are results derived from intervals between first marriage and first birth, using the approximate conversion technique given by Bongaarts (1975). The information allowing this is given by Hobcraft and McDonald (1984). The lowest estimated mean fecundability used by Bongaarts in developing his procedure was 0.18 for Crulai, corresponding to 34 per cent of women without a first birth in the nine months after marriage having a birth in the next three months. For 28 WFS countries, the highest equivalent proportion is for the Philippines at 38 per cent, but the values are below 30 per cent, and thus involve considerable extrapolation from Bongaarts' data base, for as many as 20 countries. Indeed, these percentages fall below 21 per cent, equivalent to a mean fecundability of 0.10, at the extreme of the conversion table provided by Bongaarts, for eight out of the 28 countries. Table 30.3 gives the relevant results. Taken at face value, most Third World countries appear to have lower fecundability than was observed in historical populations. Especially low estimates appear where marriage is very early, as in Nepal, Bangladesh, Pakistan, Senegal, Indonesia and Sudan: these values at least partly reflect teenage sub-fecundity. The other really low values occur in Caribbean societies, where the first union is often a visiting union, with possible consequent reduction in exposure. It is worth bearing in mind that almost all countries covered here have mean ages at first union which are much lower than in many European historical populations and that the generally lower fecundability estimates are compatible with far more marriages taking place before age 18 in the Third World. Also, coital frequency is likely to be lower early in an arranged marriage than in a 'romantic' one. (See Rindfuss and Morgan 1983 for a discussion of this for the Republic of Korea.)

However, the results presented in table 30.3 should be regarded as untrustworthy. First birth intervals have been demonstrated to be unreliably reported,

TABLE 30.2

Percentages still amenorrhoeic and abstaining at selected intervals since birth, by breastfeeding status (number of cases in brackets)

Country	4–6 months since birth: breastfeeding status				11–13 months since birth: breastfeeding status			
	Never	Not now	Still partial	Still full	Never	Not now	Still partial	Still full
A Percentages still amenorrhoeic (N)								
Benin	20 (5)	15 (26)	72 (220)	90 (30)	33 (6)	14 (58)	54 (165)	83 (12)
Cameroon	16 (4)	36 (29)	77 (215)	90 (154)	15 (16)	5 (66)	59 (269)	69 (48)
Ghana	40 (5)	44 (25)	81 (196)	96 (103)	0 (3)	19 (75)	69 (186)	75 (23)
Ivory Coast	11 (9)	8 (38)	68 (154)	85 (130)	0 (4)	3 (66)	50 (223)	63 (35)
Kenya	28 (8)	17 (43)	69 (421)	85 (40)	0 (12)	5 (105)	50 (310)	72 (7)
Lesotho	14 (7)	8 (13)	71 (134)	84 (36)	0 (6)	2 (39)	39 (162)	100 (1)
Mauritania	0 (3)	11 (16)	57 (54)	55 (126)	0 (1)	7 (64)	48 (92)	51 (51)
Egypt	13 (23)	9 (53)	41 (121)	70 (324)	0 (20)	5 (149)	37 (188)	58 (104)
Sudan (North)	0 (6)	11 (23)	64 (85)	86 (94)	0 (2)	3 (66)	62 (160)	80 (26)
Tunisia	8 (12)	2 (49)	37 (76)	60 (126)	7 (15)	4 (114)	40 (107)	40 (30)
Syria	0 (14)	10 (88)	50 (148)	70 (208)	0 (16)	2 (177)	37 (88)	56 (45)
Yemen AR	20 (9)	19 (52)	60 (52)	72 (91)	8 (13)	4 (143)	51 (51)	32 (12)
Bangladesh	15 (10)	20 (29)	– 76 (253)	–	70 (4)	9 (61)	– 62 (265)	–
Fiji	10 (30)	12 (68)	– 48 (123)	–	4 (29)	1 (134)	– 20 (68)	–
Philippines	11 (77)	13 (83)	71 (267)	79 (164)	4 (74)	6 (166)	47 (264)	0 (2)
Haiti	27 (5)	25 (8)	– 81 (137)	–	– (0)	5 (46)	– 68 (79)	–

B *Percentages still abstaining*

Benin	20	27	82	97	33	14	71	83
Cameroon	50	32	80	86	12	3	73	70
Ghana	40	26	50	81	0	4	37	51
Ivory Coast	11	5	86	92	0	5	65	73
Kenya	0	5	15	31	0	1	4	38
Lesotho	42	16	91	97	0	11	67	100
Sudan (North)	11	0	8	19	0	0	3	12
Tunisia	0	2	1	8	0	1	3	3
Syria	0	0	0	2	0	0	0	4
Yemen AR	11	7	10	26	8	3	10	0
Bangladesh	12	14	– 13 –		0	3	– 11 –	
Fiji	16	11	– 46 –		3	4	– 34 –	
Philippines	12	1	10	15	3	2	4	
Haiti	40	44	– 44 –		0	2	– 5 –	0

TABLE   30.3

Percentages having first birth between 9 and 12 months after first marriage, with no previous birth, and equivalent fecundabilities

Percentage 9–12 month first births	Mean fecundability estimate	Countries
3	(0.01)	Nepal
4	(0.02)	Bangladesh
11	(0.05)	Pakistan
13	(0.06)	Haiti, Trinidad & Tobago
14	(0.07)	Senegal
15	(0.07)	Indonesia, Jamaica
21	0.10	Guyana
23	0.11	Sudan (North), Fiji
25	0.12	Kenya, Lesotho
26/27	0.13	Costa Rica, Panama, Syria
28/29	0.14	Thailand, Paraguay, Sri Lanka, Dominican Rep.
32/33	0.17	Colombia, Jordan, Korea, Rep. of, Malaysia, Mexico .
34	0.18	Peru (Crulai)
36	0.19	Venezuela
38	0.21	Philippines, (Tourouvre au Perche)
41	0.23	(Geneva)
43	0.25	(Tunis)
49	0.31	(Canada)

Note: The population groups in parentheses constitute the base from which Bongaarts generated the above relation between births 9–12 months after marriage and mean fecundability. A coefficient of variation of 0.56 is implicit in this relation and may be untenable for very low percentages. Mean fecundabilities which involve extrapolation even beyond the range provided by Bongaarts are also in parentheses.

which makes reliance on exact allocation very hazardous. Quite high proportions of women have already had a first birth by nine months after marriage in many of these societies, which undoubtedly involves some selection for higher than average fecundability. More detailed calculations than shown here, which control for age at first marriage, generally show plausible variations with age. More refined estimates by Goldman, Westoff and Paul (1985) give broadly similar results, but give slightly higher estimates of fecundability in several instances (e.g. 0.21 for Republic of Korea, Malaysia and Costa Rica).

The other approach which has been used occasionally to estimate fecundability or mean waits to conception from WFS data involves examination of inter-birth intervals or allocation of periods of risk and pregnancies in a short reference period (see e.g. Mosley, Werner and Becker 1982; Ferry and Page 1984; Hobcraft and Little 1984). Essentially these procedures work indirectly, by blocking out periods when a woman is not at risk of conception through pregnancy or postpartum non-susceptibility, to leave a residual set of months at risk. Ideally, any periods out of a union, separated and temporarily abstaining are also removed. Moreover, either analysis is restricted to non-contraceptors or some allocation of degree of fecundability reduction is used for periods of contraception, which are usually very imprecisely defined in time. In addition, attempts are usually made to remove sterile women from such analyses in order to estimate mean waits to conception when fully at risk for those who can, but will not necessarily, conceive. Closed birth intervals omit those who will not conceive before onset of sterility or other complete removal from risk and therefore tend to bias results downwards. Last closed intervals suffer from additional bias from length-biased sampling. This is not the place for a full discussion of the details of the various measurement procedures which have been attempted, but suffice it to, say that the waiting time to conception is always derived as a residual or end-point in elaborate analysis (see also Trussell, Martin, Feldman, Concepción and Noor Laily Abu Bakar 1984) and is therefore vulnerable to reporting errors. Curiously, the mean waits derived from the analysis of Mosley, Werner and Becker for Kenya do not rise substantially with age of the mother, whereas most simulation models assume declining fecundability with age beyond about 30. Table 30.4 shows a few estimates of mean waits to conception from various sources and includes an approximate reference model adapted from REPMOD (Bongaarts and Potter 1983). The estimated mean waits are probably a little high, but the agreement of age pattern for the estimates based on the fertility ex-posure analysis approach of Hobcraft and Little with the REPMOD assumptions is surprisingly good. The Mosley, Werner and Becker estimates are superficially appealing (see Ferry and Page, who use these as a basis for questioning their own estimates) but the 35-44 estimate is clearly too low. Thus, we conclude that estimation of mean waits, while hazardous, can be achieved with care, but should not be taken as exact.

Coital frequency

Our next major grouping of proximate determinants involves variables associated with coital frequency. If we ignore biblical evidence to the contrary, no woman can conceive in a month without engaging in coitus. The timing of such coitus in the cycle is clearly crucial in determining whether conception takes place. We do not expect to have information on timing of coitus within a cycle very often, but averaging across women and assuming random timing of coitus enables useful results to be obtained from known coital frequency. The relationship between monthly coital frequency and chances of conception is generally clear, although residual doubts remain about the relationship at very high coital frequency (see Potter and Millman 1985; 1986).

More frequent coitus raises fecundability. Yet few surveys have attempted to collect information on this important variable. Coital frequency was among the recommended variables for the WFS FOTCAF module, but was usually excluded from actual questionnaires, presumably on grounds of likely sensitivity to the topic among respondents. However, a few WFS surveys did include questions on

TABLE   30.4

Some estimates of mean waits to conception (months)

Age group	Kenya (Mosley et al.)	Kenya (Page and Ferry)	Dominican Republic (Hobcraft and Little)	Korea, Rep. of, (Little and Hobcraft)	Age pattern[a] of fecundability from REPMOD f = 0.143
15–19	{ 8	{ 11.0	7.9	9.6	10.2 (at 17.5)
20–24			6.2	7.3	7.0 (at 22.5)
25–29	{ 7	{ 12.6	9.1	7.0	7.0 (at 27.5)
30–34			9.1	10.2	8.1 (at 32.5)
35–39	{ 9	{ 28.3	12.4	15.0	12.0 (at 37.5)
40–44			26.7	32.0	22.9 (at 42.5)
45–49			83.4	105.7	83.9 (at 46.5)

[a] See Bongaarts and Potter (1983). For this illustrative calculation heterogeneity has been ignored. Use of the middle of the relevant age range is probably acceptable, as age structure typically decreases with age, while the increasing mean waits by age increase: two compensating biases.

frequency in the last week or frequency in a usual week. In our view a month provides a better reference period, despite the tendency to heap on multiples of four. This preference is based upon the strong tendency to. avoid a zero response, especially for usual frequency. Fairly low coital frequencies, an average of less than two or three acts per month, can be an important source of population heterogeneity and generate long waiting times to conception (see table 30.1 for an indication of this). Reduced coital frequency with age is probably an important source of increasing waiting times with age.

Although coital frequency is of major importance in determining fertility, there are a number of problems associated with its measurement and analytic use. Of prime importance is the likely unreliability of responses: in many societies high coital frequency is regarded as a sign of virility, with consequent avoidance of reporting low frequency. For current status based analyses, which suffer from other problems such as reporting of current pregnancies, frequency in the last month may be most useful; there is some evidence that responses pertaining to the last week are more reliable than usual frequencies (Cleland and Kalule-Sabiti 1984). But responses on recent frequencies typically tell us nothing about usual frequency for longer reference periods, especially for women in post-partum abstention, temporarily separated or in the late stages of pregnancy. For analyses which span a reference period of from one to five years before a survey, it is clearly far more relevant to know something about usual frequency, perhaps even specifying certain conditions. In many societies it would be desirable, but perhaps unacceptable, to obtain this information for unmarried women, along with contraceptive information. Until recently, the analytic utility of such information was restricted to descriptive analysis, but it can now be incorporated explicitly by stratifying women into coital frequency groups in order to assess the fertility aspect (see Little and Hobcraft forthcoming).

Usually we do not obtain a measure of coital frequency for all women, especially on a month by month basis, and consequently resort to trying to identify women at low or zero risk of coitus. Thus we identify sexual exposure status, using proxies that correlate highly but usually imperfectly with zero coital frequency. This is the main justification for concentration on union histories and marital status in fertility surveys and analysis. Women outside cohabitation usually have low risks of coitus, although many societies prove exceptions to this generalization. WFS tried very hard to overcome these problems by adopting fairly wide definitions of union type. However, substantial numbers of births were still reported at earlier dates than the reported date of entry into first union, especially in parts of Africa. In the Caribbean, there is a visiting union status which is well recognized by the local inhabitants: WFS explicitly included such unions in the union histories. Yet union type may well be an important source of heterogeneity in exposure: thus Bongaarts and Kirmeyer (1982) assumed that women in visiting unions were only half as much at risk of conception as women in consensual or formal unions, although survey evidence on coital frequency suggests it was only very slightly lower for visiting unions than for cohabiting unions (Roberts and Sinclair 1978, as cited by Casterline, Singh, Cleland and Ashurst 1984); there is also clear evidence of a convergence of fertility levels over time for these union types in the Commonwealth Caribbean (Lightbourne and Singh 1982). In assessing the fertility impact of various union types, it is of considerable importance to know whether the 'contraceptive efficacy' or fecundability reduction is high or low, net of other controls such as contraception (see also Potter and Guest forthcoming). Risks of coitus to women not in a recognized union are just as likely to change with age as are coital frequencies of those in a union.

Similar problems arise with polygyny. Women in monogamous marriages are likely to experience higher coital frequency. Long periods of post-partum abstinence are more easily observed by polygynists than monogamists. Clear fertility differences emerge by rank of wife within polygyny: are these due to differing coital frequencies, the age difference at marriage, or higher sterility among low order wives? (See Lesthaeghe 1984 for detailed discussion.)

In many countries of the world, union dissolution is frequent, with high mortality levels causing widowhood and high divorce rates. What of the conception-reducing impact of spells outside marriage, again net of other factors? (Note it is conceptions, not births which are crucial at all junctures, although the pregnancy outcome matters.) Periods of separation before divorce are of major relevance here; as may be cohabitation with a future spouse during this period. Entry into a new union will almost certainly be associated with higher initial coital frequency, not necessarily aimed at achieving early conception. Answers to these difficult questions concerning the coital frequency changes associated with union dissolution and remarriage are not easily come by, but may help our understanding of fertility. As already mentioned, WFS made a major effort to obtain complete union histories. These have permitted a number of interesting studies of union dissolution and remarriage (e.g. Smith, Carrasco and McDonald 1984; Goldman 1981). Several studies have concluded that the fertility impact of dissolution is small, with a few countries proving notable exceptions, although these analyses either fail to account for other proximate determinants (e.g. the noteworthy paper by Rodríguez and Cleland 1981a) or make no attempt to deal with the likely association between periods around dissolution and the other proximate determinants, being aggregate-level analyses (e.g. Casterline, Singh, Cleland and Ashurst 1984). Elaborate adjustment using individual-level analysis would probably not provide very different answers here (for an example, in the Dominican Republic, where dissolution does have a substantial fertility-reducing impact, see Hobcraft and Little 1984). In the Republic of Korea, union dissolution seems to be the key to the relationship of fertility to rural/urban residence but not to education level, once each is controlled for. Union dissolution is higher in urban areas and thus reinforces abortion and contraception differences, dominating reverse differences in lactational infecundability. For education of the mother, though, dissolution reinforces differences in lactational infecundability, balancing out the countervailing effects of contraception and abortion (see Little and Hobcraft forthcoming).

A further distinctive contribution of WFS has been to pay due attention to other states associated with zero coital frequency. Thus, in much of sub-Saharan Africa, post-partum abstinence is widely practised, although there is evidence of considerable erosion over time (e.g. Lesthaeghe 1984). The FOTCAF module addresses this question, and WFS has provided the first national-level evidence on such practice for most countries which collected the information. In most cases, even where abstinence is typically short compared with mean duration of amenorrhoea, the mean non-susceptible period following a birth is slightly increased by inclusion of abstinence. Table 30.5, taken from Singh and Ferry (1984), shows this — for example, for Tunisia. Of course, we must be cautious here in view of likely reporting errors. If we take the larger of two numbers with a significant random component, especially where the true values are similar, we shall overstate the mean length of the non-susceptible period. The important question in assessing the fertility-reducing role of post-partum abstinence concerns just this hazardous measure: how far does it provide protection beyond the period of infecundability? The long mean post-partum abstinence for Lesotho was somewhat unexpected and may reflect temporary absences.

Temporary separations can be of considerable importance in some societies (e.g. Chen, Ahmed, Gesche and Mosley 1974 for Bangladesh). We have already instanced Lesotho, where large numbers of men are away in South Africa. Yet WFS failed to capture the expected levels of absence, despite explicit questions about separations of more than three months duration. Birth intervals in Lesotho are nevertheless unusually long (see Hobcraft and McDonald 1984). Potter and Guest (forthcoming) consider the assessment of spousal separation on fertility at some length, partly using WFS results. Such assessment is not simple, although methods now exist. In our view the major problem is that of measurement: how

TABLE 30.5

Mean durations for the five post-partum factors

Country	Per cent ever breastfed	Mean durations					No. of cases
		Full breastfeeding	Breastfeeding	Amenorrhoea	Abstinence	NSP	
Benin	97	2.6	19.2	11.9	15.5	17.2	2803
Cameroon	98	5.1	17.5	11.8	13.9	15.9	4650
Ghana	92	4.5	17.9	12.4	10.0	14.6	3335
Ivory Coast	98	5.0	17.5	10.4	13.1	14.7	3804
Kenya	98	2.2	16.9	9.9	2.9	10.3	5679
Lesotho	95	2.5	19.1	9.6	15.0	16.5	2348
Egypt	95	7.4	16.3	8.9	—	—	5667
Senegal	98	4.9	17.7	—	—	—	3438
Mauritania	98	7.9	15.6	8.8	—	—	2447
Morocco	94	5.5	14.2	—	—	—	3612
Sudan (North)	98	5.6	15.8	10.8	2.6	11.2	2242
Tunisia	95	6.2	14.0	6.9	1.6	7.4	3021
Syria	95	5.5	11.2	6.6	1.2	6.6	4025
Yemen AR	92	4.5	10.6	7.1	2.8	7.9	2216
Bangladesh	98	—	26.5	14.6	3.0	15.2	3836
Fiji	87	—	9.4	4.6	5.1	6.4	2660
Philippines	86	3.3	12.6	8.0	2.8	8.3	6667
Haiti	96	—	15.3	12.2	6.5	13.9	1489
Paraguay	93	2.9	10.9	—	1.5	—	1830
Costa Rica	75	—	5.0	—	1.3	—	1491

Source: S. Singh and B. Ferry (1984), table 5

do we reliably elicit information? Is current status and duration of separation for those currently separated the only viable collection procedure? If so, this would be of limited analytic utility: for current status, pregnancy is hard to assess; going further back in time would involve appalling sample selection problems. Yet even with the limited information available within WFS, it is sometimes possible to show clear fertility-reducing associations. For example, Nawar and Hobcraft (forthcoming) used the variable reporting whether the respondent's husband was currently working abroad to demonstrate a substantial fertility-reducing effect. So current status information, because of its correlation with past behaviour, serves to identify strata with low and high average coital frequencies, although not a group with zero frequency. Thus currently separated women often need to be regarded as at reduced rather than zero risk.

A final source of zero coital frequency is terminal abstinence. In parts of Africa and South Asia there are reported taboos associated with having a married daughter or achieving grandmotherhood. There have been attempts to address this issue indirectly using WFS data, although the results are equivocal (Tan 1983; Sathar and Alam 1983). Terminal abstinence has very high theoretical use effectiveness, but is easily reversible. As a consequence, while supporting, for sociological purposes, identification of whether couples thought they were terminally abstaining, we prefer to measure current or past abstinence in assessing its impact on fertility.

We conclude this subsection by stressing the crucial importance of coital frequency and the need to pay attention to risks of copulation both outside and within formal union. Most divisions of the population by exposure status are undoubtedly quite efficient: coital frequency is indeed usually much lower among the unmarried, for example. But we cannot continue to ignore sex outside marriage and the fertility consequences. This requires much better information about never-married women in relevant societies, including use of contraception. The sexual life history approach devised by Gaslonde is useful in this respect and explicitly tries to identify periods in or out of sexual relations rather than union types or marriage: for fertility study this is what we need – the only question is whether we can reasonably use such instruments in all societies. To this we have to add a plea for more attempts to collect, and devise improved procedures for collecting, information on coital frequency. A problem for analysts to face will then be the almost certain association between coital frequency and union duration. Analysis by age will mix women at different marital durations and hence fail to control sufficiently for the rapid changes in frequency which can occur, especially early in marriage. Related to this issue are a number of studies which examine fertility by both age and duration (e.g. Page 1977; Hobcraft and Casterline 1983; Knodel 1983).

Deliberate fecundability reduction

Conscious control of conception is usually achieved through contraception. This is especially so within the framework used here to organize the proximate determinants, where fecundability is taken to refer to a particular level of coital frequency. Hence, controls such as abstinence which act through changes in coital frequency are not here regarded as deliberate fecundability reduction. However, sterilization clearly is included here. Philosophers may wish to discuss placement of deliberate use of lactation to prolong amenorrhoea, which we include as a determinant of fecundability. Another philosophical issue covers use of the rhythm method; this essentially acts through coital timing, but is treated as a deliberate attempt to reduce fecundability. Any attempts to time intercourse in order to raise chances of conception are also ambiguous in this respect, but may be relevant to the study of volitional replacement effects for dead children.

We separate two key aspects of deliberate fecundability reduction: means of reduction and their levels of use, and the effectiveness of each means. This distinction is slightly artificial, because adequate measurement of episodes of use during a reference period can be supplemented by questions on method failures. Of course, response errors remain a problem.

In all WFS surveys, questions were asked about knowledge, ever-use and current use of a broad range of contraceptive methods. A distinctive, but by no means unique, feature was the use of elaborate probes at the stage of enquiry about knowledge (or, more correctly, awareness) of methods, including a fairly full description of each method. Vaessen (1981) demonstrates the increased levels of knowledge obtained and the implications for the ever- and current-use results. A substantial proportion of WFS surveys also used the fertility regulation module, which added questions on use in the open and last closed intervals. Typically, no information on timing or duration of use was elicited. Those surveys which did enquire concerning duration of use usually failed to place this segment of use within the interval, rendering the extra information of little analytic value. The survey in Malaysia attempted to obtain moderately satisfactory information on timing and segments of use, along with information on reasons for cessation. In Venezuela and Dominican Republic a sexual life history in the year before the survey was used to collect similar information on a month by month basis (Gaslonde and Carrasco 1982).

When examining the impact of contraception on fertility, current use is not an ideal indicator. Use levels in many developing countries are rising very rapidly. Current use can only protect those not already pregnant (who are hard to identify, see Hanenberg 1980 and Goldman and Westoff 1980). Yet fertility indicators often refer to births over a time-segment before a survey, perhaps three or five years, and to conceptions at least nine months before the survey. There is thus a mismatch of reference periods, which is potentially serious (see also Laing forthcoming for an extended discussion of issues treated in this subsection). Hobcraft and Little (1984) illustrate the contraceptive impact of such changes within the five years before the survey for the Dominican Republic, using reports from the open and last closed intervals, and probably understate the recent rises due to lack of information on timing. Rapidly changing use levels clearly invalidate the renewal process assumptions of Bongaarts (1978) in developing an index of contraceptive impact on fertility.

·In order to provide the analyst with adequate information on contraceptive use and timing, the amount of questioning has to be increased substantially. We would not be alone in questioning whether a birth interval specific approach is desirable for obtaining such information. In view of the potential for method switching, it is preferable to concentrate on obtaining a fairly detailed account of use in a recent period of from one to five or six years in length (see Gaslonde and Carrasco 1982, Little and Hobcraft forthcoming and, most fully argued, Laing forthcoming). More distant information is likely to suffer worse recall problems, and concentration on the open and last closed intervals introduces severe selection biases any earlier than three to five years before the survey.

However, detailed information for a short to medium reference period before the survey might be better derived from a series of questions relating to inter-pregnancy intervals, beginning with the pregnancy (or first union if no pregnancy) immediately prior to the reference period. At a minimum, we would want to know timing and method of first use in each interval and for the last segment of use would want to know length of use, when it terminated and a reason for the cessation of use, including an explicit question on whether pregnancy was that reason. These issues are further discussed by Page, Cleland and Hobcraft (1984) who provide several new, but unpiloted, questionnaires which would obtain the relevant information.

This final piece of information is crucial to measurement of use effectiveness, which may vary considerably between societies, perhaps especially for less effective methods. There is evidence to suggest that women are reluctant to report contraceptive failures, but careful questioning for short recent periods of up to 30 months has elicited fairly reliable responses in the Philippines (Laing forthcoming). In translating contraceptive use into an assessment of its fertility-reducing impact, a measure of use effectiveness is essential. Unless quite detailed information on segments of use and consequent failures is available, approaches which use either clinical or observed month-by-month use effectiveness will overstate the true fertility-reducing impact of contraception. Methods of translation into fertility-reducing impact which rely upon current use of contraception, with assumed permanent usage except for method failures, or upon attribution of current or past use to all exposure time in an interval, should almost certainly incorporate extended use-effectiveness measures, which account for method-switching and cessation of use for reasons not associated with desire for further pregnancy. There is even a case for using extended use-effectiveness measures which are biased downwards by inclusion of experience for women who stop use in order to become pregnant.

There are few studies which have attempted to assess use effectiveness from WFS surveys. The best potential source, the Malaysian survey, has been used by Aziz, Majumber and Tan 1981; Gaslonde and Carrasco (1982) use the direct information for Venezuela, although they cannot remove periods of post-partum infecundability; and Goldman, Pebley, Westoff and Paul (1983) have studied extended use effectiveness, making careful use of the WFS fertility regulation module, for five Latin American countries. Almost all such studies are plagued by problems of removing months when the woman was not otherwise at risk of conception through zero fecundability or zero coital frequency. An integrated and consistent measurement of the proximate determinants over a moderate length reference period before the survey is the only likely solution to this problem.

Pregnancy by outcome

Ultimately, the combination of fecundability, coital frequency and contraception determines the probability that a woman conceives in a given month, or more correctly has a recognizable conception (to avoid problems of early foetal wastage). There are three important sources of variation in determining pregnancy status. First, there is considerable variation between women at the same stage of the life-cycle in terms of all three of the key determinants of the chance of conception: use effectiveness of deliberate fecundability reduction both within and between methods, coital frequency even within identifiable exposure status groups, and, probably, fecundability when not clearly zero. Second, there is likely to be considerable variation for individual women over their life-cycle: fecundability varies with age; coital frequency varies especially with union duration; and use effectiveness may increase with birth order. Third, even given a fixed monthly probability of conception, there is a distribution associated with the conceptions which is a source of chance variation. A goal in controlling for the proximate determinants and for other demographic and socio-economic variables in fertility analysis is to account for as much of the first two systematic sources of variation as we can, leaving only the pure random variation associated with the third (some of which could be further accounted for by knowledge about timing of coital acts and of ovulation within cycles). Inevitably, we almost always fail to capture all the systematic variation of the first two types identified here. This has implications for any regression models (or tabular analyses) that we carry out; the unobserved but systematic-heterogeneity distorts our results. Some recent work has attempted to address this problem of heterogeneity when modelling birth intervals (e.g. Hobcraft and Rodríguez 1985 and, in a regression context, Trussell and Richards 1985), although not with proximate determinants explicitly incorporated; models incorporating unobserved heterogeneity often cause identification problems and are rarely especially parsimonious; the specification of the distribution for the unobserved variation can be crucial (also Trussell forthcoming).

Once a woman has recognizably conceived we want to know the outcome. Current pregnancies are typically under-reported and additionally cannot be allocated directly to outcomes. WFS surveys obtain estimated dates of each live birth: a gestation period of nine months has to be assumed for many analyses, so that incidence of prematurity cannot be detected. Almost all WFS surveys also included non-live birth histories. Spontaneous abortions and stillbirths are by no means fully reported, although Casterline and Ashurst (1984) show that differentials by age and several other variables are as would be expected. It is notoriously difficult to obtain information on induced abortion: in many countries induced abortion is illegal and women never like to be reminded of psychologically traumatic events. Table 30.6 gives summary information on reporting of non-live births from WFS surveys. Foetal wastage should probably be around 10 or 15 per cent of all recognized pregnancies (e.g. Leridon 1977; Bongaarts and Potter 1983).

In assessing the impact of spontaneous or induced abortion on fertility levels, it is essential to account for more than the actual months of pregnancy. It is evident that any period of infecundability following such a pregnancy has a fertility-reducing effect: it is common to assume one (or two) months of protection following a foetal loss and two (or three) months following a stillbirth, as it is rare for explicit questions on duration of amenorrhoea following foetal loss to be included in surveys, although this was done in the FOTCAF module. The underlying distribution of durations may be of minor consequence as a source of heterogeneity. Similarly, we know of few surveys which enquire about sexual abstinence or coital frequency after a foetal loss. Yet such losses may operate to increase or lower coital frequency: following a miscarriage, a couple may try to conceive with renewed determination; alternatively a miscarriage, and especially an induced abortion, may lead to a depression and withdrawal from sexual relations – these effects may also differ by union status.

A more important aspect of assessing the impact of non-live births upon fertility levels is that each such event effectively negates a wait to recognizable conception. The amount of time to be included as the fertility-reducing impact is debatable. Clearly any infecundability consequent upon the preceding pregnancy should not be included. But what of contraception? Our view is that abortion is a method of last resort and that the extension of waiting time achieved through contraception before the non-live birth pregnancy should thus be treated as protection derived from contraception, although the pregnancy should certainly count as a contraceptive failure. Others may differ and attribute all months when the woman was at risk of coitus and fecundable, regardless of contraceptive protection, to the protection derived from induced abortion. Similar arguments apply, though with less force, to spontaneous abortions and stillbirths. The grounds for treating such foetal loss as an explicit proximate determinant are debatable; some foetal loss is unavoidable, but there may be important variations by access to health care, socio-economic status, age and rapidity of recent childbearing, which should be incorporated in the systematic variation in fertility. (This debate is paralleled for sterility, where there is an irreducible minimum, but some populations experience excess risk through sexually transmitted diseases and, perhaps, malaria and tuberculosis.)

Although there are problems of under-reporting of abortion, both spontaneous

TABLE 30.6

Percentage of pregnancies[a] terminating in miscarriage, stillbirth and induced abortion: pregnancies conceived in the five years preceding the survey[b]

Region and country	Mis-carriage	Still-birth	Miscarriage + stillbirth	Induced abortion	Total loss	Number of pregnancies
Africa						
Cameroon	6.4	1.2	7.6	2.5	10.1	7 078
Ghana	5.2	0.4	5.7	1.1	6.8	4 942
Ivory Coast	9.2	1.4	10.6	1.5	12.1	5 954
Kenya	5.8	0.8	6.5	c	6.5	8 351
Lesotho	7.6	0.8	8.4	c	8.4	3 373
Senegal	9.0	3.0	12.0	c	12.0	4 052
Tunisia	5.8	1.6	7.5	4.1	11.6	4 713
Asia and Pacific						
Syria	10.8	1.0	11.9	c	11.9	6 202
Yemen AR	6.4	0.7	7.1	c	7.6	3 252
Bangladesh	4.6	2.7	7.4	0.2	7.6	5 827
Korea, Rep. of	5.1	1.0	6.1	24.0	30.1	5 839
Philippines	9.2	1.0	10.2	0.5	10.8	10 193
Americas						
Colombia	9.1	1.0	10.1	0.8	10.9	3 274
Paraguay	8.1	1.9	10.0	c	10.0	2 889
Peru	6.3	1.2	7.5	0.5	8.0	6 122
Venezuela	9.1	1.8	10.9	c	10.9	2 772
Costa Rica	12.5	1.5	13.9	0.5	14.4	2 574
Mexico	7.3	2.1	9.3	0.7	10.0	7 384
Panama	7.5	1.3	8.8	0.8	9.6	2 745
Guyana	17.8	2.6	20.4	c	20.4	3 700
Haiti	4.9	2.4	7.3	c	7.3	2 171
Jamaica	8.2	2.0	10.1	c	10.1	2 345

a Multiple births counted as one pregnancy.
b Excludes pregnancies conceived within nine months of the survey date.
c Miscarriages and induced losses not distinguished.
Source: J. B. Casterline and H. Ashurst (1984)

and induced, and of stillbirths, these can be of considerable consequence in determining achieved fertility levels. Correct attribution of protection requires detailed parallel information on other proximate determinants (see e.g. Little and Hobcraft forthcoming). Failure to take account of the conception waits associated with induced abortion understates the fertility-reducing impact very considerably: Little and Hobcraft (forthcoming) estimate that the fertility-reducing impact of induced abortion in the Republic of Korea is increased four-fold by including the conception waits, excluding contraceptive protection.

30.3   Integrated treatment of the proximate determinants of fertility

The frameworks

Since Davis and Blake (1956) presented their classic statement on intermediate fertility variables, demographers have become increasingly aware of the levers through which fertility behaviour is determined and altered. However, no means of conjointly assessing the impact of several proximate determinants upon fertility was available until over 20 years later, when Bongaarts (1978) first published his now well-known framework. This influential work made several key simplifications. Bongaarts grouped the intermediate fertility variables into eight factors under three broad categories. He then argued that four of these factors were generally of low importance in determining fertility levels: frequency of intercourse, sterility, spontaneous intra-uterine mortality, and duration of the fertile period. The other four factors were proportion married, contraception, induced abortion and lactational infecundability; indices were developed to assess the fertility-reducing impact of each of these. Table 30.1 touches on many of the measurement issues and assumptions involved (see Bongaarts and Potter 1983 for a recent account of this framework). The grouping and treatment of the factors identified owes more to the work of Henry (e.g. 1972) than to Davis and Blake. The Bongaarts framework has considerable attractions, not least its simplicity and low data requirements, and is by far the most widely used procedure for quantifying the impact of the proximate determinants on fertility; it has been employed very extensively in the analysis of WFS data (see especially Bongaarts (1982), Lesthaeghe, Shah and Page (1981), Casterline, Singh, Cleland and Ashurst (1984) and Singh, Casterline and Cleland (1985), all of which report on application to a large number of countries, with all but the first also examining differences for education and residence groups).

Inevitably, the widespread application of the pioneering framework of Bongaarts has raised a number of questions about its validity and assumptions. Bongaarts (1982) demonstrated impressive consistency in total fecundity estimates across a wide range of populations, using mainly WFS data. He used the average total fecundity of 15.3 to predict total fertility via his indices and accounted for 96 per cent of the cross-national variation in observed fertility levels. Applications of Bongaarts' framework by others have proved less successful. Chidambaram and Cleland (1981) showed disturbingly large discrepancies, although their derivation of the marriage index was flawed. Subsequently, Casterline, Singh, Cleland and Ashurst (1984) undertook a major piece of analysis using the framework due to Bongaarts and exploring the consequences of varying a number of the advocated measurement procedures. They explicitly examine results for the 17 countries included in their study and in Bongaarts' study. For these 17 countries, Bongaarts accounts for 91 per cent of the variation in TFRs; Casterline *et al.* account for 81 per cent of variation in TFRs using their preferred age-specific and otherwise modified version, and for 78 per cent when they construct the indices in the same manner as Bongaarts. The sources of this discrepancy seem to be in the marriage indices and the total fertility estimates, which Bongaarts usually took from non-WFS sources, whereas the Casterline *et al.* analysis relies entirely on WFS surveys for all its information.

The methodological parts of the Casterline *et al.* report address a number of methodological questions, which assess the sensitivity of the Bongaarts framework to alternative constructions of the indices. They conclude that five of the variations they assess are of no great practical importance, meaning that the simple procedures are robust: (1) use of actual fertility rate for age group 15–19 or of 0.75 times the age-specific rate for 20–24 in determining C_m; (2) age-specific or non age-specific construction of C_c; (3) adjustment for overlap with post-partum infecundability in calculation of C_c, with adjustment achieved by omitting users still breastfeeding a child under six months of age, compared with no adjustment; (4) age-specific versus non age-specific construction of C_i; and (5) use of direct information on amenorrhoea versus indirect estimates from breastfeeding in calculating C_i. These instances are reassuring in regard to the validity of Bongaarts' procedures. However, among the nine variations investigated, four were of greater consequence: (6) inclusion or exclusion of out-of-union births in calculating the total fertility rate; (7) use of current status or experience over a five-year reference period for union status in calculating C_m; (8) use of different age-specific schedules of sterility in constructing C_c; and (9) inclusion of post-partum abstinence in the non-susceptible period compared with use of information solely on breastfeeding or amenorrhoea in C_i.

With the exception of (9), which simply restresses the importance of post-partum abstinence and the need to collect and analyse information on it, these variations raise questions about some aspects of Bongaarts' framework. No doubt the next few years will see further clarification in this direction (see e.g. Menken forthcoming).

The pioneering work of Bongaarts has also stimulated other attempts to assess the fertility-reducing impact of the proximate determinants, although the approach due to Gaslonde pre-dates Bongaarts' work by several years (e.g. Gaslonde and Bocaz 1970). Gaslonde developed a sexual life history approach, which identifies, for the year preceding a survey, each month of pregnancy by outcome where known; for the remaining months, any months of absence of sexual relations are recorded by reason (e.g. permanent celibacy, temporary celibacy, temporary separation, permanent separation or divorce, illness and other, including abstinence within marriage); finally, any months of contraceptive use among the remaining months at risk are identified by method. Any pregnancies while using contraception are also recorded. Except for the serious omission of post-partum amenorrhoea, which can easily be incorporated in this scheme, this approach constitutes a valuable contribution to the measurement and accounting of the proximate determinants. Despite its exposure in CELADE publications, the approach remains largely unacknowledged in the English-speaking world. It has gained greater exposure through publication of an analysis of Venezuelan data by Gaslonde and Carrasco (1982).

A further approach to examining the proximate determinants of fertility was developed by Mosley, Werner and Becker (1982) for an analysis of WFS data from Kenya. Their approach has a number of interesting features but suffers from lack of explicit incorporation of contraception, which is relatively un-important for Kenya but a damaging problem elsewhere. It also somewhat inexplicably ignores information on post-partum abstinence which is available for Kenya and assumes no pre-marital births, which is contrary to fact in Kenya, where about 28 per cent of women in recent unions had had a first birth before their reported date of first union (see Hobcraft and McDonald 1984).

The most fully developed alternative procedure for assessing the fertility-reducing impact of proximate determinants so far is fertility exposure analysis (FEA) (Hobcraft and Little 1984; Little and Hobcraft forthcoming). This ap-proach is too recent to have yet received the detailed scrutiny accorded to the framework developed by Bongaarts. Once again, a full discussion of the approach is beyond the scope of this chapter, but FEA possesses a number of advantages. Principal among these is that it permits individual-level analysis, thus opening up the whole panoply of regression techniques for assessing how remote determinants operate through individual proximate determinants to determine fertility levels, in an integrated and coherent framework. While the present author can hardly claim to be an unbiased observer, this does seem an important step forward. Other advantages of FEA are numerous: it permits incorporation of coital frequency reports or self-reported fecundity status including an uncertain category, through its stratification approach; it is very explicit about rules of precedence between various proximate determinants; it can handle partial protection; it maintains an absolute consistency of reference periods for all inputs, unless explicit substi-tution is made; it can incorporate internal estimates of contraceptive efficacy, breastfeeding 'contraceptive' efficacy and even union-type 'contraceptive' efficacies, as estimates of the fecundability-reducing effect of each status group; it provides direct estimates of mean waits to conception; it naturally incorporates age variation; and it uses exact accounting relationships for all measures.

Naturally, such potential rewards are not without cost. FEA relies on detailed allocation of exposure on a month-by-month basis to a number of mutually exclusive categories. A woman may contribute to more than one exposure category in a month. In principle, any measurable proximate determinant can be dealt with: if it can be recorded or approximated on a month-by-month basis it can be included among the exposure states; alternatively, stratification can be used where the measure is imprecise, especially if it is likely to be an important correlate of fecundability or coital frequency. A full analysis, incorporating all the features sketched here, would require too large a sample to permit the detailed, accurate measurement required. Thus many of the efficacies which can be endogenized will be treated as exogenous in most applications: FEA has the advantage of forcing such assumptions to be explicitly and clearly stated, allowing subsequent assessment to be made. The amount of information required will always be a drawback, as will the need for special computer programs to perform the analysis, until appropriate software is fully developed and available. Ultimately, elaborate approaches such as FEA have to demonstrate a modicum of robustness to reporting and measurement errors and to justify their greater data demands through enhanced understanding; time and other observers will tell.

A final and still more recent attempt to integrate analysis of the proximate determinants into a framework that encompasses remote determinants and fertility is that developed by Palloni (forthcoming). This has even more ambitious features, disaggregating analysis by birth order but reaggregating to obtain overall indicators of the fertility-inhibiting effects of proximate determinants. The approach begins with a detailed analysis of birth intervals, using logit regression on life tables. Then formulae are derived to obtain the estimated impact on each parity progression ratio for each proximate determinant. Finally, a means of summarizing to get overall fertility-reducing effects is described. Technically, this constitutes an important contribution. Unfortunately, the preliminary results for Peru are somewhat disappointing, but further development may overcome the apparent problems when results are compared with those of Bongaarts, or alternatively confirm their greater validity.

A number of other variants which provide more or less integrated treatment of the proximate determinants have been proposed in recent years. For example, Vanderhoeft has proposed a series of regression procedures which examine the correlates of each proximate determinant in turn (Vanderhoeft 1983). These can then be used to generate predicted values for subgroups which are fed into an analysis using the Bongaarts framework (e.g. Lesthaeghe, Vanderhoeft, Becker and Kibet 1985). Partial analyses have also often made use of an assessment of determinants of starting, spacing and stopping of childbearing (e.g. Page and Lesthaeghe (eds.) 1981). This approach was heavily used in the WFS workshop on the analysis of FOTCAF information, guided by the illustrative analysis of Ferry and Page (1984). Effectively, entirely separate analyses are made, focusing on (1) age at first birth and related phenomena, such as age at first marriage and age at menarche, (2) analysis of birth intervals, paying special attention to post-partum variables and (3) the cessation of childbearing, identified by onset of sterility, widowhood, age at last birth, etc. (see also Leridon and Ferry 1985). Integration of the separate analyses is not achieved, and resort is commonly made to the framework due to Bongaarts, with modifications, for synthesis. Serious doubts are sometimes expressed about the wisdom of distinguishing spacing and stopping, as there are real problems of separation in the face of stochastic variation and changing attitudes over time (see e.g. Hobcraft 1985 and Lightbourne 1985).

Applications of the frameworks

Have the various approaches to integrated treatment of the proximate determinants of fertility made a decisive contribution to our understanding and analysis of fertility? The answer must be a qualified yes. A great deal of the gain to the profession is in the heightened awareness that the frameworks have brought, by focusing our attention on the range of levers through which fertility levels and trends are determined. Thus, we have become much more sophisticated in our ability to account for exceptions to general relationships.

A classic example occurs in the examination of educational differences in fertility. In general, within a society, more educated women have lower fertility. But, as we accrued more detailed information, a number of exceptions to this rule emerged (e.g. Cochrane 1979). The WFS and the Bongaarts framework have helped considerably in accounting for these anomalous findings. Increased education seems almost universally associated with reductions in duration of breast-feeding and erosion of other traditional fertility restraints, such as prolonged post-partum abstinence. Conversely, increased education is also almost universally associated with higher contraceptive use. The overall impact of increased education, especially incomplete primary education, can then operate to raise or lower marital fertility, depending upon the relative strength of these associations. Thus, where contraceptive use is low, the reduced protection from lactational amenorrhoea can outweigh the small increase in protection from contraception. The early stages of development can then lead to rises in fertility. However, once secondary schooling (or seven or more years of schooling) is achieved, a noticeable fertility reduction always seems to occur: the increased impact of contraception now almost always outweighs the reduced protection from lactational amenorrhoea, and delayed marriage acts as a powerful reinforcement to the impact of contraception.

An age-specific set of estimates for Bongaarts' indices is given by Lesthaeghe, Shah and Page (1981), although these are badly distorted by a failure to take account of changing sterility with age. More subtly, their Bongaarts indices for education groups are also distorted by this problem, with less educated women typically being older than the more educated: these age distributions can differ dramatically and thereby distort C_c in particular; age variations in duration of breastfeeding can also be of moderate consequence. These problems are avoided by the age-specific analysis of Casterline, Singh, Cleland and Ashurst (1984) for education and residence groups.

Lesthaeghe and his collaborators (Lesthaeghe 1982; Lesthaeghe, Shah and Page 1981) forcibly raise the spectre of potential fertility increases as a consequence of erosion of traditional fertility restraints (see also Lesthaeghe 1984). In order to address this issue, the Bongaarts framework is employed: the basic relationship $TMFR/TF = C_c C_i$ is used, where TMFR is the total of marital fertility rates, TF the total fecundity, C_c a simplified form of Bongaarts' contraceptive index and C_i the lactational infecundability index. If C_i is increased, through shorter lactational amenorrhoea, it is easy to derive the value of C_c required to neutralize the rise in fertility that would otherwise follow. On the basis of these calculations, which place trust in the exactitude of Bongaarts' approximations, they suggest, for example, that a reduction of lactational amenorrhoea from the current mean of 14.7 months to one of 10 months in Pakistan would require a rise in contraceptive use from the current level of five per cent to 20 per cent in order to compensate; further reduction of mean post-partum amenorrhoea to six months requires 33 per cent using contraception merely to prevent fertility rises. Similar illustrative calculations are made for a number of countries. Clearly, in Africa and Asia, where durations of breastfeeding are long, a substantial erosion of this practice and of post-partum abstinence taboos could indeed lead to a fertility rise unless accompanied by substantial increases in contraception. The very high levels of fertility in Jordan and Kenya could reflect the early impact of such changes. Lesthaeghe, Shah and Page (1981) conclude by stressing that rapid and substantial increases in contraceptive use among currently married women to over 40 or 50 per cent are probably required in Indonesia and Sri Lanka to compensate likely reductions in lactational amen-orrhoea. Further, 'in Kenya, Bangladesh and Pakistan a real contraceptive revolution would be needed to counteract a decline in breastfeeding. We would not be surprised if genuine increases in marital fertility were to occur in these three countries during the next decade' (Lesthaeghe, Shah and Page 1981).

Such hypothetical analyses do raise important possibilities, but there is little evidence to suggest actual substantial rises in marital fertility in many Third World countries, although exceptions can be made for parts of Africa, where sterility has been substantially reduced over time. Rapid secular changes in dur-ation of breastfeeding have been documented for several South-East Asian societies, including Republic of Korea, Malaysia, Taiwan and Thailand (Coale, Cho and Goldman 1982, DaVanzo and Haaga 1982, Freedman and Casterline 1982, and Knodel and Debavalya 1980). Yet in all these societies the fertility-increasing effects of this reduction have been overwhelmed by rapid increases in contraceptive use and by delayed marriage. Delayed marriage is an important consequence of urban residence, yet is ignored by treatment of marital fertility. In addition, the TMFR is based on marital fertility rates, which represent far smaller segments of urban or metropolitan populations at ages below 25 and thus may suffer from greater selectivity for high fertility.

Casterline, Singh, Cleland and Ashurst (1984) and Singh, Casterline and Cleland (1985) are far more sanguine about future prospects, based on their analysis of proximate determinants for 29 countries, which examines residence and education groups in detail and uses an age-specific and otherwise modified formulation of the Bongaarts framework. Among the 29 countries considered, the total of fertility rates is almost universally lower in urban than in rural areas (the only exception being Guyana); the reduction is below 10 per cent only for Jamaica, Bangladesh, Indonesia and Pakistan. There is usually a further, often substantial, reduction in metropolitan areas, although once again differ-ences are small for Guyana, Bangladesh, Indonesia and Pakistan, as well as in a number of other countries with substantial urban–rural differences. Kenya, much referred to as a source of likely rises, shows a nearly 50 per cent reduction in TFR for urban or metropolitan areas compared with rural areas. Casterline *et al.* (1984) show that sharp changes in the impact of breastfeeding on fertility as measured by Bongaarts' C_i occur with residence in any urban area or with seven or more years of schooling for the mother (which always seems to achieve reductions in fertility). Yet they also show that sharp changes in marriage behaviour occur across the same boundaries; in addition, contraception increases steadily with education and urbanity. Casterline *et al.* conclude: 'It is very clear that, cross-sectionally, the fertility-increasing effect of shorter durations of post-partum infecundability among the more modern strata is almost always more than counterbalanced by the fertility impact of nuptiality and contraceptive usage. This suggests that the time-lag between declines in breastfeeding and compensating movements in contraception and nuptiality are normally short, in the contemporary developing world. Thus alarm that radical declines in breast-feeding while marriage and contraception remain static will lead to substantial increases in fertility seems unwarranted'. Clearly they are much more sanguine about prospects than Lesthaeghe and collaborators (see also Dyson and Murphy 1985). Casterline *et al.* find that increased urbanity and schooling seem to change nuptiality, lactation and contraception less in the few African countries they were able to include than in other regions.

It is to sub-Saharan Africa that we now turn. A major project is under way at the Free University of Brussels, directed by Lesthaeghe, which is seeking to examine both individual and contextual effects of maternal education and how these act through the proximate determinants to determine fertility, using WFS surveys (see Lesthaeghe, Vanderhoeft, Becker and Kibet 1985; Gaisie forthcoming). The work also includes a much broader synthesis of the information on the proximate determinants of fertility in sub-Saharan Africa (Lesthaeghe 1984). The complexity and variability of the proximate determinants of fertility in Africa is a demographic analyst's dream come true (or perhaps a data collector's nightmare). Sterility, probably mainly from widespread venereal disease, but also from malaria, has acted as a powerful depressant of fertility in many areas, although this also is changing, for example in Cameroon (Santow and Bioumla 1984). Polygyny is common; union dissolution is often high; remarriage rates can also be high. Prolonged post-partum abstinence is widely practised and lactational amenorrhoea is often long. There is enormous regional variation, even within countries. Lesthaeghe (1984) provides an impressive overview of this diversity, but always remains sensibly concerned with the cultural and social determinants of the observed patterns. The theme of erosion of traditional fertility restraints and reduced sterility causing likely fertility rises is once again stressed, as are the problems facing family planning programmes in reaching couples and persuading them to use contraception without alienation.

An interesting development is the introduction of contextual effects of maternal education into analysis, over and above individual effects (Lesthaeghe, Vanderhoeft, Becker and Kibet 1985; Gaisie forthcoming). The approach for Kenya is a curious admixture of elaborate Bayesian discriminant analysis and informal exploratory data analysis (Lesthaeghe, Vanderhoeft, Becker and Kibet

1985). It is by no means clear what the contextual levels of education are measuring, as almost no other socio-economic or cultural determinants are included in the analysis. High contextual levels of education may proxy for local socio-economic development, including for example availability of family planning services. Thus, interpretation of the results is difficult, although due account is taken of these problems. In contrast to the earlier paper of Lesthaeghe, Shah and Page (1981), this paper concludes that 'the fertility transition in Kenya is clearly advancing and moving to a crucial stage . . . there is evidence pointing in the direction of an imminent net fertility decline in large parts of Nairobi, Mombasa and the Central and Eastern provinces. Urban populations and immigrant populations originating from the Central Highlands in the Rift Valley may be following'. Other groups 'may even exhibit a further (*sic*) fertility increase'. Once again, we must emphasize the key role played by the incorporation of the proximate determinants in these analyses. It is the countervailing impacts of shorter nonsusceptible periods and other fertility-increasing changes, compared with the reducing effects of increased contraception and delayed marriage, which are the key to determining short-term trends associated with societal change or socio-economic development.

A crucial question, not always addressed, is how far the proximate determinants that are identified and included in an analysis do completely account for observed fertility differences. This can be of considerable importance in interpreting results and inferring the correlates of change. An analysis of education and urban–rural differences in fertility (Casterline *et al.* 1984, Singh, Casterline and Cleland 1985) was plagued by such problems, with the estimated total fecundity showing a clear propensity to be lower for more developed groups. Unusually, this problem is given close scrutiny, through an examination of a number of fragmentary pieces of evidence on the proximate determinants not explicitly included in the main analysis but available from WFS surveys. The results are inconclusive, but the most plausible explanation seems to be unreported abortion in the more urbanized areas or among the most educated. An indication of the abortion rates needed to equalize the total fecundity estimates across groups is provided, assuming Bongaarts' abortion index to effect the translation. In addition, a pattern of variation in use effectiveness, lower for rural or uneducated groups, is posited. Although clearly speculative, the results are interpreted as supporting 'the argument that the analysis is deficient for many of these countries due to crude measurement (*sic*) of contraceptive effectiveness and lack of measurement of abortion' (Casterline, Singh, Cleland and Ashurst 1984). A further discrepancy sometimes occurs for total fecundity estimates referring to the uneducated (Casterline, Singh, Cleland and Ashurst 1984) or those in very backward areas (e.g. rural upper Egypt, Nawar and Hobcraft forthcoming). Perhaps the low total fecundity estimates for these groups reflect under-reporting of fertility or contraceptive use, rather than omission of abortion. Whatever the true sources of variation in total fecundity estimates, care needs to be exercised: if the frameworks inadequately account

for the effects of the measured proximate determinants, this needs to be explained and corrected; if the problem is one of unmeasured variation, this
suggests improving our coverage of the omitted proximate determinants and
refining measurement of those currently measured.

A tantalizing feature of the work on education and residence groups by
Casterline, Singh, Cleland and Ashurst (1984) and Singh, Casterline and Cleland
(1985) is the treatment of a single variable at a time. Thus, as we have seen,
urban residence is usually associated with increased contraceptive use, shorter
breastfeeding and delayed marriage; education, especially beyond seven years of
schooling, is similarly associated. Which, if either, is the decisive correlate? If the
effects of the other variable are controlled for, are variations for each of the
proximate determinants more clearly associated with education or with residence? These are the classic problems of multivariate analysis, and obviously we
want to consider more than two socio-economic variables. Analysis for separate
groups rapidly becomes infeasible with cross-classification by several variables
and resort to regression procedures is desirable. Regression of individual proximate determinants on a range of remote determinants has been part of the staple
diet of demographers for years. Putting separate regressions for each proximate
determinant on an equal footing in order to assess the resultant fertility impact
is a much more recent preoccupation. Hobcraft and Little (1984) give an example
of this kind of analysis for the Dominican Republic. After controlling for region,
urban-rural residence, mother's education and age, they assess the combined
and separate fertility impact of the proximate determinants. The range of education differences is greatest among the non-demographic controls; women with
six or more years of schooling reduce their fertility exposure by 20 percentage
points more than those with 0-2 years of schooling. The dominant source of
these education differences is delayed first sexual relations; the combined impact
of the other proximate determinants examined acts to close the differential
slightly, although this is achieved by compensating differences five and four percentage points less protection for the educated due to dissolution and lactational
infecundity respectively and six percentage points more protection from contraception. Even after controls for the other variables, rural–urban differences in
total fertility reduction also persist, with urban women achieving a nine percentage point additional reduction: this is mainly due to higher union dissolution in
urban areas, which is also featured in the results reported for the Republic of
Korea (Little and Hobcraft forthcoming). A similar analysis for Egypt showed
once again the importance of delayed marriage, but demonstrated very persistent
relationships between type of locality and fertility and the proximate determinants, even after controls for a number of other variables (Nawar and Hobcraft
forthcoming). In both of the aforementioned analyses (for the Dominican
Republic and Egypt), the relationship of at least one of the socio-economic
determinants with potential fertility remained significant, suggesting measurement errors or omitted determinants. More successful in this respect was the
analysis for the Republic of Korea, where none of several variables considered

was significantly associated with potential fertility, suggesting that the proximate determinants as measured, including induced abortion, were fairly successful in accounting for observed fertility differences (Little and Hobcraft forthcoming).

30.4 Discussion

There is no doubt that our analytic tools and understanding have been considerably enhanced by paying due attention to the proximate determinants of fertility. That WFS has made a major contribution to this heightened awareness is self-evident. A number of themes requiring more thought and careful elucidation are beginning to emerge from the flood of recent work, which we shall now briefly review.

An issue deserving more attention is the grouping of the many individual proximate determinants. This chapter has advanced yet another grouping to add to the many existing ones. But our concern now is with the criterion for grouping. Most categorizations are essentially fertility oriented and group together, say, post-partum variables, all lack of sexual exposure or all methods of contraception. In terms of the fertility impact of the proximate determinants, this makes sense; our own categorization has such features. A further possibility which cannot be ignored, though, is to group together those proximate determinants which have common antecedents or remote determinants. Thus, it may be the case that the determinants of post-partum abstinence differ from those of breastfeeding practice, as seems plausible in parts of Africa, where the abstinence taboos seem to be collapsing while breastfeeding persists (Lesthaeghe 1984). If so, it is not sensible to lump these two proximate determinants together as a combined non-susceptible period. Similarly, the determinants of union dissolution are unlikely to be the same as the determinants of entry into first union, especially where widowhood is prevalent. Conversely early entry into marriage is an important correlate of divorce in highly developed societies which persists in the face of many other controls. Contraceptive availability is often measured on a method-specific basis. Such arguments push us towards continued partition of the proximate determinants in examining the paths through which a broad range of remote determinants operate.

On the other hand, there are many issues which suggest we need to examine proximate determinants as a whole, because of substitution effects. It is clear that the cluster of variables concerning post-partum amenorrhoea, abstinence, breastfeeding and child survival require much closer conjoint scrutiny, to permit better comprehension, modelling and explanation (e.g. Santow and Singh 1984). Similarly, polygyny, sterility and post-partum abstinence taboos seem intimately interlinked (Lesthaeghe 1984). The important questions surrounding substitution of contraception for traditional spacing mechanisms require much closer examination at the individual level (e.g. Casterline, Singh, Cleland and Ashurst 1984; Singh, Casterline and Cleland 1985; Casterline 1984; Millman forthcoming; Lesthaeghe, Page and Adegbola 1981).

It is clear that many if not most of the proximate determinants respond to influences broadly associated with development; certainly observed education and residence differences generally indicate this. But many argue a critical role for ideational change in the adoption of contraception: fertility control has to be perceived as within the calculus of conscious choice (see for example the following disparate sources: Coale 1973; Casterline 1982; and Cleland 1985). Yet does not the wholesale abandonment of traditional fertility restraint also require ideational change? The major question then becomes whether the two sets of ideas can change independently, or whether they are almost inextricably intertwined: the classic survey approach is unlikely to provide relevant material for answers. A third key element usually identified in discussion of changing contraceptive practice is availability (e.g. Jones 1984 for a synthesis of WFS findings). Without the means of reliable contraception, couples are less likely to achieve fertility control. Yet, especially where distribution of contraception is integrated with maternal and child health services, as is increasingly common, the same clinic may serve to advocate bottle-feeding and contraception. Even without quite such direct links, it is nevertheless likely that service provision of all kinds is heavily clustered, with the accessibility to health services and family planning services being similar, perhaps often in market towns (which incidentally can make a nonsense of travel time as a measure of accessibility).

The issues raised in the preceding paragraph are by no means trivial. If, even in a sizeable number of societies, the links between breastfeeding reductions and increases in contraceptive use are ineluctable, we are foolish to break apart proximate determinants too mechanically. An intriguing finding in this respect was that of Hobcraft and Little (1984) for the Dominican Republic. Women seemed to achieve consistent degrees of reduction of exposure to risk of conception through the various proximate determinants at ages above 25, but the degree of reduction varied with education or type of place of residence. The mix of proximate determinants changed with age, but the overall exposure reduction did not; this may be fortuitous, but its persistence in five groups raised the possibility that women in the Dominican Republic achieve substitution of dissolution, contraception and breastfeeding.

In a similar vein is the recent work by Palloni (forthcoming), which achieves a technical advance by permitting separate analysis of the effects of some of the proximate determinants on birth interval analysis and recombination to summary measures of the impacts of the proximate determinants on parity progression ratios and total fertility. Yet there is emerging evidence that fertility behaviour is essentially unaltered beyond the second birth in a number of countries, which has intriguing implications for our understanding of fertility (see Rodríguez, Hobcraft, McDonald, Menken and Trussell 1984 and Hobcraft 1985). This again contraindicates fragmentation of the reproductive process.

Although the proximate determinants of fertility are the theme of this chapter and a great deal of valuable work on this topic has emerged in recent years, we must caution against undue emphasis. The proximate determinants have several attractions, including much common ground among demographers in their identification; they are often measurable and we at least know what we want to measure; we now have a range of analytic procedures to enable exploitation of the measurements we obtain. These are not inconsiderable assets. But we should not forget that the proximate determinants are merely the levers through which fertility levels are determined. Our main research goals still lie with the much less tractable problems of discovering the real determinants of fertility. Here there is little common ground, with almost every demographer having a pet theory; even when we understand each other's broad concepts we can rarely identify agreed measurement procedures. Explanation at this level is usually qualitative. A major research challenge over some time to come is the elucidation of common ground and development of a consensus on the real determinants of fertility and their quantification. It is, however, only realistic to accept that we may not achieve such a desirable synthesis in the foreseeable future. The further refinement, measurement and analysis of the proximate determinants with some remote determinants will no doubt continue to provide our bread-and-butter research on fertility for some time to come: doing the do-able keeps most scientific disciplines alive.

31

Reproductive Preferences and Behaviour

Robert E. Lightbourne

31.1 Introduction

The measurement and interpretation of fertility preferences data has for some time been a particularly problematic and controversial area in demography. The controversy grew particularly acrimonious in the wake of the knowledge, attitudes and practice (KAP) surveys of the 1950s and 60s, conducted in a number of countries with varying degrees of adherence to acceptable scientific standards of sampling and analysis.

These surveys indicated that in most of the countries studied, vast numbers of women preferred substantially fewer children than they were actually having. On the basis of such findings, some observers argued that the unprecedentedly high rates of population growth being observed in developing countries could be reduced relatively cheaply and painlessly by making contraceptives widely available. Others argued that the data on reproductive motives had little validity or meaning, and that reductions in population growth would come about only as a consequence of real economic and structural change, or as the result of draconian policies aimed at increasing the costs or reducing the benefits of children to parents.

Scope

One of the purposes of WFS was to collect more trustworthy data on reproductive motives, and the question naturally arises as to how far the programme has succeeded in doing so, and how the data that have been collected should be interpreted.

This chapter will first summarize evidence on the quality of the WFS fertility preference data and will then provide a selective review of substantive findings. It should be emphasized in advance that a large number of writers have contributed at both the substantive and theoretical level to analysing the WFS preference data. Owing to limitations of space, and also owing to a particular focus on the relationship between actual and desired fertility levels, this chapter does not contain a balanced review of findings, and instead attempts a highly selective synthesis.

31.2 Data quality

This discussion briefly summarizes the conclusions of a background paper on WFS fertility preference data quality (Lightbourne 1984b).

In virtually all the 39 countries considered here (Nigeria, Iran and Turkey are omitted) three 'core' items were asked, namely desire for additional children, number of additional children desired, and total number of children desired. Twenty countries asked a question on desire for last birth and 15 asked respondents who wanted additional children whether or not they wanted the next birth as soon as possible or later. A question on preferred sex of next child was asked in virtually all of the countries, but this has had limited analytical utility and is not examined here.

One important element of data quality is completeness. If a large segment of the sample does not answer a question, analysis is hampered, in large part because omitted respondents might in theory have given very different answers. The background paper on data quality (Lightbourne 1984b) showed a low frequency of 'not stated' responses, well below 5 per cent except in a few isolated cases, to all four of the preference items.

Scepticism about the capacity of respondents to provide numeric answers to the question on total number of children desired proved unjustified in most of the countries, but was justified in about one-quarter. The frequency of non-numeric answers was low in 26 countries (i.e. below 5 per cent), medium in seven countries (5–19 per cent), high in six countries (20–30 per cent) and very high in one (43 per cent). While non-numeric answering is in principle a source of possible analytical bias, the background paper presented several types of evidence to suggest that national-level estimates of preferred family size are at most negligibly affected.

The 'undecided' response to the question on desire for additional children was considered at some length. Undecidedness occurs with particularly high frequency in the African countries, and is as much as 30 per cent at some parities. One principal conclusion is that the proportion using contraception among undecideds is very close to the proportion observed in the 'want more' group and that the undecideds do not display the elevated proportions using contraception usually observed among women who want to postpone. On the other hand, the proportion undecided is typically strongly associated with parity, rising from very low levels at low parities to a maximum at one of the middle parities, then declining at the higher parities. On balance, it seems that undecideds are genuinely indifferent about whether they have additional children, and that the correct analytical choice when analysing proportions not wanting additional children is to group undecideds with women who want more rather than to exclude them from the sample. In countries that seek to reduce fertility and where there are low levels of motivation to terminate, one speculates that it may nevertheless prove useful to advocate the idea that individuals should have children only when they positively want them, with the object of motivating both postponers and the undecideds to adopt contraception.

Another topic examined in the background paper on data quality was the somewhat controversial subject of what respondents actually mean when they report not wanting additional children and yet state a desired family size in excess of the number of children living. The theory of random answering had to be rejected, since the data showed impressively high consistency among women who replied in the affirmative to the direct question on whether they wanted additional children (95 per cent were consistent, and stated a desired family size greater than actual family size). A more persuasive theory (Palmore and Concepción 1981; Pullum 1981) is that in answering the question on desire for further children, respondents stated their effective demand for an additional child under the influence of such considerations as being able to afford another, or marital problems, or being too old to start rearing another child; in answering the question on total number desired, on the other hand, they were argued to be stating their ideal family size in the absence of real world constraints. An alternative explanation (Ware 1977; United Nations 1981c) is that some women misunderstood the time referent to the question on desire for additional children, and misconstrued it as asking whether they wanted a birth in the near future. This latter view receives support from the analysis of over 2000 reinterviews with the respondents of the 1975 Costa Rican Fertility Survey, which occurred one and a half years later and showed a very low rate of switchover from wanting no more to wanting more among respondents whose desired family size was less than or equal to actual (i.e. about 5 per cent), and a much higher rate of switch-over among respondents whose desired size exceeded actual family size (i.e. about 50 per cent switched). On the other hand, comparisons of proportions using contraception among the consistent and the inconsistent respondents indicate very little difference in about two-thirds of the countries, including all the Latin American countries and a number of the Asian countries. Only in about one-third of the countries was contraceptive use substantially higher among the consistents. On balance, it seems that in some countries the inconsistency reflects an important difference of motive, while in most it does not. It is not possible from the data at hand to judge the extent to which the idealization of family size versus postponement theories are true; the theories are not mutually exclusive and it seems possible that both tendencies may contribute to the explanation. Resolution of such an issue will require reinterview data.

The background paper on data quality gave critical attention to the subject of the test–retest reliability of the preference questions. One of the conclusions drawn is that there is a need to tailor the tests to analytical purposes. For example, analytical interest in the desire for additional children question is often focused on the proportion not wishing additional children. When this is the objective, the appropriate test–retest item is the proportion remaining in the 'want no more' cell rather than proportions remaining on the main diagonal in the nine-cell table formed when desire for children is trichotomized into the WFS 'more', 'no more' and 'uncertain' categories.

When the available retest data are subjected to this more appropriate test, the reliability of the 'whether more wanted' question is often seen to be appreciably higher than the proportion on the main diagonal, and is in the range 80–90 per cent rather than the 60–70 per cent typically reported for the latter test. More detailed analysis of the reinterview data also revealed systematic variation in test–retest reliability by parity. In particular, women with one or two children who said they wanted no more additional children were particularly apt to switch to saying they wanted more, though it is not clear whether they were switching from wanting no more to wanting to postpone, or switching to wanting to have soon. This question is of more than trivial importance because switches between wanting no more and wanting to postpone do not necessarily imply any change in contraceptive use. So long as women do not switch to wanting another child soon, they are continually motivated to restrict. Future testing of response reliability to the question on whether more children are desired should take this into account, and may reveal even higher stability of the desire to restrict.

The evidence on test–retest reliability of the total number of children desired item basically confirms what we already knew, namely that a large proportion of women definitely do not have fixed desired family sizes. It is none the less true that quite a high proportion – between 40 and 60 per cent – report the same number when there are no intervening births, even after intervals as long as four years, and that 70–80 per cent of respondents give an answer within one child of their initial answer. But to the degree that current family size influences desired size, this correlation is not necessarily meaningful. Indeed, the reinterview data contain confirmation of what is clearly and unmistakeably suggested in the cross-sectional data on mean desired family size by parity, namely that women tend to shift their desired family size upwards when they have additional births. The cross-sectional information, on the other hand, has suggested that this is not simply a rationalization of undesired births, but is also the result of a tendency on the part of low-parity women to understate the number of children they will ultimately want (Lightbourne and MacDonald 1982). Despite all these problems with the desired family size item, the comparison later on with 'desired stopping point' approaches to estimating mean number of children desired suggests that the item does remarkably well in giving us a reasonable approximation at the aggregate level of the number of children women would have if there were no fecundity impairments and no postponement behaviour.

Direct information on the test–retest reliability of the desire for last birth item is available in rather imperfect form for Fiji, where the standard form of the question was not asked. The item of interest is the stability of response in the 'not want last birth' category, which was unimpressively low at 70 per cent. One should not, however, leap immediately to the conclusion that since it was unstable for individual Fijians, the desire for last birth item is generally worthless at the aggregate level. On the contrary, the results outlined in the next paragraph suggest that the question does quite well in some countries.

One of the most substantively important results in the data assessment paper is an analysis which strongly suggests the validity of the astonishingly low wanted total fertility rate of 2.2 births per woman estimated for the 1974-1975 period for Sri Lanka. Women initially interviewed in 1975 were reinterviewed in 1979, which provided a count of births between 1975 and 1979. If a woman did not want additional children in 1975 it seemed proper to count any subsequent birth in the 1975–1979 period as a 'true unwanted' birth. Confining attention to births occurring 0–2 years prior to the 1979 interview allowed estimation of the 'true proportion of births unwanted' circa 1978–1979, and provided a definitionally strong criterion for evaluating the validity of the responses to the question on the desire for the last birth, by comparing the true proportion unwanted with the proportion unwanted estimated via the question on desire for last birth. The conclusion based on this comparison — qualified only slightly by problems discussed in the background paper — is that the desire for last birth question succeeded remarkably well in the Sri Lankan case in doing what it was supposed to do. While it would be rash to argue that the Sri Lankan data can be generalized to all other countries, this result lends greater credibility to the wanted total fertility rates discussed in the substantive section of this chapter. It also provides an illustration of the vital role which re-interviews can play in assessing the quality of preference data.

Further evidence supporting the validity of data on desire for additional children is found in re-interview studies of Costa Rica (Stycos 1984), Sri Lanka (Lightbourne 1984e), and Taiwan (Coombs and Chang 1981). Women wanting more children had higher subsequent fertility than those who did not, after controlling for age or parity.

The validity of the question on number of additional children desired receives considerable support from the finding that in nearly all countries the proportion using contraception rises systematically as women approach the stated desired stopping point (Lightbourne 1984b, table 2b). In Egypt, for example, contraceptive prevalence was 41 per cent among women wanting zero additional children, 23 per cent among those wanting one more, 9 per cent among those wanting two more, and 2 per cent among those wanting three more.

One of the overall conclusions drawn in the background paper on the quality of the preference data is that the WFS data on fertility preferences are far from meaningless. This is not to say that there are no difficulties of interpretation and that we can blindly take the data at face value. They call for careful analysis based on a thorough appreciation of possible biases. But it would be throwing out the baby with the bathwater to conclude that valid interpretations are impossible. Instead, the interpretation becomes an exercise in treading the fine line between being too cautious or too rash.

The other main conclusion is that the data would have been much easier to interpret had there been more reinterview studies, at long as well as short intervals after initial interview. Questions on intensity of preference would have undoubtedly simplified assessment of the quality of the data, and helped us in deciding what the data really mean. But despite the many shortcomings, WFS preference data reflect a genuine and serious commitment to securing comparable data in an unprecedentedly large number of countries. Because of translation difficulties, the comparisons are bound to be less than 100 per cent perfect, but they nevertheless do represent the best source yet. The present writer hopes that future surveys will pursue the difficult goal of improving preference measurement without sacrificing comparability, so that changes in preferences over time can be studied.

31.3 Substantive findings

This necessarily restricted review of substantive findings will begin by commenting on the basic data and will then consider a number of more refined indicators intended to clarify the demographic implications of the preference data.

It will be argued that on balance the WFS data on reproductive motives imply that if women fully implement their stated preferences, substantial fertility decline is likely in a majority· of countries and unlikely in only a few. We will describe several definitionally correct techniques for estimating the amount of fertility change that would occur, but it will be evident that the correctness of the estimates depends heavily on the correctness of the data.

Desire for additional children

For demonstrating that demand for children is limited in most developing countries, the proportion not desiring additional children is an excellent summary indicator with formidably good face validity. Taken at face value, the WFS data imply that in most of the countries surveyed very large numbers of women do not wish to have additional children. The parity-standardized proportions not wanting additional children in table 31.1 demonstrate that of 41 countries, there are only 11 where the proportion not wanting additional children is lower than 30 per cent. Strong evidence of internal validity is found in the systematic decline in desire for additional children as parity increases, in all countries.

For purposes of rigorous analysis, however, there are several potential problems with the data on desire for additional children, namely vagueness and vulnerability to biases which do not seem to be widely understood.

It is a vague indicator inasmuch as it says nothing very definite about the desired fertility level, especially if one relies on the overall proportion not wanting additional children.

As one example of bias, holding desired family size constant, a country where women reach desired family size quickly will have higher proportions not wanting additional children than one where women reach desired family size slowly. This bias can be removed by standardizing on parity, but there are parity-specific biases described elsewhere (Lightbourne 1977). In particular, terminating behaviour at a particular parity causes women who want no more to pile up at that parity, downwardly biasing the proportion wanting more, while postponing behaviour at a particular parity causes postponers to pile up, which upwardly biases the proportion wanting more. The effects are potentially far from trivial. Parity-specific proportions wanting more children are substantially

TABLE 31.1

Proportion saying they did not want additional children (in response to direct question), by number of living children

Country	No. of living children (counting pregnancy as living)					Ordinary mean	Standardized mean	No. of cases
	0	2	4	6	9+			
Africa								
Benin	0.0	2.5	10.5	20.0	61.1[b]	7.7	11.4	2915
Cameroon	1.0	3.6	3.2	9.4	41.4[a]	3.3	7.4	2245
Ghana	0.7	3.2	15.1	34.7	54.7	11.8	15.4	3999
Ivory Coast	0.0	2.3	3.2	11.4	36.2	4.3	6.1	4207
Kenya	1.5	3.6	16.1	25.5	56.2	16.6	14.4	5119
Lesotho	0.3	7.7	26.3	45.4	70.0[b]	14.8	23.5	2730
Nigeria	2.6[b]	2.0	5.6	8.2	25.4	4.9	6.2	7154
Senegal	0.0[b]	0.8	5.2	18.2[a]	87.5[b]	8.0	7.0[c]	528
Egypt	0.5	42.5	76.0	89.9	91.7	53.7	54.0	7207
Mauritania	2.8	7.2	12.9	15.4	32.9	10.9	11.4	2648
Morocco	2.5	18.1	44.7	68.8	88.7	41.8	38.6	2818
Sudan (North)	1.1	7.8	16.6	31.7	60.4	16.9	16.5	2471
Tunisia	1.0	25.0	61.6	81.3	90.3	48.9	44.6	3287
Asia and Pacific								
Jordan	4.2	15.2	38.3	54.5	78.3	41.8	31.1	3065
Syria	1.2	13.1	44.5	53.5	71.3	36.5	30.6	3779
Turkey	0.8	51.5[i]	82.6	86.4	92.6	57.1	55.3	3742
Yemen AR	5.8	11.4	25.1	47.7	51.6[a]	19.3	23.8	2078
Bangladesh	12.3	56.3	76.7	90.4	96.0	62.8	63.7	5104
Nepal	1.5	23.9	59.5	81.3	91.8[b]	30.3	43.6	4882
Pakistan	0.1	22.7	60.5	87.4	87.7	43.0	43.9	4089
Sri Lanka	2.1	49.5	87.1	94.3	96.5	61.4	60.5	5326

Fiji	2.1	34.1	66.7	79.5	93.7	49.5	48.1	4159
Indonesia	4.2	28.5	57.4	77.6	93.9	38.9	45.2	6534
Korea, Rep. of	12.4	65.6	92.0	96.2	100.0[b]	71.6	68.1	4395
Malaysia	0.4	22.2	54.2	78.9	93.1	44.9	41.0	5102
Philippines	0.7	32.6	68.3	76.4	84.9	54.3	47.1	7893
Thailand	6.3	49.1	85.3	91.6	100.0	61.0	61.4	2924
Americas								
Colombia	8.6	52.1	79.0	85.1	90.1	61.5	57.9	2667
Ecuador	4.3	45.8	68.2	80.1	86.2	55.9	52.0	3602
Paraguay	1.4	21.1	41.2	52.7	73.2	32.3	31.6	2372
Peru	6.3	48.2	74.2	80.7	94.7	61.4	56.0	4512
Venezuela	8.8	41.1	74.3	84.5	88.9	55.0	54.7	2205
Costa Rica	5.3	35.2	68.4	77.8	85.0	52.0	49.9	2446
Dominican Rep.	4.6	38.5	69.6	73.6	78.3	51.9	50.0	1673
Mexico	9.8	42.4	69.4	81.6	91.1	57.1	52.0	4883
Panama	7.7	42.0	81.7	86.7	88.5	63.0	57.0	2524
Guyana	8.9	41.6	64.5	89.8	94.9	55.0	54.3	3029
Haiti	3.2	42.0	68.6	79.3	93.0[a]	45.9	52.4	1678
Jamaica	3.8	41.5	63.8	79.3	94.3	50.5	52.5	2099
Trinidad & Tobago	4.5	39.1	75.0	85.7	89.0	46.5	53.5	2941
Europe								
Portugal	14.4	84.9	88.6	92.3	73.2[a]	68.5	71.7	4477

a Cell based on fewer than 50 unweighted cases.
b Cell based on fewer than 20 unweighted cases.
c Standardized means where one or more of the cells had a denominator less than 10 unweighted cases, and where adjacent cells were pooled as described in the text.

Note: Age ranges are 15–49 for all countries except Costa Rica and Panama, where the range is 20–49, and Venezuela, where the age range is 15–44.

higher in the WFS survey in Trinidad and Tobago than in Jamaica, despite slightly lower preferences among Trinidadians and Tobagonians.

The postponing motive

There is ample evidence that large numbers of women wish to postpone births. In some countries, the number of women using contraception for postponing purposes exceeds the number using for terminating purposes. In Latin America, for example, between three and six out of ten contraceptors are women who want additional children. Actual proportions stating they do not want a birth soon are tremendously high in many of the countries, sometimes nearly reaching 80 per cent of non-pregnant and fecund women who want additional children, as can be seen in table 31.2.

The dominant view until recently was that desire to terminate childbearing was far more important demographically than desire to postpone. Spending precious resources on postponers was certainly in some circles regarded as a waste, since it was assumed that the postponers would go on to have their desired family size anyway. This point of view is founded on a 'target' model of human reproductive motivation which is in itself becoming increasingly questionable, for reasons given later on.

TABLE 31.2

Percentage wanting the next child soon or later among exposed women who wanted more children

Country	Want soon[b]	Want later[c]	Other
Bangladesh (CPS)[a]	28	72	
Benin (WFS)	33	55	13
Colombia (CPS)	34	66	
Costa Rica (CPS)	23	77	
Ecuador (WFS)	23	77	
Egypt (WFS)	54	40	6
Ghana (WFS)	40	60	
Ivory Coast (WFS)	62	38	
Korea, Rep. of (CPS)	64	36	
Mexico, rural (CPS)	21	79	
Mexico, urban (CPS)	28	72	
Paraguay (WFS)	25	68	8
Portugal (WFS)	24	50	26
Thailand (CPS)	25	75	

[a] Surveys marked CPS are Contraceptive Prevalence Surveys conducted by either Centers for Disease Control, Atlanta, or Westinghouse Health Systems. *Source for CPS surveys*: Nortman (1982), p. 18

[b] 'Want soon' in CPS surveys specified 'want in next year'.

[c] 'Want later' in CPS surveys included respondents uncertain about wanting more children and those who failed to answer. These groups averaged 6 per cent in the countries shown.

Note: See note 1 on p. 861 for wording of WFS questions.

It seems likely that the demographic significance of the desire to postpone births may in some countries be quite negligible, while in others it may be very important. If the desired period of postponement is relatively short and the number of children desired is modest, then contraception to delay births is unlikely to affect fertility much, except to the extent that it makes women better able to use contraception effectively when they achieve the parity where they wish to stop and helps legitimize fertility control more quickly by widening the user base and by spreading the idea that some methods are reversible.

But there are at least two cases where the desire to postpone births would have much greater impact on fertility, if it were to be fully implemented by adoption of effective contraception. As Ware (1976) has suggested, the impact of implementing the desire to postpone will be quite substantial in countries where women want an unlimited number of children but at the same time feel they should preserve maternal and child health through avoiding overly narrow birth intervals.

A second case, where the effect on fertility would be far greater, is if there are large numbers of women who begin contraception with the intention of ultimately having another child, but who then never get around to actually wanting the next birth, or who shift into the 'desire to stop' category before having any more children. While commonsense suggests that there must be at least some such women, there is at present no clear evidence of their existence in large numbers, though there are a variety of clues which taken together suggest that there are quite likely to be many countries where they do exist in fairly large numbers. Table 31.3 is presented largely because it makes the data on desire to postpone somewhat more plausible. It shows that, as we would expect, the desire to postpone births is much lower at parity zero, and much higher at subsequent parities, with remarkably little variation in desire to postpone between parities 1–8. A particularly remarkable finding is that in some

TABLE 31.3

Percentages wanting another child soon, by family size, five WFS countries, restricted to exposed women who wanted additional children

Country	Family size						
	0	1	2	3	4–5	6–8	9+
Ecuador	59	25	12	20	17	15	21
Egypt	93	44	43	48	54	56	70
Ghana	85	39	37	34	35	33	28
Ivory Coast	95	64	58	54	54	55	57
Paraguay	63	28	19	21	19	25	18
Portugal	58	26	26	26	24	cc	cc

Notes: 1. Portugal figures exclude undecideds and count women desiring birth in next 0–23 months as 'wanting soon'; this may overstate proportion wanting soon.
2. The designation 'cc' means 'cannot compute'.

countries, especially in Latin America, there are substantial numbers of childless women who wish to postpone their first births.

Table 31.4 subdivides non-pregnant women who said they want more children by number of months elapsed since last birth, and indicates for the Latin countries remarkably high proportions wanting to postpone the next birth at intervals as long as 5–7 and 7–10 years. Of course, there are a variety of selection effects that could produce misleadingly high proportions wanting to postpone at such long intervals as 5–10 years. Whenever fertility is lower among women who wish to postpone, they are selected to longer intervals. Women found at long intervals are selected either for infecundity (which introduces no bias) or lower coital frequency (which introduces moderate bias) or contraceptive use (which introduces major bias and selects for women who wish to postpone). On the other hand, some contraceptors who began an interval wishing to postpone will switch to wishing to terminate, thus reducing bias. One bias-reduction technique recently employed has been to restrict the analysis to women who have not used contraception since the last birth; this has revealed surprisingly large proportions still wishing to postpone at longer intervals in Ecuador, Ghana and Malaysia. The least biased data is found in countries with very low contraceptive practice, such as Ghana and Ivory Coast, where 'true' proportions wanting to postpone are most likely to be observed, uncontaminated by the powerful effects of contraception in selecting women who wish to postpone to longer intervals. The comparison between Ivory Coast and Ghana is particularly intriguing. In Ivory Coast one sees a classic spacing behaviour, in the form of a short-lived desire to postpone coupled with an almost universal reversion to wanting another child in the near future. In Ghana, however, one sees clear hints of something quite different, namely quite large numbers of women who seem to take a very long time before wanting another birth, and quite a few who never do. This is consistent with economic conditions at survey time, which were relatively favourable in Ivory Coast and relatively difficult in Ghana.

In sum, it is argued that the stated desire to postpone may quite often mask what is effectively a desire to terminate. If this is true in a sufficiently large number of cases, it would imply a very different view of reproductive motives in some countries in the developing world. Clearly, the only way to confirm or reject such an argument is through the medium of repeated reinterviews to determine whether large numbers of apparent 'spacers' are *de facto* terminators.

Preferred family size

Perhaps the most important objective in studying preferred family size is to estimate the fertility level that would result if women were to fully implement their stopping and postponing preferences and were subject to real world conditions such as child mortality and fecundity impairments. To set the stage for subsequent discussion of substantive findings on preferred and actual fertility, we

TABLE 31.4

Percentage wanting another child 'later' rather than 'soon' by duration of open interval: restricted to exposed women who want more children (exposed = non-pregnant, currently married and fecund)

Country		Open interval duration (months)									Total
		0–11	12–23	24–35	36–47	48–59	60–83	84–119	120–179	180–300	
Ecuador	%	90	86	82	74	67	63	35	33	18	77
	N	432	252	126	81	70	84	62	51	22	1180
Egypt	%	55	50	31	22	22	16	5	10	2	43
	N	1090	582	291	147	94	108	65	70	60	2507
Ghana	%	84	71	50	37	38	20	24	13	11	60
	N	906	610	371	224	128	139	122	85	57	2642
Ivory Coast	%	65	42	16	8	8	5	5	– 5 –		38
	N	1164	790	405	218	122	164	136	– 185 –		3184
Paraguay	%	88	85	83	71	75	62	40	27	12	73
	N	392	220	124	82	71	97	92	55	43	1176
Portugal	%	76	71	63	63	59	58	57	45	33	68
	N	215	140	104	86	68	78	49	29	12	781

Notes: 1. Undecideds excluded for Paraguay (8 per cent of sample) and Portugal (26 per cent of sample).
2. See note 1 on p. 861 for wording of questions.

now discuss three different ways of estimating the number of children preferred, namely a 'target model', a 'two-stage model' and a 'three-stage model'.

Target model. For a long time the notion that individuals have some target number of children has dominated the study of reproductive preferences. It has been assumed for purposes of simplicity and manageability of data collection that individuals are planners with a long time horizon, who carry around in their heads some definite target number of children that is sufficiently fixed to be meaningful. Advocates of this approach have long known that such an assumption is not supported at the individual level, but have been able to produce some examples where it has predicted future fertility tolerably well at the aggregate level, in developed countries. These are perhaps the principal justifications for asking people the conventional question on how many children they want, despite the knowledge that they may have difficulty in providing meaningful answers.

The desired stopping point: a two-stage model. A considerably more realistic way of thinking about size preferences, which is more conceptually appealing at the individual level, is to consider the preferred number of births as being the outcome of a sequential process in which the individual has only two motives, namely 'continue childbearing' and 'stop childbearing'. Under this model, the individual adds children one at a time, and at some time not necessarily known in advance comes to a point where she or he stops desiring additional children. One clear advantage of this is that it does not not assume any long-run planning or any particular number preference. Nor does it assume that the preference is highly crystallized or well formed. It only assumes that as an individual adds children, there comes a point where the individual has no particular desire to have additional children, and that even if such a motive is latent rather than conscious, astute communications campaigns can surely cause it to surface. A final and conclusive advantage is that the motive to stop is in principle much more susceptible to precise measurement.

The desired stopping point: a three-stage model. The prime disadvantage of the two-stage model just described is that it neglects entirely several very important real world considerations. First of all, it ignores postponement as an important reproductive motive. It is more realistic to think of a three-stage sequential model in which individuals fluctuate between the motives of 'have now', 'postpone' and 'want no more'. Postponement becomes important if there are many women who begin at a given parity by wanting to postpone, and then ultimately shift to wanting to stop, without spending any time in the intervening 'have now' phase. In such an instance, the cross-sectional survey will systematically overestimate the true level of effective reproductive demand, and will systematically misclassify women as wanting more when longitudinal observation would make it clear that they really do not. Such observation is expensive, however. A shortcoming of the three models discussed so far is that none of them takes explicit account of fecundity impairments which will prevent some women from having all the births they want.

Analytical methods. With these three alternative models in mind, we now examine three different approaches to measuring the number of wanted births that women would have over a lifetime, namely the 'wanted total fertility rate', the 'stopping point' estimate based on synthetic cohort procedures, and the 'conventional' or target model approach based on asking a direct question concerning how many children the respondent wants to bear.

Wanted total fertility rate. The total fertility rate estimates the number of births a woman would have over a lifetime if the age-specific rates prevailing at a given period of time were to continue forever, and relies on summing age-specific rates, where each rate is formed using births at each age as the numerator and person-years lived at each age as the denominator. The 'backwards deletion' form of wanted total fertility rate was first used on WFS data by Westoff (1981), and is just like the actual total fertility rate except that it deletes unwanted births. The actual amount to delete is somewhat controversial. The present writer belongs to the 'double deletion' school of thought, which says that we should delete not only births in excess of desired family size, but also unwanted last births as reported in the response to whether the last birth was unwanted. A recent analysis of re-interview data, described in more detail towards the end of section 31.2, lends some support to this approach, since it showed that the proportion of last births unwanted as estimated by double deletion was remarkably consistent with the proportion of unwanted births estimated from information on desire for additional children and the actual count of births to women who no longer wanted additional children. Also, it can be argued that if women tend to rationalize, they are more likely to underestimate the number of last births unwanted than to overestimate. The opposing school of thought holds that the wanted total fertility rates based on double deletion are implausibly low, and that it is safer to use the more conservative estimates based on deleting only births in excess of desired family size. In order to show both sides of the picture, table 31.5 presents both types of estimate. As can be seen, the wanted total fertility rates based on double deletion are indeed much lower. In subsequent discussion the single deletion method will be referred to as the 'definition 1 wanted TFR' and the double deletion as the 'definition 2 wanted TFR'. It is emphasized that the wanted TFR automatically incorporates the effects of (1) fecundity impairments, (2) any current contraception for purposes of postponing pregnancy. The wanted TFR is thus a partial step in the direction of capturing the three-stage 'have now', 'postpone', terminate' model described above, because it at least partly brings in the effects of postponement behaviour, and the real world factor of fecundity impairments.

'Stopping point' or synthetic cohort methods. An alternative approach to estimating the number of desired children a woman would have over her lifetime estimates the desired stopping point by making use of information on the

TABLE 31.5

Preferred family size, synthetic cohort estimates of desired stopping point, total fertility rates and wanted TFRs, for WFS countries

Country	'Conventional' preferred family size (based on direct question)			Synthetic cohort estimates of desired stopping point		Total fertility rates		
						Usual TFR (no birth deleted)	Birth deleted if:	
							Exceeds desired family size Defn 1	Exceeds DFS or if last unwanted Defn 2
	Age 15–19	Age 45–49	All women	Upper bound	Lower bound			
	(1)	(2)	(3)	(4)	(5)	(6)	(7)	(8)
Africa								
Benin	7.2	8.0	7.6	cc	7.7	7.3	7.3	6.9*
Cameroon	6.5	8.6	8.0	cc	7.6	6.4	6.1	6.1*
Ghana	5.2	7.3	6.0	cc	7.6	6.1	6.0	5.6*
Ivory Coast	7.5	9.6	8.4	cc	8.9	7.2	7.2	7.0*
Kenya	6.6	8.7	7.2	cc	8.4	7.9	7.6	6.9*
Lesotho	5.6	7.3	6.0	cc	6.4	6.0	5.6	5.3*
Senegal	8.3	8.4	8.3	cc	7.2	7.1	6.9	6.7*
Egypt	4.2	4.7	4.1	4.0	3.7	5.0	3.6	3.1
Mauritania	8.3	9.4	8.8	cc	9.4	7.5	7.1	6.8*
Morocco	4.3	6.6	4.9	5.5	5.6	5.5	4.4	3.7
Sudan (North)	5.4	6.5	6.4	cc	7.7	5.6	5.0	4.8
Tunisia	3.7	4.4	4.1	cc	4.4	5.5	4.1	3.6

Asia and Pacific								
Jordan	4.9	7.5	6.2	6.6	6.4	7.0	6.0	5.1
Syria	5.0	7.1	6.1	cc	6.5	7.4	6.3	5.6*
Turkey	2.8	3.1	3.0	cc	cc	3.8	cc	2.4*
Yemen AR	4.5	6.9	5.5	cc	6.5	8.9	8.2	7.4*
Bangladesh	3.7	5.0	4.1	4.3	3.9	5.4	4.6	3.1
Nepal	3.6	4.3	3.9	cc	4.5	6.1	5.4	4.5*
Pakistan	4.0	4.5	4.2	cc	4.3	6.0	4.3	3.9*
Sri Lanka	2.6	4.8	3.7	3.4	2.9	3.4	2.9	2.2
Fiji	2.7	6.1	4.2	4.9	4.1	4.0	3.6	3.6
Indonesia	3.3	5.4	4.2	4.8	4.5	4.3	4.0	3.6
Korea, Rep. of	2.7	3.8	3.1	3.1	2.6	3.9	2.8	2.5
Malaysia	3.9	4.5	4.3	cc	4.6	4.5	3.3	3.1*
Philippines	3.0	5.6	4.3	5.1	4.5	5.1	4.1	3.6
Thailand	2.9	4.4	3.6	cc	2.8	4.3	3.2	2.6*
Americas								
Colombia	2.7	5.7	4.0	3.7	3.3	4.6	3.4	2.6
Ecuador	3.1	5.6	4.1	4.5	4.2	5.2	4.1	3.1
Paraguay	3.7	7.1	5.2	6.4	6.2	5.0	4.5	4.2
Peru	3.1	4.6	3.8	4.0	3.5	5.3	3.5	2.6
Venezuela	3.0	6.0	4.3	4.2	3.6	4.3	3.6	2.9
Costa Rica	3.5	6.1	4.7	4.7	4.1	3.5	3.0	2.6
Dominican Rep.	3.4	6.0	4.7	5.0	4.4	5.2	3.8	3.0
Mexico	3.8	5.8	4.4	cc	4.0	5.7	4.5	3.6*
Panama	3.4	5.1	4.3	4.0	3.4	4.2	3.9	3.4
Guyana	3.4	5.9	4.6	3.9	3.6	4.4	3.8	2.8
Haiti	2.8	4.3	3.6	cc	3.9	5.6	4.3	3.8*
Jamaica	3.3	4.8	4.1	4.1	3.7	4.4	3.4	2.3
Trinidad & Tobago	3.2	4.8	3.8	cc	3.6	3.2	2.5	2.4
Europe								
Portugal	2.0	2.8	2.4	2.6	2.2	2.2	1.9	1.4

858 CONTRIBUTION TO KNOWLEDGE

Notes to table 31.5

Notes: The designation 'cc' means 'cannot compute'.

Columns 1–3: Means based on direct question: 'If you could choose exactly the number of children to have in your whole life, how many would that be?' The age range for Costa Rica and Panama is 20–49, for Venezuela 15–49, and for other countries 15–49; column 1 figures for Costa Rica and Panama are for age 20–24.

Columns 4–5: The 'upper bound' stopping point is estimated using the Rodríguez-Trussell synthetic cohort procedure and the 'lower bound' stopping point is estimated using the author's; both procedures estimate the number of living children respondents would have if they stop childbearing at the family size where they do not want additional children. Upper and lower bound estimates for Bangladesh based on contrast between desired and actual family size. Women undecided about having another child or last birth are counted as wanting it. The maximum parity to which calculation is carried equals either the first parity at which the proportion wanting more children is less than 10 per cent or the parity prior to the first occurrence of a denominator less than 15. The estimates are adjusted for socio-economic status: if D_i is the mean for the i-th social category, and W_i is number of women in that category, then the overall mean value of D is calculated using:

$$D = \sum_{i=1}^{14} \left(\frac{D_i \cdot W_i}{\sum_{i=1}^{14} W_i} \right)$$

This procedure was used for the 14 categories contained in the WFS standard background variables, namely respondent residence, respondent education, respondent work status and husband occupation. This weighting procedure guards against overestimation due to selection to the higher parities of social groups with atypically high preferences.

Column 6: The 'all births' total fertility rate was estimated from WFS birth histories for the period 0–2 years before survey.

Column 7: The 'definition 1' wanted total fertility rate is for 0–2 years before survey, uses the same denominators as the 'all births' rate, but deletes from the numerator births in excess of the respondent's preferred family size.

Column 8: The 'definition 2' wanted total fertility rate is for 0–2 years before survey, uses the same denominators as 'all births' and 'definition 1' rates, but deletes from the numerator (1) births in excess of preferred family size and (2) births that respondents said were unwanted in answer to the question: 'Thinking back to the time before you became pregnant with your last child, had you wanted to have any more children?' Asterisked rates have been estimated using regression or indirect methods as described in R. E. Lightbourne (1985). Desired Number of Births and Prospects for Fertility Decline in 40 Developing Countries. *International Family Planning Perspectives* 11(2): 34–39.

number of children living and whether the respondent wants additional children. With this in mind a variety of 'synthetic cohort' or 'stopping point' estimators have been proposed, by writers including Udry, Bauman and Chase (1973), Lightbourne (1977), Pullum (1981) (earlier presented at the 1979 PAA annual meeting), Rodríguez and Trussel (1981), Rosero-Bixby (1983, personal communication) and Nour (1983). The Rodríguez-Trussell and Pullum methods use not only proportions wanting additional children, but also the proportions desiring the last birth.

The concept of estimating the mean number of children women would have were they to stop childbearing on reaching the point where they want no additional children is both elegant and simple. But operationalizing it is greatly complicated by the fact that, when classified by number of living children, proportions wanting more children are very sensitive to contraceptive behaviour, a point discussed earlier in this section.

Evaluation of how well the various synthetic cohort methods perform in estimating the desired stopping point has been based on simulations that begin with a known desired family size distribution, and then generate from this distribution a set of parity-specific percentages wanting more children and wanting the last birth, under various assumptions about contraception for stopping and spacing purposes. One can then judge the relative merits of each of the synthetic cohort procedures by applying each one to the generated data to see how well it does in recovering the know true mean of the distribution. The conclusion reached from simulations by the present writer is that while none of the methods so far proposed are unbiased under all of the conditions simulated, reasonably good estimates can be secured under most conditions by combining the estimate yielded by the Rodríguez-Trussell procedure with the estimate produced by the Lightbourne procedure. This is because the former procedure typically overestimates the underlying true mean while the latter underestimates it, which provides us with an upper and lower bound outside which the true mean desired .stopping point should not fall, except when the procedures are operating outside their known safety limits. Figure 31.1 provides a summary of the known limits. One feature worth noting is that the procedures are unbiased in non-contraceptor populations.

Conventional preferred family size. The most common and conventional method of measuring preferred family size is to rely on responses to a question asking respondents how many children they want. The WFS question on this subject was worded: 'If you could choose exactly the number of children to have in your whole life, how many would that be?' As discussed elsewhere, this conventional measure has many problems, including rationalization effects. The analysis of WFS data has also revealed a hitherto unnoticed tendency for lower parity women to understate their preferred family size (Lightbourne and MacDonald 1982), while other analysts have noted that the high correlation between actual family size and desired family size could be explained if women have exactly the number of children they want (Knodel and Prachuabmoh 1973). It has also been argued that a high correlation between actual and desired family size would occur

Condition		Rodríguez–Trussell	Lightbourne
Effective use of contraception for stopping purposes	None	Unbiased	Unbiased
	Some	Slight upward bias	Slight downward bias
	High	Slight upward bias	Strong downward bias
Effective use of contraception for spacing purposes	None	No bias	No bias
	Some	Slight upward bias	Reduced downward bias
	High	Potentially severe upward bias	Potentially severe upward bias
Rationalization of last birth	None	No bias	No bias
	Some	Added upward bias	No bias
	High	Strong upward bias	No bias
Age composition of female population		No bias	Miniscule bias except under absurdly high rates of growth never observed in nature

FIG. 31.1   Operating limits of two synthetic cohort estimators

if younger women had genuinely lower desired size as a result of the impact of education and modernization, but the analysis of WFS data so far has suggested that this effect does not seem to operate, since when parity is controlled for, the relationship between desired family size and age tends to disappear in almost all the countries thus far examined.

Comparing three types of preferred family size estimate. The discussion above has described three fundamentally different ways of measuring preferred family size, namely the wanted total fertility rate, the mean desired 'stopping point' estimated via synthetic cohort procedures, and the 'conventional' mean preferred family size estimated by asking respondents to state how many children they would like to have. To investigate whether these different approaches lead to similar results, we now compare the three types of estimate with actual total fertility rates in table 31.5.

Several major conclusions emerge from the comparison of the conventional preferred family size and the stopping point estimates. Almost without exception, the lower bound estimate of the mean stopping point (column 5) is substantially higher than the conventional preferred mean based on women aged 15–19 (column 1). This is consistent with the finding reported above that young women usually seem to underestimate the number of children they will ultimately desire. Similarly, the upper bound estimate of the mean stopping point is consistently lower than the conventional mean for the oldest women (compare columns 2 and 4), usually by about one child, which suggests that 'rationalization' effects indeed upwardly bias the conventional estimates of desired size reported by higher parity women. Since in nearly àll countries there is little or no variation by age in the conventional mean once number of living children is controlled for, these two conclusions cannot be explained away on the basis of variations in family size preferences by age.

Perhaps the most important conclusion to be drawn is that the conventional mean for all women (column 3) almost invariably falls between the lower and upper bound synthetic cohort estimates of the mean stopping point, or else comes close to falling between these limits. The significance of this is that in spite of the very persuasive objections that have been raised against the conventional estimate of average number of children preferred, in respect of both its meaningfulness and validity, it becomes obvious that the conventional mean for the whole sample (as opposed to any particular group of women) does offer a reasonably good approximation to the mean number of living children that women would have if (1) they were to succeed in stopping at the family size at which they cease desiring additional children; (2) they do not suffer fecundity impairments; (3) they do not engage in prolonged postponing behaviour.

As shown in figure 31.1, stopping point estimates by either the Rodríguez-Trussell or the Lightbourne method are potentially upwardly biased if contraceptive use among women who report wanting additional children is sufficiently widespread and effective. The patterning of comparisons in table 31.5, however, suggests that the extent of spacing behaviour found in the countries concerned is insufficient to produce any recognizable upward bias.

We now turn to comparing conventional and stopping point estimates with the wanted total fertility rate estimated for the 24-month period before the survey and with the actual TFR estimated for the same time period.

To place these comparisons in proper context, we note that one fairly common and apparently reasonable approach to assessing prospects for fertility change is what might be called 'conventional equilibrium analysis', which is based on comparing the TFR with the conventional estimate of mean preferred family size (PFS). This type of analysis predicts that (1) when TFR equals PFS, preferences and fertility are in equilibrium, and there is little prospect for fertility change; (2) when TFR is less than PFS, there are prospects for a rise in fertility; (3) only when TFR exceeds PFS is there much prospect of fertility decline. These propositions may appear to be eminently reasonable. But despite the apparent reasonableness of conventional equilibrium analysis, the results in table 31.5 suggest it may often produce highly misleading conclusions.

The case of Costa Rica. The case of Costa Rica is particularly helpful in illustrating the dangers of conventional equilibrium analysis. The stopping point and conventional indicators of preferred family size range between 4.1 and 4.7 and are substantially higher than the TFR of 3.5. According to the conventional equilibrium analysis, Costa Ricans should expect a substantial rise in fertility. Yet the definition 1 (i.e. single deletion) wanted TFR in column 7 indicates that Costa Rica would have had a wanted total fertility rate of 3.0 had all births in excess of preferred family size been avoided, and the double deletion (definition 2) wanted TFR in column 8 indicates that Costa Rica would have had an even lower wanted total fertility rate of 2.6 if (1) all births in excess of preferred size had been avoided and, additionally, if (2) all last births reported as unwanted had been avoided. We attribute the difference of 4/10 of a birth between definitions 1 and 2 as to some extent reflecting the tendency of respondents to rationalize in reporting desired family size and as also perhaps reflecting a certain number whose report on desire for last birth may reflect desire to postpone.

The sizeable difference between the wanted TFR and preferred family size becomes all the more surprising when one considers that while preferred family size most likely refers to the number of living children preferred, the wanted TFR unambiguously refers to the mean number of *births* wanted over a lifetime that women would have if the preferences observed at time of survey remain constant into the future and if there is no change in fecundability or in the age at marriage.

What factors explain the wide gulf observed for Costa Rica between the conventional measure of preferred family size (4.6), the stopping point estimates (4.1–4.7) and the wanted TFR estimates (2.6–3.0), and why is the TFR (3.6) so much lower than the conventional estimate of desired family size? Reviewing the Costa Rican case in some detail, several factors seem to be implicated. The overall TFR – one of the lowest observed in WFS surveys – was being held down in large part by high levels of contraceptive use for both terminating and spacing childbearing. Out of every 100 currently married women aged 20–49, 37 per cent were using contraception and wanted no more children, and 28 per cent wanted additional children and were using contraception. Late marriage does little to explain the low TFR, since the median age at marriage of 21.4 years was only slightly higher than in most other Latin–Caribbean countries. The pattern of breastfeeding, on the other hand, favours high rather than low fertility, since the proportions ever breastfeeding were exceptionally low at 74 per cent and the median duration breastfed was exceptionally short at 1.8 months.

It is thus likely that the sizeable discrepancy between the various estimates of preferred family size and Costa Rica's actual TFR is largely explained by some combination of contraception for termination and postponement reasons plus desired births lost because of involuntary infecundity. It is also the case, however, that Costa Rica's actual TFR was 5/10 of a child higher than the definition 1 wanted TFR, and this suggests a good deal of contraceptive failure, which is not entirely surprising since 18 per cent of all contraceptors were using either rhythm, douche, abstinence, or other methods classified as ineffective. The additional difference of 4/10 of a child between the definition 1 and definition 2 wanted TFR is probably explained at least in part by contraceptive failure, though it may also be partly explained by failure to implement the preference to postpone births.

The differences observed between the wanted TFRs and the desired stopping point and the conventional estimates of preferred family size are by no means trivial. This is probably because the wanted TFRs more nearly approximate the fertility levels implied by the tri-phase 'have now', 'postpone', 'terminate' model of reproductive motivation, which does not assume uninterrupted reproduction until the stopping point is reached.

If this reasoning is correct, it illustrates the inadequacy of the binary 'keep going until you want to stop' model of reproductive motivation and also of the 'target number' model, which both assume uninterrupted reproduction until the target number or stopping point is reached, and which imply that we should expect a rise in Costa Rican fertility, and not a decline. Instead, the Costa Rican example illustrates the need to view number of desired births as the outcome of a process in which individuals oscillate back and forth between wanting immediate pregnancies, wanting to postpone and wanting to stop, with differing intensities of these wants and consequent variability in implementation.

Most important of all, Costa Rican preferences are no lower than in any of the other Latin American countries except Paraguay, yet Costa Rica has one of the lowest TFRs observed in the region. The data clearly indicate that this is explained by better implementation of preferences, and not by lower preferences. Even so, Costa Rican fertility would decline substantially if unwanted births were prevented.

Results for other countries. We now turn from the Costa Rican case to assess prospects for fertility change in the other countries, using the wanted TFRs in table 31.5. It is recalled that the definition 1 wanted TFR is based on deleting births in excess of preferred family size, and is available for 39 countries. The definition 2 wanted TFR, available for only 21 countries, deletes two categories of births, namely births in excess of preferred family size and, secondly, births not wanted at time of last pregnancy.

If assessment is based on the contrast between the definition 1 wanted TFR and the actual TFR, there are only two countries where there is no potential for fertility decline, namely Benin and Ivory Coast. Ghana and Senegal come next, with negligible potential declines of only 1/10 of a child and 2/10 of a child respectively. Countries with only moderate potential for decline, ranging between 0.3 and 0.5 births off the TFR, are Cameroon, Kenya, Indonesia and Portugal (all by 3/10 of a child), Lesotho, Mauritania and Fiji (by 4/10 of a child), and Costa Rica, Paraguay and Sri Lanka (5/10 of a child). Countries with somewhat higher potential for decline, ranging between 0.6 and 0.9 births off the TFR, are Sudan and Guyana (6/10), Yemen AR, Nepal, Venezuela and Trinidad and Tobago (7/10), and Bangladesh (8/10 of a child). Countries with relatively high potential for decline, ranging between 1.0 and 1.4 births off the TFR, include the Philippines, Jordan and Jamaica (by 1.0 births), Morocco, Syria, Republic of Korea, Thailand, Ecuador (by 1.1 births), Malaysia, Colombia, Mexico, Peru (by

1.2 births), Haiti (by 1.3 births), and Egypt, Tunisia and Dominican Republic (by 1.4 births). The largest potential decline of all is for Pakistan, where the definition 1 wanted TFR is 1.7 children below the actual TFR.

If the potential for fertility change is instead assessed using the contrast between the definition 2 wanted TFR and the actual TFR, the potential decline is, on the average, nearly twice as great, being 7/10 of a child for Indonesia, 8/10 of a child for Panama, Paraguay, Portugal and Trinidad and Tobago, and 9/10 of a child for Costa Rica. Three countries would have declines between 1.0 and 1.4 children, namely Sri Lanka, Republic of Korea and Venezuela; declines of between 1.5 and 1.9 births would be observed for Egypt, Guyana, Jordan, Morocco and the Philippines; declines of 2.0 births or more would be observed for Bangladesh (2.3), Colombia (2.0), Dominican Republic (2.2), Ecuador (2.1) and Jamaica (2.1); the highest decline of all would be observed for Peru, of 2.7 births off the TFR.

These are very different conclusions than those implied by conventional equilibrium analysis, which would rely on comparing the actual TFR with conventional estimates of preferred family size or the stopping point estimates; using this type of analysis one would predict fertility rises instead of fertility declines in Costa Rica and Fiji, and very much more moderate declines in Colombia, Dominican Republic, Jamaica, Jordan, Republic of Korea, Panama, Peru and the Philippines.

On the other hand, a number of observers have predicted fertility rises in some of the African countries, based on the expectation of reduction in prevalence of certain fecundity-impairing diseases and declines in breastfeeding. Whether or not the implementation of postponing preferences would be sufficient to counteract this expected rise remains a moot point.

Regardless of whether one relies on the definition 1 or definition 2 wanted TFR, it is apparent that if the WFS preference data are taken at face value, the full implementation of preferences would lead to substantial reductions in fertility in a number of societies that remain largely traditional and pre-industrial, and in several Islamic countries. On the other hand, it seems evident from table 31.5 that expected TFRs remain extremely high in the sub-Saharan African countries included, and substantially above replacement levels in most of the countries considered, though the deficiencies of data that prevent us from accounting completely for the desire to postpone births should not be overlooked, and mean that in some instances the wanted TFRs may overestimate the preferred fertility level and hence underestimate the potential for fertility decline.

A principal conclusion that can be drawn from these results is that 'pure' measures of preferred family size (i.e. the stopping point or conventional preferred family size questions) tend to imply a much larger number of births preferred than do the wanted total fertility rate estimates. This may seem doubly surprising in view of the fact that the wanted TFR automatically takes full account of the effect on preferences of child mortality plus preferences for children of a given sex, and that in calculating the wanted TFR we were unable to delete all the births that were either mistimed or that women wished to postpone permanently.

There are several reasons why 'pure' measures of desired family size should often greatly exceed the wanted TFR. The wanted TFR reflects the effects of fecundity impairments, reproductive time lost due to divorce, widowhood and separation, and also excludes the births of women who are successful in deliberately postponing wanted births. Also, and perhaps sometimes of greater importance, the 'stopping point' estimates assume that women keep on child-bearing without interruption until they want to stop, and make no allowance for the deliberate suppression of desired births. Just suppose, however, that current economic conditions are poor, and that prices have been rising faster than incomes. Under such circumstances couples may desire more births but not want the next birth right now, and short-run considerations override long-run desires.

Such a mechanism might go far in explaining the high proportions wanting to postpone the next birth even after long periods elapsed since the last birth, and would also help explain the large negative gap observed between current fertility and desired family size in a number of the countries at hand.

To forestall confusion, it must be stressed that the various measures are emphatically not attempts to measure the same underlying quantity. Not only are the computational procedures different, the measures have distinctly different definitions, and the reason for numerical differences cannot be mostly attributed to inconsistencies of data.

The chief reason for caution in interpreting the results described above is that they are all based on single-round surveys which did not ask all the questions we would have liked, and were not validated by reinterviews in each of the countries. Proper stopping point estimation requires information on whether or not the respondent positively wants to stop or permanently wants to postpone, rather than whether she wants to continue, and information on the stability of these desires through reinterviews. Improved wanted TFRs require identifying the parity at which respondents either explicitly stopped wanting additional children or implicitly stopped wanting them (i.e. the parity at which respondent would have stopped for postponement reasons), plus information on mistimed births.

Note

1. Questions in WFS surveys on desires to postpone varied:
   Benin: 'Do you wish to have your next child soon, say in a year, or do you prefer to wait until later?'
   Ecuador: 'Do you want to have your next child more or less soon, or to wait a few years?'
   Egypt: 'Would you prefer to have another child in the near future or would you prefer to wait a few years?'
   Ghana: 'Would you rather have a baby in the next year or so, or would you prefer to wait for several years?'
   Ivory Coast: 'Do you wish to have your next child soon, or do you want to wait for some years?'
   Paraguay: 'Do you want the next child quickly, or do you want to wait for a while?'
   Portugal: 'In how many years would you prefer your next child?'

32

Childhood Mortality

V.C. Chidambaram
John W. McDonald
Michael D. Bracher

32.1 Introduction

The World Fertility Survey programme was conceived and implemented with the primary object of assisting participating countries in their efforts to gain a better understanding of the fertility behaviour of their populations. A detailed maternity history of the respondent (usually ever-in-union or ever-married woman aged 15–49) was a compulsory part of the core questionnaire and aimed to record as accurately as possible the number and timing of all births to the respondent, the sex of each child, their survival status and, if dead, the date of, or age at, death. In the course of its activities, the programme thus obtained information which has made possible the study of levels, trends and differentials in infant and child mortality in each of the 42 participating countries. This was neither an accident nor a surprise.

From the very beginning it was recognized by the WFS that this information could be used for studying child mortality, as is evident from the discussions at the session on 'Estimation of Child Mortality' in the Seminar on Tabulation and Analysis of Survey Data held in September 1974 (WFS 1974). Moreover, the 'Guidelines for Country Report No. 1' (WFS 1977a) recommends a section on child mortality and suggests tabulations which can be expected to provide indications of the level of infant and child mortality and a background for the later sections on contraceptive use and intentions to increase or limit family size. Having said this, it must be admitted that in the earlier reports – mostly for Asian and Latin American countries – the coverage of mortality was limited to a brief discussion at the national level. The more serious exploitation of the WFS data and, in particular, of the mortality information, started only in 1979 as data from many countries started to become widely available and accessible and as the WFS analysis programme became operational.

The more recent country reports, at least 14 of them, have devoted one chapter to reporting the analysis of mortality. Moreover, mortality was selected as one of the 12 topics for the WFS programme of illustrative analyses designed to assist the countries and the resulting report on infant and child mortality in Colombia has served as a useful illustrative model for subsequent studies of mortality in many of the participating countries (Somoza 1980). In addition, the WFS evaluation programme, implemented mainly through a series of workshops, has assessed the quality of the mortality estimates, and the findings are published in the country evaluation reports. Finally, mortality has been the principal topic of at least 122 further analysis projects at the country level (see chapter 22) and of 18 comparative studies. The studies so far completed and the results emerging from them provide information on infant and child mortality hitherto not available for many of the countries and have enabled us to assess the usefulness and the limitations of the WFS data for studying child mortality. [1]

In this chapter we shall first present a brief description of the type and coverage of data collected with special emphasis on their comparability. This will be followed by a discussion of the quality and limitations of the data. We then present a summary of the findings from the analyses so far completed to highlight the contribution of WFS to the study of levels, trends and differentials in infant and child mortality.

32.2 Types and sources of mortality data

Coverage and eligibility

The fertility surveys conducted as part of the WFS programme consisted of a household survey and an individual survey. The household surveys were conducted, in the main, to provide information on the age, sex and marital status of the general population and the sampling frame for the selecting of women eligible for the individual interview. The sample size for the individual survey varied from 2500 (Yemen AR) to 10 000 (Nigeria). By and large, ever-married women in the reproductive age range — usually 15–49 years — were interviewed, though in some countries all women of reproductive age were interviewed. In most countries where single women were not sampled for the individual survey, the survey provides no information on births to single women, except insofar as single mothers married after they had a child. This omission of births to single mothers will not cause any problems for countries with little illegitimate fertility or where most illegitimate births were quickly followed by marriage. However, in Peru the household survey revealed that 8 per cent of the births to women aged 15–19, and 4 per cent to women aged 20–24, were illegitimate. Thus, in some countries this source of bias cannot be entirely dismissed, though the effect on results must be small.

Universally collected mortality data

The individual survey was the common source of information on infant and child mortality. The basic question used to obtain the date of a live birth was, 'In what month and year did your (first, second, etc.) birth occur?'. If the respondent did not know the answer, she was asked how many years ago the birth occurred. A few countries used additional probes, such as asking for the season of birth or using local calendars. A detailed discussion of this topic may be found in chapter 5.

If a child had died, the respondent was asked, 'For how long did the child live?'. For all but three countries, the interviewer was instructed to obtain the age in completed years and completed months. In Dominican Republic, Paraguay and Venezuela, age in completed years only was obtained. Moreover, several countries grouped data into broader categories for coding purposes.

When exact dates were not reported for any event, subject to relevant constraints, a date in month and year was imputed. The amount of imputation varied from country to country. It should be noted that the imputation procedure alone cannot misplace births seriously in time and that the imputation of date of birth usually has no serious effect on the age of death for non-surviving children. Moreover, the results of a special analysis (see chapter 26) suggest that substantive conclusions are unlikely to be biased by imputation.

Extended household schedules and the general mortality module

The standard WFS household questionnaire was designed to provide a listing of household members from which women eligible for interview could be selected. It is important to note that the household survey questions could have been answered by any adult member of the household. Some countries supplemented the core household schedule with questions on children ever born and children surviving and increased household sample size. This permits indirect estimation of infant and child mortality at national level and subgroup analysis for those characteristics obtained in the household survey. Other countries adopted, in whole or in part, the WFS general mortality module (see chapter 3). This was intended for use by countries with deficient vital statistics and was designed to measure adult mortality in particular. The module obtained information on deaths of household members (including children) in the 12 or 24 months preceding the survey, survival of respondent's first spouse and parents, whether the person being interviewed was the eldest living offspring, the survival of the last born child, and the number of children ever born and still living. Despite the wealth of data available from the household survey, however, the principal sources of information on infant and child mortality are the birth histories from the detailed individual interviews.

Country-specific mortality data

All WFS surveys collected information on the demographic characteristics of each child and its mother. This included the sex of the child, its birth order, multiplicity, the length of various birth intervals, the age of the mother at the birth (or death) of the child and the mother's marital status. Reasonably comparable information on such background characteristics of the mother and her current husband as education, current and childhood place of residence and work history is also available. In addition, we have information on the duration of breastfeeding for the two most recent births in all countries except Fiji (where it is available for the most recent birth only) and for every live birth in Pakistan and the Republic of Korea.

Questions on maternal and child health were added by several countries (five in Latin America and seven in Africa). Questions varied substantially from country to country and were asked to various groups of women – for example, to all women who had had a pregnancy in the previous year (Dominican Republic) or to all women about their most recent or current pregnancy (Mexico and Peru). Information collected here includes type of medical care during pregnancy, type of place of delivery, who attended the delivery, whether the child was taken to a doctor, and if so, where, and whether the child was vaccinated against any diseases.

The household and community questionnaires used by a number of countries contain additional information relevant to the study of infant and child mortality. In some household surveys, questions were asked about the source of drinking and cooking water and about toilet facilities. In the community surveys (restricted to rural areas with the exception of Mexico), questions were asked on the availability or accessibility of various health-care facilities and personnel. Questions were also asked on water supply, sewage facilities and garbage disposal in various countries. Further details on the contents of the questionnaires have been published in a separate report (Singh 1984a).

32.3   Quality of the WFS data

Maternity history data, like any data from a sample survey, are likely to contain sampling as well as non-sampling errors. Sampling errors are relatively easy to deal with since their magnitude can be estimated if the details of the sample design are known. This is true for all the WFS surveys. Our calculations show that the coefficient of variation of the infant mortality rates for the period of 1–4 years before the surveys ranges from 4–13 per cent, with 30 countries having a coefficient of variation of less than 8 per cent.

The more difficult question of non-sampling errors is addressed in chapter 24. Practically all surveys showed discrepancies on at least one of the various tests of plausibility. Particularly worrying is the severe heaping of reported ages at death at one and at two years of age and the possibility of upward bias in recent mortality in a few surveys. However, in general, WFS mortality data are of surprisingly good quality, yielding convincing trends for the 15 preceding years. Comparison with external sources usually indicates WFS data to be superior. Thus Hobcraft (1984) is able to conclude: 'A review of all known reports on infant and child mortality using WFS data, including the relevant chapters of the evaluation reports, shows that the data for the 22 countries concerned are generally of remarkably high quality. In no single instance was there a demonstrably better source of information on infant and child mortality at the national level.' A similar note of confidence also emerged from a review carried out by Preston (1985).

32.4   Summary of findings

Levels

Table 32.1 presents mortality estimates for 40 countries for the period 0–4 years before the survey (years of survey range from 1974 to 1982). Six rates of mortality are presented:

1 Infant mortality	$(_1q_0$	– Between birth and first birthday)
2 Neo-natal	(NN	– In first month of life)
3 Post-neonatal	(P–NN	– Between one and 11 months)
4 Under 5	$(_5q_0$	– Between birth and fifth birthday)
5 Toddler	$(_1q_1$	– Between first and second birthdays)
6 Child	$(_3q_2$	– Between second and fifth birthdays)

For some of the countries such information has not been hitherto available; for others the available information was known to be defective or incomplete and only for 10 countries were reliable rates known from vital registrations. In such a situation it is not easy to make any direct assessment of the accuracy of the survey estimates. In general, the infant mortality rates vary from a low level of 33 per 1000 births in Panama and Portugal to as high as 162 in Yemen AR. Twelve countries have rates above 100 while seven have rates below 50. There is some evidence of a regional pattern; in general high mortality countries are in Africa, Middle East and South Asia. Most of the Latin American and the three English-speaking Caribbean countries covered fall in the bottom half. It is surprising, however, that in Jordan and Syria the survey estimates appear to be on the low side.

In table 32.2 we present comparable estimates of infant mortality rates from vital statistics as reported in the United Nations' *Demographic Yearbook* (1974) and the rates reported by the US Bureau of the Census, the latter being largely estimated from life tables or by indirect techniques. Registration estimates are available only for 25 countries; three have data from surveys (Lesotho, Pakistan and Turkey), and for the remaining 12 no information is available. Moreover, in 15 of the 25 countries, the vital registration is known to be incomplete and hence the true values should be higher than those given in italics for these countries. Hence our comparison is limited to the 10 countries whose registration is reported to be complete. In Portugal the WFS estimate is 33, compared with 38 (1974) from vital registration and similar figures are 36 and 38 respectively in Malaysia. In the seven other countries (Sri Lanka, Paraguay, Guyana, Costa Rica, Fiji, Jamaica and Trinidad and Tobago) the survey estimated higher levels of infant mortality rates than the vital registration. In Senegal, the UN figure is for Dakar city only and hence not comparable with WFS estimates. If it can be assumed that the surveys are not likely to overestimate infant mortality rates (at least for the recent periods) and since vital registration is likely to be less than 100 per cent complete in these countries, it appears that for at least nine countries the survey estimates are nearer to the true level of infant mortality rates than the vital registration figures. It could, however, be argued that countries with reasonably good vital registration are likely to produce better survey data and hence the above findings need not necessarily imply that WFS provides better estimates in other situations.

We have indirect estimates, reported by the US Bureau of the Census, for 36 countries. Biases can be, and are, present in the indirect estimates. However, the higher status accorded to indirect procedures by many demographers, combined with the general tendency to accept higher estimates in view of the expected omission in reporting of deaths, has produced a preference for indirect estimation procedures, the results of which are rarely evaluated as critically as the direct survey estimates. While examining various studies carried out using WFS data from Indonesia, Bangladesh, Sri Lanka, Colombia and Kenya, Preston (1985) points out that 'one of the important uses of WFS data has been to provide repeated clear demonstrations of the biases in the indirect estimation procedures that have come to dominate mortality measurement in statistically poor countries'. He also concludes, based on WFS experience, that the direct information is superior to the more conventional indirect information for estimation of recent levels. Bearing in mind these limitations, if we examine the data in table 32.2, there is ample evidence to conclude that WFS has succeeded in providing what appear to be reasonable estimates of the recent level of infant mortality in 35 of the 40 countries covered. In four of them (Yemen AR, Ivory Coast, Senegal and Benin) there is no other reliable information.

We have so far looked at deaths in the first year of life; we can further decompose this into deaths in the first month and deaths between the first and eleventh month of life. In general, there is evidence from the variations in the relative contribution of neo-natal rates to infant mortality rates of shifting of the events. It is noticeable in Malaysia, for example, that some births in the first month have been moved forward, even though the overall infant mortality rate is sufficiently accurate. In contrast, in Syria there is possible omission as well as shifting.

Finally, we also look at mortality within the first five years of life among the 40 countries. As implied earlier, there is always the possibility that infant mortality rates could be underestimated by the forward shifting of some deaths to exact age one, resulting from rounding of the age by the respondent. But the under-five mortality is relatively free from that error. In the absence of independent information on under-five mortality for these countries, we examine the relationship between the components of under-five mortality. In general, as child mortality declines, one would expect more rapid reductions in the mortality after the first year of life and, after the first month, within the first year. The data in table 32.1 confirm this pattern. The percentage of deaths in the first year among all deaths in the first five years of life are found to decline with increasing chances of dying in the first five years of life. A similar relation is also observed if we replace deaths in the first year by those in the first month of life (Rutstein 1983).

TABLE 32.1

Current levels of infant and child mortality (in the period 0–4 years before the survey)

Country	Date of survey	Infant ($_1q_0$)	NN	P-NN	Under 5 ($_5q_0$)	Toddler ($_1q_1$)	Child ($_3q_2$)
Senegal	1978	111.8	49.6	62.1	262.4	73.9	103.4
Yemen AR	1979	161.5	58.4	103.1	236.5	41.6	50.0
Nepal	1976	142.3	75.4	66.9	234.6	53.7	57.0
Bangladesh	1975–6	135.0	73.7	61.3	221.6	34.6	67.9
Pakistan	1975	139.0	79.9	59.0	207.2	33.1	47.8
Benin	1981–2	107.6	49.7	57.9	204.2	36.7	74.3
Mauritania	1981–2	90.2	47.8	42.4	195.9	45.3	74.3
Cameroon	1978	104.6	45.3	59.3	191.2	40.1	59.0
Haiti	1977	122.7	60.5	62.2	191.1	29.5	49.9
Egypt	1980	132.3	58.7	73.7	190.6	37.1	31.2
Lesotho	1977	125.8	67.6	58.2	173.7	29.0	26.5
Turkey	1978	132.6	63.0	69.6	165.8	22.7	16.0
Ivory Coast	1980–1	113.1	54.0	59.2	161.8	17.2	38.4
Indonesia	1976	94.6	47.3	47.3	158.5	26.4	45.4
Sudan (North)	1978–9	78.6	41.5	37.0	150.8	37.5	42.5
Peru	1977–8	96.5	43.8	52.7	149.3	31.3	28.0
Morocco	1980	91.2	50.3	40.9	141.8	30.3	26.2
Kenya	1977–8	86.6	37.8	48.8	141.6	27.9	33.3
Dominican Rep.	1975	88.6	—	—	128.5	25.3	18.9
Ghana	1979–80	73.4	38.0	35.3	127.2	24.7	34.3

Ecuador	1979–80	75.7	37.6	38.1	117.6	24.8	21.0
Colombia	1976	69.6	33.5	36.2	107.9	18.5	23.0
Tunisia	1978	79.8	38.9	40.9	107.2	16.2	13.8
Mexico	1976–7	71.6	40.9	30.7	96.0	12.5	14.0
Philippines	1978	58.3	24.5	33.7	92.9	15.5	21.6
Thailand	1975	65.1	38.9	26.2	90.9	8.6	19.2
Sri Lanka	1975	59.9	36.9	23.0	86.1	8.2	19.7
Syria	1978	64.6	15.2	49.4	86.1	12.2	10.9
Paraguay	1979	61.2	–	–	84.9	15.1	10.3
Jordan	1976	65.6	27.5	38.1	79.7	9.3	5.8
Guyana	1975	57.6	34.3	23.2	77.2	11.7	9.2
Venezuela	1977	53.1	–	–	63.7	5.5	5.7
Costa Rica	1976	53.3	24.8	28.5	61.3	3.9	4.6
Fiji	1974	47.0	–	–	58.5	5.4	6.7
Korea, Rep. of	1974	41.7	23.0	18.7	56.1	6.9	8.1
Jamaica	1975–6	43.0	23.9	19.1	55.8	8.1	5.3
Malaysia	1974	36.1	13.9	22.2	49.8	5.5	8.7
Trinidad & Tobago	1977	41.3	30.8	10.5	49.1	2.8	5.4
Panama	1975–6	32.8	20.5	12.3	45.7	5.6	7.9
Portugal	1979–80	33.3	23.3	10.0	36.6	1.8	1.6

Notes:

(i) Countries are ordered by level of under-five mortality.

(ii) – = not available.

TABLE 32.2

Comparison of WFS estimates of infant mortality rates with rates from other sources

Country	WFS 0–4 years before survey	UN Vital registration	US Bureau of the Census
(1)	(2)	(3)	(4)
Yemen AR	162	Not available	Not available
Nepal	142	Not available	133 (1975)
Pakistan	139	124 (1968 survey)	142 (1971)
Bangladesh	135	Not available	153 (1969–74)
Turkey	133	153 (1967 survey)	125 (1974)
Egypt	132	*116* (1972)	90 (1975)
Lesotho	126	114 (1974 survey)	114 (1971)
Haiti	123	Not available	150 (1967)
Ivory Coast	113	Not available	Not available
Senegal	112	63 (1972) Dakar	Not available
Benin	108	Not available	Not available
Cameroon	105	Not available	157 (1976)
Peru	97	*65* (1970)	130 (1972)
Indonesia	95	Not available	114 (1975)
Morocco	91	Not available	162 (1972)
Mauritania	90	Not available	162–193 (1964)
Dominican Rep.	89	*49* (1972)	96 (1967)
Kenya	87	*140* (1965) Africans	83 (1977)
Tunisia	80	*75* (1971)	135 (1968)
Sudan (North)	79	Not available	141 (1970)
Ecuador	76	*76* (1973)	115 (1967)
Ghana	73	*63* (1971)	115 (1970)
Mexico	72	*51* (1973)	70 (1973)
Colombia	70	*63* (1971)	77 (1973)
Jordan	66	*23* (1973)	160 (1961)
Thailand	65	*27* (1972)	76 (1974)
Syria	65	*22* (1972)	81 (1974)
Sri Lanka	60	45 (1972)	53 (1974)
Philippines	58	*74* (1973)	80 (1970)
Paraguay	61	39 (1971)	58 (1972)
Guyana	58	39 (1968)	52 (1974)
Costa Rica	53	45 (1973)	28 (1977)
Venezuela	53	*54* (1973)	45 (1976)
Fiji	47	21 (1973)	
Jamaica	43	27 (1974)	17 (1978)
Korea, Rep. of	42	Not available	47 (1970)
Trinidad & Tobago	41	26 (1974)	29 (1978)
Malaysia	36	38 (1972)	42 (1972)
Portugal	33	38 (1974)	39 (1975)
Panama	33	*31* (1974)	37 (1975)

Trends

The data from birth histories enable us to study not only the current levels but also the past trends in infant and child mortality. There are, however, three main issues that should be recognized while studying the trends from retrospective data of the WFS type. First, the effect of truncation arising from the upper age limit of 50 imposed on the women interviewed should be considered. As we go back in time, the older, and hence higher parity, women are systematically removed from the sample and therefore the rates are based on the mortality experience of progressively younger mothers. Since birth order, and age of the mother at birth, are also found to affect the chances of survival of the child, the observed trends over time could be distorted. It is therefore recommended that, for the study of trends, the rates are limited to children born to mothers up to age 29 years at birth and for the period up to 19 years before the survey. This will provide comparable rates for a 20-year period. Secondly, we should consider selectivity, resulting from the fact that data are available only for those women who are living at the time of the survey. The child mortality experience of those women who died during the last 20 years is not available and if there are differentials by the survival status of women, this selectivity could also distort the trends. In the survey context there is no easy solution to this. Thirdly, we must look at reporting errors, as mentioned earlier. Events further back in the woman's life are particularly likely to suffer from omission of births (especially those not surviving or not resident at the time of the interview), omission of early deaths and misreporting of age at death. Also data on children born to mothers below the age of 20 years may suffer from omissions particularly in societies where premarital unions and conceptions are not rare, and hence a lower age limit of 20 years has been introduced for the purpose of trend analysis. In general one would expect the incidence of under-reporting to increase as one moves further back from the date of interview. If so, it is rather unlikely that the data would depict any spurious declining trend over time; more probably the observed quantum of decline will be an underestimate.

Table 32.3 presents infant and child mortality rates based on the experience of mothers aged 20–29 years for four five-year periods preceding the survey in 40 countries. Let us first compare the rates for the period 0–4 years before the survey presented in table 32.3 with those in table 32.1 for the same period. The infant mortality rate based on mothers aged 20–29 years (IMR_{20-29}) is invariably

TABLE 32.3

Under-five and infant mortality for five-year periods before the survey (children with mothers aged 20-29 years at birth)

Country	Date of survey	Levels of mortality for years before survey							
		Mortality under age five ($_5q_0$)				Infant mortality ($_1q_0$)			
		0–4	5–9	10–14	15–19	0–4	5–9	10–14	15–19
Senegal	1978	250.6	269.7	293.7	267.9	102.0	115.7	115.2	105.7
Yemen AR	1979	234.8	268.8	(321.9)	(367.1)	162.8	154.2	186.4	(236.8)
Nepal	1976	232.7	241.1	294.0	293.1	142.1	149.3	181.5	171.6
Bangladesh	1975–6	208.9	187.4	205.1	230.0	117.0	109.8	129.7	139.5
Pakistan	1975	203.4	187.9	219.2	251.8	132.2	127.8	129.7	156.0
Benin	1981–2	196.1	240.3	254.1	(277.1)	101.8	126.2	139.4	156.0
Mauritania	1981–2	188.5	166.3	163.3	(227.6)	82.0	68.8	68.4	111.9
Cameroon	1978	181.3	191.9	238.0	258.1	95.0	96.2	137.2	149.5
Haiti	1977	186.6	234.0	254.7	(244.3)	124.3	148.7	157.0	143.0
Egypt	1980	182.1	230.7	240.9	265.7	124.3	142.6	135.3	139.4
Lesotho	1977	165.8	176.9	188.0	169.3	121.9	123.1	138.9	115.3
Turkey	1978	150.6	176.0	206.4	267.1	119.0	127.8	146.2	176.2
Ivory Coast	1980–1	159.0	222.5	245.6	289.4	101.3	133.3	154.2	169.8
Indonesia	1976	151.6	162.6	199.0	217.7	87.7	88.6	112.5	117.2
Peru	1977–8	140.7	157.5	192.9	210.9	89.4	101.8	112.4	121.9
Morocco	1980	134.3	153.7	172.9	188.1	84.4	91.6	98.5	102.5
Sudan (North)	1978–9	129.4	123.0	140.4	(142.2)	66.6	72.2	71.3	49.1
Kenya	1977–8	134.8	148.1	156.5	193.0	83.2	88.2	96.1	121.0
Dominican Rep.	1975	120.7	135.7	162.0	(117.9)	80.9	97.7	105.2	72.3
Ghana	1979–80	116.7	124.1	157.8	147.3	64.8	67.7	85.9	78.3

Ecuador	1979–80	109.2	122.9	153.3	169.1	69.2	72.0	95.1	107.4
Colombia	1976	89.7	101.2	116.9	134.2	56.6	64.2	72.4	83.9
Tunisia	1978	101.6	126.0	138.3	186.1	74.4	74.1	78.4	105.6
Mexico	1976–7	84.4	108.8	118.6	139.1	60.2	74.8	80.5	86.3
Philippines	1978	85.4	86.3	86.3	90.9	52.3	53.6	49.6	54.6
Thailand	1975	82.9	107.5	121.6	137.5	56.8	76.5	86.4	95.4
Syria	1978	84.3	89.2	120.7	137.7	62.5	65.8	80.2	85.5
Sri Lanka	1975	81.0	81.4	87.6	102.0	57.9	56.7	58.7	60.7
Paraguay	1979	73.1	62.8	78.2	64.0	52.4	45.0	56.8	42.8
Jordan	1976	75.8	85.2	120.6	185.7	65.6	61.9	75.5	110.9
Guyana	1975	72.5	62.9	71.7	88.7	54.0	50.4	56.4	67.0
Venezuela	1977	55.0	63.3	57.7	(78.4)	45.4	45.1	41.2	44.5
Costa Rica	1976	50.5	76.2	100.1	90.0	44.2	59.0	81.2	60.1
Fiji	1974	51.5	55.9	61.0	69.8	41.5	48.0	49.6	59.3
Korea, Rep. of	1974	51.1	81.3	100.9	113.9	35.2	51.2	53.0	64.0
Jamaica	1975–6	48.4	42.7	54.3	100.2	38.8	30.0	39.7	78.7
Trinidad & Tobago	1977	40.9	49.9	46.4	60.1	33.3	40.7	38.7	53.6
Malaysia	1974	46.7	51.6	70.6	105.0	35.5	38.5	50.8	72.2
Panama	1975–6	36.1	56.0	61.6	82.7	26.5	43.1	38.7	60.3
Portugal	1979–80	36.0	46.4	52.1	83.3	32.1	41.1	43.3	64.2

Notes:

(i) Countries are ordered by level of under-five mortality.
(ii) Under-five is mortality between birth and fifth birthday ($_5q_0$); Infant is mortality between birth and first birthday ($_1q_0$).
(iii) Brackets indicate that the rate is based on less than 500 children exposed.

at least 80 per cent of that based on mothers aged 15–49 years (IMR_{15-49}). The percentage is over 100 in two countries, between 90 and 100 in 22 countries and between 80 and 90 in the remaining 16 countries. If we examine child mortality, the corresponding number of countries is 0, 30 and 9 respectively, with Panama reporting 78 per cent. Therefore, by limiting our analysis to the experience of mothers aged 20-29 years, we have captured well over 80 per cent of infant and child mortality. This increases our confidence in the trends observed.

The figures in table 32.3 show that both infant and child mortality have fallen over time in all the 40 countries and substantially in some of them. There are three countries in Latin America – Dominican Republic, Paraguay and Costa Rica – which show an increase in mortality during the period 10-19 years before the survey. This phenomenon has been confirmed by the results of a subsequent survey in the Dominican Republic (Hobcraft and Rodríguez 1982a) but it is not possible to say whether the same is true in the other two countries. Detailed analysis of the trends is beyond the scope of this chapter. In general, the relative decline in child mortality is larger than the corresponding decline in the mortality rate in the first year of life. Venezuela is the only case where no substantial fall in infant mortality rate is observed during the 20 years before the survey. Among the remaining countries, the amount of change does not seem to be related to the current level of mortality, though the relative decline is naturally higher among low-mortality countries than high-mortality countries. The observed increase during the most recent period, compared with 5-9 years before the survey in Bangladesh, Pakistan, Mauritania, Paraguay, Guyana and Jamaica, may be due to either a genuine increase or bias or both (see chapter 24). However, the fact that earlier rates are higher in all countries except Mauritania is impressive.

In general, it appears that the retrospective data from WFS can, if handled properly, be used to provide a good understanding of the trends in infant and child mortality during the period 0–19 years before the survey.

Differentials

Traditionally, the principal sources of information on infant and child mortality have been the vital registration system and the census. One problem with the study of mortality differentials from this type of data is the very limited information available on bio-demographic and socio-economic characteristics. In developing countries, the widespread lack of reliable information on mortality from conventional data sources has led to the use of retrospective questions in censuses and household surveys. The WFS has significantly increased the amount of information available in developing countries for the study of such differentials.

Bio-demographic factors. Infant and child mortality is not independent of the child's or the mother's demographic characteristics. Five bio-demographic factors have been found to be particularly important predictors of child survival. These are the sex of the child, the age of the mother at the time of the birth,

birth order, the multiplicity of the birth and the length of the previous birth interval.

Death rates during the first year of life tend to be higher for males than for females, and the differences can be expected to be apparent right from birth. In each of 29 WFS surveys examined — with the exceptions of Jordan and Syria — the infant mortality rate for males exceeds that for females, and the size of the differences ranges to as much as 25 deaths per 1000 live births (Rutstein 1983). There was no relation between size of the differences and the actual levels of mortality.

The sex ratio of mortality is more balanced after infancy and, in general, neither sex enjoys a notable advantage between the ages of one and five. Three exceptions to this pattern are Egypt, Pakistan and Bangladesh (Hobcraft, McDonald and Rutstein 1985). Indeed, in Pakistan, female death rates at ages one and 2-5 years exceeded male rates by a factor of 50 per cent, an excess that reflects, perhaps, a 'selective neglect' of female children that persists regardless of the sex composition of families (Alam and Cleland 1984).

The occurrence of a multiple birth is a rare event, and only 1.8 per cent of the half-million or so births captured in 29 surveys studied by Rutstein (1983) were the outcome of such confinements. While the deaths of children born of multiple births cannot greatly affect the overall mortality levels, the levels of mortality of these children are staggering. In no country was their infant mortality rate less than 150 per 1000, and in only five countries was it lower than 200 per 1000. Overall, infant mortality rates for multiple births were between two-and-one-half and six times higher than for single births, and the differences persisted well into childhood.

In countries with reliable vital registration, neo-natal and infant mortality are known to vary according to the mother's age at the time of the confinement, regardless of the overall level of risk in the community. The relation tends to be J- or U-shaped, with mortality high for the children of teenage mothers, relatively low for those in their twenties and then rising steeply with increasing maternal age (Nortman 1974; Omran 1981). Infant mortality rates for children born in the 10 years preceding the surveys generally vary with maternal age. Without exception, births to teenage mothers were subject to considerably higher mortality than were births to mothers aged 20-29; in the majority of the 29 countries surveyed, the discrepancies were found to continue into the second and subsequent years of life (Rutstein 1983).

As a rule, the age of minimal risk was 20-29 years, and infant death rates tended to increase at the higher maternal ages. No single pattern could be identified, however, and in a handful of countries, notably Syria, Sri Lanka and Malaysia, the period of minimal risk occurred between ages 30-39 years. Most countries showed extremely high death rates for the infants of mothers aged 40 and above, and increases in infant mortality at the older maternal ages were found to be more pronounced in countries in which overall mortality levels were low.

In most WFS surveys, birth order also proved to be an important correlate of infant mortality. In high-mortality countries, such as Nepal and Kenya, first-born children were at greater risk of dying during infancy than were their younger siblings, and there was a tendency for risks to increase again at birth orders seven and above. This U-shaped pattern was not observed in all the 29 countries examined (Rutstein 1983). Indeed, in countries in which overall child mortality levels were lower, such as the Philippines and Jamaica, the first-born appeared to be the most likely to survive and, thereafter, risks of death increased progressively with birth order.

With some modification, these observations hold true for the probability of dying during the second year of life. In virtually every country 'toddler' mortality increased with birth order, and only in one country, Senegal, did the risk for first-born one year olds exceed that of second- or third-order births by more than five deaths per 1000. An even simpler relation emerged for mortality between the ages of two and five, with the risks tending to increase monogonically with the order of birth.

The likelihood of a child's survival is known to be related to the length of the interval leading up to its birth. The relation is such that infants born after a very short birth interval, say less than 18 months, experience higher mortality risks, especially within the first month of life (Omran 1981).

In virtually all surveys examined, infants born within two years of an older sibling were found to be subject to higher death rates than were those born two to three years after the previous birth (Rutstein 1983). In several countries, notably Lesotho, Turkey and Bangladesh, the absolute difference between the rates approaches 90 per 1000, and even in countries in which overall mortality levels are low, such as Panama, Malaysia and Jamaica, the difference is seldom less than 20 deaths per 1000 live births. The relative differences in mortality are reduced if the older sibling survived for at least two years or until the birth of the reference child, but in the majority of countries it still exceeds 40 per cent. This is so whatever the underlying mortality level.

In most countries the influence of the length of the previous birth interval on a child's survival chances extends into the second year of life. This is most clear in those cases where toddler mortality rates are of the order of 30 per 1000 and above. In Turkey, for example, the risk of death for children aged one year declined from about 50, to 20, to 10 per 1000 according to whether the reference child was born less than two years, two to three or four or more years after the previous birth. Unlike infant death rates, however, mortality among toddlers born within two years of the last birth appears to be largely independent of the survival status of older sibling. In a handful of countries, especially high-mortality countries such as Pakistan, Turkey and Bangladesh, substantial birth-interval effects were evident even among death rates for children aged three to five years (Rutstein 1983).

The deleterious effects of short birth intervals on mortality early in life may be explained in part by the 'maternal depletion syndrome', whereby one pregnancy coming too soon after the previous confinement leaves the mother little time to recover her health, especially if the child is breastfed for a long time or is still unweaned when the next child is conceived. Indeed, a continouous cycle of pregnancy and lactation leads to progressively higher risks of low birth-weight babies with heightened chances of death (Jelliffe 1966). The effects of maternal depletion may be exacerbated by competition between siblings, since the attention and resources the mother is able to devote to two children very close in age may be insufficient to ensure their survival.

Nevertheless, an analysis based on the Pakistan Fertility Survey showed that elevated risks of infant and child death could not be attributed entirely to competition between closely spaced siblings since the previous birth interval was still strongly related to mortality if the older sibling had died. Moreover, this was true even after controlling for birth order and maternal age (Cleland and Sathar 1984).

Subsequent analyses suggest that both competition and depletion play a role; when children are born in rapid succession, both the younger and the older child suffer. Thus, in a comparative study which controlled not for the length of the preceding birth interval but for the number of births occurring in the specified time periods before and after the reference child, Hobcraft, McDonald and Rutstein (1983) found that the occurrence of a birth within the preceding two-year period raised the neo-natal mortality rate of the reference child by at least one-half in 24 of the 26 countries examined, and more than doubled it in 14 countries. The effects of rapid childbearing were equally apparent in the post-neonatal period, when the mortality risk for reference children was raised in 22 of the countries and actually doubled in 12. A subsequent birth occurring soon after the birth of the reference child also had an adverse effect on toddler and child mortality. The birth of a younger sibling within 18 months of the reference child raised mortality in the second year of life by one-half in 16 of 23 countries and doubled it in nine. The effect on child mortality is naturally weaker; the birth of a younger sibling within 30 months tended to raise child mortality, but by as much as one-half in only five countries.

The effects of birth spacing on infant and child mortality are not independent of those of maternal age and birth order in the sense that, for example, the births of a young high-parity mother are of necessity closely spaced. This raises the question of whether birth spacing or the inter-relation of birth order and maternal age is the primary causative agent. Results from a more recent comparative analysis (Hobcraft, McDonald and Rutstein 1985) indicate that, after controlling for the effects of birth spacing, first births and the births of teenagers were still subject to significantly higher risks of death during infancy. These were the only consistent maternal-age birth-order effects. Indeed, in many of the approximately 30 countries examined, birth-spacing effects appear to subsume those of maternal age and birth order, although in a minority of cases children of birth orders seven and above may have suffered inordinately high mortality.

One result to emerge from multivariate analyses of infant and child mortality

is that the effects of most factors on mortality are changed by introducing simultaneous controls. We might note that the intercorrelations of socio-economic
variables tend to be stronger than correlations between such variables and bio-
demographic factors, so that analyses focusing mainly on the effects of variables
of one type are likely to be fairly robust to the omission of control variables of
the other type.

Socio-economic differentials in infant and child mortality. The WFS surveys
contain a rich mine of information on socio-economic differentials in infant and
child mortality. All surveys included questions on such background characteristics as the respondent's education, current and childhood places of residence
and work history as well as the current husband's education, occupation and
labour-force status. Several surveys also included questions on religion, ethnicity
and language for women and age, income and migration for husbands.

One of the most frequently measured differentials in child mortality is that
associated with current place of residence. Thus, death rates between ages one
and five years tend to be lower in urban than in rural areas, and lowest of all in
metropolitan areas. A striking example of such differentials occurs in Peru where,
among infants born 5–15 years before the survey, the probability of dying
between ages one and five years rose from 20 per 1000 for those residing in the
capital, to 60 per 1000 for those in other urban areas, and to nearly 100 per
1000 for children in rural areas (Hobcraft, McDonald and Rutstein 1984). An
even greater absolute difference was recorded in Senegal, where the mortality
risks for children in urban and rural areas were, respectively, 116 and 222 per
1000. It is worth noting also that such differentials tend to be present whatever
the underlying mortality level although, of course, the lower the underlying
level of mortality the smaller the absolute differences in child mortality.

The picture is more complicated if we confine our attention to deaths
occurring in the first year of life. In more than half of the 40 countries for which
estimates were available at the time of writing, infant mortality (and its principal
component, neo-natal mortality) was lowest in metropolitan areas, higher in
other urban agglomerations and higher still in rural areas. In several countries,
most notably Egypt, Bangladesh, Sri Lanka, Thailand and Philippines, urban-
rural differentials did exist, but infants in metropolitan centres did not appear to
be greatly advantaged in comparison with those living in other urban areas.

In a few countries, infants in urban areas were subject to mortality risks as
high as or even higher than those experienced by infants in rural areas. Such
countries include Kenya, Lesotho, Mauritania, Tunisia, Costa Rica, Dominican
Republic and Republic of Korea. In Haiti and Guyana, infant death rates were
lower in urban than in rural areas but children in metropolitan areas were significantly disadvantaged. In Haiti, for example, infant death rates for children born
0–9 years before the survey were 100 and 120 per 1000 in non-metropolitan urban and rural areas but more than 180 per 2000 in metropolitan Port-au-Prince.

In developing countries, mortality is often thought to be higher in rural than
in urban areas because of differential standards of living and health conditions

and because of differential availability of and access to public health facilities. The variety of patterns of urban–rural infant mortality differentials recorded by the WFS does not necessarily counter such observations since the quality of urban life varies greatly both within and between countries. However, residential differences may subsume other important behavioural determinants of child mortality.

One such factor is parental education. It should be noted, however, that any consideration of the effects of education on mortality is complicated by the fact that in one country a given number of years of schooling may indicate an individual's membership of a social elite whereas in another country the same duration may indicate that a person is relatively disadvantaged. The same holds true for young women and older women within any country which has expanded its educational system within the lifetime of the respondents. It is remarkable, therefore, that in virtually every country surveyed both infant and child mortality decrease consistently with increasing years of education. In Cameroon, for example, among infants born during the 10-year period before the survey, the death rate declines from 116, to 88, to 87, to 64 per 1000, depending upon whether their mothers had no formal education, 1–3 years, 4–6 years or 7 or more years of schooling. Similarly, between the first and fifth birthdays the probabilities of dying fall from 109, to 87, to 80, and to 55 deaths per 1000 across the same durations of schooling. Overall, the ratios of infant death rates for the highest and lowest educational groups range from about one-third in Benin and Costa Rica to more than two-thirds in Bangladesh and Lesotho.

Since the better educated tend to reside in towns and cities, education can be expected to play an unseen role in maintaining urban–rural differentials in infant and child mortality, and in many cases this is in fact true. In Sri Lanka, for example, where mortality now appears to be stabilizing, a small but persistent urban–rural differential in child mortality disappeared once maternal education had been controlled (Meegama 1980). In Kenya, where mortality declines are continuing, urbanization and education act independently to depress infant mortality for younger women, but among older women urbanization has no effect independent of education (Mott 1982).

The importance of parental education in reducing mortality within the first two years of life has been documented in a study of 10 WFS countries as diverse as Jamaica, Bangladesh and Peru. The mother's attainment of primary schooling was found to have a significant impact on child survival, but more critical than the step from illiteracy to primary education was that from primary to secondary schooling. In most cases the father's education also had a bearing on mortality during early childhood quite distinct from those of father's occupation and mother's education. There were also suggestions that the impact of parental education may have been greater than both income factors and access to health facilities combined (Caldwell and McDonald 1981).

Other analyses, whether of individual WFS datasets or involving cross-national comparisons, have confirmed the overall association between parental education and early childhood mortality, and found that in general it extends into the first five years of life. For example, the results of a study of 28 WFS surveys (Hobcraft, McDonald and Rutstein 1984) indicate not only that earlier analyses may have underemphasized the importance of parental education for infant mortality but also that the father's educational level is often the strongest predictor of child survival beyond the age of one. The relative contribution of the parent's characteristics was found also to differ greatly between countries. For example, while mother's education emerged as an important determinant of child survival in most Latin American surveys, in tropical Africa and parts of South-East Asia, where there are relatively few educated women, the role of the husband's education was particularly strong. This study stressed, in addition, the interplay of such characteristics as education, income, occupation and work status; in some sense the better educated and wealthier can be expected to be better nourished and to have better housing, and to be more likely to recognize illness requiring medical intervention and to have the wherewithal to afford medical attention.

The type of marital union must also be considered in an examination of child mortality. In those (mostly Caribbean) surveys in which legal marriages were distinguished from consensual unions, children born within formal marriages generally faced lower risks of dying than did other children. In addition, children born to women not in a union at the time of confinement also experienced higher than average mortality rates.

A number of studies on WFS data have signalled the importance of the characteristics of households, as opposed to the characteristics of individuals, for child survival. Thus, in the Philippines, the availability of sanitation and electricity proved to be correlates of child mortality even after controlling for such things as birth order, maternal age and education (Martin, Trussell, Reyes-Salvail and Shah 1983). In Panama, the characteristics of the mother were the most important determinants of neo-natal mortality but housing conditions, in particular the type of water supply and sewage disposal, were almost equally important as the mother's characteristics in determining post-neonatal mortality (Guerra 1981). Access to toilet facilities also showed a clear relationship with early child survival in Sri Lanka and Mexico, but in neither country did the availability of piped water appear to have a bearing on mortality within the first five years of life (Hobcraft 1984).

Community factors. Analysis of WFS data has also been directed towards an exploration of the relationship between community factors and child mortality. Data for Cameroon, Ivory Coast, Egypt, Jordan, Bangladesh, Philippines, Ecuador and Peru have been analysed by national researchers either as part of the second-stage analysis programme in a country, or at the workshop carried out in London. A more extended discussion is given in chapter 33. The most significant finding emerging from the analysis is the absence of any impact of the density of medical personnel on levels of infant and child mortality. The only exception is the observed effect of proximity of trained midwives on neo-natal mortality. Here it must be mentioned that most WFS surveys did not inquire about the proximity of less trained personnel who form an important component of the primary-health-care systems in many countries. In one country where such personnel were singled out — the Philippines — the expected effects emerged.

The impact of proximity of health facilities was examined in six countries (Bangladesh, Cameroon, Ecuador, Egypt, Peru and Philippines) and, on balance, the view that more dense networks of health facilities can have a beneficial impact on infant and child mortality is confirmed. Of course, such conclusions do not apply to all types of facilities under all settings. For instance, the absence of any significant net mortality differentials between villages with or without at least one health clinic has raised many questions in Egypt. In some countries, such as Ecuador and Bangladesh, the impact is less on infant mortality than on mortality after the first birthday. In these studies the researchers had data on the proximity or availability of health facilities but not on access to, and the extent and frequency of, utilization of these facilities without which it is not possible to explain the relationship to and assess the impact of such facilities. A recent study has documented striking socio-economic differentials in pre-natal and post-natal health care in five Latin American countries — Dominican Republic, Ecuador, Mexico, Paraguay and Peru (Fernández 1984).

If utilization of services is related to the socio-economic characteristics of the user, the impact of service availability will possibly be eliminated by introducing socio-economic controls, so that the above findings are merely indicative of the differences in utilization of the services.

Note

1. This chapter does not cover the experience from the household surveys which collected information for either direct or indirect estimation of mortality. See chapter 4 for a comparison of household and individual survey results.

33

The Collection and Analysis of Community Data

John B. Casterline

33.1 Introduction

Community data have occupied an eccentric position within the World Fertility Survey programme. Fewer than half of the participating countries chose to collect community data, and in these countries (with two exceptions) the community survey was restricted to rural areas. In a programme criticized in some quarters for enforcing a standardized approach in varying social and demographic settings, the community survey questionnaires stand out for their diversity. And, while the value of WFS data on fertility, the proximate determinants of fertility, and infant mortality are now unquestioned, the community data have satisfied few analysts. Some analysts see no compelling reasons for relating demographic behaviour to the community setting: the pertinent theories seem either poorly articulated, weakly grounded, or not relevant to major policy concerns. Other analysts, who regard an understanding of the social, economic and cultural setting as fundamental to an understanding of demographic behaviour, find the WFS community data uninformative about the basic factors of interest.

The returns from analysis of the WFS community data have not yet matched expectations, but they have been far from negligible. In this chapter we will argue that a growing body of research incorporating the community data is yielding intriguing and important findings. This is a direct consequence of a more sober appraisal of the potential value of these data. Community data of the type collected in the WFS do not provide a basis for testing global hypotheses about demographic determinants. Nor do they offer a complete portrait of community settings, and thus in no sense substitute for intensive community studies. Only a modest set of propositions can be tested with these data, but some of these propositions are directly relevant to basic theoretical and policy concerns.

The hypotheses which can be addressed with community data fall within a general class of problems for which individual data alone are clearly inadequate. Demographic theory or policy interventions often posit, either explicitly or implicitly, that individual behaviour is conditioned by features of the community setting. We identify here three sets of issues characterized by this premise, without attempting to elaborate on them or evaluate the plausibility of the underlying arguments:

1 Effects of the provision of family planning and health services on fertility and mortality. It is difficult to exaggerate the significance of these topics from

either theoretical or policy standpoints. By their very nature, they are most appropriately examined empirically by linking information on the availability of services in geographical localities with individual experiences (such as use of contraception and child survival rates).

2 Relationships between economic and social opportunities and fertility. We refer here to a diverse set of propositions. Many theories of fertility change explicitly refer to structural changes whose locus is at a higher level of aggregation than the individual or household (although ramifications for individuals or households are the essence of the ultimate effect). Examples of such changes include such development efforts, often government-sponsored, as improved transportation, electrification, and extension of schooling; expansion of employment opportunities, for men, women and children; and transformation of the normative context — the most elusive feature of the social setting to measure but the feature with perhaps the most profound and pervasive influence on reproductive behaviour.

3 Relationships among the three basic demographic variables, namely fertility, mortality and migration. It is common to argue, on theoretical grounds, that the three variables are not independent. For example, a basic proposition in demographic transition theory is that fertility decisions are influenced by the expected probability of infant and child survival (with perceived community levels of mortality serving as one basis for formulating expectations). Levels of migration can also affect fertility decisions. Emigration of some community members will increase the knowledge of other community members about distant economic opportunities (Hugo 1985). It will also alter competition for local economic opportunities. Both of these economic effects of migration can influence fertility decisions. In addition, migration can have significant impacts on marriage markets. Changes in fertility and mortality, and the relative timing of the changes, generate changes in the age structure, which themselves affect economic opportunities (and thus fertility) and marriage markets. The nature of these relationships and others are not conveniently explored through analysis confined to the individual level alone. At issue are the *consequences* of *aggregate* demographic changes on household and individual decisions.

By their very nature, these research problems cannot be satisfactorily addressed with individual-level data alone. Community data of the type collected in WFS surveys will often not be appropriate either. An important issue in this regard is the definition of community. WFS community surveys have in every country collected data about small geographical localities, normally defined on an administrative basis. Thus, throughout this chapter we use the term 'community' with this definition in mind. For some topics, a larger geographical unit is more relevant: for example, larger units may be more appropriate when the concern is measurement of economic opportunities or cultural contexts. Moreover, for some purposes geographical criteria alone are not sufficient: the salient groups may be defined by ethnicity or kinship memberships which cut across conventional geographical boundaries (Hobcraft 1981). Nevertheless, the local community is the context for most social and economic activity, especially in traditional rural societies or where levels of geographical mobility are low. Furthermore, it is reasonable to assume that spatial proximity will ordinarily be an important determinant of the utilization of social services. For these reasons, community survey data can contribute to our understanding of the determinants of demographic behaviour.

A final question remains: with appropriate data on aggregate units, why carry out analysis at the individual level? There is a long tradition in demography of aggregate-level analysis, which has provided major insights. One can envisage addressing most of the research problems formulated above in aggregate-level analysis. What do we gain by mixing individual- and aggregate-level data (i.e. multilevel analysis)?

There are at least three compelling reasons for using individual-level analysis to test propositions about effects of aggregate-level variables. First, a practical consideration: for most countries we do not possess suitable measures for aggregate units of the dependent variables of interest, including fertility, contraceptive use, and infant mortality. Measures can be calculated from survey data by aggregation, but this represents inefficient use of the survey data as under most sample designs the aggregate measures are subject to substantial sampling error. Secondly, demographic behaviour is powerfully associated with such factors as age, union duration, and parity. Because the effects of these are often complex (and, in particular, non-linear), it is difficult to control for them properly in aggregate-level analysis. Thirdly, and most important, there are strong reasons for supposing that the effects of community factors differ among individuals, according to characteristics such as stage in reproductive career, socio-economic status, fertility aspirations, and so on. Consider, for example, the likely impact of service provision (family planning or health): certain types of community members will be more *motivated* to make use of services, and certain types will be more *able* to make use of services (where financial costs or other barriers exist). Equally, the structure of services, intentionally or not, may determine which individuals make use of the services; ascertaining the extent to which this is so is a crucial exercise in programme evaluation. The general point here is that the effects of community factors are not uniform, but rather are conditional on a variety of individual characteristics. If this generalization applies — and both theory and empirical evidence suggest it does — then the essential processes of interest can only be captured through a multilevel approach, in which the interactions among individual and community factors are explicitly modelled. Analysis at the aggregate level alone is not misdirected but risks missing relationships which offer significant insights about the underlying processes at work. Thus, although programme targets are ordinarily set in terms of community levels (of contraceptive prevalence, for example), differential impact according to individual characteristics is an indication of programme strengths and weaknesses and can provide clues about needed improvements in programme structure.

In proposing the collection of community data, Freedman (1974) emphasized the importance of examining interactions between individual and community characteristics. As we will note when reviewing the research with WFS community data, analysts have often neglected to model these interactions, but in a few instances attention to them has paid dividends.

There is a strong case, then, for augmenting individual survey data with information on the localities in which respondents reside. Our theory posits that demographic behaviour is responsive to social, economic, and normative features of the setting. The major policy efforts in recent decades have implicitly assumed that the accessibility of health and social services affects fertility and mortality. In the remainder of this chapter, we first describe the WFS efforts to collect community data and suggest improved methods of data collection. We then review the findings from analysis of the WFS data. In a final section, we summarize the WFS experience and reflect on its implications.

33.2 Community survey design and data collection

The sample

Community data were collected in 17 WFS surveys: Cameroon, Ivory Coast, Mauritania, Nigeria, Egypt, Sudan, Jordan, Syria, Bangladesh, Pakistan, Republic of Korea, Malaysia, Philippines, Thailand, Ecuador, Mexico and Peru. With the exceptions of Cameroon and Mexico, the community survey was restricted to rural areas. In Indonesia, community data obtained from administrative records were linked to the WFS data and served in place of a community survey (see Freedman, Khoo and Supraptilah 1981). In several countries where community data were collected as part of the WFS survey, analysts have augmented these data with data from other sources: Bangladesh (Alauddin 1979); the Philippines (Casterline and Engracia 1984); Ecuador (Borja 1985); and Peru (Bernedo 1984; Young, Edmonston and Andes 1983).

General practice was to take the sampling cluster as the 'community'. We suspect this was a sensible choice in most countries. Most often the sampling clusters were census enumeration districts, or segments thereof (see chapter 12). These ordinarily coincided with administrative boundaries, and, as such, they represented the most conveniently identified units approximating natural areas of social and economic interaction. In addition, other data on these formal administrative units were often available – census data, for example – which could be relatively easily recorded as part of the WFS community survey (this occurred in Egypt and Republic of Korea). Finally, the use of formal units facilitated the community survey interview in several respects: definition of community boundaries was fairly straightforward, and officials to serve as respondents could be readily identified.

These advantages, obviously, did not exist in all countries. Census enumeration districts were not always well-recognized political or social units. Where this was so, certainly the boundaries of daily social and economic interaction rarely coincided perfectly with the administrative units: for some types of activities the discrepancy may have been substantial. And where the units represented meaningful social and economic units, the independence of activities in one community from those in adjacent communities varied; the analysis, however, often implicitly assumes a high degree of independence. Topography is of particular relevance here. In countries like the Philippines and Peru, rural communities are relatively isolated due to natural barriers such as mountains and water (Casterline and Engracia 1984; Tienda 1983), whereas rural villages in Egypt are concentrated in a small area of land with relatively good transport links to other villages and towns (Casterline and Eid forthcoming). These considerations raise vexing problems for the collection of community data. More sensitive and flexible definitions of community boundaries would improve the validity of these data. For example, within the same community survey one might collect information about several different sizes and types of units. However, WFS experience provides no guidance as to the practicability of utilizing flexible and multiple definitions, for a variety of topics, in a one-visit community interview.

There is considerable variation across countries in the average population size and land area of the communities. Harpham and Scott (chapter 13) present summary statistics which indicate the amount of variation in population size. The author has collaborated on analysis of community survey data from Egypt and the Philippines: in the former country the median population size of the community survey villages was about 6000, while in the Philippines the rural *barangays* average about 1000 persons. There is also considerable within-country variation in community population size, as well as land area. Hence the existence of a school or health clinic in the community, for example, does not imply equivalent density of services in all communities surveyed. The average number of respondents per community also varied substantially across countries, from less than 10 to more than 50, with the majority of rural samples averaging between 15 and 30 respondents per cluster. Even within countries there is considerable variation in sample size per cluster, although the cross-national variability is somewhat greater (see chapter 13).

The cluster size and the number of clusters, related features of the sample design, both affect the analysis of community data. The principal objective in such analysis will ordinarily be identification of relationships between community characteristics and individual behaviour. For this objective, a larger number of communities strengthens the analyst's hand, as *between-community* variation is the primary focus. One hundred communities would seem an acceptable lower limit, with 150 or more desirable. Two counter considerations argue for fewer communities and a larger sample take per community. First, the individual survey data can provide useful community indicators (constructed by aggregation). Most investigators, in fact, have augmented the community survey data with indicators of this type (Alauddin 1979; Casterline and Eid forthcoming; Chayovan 1982; Nizamuddin 1979; Tienda 1983), and some investigators have relied entirely on community variables constructed by aggregation where community survey data were not collected (Lesthaeghe, Vanderhoeft, Becker and Kibet 1985). Clearly, aggregated individual data will be subject to sampling error and, depending on the type of measure, will be untrustworthy where the number of respondents in a community falls below 15 or 20. (Some measures are more defensible than others. Averages of responses to items which are thought to vary minimally within community – distance to a health clinic, for example – may provide precise estimates of the desired factor, whereas aggregation of items which by their nature are likely to vary – use of contraception, approval of abortion – will be subject to large sampling errors.) Secondly, some analysts are especially concerned with examining the variation in *within-community* relationships across communities. At issue are questions of the form: does the relationship between schooling and contraceptive use differ depending on the accessibility and quality of family planning services? One means of addressing this type of question is first-stage estimation of within-community relationships, and a second-stage analysis of between-community variation in the within-community relationships. This is the strategy adopted in the cross-national analysis of WFS data of Entwisle, Hermalin and Mason (1982). The statistical approach of Entwisle, Hermalin and Mason can be applied only if no community contains fewer respondents than the number of parameters in the equation to be estimated, and thus this approach requires rather large expected sample takes per community. The same objective can be accomplished, however, without recourse to separate community-by-community estimations by estimating individual-level equations containing community variables and interactions between individual and community variables (see Hermalin 1985). Hence a large number of respondents per community is not required.

Questionnaire content

Because of the substantial variation in community questionnaire content, a succinct summary of the commonalities and differences is almost impossible. Since many of the questionnaires apparently used the suggestions of Freedman (1974) as a point of departure, we can draw on his classification of community items, with some modification, to organize the review. (The reader is referred to Singh 1984a for further detail.)

A majority of items in most of the questionnaires asked for the proximity of the community to a set of amenities and services. To define proximity, some countries relied on distance, others on travel time, and others obtained both (the Philippines). Casterline and Engracia (1984) show that, in the case of the Philippines, distance and travel time are so highly correlated that the distinction can have little bearing on research findings. Mode of travel to amenities and services was also asked in many surveys, but to our knowledge little use has been made of this information, especially where travel time was also obtained. Finally, only one country, Nigeria, obtained information on the timing of the establishment of each facility (in those communities where the facility was present). (This information was obtained for selected facilities in a few other countries.)

Transportation. Proximity to the nearest 'centre' (administrative, market town, etc.) was obtained in all but three surveys (Nigeria, Ecuador, Peru). The type of road in the community (unpaved or paved, for example) was ascertained in all but three surveys (Mauritania, Republic of Korea, Thailand).

Communication. Here we refer to amenities such as postal service, telephone, telegraph, radio, television, newspaper, and cinema. Only the Ivory Coast excluded these types of items. With the exception of telegraph, almost all of these items were included in the community questionnaire for most countries.

Government and other institutions. Most surveys asked about the proximity to a police station. The proximity to some type of government office was ascertained in all countries except Nigeria, Bangladesh, Philippines, Ecuador and Peru, and in these countries this information usually was implicit in other information obtained (e.g. distance to *thana* headquarters in Bangladesh). Fewer than half of the countries asked about the existence of or proximity to courts of law and various types of co-operatives.

Health and related facilities. All countries obtained information about the proximity to more than one type of health facility or health personnel. Inquiry about hospitals and health clinics, qualified midwives and pharmacies was most common. Egypt is an exceptional case, as the community survey collected detailed information from the local health clinic about matters such as the staffing (number of days qualified personnel were present, and their qualifications) and distribution of services (numbers of vaccinations and pill cycles given out in calendar year 1979, for example).

Family-planning services. Nine countries inquired directly about the proximity to family planning services (Nigeria, Egypt, Jordan, Bangladesh, Republic of Korea, Malaysia, Pakistan, Philippines, Mexico). It might seem surprising that explicit questions about family-planning services were not asked in some countries. The explanation is that in these countries either no family-planning programme existed at the time of the WFS survey, or all official family-planning services were provided through the health service network.

Schools. All 17 countries asked about the proximity to schools. Inquiry about primary and secondary schools was standard, as well as inquiry about other types of schools – for example, vocational schools. Three countries obtained data about levels of school attendance: Egypt, Republic of Korea, and Malaysia.

Agriculture. Ten countries gathered information about agricultural activity in the area. Included in this category are data on labour-force composition (by occupation or employment sector), land distribution, main crops grown, and existence of mechanical equipment.

Aspects of development. Under this rubric we classify a set of items which do not fall within any of the above categories. Fourteen countries (Ivory Coast, Syria, and Jordan are the exceptions) included items which pertain to other aspects of modernization. For example, all 14 asked about electrification and sources of drinking water. Only four countries, however, asked about sewer systems. Seven countries included items on the proximity to market shops.

Other. A fascinating number of items, often used only in one country, fall outside the above categories. Their inclusion in the questionnaires suggests that effort was made to adapt the questionnaire to the local setting. Three countries asked about ethnic or language composition of the community. Two asked about the existence of specific types of formal social groups. Two included items about levels of migration. Registered numbers of births and deaths occurring during the five years preceding the survey were obtained for each community in Egypt. The availability of modern consumer items in the community was ascertained in Nigeria. The proximity to 10 types of skilled tradesmen was obtained in Bangladesh. The Bangladesh survey also asked about the occurrence of recent natural disasters and epidemics, and the resulting loss of life. In Ivory Coast, the midwife of the village was asked about traditional customs (weaning, post-partum abstinence, contraception, female circumcision and so on).

The relevance of some of the community questionnaire items to theories about the determinants of fertility and mortality can be questioned. It certainly seems doubtful that the potential utility of the information for testing plausible hypotheses was carefully considered at the questionnaire design stage. Furthermore, in the community data with which this author is familiar, the responses to many items show almost no distribution: the rural communities were homogeneous with respect to these characteristics, and thus they have minimal analytic utility. As a consequence of these shortcomings, which reflect lack of thought about the role of community data in further analysis or unfamiliarity with the society (Cain 1985), many of the items have proved awkward to integrate into analysis of fertility or mortality. (Poor wording of the questionnaire items has been a further problem in some instances. See Chayovan (1982: appendix B) for the case of Thailand.) The community data are also of potential value in their own right, offering a portrait of the accessibility of community amenities and services to rural residents. In many developing countries such descriptive data are not available from other sources. But several of the shortcomings noted here also detract from the descriptive value of the data. These experiences lend support to the recommendation of Freedman (1985) that future community surveys be designed by a team of demographers and social scientists who, ideally, work together through the design, fieldwork and analysis phases.

Fieldwork and quality of data

The fielding of the community surveys is not well documented. To our knowledge, in all countries the community survey was conducted while the individual survey team was interviewing in the community. Ordinarily the team supervisor served as the interviewer and the village headman as the respondent (e.g., in the Philippines over 80 per cent of the respondents were *barangay* chairmen, and most of the remainder were *barangay* council members: Casterline and Engracia 1984). As interviewing teams usually remained in communities for several days, the supervisor had a limited opportunity to familiarize himself with the community and to become acquainted with the village leaders. A recommended procedure was to fill out the community survey questionnaire during the final day in the village (see, for example, for Bangladesh, Ministry of Health and Population Control 1978).

There have been only a few efforts to assess the validity of community data. In Bangladesh, a post-enumeration survey was carried out in 54 of the 160 villages in the community survey. The results are presented in an appendix of the First Country Report for the entire survey (Ministry of Health and Population Control 1978). Most of the community items appear reasonably reliable, but there is an expected tendency for the two sets of responses to differ most when facilities and amenities are (apparently) more distant (Al-Kabir 1984). In the Philippines, the 1980 census included a *barangay* schedule, completed for all *barangays* in the country. Some of the items on this schedule resemble the items in the 1978 community survey questionnaire used in the WFS survey. Casterline and Engracia (1984) compare the responses in the two surveys and find a rather high level of discrepancy, even on items as seemingly straightforward as presence of health centres and schools. Some of the discrepancy is probably explained by variation in the wording of questionnaire items and by changes over the two-year period between 1978 and 1980. The authors conclude, however, that much of the discrepancy must be due to differential knowledge of the *barangay* on the part of respondents and differing interpretations of similar items. Chayovan and Knodel (1985) report pre-tests of community questionnaires in Thailand in which multiple respondents from a few villages, interviewed during the same survey visit, provided markedly different responses about the existence of or proximity to community services. There is growing evidence, then, that collection of valid and reliable community data requires more care than previously assumed. We provide below a set of suggestions for improving community data collection.

Recommendations for survey design and data collection

Some of the recommendations presented here repeat points made earlier, but for convenience all the recommendations are listed together. We draw heavily on the recent work of Chayovan and Knodel (1985) in Thailand.

Sample design.
1 The number of sampled communities should exceed 100; 75–80 represents a minimum acceptable number, and 150 a more desirable number. If community data are collected in urban areas (see below), this guideline applies to urban and rural areas separately, as often the analysis will be stratified by urban-rural locality.

2 The number of respondents per community is of less concern, above a minimum which we would set at 15.

Questionnaire design.

3 The questionnaire must be developed by individuals familiar with the structure of the society. Substantial adaptation of questionnaires developed elsewhere is strongly encouraged.

4 Because questionnaires must be adapted to fit local settings, extensive pretesting is essential.

5 Proximity to amenities and services should be measured in travel time alone. Mode of transport is superfluous information in most settings.

6 Information on proximity to alternative outlets for those services of particular analytic interest (medical, family planning, educational), as opposed to information on the proximity of the nearest outlet only, will permit development of more sensitive indicators of accessibility. (See Hermalin and Chayovan 1984.)

7 Wherever applicable, information on change over time in community conditions should be collected. In the case of services and amenities, this can be accomplished by asking the date of their establishment in the community, or whether they existed as of some reference date (e.g. five or ten years before the survey). Reconstruction for dates in the past of conditions of accessibility is more difficult and probably cannot be achieved successfully in a WFS-type community survey.

8 Where a recent census provides tabulations at the community level, data on the composition of the community according to demographic characteristics (age, sex, and marital status), ethnicity or religion, and economic activity (occupation) should be recorded.

9 Data on the utilization of social services (clinics, schools) should be collected, in particular where administrative records provide this information in easily accessible form and the records are considered accurate and complete. However, without data on the population size by age and sex (as proposed in 8), this information will be of limited use.

10 Items on the characteristics of social services in addition to their proximity – such as staffing, hours, cost, supplies, attitudes of staff – should be considered for inclusion in the questionnaire, especially where it is feasible to collect this information directly through visits to the facilities.

11 Many of the usual community questionnaire items can be administered in urban areas, in reference to neighbourhoods or blocks. This is strongly recommended. Some items will be inapplicable, some will require modification for the urban setting, and some will be applicable to urban areas but not rural areas. Hence, it may be sensible to develop a separate urban questionnaire. Data processing and analysis will be facilitated, however, if the rural and urban questionnaires overlap to the fullest extent possible.

Data collection.

12 Those who administer the community questionnaire should be specifically trained for this task. Those responsible for development of the questionnaire (see 3) should be involved in the training.

13 High-quality interviewing is more likely to be achieved if small teams (two or three individuals each) are assigned to this task alone, perhaps travelling independently of the main survey team. This design permits more intensive training and data collection without distraction by other responsibilities. (Individuals carrying out both individual and community survey duties will normally find that the pressure of individual survey work overwhelms attention to the community survey.) Creation of special community survey teams also increases the opportunity for involvement by those responsible for development of the questionnaire, certainly during training and possibly during the fieldwork as well (acting as team supervisors, for example). Utilization of special teams will ordinarily be more costly, however.

14 Because few, if any, community members are likely to be well informed about the full range of community features inquired about, the community survey should draw on more than one respondent per community. An attractive design is to use a group interview, which permits immediate reconciliation of the inevitable discrepant responses (Chayovan and Knodel 1985).

15 Time and resources should be allotted to visits to local service outlets (e.g. health, or family planning, clinics); see 9 and 10 above.

16 Data from other statistical sources (e.g. censuses) can be recorded in a separate operation; see 8 above.

33.3 Findings from analysis of WFS community data

From section 33.2 we conclude that WFS community surveys were not well designed and that the fieldwork was not always carried out with the necessary care. This places us in an awkward position for reviewing the findings from the analysis of these data. Failure to identify expected relationships could be the consequence of errors in the data, as random errors will attenuate relationships. There is, of course, a converse danger that errors account for some of the significant relationships which have emerged. Nevertheless, a substantial amount of analysis has been completed, and it would be irresponsible to ignore the findings from this work. In particular, the findings provide indications of which types of community survey items are likely to prove most useful analytically.

The review of findings is organized according to the three research problems identified in section 33.1: relationships between service provision and demographic behaviour; relationships between economic and social opportunity structures and fertility; and relationships between fertility, mortality, and migration.

Service provision

Two bodies of work are of interest here: analyses of the relationship between the accessibility of contraceptive services and contraceptive use, and of the relationship between the accessibility of health services and infant mortality. We review the two in turn, but first consider the expected nature of these relationships.

It goes without saying that services will show no impact unless they are utilized. Indeed, one might argue that the research question of immediate interest is whether accessibility is related to utilization, and secondarily whether utilization has any effect on behaviour (fertility, mortality). Most WFS surveys collected no information on utilization of services. Exceptions are items in the family-planning module of the individual survey in some countries on sources of most recent supplies of contraceptives, and information on pre-natal and post-natal medical care of the most recent child, gathered in a number of Latin American and West African countries.

Most analysts, therefore, have examined effects of proximity to services with no reference to their utilization. One can argue that this approach is fully justified: the basic policy question must be, does greater density of services show any impact (on contraceptive use or mortality), whatever the mechanism of the effect? But obviously this approach is naïve unless supplemented by a recognition that other unmeasured factors can act as critical obstacles to service impact. To begin with, geographical proximity is but one determinant of service utilization, although surely it is a fundamental one. (Moreover, with a bit of thought one soon realizes that the determination of geographical proximity is not at all straightforward, especially where different types of service outlets are available and where respondents have multiple·choices among outlets of the same type. For an illustration of the implications of alternative definitions of geographical proximity provided by community data from Thailand, see Hermalin and Chayovan 1984.) Other aspects of services which may influence their utilization include financial costs, hours of service, waiting time for services, quality of personnel, stock of necessary supplies, and so on. These other aspects have not been measured in WFS community surveys, but clearly must be candidates for inclusion in future surveys. Furthermore, the impact of services is a function of more than simple utilization. Clients must properly follow instructions for use of supplies received (oral contraceptives, medications). And, in the case of mortality and morbidity, when the standard of living or of nutrition falls below certain levels the impact of some medical therapies may be minimal.

These considerations, and others, temper our expectation of observing clear-cut relationships between proximity to services and demographic variables. Those assessing the impact of primary health-care programmes are increasingly aware of the complexities involved (Gwatkin, Wilcox and Wray 1980; Mosley 1983).

Even if we were interested solely in assessing the impact of geographical proximity to services on fertility or mortality, there are pitfalls in the analysis permitted by WFS data which are not well recognized. Consider the matter of family-planning services and contraceptive use. The underlying hypothesis is that the probability of utilization of the services (e.g. adoption of contraception, or continuation of use) during an interval of time is positively associated with the proximity to services. Stated in this fashion, the hypothesis requires measurement of adoption/continuation rates over a period of time, for fixed conditions of service accessibility. This is only approximated by relating cross-sectional levels of accessibility and current or ever-use. Undermining this approach are two plausible sets of circumstances: first, communities with equally proximate services may have enjoyed them for differing lengths of time; and, second, the distribution of services may be associated with exogenously determined levels of use. The former danger is widely recognized, but the latter has been largely ignored. Many health and family-planning programmes, however, are targeted to areas most in need, inducing a *negative* association between the density of public services and the prevalence of use. Artifactual relationships like this are a common hazard in research linking community features with individual behaviour: the analyst must constantly be alert to the possibility that elements of the community setting are in part a response to average levels of individual behaviour (Blalock 1985). An illustration of the problem is provided by Eid and Casterline's (forthcoming) analysis of infant and child mortality in rural Egypt. The authors conclude that it is likely that government policies of establishing basic clinics, staffed by young doctors in short-term government service, in the least developed villages is the explanation for an estimated negative relationship between the proximity to health services and levels of mortality.

Information on the length of time since the establishment of services would obviously improve the utility of the community data. The analyst could then estimate models of the form (Brown 1981):

$$Y = aP + bT + cPT$$

where Y is the demographic response (contraceptive use, probability of infant survival), P is proximity to the services, T is length of time since establishment, and a, b, and c are estimated parameters, all of which should be positive (remembering that proximity is the inverse of distance). The interaction term PT is required because the impact of service accessibility will ordinarily increase over time (e.g. little impact may be apparent after six months, but considerable impact after five years, since contraceptive adoption is a cumulative process). Direct information on the respondent's behaviour during a fixed period of time would eliminate the need for the T terms in the above equation, although data on T will be required to determine the service provision conditions during the specified period of time. For example, if one knows which services were in place two years before the survey, as well as which were established during that period, and one also knows the timing of first use of contraception (an item included in some WFS surveys), a straightforward analysis of the effect of proximity on the probability of adoption during those two years can be carried out.

The second problem identified above — a prior association between the demographic response and the density of services which is not the consequence of the effects of services — is not easily resolved. The optimal strategy is to estimate relationships with controls for the factors influencing the non-random distribution of services. Measures of these factors are difficult to generate or collect, however, so the analyst will usually be forced to rely on proxy measures. We cannot be optimistic this approach will eliminate the problem. Where there is reason to suspect that this type of bias is large, a strong case exists for the adoption of an experimental design.

Taking all these conditions into account, we are forced to conclude that an analysis of the demographic impact of service provision using WFS data is very likely to yield a mixed picture. We now turn to the findings.

Contraceptive use. Tsui (1985) provides a thorough review of these findings, and the reader is referred to her paper for details.

The relationship between accessibility and use of family-planning services has been examined using WFS community data from eight countries: Egypt, Bangladesh, Republic of Korea, Malaysia, Pakistan, Philippines, Thailand and Mexico. In Bangladesh, the community measure is the frequency of health and family-planning worker visits; in Thailand, frequency of health and family-planning worker visits and proximity to outlets are both measured. Elsewhere, the community variable measures proximity to service outlets. Expected positive effects have been identified in Bangladesh (Alauddin 1979; Tsui *et al.* 1981a; 1981b), Republic of Korea (Tsui *et al.* 1981a; 1981b), the Philippines (Engracia 1985), and Mexico (Tsui *et al.* 1981a; 1981b). No significant effects are found in Egypt (Casterline and Eid forthcoming), Malaysia (Mason and Palan 1978), Pakistan (Nizamuddin 1979), and Thailand (Chayovan 1982). It is interesting that the significant effects emerge where the estimated equations contain fewer terms. Tsui *et al.* and Engracia, for example, consider effects of single measures of accessibility of services and community development, with controls for a small number of individual socio-economic and demographic factors. A related analysis using non-WFS data from Thailand (Entwisle, Hermalin, Kamnuansilpa and Chamratrithirong 1984) also finds positive effects of greater accessibility (in this case conditioned by age and fertility preferences of the respondent). In analysis utilizing community data, adjusted effects from equations including large numbers of community variables are often unstable because the community variables tend to be highly correlated with each other (Casterline 1985). This may partially account for the failure to find significant positive effects in Pakistan and Thailand, but does not explain the outcomes in Egypt and Malaysia.

It should also be noted that a larger number of studies have utilized only individual-level data to examine the relationship between accessibility and use. Where the family-planning module was used, respondents were asked the distance or travel time to the nearest outlet. Most of the studies using these data find some effects in the expected direction, but they are not always strong and are severely attenuated by controls for other factors (Brackett 1981; Chidambaram and Mastropoalo 1981; Jones 1984; Rodríguez 1978). These studies are subject to the criticism that the direction of causality is ambiguous: non-users may report greater distances to outlets because of ignorance about the actual distance to the nearest outlet, or in order to rationalize non-use. There is, however, little evidence supporting this argument. Casterline and Engracia (1984) compare individual and community survey measures of accessibility in the Philippines separately for users and non-users. Among respondents at the same distance from an outlet according to the community data, reported knowledge of an outlet is substantially lower for non-users. But among those women knowing of an outlet, reported proximity to the outlet does not vary by contraceptive use (again controlling distance according to the community data). Despite the lack of evidence, the danger that 'perceived' accessibility may be contaminated by past utilization of services provides a strong argument for investigating this topic with data collected in a community survey.

A major conclusion which has emerged from the analysis using individual data alone is that it is essential to distinguish availability and use of specific methods (Chidambaram and Mastropoalo 1981). Some methods require more frequent re-supply (pills, condoms), and thus geographical accessibility is potentially an important variable. Moreover, the distance to outlets offering the various methods typically will differ, with condoms, for example, available in far more locations than the IUD or sterilization. In recognition of the need for method-specificity, the revised family-planning module inquired about travel time to outlets method-by-method (Jones 1984). Regrettably, with the exception of Egypt, none of the community surveys inquired about accessibility to outlets for specific methods, or, alternatively, asked about the availability of specific methods in the nearest outlet. While, in principle, method availability is determined by the type of outlet in most countries, in practice, method availability cannot be assumed and should be ascertained through the survey. Hence, we are aware of no analysis of WFS community data which has considered method-specific availability. Several analysts have examined the impact of accessibility of family-planning services on use of different types of methods. The most common approach is to distinguish efficient and inefficient methods, following the WFS definition, with use of the efficient methods presumably more dependent on proximity to outlets (Alauddin 1979; Mason and Palan 1978; Engracia 1985). In general, the results do not differ according to type of method. As this does not mesh with previous analyses of individual-level data alone, the need for more detail on the types of methods offered by outlets is emphasized.

Infant and child mortality. The relationship between the probability of infant and child survival and accessibility of health services has been examined with WFS data from eight countries: Cameroon, Ivory Coast, Egypt, Jordan, Bangladesh, Philippines, Ecuador and Peru. (See Al-Kabir 1984; Bernedo 1984; Edmonston and Andes 1983b; Young, Edmonston and Andes 1983; Borja 1985; Casterline and Engracia 1984, and Engracia 1983; Edmonston 1983; Eid and Casterline forthcoming; Njeck 1984; Tiapani 1984.) As there has been as yet no effort at a synthesis of the findings from these studies, we review them in some detail. The reports for Cameroon, Ivory Coast and Peru (Bernedo) are not yet completed, and thus we report.no findings from the Ivory Coast and Peru (Bernedo) studies and preliminary findings only from the Cameroon study.

The studies have many features in common. The probabilities of survival at different age intervals are considered separately: infant and child mortality are always distinguished, and usually the neo-natal and post-neonatal periods are also distinguished. Effects of the accessibility of health services are estimated with controls for characteristics of the child and mother and, in most of the studies, other characteristics of the community. (Except where otherwise noted, we report *net* effects.) Finally, where the data permit, the effects of different types of health services are examined individually; the analyses for Bangladesh and the Philippines exemplify this approach.

The importance of these distinctions is vividly illustrated by the findings from the Philippines. The authors examine neo-natal and post-neonatal mortality. Exploratory analysis reveals that for neo-natal mortality the important proximity criterion is whether or not the facility or personnel are located within the *barangay*, whereas for post-neonatal mortality the threshold distance is one hour of travel time. This is a sensible outcome: in the first weeks of life infants need attention more immediately, and the mother is less able to travel. When children reach the post-neonatal period, care need not be so immediate and travel is more feasible, so that facilities within an hour's travel time of the *barangay* are all relatively accessible. The types of services which show significant effects also differ. In the neo-natal period, presence in the *barangay* of a midwife or nurse, a primary health-care centre, a hospital, or a pharmacy are associated with lower mortality rates. The authors regard the effects of presence of a pharmacy as difficult to interpret, but the effects of presence of a midwife, primary health-care centre, and hospital are understandable. In the post-neonatal period, proximity to a midwife is unrelated to the probability of survival, but proximity to a health worker or a hospital is associated with better survival chances. Again the authors find the results, in particular the disappearance of effects of the midwife and the emergence of effects of the health worker, sensible.

Most of the studies have examined effects of medical personnel and health facilities separately. Although this distinction is not always meaningful — in rural areas most personnel will be attached to health facilities — we organize our review of the findings in terms of this distinction. The medical personnel most likely to influence survival during the neo-natal period are birth attendants. The community data for Cameroon, Egypt and the Philippines included items on the proximity to midwives trained in modern medical techniques. Significant net effects on neo-natal mortality are estimated in both Egypt and the Philippines. In the Philippines, the effect interacts with education of the mother: it is pronounced for mothers with primary or higher schooling but is not evident for uneducated mothers. The authors interpret this as a reflection of differentials in reliance on modern midwives as birth attendants, reasoning that less educated women will more often rely on the traditional birth attendants present in most *barangays*. (A similar interaction with literacy of the mother does not emerge in Egypt.) In Cameroon, unadjusted neo-natal rates are related to the presence of a midwife, as expected, but the effect disappears with controls for other variables.

Beyond the neo-natal period, there is little evidence that survival chances are affected by proximity to qualified medical personnel. This conclusion applies to doctors and nurses in Cameroon, medical personnel per capita in Egypt, doctors in Bangladesh (excepting significant associations with the probability of survival between the ages of one and five), and doctors and nurses in the Philippines. In the Philippines, however, travel time to a health worker (a category referring to paramedics with less training than doctors) is significantly related to post-neonatal mortality for certain socio-economic strata, as noted above.

With the important exception of effects on neo-natal mortality of proximity to trained midwives, then, the WFS findings provide little evidence of beneficial impact of the density of *medical personnel* on levels of infant and child mortality. It must be noted, however, that few WFS surveys inquired about proximity to the less trained personnel which are basic components of extensive primary health-care systems. Perhaps this was because such personnel are normally closely attached to clinics or health stations, which were asked about. In the one instance where such personnel were singled out — health workers in the Philippines — expected effects emerged.

The impact of proximity to *health facilities* was examined in all the studies. We review the results from each country. In Cameroon, neo-natal mortality is lowest in communities where there is neither a hospital nor a health centre, but post-neonatal mortality shows a reverse pattern of lowest rates where there is a hospital and highest rates where neither a hospital nor health centre are present. Infant mortality as a whole is lowest where hospitals are nearby (16 per cent of the births analysed). In Egypt, there are no significant net mortality differentials between villages with, and those without, at least one health clinic. In Jordan, infant mortality is lower in rural communities containing and MCH clinic or a pharmacy, while mortality at ages one and two is lower where any of the measured health facilities are present (health, MCH, or family-planning clinics; pharmacy; hospital). In Bangladesh, proximity to family-planning clinics (which at the time of the survey provided maternal and child health care) is associated with lower neo-natal rates, and proximity to hospitals and family-planning clinics with lower rates at ages one to four years. No effects of proximity to a government dispensary are found. In the Philippines, proximity to a hospital is associated with lower neo-natal and post-neonatal rates. A composite health facilities indicator (measuring travel time to the nearest hospital, primary health-care centre, or dispensary) shows a similar relationship with post-neonatal rates. In Ecuador, a single health facilities indicator, measuring the number of health facilities in the community, is significantly related to child mortality (ages one to four) but not infant mortality. In Peru, however, a similar measure shows no association with survival probabilities. Among these six countries, then, significant effects are estimated in four countries, but not in Egypt and Peru. It may be relevant that in both of these countries the median population size of the rural communities was over 5000: in this circumstance, presence or absence of health facilities in the community is a weak indicator of availability of services to households.

While the sample of countries is small, and the health facility indicators diverse, some common themes emerge. Effects on post-neonatal and child mortality are more pronounced than on neo-natal mortality: this is as expected. Maternal and child health-care facilities are exceptions: these show impact on neo-natal mortality (Bangladesh) and overall infant mortality (Jordan and Bangladesh). Facilities such as dispensaries and pharmacies, on the other hand, are rarely associated with survival probabilities.

The WFS findings, on balance, confirm the view that more dense networks of health facilities can have beneficial impacts on infant and child mortality. This conclusion does not apply to all types of facilities and all types of settings but we would not expect such a simple finding: health service availability is one of a complex of factors bearing on infant and child survival, perhaps among the less potent, and different types of interventions should be expected to have different magnitudes of effects (Mosley 1983). Nor, indeed, would uniform effects be as informative for policy purposes as a mixed outcome.

These studies are handicapped by our ignorance about patterns of service utilization. We can assume that often there are significant differences among community members in the capacity and willingness to make use of facilities. Fernández (1984) documents striking socio-economic differentials in pre-natal and post-natal health care in five Latin American countries. All of the analyses reviewed above include controls for socio-economic characteristics (usually maternal education). To the extent that utilization is a function of these characteristics, the impact of service availability will be eliminated by these controls. (In Ecuador and Peru, in fact, the control for maternal education has a particularly devastating effect on unadjusted effects of proximity to health facilities.) One means of taking account of this possibility is to model interactions between socio-economic characteristics and proximity to services: if utilization is concentrated among certain socio-economic strata, the estimated effects of health services should be confined to these strata. In the Philippines analysis, such interactions were tested and several emerged as significant; in Egypt and Bangladesh, however, similar interactions failed to show meaningful patterns.

Before concluding this section, we should note that several of the studies consider other community variables with plausible relationships to infant and child mortality. In Cameroon, no significant impacts of general health campaigns nor of vaccination campaigns are observed, but community water improvement projects (applicable to 14 per cent of births) are associated with substantially lower child mortality. In Bangladesh, the number of visits to the village by health and sanitation workers during the year preceding the survey shows no net relationship with infant or child mortality. Provision of piped water in the community was an item included in many of the community schedules, and several of the analyses examine its effects. This factor is better considered at the household level, however, and for a review of these findings see chapter 32. The authors conclude that piped water in the household is rarely associated with lower mortality rates, whereas presence of a toilet often shows expected effects.

Economic and social opportunity structures and fertility

We are interested here in considering the contribution of community data to the investigation of some of the major theoretical propositions in fertility research. This cannot be adequately accomplished in a brief review. The author has elsewhere attempted a more comprehensive review (Casterline 1985), on which we rely in this discussion. We consider seven sets of propositions, and summarize the evidence concerning each.

Agricultural development. The mechanization of agriculture is assumed to reduce the labour value of children, and thereby the desire for large families. The expected effects of introduction of other modern methods (high-yielding grain varieties, chemical fertilizers) are more ambiguous. Effects in the predicted direction do not emerge in analyses of data from Bangladesh (Alauddin 1979), Pakistan (Nizamuddin 1979), and Thailand (Chayovan 1982). Casterline and Eid (forthcoming), however, observe negative effects of agricultural mechanization on fertility aspirations in rural Egypt.

Industrial development. Transformation of the economy away from agriculture is expected to reduce the labour value of children and increase their cost. Industrial development may also generate employment opportunities for women which compete with childbearing. Alauddin (1979) finds the proportion of males employed in agriculture unrelated to family size desires in rural Bangladesh, but Casterline and Eid (forthcoming) obtain significant effects of the same variable on two fertility preference measures and current use of contraception in rural Egypt. Chayovan (1982) finds desired family size to be negatively associated with an index of industrial development in rural Thailand.

Village modernization and prosperity. The community indicators considered here are constructed from items on village electrification, presence of piped water, mail service, telephones, paved roads, and schools. Analysts have often termed the index which results from their combination a measure of 'level of development' of the community. Significant effects on contraceptive use are observed in Bangladesh, Republic of Korea, and Mexico (Tsui, Hogan, Teachman and Welti-Chanés 1981b), in the Philippines (Engracia, Mortel and Nartatez 1984), and, for completed fertility, in Peru (Tienda 1983). Electrification is a key item in the Philippines index (Engracia, Mortel and Nartatez 1984), but the presence of electricity in the village is unrelated to various aspects of reproductive behaviour in Syria (Alloush, Herting, Immerwahr, Maier and Pullum 1986) and in Thailand (Chayovan 1982). Finally, several analysts utilize the mean education level of the community as an indicator of development. Alauddin (1979) finds no effect of this measure on desired family size in Bangladesh, but Chayovan (1982) observes a relatively strong relationship in Thailand. Analysis of data from Peru (Tienda 1983) and Kenya (Lesthaeghe, Vanderhoeft, Becker and Kibet 1985) also reveals rather powerful effects on various aspects of reproduction. All the authors remark that the mean educational level probably reflects a diffuse set of underlying factors.

Schooling opportunities. Schooling makes child-rearing more expensive: usually there are direct and indirect costs. Moreover, as a vehicle for social mobility, it encourages parents to invest in fewer children of higher quality. Of possibly more fundamental importance, schooling may have complicated ramifications on generational relationships within the family, a theme developed by Caldwell in recent years (Caldwell 1982; see also Ryder 1983). Schools can also serve as channels for the promotion of Western ideals of family size.

Analyses of WFS community data offer intriguing findings on the relationship between schooling opportunities and reproductive behaviour. The proximity to schools shows no effects on fertility aspirations in Syria (Alloush, Herting, Immerwahr, Maier and Pullum 1986), Bangladesh (Alauddin 1979), Pakistan (Nizamuddin 1979), and Thailand (Chayovan 1982). The analyses for Pakistan and Thailand also fail to find effects on fertility. In Egypt (Casterline and Eid forthcoming), however, the proximity to a primary school is related to fertility aspirations and contraceptive use. In only two countries have analysts been able to consider effects of school attendance. Arguably this variable better measures variation in schooling opportunities, as distance is but one of the costs of schooling. There are conceptual problems, however, in modelling reproductive behaviour as a function of school attendance levels: attendance levels may respond to levels of fertility, or both may respond to related changes in generational relations. In Bangladesh, Alauddin (1979) finds a significant negative effect of village school attendance on desired family size. In Egypt, Casterline and Eid (forthcoming) identify powerful effects of school attendance levels on fertility aspirations and contraceptive use. To our knowledge, these findings are among the strongest empirical confirmations of the arguments advanced by Caldwell and others. It is a pity that WFS data do not permit replication of these analyses elsewhere.

Health services. Easily accessible health services provide opportunities for parents to invest in healthier children, with a concomitant increase in the costs of child-rearing. Both effects motivate fertility reduction. The WFS results provide only weak support for this argument. Alloush, Herter, Immerwahr, Maier and Pullum (1986) conclude that fertility preferences are not related to a summary index of the accessibility of health services. A large set of health and sanitation items are unrelated to desired family size in Bangladesh (Alauddin 1979). Similarly, fertility shows no association with health service indices in Malaysia (Mason and Palan 1978) or in Thailand (Chayovan 1982). In Egypt, however, presence of health clinics and the number of health personnel are both associated with several measures of fertility aspirations (Casterline and Eid forthcoming).

Community isolation. A long-standing hypothesis in fertility research is that expansion of communication and transportation networks, and the resulting breakdown of rural isolation, sets in motion changes which transform reproductive aspirations and behaviour. (See Casterline 1985 for further elaboration of this argument.) The WFS community data are designed to test this proposition, albeit on a cross-sectional basis. The hypothesized effects do not emerge in Egypt (Casterline and Eid forthcoming), Bangladesh (Alauddin 1979), Pakistan (Nizamuddin 1979), or Thailand (Chayovan 1982). A summary media index is strongly related to fertility preferences in rural Syria (Alloush, Herter, Immerwahr, Maier and Pullum 1986). More to the point, measures of geographical isolation show powerful effects on fertility preference in the Philippines (Casterline and Engracia 1984) and completed fertility in Peru (Tienda 1983). Rural isolation is a relevant concept in these two countries, due to their topography, and hence it is not surprising that here the expected effects emerge.

Social pressures. Many of the conventional assumptions about the social processes underlying fertility transition can only be tested in a multilevel approach. Assume, for example, that changes in fertility attitudes and behaviours of community members, neighbours, and kin modify the normative context for the reproductive decisions of individual couples. If so, then in modelling these individual decisions one must take into account the attitudes and behaviours of these other persons. If such social effects are substantial, one can describe a diffusion process in which normative change is an integral element in the societal process of adoption of newly available modern contraceptives, leading to fertility transition (Crook 1978). Research with WFS data has contributed little to the exploration of these themes. There has not been, for example, any systematic analysis of the relationship between ethnic homogeneity of communities and reproductive behaviour. However, effects of ethnicity and region of residence on contraception and fertility, net of controls for other variables, have emerged in several countries (e.g. Egypt, Philippines, Thailand; see review in Freedman 1985), and these may be the consequence of the social dynamics referred to above. Casterline (1982) derives from a similar line of reasoning the proposition that the intention to use contraception in the future (among never-users) will be positively associated with community levels of use, assuming that adoption by some community members reduces the social costs for others. Results for Indonesia, Philippines, and Thailand largely support the hypothesis, while effects in Colombia, Mexico and Peru are much weaker. The author speculates that societal differences in the level of social integration at the local community level account for the discrepancy between the Asian and Latin American findings.

Relationships among the demographic variables

Because almost no attention has been given to this set of research problems using WFS community data, our discussion will be extremely brief. The issues here warrant much fuller development and investigation, but in fact the community data collected in the WFS programme are not generally very helpful for this purpose.

Three reports examine the relationship between community levels of infant mortality (estimated from individual survey data, and thus subject to large sampling error) and fertility. Casterline and Eid (forthcoming) find more traditional behaviour (aspirations for larger families, less contraceptive use, and higher recent fertility) in those communities in rural Egypt where infant mortality rates are higher. Nizamuddin (1979) estimates positive effects of child mortality on children ever born in rural Pakistan. Chayovan (1982), on the contrary, finds no relationship between desired family size and estimated levels of community mortality in rural Thailand. Because the direction of the relationship between achieved fertility and levels of mortality is ambiguous (causes can operate in both directions), it is hazardous to interpret findings. Discounting these, the only significant effects which remain are for fertility aspirations in rural Egypt.

The most intriguing results concerning relationships among the demographic variables are reported for Egypt by Casterline and Eid (forthcoming). Using census data, the authors construct a measure of the age structure of the adult male population of the village, which they then interpret as an indicator of one component of social and economic opportunity, namely the intensity of competition within age cohorts for limited resources. The measure is significantly associated with fertility aspirations and contraceptive use: where young adult males are more numerous relative to older males, fertility aspirations are lower and contraceptive use higher, net of other individual and village variables. Obviously the finding must be regarded as largely suggestive, in the absence of further study of the possible mechanisms of the effect and of the sources of variation in the age-structure measure (e.g. past fertility and mortality, recent migration).

33.4 Concluding remarks

Demographic theory and the desire to address policy concerns drives us beyond the type of data gathered in most cross-sectional fertility surveys. Investigation of the influence on demographic behaviour of family relations (Caldwell 1982; Ryder 1983), the provision of health and family-planning services, transformations of labour and commodity markets, community-based population programmes (McNicoll 1975) – to cite general examples – require data not provided by such surveys. Indeed, for these and related topics, national surveys may be an inappropriate research instrument. Ethnographic data collection, structured in-depth interviews with small groups of women (as in Knodel, Havanon and Pramualratana 1984), intensive community studies (Cain 1985), various mixed designs (Hugo 1985), and experimental designs, are alternative approaches which are likely to prove invaluable in the future. These approaches permit more precise delineation of salient features of the institutional setting of demographic decisions than can be achieved in a brief community survey.

The first analysts of WFS community data set out with expectations that these data would fill in much of the void in our measurement of the setting of demographic decisions, correcting our exclusive reliance on a structured set of individual and household socio-economic characteristics and region of residence. We now recognize the rather limited potential of the community data compared to these initial expectations. Even well-designed and detailed community surveys will provide a sketchy impression of the social, cultural and economic setting. But similar shortcomings plague other types of data collected in national fertility surveys: measurement of important variables is often inaccurate or imprecise. Yet we recognize the substantial value of these data, the weaknesses notwithstanding, because they allow us to address questions of national importance.

The same view must be adopted concerning the potential value of community data. Specific research problems need to be formulated, and community survey instruments designed to provide the appropriate data. This is a modest and disciplined approach, lacking the all-embracing enthusiasm of some of our earlier efforts. Yet ironically there is good reason for optimism that this approach might yield genuine contributions to our understanding of demographic behaviour. We base this optimism on our review of the WFS experience, which reveals an encouraging number of intriguing and useful findings:

1 Contraceptive prevalence is higher where family-planning services are geographically more accessible. The relationship is often weaker than the relationship with simple indices of community development. Moreover, the effect of accessibility on contraceptive use differs according to such factors as age of the respondent, her fertility preferences, and her choice of contraceptive method.

2 In rural areas of Egypt and the Philippines, neo-natal mortality is lower where a trained midwife is present in the community. The proximity to other types of medical personnel — trained doctors and nurses — is, for the most part, unrelated to infant and child mortality in rural areas of seven WFS countries. The proximity to specific types of health facilities, on the other hand, is significantly related to levels of post-neonatal and child mortality in five of the seven countries.

3 Proximity to primary and secondary schools is a weak predictor of fertility behaviour, but levels of school attendance is a powerful correlate of fertility aspirations in rural Egypt and rural Bangladesh. This suggests that establishment of schools is not, in itself, sufficient to have an impact on fertility.

4 Economic indicators derived from WFS community data rarely show significant associations with reproductive behaviour. The same applies to indicators of village modernization. This raises the question of whether there are substantial and systematic effects of these facets of the development process on reproductive behaviour. One might attribute the absence of systematic effects to the crudeness of the indicators provided by the WFS data. In our view, however, the repeated failure of basic indicators of village modernization

cannot be so easily dismissed: were the measured facets of modernization actually related to fertility, we suspect a larger number of significant associations would have emerged in the analyses to date.

5 In countries characterized by difficult transportation and communication in some rural areas, such as the Philippines and Peru, fertility aspirations and fertility are higher in the more isolated localities.

Provocative conclusions can be derived from these results, some of which appear to apply in a wide variety of settings. Equally interesting is the diversity of outcomes on some matters. Is this a consequence of differences in design of the questionnaires, the samples, or the analyses? Or does the variation in outcome reflect genuine societal differences? These are intriguing questions not yet answered.

The findings cited demonstrate that community data can be employed to test propositions of theoretical and policy importance. To be sure, the propositions can be investigated through other research strategies, and indeed a complement of approaches is desirable. There are, however, several attractive features of using community data collected in conjunction with a national fertility survey. First, substantial investments are made to assure that the data on fertility and mortality are of good quality. These variables usually serve as dependent variables, and thus good measurement is essential. Secondly, the national scope of the survey ensures variability of community types (within the range set by the society) and avoids the danger of deriving conclusions for national policy on the basis of regional or local peculiarities. Thirdly, as an addition to a national survey, collection of community data is relatively inexpensive. The data can be collected while the individual survey team is in the community. Even travel by a special community survey team to all communities on an independent schedule will add little cost to the survey budget. Several other types of costs — printing of questionnaires, data processing — are minimal, since typically a few hundred villages at most are surveyed.

We are confident that future community data collection and analysis can improve on the foundation established by the WFS experience. (See the many specific recommendations of Bilsborrow 1985, Freedman 1985, and others contained in Casterline (ed.) 1985.) The success of many aspects of the WFS programme derives in part from the collective experience gained in fertility and KAP surveys throughout the developing world in the 1960s. Hopefully the WFS experience with community data will perform the same service for demographic research in the future.

34

The WFS in Developed Countries

Paolo De Sandre

34.1 Uniformity and diversity in the WFS programme

The aims of the WFS programme were to enable the fertility of different populations to be described and interpreted; to improve national capability for data collection by means of surveys; and to facilitate comparative analysis. These objectives were achieved somewhat differently in the high fertility countries (HFCs) on the one hand and low fertility countries (LFCs) on the other, although in almost all cases the surveys used the recommended core questionnaire and were based on representative samples of the particular country's population.

The demographic conditions and the problems of HFCs and LFCs are quite different: in HFCs population growth is too fast, whereas in LFCs population growth may be below replacement level.

Systems for data collection (i.e. vital registration and censuses) are efficient in the LFCs, where there are organizations experienced in taking sample surveys and in the automatic processing of data. However, the system is poor in the HFCs (Wanglee 1983; Zarkovic 1983), although in some areas different types of data collection are used, especially as far as fertility control is concerned (Srikantan 1982).

Many countries – 42 HFCs and 20 LFCs – agreed to follow the same general strategy proposed by the WFS programme in their attempt to improve their knowledge of the effects of the same type of variables on fertility in different social and economic contexts.

If the data had been collected during the same period, they would undoubtedly have been easier to interpret, and their analysis would have been clearer.

Indeed, both preliminary and further analysis of data from HFCs, which were more subject to the general guidance of WFS London headquarters, are more uniform and the data from HFCs are more comparable than those of the LFCs. Moreover, while for most HFCs the international programme of fertility surveys was conducted in accordance with externally determined rules and procedures, in some cases even artificially setting up the necessary structures to enable the surveys to be carried out, in most LFCs demographic surveys on fertility control were already well established.

34.2 Previous fertility surveys in the LFCs

Starting with their pioneer survey of Indianapolis, the USA has a long-standing history of regular and thorough sample surveys on fertility.[1] From the end of the 1960s to the early seventies, in addition to the USA, a further ten countries analysed the reproductive behaviour of their populations, using sample interview surveys. These countries were Belgium, Czechoslovakia, Denmark, Finland, France, Great Britain, Hungary, Netherlands, Poland, and Yugoslavia.

In the 1960s the pill became widely used and, a little later on, the IUD. From the mid-sixties onwards, the birth rate showed a new decline almost everywhere, a trend that continued until about 1980 and is perhaps not yet exhausted. At the same time, divorce was on the increase.

The need to improve our understanding of the methods and implications of fertility control was felt to be more pressing. In a study of fertility and family planning (UN 1976b), the UN Economic Commission for Europe tried to compare the main results of these surveys. Although the surveys had not been co-ordinated at the outset, they followed the pattern of the US surveys and have considerable comparability.[2]

34.3 Surveys and reproductive patterns

The first investigations and the strategies followed by different countries have been the subject of critical discussion. The WFS programme has enabled considerable improvement in quality to be made. For example, data collections contain the whole set of variables (intermediate or proximate and explanatory) which are linked with reproduction, contrary to the earlier practice of considering fertility only partially (Kendall 1977). There still, however, remain limitations and ambiguity arising from some of the questions used in the interviews (Simons 1978; Vaessen 1981), and from the interviews themselves in cases where the determinants of respondents' behaviour have yet to be tested (Ryder 1973).

On the other hand, surveys on family planning are an invaluable, indeed unique, means of identifying the true situation (Westoff 1975; Hermalin and Entwisle 1982). Their shortcomings can be overcome, at least in part, by making regular checks on the quality of the data. This point will be considered later.

Data from censuses and vital registration cannot be expected to do more than simply outline the essential characteristics of the population, even if censuses, by use of retrospective questions, allow past behaviour to be reconstructed and if population registers are used, as in the Swedish system (Arvidson in WGSD 1978).

The opposite is true of the study of reproductive motivation, which focuses not simply on contraceptive practice, but rather on the individual's behaviour and attitudes, which can be revealed only through detailed questions and delicate, fairly lengthy interviews (see figure 34.1, which shows how the groups of variables are linked). Such interviews require a high degree of co-operation from respondents and a high level of competence from interviewers.

We should point out that the conceptual approach which reconstructed the reproductive process, following an analytical classification of the intermediate variables (between background variables and fertility) proposed by Davis and Blake (1956), has been re-assessed (Freedman 1961–2) and put into practice

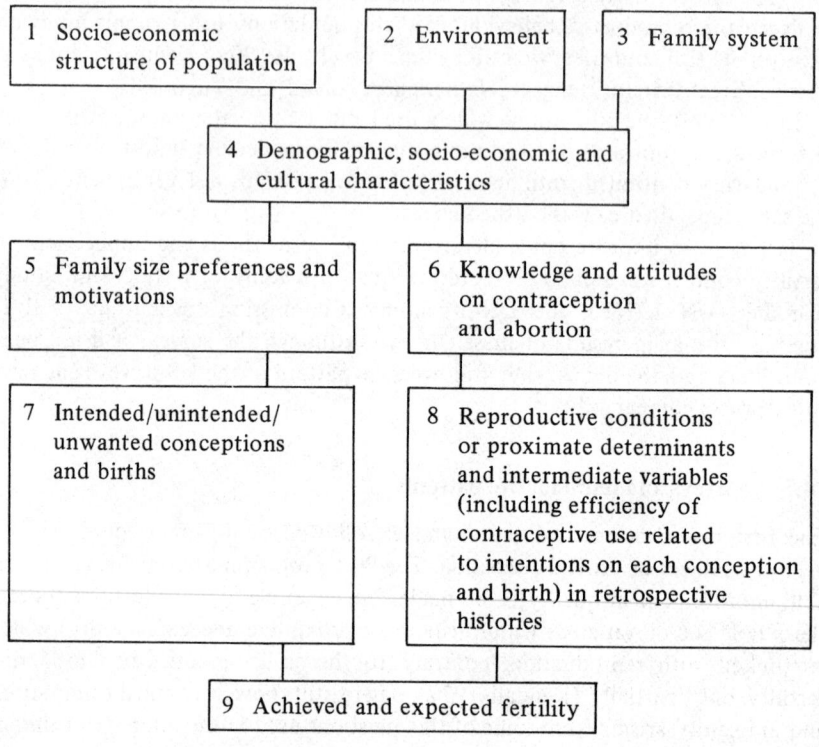

Note:
1–3: as perceived by the respondent and/or
aggregating individual factual information

FIG. 34.1. Fertility-related variables collected in WFS-type surveys in the low fertility
countries by individual questionnaire

using methods that vary in their comprehensiveness and are influenced by the
data available.

The multiplicative model of Bongaarts (1978), which is based on the prevalence of marriage, contraception, induced abortion and breastfeeding, and the
model of Gaslonde, which is similar but based entirely upon data from surveys
(Gaslonde and Carrasco 1982), have been used in survey analysis (e.g. Casterline,
Singh, Cleland and Ashurst 1984) and have lent themselves to adaptation (for
example in the age-specific versions) and further improvement, as in the development of a model based upon individual data analysis by Hobcraft and Little
(1984). Survival models with intermediate variables as covariates are applied to
parity progression ratios (Palloni 1984). A decomposition of the marital fertility
index was carried out by Ryder (1978), who introduced intentions concerning
births, and childspacing patterns have been constructed using typologies based
only on family planning behaviour (Moors 1978).

Here we are dealing with clear examples of interactions between theory and research, which have been made possible by sample surveys on birth control. These examples show how the identification of the determinants of fertility has improved, and point the way towards fruitful areas of future research.[3]

34.4   The WFS programme: national and international objectives

The 20 LFCs which participated in the WFS programme all accepted the recommended strategy; the individual slant of particular countries is a result of pre-existing interests and a need to suit local conditions.

The WFS questionnaire for ever-married women of childbearing age, in its variant for low fertility countries (see WFS Technical Paper no. 138, 1975), was intended to provide only an important outline, paying particular attention to the factors which might have influenced the present fertility decline. The intention to make these findings comparable was limited to the topics of analysis indicated in the ECE comparative project (WGSD 1976). The aims of this project were primarily to search for the causes of the recent decline in fertility and the probable trends in fertility in the near future. In examining the prevalence of unplanned or unwanted pregnancies (or births) and, as far as possible, the level of abortion and the attitudes of respondents, the ECE project was interested in additional questions concerning family size preferences and motivations (CES 1975; Berent 1977).[4]

Clearly, the two main objectives proposed by the ECE present strategic directions for sample surveys. The search for future trends relies upon the fertility expectations of the respondents as perceived in the period. It is well known that subjective attitudes towards fertility change considerably: viewed aggregately, however, the expectations of cohorts are more consistent, but have the same limitations as any other period measure (Westoff and Ryder 1977; Hendershot and Placek (eds.) 1981).

The search for the causes of the fertility decline has been established along promising lines: using structured questions focused on sequences of interconnected events, retrospective birth histories and attitudes have been ascertained, enabling more variables and patterns of behaviour and attitudes to be analysed.

Nevertheless, this type of research has grave limitations as far as international comparability is concerned. This is a result partly of the inadequacy and ambiguity of some of the questions used by the various LFCs and, more generally, of a single-round sample survey being used to study the determinants of individual decision-making processes, which may change over time and are subject to complex influences. A sample followed longitudinally, at two or more points in time, would allow a more satisfactory assessment of dynamic individual processes.

Moreover, the surveys done in countries that had already participated in the first international comparative study (UN 1976b) are not based upon panels.

Considering 16 of the LFCs, the questions asked cover the essential demographic and socio-economic characteristics in every country (WGSD 1976; Berent, Jones and Siddiqui 1982; ECE/WFS Comparative Fertility Study, draft report),[5] but important details are missing. For example, only five countries asked questions on knowledge of sterilization; eight on unwanted pregnancies, distinguishing between the pregnancies that are 'not wanted at all' and 'not wanted at that moment'; seven on religion; eight on second preference as to ultimate family size; and six countries (who are essentially interested in pronatalist policies) on the conditions that might influence women to have more children. The main reason for these differences lies in the fact that most countries used questionnaires to collect data on topics of local interest, except for five or six which were carrying out research of this type for the first time and benefited from international standardization.

As the column labelled 'Special topics' in appendix A·indicates, some countries were more interested in the biometrics of pregnancy and fertility control (France); others investigated in greater depth the history of the couple (Denmark, Great Britain and USA) or attitudes and motivations (Belgium and Netherlands); yet others explored the ways in which social norms are perceived. Thus, although the research of the different countries gives results which are nationally of great interest, international comparison of the data is restricted.

Further restrictions on the comparability of data are imposed by the specifications used for the data collected (or rather the mode of data entry). Seventy pages of the provisional comparative report of the ECE (see chapter III on production of comparable data and their limitations) are devoted to the difficult task of making compatible, where possible, the different variables of the participating countries.

34.5   The target populations

As an example, let us consider the problems that arise, both for national analysis within a country and for international comparative studies, from the criterion used to select eligible women for interview.

In order to ensure comparability between the first and second series of surveys, only married women in their first marriage were selected, rather than all ever-married women. Some countries (Czechoslovakia, Finland, Romania) adhered to this criterion for selection. This may result in the phenomenon of selectivity: there is differential fertility in ever-married women who are not currently married and there are the effects of marriage breakdown, which increases with duration of marriage and age of the woman.

On the other hand, it is difficult to define the 'married' woman: does this mean *de jure* marriage only (as at least eight countries decided) or does it also include *de facto* marriage? Some countries selected women from a list (as Finland, Italy and Netherlands did) and thus adopted the first method.

Moreover, the married state is only a *proxy* for exposure to the risk of pregnancy. For this reason it would be convenient to study the characteristics of all the women: five countries (Belgium, Denmark, France, Great Britain and Norway) included all women in the survey, but chose different age limits that ranged from 15 years (Great Britain) to 20 years (France). In this way, France eliminated the possibility of exploring the behaviour of teenagers. The omission of one simple datum, such as date of first marriage (Denmark ascertained only the most recent marriage), prevents an adequate comparison of duration of marriage.

Finally, since fertility and its control depend on the couple, it is important to also consider the husbands. This was done, but only with a reduced sample, in Belgium, France and Italy.

The age groups included in the sample have important effects on analysis and comparability, censoring the cohorts at different moments of their lives. The highest minimum age and lowest maximum were used by France (20 years) and Hungary (40 years), respectively.

Except for cases where a sample population is restricted for a specific scientific objective, the study of the causes of reproductive behaviour requires attention not to be restricted to *de jure* couples or to couples who are in their first marriage. Single women and their partners should also be interviewed.

Not enough attention has yet been paid to the behaviour of minorities who are on the increase.[6] The omission of husbands or partners has led to a neglect of the interaction among couples (INED–CSIS 1982).

34.6 The survey itself: management, data processing and publication of results

Appendix A shows that in almost all LFCs (except Italy and Switzerland), the organization of the survey was entrusted to a central institute of statistics or a centre for the study of population. As pointed out by Zarkovic (1983), this presupposes an existing infrastructure, statistical skills and experience of sample surveys. Even apart from the varying resources available to countries, the delicate nature of fertility behaviour and attitudes presents a challenge to the best-equipped organizations.

As practical experience is accumulated and analytical methods of fertility research are developed, the central organization of statistics which is involved should evaluate past achievements in order to ensure continuity, and place the survey findings within a broader framework. Clearly, such continuity must go hand in hand with detailed analysis and, previously, with a methodology which is adequate for measuring variables which relate to behaviour and are not purely objective. The adopted approaches to the point, in general, cannot be assessed yet, since we await further publication, but our impression is one of considerable diversity among countries.

A crucial aspect of the technical organization of a survey after data collection is data editing and automatic data processing, both traditionally bottlenecks which delay the analysis of results. There do not appear to have been important innovations in this area. Programs for data processing, such as Clusters for the calculation of sampling errors, as well as the usual statistical packages, were used more than cleaning programs.

The most widely adopted approaches for the publication of results are either the successive publication of different aspects of the findings, followed by a concluding summary (though in some cases this has not yet been done), or the publication of a general report, sometimes following the WFS 'Guidelines for Country Report No. 1', later supplemented by second-stage analysis. Belgium, Netherlands and USA were the first countries to adopt the former approach, while Spain, Italy and Great Britain adopted the latter. Norway attempted both a general report and single-subject analyses. In some cases, the preliminary results are provisional, that is, based on data that are unedited or incomplete.

The dissemination of the data has taken the form of partial or general reports which have appeared in different journals or in specialist publications, almost always in the language of the country. There has been no systematic communication between the countries in which the different results have been published.[7] This is something of a disappointment, and almost half the LFCs have failed to publish even a summary of findings. The summaries were intended to appear in the WFS series of country summaries.

The depository libraries, which receive copies of WFS publications, have had the reports of the HFCs but only rarely have they received publications from the LFCs. For this reason, the long-awaited ECE report is of even greater interest, because access to the original papers published by each country is quite difficult.

Publication delays have varied considerably. Obviously, some subjects call for rapid publication; others can await more thorough exploitation of the wealth of findings that emerge from a fertility survey, which one might speak of as a permanent laboratory.

The overall impression, however, is that intensive use of survey data has been made by only a minority of the LFCs.

34.7   Sampling designs and interviews

In appendix A only the sample size of the different samples used is given, revealing the great variety that exists. (Note that relatively small samples preclude any detailed analysis.) Generally speaking, a favourable opinion has been expressed in the ECE provisional report as to the reliability of the sampling designs used. However, more uniform criteria for the design and practice of sampling should be agreed upon. Attention should be drawn to the following points.

It is important for the sampling frame to be complete and up to date. Moreover, the interval between the identification of the individual respondents, the preliminary inquiry and the individual interview should, as far as possible, be reduced.

The use of unequal probabilities of eligible women, with weighting, creates difficult conceptual and technical problems for the statistical analysis of data (at least five countries have resorted to these procedures: France, Italy, Spain, USA and Yugoslavia). This needs to be studied in greater depth.

Response failure, due both to non-contact and refusal, deserves further attention (response failure is quite high – between 15 and 40 per cent – in

Belgium, France, Great Britain, Italy, Netherlands, Norway and Spain). In general, response failure óccurs more among single women; where it occurs among married women, it is found ámong younger people.

It is probably better not to replace non-respondents, i.e. the women who were not contacted and those who refused to be interviewed, as six countries did – Belgium, Czechoslovakia, Hungary, Italy, Netherlands and Spain. Indeed, one could not assume *a priori*, on the basis of a few matching characteristics, that there was a similarity between the replacements and the women who were originally selected. Rather, the survey plan must provide for a *subsample of non-respondents* for additional visits (as Great Britain and the USA did), with a view to evaluating the characteristics of the population left uncovered (NCHS 1981).

It is not clear (except in the case of two countries) if the sampling procedure used allows for return visits to the respondents to collect further information. The longitudinal technique of the panel, although unusual, is suitable for monitoring development and change in behaviour and attitudes on fertility and birth control.

The presentation of sampling errors could be extended, also by using the methods of calculation for the overall samples supplied by software of the Clusters type.

All the LFCs used women as interviewers in their surveys. The number of interviewers varied considerably, depending on the type of sample chosen, as did the skill of the individual interviewers. As some sort of relationship between the respondent and the interviewer is likely to develop, some criterion should be used to assign interviewers to the interviews. This criterion should allow an evaluation of the interviewer/respondent effect through a comparison of the differential results of their work.

34.8 Evaluation of data

Each participating country has attempted an evaluation of the quality of the data: sampling error, non-sampling error linked to response failure and the representativeness of the sample are assessed. However, as yet, this subject has only been mentioned briefly in the literature. Even less attention appears to have been devoted to the quality of the questions and to the interviewer/respondent relationship.

Reinterviews do not appear to have been done to check the quality of questions and answers. An evaluation of the effect of different sequences of the various items is possible if planned in advance. Attempts to do this have been made, as for example in Italy.

The very different conditions in which interviews are held are brought to light more by questioning the interviewer than by exploring the interview effect.

There is less opportunity to compare the data with those from other sources where they focus less on fertility matters such as births and abortion and on marriage and divorce than on sequences of behaviour and attitudes. A series of checks might be made by comparing the answers given by husbands and wives to the same questions, though this is unlikely to resolve all the inconsistencies. This option is open only to Belgium, France and Italy (see section 34.5).

The most interesting questions on opinions, motivations and expectations are also the most difficult to elucidate because of their multidimensional nature. Despite improvements in scaling, there is a wider diffusion of culturally shared stereotypes than of one-dimensional items. This is also the case for the ECE model on preferences and motivations (CES 1975). This does not mean we should abandon questions which ascertain individual feelings and cultural pressures of different types. These undoubtedly have an important influence, and we should therefore make greater efforts to assess the reliability of techniques used.

In this connection, comparable pre-tests are of value, and the results should be of general interest (for an example relative to the Cycle III of the National Survey of Family Growth, see NCHS 1982).

34.9 New knowledge

Acquiring new knowledge has been the main objective of the surveys and also the most successful. Recent changes in behaviour have been dramatic, and even a straightforward description of the differences between cohorts — their socio-economic and residential characteristics — is of interest. The pattern of sexual relations and cohabitation of couples preceding or replacing marriage (Roussel and Festy 1979) is especially marked in the northern European countries (Dunnell 1979; DNSIR 1980; SS 1981; SCBS 1982). The characteristics and effects of the increasing incidence of marriage breakdown and remarriage — less relevant for ultimate fertility — among ever-married women have been analysed (e.g. Mosher 1982).

There has been great interest in the changes in contraceptive methods which have occurred between cohorts, as well as the changes over time which may be established through the findings of successive surveys. Also of interest are individual methods: the rise and the fall in the use of the pill; the increased use of sterilization; induced abortion, which is often underestimated. There has been a reduction in some group differences in behaviour, for example between religious groups, and an increase in others, for example between various races in the USA; there is uncertainty as to the meaning of other differences linked with the woman's occupation.

Particular attention has been paid to the problems of contraceptive failure and discontinuation of contraception. Use has been made of attrition tables, introducing also relationships with explanatory variables through proportional hazards techniques. Attempts have been made (Ryder 1978) to link contraceptive efficacy with the reproductive intentions of the couple at that moment (in particular the desire not to have children or to have them later).

Another topic is now being explored in greater depth: the value of children and motivations and preferences as to family size. The costs and benefits of children should be considered as part of the conditioning and the constraints of the individual on the one hand, and as part of fertility expectations on the other.

Of particular interest in the behaviour of minorities is the phenomenon of the childless woman whose sterility is due either to fertility impairment or to a voluntary decision. This decision is not easily defined and may change over time (Mosher and Bachrach 1982; Noack and Østby 1982). The development of this phenomenon should be followed longitudinally.

Expected family size (which ranges from 2.13 children in Bulgaria to 2.80 in Spain) is not higher than that observed around 1970 and does not support the hypothesis that there may be an increase in the birth rate. In most LFCs, recent marriage cohorts are likely to have a completed family size at or below replacement level (Siddiqui 1984).

The evidence mentioned here is just part of the results which have already been published (see list of special topics in appendix A).

34.10   Progress made in data analysis

We agree with the opinion that the method of data analysis contributes to the quality of the results in a way that is often decisive (Hobcraft 1981). The efforts made by WFS central staff in London to review survey methodologies are without precedent and have yielded exceptional results. The various WFS series of publications, *Basic Documentation, Technical Bulletins, Scientific Reports, Comparative Studies* and *Occasional Papers*, together with the papers presented at the methodology sessions of the 1980 WFS Conference held in London, show the range of problems analysed and the solutions offered. We should also mention the interest of the Population Division of the UN (see in particular Hermalin and Mason 1980).

The synthesis which WFS research offers and its practical recommendations are especially valuable as regards the censoring and selection which arise in retrospective cross-sectional surveys; improvements in data processing, bearing in mind the constraints mentioned earlier and the nature of the data available; the revision of cohort–period measures; the use of multidimensional statistical methods (either by themselves or integrated into classical demographic methods, as in attrition tables); the methods of sampling; and the evaluation of sampling errors.

From the publications consulted, it appears that few countries have anticipated or followed the ideas promoted by WFS London headquarters. Most countries have adopted some of the methodology proposed, but much remains to be done.

34.11   New findings and policy implications

The knowledge provided by these surveys may lead to political action in three ways. First, it may affect policy on surveys and on national and international systems of data collection and dissemination. Second, it may lead to changes in government policy on family planning services and to initiatives to influence marital and fertility behaviour. Some countries have collected information on the use of public family planning services. However, the motivations and conditioning which influence fertility at the individual level may be studied with a view to government intervention not necessarily through family planning services. Third, other social and cultural institutions may be interested in acting upon the mechanisms of family formation, as the family-building process relates to other important changes that are taking place.

34.12 Conclusions

The fertility surveys of LFCs participating in the WFS programme were carried out primarily as a response to local needs. The experience of international co-ordination through ECE has demonstrated the willingness to work towards an interdisciplinary approach and to achieve comparability of data.

Certainly, there is much to do in the future. Changes in conceptual schemes and methodologies are made slowly. The fusion between analytical descriptions and compact, reliable models is difficult (Hobcraft 1981) since progress in modelling is also needed.

As the work done at the ECE headquarters demonstrates, there is still great scope for improving comparative analysis and the use of data, and we are likely to see more research being done in this field. There are still, however, too few workshops being organized to ascertain the usefulness of the data collected and to find better criteria for the multidimensional treatment of the information available.

We must continue to evaluate the quality of the data in terms of their validity, reliability and coverage, and to improve methods and models of data analysis, especially focused on assessing the effects of intermediate variables, and their covariates, on fertility levels and patterns, also decomposed by parity. All this goes without saying. But the debate should also focus on another point: whether data should be collected through independent samples, at successive moments in the same country, or whether the same samples should be investigated longitudinally. Variation in human behaviour depends on the history of individuals. The cohort approach, where individuals are perceived as an aggregate, builds a picture based on individual histories, albeit a partial and average one. Samples followed by panels would reflect reality better, and new surveys could give information that a comparison between independent samples cannot.

Notes

1. Growth of American Families Studies: 1955 and 1960; National Fertility Studies: 1965, 1970 and 1975. This last survey mainly consisted of re-interviews of a specific subset of women first interviewed in the 1970 study (Westoff and Ryder 1977). Czechoslovakia (FSO 1978), Great Britain, Hungary and Japan have carried out some sample interview surveys on family planning since the war (Freedman 1961–2).

2. All the national surveys included at least three major topics: levels and trends in achieved fertility; ideals, desires and intentions concerning family size; and knowledge, attitudes and practice of fertility control (UN 1976b: 2).

3. Hobcraft (forthcoming) brings up to date research and discussion on integrating proximate determinants in the analysis of fertility.

4. The ECE module introduced six new variables: two variables on ideal number of children; second preference for ultimate family size; reasons for wanting additional child; conditions for acceptance of additional children; reasons for wanting more than two children (Berent 1977).

5. Comparisons involving the husband's work status, wife's work status, wife's occupation, place of work, number of hours worked per week, proportion of work since marriage, area of living space, household density, religious denomination, intensity of religious feeling, are of limited value in generalization because they cover only a few of the 16 countries (WFS/ECE Comparative Fertility Study, draft of chapter III). *Note*: subsequent to the writing of this chapter, ECE completed its overall report on the WFS/ECE project: see UN (forthcoming c). Comparative reports on certain subjects were published as *WFS Comparative Studies* nos. 18, 20, 21, 26 and 38.

6. On the importance of cohabitation, see the reports of the countries which interviewed all women, regardless of marital status (see appendix A and the sources quoted). On the importance of divorce, see also Mosher 1982; the NCHS of the USA has recently prepared a survey which also covered adolescents, with careful pre-tests (*Vital and Health Statistics*, series 2, no. 91, 1982).

7. Subsequent to the writing of this chapter, a list of reports based on developed country WFS surveys has been published in WFS (1985), app. 11.

Appendix A overleaf

APPENDIX A – Participation of developed countries in WFS programme

Country	Sample size	Executive agency	Timing of fieldwork	Country report	Summary of main findings (in WFS series)	Special topics	Included in ECE/comparative fertility study	
							1970s	1975s
Belgium (Flemish part only)	4 877	Population and Family Study Centre, Dept. of Public Health and the Family, Brussels	1975-6	x	x	e g i k W H	x	x
Bulgaria	6 000	Scientific Research Institute of Statistics, Sofia	1976	–	–	m	–	x
Czechoslovakia	3 041	Federal Statistical Office, Prague	1977	–	x	m	x	x
Denmark	6 000	Danish National Institute of Social Research, Copenhagen	1975	–	–	d g W	x	x
Finland	6 100	Population Research Institute, Helsinki	1977	x	–	l	x	x
France	3 000 women 600 men	Institut National d'Etudes Démographiques, Paris, in co-operation with Institut National de la Statistique et des Etudes Economiques	1977-8	–	x	g i W H	x	x
Great Britain	6 589	Office of Population Censuses and Surveys, London	1976	x	–	d W	x	x
Hungary	4 009	Hungarian Central Statistical Office, Budapest	1977	x	x	g m i	x	x

Country	Sample	Institution	Year					
Israel	6 000 21 000[a]	Central Bureau of Statistics and the Hebrew University of Jerusalem	1973–5	–	–	d e k	–	_[n]
Italy	5 500 women 850 men	Universities of Padua, Florence and Rome	1979	x	x	k 1 H	–	x
Japan	2 860	Dept. of Statistics and Information, Ministry of Health and Welfare, Tokyo	1974	x	x	f	–	_[n]
Netherlands (11 marriage cohorts only)	4 522	Netherlands Interuniversity Demographic Institute, Voorburg	1975	x	x	f i j k	x	x
Norway	5 100	Central Bureau of Statistics, Oslo	1977–8	x	x	d i k W	–	x
Poland	10 000	Central Statistical Office, Warsaw	1977	x	–	–	x	x
Romania	10 000	Population Commission of Romania, Bucharest	1978	–	(x)[b]	1	–	x
Spain	6 222	Instituto Nacional de Estadística, Madrid	1977	x	x	–	–	x
Sweden	5 000	Statistics Sweden, Stockholm	1981	x	–	d k	–	_[o]
Switzerland	601	University of Zurich	1980	–	–	–	–	_[o]
USA	8 611	National Center for Health Statistics, Washington, DC	1976	–	(x)[c]	d f g i k m	x	x
Yugoslavia	7 500	Federal Institute of Statistics, Belgrade	1976	x	–	g	x	x

Notes to appendix A continued overleaf

Notes:

a   Short questionnaire.
b   Population Commission of Romania: *A Summary Report* (in French) 1981.
c   W.D. Mosher (1982). Fertility and Family Planning in the 1970s: the National Survey of Family Growth. *Family Planning Perspectives 14(6):* 314–320.

n   Survey undertaken before WFS/ECE recommendations for low fertility survey countries: not included to maintain comparability.
o   Available after the deadline for the comparative analysis.

Special topics (i.e. questions expanded or a thorough analysis planned or published)

d   Family formation (cohabitation, marriage, divorce, remarriage, etc.).
e   Motivations and preferences on family size; value of children.
f   Intentions on each conception or birth.
g   Contraception; efficiency of contraceptive use; induced abortion.
h   Breastfeeding.
i   Childlessness and sterility.
j   Fertility expected and desired.
k   Differential fertility (e.g. related to women's work, religion or race).
l   Expenses; conditions and constraints of living.
m   Family planning services, conditions likely to change expected family size.
H   Survey extended to husbands.
W   Survey extended to all women, including single women.

Sources:

WFS Annual Report 1982. WFS summaries. Personal communication from WFS of the list of publications of the LFCs in WFS programme (1983). WGSD (1978). Personal communications and offprints from A. Arvidsson (Sweden). O. Bertelsen (Denmark), D. Breznik (Yugoslavia), V. Cap (Czechoslovakia), R.L. Cliquet (Belgium), Z. Eisenback (Israel), K. Elkerton (UK), H.G. Moors (Netherlands), L. Østby (Norway), W.L. Pratt (USA). UN (1976b). Berent *et al.* (1982). ECE/WFS *Comparative Fertility Study* (1983): draft of the Report. Breznik (1980). De Sandre and Rossi (eds.) (1982). DNISR (1979–81). Dunnell (1979). INE (1978). Klinger (ed.) (1979). Leridon (1982). SCBS (1981). For the USA the main findings are published in NCHS (National Center for Health Statistics), *Advancedata* (from 1978), *Vital and Health Statistics Series 2* (no. 87), Series 23 (nos. 7 to 11), *Working Papers* (1981).

PART VIII

*Implications for Policy and
Future Data Collection*

35

Standardized Multi-National Research:
Strengths and Weaknesses

Ramesh Chander
Christiaan Grootaert[1]

35.1 Introduction

Empirical research in the social sciences is made up of four components: the development of concepts, the collection of the appropriate data to match these concepts, the analysis of the collected data and the dissemination of the findings. Each of the four areas has its own tradition of theoretical and practical approaches. Loosely speaking, the first two have been the preserve of the statistician and have led to a substantial body of literature covering, for example, sampling methodology and questionnaire design, as well as codified classification schemes such as the International Standard Industrial Classification (ISIC) and the System of National Accounts (SNA). On the whole, the statistician's task is complete when the survey findings can be presented in tabular form. Data analysis and the dissemination of research findings, on the other hand, have tended to be the preserve of the economist or demographer. The researcher who has wanted to engage in hypothesis testing has generally been faced with two alternatives, either to recognize that no suitable body of data does exist and therefore to remain confined to the theoretical development of the subject, or to use the best available data set even though the characteristics of the data as collected may not match the assumptions underlying the analytical technique. To venture into the middle ground, to try to collect and analyse data where the underlying concepts do match, is to run the risk of attracting criticism from both statistical and economic purists.

Despite the risks, many attempts to bridge the data collection to analysis gap have been made, but the difficulties are highlighted when another researcher tries to combine the data from different enquiries. As often as not, the compromises made in each individual project will be incompatible with one another and the researcher is again left with the choice of ignoring the data problems or abandoning the analysis. Against this background the achievements of WFS are a considerable landmark. Data of high quality suitable for detailed analysis of fertility and demographic factors have been collected not just in a single setting but in a variety of environments. The benefits have been not only in the quality of the final analyses and their widespread availability, but also in the improvement of practical survey techniques and the transfer of skills to the participating countries.

Without wishing to detract in any way from its achievements, WFS had one advantage that other socio-economic research undertakings may not have. At the time WFS was conceived, many demographic concepts were already well established and there was a sizeable body of experience in the analysis of fertility and demographic data. In addition, the concepts of life and death are unequivocal and the basic unit of observation in fertility study, viz. a birth, poses relatively few problems of measurement. This also holds true for several of the major demographic variables such as age and sex, and stands in contrast with the complexities associated with defining and measuring economic variables. Consider, for example, the question of income distribution. Analysts may wish to include some or all of cash income from cash crops or from other activities, to impute incomes from subsistence crops and other activities, to include transfers to a person or a household from within the country or outside the country. They may wish to consider 'full' income or disposable income, current income or permanent income. Distribution categories are also by no means easy to determine; even a simple criterion such as the distinction between urban and rural entails many conceptual difficulties. There is thus no fully agreed framework as was the case in the WFS context.

If then the considerable problems of reconciling concepts have to be added to the already extensive other problems faced by multi-national efforts such as WFS, what chance of success would attend such an enterprise? Given the difficulties, why undertake multi-national research when the problems of concepts, data collection and analysis have to be reconciled with one another, not just subject to local and national considerations, but taking international factors into account also? A fact, however well quantified, conveys little information on its own. It achieves relevance, literally, by being related to other quantified facts. For some purposes local facts are sufficient: for example, one-quarter of the population lives in urban areas and earns three-quarters of the country's income. Additional facts are required, however, to answer questions such as: Is this an 'acceptable' distribution? How might it change over time? What can be done to influence the change? The answers may come from comparisons with like situations. Cross-sectional studies across countries are an obvious analogue of studies across time. In studying countries at different stages in the development process lies one of the best hopes of understanding this process and learning how it may be influenced. The results of successful multi-national research benefit individual countries, when put in the proper socio-economic and cultural context of these countries, as they plan their development. They also guide international agencies as to which countries most need assistance and which policies are most likely to succeed.

Multi-national research, however, is inherently difficult and expensive, and a careful study of its potential contributions and costs in each of the four stages of research is in order. In this chapter we outline some of the arguments that can form part of such a study. In section 35.2 we review selected international research efforts, then in section 35.3 the benefits and disadvantages of multi-national approaches to each of the four research components, before presenting our recommendations in section 35.4.

35.2 The family of standardized multi-national research projects

The Living Standards Measurement Study (LSMS) of the World Bank is concerned with the establishment of data bases that allow the tracking over time of welfare levels of different household groups within a country and the studying of the impact of various policy measures on these groups. For that purpose the LSMS has developed a general conceptual framework for the analysis of data on levels of living, centred around a multi-dimensional concept of levels of living (Grootaert 1983). A prototype questionnaire has been developed which can be used to gather the needed data. Repeated survey operations using the same data collection methodology and the same questionnaire are to be set up in the participating countries, to ensure that the data are comparable over time and can effectively track the impact of development over time. The standardization aspect of the LSMS lies in its conceptual framework, which is the same for all participating countries. As we shall discuss below, however, flexibility is introduced at the national level to adapt the specific data collection methodology to local conditions and policy requirements.

The National Household Survey Capability Programme (NHSCP) of the United Nations Statistical Office is designed to develop or strengthen the capability of developing countries to undertake household surveys. The programme envisages a series of household surveys of which the subject matter matches the countries' own requirements and priorities. The NHSCP emphasizes country-orientation and flexibility with respect to sequence and frequency of different surveys and with respect to the degree of detail of data collection. While the NHSCP is multi-national, the extent to which it is a standardized programme is actually quite limited. In fact it purposely shies away from imposing standards or uniform procedures. No emphasis is placed on cross-country analysis and comparative research. Its main standardization lies in the approach to data collection that is recommended, viz. a series of one-topic surveys whereby integration could be achieved by including a common set of core variables in all of them (UN 1980c).

The Joint Studies on Latin American Integration (best known under their Spanish acronym ECIEL) conducted as part of their work programme a series of household income and consumption surveys in 18 cities of 10 South American countries. The goal was to obtain 'internationally uniform data and results'. In each participating country one or more statistical and/or research institutes were responsible for the implementation of the project. A general 'Co-ordination' was set up to watch over the comparability of the work as it proceeded, and to provide technical and other support where needed for that purpose. The Co-ordination was also responsible for the international analyses and comparisons of the collected data (Musgrove 1982).

The International Comparison Project (ICP) is a joint effort between several international agencies, with the United Nations Statistical Office and more recently the Statistical Office of the European Community playing a co-ordinating role. The aim of the project is to make inter-country comparisons of national account aggregates in terms of a common currency unit. Conversions based on exchange rates are unsuited for that purpose because such rates do not reflect purchasing power parities. The ICP first developed a methodology that makes possible comparisons of real product between all countries of the world, regardless of their level of income. To effectuate the actual comparisons, participating countries were asked to provide price information on selected commodities and services in 151 standard categories of final expenditures. The ICP provided precise definitions of all items to ensure that the prices pertained to comparable qualities. Of all the projects discussed so far, the ICP has imposed the highest degree of standardization on its participating countries. This follows from its strict and sole goal of achieving international comparability in its results (Kravis, Heston and Summers 1982).

It will be noted from this brief review that the goals of multi-national research range from country-focus to international comparability. The latter goal has been achieved only in part in most instances because of differences in the level of statistical development in the participating countries, and because of the trade-off that exists between the imposition of comparability on the results and their timeliness, volume and cost.

35.3   Benefits and drawbacks of standardized multi-national research

Standardization is a matter of degree. At one extreme is complete uniformity of concepts, data collection techniques, methods of analysis and data presentation — a degree of perfection unachievable in practice. At the other end of the spectrum is a mere correspondence in framework and research purpose. The pros and cons of standardization as we discuss them below will therefore also apply in differing degrees, depending upon where in the range of possibilities a particular project is situated.[2]

Concepts and design

Standardization at the design and concept stage requires the co-operation of the theoreticians who develop the concepts and the practitioners who design the data collection schemes. Too often the regrettable reality in current data collection is that data users develop concepts which are fully justified theoretically but which have data requirements far outside the technical and/or financial scope of a national statistical office. On the other hand, survey statisticians often let themselves be guided too much by the demands of the field and collect data which do not permit analysis that is relevant for policy purposes. The end result is that scarce statistical resources are often wasted. The essential feedback between data users and producers in many countries is hampered by resource constraints and limited access to expertise. Furthermore, users and producers lack the motivation to get together to provide feedback. If such feedback can be fostered, a compromise agreement can be reached to use concepts that satisfy researchers and are not forbidding to data gatherers.

There are also, however, drawbacks associated with the standardization of concepts and design. The most important one is that when the interaction process described above takes place among the designers of a multi-national research project, they will also strive to reach a compromise position which balances relevance and feasibility of concepts, relative to a multitude of countries. Such a compromise position runs the risk of not fitting any individual country. This risk clearly becomes greater the larger the number of countries involved in the research project. In addition, there is the risk of losing policy relevance if the designers are oriented towards developed countries and do not have an adequate appreciation of conditions in developing countries. This may cause resentment from researchers in the developing countries where the actual data collection is to take place, who will be quick to point out the lack of relevance of the proposed research for their countries. This is in fact an often heard criticism of international research projects and is the foundation of the concern of the NHSCP in particular to be 'country-oriented'.[3]

It is therefore important to maintain a degree of flexibility in the proposed concepts and design. WFS did this by offering countries a core questionnaire and a range of modules from which they could choose to make up what would ultimately become a national fertility survey. Similarly, the LSMS has designed prototype questionnaires which need to be adapted in each country to reflect national customs, field conditions and policy concerns. Participating countries must, however, remain within the general conceptual framework of the study and are committed to maintaining the selected adaptations for at least two rounds of surveys so as to guarantee comparability over time. WFS thus offered a flexibility to choose *among* modules while the LSMS introduces flexibility by allowing some change and adaptation *within* modules. The WFS method maximizes international comparability of a set of core concepts but loses out somewhat in the ability to do the same kinds of behavioural analyses across countries, since not all the explanatory data will be available everywhere.

Data collection

The data collection method offered to a country participating in an international research programme will embody the experience previously gained in all other participating countries. Clearly, this is more useful to a country that participates late in the programme, and the first one may not benefit in this way at all. However, the programme will usually have been preceded by thorough research into existing and tried methodologies to distil the state of knowledge, and the fruits of this exercise will benefit even the first participating country.

In some cases this research and the subsequent implementation of the data collection itself can lead to innovations in the methodology. This was the case for the ICP. The basic data required for the ICP are price information on a whole range of consumer and investment goods. These need to be carefully specified to ensure comparability and must be representative of expenditures in these categories. Organizing such price collection in several developing countries led to a rigorous review of existing price collection practices and in several cases to substantial innovation and improvement. In some cases where local resource constraints precluded it, ICP funded an examination of price variation by region. Even where such initiatives could not be pursued, an appreciation was given in the basic statistics of the order of magnitude of this deficiency which could be used subsequently in setting local priorities for future statistical development.

The key point is that the multi-national programme can introduce external inputs of a fairly critical nature which are not available in one-time undertakings. The reason lies in the economies of scale that can be realized as a result of the repetition of the surveys in many countries. No single survey – in any country, however rich – could justify the amount of research, review and piloting that went into the WFS instrument. The same applies to many other aspects of the WFS package: the computer programs, the system design, the manuals, the model final report. These items were produced to higher standards than would have been possible for a single survey because the expense could be defrayed over a large number of surveys.

This opens up the possibility that this high-quality know-how might be institutionalized in the participating country. This requires that the country's statistical office sets up an appropriate counterpart to the international sponsor's experts so that the experience can be internalized and a capability established. If the country views the survey as a one-time event, little if any permanent transfer of know-how will occur.

It is not easy to judge the extent to which transfer of technology took place in WFS. One indicator may be the number of follow-up fertility surveys that the participating countries undertook on their own initiative. It must be pointed out, though, that it is still a fairly short time since the WFS surveys were carried out and many countries may not yet have felt the need to repeat a fertility survey. This issue will obviously become clearer over the next five years or so.

Even though the extent to which the benefits from methodology standardization are internalized depends largely on the countries' own efforts, a multi-national research programme can take direct action to promote such institutionalization. Both WFS and ECIEL organized national and regional seminars to promote exchanges of views and experiences among the participating countries. The development of documentation and manuals also contributes greatly to preserving the experience gained in the programme, and keeps it available for later reference for all participating countries, and potentially also for countries which were not in the programme. The 'problem reports' that WFS produced were quite effective in achieving that goal.

On the negative side, imposing a standardized methodology in a country may disregard differences in culture or thinking which could call for differentiated approaches. For example, certain cultures are particularly sensitive to revealing information about stillbirths, or the use of contraceptives, or income, etc., relative to others, which might affect the sequencing of questions, the gender of the enumerators, or other aspects of the survey methodology. Equally, in some countries farmers will be able to report on their farm yields by crop, while in others the information will need to be gathered plot by plot. In some market settings purchases are obtained more easily by asking weights and prices as opposed to total outlay, while in others the reverse is true. Such examples suggest that some flexibility is needed not only in questionnaire content but also in methodology. Even though methodology has a direct bearing on the quality and comparability of data, we feel that some adaptation should be permissible within limits. Adaptation of *questions* to local conditions can in fact promote comparability of *answers*, which is what is required for comparability in data. However, even if adaptations would take something away from comparability, we think that the resultant gain in overall data quality would generally more than make up for this.

Another potentially negative aspect of large international programmes of data collection is that countries may feel obligated to participate in them, particularly if the programme provides most or all of the funding. This may disturb their own statistical schedules, which presumably best reflect national needs and priorities. This can of course be seen as the price the country has to pay to receive the funding and the technical know-how. Nevertheless, we feel strongly that international efforts at data collection should exhibit maximum flexibility in accommodating existing plans for data collection in the participating countries.

Analysis

The major pay-off from standardized multi-national research is the possibility of comparing key policy variables and their development over time across countries. Such data are of use in singling out those aspects of the development process that are common to all or many countries and thus constitute lessons that can be transferred to countries at earlier stages of development. Household-level data are needed to study household decision-making behaviour and to help predict the responses of household groups that are the target of government policy interventions. Testing the robustness of observed relationships across countries can contribute greatly towards the improved design of development policy programmes by building upon the experience of many countries. To do this not only must the data be comparable across countries in terms of collection practices, but standardization of research in terms of analytical techniques used is also necessary.

Data processing and analysis constitute in many countries – not only less developed countries – a more severe capability bottleneck than the actual data collection. The numerous questionnaires that lie unanalysed on the shelves of many statistical offices are evidence of this and the experience of WFS and ECIEL confirms it: the assistance of the headquarters staff was most needed at the processing and analysis stages. The potential contribution of international research is particularly great in this area – efforts like WFS, LSMS, ECIEL virtually guarantee that the results will appear and that they will be presented in a format that makes them suitable for input into policy analysis both locally and internationally.

The drawback from the countries' perspective is that the research may not always reflect their national priorities, and it may be necessary that the data tapes leave the country to be analysed at the project's headquarters. Indeed, standardization of analysis seems in practice to coincide with centralization. ECIEL, for example, whose Co-ordination had a role similar to that of WFS' headquarters with respect to analysis, experienced a steadily increasing centralization throughout its life. The heterogeneity of computers, languages and packages available in the participating countries may make the production of comparable results from decentralized analysis a very slow and costly process, and sometimes even impossible. In some cases essential programming and analytic skills and tools may not be available at all locally. All this tends to shift the analytic work towards the project's headquarters, and the more this happens the more prominently the production of comparable results figures among the goals of the project.

Such centralization runs counter to the desirability for technology transfer to the participating countries, unless — as in the case of data collection methods — a conscious effort is made by the participating countries to institutionalize the process and build the analytical know-how into the overall statistical system. To the extent that centralization is a result of the striving for international comparability, then programmes of standardized multi-national research are not the best vehicle to improve local statistical standards. The NHSCP's approach is consistent with this: it is concerned directly with capability building, and is the least standardized of the projects we discuss here.

However, even if there is a trade-off between capability building, i.e. decentralization, and the ability to produce internationally comparable research, this does not mean that projects of standardized research cannot do anything to promote know-how in their participating countries. ECIEL compensated for its tendency towards centralization of activities by organizing apprenticeships in the Co-ordination for statisticians and researchers from the participating institutes. WFS had nationals from participating countries work with headquarters staff on the analysis. The LSMS provides in its arrangements with participating countries that researchers will be invited to World Bank headquarters to work jointly with LSMS staff on the analysis of the data tapes.

International research programmes can also contribute to the capability of the participating countries to perform data analyses by assisting in the provision of appropriate software. WFS helped countries mount the Concor and Cocents packages for data editing and tabulation. The LSMS is going one step further by providing the countries that test its modules with microprocessors on which the data can be directly entered in the field. Customized software is being developed to allow instantaneous data edits and to flag any apparent inconsistencies so that the enumerators can verify the information during their next visit to the household. The microprocessor's diskettes can then be sent to the statistical office's headquarters for computer processing and initial tabulation, using another set of specially designed software. This should greatly enhance the speed with which statistical offices can produce a first report on newly collected data. The LSMS is also planning to experiment with the use of microprocessors as a means of analysing data.[4]

Dissemination

WFS augmented the national reports by undertaking and publishing further analyses of the collected data, incorporating cross-country comparisons. These reports have contributed greatly to the understanding of what happened to fertility and its determinants worldwide. They also provided policy-makers in the participating countries with a valuable tool to start the design of various demographic policies, pending more specific analyses on the data. It is fair to say that dissemination of results both within countries and internationally has been much more thorough than if it had been left to individual countries to produce the reports. Following this example, the LSMS also intends to assume a major role in report-writing and dissemination. At the current stage this is done through the production of a series of analytical topic studies, based on existing data sets, which illustrate how data on levels of living contribute to understanding the impact of policies and to designing new ones. These topic studies will be repeated on the new data once these are available, in collaboration with analysts from the participating countries.

The major potential problem arising from dissemination by the international research unit is that some countries may object to the publication of politically sensitive information. The extent to which this problem may occur depends of course on the subject matter of the research. The WFS central unit took the position that the data were the property of the country and that it was for the country to say what could be disseminated.

35.4   Recommendations for the future

WFS was a very costly operation. Any recommendation about similar undertakings in the future will have to consider the cost-benefit ratio of alternatives. Was there another way this information could have been collected? We believe not. The WFS brought survey statisticians and demographers together to design the best possible field instrument that took into account analytical requirements and feasibility in the field. The alternative to WFS would have been a number of *ad hoc* fertility surveys in individual countries. In fact, before the start of WFS, quite a number of demographic surveys and censuses had already taken place. It is clear that these had not given the same broad picture of fertility and the same range and quality of data as was obtained from WFS.

Such achievements do not of course come without costs. Standardized multinational projects add to the costs of the national surveys, the costs of the headquarters staff, of providing various forms of assistance to the participating countries, of the training component, and of safeguarding the quality and comparability of the data. These higher costs are only partly offset by economies of scale in the collection and analysis of the same or similar data sets in many countries. An important priority for future multi-national standardized research projects is to develop ways to reduce the costs of improvements in data quality, by developing survey instruments and methodologies that require less technical assistance than was the case in WFS and that can more easily be implemented by the national statistical offices themselves. In this context, it is important to indicate the special opportunity offered by multi-national research projects to improve on the state of the art in data collection by building experimentation into the programme. WFS, for example, experimented with alternative sampling designs and different incentive systems to improve response rates and overall data quality. The LSMS intends to test out alternative questionnaires and reference periods in the collection of income and expenditure data. If comparable experiments are incorporated in the data collection in various participating countries, a large enough case load can be developed from which to make international recommendations.

We believe that there are a number of subject areas other than fertility that are suitable for standardized multi-national research, such as agriculture, migration and mortality. The full conditions of the agricultural sector are not known in many countries, in spite of many agricultural production and related surveys. Agriculture is still the occupation of the majority of the population in developing countries. A better understanding of how to increase agricultural productivity could yield significant pay-offs. Again the rapid rate of urbanization is a problem faced by almost all developing countries. Solid behavioural analysis of the household decision-making process that underlies rural-to-urban migration, in a community context, is essential to designing policies that can adequately cope with the phenomenon. Finally, the success of WFS in enhancing knowledge about fertility virtually provides in itself the argument for similarly enhancing the information available about its counterpart demographic phenomenon, viz. mortality.

Levels of living is a subject of high priority for multi-national research as it provides the basic indicator to gauge the success of the development effort by. The LSMS addresses this subject and has brought together a team of economists and survey statisticians to design a survey instrument that is focused on income and expenditure but will also gather the social and economic corollary data necessary for an analysis of levels of living and for monitoring progress in raising them. The LSMS does not intend such a rigid degree of standardization as WFS since it leans more toward comparability within a country over time and between socio-economic groups than towards international comparability. The analytic emphasis is on the study of household behaviour and response to market signals. Nevertheless, the intention is that all participating countries adopt LSMS' framework of concepts and analysis. For example, it is deemed essential for an explanatory analysis of levels of living to have information on the activities of each household member both in the labour market and outside. Without such information a study of living standards would be incomplete. The LSMS thus standardizes the broad content of its survey instrument but countries adapt the specific way information is collected to their needs and conditions.

The quest for standardization and international comparability has several inherent dangers. The main danger lies in the potential conflict with local and national needs for consistent and comparable data over time. If these needs are overlooked, the local and national development of appropriate techniques and the establishment of a lasting capability will be hindered. While there are several legitimate international demands for data, such as comparable national accounts and trade statistics, domestic demands must in our opinion take precedence over international needs. The challenge, therefore, lies in evolving frameworks which can serve both. There is a legitimate cause for action at the international level to identify a limited, well-specified set of data that are necessary for international comparisons. Equally, there is need for agreement on certain basic standard international classifications. The associated data collection must be designed so that it does not exclude national uses of the data. For this to be feasible the recognition of the national priority is required from the very start of the design of multi-national data collection and research efforts as well as of international classifications.

The main advantage of WFS came from the completeness of the range of services it provided, starting from assistance in the construction of a suitable sample frame where needed, through data collection, to analysis and publication of results. We believe that this type of vertical integration of research will have to characterize any future efforts of standardized multi-national research.

Notes

1. We are grateful to Dennis De Tray, Graham Pyatt and Christopher Scott for valuable comments on an earlier draft. We are also indebted to Anne Harrison, whose many specific suggestions greatly helped to improve this chapter. We also thank the participants of session P6 of the World Fertility Survey 1984 Symposium, and in particular K. de Graft-Johnson and M. Macura, who were discussants for the paper.
2. Standardization can apply to research over time within a country, and to research across countries. We shall restrict ourselves mostly to the latter.
3. Nevertheless, the NHSCP does suggest that countries follow broad international standards and definitions but that they incorporate an internationally sponsored multi-country inquiry into their statistical programmes only if the data are of direct use to themselves (UN 1980c, pp. 4–7).
4. Microprocessors have several advantages over mainframe computers: they are a relatively cheap form of hardware and easier to operate. They are also less sensitive to temperature changes and power surges.

36

Implications for Future Demographic Enquiries

William Brass

36.1 The stage of the WFS programme

It is too early to assess the contribution of WFS to the extension of demographic knowledge, including under that heading factual description, understanding of forces and capacity to influence. As yet the mass of data has been little more than outlined, although the pilot and feasibility investigation of parts of the materials have been wide ranging and significant. In a longer time-perspective the most important findings from WFS will be about the consistency or otherwise of the relationships of social and economic markers to demographic character-istics conditioning fertility and child mortality. Only the simplest of these have been investigated systematically over the many populations, diverse in culture as well as political and economic organization, which are required for adequate generalization. The accessions of data, particularly over the past two or three years, have been too large and rapid for the population research community to digest them.

As with all sciences, the progress of demography occurs through a mix of new problems, different types of information, conceptual invention and innovative analysis techniques. WFS was stimulated by what could be called a new set of conditions — the increasing evidence of widespread fertility falls — and generated data which, although not novel in concept, were new in extent and comparability. To understand the implications it is necessary to realize how little survey ma-terial of a WFS type was available previously. Many small-scale studies had been reported but coverage was limited geographically and in detail; most notably, publication was inadequate. When Potter (1977) was investigating the 'accordion' effect in reporting of the timing of past births to mothers, he was able, with all the resources of the Office of Population Research, Princeton, to find only two or three surveys on which to test his ideas.

The provision of the data leads to the development of new models and techniques. But this is a slow, exploratory process. In the present instance it was retarded even further by the problems of familiar and unfamiliar response errors. The WFS countries included a proportion where previous experience had shown the information from retrospective demographic surveys to be badly biased. The African populations are probably the most extreme in this respect but every region is characterized by some particular uncertainty. Although for broader pur-poses useful checks of accuracy can be applied, in many analyses the only practi-cable strategy is to proceed with a rigorous consideration of how configurations and relationships may be distorted by error. The search must be for techniques which are robust as well as, or rather than, efficient. This extra dimension multiplies the difficulty of arriving at firm conclusions. In a population with, say, changing age at marriage the disentanglement of cohort–time trends in marital fertility from truncated birth histories is complex enough without the additional confounding from misstatements of ages of mothers and years at childbirth.

Response error effects cannot be deduced by abstract reasoning. Their elucidation and separation from substantive features are only possible through long, patient investigation of observations. The approach has begun to clarify important questions about the use of techniques and models, but in many instances there is still much to be done. For example, despite progress in methods for studying the components of birth intervals from pregnancy histories (see Mosley, Werner and Becker 1982), a full grasp of the intricacies of biases and errors has not been achieved. The ideas and techniques of life-table calculations of birth intervals by order from maternity histories were devised before the WFS programme. The exploration and systematization were made possible by the survey results (Rodríguez and Hobcraft 1980; Juárez 1983). Cohort parity progression ratios (or near parity progression ratios) thus estimated are critical for the detection of trends in the effects of family limitation (Brass and Juárez 1983). The calculations which earlier seemed complicated and exotic are now, with familiarity, an easily understood routine with obvious objectives and standard computing packages. Nevertheless there are still uncertainties, particularly about the practicability of using synthetic cohort life-table calculations for time periods. There could be substantial advantages in the up-to-dateness of estimates if these calculations were sufficiently accurate (Feeney 1983).

A further example of a different type comes from the study of social determinants of fertility. It has become sufficiently clear that such determinants do not act as largely independent effects on a unitary outcome. Fertility is multi-dimensional and the social factors interact in subtle ways. In these circumstances multivariate analysis for explanatory as opposed to descriptive purposes requires the construction of general, meaningful models (Brillinger 1983). Very few of the many multivariate investigations of WFS data have been of this kind. The careful, experimental examination of alternative explanatory models on large sets of observations has only just begun (Entwisle, Hermalin and Mason 1982).

There is nothing new in the conclusion that the collection and organization of data do not constitute a programme but only the first stage of one. But, however often repeated, the truism seems to be constantly forgotten. Routine descriptive measurements may be produced quickly. With modern facilities, well-tried analyses of relationships presented in accurate, familiar types of information are not greatly demanding. Much useful extraction of materials from the WFS programme falls under these headings. As noted above, however, the studies which will reveal the patterns and links to aid interpretation and understanding are still comparatively undeveloped. It is reasonable to assume that much of the most important usage of WFS material is still to come. The 1911 Census of the United Kingdom was a pioneer in the collection of data on children born to mothers and also numbers surviving. The results were effectively presented and discussed in the Census Reports. But reanalysis of the birth measures in the 1970s contributed significantly to an increased understanding of the natural fertility of females and males (Barrett 1971; Anderson 1975). Investigations of trends in child mortality from 1895-1910 by techniques invented in the 1970s are now giving new insights into the causes of the decline in death rates.

36.2 Lessons from the WFS experience

An assessment of the implications of the WFS experience must, therefore, be an interim one based not only on confirmed results but also on a forecast of how successful ongoing and prospective studies will be. The balancing of the uses of the programme outputs must depend on the stance of the evaluator; heavy weight must be given to the importance of the immediate descriptive measures for planning in individual countries. Nevertheless, in the examination of the needs for future demographic enquiries, the general returns from the WFS programme as a whole, the more speculative issue, should also play a role. The programme was not just an aggregation of individual surveys.

The purpose of this chapter is to comment on the implications of the WFS experience rather than the experience itself. Some broad indications of the relevant lessons are required, however, as a basis for the discussion. It is noted elsewhere in this volume that the most fundamental finding is that the recording of birth histories retrospectively can be successful even in populations with low standards of literacy and relatively unfamiliar with national systems of statistics. Although such a suggestion would not have been novel before the WFS programme, it would have been contested on both theoretical (social plausibility) and empirical (too many poor quality surveys) grounds. The evidence is now conclusive that efficient organization, management and staff training can ensure accuracy of answers to the extent that this is within the capacity of respondents. Of course, there may still be problems of deliberate deception (induced abortions) but these are rarer than has often been claimed. Inadequate memory of respondents in societies where this is not institutionally or culturally reinforced (ages and timing of events) may be a nuisance but knowledge of how such effects can be minimized or allowed for is improving. The reporting of happenings which do not leave any mark on the stock, for example births which have not survived or dissolved marriages, is of much higher quality than has been postulated on theoretical grounds.

There are, however, strict limits to the scope for recording series of transitions retrospectively. The episodes which are fundamentals of life (marriage and births and deaths of children) are of a different order even from such notable experiences as employment and residence histories. The WFS attempts to obtain lengths of breastfeeding retrospectively have not been too encouraging. No doubt carefully structured and lengthy interviews could lead to reasonably complete reconstitution for some of these series but many would be beyond recall and the costs would be formidable. There is still much to be learned about the extent to which a small number of past happenings can capture a substantial part of the relevant social and economic forces, for example a move from a rural to an urban area or leaving the parental home, the assumption or loss of farm ownership. The growing evidence from research in developed countries that such 'critical episodes' do exist — completion of education and home ownership may be noted — suggests that it is not over-optimistic to believe that enquiries of WFS type can make a contribution to explanations which depend on transitions far from the current time.

The time series of births, marriages and child deaths constitute a partial replacement for vital registration. The limitations are obvious. Numbers are small and severely truncated in past time because only women under fifty are included. (That this is not a necessary limitation is demonstrated by the results from some other birth history surveys; the most outstanding is the 1982 one-in-a-thousand sample of China, where the birth series was recorded for women up to age 64.) But experience with the WFS data has shown that there are advantages as well as problems. These come mainly from the greater flexibility. In developed countries there is increasing realization of the importance of tempo components in the interpretation of fertility change; these are examined through ages of mothers at first birth and by the subsequent birth intervals. Although the factors and implications may be different, such analyses are equally required for less developed countries. In principle, the observations are best obtained from birth registrations at which the appropriate auxiliary information is recorded (age of mother, birth order and time of preceding birth at least). Few countries collect these details and fewer still have series of sufficient length for effective analysis. The amendment of the registration system to obtain the required data is a cumbersome and long-term business. The quasi-registration from birth histories can be readily explored in pilot studies and modified in the light of the findings, even if sample sizes are ultimately found to be too small for the most incisive interpretation and application. For critical purposes such as population projections, the evidence of tendencies from the sample may be virtually as valuable as the more specific measures from complete registration.

A linked but slightly different feature is the extra dimension which comes from the 'natural' grouping of the births in families (whether defined through the mother only or by both parents). Traditional data for measuring population flow (registration and numbers at risk from updated census returns) have determined the types of problem which can most easily be studied. Inevitably these become the classical problems which dominate thinking. When statistics appear in a new arrangement, the first response is an attempt to manipulate them to answer the old problems. It is only gradually that their capacity for tackling new and possibly more significant questions emerges. The 'natural' grouping of births allows study, for example, of the differentials in pace of childbearing, of the extent to which series of short birth intervals are characteristic of some mothers who contribute most heavily to total births. Certain analyses have suggested that birth concentrations of this kind are a powerful element in excess child mortality. The indirect evidence is conflicting, however, and birth histories, with associated child deaths, provide the means for direct investigation.

Another topic which has advanced greatly along with the WFS programme is the integration of proximate determinants to account for the level of fertility (Bongaarts 1982). Of course, the concept of fertility as the product of a set of components in exposure to risk of conception and birth intervals is not new. The progress in empirical knowledge and technical analysis which has led to a firm specification of the relationships might have occurred without WFS. Data of the type obtained in the surveys were, however, the most valuable for the development and substantiation of the ideas and methods. Since fertility trends operate through these components and usually involve changes in more than one simultaneously, not always having effects in the same direction, the accounting process is critical for interpretation, at least in the shorter term. In particular, it is possible for small and perhaps hardly detectable falls in fertility to be the outcome of significant alterations in the effects of the proximate determinants, with future implications which need to be taken into account.

One of the main aims of the WFS programme was the provision of measures which were comparable over a wide range of populations. As noted above, the assessment of the full returns from this policy is hindered by the as yet incomplete exploration of explanatory models and theories. But the findings from the more direct, descriptive comparisons have often been illuminating. One illustration of this has been given above. Despite some inconsistencies, the degree of coherence in the relation of fertility to proximate determinants has been impressive. Another instance, as yet inadequately examined, is the variation in the interval from marriage to first birth in relation to cohabitation customs. Recent basic analysis of child mortality (Rutstein 1983) has revealed consistencies and differences among countries which in some features were in line with expectation but in others surprising. Thus the increase in infant and child mortality at higher birth orders in all countries was predictable; the diversity of the relation of the first birth probabilities of death to the others was not. Developed country experience is of a greater risk to first births than to second and third, but in several Latin American and a few other populations the lowest death rates were for the first birth. Although the rise in infant mortality as the interval to the preceding birth becomes short is in accord with past research, the size of the increase is remarkably large; the apparent continuance of the downward trend at intervals well above the average is also notable. Further investigation should help in the unravelling of the interactions of economic circumstances, child care and disease transmission as contributors to child death.

36.3 Improvements in data sources and estimation of measures

Although judgement on the implications of the WFS programme for future data collection is not the same as judgement of the contribution to the increase in demographic knowledge already made, the two issues are closely intermingled. The knowledge is largely conditional and time-limited. Methods that have been effective are likely to continue to be so unless, of course, superior approaches emerge. It is necessary then to examine in broad terms how population data sources and the capacity to extract relevant measures from them have advanced over the past 15 years or so. Attention will be focused on the less developed countries but reference will also be made, where appropriate, to populations with more sophisticated statistical systems as a standard of comparison.

The conventional, and largely correct, simple explanation of the difficulties of securing firm results about the population dynamics of the Third World is the lack of complete vital registration data. The other major traditional source of information, the census, is directed to the delineation of the population stock. Although many less developed countries have deficiencies in census-taking (in frequency, in coverage, in range of content) the resulting problems are, generally, less intractable. There have been some dramatic improvements in the quantity and quality of censuses. The most striking example of extension is, of course, China. Equally, there have been disappointing cases where the more recent censuses of a country are poorer than earlier ones. It appears that, in many less developed countries, the potential for greater accuracy of response, through higher levels of education and increased familiarity with the demands of record-keeping, is greater; the realization of that potential has, however, been frustrated by political and economic instability.

Continuous, complete vital records provide a basis for analysis which is potentially more refined and reliable than can be achieved by any survey scheme, however ingenious. In a few countries vital registration has come sufficiently near to completeness in the 1970s for the derived measures to be used without adjustment, but the populations covered are small and not among those for which knowledge is most scanty. The overall value of the gains from the greater certainty is important. On the other hand, the broad perspective is little altered. In the context of the demand for better population information to aid planning and policy, it is clear that the rate of improvement in the supply of satisfactory census and, above all, vital registration data is far too slow. The dependence of the improvement on economic and social development is too strong to offer much hope that devices designed to hurry it along faster might be more than marginally successful. The availability of data from the traditional sources is not then greatly different now from the circumstances which led in part to the arguments for establishing the WFS programme.

There has, nevertheless, been a large increase in knowledge of levels, trends and differentials in fertility and childhood mortality of less developed countries over recent years. This has been due to a combination of non-traditional sources of data and methods of analysis. Although there are a number of subvariants and combinations of systems, it is not appropriate here to enter into these in detail. Broadly, there are three approaches to the reconstitution of vital registration-based measures which have been important, apart from the recording of birth histories of a sample of women at a single-round survey. Excluded from this classification are intensive studies of small communities, in which information about the population is collected by repeated household visits at quite frequent intervals over considerable periods of time. Such studies are a diverse group and cover the observations of resident anthropologists, special health programmes often linked to medical training, follow-up surveillance, and larger projects which have expanded their aims to encompass more general demographic objectives, as in Matlab, Bangladesh. The increase in the understanding of a number of specific issues of demographic interactions from these studies has been very valuable but the overlap with the objectives and contributions of WFS-type enquiries is small. It is worth noting, however, that research into the explanations of population phenomena, for example the response to particular methods of family planning or the effects of breastfeeding practices on child mortality, where much specific detail is essential, may best be pursued by these means.

The three non-traditional approaches to the elucidation of population dynamics are the collection of vital statistics through household visits, the estimation of past fertility and mortality from 'stock' information obtained at censuses or large sample enquiries, and the reconstruction of birth histories from the same type of data. The classification is an operational one rather than the consequence of a clear principle. There are cross-breeds which link the categories (and also those with WFS-type procedures). Nevertheless, the essential features of each class are clear enough and their main merits and limitations must be briefly examined.

Multi-visit household surveys include schemes of 'active' registration, where the registrar is responsible for the detection of vital events if the relatives do not report them. There may be checks through more regular visits to the households with various degrees of independence from the original recording. In the extreme case, the vital events from two clearly different sources may be matched and omissions estimated, usually on the assumption of independence and by application of the Chandrasekar-Deming formula (Marks, Seltzer and Krotki 1974). To produce large enough numbers of events for the analysis of trends and differentials the samples must be large; for management control the households must be in substantial geographic aggregates since formations, dissolutions and migration are usually a severe complication.

The observations and derived measures from these schemes are similar in nature to the results from traditional registration, although there may be some theoretical advantages in the direct relation between the collection of data on events and populations at risk. In principle, the derivation of measures for sub-groups and hence the analysis of differentials is straightforward. Nevertheless, the contribution from many of the multi-visit surveys has been disappointing in relation to the effort and resources expended. It is in fact virtually impossible to cost the schemes since much of the expenditure is carried by existing government services. But the events recorded are sufficiently infrequent for the return per household visit to be small, particularly if elaborate checking by dual recording and verification of doubtful matches is adopted.

On a limited geographical scale valuable results have been achieved, particularly on mortality. In these examples the dividing line from the intensive studies of small communities, excluded as being not sufficiently relevant to the present assessment, is slight. At the national level the accuracy of the derived measures, whether adjusted by checks or not, has usually been suspect. Most important of all, the strength of the traditional, complete vital registration lies in the provision of a long, regular series of rates extending to near the current time. Few of the national multi-visit programmes have been able to sustain either continuity or up-to-date publication of statistics. The failure has been due to a variety of reasons but the main one is probably that the problems of continuous management are too formidable. This applies to the processing of the data in addition to their collection. The theoretical advantages of the approach for the investigation of differentials have nowhere been exploited, presumably because the sample sizes have been too small or the processing too demanding. Despite these broad criticisms there is at least one country, India, in which the Sample Registration Scheme, incorporating dual recording of events with multi-visits to households and checking, has been notably successful. In many Indian states the observations have been sufficiently accurate to provide acceptable series of fertility and mortality measures from the beginning of the 1970s. It may be deduced that there is a stage in the development of countries when the organization and acceptance of central statistical systems makes it possible to operate successfully a sample registration scheme of the class considered. It seems likely that, in some countries at least, that stage will precede the conditions which make it practicable to establish complete registration. However, experience suggests that the return for resources expended in the many countries which are not yet ready for activity of this type is poor.

The utilization of information related to population dynamics but collected at a census or largish demographic enquiry has steadily increased over the past 10 years. (The same questions can be usefully asked in small sample surveys but the problems and gains are notably different; no special attention will be paid to them here.) The surveys can be called retrospective but, in most cases, the measures derived are from a cumulation of events in the past which characterize the respondent in the present, e.g. the total children born to each woman, how many of these have died, whether parents of sample members are alive or dead. The aim is to achieve accuracy in simple, comparatively cheap surveys with particular emphasis on the addition of the useful questions to censuses, or linked enquiries which have a variety of purposes in addition to the estimation of fertility, mortality and population growth.

With parallel improvements in the design of the questions, the conduct and management of the fieldwork and the techniques of analysis, the approach has achieved remarkable success in the estimation of fertility and mortality levels, trends and differentials. The key has been the construction of demographic models which are efficient in the sense that they describe patterns and relationships well but depend on only a few parameters which can be determined from the modest current observations. The most recent developments have provided tools for determining past trends in mortality for both children and adults over a substantial period. A very large body of work on mortality differentials has also been undertaken over the past few years. The main problem here is not the estimation but the relevance of the classification (based on current characteristics of respondents such as education, religion, occupation, residence, housing conditions and so on) to deaths of relatives (children, parents, spouses) over past time. All attempts to generate vital statistics by survey, however, are burdened by the difficulty of classifying those at risk by contemporary features. The gains from the fertility questions have been less impressive for a number of reasons, including larger errors in reports by older women and the availability of alternative analysis approaches, for example quasi-stable population methods and reverse survival. There has been little application to the derivation of trends. On the other hand, recent research has shown that it is possible to make fairly robust estimates of parity progression ratios for cohorts (Brass 1984). From the ratios for middle birth orders (say 3-6) and women around the centre of the reproductive period, good indications of trends in fertility components strongly affected by family planning use can be obtained. The achieved mean parities of women by age group which are found from the responses on total children born can also give valuable, although rather inflexible, information on fertility differentials by characteristics such as education which are fixed largely before the start of reproduction. The examination of these measures at two time points (say censuses or linked demographic enquiries) at a ten-year interval is particularly direct and powerful for tracing the major features of trends.

The limitations of the class of survey described lie, in a sense, in the strengths. Summary robust measures interpreted through simple models are excellent if the data are accurate and the assumptions valid. If either of these criteria fails there is not the detail to assess and adjust for the errors. Inconsistencies may be difficult to explain and interpretation must then be tentative. It is not clear that the measures obtained from more intensive birth history surveys of (say) mean parities are necessarily of improved accuracy, but more effective checking and adjustment is possible. The strength of two similar surveys in sequence is far more than double that of one alone because of the capacity for cross-checking fertility, mortality and indeed other dynamic inputs.

The final approach to be considered is the technique known as the 'own-children' method. It would have been logical, in some respects, to include it in the previous paragraphs since the data used are of census or large enquiry type, most conveniently organized with the help of 'cumulated event' reports. On the other hand, its development and use have been largely separate and the outcome appears as a population flow. The method is a form of reverse survival in which children recorded on a household schedule by age are linked to their mothers (preferably through a specific question but, if need be, by general rules for selecting the most likely of the candidates). Tabulations can then be produced of the children born in each past year by the age and characteristics of their mothers. These differ from birth history tabulations only by the deaths of children and separation of offspring and mothers. Aggregate allowances can be made for births which do not survive through questions on children born and dead or other mortality information. Widespread adoption can complicate the birth history reconstruction. Experiments on the insertion of births to allow for the dead children have been tried (Cho and Bussen 1985) with some success. It appears that when child mortality is low at least, the distortions of interval analysis which result are not very important.

One of the most valuable features of the 'own children' method is the ease with which differentials in fertility by the characteristics of the mother (including those which are household and husband-based) can be investigated. The sample sizes are usually large enough for significant cross-tabulations to separate out confounding influences. However, the usable birth histories cannot be extended too far into the past since the method breaks down when children begin to live apart from the mother in appreciable numbers. Any auxiliary events which have not left an unambiguous mark on the present, the dissolution and re-formation of marriages for example, must be recorded through specific questions as in any other retrospective survey; the large sample sizes restrict the possibilities of doing this extensively because of the high costs of interview time.

36.4 Population data needs

The data collection systems have been discussed. What are the needs? Fifteen years ago the answer to that question was reasonably simple and sufficiently general. A dogmatic review was given in a paper by the present writer (Brass 1968). It dealt with Africa but the discussion and conclusions would have applied to most of the less developed world. The primary aim was stated to be a regular series of good quality censuses. The numbers of persons by location, sex, age and the major social and economic divisions were the basic population ingredients for administration, planning and policy. Sample estimates of the stock were a poor second best because many of the measures of significance were for quite small subgroups, such as the secondary educated in an age group for a limited area. Next in importance came guidance on the population dynamics for assessing the future. The suggestion was that, in the absence of adequate vital registration (the usual condition), the most cost-effective procedure was estimation of fertility and mortality through the simple, retrospective-type information on births and survival of relatives collected at a census or linked demographic enquiry. In fact, at the time, the methods for analysing such data were primitive compared with the current, sophisticated efficiency. It was, however, believed with justification that in nearly all the relevant populations fertility was relatively constant and mortality falling fairly slowly. Rough measures would suffice.

By the time WFS was established the scene had changed. There had been many good censuses in the late 1960s and early seventies; the retrospective-type questions had become much more widely used and their strengths and limitations could be better assessed. By far the most important movement, however, was in the demographic trends themselves. It was beginning to become clear that, in many countries, mortality was improving rapidly and that fertility might be falling, although the size and correlates of the trends were usually controversial. It was, of course, to the elucidation of the latter issue that WFS was mainly devoted.

The large amount of data generated by WFS is one of the factors in a current reassessment of the needs, but there are others. Again the population dynamics must have primacy. Although mortality may not be decreasing faster now than ten years ago, the most notable falls are occurring in countries which would previously have been regarded as closer to demographic stagnation. Kenya, Ghana, Indonesia, Syria and Peru are examples. Downward trends in fertility have accelerated in populations where they were slight around 1970 (Mexico, Brazil, India, Indonesia, etc.) and are beginning to appear in many other places. Forecasting, and indeed keeping a satisfactory account of current numbers which is a primary administrative requirement, becomes increasingly difficult.

Another important element is the rise in expectation or ambition. Much of this stems from progress in demographic science and the greater demands in the developed countries. It is not clear which of these factors was the initial stimulus since they are so closely intertwined. Countries with sophisticated statistical systems are no longer content to rely on vital registration as the sole source, supplementing the census, for the derivation of flow measures. The increased weight given to proximate determinants (marriage, divorce, remarriage, contraceptive behaviour), tempo (ages at births, intervals) and the interpretation of reproductive behaviour (female employment, housing, birth intentions) comes partly from real changes in impact and partly from recognition of their influence. In many Third World countries similar issues arise even if the mode of operation is sometimes different. Thus alterations in breastfeeding customs and the adoption of family planning may cause even faster and more complex changes in birth intervals than the deliberate spacing prompted by economic fluctuations of the low fertility populations.

The more developed countries have attempted to meet these newer concerns in a variety of ways. In some, extra information has been sought at registration of births, although the scope of the detail has been and is limited. Minimum birth histories, that is with little recording of associated events, have been collected at censuses. There are attempts to establish longitudinal surveys of individuals over time, both with large samples and a modest range of items and with small samples but full and rich series of events. In a few countries it has been possible to institute complete registers of the population in which the basic characteristics such as residence, married state and numbers of children are recorded when the transitions occur. The most commonly used method, however, has been retrospective surveys. They include general household surveys or micro-censuses, in which data are collected by interview in a continuous or near-continuous system. The questionnaires are regularly altered to cover new topics but the basic demographic items of census type (residence, sex, age, household relationships, source of livelihood) normally remain. Among the possible, alternating topics are births to women. Many surveys in the class considered, however, have been single, specialized endeavours with an emphasis on particular facets of reproductive behaviour, for example methods and effectiveness of family planning, competition of childbearing and female employment, family size intentions and achievement. Others are reasonably described as of a more general WFS type, although there is much variability in detail and the borderlines between categories depend on the features which are regarded as critical for classification.

It is not now sensible to be as dogmatic and general about the population data needs of less developed countries as it was 15 years ago. On the other hand, it is arguable that a prescription for the future can be given with more confidence than at the start of the WFS programme. The scene is now far more diverse than in the past, particularly with respect to the quality of censuses and the range of retrospective information from them. In a few countries vital registration has improved sufficiently to be near reliable, in others checks and adjustments can be applied effectively and, as noted, sample registration has been successful in significant examples. Thus the discussion on the best means to advance knowledge further for a particular population depends on a close assessment of the extent and accuracy of the data available through the routine statistical system.

The primary necessity, as explained previously, is for good quality, regular, full censuses. Nothing in the experience of WFS has any bearing on that. No procedure has emerged by which vital registration, complete or sample, with the accuracy of detail to trace inter-censal population numbers by location and biological subgroups, can be achieved quickly and cheaply. It must await social and administrative development. However, the broad features of the population dynamics can be outlined quite well through censuses which include appropriate retrospective questions, possibly in a post-enumeration enquiry. A large amount of recent research on the analysis of data of this type from two or more successive censuses has established the techniques and the most useful questions. It appears that these can be very few. In effect, therefore, the topic has become part of census planning and design. The 'own-children' method can, in principle, be linked and regarded as an aspect of census tabulation. It is, of course, possible for both retrospective questions and 'own-children' data extraction to be incorporated in a demographic enquiry inter-censally. On a national basis, there would seem little to be gained unless the sample size was large. The operation would then be of census type. Because of the broad, averaged estimates of fertility, mortality and growth rates which come from this approach, the argument about frequency becomes inseparable from a consideration of intervals between censuses. The idea of full censuses every 10 years with a large sample enquiry at the mid inter-censal point is attractive but many factors would have to be taken into account for a particular country, pre-eminently the rate of social and demographic change and the organization of statistical services.

The gaps which remain in the population knowledge required for effective utilization in planning and policy are of currency, pattern and proximate determination. Of course, the explanation of trends in fertility, mortality and migration in social and economic terms is more important still, but this depends on much that cannot be encompassed in a data collection programme. If these trends can be traced in significant detail, there is a vastly increased chance that the explanations of deeper causes will be relevant and helpful. Even without the explanations, the measurement of the present and extrapolation to the future will be improved. As noted above, the developed countries have used a number of means to supplement censuses and vital registration for the delineation of the significant detail of the dynamics. Most of these approaches are impracticable in less developed countries for reasons which have been already indicated or are sufficiently obvious. Updated population registers and longitudinal surveys are hugely demanding on administration and management; the addition of more items in registration could only affect a few places; birth histories in full censuses are very expensive and little of serial detail is usually included. There remain the small-sample, retrospective surveys of different types.

36.5 WFS experience and future demographic enquiries

The implications of the WFS experience can now be assessed in relation to the gaps in population knowledge which should be filled and the alternative ways, largely explored in the more developed countries, which might be adopted to fill them. There are populations, mainly in Africa, in which demographic characteristics are, as yet, comparatively static and others, mostly of modest size, in Asia or Latin America, where data sources approach those of Europe. In the majority, however, the tracing of trends in fertility and mortality with appropriate detail would be valuable and this can only be done through retrospective surveys. Although these were divided above into different types according to the range of topics covered (broad or narrow) and the organization of collection (regular, general household or specifically demographic), the distinctions are not central to the present evaluation. By a WFS-type survey is meant the collection of complete birth histories from a modest-sized sample of women, along with related information on the proximate determinants of the quantum and tempo of fertility, including child mortality and contraceptive use, and on social and economic characteristics.

The earlier discussion of the experience from the WFS programme shows a close agreement between what the surveys can provide and what is needed to supplement knowledge from well-designed censuses. The fit of the attainable to the desirable is not ideal. Adult mortality trends and, indeed, at old ages, levels are not well captured by WFS methods. The subgroup details of births and child deaths (by geographical areas, cultural divisions, educational levels, etc.) are normally less reliable because of sample errors than would be wished. But apart from simply increasing the sample size by a substantial multiplier, with prohibitive costs, there is no practicable way of achieving the ideal. The assumption that the surveys supplement well-designed censuses, that is with appropriate retrospective questions (including those from which adult mortality is derived), goes a long way towards the specification of the cheapest combination of data sources for the estimation of the components of population change. A considerable number of censuses now fall within the desired category. The integration of the census and survey results can overcome most of the limitations of time extension of the former and subgroup detail of the latter.

As indicated earlier, the strength of the WFS-type data is in the 'natural' grouping of births and child deaths in families with the related proximate determinants. In many less developed countries the most important knowledge is of how trends in fertility over time are mediated by the proximate determinants in the major social groups. The experience of the WFS programme is that in favourable circumstances most of this knowledge can be extracted, and in less favourable a useful part of it. It seems likely that with further comparative analysis and verification of models even more will be possible. There is a fair correlation between favourable and valuable in the sense that the better data have tended to come from populations in which social and demographic changes were most rapid. There are exceptions, however.

Since the comments imply that future demographic enquiries of WFS type should be closely fitted to the other data sources in the country and these remain very variable, the conclusion is that a flexible, rather than a rigid approach should be adopted. The search for consistencies in the relation of social and economic factors to reproduction, and hence explanations through comparative analysis, has as yet not progressed far enough for it to be clear what information, which can be obtained, would be most powerful in the next worldwide attack. Until the lessons have been digested, the objective should be a major contribution to the more immediate needs of individual countries. Of course, where the same kinds of data are collected in different surveys it is important to make them as comparable as practicable.

What is collected should be fitted to the population's demographic condition and statistical organization. If there has already been a WFS-type enquiry, this becomes a part of the sources to which a new survey should be related. There are obviously gains if classification and measurement definitions in the two similar surveys are the same from the point of view of fixing points in time series. It does not appear, however, that any very strong advantages come from direct comparisons of measures for the same cohort members at the times of the surveys. These provide some checks on the accuracy of recording and indications of change in state but the sample sizes are probably too small for much to be derived. Similar comparisons with census data could be much more powerful.

Probably, on the principles suggested here, sample sizes should be larger in some surveys and the detail of factors associated with the determination of births reduced. This would be particularly the case in countries with weaker data from censuses and large demographic enquiries. Again, what has been said implies that no universal rules about the frequency of the surveys required can be laid down. It seems unlikely that there would be a sufficient return for survey intervals of less than five years. There are clearly countries where demographic change is so rapid that a strong case can be made for a five-year interval in terms of the criteria of current accuracy and reduced errors of forecasts for planning. Whether the costs would be justified by the usage of the data cannot, however, be given a general answer. A timing near the middle of a ten-year inter-censal period is a tidy and attractive prospect.

Increasingly, however, there are likely to be surveys with an emphasis on the economy, the labour force, agricultural production and so on which will contain demographic information which can be put to use in the reconstruction of the population dynamics. The availability of such evidence must be taken into account. There is scope for the embedding of the demographic enquiry within a regular system of household interviews or for relating it to other surveys focused on different subjects but using units from the same sample at some degree of aggregation. But it should be noted that the practical problems of incorporating measures from the common aggregates in analyses of the demographic responses have proved formidable; the demands on data management and processing are high.

To summarize, surveys of WFS type (where the class is defined broadly) should be widely used for the collection of demographic data in less developed countries. Their main contribution will be in the estimation of trends in fertility and child mortality, detailed in time and component parts, in close relation to proximate determinants. The design of the surveys, in questions, sample sizes and timing should be fitted to the other sources of population data, notably censuses. Since censuses are the cumulated outcome of flows, they contain some information on the population dynamics which can be linked to birth history data. Where the system of census-type enquiry questions on cumulated fertility and mortality, devised to give the maximum capacity to estimate these measures effectively, is in operation, an extensive reconstruction of the dynamics is possible. The replacement of reliance on enquiries of WFS type by a mixture of sources (vital registration, longitudinal studies, general household surveys, a variety of specialist sample enquiries) as in the developed countries is likely to be slow over a large part of the world. The emphasis on the contribution of the WFS-type surveys to the data needed in planning and policy in the individual populations does not imply that their function in advancing research into social and economic explanations of demographic processes will be less important. The integrated results will provide wide scope for such studies and the flexibility advocated is not of the kind which should seriously damage comparability. As the comparative analyses of the existing WFS datasets continue, it will become clearer what social and economic characteristics, measured in what way, should be common to the bulk of the future surveys.

37

Dissemination and Utilization of Findings and Methodology within Countries

Manuel Ortega
Martin Vaessen

37.1 Introduction

This chapter presents the results of a postal survey about the *dissemination* of National Fertility Survey (NFS) findings in nine countries and the *utilization* of NFS findings and methodology in 25 countries. The survey was carried out under contract with the WFS. The countries intended for inclusion in this study were those which had published their First Country Report by December 1982, 28 in total. Bangladesh, Indonesia and Nepal did not, however, reply.

Questionnaires were sent out in mid-1983 and the deadline for returns was the end of November 1983. Responding countries, together with the year of publication of the First Country Report, are listed below for the two categories of questionnaire.

Questionnaire on dissemination and utilization	Questionnaire on utilization only	
Colombia (1978)	Costa Rica (1978)	Panama (1978)
Jamaica (1979)	Dominican Rep. (1976)	Paraguay (1981)
Jordan (1980)	Fiji (1976)	Sri Lanka (1978)
Kenya (vol. 1: 1980)	Guyana (1979)	Sudan (1982)
(vol. 2: 1981)	Haiti (1981)	Syria (1982)
Mexico (1979)	Korea, Rep. of (1978)	Thailand (1977)
Pakistan (1977)	Lesotho (1981)	Trinidad and Tobago (1981)
Peru (1979)	Malaysia (1978)	Turkey (1980)
Philippines (1979)		
Senegal (1981)		

In each country one respondent connected with the NFS was selected to take responsibility for collecting the information. These respondents were asked to consult various specified informants, including the national director and the survey director of the NFS. The responses therefore represent assessments and opinions as expressed by these various persons. Responses of a factual nature have not been checked by us but in the one or two cases where a statement was known to be mistaken it has been excluded.

A complete account of the survey methodology and results can be found in Ortega and Vaessen (1984): only a summarized version of the results will be presented here.

37.2   In-country dissemination of NFS findings

The dissemination of findings was achieved by three main means: publication and distribution of a First Country Report, publication and distribution of a Summary of Findings and the organization of a national meeting.

The First Country Report

In the nine countries included in the dissemination study, the within-country distribution of the First Country Report varied from 100 copies in Peru to 642 copies in Colombia. Only Peru, Jordan and Senegal distributed less than 150 copies. Distribution generally covered all top-priority audiences such as national population programmes, ministries of health and education, national statistical and development planning systems, academic circles and programmes on the status of women where they existed.

The Summary of Findings

In-country distribution of the Summary was not as widespread as that of the First Country Report. The number distributed varied from 30 in Peru to 200 in Pakistan, with about half the countries distributing less than 50 copies and the other half 100 or more. Coverage of top-priority audiences was also less than for the First Country Report. Several ministries of health and education and one national population programme did not get any copy at all. Similarly, top political leaders and leaders of key professional groups were omitted from the distribution in more than half the cases.

The main cause of the discrepancy in distribution between the First Country Report and the Summary seems to be that the WFS did not send enough copies of the latter to the countries. Often, 50 copies were sent and this number was increased only on request. Distribution of the Summary was also hampered by the fact that it often came out at a time when most survey personnel had been redeployed and, more often than not, it was only distributed during the national meeting.

The national meeting

The objectives of the national meeting were to disseminate WFS findings, to stimulate the submission of national research projects for second-stage analysis, to pinpoint top-priority areas for these analyses and to discuss the implications of the NFS findings for decision-making. Of the nine countries under study, seven had a national meeting. One did not take place in Kenya or Pakistan. In Kenya the data were presented during the 1980 Regional African Conference organized by the WFS and the Pakistan First Country Report was published more than a year before WFS decided to sponsor national meetings.

The number of participants in the remaining seven countries varied from 35 in Jamaica and Jordan to 114 in Philippines. Between 40 and 70 participants attended the meeting in the other five countries.

The reports of these meetings show that there were two top-priority subjects:

1   First, in-depth analyses to be undertaken following the publication of the first NFS results. Some of the remarks and specific recommendations included in the questionnaire replies on this topic, with the respondent country shown in parentheses, are given below:

(a) Government support was requested to enable researchers to carry out analyses (Peru).

(b) The need for international financing for these analyses, for instance from USAID and UNFPA, was mentioned (Senegal).

(c) The importance of in-depth analyses was emphasized: (i) in general (Philippines); (ii) because they provide the figures for a greater understanding of the society concerned (Senegal); and (iii) together with data from other studies, for their contribution to the evaluation of population programmes (Philippines).

(d) Top-priority areas or topics for such analyses were identified: (i) peri-natal and infant mortality, contraceptive use and nuptiality patterns (Jordan); (ii) the importance of mother–child health care in national population policies (Peru); (iii) comparisons between NFS data and those from other sources (Senegal and Mexico); and (iv) the inter-relationship between demographic and socio-economic variables with a view to designing a population policy and integrating demographic factors into development planning (Senegal).

(e) Specific analysis projects were submitted (Senegal and Jordan).

(f) Students of demography at university level should be encouraged to carry out this type of analysis (Jamaica).

(g) It was recommended that official statistical departments should make use of data already provided by the NFS (Jamaica).

(h) Finally, it was proposed that a working party be created within the Universidad Nacional Autónoma to carry out such analyses (Mexico).

2   The second priority area mentioned was an evaluation of the experience gained by the country from the NFS. Among the specific conclusions on this subject should be mentioned:

(a) The importance of carrying out demographic sample surveys was recognized (Peru).

(b) A tentative evaluation of the NFS was made, and it was concluded that it was a good quality survey (Mexico).

(c) It was stated that the NFS had produced a large number of very valuable data, thus helping to fill gaps at the national level (Jamaica).

(d) Without consideration of its limitations, the NFS experience could be useful in designing future surveys (Philippines).

(e) A second 'round' of the NFS was requested (Jordan).

Dissemination through the mass media

In addition to the three methods of dissemination described above, some countries tried to use the mass media to give a wider dissemination to the survey results. Six of the nine countries prepared press releases, generally only one or two. Only in Senegal was a release sent to all the main mass media.

Pakistan was the only country where survey staff were invited by radio and television to speak about their survey. Press reports on survey results were more frequent, but even so Kenya, Colombia and Jordan stated that there had not been any press reports at all.

In seven cases in four countries the press expressed arguments in favour of some public policy, on the basis of NFS data:

1 In Senegal, reference was made in the national newspaper to NFS data in defence of polygamy in the course of a debate on the subject.

2 In the Philippines the two points reported were that breastfeeding is an effective means of preventing pregnancies and that postponing the age at marriage is the main reason for the decrease in fertility in the country.

3 In Mexico, two national newspapers – *El Universal* and *El Excelsior* – agreed that the success of family planning campaigns run by the Mexican government was proved by NFS findings.

4 In Peru, arguments were presented in favour of: (*a*) health policies such as hospital care and mother and child programmes; and (*b*) population policies including responsible parenthood, family planning and greater access by Peruvian women to education and work.

Other types of dissemination

Information was gathered on reference to or use of NFS data and analysis in three types of publications: those produced by statistics and planning offices, those produced by family planning and health programmes, and articles in scientific journals.

The impact of the NFS detected in these three types of publication was very limited in the nine countries, at least in terms of the number of publications. However, NFS data were given wider use than mere reference in five of the nine countries in publications by the statistical and economic planning offices. Also, in five countries, NFS data were used in publications by family planning or public health programmes but they were used in scientific journals (apart from reference) only in one country.

It should be remembered, however, that a considerable number of papers on the NFS have been published by the WFS and other international organizations, such as the United Nations, and also by several international journals and many university reviews. The authors or co-authors of these papers are often nationals of the participating countries. Various sources of analysed data are, therefore, actually available in all these countries, and this may explain the fact that national agencies have not made greater efforts to analyse and publish NFS data themselves. In some cases, also, publication has occurred, or is planned, after the date of the questionnaire return.

Direct and personal communication of information from the NFS was made to: (a) academics (eight countries); (b) officials in the area of population and family planning (seven countries); and (c) officials in the area of health, statistics and socio-economic planning (six countries). On the other hand, such person-to-person communication was not much used with: (a) other government leaders at the highest level, leaders in key professional groups and leaders of programmes on women's status (three countries only); (b) officials in the area of education (two countries); and (c) least of all, leaders in industry and trade-union organizations (one country).

Availability of data

Tapes with both the raw and the recoded data are available in all the countries, usually in institutions situated in the capital city. Only in four of the nine countries are raw data tapes available at more than one institution, and this is also the case with recoded data in six of the countries.

Lessons from the NFS dissemination

On particular lessons to be learned from the NFS dissemination, countries reported:

Kenya: (a) All the institutions, ministries and other persons involved should be briefed about the more significant findings of any survey; and (b) all significant findings should be incorporated into the new projects undertaken by the Central Bureau of Statistics.

Senegal: Particular care should be taken in selecting individuals to whom the reports on an investigation are sent since, unfortunately, in the majority of cases executives do not take the trouble to circulate documents they receive.

Philippines: Prompt dissemination of survey results gives them a greater impact in terms of their utilization in decision-making and planning.

Colombia: (a) Funds for the dissemination of results and in-depth analyses should be allocated at the planning stage; (b) clear regulations should be set out regarding use of data to achieve a more widespread utilization; and (c) meetings should be held with the mass media and results couched in less technical terms.

Mexico: (a) The dissemination of results should be carried out mainly through the academic sector; and (b) a special budget item is required for the dissemination of results.

Peru: (a) More intensive use of the mass media is desirable; (b) greater emphasis should be placed on the dissemination of results, and this should be done in a more systematic and continuous manner; and (c) in addition to reports aimed at experts, documents of a simpler nature, aimed at the layman, are required.

Jordan: It is important that a high-level political leader in the country should open the national meeting.

Finally, six of the nine countries considered that the dissemination of the NFS was better than that of other surveys. One (Jamaica) reported that it was worse, one similar (Kenya) and one (Mexico) that it was better than most other surveys but worse than other projects undertaken by the statistical office.

37.3 Utilization of NFS data and analyses

Data were collected from all 25 countries on this subject. Many countries reported specific types of utilization and in this summary only a few examples will be given in each case. The full account can be found in Ortega and Vaessen (1984).

Utilization in government family planning programmes

Eighteen of the 19 countries with government family planning programmes made some kind of utilization of the NFS data. Examples include:

Lesotho: (a) NFS findings were used to redefine programme objectives, for example in the project on strengthening and upgrading the MCH/FP programme; (b) training of field staff and service providers in FP skills and techniques is being emphasized as a result of NFS findings; (c) more donor help is being sought by the government; (d) public attention is being increased through government efforts to provide information and education.

Haiti: (a) NFS led to changes in programme tactics, with greater emphasis being placed on the education of women and their economic status, instead of continuing to insist solely on a massive distribution of contraceptives; and (b) the NFS was used to evaluate the achievements of the programme, with particular attention to the great gap observed between rates of contraceptive distribution and actual use.

Korea, Rep. of: (a) NFS findings were utilized for the revision of demographic targets, to reduce the annual rate of population increase to 1.6 per cent by 1981 (see fourth five-year development plan); (b) the estimate of the level of fertility has been compared with earlier estimates in order to observe the achievement of fertility decline; (c) as a result of NFS findings, the programme authority emphasized strengthening the campaign for birth spacing in relatively young childbearing ages; (d) as a result of NFS findings about preference in number and sex of children, and in order to foster equal opportunity for males and females, a study of current Korean civil law, including traditional inheritance systems, was recommended.

Dominican Republic: The partly unexpected findings of NFS, such as a decline in fertility, universal knowledge of FP methods, higher levels of use than known so far and wide acceptance of female sterilization, resulted in modifications of programmes and initiation of new ones. Specifically, a female sterilization programme was started in 1977, the education and information programme of CONAPOFA was re-oriented, there was re-inforcement of FP services in rural areas, and, finally, modifications and extensions of maternal and child health-care programmes occurred.

Turkey: (a) NFS findings have been used to redefine the objectives of regional programmes; (b) its findings served as the basis for a change in programme tactics; (c) the NFS was used as a reference document in various reports and briefings submitted by the government; (d) the General Directorate of Mother and Child Care and Family Planning of the Ministry of Health frequently uses data from NFS to give a demographic picture of the country in public talks.

Utilization in private family planning programmes

Twenty-three of the 25 countries reported the existence of private family planning programmes. In 15 countries, private programmes utilized, in one way or another, data and analyses of the NFS while four countries (Sudan, Fiji, Pakistan and Jamaica) reported that there was no utilization of their NFS by private programmes and another four could not provide the answer.

Senegal: The Association Sénégalaise pour le Bien-Etre Familial has used NFS data to demonstrate that Senegalese women's fertility is relatively high and that such levels are not compatible with the aims of the Association.

Malaysia: (a) The NFS contributed to defining the objectives of the programme by providing knowledge about patterns of contraceptive use and also about the reproductive behaviour of women at risk of pregnancy: and (b) to a certain extent its data also helped to assess the current programme and in the formulation of new and more efficient programmmes.

Trinidad and Tobago: (a) NFS indicated the percentage of women who were not contracepting, yet not wanting to have more children – this made the Association review its programmes, particularly in rural areas, by trying to identify those women; (b) NFS showed that the percentage of women who were using contraceptives was falling, which indicated the need to intensify FP motivational programmes; (c) statistical information from the NFS was used in the Family Planning Association's publications; and (d) NFS gave a nationwide view of fertility patterns which helped the FPA to analyse and identify unmet needs and determine its direction over the next three years.

Paraguay: (a) NFS data helped to select areas of greater potential demand; (b) in particular, they showed the need for greater attention to be focused on rural areas; and (c) the NFS was taken as a source of baseline data for debates on population and development.

Turkey: (a) NFS data served to make a short-term project of the Family Planning Association of Turkey give priority to eastern and south-eastern areas of the country, where the NFS had shown the existence of high fertility rates and low contraceptive use; (b) the FPA gives priority to education in family planning aimed at those groups identified by the NFS as in greater need; (c) NFS data have been used in proposals for projects submitted by the FPA to the IPPF; and (d) likewise, in the annual reports submitted by the FPA to the IPPF, to describe the demographic situation in the country.

Utilization in the public health programme

Another major area for the utilization of NFS findings is the national public health programmes.

Nineteen of the 25 countries studied reported some kind of utilization of the NFS by their public health programmes while an additional five reported no utilization. It should be noted that three of these five countries (Dominican Republic, Mexico and Peru) are Latin American. Finally, in one country (Panama) it was not possible to find out whether there had been use by the public health programme or not.

Most of the countries backed their replies with concrete examples of the utilization of NFS data, among which were included:

Kenya: NFS findings helped to formulate the integrated rural health and family planning programme 1982-8. The finding by the NFS of a national preference for large families led to the programme being divided into two sections: (a) demand creation through information and education; and (b) the services themselves.

Pakistan: The high levels of infant and child mortality came as a surprise to health planners. Consequently, the sixth five-year plan emphasizes the need to improve the infant and child health-care system.

Guyana: (a) NFS data on current and future levels of fertility were used to redefine the programme objective (i.e. coverage) of infant immunization and inoculation programmes and programmes concerning maternal care; (b) the coverage of infant and maternal care programmes was evaluated against expected births and number of women giving birth as shown in NFS; (c) total and areal distribution of births (actual and expected) provided by the NFS were used to plan coverage and efficient management of maternal and child care programmes. Tactics were changed in areas where programme coverage or effectiveness were considered unsatisfactory.

Colombia: (a) NFS data were helpful in a comparison with coverage rates found by the ministry and thus served to evaluate the quality of information used by the health system; (b) strategies were redesigned in accordance with NFS data to increase coverage and improve quality; and (c) on the other hand, these data were not used in defining programme objectives. The national health plan and national development and health policies define programme objectives. Since the government draws up these policies, surveys are useful only for re-orienting programmes, and not for defining policies or objectives.

Jordan: NFS data were utilized (*a*) to redefine the objective of reducing mortality rates in rural areas; (*b*) to pay greater attention to rural areas by opening more clinics in the villages; and (*c*) to attract more governmental attention by presenting the case to the Ministers' Council.

Utilization in programmes on status of women

In three of the six countries (out of nine only) where such programmes existed, utilization was reported as follows:

Pakistan: The data were of no direct use. The Women Division used them to show the low rate of participation by females in the labour force.

Mexico: Until quite recently, the basic objectives of the programme on the status of women in Mexico were still being defined. However, there was an indirect contribution by NFS findings to strengthening the original project because publication of NFS data created a favourable atmosphere for the development of the programme.

Peru: (*a*) NFS analyses have been of use to three of the most active feminist groups in the country in the task of redefining their objectives regarding women's socio-economic status; (*b*) they have also been of help in making women aware of their·freedom to opt for a desired number of children; (*c*) it should be noted, however, that in Peru there is as yet no national official programme on women's status. A number of women's associations, which receive support from private sources or international grants, exist and a number of these associations make use of NFS information, particularly with regard to women's incorporation in the economically active population and in reassessing women's roles.

Utilization in official population projections

NFS data were used, in one way or another, in official population projections by 19 of the 25 countries. In five of the remaining six countries, they were either used in less important projections or there are plans to use them when official national projections are prepared. The following examples of use were indicated:

Senegal: Used in projections at national and regional level by the Direction de l'Aménagement du Territoire, prepared with the technical assistance of the Direction de la Statistique.

Malaysia: Official demographic projections are based on the census and vital statistics systems. NFS data were used only to supplement the above in mid-census estimates for the projections.

Jamaica: Projections prepared in 1981 by T. Frejka, with the technical assistance of a demographer from the National Planning Agency, and including NFS data, were accepted as official.

Panama: NFS data were used in projections prepared by a government team covering the period 1950–2025.

Jordan: Life tables were used to project the size of the labour force. NFS was also used in projections of total population and population by sex.

Utilization for teaching purposes

Of the nine countries from which information was obtained on this issue, all reported that NFS data and analyses were being used for teaching demography, while four reported that they were being used for teaching in public health.

Utilization for further analysis

Further analysis of national datasets is discussed in chapter 22. The total number of nearly 700 further analysis projects is ample testimony to the use of WFS data.

37.4 Subsequent use of the NFS/WFS methodology

Of the 17 countries which attempted to answer the question, five reported use of the WFS sample, or sampling frame, for subsequent surveys and listed between them 10 such surveys.

Countries were also asked about their use of WFS methodology. Six specific WFS methodological features were singled out and countries were asked whether these represented standard practice for their organization before the NFS and, if not, whether the practice had been used again by their organization since the NFS. The responses are summarized in table 37.1. They should be interpreted with caution: in some cases data from independent sources suggest that misunderstanding may have occurred.

37.5 General assessment of the NFS/WFS experience

Benefits of the NFS experience

The following are examples of the major benefits derived from the NFS experience as reported by the respondents from 24 of the 25 countries. Kenya did not reply to the question. It should be noted that without exception the countries all mention at least one benefit:

1 The NFS produced demographic information about fertility and related subjects that:

(*a*) Provided the country for the first time with certain data: four countries (Sudan, Sri Lanka, Mexico and Paraguay).

TABLE 37.1

Prior and subsequent use of specified WFS techniques by
NFS executive agency (number of countries)

Techniques	Was standard practice before NFS?		If no: Has been used since NFS
	Yes	No	
Local language questionnaires[a]	7	4	1
Female interviewers	19	5	5
Team organization of interviewers	20	4	2
Tape-recorded interviews	4	20	2
Field editors	19	5	2
Exhaustive computer cleaning of data	13	11	8

[a] Not applicable in 13 countries, which used only one language.

(b) Updated valuable basic demographic data: nine countries (Lesotho, Trinidad and Tobago, Colombia, Dominican Republic, Panama, Paraguay, Jordan, Syria and Turkey).

(c) Could be used in development planning and for designing and evaluating programmes: 12 countries (Malaysia, Thailand, Haiti, Jamaica, Trinidad and Tobago, Colombia, Costa Rica, Dominican Republic, Mexico, Panama, Paraguay and Peru).

2 The NFS contributed to the development of research methodology:

(a) It developed capabilities in design, fieldwork, data processing and analysis: 15 countries (Sudan, Fiji, Malaysia, Sri Lanka, Thailand, Guyana, Jamaica, Trinidad and Tobago, Costa Rica, Dominican Republic, Mexico, Panama, Peru, Jordan and Syria).

(b) It increased analytical capabilities of local researchers: four countries (Lesotho, Philippines, Haiti and Republic of Korea).

(c) It contributed to the acquisition or utilization of software for fertility analysis and to the dissemination of this software in the country: three countries (Senegal, Philippines and Trinidad and Tobago).

3 The NFS was the first survey in the country:

(a) To be concluded, including the publication of its technical report, less than a year after fieldwork was finished: one country (Pakistan).

(b) Of such scope and sophistication to be successful in its aims: one country (Guyana).

4   The NFS demonstrated the capability of the country to carry out such studies: one country (Colombia).

5   NFS data had several practical uses:

(a) The decline in fertility was corroborated: one country (Colombia).

(b) These data were presented at a very opportune moment when population programmes were under attack: one country (Costa Rica).

(c) Results of the NFS led to more realistic population programmes (Dominican Republic).

Negative effects of the NFS experience

Replies received from 24 of the 25 countries — Kenya failed to reply to this question — report the following negative effects:

1   No negative effects were observed: 15 countries (Senegal, Fiji, Pakistan, Thailand, Guyana, Haiti, Jamaica, Trinidad and Tobago, Costa Rica, Dominican Republic, Mexico, Paraguay, Peru, Jordan and Syria).

2   Attention being focused on the NFS affected other projects by the executing agency due to its limited human resources: one country (Lesotho).

3   The survey did not cover the whole of the country while its sample size did not allow analyses to be made at the regional level: one country (Sudan).

4   Limitations in connection with NFS financing — five countries:
— Initial financial controls were too rigid (Malaysia).
— Financing was too limited, particularly for analysis (Colombia).
— Costs exceeded the real autonomous possibilities (Republic of Korea and Panama).
— WFS did not support a second round of surveys (Turkey).

5   There was no possibility of innovation in the formulation of questionnaires because of the standard core questions: one country (Philippines).

6   Official working communications were imperfect: one country (Panama).

7   A tendency to reinforce the current preoccupation with research on fertility and associated themes, sometimes to the neglect of other important subjects in population studies: one country (Sri Lanka).

How adequate is the NFS model for future national research projects?

1   Most countries (16 out of 24) found the NFS model adequate for future research projects. Some examples are:

(a) All subsequent demographic studies have been based on the NFS organizational model (Senegal).

(b) It can be adopted with some modifications by the programme of household surveys (Fiji).

(c) WFS model used in NFS has been utilized for 1976 survey of fertility and family planning and occasionally by small-scale inquiries made by local universities (Republic of Korea).

(d) The country has undertaken a second NFS in 1979–80 (Pakistan).

(e) The Institute of Population Studies is planning to conduct the second round of the NFS model in 1985 using the experiences gained with the WFS (Thailand).

(f) It is felt that the NFS model can and will serve as a basis for future research projects in demography (Guyana).

(g) With appropriate modifications, the model will continue to be useful in devising survey instruments in a number of areas of inquiry, e.g. health (Trinidad and Tobago).

(h) The NFS model may be adequate for certain future national research projects not *per se*, but because it contains all the indispensable basic, scientific and methodological elements for carrying out a sample survey (Costa Rica).

(i) In general, the NFS model was adequate because the original model was adapted to the conditions prevailing in the country, at the same time, respecting the basic structure and thus ensuring international comparability (Mexico).

(j) In fact, the NFS model was adequate. I wish we could do another round (Jordan).

2   Four countries thought the NFS model was not adequate:

(a) The manpower mobilized for the NFS effort and the collaboration effected among participating agencies can no longer be duplicated. The costs of maintaining a WFS staff to render technical assistance to participating countries cannot be matched in demography or any other field (Philippines).

(b) The costs of the model exceed the actual autonomous possibilities (Panama).

(c) It is a costly model and difficult to implement at the local level (Paraguay).

(d) It would probably be better if the NFS model was simpler since it is difficult for national research personnel to carry out similar projects in the future without outside assistance (Syria).

3   Four countries had mixed reactions to the model:

(a) The sampling techniques are appropriate and training and experience gained will be capitalized upon. However, this type of retrospective survey in an illiterate society may not be appropriate (Sudan).

(b) The NFS model is excellent for future national research projects in family planning, demography and health, only if its costs can be scaled down (Malaysia).

(*c*) The NFS model was very efficient only for countries which already had an infrastructure for statistical data collection and analysis (Sri Lanka).

(*d*) In general, the model is quite adequate. The chief objection is that the questionnaire does not focus sufficiently on certain aspects of interest to the country, thus making the basic WFS questionnaire a bit of a 'strait-jacket' (Dominican Republic).

Contribution of the NFS experience to the institutionalization of research activities

Nine countries felt that the NFS experience contributed to the institutionalization of their research activities. Five of the 16 countries which did not see such an effect reported, however, that the NFS/WFS experience had very positive effects on national research activities.

37.6 Conclusions

Dissemination

(*a*) Dissemination of the First Country Report in the nine countries studied ranged from a maximum of 642 copies to minimum of 100. In three of the countries, less than 150 copies were distributed, clearly an insufficient number in most countries. The First Country Report was sent in all countries to the high-priority audiences for any demographic study: officials of national population programmes, ministries of health and education, official statistical and development planning systems, academics and leaders of programmes on women's status where such programmes existed.

(*b*) The distribution of the Summary of Findings, on the other hand, was a much more restricted affair. Inexplicably, in only one country did the number of copies of the Summary distributed exceed the number of copies of the First Country Report. Possible contributory factors to such a poor dissemination of the Summary may include: the small number of copies often sent by the WFS to the countries; the long time which often elapsed between the execution of the NFS and the publication of the Summary; and, perhaps, the fact that these summaries were produced in London and not by the countries themselves.

(*c*) The inquiry into the number of studies based principally on NFS data, either written by national authors or co-authors, or published by institutions in the nine countries, shows that the NFS in all countries has already produced a 'second generation' of scientific papers of an analytical nature which no doubt helped to disseminate information generated by the NFS.

(*d*) The number of participants at the national meetings held in seven of the nine countries ranged from 35 to 114. Generally speaking, they represented the high-priority audiences among whom the First Country Report was circulated in the country. Thus, the majority of participants at the national meetings were officials from population programmes and ministries of health and education, specialists from the official statistical and planning systems, and academics.

(e) The dissemination of NFS results through the national mass media appears to have been insufficient in the nine countries. Both the number and intensity of the methods employed by the national NFS executing agencies to obtain media coverage, as well as their achievements, appear to have been extremely meagre.

(f) The 'echo' of NFS data and analyses in national publications of statistical and socio-economic planning systems, family planning and public health programmes and the academic world, would appear to be quite substantial, if we take into account the larger number of international publications (by WFS, United Nations, international circulation journals, universities, etc.) continually arriving in the countries. This would appear to have made any national effort to publish material already available at the international level less necessary.

(g) NFS data are available in the nine countries in the form of raw and recoded data files. However, in five countries tapes with raw data can only be found in one institution, as is also the case with recoded data in three countries. This would suggest an excessive concentration of the data files in very few institutions.

(h) Among lessons learnt by the countries from their respective dissemination processes we find: the need for specific budgets for the dissemination of results phase; earlier production and prompt publication of the findings; early planning for dissemination by preparing a detailed list of potential audiences; more intense and effective use of the media and preparation of reports more accessible to audiences not specializing in demography; and, lastly, the holding of briefing sessions with high level decision-makers.

(i) In spite of limitations found in the dissemination process in the nine countries, six of them considered that NFS dissemination had been better than that for other surveys by the same executing agencies. In this respect, the dissemination of NFS may be considered as a tentative step in the right direction.

Utilization

(a) Utilization of NFS data and analyses in action programmes was reported as follows: 18 of the 19 countries with official family planning programmes made use of NFS findings in these programmes; findings were also applied in 15 of the 23 countries with private family planning programmes. Nineteen of the 25 countries made use of NFS findings in their public health programmes and in their programmes on women's status, use was made of the NFS in three of the six countries where such programmes existed. In all these cases, with the exception of programmes on women's status, NFS results were mainly used to define or redefine objectives, to evaluate programmes, to increase efficiency of programmes and to obtain more government support.

(*b*) Other major areas of utilization of NFS data were: in population projections, in 19 of the 25 countries, with a further five planning to use them for this purpose in the near future; in the teaching of demography in all the nine countries addressed; and in the teaching of public health in four of these nine countries.

(*c*) With regard to future use of NFS data, 13 of the 25 countries reported specific plans for further analyses. Others reported that, because of the time that had elapsed since their NFS, data analysis had been concluded, or was about to be concluded.

(*d*) As far as the methodology used by the NFS was concerned, it was reported that five countries had already made use of the NFS sampling frame in a total of ten studies. Other methodological aspects of the NFS with a significant impact were the translation of questionnaires into local languages and the utilization of female interviewers, especially in Africa. The tape-recording of interviews was an innovation in 20 countries, but was reported to have been used subsequently in only two. Field editing of questionnaires and exhaustive computer cleaning of data were reported to be non-standard practice in five and 11 countries, respectively.

At this point, it should be noted that although the dissemination of NFS data appears insufficient, their utilization was quite widespread. There is no country where data have not been used in major population programmes, and use of these data as a rule occurred in more than one programme. Similarly, there has been good utilization of data in analytical papers, as well as of the NFS methodology in later research.

The value of the NFS experience

The evaluation of the NFS experience by the countries leads to the following conclusions regarding benefits, negative effects and usefulness of the NFS as a model for future research:

(*a*) Among the benefits may be noted: the abundant production of reliable data on fertility and related subjects; the contribution by the NFS to the development of electronic data processing and in-depth analyses; and the practical significance of the NFS data and analyses for population and health programmes and, to a lesser degree, for development planning.

(*b*) Among negative effects or limitations reported by nine of the 24 countries replying to the question, we should mention: the financial limitations which either presented obstacles for various aspects of the NFS experience or lessened the expectation that a similar investigation could be undertaken autonomously in the future by the countries; the WFS standard 'core questionnaire' which, although it ensured international comparability, precluded a greater focusing on subjects of national interest; and, finally, complaints were expressed – both at this point and at other stages of the questionnaire – regarding the excessively strict (national) regulations governing access to NFS tapes.

(*c*) It is, however, significant that not a single country has given a negative over-all assessment of the NFS experience after weighing both the quantifiable and non-quantifiable costs and benefits.

(*d*) The majority of countries (16 out of 24) considered the NFS model adequate for future national investigations. Only four expressed doubt. Once again, the main reservations concerned the viability of the model for developing countries in the absence of financial and technical assistance of the type available for the WFS programme.

(*e*) Finally, it would appear that the NFS experience should not be considered as a milestone in the process of institutionalization of national research activities. According to replies received, only nine countries out of the 25 were of the opinion that their NFS had made a significant contribution in this respect. However, 14 of the countries agreed that the NFS experience did have a clearly positive effect on research activities in their country.

37.7 Recommendations

A considered analysis of the information collected leads us to the following recommendations:

1 It would appear highly desirable, and even necessary, that the design and particularly the budget for any research project should explicitly provide for the dissemination phase of its analyses and data. An investigation should not be considered concluded with the publication of its 'final report', since it is necessary to take into consideration the way its results will be communicated to individuals and institutions.

2 In designing a dissemination strategy which will contribute to a wider subsequent utilization of the study the following points should be kept in mind:

(*a*) Careful identification should be made of the top-priority audiences to which data, conclusions and recommendations of the research should be conveyed.

(*b*) A selection should be carried out, with these audiences in mind, of the most adequate channels of communication in each case. Even in the least developed countries a number of such channels exist which are often neglected by researchers.

(*c*) Press releases should be prepared to ensure that information is clear and exact.

(*d*) Availability of basic data (tapes, documents, etc.) to *all* national researchers and potential users of these data should be ensured.

(e) The following suggestions on the format of the Summary may be helpful: clarity of language, to make reports accessible to the specific target audience – this may involve the use of local languages; use of an attractive format even if more expensive; and, lastly, if high-level executives are to be approached, it should be remembered that brevity and conciseness are essential.

(f) The national meetings as organized by the WFS seem to have been much appreciated, and should stand as an example for the dissemination of research results.

(g) Consideration should be given to employing policy analysts as a link between research and decision-makers.

(h) Finally, every effort should be made to ensure that the period between the execution of an investigation and the publication of its findings is as short as possible.

38

Contribution to Survey Capability in Developing Countries

Vijay Verma
V. T. Palan

38.1 An unarticulated objective

The success of the World Fertility Survey is often measured – and not unreasonably – by the fact that in the decade or so of the programme's existence, 41 developing (and 20 developed) countries successfully completed 'nationally representive, internationally comparable and scientifically designed and implemented sample surveys on human fertility and family planning behaviour and attitudes' (Gille and van de Kaa 1983). The achievements of the WFS are clearly outstanding in this respect. Most surveys conducted under the WFS are recognized as being of high quality and almost all have resulted in published reports within a reasonable time after fieldwork. Assisting countries to acquire the scientific information that will permit them to describe and interpret their populations's level of fertility was always stated to be the most basic requirement, and always listed as the first objective, of the WFS. Reference libraries of statistical offices, universities and other national and international institutions, and private collections of users and researchers all over the world display ample proof of the WFS's ambitious publications programme. Apart from country reports and summaries, over 150 technical manuals and bulletins, illustrative and comparative analyses, and research papers have been directly prepared and published by the WFS. Furthermore, numerous analysts, at national and international level, have access to standardized micro-level data tapes with full documentation. This has already facilitated a great deal of intensive demographic research, and will continue to do so for some time to come. By the middle of 1984, about 650 national (country-level) and 260 comparative or multinational studies had been completed, and a large number were in preparation (WFS 1985). Hence, much headway has also been made towards meeting the stated WFS objective of promoting international comparisons and comparative analysis of the data.

But let us also remind ourselves that, as originally formulated, the WFS had *three* major objectives:

1 to assist countries in acquiring scientific information on fertility and fertility regulation including levels and differentials;

2 to build up national fertility and other demographic survey capability; and

3 to promote international comparisons of the data.

Note also the *order* in which these objectives have usually been listed: the enhancement of national capabilities is the second of the three objectives, after the main objective of assisting countries in acquiring information on fertility and related factors, but *above* the objective of comparative analysis. This was not an unreasonable ordering, since WFS, though often described (merely) as a programme of fertility research, was bound simultaneously to be a major programme of technical assistance, absorbing and disbursing as it did more than US$50 million over a period of 12 years or so. WFS represents an international investment in survey-taking in developing countries without precedent in scale or nature, and ignoring the enhancement of national capability would constitute a most serious flaw in any international programme of this magnitude.

However, it remains true that the WFS approached its stated objective of enhancing national fertility survey and research capabilities in a rather peculiar manner. This was quite different from the way the other two objectives, both concerned with generating data of a particular type, were tackled. A great deal of time and effort was devoted to developing detailed technical and operational plans and standard procedures with the aim not only of achieving high-quality national surveys but also of safeguarding their international comparability. There evolved a fairly clear, well-articulated and explicit 'WFS philosophy' and 'WFS approach' to meet these objectives of data collection and analysis but, by contrast, no such coherent philosophy or approach emerged in relation to the objective of enhancing national capability.[1] It would not be too far from the truth to claim that whatever the level of WFS contribution to enhancing national capabilities, it has been achieved more as a result of spontaneous factors than of deliberate plans. Often, it has been an indirect result of activities carried out primarily for other purposes; and not infrequently, a consequence of the personal philosophies of the exceptionally high quality staff involved in shaping and implementing the WFS programme, to the extent that the pressure of getting the job done well and on time would permit.

The lack of articulation by the WFS itself makes an evaluation of its success or otherwise in meeting the objective of enhancing national capabilities more difficult. Often, one can judge programmes and organizations against their own stated objectives since, unless they are merely an insincere exercise in public relations, the stated objectives are an expresssion of what could potentially be achieved under 'ideal' but not altogether unrealistic conditions, i.e. achievements which can be considered feasible under the circumstances, given sufficient effort and will and barring accidents and unfortunate combinations of circumstances.

Since the WFS does not provide its own definition of building national capability, it is necessary for us to begin from a broad definition and to narrow it down to what could be considered a feasible ideal for the WFS, given the specific context in, and the objectives for, which the programme was created, and the conditions under which it had to be implemented. In a sense we are trying to address an issue which should have been addressed much earlier and in much greater detail by the WFS as an organization.

38.2   Essential elements of national statistical capability

In general terms, we take the concept of 'national statistical capability' to refer to the capacity of all the indigenous organizations engaged in the production of statistical information to *identify* what information is needed and to *deliver* that information in a manner which maximizes both its usefulness to the diversity of national needs and its chances of being used.

A statistical organization cannot be a passive collector of figures in response to predetermined and clearly expressed 'needs' of users. To be able to participate in the articulation, refinement and even prediction of the needs is an essential part of the capability of the statistical system. First, the potential users may not always be aware of the objective needs for statistical information; they may, for example, not realize that improved information on the impact of a programme or project is needed to improve certain aspects of its design and operation. Even with this awareness, the need may go unexpressed, in terms of the specific statistical inputs required. Then, it is necessary to prune these expressed needs to what is feasible to collect and actually use; to determine priorities and develop a balanced programme to meet the diversity of needs in the best possible way within the available resources; and gradually to make permanent arrangements for generating data on a continuous basis, and secure necessary resources to sustain and enhance this capability.

In short, it is an essential part of the capability and function of a statistical organization to be able to assist users in defining and expressing needs which are realistic and pertinent, and to be able to specify the steps or activities, time, skills and resources needed to meet them. This capacity is dependent on the existence of appropriate organizational arrangements and channels for effective user-producer interactions, on necessary expertise in various subject fields to facilitate communication with users, and on technical skills in the general planning of statistical operations.

The essential requirements for producing and delivering the necessary statistical information include technical staff equipped with skills and tools for statistical design, processing and analysis; interviewing and data processing staff; adequate infrastructural facilities such as suitable sampling frames, field transport, computer hardware and software, printing and publication facilities; and, above all, funds to execute the operations.

It is also necessary to develop a capacity to utilize these facilities in a manner that maximizes the quality and quantity of information produced within given resources. It is essential to view these elements as integrated or common facilities for defining and meeting all needs for statistical information, cutting across the often arbitrarily delineated subject fields. It is neither desirable nor, in the long run, possible to emphasize only a single subject area or a single source or method of obtaining statistical information at the expense of others. Censuses, household surveys, surveys of establishments, registration systems and other administrative sources have to be utilized in a balanced manner, in conjunction with each other, recognizing the strengths and weaknesses of each source. Data on agriculture, economic activity, social conditions, demographic trends and so on all represent inter-related aspects of the same basic situation to be explained, managed and hopefully improved.

A degree of endurance and continuity are, by definition, concomitant with 'capability', not only in statistics but also in other fields of activity. Statistical capability involves the creation of reasonably enduring facilities and arrangements to ensure some continuity and co-ordination between statistical operations. Co-ordination encompasses investments to develop and utilize common sampling frames and arrangements, data processing, printing and other facilities; to set up regular supervisory, field and office staff to meet the requirements of diverse operations; to develop and plan the various operations to facilitate utilization of inter-relationships both at the functional and substantive levels, and so on. Without some attention to continuity and co-ordination, it makes little sense to talk of 'national capability'.

We have tried to sketch some broad requirements. In practice, however, the process of building capability is much more complex and uneven. At different stages, it may involve more or less emphasis in particular directions, on particular modes or sources of obtaining statistical data, on particular subject areas. For instance, focused attention on undertaking the population census has in many countries provided a tremendous boost to the overall development of statistical capability. Similarly, the establishment of infrastructural facilities for undertaking sample surveys of the household sector can constitute in many situations a leading or dynamic component in the process of overall development. This is because properly planned and executed programmes of household surveys can generate interconnected data of great variety, broadening the range of users which statistical organizations can satisfy. At the same time, the statistical agency is in general able to design and undertake sample surveys with less dependence on wider administrative support which full-scale censuses and collection from adminstrative sources require – a type of support which is often not easy to secure (Rao and Verma 1982).

In a similar manner, it may be necessary to pursue the development of statistical capacity in particular sectors before the subject-matter scope can be broadened to cover other areas in a balanced way. For instance, many developing countries have tried to establish regular surveys in particular areas such as population, labour force and agriculture, and only later expanded the scope to include other topics, possibly around the established regular surveys which serve as the core. There is, of course, a limit to which capability in any one field can be developed in isolation from and independently of other fields.

The development of infrastructural facilities and skills is also a step-by-step process. Even more important, it can only be an *ongoing* process with no permanent solutions. Vehicles, computers, printing facilities, even buildings and all sorts of other 'durable' equipment need to be constantly replenished. Sampling frames and designs need periodic updating and revision. Resources for survey operations need to be secured and resecured year after year, survey after survey. There is a constant loss of trained statisticians to non-statistical responsibilities, to the commercial sector, to other organizations and to other countries.

Given the breadth and complexity of the process of development of national statistical capacity, no single programme, approach or set of activities can provide the sole or lasting solution. Even so, the role of the World Fertility Survey in this context was meant to be, and could only be, a relatively limited one. The WFS was designed to assist countries in obtaining high quality information, comparable across countries as far as possible, on a very specific topic. Furthermore, the time horizon of the programme, and especially of any country project under it, was strictly limited. Consequently, even under ideal circumstances, WFS could not be expected to make a fundamental contribution to setting up new arrangements, nor could it be expected to help set up enduring infrastructural facilities for survey-taking and analysis, whether in fertility or in any other field. The funding agencies had explicitly placed constraints on the form in which resources provided through WFS could be delivered to participating countries: they had to be devoted primarily to developing tools and techniques for conducting surveys of a specified type, providing intensive technical assistance to countries to ensure successful implementation of the surveys, meeting some in-country operational costs, imparting on-the-job project-specific training, and undertaking and supporting analytical research on the data collected. Little provision could be made for long-term training, providing 'durable' equipment such as new computers or vehicles, setting up permanent cadres for data collection and processing, or for supporting any other operations not clearly linked to the requirements of the particular survey. Chapter 10 on survey costs serves to reinforce this point.

For a programme representing 'international investment in survey-taking in developing countries without precedent in scale or nature', these are indeed very serious limitations in so far as the building of national capabilities is concerned. Given that the WFS in many respects has been an outstandingly successful programme, there is a danger of forgetting these inherent limitations in the scope and possible impact of the programme on national capabilities. Yet these limitations do not, as such, reflect shortcomings in the implementation of WFS. Rather, they were inherent given the primary objective of WFS to 'assist countries to describe and interpret the fertility of their populations by conducting scientifically designed sample surveys'. It can indeed be claimed that the manner in which WFS was implemented seriously attempted to transcend some of these limitations.

38.3   Some positive features of the WFS approach

We have lamented the lack of articulation and limited scope and time horizon of WFS in relation to the objective of enhancing national capabilities in survey research. Yet this lack of articulation does not mean that issues of national survey capability were completely forgotten or ignored in determining the WFS's mode of implementation. It is necessary to remember and emphasize several positive features of the manner in which WFS went about promoting fertility surveys and research in developing countries (and in developed countries as well). The WFS promoted a standardized approach, but it was far from a series of prepackaged questionnaires and survey procedures simply taken to and implanted in countries, with countries acting merely as collection agencies re-exporting the data collected for processing and analysis by foreign individuals and institutions. There have been, and probably will continue to be, international projects of that nature, despite some raising of consciousness of developing countries by efforts such as the United Nations' National Household Survey Capability Programme, but the WFS was not such an international project. WFS managed to achieve considerable success in four major areas: (*a*) completion of as much work as possible *in situ*, within countries; (*b*) active participation by national staff in survey implementation; (*c*) successful completion of all phases of the survey, providing countries with the rich (and often memorable) experience of a well-conducted survey; and (*d*) providing valuable experience and training not only in collection but also in analysis and reporting of the data — a feature sadly lacking in a great deal of survey-taking. Let us consider these points a little further.

Much time and effort was devoted in WFS operations to ensure that as much work as possible was completed in the countries themselves. Serious attempts were made to adhere to this policy, even in situations where the cheaper and quicker alternative might have appeared to be a direct execution of the task by WFS headquarters. In no case were completed questionnaires removed from the country. All manual editing and coding and (with one exception) all data entry was done in the countries themselves. The same applies to machine editing, even though this involved very prolonged and sophisticated procedures and turned out to be a major cause of delay in the publication of final results in some countries (see chapter 18). At a later stage, WFS directly undertook some further editing and corrections of country data and reformulated data files into a standard format, but this was done to facilitate wider dissemination and comparative analysis of the data and was undertaken generally after the major descriptive report of the survey had been issued by the country concerned. The initial policy of WFS was also to have all tabulation and report-writing done in the countries. In fact, little provision was made for several years to equip WFS headquarters to undertake processing work directly; rather, the organization concentrated on developing and installing in countries the necessary computer software packages for this purpose. This policy was fairly successfully implemented in the first years of the programme, even though it resulted in delays and proved more, not less, taxing on WFS technical resources. Gradually, however, these problems became more critical, and the policy of completing processing and report-writing in countries was increasingly compromised due to the mounting pressure from all quarters to get the basic task of producing First Country Reports for all participating countries finished in reasonable time, or at least within the lifetime of the WFS. This failure is indicative more of the problems many developing countries face in timely processing and reporting of survey data, than of a flaw in WFS institutional philosophy or any inherent callousness towards the issue of enhancing national capabilities.

The second positive feature of the WFS approach has been the efforts made to ensure close participation of national staff in the execution of their fertility surveys. Several factors facilitated this. Generous support by the funding agencies for a relatively large central staff meant that the WFS could also be generous (sometimes even on the verge of wasteful) in providing technical assistance to country surveys. In fact it has never failed to surprise us how substantial a part of the total cost of externally supported projects, WFS or others, technical assistance usually forms. This appears to be the case at least in the area of statistics. But even so, WFS may have been an atypical 'ivory tower' in this respect: the project provided, for a single one-time survey operation of a fairly standardized type, an average of around 2.2 person-years of direct in-country technical assistance, plus a substantial amount of additional time spent at London headquarters (see chapter 8). There are some advantages in this generosity. It is our contention that, with an appropriate institutional philosophy and a determination to get the job finished, the relationship (for a given level of existing capability in the country) between the intensity of technical assistance and the extent of country participation is a U-shaped curve. National staff, of course, 'participate' fully in their work when there is little external assistance available, the limiting factor being their ability to undertake and complete the task. This situation prevailed, for instance, with respect to data processing in some of the first participating countries before the WFS became adequately equipped to provide the necessary assistance in this field. At the other end, with generous provision of technical support, it becomes more feasible to take a liberal approach, with the foreign 'expert' taking on a more advisory, as opposed to an executive, responsibility and paying greater attention to transmitting skills – the sort of arrangement conducive to enhancing national capabilities. The WFS enjoyed this advantage in many of its operations owing to the exceptionally favourable material conditions in which the programme was implemented. In less favourable circumstances, an international agency pressed to get the job finished would tend, in the interest of short-term expediency, to take upon itself direct execution of as much work as possible and hence minimize participation by the country staff, as indeed tended to happen more and more during processing and reporting stages of the later WFS surveys.

Country participation and the development of a partnership was also facilitated by other circumstances. On the public relations side, carrying out a WFS survey often turned out to be a 'high profile' activity both within a country and to some extent internationally, with a bit of fanfare and, more seriously, with a lot of interest in the successful completion of a survey and in the timely publication of its results. This, and the intensive technical inputs by WFS staff, helped to develop a close partnership between the national and international staff involved since both sides had a clear stake in the successful completion of the country project.

Thirdly, a determination to produce high-quality final results for each and every national survey (by no means a universal virtue in survey practice) has been another crucial factor. This emphasis is, of course, a two-edged sword in relation to capability building. On the negative side, pressure from outsiders for timely completion tends to take some aspects of the work out of the hands of national staff; and emphasis on high quality can result in adoption of procedures and practices which are irrelevant, or at best of limited applicability, to conditions under which most other survey work has to be carried out in the country. These are very serious concerns. However it is equally important to appreciate the positive side of the equation. Our close contact and discussion with a wide spectrum of national staff has convinced us that the contribution of WFS in transferring skills and good practice in survey work has been far from trivial. Emphasis on quality went hand in hand with the production by WFS of detailed manuals on survey methodology, as well as detailed documentation of survey implementation and outcome. These are useful contributions to enhancing survey capability, and provide examples which can be studied and emulated. Even more important, participation in the WFS provided countries with *direct experience* of a high-quality, well-executed, large-scale national survey. The completion of a national survey included not only data collection and production of basic tables, but also a programme of analysis of survey results – which again is not a universal virtue of survey practice, especially in developing countries. Successful completion and publication of results also enhances the morale of the statistical organization involved and raises its image and general standing with the user community and with the outside world in general; these are important elements of what has been termed 'external capability'.[2]

The fourth positive factor which should be highlighted is that, in line with its emphasis on data analysis as an integral part of survey-taking, WFS headquarters provided facilities for intensive and task-oriented training in data processing, evaluation and analysis. The 'analysis workshops', in which country researchers analysed their own data at London headquarters or elsewhere in intensive interaction with WFS staff, are a fine example of this. Indeed these workshops and other arrangements for prolonged stay in London by individuals from developing countries to participate in data processing and analysis became an increasingly important activity of WFS, compensating to some extent for the unfortunate tendency to shift some of these activities away from the countries in the later years of the programme.

38.4 General assessment of WFS contribution

Let us return to some of the essential elements of survey capability sketched earlier and see how WFS fared in general in relation to them. Five areas of capability are relevant:

(a) Development of appropriate organizational arrangements for communication between users and producers of statistical information; the capacity of producers to assist in identification and definition of statistical needs, and to plan operations necessary to meet those needs.

(b) Development of material infrastructure and common tools and arrangements on the basis of which diverse needs can be readily met, and continuity and a degree of permanence assured.

(c) Development of necessary professional skills for survey planning, design and management, for evaluation and for research and analysis; establishment of trained and experienced cadres for data collection and processing.

(d) Specifically in the context of WFS, capability to collect and analyse fertility and related demographic data.

(e) Capability to report and disseminate statistical information in the appropriate form, at the appropriate time and to the appropriate audiences.

The first and the last points pertain to the 'external capability' of an organization, i.e. to its relationship with the outside world. The development of appropriate organizational arrangements and 'standing' of the organization is a long-term process, and depends not only on the organization's capacity to deliver what it is supposed to deliver and what it promises, but also on prevailing legal structures, arrangements and traditions. By and large, it is beyond the capacity of externally supported projects of limited scope and focus to fundamentally influence these factors. This is certainly. the case for a one-time project of strictly limited duration, such as a fertility survey under WFS. Before discussing the WFS in this respect, however, it should be noted that in many countries the model provided by WFS could and did help to raise the users' awareness of the extremely important issue of human fertility. Its promotion on an international scale and especially in neighbouring countries provided a catalyst in many cases. Nations are becoming increasingly aware of the significance of their demography, even though there remains a gap between this objective significance and its subjective realization and acceptance by governments, other organizations and people at large. WFS contributed to the narrowing of this gap. More specifically, the successful conduct of fieldwork, preparation of comprehensive reports and analyses, wide dissemination of the results, and especially the organization of WFS national seminars at the conclusion of the survey, contributed towards improving user-producer contact and hence the chances of actual utilization of results. The significance of this contribution is enhanced by the fact that three-quarters of the WFS surveys were carried out by national statistical offices which in many countries are the exclusive or primary source of official statistics. In several cases these institutions collaborated with universities, health and family planning organizations or other national institutions — which again is a good thing.[3]

We have already noted the very limited scope of WFS's contribution to the development of a survey infrastructure. The provision of equipment was largely precluded by its terms of reference, and of course the use of *ad hoc*, specially recruited female interviewing staff seriously limited any contribution WFS could have made towards the building of a permanent survey machinery.

However, where a survey machinery existed, in some cases WFS's contribution to its enhancement was considerable. Existing staff generally acted as supervisors and received valuable experience and training. In addition, coders, editors and other office workers usually came from existing staff. In a few countries some of the newly recruited staff could be retained in the organization on a regular basis, or could be absorbed in other national organizations engaged in statistical or related work. In a survey of participating developing countries (response rate about 60 per cent), just over one-half reported such retention of staff (see chapter 37). As argued in chapter 14, the WFS experience may also have made an important contribution in the rightful acceptance of females as survey interviewers, quite capable of undertaking the exposure and hardship of fieldwork.

WFS could not directly support long-term training fellowships for the development of professional skills. However, data collected through the WFS formed the basis of many postgraduate research theses by scholars from participating countries, and sometimes the WFS was able to act as a 'broker' in arranging for long-term training fellowships from other sources. An important contribution of WFS came in the form of analysis projects undertaken by national researchers and the short-term but intensive analysis and training workshops organized by WFS directly, or sponsored by it in collaboration with other reputable institutions. In addition, a partial analysis of responses from countries indicates that WFS materials and data have been used for some sort of training and general research at national institutions in nearly two-thirds of the participating countries, though only one in three reported that WFS had contributed towards 'institutionalization of research' (excluding those who stated that such capability already existed).

Direct experience through participation in a well-conducted survey is, of course, the main contribution of WFS. The problem in this context is the well known one of loss of trained staff. In the survey of participating developing countries, the percentages of national directors (responsible for overall policy direction), survey directors (responsible for technical direction), field directors, principal persons responsible for data processing, and principal analysts who were still with the survey organization by the end of 1983 were approximately as follows: 30, 40, 50, 40 and 60 per cent respectively. Between 20 and 25 per cent in each category were reported to have left the country, the rest having gone to other organizations within the country.

Apart from providing on-the-job training in various aspects of survey work, the major contribution of WFS lies in the area of developing and disseminating tools and techniques of survey-taking and analysis.

38.5   Contributions to survey methodology

That WFS has made important contributions to the practice of survey-taking is by now a widely accepted view. Yet in assessing this contribution, it needs to be remembered that, with minor exceptions, WFS has not had at its disposal any funds for purely methodological research or experimentation, and no breakthroughs in methodology were expected of the programme. The contribution lies primarily in successful survey implementation using what may be considered state-of-the-art technology, and in promoting wider and more systematic application of that technology. The significance of this lies in the fact that many of these techniques were innovative as far as many of the participating countries were concerned. As the existence of this volume implies, its contribution also lies, though perhaps to a lesser extent, in the area of assessment and documentation of survey procedures and outcome, and evaluation and analysis of data. The availability of a substantial and competent staff at WFS headquarters made this possible, especially in the later years of the programme when the pressure of country work had eased somewhat.

It is necessary to take a balanced view of WFS methodological contributions. On the one hand, several factors limit the generalizability of WFS techniques and procedures: for example, its highly standardized nature, the absence of experimental evaluation of alternatives, the generally *ad hoc* approach to design, and the relative lack of financial constraints. On the other hand, the significance of the contribution is hard to overstate since, in our experience, the most common cause of wastage of enormous resources in survey work is the use of poor methods and techniques, resulting in equally poor or even useless data.

First let us consider some limitations of WFS methodology.[4] The WFS has applied a standardized approach across diverse circumstances so as to generate more or less comparable data on a very specific topic. It is important to appreciate the nature, extent and rationale of this standardization as it defines both the strengths and limitations of the WFS. Of course the standardization is by no means complete and there has been considerable flexibility in its application. The central staff of WFS were directly involved in the development and provision of common concepts, definitions, survey instructions and the main statistical outputs as well as of detailed survey designs and their implementation at the country level. Furthermore, as noted earlier, the pressure for speed and high quality invariably encouraged concentration of activities at WFS headquarters, increasing further the degree of standardization.

On the one hand, standardization has had the advantage of efficiency. For an international organization, there is considerable economy of effort in designing a uniform package of procedures for data collection, processing and analysis, in contrast to custom-designing survey tools and procedures for each country. For given resources, it can provide a much more intensive technical support to country surveys. This element has been crucial in the successful completion of country surveys under WFS. Outside WFS, there are countless examples of poor quality surveys, yielding poor quality data, which are published after long delays, if at all. The main cause of this state of affairs has been the lack of time and of the professional skills necessary for detailed and careful planning in many developing countries' organizations. The WFS has done well on this score.

On the other hand, there are certain fundamental limitations of the standardized approach. Standardization results in neglecting the broader issues of planning, design and implementation of statistical surveys which, even if not narrowly technical, constitute an essential part of survey capability. As noted earlier, participation in the WFS did not provide countries with experience in developing user-producer interactions and the organizational forms necessary for identifying, expressing and enumerating priorities in user requirements. The scope and content of the survey was largely predetermined in the form of a fairly elaborate 'minimum' core which all countries were required to follow. Of course, to facilitate the inclusion of additional topics in country surveys, a series of 'modules', described in chapter 3, were developed which, at the country's discretion, could be added in whole or in part to the core. In principle, countries could also add other relevant topics of special concern but, in practice, the possibilities of broadening the scope of the survey were severely limited to what could be accommodated in a retrospective single-round survey with the major part of the content already fixed in the form of the WFS core. The only substantial additions to this arrangement were the collection of information on (i) current age-specific fertility and mortality on a larger sample of households; (ii) availability of various facilities at the community level; (iii) attitudes and behaviour of husbands of women interviewed in the main survey; and (iv) response errors by re-interviewing a subsample of the women. Of 42 developing countries which participated in the WFS, the numbers which introduced these additions were, respectively, 13, 17, 3 and 9, i.e. a minority in all cases. Although a number of surveys in Latin America included questions on maternal and child health, insufficient attention was paid to this topic, or to such related subjects as nutrition. Our general conclusion is that, given the diverse conditions and requirements of countries, and the intellectual and material resources at its disposal, WFS provided inadequate opportunity for user-producer interaction and country-specific determination of survey content. Greater effort in this direction would have been entirely compatible with the WFS primary objective of assisting countries in describing and interpreting the fertility of their populations.

A further limitation of WFS methodology is that fixing the approach in the form of a single-round survey of women in the reproductive age range also precluded the study, evaluation and adoption by countries of any alternative survey arrangement. Yet it is possible that, even within the specific context of a fertility survey, different approaches would have been more appropriate in terms of cost or precision and relevance of the information generated. For example, it is possible that a multi-round survey or a 'dual record' system would have fitted more economically and conveniently into existing statistical operations of particular countries; in other countries, the experience gained by participating in and the results obtained through a larger-scale, simpler demographic survey of the conventional type might have been more relevant to national needs and served them better.

The 'portability' of WFS methodology is also limited by the fact that, in spite of some variation in the approach followed in different countries, the experience of the WFS sheds little light on the relative efficiency of these various approaches. It is true that large scale experimentation was precluded in WFS's mandate. Even so, WFS does not provide a good example to follow in its almost total neglect of experimentation. In spite of the large size of the operation, little can be said, for example, about which of the various approaches to collecting birth history data tried in different countries is better. To obtain an indication of the direction in which the answer lies does not necessarily involve split-panel experiments on a national scale! WFS failed to give countries experience of how alternative design and operational strategies may be formulated and evaluated. Such experience is an extremely important element of general survey capability.

In many countries, the fertility survey was conceived and designed as a special operation, requiring specially recruited interviewers and other *ad hoc* arrangements. The designs and procedures for the fertility survey were often – though certainly not always – chosen without considering seriously the broader requirements of operational co-ordination and substantive integration of related surveys. But these requirements ought increasingly to be considered critical in choosing appropriate designs and methodologies of statistical surveys, especially in developing countries where, despite very limited resources, data requirements are becoming more extensive and diverse and the number of surveys being undertaken is on the increase. It is important to consider to what extent the approaches and procedures developed within the particular context of a fertility survey are useful and applicable to future surveys on other topics. Are there elements which can be regarded as models of excellence, comprising a more lasting and general contribution to survey methodology, portable beyond the immediate concern of fertility surveys? To what extent have countries actually retained and absorbed the survey practices introduced through WFS? And how realistic and relevant are these contributions for general survey work in countries, given that that work has usually to be carried out under less favourable material circumstances than was WFS?

There is another limitation which needs to be recognized, even though its significance has been often exaggerated. The usefulness of some aspects of WFS methodology towards national survey capability may certainly be limited because these surveys were often carried out under favourable conditions in terms of available material and intellectual resources and the provision of liberal operational and technical assistance – conditions which are not easily repeated or sustained in survey work in developing countries. Indeed, what may appear to be an optimal or at least a good methodology in favourable circumstances may sometimes be far from sensible when resources are scarce. It is important to emphasize that this limitation has often been overstated. Certainly the *operational* costs of WFS surveys have, for a given sample size, been notably above average, but not outstandingly so, especially when one considers the mean square error and elapsed time before publication, and remembers that many surveys yield nothing. These costs are comparable to numerous surveys of similar size, and lower than many. What is exceptional in the case of WFS is the cost and intensity of technical assistance provided, although that in itself does not reduce the relevance or applicability of the many excellent contributions of WFS to the methodology of survey-taking in developing countries. It is to be hoped that some of the methodology can be applied with less technical assistance in the future, as shown by the Dominican Republic in its second fertility survey, for example. Numerous surveys are badly conducted and yield poor or unusable results not so much because of lack of operational resources, but largely because of lack of the technical and managerial skills to design and execute surveys properly. Indeed, some of the 'methodological sophistication' promoted by the WFS is important precisely because it can be an instrument of *saving* costs through more efficient design and procedures. Appropriate methodology is an essential element of survey capability.

Specific WFS contributions to survey design, execution and analysis capability have been described in the chapters of this volume and in the numerous manuals, technical bulletins, illustrative and comparative analyses, case studies, occasional papers and other scientific publications, mainly by the WFS but also by other organizations. Below we list briefly the five most outstanding areas of contribution.

Questionnaire design

If we were to identify one area where the basic WFS characteristics of centralized support, standardization across countries and concern with high technical standards are most manifest, this would be in the area of design and development of survey questionnaires. The care and attention with which the basic instrument was developed is exemplary, and in design if not in content the WFS questionnaire has served as a model for many other surveys on different topics. Even so the process of review and refinement continued throughout the WFS's own existence.

One of the fundamental sources of trouble in many surveys is the use of poorly formulated, designed and tested questionnaires. Often questionnaires are unnecessarily bulky, contain irrelevant and unusable material, are not properly tested and evaluated, and make little provision for editing, coding and data processing requirements. We have already noted the undesirable rigidity with which the WFS questionnaire was sometimes applied in countries, but whatever its shortcomings, a critical study of the documents ought to be a compulsory part of the training of practising survey statisticians.

WFS promoted painstaking work in the area of translation of questionnaires into the languages of the interviews. Further details may be found in chapter 6. This practice was a new departure in survey-taking. Its neglect in past surveys may in part have been due to lack of resources, but in part it may also be the result of lack of attention to an important issue. A senior member of one national staff remarked that it was illuminating for his organization to undertake a multi-lingual survey. The practice has not been repeated in that country since the fertility survey but the experience exists to be made use of as appropriate.

Training, pre-testing, supervision and fieldwork

The WFS can claim with justification to have encouraged and introduced several major improvements in data collection. Not all these are innovative, but the credit lies in their elaboration and systematic application. We have already noted the use of well-designed verbatim questionnaires and written translations. Other improvements include thorough training and pre-testing, the use of female interviewers and mobile teams, high supervisor-interviewer ratio, prompt editing in the field, spot-checks and re-interviews, tape-recording and analysis of a sample of interviewers' work, rigorous rules for callbacks to follow-up non-responding units, and so on. The WFS training manuals for interviewers and supervisors, as well as trainers, contain a great deal of useful material which can be adapted to diverse surveys and survey conditions. The same applies to training courses developed in WFS surveys, with their emphasis on demonstration and role-playing exercises and field practice, use of audio-visual aids, especially tape-recorders, and, above all, on the length of training – usually three weeks for interviewers and up to five weeks for field supervisors. In so far as WFS has demonstrated and convinced countries that longer training of operative staff can contribute towards substantial improvements in the quality of the data collected, it has made a significant contribution to the improvement of survey practices.

Sampling

WFS samples were designed within the specific context of a one-off survey, yet a great deal can be learned from the simple and clear strategy adopted. The experience of countries participating in WFS has demonstrated that it is feasible to conduct, and conduct fairly well, surveys based on strict probability samples; and that it is possible to have measurable samples, to keep records of sample structures, and to estimate and present sampling variances along with the publication of substantive results. The designs were simple in several respects. They were often self-weighting, avoided multiple-area stages and cumbersome stratification and, relatively speaking, the sample sizes were small to moderate, emphasizing the importance of controlling non-sampling errors. The WFS 'Manual on Sample Design' (WFS 1975c), as didactic material for the general survey practitioner, should be counted among the significant contributions of WFS to the art of survey-taking in developing countries. But most important is the WFS contribution to computation and analysis of sampling errors. The WFS developed and distributed free of charge a special package program for the purpose (Clusters), and provided technical and empirical material on analysis of sampling errors and evaluation of the sample designs used. Most survey reports include detailed information on sampling errors; the participating developing countries in this respect have excelled the usual practice of neglect by many developed country organizations.

Data processing

The WFS contribution in the area of data processing is sometimes underestimated, at least in part because the programme originally underestimated the complexities of the task and its strategy and methodology evolved rather slowly. Considerable resources were ultimately devoted to the development and free distribution of useful software packages for survey data processing. While some of these were designed for very specific WFS applications, others such as Cocgen, Clusters, Assembler, Concor, Update, Corrector, MARG and Codbox provided a valuable arsenal for countries in a very critical area of survey work. The usefulness of the packages goes beyond specific WFS applications. WFS also developed and carefully documented detailed procedures for data editing, tabulation and archiving. The comprehensive WFS publication, 'Data Processing Guidelines' (WFS 1980a), is an outstanding document on how to plan and specify the various data processing steps; in fact we know of no other document of comparable quality on the subject.

Reporting, analysis, assessment and evaluation

Perhaps the most outstanding contribution of the WFS lies in the fact that it took the tasks of data analysis, assessment, evaluation and reporting most seriously, as an integral part of the total survey operations. This is not because WFS paid any less attention to data collection and processing, but because insufficient attention is paid in most other survey work to data *analysis*. WFS has made some important contributions in this area. We need not comment on specific techniques developed and tested, some of which are described in chapter 25, except to note that the large number of scientific publications by WFS, or others in association with WFS, constitute an important contribution to the development of survey methodology and analysis techniques, some of which go beyond the specific concern of a fertility survey. It is important to note that many of the exemplary analyses and technical papers were done by researchers from developing countries in collaboration with or under contract from the WFS.

WFS has also been able to set up excellent standards in the areas of assessment and evaluation. Approximately one in four of the participating countries carried out re-interview surveys for quantitative assessment of non-sampling errors. Numerous investigations have also been undertaken for a more general assessment of WFS survey methodology and implementation, and we have little doubt that for many years to come these painstaking investigations will provide guidance and encouragement to practising survey statisticians to look more closely and critically at the quality of the work they do. A major contributing factor in this respect has been the high standard achieved and reliability of the services provided by WFS data archives.

Special mention should be made of the analysis and evaluation workshops conducted by WFS to help train a large number of researchers from developing countries.

38.6   Capacity to absorb

It is important to question the extent to which countries are willing or able to absorb some of the desirable survey practices promoted by WFS. In other words, has there been a lasting effect?

Such questions are, of course, extremely difficult to answer. In the main one can form only subjective impressions by talking to the individuals involved. On that basis, we may answer the above questions affirmatively, since almost always ex-directors of WFS surveys have been complimentary to the WFS in their remarks to us. Generally, criticism of WFS has come from other, non-ex-directors, who no doubt are equally wise and objective.

The WFS was itself, at least latterly, quite conscious of the importance of these questions and in 1983 arranged for a survey of senior national staff in participating countries (see chapter 37). Again responses were, generally, positive. Perhaps people are polite, or we have a biased population of those who may have personally benefited from participation in the WFS experience; nevertheless, we present here a typical sample of responses to a question on general appraisal of the WFS (on the basis of a 60 per cent response rate):

Question: How appropriate is the WFS model for fertility and other similar surveys?

Sample responses:

- Very appropriate; want to repeat
- Appropriate; in fact have repeated fertility survey on same model
- Too expensive; not sensitive to national needs
- High fieldwork cost; too much emphasis on data editing
- Very appropriate
- Better than most surveys, but cost high
- Follow-up prospective approach would have been preferable in this country
- High marks for thorough training, planning, fieldwork and editing
- Very appropriate
- Need to follow a simpler approach
- Will follow the WFS approach in future
- Good for countries which already have a capability (like the country concerned).

Responses to specific questions relating to particular aspects of WFS practice indicate that in the promotion of translation, in the use of female interviewers, and in the team approach, the WFS was not particularly innovative although it should be noted that six countries (out of 24) introduced female interviewers following experience with the WFS, and eight introduced more thorough machine editing of the data. The use of tape-recorders has not caught on, probably due to the substantial extra work required in the analysis of tape-recordings, and because appreciation of the practical significance of methodological research and evaluation still remains inadequate.

38.7   Concluding remarks

We have argued that the major limitations of WFS in making a contribution to the enhancement of national survey capability sprang largely from the limited time horizon and rather predetermined content and scope of the programme. These features – dictated in great part by the limited mandate given to WFS by its donor agencies – precluded much significant contribution to institution building, strengthening survey-taking infrastructural facilities, and long-term formal training of national staff. WFS must, however, bear the responsibility for a certain lack of flexibility in adapting survey procedures and content to country requirements and for refraining from methodological experimentation beyond what was dictated by its limited mandate.

However, on the whole, the orientation and manner with which WFS implemented national fertility surveys seriously attempted to transcend some of these inherent limitations. The WFS staff, as individuals and as a group, demonstrated a clear commitment to improving survey research methods and supporting the growth of survey capability in developing countries. WFS managed to get as much work as possible done within countries; to ensure active participation by national staff in survey implementation; to ensure successful completion of all phases of the survey; to provide countries with the rich experience of a well-conducted survey; to make significant contributions to the art of survey data collection, processing and analysis with relevance far beyond the specific fertility survey; and to get scholars from developing countries to participate in analysis and reporting of survey results. These are significant contributions to the enhancement of national survey capability. Furthermore, the full WFS contribution to survey research in developing countries cannot yet be assessed, since the research and analysis process generated by the WFS will continue to flow for many years after the formal conclusion of the project.

Notes

1. There have, of course, been isolated discussions of the issue. For an explicit consideration see Smith *et al.* (1980), which was prepared by independent consultants to the main WFS funding agencies under the auspices of the American Public Health Association.
2. The concepts of 'external' and 'internal' capability are expounded in United Nations (1977b); (1979b).
3. For information on the national agencies involved in executing WFS surveys, see WFS (1985), app. 3.
4. For a fuller discussion of the broader issues and specific illustrations of WFS contributions to survey methodology, see Verma (1985).

39

Social and Economic Implications

Halvor Gille

39.1 Introduction

A realistic population policy cannot be formulated and carried out without considerable information about the levels and trends of the demographic variables and their inter-relationships with economic and social factors. Such information is needed not only to enable governments to formulate and implement population policy but also to judge if a policy is needed. Most governments have some policies or programmes related to fertility — not necessarily with the specific aim of reducing or increasing fertility but to enable families to accomplish the birth spacing and childbearing pattern they want. Where no policies or activities have been adopted, particularly in Africa, the main reason given is insufficient information on which to develop a policy position (United Nations 1979c). Adoption of a *laissez-faire* attitude, however, is in itself an important policy decision, requiring considerable data and understanding of socio-economic and demographic inter-relationships, and ought to be taken only after consideration of the socio-economic consequences of present and expected future population trends and the various policy options.

The primary focus of WFS, established in 1972, was to provide reliable and detailed information on human fertility and family planning practice, but data have also been obtained on related topics such as infant and early childhood mortality, nuptiality and breastfeeding patterns. In this way the programme has contributed to policy-making, not only in the fields of fertility and family planning but also with regard to maternal and child health and health planning in general. WFS data have in many countries contributed greatly to improving the data base for determining current and future population trends by providing information which was not previously available in any detail or in reliable form, or indeed at all. An introduction to a United Nations comparative analysis of WFS data noted the following:

At the national level, planning agencies must try to assure that strategies for socio-economic development are based on appropriate research findings. Demographic theory has not yet reached the point of propounding universally applicable theories and a more cautious approach of allowing for the possibility of cultural or regional differences is preferable. Unfortunately, in the past, findings from one setting have often been used as a basis for policy formulation in another setting, because no other alternative was available. Findings from the comparative analysis of WFS data can be used to test such assumptions and better-founded population policy can be expected to follow. (United Nations 1983d)

The background documentation prepared for the 1984 International Conference on Population demonstrates the importance of and the extensive dependence on WFS data in a worldwide review and appraisal of population trends and policies (United Nations 1985c; World Bank 1984). WFS data have played a major role in eliminating doubts or controversy about whether a clear and significant decline in fertility had set in on a wide scale in a large number of developing countries or whether it was just a few special cases of small countries or areas. A mail inquiry undertaken by WFS indicates that survey data have been used by government departments in a number of ways in the countries concerned (see chapter 37). In many countries WFS results have led to the revision of current estimates of fertility, infant mortality and population growth and of population projections forming the basis for economic and social development planning for the future. WFS data are important in this regard not only in developing countries, which generally have a dearth of demographic data, but also in developed countries, as one analyst noted:

The official population projections prepared in the mid and late 1960s would have been quite different in many countries of Europe had the governments and the responsible agencies had at their disposal replies from a small sample of women to the question of how many children they expected to have in the future. Instead, they usually relied on mechanical extrapolations of past fertility trends, often with disastrous results. It was this usefulness of questions on family size preferences which was mainly responsible for the support European governments gave to WFS-type surveys in the 1970s. (Berent 1983)

Overall population policies have sometimes been reaffirmed or changed by taking into account new and better information on fertility, demonstrating a substantial, and unsuspected, declining trend in fertility as in some countries of Asia, Latin America and the Mediterranean region, or indicating no decline but rather an upward trend as in many sub-Saharan African countries. Sometimes WFS has clearly shown that the level of fertility was much higher than had been thought in the absence of reliable census or other data, or than what was deemed desirable from the point of view of development.

The influence of WFS findings on government attitudes towards population growth and the provision of family planning services may well have been critical in a number of countries. In Kenya the results came as a great surprise, portraying as they did a nation with one of the highest population growth rates in the world (nearly 4 per cent per annum, implying a doubling of the population every 18 years) and demonstrating that the family planning programme had had little impact, The result was that an appreciable change towards approaching family planning with a greater sense of urgency took place in the climate of political opinion. In Haiti the fertility survey data led to the recognition of the need for a national population policy. In Cameroon the establishment of a new Population Commission was announced at the national meeting where the main survey findings were presented. In Nigeria the fertility survey was recognized as providing, for the first time, demographic data urgently needed for policy planning, implementation and evaluation after a number of past attempts to carry out population censuses and enumerations had given only questionable results. In several of the African francophone countries survey results have provoked widespread discussion in government circles that may well mark the beginning of a decisive shift away from indifference or even hostility towards a confrontation of the population problems.

One of the most important contributions of WFS has been to provide basic demographic and related information required to formulate, organize, evaluate and monitor population policies on fertility and family planning. The surveys have contributed greatly merely by providing detailed descriptive and usually reliable data for the countries concerned and for major geographical and socio-economic population groups within them on such topics as, for example, age at and duration of marriage, levels of fertility and infant mortality, family building patterns, knowledge and use of various methods of contraception, availability of family planning services and extent of breastfeeding. The above-mentioned mail enquiry showed that the most frequent use countries made of WFS data in the field of family planning was to assess programme achievements, then to define or redefine objectives and goals, to increase efficiency, to determine where there was most unmet need for family planning and to identify prevailing preferences with regard to methods of contraception.

Policy-makers would be interested not only in information about the actual levels of the various variables but also in their trends. A one-round survey like WFS has limitations in this regard but it does provide some estimates of trends concerning age at marriage, fertility, infant and child mortality and breastfeeding. In one country, Dominican Republic, a repeat survey was carried out after five years, clearly demonstrating the additional information which could be obtained on fertility change and its determinants, information of considerable policy and programmatic significance (Hobcraft and Rodríguez 1982a).

Some of the most surprising data revealed by WFS are on infant and child mortality. The surveys have demonstrated that information available from vital statistics registration or any other sources underestimated the level of infant and early childhood mortality to a considerable extent in a number of countries, particularly Africa and South and West Asia (see chapter 32). Perhaps the contribution of WFS to demographic knowledge has been even greater for child-hood mortality than for fertility, providing a rich source of information needed by various national and international agencies and organizations. The detail and high quality of WFS data on this topic provide a more convincing demonstration of need for policy measures than mortality estimates often based upon incom-plete or unreliable sources.

Furthermore, WFS has made considerable contributions to the knowledge of breastfeeding patterns and trends, with important policy ramifications and guidance for health programmes for women and infants. Data have been obtained on the prevalence and duration of breastfeeding on a wider scale and in more depth than ever before for some 41 developing countries as well as for major population groups within them.

From a policy-making and programmatic point of view, it is of great importance that the WFS data are available for major geographical and socio-economic groups of the population in the countries concerned. The planners and administrators want to know which population groups require their special attention, where needs are greatest, who will be most receptive to programmatic efforts and where impact will be most significant in terms of cost effectiveness. Information on differentials in fertility and family planning as well as nuptiality, infant mortality and breastfeeding makes it possible to identify target groups which should be given programmatic priority. In this regard, urban–rural and regional differentials may be the most important as the population groups concerned are fairly easily identifiable. WFS data may suggest different policies and approaches in different parts of a country, as demonstrated, for example, in the case of Egypt, where important regional differentials in use of family planning cannot be accounted for by differentials in socio-economic characteristics of the population and access to supplies alone; the principal reason may be differences in basic values concerning family life and childbearing (El-Deeb and Casterline forthcoming).

An assessment of the policy implications of WFS surveys carried out in developing countries is a difficult undertaking for several reasons. The surveys and their findings are country-specific, and generalizations cannot easily be made. Social and economic conditions vary from country to country and within countries. Concern about population issues and policy objectives as well as willingness to make interventions also vary. Certain findings may be very relevant for the promotion of one type of policy but not for another. Although WFS is a standardized international research programme, there are sometimes important differences in coverage, content and question formulation, and not all surveys produce findings of equal relevance to policy. Furthermore, it is premature to draw conclusions about policies for countries with recent surveys in view of the fact that the detailed analysis of the results necessary has not yet been undertaken. For other countries many aspects of the data have not yet been fully studied and analysed, and there are a number of country-specific as well as cross-national comparisons or analyses underway or still to be initiated which may suggest more or different policy implications than can be indicated at present.

The following discussion focuses on the implications of the available survey findings, and the alternative strategies they may suggest for planning and implementing population policies of developing countries aimed at promoting fertility decline and bringing about acceptable levels of infant and early childhood mortality. Only those variables which lend themselves to manipulation in practice or which are anticipated to influence policy-making decisions or directions will be considered.

39.2   Socio-economic factors in fertility decline

The early 1970s saw a lively debate between those who argued that general development, improved levels of living, education, health and communication facilities, as well as industrialization, urbanization and increased employment of women, would bring about fertility decline with little or no promotion of organized family planning and those who maintained that development itself was threatened by rapid population growth but family planning programmes could make an appreciable independent impact on fertility. The debate culminated at the 1974 World Population Conference, when the slogan 'development is the best contraceptive' was coined by some developing countries. More recently, this fundamental conflict has been transformed into a positive co-existence, with the realization that organized family planning can never replace general development aims but can be a useful adjunct, not only for demographic reasons but also as an extension of individual freedom of choice. Still at issue is the question of which particular components of development, if any, independent of family planning efforts, may most effectively promote fertility decline. The advent of WFS data provides an unprecedented opportunity to re-examine the relationship between modern attributes and fertility at the level of the individual family rather than relying on macro data with a high degree of aggregation at the national or provincial level. Modernization may influence fertility in two different ways: it may affect parental demand, desire or need for children and it may affect willingness to translate these desires into appropriate forms of reproductive control.

Formal education and rising literacy, particularly of young women, are often mentioned as factors most likely to lead to fertility decline. In general, the results from WFS support this contention. Women who have completed primary education have fewer children than women with no education, and family size declines consistently in all countries with increased secondary or higher schooling. Education contributes to changing attitudes and values in favour of a small family norm. Better educated women tend to marry later than women with little or no education. Couples who are better educated are more likely to be exposed to, know about and use family planning services and will, therefore, usually have smaller families than their less educated counterparts. Furthermore, education of women contributes to reduction in infant and child mortality and may thereby reduce fertility.

A detailed analysis of the data, however, suggests that rising education may not be consistently associated with reduction in fertility. Modest increases in exposure to formal schooling do not always lead to lower fertility. In a number of WFS countries, such as, for instance, Bangladesh, Benin, Kenya, Philippines and Senegal, women with a few years' schooling have a slightly higher current fertility than uneducated women. An educational 'threshold' seems to exist, particularly in countries at an early stage of development and in rural areas, prior to which fertility either remains stationary or increases as level of education rises

(United Nations 1983d). The reason is not that such women desire more children or are less ready to use contraception. On the contrary, they report evidently higher levels of contraceptive use than completely uneducated women. But increased education seems associated with reduction in duration of breastfeeding and other fertility-reducing restraints such as prolonged post-natal abstinence. The overall impact of increased education, especially incomplete primary education, may operate to raise or lower fertility depending upon the relative strengths of these associations. Where contraceptive use is low, the reduced protection due to shortened length of breastfeeding may offset the small impact of contraception (chapter 30). Other factors not captured in survey results may also play a part, such as better nutrition and health, leading to a lower level of sterility and spontaneous foetal loss. Furthermore, in certain parts of Africa, a lower level of polygamy among women with some primary schooling may have some pronatalist effect (Casterline, Singh, Cleland and Ashurst 1984).

The policy implications of these findings are that universal education should be promoted to provide for at least complete primary schooling and in so far as possible secondary education. A few years only of education, due to high drop-out rates such as are common in many developing countries at an early stage of development, may not contribute to fertility decline although they may have various other socio-economic effects which are most desirable. In those countries it is important for policy-makers to be aware of an educational threshold level, if it exists, and take steps to surmount it or find ways and means of neutralizing its effects. Developing countries which have reached an intermediate or higher level of development should be aware of the high level of fertility usually prevailing in population groups with little or no education and special programmes should be promoted towards meeting their educational needs, including functional literacy and adult education activities to reinforce other fertility-reducing factors.

The existence of a generally negative relation between education and fertility does not necessarily mean that raising educational attainment is either necessary or sufficient to bring about fertility decline. United Nations studies based on WFS data show that both actual and desired fertility of educated women vary greatly among countries; thus, advanced education does not by itself guarantee uniformly low fertility. Furthermore, if only marital fertility is considered, there are some developing countries where fertility is no lower for the highly educated than for those with no schooling. Where fertility *is* much lower for the highly educated, this may have less to do with education's effect on desired family size than with greater success of the highly educated at preventing unwanted births (United Nations 1983d; forthcoming b).

Recent demographic changes in some countries show that reasonable educational levels are not always necessary for bringing about fertility decline. The rapid diffusion of family planning in such countries as Indonesia and Thailand, and some states of India, where a large proportion of couples have received little or no formal education, testifies to the truth of this assertion. Even in Latin

America, fertility is now declining among the least educated sectors of the population. Illiteracy or a total lack of formal education cannot therefore be regarded as an unconquerable impediment to radical changes in reproductive behaviour. This realization should be welcome to the family planning movement, for progress in the provision of formal education often cannot be achieved rapidly without incurring high costs and it will be a decade or so before today's schoolchildren enter their reproductive careers.

The survey data available for the study of the impact of education upon fertility are limited to educational attainment in quantitative terms. Other aspects of education such as content, particularly whether family life or population education is a part of the curriculum, quality of education, availability of teaching materials, etc., may be relevant. Such factors could have appreciable impact and should be kept in mind. Unfortunately, little of this information, which could give important guidance for educational efforts in support of population policies, is available from WFS.

It has often been suggested that improving the status of women will lead to more rapid declines in fertility in developing countries than would otherwise be the case. In the World Population Plan of Action (WPPA) adopted by the 1974 World Population Conference, full integration of women in the development process, including elimination of discrimination in education and employment, was recommended as one way to moderate fertility levels, and the importance of research on the interrelationships between women's status and population trends was emphasized. Ten years later, the International Conference on Population at Mexico City devoted one of the five main sections of the recommendations exclusively to the topic of improvement in the status of women as an important goal that should be pursued as an end in itself as well as a means among others of reducing the level of fertility.

WFS can only make a minor contribution to the important issue of the impact of the integration of women upon fertility since no attempt was made in surveys to obtain direct measurements of the status of women – a term which includes various social and economic factors affecting women's life in the family and the community. Evidence, however, is available from analyses of the relationship between maternal education, employment and fertility, after controlling for the socio-economic status of the husband. The relationship between education and fertility appears to be essentially of the same magnitude for the husband and the wife but female education exerts a stronger influence upon contraceptive use, particularly in the least developed countries, which may eventually be reflected in greater impact upon fertility as contraception increasingly becomes a major determinant affecting fertility levels (United Nations 1983d). This finding suggests that preference in educational policies should be given to the promotion of girls' education and correction of the imbalance between school enrolment rates for girls and boys (the former still being between one-half and three-quarters of the latter in most developing countries). Measures should be taken not only to promote school enrolment of girls but also to maintain actual attendance by identifying and dealing with some of the constraints operating to prevent them completing their schooling.

Comparative analysis of WFS data indicates that the extent of the association between women's work and fertility depends upon the overall level of development (United Nations 1985c). In the least developed societies, it appears that there are no significant and consistent fertility differentials between various work status groups, particularly in the traditional sector of the economy. In more advanced developing countries (and in industrialized countries), the relationship between women's work and childbearing is stronger and more consistent. It is likely that conflicts between employment and childbearing arise increasingly as education, urbanization and socio-economic development in general are advanced. WFS results have not established a definite association between work status and contraceptive use but in some countries employment outside the home does appear to engender higher levels of use even after controlling for education and rural–urban residence (Sathar and Chidambaram 1984). Even if a consistent direct influence of women's work upon childbearing is not proven, improved employment opportunities for women are likely to contribute indirectly to fertility decline by increasing the incentive to give girls an education, strengthen their position in the family if they can make an income, increase communication with others and raise the opportunity cost of women's time.

High level of fertility is often explained as being due to a large demand for children. One way of reducing parents' demand for children or desired family size is to limit the economic benefits of children. The large majority of the adult population in developing countries, particularly in rural areas, are not covered by any social security system but have to rely upon their children for economic support in old age and in time of need, such as during prolonged illness, invalidity and unemployment. Only a few of the WFS surveys provide information on the significance of children for the family economy. According to one such survey — in Egypt — women expecting financial support from their children want on average 0.5 more children than other women, and women who expect to live with their children want 1.6 more children than those who do not.

In due course the labour and other values of children tend to diminish with economic and social development such as urbanization, industrialization and higher levels of living. The demand for children may, however, be reduced by promoting social welfare, social security schemes and mutual aid societies, but such institutions are not easily established in a subsistence economy. The value of child labour declines if production functions are transferred from the family or household to market enterprises, co-operative establishments or other non-household undertakings. Various institutional changes, provision of credit facilities and the strengthening of management can be promoted to accelerate this process. However, to restrict child labour through legislation or to introduce compulsory education may not be effective in this regard unless the political, economic and social climate for such measures is generally favourable.

Another way of reducing the demand for children would be to increase the costs of children to their parents. It would in general hardly be acceptable, in support of a demographic policy, to increase the direct costs of having children, for food, clothing, education, etc. But the indirect costs of children may be increased by policy measures. Women may be given other options than childbearing by providing employment or income-generating activities for them outside the home and facilitating their access to educational and vocational training programmes. In conditions of severe unemployment or underemployment prevailing in many countries, emphasis should be given to training and production activities, particularly in the informal sector and in small-scale enterprises. Such programmes should aim particularly at unmarried and young married women with only a few children in order to have the desired results of delayed childbearing and reduced family size. These measures will at the same time promote general development goals, in particular the integration of women in the development process and the improvement of their status in the family and in society. However, in so far as such employment and income-generating opportunities can be exercised in or near the home, they may lose some of their fertility-reducing effect by making children's participation possible and increasing the value of child labour.

The level of fertility in most countries with WFS data is lower in urban than in rural areas and usually lower in metropolitan districts than in other urban areas (Singh *et al.* 1985). These differentials are clearly an effect of urban–rural differentials found in contraceptive use. A strong positive association exists between the level of urbanization and use of contraceptives, and women classified as 'lifetime' urbanites are more likely contraceptors than rural dwellers, with rural–urban migrants in between (Sathar and Chidambaram 1984). Other intermediate determinants of fertility, such as extent and duration of breastfeeding and post-natal abstinence, seem to be generally negatively related to urbanization, which means that differentials in contraceptive use play a more dominant role.

The influence of urbanization upon fertility should be taken into account by policy-makers in assessing the impact of urbanization and deciding on measures, if any, to influence rural–urban migration. It should be recognized, however, that the relationship between urbanization and fertility is far from uniform in magnitude and sometimes even in direction. It varies from country to country and between major regions of the developing world. It seems that the fertility differentials are most pronounced in countries which have advanced somewhat in social and economic development, but are far less important, sometimes insignificant or maybe even display reversed relationships, in countries which are at an initial stage of development. It will therefore be particularly in countries which are already quite urbanized, as in Latin America and East Asia, that further urbanization can be expected to contribute significantly to reducing fertility.

Other socio-economic factors may be related to fertility as indicated by various studies. The general conclusion, based upon analysis of WFS data so far, seems to be that no single aspect of development which from a policy point of view can be considered a key factor in bringing about fertility decline and demographic change has been identified. Fertility decline can and does occur in widely differing socio-economic contexts. Its onset may be determined more by a composite of several socio-economic factors or by ill-understood cultural factors than by any particular objectively ascertainable development indicator. As far as many factors, such as education, employment of women and urbanization, are concerned, it seems that certain thresholds have to be reached and passed before they have a significant fertility-reducing impact and that before reaching such minimum levels there may be no such impact, sometimes even the opposite. However, with sufficient socio-economic development and structural changes in the community fertility can in due course, perhaps after some delay, be expected to decline, although it may not be known which particular factors are most important in this regard. It will be for the policy-makers to select those which, on the available evidence, are most likely in a given situation to work together to promote the policy objectives concerned.

39.3 Family planning

The impact of socio-economic development upon the reduction of fertility can be considerably sustained and reinforced by family planning facilities. An important question carrying policy implications is whether legitimation of family planning and provision of supplies will suffice to lower fertility. If, for instance, it is true that high fertility is deeply embedded in the socio-economic structure of the society, family planning provision without structural changes is unlikely to bring about a major fertility reduction. The family size norms and attitudes have to be investigated and changed, for example by discouraging child labour, enforcing school attendance, promoting forms of security against illness, old age and other calamities and providing women with increased economic opportunities.

WFS data cannot provide direct and definitive answers to questions about the nature of institutional supports for high fertility. But, outside sub-Saharan Africa and some Middle East countries, WFS surveys have helped to reaffirm that couples do not consciously want very large families. In most countries, half or more married and fecund women indicated that they did not want any more children than they already had. In Asian countries included in WFS, preferred family sizes were on the average 4.0 children, in Latin America 4.3 and the Middle East 5.8 (but considerably higher in Africa, as discussed below). These levels of desired fertility are, of course, far above replacement levels, even after allowing for childhood mortality. However, some are appreciably lower than prevailing fertility levels and thus run counter to the contention that high fertility in these settings is generally considered beneficial by parents.

The validity of this impression of a huge untapped market for family planning is somewhat controversial. It may be argued, for instance, that if the desire for small families was felt with sufficient intensity, couples would adjust their behaviour. Furthermore, preferences or need may be more inferred from what people do rather than what they say. On the premise that the modest desired family sizes measured in WFS surveys in many countries provide a genuine indication of at least latent motivation for lower fertility, can the surveys throw any light on the reasons why family planning is not more widely practised in a number of countries and will the findings provide any guidance for future policy?

Use of contraception for spacing purposes is usually proclaimed as a major objective of family planning, but in actual fact many programmes in developing countries are directed mainly at couples with several children already, with the emphasis on family limitation. Many governments, particularly in Africa, are interested in family planning only as a means of birth spacing and improvement in health of mothers and children and this concept is more readily acceptable and understood by the population at large. WFS data show that while the majority of contraceptive use in developing countries is for the purpose of family limitation, a substantial minority in most countries, amounting on average to over one-third of the contraceptors, wanted another child although many of them did not want it soon. This finding suggests that family planning programmes should focus on potential users of contraception for childspacing as well as on couples who do not want more children. Promotion of contraceptive use for spacing purposes can actually contribute to fertility decline. WFS data show that a fairly high proportion of women who had ever used contraception were continuing to use it at the time of the survey (on average 61 per cent of all ever-users and 57 per cent of women wanting more children). Women who use contraception for spacing purposes are more likely to use it successfully if they want to cease childbearing later on. Spacing also has a demographic impact by reducing fertility of women in the younger and more fertile age groups and by increasing the average birth intervals and thereby extending the interval between generations. Therefore, family planning programmes should aim at informing, educating and servicing all individuals from the beginning of their reproductive lives.

Total ignorance of contraceptive methods does not appear to be a barrier in most of the surveyed countries, as large majorities of women claim to know at least one method; typically, modern methods such as the pill or intra-uterine devices are most familiar. Among the Asian countries, knowledge fell below 50 per cent only in Nepal; in the Arabic-speaking world, only women of Yemen AR and Mauritania were largely ignorant of contraception. In much of sub-Saharan Africa, however, knowledge of contraception is still at very low levels.

Superficial awareness of the existence of methods is hardly sufficient for actual practice, since this does not imply knowledge of how to use particular methods and/or where to obtain them. WFS did not enquire about knowledge of how to use various methods but, in an appreciable number of surveys, respondents were asked whether they knew of any source of supply. Knowledge of sources is often well below general awareness of methods and varies greatly between the diverse societies; but it is worth noting that even in countries such as Colombia, Venezuela, Mexico and Indonesia, where contraceptive awareness is high, substantial minorities are apparently ignorant of any places where they can obtain advice and supplies. Non-medical and non-appliance methods such as withdrawal and rhythm are, of course, available in principle to all, but such methods do not appear to be widely used in most developing countries. The so-called contraceptive revolution over the last decade has derived its impetus almost entirely from increased use of modern methods, with few reliable recorded instances of increased popularity of traditional methods.

As expected, ignorance of supply sources is concentrated among the rural and least well-educated population groups. The disparities are sometimes startling. In Mexico, for instance, only 27 per cent of rural women compared to about 70 per cent of urban residents knew of a source; and only a quarter of uneducated women, in contrast to nearly 90 per cent of those with secondary or higher schooling, were aware of any place to visit for advice or supplies. Similarly sharp differences are apparent for other Latin American countries and in Nepal. Thus in these societies, differences between sectors of the population in the adoption of contraception reflect to some extent differential knowledge. But for countries like the Republic of Korea, Malaysia, Indonesia and Costa Rica, the findings show that knowledge of family planning outlets is widely and equally diffused among all sectors of the population.

To the extent that couples have distinct aversions to or preferences for particular methods, knowledge of where to obtain specific methods is a better criterion of access than knowledge of sources in general. A number of WFS surveys enquired about method-specific knowledge of sources. In general, places where the oral pill can be obtained are more widely known than sources for intra-uterine devices or sterilization, but, as might be expected, condom sources were not well known among female respondents in the surveys.

These results demonstrate the point that for many couples the effective choice of methods of contraception is extremely limited. To ensure the individual's free choice and strengthen the acceptability and practice of family planning, all available methods should not merely be provided for in service programmes but also be dealt with fully in information and educational activities as well as in the training of service personnel.

WFS, like most other surveys on fertility and family planning, relied almost exclusively on the testimony of women. However, in four surveys a subsample of husbands was also interviewed and results are available for two countries, Thailand and Egypt. In these two settings the attitudes of husbands towards family size and limitation are not radically different from those of wives. Perhaps this is not surprising in Thailand, considering the comparatively high status and independence of women in that country. The similarity is less predictable in Egypt, a predominantly Muslim country. Whether similar findings would have been obtained in other countries or other regions must remain in doubt, but this limited evidence suggests that men as well as women should be targets in programmes aiming at reducing fertility.

A problem facing many family planning programmes and revealed in survey results is the side-effects of some contraceptive methods which often contribute to users' high discontinuation rates. Thus, in one WFS survey (Philippines), side-effects was the reason given by one-third of all women for discontinuation, and it was estimated that if a contraceptive method free from side-effects and fully effective had been available, discontinuation rates could have been cut by over one-half and the birth rate substantially reduced. It is essential, therefore, to provide for follow-up service and advice as a part of family planning and health services.

The degree of dispersion and density of contraceptive sources needed to promote and sustain high levels of contraceptive practice is a key issue for family planning programmes. Though various indicators of proximity have been obtained in WFS surveys, the data have proved analytically complex. The effect of distance on propensity to use no doubt partly operates through awareness of the sources and partly relates to the cost and inconvenience of travel. It also depends on the nature of specific methods, such as whether it requires a single or a continued effort, is reversible, etc.

For those who are permanent spacers – unwilling to accept that they will never want another child yet never actually reaching a point when they want one – as well as for couples who are interested only in temporary spacing, reversible methods such as the pill, condom, intra-uterine device or injection are needed. An important question is whether travelling time to a source of these methods may be a critical factor in the decision to adopt and continue using them. Survey results seem to indicate that once confounding variables such as urban–rural residence, education and desire to limit fertility are controlled for among those aware of a source, the relationship between proximity to source and actual use is only weakly positive. Thus it might appear that women are not deterred by the need to travel to obtain supplies or for check-ups. This finding may not be so surprising as it would appear at first glance when it is realized that travel time may not be a major problem in communities where family planning services are already well developed and widely accessible. Furthermore, where a family planning programme is only at an early stage, the actual users will be limited to those highly motivated and therefore likely to be prepared to overcome travel barriers. But this does not mean that where family planning is not yet fully developed potential users less determined to control fertility will be able and willing to overcome travel difficulties. Most health care studies have shown strong declines in the utilization of services with increasing distance from facilities.

The policy implications are several. First, there is in many countries and in selected population groups considerable scope for increased efforts to promote publicity about family planning, including information about types of methods, their advantages and disadvantages, where facilities are available, follow-up services and how they can be reached. Second, increasing the accessibility of services may have a positive effect on the use of supply methods, particularly in the early stages of programme development, but a well-planned distribution system making facilities available at convenient locations and opening days and hours, supplemented by visits to the families by 'outreach' fieldworkers and by social marketing programmes, may be, more effective than simply saturating an area with outlets. Third, *all* methods of family planning, in so far as their use is legal and in accordance with prevailing social values, should be made available, promoted and be dealt with in all aspects of family planning programme activities.

A combination of low desired fertility and reasonably widespread family planning services is no guarantee of the acceptance and practice of birth control and declining fertility. In many states of India, in Bangladesh and in Pakistan (in the period 1965-69) these two conditions appear to have been fulfilled but achievements have been modest. It seems that full explanations have not yet been advanced for the apparent limited success of family planning programmes in these settings or for their dramatic success in countries such as Thailand and Indonesia. One of the reasons is probably that availability and accessibility of family planning facilities are usually not sufficient for success: strong leadership, trained personnel and other elements which constitute major programmatic efforts are also needed. A study of birth rate declines, 1965-80, in a large number of developing countries with various types and contents of family planning programmes has identified a set of such programme effort indicators, which include good supervision, effective personnel, use of evaluation findings in management, mass media support and post-partum facilities in addition to availability and accessibility of family planning methods (Lapham and Mauldin 1984). Perhaps another reason is that a major behavioural innovation like family planning can only flourish where many other attitudes are changing at the same time. The crust of custom and conservatism has to be broken by a modicum of social, economic or political change before contraception becomes widely acceptable.

The problems of and policies for fertility decline in sub-Saharan Africa have to be considered separately. WFS survey results, so far available for eight of these countries, portray a culture which is strongly pronatalist in attitude. The average desired family size ranges from six to eight and a half children, and large proportions of women in some of these countries decline to provide any numerical boundary to their reproductive wishes. Only small minorities of women want to avoid further childbearing and levels of contraceptive practice are negligible. The general impression is quite different from attitudes prevailing in other regions, which have persistently shown more modest desired family sizes. The reasons for the disparity may to some extent be difficult to explain but it has important policy implications.

In Africa, family planning programmes cannot be framed on the assumption of a massive latent demand for smaller sizes of family. There appear to be two main feasible policies – to attempt to change people's views about the desirability of large families or to stress the benefits of birth spacing through contraception. The former course of action presents a formidable challenge. There are few instances where government action has been effective in changing family size ideals. China, perhaps, is one such case but the political structure of China is very different from that in Africa. Elsewhere there is little evidence that family size ideals declined prior to the mass adoption of family limitation, which itself may reduce desired fertility as couples realize that fertility can be controlled effectively. The second course of action is perhaps more likely to succeed. There are already in most African societies strong beliefs in the benefits of birth spacing and a rapid succession of births is often considered shameful. As traditional means of birth spacing such as prolonged lactation and post-natal abstinence are weakening, a process which may be difficult to arrest, a strong demand for contraception as a substitute may emerge. Programme efforts should focus on the period following delivery, to encourage women to substitute contraception for lost protection against pregnancy. This clearly suggests that, particularly in Africa, family planning activities to be effective have to be integrated with and be part and parcel of maternal and child health services.

In parts of sub-Saharan Africa, the only way that contraception can gain acceptance is by focusing on birth spacing as a major target, because of the high prevailing family size preferences. However, there are considerable practical difficulties in delivering family planning services designed primarily for spacing needs. Owing to prolonged lactational amenorrhoea and, in West Africa, to extended post-partum abstinence, many women are not at risk for many months following childbirth. In these circumstances, adoption of contraception in the immediate post-partum period is otiose. However, it is more difficult to identify and canvass women one year or so after childbirth than at the time of delivery, when contact with health services is at its greatest.

An effective birth spacing programme has to deal with the problem of high fertility as well as of low fertility due to subfecundity and sterility. Childlessness and low fertility are common phenomena in some ethnic or regional population groups in several countries and are considered as major population problems by their governments. The WFS survey in Cameroon indicated that about one-fifth of all ever-married women were childless at the end of their reproductive period and higher national figures have been reported in several other countries in West Africa. The causes of widespread sterility and subfecundity are not always clear but they include poor health, early sexual union, taboos and, in particular, venereal diseases. A population policy aiming at reducing fertility in the long run has to deal with this problem, particularly in population groups where it is most serious, in order to obtain the confidence of the population at large even if it may mean some increase in fertility in the short run. Therefore, health and other measures, particularly directed towards controlling venereal diseases, should be promoted as a population policy; the scope for an early impact should be considerable in view of the fact that, according to the WHO, no major campaign to eradicate venereal diseases has been conducted in sub-Saharan Africa in over 20 years.

39.4   Age at marriage

Marriage is defined here as any cohabitation or sexual union irrespective of whether it is legally recognized. Almost all women in developing countries marry and most of them begin their married life earlier than in industrialized countries. In several countries like Bangladesh, India, Nepal and Senegal the median age at first marriage is 16 years or less and in most Asian and African countries it is under 20 years, but in Latin America the typical median age at marriage is around 19-21 years. Evidence from WFS data indicates a dramatic rise in age at marriage in a number of developing countries in Asia, mainly in the 1970s, but only minor increases in Latin America and no change in Africa.

Of particular relevance to policy-makers are the WFS findings on the role of age at first union in achieving reduction in fertility. It is often assumed that women marrying late would have fewer children than women marrying earlier and having a longer exposure to the risk of pregnancy, and that a policy promoting postponement of marriage would contribute to fertility decline. But WFS surveys have shown that women marrying late do not always have fewer children on average than those who marry at younger ages. Women who marry below age 20 tend to end up with higher completed fertility than women marrying later, particularly above age 25, but women who marry very young, particularly in some Asian countries, have lower completed fertility than those marrying at ages 17-20, due to the greater risk of complications and miscarriages from early pregnancies, sometimes resulting in fecundity impairment. These findings suggest that policies aimed at delaying marriage, although desirable on social grounds, may have little fertility-reducing effect unless postponement into the twenties becomes prevalent.

It is hard to determine to what extent fertility reductions associated with higher ages at marriage are directly caused by the later marriage. It is likely that at least some of this apparent reduction is actually linked to some of the factors which contribute to delay in marriage. Among socio-economic measures contributing to postponement of marriage are education, vocational training, employment and other social and economic opportunities for women. Measures having the effect of raising age at marriage may at the same time reinforce social changes which reduce fertility, such as the transformation of the extended family pattern into a nuclear one and the acceptance of full responsibility by parents for bringing up their own children. A United Nations study of WFS data in 22 developing countries found consistent positive effects of education upon age at marriage except in one country (Nepal) and in rural subsamples in a few countries (United Nations 1983d). It seems, however, that improvement in primary education as such may have only limited effect upon girls' age at marriage but that raising of the attainment level to secondary education may have such an effect, particularly if improved employment opportunities outside the home are made available at the same time.

It is, therefore, questionable whether raising age at marriage *per se* will reduce overall fertility levels significantly. A number of developing countries have tried to raise age at marriage by legislation, but often with little success. The administrative structure in many countries is too weak to enforce such legislation, and until reasonably reliable registration of vital events has been developed implementation is likely to be weak and enforcement difficult. Raising age at marriage by law is unlikely to be effective unless the social, economic and cultural climate is also changing and other fertility-reducing factors are in operation.

39.5   Breastfeeding

WFS surveys have provided considerable evidence that breastfeeding is a widely adopted practice in most developing countries. A large majority of women, particularly in Africa and Asia, breastfeed their children for long periods, usually between one and two and a half years. There is considerable survey evidence that infant and early childhood mortality is substantially reduced for breastfed children, especially if fully breastfed during the first six months of infancy (Plank and Milanesi 1973; DaVanzo, Butz and Habicht 1983). Breast milk, particularly in the early days of lactation, provides immunity from various infections, is adequate as a sole source of nutrition for up to about six months of a child's life and is of nutritional value for older children as it provides greater protein and caloric contributions than most other sources of food. Furthermore, breastfeeding may be beneficial to the mother due to its birth spacing effect. Lactation has a contraceptive effect because frequent stimulation of the nipple during suckling inhibits ovulation and promotes amenorrhoea. In some cultures it also acts as a contraceptive due to taboos against sexual intercourse during breastfeeding.

WFS surveys have clearly shown that the average duration of breastfeeding is shorter for women who are younger, more educated, urban and work away from home than for the more traditional groups (Smith and Ferry 1984). These findings suggest that educational advancement, employment for women, urbanization and development in general will be accompanied by a decline in breastfeeding. This circumstantial evidence of a declining trend in breastfeeding as an effect of modernization is reinforced by survey information on recent trends in lactation from such countries as, for example, the Republic of Korea, Philippines and Thailand.

The role of breastfeeding in limiting fertility by prolonging birth intervals is often buttressed by other traditional fertility-inhibiting practices. Principal among these is sexual abstinence after a birth, usually applied to ensure the survival and health of children born rather than to limit family size. In several sub-Saharan countries these periods of abstinence are longer on average than post-partum amenorrhoea, despite prolonged breastfeeding. Once again, WFS surveys provide clear evidence that abstinence is typically less prolonged among the modern sectors of many countries, such as, for example, Ivory Coast, where women with seven or more years of education abstain on average for half as long (seven months) as women with no education. Erosion of these traditional restraints will tend to shorten birth intervals and raise fertility.

The declining trend in breastfeeding in many developing countries confronts policy-makers with a difficult problem. Unless determined efforts are made to counteract this or measures are taken which will successfully increase the use of contraceptives to neutralize the effect of the decline in breastfeeding, the period of infecundity after childbirth will shorten, birth spacing will be reduced and fertility will tend to increase.[1] Studies of WFS data have shown that a one-month increase in breastfeeding lengthens the birth interval by three-quarters of a month (Lightbourne, Singh and Green 1982). However, the fertility impact of a decline in duration of breastfeeding depends to some extent upon whether the infants are exclusively breastfed or whether supplementary foods are provided at the same time. The use of supplementary food will tend to bring about resumption of fecundity, and therefore decline in breastfeeding of long duration when supplements are used will not tend to increase fertility to the same extent as decline in breastfeeding of shorter duration, say under one year.

The obvious response to the current declining trend in breastfeeding in many developing countries is to strengthen maternal and child health and family planning programmes aimed at arresting this trend, as well as adjusting to it by developing consistent and mutually reinforcing policies on lactation and family planning. The importance of lactation for the health of mothers and children should be emphasized through health education and other educational programmes. The fact that infants are more vulnerable to infection, retarded growth and other health risks during their first six months suggests that special educational efforts be directed mainly at women who already have comparatively short durations of breastfeeding, with the aim of arresting any further decline and possibly reversing the trend. It is therefore important to identify the factors which influence mothers' decisions to extend breastfeeding from a fairly short to a moderate duration. Health considerations as well as costs of purchasing infant food would justify efforts to continue breastfeeding as a partial source of food for some time after the introduction of supplementary food. The WFS findings that infant and child mortality are clearly related to the level of the mother's education would indicate that lactation promotion and other maternal and child health measures should pay particular attention to the needs of women with no or little education irrespective of whether they currently breastfeed for short or long periods. But educational programmes aiming at increasing duration of breastfeeding or preventing it from declining will tend to have less fertility impact among women in rural areas, who are illiterate and poor and who tend to breastfeed for longer durations than women elsewhere. Other considerations than the fertility effect, such as the health of the child, may, however, suggest that educational programmes be directed to all population groups, reinforced by the WFS findings that infant and child mortality is strongly inversely related to level of education, particularly mother's education and to a lesser extent father's.

It is obvious that the beneficial effects upon the health of the infant should be stressed in all maternal and infant care educational and promotional activities and in the training of health personnel, including curricula development. Women should be informed about the importance of breastfeeding well in advance of childbirth and be educated about the proper techniques. The desirability of frequent suckling should in particular be pointed out as important for maintaining milk production and delaying resumption of ovulation. At the same time, it should be made clear that breastfeeding alone is not sufficient food intake for a child over four to six months of age, as prolonged breastfeeding without supplementary food will result in malnutrition. Good weaning practices are important for healthy child growth and advice should be given about the use of locally produced food and low-cost methods of preparing it.

Information and education are not enough. A favourable environment should be created in the community for breastfeeding mothers. Legislation might be enacted requiring industrial and commercial enterprises above a certain size to establish a nursery where women can breastfeed their children and leave them during working hours or to grant paid leave during absence from work due to nursing. Income-creating programmes should be promoted which will provide employment for women in their home or nearby to allow them to continue their nursing and other child responsibilities. Further, community facilities for nursing mothers and production of supplementary food could be organized.

Health education programmes and promotional efforts should be provided through the maternal and child health services but not limited to them. A WFS-type survey in north-eastern Brazil indicates a strong inverse relationship between use of health services and prevalence of breastfeeding (Anderson, Rodrigues and Thome 1983). Women who had pre- and post-natal care, who gave birth at a hospital or clinic and whose child was under medical care were much less likely to breastfeed and had much shorter breastfeeding durations, irrespective of their socio-economic background. Studies in Thailand and Malaysia also found that women who delivered in medical facilities were less likely to breastfeed than women who delivered at home, even when taking the influence of socio-economic status into account (McCann et al. 1981). These findings suggest that an educational programme should first of all impress upon the staff of the medical services the importance of breastfeeding and the shortcomings of powdered or condensed milk and the associated risk of infection. Educational activities could successfully be directed towards the women attending health services, particularly those who had shown concern about their child's and their own health and were therefore likely to be responsive to advice. Women who are not using health services should be approached through other channels, such as mothers' clubs, community centres, teachers and mass media.

The WFS has proved an important vehicle for studying the extent to which rises in contraceptive use compensate for the effects of erosion of traditional restraints. Two studies on this theme reach somewhat similar conclusions, although differing in emphasis (Lesthaeghe, Shah and Page 1981; Casterline, Singh, Cleland and Ashurst 1984). The fertility-increasing effect of shorter durations of lactation among the more modern strata seems almost always more than counterbalanced by the fertility-reducing impact of institutional factors promoting postponement of marriage and contraceptive use. This suggests that the time-lag between decline in breastfeeding and compensatory movements in contraception and nuptiality may not be long lasting, although not necessarily insignificant in a transitional period in many African and Asian societies with high total fertility rates.

Maternal and child health activities promoting breastfeeding should be closely co-ordinated and consistent with family planning programmes. Advice on breast-feeding and family planning should be provided, in so far as possible, by the same health personnel in view of the fact that they are very much interconnected and must be promoted in a co-ordinated way to be effective. It should be kept in mind that the fertility-inhibiting impact of efforts to promote breastfeeding will be more pronounced if no supplementary food is introduced and full breast-feeding is applied during the first four to six months. WFS data indicate that women in developing countries appear not to be deliberately using breastfeeding as a means of spacing births: women with large families did not breastfeed more or longer than women with fewer births. This suggests that there may be scope for improving educational and promotional programmes pointing out the impact breastfeeding may have upon birth spacing.

In choosing the most suitable method of contraception and the time for introducing it, the possible effect upon lactation in particular has to be fully considered. Non-hormonal contraceptives are preferable during lactation as they do not interfere with milk production, thereby reducing the duration of breast-feeding. At least one WFS survey supported the belief that pill use, but not other methods, has a negative effect upon breastfeeding (Akin *et al.* forthcoming). WHO recommends that use of combined hormonal contraceptives be discouraged and only progestogen methods — oral or injectable — be made available to lactating mothers or to mothers in the early months of lactation if they clearly want to use hormonal methods (World Health Organization 1983). Contraception other than lactation should be introduced at a time after childbirth when the risk of pregnancy for breastfeeding women begins to become significant. It would be a waste of resources to introduce it to amenorrhoeic women and too early an introduction could, where discontinuation is common, result in pregnancy later on. But it is a difficult programmatic task for health service personnel to deter-mine, in practice, all factors considered, the right time for recommending the application of effective contraception, which may not be the same for all coun-tries and societies. The post-partum period of reliable pregnancy protection due to breastfeeding is rather brief, as illustrated by WFS data from 16 developing countries indicating that in half of the countries one-fifth or more of women breastfeeding four to six months after childbirth were no longer amenorrhoeic, and for some women ovulation may have taken place shortly before resumption of menstruation (chapter 30).

39.6 Infant and child health

WFS has contributed a great deal to improved knowledge of the inter-relation-ships between infant mortality and fertility in the developing world. In general, countries with comparatively low fertility tend in the long run to have relatively low infant mortality and countries with exceptionally high fertility appear also to have high infant mortality rates. This association at the aggregate level is often believed to reflect common antecedent conditions, such as levels of economic development, health conditions and general levels of living.

At the individual level, survey data from a number of countries show that fertility consistently increases as the number of child deaths increases. A body of research suggests that infant and child mortality and fertility are causally linked. High fertility increases the probability of child death due to the close spacing of births, giving the mother limited opportunity and ability to care adequately for any one of her children. Depletion of the mother's health and nutritional status is probably the key factor; when a pregnancy occurs before the mother has had time to recover from an earlier delivery and period of lactation, foetal growth and development may be retarded resulting in a low birth weight and perhaps other deficiencies.

The importance of fertility and birth spacing for child health and survival has generally been recognized but has sometimes been questioned because of the lack of supporting evidence from research (Winikoff 1983). But WFS findings show conclusively that the chances of dying in infancy and childhood are higher for babies born within two years of an older brother or sister than for babies born after a longer interval. In Bangladesh, Pakistan and Nepal, where childhood mortality is still extremely high, the harmful effects of inadequate spacing are particularly severe — babies born after short intervals are two and a half times more likely to die before their fifth birthday than babies born after a gap of four years or more. Even in countries where standards of nutrition and health are higher and childhood mortality is moderate, the risks of death are still 30–50 per cent higher for closely spaced babies than for widely spaced births. A number of detailed country studies have shown that the increased mortality risk for infants and children related to short birth spacing is largely independent of mother's education, rural or urban residence, family size or maternal age at the birth of the child.

The important policy implication is that family planning and other measures promoting birth spacing can contribute to reducing infant and child mortality, but to the extent that the strong association between birth spacing and infant mortality is due to a common factor such as breastfeeding, it is rather the common factor which should be tackled. Family planning may have a mortality effect not only by lengthening of birth spacing but also, in so far as it reduces family size, by decreasing the number of high birth order childbirths. In most WFS surveys infant mortality was recorded to be considerably higher for seventh and higher birth orders than for second and third, on average 40 per cent higher and in some countries nearly double. An analysis of WFS data available for three countries in the Caribbean region concluded that fertility will remain relatively high as long as infant and child mortality remain at or near their current levels (Ebanks 1985). A review of survey results for ten Asian countries suggested that reduction of child mortality may still be an important factor in reducing fertility, particularly in countries like Bangladesh, Nepal and Pakistan.

On the other hand, infant mortality may cause higher fertility by cutting off lactation when an infant dies, thereby advancing the return of ovulation and increasing the probability of another pregnancy, or by motivating parents to have another child as a replacement. New and more substantial evidence has been provided of this so-called replacement effect whereby women consciously attempt to replace a deceased child. A World Bank study on WFS data from 25 developing countries showed a replacement on average of well over one-half of an additional child after a child's death, although the magnitude of the impact varied considerably from country to country (World Bank 1983). The analysis indicated that a woman experiencing a child death has lower contraceptive use in all countries and that the reduction is statistically significant in almost all of them. Some policy guidance for allocation of resources between competing claims of family health and child care was obtained in the study by applying the findings to estimates of costs per birth averted through family planning and costs per infant death prevented. It was found that even with the high estimates of the fertility effect of infant mortality, the most cost-effective way of reducing fertility would be through family planning rather than by reducing infant mortality. Only in one country, Kenya, did the cost of preventing births exceed the cost of reducing fertility through mortality reduction, largely because the current low acceptance rates of family planning raised the cost per user to a very high level, making mortality reduction the most cost-effective approach. When detailed WFS data from West African countries become available in due course, it is possible they may indicate conclusions similar to those drawn for Kenya, because of low demand for family planning and the prospects for low-cost measures to reduce mortality from its present high levels.

Beyond the series of valuable findings on demographic and biological factors associated with infant and child mortality and their fertility consequences, a number of WFS-based analyses have begun to raise important questions about the relative roles of socio-economic development and health provision in the developing countries. Circumstantial evidence on this issue emerges from a number of studies which concentrate on socio-economic correlates of infant and child mortality, with or without demographic controls (Hobcraft, McDonald and Rutstein 1984).

In most countries infant and early childhood mortality is lower in urban than in rural areas and lowest in metropolitan areas, but urban–rural differences in child survival disappear to a large extent once other socio-economic correlates are controlled for, especially education of the mother and the occupation and educational level of her husband. This may lead to the conclusion that rather than try to eliminate the great disparity in provision of health services between metropolitan and rural areas by promoting urban types of costly health care centres, the primary aim of a policy to reduce infant and child mortality in rural areas should be to promote primary health care utilizing existing resources and personnel with the participation of the population at large.

The close relationship between infant and child mortality and the level of parental education found in most surveys mainly suggests that promoting education will help to achieve the objective of reducing mortality. A detailed study on estimates of child mortality and information on health services for administrative districts in Kenya concluded that mother's education has far greater impact than health service provision (Mosley 1983). A review of the findings for some ten WFS surveys concluded that the impact of parental education upon chances of child survival is probably greater than both access to health facilities and income combined (Caldwell and McDonald 1981). But it should be noted that the most significant impact came from education to secondary school level, while the attainment of primary education did not contribute very much as compared with no education. The strong emphasis in development programmes in developing countries upon the eradication of illiteracy may therefore have a limited impact on reducing mortality unless it goes beyond primary education. Yet simpler educational programmes with a more direct health focus may help to reduce mortality significantly. The importance of personal hygiene, storage of food and drinking water, provision of safe water supply, treatment of child diseases and benefits of lactation for mothers and children are just a few topics which should be covered by health education. Such education may be introduced in school curricula as well as in adult programmes carried out by social welfare organizations, community institutions and mass media. It should also be adequately provided for in the training of various types of field personnel, including social workers, agriculture extension personnel, community development workers, nurses, midwives and family planning workers.

A number of WFS surveys obtained information about health service provision at the community level in addition to the individual and household data. This information has provided the opportunity to examine whether having health services easily accessible is associated with substantial reductions in infant and child mortality and how far such links may interrelate with socio-economic factors. The data obtained in many different settings seem to indicate that proximity of these services alone may not have an important impact. The most consistent positive finding to date has been the reduction in neo-natal mortality associated with availability of trained midwives, although in the Philippines it was only the better educated mothers who achieved this gain, demonstrating an important interplay between education and effective use of services. In rural Bangladesh, infant and child mortality were lower when a primary school or family planning clinic was nearby, but distance to health services, such as a hospital, primary health centre, dispensary and qualified doctor, was not strongly associated with levels of mortality. Favourable effects upon mortality of short distance health facilities may not necessarily be due to greater use of them but have a common cause like overall social and/or economic development of the area concerned, resulting in widespread facilities as well as a relatively low level of mortality. Therefore, expansion of coverage of various health and educational facilities in terms of geographical proximity of services may not necessarily contribute substantially to lowering of mortality but should be a part of overall development strategy including education, family planning and other community facilities.

The largest cause of death of children in developing countries is diarrhoeal infection, due to lack of clean water, poor nutrition, unsafe sanitation, etc. Medical facilities are required but it is not sufficient that technology for dealing with diseases is available; the proper application of preventive and curative means must be ensured through communication and education of women. Diarrhoeal diseases often become a serious problem at the time when breast milk ceases to be an infant's sole source of food and liquid but mortality can be reduced by introducing oral rehydration therapy, including use of home-made solutions, especially if given at an early stage.

Several studies based on WFS data have failed to uncover any substantial differences in mortality under age five by household type of water supply. Although these findings are not yet definitive in view of various methodological problems, a *prima facie* case exists that availability of piped water alone may have little impact on infant and child mortality. Most important, no doubt, is the source of the water supply and the availability of safe drinking water. More positive findings have emerged with regard to toilet provision. Availability of sanitation within a household is strongly associated with gains in infant and especially child survival, even after controls for a number of socio-economic factors. But perhaps having a flush toilet is partly reflective of wealth, and hence of socio-economic factors which have a beneficial impact upon infant and child mortality.

39.7 Conclusions

The World Fertility Survey has made important contributions to the planning, implementation and monitoring of health care, education, family planning and related programmes. In many developing countries survey findings have taken some of the guesswork out of policy-making and programme implementation and evaluation in the field of population. In some areas the survey findings and the causal explanations provide clear policy guidance. In others certain relationships have been readily established but the causal explanations are uncertain. Such findings may, nevertheless, be relevant for policy-makers who do not always need to know and fully understand how causal factors work and what motivations may lie behind them. Sometimes survey findings are such that the conclusions do not suggest any effective and realistic policy or programmatic measures, but they may still be useful for policy-makers. The additional value of the WFS is that policy-relevant comparisons of data for a large number of countries in all parts of the world can be made.

Many of the WFS data have still to be interpreted and analysed, particularly those from surveys completed only recently in Africa, and, no doubt, further important conclusions of significance for policies and programmes will materialize in due course. More can be accomplished in the future with surveys of this kind by applying the framework and scope of WFS not only in countries which have not yet had a survey but also, and even more important, in countries wanting to carry out repeat surveys enabling them to measure changes and programme impact. Modifications in survey instruments and methodology may be made to take the experience gained fully into account. A number of suggestions have been made in this regard in some of the scientific and technical documents issued by WFS, in many of the earlier chapters of this book and in papers and comments which have appeared elsewhere.

The population problems in developing countries remain, today and for many years to come, some of the most vital development issues for these countries, as well as for the world as a whole. Major shifts of emphasis are occurring in provision of health care and family planning. National surveys and major internationally co-ordinated efforts like the WFS can contribute greatly in assisting implementation and monitoring of these important activities. The International Conference on Population convened by the United Nations in Mexico City in August 1984 fully recognized this in adopting by consensus a recommendation about well-designed national sample surveys, and pointing out 'in particular that surveys should be carried out periodically on fertility, family planning, health of mothers and children, mortality and migration and that technical assistance should be made available from international sources'.[2]

Notes

1. It has been estimated that if, for example, in Bangladesh the breastfeeding patterns were to change to those currently typical of industrialized countries (from 31 to 3 months' average duration), the level of fertility would increase by over 50 per cent; to prevent fertility from rising would require a more than fivefold increase in contraceptive use (from 9 to 52 per cent) (Lesthaeghe 1982).
2. Recommendations for the Further Implementation of the World Population Plan of Action. United Nations *International Conference on Population, Mexico City, August 1984, Proceedings*, recommendation 66.

REFERENCES AND BIBLIOGRAPHY

Note: The place and name of publisher for World Fertility Survey publications, and International Statistical Institute publications generally, are:
Voorburg, Netherlands: International Statistical Institute.
This material is not repeated in individual references. However, 'ISI' is added in cases when the provenance of the work might not otherwise be clear.

Abdel-Aziz, A. (1983). Evaluation of the Jordan Fertility Survey 1976. *WFS Scientific Reports* no. 42.

Acsádi, G. T. (1979). Strategies for Comparative Demographic Analysis: Applications for WFS Data. United Nations Working Group on Comparative Analysis of World Fertility Survey Data. UN/UNFPA/WFS III/7.

— and G. Johnson-Acsádi (1983). Demand for Children and Spacing in Sub-Saharan Africa. Report prepared for the World Bank.

Adelman, I. (1963). An Econometric Analysis of Population Growth. *American Economic Review 53 (3)*.

Akin, J. *et al.* (1981). The Determinants of Breastfeeding in Sri Lanka. *Demography 18 (3)*: 287–307.

— (forthcoming). Breastfeeding Patterns and Determinants in Egypt. In A. M. Hallouda and S. M. Farid, eds. *Egypt: Demographic Responses to Modernization*. Central Agency for Public Mobilisation and Statistics.

Alam, I. and J. G. Cleland (1981). Illustrative Analysis: Recent Fertility Trends in Sri Lanka. *WFS Scientific Reports* no. 25.

— — (1984). Infant and Child Mortality: Trends and Determinants. In I. Alam and B. Dinesen, eds. *Fertility in Pakistan: a Review of Findings from the Pakistan Fertility Survey*. ISI.

— and B. Dinesen (eds.) (1984). *Fertility in Pakistan: a Review of Findings from the Pakistan Fertility Survey*. ISI.

Alauddin, M. (1979). Rural Development and Family Planning Behaviour in Bangladesh Villages. Doctoral dissertation, Department of Population Planning, School of Public Health, University of Michigan, Ann Arbor.

Al-Kabir, A. (1984). Effects of Community Factors on Infant and Child Mortality in Rural Bangladesh. *WFS Scientific Reports* no. 56.

Alloush, K., J. S. Herting, G. E. Immerwahr, A. Maier and T. W. Pullum (1986). Fertility Preferences and Contraceptive Use in Syria. In S. M. Farid and K. Alloush, eds. *Determinants of Fertility in Syria*. ISI.

Alwani, M. and G. Santow (1986). The Proximate Determinants of Fertility and their Effect on Fertility Patterns in Syria. In S. M. Farid and K. Alloush, eds. *Determinants of Fertility in Syria*. ISI.

Anderson, B. A. (1975). Male Age and Fertility Results from Ireland prior to 1911. *Population Index 41 (4)*: 561–566.

Anderson, J. E. and J. G. Cleland (1984). The World Fertility Survey and Contraceptive Prevalence Surveys: a Comparison of Substantive Results. *Studies in Family Planning 15 (1)*: 1–13.

—, W. Rodrigues and A. M. T. Thome (1983). Analysis of Breastfeeding in Northeastern Brazil: Methodological and Policy Considerations. *Studies in Family Planning 14 (8/9)*: 210–217.

Andrews, F., J. Morgan and J. Sonquist (1969). *Multiple Classification Analysis*. Institute for Social Research, University of Michigan, Ann Arbor.

Anker, R. (1977). The Effect of Group Variables on Fertility in a Rural Indian Sample. *Journal of Development Studies 14 (1)*: 63–76.

Arnold, F. and C. Pejaranonda (1977). Economic Factors in Family Size Decisions in Thailand. *SOFT Report* no. 2. Bangkok: Chulalongkorn University, Institute of Population Studies.

Aziz, Noor Laily, P. Majumber and B. A. Tan (1981). Contraceptive Effectiveness in Delaying a Birth: the Malaysian Experience. Paper presented at IUSSP/National Family Planning Board of Malaysia Seminar on Analysis of the WFS Family Planning Module, Genting Highlands, Malaysia.

Baldion, E. W. (1981). Colombia: aspectos socio-demograficos relevantes en el estudio de la mortalidad infantil y su asociación con la fecundidad. *Serie D* no. 102. Santiago: CELADE.

Barrett, J. C. (1971). Use of a Fertility Simulation Model to Refine Measurement Techniques. *Demography 8 (4)*: 481–490.

Baum, S., K. Dopkowski, W. G. Duncan and P. Gardiner (1974). WFS Inventory: Major Fertility and Related Surveys 1960–73. *WFS Occasional Papers* nos. 3–6.

Becker, S. and S. Mahmud (1984). A Validation Study of Backward and Forward Pregnancy Histories in Matlab, Bangladesh. *WFS Scientific Reports* no. 52.

Berent, J. (1977). Directions and Methods of Analysis of WFS Data in Low Fertility Countries. In *International Population Conference, Mexico 1977 1*: 67–86. Liège: IUSSP.

— (1983). Family Size Preferences in Europe and USA: Ultimate Expected Number of Children. *WFS Comparative Studies* no. 26.

—, F. Jones and M. Siddiqui (1982). Basic Characteristics, Sample Designs and Questionnaires. *WFS Comparative Studies* no. 18.

Bernedo, J. (1984). The Effect of Community Factors on Infant and Child Mortality in Peru. WFS unpublished manuscript.

Bhatia, S. (1982). Contraceptive Intentions and Subsequent Behaviour in Rural Bangladesh. *Studies in Family Planning 13 (1)*: 24–31.

Bilsborrow, R. E. (1985). Collecting Community-Level Data for Fertility Analysis. In J. B. Casterline, ed. *The Collection and Analysis of Community Data*. ISI.

—, A. Adlakha, A. Cross, D. Chao and M. Nizamuddin (1982). Analyzing the Determinants of Fertility: a Suggested Approach for Data Collection. *Manual Series* no. 9, Laboratories for Population Statistics, University of North Carolina at Chapel Hill.

Blacker, J. G. C. (1984). Experiences in the Use of Special Mortality Questions in Multi-Purpose Surveys: the Single-Round Approach. In United Nations *Data Bases for Mortality Measurement*, UN Population Studies no. 84; ST/ESA/SER. A/84.

— and W. Brass (1979). Experience of Retrospective Demographic Enquiries to Determine Vital Rates. In L. Moss and H. Goldstein, eds. *The Recall*

Method in Social Surveys. London: University of London, Institute of Education.

—, A. G. Hill and K. A. Moser (1983). Mortality Levels and Trends in Jordan Estimated from the Results of the 1976 Fertility Survey. *WFS Scientific Reports* no. 47.

—, R. Fernández and I. Timæus (1984). The Estimation of Adult Mortality from the Mortality Module of the WFS Household Schedule. WFS unpublished manuscript.

Blalock, H. M. (1985). Cross-Level Analyses. In J. B. Casterline, ed. *The Collection and Analysis of Community Data*. ISI.

Blanc, A. K. (1982). Unwanted Fertility in Latin America and the Caribbean. *International Family Planning Perspectives 8 (4)*: 156–162.

Bogue, D. J. (1970). A Model Interview for Fertility Research and Family Planning Evaluation. Community and Family Study Center, University of Chicago.

— and E. J. Bogue (1970). Techniques of Pregnancy History Analysis. *Family Planning Research and Evaluation Manual* no. 4. Community and Family Study Center, University of Chicago.

Bongaarts, J. (1975). A Method for the Estimation of Fecundability. *Demography 12 (4)*: 645–660.

— (1978). A Framework for Analyzing the Proximate Determinants of Fertility. *Population and Development Review 4 (1)*: 105–132.

— (1982). The Fertility-Inhibiting Effects of the Intermediate Fertility Variables. *Studies in Family Planning 13 (6/7)*: 179–189.

— and S. Kirmeyer (1982). Estimating the Impact of Contraceptive Prevalence on Fertility: Aggregate and Age-Specific Versions of a Model. In A. I. Hermalin and B. Entwisle, eds. *The Role of Surveys in the Analysis of Family Planning Programs*. Liège: Ordina.

— and R. G. Potter (1983). *Fertility, Biology and Behaviour: an Analysis of the Proximate Determinants*. New York: Academic Press.

Borja, E. (1985). Factores determinants de una mortalidad prematura en Ecuador. *WFS Scientific Reports* no. 74.

Brackett, J. W. (1978). Family Planning in Four Latin American Countries – Knowledge, Use and Unmet Need: Some Findings from the World Fertility Survey. *International Family Planning Perspectives 4 (4)*: 116–123.

— (1981). The Role of Family Planning Availability and Accessibility in Family Planning Use in Developing Countries. In *World Fertility Survey Conference 1980: Record of Proceedings 2*: 13–49.

—, R. T. Ravenholt and J. C. Chao (1978). The Role of Family Planning in Recent Rapid Fertility Declines in Developing Countries. *Studies in Family Planning 9 (12)*: 314–323.

Brass, W. (1968). The Improvement of the Quantity and Quality of Demographic Statistics. In J. C. Caldwell and C. Okonjo, eds. *The Population of Tropical Africa*. London: Longmans.

— (1971). On the Scale of Mortality. In W. Brass, ed. *Biological Aspects of Demography*. London: Taylor and Francis.

— (1975). Methods for Estimating Fertility and Mortality from Limited and Defective Data. *POPLAB Occasional Publication*. Chapel Hill: University of North Carolina.

— (1982). A Simple Approximation for the Time Location of Estimates of Child Mortality from Proportions Dead by Age of Mother. Centre for Population Studies, London School of Hygiene and Tropical Medicine. Mimeo.

— (1983). The Derivation of Life Tables from Retrospective Estimates of Child and Adult Mortality. Centre for Population Studies, London School of Hygiene and Tropical Medicine. Mimeo.

— (1984). P/F Synthesis and Parity Progression Ratios. Research Paper, Centre for Population Studies, London School of Hygiene and Tropical Medicine.

— and E. A. Bamgboye (1981). The Time Location of Reports of Survivorship Estimates for Maternal and Paternal Orphanhood and the Ever-Widowed. *CPS Working Papers* no. 81-1. Centre for Population Studies, London School of Hygiene and Tropical Medicine.

— and A. J. Coale (1968). Methods of Analysis and Estimations. In W. Brass *et al. The Demography of Tropical Africa*. Princeton: Princeton University Press.

— and F. Juárez (1983). Censored Cohort Parity Progression Ratios from Birth Histories. *Asian and Pacific Census Forum 10 (1)*: 5-13.

— *et al.* (1968). *The Demography of Tropical Africa*. Princeton: Princeton University Press.

Breznik, D., ed. (1980). *Fertility and Family Planning in Yugoslavia*. Belgrade: Institute of Social Sciences.

Brillinger, D. R. (1983). Statistics in Fertility Research: Value and Limitations. Committee on Population and Demography *Report* no. 19. Washington, DC: National Academy Press.

Brown, L. A. (1981). *Innovation Diffusion: A New Perspective*. New York: Methuen.

Bulatao, R. A. and J. T. Fawcett (1983). Influences on Childbearing Intentions Across the Fertility Career: Demographic and Socioeconomic Factors and the Value of Children. East-West Population Institute, Honolulu.

Bumpass, L., and C. F. Westoff (1969). The Prediction of Completed Fertility. *Demography 6 (4)*: 445-454.

—, R. R. Rindfuss, J. A. Palmore, M. B. Concepción and B. M. Choi (1982). Intermediate Variables and Education Differentials in Fertility in Korea and the Philippines. *Demography 19 (2)*: 241-260.

Bureau of Statistics (1976). *Fiji Fertility Survey 1974: Principal Report*. Suva.

Cain, M. (1981). Risk and Insurance Perspectives on Fertility and Agrarian Change in India and Bangladesh. *Population and Development Review 7 (3)*: 435-474.

— (1985). Intensive Community Studies. In J. B. Casterline, ed. *The Collection and Analysis of Community Data*. ISI.

Caldwell, J. C. (1979). Education as a Factor in Mortality Decline: an Examination of Nigerian Data. *Population Studies 33 (3)*: 395-413.

— (1980). Review of: World Fertility Survey, *Bangladesh Fertility Survey 1975. First Report. Population Studies 34 (3)*: 581-583.

— (1982). *Theory of Fertility Decline*. New York: Academic Press.

— and P. McDonald (1981). Influence of Maternal Education on Infant and Child Mortality: Levels and Causes. In *International Population Conference, Manila 1981 2*: 79-96. Liège: IUSSP.

— and K. Srinivasan (1984). Review of: State Family Planning Commission of China, An Analysis of a National One-per-Thousand Sample Survey of the Birth Rate. *Population and Economics* (special issue), Beijing. *Population and Development Review 10 (1)*: 71-79.

—, G. Immerwahr and L. T. Ruzicka (1982). Illustrative Analysis: Family Structure and Fertility. *WFS Scientific Reports* no. 39.

—, P. H. Reddy and P. Caldwell (1982). The Causes of Demographic Change in Rural South India: a Micro Approach. *Population and Development Review 8 (4)*: 689-727.

— — — (1984). The Determinants of Fertility Decline in India. In T. Dyson and N. Crook *India's Demography: Essays on the Contemporary Population.* New Delhi: South Asia Publishers.

Cannell, C. and R. Kahn (1953). The Collection of Data by Interviewing. In L. Festinger and D. Katz, eds. *Research Methods in the Behavioural Sciences.* New York: Holt, Rinehart and Winston.

Carrasco, E. (1981). Contraceptive Practice. *WFS Comparative Studies* no. 9.

Casterline, J. B. (1981). Community Effects on Individual Demographic Behaviour: Multilevel Analysis of WFS Data. In *International Population Conference, Manila 1981 5*: 405-421. Liège: IUSSP.

— (1982). Community Effects on Fertility Intentions: the Effect of Aggregate Levels of Contraceptive Use on Individual Intentions to Use. WFS Technical Paper no. 1952.

— (1984). Patterns of Cross-National Variation in the Proximate Determinants of Fertility. Paper presented at IUSSP/WFS Seminar on Integrating Proximate Determinants into the Analysis of Fertility Levels and Trends, London.

— (1985). Community Effects on Fertility. In J. B. Casterline, ed. *The Collection and Analysis of Community Data.* ISI.

— (ed.) (1985). *The Collection and Analysis of Community Data.* ISI.

— and H. Ashurst (1984). Pregnancy Loss: Evidence from WFS Surveys. WFS Technical Paper no. 2381.

— and V. C. Chidambaram (1984). The Presence of Others During the Interview and the Reporting of Contraceptive Knowledge and Use. In J. A. Ross and R. McNamara, eds. *Survey Analysis for the Guidance of Family Planning Programs.* Liège: Ordina.

— and I. Eid (forthcoming). Community Characteristics and Reproductive Patterns. In A. M. Hallouda and S. M. Farid, eds. *Egypt: Demographic Responses to Modernization.* Central Agency for Public Mobilisation and Statistics.

— and L. T. Engracia (1984). Community Effects on Demographic Behaviour in the Rural Philippines. WFS unpublished manuscript.

— and P. F. McDonald (1983). The Age Difference Between Union Partners. WFS Technical Paper no. 2070.

— and J. Trussell (1980). Age at First Birth. *WFS Comparative Studies* no. 15.

—, S. Singh, J. G. Cleland and H. Ashurst (1984). The Proximate Determinants of Fertility. *WFS Comparative Studies* no. 39.

Center for Policy Studies, The Population Council (1980). Population Brief: Latin America. *Population and Development Review 6 (1)*: 126-152.

Central Agency for Public Mobilisation and Statistics (1983). *The Egyptian Fertility Survey 1980 III.* Cairo.

Chayovan, N. B. (1982). A Contextual Analysis of Demographic Phenomena in Rural Thailand. Ph.D. dissertation, Department of Sociology, University of Michigan, Ann Arbor.

— and J. Knodel (1985): Improving the Collection of Village-Level Data: an Experience for Thailand. In J. B. Casterline, ed. *The Collection and Analysis of Community Data*. ISI.

Chen, L. C., S. Ahmed, M. Gesche and W. H. Mosley (1974). A Prospective Study of Birth Interval Dynamics in Rural Bangladesh. *Population Studies 28 (2)*: 277–297.

Chidambaram, V. C. (1979). Report of the WFS Expert Group Meeting on Methodology of Comparative Fertility Studies. WFS Technical Paper no. 1198.

— (1981). Findings from Second Stage Analysis of Pakistan Fertility Survey Data. In *World Fertility Survey Conference 1980: Record of Proceedings 2*: 617–636.

— and J. G. Cleland (1981). The Contribution of the World Fertility Survey to an Understanding of Fertility Determinants and Trends. In *International Population Conference, Manila 1981 5*: 381–404. Liège: IUSSP.

— and L. V. T. Mastropoalo (1982). The Role of WFS Data in the Analysis of Family Planning Programs. In A. I. Hermalin and B. Entwisle, eds. *The Role of Surveys in the Analysis of Family Planning Programs*. Liège: Ordina.

— and T. W. Pullum (1981). Estimating Fertility Trends from Retrospective Birth Histories: Sensitivity to Imputation of Missing Dates. *Population Studies 35 (2)*: 307–320.

— and Z. A. Sathar (1984). Age and Date Reporting. *WFS Comparative Studies no. 5*.

—, J. G. Cleland and V. Verma (1980). Some Aspects of WFS Data Quality: a Preliminary Assessment. *WFS Comparative Studies* no. 16.

Cho, L. -J. (1973). The Own-Children Approach to Fertility Estimation: an Elaboration. In *International Population Conference, Liège 1973 2*: 263–279. Liège: IUSSP.

— and R. Bussen (1985). Use of Own Children for Reconstruction of Maternity Histories. In W. Brass and A. G. Hill, eds. *The Analysis of Maternity Histories*. Liège: Ordina.

— and L. Kantrow (1981). Comparative Analysis of Fertility Orientations: World Fertility Survey Findings. In G. E. Hendershot and P. J. Placek, eds. *Predicting Fertility: Demographic Studies of Birth Expectations*. Lexington, Mass.: Lexington Books, D. C. Heath and Company.

Cleland, J. G. (1985). Marital Fertility Decline in Developing Countries: Theories and the Evidence. In J. G. Cleland and J. N. Hobcraft, eds. *Reproductive Change in Developing Countries: Insights from the World Fertility Survey*. Oxford: Oxford University Press.

— and I. Kalule-Sabiti (1984). Sexual Activity within Marriage: the Analytical Utility of World Fertility Survey Data. WFS Technical Paper no. 2265.

— and Rodríguez, G. (1980). How Women's Work and Education Affect Family Size. *People 7(4)*: 17–18.

— and Z. Sathar (1984). The Effect of Birth Spacing on Childhood Mortality in Pakistan. *Population Studies 38 (3)*: 401–418.

—, R. J. A. Little and P. Pitaktepsombati (1979). Illustrative Analysis: Socio-Economic Determinants of Contraceptive Use in Thailand. *WFS Scientific Reports* no. 5.

—, J. E. Verrall and M. Vaessen (1983). Preferences for the Sex of Children and their Influence on Reproductive Behaviour. *WFS Comparative Studies* no. 27.

Cliquet, R. L. (1980). Progress Report on the Flemish Fertility Surveys. Population and Family Study Centre, Brussels.

Coale, A. J. (1973). The Demographic Transition Reconsidered. In *International Population Conference, Liège 1973 1*: 53–71. Liège: IUSSP.

— (forthcoming). A Reassessment of Fertility Trends in Egypt, Taking Account of the Egyptian Fertility Survey. In A. M. Hallouda and S. M. Farid, eds. *Egypt: Demographic Responses to Modernization*. Central Agency for Public Mobilisation and Statistics.

— and D. R. McNeil (1972). The Distribution by Age at First Marriage in a Female Cohort. *Journal of the American Statistical Association 67*: 743–749.

—, L. -J. Cho and N. Goldman (1982). Nuptiality and Fertility in the Republic of Korea. In L. T. Ruzicka, ed. *Nuptiality and Fertility*. Liège: Ordina.

—, A. G. Hill and T. J. Trussell (1975). A New Method of Estimating Standard Fertility Measures from Incomplete Data. *Population Index 41 (2)*: 182–210.

Cochrane, S. H. (1979). Fertility and Education: What Do We Really Know? Baltimore: Johns Hopkins University Press.

— (1983), Effects of Education and Urbanization on Fertility. In R. A. Bulatao and R. D. Lee, eds. *Determinants of Fertility in Developing Countries 2*. New York: Academic Press.

Collver, A. O. (1965). Birth Rates in Latin America: New Estimates of Historical Trends and Fluctuations. *Research Series Monographs* no. 7, Institute of International Studies, University of California, Berkeley.

Committee on Population and Demography (1980a). Estimation of Recent Trends in Fertility and Mortality in the Republic of Korea. *Report* no. 1. Washington, DC: National Academy Press.

— (1980b). Fertility and Mortality Changes in Thailand, 1950–1975. *Report* no. 2. Washington, DC: National Academy Press.

— (1980c). Fertility and Mortality Changes in Honduras, 1950–1974. *Report* no. 3. Washington, DC: National Academy Press.

— (1981a). Estimation of Recent Trends in Fertility and Mortality in Bangladesh. *Report* no. 5. Washington, DC: National Academy Press.

— (1981b). Collecting Data for the Estimation of Fertility and Mortality. *Report* no. 6. Washington, DC: National Academy Press.

— (1982a). Trends in Fertility and Mortality in Turkey, 1935–1975. *Report* no. 8. Washington, DC: National Academy Press.

— (1982b). The Estimation of Recent Trends in Fertility and Mortality in Egypt. *Report* no. 9. Washington, DC: National Academy Press.

— (1982c). Levels and Trends in Fertility and Mortality in Colombia. *Report* no. 12. Washington, DC: National Academy Press.

— (1982d). Fertility in Thailand: Trends, Differentials, and Proximate Determinants. *Report* no. 13. Washington, DC: National Academy Press.

— (1982e). The Determinants of Fertility in the Republic of Korea. *Report no. 14*. Washington, DC: National Academy Press.

Concepción, M. B. (1981). Family Formation and Contraception in Selected Developing Countries: Policy Implications of WFS Findings. In *World Fertility Survey Conference 1980: Record of Proceedings 1*: 197–260.

Conference of European Statisticians (CES) (1975). Meeting on Fertility Surveys. CES/AC/43/12. Geneva.

Conning, A. M. and A. M. Marckwardt (1982). Analysis of WFS Data in Colombia, Panama, Paraguay and Peru: Highlights from the CELADE Research and Training Seminar. *WFS Occasional Papers* no. 25.

Coombs, C. H., L. C. Coombs and G. H. McClelland (1975). Preference Scales for Number and Sex of Children. *Population Studies 29 (2)*: 273–298.

Coombs, L. C. (1974). The Measurement of Family Size Preferences and Subsequent Fertility. *Demography 11 (4)*: 587–611.

— and M. -C. Chang (1981). Do Husbands and Wives Agree? Fertility Attitudes and Later Behavior. *Population and Environment 4 (2)*: 109–127.

Cornelius, R. M. and A. Novak (1983). Contraceptive Availability and Use in Five Developing Countries. *Studies in Family Planning 14 (12)* pt. 1: 302–317.

Cox, D. R. (1972). The Analysis of Multivariate Binary Data. *Applied Statistics 21*: 113–120.

Crook, N. (1978). On Social Norms and Fertility Decline. *Journal of Developmental Studies 14 (4)*: 198–210.

Curtin, L. B. (1982). Status of Women: a Comparative Analysis of Twenty Developing Countries. *Reports on the World Fertility Survey* no. 5. Washington, DC: Population Reference Bureau.

Cutright, P. (1983). The Ingredients of Recent Fertility Decline in Developing Countries. *International Family Planning Perspectives 9 (4)*: 101–109.

Danish National Institute of Social Research (DNISR) (1979, 1980, 1981). *Publikation 87* (by J. Ussing, on abortion), *Publikation 99 and 104* (by O. Bertelsen, on young families and falling birth rate).

DaVanzo, J. and J. Haaga (1982). Anatomy of a Fertility Decline: Peninsular Malaysia, 1950–1976. *Population Studies 36 (3)*: 373–393.

—, W. P. Bucht and J. -P. Habicht (1983). How Biological and Behavioural Influences on Mortality in Malaysia Vary During the First Year of Life. *Population Studies 37 (3)*: 381–402.

Davis, K. (1955). Institutional Patterns Favoring High Fertility in Underdeveloped Areas. *Eugenics Quarterly 2*: 33–39.

— and J. Blake (1956). Social Structure and Fertility: An Analytic Framework. *Economic Development and Cultural Change 4*: 211–235.

Debavalya, N. (1981). Patterns of Fertility Decline in Asia with Special Reference to Thailand. In *International Population Conference, Manila 1981 1*: 55–69. Liège: IUSSP.

Demeny, P. (1981). Discussion of a paper by L. Tabah. In *World Fertility Survey Conference 1980: Record of Proceedings 1*: 137–144.

Department of Statistics (1982). *The Sudan Fertility Survey 1979. Principal Report*. Khartoum: Ministry of National Planning.

De Sandre, P. and F. Rossi (eds.) (1982). Indagine sulla fecondità in Italia —

Rapporto Generale. (With English tables and summary.) Universities of Padua, Florence and Rome.

Diamond, I. D., J. W. McDonald and I. H. Shah (1984). Proportional Hazards Models for Current Status Data: Application to the Study of Age at Weaning Differentials in Pakistan. Paper presented at Population Association of America Annual Meeting.

Dow, T. E. and L. H. Werner (1981). Family Size and Family Planning in Kenya: Continuity and Change in Metropolitan and Rural Attitudes. *Studies in Family Planning 12 (6/7)*: 272–277.

Downing, D. C. and D. Yaukey (1979). The Effects of Marital Dissolution and Remarriage on Fertility in Urban Latin America. *Population Studies 33 (3)*: 537–547.

D'Souza, S. (1982). Nuptiality Patterns and Fertility Implications in South Asia. In L. T. Ruzicka, ed. *Nuptiality and Fertility*. Liège: Ordina.

Duncan, W. G. (1973). Fertility and Related Surveys. *WFS Occasional Papers* no. 1.

Dunnell, K. (1979). *Family Formation 1976*. London: Office of Population Censuses and Surveys.

Durch, J. S. (1980). Nuptiality Patterns in Developing Countries: Implications for Fertility. *Reports on the World Fertility Survey* no. 1. Washington, DC: Population Reference Bureau.

Dyson, T. and M. J. Murphy (1985). The Onset of Fertility Transition. *Population and Development Review 11 (3)*: 399–440.

Easterlin, R. A. and E. M. Crimmins (1982). An Exploratory Study of the 'Synthesis Framework' of Fertility Determination with World Fertility Survey Data. *WFS Scientific Reports* no. 40.

Ebanks, G. E. (1985). Infant and Child Mortality and Fertility: Trinidad and Tobago, Guyana and Jamaica. *WFS Scientific Reports* no. 75.

Edmonston, B. (1983). Community Variations in Infant and Child Mortality in Rural Jordan. *Journal of Developing Areas 17*: 479–490.

— and N. Andes (1983a). Community Variations in Infant and Child Mortality in Peru. In *Infant and Child Mortality in the Third World*: 71–90. Paris: CICRED.

— — (1983b). Community Variations in Infant and Child Mortality in Peru. *Journal of Epidemiology and Community Health 37 (2)*: 121–126.

Eid, I. and J. B. Casterline (forthcoming). Socio-Economic Determinants of Infant and Child Mortality. In A. M. Hallouda and S. M. Farid, eds. *Egypt: Demographic Responses to Modernization*. Central Agency for Public Mobilisation and Statistics.

El-Deeb, B. (1984). Evaluation of the Egyptian Fertility Survey 1980. Central Agency for Public Mobilisation and Statistics.

— and J. B. Casterline (forthcoming). Contraceptive Use in Egypt. In A. M. Hallouda and S. M. Farid, eds. *Egypt: Demographic Responses to Modernization*. Central Agency for Public Mobilisation and Statistics.

Engracia, L. T. (1983). Infant Mortality and Health Services in Rural Philippines. Paper presented at Sixth National Population Welfare Congress, Manila.

— (1985). Community Effects on Contraceptive Use in the Philippines. In J. B. Casterline, ed. *The Collection and Analysis of Community Data*. ISI.

—, D. M. Mortel and L. B. Nartatez (1984). Accessibility of Family Planning, Community Development, and their Impact on the Birth Rate of Rural Philippines. In L. T. Engracia, C. Raymundo-Mejia and J. B. Casterline, eds. *Fertility in the Philippines: Further Analysis of the Republic of the Philippines Fertility Survey 1978.* ISI.

Entwisle, B. and Mason, W. M. (1983). Multilevel Effects of Socio-Economic Development and Family Planning Programs on Children Ever Born. Research Report no. 8353, Population Studies Center, University of Michigan.

—, A. I. Hermalin and W. M. Mason (1982). *Socioeconomic Determinants of Fertility Behavior in Developing Nations: Theory and Initial Results.* Washington, DC: National Academy Press.

—, W. M. Mason and A. I. Hermalin (1984). Multilevel Dependence of Contraceptive Use on Socio-Economic Development and Family Planning Program Strength. Research Report no. 8460, Population Studies Center, University of Michigan.

—, A. I. Hermalin, P. Kamnuansilpa and A. Chamratrithirong (1984). A Multilevel Analysis of Family Planning Availability and Contraceptive Use in Rural Thailand. *Demography 21 (4):* 559–573.

Ewbank, D. C. (1981). Age Misreporting and Age-selective Underenumeration: Sources, Patterns and Consequences for Demographic Analysis. Panel on Data Collection, Committee on Population and Demography, *Report* no. 4. Washington, DC: National Academy Press.

Federal Statistical Office (FSO) (1978). The Czechoslovak Fertility Survey 1977. *WFS Summaries of Findings* no. 16.

Feeney, G. (1976). Estimating Infant Mortality Rates from Child Survivorship Data by Age of Mother. *Asian and Pacific Census Newsletter 3 (2):* 12–16.

— (1980). Estimating Infant Mortality Trends from Child Survivorship Data. *Population Studies 34 (1):* 109–128.

— (1983). Population Dynamics Based on Birth Intervals and Parity Progression. *Population Studies 37 (1):* 75–89.

Fernández, R. E. (1984). Análisis de la información sobre atención materno-infantil de las Encuestas de Fecundidad en América Latina. WFS Technical Paper no. 2296.

Fernando, D. F. S. (1980). The Continuing Fertility Decline in Sri Lanka. *Journal of Biosocial Science 12 (1):* 51–60.

Ferry, B. (1981). Breastfeeding. *WFS Comparative Studies* no. 13.

— and H. J. Page (1984). The Proximate Determinants of Fertility and their Effect on Fertility Patterns: an Illustrative Analysis Applied to Kenya. *WFS Scientific Reports* no. 71.

— and D. P. Smith (1983). Breastfeeding Differentials. *WFS Comparative Studies* no. 23.

Flórez C. E. and N. Goldman (1980). An Analysis of Nuptiality Data in the Colombia National Fertility Survey. *WFS Scientific Reports* no. 11.

Fortunat, F. (1984). Les déterminants proches de la fécondité en Haïti. *WFS Scientific Reports* no. 61.

Freedman, R. (1961–2). The Sociology of Human Fertility. *Current Sociology 10/11 (2).*

— (1974). Community-Level Data in Fertility Surveys. *WFS Occasional Papers* no. 8.

— (1985). Summary Observations on the WFS Seminar. In J. B. Casterline, ed. *The Collection and Analysis of Community Data*. ISI.

— and J. B. Casterline (1982). Nuptiality and Fertility in Taiwan. In L. T. Ruzicka, ed. *Nuptiality and Fertility*. Liège: Ordina.

—, M. -C. Chang and T. -H Sun (1982). Household Composition, Extended Kinship and Reproduction in Taiwan: 1973–1980. *Population Studies 36 (3)*: 395–411.

—. L. Coombs and L. Bumpass (1965). Stability and Change in Expectations about Family Size: a Longitudinal Study. *Demography 2 (2)*: 250–275.

—, S. -E. Khoo and B. Supraptilah (1981). Modern Contraceptive Use in Indonesia: a Challenge to Conventional Wisdom. *WFS Scientific Reports* no. 20.

Friedlander, S. and Silver, M. (1967). A Quantitative Study of the Determinants of Fertility Behavior. *Demography 4 (1)*: 30–70.

Gaisie, S. K. (1981). Mediating Mechanisms of Fertility Change in Africa – The Role of the Post-Partum Variables in the Process of Change: The Case of Ghana. In *International Population Conference, Manila 1981 1*: 95–112. Liège: IUSSP.

— (1984). The Proximate Determinants of Fertility in Ghana. *WFS Scientific Reports* no. 53.

— (forthcoming). The Proximate Determinants of Fertility in Ghana. In J. N. Hobcraft, ed. *The Measurement of Fertility: Incorporating the Proximate Determinants*. Oxford: Oxford University Press.

— and B. Gyepi-Garbrah (1976). Report of the 1975 Ghana Pilot Survey (The Multilingual Approach). WFS manuscript.

Garma, I. O. Y. G. (1983). Some Factors Associated with Infant Mortality in Mexico. In *Infant and Child Mortality in the Third World*: 91–128. Paris: CICRED.

Gaslonde, S. (1972). Programa de estudios comparativos sobre aborto inducido y uso de anticonceptivos en América Latina. *Serie A* no. 118. Santiago: CELADE.

— and A. Bocaz (1970). Método para medir varaciones en el nivel de fecundidad. *Serie A* no. 107. Santiago: CELADE.

— and E. Carrasco (1982). The Impact of Some Intermediate Variables on Fertility: Evidence from the Venezuela National Fertility Survey 1977. *WFS Occasional Papers* no. 23.

Gilks, W. R. (1984). The Relationship between Birth History and Current Fertility in Developing Countries. WFS unpublished manuscript.

Gille, H. and D. J. van de Kaa (1983). Contributions of the WFS to Survey Methodology and Analysis. In *Bulletin of the International Statistical Institute 50 (2)*: 910–930. (Proceedings of ISI 44th Session, Madrid.)

Goldberg, D. (1974). Modernism. *WFS Occasional Papers* no. 14.

Goldman, N. (1981). Dissolution of First Unions in Colombia, Panama and Peru. *Demography 18 (4)*: 659–679.

— and J. N. Hobcraft (1982). Birth Histories. *WFS Comparative Studies* no. 17.

— and C. F. Westoff (1980). Can Fertility be Estimated from Current Pregnancy Data? *Population Studies 34 (3)*: 535–550.

—, A. J. Coale and M. Weinstein (1979). The Quality of Data in the Nepal Fertility Survey. *WFS Scientific Reports* no. 6.

—, A. R. Pebley and C. F. Westoff (1982). Probabilities of Conception in Latin America. Paper presented at Population Association of America Annual Meeting, San Diego.

—, S. O. Rutstein and S. Singh (1985). Assessment of the Quality of Data in 41 WFS Surveys; a Comparative Approach. *WFS Comparative Studies* no. 44.

—, C. F. Westoff and L. E. Paul (1985). Estimation of Fecundability from Survey Data. *Studies in Family Planning 16 (5)*: 252–259.

—, A. R. Pebley, C. F. Westoff and L. E. Paul (1983). Contraceptive Failure Rates in Latin America. *International Family Planning Perspectives 9 (2)*: 50–57.

Gomez Barrantes, M. G. and J. McCarthy (1982). Female Sterilization in Costa Rica. *Studies in Family Planning 13 (1)*: 3–11.

Grootaert, C. (1983). The Conceptual Basis of Measures of Household Welfare and Their Implied Survey Data Requirements. *The Review of Income and Wealth*, Series 29, no. 1.

Gubhaju, B. (1983). Differential Fertility in Nepal. *Journal of Biosocial Science 15 (3)*: 325–331.

— (1984). Demographic and Social Correlates of Infant and Child Mortality in Nepal. Unpublished Ph.D. thesis, Australian National University.

Guerra, F. (1981). Determinantes de la mortalidad infantil en Panamá (1940–1974). *Serie D* no. 99. Santiago: CELADE.

— (1982). Determinants of Infant Mortality in Panama. *Serie D* no. 99, Santiago: CELADE, as summarized by A. M. Conning and A. M. Marckwardt in Analysis of WFS Data in Colombia, Panama, Paraguay, and Peru: Highlights from the CELADE Research and Training Seminar, *WFS Occasional Papers* no. 25: 24–25.

Guzman, J. M. (1980). Evaluation of the Dominican Republic National Fertility Survey 1975. *WFS Scientific Reports* no. 14.

Gwatkin, D. R., J. R. Wilcox and J. D. Wray (1980). Can Health and Nutrition Interventions Make a Difference? Washington: Overseas Development Council.

Habicht, J. P., W. P. Butz, L. Meyers and J. DaVanzo (1984). The Contraceptive Role of Breastfeeding. Rand Corporation. Mimeo.

Hanenberg, R. (1980). Current Fertility. *WFS Comparative Studies* no. 11.

Heer, D. M. and D. O. Smith (1967). Mortality Level, Desired Family Size and Population Increase. *Demography 4 (1)*: 104–121.

Hendershot, G. E. and P. J. Placek (eds.) (1981). *Predicting Fertility: Demographic Studies of Birth Expectations*. Lexington, Mass.: Lexington Books, D. C. Heath and Company.

Henry, L. (1972). *On The Measurement of Human Fertility*. (Translated and edited by M. C. Sheps and E. Lapierre-Adamcyk). Amsterdam: Elsevier.

Hermalin, A. I. (1983). Fertility Regulation and Its Costs: a Critical Essay. In R. A. Bulatao and R. D. Lee, eds. *Determinants of Fertility in Developing Countries 2*. New York: Academic Press.

— (1985). Integrating Individual and Community Data in the Study of Contraceptive Behaviour. In J. B. Casterline, ed. *The Collection and Analysis of Community Data*. ISI.

— and N. B. Chayovan (1984). The Effects of Individual, Village and Program Characteristics on Contraceptive Use in Rural Thailand. Paper presented at IUSSP/WFS Seminar on Integrating Proximate Determinants into the Analysis of Fertility Levels and Trends. London.

— and B. Entwisle (1982). Surveys and their Use in Family Planning Analysis. In A. I. Hermalin and B. Entwisle, eds. *The Role of Surveys in the Analysis of Family Planning Programs*. Liège: Ordina.

— and W. M. Mason (1980). A Strategy for the Comparative Analysis of WFS Data with Illustrative Examples. In United Nations Fund for Population Activities *The United Nations Programme for Comparative Analysis of World Fertility Survey Data*: 90–168. New York: United Nations.

—, R. Freedman, T. -H. Sun and M. -C. Chang (1979). Do Intentions Predict Fertility? The Experience in Taiwan, 1967–74. *Studies in Family Planning 10 (3)*: 75–95.

Herrera de Rivadeneira, M. I. (1984). Evaluación de la Encuesta Nacional de Fecundidad de 1979 de Ecuador. *WFS Scientific Reports* no. 51.

Hill, K. (1981). An Evaluation of Indirect Methods for Estimating Mortality. Paper presented at the IUSSP Seminar on Methodology and Data Collection in Mortality Studies, Dakar.

Hirschman, C. (1980). Demographic Trends in Peninsular Malaysia, 1947–75. *Population and Development Review 6 (1)*: 103–125.

Hobcraft, J. N. (1980). Illustrative Analysis: Evaluating Fertility Levels and Trends in Colombia. *WFS Scientific Reports* no. 15.

— (1981). Strategies for Comparative Analysis of WFS Data. In *World Fertility Survey Conference 1980: Record of Proceedings 3*: 501–561.

— (1984). Use of Special Mortality Questions in Fertility Surveys: the WFS Experience. In United Nations *Data Bases for Mortality Measurement*, UN Population Studies no. 84. ST/ESA/SER.A/84.

— (1985). Family-Building Patterns. In J. G. Cleland and J. N. Hobcraft, eds. *Reproductive Change in Developing Countries: Insights from the World Fertility Survey*. Oxford: Oxford University Press.

— (ed.) (forthcoming). *The Measurement of Fertility: Incorporating the Proximate Determinants*. Oxford: Oxford University Press.

— and J. B. Casterline (1983). Speed of Reproduction. *WFS Comparative Studies* no. 25.

— and R. J. A. Little (1984). Fertility Exposure Analysis: a New Method for Assessing the Contribution of Proximate Determinants to Fertility Differentials. *Population Studies 38 (1)*: 21–45.

— and J. W. McDonald (1984). Birth Intervals. *WFS Comparative Studies* no. 28.

— and G. Rodríguez (1982a). The Analysis of Repeat Fertility Surveys: Examples from Dominican Republic. *WFS Scientific Reports* no. 29.

— — (1982b). The Dominican Republic – Trends from Two Fertility Surveys. *International Family Planning Perspectives 8 (2)*: 57–63.

— — (1985). Methodological Issues in Life Table Analysis of Birth Histories. In W. Brass and A. G. Hill, eds. *The Analysis of Maternity Histories*. IUSSP.

—, N. Goldman and V. C. Chidambaram (1982). Advances in the P/F Ratio Method for the Analysis of Birth Histories. *Population Studies 36 (2)*: 291–316.

—, J. W. McDonald and S. O. Rutstein (1983). Child-Spacing Effects on Infant and Child Mortality. *Population Index 49 (4)*: 585–618.

— — — (1984). Socio-economic Factors in Infant and Child Mortality: a Cross-national Comparison. *Population Studies 38 (2)*: 193–223.

— — — (1985). Demographic Determinants of Infant and Early Child Mortality: a Comparative Analysis. *Population Studies 39 (3)*: 363–385.

Hodgson, M. and J. Gibbs (1980). Children Ever Born. *WFS Comparative Studies* no. 12.

Hughes, E. (1923). Infant Mortality. Results of a Field Study in Gary, Indiana, Based on Births in One Year. *Children's Bureau Publications* no. 112. Washington, DC: Government Printing Office.

Hugo, G. (1985). Investigating Community-Level Effects on Population Movement. In J. B. Casterline, ed. *The Collection and Analysis of Community Data*. ISI.

Hunte, D. (1983). Evaluation of the Trinidad and Tobago Fertility Survey 1977. *WFS Scientifc Reports* no. 44.

Immerwahr, G. (1981). Contraceptive Use in Sri Lanka. *WFS Scientific Reports* no. 18.

INED-CSIS (1982). Les pères d'aujourd'hui. (Personal communication of P. De Sandre and H. Leridon on male attitudes to parenthood). Paris.

Institute of Population Studies, Chulalongkorn University (1977). *The Survey of Fertility in Thailand: Country Report I*. Bangkok.

Instituto Nacional de Estadística (INE) (1978). Encuesta de Fecundidad (Diciembre 1977). Metodología y resultados. Madrid: Ministerio de Economía.

IUSSP (1981). *International Population Conference, Manila 1981: Solicited Papers*. Liège.

Jain, A. K. (1981). The Effects of Female Education on Fertility: a Simple Explanation. *Demography 18 (4)*: 577–595.

— and J. Bongaarts (1981). Socio-Biological Factors in Exposure to Childbearing: Breastfeeding and its Fertility Effect. In *World Fertility Survey Conference 1980: Record of Proceedings 2*: 255–321.

Jelliffe, D. B. (1966). The Assessment of Nutritional Status of the Community. *WHO Monograph Series* no. 53. Geneva: World Health Organization.

Jones, E. F. (1982). Socio-Economic Differentials in Achieved Fertility. *WFS Comparative Studies* no. 21.

— (1984). The Availability of Contraceptive Services. *WFS Comparative Studies* no. 37.

Jones, G. W. (1981). Malay Marriage and Divorce in Peninsular Malaysia: Three Decades of Change. *Population and Development Review 7 (2)*: 255–278.

Juárez, F. (1983). Family Formation in Mexico: a Study Based on Maternity Histories from a Retrospective Fertility Survey. Ph. D. thesis, University of London.

Kabir, M. (1980). The Demographic Characteristics of Household Populations. *WFS Comparative Studies* no. 6.

Kendall, M. G. (1976). Some Notes on Statistical Problems Likely to Arise in the Analysis of WFS Surveys. *WFS Technical Bulletins* no. 1.

— (1977). The Analysis of World Fertility Survey Data. In *International Population Conference, Mexico 1977 1*: 55–66. Liège: IUSSP.

— and C. A. O'Muircheartaigh (1977). Path Analysis and Model Building. *WFS Technical Bulletins* no. 2.

Kent, M. M. (1981). Breastfeeding in the Developing World: Current Patterns and Implications for Future Trends. *Reports on the World Fertility Survey* no. 2. Washington, DC: Population Reference Bureau.

— and A. Larson (1982). Family Size Preferences: Evidence from the World Fertility Survey. *Reports on the World Fertility Survey* no. 4. Washington, DC: Population Reference Bureau.

Khalifa, M. A. (1983). Age Pattern of Fertility in the Sudan. *Journal of Biosocial Science 15 (3)*: 317–323.

Kim, N. I. and B. M. Choi (1981). Preferences for Number and Sex of Children and Contraceptive Use in Korea. *WFS Scientific Reports* no. 22.

Kish, L. (1975). *Survey Sampling*. New York: Wiley.

— (1980). Discussion of the Paper by Drs Verma and Scott and Mr O'Muircheartaigh. *Journal of the Royal Statistical Society, A 143 (4)*: 463–464.

Klinger, A. (ed.) (1979). *Main Results of the 1977 Hungarian Fertility, Family Planning and Birth Control Study*. Hungarian Central Statistical Office.

Knodel, J. (1983). Natural Fertility: Age Patterns, Levels and Trends. In R. Bulatao and R. Lee, eds. *Determinants of Fertility in Developing Countries 2*. New York: Academic Press.

— and N. Debavalya (1978). Thailand's Reproductive Revolution. *International Family Planning Perspectives 4 (2)*: 34–49.

— — (1980). Breastfeeding in Thailand: Trends and Differentials, 1969–1979. *Studies in Family Planning* 11 (12): 355–377.

— and V. Prachuabmoh (1973). Desired Family Size in Thailand: Are the Responses Meaningful? *Demography 10 (4)*: 491–506.

—, N. Havanon and A. Pramualratana (1984). Fertility Transition in Thailand: a Qualitative Analysis. *Population and Development Review 10 (2)*: 297–328.

Kravis, I. B., A. Heston and R. Summers (1982). *World Product and Income – International Comparisons of Real Gross Product*. Baltimore: The Johns Hopkins University Press.

Laing, J. (1978). Estimating the Effects of Contraceptive Use on Fertility. *Studies in Family Planning 9 (6)*: 150–175.

— (forthcoming). Measurement of Contraceptive Protection for Fertility Analysis. In J. N. Hobcraft, ed. *The Measurement of Fertility: Incorporating the Proximate Determinants*. Oxford: Oxford University Press.

Langford, C. M. (1982). The Fertility of Tamil Estate Workers in Sri Lanka. *WFS Scientific Reports* no. 31.

Lapham, R. J. and W. P. Mauldin (1984). Conditions of Fertility Decline in Developing Countries, 1965–80. Background paper to World Bank *World Development Report 1984*.

Lee, C. F. and R. Amin (1981). Socioeconomic Factors, Intermediate Variables and Fertility in Bangladesh. *Journal of Biosocial Science 13 (2)*: 179–188.

Lee, R. D. and R. A. Bulatao (1983). The Demand for Children: a Critical Essay. In R. A. Bulatao and R. D. Lee, eds. *Determinants of Fertility in Developing Countries 2*. New York: Academic Press.

Leridon, H. (1973). Aspects Biométriques de la Fécondité Humaine. *INED Travaux et Documents* no. 65. Paris.

— (1977). *Human Fertility: the Basic Components*. (Translated by J. F. Helzner.) Chicago: University of Chicago Press.

— (1982). Stérilité, hypofertilité et infécondité en France. *Population 4-5*: 807–836.

— and B. Ferry (1985). Biological and Traditional Restraints on Fertility. In J. G. Cleland and J. N. Hobcraft, eds. *Reproductive Change in Developing Countries: Insights from the World Fertility Survey*. Oxford: Oxford University Press.

Lesthaeghe, R. J. (1982). Lactation and Lactation Related Variables, Contraception and Fertility: an Overview of Data Problems and World Trends. Paper presented at WHO/US National Academy of Sciences Seminar on Breastfeeding and Fertility Regulation, Geneva.

— (1984). Fertility and its Proximate Determinants in Sub-Saharan Africa: The Record of the 1960s and 70s. Paper presented at the IUSSP/WFS Seminar on Integrating Proximate Determinants into the Analysis of Fertility Levels and Trends, London.

—, H. J. Page and O. Adegbola (1981). Child-Spacing and Fertility in Lagos. In H. J. Page and R. J. Lesthaeghe, eds. *Child-Spacing in Tropical Africa: Traditions and Change*. London: Academic Press.

—, I. H. Shah and H. J. Page (1981). Compensating Changes in Intermediate Fertility Variables and the Onset of Marital Fertility Transition. *International Population Conference, Manila 1981 1*: 71–94. Liège: IUSSP.

—, C. Vanderhoeft, S. Becker and M. Kibet (1983). Individual and Contextual Effects of Female Education on the Kenya Marital Fertility Transition. IPD Working Paper no. 1983-9. Interuniversity Programme in Demography, Vrije Universiteit Brussel.

— — — — (1985). Individual and Contextual Effects of Education on Proximate Fertility Determinants and on Life-Time Fertility in Kenya. In J. B. Casterline, ed. *The Collection and Analysis of Community Data* ISI.

Lieberman, S. S. (1982). Demographic Perspectives on Pakistan's Development. *Population and Development Review 8 (1)*: 85–120.

Lightbourne, R. E. (1977). Family Size Desires and the Birth Rates They Imply. Ph.D. thesis, University of California at Berkeley.

— (1980). Urban-Rural Differentials in Contraceptive Use. *WFS Comparative Studies* no. 10.

— (1981). Some Improved Measures of Desired Family Size: an Application to 14 Developing Countries. Paper presented at Population Association of America Annual Meeting, Washington, DC.

— (1984a). Fertility Preferences in Guyana, Jamaica and Trinidad and Tobago, from World Fertility Survey 1975-77 – a Multiple Indicator Approach. *WFS Scientific Reports* no. 68.

— (1984b). Quality of the WFS Fertility Preference Data. Background Paper for WFS Symposium, London.

— (1984c). Socio-Economic Differentials in Current Fertility and Standardized Desired Family Size: Provisional Tables for 39 Countries. WFS Technical Paper no. 2262.

— (1984d). Test-Retest Reliability of WFS-Type Preference Data: the Case of the Dominican Republic. WFS Technical Paper no. 2309.

— (1984e). The Value of Re-interviews in Interpreting Fertility Preference Data: the Case of Sri Lanka 1975-1979. WFS Technical Paper no. 2299.

— (1985). Individual Preferences and Fertility Behaviour. In J. G. Cleland and J. N. Hobcraft, eds. *Reproductive Change in Developing Countries: Insights from the World Fertility Survey*. Oxford: Oxford University Press.

— and A. L. MacDonald (1982). Family Size Preferences. *WFS Comparative Studies* no. 14.

— and S. Singh (1982). Fertility, Union Status and Partners in the WFS Guyana and Jamaica Surveys 1975-1976. *Population Studies 36 (2)*: 201-225.

— — and C. P. Green (1982). The World Fertility Survey: Charting Global Childbearing. *Population Bulletin 37 (1)*. Washington, DC: Population Reference Bureau.

Little, R. J. A. (1978). Generalized Linear Models for Cross-Classified Data from the WFS. *WFS Technical Bulletins* no.5.

— (1980). Linear Models for WFS Data. *WFS Technical Bulletins* no. 9.

— (1981). Statistical Models for World Fertility Survey Data. In *World Fertility Survey Conference 1980: Record of Proceedings 3*: 189-237.

— (1982). Sampling Errors of Fertility Rates from the WFS. *WFS Technical Bulletins* no. 10.

— and J. N. Hobcraft (forthcoming). Fertility Exposure Analysis: Further Developments. In J. N. Hobcraft, ed. *The Measurement of Fertility: Incorporating the Proximate Determinants*. Oxford: Oxford University Press.

— and S. Perera (1981). Illustrative Analysis: Socio-Economic Differentials in Cumulative Fertility in Sri Lanka — a Marriage Cohort Approach. *WFS Scientific Reports* no. 12.

— and T. W. Pullum (1979). The General Linear Model and Direct Standardization: a Comparison. *Sociological Methods and Research 7*: 475-501.

Lloyd, C. B. (1974). An Economic Analysis of the Impact of Government on Fertility: Some Examples from the Developed Countries. *Public Policy 22(4)*: 489-512.

Lorimer, F. (1954). *Culture and Human Fertility*. Paris: UNESCO.

McCann, M. F. *et al.* (1981). Breastfeeding, Fertility and Family Planning. *Population Reports Series J* no. 24. Baltimore: Population Information Program.

McCarthy, J. (1982a). Contraceptive Sterilization in Four Latin American Countries. *Journal of Biosocial Science 14 (2)*: 189-201.

— (1982b). Differentials in Age at First Marriage. *WFS Comparative Studies* no. 19.

McClelland, G. H. (1979). Determining the Impact of Sex Preferences on Fertility: a Consideration of Parity Progression Ratio, Dominance and Stopping Rules Measures. *Demography 16 (3)*: 377-388.

MacDonald, A. L., P. M. Simpson, and A. M. Whitfield (1978). An Assessment of the Reliability of the Indonesia Fertility Survey Data. *WFS Scientific Reports* no. 3.

McDonald, J. W. (1981). A New Methodological Approach for the Analysis of WFS Current Status Breastfeeding Data. WFS Technical Paper no. 1732.

McDonald, P. F. (1981). The Measurement of Differential Mortality in the Absence of Complete Death Registration Statistics. In *Mortality in Asia: a Review of Changing Trends and Patterns, 1950–1975*. Geneva: World Health Organization.

— (1985). Social Organizations and Nuptiality in Developing Societies. In J. G. Cleland and J. N. Hobcraft, eds. *Reproductive Change in Developing Countries: Insights from the World Fertility Survey*. Oxford: Oxford University Press.

—, L. T. Ruzicka and J. C. Caldwell (1981). Interrelations between Nuptiality and Fertility: the Evidence from the World Fertility Survey. In *World Fertility Survey Conference 1980: Record of Proceedings 2*: 77–126.

McNicoll, G. (1975). Community-Level Population Policy: an Exploration. *Population and Development Review 1 (1)*: 1–21.

Macura, M. (1981). Contribution of the WFS to an Understanding of the World Population Situation. In *World Fertility Survey Conference 1980: Record of Proceedings 1*: 157–190.

Makinson, C. (1984). Age Overstatement among Young Women and its Effect on Estimates of Fertility and Proportions Married at Young Ages. Unpublished manuscript.

Mamlouk, M. (1982). Knowledge and Use of Contraception in Twenty Developing Countries. *Reports on the World Fertility Survey* no. 3. Washington, DC: Population Reference Bureau.

Marckwardt, A. M. (1975). The World Fertility Survey: its Demographic and Sociological Content. *Population Index 41 (2)*: 171–181.

— (1984). Response Rates, Callbacks and Coverage: the WFS Experience. *WFS Scientific Reports* no. 55.

Marks, E. S., W. Seltzer and K. J. Krotki (1974). *Population Growth Estimation: a Handbook of Vital Statistics Measurement*. New York: The Population Council.

Martin, L., J. Trussell, F. Reyes-Salvail and N. Shah (1983). Co-variates of Child Mortality in the Philippines, Indonesia and Pakistan: an Analysis Based on Hazard Models. *Population Studies 37 (3)*: 417–432.

Mason, K. O. and V. T. Palan (1981). Female Employment and Fertility in Peninsular Malaysia: the Maternal Role Incompatibility Hypothesis Reconsidered. *Demography 18 (4)*: 549–575.

Mason, W. M. and V. T. Palan (1978). Community-Level Variables and their Effects on Reproductive Behavior in Malaysia. Paper presented at Conference on Comparative Fertility Transition in Asia, Tokyo.

Mati, J. K. G., A. Hatimy and D. A. M. Gebbie (1971). The Importance of Anaemic Pregnancy in Nairobi and the Role of Malaria in the Aetiology of Megaloblastic Anaemia. *Journal of Tropical Medicine and Hygiene 74 (1)*: 1–8.

Mauldin, W. P. (1981). Fertility Declines in Developing Countries. *World Fertility Survey Conference 1980: Record of Proceedings 1*: 373–398.

— and B. Berelson (1978). Conditions of Fertility Decline in Developing Countries, 1965–75. *Studies in Family Planning 9 (5)*: 90–147.

— and Lapham. R. (1984). Conditions of Fertility Decline in the LDCs, 1965–80. In Staff Paper *Two Cross-Country Analyses of the Effect of Organized Family Planning Programs on Fertility*. Washington, DC: World Bank.

Meegama, S. A. (1980). Socio-Economic Determinants of Infant and Child Mortality in Sri Lanka: an Analysis of Post-War Experience. *WFS Scientific Reports* no. 8.

Menken, J. A. (forthcoming). Existing Frameworks: an Analytic Review. In J. N. Hobcraft, ed. *The Measurement of Fertility: Incorporating the Proximate Determinants*. Oxford: Oxford University Press.

Millman, S. (forthcoming). A Note on Redundant Contraceptive Protection. In J. N. Hobcraft, ed. *The Measurement of Fertility: Incorporating the Proximate Determinants*. Oxford: Oxford University Press.

Ministry of Health and Population Control (1978). *Bangladesh Fertility Survey: First Report*. Dhaka.

Miró, C. (1981). The Potential of the WFS to Clarify the Socioeconomic Determinants of Fertility in Developing Countries. *World Fertility Survey Conference 1980: Record of Proceedings 1*: 337–350.

Moors, H. G. (1978). Prognostic Implications of Early Family Building Behaviour. In H. G. Moors *et al.*, eds. *Population and Family in the Low Fertility Countries II. Leyden*. Nijhof.

— (ed.) (1983). *Netherlands Survey on Fertility and Parenthood Motivations 1975*. Voorburg, Netherlands: Netherlands Interuniversity Demographic Institute.

Morris, L. *et al.* (1981). Contraceptive Prevalence Surveys: a New Source of Family Planning Data. *Population Reports Series M* no. 5. Baltimore: Population Information Program.

Moser, C. A. and G. Kalton (1971). *Survey Methods in Social Investigation*. Second Edition, London: Heinemann Educational Books Ltd.

Moser, K. A. (1985). Levels and Trends in Child and Adult Mortality In Peru. *WFS Scientific Reports* no. 77.

Mosher, W. D. (1982). Fertility and Family Planning in the 1970s: the National Survey of Family Growth. *Family Planning Perspectives 6*: 314–320.

— and C. A. Bachrach (1982). Childlessness in the US: Estimates from the NSFG. *Journal of Family Issues 4*: 517–543.

Mosley, W. H. (1983). Will Primary Health Care Reduce Infant and Child Mortality? A Critique of Some Current Strategies, with Special Reference to Africa and Asia. Paper presented at IUSSP Seminar on Social Policy, Health Policy and Mortality Prospects, Paris.

—, L. H. Werner and S. Becker (1982). The Dynamics of Birth Spacing and Marital Fertility in Kenya. *WFS Scientific Reports* no. 30.

Mott, F. L. (1982). Infant Mortality in Kenya: Evidence from the Kenya Survey. *WFS Scientific Reports* no. 32.

Mpiti, A. M. and I Kalule-Sabiti (1985). The Proximate Determinants of Fertility in Lesotho. *WFS Scientific Reports* no. 78.

Musgrove, P. (1982). The ECIEL Study of Household Income and Consumption in Urban Latin America: An Analytical History. Living Standards Measurement Study Working Paper no. 12. Washington, DC: World Bank.

National Center for Health Statistics (NCHS) (1981). NSFG, Cycle III: Sample

Design, Estimation Procedure and Variance Estimation. *Vital and Health Statistics, Series 2* no. 87.

— (1982). Consent and Privacy in the National Survey of Family Growth. A Report on the Pilot Study for Cycle III. *Vital and Health Statistics, Series 2* no. 91.

Nawar, L. and J. N. Hobcraft (forthcoming). Proximate Determinants of Fertility. In A. M. Hallouda and S. M. Farid, eds. *Egypt: Demographic Responses to Modernization*. Central Agency for Public Mobilisation and Statistics.

Nizamuddin, M. (1979). The Impact of Community and Program Factors on the Fertility-related Behavior of Rural Pakistani Women. Ph.D. dissertation, Department of Population Planning, School of Public Health, University of Michigan, Ann Arbor.

Njeck, R. A. (1984). The Effect of Community Factors on Infant and Child Mortality in Cameroon. WFS unpublished manuscript.

Noack, T. and L. Østby (1982). Childless or Childfree? *Scandinavian Population Studies 6*, Stockholm.

Nortman, D. (1974). Parental Age as a Factor in Pregnancy Outcome and Child Development. *Reports on Population/Family Planning* no. 16.

— (1982). Estimating Potential Contraceptive Demand: an Improved Method of Measurement. Working Paper no. 82. Center for Policy Studies, The Population Council.

— and E. Hofstatter (1980). *Population and Family Planning Programs: a Compendium of Data through 1978*. 10th edition. New York: The Population Council.

Notestein, F. W. (1945). Population: the Long View. In T. W. Schultz, ed. *Food for the World:* 36–57. Chicago: University of Chicago Press.

— (1953). Economic Problems of Population Change. In *8th International Conference of Agricultural Economists:* 13–31. London: Oxford University Press.

Nour, E. -S. (1983). On the Estimation of the Distribution of Desired Family Size for a Synthetic Cohort. *Population Studies 37 (2):* 315–322.

Ochoa, L. H. (1981). Patterns of Fertility Decline in Latin America with Special Reference to Colombia. *International Population Conference, Manila 1981 1:* 25–53. Liège: IUSSP.

Ogawa, N. (1982). Differential Fertility in Indonesia and the Philippines: a Multivariate Analysis. *Southeast Asian Studies 20 (2):* 179–205.

Omran, A. R. (1981). Review of the Evidence: an Update. In A. R. Omran and C. C. Standley, eds. *Further Studies on Family Formation Patterns and Health*. Geneva: World Health Organization.

— and C. C. Standley (eds.) (1976). *Family Formation Patterns and Health*. Geneva: World Health Organization.

— — (eds.) (1981). *Further Studies on Family Formation Patterns and Health*. Geneva: World Health Organization.

O'Muircheartaigh, C. A. (1982). Methodology of the Response Errors Project. *WFS Scientific Reports* no. 28.

— (1984a). The Magnitude and Pattern of Response Variance in the Lesotho Fertility Survey. *WFS Scientific Reports* no. 70.

Comparative Fertility Study. In *Indagine sulla Fecondità in Italia-Rapporti monografici* no. 3. Universities of Padua, Florence and Rome.

Simons, J. (1978). Opinions and Attitudes. In Conseil de l'Europe *Incidences d'une population stationnaire ou decroissante en Europe*: 243–268. Liège: Ordina.

Singh, S. (1980a). Background Characteristics Used in WFS Surveys. *WFS Comparative Studies* no. 4.

— (1980b). Comparability of First Country Report Tabulations. *WFS Comparative Studies* no. 3.

— (1980c). Comparability of Questionnaires. *WFS Comparative Studies* no. 2.

— (1982). Evaluation of the Jamaica Fertility Survey 1975–76. *WFS Scientific Reports* no. 34.

— (1984a). Comparability of Questionnaires: Forty-One WFS Countries. *WFS Comparative Studies* no. 32.

— (1984b). Guyana, Jamaica and Trinidad and Tobago: Socio-Economic Differentials in Cumulative Fertility. *WFS Scientific Reports* no. 57.

— and J. B. Casterline (1985). The Socio-Economic Determinants of Fertility. In J. G. Cleland and J. N. Hobcraft, eds. *Reproductive Change in Developing Countries: Insights from the World Fertility Survey*. Oxford: Oxford University Press.

— and B. Ferry (1984). Biological and Traditional Factors that Influence Fertility: Results from WFS Surveys. *WFS Comparative Studies* no. 40.

— and P. Platridis (1980). Characteristics of the Surveys. *WFS Comparative Studies* no. 1.

—, J. B. Casterline and J. G. Cleland (1985). The Proximate Determinants of Fertility: Sub-National Variations. *Population Studies 39 (1.)*: 113–135.

Smith, D. P. (1980a). Age at First Marriage. *WFS Comparative Studies* no. 7.

— (1980b). Life Table Analysis. *WFS Technical Bulletins* no. 6.

— (1981a). Illustrative Analysis: Marriage Dissolution and Remarriage in Sri Lanka and Thailand. *WFS Scientific Reports* no. 17.

— (1981b). Regression Analysis of 'Current Status' Life Tables on Duration of Breastfeeding. WFS Technical Paper no. 1612.

— and B. Ferry (1984). Correlates of Breastfeeding. *WFS Comparative Studies* no. 41.

—, E. Carrasco and P. F. McDonald (1984). Marriage Dissolution and Remarriage. *WFS Comparative Studies* no. 34.

Smith, P. C., M. Shahidullah and A. N. Alcantara (1983). Cohort Nuptiality in Asia and the Pacific: an Analysis of WFS Surveys. *WFS Comparative Studies* no. 22.

Smith, T. E. *et al.* (1980). Evaluation Report of the World Fertility Survey. UNFPA/USAID.

Somoza, J. L. (1980). Illustrative Analysis: Infant and Child Mortality in Colombia. *WFS Scientific Reports* no. 10.

Srikantan, K. S. (1979). An Evaluation of the Fiji Fertility Survey Based on the Post-Enumeration Survey. *WFS Occasional Papers* no. 21.

— (1982). Quality and Comparability of Family Planning Data from Survey and Service Statistics. In A. I. Hermalin and B. Entwisle, eds. *The Role of Surveys in the Analysis of Family Planning Programs*. Liège: Ordina.

Srinivasan, K. and K. B. Pathak (1981). The Nature of Stable High Fertility and the Determinants of its Destabilization: Process in Selected Countries of Asia. In *International Population Conference, Manila 1981 1*: 115–135. Liège: IUSSP.

—, P. H. Reddy and K. N. M. Raju (1978). From One Generation to the Next: Changes in Fertility, Family Size Preferences and Family Planning in an Indian State between 1951 and 1975. *Studies in Family Planning 9 (10–11)*: 258–271.

Statistik Sentralbyra (SS) (1981) *Fruktbarhets-Undësøkelse 1977* (Fertility Survey 1977) (by L. Østby and T. Noack). Oslo.

Stevenson, T. H. C. (1923). *Fertility*. Census of England and Wales 1911, vol. 13: Fertility and Marriage, part II. London: HMSO.

Stycos, J. (1984). Putting Back the K and A in KAP: a Study of the Implications of Knowledge and Attitudes for Fertility in Costa Rica. *WFS Scientific Reports* no. 48.

Sukdeo, F. (1973). *Malaria Eradication and Population Growth in Guyana*. University of Guyana, Georgetown, Guyana.

Swedish Central Bureau of Statistics (SCBS) (1982). *Kvinnor och barn* (Women and Children: Interviews with Women about Family and Work). Stockholm.

Tabah, L. (1980). World Population Trends: a Stocktaking. *Population and Development Review 6 (3)*: 355–389. (English translation of Tabah 1981.)

— (1981). Quelques traits de l'évolution démographique récente. In *World Fertility Survey Conference 1980: Record of Proceedings 1*: 61–136.

Tan, J. -P. (1983). Marital Fertility at Older Ages in Nepal, Bangladesh and Sri Lanka. *Population Studies 37 (3)*: 433–444.

Tardieu, C. (1984). Evaluation des données de l'Enquête Haïtienne sur la Fécondité. *WFS Scientific Reports* no. 50.

Technical Advisory Committee (1973). Report of the First Meeting.

— (1974a). Report of the Fourth Meeting.

— (1974b). Report of the Fifth Meeting.

— (1977). Report of the Eighth Meeting,

Tekse, K. (1967). *Population and Vital Statistics in Jamaica, 1832–1964*. Kingston, Jamaica: Department of Statistics.

Tey, N. P. and I. Abdurahman (1981). Factors Affecting Contraceptive Use in Peninsular Malaysia. *WFS Scientific Reports* no. 23.

Thapa, S. and R. Retherford (1981). Infant Mortality Estimates Based on the 1976 Nepal Fertility Survey. *Population Studies 36 (1)*: 61–80.

Thompson, L. V., M. N. Ali and J. B. Casterline (1982). Collecting Demographic Data in Bangladesh: Evidence from Tape-Recorded Interviews. *WFS Scientific Reports* no. 41.

Tiapani, L. (1984). The Effect of Community Factors on Infant and Child Mortality in Ivory Coast. WFS unpublished manuscript.

Tienda, M. (1983). Community Socioeconomic Differentiation and the Education-Fertility Relationship in Peru. Center for Demography and Ecology Working Paper no. 83–36. University of Wisconsin.

Timæus, I. (1984). Mortality in Lesotho: a Study of Levels, Trends and Differentials based on Retrospective Survey Data. *WFS Scientific Reports* no. 59.

— and K. Balasubramanian (1984). Evaluation of the Lesotho Fertility Survey 1977. *WFS Scientific Reports* no. 58.

Trussell, J. (1980). Illustrative Analysis: Age at First Marriage in Sri Lanka and Thailand. *WFS Scientific Reports* no. 13.

— (forthcoming). Estimating the Determinants of Birth Intervals. In J. N. Hobcraft, ed. *The Measurement of Fertility: Incorporating the Proximate Determinants*. Oxford: Oxford University Press.

— and D. E. Bloom (1983). Estimating the Co-variates of Age at Marriage and First Birth. *Population Studies 37 (3)*: 403–416.

— and C. Hammerslough (1983). A Hazards-Model Analysis of the Covariates of Infant and Child Mortality in Sri Lanka. *Demography 20 (1)*: 1–26.

— and T. Richards (1985). Correcting for Unobserved Heterogeneity in Hazards Models: an Application of the Heckman-Singer Model to Demographic Data. In N. B. Tuma, ed. *Sociological Methodology, 1985*. San Francisco: Jossey-Bass.

—, L. Martin, R. Feldman, M. Concepción and Noor Laily Abu Bakar (1984). Determinants of Birth Interval Length in the Philippines, Malaysia and Indonesia: a Hazard Model Analysis. Paper presented at Population Association of America Annual Meeting, Minneapolis.

Tsui, A. O. (1982). Contraceptive Availability and Family Limitation in Mexico and Rural Korea. *International Family Planning Perspectives 8 (1)*: 8–17.

— (1985). Community Effects on Contraceptive Use. In J. B. Casterline, ed. *The Collection and Analysis of Community Data*. ISI.

—, D. P. Hogan, J. D. Teachman and C. Welti-Chanés (1981a). Community Availability of Contraceptives and Family Limitation. *Demography 18 (4)*: 615–625.

—, D. P. Hogan, C. Welti-Chanés and J. D. Teachman (1981b). Contraceptive Availability Differentials in Use and Fertility. *Studies in Family Planning 12 (11)*: 381–393.

Tukey, J. (1971). *Exploratory Data Analysis*. Reading, Mass.: Addison-Wesley.

Udry, J. R., K. E. Bauman and C. L. Chase (1973). Population Growth in Perfect Contraceptive Populations. *Population Studies 27 (2)*: 365–371.

United Nations (1969). Department of International Economic and Social Affairs. *Variables and Questionnaires for Comparative Analysis*. Population Studies no. 45; ST/SOA/SER.A/45. (Sales no. E.69.XIII.)

— (1971). Department of International Economic and Social Affairs. *Human Fertility and National Development: A Challenge to Science and Technology*. (Sales no. 71.II.A.12.)

— (1973). Department of International Economic and Social Affairs. *World Population Prospects as Assessed in 1968*. Population Studies no. 53; ST/ESA/SER.A/53. (Sales no. 72.XIII.4.)

— (1974). Economic Commission for Africa/UNESCO. *Manual on Demographic Sample Surveys in Africa*. E/CN.14/CAS.7/17/Rev.2.

— (1975). *Report of the United Nations World Population Conference, 1974, Bucharest, 19–30 August 1974*. E/CONF.60/19. (Sales no. E.75.XIII.3.)

— (1976a). Department of International Economic and Social Affairs. *Manual IV: Methods of Estimating Basic Demographic Measures from Incomplete Data*. Population Studies no. 42; ST/SOA/SER.A/42. (Sales no. E.67.XIII.2.)

— (1976b). Department of International Economic and Social Affairs. *Fertility and Family Planning in Europe Around 1970: A Comparative Analysis of*

Twelve National Surveys. Population Studies no. 58; ST/ESA/SER.A/58. (Sales no. E.76.XIII.2.)

— (1977a). Department of International Economic and Social Affairs. *Levels and Trends of Fertility Throughout the World, 1950–1970.* Population Studies no. 59; ST/ESA/SER.A/59. (Sales no. E.77.XIII.2.)

— (1977b). Department of International Economic and Social Affairs. Statistical Office. *The Organization of National Statistical Services: A Review of Major Issues.* Studies in Methods, Series F, no. 21; ST/ESA/STAT/SER.F/21. (Sales no. E.77.XVII.5.)

— (1977c). Department of International Economic and Social Affairs. *World Population Prospects as Assessed in 1973.* Population Studies no. 60; ST/ESA/SER.A/60. (Sales no. E.76.XIII.4.)

— (1979a). Department of International Economic and Social Affairs. *Factors Affecting the Use and Non-Use of Contraception: Findings from a Comparative Analysis of Selected KAP Surveys.* Population Studies no. 69; ST/ESA/SER.A/69. (Sales no. E.79.XIII.6.)

— (1979b). Department of International Economic and Social Affairs. Statistical Office. *Handbook of Statistical Organization* vol. I. Studies in Methods, Series F, no. 28; ST/ESA/STAT/SER.F/28. (Sales no. E.79.XVII.17.)

— (1979c). *Review and Appraisal of the World Population Plan of Action.* Population Studies no. 71; ST/ESA/SER.A/71.

— (1980a). Department of International Economic and Social Affairs. Population Division. *Some Factors Affecting Fertility in Eight Developing Countries.* New York: UNFPA.

— (1980b). Some Implications of Variations in Type and Duration of Work for the Analysis of WFS Data. UN/UNFPA/WFS.IV/16. Paper prepared by the Population Division of the Department of International Economic and Social Affairs, United Nations Secretariat, for United Nations Working Group on Comparative Analysis of World Fertility Survey Data, Fourth Meeting, Geneva.

— (1980c). *The National Household Survey Capability Programme: Prospectus.* DP/UN/INT–79–020/1.

— (1980d). *The United Nations Programme for Comparative Analysis of WFS Data.* New York: UNFPA.

— (1981a). Department of International Economic and Social Affairs. Population Division. An Educational Coding System Constructed for Application in the United Nations Programme of International Comparative Analysis of World Fertility Survey Data. ESA/P/WP.71. Working paper.

— (1981b). Department of International Economic and Social Affairs. Population Division. Occupational Classification Systems Constructed for Application in the United Nations Programme of Comparative Analysis of World Fertility Survey Data. ESA/P/WP.70. Working paper.

— (1981c). Department of International Economic and Social Affairs. *Selected Factors Affecting Fertility and Fertility Preferences in Developing Countries.* ST/ESA/SER.R/37.

— (1981d). Department of International Economic and Social Affairs. *Variations in the Incidence of Knowledge and Use of Contraception: A Compara-*

tive Analysis of World Fertility Survey Results for Twenty Developing Countries. ST/ESA/SER.R/40.

— (1982a). Department of International Economic and Social Affairs. *Demographic Indicators of Countries: Estimates and Projections as Assessed in 1980.* Population Studies no. 82; ST/ESA/SER.A/82 and Corr. 1. (Sales no. E.82.XIII.5.)

— (1982b). Department of International Economic and Social Affairs. *World Population Trends and Policies: 1981 Monitoring Report* vol. I. Population Studies no. 79; ST/ESA/SER.A/79. (Sales no. E.82, XIII.2.)

— (1982c). Department of International Economic and Social Affairs. *The Impact of Population Structure on Crude Fertility Measures: A Comparative Analysis of World Fertility Survey Results for Twenty-one Developing Countries.* ST/ESA/SER.R/49.

— (1983a). Department of International Economic and Social Affairs. *Fertility Levels and Trends as Assessed from Twenty World Fertility Surveys.* ST/ESA/SER.R/50.

— (1983b). Department of International Economic and Social Affairs. *Manual X: Indirect Techniques for Demographic Estimation.* Population Studies no. 81; ST/ESA/SER.A/81. (Sales no. E.83.XIII.2.)

— (1983c). Department of International Economic and Social Affairs. *Marital Status and Fertility: A Comparative Analysis of World Fertility Survey Data for Twenty-one Developing Countries.* ST/ESA/SER.R/52.

— (1983d). Department of International Economic and Social Affairs. *Relationships between Fertility and Education: A Comparative Analysis of World Fertility Survey Data for Twenty-two Developing Countries.* ST/ESA/SER.R/48.

— (1984). Department of International Economic and Social Affairs. *Some Relationships between Nuptiality and Fertility in Countries of the West Indies.* ST/ESA/SER.R/46.

— (1985a). Department of International Economic and Social Affairs. Population Division. Socio-Economic Development in Relation to Fertility Decline: A Review of Methodological Developments and Recent Empirical Studies. ESA/P/WP.86. Working paper.

— (1985b). Department of International Economic and Social Affairs. *Women's Employment and Fertility: A Comparative Analysis of WFS Data.* Population Studies no. 96; ST/ESA/SER.A/96.

— (1985c). Department of International Economic and Social Affairs. *World Population Trends, Population and Development Interrelations and Population Policies; 1983 Monitoring Report.* Population Studies no. 93; ST/ESA/SER.A/93.

— (1986). Department of International Economic and Social Affairs. *Policy Relevance of Findings of the World Fertility Survey for Developing Countries.* ST/ESA/SER.R/59.

— (forthcoming a). Department of International Economic and Social Affairs. *A Comparative Evaluation of Data Quality in Thirty-eight World Fertility Surveys.* ST/ESA/SER.R/50/Rev.1.

— (forthcoming b). Department of International Economic and Social Affairs. *Fertility Behaviour in the Context of Development: Evidence from the World Fertility Survey.* ST/ESA/SER.A/100.

— (forthcoming c). Economic Commission for Europe. *Fertility and Family Planning in Europe and the USA: A Comparative Study of National Surveys.*

United Nations/World Health Organization (1979). *Proceedings of the Meeting on Socioeconomic Determinants and Consequences of Mortality, Mexico City, 19-25 June 1979.* Geneva: World Health Organization.

US Bureau of the Census (1978). World Population 1977: Recent Demographic Estimates for the Countries and Regions of the World. Washington, DC: US Department of Commerce.

— (1980). World Population 1979: Recent Demographic Estimates for the Countries and Regions of the World. Washington, DC: US Department of Commerce.

— (1981). Demographic Estimates for Countries with a Population of 10 Million or More: 1981. Washington, DC: US Department of Commerce.

Vaessen, M. (1980). Knowledge of Contraceptive Methods. *WFS Comparative Studies* no. 8.

— (1981). Knowledge of Contraceptives: an Assessment of World Fertility Survey Data Collection Procedures. *Population Studies 35 (3):* 357-373.

— (1984). Childlessness and Infecundity. *WFS Comparative Studies* no. 31.

Vanderhoeft, C. (1982). Accelerated Failure Time Models: an Application to Current Status Breastfeeding Data from Pakistan. *Genus 38:* 135-157.

— (1983). A Unified Approach to Models for Analysis of Zero-One Data with Applications to Intermediate Fertility Variables. Working Paper no. 1983-5, Interuniversity Programme in Demography, Vrije Universiteit, Brussels.

Verma, V. (1981). Sampling for National Fertility Surveys. In *World Fertility Survey Conference 1980: Record of Proceedings 3:* 389-436.

— (1985). WFS Survey Methods: an Assessment. In J. G. Cleland and J. N. Hobcraft, eds. *Reproductive Change in Developing Countries: Insights from the World Fertility Survey.* Oxford: Oxford University Press.

— and M. Pearce (1978). User's Manual for Clusters. WFS Technical Paper no. 770.

—, C. Scott and C. O'Muircheartaigh (1980). Sample Designs and Sampling Errors for the World Fertility Survey. *Journal of the Royal Statistical Society A 143 (4):* 431-463.

Wanglee, A. (1983). The Contribution of the WFS to Survey Capability in Developing Countries. In *Bulletin of the International Statistical Institute 50 (2):* 896-909. (Proceedings of ISI 44th Session, Madrid.)

Ware, H. (1974). Ideal Family Size. *WFS Occasional Papers* no. 13.

— (1976). Motivations for the Use of Birth Control: Evidence for West Africa. *Demography 13 (4):* 479-493.

— (1977). Language Problems in Demographic Field Work in Africa: The Case of the Cameroon Fertility Survey. *WFS Scientific Reports* no. 2.

Westlake, A. (1984). EHP-Processing Event-Based Data: Preliminary Concepts and Examples. WFS Technical Paper no. 2302.

Westoff, C. F. (1975). The Yield of the Imperfect: the 1970 Fertility Study. *Demography 12 (4):* 573-580.

— (1978). The Unmet Need for Birth Control in Five Asian Countries. *International Family Planning Perspectives 4 (1):* 9-18.

— (1981). Unwanted Fertility in Six Developing Countries. In *World Fertility Survey Conference 1980: Record of Proceedings* 2: 707–759. Shortened version published in *International Family Planning Perspectives 7 (2)*: 43–51.

— and A. R. Pebley (1981). Alternative Measures of Unmet Need for Family Planning in Developing Countries. *International Family Planning Perspectives 7 (4)*: 126–136.

— and N. B. Ryder (1977). The Predictive Validity of Reproductive Intentions. *Demography 14 (4)*: 431–453.

—, J. McCarthy, N. Goldman and F. Mascarín (1979). Illustrative Analysis: Contraceptive Sterilization and Births Averted in Panama. *WFS Scientific Reports* no. 4.

Whitten, W. B. and J. M. Leonard (1981). Directed Search Through Autobiographical Memory. *Memory and Cognition 9 (6)*.

Winikoff, B. (1983). The Effects of Birth Spacing on Child and Maternal Health. *Studies in Family Planning 14 (10)*: 231–245.

(UN) Working Group on Social Demography (WGSD) (1976). *A Comparative Study of Fertility and Family Planning in LFCs around 1975*. SOA/WG/2/CONF.8/WP.1.

— (1978). Meeting Report, Varna. SOA/ESDP/1978/4.

World Bank (1980). *World Tables, the Second Edition*. Washington, DC: The World Bank.

— (1983). Infant and Child Mortality as a Determinant of Fertility. Paper presented at UN Expert Group Meeting on Fertility and Family, New Delhi.

— (1984). *World Development Report 1984*. New York: Oxford University Press.

World Fertility Survey (1974). Report of the Seminar on Tabulation and Analysis of Survey Data. WFS Technical Paper no. 104.

— (1975a). *Annual Report*.

— (1975b). Interviewers' Instructions. *WFS Basic Documentation* no. 6.

— (1975c). Manual on Sample Design. *WFS Basic Documentation* no. 3.

— (1975d). Supervisors' Instructions. *WFS Basic Documentation* no. 5.

— (1975e). Survey Organization Manual. *WFS Basic Documentation* no. 2.

— (1976a). Editing and Coding Manual. *WFS Basic Documentation* no. 7.

— (1976b). Training Manual. *WFS Basic Documentation* no. 4.

— (1977a). Guidelines for Country Report No. 1. *WFS Basic Documentation* no. 8.

— (1977b). Selected Topics for Further Analysis of WFS Data. WFS Technical Paper no. 637.

— (1977c). Strategies for the Analysis of WFS Data. *WFS Basic Documentation* no. 9.

— (1977d). WFS Modules: Abortion, Factors Other Than Contraception Affecting Fertility, Family Planning, General Mortality. *WFS Occasional Papers* no. 19.

— (1980a). Data Processing Guidelines. *WFS Basic Documentation* no. 11.

— (1980b). Regional Workshop on Techniques of Analysis of World Fertility Survey Data. *WFS Occasional Papers* no. 22.

— (1981). *World Fertility Survey Conference 1980: Record of Proceedings*.

— (1982). *Annual Report.*

— (1984). Software User's Manual. *WFS Basic Documentation* no. 12.

— (1985). *Final Report.*

World Health Organization (1975). The Epidemiology of Infertility. *Technical Report Series* no. 582. Geneva: WHO Press.

— (1981). *Contemporary Patterns of Breastfeeding.* Geneva: WHO.

— (1983). Breastfeeding and Fertility Regulation: Current Knowledge and Programme Policy Implications. *Bulletin of the WHO.* Geneva.

Young, F. W., B. Edmonston and N. Andes (1983). Community-Level Determinants of Infant and Child Mortality in Peru. *Social Indicators Research 12 (1):* 65–81.

Yusuf, F. and R. D. Retherford (1981). Urban-Rural Fertility Differentials in Pakistan. *Journal of Biosocial Science 13 (4):* 491–499.

Zaba, B. (1981). Use of the Relational Gompertz Model in Analysing Fertility Data Collected in Retrospective Surveys. *CPS Working Paper* no. 81–2, Centre for Population Studies, London School of Hygiene and Tropical Medicine.

Zablan, Z. (1984). The Proximate Determinants of Fertility and Their Effects on Fertility Patterns in the Philippines. WFS unpublished manuscript.

Zarkovic, S. S. (1983). The Management of the WFS. Paper presented to ISI 44th Session, Madrid.

Zoughlami, Y. and D. Allsopp (1985). The Demographic Characteristics of Household Populations. Revised edition. *WFS Comparative Studies* no. 45.

WFS PUBLICATIONS

In English only unless otherwise stated; some scientific reports are in Spanish or French, as their titles indicate. Year of publication is given in brackets.

GENERAL BROCHURE (1979)   (English, French, Spanish, Arabic)

ANNUAL REPORTS

A series of reports covers the period 1972–82.
The World Fertility Survey: Final Report (1985).

NON-SERIES TITLES

Alam, Iqbal and Betzy Dinesen, eds. (1984). Fertility in Pakistan: a Review of Findings from the Pakistan Fertility Survey.
Casterline, John B., ed. (1985). The Collection and Analysis of Community Data.
Cleland, John and Chris Scott, eds. (1986). The World Fertility Survey: an Assessment (OUP)
Engracia, Luisa T., Corazon Mejia-Raymundo and John B. Casterline, eds. (1984). Fertility in the Philippines: Further Analysis of the Republic of the Philippines Fertility Survey 1978.
Farid, S.M. and K. Alloush, eds. (1986). Determinants of Fertility in Syria.
Grebenik, E. (1981). The World Fertility Survey and its 1980 Conference.
Nuptialité et fécondité au Sénégal. Etudes coordonnées par Yves Charbit, Lamine Gueye et Salif Ndiaye (1985). (INED)
Rosero, L., M. Gómez and V. Rodríguez (1982). The Determinants of Fertility Decline in Costa Rica 1964–76.
Singh, Susheela, John Y. Owusu and Iqbal H. Shah, eds. (1985). Demographic Patterns in Ghana: Evidence from the Ghana Fertility Survey.
World Fertility Survey Conference 1980: Record of Proceedings (1981).
World Fertility Survey: Fertility in the Developing World (1984).
World Fertility Survey: Major Findings and Implications (1984).

WFS BASIC DOCUMENTATION

1   Core Questionnaires (1975) (English, French, Spanish, Arabic)..
2   Survey Organization Manual (1975) (English, French, Spanish, Arabic).
3   Manual on Sample Design (1975) (English, French, Spanish, Arabic).
4   Training Manual (1976) (English, French, Spanish, Arabic).
5   Supervisors' Instructions (1975) (English, French, Spanish, Arabic).
6   Interviewers' Instructions (1975) (English, French, Spanish, Arabic).
7   Editing and Coding Manual (1976) (Revision of appendix 4 available in English only) (English, French, Spanish, Arabic).
8   Guidelines for Country Report No. 1 (1977) (English, French, Spanish, Arabic).
9   Strategies for the Analysis of WFS Data (1977) (English, French, Spanish).
10 Modifications to the WFS Core Questionnaires and Related Documents (1977) (English, French, Spanish).
11 Data Processing Guidelines (2 vols.) (1980). (English, both vols.: French, vol. 1 only)
12 Software User's Manual (1984).
    – Core Questionnaire for Husbands (working version only) (1977) (English, French, Spanish).

TECHNICAL BULLETINS

1   Kendall, Maurice (1976). Some Notes on Statistical Problems Likely to Arise in the Analysis of WFS Surveys.
2   Kendall, M.G. and C.A. O'Muircheartaigh (1977). Path Analysis and Model Building.
3   Pullum, T. W. (1978). Standardization.
4   Verma, Vijay (1980). Basic Fertility Measures from Retrospective Birth Histories.
5   Little, Roderick J.A. (1978). Generalized Linear Models for Cross-Classified Data from the WFS.
6   Smith, David P. (1980). Life Table Analysis.
7   Rodríguez, Germán and James Trussell (1980). Maximum Likelihood Estimation of the Parameters of Coale's Model Nuptiality Schedule from Survey Data.
8   Ryder, Norman B. (1982). Progressive Fertility Analysis.
9   Little, Roderick J.A. (1980). Linear Models for WFS Data.
10 Little, Roderick J.A. (1982). Sampling Errors of Fertility Rates from the WFS.
11 Verma, Vijay (1982). Estimation and Presentation of Sampling Errors.

SCIENTIFIC REPORTS

1   Rodríguez, Germán (1977). Assessing the Availability of Fertility Regulation Methods: Report on a Methodological Study.
2   Ware, Helen (1977). Language Problems in Demographic Field Work in Africa: the Case of the Cameroon Fertility Survey.
3   MacDonald, A.L., P.M. Simpson and A.M. Whitfield (1978). An Assessment of the Reliability of the Indonesia Fertility Survey Data.
4   Westoff, Charles F., James McCarthy, Noreen Goldman and Felix Mascarín (1979). Illustrative Analysis: Contraceptive Sterilization and Births Averted in Panama.
5   Cleland, J.G., R.J.A. Little and P. Pitaktepsombati (1979). Illustrative Analysis: Socio-Economic Determinants of Contraceptive Use in Thailand.
6   Goldman, Noreen, Ansley J. Coale and Maxine Weinstein (1979). The Quality of Data in the Nepal Fertility Survey.
7   Srinivasan, K. (1980). Birth Interval Analysis in Fertility Surveys.
8   Meegama, S.A. (1980). Socio-Economic Determinants of Infant and Child Mortality in Sri Lanka: an Analysis of Post-War Experience.
9   Pullum, Thomas W. (1980). Illustrative Analysis: Fertility Preferences in Sri Lanka.
10 Somoza, Jorge L. (1980). Illustrative Analysis: Infant and Child Mortality in Colombia.
11 Flórez, Carmen Elisa and Noreen Goldman (1980). An Analysis of Nuptiality Data in the Colombia National Fertility Survey.
12 Little, Roderick J.A. and Soma Perera (1981). Illustrative Analysis: Socio-Economic Differentials in Cumulative Fertility in Sri Lanka – A Marriage Cohort Approach.
13 Trussell, James (1980). Illustrative Analysis: Age at First Marriage in Sri Lanka and Thailand.
14 Guzmán, José Miguel (1980). Evaluation of the Dominican Republic National Fertility Survey 1975.
15 Hobcraft, John N. (1980). Illustrative Analysis: Evaluating Fertility Levels and Trends in Colombia.
16 Rodríguez, Germán and John N. Hobcraft (1980). Illustrative Analysis: Life Table Analysis of Birth Intervals in Colombia.
17 Smith, David P. (1981). Illustrative Analysis: Marriage Dissolution and Remarriage in Sri Lanka and Thailand.
18 Immerwahr, George (1981). Contraceptive Use in Sri Lanka.
19 Reyes, Florentina (1981). Evaluation of the Republic of the Philippines Fertility Survey 1978.
20 Freedman, Ronald, Siew-Ean Khoo and Bondan Supraptilah (1981). Modern Contraceptive Use in Indonesia: a Challenge to Conventional Wisdom.
21 Ordorica, Manuel and Joseph E. Potter (1981). Evaluation of the Mexican Fertility Survey 1976-77.

22   Kim, Nam Il and Byoung Mokh Choi (1981). Preferences for Number and Sex of Children and Contraceptive Use in Korea.
23   Tey Nai Peng and Idris Abdurahman (1981). Factors Affecting Contraceptive Use in Peninsular Malaysia.
24   Soeradji, Budi and Sri Harijati Hatmadji (1982). Contraceptive Use in Java–Bali: a Multivariate Analysis of the Determinants of Contraceptive Use.
25   Alam, Iqbal and John Cleland (1981). Illustrative Analysis: Recent Fertility Trends in Sri Lanka.
26   Balkaran, Sundat (1982). Evaluation of the Guyana Fertility Survey 1975.
27   Mohd. Yatim, Masitah (1982). Evaluation of the Malaysian Fertility and Family Survey 1974.
28   O'Muircheartaigh, C.A. (1982). Methodology of the Response Errors Project.
29   Hobcraft, John and Germán Rodríguez (1982). The Analysis of Repeat Fertility Surveys: Examples from Dominican Republic.
30   Mosley, W. Henry, Linda H. Werner and Stan Becker (1982). The Dynamics of Birth Spacing and Marital Fertility in Kenya.
31   Langford, C.M. (1982). The Fertility of Tamil Estate Workers in Sri Lanka.
32   Mott, Frank L. (1982). Infant Mortality in Kenya: Evidence from the Kenya Fertility Survey.
33   Céspedes, Yolanda (1982). Evaluation of the Peru National Fertility Survey 1977–78.
34   Singh, Susheela (1982). Evaluation of the Jamaica Fertility Survey 1975–76.
35   Vielma, Gilberto (1982). Evaluation of the Venezuela Fertility Survey 1977.
36   Henin, Roushdi A., Ailsa Korten and Linda H. Werner (1982). Evaluation of Birth Histories: a Case Study of Kenya.
37   Page, H.J., R.J. Lesthaeghe and I.H. Shah (1982). Illustrative Analysis: Breastfeeding in Pakistan.
38   Supraptilah, Bondan (1982). Evaluation of the Indonesian Fertility Survey 1976.
39   Caldwell, John C., George Immerwahr and Lado T. Ruzicka (1982). Illustrative Analysis: Family Structure and Fertility.
40   Easterlin, Richard A. and Eileen M. Crimmins (1982). An Exploratory Study of the 'Synthesis Framework' of Fertility Determination with World Fertility Survey Data.
41   Thompson, L.V., M. Nawab Ali and J.B. Casterline (1982). Collecting Demographic Data in Bangladesh: Evidence from Tape-Recorded Interviews.
42   Abdel-Aziz, Abdallah (1983). Evaluation of the Jordan Fertility Survey 1976.
43   Üner, Sunday (1983). Evaluation of the Turkish Fertility Survey 1978.
44   Hunte, Desmond (1983). Evaluation of the Trinidad and Tobago Fertility Survey 1977.
45   O'Muircheartaigh, C.A. (1984). The Magnitude and Pattern of Response Variance in the Peru Fertility Survey.
46   Abdel-Aziz, Abdallah (1983). A Study of Birth Intervals in Jordan.
47   Blacker, J.G.C., Allan G. Hill and Kath A. Moser (1983). Mortality Levels and Trends in Jordan Estimated from the Results of the 1976 Fertility Survey.
48   Stycos, J. Mayonne (1984). Putting Back the K and A in KAP: a Study of the Implications of Knowledge and Attitudes for Fertility in Costa Rica.
49   Gueye, Lamine (1984). Enquête Sénégalaise sur la Fécondité: Rapport d'évaluation.
50   Tardieu, Camille (1984). Evaluation des données de l'Enquête Haïtienne sur la Fécondité.
51   Herrera de Rivadeneira, M. Ines (1984). Evaluación de la Encuesta Nacional de Fecundidad de 1979: Ecuador.
52   Becker, Stan and Simeen Mahmud (1984). A Validation Study of Backward and Forward Pregnancy Histories in Matlab, Bangladesh.
53   Gaisie, S.K. (1984). The Proximate Determinants of Fertility in Ghana.
54   Pullum, Thomas W., Nuri Özsever and Trudy Harpham (1984). An Assessment of the Machine Editing Policies of the WFS.
55   Marckwardt, Albert M. (1984). Response Rates, Callbacks and Coverage: the WFS Experience.
56   Al-Kabir, Ahmed (1984). Effects of Community Factors on Infant and Child Mortality in Rural Bangladesh.

57   Singh, Susheela (1984). Guyana, Jamaica and Trinidad and Tobago: Socio-Economic
      Differentials in Cumulative Fertility.
58   Timæus, Ian and K. Balasubramanian (1984). Evaluation of the Lesotho Fertility Survey
      1977.
59   Timæus, Ian (1984). Mortality in Lesotho: a Study of Levels, Trends and Differentials
      Based on Retrospective Survey Data.
60   Abdulah, Norma and Jack Harewood (1984). Contraceptive Use and Fertility in the
      Commonwealth Caribbean.
61   Fortunat, F. (1984). Les déterminants proches de la fécondité en Haïti.
62   Schoemaker, Juan F. (1984). Evaluación de la Encuesta Nacional de Fecundidad del
      Paraguay de 1979.
63   Rodríguez Sepúlveda, Bienvenida (1984). Evaluación de la Encuesta Nacional de
      Fecundidad de la República Dominicana de 1980.
64   Santow, Gigi and A. Bioumla (1984). An Evaluation of the Cameroon Fertility Survey
      1978.
65   Charbit, Yves (1984). Caribbean Family Structure: Past Research and Recent Evidence
      from the WFS on Matrifocality.
66   Courbage, Youssef (1984). Méthodes d'estimation du niveau futur de la fécondité à
      partir du nombre d'enfants désirés et des facteurs socio-économiques en Haïti.
67   Harewood, Jack (1984). Mating and Fertility: Results from Three WFS Surveys in
      Guyana, Jamaica and Trinidad and Tobago.
68   Lightbourne, R.E. (1984). Fertility Preferences in Guyana, Jamaica and Trinidad and
      Tobago, from World Fertility Survey 1975–77 – a Multiple Indicator Approach.
69   Owusu, John Y. (1984). Evaluation of the Ghana Fertility Survey 1979–80.
70   O'Muircheartaigh, C.A. (1984). The Magnitude and Pattern of Response Variance in
      the Lesotho Fertility Survey.
71   Ferry, Benoît and H.J. Page (1984). The Proximate Determinants of Fertility and their
      Effect on Fertility Patterns: an Illustrative Analysis Applied to Kenya.
72   Rizgalla, M.K. (1985). Evaluation of the Sudan Fertility Survey 1979.
73   El Nasr, I.A. and I. Kalule-Sabiti (1985). The Proximate Determinants of Fertility in
      Sudan.
74   Borja M., Eduardo (1985). Factores determinantes de una mortalidad prematura en
      Ecuador.
75   Ebanks, G. Edward (1985). Infant and Child Mortality and Fertility: Trinidad and
      Tobago, Guyana and Jamaica.
76   Al-Tohamy, A.-M. and I. Kalule-Sabiti (1985). Evaluation of the Yemen Arab Republic
      Fertility Survey 1979.
77   Moser, Kath (1985). Levels and Trends in Child and Adult Mortality in Peru.
78   Mpiti, A.M. and I. Kalule-Sabiti (1985). The Proximate Determinants of Fertility in
      Lesotho.
79   Sombo, N'Cho (1985). Evaluation de l'Enquête Nationale Ivoirienne sur la Fécondité
      1980–81.
80   Morah, Benson C. (1985). Evaluation of the Nigeria Fertility Survey 1981–82.
81   Cónim, Custódio (1986). Evaluation of the Portugal Fertility Survey 1979–80.
82   Rousseau, J.A. (1985). La mortalité infantile et juvénile en Haïti.

COMPARATIVE STUDIES

1   Singh, Susheela and Pat Platridis (1980). Characteristics of the Surveys.*
2   Singh, Susheela (1980). Comparability of Questionnaires.*
3   Singh, Susheela (1980). Comparability of First Country Report Tabulations.*
4   Singh, Susheela (1980). Background Characteristics Used in WFS Surveys.*
5   Chidambaram, V.C. and Zeba A. Sathar (1984). Age and Data Reporting.*
6   Kabir, Mohammad (1980). The Demographic Characteristics of Household Populations.*
7   Smith, David P. (1980). Age at First Marriage.*

8   Vaessen, Martin (1980). Knowledge of Contraceptive Methods.*
9   Carrasco, Enrique (1981). Contraceptive Practice.*
10 Lightbourne, Robert E. (1980). Urban–Rural Differentials in Contraceptive Use.*
11 Hanenberg, Robert (1980). Current Fertility.*
12 Hodgson, Maryse and Jane Gibbs (1980). Children Ever Born.*
13 Ferry, Benoît (1981). Breastfeeding.*
14 Lightbourne, Robert E. (1980). Urban–Rural Differentials in Contraceptive Use.*
15 Casterline, John B. and James Trussell (1980). Age at First Birth.*
16 Chidambaram, V.C., J.G. Cleland and Vijay Verma (1980). Some Aspects of WFS Data Quality: a Preliminary Assessment.[+]
17 Goldman, Noreen and John Hobcraft (1982). Birth Histories.*
18 Berent, Jerzy, Elise F. Jones and M. Khalid Siddiqui (1982). Basic Characteristics, Sample Designs and Questionnaires.[‡]
19 McCarthy, James (1982). Differentials in Age at First Marriage.*
20 Berent, Jerzy (1982). Family Planning in Europe and USA in the 1970s.[‡]
21 Jones, Elise F. (1982). Socio-Economic Differentials in Achieved Fertility.[‡]
22 Smith, Peter C., M. Shahidullah and Adelamar N. Alcantara (1983). Cohort Nuptiality in Asia and the Pacific: an Analysis of WFS Surveys.[+]
23 Ferry, Benoît and David P. Smith (1983). Breastfeeding Differentials.*
24 Rutstein, Shea Oscar (1983). Infant and Child Mortality: Levels, Trends and Differentials.*
25 Hobcraft, John and J.B. Casterline (1983). Speed of Reproduction.[+]
26 Berent, Jerzy (1983). Family Size Preferences in Europe and USA: Ultimate Expected Number of Children.[‡]
27 Cleland, John, Jane Verrall and Martin Vaessen (1983). Preferences for the Sex of Children and their Influence on Reproductive Behaviour.*
28 Hobcraft, John and John McDonald (1984). Birth Intervals.*
29 Rindfuss, Ronald R. et al. (1984). Childspacing in Asia: Similarities and Differences.[+]
30 Rodríguez, Germán, John Hobcraft, John McDonald, Jane Menken and James Trussell (1984). A Comparative Analysis of Determinants of Birth Intervals.*
31 Vaessen, Martin (1984). Childlessness and Infecundity.*
32 Singh, Susheela (1984). Comparability of Questionnaires: Forty-one WFS Countries.*
33 Alam, Iqbal and J.B. Casterline (1984). Socio-Economic Differentials in Recent Fertility.*
34 Smith, David P., Enrique Carrasco and Peter McDonald (1984). Marriage Dissolution and Remarriage.*
35 McDonald, Peter (1984). Nuptiality and Completed Fertility: a Study of Starting, Stopping and Spacing Behaviour.[+]
36 Sathar, Zeba A. and V.C. Chidambaram (1984). Differentials in Contraceptive Use.*
37 Jones, Elise F. (1984). The Availability of Contraceptive Services.[+]
38 Ford, Kathleen (1984). Timing and Spacing of Births.[‡]
39 Casterline, John B., Susheela Singh, John Cleland and Hazel Ashurst (1984). The Proximate Determinants of Fertility.[+]
40 Singh, Susheela and Benoît Ferry (1984). Biological and Traditional Factors that Influence Fertility: Results from WFS Surveys.*
41 Smith, David P. and Benoît Ferry (1984). Correlates of Breastfeeding.[+]
42 Ashurst, Hazel, Sundat Balkaran and J.B. Casterline (1984). Socio-Economic Differentials in Recent Fertility. Revised edition.*
43 Rutstein, Shea Oscar (1984). Infant and Child Mortality: Levels, Trends and Demographic Differentials. Revised edition.*
44 Goldman, Noreen, Shea Oscar Rutstein and Susheela Singh (1985). Assessment of the Quality of Data in 41 WFS Surveys: a Comparative Approach.[+]
45 Zoughlami, Younes and Diana Allsopp (1985). The Demographic Characteristics of Household Populations. Revised edition.*

OCCASIONAL PAPERS

1   Duncan, William G. (1973). Fertility and Related Surveys.
2   Caldwell, J.C. (1973). The World Fertility Survey: Problems and Possibilities.
3-6 Baum, Samuel, Kathleen Dopkowski, William G. Duncan and Peter Gardiner (1974). WFS Inventory: Major Fertility and Related Surveys – 3. Asia; 4. Africa; 5. Latin America; 6. Europe, North America and Australia.
7   Caldwell, John C. (1974). The Study of Fertility and Fertility Change in Tropical Africa.
8   Freedman, Ronald (1974). Community-Level Data in Fertility Surveys.
9   Freedman, Ronald (1974). Examples of Community-Level Questionnaires.
10 Acsádi, György T. (1974). A Selected Bibliography of Works on Fertility.
11 Freedman, Deborah S. (with Eva Mueller) (1974). Economic Data for Fertility Analysis.
12 Freedman, Deborah S. and Eva Mueller (1974). Economic Modules for Use in Fertility Surveys in Less Developed Countries.
13 Ware, Helen (1974). Ideal Family Size.
14 Goldberg, David (1974). Modernism.
15 Sahib, M.A., N.B. Navunisaravi, R. Chandra and J.G. Cleland (1975). The Fiji Fertility Survey: a Critical Commentary.
16 Sahib, M.A. *et al.* (1975). The Fiji Fertility Survey: a Critical Commentary – Appendices.
17 Kish, L., R.M. Groves and K.P. Krotki (1976). Sampling Errors for Fertility Surveys.
18 Ramírez, N., P. Tactuk, E. Hardy and M. Vaessen (1976). The Dominican Republic Fertility Survey: an Assessment.
19 WFS Central Staff (1977). WFS Modules: Abortion, Factors other than Contraception Affecting Fertility, Family Planning, General Mortality (English, French, Spanish).
20 Little, Roderick J.A. and Thomas W. Pullum (1979). The General Linear Model and Direct Standardization: a Comparison.
21 Srikantan, K.S. (1979). An Evaluation of the Fiji Fertility Survey Based on the Post-Enumeration Survey.
22 Regional Workshop on Techniques of Analysis of World Fertility Survey Data (1980).
23 Gaslonde, Santiago and Enrique Carrasco (1982). The Impact of Some Intermediate Variables on Fertility: Evidence from the Venezuela National Fertility Survey 1977.
24 Ortega, Manuel M. (1982). Utilization of Research in Dominican Republic.
25 Conning, Arthur M. and Albert M. Marckwardt (1982). Analysis of WFS Data in Colombia, Panama, Paraguay and Peru: Highlights from the CELADE Research and Training Seminar.

SUMMARIES OF COUNTRY REPORTS

The summaries for developing countries are generally available in English, French and Spanish.

1 Fiji	18 Guyana	35 Syria
2 Dominican Republic	19 Costa Rica	36 Sudan
3 Pakistan	20 Jordan	37 Italy
4 Malaysia	21 Peru	38 Paraguay
5 Nepal	22 Guadeloupe and Martinique	39 Ghana
6 Thailand	23 Spain	40 Portugal
7 Sri Lanka	24 Belgium (Flanders)	41 Cameroon
8 Republic of Korea	25 Hungary	42 Egypt
9 Colombia	26 Kenya	43 Sweden
10 Panama	27 Jamaica	44 Mauritania
11 Indonesia	28 Turkey	45 Venezuela
12 Netherlands	29 Norway	46 Tunisia
13 Bangladesh	30 Senegal	47 Morocco
14 Japan	31 Haiti	48 Benin
15 Philippines	32 France	49 Nigeria
16 Czechoslovakia	33 Trinidad and Tobago	50 Ivory Coast
17 Mexico	34 Lesotho	51 Ecuador

FIRST COUNTRY REPORTS

Bangladesh (1979)
Benin (French) (1984)
Cameroon (French) (1983)
Colombia (Spanish) (1978)
Costa Rica (Spanish) (1978)
Dominican Republic (Spanish) (1976)
Ecuador (Spanish) (1984)
Egypt (1983)
Fiji (1976)
Ghana (1983)
Guadeloupe and Martinique (French) (1980)
Guyana (1979)
Haiti (French) (1981)
Hong Kong (1979)
Indonesia (1979)
Ivory Coast (French) (1984)
Jamaica (1979)
Jordan (1980)
Kenya (1980/81)
Korea, Republic of (1978)
Lesotho (1981)
Malaysia (1978)

Mauritania (French) (1984)
Mexico (Spanish) (1979)
Morocco (French) (1984)
Nepal (1977)
Nigeria (1984)
Pakistan (1977)
Panama (Spanish) (1978)
Paraguay (Spanish) (1981)
Peru (Spanish) (1979)
Philippines (1979)
Portugal (Portuguese) (1983)
Senegal (French) (1981)
Sri Lanka (1978)
Sudan (1982)
Syria (1982)
Thailand (1977)
Trinidad and Tobago (1981)
Tunisia (French) (1983)
Turkey (1980)
Venezuela (Spanish) (1980/82)
Yemen AR (1984) (English and Arabic)

Notes

*   In the subseries *Cross-National Summaries*.
+   Comparative Study, not part of a subseries.
‡   In the subseries *ECE Analyses of WFS Surveys in Europe and USA*.

INDEX